Good Housekeeping's

Cookery Book

Compiled by Good Housekeeping Institute
with a chapter on Wines by
ANDRÉ L. SIMON
President of the
Wine & Food Society

The National Magazine Company Limited London

First published 1948
Second Impression 1949
Third Impression 1949
Fourth Impression 1950
Revised Edition 1951
Reprinted 1952
Revised Edition 1954
Reprinted 1955
Reprinted 1956
Reprinted 1957
Reprinted 1958
Revised Edition 1959

Printed in Great Britain by
Morrison and Gibb Limited, London and Edinburgh

Colour Plates Printed by
Sun Printers Limited, Watford

Contents

Section Two (contd.)

Section Three

List of Colour Plates

Foreword

Good Housekeeping's Cookery Book has come to be known all over the world as the standard book for every woman. First published in 1948, it has been reprinted many times, and in its present, completely revised edition, with large pages, clearly set out recipes, and attractive pictures, it provides a volume that will be treasured in every home.

The book covers the whole field of domestic cookery, and caters for every need. The novice will find even the simplest basic processes carefully described, while the skilled cook will enjoy experimenting with the more elaborate recipes; the mother catering for her family will appreciate the menus and recipes for meals that are both satisfying and nourishing; the hostess will find helpful advice on entertaining; and for the housekeeper there are notes on storing food, and full instructions in all branches of preserving.

The recipes in this edition have been carefully revised, and new ones added. The chapter on Iced and Decorated Cakes is considerably augmented, with many original ideas for party cakes—a subject of interest to every hostess. Other sections in which additional recipes and information are given include Herbs and Spices, Home-made Wines, and the use of Wine in Cookery. In response to numerous requests, entirely new chapters have been added on Vegetarian Cookery and on Diet and Weight, which includes menus and recipes for slimming and fattening.

Good Housekeeping recipes are easy to follow, every step being fully described. The ingredients are clearly set out at the head of the recipes in the order in which they are to be used. As a rule the quantities given are suitable for a family of three or four, but the recipes can usually be adapted for smaller or larger numbers; in many cases alternative versions are given, one using plain and the other richer ingredients. The very extensive Index not only makes it easy to find any recipe or information, but also gives many new ideas for planning daily meals (see page 576).

The black-and-white plates are arranged in a complete 64-page section, following on page 560 of the book. This is to facilitate easy reference to the pictures, the marginal numbers against the recipes corresponding to the plate numbers in this pictorial supplement. Colour plates, which are a characteristic feature of all Good Housekeeping publications, appear throughout the book. Line drawings and decorations for chapter headings and tailpieces are by Fred Reeves and Douglas Woodall.

You can use Good Housekeeping's Cookery Book with every confidence; it is the outcome of thirty years of experience and research in Good Housekeeping Institute kitchens. Here recipes are tested, new ideas tried out, and highly trained experts are continually conducting experiments, not only with new food products, but also with the most up-to-date kitchen equipment. The Good Housekeeping Seal of Guarantee is awarded only to manufacturers of domestic equipment and products which fulfil the high standard required by the Institute. (See chapter on Cookers and Cooking Tools.)

The Institute exists to serve all readers of Good Housekeeping magazine and books, hundreds of enquiries being answered daily. If, therefore, you have any cooking or catering problems, write to the Institute at 30 Grosvenor Gardens, London, S.W.1, and our Staff will gladly give you any help or advice you need.

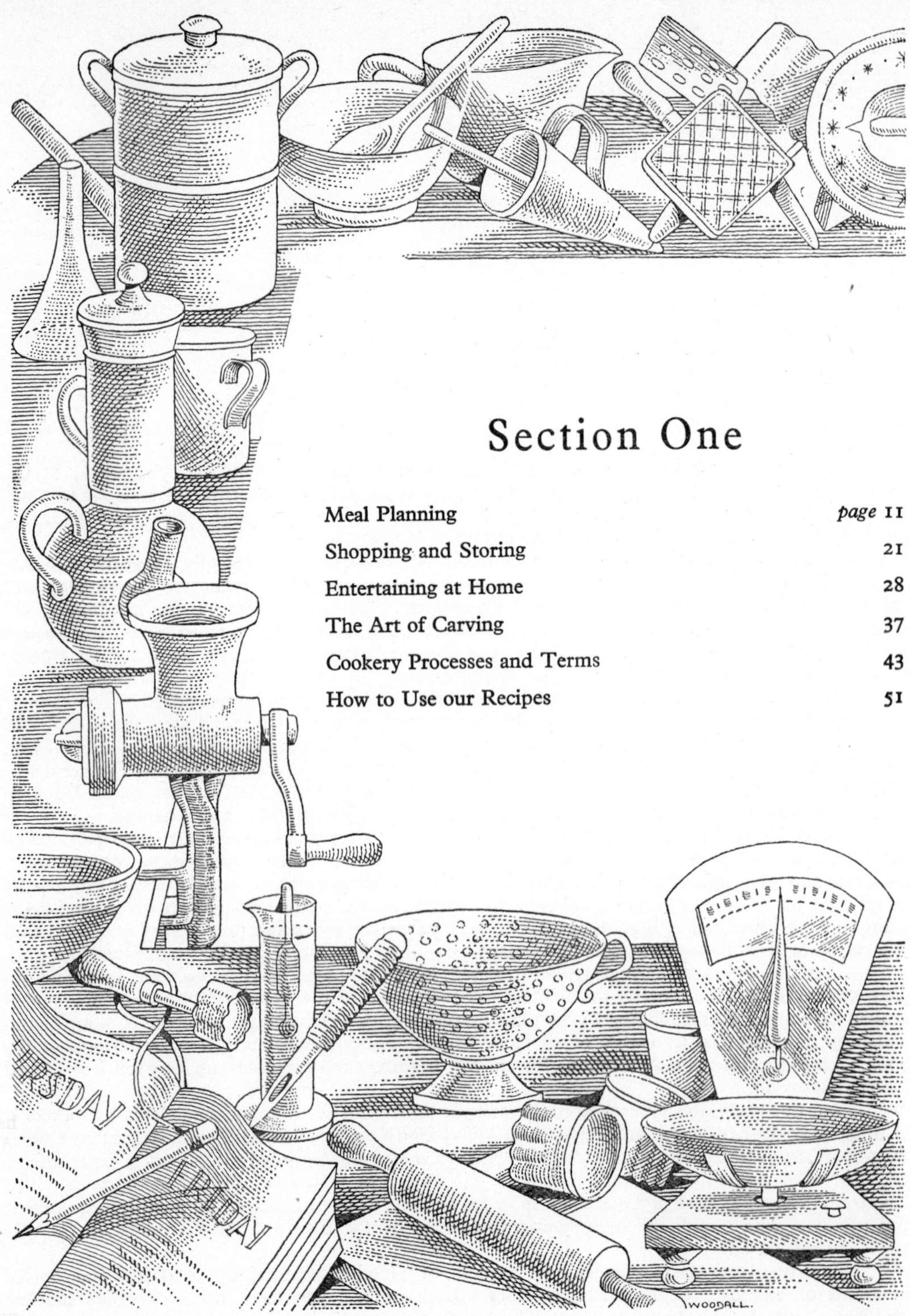

Section One

MEAL PLANNING

Planning family meals, day in, day out, and often doing the shopping and cooking the food as well, is a big task, especially when the housewife is single-handed. But it can be enjoyable too. Indeed, every housewife who finds it an inevitable part of her daily work should set out to study the subject carefully, so that she may make it a pleasure rather than a burden.

One aim must be to avoid monotony, for monotonous meals are both boring for the cook and disappointing for the family. Admittedly, variety is more difficult to achieve where cost has to be a prime consideration, but even thrifty meals, prepared from the simplest ingredients, can be varied and interesting if they are carefully thought out, well cooked and attractively served. Foodstuffs should be bought when they are at their cheapest and best—a watchful eye kept on market prices, enabling the housewife to take advantage of any drop in price of some normally expensive item, makes it possible to include a wide variety of foods, while yet keeping within a moderate budget. Ideas gleaned when dining with friends or in restaurants or when travelling, and suggestions from cookery books, all help to provide new ways of serving foods ; a notebook kept handy for jotting down any new ideas as they occur, will ensure that they are not forgotten.

The kind of meals served in any home must be influenced by the tastes and special circumstances of the family, and by nutritional considerations, but the housewife must also bear in mind the time and help she has available ; if these are small, it is all the more important that the meals should be carefully planned. She must strike a balance between, on the one hand, over-simplifying the catering to the extent of not providing a well-balanced diet, and on the other hand attempting so ambitious a programme that she becomes overwhelmed, tired and disheartened. This applies also to entertaining : a simple but well chosen and perfectly cooked meal, served in a calm, unruffled manner, is far more enjoyable than would-be elaborate dishes, and a flustered, exhausted hostess.

Some people find it easiest to plan the whole week's meals at the beginning of each week, writing down the main items of the menus. This practice can indeed be very helpful, especially where there is a cook, or when shopping facilities are very limited, though it might well prove an impracticable method, more tiresome than time-saving. It is wise, however, to plan the family meals for at least two or three days ahead, and such a plan, whether the menus are written down or just carried in the head, can be enormously helpful, simplifying shopping, saving anxiety and making things easier for the cook. There is no need, of course, to adhere rigidly to the planned menus—in fact, flexibility is important, for circumstances often change, making it necessary to rearrange the meals or alter them completely.

FOOD VALUES

Absorbing though the science of food and nutrition is to those who have time to study it the housewife's day is far too short for " counting calories "—nor is this necessary. But she should realise her responsibility towards her family, and she can do much towards keeping them in good health by feeding them properly. A deficiency or lack of balance in the diet soon shows its ill effects on health—constipation, pimples, headache, lassitude, sleeplessness and dental decay are a few of the disorders often attributable to a faulty diet, while a real lack or shortage of one of the dietary essentials can lead to serious deficiency diseases.

The housewife ought to know, therefore, in terms of the food she handles, what the body needs and where to find it, and then to ensure that the meals she plans and serves to her family are well balanced.

Proteins

Protein is the material that makes and repairs body tissue, and is therefore of particular importance for growing children, though rather less so for adults.

The principal sources are animal foods, i.e., meat, fish, eggs, milk, cheese; also some vegetables, notably pulses, e.g., peas, beans, lentils, and nuts. Protein of a vegetable type also occurs in whole-grain cereals.

Fats

These give heat and energy and are particularly necessary in cold weather.

The principal sources are butter, margarine, cheese, milk (also cream), cooking fats, bacon, fat meat, oily fish and fish liver oils, nuts and nut oils, olive oil.

Carbohydrates

Starchy foods and sugars come under this heading, and they too give heat and energy. The principal sources are :

1. Farinaceous foods, which include flour (and therefore bread, cakes, biscuits), cereals of all kinds, potatoes and pulses.

2. Sugars, which include honey, jam, marmalade, syrup, treacle, sweets and chocolate, sweet fruits and some root vegetables, e.g., beetroots.

Mineral Salts

These salts, often known as the " regulating " substances, are essential constituents of the blood and are necessary in the formation of healthy teeth and bones. The chief ones are :

Calcium, obtained from milk, cheese, green vegetables and fish (especially if the bones are eaten, as with tinned salmon and sardines). Nowadays flour is " fortified " with calcium salts.

Iron, obtained from liver, meat, egg yolks, beans, wholemeal bread, peas.

Chlorine : the body obtains most of the necessary chlorine from common salt. Most people do not need more salt than is contained in prepared foods—the actual need depends in part on the daily consumption of water.

Iodine : this element is essential to health; it is particularly important in adolescence and pregnancy; shortage of it leads to glandular abnormalities. Iodine occurs in milk and vegetables, and table salt sold in this country is now iodised.

Vitamins

Though present in food in minute quantities, these substances play a vital part in promoting and maintaining good health.

Vitamin A maintains a healthy condition of the mucous membranes, also of the skin, glands, and teeth, and is necessary for normal growth, development and eyesight. Deficiency sometimes results in loss of appetite, frequent colds and other infections.

The principal sources are carrots, spinach, tomato, kidney, watercress, dried apricots, prunes, butter, margarine, egg, milk and canned fish.

Vitamin B (i.e., the Vitamin B complex, including Vitamins B_1, B_2, etc.), is necessary for promoting and maintaining good general health, for normal appetite and digestion, and for good condition of the nervous system.

The principal sources are yeast and yeast extracts, whole-grain cereals and wheat-grain preparations, liver and other internal organs, lean meat (particularly pork), egg yolk, milk, vegetables (including pulses), nuts and fruits.

Vitamin C increases resistance to infection, and maintains a healthy condition of the skin (in a deficiency, wounds are slow to heal), improves circulation, the condition of the gums and other body tissues. Dental decay is less likely to occur.

The principal sources are fresh vegetables and fruits, but the distribution is uneven. The following fruits are good sources of this vitamin : black-currants, orange juice concentrate, rose-hip syrup, oranges, strawberries, lemon juice, gooseberries and other soft fruits. Green vegetables are particularly rich in Vitamin C, especially sprouts, turnip tops, cauliflower, spinach, watercress; nasturtium leaves and stems add considerably to the Vitamin C content of a salad.

On the other hand, some fruits and vegetables are of little value, e.g., some apples, cherries, the plum family, grapes, apricots, peaches, pears and vegetables such as lettuce, cucumber, beetroot, French beans, carrots, onions, parsnips, marrow and celery, etc.

Vitamin D directly influences the structure of bones and teeth, ensuring the proper utilisation of calcium and phosphates. It is thought also to help in maintaining general good health.

The principal sources are fish liver oils, oily fish, egg yolk, butter (and vitamin-enriched margarine). It can also be manufactured in the body by the action of sunlight and ultra-violet light on the skin.

Roughage

Roughage is the name given to the fibrous part of foods, which is not ordinarily digested (such as fruit peel, vegetable fibres, and grain husks) but which, though it does not provide energy, is of great importance in supplying the necessary bulk. Much constipation is due to insufficient quantities of roughage in the diet. Under modern conditions the tendency is to over-refine foodstuffs, particularly cereals, and this may result in too small a bulk for the efficient working of the lower intestine.

Water

Adequate water is just as essential for health as proper food. It is necessary for building and repairing body tissues; for the normal action of body functions; for regulating body temperature, carrying food and removing waste products.

For temperate climates a daily intake of about 5 pints is generally considered the right amount. Much of this will be taken in the form of cooked dishes, as well as raw fruits and vegetables, which always contain a large percentage of water.

PROVIDING A WELL-BALANCED DIET

1. See that each day's meals contain an adequate amount of protein foods. The average adult requires approximately 70 grammes (i.e., 2½ oz.) of protein in one day. The following assortment of foods gives approximately the day's requirement:

1 egg	1 pint milk
1 oz. cheese	½ lb. bread
4 oz. meat or fish	

2. Avoid very starchy meals; if pastry is served in a main meal, cut out steamed puddings, rice, spaghetti, etc., from the same meal. For example, beefsteak and kidney pie should be served with, say, spring greens and swedes, and followed by a light sweet such as fruit and junket or a similar dish, rather than by a steamed pudding or pastry. Again, a sweet such as steamed pudding or a pastry dish should be preceded by a first course low in starch, for example, meat stew or curry with the usual vegetables.

Tea tends to be a starchy meal, so balance it by serving such items as tomato or salad sandwiches; a dish of watercress, celery or radishes (with bread and butter); fresh fruit in season, or a fruit flan or tartlets as an alternative to cake. This meal is best omitted or at least reduced to very small portions for adults who have a tendency to put on weight; it is of value chiefly for active children who expend a considerable amount of energy.

3. During cold weather allow plenty of fats in the diet, but remember that the body cannot make proper use of fat unless sufficient sugar is taken in the diet. (Hence the habit of serving apple sauce with pork or goose, jam or marmalade with bread and butter, lemon juice or vinegar with fried foods, tomatoes with bacon.) So see that the meals are well-balanced from this point of view—a diet which is too rich in fat, or without adequate sugar, may cause biliousness.

4. Include some raw salad plants or vegetables each day (either in salads or as a garnish to cooked dishes, or in sandwich fillings, etc.), to ensure an adequate supply of Vitamins A and C and mineral salts. Two servings daily are ideal, in addition to cooked vegetables, which should be included at least once a day. Be sure to cook vegetables carefully so as to conserve the maximum vitamin content.

Serve raw fruit daily when this is available, particularly the citrus fruits and other fruits rich in Vitamin C. Tinned, bottled and frozen foods are good too, but it must be remembered that dried fruits do not contribute Vitamin C to the diet. They are, however, useful when fresh fruits are not available.

5. Start the day with a good breakfast, especially in the winter.

6. Include as much variety as possible in the menu. This makes the meals more interesting and consequently of greater value—for food that is enjoyed is more readily digested.

NOTES ON MENU PLANNING

1. Always serve dishes with their correct accompaniments. There is usually a good reason for the food habits that have grown up and become established, and combining the right ingredients brings out the flavour of the food and helps to make the meal digestible. For example, mint sauce with roast lamb or red-currant jelly with mutton, greatly improves the flavour of the meat, and at the same time, the sugar in the sauce helps to balance the meat fat. Again, a dressing, generally containing oil and vinegar, is served with salad; not only does this improve the flavour of the salad, but also the oil in the dressing aids in the absorption of the Vitamin A contained in the salad plants.

2. The character, texture and flavour of the dishes served in any meal should contrast—this makes the meal more appetising and easier to digest. Generally speaking, a "wet" course should follow a "dry" one or vice versa; for example, a crisp fried main dish preceded by soup and followed with a creamy sweet would be a happy choice, whereas soup, followed by stew and finishing with fruit and custard would be too liquid to be really appetising. By the same token, a meal such as meat pasties with vegetables, followed by apple charlotte, finishing with cheese and biscuits, would be unappetisingly dry and stodgy. A sauce should always be served with a "dry" dish (e.g., fish cakes, rissoles, etc.), and conversely, a crisper ingredient should accompany a "wet" or very soft dish, for example, a crisp green salad with macaroni cheese, croûtons with a cream soup, toast with mince.

So far as flavour is concerned, something piquant should be served with a dish that is very bland, as in the case of Hollandaise sauce with turbot, lemon sauce with steamed sponge pudding, or with one that is very rich, as in the case of mustard sauce with fried or grilled herrings. On the other hand, something smooth and bland is a good accompaniment for sharp or piquant dishes—custard with stewed fruit, and boiled rice with curry.

3. Colour, too, should be considered so that the meal may be made interesting in appearance, for if it appeals to the eye, it will be eaten with more relish than if it looks unappetising, however well-balanced and skilfully cooked it may be. A dish of fried or grilled chops with chipped potatoes (or with new potatoes tossed in butter and a little chopped parsley), with grilled tomatoes and sprigs of watercress, makes a combination which would never fail to delight the eye, and is also delicious to eat. The same dish—chops—is equally good served with creamed potatoes and cauliflower with white sauce, but this combination will tend to be unappetising in colour unless garnished with, say, parsley on the potatoes, a little paprika pepper on the cauliflower and possibly a slice or so of tomato with the chops.

Whenever possible, ingredients that are similar in colour should not be served at the same meal, but if for any reason this is unavoidable, some other item should be included to give colour interest. For example, creamed fish with marrow and potatoes, though they make an appetising combination, might look very anaemic if plainly dished, but quite interesting with a garnish of lemon fans, small sprigs of parsley and coralline pepper.

MEALS FOR GROWING CHILDREN

Sound nutrition in childhood is a safeguard to health and happiness in adult life. Growing children need plenty of protein and vitamin foods to build up new tissues for growth and to supply the energy they expend so freely in all their activities. A child of 7–9 years requires as much as a woman, and the child of 10–12 years needs as much as a man; over this age, the adolescent requirement is greater than for adults.

Meals of the well-balanced family type are suitable, but foods should be simply cooked, by methods which preserve their full goodness. Fried foods delay the action of digestion and are therefore best avoided for children who have delicate stomachs. Some raw food should be given to children every day, and they must learn to chew hard foods thoroughly, so that their jaws and teeth develop and food is fully digested. Toast, rusks, crusts, raw apples, nuts and celery give good opportunities for chewing.

Serve meals as attractively as possible and give food in small helpings, so that children get into the habit of eating up all their food without toying with it. They should be encouraged to ask for a second helping as desired. Meals should be served regularly at the same time each day, and no food should be given between meals, though a snack such as a glass of milk is generally necessary in the middle of the morning, to bridge the gap between breakfast and dinner, but this, like other meals, should be given regularly.

[*continued on page* 19

FAMILY MENUS FOR ONE WEEK IN EACH SEASON OF THE YEAR

The menus which follow are intended merely as a guide to the planning of well-balanced meals during the four seasons of the year; they are, of course, subject to adaptation to individual taste and circumstances. Some of the menus show lunch and supper, and some lunch and dinner, to cater for different types of households. Although it is the custom nowadays for many people to have a very light tea, in some households this meal is important (particularly in families with growing children) and suggestions for tea are therefore included in the menus.

It is taken for granted that toast and marmalade and coffee or tea are served at breakfast, and tea to drink at tea-time.

SPRING MENUS

Breakfast	*Lunch*	*Tea*	*Supper*
	SUNDAY		
Cereal Boiled Eggs	Roast Chicken Ham Bread Sauce Potatoes Spring Greens Rhubarb Tart Custard	Chocolate Sponge Sandwich	Glazed Beef Loaf Sauté Potatoes Salad Prune Mould
	MONDAY		
Fruit Bacon Fried Bread	Cold Chicken and Ham Potatoes Salad Steamed Sponge Pudding Jam Sauce	Savoury Sandwiches Chocolate Sandwich	Risotto Green Salad Canton Cream
	TUESDAY		
Cereal Ham	Meat Croquettes Chipped Potatoes Spinach Gooseberry Fool	Batch Cakes	Chicken Soup Cheese Charlotte Salad
	WEDNESDAY		
Fruit Bacon	Stuffed Breast of Lamb Potatoes Sprouting Broccoli Baked Fruit Sponge Custard	Scones Sponge Sandwich	Stuffed Eggs Salad Bakewell Tart
	THURSDAY		
Fruit Scrambled Eggs	Liver and Bacon Potatoes Asparagus Coffee Junket	Sandwiches and Radishes Sponge Sandwich	Shepherd's Pie Salad Milk Pudding
	FRIDAY		
Cereal Grilled Tomatoes on Toast	Fried Fillets of Fish Potatoes Spring Greens Chocolate Mould	Lettuce Sandwiches Gingerbread	Scotch Eggs Salad Stewed Fruit Custard
	SATURDAY		
Fish Cakes	Beef Roll Potatoes Young Carrots and Turnips Syrup Tart	Sandwiches Gingerbread	Macaroni Cheese Tomato Salad Trifle

SUMMER MENUS

Breakfast	Lunch	Tea	Dinner
	SUNDAY		
Fried Eggs and Bacon	Roast Loin of Lamb Mint Sauce New Potatoes Green Peas Cherry Pie Custard	Tomato and Cucumber Sandwiches Strawberries and Cream	Salmon Mayonnaise Salad Fruit Cream Biscuits
	MONDAY		
Cereal Scrambled Eggs	Fish Cakes Parsley Sauce Potatoes Jam Tart	Cress Sandwiches Fresh Raspberries	Cold Lamb Mint Sauce New Potatoes Green Salad Caramel Custard
	TUESDAY		
Bacon and Fried Tomatoes	Pork Pie Salad Fruit Fool	Egg and Cress Sandwiches	Fricassee of Veal Young Carrots and Potatoes Summer Pudding
	WEDNESDAY		
Kippers	Grilled Ham Tomatoes Potato Crisps Ice Cream Biscuits	Sandwiches Fresh Fruit	Lamb Cutlets New Potatoes Peas Green Salad Fruit Salad
	THURSDAY		
Fruit Tomatoes on Toast	Steamed Cod Egg Sauce Potatoes Steamed Jam Sponge	Salad Sandwiches	Braised Tongues Potatoes Spinach Black-currant Tart
	FRIDAY		
Cereal Fish Cakes	Baked Stuffed Marrow Potatoes Salad Milk Pudding	Tomato Sandwiches Fresh Cherries	Mince and Toast Croûtons Potatoes Runner Beans Welsh Rarebit
	SATURDAY		
Cereal Kidneys on Toast	Hot Salmon Parsley Sauce New Potatoes Green Peas	Cucumber Sandwiches Fruit	Cheese and Vegetable Flan Salad Chocolate Soufflé

AUTUMN MENUS

	Breakfast	*Lunch*	*Tea*	*Supper*
SUNDAY	Tomato Omelette	Roast Shoulder of Mutton Onion Sauce Roast Potatoes Artichokes Plum Tart Cream or Custard	Anchovy Toast Watercress Raisin Cake	Liver Pâté Salad Chocolate Trifle
MONDAY	Fruit Bacon and Sauté Potatoes	Cold Mutton Creamed Potatoes Salad Pancakes	Tomato Sandwiches Raisin Cake	Cauliflower au Gratin Potatoes Bakewell Tart
TUESDAY	Cereal Mushrooms on Toast	Baked Stuffed Marrow Potatoes Gravy Rice Pudding Stewed Fruit	Almond Tartlets	Poached Egg on Toast Green Salad Coffee Junket
WEDNESDAY	Fruit Bacon and Tomatoes	Boiled Ham Parsley Sauce Spinach Potatoes Castle Puddings Jam Sauce	Paste Sandwiches Watercress Chocolate Cake	Celery Soup Cheese Salad Apple Turnover
THURSDAY	Porridge Kippers	Cold Ham Baked Potatoes Salad Baked Apples Custard	Gingerbread Chocolate Cake	Stuffed Onions Curly Kale Lemon Meringue Pudding
FRIDAY	Porridge Ham	Baked Fish Tomatoes Creamed Potatoes Baked Fruit Sponge Pudding Custard	Gingerbread Swiss Roll	Shepherd's Pie Parsnips Fresh Plums
SATURDAY	Fruit Scrambled Eggs	Liver and Bacon Potatoes Cabbage Steamed Chocolate Pudding Chocolate Sauce	Scotch Pancakes Swiss Roll	Fish Cakes Parsley Sauce Chipped Potatoes Fruit Salad

WINTER MENUS

	Breakfast	*Lunch*	*Tea*	*Dinner*
SUNDAY	Omelette Sauté Potatoes	Roast Pork Apple Sauce Sage and Onion Stuffing Roast Potatoes Brussels Sprouts Lemon Curd Tart	Muffins Chocolate Shortbread	Cheese Charlotte Watercress Beetroot Stewed Fruit Cream
MONDAY	Cereal Scrambled Eggs	Macaroni Cheese Macedoine of Vegetables Fruit Jelly	Buttered Toast Watercress Shortbread	Ox-tail Soup Cold Roast Pork Potatoes Salad Apple Dumplings
TUESDAY	Bacon and Fried Potato Cake	Meat Pasty Sauté Potatoes Beetroot Apple Charlotte	Scones	Beefsteak Pudding Sprouts Carrots Stewed Prunes Blancmange
WEDNESDAY	Porridge Bacon Fritters	Welsh Rarebit Salad Hot Chocolate Semolina Cream	Toasted Teacakes	Liver à la Française Sprouts (or Sprout Tops) Potatoes Apple Tart Custard
THURSDAY	Porridge Liver Pâté	Grilled Sausages Mashed Potatoes Cabbage Jam or Syrup Tart	Currant Bread Jam Sponge Sandwich	Curried Breast of Mutton Potatoes Spinach Queen of Puddings
FRIDAY	Bacon and Scrambled Egg	Grilled Cutlets Sauté Potatoes Peas Black-currant Pudding	Dripping Toast Watercress Sponge Sandwich	Tomato Soup Fried Fillets of Fish Chipped Potatoes Mushrooms Watercress Caramel Custard
SATURDAY	Fish and Potato Scallops	Braised Ox-tail Carrots Potatoes Sultana Pudding Custard Sauce	Iced Buns	Spaghetti with Tomato and Cheese Salad Baked Apples

continued from page 14]
Sweets eaten just before a meal take away the appetite for other foods essential to health.

Nursery meals should be leisurely and happy; good manners and self-reliance are developed at mealtimes, but they should be quietly encouraged and the necessary corrections made calmly.

Meat and Fish

All flesh foods are suitable for children, but those with a high proportion of fat are digested more slowly. Boys and girls over the age of 12 need more meat than men. For very young children, cut meat up small or mince it.

Liver is a very valuable food, and can be given either lightly fried or cooked in a casserole. Stewed sweetbreads and tripe are good too. Kidney is rather less easily digested, but can be given to the older child.

White fish steamed in water or milk is popular with most children. Herrings and sprats have good food value and can be given to children, and, if boned and broken up, to toddlers.

Milk, Butter and Margarine

A pint of milk a day should be regarded as the minimum for children, but a child that likes more and can tolerate it without having any digestive upsets, should be encouraged to have as much as possible, for most of the leading nutritionists consider a quart of milk a day per child none too much for health. The toddler should be given the specially graded milks, but if this is not possible, boil the milk until he is at least three years old.

Butter and margarine are very valuable foods and should be given freely.

Eggs and Cheese

Eggs are a valuable food, and any child above the age of one year should be able to enjoy a whole egg two or three times a week. This is best given lightly boiled, poached, coddled or scrambled. Fried eggs should be cooked gently, without toughening the edges, and a child of four or five will probably like them very much.

Most children like cheese, and it is a good protein and calcium food. Give it thinly sliced or grated in sandwiches, on biscuits or rye crispbread or with salad. Cooked cheese in concentrated form is not easily digested, but the older child usually likes it in dishes such as macaroni cheese and cauliflower cheese. Cream cheese is good to use from quite an early age as a filling for sandwiches.

Bread, Cakes, etc.

White and wholemeal bread should both be included in the diet. Cakes and biscuits should be given sparingly, and bought ones should always be of a good standard quality. Rye or wheat crispbread makes a good alternative to the more usual sweet biscuit, and children usually like it if it is buttered.

Jams, Honey and Syrup

These give easily absorbed sugars and are therefore useful as sources of energy. They can be given at tea and breakfast with other foods. If the diet contains a high proportion of these foods, however, it is important to have a plentiful supply of foods containing vitamin B_1, such as pork, bacon, potatoes, mutton, eggs, milk, peas, and beans, lentils, spinach and cabbage, and offal, when available.

Vegetables, Fruit and Tomatoes

Spring greens, cabbages, sprouts, savoys, cauliflowers and spinach are all good provided they are not over-cooked. Raw cabbage, lettuce and watercress can be used in salads or to fill sandwiches.

Carrots, turnips and swedes are all useful; carrots are especially valuable for their Vitamin A content—they can be given either cooked or raw. Onions and leeks must be given with discretion. Celery is another acquired taste, but many young children like it, especially a nice, crisp, crunchy piece to eat raw.

Children under a year old need to have their vegetables sieved, but once they are over this age, it is wise to stop sieving and to give vegetables either cooked and mashed, or root vegetables raw and grated.

Oranges and grapefruit are good fruit for children to have, and can be given without any special precaution except that of removing the skin and pips. Apples, either raw or cooked, are good, especially Bramley Seedlings, and stewed apple and custard or junket make an excellent second course at dinner-time. A piece of raw apple at the end of each meal helps to keep the teeth clean. Bananas are usually popular, but they must be ripe, without any traces of green on the skin; it is often best to serve them mashed to make them more easily digested. Strawberries and gooseberries are also permissible, but must be given carefully to the very young child, and sieved if necessary, to remove the pips.

Tomatoes are a valuable source of Vitamin A and C and can be given raw or cooked. Here again, it may be necessary to skin and sieve for very young children.

Drinks

The main drink of a child should be water, or fruit drinks, for milk really ranks as a food and has already been considered. Always allow the tap to run well before filling the jug or cup, to make sure the water is fresh. Water can be given between meals, and is especially necessary if a child is constipated or when the weather is warm. A child needs about three tumblers full of water every day, with or without fruit juice.

If a child dislikes milk, weak tea, made with half milk and half water, is a good alternative.

Cocoa and patent drinks made with milk are good foods, but do not quench the thirst.

MEALS FOR THE EXPECTANT MOTHER

When a woman is going to have a baby, she needs a simple, well-balanced diet of fresh, natural foods, particularly those rich in vitamins and minerals. Also she needs extra amounts of the body-building foods such as milk, eggs, meat and fish—more than those needed by a man who is actively employed. She should take a liberal supply of vegetables (especially plenty of leafy greens), with salads and fruits in season. The foods should be fresh, and quite simply cooked, and the meals eaten at leisure.

As a rule there is no need for her to have different dishes from the rest of the family, so long as she remembers that plain foods and simple methods of cooking are best for her and substitutes a simple dish for herself when the meal includes fried or highly seasoned foods, or any other indigestible item. Also, she must be careful to see that her portions include extra meat, eggs, fish and milk.

Fresh green vegetables supply Vitamins A and C (some also contain B) and mineral salts; eating such vegetables daily is the most natural way of helping to avoid constipation. Salads should be included freely in the diet: parsley sandwiches, watercress or lettuce with bread and butter for tea, or a green salad for lunch or supper give an additional daily supply of green vegetables. Salads should be eaten in winter and summer, as well as cooked vegetables. Root vegetables should, of course, be included daily, for they also contain valuable vitamins and mineral salts and help in preventing constipation.

The following should be avoided: twice-cooked vegetables or over-cooked meat, stodgy puddings, too much pastry or batter, fried foods, too highly seasoned dishes, vinegar, spices, onions, alcohol, foods that are not easily digested, such as shell fish or any other food that seems to disagree in a particular case.

The expectant mother will probably find that she takes more liquids than usual. This is as it should be, provided that she cuts out strong tea and coffee and alcohol.

Meal-Planning Guide

Meat: Eat more meat than usual, supplementing it when possible with internal meats (liver, kidney, etc.). Liver is especially valuable. A normal healthy woman requires extra body-building proteins during pregnancy—the doctor will say if it should become necessary to cut down these items.

Fish: Include fish two or three times a week. For one of the meals use an oily fish such as herring, mackerel or salmon (fresh or tinned).

Cheese: Make full use of cheese, both raw and lightly cooked. It is a valuable source of the much-needed calcium.

Eggs: Eggs may be taken in many ways—fresh eggs poached, boiled or scrambled for breakfast; in omelettes, baked custards and so on for lunch or supper.

Milk: Set aside a daily allowance of 1 pint or more for drinking, and use plenty in cooking.

Fats: Eat a liberal allowance of butter or margarine. Cod liver oil or halibut liver oil must also be taken, as it is difficult to include enough Vitamin A or D in the diet, unless the fat intake is high.

Vegetables: Allow a plentiful supply of all vegetables, both raw and cooked. Take cooked green vegetables once daily, or twice daily if salad is not included. Serve potatoes twice daily, and other root vegetables once daily. Have salads at least once daily in the summer, and include them frequently during the colder months of the year. Serve watercress or lettuce for tea. Sprinkle freshly chopped parsley liberally on savoury dishes and in soups.

Fruit: Take plenty of fresh fruits and tomatoes when in season and drink orange juice every day.

Bread: Wholemeal is important because of its roughage, but white bread should be included for contrast and variety of flavour.

SHOPPING AND STORING

The money spent on food is the most important part of the total housekeeping expenditure. When starting housekeeping for the first time, it is well to keep the food budget flexible for a few weeks; then, by keeping careful accounts, it can be seen how much is needed per week for the different items, and the allowance can be planned accordingly. Having set aside an adequate sum to be spent on food, aim at getting the best possible value for money while keeping within the budget.

It is obviously wise to deal with reliable tradespeople whose goods are of sound quality. You will find it worth while taking the trouble to compare the quality and price of food in the different shops in the district, bearing in mind that it is false economy to buy inferior food in order to save a few pence. It is worth while to get acquainted with the shopkeepers: they soon become interested, get to know one's likes and dislikes, and give better service.

BUYING AND STORING GROCERIES

It is a wise plan to keep a small nucleus of dry stores on hand in case of emergencies, as well as a reasonable supply of tinned and packaged goods, preserves and so on. A complete list of dry stores in common use is given in this chapter, and this will serve as a guide when ordering groceries. You may also like to keep a few delicacies in reserve, so when visiting the grocer's look round for any interesting or unusual foods to put aside for special occasions.

The quantities to buy will naturally vary according to the size and needs of the household. If there are adequate facilities for storing, the supply of cereals and grains should be sufficient, say, for 1–2 months. Whole-grain cereals, such as wholemeal flour and oatmeal, contain a fairly high proportion of fat, and therefore do not keep very well, so do not attempt to store them longer than 2 months. (For other details, see list of dry stores.)

The Store Cupboard and Pantry

As these groceries are for the most part dry, deterioration during storage is not a serious consideration. They must, however, be protected from heat and damp and from attack by weevils and mites. The store cupboard, therefore, should be cool, dry and well-ventilated.

There should be a cupboard in the kitchen for stores in daily use, and this should be placed in a convenient position near the working table and away from steam and heat. Ideally, jars should be arranged in single rows; in any case, not more than two deep. Much time is wasted when stores are not easy to see at a glance. Single rows of jars also make it possible for the shelves to be placed closer together. Plastic or glass storage jars are excellent for cereals, grains, dried fruits and so on, as they enable one to see at a glance how much there is in stock. They should, of course, have lids, but for these stores it is not necessary for the containers to be airtight (except in the case of biscuits, coffee, baking powder and salt); in fact, ventilation is desirable for these foods. Smaller glass jars with well-fitting lids are good for spices and herbs, and enamel bins for flour and bread. Containers with tightly fitting lids should be used for biscuits and cakes—either tins or the plastic containers which are now available.

Keep reserve stores in a cool, dry, well-ventilated pantry or cupboard with fairly wide shelves. If there is no window, there should be a ventilator and good artificial light. The shelves should be lined with waxed shelf-paper or special plastic adhesive covering, laminated plastic or linoleum. All of these can be easily wiped down, and they are obtainable in many attractive designs and colours. A stool for reaching the higher shelves and a pencil and pad for noting replenishments are useful.

LIST OF DRY STORES

FLOURS AND RAISING AGENTS

Plain Flour is generally considered best for the richer type of cakes and for pastry, and should always be used for sauces, gravies, etc. The white (or fortified) flours keep well, but the darker (or high-extraction) flours if stored for too long are subject to attack by weevils and mites and tend to become musty on long storage, so they should not be kept for more than a month or two.

Self-Raising Flour : Handy for puddings and cakes which require baking powder as a raising agent, since this is included in this type of flour. Buy and use as required and keep perfectly dry, otherwise the flour's raising properties will be impaired.

Wholemeal Flour : Useful on account of its food value. Finely milled wholemeal flour can replace white flour in most recipes ; the coarser varieties can be mixed with a proportion of white flour. Buy wholemeal in small quantities only and use within a few weeks—the fat contained in it goes rancid on prolonged keeping.

Baking Powder : Buy in fairly small quantities and keep tightly covered ; on no account allow it to get damp, or its raising properties will be destroyed.

Bicarbonate of Soda ; Cream of Tartar : Useful in addition to baking powder. Buy in small quantities and label clearly.

CEREALS AND PULSES

Barley (pearl barley and barley meal).
Beans (haricot and butter).
Cornflour, custard powder.
Lentils.
Macaroni, spaghetti, vermicelli.
Oatmeal (fine, medium, coarse, rolled oats).
Peas (dried and split).
Rice and ground rice.
Sago.
Semolina.
Tapioca (large, seed).

These cereals and pulses being dry, keep in good condition for several months (with the exception of oatmeal). However, since they are subject to attack by weevils and mites and will mould and become musty if allowed to get damp, it is not advisable to store them for indefinite periods. Oatmeal contains fat and becomes rancid on prolonged storage, so it should be bought in small quantities and used within a few weeks.

SUGARS

Sugars will keep in good condition indefinitely so long as they are kept dry (this applies particularly to icing sugar, which forms hard lumps if allowed to get damp).

Granulated Sugar : For general cooking and sweetening purposes.

Caster Sugar : For cooking purposes where a fine sugar is preferable (e.g., in creamed mixtures), and for table use.

Loaf Sugar : Convenient for table use.

Icing Sugar : Buy good quality icing sugar, and keep it tightly covered, which will help to prevent lumps forming.

Brown Sugars : Unrefined sugars containing a varying percentage of molasses. They include Demerara sugar, which is light in colour with coarse crystals ; soft brown sugar (sugar " pieces "), also light in colour, but with a very fine crystal, and Barbadoes sugar, which is very dark in colour, with fairly fine crystals and a pronounced treacly flavour.

Brown sugars are useful for gingerbreads and plum cakes, and for puddings (such as steamed puddings, apple charlotte and so on), and are preferred to white sugar by many people for sprinkling on porridge and such dishes.

SYRUPS

Syrups will keep in good condition for several months, but tend to crystallise if stored indefinitely, particularly in the case of clear honey.

Golden Syrup : Good for both cooking purposes and table use.

Black Treacle : For gingerbreads, rich fruit cakes and puddings, treacle toffee, etc.

Honey : Obtainable clear or crystallised. Chiefly for table use, but employed occasionally in cooking.

DRIED FRUITS

Currants, sultanas, raisins (seedless and Valencia).
Candied peel, glacé cherries.
Prunes, apricots, figs, dates.

Under ideal conditions, dried fruits keep well, but are liable to ferment if allowed to get damp, while a warm, dry atmosphere will cause them to wither unduly ; so use within 2–3 months—do not store for indefinite periods.

NUTS

Almonds (whole and ground).
Hazelnuts, pistachio nuts, walnuts.
Coconut.

Nuts contain oil and so become rancid on prolonged storage. Keep cool and dry, and use within a few weeks.

COLOURINGS, FLAVOURINGS AND DECORATIONS

Almond, vanilla, lemon and other essences.
Angelica.
Block chocolate (sweet and bitter).
Coffee essence.
Colourings (carmine, cochineal, green, etc).
Crystallised fruits, violets, rose leaves.
Mimosa balls, silver balls.

Buy good quality essences and flavourings and use them sparingly. Keep them tightly corked.

HERBS AND SPICES

Allspice.
Bay leaves.
Carraway seeds.
Celery seed.
Cinnamon (stick and powdered).
Cloves (whole and powdered).
Dried herbs (thyme, sage, marjoram, etc.).
Ginger (root and ground).
Mace (blade and powdered).
Mixed spice.

Spices and herbs, should be bought in small quantities and kept tightly covered, or they lose their aroma and flavour.

SEASONINGS

Curry powder and paste.
Mustard (dried, Continental, mustard seeds).
Pepper (white, black, cayenne, coralline, paprika).
Peppercorns (white and black).

Buy these aromatic condiments in small quantities and keep tightly covered.

Salt (table and block) : Keep very dry.

PACKET GOODS

Breakfast cereals (cornflakes, wheatflakes, etc.).
Gelatine (powdered or leaf).
Jellies, creams and other prepared desserts and junket powder or tablets.
Soups.

Keep in a cool, dry place ; do not store for indefinite periods.

BOTTLED GOODS

Anchovies and anchovy essence.
Gravy browning.
Mayonnaise and salad cream.
Olive oil.
Pickles (capers, gherkins, olives, etc.).
Relishes and ketchups.
Rennet essence.
Sauces (table sauce, tomato sauce, piquant sauce).
Vinegars (malt, wine, tarragon, chilli, cider).

It is a good idea to buy in large-sized bottles products which are used frequently, as these are more economical. Buy and use mayonnaise and salad creams as required, as they tend to go rancid on long storage. Do not attempt to store olive oil for long periods and keep it in the dark, since the light tends to hasten rancidity. Buy rennet essence in fairly small quantities and keep very cold.

BEVERAGES

Tea, coffee, cocoa.

Cup chocolate, patent milk drinks : Buy and use as required and keep tightly covered (particularly coffee—see chapter on Hot and Cold Drinks).

Yeast extracts and meat extracts.

PRESERVES

Bottled fruits and vegetables.
Jams and jellies, lemon curd, marmalade, mincemeat.
Pickles and chutneys.

For storage details see chapters on Bottling, Jam Making and Pickling.

TINNED GOODS

Fish (salmon, lobster, crab, sardines, pilchards, etc.).
Fruits (various).
Meats (ham, tongue, corned beef, spiced meat, etc.).
Soups (various).
Vegetables (various, including tomato juice and tomato purée).

Storing Tinned Foods

The life of a tin of food depends not only on the contents but also on the kind of lacquer, if any, used inside the tin, and the temperature and humidity of the storage place. Generally speaking, the quality of the food tinned under modern scientific conditions is very good, and a reputable manufacturer takes care to use sound quality tins and suitable lacquer, so choose good brands and keep them in a cool, dry place ; damp causes rusting, which may eventually lead to perforation.

When a tin of food is bought for storage rather than immediate use, it is a good idea to write the date of purchase on the label.

Tinned fruits : 1 year is the usual time for storing. If kept longer, the food value is not impaired, though the fruit may appear less attractive, but the natural acidity of the fruit may attack any scratch or otherwise damaged parts of the lacquer inside the tin. In this case, a metallic flavour develops and a gas (hydrogen) is produced which will eventually cause the tin to bulge, and the fruit will be very unpalatable if not actually unwholesome.

Honey and *jam* should keep at least 3 years in lacquered tins.

Vegetables will store well for at least 2 years. If kept longer they may become less attractive in appearance, but the food value remains unchanged.

Fish and *meat* will keep in good condition for several years.

Hams present a special problem in food preservation, and the packer's guarantee is usually only 6 months. If, however, after longer storage the tin has not bulged, the contents are usually sound.

Unsweetened evaporated milk keeps in good condition for about 3 years.

Sweetened condensed milk remains unchanged for 6–9 months, after which time it may become sugary, though this is not objectionable.

Dried milk in tins is best used within a few weeks. It tends to form hard lumps and develop a rancid flavour on long storage.

Using Tinned Foods

Always follow the manufacturers' directions given on the tins for heating the contents. It used to be considered advisable to turn the contents of a tin into a glass or earthenware receptacle immediately on opening, but this is not as a rule necessary—foods do not deteriorate more quickly in open tins than in glass or china.

" Blown " tins (i.e., with one or both ends bulging), or leaking tins, should always be discarded. It is unwise to eat the contents of a tin if they have an unusual smell or colour, even though the tin itself appears sound.

BUYING AND STORING PERISHABLE FOODS

Foods such as meat, fish, milk, fats and eggs and so on, are termed " perishable " because changes due to bacterial and enzyme action take place in them on keeping, causing milk to sour, fats to become rancid, and meat, fish and eggs to decompose. The lower the temperature the less bacterial and enzyme activity there will be ; for this reason these foods should, ideally, be stored at a temperature low enough to delay this activity—that is to say, between 42° and 45° F., as in a domestic refrigerator, or failing that, in a cold larder. In any case, a good larder is desirable, in addition to a refrigerator, for storing less perishable foods. No attempt should be made to store perishable foods for a long time, unless a deep-freeze cabinet is available (see next page).

Shopping facilities naturally vary, but whenever conditions allow, stores of bacon, cheese, eggs and fats should be purchased weekly, or twice a week in hot weather, with a small reserve for emergencies. Meat, fish, poultry, fruit and vegetables (except potatoes) should be purchased in fairly small quantities as required.

Meat : Whereas in the shop meat should be hung to allow air to circulate freely, at home, if no refrigerator is available, meat (and fish) should be placed on a grid, with a plate underneath, and covered loosely either with greaseproof paper or with a ventilated meat cover. In no case should meat or fish be left tightly wrapped, nor should they be left standing in their own juices.

Cream, custard, etc., should be kept in jugs or basins and covered to protect them from flies and dust : muslin is suitable for this purpose.

Milk is best kept in the bottle in which it is delivered. When it is stored in a larder it can be kept cooler in hot weather if the bottles are stood in a dish containing water and covered with a wet cloth or muslin (densely woven), the ends of which must be in the water, and the whole placed in a current of air. (Thin, openweave material is not suitable for this purpose, because absorption of the water by the fabric does not keep pace with evaporation, so the material dries and the cooling action ceases.)

Yoghourt, a fermented milk which is reputed to have a beneficial action on harmful toxins in the body, can be used as a beverage, as an accompaniment to fresh or stewed fruit, and in a wide variety of other ways. It should not be heated. It may be obtained plain or flavoured, and may also be made at home from a culture, which in some parts of the country can be delivered weekly. It should not be kept for more than a day or two, and should be stored like ordinary milk.

Fats and *oils* should be kept in the dark, if possible, since the light has a destructive effect on their vitamin content and tends to hasten rancidity.

Cheese **for table use should be stored in conditions that prevent both mould growth and excessive drying. A cheese dish with a ventilated cover is good, since it allows ventilation without undue drying. It should be kept in a cool, dry, well-ventilated place. A very low temperature is not necessary for storing cheese. Cheese for cooking should be allowed to harden, especially if it is soft or immature when purchased. If hung in a muslin bag for a few days (again in a cool, dry, well-ventilated place) it becomes easier to grate.**

Eggs should be kept in a cold place, either the larder or the refrigerator. Store them in a special egg rack or in a bowl.

Fruits and *vegetables* also come under the heading of perishable foods. Many vegetables contain Vitamin C, and since the vitamin content rapidly diminishes on storing, these foods should be eaten absolutely fresh ; in fact, ideally, they should be prepared and served immediately after gathering. Where this is not practicable, however, they should be used as fresh as possible, and if storage for a short time is unavoidable, they should be kept cool. A vegetable rack with slatted shelves should be provided for root vegetables. Green vegetables and salad plants should be washed, put in a covered container or plastic bag, and stored in a refrigerator, if available.

Frozen Foods : Packaged frozen foods may be bought from many grocers and greengrocers. They are convenient and quickly prepared, and can be substituted for fresh foods in almost any recipe. The frozen food may be kept for a short time, not more than a day in cold weather and less in hot weather—but are best used immediately. Any directions for thawing out and cooking given by the manufacturers should be very carefully followed.

Frozen foods cannot be stored in an ordinary refrigerator unless there is a specially constructed compartment for this purpose ; the freezing cabinet of an ordinary domestic refrigerator should not be used for keeping them longer than three days.

THE LARDER

Good ventilation in the larder is important, especially in hot weather, but cover the window opening with perforated zinc or fine gauze to keep out flies and other insects. If the larder is on the warm side of the house, shelter the window in summer by a sun-blind, to prevent its becoming too hot.

Wipe up spilt food immediately and clear the larder shelves about once a week, so that they **can be cleaned. A wash with a cloth wrung out of warm soapy water will be enough if the shelves are covered with American cloth, vitreous enamel, laminated plastic, etc. If the shelves are of bare wood, they will need scrubbing.**

THE REFRIGERATOR

The domestic refrigerator, kept normally at approximately 45° F., is suitable for the storage of meat, fish, fats, eggs and milk for short periods, and is useful for crisping salads and green vegetables.

It should not be regarded as a place in which foods can be stored over a long period. It does, however, enable perishable foods to be kept in better condition than in a larder.

It should be situated in as cool a place as possible, and should be set to maintain the main food compartment at a temperature of about 40°–45° F. The door should not be opened unnecessarily. Nothing hot should be placed in a refrigerator, as this not only raises the temperature of the compartment but also causes excessive frosting.

Use covered containers whenever possible to prevent drying. Rectangular boxes fitted with lids are the most convenient and most economical of space. Alternatively, use basins covered with plates, or the specially made transparent bags.

Strongly smelling foods should be placed towards the top of the refrigerator, but not under the freezing compartment ; in this position they are not likely to contaminate the other contents. Foods requiring the lowest temperature should be placed directly under the freezing compartment. Cooked foods, particularly meat, should be removed from the refrigerator and placed in a cool larder for a short time before serving. If served straight from the refrigerator, these foods will lack flavour.

The refrigerator must be defrosted regularly, following the manufacturers' instructions ; after defrosting, wash out the refrigerator with a cloth wrung out of lukewarm water with a little bicarbonate of soda added. Obstinate marks may be removed with a mild abrasive, but plastic interiors respond better to neat liquid detergent.

Always fill and replace the ice drawers immediately after removing the ice.

THE DEEP FREEZE CABINET

As already mentioned, the ordinary domestic refrigerator is not intended for long-term storage, for which deep or quick freeze refrigeration is necessary. A deep freeze cabinet which maintains a temperature of zero or lower will keep the food fresh for months, provided it is in good condition when frozen, carefully prepared, and adequately packaged. This equipment is invaluable for people with large fruit or vegetable gardens; six months or more after picking, the products have been found to retain the same flavour and the same nutritional value as when freshly gathered. The deep freeze cabinet thus enables a family to enjoy their home-grown fruit and vegetables during the greater part of the year.

The exact degree of temperature required for deep freezing depends on the equipment and on the kind of food frozen; for instance, zero is perfectly satisfactory for fruit and vegetables and for such things as raw meat and poultry, since in the latter case the subsequent cooking is effective in sterilising the food. More care must be taken in the storing of flesh foods which are already cooked before freezing, as they may merely be heated before eating.

Some refrigerators combine compartments of ordinary refrigerator temperature (about 40°–45° F.) with a deep freeze compartment which maintains a temperature of −15° to 0° F., and has a deep-frozen-food capacity of about 2 cubic feet. Another type of cabinet maintains a temperature of zero or a little lower, throughout, and has a capacity of about 2–11 cubic feet. (A rough idea of the number of lbs. of food that can be stored is obtained by multiplying the cubic capacity by 35).

The length of time the food can be stored obviously depends upon its freshness when frozen, the cleanliness and care used in handling, and the temperature of the cabinet. Generally speaking, however, fruit and vegetables can be safely stored for up to twelve months, and this is also true of some meats (raw) although pork and ham are probably only safe for a shorter period. Fish is a still more doubtful proposition, and oily fish should only be kept for 2–3 months. (It must be borne in mind that frequently a considerable time has elapsed between catching and retailing the fish.)

There is little or no loss of vitamin C during storage at 0° F. or just below. Frozen vegetables, therefore, if plunged immediately into boiling water, will have approximately the same food value as fresh vegetables. Frozen fruit should be used as soon as it is thawed, otherwise it loses its vitamin C value.

For notes on the preparation of foods for deep freeze storage, see the chapter on Bottling, Canning and Deep Freezing.

SHOPPING AND CATERING GUIDE

1. Choose foods in season whenever possible, as they are cheaper and better then. Forced foods, such as fruits, besides being very expensive, lack flavour.

2. Shop early in the day, when the choice is better.

3. Shop in person where this is practicable. Personal contact with one's shopkeepers ensures their interest and attention.

4. Buy reserve stores weekly or fortnightly. Order them in good time to avoid running short.

5. Purchase fresh stores, such as fats, eggs, butter, bacon and cheese, weekly, or twice a week in the hot weather.

6. Buy vegetables, particularly greens, as they are required. Do not store them, as their flavour spoils and also their vitamin content diminishes during storage.

The amounts given below are the approximate quantities per head per meal to allow for family catering, and will serve as a guide to the young wife who is catering for the first time.

Meat

With bone	4–6 oz.
Boneless	3–4 oz.

(For made-up dishes, 2–3 oz.)

Fish

With much bone	6–8 oz.
Little or no bone	3–4 oz.

(For made-up dishes, 2–3 oz.)

Vegetables (weight as purchased)

Artichokes (Jerusalem)	6 oz.
Beans (broad)	½–¾ lb.
Beans (runner)	6 oz.
Beans (butter or haricot)	2 oz.
Beetroot (as a vegetable)	4–6 oz.
Brussels sprouts	6 oz.
Cabbage	½ lb.
Carrots	4–6 oz.
Celeriac	4–6 oz.
Celery	1 large head serves 4–5 persons
Curly kale	6–8 oz.
Greens (spring)	½ lb.
Kohl Rabi	6 oz.
Onions (as a vegetable)	6 oz.
Parsnips	6 oz.
Peas (green)	½ lb.
Peas (dried)	2 oz.
Potatoes	6–8 oz.

Savoy	6–8 oz.
Seakale	4 oz.
Spinach	$\frac{1}{2}$–$\frac{3}{4}$ lb.
Swedes	$\frac{1}{2}$ lb.
Turnips	$\frac{1}{2}$ lb.
Turnip tops	$\frac{1}{2}$ lb.

Puddings

Sponge and suet puddings	1$\frac{1}{2}$ oz. flour, etc.
Pastry (for pies and puddings)	1$\frac{1}{2}$ oz. flour, etc.
Milk puddings, moulds, jellies	$\frac{1}{4}$ pint milk, etc.
Batter	1 oz. flour
Junket	$\frac{1}{4}$ pint milk
Fruit (pies, puddings, stewed)	4–5 oz. of fruit
Custard, as sauce	$\frac{1}{2}$ pint milk per 4 people

Cereals

Rice (for curry, etc.)	1–1$\frac{1}{2}$ oz.
Macaroni	1–1$\frac{1}{2}$ oz.
Oatmeal (for porridge)	1–1$\frac{1}{2}$ oz.

Beverages

Coffee (breakfast)	6 tbsps.	per 4 people
Coffee (after dinner)	3 tbsps.	per 4 people
Milk (in tea)	$\frac{1}{2}$ pint	per 4 people
Tea	1 tsp. per person	

Miscellaneous

Soup	$\frac{1}{4}$–$\frac{1}{3}$ pint
Sauces and gravies	$\frac{1}{8}$ pint

ENTERTAINING AT HOME

The modern hostess has often to play several rôles : she and her husband between them may have to cook and serve the meal, receive the guests and look after the many details that make for a successful party ; consequently, entertaining nowadays tends to become simpler. There are occasions, however, when a formal dinner party is appropriate, and while it is perfectly possible for a host and hostess to serve the dinner correctly, for those who feel the need for professional help there are in many towns agencies which can supply well-trained servants by the hour or by the evening. The following notes on giving a formal dinner party assume that some domestic help is available, while suggestions for single-handed entertaining are given on page 32.

THE FORMAL DINNER

The dining-room should look as charming as possible, and be evenly warmed. All interest is centred on the table, so this should be carefully laid, with spotless linen, well polished silver, sparkling glass, and an attractive (though not over-large) centrepiece or other decorations as appropriate.

The Linen, Centre Piece, and Candles

The choice between mats or an all-over cloth depends to some extent on the dining table. If the table has a beautifully polished wood surface, mats will show this off to advantage ; a table
1 with a poor surface will be best covered with a long tablecloth.

For dinner the tablecloths (or mats) and the table napkins should be of fine quality, and more elegant than those used for luncheon.

In laying the cloth, have the long centre crease running exactly down the centre of the table. A silencing pad placed underneath is an asset.

The centre piece depends upon the importance of the dinner—for a small dinner of six or eight, a low bowl of flowers is suitable ; for a large dinner, a more elaborate decoration may be arranged. Ornaments of silver, china, and glass may be used, but none of these lends so much charm to the dinner table as do flowers.

To arrange table flowers effectively, choose vases which are suitable in relation to the size and shape of the table itself, as well as to the flowers. Always keep the decoration low, especially if the table is a small one, so that the guests may see each other. If space allows, a tiny posy bowl of small flowers, set at each corner of the table, can look very charming.

Candles are attractive on the dinner table, set either in candlesticks or in two branching candelabra. The flames should be above eye level, for the flicker is annoying if directly in the line of vision.

Laying the Table

Cutlery should be placed with the handles about 1 inch from the edge of the table, and should be laid in order of use. Always make quite sure at the last moment that all silver is placed absolutely straight and in line.

In arranging the covers, see that each person has plenty of elbow room. Some people allow 27 inches for each place, while others think that 24 inches is sufficient. This very largely depends on the size and shape of the cutlery and china, and also on the width of the dining-room chairs.

Cruets : Place these at convenient positions along the table, allowing one set to each two or three people. If there are only two sets, place them at opposite ends of the table.

Placing the Glasses : Glasses vary according to the wine to be served, but the usual ones are a small glass for sherry, placed to the right of the soup spoon ; a large glass for water, beyond the sherry glass in a straight line ; and a medium-sized glass for white or red wine, forming a triangle with the other glasses.

Table Napkins : Napkins can be folded in
various ingenious ways, and favourite designs 2
are the water lily and the mitre, with a roll or

piece of bread placed in the middle. The tendency, however, is now towards much simpler folding, and a damask napkin, folded so that the width is one-third the length, can be laid flat at each place.

Finger Bowls : The finger bowl, if used, is presented standing on the dessert plate, with a fine lace mat beneath the finger bowl and a dessert knife and fork on either side; the guest arranges the lace mat and bowl to the left of the plate. The water may be delicately perfumed—rose water or verbena are good scents for this purpose—and each bowl may contain one or two very small flowers.

Dessert : This should be placed on a side table (see below) in the dining-room before the dinner is served.

Bon-Bon Dishes : Small silver compotes for salted almonds, olives, and bon-bons are an integral part of the table decoration, and should be placed at intervals along the table.

Ash Trays : Ash trays are brought to the table after or with the port. A liberal number should be provided, and they should be in keeping with the other table appointments.

Menu and Place Cards : Printed menus are used in a private house only for very large and formal dinner parties, and then only the name of each course and the main accompaniments are stated: sauces and dressings are taken for granted, and so are dessert, coffee, and wine.

Place cards, however, are almost a necessity when more than eight guests are invited—it is obviously a little difficult for a hostess to indicate without confusion to more than eight people where they are to sit. The place card can be of thin or heavy paper in white or light cream, never in colours. It is laid either on the napkin or on the table directly above the plate.

The Side Tables

The Sideboard : Wines are served from the sideboard. Water, glasses, bread, and extra serving table silver may be placed here or on the serving table.

The Serving Table : This must be well lighted and conveniently placed for the serving and carrying of food.

Place the carvers and serving utensils on this table, with room at the side for plates and vegetable dishes, also salvers for sauce-boats, cream, sugar, and so on. A hot-plate is useful for keeping the dishes hot during the serving.

Extra silver can be kept ready in case it is needed for replenishment, also crumb tray and brush, or napkin, a small tray for clearing away salts and peppers, etc.

Butler's Tray or Trolley : Have this conveniently placed for removing used dishes, etc. It may facilitate service if the trolley is placed first outside the dining-room door, so that used dishes can be removed from it, and the next course placed in readiness.

Announcing Dinner and Entering the Dining-room

The butler or maid at the door counts the number of guests as they enter, and when all have arrived goes to the kitchen to make sure that dinner is ready, sees that the table is complete, with the candles lighted, then goes to the drawing-room to announce "Dinner is served." Leaving the doors open, the servant returns to the dining-room and takes up position next to the serving table.

The host then leads the way to the dining-room with the guest of honour. The other guests follow, and the hostess and her escort come last. The host usually takes in the lady holding the highest social position or the one who is the greatest stranger. If the lady is married and her husband is present, the latter usually takes in the hostess.

At less formal dinners the guests enter the dining-room in groups and find their places themselves by means of the place cards.

At an informal dinner, when there are no place cards, the hostess indicates where the guests are to sit, beginning always with the woman at the right of the host. After each woman's place has been designated, the hostess then indicates where the men are to sit.

Serving the Dinner

The guest seated at the right of the host is served first, and then the other guests in rotation.

Food is served and plates are removed from the left, with the left hand, while beverages of all kinds, with their glasses or cups, are served and removed from the right, with the right hand.

All plates or cutlery should be removed very quietly, not more than two at a time, and placed at the side; they are then removed from the dining-room as soon as possible.

The various courses are served from the serving table or handed (see notes on different courses on the next page), and vegetables quickly follow. Sauces in sauce-boats and other accompaniments are placed on a silver salver and offered to the guests from the left. Second helpings are not offered at formal meals.

All glasses, condiments, and cutlery are removed after the savoury, a small tray being used to collect them. Crumbs are unobtrusively brushed from the table with a napkin on to a plate or salver.

The dessert plate, with fruit knife and fork and a finger bowl, are now placed in front of each guest, and the port glass is put in position at each cover. When all guests have been served with port, the decanter is placed before the host, together with cigarettes and matches on a salver.

Notes on Serving the Courses

Hors d'Œuvre : If arranged on individual dishes, these are placed on the table before dinner is announced.

If a choice is offered, a plate is placed at each cover, and the hors d'œuvre, arranged in a divided dish, or on a small tray, are handed round, with any accompaniments.

Soup : A filled soup plate or cup is placed before each person, and croûtons, grated cheese, etc., offered, the maid taking the soup plate in one hand, the accompaniments in the other.

Fish : When this is served from the side table, the maid places the helping of fish before the guest with her right hand and offers the sauce or other accompaniment with her left hand. A fish entrée is always handed with a spoon and fork.

Entrée : An entrée is always handed in the dish, however simple the dinner : a hot or cold plate is placed at each cover, then the servant hands the entrée dish on a folded napkin in the left hand, with serving spoon and fork.

Joints and Game : These are carved at the side table, by the host. The portions are handed, the maid then offers vegetables (one in each hand), sauces, and lastly, any other accompaniments.

Salad : When served as an accompaniment, the salad plate is placed to the left of the cover ; the servant offers the bowl of freshly mixed salad with salad spoon and fork in readiness. If salad is not taken, the extra plate is removed. (Have salad mixed just before serving, either in the kitchen, at the side table, or by the hostess at the head of the table.)

When salad is served as a separate course, a cold plate is placed at each cover round the table and it is offered as above. If preferred, serve individual salads.

Sweets : Sweets are usually offered in the same way as entrées. When the sweet requires cutting, as in the case of a tart, Christmas pudding etc., it is served from the side table. Individual sweets, ices, etc., are placed before each person, usually with the necessary spoon or fork on the plate.

When everyone has been served with the sweet, cream and sugar are handed, if required ; the cream jug and caster sugar should be placed on a silver salver.

Savoury : Savouries are usually offered in the same way as entrées.

Bread : This is cut in thick slices, and handed in a bread basket or on a plate.

Cheese : Different kinds of cheese (served only at luncheon) are placed on the table, with butter and plain biscuits, or rolls.

Wine : As soon as each person has been served with the first course, the wine is handed round. Each guest should be asked in the first instance whether he will take wine or not ; afteawards his glass should be replenished without further question. (For appropriate wines to serve, see chapter on Wine.)

Water : The maid fills the water glasses after the first course is served. They are filled three-quarters full, and refilled when empty. A napkin is held in the left hand to catch drops from the jug.

After-Dinner Coffee and Refreshments

Coffee is seldom served at the table. The butler or maid carries the coffee tray into the drawing-room, when everyone has assembled there, and offers it to each guest to pour out his own coffee.

It is customary now for a tray of drinks to be brought in at about 10 o'clock before any of the guests are ready to leave. This should be set with suitable glasses, iced water, soft drinks, whisky and soda water, and so on.

Some Menus for Formal Dinners

Even for the more formal dinner party menus nowadays are much simpler than of old, and seldom include more than five courses. The following are suggested as menus for dinner parties at the different seasons of the year.

SPRING

Artichoke Soup
Scalloped Salmon
Roast Gosling
Orange Salad Potato Balls
Vanilla Soufflé
Cheese Straws

SUMMER

Cucumber Soup
Eggs in Aspic
Pigeon Pie Salad
Raspberry Chartreuse
Stuffed Prunes Salted Almonds

AUTUMN

Oysters
Cream of Tomato Soup
Roast Pheasant
Chipped Potatoes Green Salad
Stewed Peaches Honeycomb Mould
Mushroom Croûtes

WINTER

Minestrone
Fillets of Brill Tomato Sauce
Beefsteak and Kidney Pie
Brussels Sprouts Duchesse Potatoes
Coconut Castle Puddings
Loganberry Sauce
Cream Cheese and Celery Canapés

LUNCHEON PARTIES

A formal luncheon is served exactly like a formal dinner. In a household in which such service is a matter of daily routine, there is little to be changed when guests are present.

The chief difference between luncheon and dinner is in the setting of the table and in the simpler menus. The silver should be as bright, the glass as sparkling, and the linen as immaculate, no matter what the meal, but the flowers are usually less elaborate, candles are not used, and there are fewer accessories on the table; plainer linen, glass, and silver are used.

There is no formality about entering the dining-room, and place cards are seldom used.

Luncheon Party Menus

SPRING

Melon Slices
Sole Matelote
Scalloped Potatoes Stewed Tomatoes
Gooseberry Flan

SUMMER

Asparagus Omelette
Summer Stew
Strawberries and Ice Cream
Sardine Snacks

AUTUMN

Hollandaise Soup
Prawns in Aspic
Mixed Green Salad
Damson Tart Junket

WINTER

Grapefruit Cocktail
Curried Beef with Rice
Apple Charlotte
Cheese Biscuits and Celery

INFORMAL DINNERS AND LUNCHEONS

It is quite possible for one quick and intelligent parlourmaid to wait on six persons efficiently, but if it is a larger party, or if the maid has not had much experience, it is wise to simplify the service to what she is capable of doing.

With an untrained maid, *very* clear step-by-step directions must be given beforehand, for although most young servants like the idea of waiting at table and are anxious to do it well, it naturally takes much practice to become a quick and deft parlourmaid. Here are some suggestions for giving a party with an inexperienced maid:

1. Let her have as much practice in waiting as possible before the party, so that the routine becomes familiar to her.

2. When giving instructions, *show* her how to do things as well as telling her. Show her where she is to stand in the dining-room, how to hold and offer dishes, how to place and serve potatoes, etc.

3. Arrange the menu so that the service is easy; have a first course which can be placed in readiness on the table before dinner, and choose a sweet which can be served in individual glasses.

4. Set the table yourself—but let the maid help you, so that she may learn to appreciate a well-laid table with gleaming silver, sparkling glass, and dainty linen.

5. Lay out the necessary serving dishes and plates in the kitchen, checking them with the maid so that she knows exactly what is being served in each dish.

6. Have the sauces and any extras put on the table and let people help themselves to these.

7. Have the coffee tray on a low table before you in the drawing-room, and serve coffee yourself.

8. Do not keep the maid in the room between

courses, but use a bell to summon her when necessary.

9. On the day of the dinner party go over the menu and the order of service with her, step by step, giving her clear and simple directions.

10. An untrained servant often forgets one point, so spare ten minutes before the guests arrive to check everything—the table, the trays, and if you have no cook, the final dishing of food and heating of plates, etc.

Informal Dinner Party Menus

SPRING

Grape and Orange Juice Cocktail
Risotto Baked Mushrooms
Spiced Apple Tart
Cup Custard

SUMMER

Green Pea Soup
Egg and Lobster Mayonnaise
Potato and Tomato Salad
Raspberries and Cream

AUTUMN

Chestnut Purée
Curried Rabbit
Boiled Rice Chutney
Blackberry Pudding Custard

WINTER

Celeriac Soup
Stewed Ox-heart
Creamed Potatoes Brussels Sprouts
Baked Stuffed Apples
Shortbread Biscuits

SINGLE-HANDED ENTERTAINING

In many households to-day no domestic help is available, and it is advisable in this case to simplify the dinner so that the host and hostess are free to enjoy the party without being too overburdened with arrangements once the guests have arrived. The following suggestions may be useful :

1. Limit the meal to two or three courses, and have at least one course completely finished and ready to serve beforehand. If you have a chafing dish, use this when entertaining small parties.

2. Serve savoury biscuits, or a small savoury, with the cocktails, to replace an extra course.

3. Cut down the number of dishes to be handed round by arranging one of the vegetables on the dish with the meat or fish, or serve a composite dish with the meat and vegetables together (e.g., fillets of beef flanked with creamed potatoes, new carrots, and green peas), or use a divided dish to hold vegetables.

4. Serve foods in the dish in which they are cooked, using the many kinds of attractive glassware and earthenware now available.

5. Avoid jumping up and down from the table by having things at hand in the dining-room. Place a small side table or trolley within easy reach for holding the water jug, bread basket, relishes, etc. A hot-plate is particularly useful when entertaining single-handed, to keep the dishes hot and so save journeys to the kitchen.

6. To speed up clearing the table, have a tray or a trolley to hold all the used dishes, ready to your hand. Collect dishes on this and place it in the kitchen without waiting to unload. Dishes for the last course will be left on the table when the party goes to the drawing-room for coffee.

7. To avoid delay in the kitchen, have trays laid ready for carrying in each course, complete with the necessary silver, plates, etc. Individual helpings of cold foods, salads, sweets, etc., placed on a tray ready for handing, can be put on the side table in the dining-room if more convenient.

8. The host and hostess should not be moving about at the same time, so arrange beforehand exactly what each one is going to do : for example, let the host be responsible for looking after the drinks and for serving the main course and vegetables, while the hostess is responsible for clearing the table, fetching food from the kitchen, and serving the sweet or savoury.

Suggested menus for such informal meals appear below.

Menus for Single-handed Entertaining

SPRING

Asparagus with Melted Butter
Spiced Lamb Roll
New Carrots and Potatoes
Salad
Caramelled Bananas Sponge Fingers

SUMMER

Tomato Juice Cocktail
Chicken Breasts in Port Wine
Green Peas Duchesse Potatoes
Charlotte Russe

AUTUMN

Grapefruit
Boston Casserole with Bacon
Brussels Sprouts
Lemon Meringue Pie

WINTER

Celery Cream Soup
Liver à la Française
Creamed Potatoes
Baked Tomatoes
Mince Pies

CHAFING DISH COOKERY FOR PARTIES

This method of cooking food at the table and serving it at once has a decided fascination for both hostess and guests, and is a most sociable way of serving a hot dish. A chafing dish is also a boon to the person living alone, with only a gas ring or electric hot-plate for cooking.

The chafing dish may be used to cook the food completely just before it is to be served, provided it does not require long cooking. Alternatively, a previously cooked dish can be reheated or finished, or cooked food kept hot until required. As much preparation as possible should be done before the meal is begun, to avoid undue waiting at table. When intense heat is required, use the upper pan or blazer by itself—that is, like a frying, omelette, or sauté pan. For slow cooking, or for keeping foods hot, use the blazer over the water-bath.

Omelettes, creamed dishes, and réchauffés, cheese fondue, and similar dishes, Welsh rarebit, and reheated tinned foods are particularly suitable for cooking in a chafing dish, as they require only a short time. A few chafing dish recipes which are especially good for entertaining will be found in other chapters, namely Chicken Breasts in Port Wine (page 164), Savoury Sweetbreads (page 154), Réchauffé of Tongue (page 156), Cinnamon Apples and Caramelled Bananas (page 327).

TEA AND BRIDGE PARTIES

For a light afternoon tea, have an adequate supply of good Indian or China tea, whichever you prefer—both, if the party is large enough to justify it—and hand round plates of daintily cut bread and butter, and some of the following: open savoury scones, thin layer sandwiches or rolled sandwiches, assorted fancy pastries and gâteaux, fingers of fruit cake, and assorted biscuits. In winter, fingers of hot savoury toast or hot buttered scones or tea cakes can be included.

B

Bridge parties are planned to suit the time of day—for an afternoon gathering serve a light tea; if the guests arrive after dinner, serve coffee or tea, small sandwiches, pastries, or biscuits during an interval. The guests usually remain at the tables when refreshments are served.

COCKTAIL AND SHERRY PARTIES

This type of party is a convenient and popular way of entertaining a fairly large number of people with the minimum of trouble and in a limited space.

Although for a large party it may be best to have an outside caterer or a waiter to manage the mixing of the drinks, this is by no means essential for smaller and less formal occasions, when the host usually manages this side of the party. For a party in your own home you are not expected to offer the wide selection of drinks available in an hotel cocktail bar, so choose two or three of the better known cocktails, which you know you can mix satisfactorily, and also serve a choice of soft drinks and sherry for those who do not care for cocktails. (See the chapter on Hot and Cold Drinks for cocktail recipes.)

To accompany the drinks serve dishes of small savoury titbits, choosing these from among the cocktail savouries suggested in the chapter on After-Dinner and Cocktail Savouries, and arrange them in convenient places.

The following notes may help in the planning for a party of this type:

1. Be sure you have enough space to accommodate comfortably the number of guests you invite.

2. Improvise the "bar" in a convenient place; avoid putting it in a corner, as this usually means that people tend to linger there instead of moving away when they have been given their drink.

3. Supply plenty of ash trays, and provide places where your guests can conveniently put down their glasses.

BUFFET PARTIES

Buffet parties, like cocktail parties, are a result of modern living conditions, for this type of entertaining is very much easier for the single-handed hostess than the more formal dinner, and it also permits more guests to be entertained at a time. Another advantage is that all preparations can be made in advance, and the buffet arranged before the guests arrive.

Any food is suitable that can be eaten with a fork or spoon or in the fingers, for example, cold meats, galantines, bouchées, tartlets, trifles, cold sweets, and petits fours. The dishes can be quite elaborate, as for an engagement party, a wedding, a twenty-first birthday, or a silver wedding celebration; choose simple and easily prepared food for lesser occasions, such as a party for 'teen-age children, who always enjoy being able to help themselves.

Arrange your buffet table in the most convenient place, according to the room you are using. Bear in mind the fact that a fair number of people will need to reach the buffet at the same time, without undue crushing, so avoid placing it in a corner. Cover the table with a cloth, if possible carrying out some attractive colour scheme with the flower arrangements. Supply piles of plates, and sufficient forks, spoons, glasses, cups, etc., as required; do not have these all in one place, but arrange them at intervals along the buffet. If there is any specially elaborate or important dish or cake, make this the central feature of the buffet, and arrange the other food on each side. Serve drinks from a separate improvised "bar," as well as the soup and coffee, if these are included.

If possible, have a number of chairs, so that at any rate the older guests may sit down.

WEDDING RECEPTIONS

The present-day trend—whether the reception is held at home or at an hotel—is towards an elegant simplicity. A reception held at the bride's home has a pleasant charm and intimacy, and if the details are carefully planned in advance, a party for up to fifty people need not overtax the hostess.

For a summer wedding, a garden setting is delightful, but it is wise to have a marquee, or to make some alternative arrangement for an indoor reception in case of bad weather.

The following arrangements should be made well in advance:

1. Decide on the type of reception and number of guests, and send out the invitations. A buffet service of refreshments is easy to arrange, especially for a large number of guests, and it is suitable for any time of day. On the other hand, a sit-down meal, which is especially appropriate after an early wedding, ensures that every guest is attentively served, and makes a more dignified setting for the ceremonies of cutting the cake and proposing the toasts.

2. Check linen, table appointments, and cooking utensils, and supplement as necessary by buying, borrowing, or hiring from a catering firm.

3. If a catering firm is to provide the refreshments, settle this well in advance.

4. Make or order the cake well in advance. (See recipe for Wedding Cake.)

5. If the refreshments are to be prepared at home, include some dishes which can be made beforehand, e.g., meringues, which can be made a week before the wedding, stored in a tin and filled at the last minute. Buy the non-perishable foods in advance; order ice cream to be delivered on the day.

6. Order the wines and beverages, choosing them to suit the food served; champagne or a sparkling white wine is best for the toasts—allow at least one glass per guest, and more if possible. Cocktails and sherry may be served while the guests are being received. Fruit cups, punches, or squashes should be available at either a buffet or a sit-down meal. Black and white coffee (hot or iced) is served at morning receptions, tea and coffee in the afternoon.

Whatever type of reception is arranged, the bridal cake may form the centre piece of the main table, or it may stand on a small side-table. The bride, helped by the groom, cuts the first slice, then a waiter (or other helper) cuts it into small pieces and hands it round.

The first toast, to the bride and groom, is usually proposed by a friend of long standing, or the bride's father. The groom replies, making a reference to the bride's parents, and concluding by proposing the health of the bridesmaids. To this the best man replies; he may also propose the health of the bridegroom's parents, or old family friends may in turn propose the health of the respective parents, though these toasts are not strictly necessary, and are often omitted.

Wedding Breakfast Buffet

For general arrangements, see Buffet Parties; suggested menus are given below, the first one being for a mid-day reception and the second for an afternoon function. (For quantities required, see the list at the end of the chapter.)

Assorted Sandwiches
Lobster and Avocado Salad
Chicken Patties Crab Éclairs
Assorted Pastries
Chocolate Biscuits
Wedding Cake
Champagne Punch Tea Coffee

Tomato Juice Cocktail
(or Iced Consommé)
Salmon Mayonnaise
Chicken, Ham, Sausage Rolls
Mushroom Bouchées
Assorted Sandwiches
Meringues Fruit Sundaes
Wedding Cake
Champagne Coffee Fruit Cup

Sit-down Wedding Breakfast

The bridal party are usually seated at one long table, with smaller ones set at right angles to it for the other guests. The bride sits on the groom's left, her mother on his right, and the groom's father on the bride's other side. The bride's father (or the relative who has given her away) sits to the left of the bride, with the groom's mother next to him. The best man and chief bridesmaid are seated together, and places of honour are reserved for the Vicar and his wife, if present, and for other close relatives and important guests. The tables are laid as for a formal luncheon ; the decorations must harmonise with the colour scheme of the bridal retinue.

Either a hot or cold luncheon may be served—see the suggested menus below, also the quantities given at the end of the chapter.

Consommé Julienne
Baked Salmon Hollandaise Sauce
Cold Meats
Salad Asparagus
Wedding Cake
Petits Fours
Sherry Champagne Black Coffee

Oysters
Iced Consommé
Smoked Trout Piquant Sauce
Cold Roast Duck
Orange and Lettuce Salad
Potato Salad
Ices Raspberry Soufflé
Wedding Cake
Champagne Burgundy
Black Coffee

CHILDREN'S PARTIES

Thorough organisation is particularly important to ensure success. Essential points to remember are the following : do not try to mix children of very different ages ; send invitations giving the exact times for the beginning and end of the party ; provide adequate cloakroom arrangements ; plan gay but simple table and room decorations ; arrange suitable games for "breaking the ice" and a full programme of entertainment, so that the children have no time to feel shy or bored. For all except the very young, a party meal is best enjoyed without grown-ups, though it is often a good idea to let them wait on the children.

The refreshments should be suited to the age of the guests.

Young children appreciate such novelties as biscuits in the shape of animals, "alphabet brick" cakes, and so on. The sandwiches, cakes, buns, etc., should be small, as children like to taste nearly everything. Festive cakes, especially for a birthday, should be designed to appeal to the children and not the grown-ups. Some children like savoury food, and some only like very plain fare, so do not forget to cater for both tastes. Jellies, fruit salads, and simple trifles have a particular appeal if prettily decorated or served in new forms. Milk and fruit drinks as well as tea should be served.

A GUIDE TO QUANTITIES FOR PARTIES

Sandwiches .	A quartern loaf gives about 50–60 slices. Allow approximately 4 small sandwiches per person.
Chicken . .	1 large bird will serve 6–8 persons.
Turkey . .	Allow 2–3 oz. (cooked, without bone) per person.
Lobster . .	1 lobster will serve 3–5 people when made into a salad. Made into lobster patties, it will give 2–3 dozen, according to size.
Oysters . .	4–5 per person.
Smoked Salmon .	1–2 oz. per person.
Cocktail Savouries	½ lb. cheese pastry makes 80 to 100 biscuits or croûtes.
Patties . .	1½ lb. puff pastry makes 75 small patties.

Sausage Rolls .	$1\frac{1}{2}$ lb. shortcrust pastry and 2 lb. sausage meat make 50 small rolls.
Meringues . .	10 egg whites, $1\frac{1}{4}$ lb. sugar, and 1 pint cream give 75 meringues.
Ice Cream . .	1 quart gives about 12 servings, varying according to the manner in which it is to be served.
Creams . .	1 quart of moulded cream gives 10 servings.
Champagne .	1 bottle serves 5 persons. (This is the ordinary size bottle, not to be confused with a magnum, which is larger, 2 reputed quarts.)
Sherry . .	1 bottle gives a maximum of 16 glasses.
Wine . .	1 bottle serves an average of 4–6 persons.
Cocktails . .	1 bottle of gin or whisky makes a maximum of 32 cocktails.
Tea . . .	$\frac{1}{2}$ lb. tea, 20 pints water, and $3\frac{1}{2}$ pints milk give approximately 100 teacupfuls.
Coffee . .	$1\frac{1}{2}$ lb. coffee, 12 pints water, and 6 pints milk make enough for 90 small cupfuls or 45 larger cupfuls.
Sugar . . .	$\frac{3}{4}$ lb. per 100 persons.
Lemon for tea .	Each lemon gives 9–10 slices.

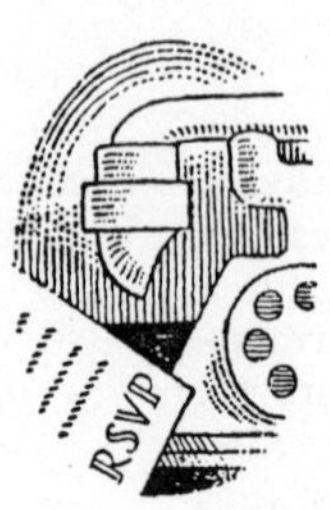

THE ART OF CARVING

The aim in carving is to cut the meat as neatly and skilfully as possible, in the way most suitable for the particular joint. Skilful carving is also economical, for by cutting the joint carefully, it can often be made to yield an extra meal. Furthermore, if the meat or bird is neatly carved when hot, its appearance will be better when it is served up cold.

Carving Tools

To make a success of carving, the right tools are a great advantage, and they should be kept in good condition.

Knives : For most joints, a carving knife with a long, fairly broad blade, slightly curved, and pointed at the end, is generally satisfactory. It can be of ordinary or of stainless steel. Some modern stainless steel carving knives have a hollowed-out, grooved blade ; such knives do not require sharpening, and are perhaps easier for an inexperienced carver to use, but a skilful carver prefers a blade with a plain edge.

For carving poultry and game, a knife with a short, straight, stiff blade, pointed at the end and with a comparatively long handle, is preferable. With such a knife, it is easier to sever the joints of the bird, the long handle giving more purchase. Failing this, a kitchen knife or ordinary carving knife will serve.

For carving boned hams, pressed tongue, pressed brisket and brawn, a carving knife with a very long, thin, straight blade, slightly flexible, is found the most practical. The blade is usually rounded at the end, for the cuts are invariably made horizontally, and a sharp point is therefore unnecessary.

Forks : A carving fork has two sharp prongs, so that it enters the meat easily, and a guard to prevent the hand from being cut should the knife slip. Forks for carving hams, tongues, etc., generally have a square or circular guard, similar to that of a sword. The guard must be kept up when carving is in progress.

Steels, Stones and Other Sharpeners : Whatever shaped carving knife is used, it must always be very sharp. The old-fashioned steel is good, especially for non-stainless knives, but it requires using with some skill. The handle end of the knife blade is placed to the top of the steel and the blade drawn smoothly down until the tip of the blade reaches the base of the steel. This is

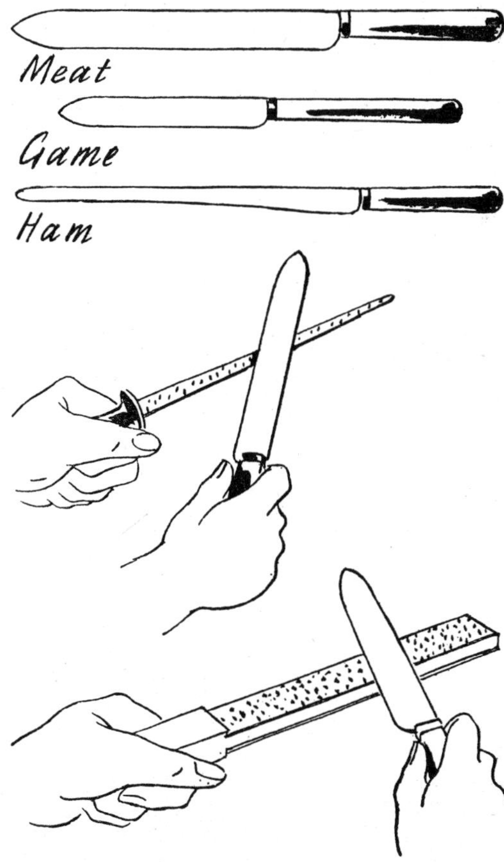

done first on one side, then on the other side of the blade, with rapid strokes, until the knife is sufficiently sharp. The inexperienced are advised to use a steel with a guard.

A sharpening stone is also very efficient and

particularly suitable for non-stainless knives, but this also requires using with some skill and, of course, has no guard. It is used in the same way as the steel.

Patent knife-sharpeners produce a very keen edge, if perhaps a rather less permanent one. They are particularly suitable for stainless steel blades, and are found very handy by those who are not expert with a steel or stone.

A very simple knife-sharpener can easily be made at home with a piece of wood, some emery paper and a strip of chamois leather. Cut the wood about the width and length of a table knife and have it about ½ inch thick for the handle, the rest slightly thinner. Cut a piece of emery paper to fit the " blade " and stick this firmly on to one side with some good adhesive. Cut a piece of chamois leather the same size as the emery paper and stick this to the other side of the " blade." To use this sharpener, place the handle end of the knife blade to the top of the emery paper and draw it smoothly down until the point of the blade reaches the handle end of the emery paper. Turn the knife over and repeat with the other side of the blade. Continue, stroking alternate sides of the blade, until the knife is sufficiently sharp. The chamois leather surface is found useful for polishing the knife after sharpening.

Simplifying Carving

The job of carving can be much simplified if attention is paid to the following points :

1. Secure the joint, if necessary, with skewers or string (or both), so that it keeps its shape during cooking. This is particularly important when the joint is boned, as in rolled rib of beef or boned sirloin ; or when stuffed, as in stuffed breast of lamb. Care should be taken, too, when trussing birds, to give them a good shape.

2. Always use metal skewers, as these can be removed with ease when the meat is cooked. Never use wooden skewers ; these swell during cooking, making it very difficult, if not impossible, to remove them neatly once the joint is cooked. If the butcher sends the meat skewered with wooden skewers, replace these with metal ones before cooking.

3. Get the butcher to *chine* joints such as loin or neck of lamb, mutton, veal or pork, rather than having them chopped. By chining is meant severing the rib bones from the backbone by sawing through the ribs close to the backbone ; it is then easy to carve the joint into regular-sized chops or cutlets. When the joint is merely chopped through the backbone, this is often done very unevenly, which makes it extremely difficult to carve neatly and economically.

4. Bone and stuff a joint such as loin or shoulder of lamb, mutton, etc., before cooking, if it must be made to serve a number of portions ; it can then be carved much more economically.

5. Be sure that the crackling of pork is properly scored before cooking : it is difficult to carve if left in thick pieces.

6. In the case of game birds that require cutting in half, carve them in the kitchen before dishing them—it is much easier to cut them on a board than on the dish.

7. Choose a large enough dish for the joint, see that it is not overcrowded, and keep the garnishes small. If any gravy or sauce is placed on the dish with the meat, it should be a small amount only, the rest being served separately.

8. Arrange for carving to be done at the side table if the carver is inexperienced or if the dining table tends to be crowded. If it is preferred to carve at the table, it is wise to place a carving cloth or table napkin under the dish, to protect the table from splashes.

9. Have everything ready, and the knife sharpened, before beginning.

CARVING MEAT

(*See sketches opposite*)

Meat is almost invariably cut across the grain, as it eats more tenderly when carved in this way. It is necessary, therefore, for the carver to understand the structure of the joint, also to know where the lean and fat are to be found, so that they can be distributed evenly or according to individual preference.

Generally speaking, beef is sliced very thinly (especially when cold) ; mutton and lamb should be fairly thick, while a medium thickness is best for pork and veal. Ham, tongue and brawn are sliced thinly.

Boneless Joints of Beef

Carve thinly and across the grain, which in a boneless joint is usually horizontally. Roast fillet of beef is an exception, in that it is usually sliced rather thickly. Again, this should be carved across the grain, which in the case of a long piece means carving downwards.

Sirloin or Rib of Beef (with bone)

First cut the meat from the top of the joint in thin slices downwards from the outside layer

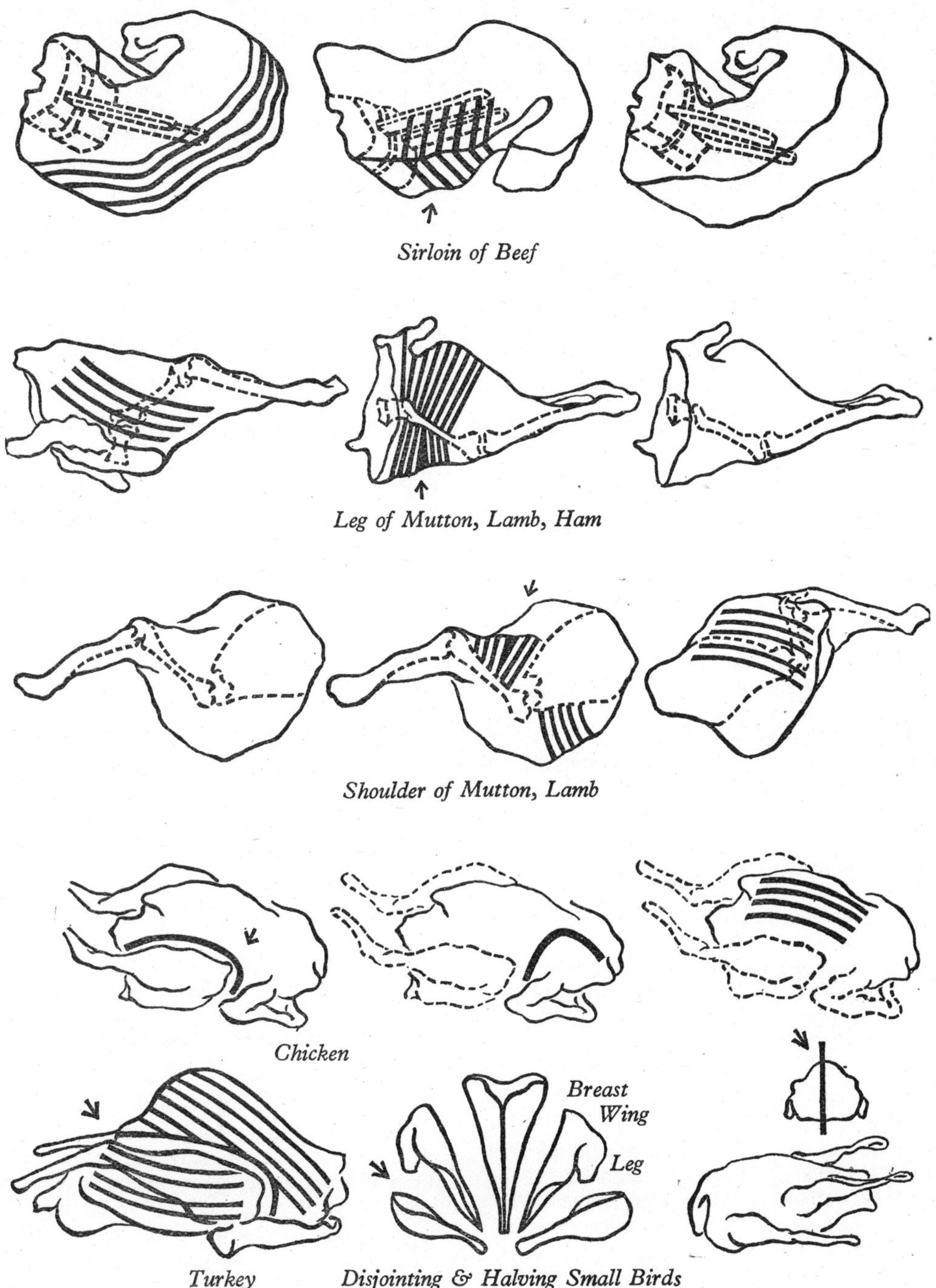
Sirloin of Beef
Leg of Mutton, Lamb, Ham
Shoulder of Mutton, Lamb
Chicken
Breast
Wing
Leg
Turkey
Disjointing & Halving Small Birds

of fat to the rib bone, cutting parallel to the bone. To carve the undercut (of sirloin), turn the joint over and slice the meat downwards, again in thin slices, but this time at right angles to the rib bone.

Leg of Mutton or Lamb

Slice the meat downwards in thick slices from the surface to the bone starting at the thick end. When all the meat is taken from the top of the joint, turn it over and carve the meat on the underside in a similar way. Here again, the knuckle is much appreciated by some people.

Shoulder of Mutton or Lamb

Place the joint so that the blade-bone points away from the carver. Insert the fork securely in the meat, and with the aid of the fork, raise the far side of the joint slightly, then make a vertical cut through the centre of the meat up to the bone; this will cause the joint to open out slightly, making it appear as if a slice had already been removed. Cut thick slices from each side of this gap, as far as the blade-bone on the one side and the knuckle on the other. Slices of the knuckle also may be carved for those who appreciate it. Next turn the joint so that the blade-bone faces the carver, and carve the meat on top of the blade-bone downwards in strips, parallel with the central "fin" of the bone. Finally, turn the joint upside down and carve the meat from the underside horizontally in slices.

Loin of Mutton, Lamb or Pork

Cut the joint right through, downwards, into chops—this is easier if the bone has been chined, as already described.

Best End of Neck of Mutton or Lamb

Cut the joint right through, downwards into cutlets. Again this is easier if the joint has been chined.

Saddle of Mutton or Lamb

First carve the meat from the top of the joint, in long slices, cutting downwards and parallel with the backbone. Do this on each side of the backbone. When all this meat is removed, turn the joint upside down and slice the meat from the underside in a similar manner.

Leg of Pork

Use the point of the knife to cut through the crackling and include some with each serving. If necessary, that is, if the crackling has not been carefully scored before cooking, lift it off and cut it on the dish. Cut the meat as for leg of mutton or lamb, but in slices of medium thickness.

Stuffed Breast of Mutton, Lamb or Veal

Cut downwards in fairly thick slices, right through the joint.

Fillet of Veal

(Remove the bone before cooking and replace with stuffing.) Cut across the grain, i.e., horizontally, in medium slices, right across the joint.

CARVING VENISON

The haunch is the joint most usually encountered, and consists of the hindquarter or leg and loin in one piece. Start with the knuckle end farthest away and make a deep cut from the thin end to the end of the loin, using the point of the knife, and slanting the cut downwards sufficiently to prevent the gravy from escaping. Carve each successive long slice in the same slanting fashion. With each portion serve a little of the fat. Do not slice the venison too thickly, and be as quick as possible over the carving, as the fat is not very palatable when it cools, so the meat should be served very hot.

The saddle and leg are carved in the same way as saddle and leg of mutton.

CARVING RABBITS AND HARES

These are awkward to carve at table, and it is better to cut them up before cooking, or to send them to table ready carved—in the latter case, see that they are really hot when served.

Rabbits

First remove the hind legs, cutting them away with a slicing and pressing movement, while holding the fork firmly across the back, repeat for the fore legs, running the knife under the blade-bone. Divide the rabbit across the middle of the back, and sub-divide each of these portions into two pieces. If the rabbit is small, the back will give only two or three portions. In the case of a large animal the legs may be divided lengthwise, but all the bone will then be in one portion.

Hares

Arrange the hare with the head pointing away from the carver. Insert the knife under the shoulder and cut along the backbone down to the rump ; the dish may then be turned sideways and long, moderately thick slices cut along the back on both sides.

If the animal is young, it may be treated as follows : Cut off the fore and hind legs, then cut the back crosswise into six equal pieces. The back is considered the best part, then the hind legs, and finally the shoulders.

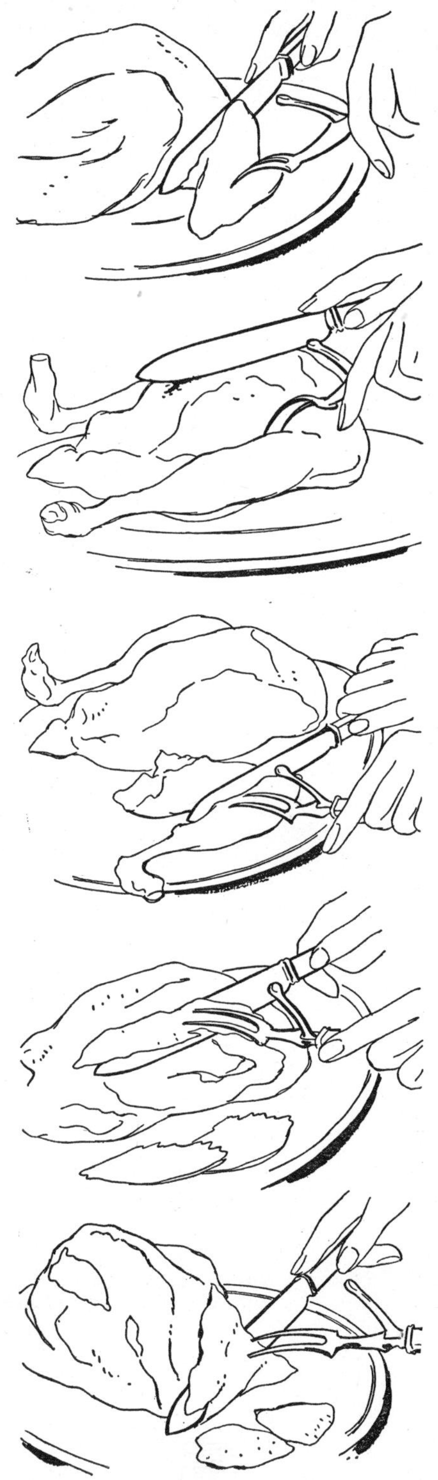

CARVING POULTRY AND GAME

For carving a bird, use a sharp knife with a short, stiff blade, as already described. If a game carver is not available, use a sharp, pointed kitchen knife ; this will be found easier to use than an ordinary meat carver. Be sure to use a carving fork, with the guard up.

Chicken (see sketches)

To remove a wing, place the bird so that the wing is on the carver's left-hand side. Holding the pinion with the fork, cut through the outer layer of the breast, judging the direction of the cut so that the knife enters the wing joint. Gently ease the wing away from the body of the bird, and firmly cut through the joint gristle. Repeat for other wing.

To remove the leg, this should be on the carver's left-hand side. Steadying the bird with the flat of the knife held against the breast, prise the leg outward with the fork, thus exposing the thigh joint—one clean cut through the joint will sever the leg.

It is usual to divide the thigh from the drumstick by cutting through the joint. In a big bird the thigh is further divided.

Cut the breast in thin slices, parallel with the breast-bone.

When stuffing has been cooked in a bird, this is sliced from the front of the breast, the remaining stuffing being scooped out with a spoon.

Turkey

A turkey is carved in the same manner as a chicken, but as it is larger and more fleshy, the meat is generally sliced off the legs and wings—these joints themselves are too large to serve as individual portions.

Duck

Cut through the skin with the point of the knife and cut the meat from each side of the breast in long slices, parallel with the breast-bone. Cut through the legs and wings at the joint.

Goose

A goose is carved in the same manner as a duck, but the meat is generally sliced from the legs and wings—these joints being rather large for individual portions.

Game Birds, etc.

A pheasant, or other game bird, if large, is carved in the same manner as a chicken.

Partridges, pigeons and birds of similar size are generally cut in half, or if very small, the whole bird may be served as one portion. Special scissors, rather like small secateurs, are made for cutting birds in half, or it can be done with the game carver or with a short, pointed kitchen knife, by inserting the point of the knife in the neck end of the breast and cutting firmly through the bird in the direction of the breast-bone.

Small birds, such as woodcock, snipe, quail, etc., are served whole.

CARVING FISH

The aim in carving fish is to serve it in neat portions without breaking up the flakes or mixing them with the bones or skin. A keen-edged blade is not necessary for this purpose—in fact a blunt edge is preferable. Special fish servers consist of a knife and fork, the knife having a short, wide, slightly pointed blade ; the fork is also wide, with short, wide prongs. They are generally silver or silver-plated, or they may be of stainless steel ; non-stainless steel servers should not be used, as this metal imparts an unpleasant flavour to the fish.

Cod

The fish is laid flat on the dish, on its side. First run the knife from head to tail through the middle of the flesh on the side uppermost, taking the knife down as far as the backbone, but not through it. Then cut slices of the flesh from each side of this centre cut, cutting at right angles to it. When all the fish is served from the upper half, remove the backbone and cut the lower half in a similar fashion.

Sole

When the fish is dished whole (i.e., not filleted), it is usual to cut it right through the bone into sections across the fish. First cut off the head, then cut through, widthways, into two, three or even four portions, according to the size of the fish.

Plaice

If plaice is served whole (i.e., not filleted), it is carved in the same manner as a sole.

Turbot

The fish is laid flat on the dish. First cut through the flesh down the middle of the fish (i.e., down the backbone), up to the bone but not through it. Then cut fairly wide slices from each side of the centre cut, cutting them at right angles to the centre. When all the fish is served from the upperside, remove the backbone and then serve the underside, cutting it in a similar fashion.

Salmon

The fish is laid flat on the dish, on its side. First cut right through the middle of the flesh from top to bottom, cutting up to, but not through, the bone. Carve the thick part of the fish (i.e., the back), in slices lengthwise, making the cuts parallel to the first cut. With each serving include a slice of the thin part of the fish (i.e., the belly), cutting the slices widthways from this part.

Mackerel

The fish is laid flat on the dish, on its side. If large, cut through the flesh across the middle of the fish and also just below the head. Slip the knife under the flesh and lift it off the bone on each side of the centre cut, making two neat servings. Remove the backbone and cut the underside of the flesh into two in a similar fashion. If the fish is small, cut through the flesh just below the head, then lift the whole of the flesh from one side without cutting, to make one serving. Now remove the bone, and serve the underside also as an individual portion.

COOKERY PROCESSES AND TERMS

In cookery books it is obviously impracticable to describe in detail every process in every recipe, so terms which embrace a whole process or sequence of operations are frequently employed. Some of the commonest are given here.

PROCESSES

TO BAKE

To cook in an oven by dry heat. This is the method of cooking most cakes, biscuits, pastries and many other dishes.

TO BAKE BLIND

The term applied to the method of baking a pastry case with a filling of baking beans, rice or

stale crusts of bread to keep it a good shape. Used when making tarts and flans in which a cold or uncooked filling is to be used, or a filling which requires only slight cooking or merely heating through. Useful also when making pastry cases to be kept for a few days, as the unfilled cases can be easily reheated to crisp them before filling.

Line the required number of flan rings, sandwich tins or patty pans with pastry. Cut rounds of greaseproof paper slightly larger than the pastry, grease them and place, greased side down, in the cases. (If the tins are very deep, snip the paper from the outside edge towards the centre about 1 inch deep and at intervals of about 1 inch.) Now fill the paper with haricot beans or rice (which can be used again and again for the same purpose) or with stale crusts cut into small pieces. Bake in a hot oven (450° F., mark 8) until the pastry is nearly cooked—about 15 minutes when a flan or sandwich tin is used, and about 10 minutes for tartlets. Then remove the filling, and return the pastry to the oven for a further 5–10 minutes to dry off.

Small pastry cases can be baked without any filling, though if this is done the pastry should be pricked well with a fork before cooking; even so, the shape of the cases is not so good as when they are baked blind.

TO BARD

Covering the breast of a bird with slices of fat bacon prior to roasting, to prevent the flesh drying during cooking (see sketch). Barding is necessary with birds lacking in fat, such as a fowl, turkey or pheasant.

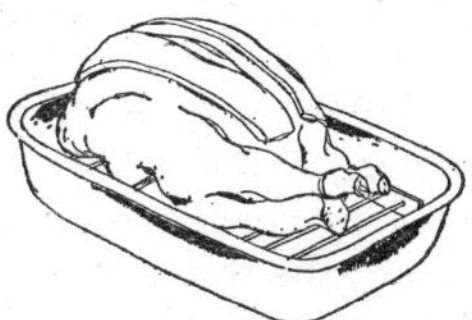

Barding a Fowl

TO AASTE

To ladle hot fat (or liquid) over the food (meat, poultry, etc.) at intervals during cooking, to prevent the outside from becoming dry.

TO BLANCH

To put food in cold water and bring to the boil, after which it is drained and usually put into cold water.

Almonds and chestnuts are blanched to facilitate removing their skins; salted and pickled meats to remove excess salt and soften the flavour; white meats and vegetables to preserve their white colour. Haricot and other dried beans cook more easily if first blanched; Brussels sprouts may be blanched to soften their flavour.

A variation of this process is used for vegetables which are to be bottled or canned. (See the chapter on this subject.)

TO BLEND

(*Sometimes also called* TO LITHE *or* TO SLAKE)

To mix flour, cornflour, rice flour and similar ground cereals to a smooth cream with a liquid, e.g., water, stock or milk. This is usually a preliminary to adding the boiling liquid, and prevents the cereal from forming lumps.

Always add the liquid to the cereal, and use a wooden spoon for mixing. Ground rice, cornflour, etc., are easy to blend. Flour, however, contains gluten, and beginners often experience difficulty in blending this cereal smoothly. The secret is to add just the right amount of liquid at first (about 2 tbsps. liquid to 2 level tbsps. flour). Too little liquid makes hard, doughy lumps which are difficult, if not impossible, to beat out. To much liquid makes lumps which, though smaller and softer, are equally difficult to smooth away. The method of mixing, too, is important—make a well in the centre of the flour, pour in a little of the liquid and stir round, gradually drawing in the flour, and adding more liquid as it becomes necessary.

TO BOIL

To cook in boiling liquid, usually stock or water. This is the method generally used for cooking vegetables, rice, suet puddings and other foods, the water being allowed to boil rapidly all the time. Although we also speak of boiled fish and meat, the expression is not really accurate, as in these cases the liquor is only allowed to simmer after the food has been put into it.

TO BRAISE

A combination of roasting, stewing and steaming, suitable for meat, rabbit, etc. The meat is first browned lightly in hot dripping, then placed on a bed of vegetables with just enough liquid to cover the vegetables. It is then covered with a lid and may be cooked either in a slow oven or over a gentle heat. (See the chapter on Meat Cookery.)

TO CASSEROLE

To cook food in the oven in a covered casserole dish, usually with vegetables and a sauce. This is a slow method of cooking, suitable for meat, rabbit, chicken, pigeons, etc. The food is frequently served in the casserole.

TO CLARIFY

The term applied to the process of separating fat from water, salt, meat juices and other ingredients that may be contained in it.

Dripping: Meat dripping is likely to contain meat juices and small pieces of meat and skin; if it has already been used for frying it may also contain small specks of food. When a pure fat is required, i.e., for pastry-making or for frying, these ingredients must be removed.

Melt the fat and strain it into a large basin; the straining will remove any large fragments. Now pour over the fat two or three times its own bulk of boiling water, stir well and allow to cool. The clean fat will rise to the top and the residue will settle—some at the bottom of the bowl and some underneath the fat. When the fat has solidified, lift it off and dab the underside dry with a clean cloth or piece of muslin. Scrape off any sediment from the fat with a knife.

Salted Margarine or Butter: These fats contain not only salt but also water, both of which must be removed if the fat is required pure for such purposes as omelette-making, for Genoese sponge mixture and so on.

Heat the fat gently until it is melted, then continue heating slowly without browning until all bubbling has ceased. When the fat is silent it indicates that the water has been driven off. Now remove it from the heat and let it stand for a few minutes, for the salt and any sediment to settle to the bottom, then gently pour off the fat. If much sediment is present, the clarified fat may be strained through muslin, but this is not as a rule necessary.

Rancid Fat: To improve the flavour of fat (especially butter) that has gone slightly rancid, heat it with water containing some bicarbonate of soda (about 1 tsp. to 1 pint); allow the fat to solidify again, then strain off the liquid, wash the fat and dry it with a piece of muslin.

Although this treatment will not restore very rancid fat, it should, in most cases, improve the flavour considerably.

TO CREAM

Working a mixture of fat and sugar together until it resembles whipped cream in colour and texture; this method is used when making cake and pudding mixtures containing a high proportion of fat, for butter cream fillings, and so on.

Put the fat and sugar together in a mixing bowl. With a wooden spoon, first crush the fat into the sugar, then work both together until soft, finally beating the mixture until light and creamy in colour and texture.

An electric mixer may be used for creaming. First soften the fat at room temperature, then put it in the basin, switch on the current at the speed recommended by the manufacturer, and beat the fat until it is soft. Add the sugar and beat for the required time.

Important points to remember are :

(*a*) Creaming must be done by beating, not by melting the fat. In very cold weather it is advisible to warm the basin containing the fat before the fire or by placing it over warm water. Do not heat the fat until it " oils."

(*b*) Do not cream the mixture until it is required for use. If left for any length of time it sets firmly and requires to be re-creamed again before use.

(*c*) Do not curtail the creaming process. The lightness and fine texture of mixtures made by this method are largely dependent on thorough creaming.

(*d*) Caster sugar creams more readily than granulated, and gives a finer texture.

TO EGG-AND-CRUMB

To dip food in beaten egg or egg and milk and then toss in fine breadcrumbs. The breadcrumbs adhere to the egg, forming a complete coating around the food. Used for coating fish, cutlets, rissoles, croquettes, and so on. After thus coating, the food is either fried or baked.

Prepare and sieve some fine breadcrumbs (fresh if the food is raw ; browned breadcrumbs or raspings for food that is already cooked), and put them on a piece of kitchen paper. Put some beaten egg (or, for economy, beaten egg mixed with an equal quantity of milk or water), on to a plate or dish. Toss the food to be coated in a little flour (seasoned, if a savoury dish) then put it, one piece at a time, in the egg. Brush all over with the egg, then lift with a flat-bladed knife, hold it for a moment to drain and lay it on the breadcrumbs. Holding opposite corners of the paper, toss the crumbs over the food, then lift it out, with the hand this time, and pass from one hand to the other until all loose crumbs have fallen off. Repeat with the remaining pieces, then fry or bake.

Important points to remember are :

(*a*) See that the food is completely coated with the egg before putting it into the crumbs. This is particularly important if the food is to be fried in deep fat, otherwise the fat is likely to splutter, and flavour from the food will pass into the fat.

(*b*) Use a pastry brush to apply the egg, and a knife to lift the food out of it—not the fingers, or the crumbs will stick to them, which is both messy and wasteful.

(*c*) Browned breadcrumbs, as stated above, are suitable only when the food is cooked and merely requires heating through, e.g., fish cakes and rissoles. Raw foods, such as fillets of fish, require longer frying and must therefore be coated with light-coloured breadcrumbs.

TO FOLD IN

A method of combining whisked mixtures with other ingredients so that they retain their lightness. Used for mixing meringues, soufflés and whisked cake mixtures such as sponge cakes and Swiss roll. It consists essentially of folding the mixture over the added ingredients, and a large metal spoon is used. (An electric mixer cannot be used for this particular operation.)

A typical example is folding dry flour into a whisked sponge cake mixture. First, sift some of the flour on top of the whisked mixture. Take a large metal spoon and, drawing it across the bottom of the bowl, take up a spoonful of the sponge mixture from the bottom and fold it over the top, thus enclosing the dry flour between. Repeat until all the flour is incorporated, occasionally cutting through the mixture with the spoon at right angles to the direction of the folding.

Important points to remember are :

(*a*) Fold the mixture very lightly.

(*b*) Remember that with every movement of the mixture some of the air bubbles are broken down ; therefore, do not agitate the mixture more than is absolutely necessary.

TO FRY IN DEEP FAT

To cook foods in sufficient fat to submerge them completely.

For this method a deep frying pan fitted with a wire basket is required, and there must be sufficient fat in the pan to cover the food, i.e., it should be about three-quarters filled.

Suitable fats for this method of frying are olive oil, lard, melted block suet, or clarified dripping. The fat, if properly looked after (see below), can be used again and again, with the addition of a little more from time to time as it becomes used up.

All food cooked in deep fat, with the exception of potatoes and pastry, must be coated either with egg and breadcrumbs or with batter—flour is not a suitable coating for deep frying. The food must never be wet.

The temperature of the fat is of great importance: if it is not hot enough the food becomes sodden with grease, and if too hot will be burnt on the outside before it is cooked through. The pan of fat should be heated until a faint blue smoke rises from the top. Any bubbling which is noticed during heating shows that the fat contains water. If this is the case, it should be heated gently until all the water has evaporated and bubbling ceases, and the heating then continued until a faint blue smoke is seen.

The prepared food is placed in the wire basket and lowered *gently* into the fat. It is a wise plan to draw the pan of fat away from the heat when first adding the food; replace it immediately over the heat and continue heating until the food is golden-brown. Gently lift out the basket and allow the fat to drain off into the pan. Transfer the contents to a piece of crumpled kitchen paper to finish draining, then dish and serve immediately.

After use, the fat should be strained into a deep container (heatproof) kept specially for the purpose, and the pan wiped out with paper to remove all crumbs or traces of food. The basket should be thoroughly washed and dried.

TO FRY IN SHALLOW FAT

To cook in a small quantity of fat in a shallow pan. The quantity of fat varies with the type of food—fillets of fish, chops, pancakes and fritters need just enough fat to prevent them from sticking to the pan. For made-up dishes, such as fish cakes and rissoles, there should be enough fat to about half-cover the food.

For shallow frying, heat the fat in the pan until just smoking hot before putting the food in. Cook the food quickly for a few moments until the surface is lightly browned on each side. Reduce the heat and finish cooking very gently. When it is cooked, lift carefully from the pan, allowing the fat to drain off, place upon a piece of crumpled kitchen paper to finish draining, transfer to a hot dish and serve at once. Any fat remaining in the pan should be strained off into the fat pot, and the pan can then be wiped out with paper.

TO GLAZE

To give a glossy surface:

(*a*) By brushing with milk, egg or a sugar solution to give a shiny surface to the cooked dish. Used as a finish for pastry, scones and yeast mixtures. Use a soft-bristled pastry brush, and brush on the glaze thinly.

Egg or milk are suitable glazes for sweet or savoury pastry dishes: both require cooking.

Sweet pastries may be glazed with sugar and water (2 tsps. sugar to 1 tsp. water), or brushed over with beaten egg white and dredged with sugar. Brush the glaze on to the raw pastry just before baking.

Yeast mixtures—buns and so on—may be glazed before or after cooking. For sticky buns, glaze with sugar and water after removal from the oven, or when nearly cooked. Melted butter is sometimes brushed over yeast buns after cooking.

(*b*) By tossing cooked vegetables, e.g., carrots, in margarine or butter before dishing. Another method of glazing vegetables, particularly suitable for small onions, is to brown them in hot butter and sugar, then add a very little stock and cook until tender, by which time the liquid should be absorbed or evaporated, leaving the onions coated with a caramel glaze.

(*c*) By coating cooked dishes with semi-transparent or glossy sauce to give a glazed effect. Puddings and gâteaux are coated with a jam glaze or concentrated fruit syrup; savoury galantines are covered with a meat glaze or aspic jelly.

TO GRILL

To cook in a direct heat, either under a griller or over a hot coal or charcoal fire. Used for choice cuts of meat (steak, chops, young chickens, etc.), bacon, sausages and fish, also for browning dishes "au gratin," making toast, and so on. (See the chapters on Meat and Fish Cookery for detailed instructions.)

TO INFUSE

To extract flavour by steeping in a liquid, as when preparing milk for sauces, such as bread sauce and Béchamel sauce; to extract flavour from lemon rind when making lemonade, and so on. Tea and coffee are also infusions.

An infusion is usually made by pouring on boiling liquid, covering, and leaving to stand in a warm place, without further cooking.

TO LARD

To insert small strips of fat bacon into the flesh of game birds or meat, to prevent it from drying during cooking. A larding needle is used for this.

TO MARINADE

To stand meat or fish in a well-seasoned mixture of oil, vinegar and herbs for a short while before cooking, in order to give flavour.

TO POACH

To cook lightly in water which is kept just below boiling point.

TO POT-ROAST

To cook meat in fat and a little water in a strong saucepan. The method is only suitable for small joints, but it is a useful way of cooking them when no oven is available. The meat is first browned in the hot fat, then if possible put on a small, low trivet; add a small quantity of water and some root vegetables, and cook gently for about $1\frac{1}{2}$–2 hours, or until the meat is tender, turning it occasionally.

TO PURÉE

To rub (vegetables and fruit) through a sieve to remove skins, fibres and pips and give a smooth, even texture. Used in making soups and sauces and for vegetable purées such as spinach and potatoes. Fruit purée forms the basis of fruit creams, fools and fruit ices.

Take a sieve, a basin large enough for the sieve to fit into it and a wooden spoon. Avoid using a non-stainless wire sieve for acid fruits, since the metal will affect the flavour and may spoil the colour of the purée. A hair sieve or a stainless wire sieve can be used for all foods, including acid fruits and vegetables. A hair sieve gives a finer texture but is a little more tedious to use.

Put the mixture to be sieved, a little at a time, into the shallow end of the sieve. First crush with a wooden spoon, then press and rub with the back of the spoon until nothing remains in the sieve but fibres, skins and pips. Add a little more of the liquid if the purée becomes very stiff and unmanageable. Occasionally scrape the purée from the underside of the sieve, but when doing this take care not to upset the contents from the top of the sieve; and either use a clean spoon, or, if the sieving spoon is used, free it from pips, etc., otherwise they will get into the purée and spoil its smoothness.

A small round strainer, though tedious for sieving when handling large quantities, may be used for sieving a small amount, e.g., a sauce.

TO REDUCE

To boil a mixture (e.g., meat glaze) in an uncovered pan to evaporate the liquid, thus reducing its bulk and concentrating its flavour.

TO RENDER FAT

The term applied to the process of extracting fat from fat trimmings, bacon rinds and suet, to use for frying, etc. There are two methods:

(*a*) Cut the fat into small pieces and put it into a baking tin. Put the tin into a slow oven while cooking is in progress. Allow to cook slowly until all the fat is extracted, leaving the crisp skin. Press the skin well with a fork, then strain off the liquid fat.

(*b*) This method is really a combination of rendering and clarifying. Cut the fat into small pieces, removing any scraps of meat or gristle, put into a pan, cover with water, and allow to boil slowly for several hours, until the water is driven off and the pieces of fat are dry and shrivelled. Strain off the fat.

TO ROAST

Strictly speaking, to roast is to cook (meat, poultry, game, etc.) by direct heat in front of an open fire, the meat being hung on a revolving spit and basted with hot fat from time to time. Nowadays, however, the term is applied to cooking meat in hot fat in a closed oven, which is more correctly described as "baking." (For Roasting, see chapter on Meat.)

TO RUB IN

A method of incorporating fat and flour, used in shortcrust pastry, plain cakes, etc., where a short texture is required.

First, cut the fat into small pieces in the flour, then, using both hands, rub the fat and flour between the thumb and finger-tips. Lift the hands well above the bowl when doing this, allowing the mixture to fall back into the bowl. The rubbing process combines the fat and flour, and lifting the mixture helps to keep it cool. Continue until the mixture is even throughout. To test this, shake the bowl; any lumps of fat will be easily seen on the surface and dry flour will collect at the bottom of the bowl. If the mixture contains half as much fat as flour it should resemble fine breadcrumbs after the rubbing-in is completed.

Important points to remember are:

(*a*) Do not attempt to rub in more than half as much fat as flour.

(*b*) Have the fat cold and firm.

(*c*) Do not curtail the rubbing-in process: thorough rubbing-in is necessary for a short and even texture.

TO SAUTÉ

To cook (vegetables) in fat without browning, as in making soups, stews and sauces. Derived from the French *sauter*, to jump, it suggests the action of tossing the food while in the hot fat; the flavour of the vegetables is improved without spoiling the colour of the finished dish.

Sauté potatoes are boiled potatoes cut into slices and cooked in a little hot fat until hot through and (in this case) lightly browned.

TO SCORE

To make shallow cuts in the surface (of fish, meat, etc.) to improve its flavour or appearance when cooked. For example, fish is improved in flavour if scored before marinading; the crackling of roast pork is scored before cooking to prevent it spoiling the shape of the joint as it shrivels, and also to facilitate carving.

TO SIMMER

To keep a liquid just below boiling point, i.e., at approximately 190° F. (Boiling point is 212° F.) Used when long, slow cooking is required (as distinct from rapid boiling), e.g., for stews, soups and sauces.

First, bring the liquid to the boil, then adjust the heat so that the surface of the liquid is kept just moving. It should be gently rippling only —bubbling indicates boiling.

TO STEAM

To cook over boiling water, usually in a special steamer with holes or a funnel to allow the steam to reach the food. Small items, such as fillets of fish, can be steamed satisfactorily on a deep plate placed over a pan of boiling water and covered with the pan lid.

TO STEW

To cook slowly, i.e., just below boiling point, in a covered stew pan or casserole with only enough liquid barely to cover the food. Used for coarse cuts of meat which require long, slow cooking to make them tender; also for vegetables and fruits. (See chapter on Meat and recipes in Index.)

TO TAMMY

To pass (soup or sauce) through a tammy cloth to obtain a very smooth texture. A tammy cloth is made of a fine woollen material.

TO WHIP OR WHISK

To beat up cream, jelly, eggs or liquid foods rapidly, in order to incorporate air (thus incidentally increasing the bulk), or to produce a pleasing fluffy texture.

The whipping may be done with a fork, a wire whisk, a special rotary whisk or an electric mixer (follow the manufacturer's directions regarding speed, etc.), and it should usually be continued until the food is quite stiff.

The method of whipping fresh cream and evaporated milk is described in the chapter on Iced and Decorated Cakes, and the whisking of egg whites is given in connection with the making of Meringues.

The term whisking also used to describe the mixing together of eggs and sugar for sponge cake mixtures. (See the Cake Making chapters for fuller details.)

COOKERY TERMS

AU GRATIN

Derived from the French *gratiner*, to brown, this term implies that the dish has been browned on the top. In many people's minds it is associated with cheese, but although dishes "au gratin" often contain cheese, this is not an essential ingredient.

In order that there may be plenty of the characteristic crisp, brown top, a shallow dish is used, hence the "au gratin" dish, which is essentially shallow and usually heatproof. The food (cooked vegetables, meats, fish, etc.) is arranged in an "au gratin" dish, coated with a sauce, sprinkled liberally with breadcrumbs (and sometimes cheese), dotted with butter, margarine or dripping, and browned under the grill or on the top shelf of a hot oven.

BOUCHÉES

Very small pastry cases filled with a savoury mixture, and served as after-dinner savouries, or with cocktails. Special tins, like miniature patty pans (called bouchée moulds), are used to bake the pastry cases.

BOUQUET GARNI

A bunch of herbs, used in soups, stews, sauces, and so on, to give flavour. (See the section on Herbs.)

When fresh herbs are not available, a pinch or so of mixed dried herbs may be used instead. If the dish calls for spices such as cloves, peppercorns and mace, these are usually included in the bag of herbs.

CARAMEL

Sugar syrup boiled until it has a rich brown colour and a caramel flavour. Used for flavouring cakes and puddings, lining pudding moulds, etc. (For example, see Caramel Custard.)

If boiling is continued beyond a certain stage, the caramel becomes very dark and loses its sweet taste; it may then be used as gravy browning, or to darken Christmas pudding mixtures.

COATING BATTER

Batter is a suitable coating for fritters (fruit or vegetable), fillets of fish, kromeskies, etc. Any coating batter recipe can be used, and the batter should be mixed to the consistency of thick cream. Place the food to be cooked, a piece at a time, in the batter, lift out, allow any excess batter to drip off, then place immediately in the hot fat.

CROQUETTES

Savoury mixtures (of meat, fish, egg or vegetables) rolled into a cylindrical shape, then coated with egg and breadcrumbs and fried.

CUTLETS

1. Chops cut from the best end of the neck of mutton, lamb, veal or pork.

2. Savoury mixtures of meat, fish, egg or vegetables shaped like cutlets, then egg-and-crumbed and fried. A piece of (uncooked) macaroni is sometimes stuck into the thin end, to imitate the bone.

DARIOLES

Savoury mixtures cooked (i.e., steamed or baked) in dariole moulds, which are very small tin moulds shaped like a flower-pot. These dariole moulds are sometimes also used to make sweet dishes such as castle puddings, steamed custards, and so on.

DOUGH

The term used to described the texture of mixtures (cakes, biscuits, bread, pastry) that are handled. Shortcrust pastry and biscuit mixtures containing a good proportion of fat are mixed to a *stiff* dough; flaky and puff pastry to a softer though still *firm* dough; spongy mixtures, such as scones, suetcrust pastry and yeast mixtures, should be mixed to a light, *soft* dough—the softer the better, though, of course, the texture must not be sticky.

DROPPING CONSISTENCY

The term used to describe the texture of a cake or pudding mixture before cooking. To test this, well fill the spoon with the mixture, hold the spoon on its side above the basin and count slowly; the mixture should drop in about 5 seconds without your having to jerk the spoon.

The majority of cakes and puddings are mixed to this consistency. Some steamed puddings—for example, suet puddings cooked in a basin—require to be rather slacker (*soft* dropping consistency), while fruit cakes should be a little stiffer (*stiff* dropping consistency).

Rock buns and similar small cakes that have to keep their shape without support (that is to say, are baked on a flat baking sheet) are mixed even drier, to a stiff paste. Gingerbreads and whisked sponge mixtures, on the other hand, are mixed very slack, almost to a batter.

ESCALOPES

Thin slices of meat (usually veal) or fish, free from skin and bone.

FILLET

1. A piece of fish cut away from the bone, such as fillets of plaice, sole, cod, etc.

2. In the case of meat it refers to the undercut of beef, or the top of the leg of mutton, lamb, veal or pork.

PANADA

A mixture of fat, flour and liquid (milk, stock, etc.) in the proportion of 2 oz. fat and 2 oz. flour to $\frac{1}{2}$ pint liquid, i.e., twice as thick as a coating sauce. It is made by the roux method, i.e., the fat is melted, the flour added and mixed well together, and the liquid stirred in by degrees, heating and stirring continuously. A panada is used for binding mixtures, such as meat croquettes, quenelles and so on, and forms the basis of hot soufflés and choux pastry. (For recipe for Panada Sauce, see chapter on Sauces.)

PETITS FOURS

Very small fancy cakes, iced cakes, almond biscuits, etc., served at the end of the formal dinner. Crystallised fruits, and caramellised and fondant-coated fruits are often included in the petits fours.

QUENELLES

Portions of a savoury mixture (such as fish or chicken, bound with a panada and sieved) shaped like small eggs and poached in hot stock or water.

RASPINGS

Fine browned breadcrumbs, which can be dried and kept in stock. Used for coating boiled ham or bacon, for sprinkling on scalloped dishes au gratin, and for coating rissoles, fish cakes and so on, prior to frying.

To make raspings, cut or break crusts of stale bread into small pieces, and put them into the bottom of a slow oven (300°–325° F., mark 1–2). Continue cooking until they are quite crisp and pale golden-brown. Break down with a rolling pin, pass through a coarse wire sieve and keep in a store jar.

RISSOLES

The strict definition is small portions of a savoury (meat, fish or egg) mixture enclosed in rounds of pastry, folded over to make crescents, and fried in hot fat. The term is often loosely applied to a type of croquette.

ROUX

A mixture of fat and flour cooked together. Used for thickening many sauces, soups and stews.

Melt the fat, sprinkle in an equal weight of flour, and stir well, then cook gently for a minute or so, stirring continuously. The roux is now ready for the addition of the hot liquid (see chapter on Sauces).

Important points to remember are :

(*a*) Allow at least as much fat as flour, otherwise the roux will be too stiff and likely to go lumpy when the liquid is added. In very rich sauces the amount of fat may exceed the flour.

(*b*) Always melt the fat before adding the flour, otherwise the flour is likely to burn.

(*c*) For white or light-colour sauces, soups and stews, the roux must not be allowed to brown at all, or the colour of the finished dish will be spoilt. For dark sauces, etc., the roux may be browned lightly, but over-cooking gives an unpleasant bitter flavour.

SEASONED FLOUR

Flour to which salt and pepper have been added. Used for coating fillets of fish and cutlets before frying : also for coating pieces of meat, joints of rabbit, etc., when making stews and when braising.

Put 2 tbsps. flour on to a plate, add 1 tsp. salt and ½ tsp. pepper, and mix well.

STOCK

The liquid in which bones and meat scraps have been cooked to extract their flavour. Stock is also made from fish bones and skin, and from vegetables. (For meat, fish and vegetable stocks, see chapter on Soups and Broths.)

TOURNEDOS

Fillets of beef (i.e., slices from the undercut, or fillet) generally trimmed into rounds and served, grilled or fried, as an entrée. (See colour picture facing page 97, where they are served on fried bread and topped with mushrooms.)

HOW TO USE OUR RECIPES

GOOD HOUSEKEEPING recipes are carefully worked out and tested. All measurements are given, and directions for making are simple, clear and detailed, so that even a beginner should be able to follow them easily. Any general instructions which apply to all or most of the dishes in any one group are given in full at the beginning of the particular chapter, and such points are then only mentioned briefly in the individual recipes. For example, in the chapter on Soufflé Making the preparation of soufflé cases is described in detail at the beginning, and not in each recipe. It is therefore essential to read through the introduction before attempting any recipes.

The Amount of Liquid

Whenever possible, the exact amount of liquid required to make a mixture is indicated, but this is often difficult to estimate exactly, since there are so many factors involved. For example, eggs vary in size, some flours absorb more moisture than others, the yield of juice from lemons varies in quantity, and so on, so in this matter you will often have to use your own discretion. However, in all recipes the approximate amount of liquid is given and also a description of the texture to be aimed at—such as "dropping consistency," "stiff paste," "dough"—to give you all possible help. Full details of these textures, etc., are given in the chapter on Cookery Processes and Terms.

Oven Temperatures

Only an approximate time for baking can be given, since this will depend on the consistency of the mixture, the size, shape or depth of the dish (or tin), position in oven, and so on; as an additional guide a description of how the finished dish should appear is usually included.

In the recipes in this book the method of quoting oven temperatures reads: Moderately hot oven (400° F., mark 6). The degrees Fahrenheit give the temperature of the oven and also the corresponding electrical setting, while the phrase "mark 6" applies to the standard thermostatic setting of a modern gas cooker. The following table shows the range of temperatures:

Oven Description	*Approx. temp., also electric oven setting*	*Standard gas thermostat*
Very slow	250° F., 275° F.	¼, ½
Slow	300° F., 325° F.	1, 2
Moderate	350° F., 375° F.	3, 4, 5
Moderately hot	400° F., 425° F.	6, 7
Hot to very hot	450° F., to 475° F.	8, 9

It must be emphasised that these gas settings apply only to modern cookers; if you have an old model and are in doubt about the settings, seek advice from your local Gas Board.

The inexperienced cook is advised to follow exactly the oven temperatures and cooking times given in the recipes; but since no two ovens are exactly alike, you will gradually learn to make any slight adjustment necessary to suit your own particular cooker.

Working from a Recipe

1. Before you start to make a dish, read the recipe all the way through, and read also the general instructions at the beginning of the chapter concerned. If any cookery term or method is new to you, you can look up its meaning in the chapter on Cookery Processes. Then you will be able to go straight through with making the dish—stopping in the middle of a process may have disastrous results.

2. Next, assemble the cooking utensils you will need, and do any preparation necessary, such as greasing dishes, lining cake tins, preparing soufflé moulds and so on. If the dish is to be baked, turn on the oven heat and set the oven control so that it will be at the correct temperature when required.

3. Finally, collect and measure out all the ingredients needed. If you are a beginner, you will be wise to follow the recipe exactly, carefully weighing and measuring the ingredients, and to leave guesswork to the more experienced cook. Directions for measuring are given below. Good kitchen scales and weights and graded liquid measures are a great asset, but for those who do not possess these, we include a table of

homely measures. Follow the directions closely—seemingly slight changes in procedure may make all the difference between an outstanding dish and one that is only mediocre.

Altering Recipes

Do not alter the amounts of such ingredients as fat, flour or baking powder, for they have been carefully proportioned to give successful results. In the case of flavourings, seasonings and spices, or other ingredients which affect only the flavour of the dish (for example, onion, garlic, etc.), the amounts indicated are those which are likely to please the average taste.

For the most part, the amounts given in these recipes are sufficient for a family of three or four. (For quantities to allow per head, see the Catering Guide given in the chapter on Shopping.) For smaller dishes, you will generally find it quite simple to halve the ingredients. Do not, however, just halve cooking times: a stew takes the same length of time to cook even though half quantities are used, and for a baked dish, the cooking time will need to be reduced only by about a quarter when the recipe is halved. For boiling or steaming meat or fish, the cooking time adjusts itself, since it depends on the size of the piece to be cooked. For cakes, see the table in the Cake Making chapter.

Generally speaking, we do not recommend making more than a double quantity of the recipe. If you need a larger amount than this, it is better to make several batches.

WEIGHTS AND WEIGHING

It is essential that the quantities of ingredients required for any recipe should be measured accurately, and Good Housekeeping Institute considers that weighing is the most reliable method for all but the smallest quantities. In the recipes in this and other GOOD HOUSEKEEPING books, therefore, quantities are stated by weight wherever practicable, but for the benefit of those who have no scales, some tables of useful equivalents are given in this chapter.

Table of Avoirdupois Weights

16 drm.	=1 oz.
16 oz.	=1 lb.
14 lb.	=1 stone
2 stones (28 lb.)	=1 quarter
112 lb. (4 quarters)	=1 hundredweight (cwt.)
20 cwt.	=1 ton
1 kilogram (Kg.)	=1000 grams (2.2 lb. approx.)

To weigh Syrup and similar ingredients: First dredge the scale pan with flour, then pour the syrup from the tin or jar, and cut off the "trail" with a knife when the required amount is registered. The syrup will slide easily off the floured pan. Alternatively, first balance a saucepan or basin on the scales, noting the weight, and then weigh in the usual manner, measuring the ingredient straight into the saucepan or basin.

MEASURES

When very small quantities are involved, or where kitchen scales are not available, the ingredients must be measured. The most common units of measurement are spoonfuls. When the term spoonful is used in recipes in this book it is taken to mean a level spoonful. A half spoonful is a level spoonful halved lengthwise with a knife.

Sizes of teaspoons and tablespoons vary considerably, so it is not possible to give exact equivalent weights. However, the following table will serve as a guide to the approximate weights of spoonfuls of the most frequently used ingredients.

Flour, cornflour, cocoa, custard powder:

2 tsps.	¼ oz.
2 dessertsps.	½ oz.
2 tbsps.	¾–1 oz.

Sugar, rice, lentils, etc.:

2 tbsps.	1¼ oz.

Breadcrumbs:

2 tbsps.	½ oz.

Standard Spoon and Cup Measures

The British Standards Institution has introduced sets of standard spoons and measuring cups. Standard spoons are always measured level, so two of them will correspond to one rounded spoonful. A standard cup is taken to mean a cup lightly filled with the ingredient and not shaken or pressed down. 1 level standard tbsp. is 1/16th of a standard cup, and 3 tsps. are equivalent to 1 tbsp.

The following table shows the number of level B.S.I. spoonfuls needed to make up 1 oz. of various foodstuffs:

Baking powder	2⅓	Lentils	2
Cocoa	3	Raisins	2
Coffee	3½	Rolled oats	4

Cornflour	3	Salt	1¾
Custard powder	3	Semolina	2½
Currants	2	Sugar	
Flour	3	Granulated	1¾
Gelatine	3	Demerara	2
Jam	1	Caster	1½

The B.S.I. cup measure holds ½ pint (10 oz. liquid measure) and the following table gives the approximate weight in oz. of 1 level B.S.I. cupful of various ingredients. (Dry foods should be spooned in lightly; jam, syrup, etc., should be well packed.)

Breadcrumbs, fresh	3 oz.
Breadcrumbs, dry and sifted	6 oz.
Cheese, grated	4 oz.
Flour, unsifted	5 oz.
Haricot beans	8 oz.
Jam	12–16 oz.
Lentils	8 oz.
Minced beef	8 oz.
Oatmeal, medium	8 oz.
Oatmeal, coarse	7 oz.
Oats, rolled	4 oz.
Peas, dried	8 oz.
Potato, cooked and mashed	8 oz.
Semolina	6 oz.
Sugar, granulated	8 oz.
Sultanas	6 oz.
Syrup or treacle	16 oz.

American Cup Measures

American recipes are sometimes followed by people in this country, and since the American cup measure differs from the British one (it holds an American ½ pint, that is, 8 oz. liquid measure) a table is given here of equivalents in oz. of American cups :

Flour	4 oz.
Sugar, granulated	6½ oz.
Fat	6½ oz.
Breadcrumbs, fresh	2½ oz.
Breadcrumbs, dry	5 oz.
Syrup	13 oz.
Currants, sultanas, etc.	5 oz.
Chopped suet	4¼ oz.
Grated cheese	3½ oz.
Rolled oats	3½ oz.
Coconut	2¼ oz.

Liquid Measures

A graduated measure or a set of measures is of great assistance when measuring liquids. The following is the liquid measure table. (The British pint contains 20 fluid oz., whereas the American one contains 16 fluid oz.).

*4 gills = 1 pint	2 gallons = 1 peck
2 pints = 1 quart	8 gallons = 1 bushel
4 quarts = 1 gallon	8 bushels = 1 quarter

* In the north of England a gill means ½ pint, but in all the recipes in this book it is taken to mean ¼ pint.

As a rough-and-ready guide, it can be taken that :

1 teacupful = ⅓ pint
1 tumblerful or 1 breakfastcupful = ½ pint

Miscellaneous Measures

Essences and Colourings : Add in very small quantities, usually a drop at a time. To measure a drop, pour a little of the liquid into a clean teaspoon, then pour it back into the bottle, leaving one drop in the spoon. Shake this into the mixture. If necessary, repeat the process. In this way there is little danger of spoiling the mixture by over-flavouring it or colouring it too highly. Another method is to use a skewer, dipping it into the liquid and shaking a drop at a time into the mixture.

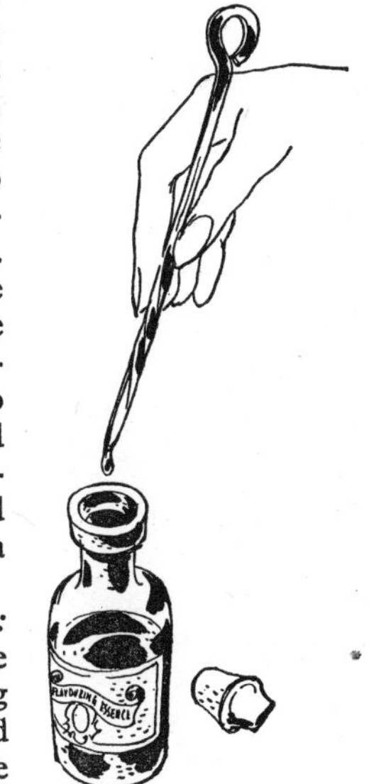

Syrup and Treacle : The most practicable method of measuring syrup is to use a warmed spoon, which will enable 1 level tbsp. to be extracted from the tin without the syrup adhering to the underside of the spoon. When measured in this way 1 tbsp. of syrup weighs approximately 1½ oz.

A Pinch is generally accepted to mean as much (of a powder, salt, etc.) as can be held between the thumb and forefinger.

A Good Pinch is as much of an ingredient such as salt as can be held between the thumb and first two fingers.

Pastry : Where pastry is called for in a recipe, the quantity stated refers to the amount of flour used to make the pastry; thus ½ lb. shortcrust pastry is made with 8 oz. flour, and so on.

Section Two

HORS D'ŒUVRE

Hors d'œuvre are served to introduce the meal; they should therefore be very appetising, small and attractively presented. Their main ingredients should contrast with the savoury (if any) to be served at the end of the meal.

The plain hors d'œuvre, such as oysters, caviare, smoked salmon, potted shrimps, etc., which are usually served *au naturel*, are delicious and generally very popular, but they are also very expensive. However, a dish of simple dressed hors d'œuvre or hors d'œuvre variés, composed of a selection of vegetables, fish, meat, eggs and so on, makes quite a decorative and appetising first course, which can be prepared very easily from quite simple ingredients—often mainly from left-overs.

More elaborate dressed hors d'œuvre, such as cassolettes and canapés, can, of course, be made if preferred; several recipes for such dishes are included here and also in the chapter on Savouries.

A fish cocktail makes an interesting beginning to a meal, especially in summer weather. Both fish and fruit cocktails are particularly good dishes to serve when entertaining, for they can be prepared and dished beforehand and, when served daintily garnished in pretty stem glasses, they help to make the table look decorative.

Fruit is a form of hors d'œuvre which is popular nowadays, served either *au naturel* as are melon and grapefruit, or in the form of a mixed fruit cocktail, attractively dished and garnished, or simply as fruit juice, such as grapefruit, orange or pineapple juice, sweetened and served ice-cold.

Cocktails made from tomato juice or other vegetable juices are often used as appetisers before a meal. Some like a plain, naturally flavoured cocktail, consisting chiefly of tomato juice, with a little lemon juice to give it a fresh, sharp flavour, while others prefer a more elaborate and highly seasoned drink. Recipes for both types are given in this chapter.

Hot hors d'œuvre as appetisers are becoming popular, especially to precede a cold meal, and a few recipes are included here.

CAVIARE

This is served ice-cold, with freshly made toast and butter. Lemon juice may be sprinkled over the caviare if liked. An alternative is to spread the caviare on croûtes of fried bread and sprinkle with a few grains of cayenne pepper.

OYSTERS

Oysters should be served in their shells, and these should be embedded in chopped ice. Thin brown bread and butter, slices of lemon and 3
cayenne pepper are the correct accompaniments. Tabasco sauce may also be served with oysters.

PÂTÉ

Liver and other savoury pâtés may be served as an hors d'œuvre. Cut into thick slices or sections, and serve with freshly made dry toast and butter.

PLOVERS' AND GULLS' EGGS

Hard-boiled plovers' eggs make a delicious hors d'œuvre, but when these are not obtainable gulls' eggs are a good substitute. Hard-boil the eggs, shell them and serve cold, on a bed of small cress.

POTTED SHRIMPS

Potted shrimps make an excellent beginning to a meal. Unless they are in attractive pots, turn them out on to a dish; serve with dry toast, butter and freshly ground black pepper.

SMOKED SALMON

Slice the salmon very thinly, and serve with thin brown bread and butter, lemon wedges and freshly ground black pepper.

MIXED HORS D'ŒUVRE

(HORS D'ŒUVRE VARIÉS)

Special divided dishes are made for serving 4
mixed hors d'œuvre, but failing one of these, you

can use a set of small dishes, placing them on a large dish or on a tray, or you can set the hors d'œuvre on a large platter, separating the individual items with a garnish of small cress, watercress or parsley. The important thing is that the various items should all be together, as this simplifies serving and ensures that each person at the table can see the choice at a glance and select accordingly.

It is usual to serve at least four varieties, preferably more. They should be served very cold, and accompanied by fresh crusty rolls and pats of butter.

Here is a list of suitable ingredients for mixed hors d'œuvre

Salad and other Vegetables

Lettuce : Crisp lettuce heart, lightly coated in French dressing.

Endive : Shredded, or torn into small pieces, and tossed in French dressing.

Chicory : Sliced and tossed in French dressing.

Radishes : Either left whole or cut into fancy shapes such as lilies or rosettes. Alternatively, they may be sliced, dressed with French dressing and sprinkled with chopped parsley.

Cucumber : Peeled, thinly sliced and laid in vinegar. Alternatively, it may be cut into small dice and dressed with French dressing.

Tomatoes : Peeled if liked, sliced, then coated with French dressing and garnished with chopped parsley.

Spring Onions : Either left whole (cut to uniform length) or sliced and tossed in French dressing.

Beetroot : Sliced or cut into dice, sprinkled with finely chopped onion or chives and coated with French dressing or plain vinegar.

Celery : Usually sliced, tossed in French dressing, and garnished with chopped parsley. Alternatively, the celery stalks may be cut into short lengths and stuffed with cream cheese or other savoury filling. Celery is sometimes served cooked, when it is sliced and dressed as above.

Red or Green Peppers : Use raw, shredded or chopped, and mixed with French dressing or tomato ketchup.

Potato : Cooked and sliced or diced, then coated with mayonnaise and garnished with chopped parsley or chopped chives.

Peas, French and Runner Beans : Cooked and tossed in French dressing or included in mixed vegetable mayonnaise.

Asparagus Tips : Cooked and dressed with vinaigrette dressing.

Carrots, Turnips, Artichokes : Cooked and diced, these are included in Russian salad or may be used alone as an ingredient in mixed hors d'œuvre. These vegetables are usually tossed in mayonnaise dressing, but a simple French dressing may be used if preferred.

Cabbage : Shredded raw cabbage (with carraway seeds if liked), dressed with French dressing, or pickled red cabbage served in its own liquor.

Olives : Either whole, or stoned and stuffed. Chopped olives are sometimes mixed with other hors d'œuvre such as vegetable mayonnaise, to give piquancy.

Pickles : Relishes such as gherkins, mixed pickles, piccalilli and so on, served in their own liquor.

Mustard and Cress, Watercress, Parsley : Used as a garnish.

Herbs : Chopped chives, tarragon, parsley or mint, etc., may be used to mix with, or sprinkle over, the hors d'œuvre.

Fish

Salted and Pickled Fish, such as sardines, anchovy fillets, rollmops, soused herrings and so on. These fish are usually served in their own liquor or with a simple dressing.

Shell Fish also are popular—shrimps, prawns, mussels, lobster, crab or crayfish. They are usually served dressed with mayonnaise dressing.

Other fish suitable for hors d'œuvre include cold salmon, dressed with mayonnaise, cold smoked haddock with piquant cream sauce or mayonnaise, and so on. White fish may be used, but in this case, the dressing should include a piquant ingredient such as capers or chopped pickled gherkins to give flavour.

Meats

Cold cooked sausages of all kinds can be used—liver, breakfast or luncheon sausage, garlic sausage, salami, or even cold cooked pork or beef sausages. These are usually served sliced, and being well flavoured, do not require dressing.

Cold cooked meats can be included, such as cold roast beef, ham or tongue, scraps of cold chicken, game and so on. These are usually cut up neatly and soaked in a marinade of oil and vinegar, with chopped parsley and sometimes chopped onion or chives added.

Eggs

Hard-boiled eggs neatly sliced, coated with mayonnaise and garnished with capers.

Pulses and Cereals

Haricot Beans : Cooked, mixed with tomato sauce or ketchup and garnished with chopped parsley or chopped chives.

Macaroni : Cooked, cut into short lengths, mixed with chopped ham and moistened with sharp sauce.

Rice : Dry boiled rice, mixed with chopped raisins and moistened with curry-flavoured dressing.

DRESSED HORS D'ŒUVRE

ANCHOVY MEDALLIONS

Rounds of cooked potato, ½ inch in diameter	Anchovies
Rounds of cooked pickled beetroot, ½ inch in diameter	Some thick mayonnaise sauce
	Cayenne pepper

Lay a round of cooked potato on one of beetroot, place a ring of anchovy round the two, fill in the centre with stiff mayonnaise, and sprinkle with cayenne pepper.

BEEF CORNETS

Cut thin slices of cold roast beef into triangles, fold, press firmly into cornet shapes and fill the centre with whipped cream flavoured strongly with grated horseradish and seasoned with pepper and salt.

CABBAGE SALAD

Shred pickled cabbage, lettuce and white of egg, into thin Julienne strips. Mix with a small quantity of cold veal or chicken and blend with mayonnaise.

CUCUMBER CREAMS

Cut a small cucumber into ½-inch lengths, scoop out the centre and fill with a cream made of pounded chicken mixed lightly with Béchamel sauce. Garnish with paprika.

DRESSED FRENCH BEANS

Drain the beans well when they are cooked, season and allow to cool. Dress with the following :

2 tbsps. salad oil	1 tbsp. tarragon or white vinegar
½ tsp. mustard	¼ tsp. sugar
½ tsp. salt	

FISH MAYONNAISE

Flake a small quantity of white fish. Chop a hard-boiled egg, and add a small quantity of cooked peas and beans. Blend with cold Tar are sauce, and serve on a bed of lettuce.

MAYONNAISE OF VEGETABLES

Cut cold cooked carrots and potato and fresh tomato into neat dice. Mix with some cold cooked peas and a few capers, and blend with a little mayonnaise sauce. Pile on a bed of lettuce, and sprinkle a very little finely chopped parsley on top.

OILED OLIVES

These should be prepared the day before, or at least several hours before required. Take the amount of olives necessary, give each a smart tap with a hammer (a wooden mallet is ideal), so as to crush but not break them. Put them on a deep plate, cover with olive oil, and for every 12 olives sprinkle with 2 tbsps. fennel seed or aniseed, 2 tsps. dried marjoram, 2 pinches of chopped garlic and a pinch of pepper. When ready, put the olives on to a plate, taking up as little oil as possible. These olives should be eaten with a wooden pick or cocktail stick.

SAVOURY RADISHES

Cut off the radish leaves, wash the radishes well and scrape them. Cut into thin slices. Pour over a dressing made with 2 tbsps. olive oil, 1 tbsp. vinegar, 1 tsp. chopped garlic and 2 tbsps. chopped parsley, seasoned with salt and pepper. Mix well, and put on to a glass dish.

FRUIT HORS D'ŒUVRE AND COCKTAILS

CHILLED FRUIT COCKTAIL

1 grapefruit	A little sugar
6 raspberries	3 cherries (fresh or maraschino)
2 tbsps. pineapple or other fruit syrup	A few mint leaves
Maraschino to flavour	

Peel the grapefruit, remove the pith and cut into neat pieces. Add the hulled raspberries, pineapple juice and Maraschino. Sprinkle with sugar, and chill in the refrigerator. Remove some ice from the drawers and break it up finely with an ice pick. Select three small, straight-sided cocktail glasses and stand each in a grapefruit or champagne glass. Pack the finely chipped ice around the cocktail glasses and fill with the chilled fruit, put a cherry on each and garnish with a sprig of mint leaves.

FRUIT COCKTAIL

1 large grapefruit
2 tbsps. sliced apricots
1 tbsp. apricot syrup
2 tsps. sugar
2 tbsps. Maraschino (if desired)
6 fresh cherries

Cut the grapefruit in half and remove the flesh from the skin. Cut into pieces, and add the sliced apricots, the apricot syrup, sugar and Maraschino. Put into cocktail glasses, top with a cherry and chill before serving.

GRAPE AND ORANGE JUICE COCKTAIL

½ lb. grapes
Juice of 3 oranges (approximately ½ pint)
2 tbsps. lime juice
Sugar to taste
Fresh mint

Skin and stone the grapes, then chill thoroughly. Half an hour before serving, arrange the grapes in individual glasses. Cover with the orange juice and lime juice, mixed, and sweeten to taste. Chill thoroughly, and when ready to serve, garnish with a sprig of mint.

GRAPEFRUIT

Wipe the grapefruit, cut it in half, cut out the centre core and separate the flesh from the individual sections, using a grapefruit knife for preference. Place in a grapefruit glass, add a
5 little sugar to the centre of the grapefruit, and a few drops of Maraschino. Add a cocktail cherry.

Preparing Grapefruit

If preferred, tinned grapefruit can be served. Chill the tin before opening. Place 2 tbsps. fruit in a cocktail glass, add a little Maraschino, and decorate with a cocktail cherry, if available. In hot weather a little chipped ice may be sprinkled over the grapefruit.

MELON

Cut wedge-shaped slices from a thoroughly chilled melon, and serve with caster sugar and
6 powdered ginger; if preferred, quartered lemons can take the place of the ginger. Serve on ice.

MELON BALLS AND GRAPEFRUIT JUICE

Remove the seeds from ½ a small water-melon, then scoop out balls from the soft melon pulp, using a Parisian potato cutter or a small teaspoon. Arrange in individual stem glasses and add ½ pint fresh or tinned grapefruit juice, sweetened to taste. Chill thoroughly, and before serving garnish with mint leaves.

MELON COCKTAIL

Cubes of ripe melon
Cubes of preserved ginger
¼ pint ginger syrup
2 dessertsps. lemon juice
A little Kirsch or Maraschino if liked

The proportion of melon and ginger must be a matter of personal taste, but three parts melon to one of ginger is a good mixture. Put the fruit into a basin, and cover with the blended syrup, lemon juice and liqueur, and allow to stand for at least half an hour for the flavours to blend. Chill, and serve very cold in cocktail glasses.

RASPBERRY AND PINEAPPLE COCKTAIL

½ lb. fresh raspberries
1 breakfastcupful diced pineapple (fresh or tinned)
Juice of 1 large or 2 small oranges
Fresh mint

Arrange the fruit in layers in stem glasses, pour the orange juice over and garnish with mint. Chill before serving.

SPICED GRAPEFRUIT COCKTAIL

1 medium-sized tin of grapefruit
6 cloves
A 3-inch stick cinnamon
¼ tsp. ginger

Strain the syrup from the grapefruit and make it up to 1½ gills with water. Add the spices, cover, and simmer for 15 minutes. Then cool, and strain over the grapefruit. Dish in individual glasses and chill before serving.

FISH COCKTAILS

For fish cocktails, fresh or tinned shell fish of any kind may be used—lobster, crab, crayfish, prawns or shrimps. A mixture of any of these is equally good.

Separate the flesh from the shell and cut into small pieces. Reserve for garnishing a few heads of prawns or shrimps or the smallest claws of a crab. Dust the flesh with pepper and squeeze a
few drops of lemon juice or vinegar over it. Add 7
1 tbsp. or so of tomato ketchup, or sieved fresh tomatoes with a dash of piquant sauce and enough mayonnaise or salad cream to bind. Line some cocktail glasses with crisp lettuce, well dried, and fill with a spoonful of the fish

mixture. Dust with a little paprika pepper, and garnish each glass with a prawn or shrimp head, tiny crab claw, or lobster coral. Serve chilled.

MUSSEL COCKTAIL

½ pint mussels
½ tsp. tabasco sauce
Pepper and salt
1 tbsp. lemon juice
1 tbsp. tomato ketchup
½ tsp. piquant sauce
2 tsps. mayonnaise

Open the mussels and reserve some of the liquor from the shells. Mix all the other ingredients together and add some of the mussel liquor with the mussels. Chill, and serve in small glasses.

SHELL FISH AND TOMATO JUICE COCKTAIL

6 oz. shell fish meat
1 small tin of tomato juice
1½ tbsps. lemon juice
3 tsps. granulated sugar
1½ tbsps. piquant sauce
1½ tsps. bottled horse-radish
Garnish of small cress

Flake the cooked fish, combine all the ingredients, chill and serve in cocktail glasses, garnished with small cress.

VEGETABLE JUICE COCKTAILS

MIXED VEGETABLE JUICE COCKTAIL

½ pint of mixed tinned vegetable juices
1 tbsp. lemon juice
Salt and pepper
1 tsp. piquant sauce

Combine all the ingredients, then cover and chill. Serve in cocktail glasses.

TOMATO COCKTAIL

Choose ripe, well-shaped tomatoes and scoop out the centres, leaving a hollow case, not too thin. Chop up the centre part, removing as many of the seeds as possible, and add to it an equal amount of chopped cucumber and the white part of celery finely chopped. Add a little piquant sauce and fill up the tomatoes with the mixture. Serve on individual dishes surrounded with shredded lettuce or chipped ice.

TOMATO JUICE COCKTAIL—I

½ pint tomato juice (bottled tomato juice or crushed ripe tomatoes)
4 tsps. sugar
½ tsp. piquant sauce
1 dessertsp. lemon juice

Mix all the ingredients together, and serve ice-cold in small glasses.

Note: 1 tbsp. cream may be added, and if fresh tomato juice is used, a few drops of carmine can be added to improve the colour of the cocktail.

TOMATO JUICE COCKTAIL—II

½ pint tomato juice
1 tbsp. lemon juice
½ tsp. salt
1 tsp. granulated sugar
1 small onion (finely sliced)
1 bay leaf
1 piece of celery
2 tsps. chopped parsley
1 tsp. piquant sauce
2 tsps. grated horse-radish

Combine all the ingredients and chill for several hours. Strain, and serve in glasses.

HOT HORS D'ŒUVRE

SCAMPI

24 Dublin Bay prawns
4 oz. flour
1 egg
¼–½ pint milk
Salt
Fat or oil for frying
Tartare sauce

Discard the heads of the prawns, remove the flesh from the shells, remove the dark vein, and if the prawns are very large, cut each in half lengthways. Make a coating batter with the flour, egg and milk, and season it with salt. Heat the fat or oil until smoking hot; dip the prawns into the batter and fry until crisp and golden-brown. Drain well on absorbent paper, and serve piled in a dish, with the sauce.

EGGS EN COCOTTE

2 rashers of bacon
4 eggs
Salt and pepper
Margarine

Cut the bacon in small pieces and divide it between 4 cocotte dishes. Put into a hot oven (450° F., mark 8) partly to cook it (about 5 minutes). Break an egg into each dish and sprinkle with salt and pepper, put a few dabs of margarine on each, and bake until the eggs have just set—7–10 minutes.

SPAGHETTI À LA BOLOGNAISE

(*See colour picture facing page* 64)

1 onion, 1 carrot, and 1 stick celery
1 clove of garlic
2 tbsps. olive oil
1 oz. margarine
1 bay leaf
4 oz. minced raw beef
1 glass dry Italian wine
8 peeled tomatoes
2 tbsps. tomato paste
Meat extract
Seasoning
12 oz. spaghetti
Grated Parmesan cheese

Put finely chopped vegetables and garlic in a pan with oil, fat and bay leaf, and fry for 5 minutes; then add all ingredients except spaghetti, and cook slowly ½ hour. Meanwhile, cook spaghetti in plenty of boiling salted water 20 minutes, drain, put in a hot dish, add sauce, and serve with cheese.

SOUPS AND BROTHS

SOUP MAKING

Soups are often served as the beginning to a meal, but may form the main part of a lunch or supper, especially during the winter. Main-dish soups should include some protein ingredient such as lentils, haricot beans or peas, or meat such as kidney or neck of mutton, or may be supplemented with cheese. The other items in the menu must be carefully chosen to give a well-balanced and satisfying meal.

Many tasty soups can be made by using vegetables only. Meat stock, though a great improvement, is not necessary, provided that the vegetables are carefully selected for their flavour, and that attention is paid to seasoning.

Stocks and soups are improved by the addition of a "bouquet garni." To prepare a fresh bouquet garni, take a small sprig each of as many of the following herbs as you have in your garden: parsley, thyme, lemon-scented thyme, marjoram, balm and savory. This will give a well-blended flavour. In the absence of fresh herbs, a small pinch each of the same herbs dried will give a good result, or you can use $\frac{1}{4}$–$\frac{1}{2}$ tsp. of "mixed herbs." This is a blend of herbs, usually prepared from those mentioned above, and has the advantage of being handy when fresh herbs are not available. The leaves of the sweet bay tree give a pleasant flavour to soups and sauces, and one small leaf should be included in the bouquet garni. The herbs are usually tied together (in muslin very often, especially if dried or powdered), so that they may be removed easily when their purpose is served. If the soup or sauce is to be sieved, there is no necessity to tie the herbs in muslin.

When time is limited, it is not convenient to sieve a soup. A soup made of grated or minced vegetables, however, can be cooked quickly and served without sieving. The minestrone type of soup, which does not need sieving, is generally well liked—this is made by cooking a good variety of diced or thinly sliced vegetables with stock, together with a bunch of herbs and some macaroni or noodles, if possible.

Grated cheese is an excellent accompaniment to soups, improving both its flavour and its food value. It may be added to the soup just before serving, or handed separately. Chopped parsley and watercress are also valuable additions. They should be freshly chopped, and added immediately before serving. A little cream, stirred in at the last moment, greatly improves any purée or cream soup, or unsweetened evaporated milk may be used when cream is not available. Egg yolks also help to enrich a soup—they should be added when the cooking is completed, and the soup must not be allowed to boil again, or the egg may curdle.

The basis of most soups is stock, made from meat, poultry, fish or vegetables. This may be made in a special stock pot, a large saucepan or a pressure cooker.

Note: When stock is made in a pressure saucepan or cooker, the time is considerably shorter. Do not have the saucepan more than two-thirds full with liquid, then bring to the boil and remove any scum before securing the lid, otherwise the scum is likely to be ejected through the pressure regulator. (See Pressure Cookery chapter.)

STOCKS

MEAT STOCK

2 lb. shin of beef	1 small carrot
2 quarts cold water	A piece of turnip
1 onion	A bouquet garni

Brown Meat Stock—First Stock

Cut the meat into fairly small pieces, removing any fat, and chop the bones if very large. Put into a large saucepan or stewpan and cover with the water. Bring slowly to simmering point, remove any scum that rises, then add the vegetables (previously prepared and cut into three or four large pieces) and the bouquet garni. Cover and simmer gently for 4–6 hours, then strain into a basin and allow to cool. The following day, or when the stock is quite cold, remove any fat from the surface.

This "first stock," which is of best quality, forms the foundation of good quality clear soups.

Second Stock

Second stock, used for general household purposes, is prepared from the original meat and bones used for first stock. Return the meat and bones to the stock pot, together with any other bones or meat trimmings available. Add fresh flavouring vegetables, herbs and cold water in the same proportions as for first stock. Bring to the boil and skim if necessary, then cover and simmer for 2–3 hours.

White Meat Stock

Make as above, 2 lb. of knuckle of veal being used in place of the shin of beef.

BONE STOCK

To prepare the stock, place the uncooked bones (2-3 lb.) in a saucepan with a few flavouring vegetables (e.g., carrot, onion, celery, a comparatively small amount of turnip), and add a few peppercorns, a clove, blade of mace, bay leaf, pinch of mixed herbs and a few parsley stalks. Cover with cold water, bring to the boil, skim, then simmer, covered, for 2–3 hours. If you do not use all the stock at once, boil up the pot every day, adding any extra bones (both raw or cooked) or vegetables and more water as required; empty the pot after three or four days and start afresh. Green vegetables and starchy foods should not be included in the stock pot, as they cause the stock to sour rapidly. If they have been added, the stock should be used at once.

If the bones or scraps of meat are fatty, the liquid should be strained off after cooking and allowed to cool, so that the fat may be removed before the stock is used. The fat is useful as dripping, of course.

VEGETABLE STOCK

When no bones are available, a very good stock can be made with vegetables only. Use a mixture of several vegetables—onions, celery, carrots, etc.—adding spices and herbs as with bone stock. Cover with cold water and cook until a good mellow flavour is obtained. This stock should be strained off and used while fresh—do not keep it from day to day, especially when starchy and green vegetables are used. A few bacon rinds help to give flavour and richness, but be careful not to add too many, or you will mask the flavour of the vegetables.

FISH STOCK

Bones and skin from fresh or cooked fish may be used to make fish stock. Flavouring vegetables, herbs and spices should be included, as with bone and vegetable stocks, but it does not require cooking so long—1–1½ hours is usually sufficient. Fish stock does not keep well, and should be used the day it is made.

SOUP GARNISHES

Bacon

Rind the bacon, cut into small strips or dice and fry lightly. This garnish is most suitable for thick soups.

Cheese

Finely grated cheese is a pleasant accompaniment to almost any vegetable soup. Leave the cheese to dry in a cool place for a few days before using it: this improves the flavour and makes it easier to grate. To give an interesting colour and flavour, and to add vitamins, mix freshly chopped parsley or watercress with grated cheese before serving. Grated cheese is usually handed separately, but may also be sprinkled on the soup just before sending to table.

Cheese Dumplings

Mix together breadcrumbs and grated cheese in equal proportions. Season with salt, pepper, mustard and mixed herbs and bind with beaten egg. Form into small balls and poach in the soup 15–20 minutes before serving. If liked, a few drops of piquant sauce may be added to the dumplings together with the egg.

Fried Croûtons

Cut the bread about ½ inch thick and fry until golden-brown in a little dripping, bacon fat or lard. Cut into cubes and serve immediately. If preferred, the bread can be cubed before frying.

Herb Dumplings

Make these according to the recipe on page 189, and add them to any thin soup or broth.

Leek

Fried chopped leek is a particularly good addition to potato soup.

Macaroni and Spaghetti

These are good with minestrone or any thin soup. They should be broken into short lengths and are added to the soup about ½ hour before serving. Other varieties of Italian pasta, such as alfabeto, small conchiglia, cappellini or tagliatelle (broken in small pieces), are more unusual for special occasions; use them in small quantities only.

Mushrooms

Cut these into thin slices and sauté in a little butter, bacon fat or dripping. Add to thick soups.

Noodles

A recipe for home-made noodles is given in the chapter on Cereals. They make an interesting and nourishing addition to thin soups, such as Chicken Broth (made without tapioca or rice).

Onion

If the soup lacks flavour, add a little finely chopped onion, and cook for a further few minutes before serving.

Onion rings cut thinly and fried in a little dripping, bacon fat or butter until golden-brown and crisp, give a good flavour. They can be added just before serving.

Rice

Left-over dry boiled rice may be added to soup shortly before serving, together with freshly chopped parsley or chives. Rice may also be cooked in a soup or broth; in this case it is added to the soup about ½ hour before cooking is completed.

Sausages and Sausage-meat

Left-over cooked sausages may be cut into rounds or small strips. They go well with vegetable soups such as spinach, and should be heated through in the soup just before serving. Raw sausage-meat may also be used. Roll into pieces about the size of a marble, dust with flour and grill, fry or bake them. Alternatively, they may be poached in the soup for 10–15 minutes.

Savoury Fritters

Make savoury fritters, season well with salt, pepper, mixed herbs and, if liked, a little chopped fried bacon or onion, and fry in a little hot fat until golden-brown on both sides. Cut into neat strips, and add to the soup just before serving.

Toast Croûtons

Make the toast just before serving the soup, and cut into small dice.

MEAT SOUPS

CALF'S HEAD SOUP

(*Also called* MOCK TURTLE SOUP)

½ a calf's head
2–3 quarts stock
Salt and pepper
2 oz. butter
2 oz. lean ham or bacon
1–2 onions
2 shallots
A few mushrooms
A bouquet garni
1 bay leaf
2 oz. flour
¼–½ pint sherry
Lemon juice
Forcemeat balls

Thoroughly wash the head, then put it into a pan with the stock. Bring to the boil, add salt and simmer for 3–4 hours, skimming occasionally. Strain off and reserve the liquor, then take the meat from the bones and cut it into small pieces. Meantime, melt the butter, add the ham or bacon, cut into dice, and the prepared vegetables, and sauté for a few minutes, then add the herbs and seasoning and enough of the calf's head liquor to cover. Cover and simmer gently for about an hour. Stir in the flour, blended with a little more of the calf's head stock, bring to the boil, stirring, and cook for about 5 minutes, then strain this mixture into the remaining stock. Add the calf's head meat, more seasoning if necessary, and the wine and lemon juice; then bring to the boil. Add the forcemeat balls, simmer for a few minutes, then serve.

CHICKEN BROTH

1 chicken
Cold water to cover (approximately 2 quarts)
1 onion
2 dessertsps. seed pearl tapioca or rice
2 heaped tsps. chopped parsley
Salt

If using a whole chicken, cut in half, after the usual preparation, wash thoroughly and remove any fat or grease, but retain the skin. Put into a pan, add the water and salt to taste, peel the onion, cut in half and add to contents of the saucepan. Simmer slowly for 3½–4 hours, and if the water boils away, add more. Strain, stand it aside until cold, and remove any grease that may have settled on the top of the stock. (If time will not permit waiting for the stock to get cold, the grease may be removed with a spoon or by passing a sheet of kitchen paper over the top of the broth.) Return the stock to the saucepan, bring to the boil, sprinkle in the seed pearl tapioca or the rice and cook until the grain is tender—10–20 minutes. Put the chopped parsley in the bottom of a soup tureen and pour the broth over it.

This is an excellent method of utilising an old chicken, but if young ones are used, the breast and wings may be removed before making the broth, and used for grilling or frying.

COCK-A-LEEKIE SOUP

- 1 boiling fowl
- 2 lb. neck of mutton or knuckle of veal
- 3 quarts cold water
- Pepper and salt
- 2 cloves
- 4 leeks
- 1 oz. rice

Wash the fowl carefully, and put it with the meat into a saucepan, then add the water and seasoning. When it boils, add the leeks, previously prepared and cut into pieces, and simmer for $1\frac{1}{4}$ hours. Wash the rice, sprinkle it into the soup, add additional seasoning if necessary, and continue to simmer for $\frac{3}{4}$ hour. The chicken and meat can be served separately, with parsley sauce made with a little of the broth, or with the soup.

CONSOMMÉ

- $\frac{1}{2}$ lb. lean beef
- 1 small carrot
- 1 small onion
- A piece of turnip
- A small stalk of celery
- 2 quarts best quality (or first) stock
- A bouquet garni
- 12 peppercorns
- 2 cloves
- A blade of mace
- The whites and shells of 2 eggs
- Salt, if necessary
- A little sherry

Shred the meat very finely, put it into a bowl with enough cold water just to cover, and allow it to soak for about $\frac{1}{2}$ hour. Prepare all the vegetables and cut each into four. Put the stock, from which all trace of fat has been removed, into a deep, lined saucepan, add the meat and the water in which it has soaked, the vegetables, herbs and spices. Lastly, add the whites and crushed shells of the eggs. Put over a gentle heat, whisk continuously and bring almost to boiling point: a thick froth should form on the top of the liquid. Stop whisking and continue heating until the froth rises in the pan, then reduce the heat and allow the soup to simmer for a few minutes. Tie a clean white cloth to a jelly stand or to the four legs of an upturned chair and scald with boiling water, then gently pour in the soup. When the consommé has dripped through, strain it a second time—passing it through the frothy egg whites, etc., to make it clear and sparkling. If necessary, the consommé may be strained a third time.

Reheat the consommé, add salt if necessary, and a little sherry to improve the flavour, but add nothing that would make it cloudy.

Consommé may be served plain or may be varied by adding a garnish, for example:

Consommé Julienne

Add very fine shreds of vegetables, such as 8
carrot, turnip, etc., boiled separately and rinsed before adding.

Consommé à la Royale

Garnish with steamed savoury custard cut into tiny fancy shapes.

Consommé à la Célestine

Garnish with shredded savoury pancake.

Consommé à la Jardiniere

Prepare a mixture of vegetables such as carrots and turnips cut into pea shapes, tiny sprigs of cauliflower, green peas and so on. Boil until tender, rinse well, then add to the soup just before serving.

Consommé à la Brunoise

Prepare a mixture of carrot and turnip (cut into small dice) and celery and leek (sliced neatly). Cook in boiling salted water until tender, rinse well, and add to the consommé just before serving.

Consommé au Riz

Put some plained boiled rice, well rinsed, into the tureen and pour the consommé over it.

Consommé à l'Italienne

Cook some Italian paste (tiny letters, shells and so on) until tender in boiling salted water. Drain and rinse well and add to the soup just before serving.

GAME SOUP

- A game carcase
- 1 onion
- 1 small carrot
- A small piece turnip
- Butter or dripping for frying
- 4 tsps. flour
- Stock (about 1 pint)
- A bouquet garni
- 1–2 bacon rinds
- Salt and pepper
- A little red wine

Cut or break up the game. Prepare and cut up the vegetables. Melt a little dripping or butter in a saucepan and fry the game and vegetables lightly. Stir in the flour and fry this also. Then cover with stock and add a bunch of herbs and one or two bacon rinds. Season with salt and pepper, cover, and simmer gently for 1-2 hours, then strain and return the soup to the pan, with any meat from the bones cut into neat dice. Add more seasoning if necessary and make very hot. A little red wine may be added just before serving.

GIBLET SOUP

Giblets from 2 chickens, geese or ducks
2 quarts stock
A few bones
1 onion
1 carrot
A bouquet garni
Salt and pepper
1 oz. butter or dripping
1 oz. flour
Port wine (optional)

Wash the giblets thoroughly, put them into a pan with the stock, and add the bones, vegetables, herbs and seasoning. Cover, and simmer gently until the giblets are tender—about 2 hours—skimming occasionally. Then strain the soup and cut up the giblets (except the necks) into small pieces and reserve them. Melt the butter or dripping in the pan, stir in the flour to make a "roux" and add the hot soup gradually, stirring well to keep it smooth. Bring to the boil and cook for about 5 minutes, then add the meat and season to taste. A little port wine may be stirred in just before serving.

GRAVY SOUP

1 lb. lean gravy beef
3 pints stock
1 oz. dripping
1 onion (sliced)
1 carrot
A piece of turnip
2 cloves and a blade of mace
Pepper and salt
½ oz. cornflour or fine sago, if required
Croûtons of toast

Pass the meat through a mincing machine and add it to the cold stock, which should include any left-over gravy. Melt the dripping in a saucepan and fry the thinly sliced onion until browned. Add the other vegetables, sliced, and fry lightly, then add the stock, meat, the herbs and seasoning. Cover, and simmer gently for 2–3 hours. If a thin soup is required, pour through a strainer, skim off any fat, then reheat; reseason if necessary.

If a thick soup is required, pass the meat and vegetables through a sieve, then return to the saucepan and reheat. Blend the cornflour or sago with a little cold water, stir into the soup, then bring to the boil, stirring, and cook for about 10 minutes. Serve with croûtons of toast.

KIDNEY SOUP

8 ½ lb. ox kidney
1½ oz. flour
Pepper and salt
1½ oz. dripping
1 onion
3 pints stock
Flavouring vegetables (carrot, turnip, celery, etc.), if required
A small bouquet garni
1 tbsp. ketchup
A little sherry, if desired

Wash the kidney in salt and water, rinse, and dry it well. Then cut it into small pieces away from the fatty core. Put the flour on a plate and mix with it some pepper and salt. Toss the kidney in this until each piece is well coated. Melt the dripping in a saucepan; when smoking hot, put in the prepared kidney and finely chopped onion, and fry these until well browned, turning them at intervals. Pour in the stock, and if not well flavoured, add a cupful of diced vegetables as well. Stir for a minute or two, add the bouquet garni, and then allow the soup to cook slowly for 3–4 hours, skimming and stirring occasionally. When the kidney is tender, strain the soup, remove any fat from the top, and return it to the saucepan to reheat. Rinse the pieces of kidney free from all vegetable, and return them to the soup, together with the ketchup, and salt to taste. A little sherry may also be added if desired.

HARE SOUP

½ a hare
2 oz. beef dripping
1 onion
2 oz. lean ham
A stick of celery
Carrot and turnip
A bouquet garni
Seasoning
3 pints stock
2 tsps. flour
1 glass port
1 dessertsp. red-currant jelly
Lemon juice
Forcemeat balls

The less choice parts of the hare may be used for making soup. Cut them into pieces, and break or chop the bones. Melt the dripping in a saucepan, and when it is smoking hot, put in the hare, the sliced onion, and the ham, cut in small pieces. Turn them over in the fat until well browned. Then add the other vegetables, the bouquet garni (which should include bay leaf and a piece of lemon rind), seasoning and stock. Mix well, cover, and simmer gently for 3–4 hours. When sufficiently cooked, strain through a sieve, and rub some of the meat through also. Let stand until cold. Next day remove all fat from the top and return the soup to a saucepan to reheat. Brown the flour, mix it with the wine and add to the soup. Add also the red-currant jelly, a squeeze of lemon juice and more seasoning if necessary. Stir until boiling and simmer for 5 minutes. If the blood from the hare has been kept, add it to the soup at the last, but do not boil again or the soup will curdle. Put some forcemeat balls into the soup tureen, and then pour the boiling hot soup over them.

The recipe for the forcemeat balls is given in Jugged Hare, in the chapter on Game.

Spaghetti à la Bolognaise

Grapefruit Cups and Dressed Salad

TIO PEPE
JEREZ

LAMB AND CARROT HOTCHPOTCH

About 1 lb. lamb (scrag-end or middle neck)
Cold water
Salt and pepper
1 lb. young carrots
A few spring onions
½ lb. potatoes
Chopped parsley

Wash or wipe the meat and cut it into small pieces of joints, trimming off any excess fat. Put the meat into a pan, just cover with cold water and bring to the boil. Add salt and pepper, then cover, and simmer gently for about 1 hour, removing any scum that collects on the top of the liquid. Meanwhile prepare the carrots, onions and potatoes, and add them to the pot, cover, and simmer gently for a further ½–¾ hour, until the vegetables are tender. Some of the fat will be absorbed by the potatoes, but if the broth appears at all greasy, skim off the excess fat from the top. If liked, the bones can be removed and the meat taken off them, chopped, and returned to the soup. Before serving, sprinkle liberally with freshly chopped parsley.

MUTTON BROTH

2½ lb. scrag-end of mutton
2 quarts cold water
1 oz. pearl barley
1 turnip
1 carrot
1 onion
1 leek
Pepper and salt
1 tbsp. finely chopped parsley

Cut the meat into neat joints, removing all the fat. Put into a saucepan and cover with cold water. Bring to the boil, add the barley and simmer for 1½ hours. Add the vegetables, previously cut into dice, and the seasoning. Cover, and cook for another hour. Place the chopped parsley in the tureen and pour on the soup.

OXTAIL SOUP

1 oxtail
2 onions
1 carrot
2 stalks of celery
1 oz. butter or dripping
3–4 pints stock
1 oz. lean ham or bacon
A bouquet garni
1 bay leaf
2 cloves
6 peppercorns
Salt and pepper
1 oz. flour
A little port wine, if liked
A squeeze of lemon juice or a little ketchup

Wash the oxtail, then joint it and dry the joints. Prepare and cut up the vegetables. Melt the fat in a saucepan and sauté the jointed oxtail and the prepared vegetables in it for a few minutes. Well cover with stock and bring to the boil. Add the ham or bacon, the herbs and seasoning, then cover and simmer gently for about 4 hours, or until the tail meat is tender, skimming occasionally. Strain the soup, remove the meat from the tail joints, cut it up neatly and replace it in the strained liquor. Return it to the saucepan and stir in the flour, blended to a smooth cream with a little water or port wine. Bring to the boil, stirring, and cook for about 5 minutes. Add more seasoning, if necessary, and a squeeze of lemon juice or ketchup to taste.

POT-AU-FEU

2 lb. lean beef
2½ quarts water
Salt
1 carrot
1 turnip
1 onion
1 parsnip
1 small cabbage
2 small leeks
2 stalks celery
A bouquet garni (including a small blade of mace, 12 peppercorns, 2 cloves)
1 oz. seed pearl tapioca or semolina

Tie the meat into a neat shape, put into a large saucepan, add the water and 2 tsps. salt and simmer for 2 hours. Prepare the vegetables, cut each into quarters, with the exception of the cabbage, and add to the broth with the bouquet garni. Continue to cook for another 2 hours. Cut the cabbage in two, but tie together so that it does not break whilst boiling, put into the pot and boil until tender. Serve the meat on a dish with some of the liquor, and garnish with the vegetables. If liked, the cabbage may be dished separately.

To make soup from the liquor, sprinkle in the seed pearl tapioca or semolina, cook for 15 minutes and serve.

RABBIT SOUP

¼ lb. onions
1 carrot
A piece of turnip
2 stalks of celery
1 small apple
½ oz. dripping or margarine
1 bay leaf
2 cloves
1 blade of mace
1 rabbit carcase, the giblets and the neck
1 quart water
1 oz. sultanas
1 oz. pearl barley
Salt and pepper
1 tbsp. chopped parsley

Prepare the vegetables and the apple and cut them up finely or mince them. Fry lightly, without browning, in the fat. Add the herbs and the rabbit bones, neck and giblets tied very loosely in muslin. Pour on the water and add the sultanas and pearl barley. Bring to the boil and simmer for 2–3 hours, then remove the bones, herbs, etc. Season with salt and pepper and add the chopped parsley just before serving.

Minestrone

Cream of Mushroom Soup

SCOTCH BROTH

1½–2 lb. lean beef	2 leeks
2 quarts water	1½ oz. pearl barley
Salt and pepper	1 tbsp. finely chopped parsley
1 carrot, turnip and onion of medium size	

Put the meat into a pan, add the water and salt, bring to boiling point slowly, then simmer gently for 1½ hours. Add the vegetables, previously cut into dice, and the barley. (To prevent the broth becoming cloudy, it is advisable to blanch the barley before adding it to the stock. To do this, put the grain into cold water and bring it to boiling point, strain and add to the soup.) After adding the barley and vegetables, continue to simmer until both are cooked—this will take approximately 1 hour. Serve the meat separately on a dish with a little of the broth. Put the chopped parsley into the soup tureen—it should not be cooked, as the attractive green colour is thereby lost—and pour in the broth. Should any fat appear on the surface of the broth, it must be removed with a spoon or with kitchen paper.

SHEEP'S HEAD BROTH

1 sheep's head	1 carrot
2½–3 quarts water	1 turnip
Pepper and salt	2 oz. pearl barley
1 large onion	1 level tbsp. chopped parsley
1 leek	

Wash the head, split it in half, remove the brains and soak in cold, salted water for half an hour. Scrape the bone and teeth, put the head into a saucepan, cover with cold water, bring slowly to the boil, remove the head and throw the water away. This process is called "blanching." Return the head to the saucepan, add sufficient cold water to cover (2½–3 quarts), season to taste, bring to boiling point, removing the scum as it rises, and simmer for 2½–3 hours. Prepare the vegetables, cut into dice of even size and add to the contents of the saucepan. Add also the barley (previously parboiled for about ½ hour), and continue to cook for ¾ hour. Remove the head and any grease that may be on the top of the broth—if there is a large quantity, use a flat metal spoon; a small quantity may be removed by passing over a sheet of unglazed kitchen paper. Add more pepper and salt, if required, place the finely chopped parsley in the tureen and pour over the hot broth. The tongue may be cooked with the head, skinned and sliced, and served separately or as a garnish in the soup.

Note: The meat on the head will make a separate dish, and should be served with a sauce made with the brains. (See recipe for Dressed Sheep's Head.)

TURKEY SOUP

1 turkey carcase	Cornflour to thicken
1 small ham-bone	A little ketchup
Stock or water to cover	A squeeze of lemon or orange juice
1 onion	
Salt and pepper	A few boiled chestnuts
A bunch of herbs	A little sherry (optional)

Remove any traces of the stuffing from the carcase, and reserve a little of the meat, cut in dice, to serve as a garnish. Break up the bones and put them and the ham-bone in a saucepan. Add enough stock or water to cover, then add the peeled and sliced onion, salt, pepper and herbs, and simmer gently for 2–3 hours, skimming occasionally. Strain, and allow to become cold. Remove all fat from the surface and return the soup to the saucepan to reheat. Blend the cornflour with the ketchup (allowing 1 oz. cornflour and 1 tbsp. ketchup to each quart of liquor) and stir into the soup. Bring to the boil, stirring, and cook for about 5 minutes. Add a squeeze of lemon or orange juice and reseason carefully. Add the diced turkey meat and a few chestnuts, boiled and shelled, and make very hot. Just before serving, add the sherry.

VEGETABLE SOUPS

ARTICHOKE SOUP—I

1½ lb. Jerusalem artichokes	½ oz. cornflour
	½ pint milk
1 oz. butter	Croûtons of fried bread or toast
1½ pints light stock	
Pepper and salt	

Prepare the artichokes and slice them: to prevent them from becoming discoloured, the peeling should be done as far as possible under water, and they should be kept covered with water until ready to be cooked. Melt the butter, add the artichokes, and sauté until all the butter has been absorbed, then pour on the stock and add the seasoning. Simmer for about 45–50 minutes, or until the artichokes are quite tender. Rub through a sieve, return to the saucepan and reheat. Mix the cornflour to a paste with a little of the cold milk, stir it into the soup, continue stirring until it boils, then add the rest of the milk and simmer for about 8 minutes. Serve with croûtons

ARTICHOKE SOUP—II

1½ lb. Jerusalem artichokes
1 stalk of celery
1 small onion
2–3 bacon rinds
A little butter, if necessary
1 quart stock
Salt and pepper
1 oz. flour
¼ pint milk
Chopped parsley
1 tbsp. cream

Peel and slice the artichokes, cut up the celery and onion and sauté them in the fat from the bacon rinds, adding a little butter if necessary. Add the stock and seasonings, bring to the boil, cover, and simmer until tender. Pass through a sieve and return to the saucepan. Add the flour, blended to a smooth cream with the milk, return to the boil, stirring, and cook for 2–3 minutes, reseasoning if necessary. Add the finely chopped parsley and the cream just before serving the soup.

ASPARAGUS SOUP

1 bundle asparagus
1 quart of white stock
Salt and pepper
1 oz. butter
1 oz. flour
¼ pint milk
A little cream

Prepare the asparagus in the usual way, discarding the woody part of the stem, and cut into short lengths. If liked, a few of the tips can be cut off and tied in muslin : these can then be removed from the soup when tender and used later as a garnish. Put the asparagus into a pan with the stock, add salt and pepper, cover, and boil gently until tender. Remove the tips that have been tied in muslin, reserve these and pass the rest through a sieve. Melt the butter and stir in the flour to form a " roux." Add the asparagus purée and bring to the boil, stirring, then cook gently for 2–3 minutes. Add the milk, reseason if necessary, and lastly stir in the cream and asparagus tips.

SAVOURY BEAN SOUP

4 oz. butter beans
½ pint water
1¼ pint stock
2 stalks celery
¼ onion
½ lb. tomatoes (or 1 small tin)
½ oz. butter
2 tsps. flour
Pepper and salt
1 dessertsp. tomato chutney or sauce

Soak the beans overnight, then place in a casserole or covered pie dish with the water, and bake in a moderate oven until tender—about 1½–2 hours. Add the stock and other vegetables, and simmer for ½ hour. Rub through a sieve. Melt the butter, add the flour and stir in the sieved soup. Season, add the tomato chutney or sauce and cook for about 10 minutes.

BEETROOT SOUP

2 large uncooked beetroots
1 oz. butter
1½–2 pints good stock
Pepper and salt
2–3 tsps. vinegar
Cooked sausage

Wash and peel the beetroots and shred them finely. Melt the butter in a saucepan and sauté the shredded beetroot for about 10 minutes, then stir in a little of the hot stock, and cook gently. When this stock is absorbed, add the remainder of the stock, the seasonings and vinegar, then cover and simmer until the beetroot is quite tender. Sieve, and serve with a few thin slices of cooked sausage as a garnish.

CURRIED BEETROOT SOUP

1 lb. beetroot (raw)
1 apple
1 onion
2–3 tomatoes
1 oz. butter or dripping
2 tsps. curry powder
Salt and pepper
1 bay leaf
1 dessertsp. sultanas
1½ pints stock
½ oz. flour
¼ pint milk

Peel the beetroot, apple, onion and tomatoes, and chop into small pieces. Fry lightly, without browning, in the hot fat. Add the curry powder, seasoning, bay leaf, sultanas and the stock, bring to the boil and simmer gently until well cooked. Remove the bay leaf. Blend the flour with the milk and add to the soup. Reboil, and simmer for a few minutes before serving.

BRUSSELS SPROUT PURÉE

1½ lb. Brussels sprouts
1 quart stock (or 1 pint stock and 1 pint milk)
Salt and pepper
¼ oz. cornflour
A little milk
Croûtons of fried bread or toast

Prepare the Brussels sprouts and cook them in a large pan of boiling salted water. When tender, strain, and rub the sprouts through a sieve. Return the purée to the saucepan, pour on the liquid, season, and when nearly boiling, strain in the cornflour, previously blended with a little cold milk. Bring to the boil, stirring, and continue to simmer for at least 8 minutes. Serve with croûtons of fried bread or toast.

CREAM OF CARROT SOUP

1 lb. carrots
Pieces of celery, turnip and onion
1 oz. butter or dripping
1½ pints stock
A bouquet garni
Pepper and salt
1 oz. flour
¼ pint milk
1–2 tbsps. cream
Chopped parsley, if desired

Prepare the vegetables and cut them into small pieces, then sauté them in the butter or dripping for about 10 minutes without browning.

Add the stock, the bouquet garni and pepper and salt. Cover and allow to simmer gently for about 1 hour, or until the vegetables are quite tender. Remove the bouquet garni and pass the soup through a sieve. Blend the flour with the milk, add to the soup and bring to the boil, stirring. Cook for 2–3 minutes, reseason if necessary, and stir in the cream just before serving, also the parsley, if used.

GRATED CARROT SOUP

1 lb. carrots	Seasoning
A small piece of turnip	A bouquet garni
2 medium-sized onions	½ pint milk
1 oz. butter	1 tbsp. chopped parsley
1 pint stock	

Prepare and grate finely the carrots, turnip and onions and sauté together in the butter. Add the stock, seasoning and the herbs, tied in muslin. Simmer gently for a few minutes until tender. Remove the herbs, add the milk and bring to the boil. Reseason, if necessary, and add the finely chopped parsley just before serving.

CAULIFLOWER SOUP

1 medium-sized cauliflower	1 blade of mace
1 onion	Salt and pepper
2–3 bacon rinds	½ oz. flour
½–1 oz. butter	½ pint milk
1½ pints stock or water	A little chopped parsley

Wash the cauliflower and boil for a few minutes, then drain and cut into pieces. Prepare and slice the onion and sauté in the fat from the bacon rinds, adding the cauliflower and a little butter, if necessary. Pour on the stock and add the mace and seasonings, bring to the boil and simmer for about ¾ hour, until tender. Rub through a sieve, return to the saucepan and stir in the flour, blended to a smooth cream with the milk. Bring to the boil, stirring, and allow to boil for 2–3 minutes. Add the chopped parsley, and reseason if necessary.

CAULIFLOWER SOUP WITH DUMPLINGS

1 cauliflower	1 pint cauliflower liquor
1–2 stalks of celery	1 pint milk
1 small onion	A small piece of mace
2 oz. butter	Seasoning
2 oz. flour	Dumplings or croûtons

Choose a medium-sized cauliflower, remove the outer leaves and cut it in quarters. Wash well and put into a saucepan of boiling salted water, boil for 10 minutes and pour off the water. Cover again with boiling water and cook the cauliflower until nearly tender. Then strain, but keep 1 pint of the water for the soup. Reserve one cupful of tiny flowerets, and chop the rest of the cauliflower. Chop also the celery and onion. Now melt the butter in the saucepan, add the flour and stir for a few minutes. Add gradually the 1 pint cauliflower water and the milk, and stir until boiling. Add the chopped vegetables, mace and seasoning to taste, and simmer slowly for 15 minutes. Meanwhile, prepare some small dumplings, add them to the soup, together with the pieces of cauliflower, and cook for 15 minutes longer. Croûtons of fried bread may be served separately, and the dumplings omitted, if preferred.

CELERIAC SOUP

1lb. celeriac	Pepper and salt
1 large potato	½ oz. flour
1 small onion or leek	2–3 tbsps. milk or cream
1 oz. butter	Thin slices of toast
1½ pints stock, or milk and stock mixed	Grated cheese, if liked

Peel the celeriac and cut into slices. Peel and slice the potato and onion. Melt the butter, then add the vegetables and cook for 5 minutes. Add the stock and seasoning, cover, and simmer gently until all the vegetables are tender. Blend the flour smoothly with the milk or cream. Sieve the soup, return it to the pan with the blended flour and stir until boiling, when the soup should be of a creamy consistency. Reseason, and serve with thin slices of toast. A little grated cheese stirred into the soup just before serving gives a delicious flavour.

CELERY CREAM SOUP

Outside stalks of 1 large head of celery	Salt and pepper
1 medium-sized onion	A bouquet garni
1 oz. butter	1 oz. flour
1 quart stock (or milk and stock mixed)	½ pint milk
	Chopped parsley
	A little cream

Prepare and slice the celery and onion and sauté in the butter for about 10 minutes. Add the stock (or milk and stock), seasoning and bouquet garni, bring to the boil, and simmer until the vegetables are quite tender. Pass the soup through a sieve and return to the saucepan. Stir in the flour, blended to a smooth cream with the milk, and allow to boil for a further 2–3 minutes. Reseason, if necessary, and add the freshly chopped parsley just before serving. A little cream added at the last is an improvement.

SIMPLE CELERY SOUP

1 head of celery	6 peppercorns
1 onion	A blade of mace
1–2 carrots	Salt and pepper
1½ pints stock or water	1 oz. flour
2–3 bacon rinds	¼ pint milk
A sprig of fresh thyme or a pinch of mixed herbs	Butter
1 clove	2 tsps. chopped parsley

Wash the celery and cut it into small pieces. Prepare and slice the onion and the carrots, and put them into a saucepan with the liquid, bacon rinds, herbs and spices tied in muslin. Add salt and pepper, cover, and simmer gently until tender—about 1 hour. Remove the bacon rinds and the bag of herbs, and stir in the flour, blended to a smooth cream with the milk. Boil for a further 2–3 minutes to cook the flour. Just before serving, add a few knobs of butter and the freshly chopped parsley.

Note: If preferred, a half rasher of bacon can be used in place of bacon rinds. In this case rind and dice the bacon and fry it lightly in the pan before adding the vegetables and liquid, etc.

CREAM OF CORN SOUP

1 oz. butter	½ pint white stock
1 tin sweet corn	1 dessertsp. cornflour
1 tsp. chopped onion	¼ pint milk
¼ of a bay leaf	Seasoning
2 peppercorns	

Melt the fat, add the corn and onion, bay leaf and peppercorns, and cook gently for 5 minutes; then add the stock, bring to the boil, cover, and cook for 25 minutes. Rub through a a hair sieve, reheat, add the cornflour, blended with the milk, and cook, stirring, for 5–8 minutes. Finally, season to taste.

CUCUMBER SOUP

2 cucumbers	1 quart white stock
2 oz. butter or margarine	½ dessertsp. cornflour
	½ pint milk
A little spinach	Croûtons of fried bread
1 Spanish onion	A few lettuce leaves

Peel the cucumbers and cut them in slices. Scald them in boiling salted water for 10 minutes and then drain. Melt the butter in a saucepan and put in the cucumber, with a handful of well-washed spinach leaves and the onion, thinly sliced. Put on the lid and allow the contents of the saucepan to cook slowly for a few minutes without browning, then pour in the white stock, cover, and simmer gently until the vegetables are quite tender. Sieve, and return the purée to the saucepan. Add the cornflour, mixed smoothly with the milk, and stir until boiling. Boil for 5 minutes, season to taste and serve with fried croûtons of bread. A few leaves of lettuce, finely shredded, may be added to the soup as a garnish.

CUCUMBER CREAM SOUP

1 large or 2 medium-sized cucumbers	1 pint milk
	1 egg yolk
1 oz. butter	2–3 tbsps. cream
1 blade mace	Pepper and salt
1 pint white stock	Croûtons of fried bread
1 oz. flour	

Slice the cucumber, rejecting the stalk end, which might impart a bitter flavour, parboil in salted water, and strain. Melt the butter and add the partly cooked cucumber, the blade of mace and the boiling stock. Blend the flour with a little cold milk, and strain, with the remainder of the milk, into the boiling stock, stirring meanwhile. Simmer gently for 30 minutes. Blend the egg yolk with the cream and add to the soup. Season to taste and reheat, bringing slowly almost to boiling point, but do not allow the soup actually to boil, or it will curdle. Serve with croûtons of fried bread.

GOLDEN SOUP

1 oz. butter or dripping	1½ pints stock or water
	Salt and pepper
1 onion or leek	A few drops of vinegar
2 tsps. curry powder	1 tsp. tart jelly or jam
2 lb. potatoes	Toasted rolled oats
1 apple	

Melt the butter or dripping in a saucepan and fry the sliced onion or leek for a few minutes. Stir in the curry powder and fry for a further 1–2 minutes, then add the potatoes and the apple, roughly sliced, and just enough stock or water to cover. Add salt and pepper, cover closely and simmer gently until the vegetables are tender and the potatoes break up. Mash well with a wooden spoon or masher and reseason if necessary, adding the vinegar and tart jelly or jam. Serve with rolled oats which have previously been "toasted" in a quick oven or under a slow grill.

HARICOT BEAN SOUP

½ lb. haricot beans	2 tsps. flour
1 quart white stock	½ pint milk
1 onion	Seasoning
A small piece of turnip	A little meat or vegetable extract
½ lb. potatoes	

Wash the beans and soak them overnight in cold water. Strain, and put in a saucepan with the stock, onion, turnip and potatoes. Bring to the boil, skim carefully, and allow to simmer gently for 2 hours, or until the beans are quite tender. Rub through a sieve and return to the saucepan. Blend the flour with a little of the milk, add the remainder of the milk, and stir into the soup. Boil up again, stirring, and season, adding a little meat or vegetable extract to taste.

LEEK AND POTATO SOUP

½ rasher of bacon
½ oz. butter
2 large leeks
1 lb. potatoes
A small clove of garlic
¾ pint stock
Salt and pepper
¼ pint milk
Chopped parsley
Grated cheese

Rind and dice the bacon and fry it lightly in a saucepan to extract the fat. Add the butter and sauté the sliced leeks, potatoes and garlic in this for a few minutes. Add the stock and seasoning, cover, and simmer gently for 20–30 minutes. When the vegetables are tender but not broken up, add the milk, reheat, and serve immediately with the parsley and cheese.

LEEK AND SPAGHETTI SOUP

6–7 leeks
1 oz. butter
1 quart stock or water
2 oz. spaghetti
1 pint milk
Seasoning
Grated cheese

Choose medium-sized leeks, remove the roots, outer skin and ends of the green leaves, and wash in cold water. Then slice them thinly, wash again, and drain in a colander. Melt the butter in a saucepan, add the leeks, put on the lid and cook gently for 10 minutes, shaking the pan occasionally, until the vegetable has absorbed the fat. Then pour on the stock or water, bring to the boil and cook for 20 minutes. Wash the spaghetti and break it in small pieces, put it into the saucepan, and cook the soup for about 15 minutes longer, or until the spaghetti is soft. Add the milk to the soup just before serving, reheat, season to taste and serve with a dish of grated cheese.

LENTIL POTTAGE

1 oz. dripping
1 rasher of bacon
1 onion
2–3 stalks of celery
½ lb. lentils
Tomato purée or ketchup
Salt and pepper
Stock or water
2 cloves
6 peppercorns
A blade of mace
2 bay leaves
½ tsp. coriander seed

Melt the dripping and fry the chopped bacon, onion and celery in it for a few moments, until a good savoury smell comes from the pan. Add the washed lentils, the tomato purée or ketchup, salt and pepper, enough liquid to cover, and the spices, tied in muslin. Cover, and cook gently until the vegetables are tender, adding more liquid if necessary—when cooked it should be of the consistency of thin porridge. Remove the bag of spices before serving.

LENTIL SOUP

4 oz. lentils
¼ lb. carrots
¼ lb. onions
A stalk of celery
A small piece of turnip
2 potatoes
1 oz. dripping
1 quart stock
Salt and pepper
A bouquet garni
¼ pint milk
Chopped parsley

Wash the lentils, prepare and slice the vegetables and sauté all together with the fat for about 10 minutes, stirring frequently to prevent sticking. Add the stock, the seasoning and the bouquet garni. Bring to the boil, cover, and allow to simmer gently until the lentils and vegetables are tender. Mash or pass through a sieve, return to the saucepan and reheat, adding the milk and more seasoning if necessary. Add the chopped parsley just before serving.

Note : If liked, 1 tbsp. flour may be blended with the milk before adding it to the soup ; boil for 2–3 minutes before serving, to cook the flour.

LENTIL CREAM SOUP

1 cupful lentils
5–6 cupfuls water or stock
1 oz. dripping
1–2 onions
½ cupful each of carrot, turnip and celery
A sprig of thyme
A pinch of sugar
Seasoning
½ pint milk
A little cream
Croûtons of toast

Wash the lentils, put them into a basin with the measured water or stock, cover, and leave to stand for a few hours or overnight, then strain off, reserving the liquid. Melt the fat in a saucepan, put in the lentils, the onion, thinly sliced, and the other vegetables cut in dice. Stir over the heat for a few minutes, pour on the liquid, and bring to the boil. Skim, if necessary, and add the thyme, sugar and seasoning. Allow the soup to simmer slowly until the lentils are quite soft (about 1 hour or longer), stirring occasionally, and adding more water if required. When ready, rub through a sieve and return to the saucepan to reheat. Heat the milk and add it with the cream just before serving. Reseason, if necessary, and serve with croûtons of toast.

Pea soup can be made in the same way, but longer time must be allowed for cooking.

The liquid in which a piece of ham or salt beef has been cooked can be used for making this soup.

LETTUCE SOUP

2–3 lettuces (about 1 lb.)
$\frac{1}{2}$ pint white stock
Salt and pepper
1 oz. butter
1 oz. flour
1 pint milk
A pinch of sugar
1 egg yolk
Croûtons of fried bread

Wash the lettuces carefully and blanch them in boiling salted water for 3–5 minutes, then drain thoroughly and press lightly to remove the water. Chop them and put into a pan with the stock and seasoning, cover, and simmer gently until tender, then rub through a sieve. Melt the butter in the saucepan, stir in the flour to form a roux, then gradually add the sieved soup and the milk, stirring carefully to keep it smooth. Return to the boil, stirring, and cook for about 5 minutes. Add more seasoning if necessary, and a pinch of sugar, then cool slightly and stir in the beaten egg yolk. Reheat, but do not boil, and serve at once with the croûtons.

VEGETABLE MARROW SOUP

1 marrow (weight about 2 lb. when prepared)
1 pint stock or water
Salt and pepper
1 bay leaf
$\frac{1}{2}$ oz. flour
$\frac{1}{2}$ pint milk
Grated cheese

Prepare the marrow by peeling and removing the seeds; cut into very small cubes and put into a saucepan with the stock or water, salt and pepper and a bay leaf. Cover, and simmer until very soft, then mash with a wooden spoon, removing the bay leaf. Blend the flour with a little of the milk, add with the remainder of the milk to the marrow and bring to the boil, stirring. Cook for 2–3 minutes, season well, and serve with finely grated dry cheese.

MINESTRONE

2 tomatoes
$\frac{1}{2}$ lb. carrots
A small piece of turnip
2 stalks of celery
1–2 leeks or onions
1 rasher streaky bacon
1 oz. butter or olive oil
1 clove of garlic
1 quart good stock
Seasoning
A bouquet garni
2 tbsps. macaroni
A small cabbage heart
2 tbsps. chopped parsley
Grated cheese to serve separately

Prepare the vegetables and cut them into small, neat pieces. Rind and dice the bacon. Heat the fat and sauté first the bacon, then the vegetables for 10 minutes. Add the crushed garlic, the stock, seasoning and bouquet garni, cover, and simmer for about $\frac{1}{2}$ hour. Then add the macaroni and the shredded cabbage heart, and continue cooking for a further $\frac{1}{2}$ hour, or until the vegetables are quite tender. Reseason and remove the bouquet garni. Just before serving, add the finely chopped parsley. Serve with grated cheese handed separately—see colour picture facing page 65.

CREAM OF MUSHROOM SOUP

$\frac{1}{2}$ lb. mushrooms
$\frac{1}{2}$ pint stock
1 small onion
1 oz. butter
1 oz. flour
$\frac{3}{4}$ pint milk
Pepper and salt
1 egg yolk

Wash and peel the mushrooms, chop them finely and cook for $\frac{1}{2}$ hour in the stock with the sliced onion; when tender, rub through 8
a sieve. Melt the butter in a saucepan, stir in the flour and add the milk gradually. Bring to the boil, stirring meanwhile, add the mushroom purée and seasoning, and simmer for $\frac{1}{4}$ hour. Remove from the stove, allow to cool slightly, then stir in the beaten egg yolk. Cook for a few minutes, but do not boil, or the egg is likely to curdle.

If desired, add a garnish of cooked mushrooms—see colour picture facing page 65.

ONION SOUP—I

3 Spanish onions
2 oz. butter or $1\frac{1}{2}$ oz. beef dripping
1 quart light stock or water
A little stale bread
A few rinds of bacon
White pepper and salt
1 French roll
Grated cheese, if desired

Peel the onions and cut them in thin slices, put them into a saucepan with the fat, and cook very gently with the lid on for about $\frac{1}{2}$ hour: shake the pan occasionally, and let the onions become a rich brown colour. Then add the stock or water, the bread and rinds of bacon, carefully washed, and cook for another hour. Now sieve the soup, season to taste, and reheat. (The sieving may be omitted, but the soup will not look so appetising, nor be so agreeable to eat.) Cut the French roll into thin slanting slices, put into the soup tureen and pour the soup over it, cover, and leave for a few minutes before serving. Grated cheese may be served separately, or is added very slowly to the soup.

To make white onion soup, do not brown the onions, and add a little hot milk before serving.

ONION SOUP—II

1 lb. onions	1 bay leaf
1 oz. butter	A few parsley stalks
½ pint stock or water	Salt
1 pint milk	1 oz. flour
4 peppercorns	1 slice of toast
A blade of mace	Grated cheese

Peel and slice the onions, melt the butter and cook the onions in it over gentle heat until they are soft and yellow. Add the stock, half of the milk, the herbs, tied in muslin, and salt to taste. Cover, and simmer gently for about ½ hour, or until the onions are tender, then remove the bag of herbs. Blend the flour with the remaining milk, add to the soup, and stir until boiling. Reseason, if necessary. Put the diced toast in a hot soup tureen and pour the soup over. Serve with cheese, handed separately or sprinkled into the soup before serving.

PEA SOUP (USING DRIED PEAS)

6 oz. dried peas	1 oz. dripping
1 quart water	Seasoning
1 large onion	A bouquet garni
1 small carrot	¼ pint milk
A small piece of turnip	

Wash the peas and soak overnight in the water. Cut the vegetables into small pieces and fry lightly in the melted dripping, add the soaked peas, the water in which they were soaked, seasoning and bouquet garni. Allow to simmer gently for 1½–2 hours, until the vegetables are reduced to a pulp. Remove the bouquet garni, add the milk, reheat, and serve. If liked, the soup may be sieved before the milk is added.

GREEN PEA SOUP—I

1 lettuce	2 quarts white stock
1 onion	1 oz. flour
1 sprig of mint	Salt and pepper
A little parsley	1 lump sugar
3–4 oz. butter	Green colouring, if necessary
1 quart shelled green peas	

8 Wash and trim the lettuce, shred it finely, and slice the onion. Wash the mint and parsley. Melt half the butter in a saucepan, add the vegetables, and sauté them until the butter is absorbed. Add the stock, bring to the boil, skim carefully, and simmer for about 1 hour, or until the vegetables are thoroughly cooked; then pass through a sieve. Melt the remaining butter in a saucepan, add the flour, and fry lightly. Pour on the sieved stock and vegetables, and stir carefully until boiling. Add the seasoning and sugar, and serve. If the soup is not a good colour, a little green colouring may be added.

GREEN PEA SOUP—II

2 lb. peas	Salt and pepper
1 quart stock or water	1 oz. flour or ¾ oz. cornflour
A sprig of mint	½ pint milk
Sugar	

Shell the peas and wash the pods in several waters. Place the pods in a pan, cover with the stock or water and allow to simmer gently for about ½ hour, to extract flavour and colour. Strain off the stock, return it to the pan with the peas, mint, sugar and seasoning, and simmer until the peas are tender, then pass through a sieve. Blend the flour or cornflour with the milk, add to the soup, then reheat, stirring all the time. Cook for several minutes, reseason if necessary, adding a little sugar, and serve.

POTATO SOUP

2 lb. potatoes	1 bay leaf
1 onion	1 blade of mace
A stalk of celery	½ oz. flour
½–1 oz. fat	¼ pint milk
1 quart stock or water	1 tbsp. chopped parsley
Salt and pepper	

Peel and slice the potatoes and chop the onion and celery. Melt the fat and sauté the vegetables in it for 5–10 minutes. Add the stock, seasoning and the herbs, bring to the boil and simmer until the vegetables are tender and the potato breaks up. Mash with a fork or potato masher, removing the herbs. Stir in the flour, blended to a smooth cream with the milk, and allow to boil for a further 2–3 minutes. Add the chopped parsley just before serving.

DICED POTATO SOUP

½ oz. bacon fat	Seasoning
1 large leek (or onion)	½ oz. flour
1 lb. potatoes	¼ pint milk
1 quart stock or water	

Melt the fat in a saucepan and fry the chopped leek (or onion) until golden-brown and crisp. Remove from the pan and set aside. Meanwhile, peel and dice the potatoes, then place in the saucepan, together with the stock and seasoning. Allow to simmer gently until just tender—about 30 minutes. Blend the flour with the milk and add it to the soup, together with the fried leek or onion. Stir for 3–4 minutes, to cook the flour, and serve immediately.

MASHED POTATO SOUP

½ oz. butter or dripping
1 onion or leek
½ pint good stock
½ pint milk
½ lb. mashed potato
Salt and pepper
A little chopped parsley
A little grated cheese

Melt the fat in a saucepan, add the finely chopped onion and cook without browning for about 5 minutes. Add the stock, bring to the boil and simmer for 5 minutes. Meanwhile add the milk gradually to the mashed potatoes, smoothing out any lumps. Add to the saucepan, season well and bring to the boil. Just before serving, add a little freshly chopped parsley and finely grated cheese.

POTATO, PARSLEY AND CHEESE SOUP

2 lb. potatoes
1 quart stock or water
½ oz. flour
¼ pint milk
Seasoning
2 tbsps. finely chopped parsley
2 tbsps. finely grated cheese

Peel and slice the potatoes and cook them in the salted stock until really soft, then mash with a fork. Stir in the flour, blended with a little milk, and boil for several minutes, stirring constantly and adding extra milk if necessary to give a creamy consistency. Season to taste and stir in the parsley. Put the grated cheese in a hot soup tureen and pour the boiling soup on to it.

CREAM OF PUMPKIN SOUP

2 small onions
1 oz. butter
Cooked pumpkin (weight about 3 lb. before cooking)
1 pint water
Salt and pepper
2 eggs
1 pint milk
A little grated cheese
Chopped parsley, if liked

Prepare the onions, chop them finely and fry lightly in the butter. Put into a stewpan with the cooked sieved pumpkin, the water and seasoning, and simmer for about 2 hours. Mix the beaten eggs with the milk, add to the soup and heat very gently for a further few minutes to cook the egg, taking care to prevent curdling. Add the grated cheese and, if liked, a little chopped parsley, just before serving.

SPINACH SOUP—I

½ pint spinach purée (2½–3 lb. spinach)
1 pint chicken or veal stock
1 pint thin white sauce
1 egg yolk
1 tbsp. cream
Seasoning
Croûtons of toast

Wash the spinach well, cook it and rub through a sieve. Return it to the saucepan, add the stock and the sauce, bring to the boil, and boil for 5 minutes. Meanwhile, beat the egg yolk with the cream. Remove the soup from the heat, allow to cool slightly and stir in the egg yolk and cream. Reheat gently to cook the egg, but do not allow to boil. Season, and serve with croûtons of toast.

SPINACH SOUP—II

1 lb. spinach
1 onion
1 oz. butter
1½ pints stock or water
Salt and pepper
1 oz. flour
¼ pint milk
Fried croûtons

Wash the spinach thoroughly. Prepare and slice the onion and sauté it in the butter for a few minutes. Add the spinach, stock and seasoning, bring to the boil and simmer for 30–40 minutes. Pass it through a sieve and add the flour, blended to a smooth cream with the milk. Return it to the saucepan, bring to the boil, stirring, and cook for 2–3 minutes. Re-season to taste, and serve with fried croûtons.

SPINACH AND RICE SOUP

½ lb. fresh spinach
2 small onions
1 oz. butter
1 quart water or stock
2 tbsps. rice
1 bay leaf
Pepper and salt
1 egg
1 teacupful milk

Wash the spinach, remove the stalks, and cut it in fine shreds. Slice the onions. Put the prepared spinach and onion into a saucepan with the butter and cook for a few minutes. Stir in the water or stock and bring to the boil. Add the rice, bay leaf, and pepper and salt to taste, and cook slowly until the rice is tender—about ½ hour. Remove the bay leaf. Just before serving draw the pan to the side of the heat; when the soup has ceased to boil, add the egg beaten with the milk, then heat gently to cook the egg, but do not boil again.

TOMATO SOUP

2 slices of bacon
½ oz. butter
1 onion
1 carrot
1 stalk of celery
1 small tin tomatoes
1 quart stock or water
2 tsps. sugar
Salt
A bouquet garni (including 1 blade of mace, 2 cloves, 1 bay leaf, 10 peppercorns)
1 oz. flour
A little cold milk

Fry the bacon and remove it from the pan. Melt the butter, slice the onion and fry lightly in the butter and bacon fat. Then add the other vegetables, previously cut into slices, and fry for a few minutes. Add the stock or water, sugar, seasoning and bouquet garni, bring to the boil and simmer for $\frac{3}{4}$ hour, or until the vegetables are tender. Rub the soup through a sieve and return it to the saucepan. Blend the flour with a little cold milk, stir into the soup, bring to the boil and simmer for 15 minutes.

CREAM OF TOMATO SOUP

1 lb. tomatoes	A bouquet garni
1 onion	1 oz. flour or $\frac{3}{4}$ oz. cornflour
1 carrot	$\frac{1}{4}$–$\frac{1}{2}$ pint milk
1 stalk of celery	A pinch of sugar
A little fat bacon or bacon rinds	Chopped parsley or watercress
1$\frac{1}{2}$ pints stock or water	
Salt and pepper	

Prepare and slice the tomatoes and vegetables. Fry the bacon or rinds slowly to extract the fat, add the prepared vegetables and sauté all together for about 10 minutes. Add the stock, seasoning and bouquet garni, bring to the boil and simmer gently until tender—about 1 hour. Remove the bacon rinds, if used, and the bouquet garni. Rub it through a fine sieve, then add the flour or cornflour, blended to a smooth cream with the milk. Return it to the saucepan, bring to the boil, stirring well, and allow to boil for 2–3 minutes. Reseason with salt, pepper and sugar and add some chopped parsley or watercress just before serving.

SIMPLE TOMATO SOUP (THIN)

1 lb. tomatoes	1 bay leaf
1 onion	1–2 bones
2–3 bacon rinds	1 pint stock
2 cloves	Salt and pepper
6 peppercorns	A little milk
A blade of mace	A pinch of sugar
A pinch of mixed herbs	Chopped parsley

Slice the tomatoes and onion and put them into a pan with the bacon rinds, spices, herbs, bones and the stock. Season, then cover, and simmer gently until well flavoured. Strain off the liquid, pressing the vegetables against the side of the strainer, but do not sieve. Return the soup to the pan, add a little milk and a pinch of sugar, and make very hot. Just before serving, sprinkle in a little freshly chopped parsley.

SIMPLE VEGETABLE BROTH

Make this when you are cooking potatoes and a green vegetable such as spinach.

Have ready a little chopped parsley, chopped chives and chopped watercress. Strain the cooking water from the spinach and mix with some of the potato water. Add a little vegetable extract, a sprinkling of pepper and more salt, if necessary, but remember that the vegetable water is already salted. Add any left-over vegetables you may have, cut up small. Make very hot, and just before serving add the chopped parsley, watercress and chives. Serve the broth at once.

VEGETABLE BROTH

1 carrot	1 quart good stock
1 onion	2 oz. barley
1 leek	Salt and pepper
1–2 celery stalks	1 tsp. finely chopped parsley
$\frac{1}{2}$ turnip or swede	Finely grated cheese
1 potato	

Cut the vegetables into neat dice or strips and put with the stock, the washed barley, salt and pepper into a saucepan. Bring to the boil, cover, and allow to simmer gently for 1$\frac{1}{2}$–2 hours. Add the chopped parsley, reseason if necessary, and pour into a hot tureen. The finely grated cheese may be added immediately before serving or handed separately.

CREAM OF VEGETABLE SOUP

1$\frac{1}{2}$ lb. potatoes	2 cloves
Lemon juice or vinegar	1 bay leaf
1 oz. butter	$\frac{1}{4}$ oz. cornflour
1 small onion	1 pint milk
$\frac{1}{4}$ lb. shelled peas	A little cream
1 quart light stock	Croûtons of fried bread or toast
Pepper and salt	
1 blade mace	

Prepare the potatoes, cut into slices and put immediately into cold water to which a little lemon juice or vinegar has been added (thus preventing the potatoes becoming a bad colour and spoiling the appearance of the soup). Melt the butter, stir in potatoes, sliced onion and shelled peas. Add stock, seasoning, mace, cloves and bay leaf, cover, and simmer gently until the vegetables are thoroughly tender, then pass the soup through a sieve and return it to the saucepan. Mix the cornflour to a thin cream with a little of the milk. Add the remainder of the milk to the soup and reheat; when nearly boiling, stir in the blended cornflour and boil for 5 minutes, stirring meanwhile. Add more seasoning if necessary, and lastly, stir in a little cream. Serve the soup with the croûtons of fried bread or toast.

WATERCRESS SOUP

2 bunches watercress (about ½ lb.)
½ oz. butter
1 pint light stock
Salt and pepper
1 tbsp. cornflour
¼ pint milk
2–3 tbsps. cream

Wash the watercress very thoroughly and remove the coarse stalks. Melt the butter in a saucepan, add the watercress (reserving a few sprigs for garnish) and toss over very gentle heat for 2–3 minutes. Add the stock, salt and pepper, then cover, and simmer gently for 20–30 minutes. Rub through a sieve, then return it to the saucepan, add the cornflour, blended with the milk, bring to the boil, stirring, and cook for 5–8 minutes. Add more seasoning if necessary, and just before serving stir in the cream. Garnish with very small sprigs of watercress.

A SIMPLE WINTER SOUP

1½ lb. potatoes
2 leeks or onions
4 tbsps. lentils
1 clove
6 peppercorns
A blade of mace
A pinch of mixed herbs
Stock or water
Salt and pepper
About ¼ pint milk
1 tsp. chopped parsley
Grated cheese, if liked

Peel and slice the potatoes, wash and slice the leeks or onions, and wash the lentils. Put all together in a pan with the herbs and spices (tied in muslin), and add enough stock or water just to cover. Season well with salt and pepper, cover, and simmer gently until tender, adding more liquid if it becomes too thick. Remove the bag of herbs, stir in the milk, make the soup very hot, and just before serving stir in the chopped parsley.

This soup is nicest if served thick, with the vegetables left in pieces, and not sieved. It can, if liked, be sprinkled with grated cheese.

WINTER HOTCHPOTCH

1 lb. carrots
½ lb. artichokes
½ lb. turnips
2 onions or leeks
2–3 stalks celery
½ a small cabbage
1 rasher of bacon
1 oz. dripping
2 cloves
6 peppercorns
2 bay leaves
A blade of mace
1 tsp. mixed herbs
Stock or water
Salt and pepper
¼ lb. macaroni
Piquant sauce
Tomato ketchup
Chopped parsley
Grated cheese

Prepare the vegetables and cut them (except the cabbage), into fairly small pieces. Rind and dice the bacon, and fry it lightly, then add the dripping, and when this is melted, sauté the cut vegetables in it for 5–10 minutes. Add the herbs and spices (tied in muslin), and enough stock or water to cover. Season well, cover closely, and simmer for ¾–1 hour. Then add the macaroni and coarsely shredded cabbage and cook for a further 20–30 minutes, adding more liquid as required. When all the ingredients are tender, remove the muslin bag, and season to taste with more salt and pepper if necessary, and add a little piquant sauce and tomato ketchup. Serve with freshly chopped parsley and grated cheese.

If preferred, the cabbage can be shredded and added just before serving, instead of being cooked in the soup: this gives a pleasant crispness.

MISCELLANEOUS RECIPES FOR SOUPS

CHEESE SOUP

½ oz. butter
1 small onion
A stalk of celery
Salt and pepper
¾ pint milk
¼ pint stock or water
½ oz. cornflour
2 oz. finely grated cheese

Melt the butter and toss the finely chopped onion and celery in it until it is all absorbed, but do not fry or brown. Add the seasonings, milk and the stock, and simmer gently for ½ hour. Mix the cornflour to a smooth paste with 2 tbsps. water, and strain on the hot liquor. Boil up, stirring well all the time, and cook for 5 minutes. Add the grated cheese, and simmer for a minute or so until it is melted.

CHESTNUT PURÉE

1 lb. chestnuts
1 oz. butter
1 small onion
1½ pints good stock
Salt and pepper
½ oz. flour
¼ pint milk
¼ tsp. sugar
2–3 tbsps. cream

Make a slit in the chestnuts at both ends with a sharp knife (this facilitates removing the skins later on). Boil them for about 10 minutes, then skin them. Melt the butter in a saucepan and sauté the chestnuts and the sliced onion for a few minutes. Add the stock, salt and pepper. Cover, and simmer until the chestnuts are quite tender—about 1 hour—then rub through a sieve. Blend the flour with the milk and add to the purée. Bring to the boil, stirring, and cook for 2–3 minutes, then reseason if necessary, and add the sugar. Lastly, stir in the cream

QUICKLY PREPARED CREAM SOUP

2 oz. butter or margarine	Pepper and salt
2 oz. flour	Celery salt, if liked
2 quarts white stock	1 teacupful cooked or bottled green peas
2 egg yolks	Croûtons of toast

Melt the butter in a saucepan, stir in the flour and blend well. Pour on the stock, bring to the boil, allow to simmer for 15–20 minutes, draw away from the heat and allow to cool slightly. Beat the egg yolks, add to the soup, stirring meanwhile, and cook for a few minutes, but do not allow the soup to boil, otherwise the eggs are liable to curdle. Season to taste with pepper and salt (or celery salt if preferred). Place the previously heated peas in a hot soup tureen, pour the soup over, and serve with croûtons of toast.

HOLLANDAISE SOUP

Carrot	1 quart white stock (preferably chicken)
Turnip	1 egg yolk
Cucumber	¼ pint cream
1 teacupful green peas (shelled)	1 tsp. caster sugar
2 oz. butter	Salt and pepper
1 oz. flour	

Prepare the carrot, turnip and cucumber, and from them cut tiny balls with a small vegetable scoop, making about ¼ pint of each, then cook these and the peas in boiling water until soft but not broken. Melt the butter in a saucepan, add the flour, and fry lightly without browning. Add the stock, bring to the boil, stirring all the time, then skim carefully, and simmer for about 15 minutes. Beat the egg yolk and the cream together. Remove the pan from the heat, cool slightly, add egg yolk and cream, stirring meanwhile. Continue to stir over a gentle heat, but on no account let it boil or the soup will curdle. Add the sugar and seasoning to taste. Put the prepared vegetable garnish into a hot tureen and pour the soup over.

MACARONI SOUP

1½ oz. butter or margarine	1 cupful cooked macaroni
1 oz. rice flour	Seasoning
1 pint milk	2–3 tbsps. grated cheese
1 pint light stock	1 egg yolk

Melt the butter in a saucepan, stir in the rice flour, and cook for a minute or two. Then draw the saucepan to one side of the stove and pour in the milk and stock. (The macaroni liquid may be used in place of the stock.) Stir until boiling, and cook slowly for 10 minutes. Add the cooked macaroni, cut in short lengths, season to taste and sprinkle in the freshly grated cheese. Pour the soup on the slightly beaten yolk of egg, stirring all the time, and serve at once.

MILK AND MACARONI SOUP

2 onions	1 pint white stock or water
1 oz. butter	1 pint milk
1 lb. potatoes	2 oz. macaroni
Pepper and salt	Finely chopped parsley
A little nutmeg	

Peel and slice the onions. Melt the butter, add the onions, sliced potatoes, pepper, salt and a little grated nutmeg. Stir over gentle heat until the butter is absorbed, then pour on the stock or water, bring to the boil, and simmer until the potatoes are cooked : this will take about 20–30 minutes. Pass the soup through a coarse sieve, then return it to the saucepan, add the milk and bring to the boil. Meanwhile, the macaroni should be cooked in salted water, strained, and placed in the bottom of the soup tureen. Sprinkle in the chopped parsley and pour the tomato soup over.

MULLIGATAWNY SOUP

2 onions	1 tsp. curry paste
1 carrot	2 oz. flour
A piece of turnip	1 quart stock
A sour apple	Salt and pepper
A rasher of bacon	A bouquet garni
1 oz. butter	A squeeze of lemon juice
1 tbsp. curry powder	A little cream
	Dry boiled rice

Prepare and cut up the vegetables ; peel and chop the apple. Rind and dice the bacon and fry it lightly to extract the fat, add the butter, and when this has melted, fry the vegetables and chopped apple ; fry also the curry powder and paste. Stir in the flour, then gradually add the stock. Bring to the boil, stirring, add salt and pepper and the herbs, then cover and simmer gently for about 1 hour, skimming occasionally. Pass the soup through a sieve, then return it to the saucepan and boil up. Add more seasonings if necessary, and stir in a squeeze of lemon juice and a little cream. Serve with the rice.

YOUNG NETTLE SOUP

1½ lb. young nettles	A little cold milk
1 lb. spinach	A few cooked sausages, cut in small pieces
1 pint bone stock	2 tbsps. yoghourt or sour cream
Seasoning	
1 oz. flour	

Blanch the nettles and mix them with the washed spinach. Pour the boiling stock over them, add seasoning, and simmer gently for 40 minutes, adding more stock as it becomes necessary. Sieve the soup and return it to the saucepan, then stir in the flour, blended to a smooth cream with the milk. Boil for 2–3 minutes, stirring, and reseason if necessary. Serve with a garnish of sausage and add the yoghourt or sour cream just before serving.

PURITAN SOUP

3 potatoes	½ oz. flour
2 bunches watercress	2–3 tbsps. cold milk
2 cupfuls hot milk	1 oz. butter
Seasoning	Toast

Choose good-sized potatoes. Wash and peel them, cut in quarters, cook them in boiling salted water until tender, then drain, reserving the liquid. Press them through a sieve or vegetable presser while still hot, and return them to the saucepan. Add 3 cupfuls of the water in which the potatoes were boiled, and bring this to simmering point. Meanwhile, wash the leaves of the watercress, drain, and chop them finely. Add them to the soup mixture together with the hot milk, and season with pepper and salt to taste. Mix the flour to a smooth paste with about 2–3 tbsps. cold milk, add to the soup, and stir until boiling. Put in the butter, broken in small pieces, and cook for a few minutes longer. Serve with toasted bread.

RICE SOUP

½ oz. butter	A small piece of turnip
1 shallot	2 oz. rice
2 tsps. curry powder	A sprig of parsley
1 quart stock and milk	A pinch of salt
A small piece of carrot	

Melt the butter and fry the sliced shallot in it to a golden-brown. Remove the shallot and fry the curry powder. Pour the stock and milk into the pan and bring to the boil. Slice the vegetables, and add them, together with the fried shallot, washed rice, parsley and the salt. Simmer for 1½ hours, rub through a sieve, reheat and serve. This makes a fairly substantial soup; if preferred, reduce the amount of rice to 1 oz.

SEMOLINA CREAM SOUP

¼ lb. onions	Seasoning
2 stalks of celery	1 oz. semolina
A piece of turnip	¼ pint milk
1 artichoke	Chopped parsley to garnish
1 pint stock	

Prepare and mince the vegetables and place in a stewpan with the stock and seasoning. Bring to the boil, cover, and simmer gently until tender. Blend the semolina with the milk, add to the soup, reboil and cook for about 10 minutes, or until the grain is tender. Add the parsley just before serving.

WINTER PURÉE

2 lb. chestnuts	Pepper and salt
1 small onion	1 quart milk
½ a head of celery	½ oz. semolina
1 quart stock	Croûtons of fried bread
A bouquet garni	

Slit the chestnuts, put them in cold water and bring to the boil. Boil for 5–10 minutes, then remove the skins and cut into slices. Prepare and slice the onion and celery, put with the nuts and vegetables into a pan, and pour on the boiling stock. Add the bouquet garni and seasoning, and simmer gently until the vegetables and nuts are tender. Rub the soup through a sieve, return it to the saucepan, add the milk and bring to boiling point. When boiling, sprinkle in the semolina, stirring briskly meanwhile to prevent lumps forming. Cook for about 8 minutes, and serve hot with croûtons of fried bread.

FISH SOUPS

FISH SOUP

1 cod's head	¾ pint milk
1 onion	2 oz. butter
1 carrot	1½ oz. flour
A bouquet garni	1 tsp. white vinegar
4 peppercorns	2 tsps. finely chopped parsley
Salt	

Put the cod's head in a saucepan with the vegetables, herbs, seasonings and enough water to cover. Cook gently for 1 hour, then remove the head and cut the white flesh into neat pieces. Strain the stock, measure off 1¼ pints, and add this to the ¾ pint milk. Melt the butter, stir in the flour, and add the liquid gradually, then stir until boiling. Add the pieces of fish, the vinegar and the parsley, and reheat without boiling. Season carefully and serve.

SHRIMP CHOWDER

1 large onion	1 pint shrimps or prawns
½ oz. butter	1 pint milk
¼ pint boiling water	1–2 oz. grated cheese
3 medium-sized potatoes	Chopped parsley
Salt and pepper	

Slice the onion and cook it in the hot fat for a few minutes until tender ; toss during cooking to prevent browning. Add the boiling water, the sliced potatoes and a sprinkling of salt and pepper. Cover, and simmer gently for about 15 minutes, or until the potatoes are tender. Add the shrimps (picked) and the milk, and bring again to the boil. Stir in the grated cheese and parsley, and serve at once.

LOBSTER BISQUE

1 cooked hen lobster	1 oz. butter
1 quart stock or water	1 oz. flour
A small carrot	A squeeze of lemon juice
1 onion	A little cream
1 bay leaf	½ glass sherry
A sprig of parsley	Lobster butter (page 447)
Salt and pepper	

Remove the meat from the lobster and cut it into neat pieces, reserving the coral to make the lobster butter. Break up the shell and cook it with the stock or water, carrot, onion, bay leaf, parsley and seasoning for ¾–1 hour, then strain. Melt the butter in the saucepan, add the flour and stir in the strained lobster stock by degrees. Bring to the boil, stirring, and cook for about 5 minutes. Add more seasoning, if necessary, the lemon juice, cream and sherry. Add the pieces of lobster meat, whisk in the lobster butter and serve at once.

SIMPLE LOBSTER SOUP

1 medium-sized lobster	Salt and cayenne pepper
2 oz. butter or margarine	Hot buttered toast or water biscuits
2 tbsps. flour	A little sherry
1 quart fresh milk	

Cut the meat from the lobster into small pieces. Melt the butter in a saucepan and stir in the flour, cook until beginning to bubble, then draw the saucepan away from the heat, beat in the milk a little at a time, and stir again over the heat until boiling. Add the prepared lobster, and cook very slowly for 15 minutes. Season rather well with salt and cayenne, and serve with hot buttered toast or water biscuits. If liked, a little sherry can be added at the last.

FRUIT SOUPS

Fruit soups are well known abroad and are very popular in summer. They are made with the diluted juice of fruit such as rhubarb, gooseberry, red-currant, raspberry, orange, lemon, etc., slightly thickened with cornflour, potato flour, or sago meal, and sweetened to taste. A little white wine may be added, and sometimes a touch of spice. Before serving, the fruit soup is either poured on to 1–2 egg yolks, or a spoonful of whipped cream is put on the top of each plateful. These soups are often served with bread cut in dice and baked until brown, with a little butter and sugar, or with a special kind of pastry.

RED CHERRY SOUP

2 lb. cherries	A little red wine, if liked
2 quarts water	Whipped cream
¾ oz. cornflour	Unsweetened biscuits or rusks
2 oz. sugar	
Lemon juice	

Wash and stem the cherries, reserving a few of the best for garnishing, and put the remainder in a saucepan with the water. Simmer gently until tender, then rub through a sieve. Reheat to boiling point, add the cornflour and sugar, mixed with a little water, and cook for about 10 minutes longer. Lastly, add the lemon juice and the reserved cherries (stoned). A little red wine may also be added. Allow the soup to become quite cold, and serve it in glasses or in cups. A small spoonful of whipped cream may be put on the top, and unsweetened biscuits or rusks should be served separately.

FISH COOKERY

Fish is a highly nutritious food, valuable as a source of protein, rich in calcium, iron and phosphorus, and containing Vitamins A, B and D. In addition, salt-water fish and shell fish are our best common source of iodine.

In the flesh of white fish, which contains little or no fat, the protein is present in a very easily digestible form, which makes it a first choice for invalids.

The darker flesh of oily fish is interspersed with fat, which is rich in Vitamins A and D, giving an extra protective food which should be included in the family meals by using such fish in either fresh or tinned form at least once a week.

BUYING AND COOKING FISH

Buy fresh fish when it is really fresh and on the day you intend to use it. The difference in flavour between fish fresh from the sea or river and fish that has lain in cold storage for a day or longer is very marked. Firm flesh, sparkling silvery scales and bright markings, red gills, bright and bulging eyes and a sweet, fresh smell, are all signs that fish is fresh. With cut fish, look for flesh with a firm appearance and grain.

To enjoy fish at its best, eat it while it is in season. Its quality is very much influenced by spawning, and during the spawning season all fish is poor and flavourless, although it is supposed to be at its best just before this takes place. Some kinds of fish are sold all the year round, but for others, such as salmon and trout, there is a close season.

When it comes to the cooking, it should be borne in mind that all fish requires a certain amount of seasoning and flavouring. The more highly flavoured varieties, such as salmon, mackerel, and herring, though they are often served with piquant or highly flavoured accompaniments, need comparatively little flavouring in themselves; but the less flavoursome kinds, such as haddock, whiting, cod, etc., need high seasoning. Nearly every kind of fish requires a good sauce or special accompaniment to bring out its best properties, and it is here that the inexperienced cook often fails. The French make a special study of sauces and butters; their fish is no better than ours, but by giving it just the necessary finish, they are able to present it more attractively.

There are many different flavours which are suitable for combining with fish; these include anchovy essence, tomato or piquant sauce, chutney, curry powder or horseradish; chopped mushrooms, parsley, tarragon, capers or gherkins; nutmeg, mace or cloves (the last three should be used in minute quantities); grated cheese or lemon rind; oysters, prawns and shrimps, etc.

Then again, fish should be made to look attractive by using a suitable garnish. No fish need be sent to table perfectly plain, as there is quite a variety of decorations to choose from. Any of the following can be utilised—parsley, chervil, hard-boiled egg, tomato, lemon, curled celery, prawns, shrimps or lobster coral.

Serve the fish very hot and have hot plates.

PREPARATION OF FISH

To Clean Whole Fish

Scrape off any scales on both sides of the fish, using a knife and scraping from tail to head, with frequent rinsing to loosen the scales.

To remove entrails from round fish, make a slit along the abdomen of the fish from the gills half-way to the tail, draw out the insides and clean away any blood. Rub with a little salt to remove black skin.

With flat fish, such as sole and plaice, open the cavity which lies in the upper part of the body under the gills and clean out the entrails as above.

Cut off fins and gills, and if the fish is to be served whole, remove head and tail or not as desired. If the head is left on, the eyes must be taken out. Finally, rinse thoroughly in cold water.

To Clean Cut Fish, Fillets of Fish and Fish Cutlets

Wipe with damp muslin. Do not wash the fish or leave it lying in water, as this draws out the juices and impairs the flavour.

To Skin Flat Fish Whole

As a sole skins easily, it is usually done before filleting, whereas a plaice is filleted first. First wash the fish and cut off the fins. Then make an incision across the tail, slip the thumb
9 between the skin and the flesh, and loosen the skin round the sides of the fish. Now hold down the fish firmly with one hand, and with the other take hold of the skin, and draw it off quickly, upwards towards the head. The white skin can be removed in the same way, but unless the fish is large, it is generally left on.

To Fillet Flat Fish

When the flesh of the fish is removed from the bones in neat pieces, it is said to be filleted. Four fillets should be taken from a flat fish, two from each side. A sharp, pliable knife should be used. First make an incision straight down the back of the fish, following the line of the bone.
10 Then insert the knife under the flesh and carefully remove it with long, clean strokes. Take the first fillet from the left-hand side of the fish, working from head to tail, then turn the fish round, and cut off the second fillet from tail to head. Fillet the other side of the fish in the same way. When finished, no flesh should be left adhering to the bone.

To Skin Fillets of Flat Fish

Lay the fillet on a board, skin side down, salt the fingers and hold the tail end of the skin firmly with the fingers. Then separate the flesh
11 from the skin by sawing with a sharp knife from side to side, pressing the flat of the blade against the flesh. Keep the edge of the blade close to the skin while cutting, but do not press heavily, or the skin will be severed.

To Skin Round Fish

Round fish are skinned from head to tail. Cut off a narrow strip of skin along the spine and cut across the skin just below the head, loosen the skin under the head with the point of a sharp knife, then dip the fingers in coarse salt and gently pull the skin down towards the tail, working very carefully to avoid breaking the flesh. Skin the other side of the fish in the same way. Finally, dry the fillets.

To Fillet Round Fish

Cut down the centre back to the bone with a sharp knife and cut along the abdomen of the fish. Remove the flesh cleanly from the bones, working from the head down, pressing the knife against the bones and working with short, sharp strokes. Remove the fillet from the other side in the same way, giving two fillets altogether, which may be cut slantwise into two or three pieces if desired.

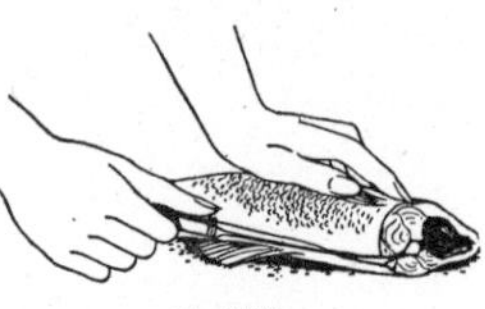

To Fillet

BOILING

This method of cooking is only to be recommended for large pieces of fish. The fish should be rubbed over with lemon juice to keep it white and firm, and then placed in sufficient hot salted water or court-bouillon (below) to cover it: a very common fault is to omit to put enough salt in the water. It is advisable to use a fish-kettle, to enable the fish to be lifted out on the drainer without breaking. Failing this, it should be tied in muslin and placed on a plate at the bottom of a saucepan. A small bunch of herbs, and a little cut-up carrot, onion and celery can be added to the water if the fish is of a tasteless kind. Bring the water to boiling point and then simmer very slowly (removing any scum as it rises) until the fish is cooked. The time depends very much on the shape and thickness of the fish; the average is 10 minutes to the pound and 10 minutes over. When the flesh comes away easily from the bone, it is sufficiently cooked. Drain well, dish on a hot dish, garnish with parsley and lemon, and serve with a suitable sauce.

Note: Although this method of cooking fish is referred to as boiling, it is more accurately described as poaching, since the water should be kept only simmering, not actually boiling, while the fish is in it. When cooking small pieces of fish, the term poaching is generally used, but the method is very similar (see next page).

COURT-BOUILLON

To each quart water (or water and white wine mixed):

1 onion	A small clove
1 clove of garlic	1 tbsp. vinegar
1 carrot	1 tsp. salt
A small stalk of celery	Freshly ground or crushed black pepper
A bunch of herbs	

Put all the ingredients into a pan, cover, and simmer for ½ hour or longer. Strain, and use this liquor for cooking fish.

POACHING

Suitable for cuts of fish, particularly for small pieces and also for small whole fish.

Prepare the fish by rolling or folding thin fillets. Have sufficient fish stock and milk, or milk and water, in a saucepan or casserole to half-cover the fish. When this is simmering lay the fish in the pan, season, cover and simmer very gently until tender, allowing 10–15 minutes to the lb., according to the thickness of the cut. Lift out the fish, drain, place on a hot dish and serve coated with a sauce made with the liquor in the pan.

STEAMING

Prepare the fish as for boiling. Place large cuts or whole fish directly in the steamer. Small fillets or thin cutlets will cook satisfactorily if laid on a greased deep plate with 1 tbsp. milk and seasoning, placed over a saucepan of boiling water and covered with the lid or a second plate.

For a large fish allow 15 minutes to the lb. and 15 minutes over; cook fillets for about 10–15 minutes.

FRYING

The Preparation

Almost any kind of fish is suitable for this method of cooking. Small fish can be fried whole, while the large ones should be filleted and cut into convenient-sized pieces. The fish must be made quite dry, and the outside coated so as to prevent the fat soaking into the fish itself. There are several different methods of coating fish for frying:

For shallow frying, the simplest method is to coat it with flour, seasoned with pepper and salt. Fine oatmeal may also be used, and this is particularly applicable to herring and mackerel.

A slightly more elaborate method for shallow frying is to dip the fish into seasoned flour, then into milk, and in flour again.

For deep frying, small pieces of fish may be dipped in batter, after being seasoned first with pepper, salt and a little lemon juice. Drop the pieces of fish into the batter, lift out with a skewer to drain off any surplus batter and put straight into the frying fat. This is a very good method of coating the fish, which, when cooked should look like nice, crisp fritters.

Perhaps the best method of all, however, is to egg-and-breadcrumb the fish, which many people find more digestible, and which looks very attractive when cooked. 12

Fish that is coated with flour or batter must not be prepared until just before frying, but if egg-and-breadcrumbed it may be made ready beforehand, as it becomes drier by standing, and fries all the better.

The Cooking

There are two different methods of frying fish: in deep fat, and in shallow fat.

The first method should be adopted when cooking all small pieces of fish, as it is by far the more successful. The initial outlay is more, as 2–3 lb. of fat will be required to start a deep fat bath, but with care this can be used many times and will keep for months. Clarified beef fat, oil, or lard may be used. Heat it in an aluminium or iron saucepan until it reaches 350°F., or until a faint blue smoke begins to rise from it, then use it at once. Do not put in too much fish at one time; if the fat is cooled below a certain temperature it will soak into the fish and make it sodden. When the fish is a golden-brown colour, lift it out with a perforated spoon, or use a frying basket, and allow the fat to drip from it.
Turn the fish on to crumpled kitchen paper to 13
absorb any remaining grease, then dish up neatly and garnish with lemon and parsley. When the cooking is finished, allow the fat to cool slightly, then strain it through muslin or a fine strainer to remove any crumbs or sediment and put aside for future use.

Frying in shallow fat is suitable for thick slices of fish, such as a cod steak, and whole fish, such as a sole, which require longer time to cook. Melt a small quantity of fat in a frying pan, and watch carefully to see that it does not become overheated. When it is hot, lay in the prepared fish and let it brown on the underside, then turn it carefully with a broad-bladed knife without destroying the outer coating, and brown the second side. Sufficient time must be allowed to cook the fish thoroughly. Drain, and serve garnished with lemon and parsley.

Fried fish may be served either with or without a sauce, which must always be served separately.

GRILLING

Herrings, mullet, mackerel, plaice and sole are suitable fish to grill, and may be cooked whole. Cuts of thick fish, such as halibut, cod, salmon, etc., are also suitable (see below).

To grill whole fish, wash, remove scales, score with a sharp knife in three or four places, and brush with melted fat. Place on the hot greased grid and cook rather slowly, so that the fish is thoroughly cooked without burning. Turn once or twice, but handle the fish very carefully, as the flesh breaks easily. Insert the back of the knife next to the bone to see when the fish is cooked. Serve with lemon juice and chopped parsley sprinkled over the fish. A sauce may be served separately.

Flat fish, such as plaice and sole, may be wrapped in well-greased greaseproof paper before grilling—this keeps the flesh from becoming dry during cooking, and facilitates turning.

A slice through a thick fish, such as halibut or cod (i.e., a steak), is very good grilled. Cut the steaks about 1–1½ inches thick, wash them, dry thoroughly and trim if necessary. Sprinkle with salt and pepper and a few drops of lemon juice or vinegar, then brush over with melted butter, and dredge lightly with flour. Have the grill hot, lay the fish on the greased grid, place it under the hot grill, and reduce the heat slightly. Turn the fish after 2 or 3 minutes, and continue cooking until the flesh is opaque and comes away easily from the bone—about 10 minutes in all. Garnish with lemon and parsley, and serve with a good sauce, such as parsley or Hollandaise sauce. Tomatoes or mushrooms may be grilled with the fish, and make a good accompaniment to it.

BAKING

Weigh and wipe the fish, place in a shallow tin or earthenware dish with a little milk or water poured round, and cover with greased paper. Bake in a moderately hot oven (400° F., mark 6) until the flesh is white and firm, with a creamy curd between the flakes, and comes easily away from the bone.

The time to allow is 6–10 minutes to the lb. and 6–10 minutes over, according to the thickness. Thin fillets take about ¼ hour.

BAKED WHOLE FISH

A whole fish such as a large sole or plaice, or a small cod, hake or fresh haddock, served on a long platter and daintily garnished, makes a decorative dish.

Wash the fish, remove any scales, clean it carefully, but leave the head on (removing the eyes). Stuff it with a good forcemeat, made from 2 oz. or so of fresh breadcrumbs, salt and pepper, a little chopped fat bacon, some chopped parsley and a pinch of mixed herbs, moistened with beaten egg and a little milk. With a round fish, such as cod or hake, place the stuffing in the cavity from which the entrails have been removed; roll any stuffing that remains into small balls and dust with flour. Place the fish on a greased baking tin with some firm tomatoes and the balls of stuffing. In the case of a flat fish, such as plaice or sole, lay the fish on a board and cut through the flesh right down to the backbone; then, using the point of a sharp knife, loosen the flesh from the bone on each side as far as the fins, but not right through the skin. Fill the stuffing into the cavity thus formed, lay some small tomatoes along the centre of the fish, and place on a greased baking sheet.

Dot the stuffed fish with some shavings of butter, cover with greased paper, and bake in a moderate oven (350° F., mark 4) for ¾–1 hour (according to size and thickness). Lift carefully on to a hot dish, using a palette knife and fish slice; garnish with lemon fans and fresh parsley or fennel. Serve with a good parsley sauce, or with fennel sauce.

BAKED ROLLED FILLETS OF PLAICE OR SOLE

Instead of being fried, fillets of plaice or sole may be cooked this way:

First, skin the fillets. Now lay them (skinned side uppermost) on the board, sprinkle with salt and pepper and a squeeze of lemon juice, and roll up neatly. Brush over with beaten egg and toss in brown breadcrumbs. Place on a greased baking sheet, with a knob of butter on each fillet, and bake in a moderately hot oven (400° F., mark 6) for 15–20 minutes. Serve hot with a good sauce.

Rolled Fillets of Plaice

A DICTIONARY OF FISH

ANCHOVIES

These small fish, though uninteresting when fresh, are very good cured. They are generally filleted and packed in bottles or tins, either in brine or in olive oil. They are used—in small quantities only, as they are very salty—in hors d'œuvre and savouries, and as a garnish. They

Anchovies

are also used to make anchovy butter (see recipe in Sandwiches chapter), which is useful for small savouries, sandwiches, anchovy toast and so on.

Essence of anchovies is added to fish dishes to give extra flavour, and is used to make a sauce to serve with fish.

BARBEL

See FRESH-WATER FISH.

BASS

In season May to August.

Bass is not unlike salmon in shape, but the flesh is very white. Large bass are usually boiled in court-bouillon and served with a good sauce or maître d'hôtel butter, or they can be cooked according to any recipe for salmon. Small bass can be grilled, fried or cooked in any way suitable for trout.

BLOATER

See HERRINGS.

BREAM (SEA)

At its best from June to December.

Bream has white flesh, a rather delicate flavour and a coarse skin. It is often served baked with stuffing, but may also be boiled, fried or grilled.

Bream

BRILL

In season all the year, but at its best from April to August.

A fish of good flavour and texture, not unlike turbot. It may be served boiled with a good sauce, cold with mayonnaise, or cooked according to any recipe for turbot.

CARP

See FRESH-WATER FISH.

COD

In season all the year, but at its best from October to January.

This is an excellent fish and very useful, since it may be cooked by any method. It is often boiled or steamed, and should be served with a very good sauce. It may also be baked, with or without stuffing; small cuts can be grilled, fried or poached, etc.

Salt Cod

This is a staple food in Portugal and Spain, and can be served in many appetising dishes. It requires soaking to remove the salt, and very careful cooking to make it palatable. Choose thick fillets of salt cod with firm, close flesh, avoiding stringy or yellow pieces. To prepare it, soak in cold water for 24 hours, changing the water several times, and place the fish skin side uppermost in the water, to allow the salt to drain out. To cook salt cod, put into a pan with enough cold liquid (milk or milk and water) to cover, bring just to the boil, then draw the pan aside and cook slightly *below* boiling point until tender. Drain thoroughly and use as required. It may be served with maître d'hôtel butter or a tasty sauce, or better still, dressed with a sauce and served au gratin, or creamed, curried, in fish pie, and so on.

DRIED CODFISH (BISCAY STYLE)

Cut 1 lb. dried cod into 2-inch squares and soak it overnight in plenty of cold water, adding about 5–6 dried pimentos. The next day, bone the fish and put it in a saucepan, cover with cold water and bring slowly to the boil; strain it, and put it in a pan, skin side up.

Prepare a sauce as follows: Heat $\frac{1}{2}$ cup olive oil in a frying pan, and add 1 chopped onion, 1 small clove of garlic, 1 oz. bread, and 1 tbsp. flour, and brown gently; add a lump of sugar, the flesh of 2 tomatoes and the flesh of the pimentos, pour in about $\frac{1}{4}$ cup of the fish stock and cook slowly for $\frac{1}{2}$ hour, until creamy. Strain the sauce over the cod and stew for $\frac{1}{4}$ hour, shaking the pan occasionally to prevent sticking.

Smoked Fillets

Filleted cod is sometimes smoked and dyed yellow, when it is nicknamed "Painted Ladies." These fillets resemble smoked haddock somewhat in appearance, though without skin or bone, but are much inferior in flavour. They may be treated as suggested for smoked haddock.

BAKED STUFFED COD CUTLETS

2 cutlets of cod or other white fish
1 rasher of bacon 14

For the Stuffing

1 oz. breadcrumbs
1 tsp. finely chopped parsley
1 oz. chopped bacon
Pepper and salt to season
A little made mustard
Egg or milk to mix

Wipe the cutlets and remove the backbone. Put the other ingredients, except the rasher, into a basin and blend with a little beaten egg or milk. Fill the hole left by the removal of the bone with the stuffing, and place the remainder on top of the cutlets. Tie round with string, cover each with a half rasher of bacon and bake in a moderately hot oven (400° F., mark 6) for about 15–25 minutes, according to thickness.

CODS' ROE

This can be bought either cooked or raw. To cook raw cods' roe, tie in muslin and cook gently in boiling salted water, with a few peppercorns added, until tender (½–1 hour, according to thickness). Lift out, and allow to cool.

The boiled cods' roe is usually fried. Cut it in slices, dip in seasoned flour or in fine oatmeal, and fry in hot fat until golden-brown. Serve on toast or with sautéed potatoes.

Cods' roe can also be used in various réchauffe dishes. Many of the recipes at the end of this section may be used, though it may be found advisable to adapt the proportions slightly, using rather less roe than the quantity given for white fish. Alternatively, a mixture of roe and white fish may be used.

DABS

Dabs, small flat fish of the plaice family, are excellent either fried or baked.

To fry them, clean and dry, then dip in seasoned flour, or in a coating batter. Fry lightly in a little hot fat (or deep fat, if batter is used for coating) until golden-brown on both sides. Drain, and serve at once.

To bake dabs, lay the cleaned fish in a greased fireproof dish and pour over a little milk or good stock. Add a knob of butter, cover with greased paper and bake in a moderate oven (350° F., mark 4) for 15 minutes. Serve in the same dish.

To vary the flavour, add a chopped mushroom or a little parsley and onion before baking.

DACE

See FRESH-WATER FISH.

EEL

At their best during autumn and winter months. There are two types of eel, found in fresh water and salt water respectively. The latter, known as conger eels, are cooked like the fresh-water ones when small; when large they are somewhat coarse, and are best used for soups, stews, etc.

BAKED EEL

1 lb. eels	Salt and pepper
¾ pint stock	Capers
A bunch of herbs	A little port wine
1 onion	Flour for thickening (optional)
2–3 cloves	Lemon to garnish
A little lemon juice	

The eels must first of all be skinned. To do this, cut off the heads, turn back the skin at the top of each and peel it off. Clean the fish thoroughly and wash them in salted water, then cut them into pieces 2–3 inches long, and soak these in salted water for about 1 hour. Meanwhile, put the fish heads, tails, and trimmings into a pan together with the stock, herbs, onion (stuck with the cloves), a squeeze of lemon juice and seasoning; simmer for 1 hour, then strain the liquor. Rinse the pieces of eel and arrange them in a fireproof dish, pour the liquor over and sprinkle with capers. Cook gently in a moderately hot oven (400° F., mark 6) 1½ hours, or until tender. Before serving, add a little port wine. If desired, the liquor may be thickened with ½ oz. flour blended with water. Garnish with thinly sliced lemon.

JELLIED EELS

2 lb. eels	1 pint stock
Pepper and salt	Flavouring vegetables
Nutmeg	A bouquet garni
Chopped herbs	¼ oz. gelatine
Juice and rind of ½ lemon	

Skin and bone the eels and clean very thoroughly. Lay on the table skinned side down, and sprinkle with seasonings and chopped herbs and a little grated lemon rind. Cut the fish into pieces about 4 inches long, roll up each piece and tie with tape. Put the stock, vegetables and bouquet garni into a saucepan, and bring to boiling point. Put in the eels and simmer very gently until tender—about 30 minutes. Lift out the fish, take off the tape, and place the fish in a basin. Measure the stock, and make up to ¾ pint with water. Add the lemon juice and the gelatine, and heat until the gelatine is dissolved. Strain over the fish and leave to set. Turn out when cold, and serve with green salad and sliced gherkins.

FLOUNDERS

Flounders are at their best from February to December.

Flounders resemble plaice, but are of less good texture and flavour. They may be fried or cooked in any way suitable for plaice.

FRESH-WATER FISH

(Barbel, Carp, Dace, Gudgeon, Perch, Pike, Roach, Tench, Trout)

To counteract the muddy flavour, fresh-water fish should be rubbed well all over with salt (or hung up with salt in the mouth), and left for a while. Clean and wash thoroughly, then soak in salt water for 2–3 hours before cooking. They are usually fried or grilled, but pike is particularly good stuffed and baked; carp is delicious cooked in red wine.

GRILLED TROUT

Clean and dry the fish, split them open, and remove the bone. Then brush them over with melted butter or olive oil, and season with pepper, salt and a little lemon juice. Lay them on the grill, previously heated, and cook for 5–10 minutes on each side. Serve them very hot, garnished with cut lemon and watercress.

Trout

BLUE TROUT

(See colour picture facing page 96.)

For this dish choose small river trout, and cook them as soon as possible after being caught—when circumstances allow, take the trout straight from the river, and kill them just before they are cooked. Clean the fish, but do not scale or wash them, or the blue colour will be spoilt. Place them in a fireproof dish and sprinkle each trout with 1 tbsp. boiling vinegar, add some seasoned fish stock and cook in a moderate oven (350° F., mark 4) for 5 minutes, or until just tender. Drain, and serve with parsley, lemon, and a separate dish of melted butter.

GUDGEON

This resembles small carp, and is best fried or grilled. See Fresh-water Fish for method of soaking before cooking.

GURNET

At its best from July to April.

A small fish with a large, bony head and firm, white flesh of good flavour. There are two varieties, red and grey, the red being considered superior.

Gurnet may be cooked according to any recipe for haddock, and are particularly good baked and served with a good sauce, as in the following recipe, in which white wine is added.

GURNET WITH WHITE WINE

2 or 3 gurnet	¼ of a Spanish onion
Pepper and salt	A little butter
1 tomato, skinned	¼ pint white wine
½ lemon	Potato garnish

Wash and clean the fish carefully, removing the head and fins. Score the skin across three times on each side, lay the fish in a well-greased flat baking dish, and sprinkle them with pepper and salt. Then slice very thinly the tomato, lemon and onion. Lay these slices neatly over the fish, sprinkle with more seasoning and put a few pieces of butter on the top. Pour the white wine round, put the dish in a moderately hot oven (400° F., mark 6) for about 20 minutes, basting fish occasionally with the liquid. Meanwhile prepare 3–4 potatoes, cutting them in small pieces, and boil in salted water until nearly tender; drain, add a small piece of butter and finish cooking at the side of the stove. Use these potatoes to garnish the fish before taking it to table.

HADDOCK

Fresh haddock is at its best from September to February.

This fish may be cooked by almost any method. Small ones are good fried whole; larger ones are often stuffed and baked.

Smoked or Finnan haddock, which is creamy-yellow in colour, is usually poached or grilled, and served as a breakfast or supper dish. Being very tasty, it also makes a good basis for kedgerees, fish savouries, soufflés, etc.

BAKED STUFFED HADDOCK

1 fresh haddock	Dripping
Egg and breadcrumbs	Anchovy sauce

For the Stuffing

2 tbsps. breadcrumbs	A few drops of anchovy essence
1 tsp. chopped parsley	A little beaten egg or milk to mix
¼ tsp. mixed herbs	
Pepper and salt	
1 tsp. chopped onion	

Wipe the fish and cut off the fins, scraping to remove the scales, and wipe the inside with a moistened cloth dipped in salt. Put all the dry stuffing ingredients into a basin, add the anchovy essence, blend with a little beaten egg or milk, and mix thoroughly. Stuff the inside of the fish with the filling, and close by sewing with thin string and a trussing needle; tie a bow which can be easily untied when the fish is cooked. Brush over the outside of the fish with beaten egg and sprinkle with breadcrumbs. Place small pieces of dripping on top of the fish and cover with greased paper. Bake in a moderately hot oven (400° F., mark 6) for about 30 minutes. Serve with anchovy sauce.

GRILLED SMOKED HADDOCK

1 haddock	1 tsp. finely chopped parsley
1 oz. butter	
Pepper	

Trim the fish by removing the fins, put into a dish, pour boiling water over and allow to soak for about 5 minutes. Remove from the water and drain. Melt half the butter and brush over the haddock, place under a grill and cook on both sides until well browned. Sprinkle lightly with pepper. Melt the remainder of the butter, mix with the chopped parsley and pour over the haddock.

HADDOCK SOUFFLÉ

6 oz. cooked smoked haddock	¼ pint milk
1 oz. butter	Cayenne and salt
1 oz. flour	2 eggs

Flake the fish finely, removing all bone and
15 skin. Melt the butter, stir in the flour and gradually add the milk, beat well until boiling, and cook for a few minutes. Cool slightly. Add the fish and seasoning and beat in the egg yolks thoroughly. Whip up the whites very stiffly and fold them into the fish mixture as lightly as possible, turn into a greased soufflé dish and bake in a moderate oven (350° F., mark 4) for about 30 minutes. Serve immediately.

POACHED SMOKED HADDOCK

Cut off the fins, and if desired, remove the skin, after dipping the fish in boiling water. If the fish is big, cut it in neat pieces, barely cover with milk or milk and water, and add pepper and a knob of butter, and gently simmer (or bake) until tender—10–15 minutes. Serve with the liquor in which it was cooked, accompanied by plain boiled or steamed potatoes, if desired.

CREAMED HADDOCK TOASTS

Cook some smoked haddock in enough milk to just cover it; when tender, strain off the liquid (reserving this) and flake the fish finely, removing any skin and bones. Make some thick white sauce with butter, flour and the liquid from the haddock; add pepper, a little powdered mace and a squeeze of lemon juice. Combine with the haddock, make thoroughly hot and serve on rounds of buttered toast, garnished with capers.

HAKE

In season all the year, but at its best from June to January.

Hake is somewhat like cod in shape and flavour, but the flesh is closer in texture. When the fish is cooked, the bones are very easy to remove, which makes it a useful fish for made-up dishes. It is cooked in any way suitable for cod.

HALIBUT

In season all the year, but best from August to April. The very young fish are best from March to October.

A very large fish with a delicate flavour; it is not unlike turbot, but cheaper and not quite so good. It is very good steamed or grilled, served with Hollandaise or other sauce, or may be cooked by any recipe for turbot or cod.

HALIBUT STEAKS IN MILK

2 halibut steaks of about 1 lb. each	2 Spanish onions
1 tbsp. flour	Oil or butter
Pepper and salt	4 strips of bacon
½ pint milk	1–2 tomatoes

Wipe or wash the fish and dry in a cloth. Mix the flour, pepper and salt, then coat the fish with the seasoned flour and place the slices in a greased baking dish. Cover with milk and put in a moderate oven (350° F., mark 4). Then cut the onions into thick slices and fry them in oil or butter until a delicate brown, keeping each slice in one whole piece, if possible. After the fish has baked for 10 minutes, remove from the oven, cover the slices with the browned onions, and lay strips of bacon on the top. Return it to the oven and continue baking till the fish is done—about 15 minutes. Serve garnished with tomatoes, cut in sections and cooked lightly in the oven, or with a garnish of potatoes, made by slicing some cold cooked potatoes and browning them in a small quantity of fat in the oven.

Halibut

HERRINGS

In season all the year, but best from June to December.

The common herring is the most valuable

fish to be found in our seas, and offers more nourishment for a given sum than any other animal food. It is wholesome and nutritious, abundant and cheap, and rich in flavour. Herrings may be cured in various ways, as salt herrings, kippers, etc.

When choosing fresh herrings, select those that are plump in form and well covered with scales. They should be bright and silvery-looking, and undamaged by packing.

To Prepare Herrings

To clean the fish, cut off the head with a sharp
knife, removing the inside with it (if this has
16 not been done by the fishmonger), scrape away
any black skin from inside, and wash clean.
Scrape off the scales with the back of a knife and
trim off fins and tail with scissors. Rinse
thoroughly and wipe dry.

To Bone Herrings

Split open neatly down the underside, place
flat on the board cut side down, press lightly
down the middle of the back with the fingers to
loosen the bone but without bruising the flesh.
17 Turn the fish over and, easing the backbone up
with the fingers, gently remove it and as many
of the small bones as will come with it. (If there
are roes, take them out, wash and cook them and
serve them with the fish, or use them separately
as a savoury.)

Kippered Herrings

To prepare kippers, wash them well, cut off the head, then just cover with boiling water and cook gently for 2–3 minutes. Then drain off the water and serve with a pat of butter, or brush over with butter or margarine, and cook in any of the following ways: (1) Grill for 5–7 minutes; (2) cover with greased paper and bake in a moderately hot oven (400° F., mark 6) for 10–15 minutes; (3) fry in a little hot fat.

Red Herrings

Open and clean the fish, then cover with boiling water and leave to soak for about 5 minutes, to remove the salt. Drain well, then cook in the same way as for kippers.

Bloaters

Cover with boiling water and soak for 1–2 minutes. Drain and remove the head and fins, split open, remove the roe and cook as for kippers. If liked, the backbone may be removed before the bloaters are cooked.

Salt Herrings

Salt herrings are kept in barrels, covered with brine. If the air comes in contact with the fish the oil turns rancid, so it is essential to keep the herrings under the brine all the time. If any fat collects on the top, this must be skimmed off.

When the herrings are required for use, remove them from the brine and wash very thoroughly. Cut off the head and fins, clean out the inside and bone if liked. Soak in cold water for 12–24 hours. After soaking, remove the skin, and use the fish as required.

SALT HERRING PIE

4 salt herrings	Pepper
2 oz. breadcrumbs	About ¼ pint milk
2 gherkins or a few capers	½ lb. tomatoes
	Mashed potato

Clean and soak the herrings as described above, and steam them for about 15–20 minutes. Flake them with a fork and add the breadcrumbs, chopped gherkins or capers, a shake of pepper and enough milk to moisten well. Put into a greased fireproof dish and cover with the tomatoes, skinned and sliced. Finally, cover with a thick layer of creamy mashed potato, rough up with a fork, and bake in a moderate oven (350° F., mark 4) for about ½–¾ hour.

HERRINGS FRIED SCOTS FASHION

Prepare and bone the herrings, and dry well by letting them lie in the folds of a cloth for an hour or two. Then sprinkle them with pepper and salt and dip each fish into coarse oatmeal, pressing it on to both sides. Put a small quantity of fat into a frying pan, and when smoking hot, put in the herrings and brown them nicely on both sides. When the fish are ready, drain them on paper, and serve garnished with parsley and cut lemon, or with small pats of maître d'hôtel butter on top.

GRILLED HERRINGS WITH MUSTARD SAUCE

Clean the fish as directed above, but without
cutting them open. Score the skin across
diagonally two or three times on each side,
season the fish with pepper and salt, and let them
lie for a short time before cooking. Then 18
brush them over with melted butter or dripping,
place on a hot grid and cook under the grill of a
gas or electric stove. When the fish are nicely
browned on one side, turn and brown them on
the other. Be sure to cook them thoroughly,
and to moderate the heat if the fish are large and
thick. Serve at once on a hot dish with a dish

paper under them. Mustard sauce is a good accompaniment.

HERRINGS AU GRATIN

3 fresh or salt herrings	A little chopped parsley
½ lb. tomatoes	1 oz. breadcrumbs
Pepper and salt	

Cut off the heads, then clean and bone the herrings. Soak overnight, if salted. Skin and slice the tomatoes and place in a fireproof dish, sprinkling with pepper, and a little salt if fresh herrings are used. Lay the fillets of herrings on the tomatoes and cover with the parsley and breadcrumbs. Bake in a moderate oven (350° F., mark 4) for about ½ hour. If liked, finish cooking under the grill.

HERRING HOT-POT

3 herrings	3 bay leaves
1 onion	4 tbsps. vinegar
2 tbsps. capers	Cold water
Salt and pepper	1 lb. potatoes

Scale the fish, remove the heads and fins and slit open. Remove the roes, if any, flatten the fish and remove the backbone. Cut each fish into four. Place the pieces in a hot-pot, with the roes, grated onion, capers, seasoning, bay leaves and vinegar, and add sufficient water to cover. Peel and slice the potatoes and put them on the top of the fish. Cover and cook in a moderate oven (350° F., mark 4) for 1–1½ hours.

STUFFED AND BAKED HERRINGS

6 herrings	A little chopped onion (optional)
4 tbsps. breadcrumbs	A little flour
1 dessertsp. parsley	Dripping or butter
Grated rind of ½ a lemon	Parsley and cut lemon
Pepper and salt	Mustard sauce (optional)
2 tbsps. milk	

Prepare and bone the fish, dry them, sprinkle with salt, and score the skin across three times with a knife. Put the breadcrumbs, parsley, lemon rind and seasoning into a basin, mix together and bind with the milk. A little finely chopped onion may also be added, if liked. Spread this stuffing equally over three of the fish and cover with the other three—making a sandwich, as it were, with the skin side outside. Place the fish on a greased baking dish, sprinkle them with flour, put a few pieces of dripping or butter on the top, and bake in a moderate oven (350° F., mark 4) about ½ hour, or until cooked. Serve on a hot dish with a paper under, and garnish with parsley and cut lemon. If there are roes in the fish, bake them also and use as a garnish. Mustard sauce may be served separately.

SOUSED HERRINGS

Clean and scale the fish, remove the roes, split down the front, and remove the backbone. Sprinkle each fish with a little coarsely ground black pepper and salt, and put a very small piece of bay leaf on the top, then roll up, and pack in a glass or fireproof dish. Cover with equal quantities of vinegar and water—half tarragon and half malt vinegar, mixed with an equal quantity of water, gives a good flavour; other- 19
wise, sprinkle a little chopped tarragon on the fish, with the pepper and salt. Bake in a moderate oven (350° F., mark 4) until cooked—¾–1 hour, depending on size of herrings. Remove from oven, allow to get cold, and serve in the liquor.

A more piquant flavour is obtained with soused herring by introducing finely chopped sliced onion or shallot. A little can be sprinkled over the fish before they are rolled up, and the remainder put in the dish.

NORWEGIAN FISH SALAD

½ lb. cold cooked potatoes	1 bunch radishes
½ lb. tart apples (weighed after peeling)	3 cooked herrings

For the Dressing

¼ tsp. made mustard	1 tsp. chopped parsley
Salt and pepper	1 tsp. chopped onion
A little sugar	2 tbsps. oil
2–3 drops Tabasco sauce	1 tbsp. vinegar
1 tsp. table sauce	

Cut the potatoes and apples into neat dice. Wash and trim the radishes. Remove the skin and bone from the fish, and flake. Make a dressing by mixing the seasonings in a basin and stirring in the sauces, parsley, onion, oil and vinegar. Toss the fish, apples and vegetables in the dressing, pile in a salad bowl and serve very cold.

HERRING ROES ON TOAST

6 soft roes	Toast
Salt	Cayenne pepper
A little flour	Lemon juice
Melted butter	Parsley to garnish

Wash the roes, dry, sprinkle with salt and dredge with a little flour. Brush over with melted butter, place under a grill and cook first on one side and then the other. Meanwhile, prepare some hot buttered toast. When ready to serve, place the roes on the toast, sprinkle with a little cayenne, add a squeeze of lemon juice and garnish with parsley. Serve immediately.

HERRING ROE FRITTERS

Herring roes | Fat for frying
Salt and pepper | Lemon wedges
Coating batter

Wipe the roes, season them, then dip in the batter and fry in smoking-hot fat until golden-brown. Drain and serve very hot, with lemon wedges.

HERRING ROE FINGERS

2 oz. shortcrust pastry | Fat for frying
2–3 cooked herring roes

Roll out the pastry very thinly and cut in squares. Lay a herring roe on each piece of pastry, damp the edges and fold over. Press the pastry lightly with a rolling pin, then fry the fingers in a little hot fat until the pastry is cooked and lightly browned. Drain and serve hot as a savoury or snack.

JOHN DORY

An ugly fish, but the firm, white flesh has a delicious flavour. With the head and fins removed the fish can be boiled or baked whole, but is usually filleted and cooked according to any recipe for sole.

LING

Ling is somewhat similar to cod but not so good. It is usually salted, and should be treated as for salt cod. Treat fresh ling as for fresh cod.

MACKEREL

In season from October to July, but at its best during April, May and June.

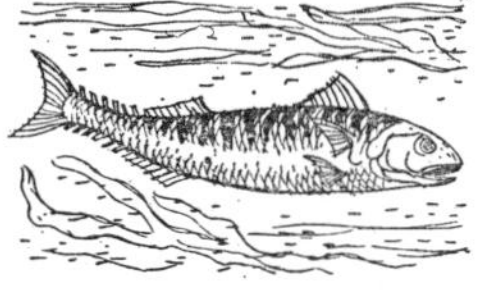
Mackerel

Mackerel should only be used when in season, and must be perfectly fresh. Serve boiled, fried or baked or according to any recipe for herrings. Boiled mackerel is very good with fennel sauce or gooseberry sauce (See Sauces chapter.)

GRILLED MACKEREL

2 or 3 mackerel | Parsley or chervil
Slices of lemon | Maître d'hôtel butter

For the Marinade

1 tbsp. olive oil | 1 tsp. chopped parsley
1 tbsp. lemon juice | Salt
1 tsp. finely chopped shallot | Freshly ground black pepper

Clean the mackerel, and fillet if large, but do not remove the skin. Mix all the ingredients for the marinade and soak the fish in this for 1 hour or so, turning them occasionally. Drain, and cook under a hot grill until tender, turning once. To serve hot, arrange on a hot dish, garnish with lemon and parsley and place a small pat of maître d'hôtel butter on each fish. To serve cold, allow to cool, then dish up; garnish with lemon and parsley or chervil and hand mayonnaise separately.

SOUSED MACKEREL

4 mackerel | A few parsley stalks
4 cloves | 1 large onion
Red pepper | Salt
12 peppercorns | Vinegar and water
1 bay leaf | Lemon and gherkins
A blade of mace | to garnish

Clean and wash the mackerel and cut off the heads and fins. Lay in a baking dish with the spices and herbs, the onion, thinly sliced, and some salt. Cover with vinegar and water in equal quantities, and bake in a moderate oven for 1–1½ hours. Lift the fish carefully into a deep dish, strain the liquor over them and leave until cold. Serve garnished with thin slices of lemon and chopped gherkins.

MULLET

Mullet is at its best from April to October.

There are two varieties, red and grey. Red mullet has firm, white flesh and a very delicious flavour. The liver is considered a great delicacy, and is always cooked and served with the fish. Do not scale the fish, but wipe it, cutting off the fins and removing the eyes. Served baked, grilled or fried; red mullet is not good steamed or boiled.

Red Mullet

Grey mullet is coarser than the red. Cook it in any way suitable for white fish.

BAKED RED MULLET IN CASES

This is a simple and popular method of cooking red mullet and is particularly suitable, since the skin is very delicate and the flesh is apt to break when cooked, making it difficult to dish the fish neatly.

To prepare the fish, wipe it, trim off the fins and tail with scissors and remove the eyes. The entrails may be left in or removed according to taste; the liver should remain in either case. Season well with salt and pepper and sprinkle with lemon juice and chopped parsley. Put each fish in an individual paper "envelope," well buttered, and fold over the top several times so that the fish is completely enclosed. Lay in a greased fireproof dish, cover the whole with a piece of greased paper and bake in a moderately hot oven (400° F., mark 6) for about 15–20 minutes, according to size. Arrange the fish, still in their cases, on a hot dish, and garnish with parsley and slices of lemon.

PERCH AND PIKE

See FRESH-WATER FISH.

PILCHARDS

Pilchards (which are in fact large sardines) should be eaten very fresh, and are very good when simply grilled. Pilchards are also sold tinned, and these may be served cold with salad or as an ingredient in hors d'œuvre, or they may be used to make savouries and sandwich fillings, and in made-up fish dishes. Fresh pilchards may be treated in the same way as herring, that is they can be grilled or fried.

PLAICE

In season from May to December.

Plaice is one of our commonest flat fish. It is usually filleted and fried (see colour picture facing page 96), or it can be cooked by any of the usual methods and served with a well-flavoured sauce, as the fish lacks flavour.

BAKED STUFFED FILLETS OF PLAICE

4 fillets of plaice
Salt and pepper
2 oz. mushrooms
1 rasher of bacon
Tomato sauce

For the Stuffing

4 oz. mashed potatoes
1 tbsp. chopped parsley
1 egg
Salt and pepper

Prepare and wash the fillets and sprinkle with salt and pepper, then lay flat in a greased casserole or on a greased tin. Mix together the ingredients for the stuffing, which should be of a fairly stiff consistency. Divide into four portions and place on the fillets. Skin the mushrooms and cut into slices; chop the bacon, mix with the mushrooms, season and sprinkle on the stuffing. Cover with a lid or a greased paper and bake in a moderately hot oven (400° F., mark 6) about ½ hour. Serve with tomato sauce, handed separately.

PLAICE AND MUSHROOM HOT-POT

1 large plaice
1 oz. butter
1 oz. flour
¾ pint milk and fish liquor
Salt and pepper
½ lb. mushrooms
1 lb. parboiled potatoes

Fillet and skin the fish and wash the fillets. Cover the fish-bones with water and cook for 15 minutes. Melt the butter, add the flour, cook for 1–2 minutes, then stir in the liquid gradually. Bring to the boil, and boil for 5 minutes, then season. Cut the fillets in half and put a layer of fish at the bottom of the hot-pot, then the peeled mushrooms, then the rest of the fish. Pour the sauce over and cover with the sliced potatoes. Put the lid on and cook in a moderate oven (350° F., mark 4) for ¾–1 hour. When half cooked, remove the lid to allow the potatoes to brown.

ROACH

See FRESH-WATER FISH.

SALMON

Salmon is at its best from February to August.

When choosing a salmon, it is well to select one with a small head and tail and broad shoulders. To have it in perfection, it should be cooked as soon as drawn from the water, for a white creamy substance will then be found between the flakes, which soon disappears when the fish is kept. On the other hand, many people consider that salmon is better if not cooked for two or three days. The flesh is naturally rich in oil, and is not so easily digested as the lighter kinds of fish.

The more simply salmon is cooked the better, as nothing must destroy the fine flavour of the fish itself. It must also be well cooked, as when underdone it is uneatable. Boiling, steaming or grilling are perhaps the best three methods of cooking salmon.

GRILLED SALMON

When only a small piece of salmon—a cutlet or slice—has to be prepared, grilling is one of the best methods of cooking it. The slices should be about 1 inch in thickness; wipe them dry and then dip them in salad oil or melted butter. Make the grill-pan thoroughly hot, grease it, and cook the fish under the grill, allowing about 10 minutes for each side, and brushing it over occasionally with more fat. Serve garnished with cut lemon and watercress or parsley. Any suitable sauce may be served separately, or a small pat of maître d'hôtel butter may be laid on the top of each slice.

TO BOIL SALMON

The middle cut, or head and shoulders, are the best cuts to use, although any part may be cooked in this way. Scrape the scales from the fish, wash it free of all blood, and then weigh it. Put as much fresh cold water into the fish-kettle as will cover the fish, add about 1 tsp. salt to the pint, and bring to the boil. Skim if necessary, put in the fish, and allow to simmer gently until sufficiently cooked. The time will depend on the thickness of the fish, but the average time to allow is 8–10 minutes to the lb. and 8–10 minutes over. Vinegar must not be added to the water, as it destroys the colour of the fish. Any scum that rises must be removed.

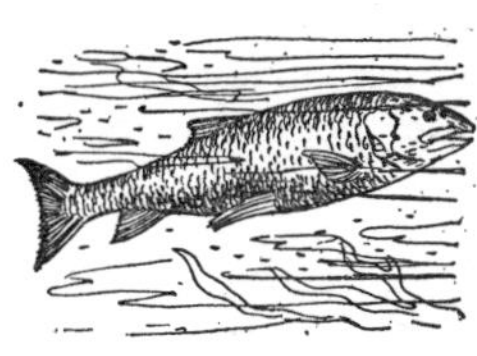

Salmon

For steaming, prepare as above, and allow about half as long again for cooking.

When the fish is cooked, the flesh should come away easily from the bone. Remove it from the pan, and if it is not required for a few minutes, cover it with a hot folded cloth. Serve it with a dish paper under it, and garnish with cut lemon and sprigs of fresh parsley. Plain melted butter is perhaps the best sauce, but Hollandaise or parsley sauce is also suitable. The imported salmon can do with something more tasty, such as Cardinal or mussel sauce. Boiled potatoes, green peas and cucumber salad are the usual accompaniments.

MAYONNAISE OF SALMON

This dish is very highly esteemed, as many people prefer to eat the fish cold rather than hot. Cook a nice piece of the fish, remove the skin, and let it become quite cold, then wipe it with a
20 dry cloth and coat it evenly with mayonnaise. Garnish with some fresh green salad around the fish, and decorate the top with cucumber, sliced gherkin, radish, tomato or lobster coral, according to individual taste.

BAKED SALMON

This is a good alternative to the more usual methods of cooking. Wrap the salmon in buttered greaseproof paper or place it in a well-greased fireproof dish, and cover closely with greased paper. Put in a moderate oven (350° F., mark 4) and allow 10 minutes to the lb. and 10 minutes over. Serve with butter or mustard sauce, or with plain melted butter.

CHAUDFROID OF SALMON

- 1 small whole-cooked salmon
- 1 pint chaudfroid sauce
- Aspic jelly
- Cucumber
- Chilli skins
- Truffles
- Hard-boiled egg
- Tomato, lettuce or endive

Coat the salmon entirely with the chaudfroid sauce, then pour over some cold aspic jelly. When set, decorate the centre and the sides of the salmon with cucumber, chilli skins, truffles, spots of yolk of egg, etc. A conventional design may be used, or sprays of flowers, leaves and so on. Set the decoration with a little aspic, and put aside till quite firm, then wipe the edges of the dish. Garnish with salad, chopped aspic and if liked, quarters of hard-boiled eggs.

The mayonnaise sauce may be coloured if desired, the decoration being chosen to tone with the colour of the sauce.

SCALLOPED SALMON

This can be prepared from left-over cooked fish. Flake the fish fairly finely and arrange in the centre of the scallop shells. Pour over each about 1 tbsp. fish stock, to which a little lemon juice has been added, and sprinkle with salt and pepper. Boil some potatoes, mash, season, and mix with butter and a little milk to a soft consistency, then pipe a border of potatoes round the fish. Cover the fish with thinly cut slices of cucumber, sprinkle with breadcrumbs, and put a few small pieces of butter on top. Place under a hot grill, or in a hot oven (450° F., mark 8) for about 5 minutes, until hot through and browned.

KEDGEREE OF SALMON

- 3 oz. rice
- 1 tin salmon (small size)
- ½ pint white sauce
- Salt and pepper
- Cayenne pepper
- A pinch of allspice
- A little grated lemon rind
- 1 hard-boiled egg

Boil the rice in salted water until tender, drain well and keep hot. Remove skin and bones from the salmon and heat in the white sauce.

Mix together the rice, fish, white sauce, seasoning, allspice, lemon rind and chopped hard-boiled white of egg. Turn into a hot dish and garnish with sieved yolk of egg.

PINK CREAM OF SALMON

4 oz. tinned salmon
¼ pint white sauce
1 tbsp. vinegar
A few drops of piquant table sauce
Salt and pepper
½ oz. gelatine
¼ pint vegetable stock
Pink colouring
Watercress or mustard and cress

Remove any skin and bones from the salmon and flake it finely. Mix the sauce with it, add the vinegar and piquant sauce, and season to taste with salt and pepper. Meanwhile, dissolve the gelatine in the strained vegetable stock over a gentle heat and stir it into the salmon mixture. Colour a delicate pink with carmine or cochineal and pour into a wetted mould. When set, turn out and decorate with watercress or mustard and cress. Serve with salad and potatoes.

SALMON AND EGG PIE

1 small tin salmon
1 oz. margarine
1 oz. flour
½ pint milk (short measure)
Pepper and salt
Mustard
A little grated cheese
1 tbsp. vinegar
2 eggs
Mashed potatoes

Drain the salmon, reserving the liquor. Lay the fish in a casserole.

Melt the margarine and stir in the flour, then gradually add a short ½ pint of milk. Cook for 2–3 minutes, stirring. Add the fish liquor, pepper, salt and mustard, and a little grated cheese. Stir in the vinegar and the eggs. Beat well and pour over the fish. Cover with creamy mashed potatoes, and rough up with a fork. Put in a moderately hot oven (400° F., mark 6) to heat through and brown top—about ½ hour.

SALMON PIE AU GRATIN

8 oz. tinned salmon
Mixed cooked root vegetables
1 oz. flour
Liquor from the salmon
¾ pint milk and vegetable water
A little grated cheese
A few drops vinegar or piquant sauce
Salt, pepper and mustard
1 lb. mashed potatoes
Browned breadcrumbs

Drain and flake the salmon and mix it with some cooked vegetables, cut into neat pieces. Make a sauce thus: blend the flour to a cream with the liquor from the salmon, add the milk and vegetable water (hot) and bring it to the boil, stirring. Add the grated cheese and vinegar or piquant sauce, and season with salt, pepper and a little mustard. Combine this sauce with the salmon and cooked vegetables, and place in a pie dish or au gratin dish. Cover with mashed potatoes, well seasoned, and sprinkle the top with browned breadcrumbs. Heat through in a moderately hot oven (400° F., mark 6) for a few minutes, and serve very hot.

SALMON CREAM RING

1 tin of salmon or some cooked fresh salmon
½ pint thick white sauce
2 tbsps. cream
Seasoning
Creamed potatoes
Chopped parsley for garnish

Flake the salmon finely, mix with the sauce, heat thoroughly, then add the cream, and season to taste. Dish up in a border of hot creamed potatoes, and sprinkle the potato with the chopped parsley.

SALMON ROLLS

6 oz. shortcrust pastry
1 tin salmon
Salt and pepper
1 tsp. finely chopped onion
1 tsp. chopped parsley
4 tbsps. breadcrumbs
1 beaten egg
2 tbsps. milk

Roll out the pastry into a strip and cut into six squares. Flake the salmon, add the seasonings, breadcrumbs, beaten egg and milk. Place 1 tbsp. of salmon mixture on each square of pastry, damp the edges of the pastry and fold over as for sausage rolls. Make three cuts in the top, glaze with milk or beaten egg, and bake in a hot oven (450° F., mark 8) until the pastry is cooked—about 20 minutes. Serve hot or cold.

SALMON TROUT

In season from March to August.

It is cooked in the same way as salmon, but is always left whole.

SARDINES

Sardines are very young pilchards. They can be eaten fresh (in which case they are grilled or cooked as for sprats), but are best known tinned, in either olive oil or tomato sauce. Tinned sardines are used in hors d'œuvre, as a sandwich spread and also in making many savouries.

SHAD

In season during the winter months, but not much known in this country. It is usually served baked, with stuffing, or boiled, with a good sauce. The roe is usually served separately.

SHAD ROE

Shad roe should be parboiled before being fried or grilled. To parboil the roe, first wash it, then put it in boiling water with 2 tsps. of salt and 1 tbsp. vinegar or lemon juice to a quart of water. Cover, and simmer for 5–15 minutes, according to size. Remove from the pan and place in cold water, then drain well, and carefully remove the membrane covering the roe.

GRILLED SHAD ROE

Brush the parboiled roe with melted butter, sprinkle with salt, pepper and lemon juice, and cook under a slow grill until golden-brown on both sides, from 5–10 minutes, brushing with more butter if necessary.

FRIED SHAD ROE

Coat parboiled roe in seasoned flour and fry in a little hot fat, until golden-brown. Serve with fried or grilled bacon and maître d'hôtel butter or Tartare sauce.

SKATE

At its best from October to April.

Unlike most fish, skate should not be absolutely fresh, but is more tender if kept for a day or two. It is usually sold cut into pieces ready prepared for cooking. The wings and the liver are the only edible parts. Cut the wings into large pieces and boil until tender in water with salt and vinegar added. Then drain, remove the skin and trim off the very bony parts. Reheat in the liquor before serving, or serve fried (see recipes below).

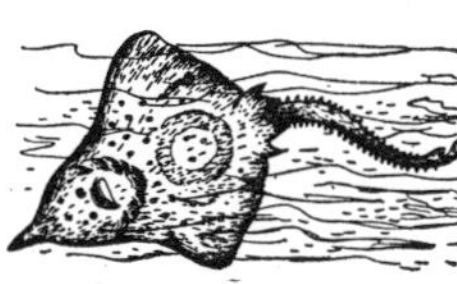

Skate

SKATE LIVER

Boil the liver separately, then drain and skin it and use as a garnish for the fish, or serve as a savoury with parsley and lemon juice and croûtes of fried bread or buttered toast.

FRIED SKATE

About 1 lb. prepared skate
Coating batter
Fat for frying
Parsley

For the Marinade

2 tbsps. olive oil
1 tbsp. lemon juice
1 tsp. chopped parsley
1 tsp. finely chopped onion
Salt and pepper

Mix the ingredients for the marinade on a deep plate or in a shallow dish. Cut the skate into even-sized pieces and soak in the marinade 2–3 hours. Drain each piece well, dip in coating batter and fry in deep fat. Drain on crumpled paper and serve very hot, garnished with parsley and accompanied by sharp sauce.

SKATE WITH BLACK BUTTER

About 1 lb. of prepared skate (see above)
Salt and pepper
1 tbsp. chopped parsley

For the Black Butter

2 oz. butter
1 tbsp. vinegar
1 tbsp. chopped capers

Reheat the prepared skate in the liquor in which it was cooked. Meanwhile, make the black butter (see below). When the skate is hot through, lift from the pan, drain, dry with a piece of muslin and place on a hot dish. Sprinkle with salt, pepper and the chopped parsley, and pour the hot black butter over.

To Make the Black Butter

Melt the butter in a small saucepan and heat gently until it turns a dark brown. Shake the pan occasionally and watch it carefully all the time, so that it does not burn. Carefully add the vinegar and the capers, shake in the pan, and pour at once over the fish.

SMELTS

In season from April to September.

These small silvery fish should be used very fresh. To prepare them, make a small cut with scissors just below the gills and gently press out the entrails, then wash well, handling carefully, as the flesh is easily damaged.

Small smelts are usually fried; larger ones may be baked or served au gratin. To fry smelts, cut off the fins and tails and dry well; toss in flour, then coat with egg and crumbs and fry in deep fat. Drain, and serve garnished with parsley and lemon wedges.

PIQUANT SMELTS

Smelts
Lemon juice
Salt
Paprika
A little flour
Fat for frying
Mashed potato
Sprigs of parsley

For the Sauce

1 oz. flour
½ pint milk or fish stock
1 tbsp. lemon juice
Pepper and salt
Paprika
1 tsp. anchovy essence
1 tsp. finely chopped parsley

Select as many fine, rather large smelts as are required; clean them, and cut diagonal gashes in each side. Sprinkle lemon juice over them and a little salt and paprika. Turn them once or twice so that they are well seasoned, and let them stand for 15 minutes, then dip in flour and sauté in any good fat until brown and crisp. Arrange neatly on a hot dish, and garnish with rosettes of mashed potato and sprigs of parsley.

Serve the following sauce separately: Add 1 oz. flour to the fat left in the pan, and stir until smooth. Add the milk or stock gradually, and stir until boiling. Season with lemon juice, pepper, salt, paprika and anchovy essence. Strain, and add the finely chopped parsley.

SOLE

In season all the year round.

Next to the turbot, the sole is considered the finest of all the flat fish. Its flesh is firm and delicate, with a delicious flavour. It is very easily digested, and so is often given to invalids and convalescents. The real sole, called the Dover sole, is easily recognised by the dark brownish-grey back skin. The lemon, witch and Torbay sole are not considered to have such a fine flavour as the Dover sole. When fresh, soles are shiny and firm to the touch. Those without roes are superior in flavour.

21

Sole

Soles are cooked by any of the usual methods, particularly frying and grilling. Fillets of sole are delicious steamed, baked or poached, served with a rich cream, white wine, mushroom or similar sauce.

BAKED SOLE WITH ITALIAN SAUCE

Choose a plump, medium-sized sole; cut off the head and fins, and remove the black skin. Grease a baking dish and lay the sole on it. Season with pepper and salt, and sprinkle with a little water and a good squeeze of lemon juice, cover with greased paper, and bake for about 15 minutes in a hot oven. Meanwhile, prepare the sauce. When the fish is ready, lift it out carefully on to a hot serving dish and add any liquid to the sauce. Pour the sauce round and over the fish, and garnish with lemon and green peas. The garnish may be varied — mushrooms, tomatoes or French beans may take the place of the peas.

Alternatively, the fish may be coated with white sauce, and a garnish of mussels, oysters or shrimps added; or, for a variety in flavour, a cheese and tomato sauce may be used for coating the fish.

GRILLED SOLE

Choose a sole of about $\frac{3}{4}$ lb. in weight, cut off the fins, remove the skin, and wipe it dry. Then brush the fish over with melted butter and season it with pepper and salt. Place it on a hot grill and cook it for 7–10 minutes, turning the fish so that it is browned on both sides. Make the grill very hot before putting the fish under it. Serve very hot, garnished with lemon and parsley or watercress. Plain butter or parsley butter may be served separately.

This is one of the best ways of cooking sole.

DOVER SOLES À LA COLBERT

Wash and trim the soles and skin them, then cut the fish about 3 inches down the centre on one side, raising the fillets from the bone, but not removing them. Break the bone at the top and bottom and also down the sides, thus making it easier to remove when cooked.

Dry the soles well, then egg and crumb them, folding back the loosened fillets. Fry in hot fat for 2–3 minutes. (A strong, oval-shaped saucepan should be used for frying, in order to keep the fish quite flat.) Drain, carefully remove the bone, and fill the centre cavity with maître d'hôtel butter and fried parsley. Garnish the dish with slices of lemon, cut into fancy shapes.

FILLETS OF SOLE WITH WHITE WINE SAUCE

Trim the fillets neatly, lay a little parsley and breadcrumb stuffing in the centre of each and fold them over lengthwise. Season with white pepper, salt and a little lemon juice, then poach the stuffed fillet thus: place in a greased baking dish, pour round a little fish stock or water, cover with greased paper and cook in the oven or on the top of the stove until the fish is ready. Arrange the fillets neatly on a hot serving dish, coat with white wine sauce and garnish with small pieces of baked tomato.

As a variation, the fillets may be stuffed with shrimps, oysters or a fish farce, and a different sauce and garnish may be used. Cheese sauce is very good over plain fillets: after coating, they should be sprinkled with grated cheese and browned in the oven or under the grill.

GLAZED PAUPIETTES OF SOLE

1 filleted sole	¼ pint tomato sauce
Anchovy paste	4 rounds of tomato
Fish stock or water	1 head of lettuce
¼ pint stiff aspic jelly	2 stoned olives

Season the fillets, spread with anchovy paste, roll up neatly and place on a greased tin. Pour on sufficient fish stock or water to come half-way up the fish. Cover with greased paper and bake in a moderate oven for 10–15 minutes. Lift on to a rack and leave to cool. Mix the aspic jelly with the tomato sauce. When cold and on the point of setting, glaze the fish with the mixture. Place each fillet on a round of tomato, garnish with crisp lettuce leaves and any remaining aspic jelly, chopped and placed round the dish. Lay half a stoned olive on top of each paupiette of fish.

SOLE À LA CRÈME AUX CHAMPIGNONS

Skin and trim a medium-sized sole and place it in a greased fireproof dish. Cover with mushrooms, trimmed, washed and cut in slices.
22 Moisten with a little white wine and a squeeze of lemon juice, and season with pepper and salt. Dot a few pieces of butter here and there over the top. Place the dish on the stove until the cooking is started, then in the oven to finish. Baste occasionally. When ready, pour over a little cream, and brown in the oven or under the grill.

SOLE BONNE FEMME

1 large sole	1½ oz. butter or margarine
2–3 tbsps. white wine	Seasoning
½ pint water	¾ oz. flour
2 slices of onion	2–3 tbsps. milk
A bouquet garni	2–3 tbsps. cream
4 oz. mushrooms	

Fillet the sole and put the bones into a pan with the wine and water. Add the onion and bouquet garni, bring to the boil and simmer for ½ hour, then drain. Arrange the sole fillets in a fireproof dish and cook in the prepared stock in a moderate oven for ¼ hour. Sauté the sliced mushrooms in a little melted butter until tender, and add seasoning to taste. Prepare a sauce from the remaining butter, the flour, ¾ pint of the fish liquor and the milk. Add the cream, and season to taste. Arrange the fillets on a dish, cover with mushrooms, and coat with the sauce.

SOLE MATELOTE

In Normandy this is a favourite way of preparing sole, or any other flat fish : it is very simple and very good. Remove the dark skin from the fish and trim off the head and fins. Grease a fireproof dish and place the fish on it with the skinned side downwards. Half-cover the fish with cider and water mixed in equal quantities, sprinkle with salt, and lay one or two sprigs of parsley at the sides. Cook in a moderate oven for 20 minutes or rather less, according to the size of the fish. Remove the parsley, and thicken the liquid with a piece of butter the size of a small egg, and 2 tsps. flour mixed smoothly together. Pour the sauce over the fish and sprinkle very lightly with some fine, browned breadcrumbs.

SOLE VÉRONIQUE

6–8 fillets of sole	Salt and pepper
1 shallot	¼ pint thick cream
1–2 button mushrooms	1 cupful white grapes
Fish stock	½ oz. butter
Dry white wine	

Skin the fillets and fold them neatly in three. Lay them in a pan with the sliced shallot and mushrooms, and enough fish stock and wine barely to cover the fish—about ½ pint. Season with salt and pepper, cover and simmer very gently until the fish is tender. Lift out the fillets, drain them well and keep warm. Boil the liquor in the pan until reduced by about half, then strain and return to the pan with the cream and the grapes (skinned and stoned). Heat gently, stirring constantly until the sauce thickens. Just before using, shake in the butter in small pieces. Arrange the fillets on a hot dish, pour the sauce over and serve at once.

SPRATS

In season from October to March.

To prepare sprats, wash them and draw through the gills as for smelts. They are usually fried or grilled and served with a mustard sauce.

Sprats are also bought smoked and dried. These should be brushed with melted butter and grilled for a few minutes or fried lightly. Serve with lemon and brown bread and butter.

FRIED SPRATS

Wash the sprats and dry carefully. Dip in seasoned flour, coating them very lightly (or dip in batter). Run a skewer through the heads of about a dozen at a time. Have ready sufficient smoking-hot fat to cover them, and fry until crisp and golden-brown. Drain and serve very hot, garnished with lemon and parsley, and with brown bread and butter handed separately.

STURGEON

In season August to March.

Sturgeons are not much eaten in this country. The flesh is firm and well flavoured, but rather close and dry. The roe of the sturgeon is known as caviare.

TENCH AND TROUT

See FRESH-WATER FISH.

TURBOT

In season all the year, but is at its best from March to August.

Turbot has a creamy-white flesh with a very delicious flavour, and is considered to be the finest of the flat fish. It grows to a very large size and is usually sold cut into thick slices or cutlets. It is very good steamed or boiled, or may be cooked by any of the usual methods. Small or " chicken " turbot may be boiled whole or cooked as for sole.

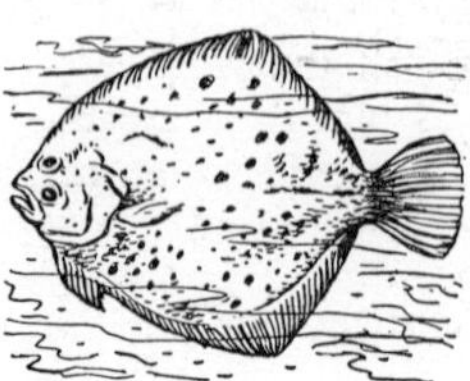

Turbot

WHITEBAIT

These small silvery-looking fish are highly esteemed by epicures. Whitebait comes into season in the early spring, and is to be had in perfection during the months of May, June and July.

FRIED WHITEBAIT

Frying is the usual method of cooking white-bait, and some cooks find this a difficult performance, but the following is a well-tried method and should produce good results.

Wash the fish, handling lightly, and remove all pieces of weed or other foreign matter. Drain in a colander and spread out on a cloth to dry. On a second cloth put 2–3 tbsps. flour,
23 place a few of the fish on the cloth and toss them
about until evenly coated, and separate one from the other. Then turn them into a frying basket and shake out all the loose flour. Place some of the fish in a frying basket and fry in smoking-hot, deep fat until they are crisp and golden-brown in colour. Take care to fry only a few at a time, and keep the cooked fish very hot while the others are frying. If a large quantity is being cooked, the fish may be returned to the basket after the first frying is completed, and fried for a further 3 minutes to make them crisp. Drain well on paper, sprinkle with salt and garnish with lemon and parsley. Serve with thin slices of brown bread and butter; no sauce is required.

Devilled whitebait is prepared in the same way, but the fish are sprinkled with black pepper before the second frying, and then drained and sprinkled lightly with cayenne pepper before serving.

WHITING

In season all the year, but at its best from December to March.

A small fish with a delicate flavour. Being easily digested, it is often given to invalids. As the flesh breaks easily the fish is usually cooked whole, but it may also be filleted. Whiting is generally poached in milk, or fried, but may be cooked by any of the usual methods.

Whiting

FRIED WHITING

Clean, wash and skin the whiting, removing eyes but not the head of the fish; dry well in a cloth. A few minutes before frying the fish, remove from the cloth and put the tail of each whiting into its mouth. Brush over with beaten egg, roll in breadcrumbs and shake off any loose crumbs. When the fat is smoking hot, put in the fish and fry until a golden-brown. Drain well on paper before dishing up, garnish with fried parsley, and serve immediately, with anchovy or other good sauce.

WHITING À LA COLBERT

Whiting	Egg and breadcrumbs
A little milk	Maître d'hôtel butter
White pepper and salt	Lemon and parsley
Flour	Anchovy sauce

Allow one fish for each person. Have the fish cleaned and skinned, remove the head and trim the tail. Make a slit down the back of each, and, by raising the flesh slightly from the bone, make a little pocket. Dip the fish in milk seasoned with white pepper and salt, and coat them lightly with flour. Then egg and breadcrumb them, pressing the crumbs on with a knife, and making the whiting tidy and even in shape.

Blue Trou

Fried Plaice, Scalloped Fish, Fish Cake

Now fry the fish in hot fat until golden-brown, being particular to see that they are thoroughly cooked. Open up the pocket at the back of each and slip into it a good pat of maître d'hôtel butter. This will soak into the fish, making it less dry and giving it a more delicious flavour. Arrange thin slices of lemon round the edge of the dish, lay the fish on a dish paper in the centre, and garnish with parsley. Serve anchovy sauce separately.

Note: Other small fish, such as haddock, gurnet or mullet, may be prepared in the same way, which is particularly good for dry fish.

SHELL FISH

CRAB

A medium-sized crab is best; it is richest in flavour and sweetest for eating. It should also weigh heavily, and have all its claws—five pairs, the first pair, ending in nippers, being much more massive than the others. The edible portion of the crab consists of two distinct parts—the white flesh of the claws, and the liver, or soft, rich, yellow substance, which nearly fills the interior of the shell. The male has larger claws and a smaller body than the female, so selection should depend upon whether the claw meat or the brown meat is liked best. A crab is usually bought ready cooked; in fact, many fishmongers will prepare and dress it as well. If alive when it comes into the cook's hands, it should be boiled in the same way as a lobster, for 10–20 minutes according to size. If over-cooked, it becomes hard and thready.

There are many different ways of serving crab, but it is always best when made up in a simple manner.

CRAB, SIMPLY DRESSED

Lay the crab on its back. Hold the shell firmly with one hand, and the body (to which the claws are attached) in the other hand, and pull apart.

Take the shell part, and with a spoon remove the stomach bag (which lies just below the head);
4 discard this. Then carefully scrape all the meat from the shell into a basin and reserve it—this is called the "brown meat." Wash and dry the shell. Then knock away the edge of the shell up as far as the dark line round the edge. Add 1 tbsp. or so of fresh breadcrumbs to the brown meat, season with salt, pepper and vinegar, and a little chopped parsley, and pack it into the sides of the prepared shell, leaving a space in the middle for the white meat.

D

Take the body and remove from it all the greyish-white frond-like pieces—these are called "dead men's fingers" and are inedible, so discard them. Crack the claws (except the very tiny ones) with nut-crackers or a weight, and take out all the flesh (the white meat) from both claws and the body. Use the handle of a teaspoon to get into the crevices, and take great care not to get splinters of shell amongst the meat. Season the flesh with salt, pepper, cayenne and vinegar, and pile it into the centre of the shell.

Decorate the crab with a little chopped parsley or small cress, then lay it on a glass dish and garnish with the small claws.

SPAGHETTI RING WITH CRAB FILLING

8 oz. spaghetti
3 eggs
6 tbsps. button mushrooms
6 tbsps. tomato sauce
5 tbsps. finely chopped onion
1 tbsp. piquant sauce
1 oz. finely grated cheese
2 tbsps. finely chopped celery or green peppers, if available
$\frac{1}{2}$ pint milk
1 tin of crab
White sauce

Cook the spaghetti in boiling, salted water until tender, and then drain. Add all the remaining ingredients, except the crab and white sauce, and mix well. Put into a well-greased ring mould and bake in a moderate oven (350° F., mark 4) for $\frac{3}{4}$–1 hour. Turn on to a hot dish, and fill the centre with flaked crab heated in white sauce.

CRAWFISH

The crawfish resembles the lobster (but without the big claws) and is prepared and cooked in any way suitable for lobster.

CRAYFISH

These river shell fish are like lobsters in appearance (though much smaller), and are very delicate in flavour. The shells turn a brilliant red colour when boiled. Small crayfish are used for soups and garnishes; the larger ones can be boiled and served either hot, in a good cream sauce, or cold with brown bread and butter. To cook, wash thoroughly and remove the intestinal tube under the tail, as this has a bitter flavour, then cook in boiling salted water or court-bouillon for about 10 minutes.

DUBLIN BAY PRAWNS

Prepare and cook as for crayfish, if bought alive. When cooked, remove bodies intact from shell, cut in half and serve with a good cream sauce in scallop shells or with dry boiled rice.

'ournedos with Savoury Rice; Spinach Timbales

They are also delicious coated with egg and breadcrumbs and fried, or may be served cold with salad.

LOBSTER

Great care must be taken in choosing a lobster, as it is most important to have it perfectly fresh and in good condition—the same applies to the choosing of all crustacea. Lobsters are generally sold ready boiled. A medium-sized one is best; it should be heavy in proportion to its size, and the tail should have plenty of "spring." Those with white shell-like incrustations on the back should be avoided, as these are an indication of age. For eating purposes, the male or cock lobster is superior to the hen and more delicate in flavour. It does not grow to so large a size, and is generally narrower in the back part of the tail. On the other hand, the hen lobster is prized for its red coral and spawn, which are so useful for garnishing and for making the delicious Cardinal sauce. If the lobster is bought alive, tie up the claws securely and wash it in clean water. Then place it in cold, salt water, bring slowly to boiling point, and let it boil fairly quickly and without stopping from 15–25 minutes, according to size, and allow to cool in the water. (This is a more humane way of cooking lobsters than the older method of plunging them into boiling water.) If boiled too long, the flesh becomes hard and thready. Remove any scum before lifting out the lobster, and if the shell is to be used, rub it over with a little oil to give it a gloss.

A few parsley stalks, a sprig of lemon thyme, a bay leaf, and a very little vinegar may be added to the water in which the lobster is boiled, if extra flavour is desired.

LOBSTER, SIMPLY SERVED

Lobster is never better than when served quite simply, with an oil and vinegar dressing, or mayonnaise or Tartare sauce used as an accompaniment.

First twist the large claws off the lobster and crack them without injuring the flesh. Remove
25 also the smaller claws, which are only used for garnishing. Then split the lobster right down the middle of the back from head to tail, using a strong, pointed knife. Remove the intestine (which looks like a small vein running through the centre of the tail), the stomach, which lies near the head, and the spongy-looking gills, which are not good.

To serve, stand the head upright on a dish, arrange the cracked claws and split tail round it, and garnish with parsley or salad. Serve the sauce or condiments separately. Another popular way of serving lobster is *en salade*. For this the meat should be removed from the claws and shell, cut into small pieces and mixed, with salad vegetables, with a mayonnaise dressing.

Lobster can also be served hot, au gratin, or the remains can be devilled, curried, scalloped, or served up in the form of cutlets, patties, or an omelette; but there is really nothing to equal the plainly dressed lobster.

LOBSTER CREAM

¼ pint stiff aspic jelly	½ pint cream or unsweetened evaporated milk
¼ lb. cooked lobster, fresh or tinned	
1 tbsp. mayonnaise	Lettuce
Cayenne pepper, salt, lemon juice	French dressing
	Watercress

Put a thin layer of aspic jelly in the bottom of a mould. Chop the lobster and add mayonnaise and seasonings. If a smooth cream is required, rub through a coarse sieve. Half-whip the cream or evaporated milk. Stir in the rest of the aspic jelly and the lobster. Colour if liked, and pour into the mould. Turn out when set, and decorate with shredded lettuce tossed in French dressing, and bunches of watercress.

LOBSTER MAYONNAISE

¼ pint mayonnaise	Endive
1 lobster	2 lettuces
1 hard-boiled egg	

First prepare the mayonnaise sauce. Remove all the meat from the lobster, retaining the coral for garnishing. Flake the flesh or cut up neatly into small pieces; slice the hard-boiled egg. Wash and dry the endive and lettuce carefully and tear into pieces of moderate size, with the exception of the hearts and a few good leaves. Arrange the lettuce leaves and pieces of endive alternately round the inside of a salad bowl Mix the lobster meat with the mayonnaise sauce. Pile this on the lettuce leaves already in the basin. Decorate with the hearts of lettuce, sliced egg and lobster coral. The claws and head of the lobsters may also be used for decoration.

LOBSTER À L'AMÉRICAINE

1 lobster	¼ pint tomato sauce
1 oz. butter	¼ pint dry white wine
1 tbsp. olive oil	Salt and pepper
2 shallots	A little butter
¼ pint Espagnole sauce	Chopped parsley

A live lobster should be used for this dish. Kill it by piercing through the spinal cord in the back, where the head joins the body, with a skewer or sharp-pointed knife (this kills it instantaneously). Break the claws and cut the body into several pieces, reserving the coral and the greenish liver. Melt the butter, add the olive oil, and when thoroughly hot, put in the pieces of lobster and sauté for a few minutes, shaking the pan meanwhile. Add the sliced shallots and sauté together for a further few minutes. Then add the sauces and the white wine and salt and pepper if necessary. Cover, bring to the boil and simmer gently for a few minutes. Meanwhile, pound the coral and the liver with a little butter. Arrange the pieces of lobster on a hot dish, add the coral butter to the sauce and pour over the lobster. Garnish with chopped parsley and serve at once.

LOBSTER CUTLETS

12 oz. cooked or tinned lobster	Salt
	Cayenne
1 oz. butter	Lemon juice
1 oz. flour	Egg and breadcrumbs
¼ pint fish stock, water, or milk	Fat for frying
	Fried parsley

If tinned lobster is used, drain off the liquid, which can then be used for the sauce: fresh lobster must be very finely chopped. If there is any coral, pound it with ½ oz. butter, sieve, and use for the sauce. Make a thick sauce with the butter, flour and liquid, and cook well until it leaves the sides of the pan, beating hard meanwhile. Add the lobster to the sauce, season, add the lemon juice, and spread the mixture on a plate to cool. Shape into cutlets, egg-and-crumb them and fry in smoking-hot, deep fat. Put a lobster feeler in the end of each cutlet, or if tinned lobster is used, put a stick of macaroni to take the place of the bone. Serve on a hot dish, garnished with fried parsley.

MUSSELS

In season from September to March.

Mussels must be alive when they are bought. If any of the shells gape, discard them, as the mussel inside is dead, unless the shell closes when tapped sharply. As mussels are cooked in their shells these must be very carefully cleaned. Wash the mussels in several waters, scraping and scrubbing each shell separately until it is perfectly clean. Lift the shells out of the water with the hands, leaving any sandy sediment, etc., behind in the basin.

To Open Mussels

Choose a wide pan with a lid. Place the mussels in this, add a small quantity of water, and to improve the flavour put in a slice of onion, some parsley stalks, thyme, bay leaf and pepper. Cover the pan tightly, put over the heat and cook for about 5–6 minutes, shaking the pan frequently. By this time all the shells should have opened and the mussels will be ready. Drain the mussels, reserving the liquor, and with a pair of scissors remove the beard—and little black part like a weed—from each mussel. Use as required.

MOULES MARINIÈRE

1 pint court-bouillon	2–3 tbsps. cream
1 quart fresh mussels	1 tsp. chopped parsley
2 egg yolks	

Make the court-bouillon as described earlier in this chapter, including the white wine, if possible. Wash the mussels thoroughly in several waters, scrubbing or scraping the shells if necessary. Strain the court-bouillon and add the washed mussels. Cover, bring to the boil and cook gently for a few minutes, shaking the pan over the heat. As the shells open, remove the mussels, keeping them on the half shell. Place them in a dish and keep covered to prevent them from drying. Reduce the liquid somewhat, then remove from the heat and stir in the egg yolks, beaten with the cream. Reheat gently but do not boil, then pour over the mussels in the dish, sprinkle with parsley and serve at once.

OYSTER

In season from September to April. The Kentish and Essex oysters are regarded as particularly good, but some excellent types are produced in French and Dutch oyster beds.

OYSTERS AU NATUREL

The true oyster-lover prefers them just out of the shell—opened on the deep shell so as to conserve as much of the natural liquid as possible. They should be served very cold, iced if need be, but never to the point of tastelessness. A sprinkle of salt, a touch of cayenne, a dash of lemon juice on each oyster, is all this is required by way of condiment. If vinegar is preferred, it should be the very best French wine vinegar, or perhaps a drop or two of tarragon, but to drown an oyster with any coarse sort of vinegar is to brutalise it. Thin, wafer-like slices of brown bread and butter should accompany the oysters; some people like grated horseradish.

FRIED OYSTERS (PIGS IN BLANKETS)

Cut thin rashers of bacon in half. Wrap each oyster, previously dried, in a slice of bacon, and fasten together with a tiny wooden skewer. Lay them on a cloth till the last minute to get entirely dry, and brown very quickly in a hot frying pan. Place two "pigs" on a square of hot toast, and serve with a little of the liquid from the pan poured over; garnish with parsley and serve at once.

OYSTERS IN GOLDEN SAUCE

Drain half a dozen oysters, or more, and cook them in a little butter until they are plump and the edges begin to curl. Add seasoning and 1 egg yolk, beaten with a little milk or cream. Stir constantly over gentle heat, without boiling, until thick. Serve on rounds of hot toast and garnish with parsley.

OYSTER PATTIES

12–18 oysters	Juice of ½ lemon
1½ oz. butter	Pepper and salt
1 oz. flour	¼ pint cream
¼ pint milk	Puff pastry
2–3 tbsps. oyster liquor or fish sauce	A little beaten egg

Blanch the oysters in their own liquor, then beard and cut them into small pieces. Melt the butter, stir in the flour, add the milk and oyster liquor, and cook for 5 minutes; then add the lemon juice and seasoning, and lastly, the cream and oysters. Heat, but do not allow the sauce to boil. Fill the patty cases (see below) with this mixture, and serve either hot or cold.

The patty cases are made by cutting out rounds of puff pastry ½ inch thick and 2 inches in diameter. Use a small sharp cutter of ¾ inch diameter for the centre cavity, pressing it lightly so that the pastry is only cut through three-quarters of its thickness. Brush over the top only with beaten egg and bake in a very hot oven (475° F., mark 9) until well risen and browned—15–20 minutes. When cooked, remove centre cap, scoop out some of the soft pastry from the centre; add the oyster filling and replace cap.

OYSTER SCALLOPS OR AU GRATIN

This dish is delicious when properly prepared. Place a layer of fine white breadcrumbs in well-greased scallop-shells or an au gratin dish. Place a layer of oysters on the top of the crumbs, the number depending on the size of the dish. Season with pepper, salt, and a tiny pinch of mace. Then add a layer of good white sauce, with more breadcrumbs on the top. Dot with butter, and bake in hot oven (450° F., mark 8) until the crumbs are a rich brown—15–20 minutes. Celery and oysters are a good combination, so a little of the white celery, finely shredded and cooked until tender, may be added to the dish as a variation. Serve with brown bread and butter, and garnish with parsley.

PRAWNS

These are very delicate little shell fish, rather larger than shrimps and finer in flavour; they are also less common and more expensive. When freshly caught, the colour of the prawn is a sort of greyish-orange, and the body is almost transparent, but it changes to a beautiful pink when boiled, and becomes more opaque. Prawns only require a few minutes' cooking, but when bought in the shops they are already boiled. They are usually served as an hors d'œuvre or as a garnish for other dishes. Curried prawns and prawns in aspic are also popular.

CURRIED PRAWNS

See the chapter on CURRIES.

PRAWN COCKTAIL

See the chapter on HORS D'ŒUVRE.

SCALLOPS

These shell fish are delicate in flavour and make excellent eating. Care must be taken, however, to use them only when they are very fresh and in full season, from October to March; they are at their best in January and February. The roe should then be a bright orange colour and the flesh very white.

Remove the scallops from their shells and wash them very thoroughly until free from all grit. Remove the beard and black part and let them drain on a cloth, then cook as desired. There are several ways of preparing scallops, some of the most popular being given below.

FRIED SCALLOPS

Let them soak for ½ hour in a mixture of salad oil and lemon juice, seasoned with pepper and salt. Then drain, roll in flour, egg-and-breadcrumbs, and fry in boiling fat to a golden-brown.

FRICASSEE

Stew the scallops in a little milk, then use the liquor to make a white sauce to cover them. Serve with dry toast.

SCALLOPS AU GRATIN

Cook them in sauce, then turn them into a fireproof dish and sprinkle with grated cheese and breadcrumbs mixed. Dot with butter on the top, and brown in a hot oven (450° F., mark 8).

SHRIMPS

There are several different varieties, the brown and the pink being the most familiar. The brown or common shrimp is very plentiful, and is caught in large numbers on our sandy coasts. It has a translucent grey colour—the colour of the sand—when caught, but changes to a reddish-brown when boiled. The rose or pink shrimp is caught in deeper waters; its flavour is more delicate, and it is considered the finer of the two. Shrimps are excellent when freshly boiled, but become indigestible when stale. They form a very good hors d'œuvre with bread and butter; they are also useful for garnishing, or for flavouring a sauce to be served with fish.

POTTED SHRIMPS

1 pint picked shrimps
4 oz. melted butter
A pinch of powdered mace
A pinch of cayenne pepper
A pinch of grated nutmeg

Heat the shrimps very slowly in the butter, but do not allow them to come to the boil. Add seasonings, then pour into small pots or glasses. Leave them to become quite cold, and then cover them with a little clarified butter. Use within a few days. Serve with dry toast, butter and freshly ground black pepper.

DISHES MADE WITH WHITE FISH

BROWN CASSEROLE OF FISH

About 1 lb. filleted white fish (cod, hake, etc.)
1 oz. flour
Salt and pepper
1–2 oz. dripping
1–2 onions
2 oz. mushrooms
2 tomatoes
1 cupful water or fish stock
A pinch of mixed herbs
Vinegar
Gravy browning

A casserole of fish can be very delicious, and this method of cooking is particularly good if the fish is inclined to be coarse.

Wash and trim the fish and cut into neat portions. Toss in the seasoned flour and fry lightly in a little hot dripping; when lightly browned, lift from the pan and lay in a casserole. Now fry the sliced onions in the dripping, and when well browned add to the fish. Fry also the sliced mushrooms and tomatoes and place in the casserole. Sprinkle the rest of the seasoned flour into the frying pan to form a roux, then add a cupful of water or fish stock, salt, pepper, herbs, and a dash of vinegar, and bring to the boil, stirring. Colour with gravy browning, and pour over the fish in the casserole. Cover, and cook in a moderately hot oven (400° F., mark 6) about ½ hour. Serve hot, with boiled potatoes.

CREAMED FISH AU GRATIN

¾ lb. white fish
¼ pint water
½ pint milk
1 small onion
A bunch of herbs
Salt and pepper
Boiled potatoes
2–3 tomatoes
1 oz. butter
1 oz. flour
2–3 oz. cheese
Mustard
A few drops of vinegar or lemon juice
Chopped parsley

Place the fish in a saucepan with the water, milk, sliced onion, herbs (tied in muslin), and salt and pepper, and simmer gently for 10–15 minutes, or until the fish is cooked. Lift out the fish, remove any bones and thick skin, and place in flakes in a fireproof dish lined with a layer of the sliced boiled potatoes. Skin and slice the tomatoes and arrange in a layer on the fish, sprinkling with salt and pepper. Melt the butter and add the flour to make a roux. Add the strained liquor in which the fish was cooked and bring to the boil, stirring continuously; boil for 2–3 minutes. Then add half the cheese, season with salt, pepper, mustard and vinegar or lemon juice, and pour over the fish. Sprinkle with the remainder of the cheese and place in a moderate oven (375° F., mark 5) for a few minutes to heat through. Before serving, brown the top under the grill and garnish with chopped parsley.

DEVILLED FILLETS OF FISH

4–5 small fillets of hake or cod
1 tbsp. olive oil
½ tsp. mustard
Cayenne and salt
1 dessertsp. chutney or ketchup
A little vinegar
2 tbsps. browned crumbs
1 oz. butter

Wash and dry the fillets and brush them over with olive oil. Mix together the mustard, seasonings and the chutney and add sufficient vinegar to mix (about 1 tsp.). Spread the mixture on the fillets and place them on a well-greased ovenware dish. Sprinkle with browned crumbs and place a portion of the butter on top of each. Cover with greased paper and bake in a moderate oven (375° F., mark 5) 25–30 minutes. Serve hot, with mashed or chipped potatoes and a sauce.

FISH IN BATTER

Slices or fillets of fish
4 oz. flour
¼ tsp. salt
1 egg
1 tbsp. oil
2–3 tbsps. tepid water
1 dessertsp. seasoned flour
Fat for frying

Prepare the fish, and make the batter; sieve the flour and salt, make a well in the centre and add the egg yolk and oil, together with sufficient water to make a smooth coating batter. Dip the fish in the seasoned flour. Whip up the egg white very stiffly and fold into the batter. Dip the fish into the batter, using a skewer, and fry until golden-brown in fat from which a faint blue smoke arises. Drain well and serve at once, with a good sauce.

FISH HOT-POT

¾ lb. white fish
1½ lb. potatoes
2 small onions
½ lb. tomatoes
Salt and pepper
A bunch of fresh herbs (thyme, marjoram, parsley, bay leaf) tied in muslin

Cut the fish into neat pieces; use the bones and skin to prepare a little fish stock. Peel and slice the potatoes, onions and tomatoes, and arrange in layers in a deep casserole, sprinkling with salt and pepper. Add the bunch of herbs, half-cover with the fish stock or water, and finish with a layer of potatoes on top. Cover, and cook in a moderate oven (350° F., mark 4) about 1 hour, removing the lid for the last 15–20 minutes. Remove herbs before serving.

FISH LAYER CASSEROLE

1 lb. white fish
1 lb. marrow
1 lb. potatoes
1–2 stalks celery
1 oz. butter
Salt and pepper
2 oz. grated cheese
2–3 tbsps. milk
Browned breadcrumbs

Prepare the fish by removing the bones and cutting into fairly thin slices. Peel the marrow, remove the seeds and cut it into sections. Wash and peel the potatoes and cut up the celery. Take a deep casserole, rub it round with butter and put a layer of sliced marrow, grated potato and celery in the bottom. Cover with half the fish, sprinkle with salt and pepper, then cover with a layer of grated cheese. Next, put another layer of the vegetables, the rest of the fish, more seasoning, and the milk. Finally, cover with the remainder of the grated cheese and the vegetables, sprinkle the top with browned breadcrumbs and dot with the remainder of the butter. Cook in a moderate oven (350° F., mark 4) for about 1 hour, until tender. Serve hot.

FISH QUENELLES

8 oz. raw whiting or other white fish
1 oz. butter
2 oz. soft white breadcrumbs
¼ pint milk
1 egg
Pepper and salt
A pinch of nutmeg
Lemon juice

Remove all skin and bone from the fish, and shred finely. Put the butter, breadcrumbs and milk together in a saucepan and cook until thick and smooth. Turn the sauce into a mortar, add the fish and the egg and pound well together; then rub the mixture through a wire sieve. Season, add a pinch of nutmeg and a squeeze of lemon juice. Shape into quenelles (i.e., shape like small eggs), by using two dessertspoons dipped in water. Have a greased frying pan half-full of gently boiling water. Lay the quenelles in this—the water should barely cover them—and poach gently for about 15 minutes. When firm, lift out with a perforated spoon, drain on a piece of folded muslin, and dish in a border of creamy mashed potatoes or on a bed of spinach. Coat with a cream sauce.

RUSSIAN FISH PIE

6 oz. flaky pastry
8 oz. filleted white fish
1 hard-boiled egg
3 tbsps. picked shrimps (optional)
4 tbsps. white sauce
Pepper and salt
Beaten egg
Parsley

Make the pastry. Cut the fish in neat pieces, and slice the egg. Mix with the picked shrimps and the sauce, and season to taste. Roll the pastry fairly thin into a square, trimming the edges, and reserving trimmings for decoration. Place the fish mixture in the centre, brush the edges of the pastry with beaten egg, and fold to the centre, over-lapping one on the other in an envelope shape. Glaze with beaten egg; cover the joins with pastry leaves cut from the trimmings; and make a cut in the centre to allow steam to escape. Place on a baking sheet, and bake in hot oven (450° F., mark 8) 30–45 minutes, until pastry is browned and the fish cooked. Garnish with parsley and serve hot.

This dish can also be made with left-over cooked fish, if preferred.

SPAGHETTI RING WITH FISH FILLING

¾ lb. cod or other white fish, or crab
¼ pint white sauce
1 tsp. anchovy essence
1 tsp. vinegar
Seasoning
6 oz. spaghetti
1 oz. butter
1 tbsp. chopped parsley

Steam or bake the fish, then separate it into flakes. Heat some good white sauce and add to it any liquid from the fish, the anchovy essence, enough vinegar to sharpen, and seasoning. Add the flaked fish and keep hot. Meanwhile, cook the spaghetti in boiling, salted water until tender (about 20 minutes). Drain, and mix with the butter and parsley, press into a warm border mould, turn on to a hot dish and pile the fish mixture into the centre.

To vary this dish, use a differently flavoured sauce and serve in a rice ring.

FISH IN JELLY

1 lb. white fish	1 oz. gelatine
2 oranges	Salt and pepper
3 lemons	1 small bay leaf
$\frac{1}{4}$ pint white vinegar	Lemon and parsley
$\frac{1}{4}$ pint water, approx.	to garnish

Fillet the fish, or cut in neat slices if a thick fish. Squeeze the oranges and lemons, strain through muslin or a fine strainer, add the
26 vinegar and make up to 1 pint with water. Add the gelatine, salt, pepper and bay leaf, and bring to the boil. Remove any scum that rises. Put in the fish and simmer gently for 15 minutes, lift it carefully into a deep dish or several individual dishes and strain the liquid over, so that it covers the fish completely. Allow to set, then decorate with lemon fans and sprigs of parsley.

Any white fish can be used for this dish, but fillets of sole are particularly suitable.

FISH MAYONNAISE

Fish and mayonnaise are a good mixture, and a little fish goes a long way served with salad. Boil, grill, steam or bake the fish, as convenient, and while it is still hot, carefully remove any bones or skin, without breaking up the fish. Sprinkle with salt and pepper, and leave to cool. When quite cold, arrange neatly on a dish, and coat with mayonnaise or salad cream. Garnish with slices of cucumber and tomatoes and little bunches of mustard and cress, and serve with a crisp green salad.

DISHES MADE WITH COOKED FISH

USING FISH LEFT-OVERS

The remains of almost any kind of cooked fish can be re-dressed and made up in some dainty way. White fish is, perhaps, the most suitable, although a mixture of white and smoked fish will sometimes make a dish more tasty. Salmon is best treated by itself, and the more simply it is served the better. Oily fish, such as herring and mackerel, can also be used, and may either be combined with a drier sort of fish, or made up into a savoury on croûtes of bread or toast.

When fish has been cooked and some is left over, it is always better to remove the bones and skin while it is still hot. As it cools, the gelatine in the fish hardens, and it becomes much more difficult to separate the different parts. The bones and skin can often be utilised for making a little fish stock, and this will make a sauce of better flavour than when milk alone is used.

When chopped fish is required, it should not be put through the mincer, as this makes it heavy, but it should be shredded down with a fork, or chopped lightly with a knife. The amount of fish indicated in the following recipes should be weighed free from skin and bone.

COLD FISH SCALLOPS

$\frac{1}{2}$ lb. cooked white fish	$\frac{1}{2}$ tsp. each chopped
Vinegar	parsley, chives, tarra-
Seasoning	gon, chervil
1 tbsp. cooked spinach	2 tbsps. mayonnaise
$\frac{1}{2}$ oz. butter	Watercress

Flake the fish and mix with a little vinegar and seasoning. Lay in scallop shells. Mix together the spinach, butter and herbs, rub through a coarse sieve, and blend with the mayonnaise. (The proportions of mayonnaise and green mixture may be varied according to taste.) Place 1 tsp. of the green sauce in each scallop shell to coat the fish, and garnish with watercress. Serve very cold.

EAST INDIA FISH

$\frac{1}{2}$ lb. cooked fish	2 hard-boiled eggs
2 oz. butter	2 tbsps. chopped
2 small onions	coconut
1 tbsp. rice flour	Lemon juice
1 dessertsp. curry powder	Pepper and salt
1 pint milk	Toast or fried bread

East India fish is quickly made, and is tasty and delicious for luncheon. Melt the butter in a frying pan, add the onions, finely chopped, and cook them until they become yellow. Stir in the rice flour and curry powder, mixing them until smooth; then add the milk gradually and stir until boiling. Continue stirring and boiling for 4–5 minutes. Draw the pan to the side of the heat and add the eggs, cut in small pieces, the fish, in flakes and free from bone, and the chopped coconut. Season to taste with lemon juice, pepper and salt, and allow all to become thoroughly hot. Garnish with small pieces of toast or fried bread, and serve boiled rice separately, also chutney, etc., if desired.

FISH À LA MORNAY

½–¾ lb. cooked fish	½ pint fish stock
1 oz. butter	2–4 oz. grated cheese
1 oz. flour	Seasoning
¼ pint milk	Mashed potatoes

Any white fish may be used. Break it into flakes, but do not chop it. Make a sauce with the butter, flour, milk and fish stock. Cook it thoroughly and add the cheese and seasoning. Cook for a few minutes longer, but do not boil after the cheese is added. Arrange the fish in a greased fireproof dish, pour the sauce over and leave for a few minutes, to let it soak through. Prepare some nicely mashed potatoes, well seasoned and moistened with a little milk and butter, put into a forcing bag with a large pipe, and decorate the top of the fish. Put in a hot oven (450° F., mark 8) for about 15 minutes, to heat through and brown the top.

FISH BALLS

6–8 oz. cooked white fish	Lemon juice
2 oz. butter	A little chopped parsley or anchovy essence
2 oz. flour	Egg and breadcrumbs or batter for coating
Salt and pepper	
½ pint milk	Fat for frying

Flake the fish finely, removing all skin and bones. Melt the butter in a pan, add the flour and seasoning, and cook slightly. Add the milk and bring to the boil, beating well all the time: the mixture should be of a soft paste consistency. Stir in the fish, lemon juice and chopped parsley or anchovy essence. Blend together and spread the mixture on a plate to cool. Divide into equal-sized portions and form into balls, coat with either egg and breadcrumbs or coating batter and fry in hot fat. Drain well.

FISH CAKES

(*See colour picture facing page* 96.)

1 tbsp. flour	About ½ lb. mashed potatoes
2–3 tbsps. milk	
2–3 tbsps. fish stock	½ lb. cooked fish
Salt and pepper	2 tsps. chopped parsley
½ tsp. mustard	Egg and crumbs, if desired
A knob of butter	
A few drops of vinegar	Fat for frying

Blend 1 tbsp. flour to a smooth cream with the milk, add the fish stock and bring to the boil, stirring. Cook for 2–3 minutes, then season with salt, pepper and mustard and beat in the butter and vinegar. Mix well and cool slightly.

Mash the potatoes, rubbing them through a sieve if necessary, and mix them with the flaked fish and chopped parsley. Bind with the sauce, adding more seasoning if required, then spread the mixture on a plate and allow to cool. Divide into 6–8 portions and shape into flat cakes or croquettes. Dust with flour and fry in a little hot fat until well browned and crisp on both sides, or coat with egg and crumbs and fry in deep fat. Drain well, dish on a hot dish and garnish with parsley. Serve with a good sauce—parsley or mustard.

FISH PIE

1 oz. butter	4 tbsps. grated cheese
2 tsps. chopped onion	A few drops of vinegar or piquant sauce
1 oz. flour	
½ pint milk and fish stock mixed	Anchovy essence, if liked
	About 1 lb. of flaked cooked white fish
Salt, pepper, mustard and cayenne	
	2 lb. creamy mashed potatoes
2 tbsps. chopped parsley	

Melt the butter and fry the finely chopped onion for a few minutes until tender, but without browning it. Stir in the flour, then add the liquid by degrees and bring to the boil, stirring. Cook for 2–3 minutes, stirring and beating with a wooden spoon to make it smooth and glossy. Add salt, pepper, mustard and a dash of cayenne, if liked, then stir in the chopped parsley, grated cheese and a few drops of vinegar or piquant sauce: a little anchovy essence may be added, in which case add less salt.

Add the fish, reheat and pour into a fireproof pie dish or casserole. Cover with a thick layer of creamy mashed potatoes, well seasoned and beaten until smooth. Before serving, brown in the oven or under the grill and be sure it is very hot. A few sliced tomatoes or fried mushrooms could be mixed with the fish, or a little tomato purée or mushroom ketchup may be added to the sauce.

FISH PIE WITH RICE

1 lb. cooked fish	2 hard-boiled eggs
½ pint white sauce	2 cupfuls boiled rice
Chopped capers or anchovy essence	A few breadcrumbs
	Butter
Seasoning	

Remove all skin and bone from the fish and break it into flakes. Make a good white sauce, flavour it with chopped capers or a little anchovy essence, and season rather highly with pepper and salt. Cut the eggs in slices, and have the rice well boiled and dry, as for curry. Grease a pie dish or fireproof dish, and put in first a layer of fish, then some rice, and moisten with the sauce

Lay some of the sliced egg on the top, and repeat these layers until all the ingredients are used. Sprinkle the top with a few breadcrumbs, dot with a few small pieces of butter, and bake in a moderately hot oven (425° F., mark 7) until thoroughly hot and brown.

FISH AND POTATO TIMBALE

1 oz. butter	½ lb. cooked fish
¾ lb. cooked potatoes	2–3 tbsps. white sauce
4 tbsps. grated cheese	Some chopped parsley
Seasoning	1 egg yolk
A few browned bread-crumbs	Grated rind of ½ lemon

Melt the butter in a saucepan, add the potato (sieved), grated cheese and seasoning. Mix together until thoroughly blended. Grease a plain mould or basin (about 1½-pint size) and sprinkle the inside with browned breadcrumbs. Then line it with the potato mixture, reserving enough to cover the top. Have the fish carefully prepared and broken in flakes, moisten it with sauce, add parsley, egg yolk, lemon rind, and season with pepper and salt. Place this in the lined mould, cover the top with more potato mixture, and smooth over with a knife. Cover with greased paper and bake in a moderate oven (375° F., mark 5) for 30–40 minutes. Turn out on a hot dish, and pour a thin fish sauce round, or serve it separately.

FISH PUDDING—I

8 oz. cooked white fish	½ pint anchovy or parsley sauce
1½ oz. breadcrumbs	Seasoning
2 tsps. chopped parsley	
1 egg	

Flake the fish, carefully removing any bones and thick skin, and mix it with the breadcrumbs. Add the chopped parsley and the beaten egg and moisten with some of the sauce, until it is of a stiff dropping consistency. Season well and turn into a greased basin. Cover with greased paper and steam for about 1 hour. Turn out carefully, and serve with the remainder of the sauce.

FISH PUDDING—II

8 oz. cooked fish	¼ pint milk
8 oz. cold boiled rice	A few drops of anchovy essence
Salt and pepper	
2 tsps. chopped parsley	Anchovy or other sauce
1 egg	

Cut up the fish finely, removing all bones, and mix it with the rice, seasoning and chopped parsley. Mix the beaten egg and milk and add to the fish mixture, together with a few drops of the anchovy essence, if liked. Put into a greased basin, cover with greased paper, and steam for about 40–60 minutes. Turn out on to a hot dish and pour a suitable sauce round.

FISH RAREBIT

1 oz. butter	1 egg
4 tsps. cornflour	1 tbsp. sherry
¼ pint milk	Seasoning
4 tbsps. grated cheese	Hot buttered toast
1 teacupful cooked flaked fish	Watercress

Melt the butter in a saucepan and stir in the cornflour. Pour on the milk and stir until boiling. Add the grated cheese, fish, the egg (beaten with the sherry) and seasoning to taste. Heat through, and serve on hot buttered toast, garnished with watercress.

FISH AND SPAGHETTI ROLLS

2 oz. spaghetti	Seasoning
¼ lb. cooked fish	A little flour
1 oz. butter	1 egg
1 oz. flour	Breadcrumbs
4 tbsps. fish stock or milk	Fat for frying
1 dessertsp. anchovy essence	Parsley or celery to garnish

Cook the spaghetti in boiling salted water until tender—about 20 minutes. Drain and let it dry, then chop finely. Shred the fish and weigh it. Melt the butter in a saucepan without allowing it to brown, add the flour and cook for a minute or two, add the liquid gradually and stir over the heat until the mixture forms one lump and draws away from the sides of the saucepan. Now add the fish and spaghetti, the essence and seasoning. Mix thoroughly and spread out on a plate: when cool this will be firm enough to make up into rolls or any other shape desired. Use a little flour when shaping them, then egg and breadcrumb and re-shape neatly. Have ready a saucepan with enough boiling fat to cover the rolls, and fry them a golden-brown. It is very important to have the fat hot enough, or the rolls will burst in the cooking. Drain on paper, and serve garnished with parsley or a little curled celery.

FLAKED FISH AND SCRAMBLED EGG

Cooked white fish (left-overs will do)	1½ oz. butter
	Salt and pepper
A little milk	2 tsps. chopped parsley
2 eggs	Hot toast

Flake the fish finely, removing skin and bones, and make hot by heating in a little milk in a pan or by steaming between two plates. Scramble the eggs, using the milk and some of the butter, and season well. Mix the fish and egg together. Add the chopped parsley and more seasoning if necessary. Serve on hot toast spread with the rest of the butter.

KEDGEREE

12 oz. cooked smoked haddock or white fish	6 oz. cooked rice
1–2 hard-boiled eggs	Salt
3 oz. butter or margarine	Cayenne pepper
	Chopped parsley

Remove the bones and skin from the fish while it is hot, and flake it coarsely with a fork. Chop the whites and part of the egg yolks, reserving a little of the latter for garnishing. Melt the butter in a saucepan, add the fish, rice, chopped egg and seasoning, and stir thoroughly over a moderate heat until hot. Pile on a hot dish and garnish with lines of chopped parsley and a little sieved egg yolk.

SCALLOPED FISH

(*See colour picture facing page* 96.)

This is an inviting way of serving the remains of cooked fish. The natural scallop shells can generally be obtained from the fishmonger—choose ones that are as deep as possible. Wash and scrub the shells, and, when perfectly clean,

grease them with a little butter or dripping. Put into each some flakes of fish, free from skin and bone, and then cover with suitably seasoned white sauce. Have ready some cooked potatoes, mash them with a little milk, and season with salt. Pile this on the top of the fish, mark with a fork (or pipe, using a large vegetable nozzle), and place the shells in a hot oven (450° F., mark 8) until brown and thoroughly hot—10–15 minutes. Garnish with sprigs of parsley.

RÉCHAUFFÉ OF FISH

Cold fish	Seasonings
Grated cheese	Celery sauce

Remove all skin and bone from the fish and flake finely, then butter a baking dish and cover the bottom with a good layer. Season, sprinkle with grated cheese, and cover with celery sauce. Repeat these alternate layers until the dish is full. Bake for 15–20 minutes in a moderate oven (350° F., mark 4).

SAVOURY FISH TOAST

½ lb. cooked fish	Seasoning
A little fish sauce	6 rounds fried or toasted bread
1½ tbsp. capers	Browned breadcrumbs
2 tsps. parsley	A little butter
1 tsp. vinegar	Parsley and lemon for garnish
A pinch of cayenne	
A pinch of curry powder	

Smoked haddock is excellent for this dish, but any white fish will do. Shred it finely and mix it with 2–3 tbsps. sauce: this should be rather thick, as the mixture must on no account be made too moist. Chop the capers and parsley and add them with the vinegar and other seasonings. Pile this, cone-shaped, on the rounds of toast or fried bread, and sprinkle with browned breadcrumbs. Put a small piece of butter on the top of each and heat thoroughly in a hot oven. Serve hot, garnished with parsley and a few slices of lemon. This makes a tasty savoury for luncheon or supper, and is quickly prepared.

MEAT COOKERY

Meat is an important source of body-building protein. In addition, it supplies valuable amounts of the health-guarding B vitamins and the minerals, iron, copper and phosphorus, which help to make blood and bones. The fat gives the meat flavour and is of high energy value.

The price varies very much according to the type of cut, the most expensive joints of meat being those which are least muscular, and therefore tender and well-flavoured. These cuts can be roasted, fried or grilled, while the more muscular parts need slower methods of cooking to make them tender. The cheaper cuts are, however, just as nutritious as the dearer ones, and can be made very palatable.

CHOICE OF MEAT

Modern methods of transport and cold storage have largely done away with " seasons " for meat. Nowadays it is possible to purchase lamb at almost any time of the year, and pork is often available in the summer months.

Most butchers nowadays sell both fresh home-killed meat and chilled or frozen imported meats. Imported meat is less expensive than meat from our own farms, and this difference may make a considerable saving if you are catering for a family on a limited allowance. While the quality and flavour may not always be so excellent as in home-killed meat, this can usually be overcome by skilful cooking. Much imported frozen meat is excellent for braising, pot-roasting and stewing, while the best of it can of course be roasted, grilled or fried.

Try to find a good butcher who sells meat only in prime condition for cooking; even the highest quality meat, if offered for sale without the proper hanging, will lack flavour and be tough. Don't be afraid to ask for the butcher's advice, remembering that he is an expert and will gladly help you to select the meat which is best suited to your particular purpose.

Generally speaking, select meat which has not got an undue amount of fat; what fat there is should be firm, and free from dark marks or discoloration. Lean meat should be finely grained, firm and slightly elastic.

Methods of cutting meat vary in different parts of the country, but those most widely used are shown in the charts in this chapter.

ROASTING AND BAKING

In its real sense, roasting means cooking by direct heat in front of an open fire, while the more modern method of cooking in a closed oven is really baking, though it is usually referred to as roasting.

Best quality meat and the best cuts should be used for roasting, for example, sirloin of beef, best end neck of mutton, fillet of pork, etc. (see notes under Beef, Mutton, Lamb, etc.).

Preparation of Meat

If the meat is frozen, allow it to thaw thoroughly and slowly before cooking, or it will be tough to eat. Thaw it by leaving in the warm kitchen for a few hours—*not* in warm water.

Wash or wipe the meat and remove any marrow, if a joint with a bone is being used. Weigh in order to ascertain cooking time.

If the joint is deficient in fat, place a little extra dripping on the meat before it goes into the baking tin.

Joints such as breast of lamb or veal can be boned and rolled with stuffing inside, in which case stuffing must be prepared (see recipes).

Tie the meat or skewer it, in order to retain its shape.

Times and Temperatures for Roasting

There are two ways of roasting meat. The first is to cook the meat fairly quickly, putting it into a hot oven (425° F., mark 7) for the first ½ hour to seal the surface, and then to continue the cooking at a temperature of 375°–400° F. (mark 5–6).

The second method is the more modern one, and is especially suitable for small cuts. The meat is put into a cold oven, the temperature is then raised quickly to 350° F. (marks 3–4), and the cooking continued at this temperature. The advantage is that the meat shrivels less and remains more juicy—any juices which are not retained in the meat due to the surface not being sealed quickly, will, of course, go into the gravy which is made in the meat tin.

Method I

Beef and Mutton : Thin joints, 15 minutes per lb., plus 15 minutes; thick joints, 20–25 minutes per lb., plus 20–25 minutes.

Veal and Pork : 25–30 minutes per lb., plus 25–30 minutes. Never serve underdone.

Method II

Allow at least one-third as long again as the times given above.

The best position in the oven for meat is the middle. About every 20 minutes baste it, i.e., pour the hot fat over the top of the meat, using a metal spoon. If a double roaster is used, basting is not necessary.

To Serve Meat

Lift the meat on to a hot serving dish and keep hot while making the gravy. Be certain that all the accompaniments are ready.

Roast beef requires Yorkshire pudding and
28 horseradish sauce. Roast mutton may be served with red-currant jelly or onion sauce; roast lamb with mint sauce. The richness of roast pork may be counteracted by serving apple sauce and sage and onion stuffing with it. Veal usually has veal forcemeat served with it.

Gravy

Gravy, either clear or thickened, is always served with roast meat. Try not to use plain water for it. Failing stock, use fresh vegetable liquor.

To make thick gravy pour off the dripping, reserving $\frac{1}{2}$–1 tbsp. fat in the roasting tin, and add to this 2 tsps. flour for beef or 4 tsps. for mutton or lamb, veal, or pork. Stir this over a low heat until smooth and lightly browned. Remove from the heat and, a little at a time, add $\frac{1}{2}$ pint stock. Stir again over the heat until boiling, and for 2–3 minutes more. After it boils, season to taste, and if necessary add sufficient gravy browning to make the gravy a good rich colour, but not too dark.

A clear gravy is more easily made, and is sometimes preferred with meat which is not stuffed.

All the fat should be poured from the roasting tin and 2–3 tbsps. of boiling stock added to the pan and stirred well round the sides, in order to remove any meat juices on the sides of the pan. Then add more stock according to the amount of gravy required. Season to taste, and bring to the boil. Here again a little gravy browning may be added, but sufficient colouring should be obtained from the meat juices.

POT ROASTING

This is an alternative to roasting meat in the oven, and is particularly suitable for small joints or for pieces which are inclined to be tough.

Flour the meat lightly and brown it in a little hot fat in the pan, then slip a low trivet under the meat, add about $\frac{1}{2}$ pint water, cover the pan with a well-fitting lid and cook slowly, turning it occasionally. Allow $1\frac{1}{2}$–2 hours for a joint weighing about 3 lb.

Vegetables may be added for the last $\frac{1}{2}$ hour of the cooking time, and when the meat and vegatables have been removed to the serving dish, the liquor in the pan may be thickened to make gravy.

BRAISING

Braising is a combination of stewing, steaming and roasting. The meat is cooked over a bed of vegetables, either in a saucepan, or in a casserole in a slow to moderate oven, which consequently gives it a delicate flavour and moist texture. For the last $\frac{1}{2}$ hour of cooking, bake or roast in the oven, or, if already in the oven, remove casserole lid and increase temperature to hot, so giving the joint the flavour of roast meat.

This method is suitable for small or large joints of meat; a delicious variation is obtained by boning and stuffing the meat before cooking.

Preparation and Cooking

Prepare the meat according to kind, boning and stuffing it if liked. Weigh it to gauge the cooking time, which is 25–30 minutes to the lb. plus 30 minutes. Then prepare a bed of vegetables on which to cook the meat: the following make a good basis—1 onion, 1 carrot, 1 small turnip, 2 stalks celery, bouquet garni, seasoning. Prepare as usual and cut into pieces.

If possible, use a fireproof casserole or pan with two handles, which may be placed in the oven. Place about 1 oz. of dripping in the pan together with a few bacon rinds and, when melted, fry the vegetables lightly in the fat.

There should be sufficient vegetables to well cover the bottom of the pan. Then add the bouquet garni, and fresh herbs such as thyme and parsley, and sufficient stock or water to three-quarters cover the vegetables. Bring to the boil, and then place the meat on top. Cover and allow to simmer gently, basting every 15–20 minutes with the liquor. Steam in this way for half the cooking time, then remove the lid and complete the cooking in a hot oven (450° F., mark 8), basting frequently. Lift the meat on to a hot plate and pour a good sauce (made from the liquor) round the meat. Garnish with the vegetables, from which the bacon rinds and bouquet garni must be removed.

An Alternative Method of Braising

Prepare the meat by coating it with seasoned flour. Melt a little dripping, and when smoking hot fry the meat in it, turning it so that it is brown all over, then remove it from the pan. If necessary, add a little more dripping, and in this fry a mixture of vegetables (onions, carrots, celery if in season, etc.) until lightly browned. Put the vegetables into a meat tin, place the meat on top, and add enough stock or water just to cover the vegetables. Add more salt and pepper if necessary, and some chopped mixed herbs. Cover, and cook in a slow to moderate oven (325°—350° F., marks 2–3) until the meat is tender. The time taken will vary according to the kind of meat (see below). When the meat is cooked, lift it on to a hot dish, arrange vegetables each end and pour liquor round.

Joints suitable for roasting	Allow half as long again as for roasting
Stewing meat (scrag end of neck, etc.)	2–3 hours
Rabbits	1–2 hours
Chicken	1 hour
Fowl	2 hours

STEWING

This means the cooking of meat in a small amount of liquid in a covered saucepan or casserole. It is an excellent method of treating the cheaper cuts of meat, as the long, slow cooking makes coarse meat tender. Vegetables are usually added to the stew, and as all the liquid is served, none of the excellent flavour is lost. There are two kinds of stews :—

White Stews

For these, mutton, veal or rabbit is generally used. Irish stew is a good example of a thin white stew; a fricassee is a thickened white stew. There is no preliminary frying.

Brown Stews

The meat and vegetables are fried first for this type of stew. When they have been removed from the fat, the flour is fried until golden-brown before addition of the liquid (see Ragoût of Beef). Stewing steak is commonly used, but other meats (kidney and liver) may be cooked in this way.

Preparation and Cooking

The meat should be wiped and any excess fat and skin removed. Then cut into neat pieces or chops (for neck of mutton), and proceed according to recipe.

Stewing is a long, slow process of cooking—remember the old but true motto : "A stew boiled is a stew spoiled." The meat must be allowed to become tender slowly, and so the stew must only simmer very gently at one side of the pan, which should be kept covered. The cheaper and coarser the meat, the longer it takes to cook. Most stews require at least 2 hours' cooking time, and some varieties, such as oxtail and brisket, may take 3 or exen 4 hours.

If cooking the stew in the oven, a temperature of 300° F. (mark 1) is ideal. Often it has to be used at the same time for baking other foods requiring a higher temperature; in this case place the stew near the bottom of the oven.

Note : When stews are made in a pressure saucepan, cooking time is considerably shorter. The thickening should be added after the pressure has been released and a few minutes before dishing. It is as well to bring the meat, vegetables and liquid to the boil and skim off any froth before securing the lid, otherwise the froth is likely to be ejected through the pressure regulator, particularly if kidney is included.

BOILING

Time to Allow for Cooking

Mutton : 20 minutes per lb. plus 20 minutes.

Salt beef and salt pork : 25 minutes to the lb. plus 25 minutes.

Bacon and ham : Bacon and small pieces of ham, 20 minutes to the lb., plus 20 minutes; whole hams (12 lbs. upwards) 15 minutes per lb., plus 15 minutes.

Preparation of Meat for Boiling

Wipe the meat thoroughly and remove any superfluous fat. (This may be rendered down and used for frying and roasting purposes.)

When boiling a large joint such as silverside of beef, tie it securely to prevent it from losing shape during the boiling.

From the hollow bone part of mutton remove the yellowish fat called marrow, as its presence tends to toughen the meat. The marrow may be rendered down (though it has a rather distinctive flavour), or it may be used for marrow dumplings or as a spread on toast.

Cooking

Put fresh meat into boiling water to which salt has been added, in the proportion of 2 tsps. salt to 1 lb. of meat. Allow it to simmer gently (i.e., the water should bubble slightly on one side of the pan only) for the required length of time.

In the case of salt meat, place it in cold water and bring quickly to boiling point, throw away this water and commence again with cold. When boiling point has been regained, allow the water round the meat to simmer gently as for fresh meat. No additional salt should be added at this stage.

Onions (or leeks), carrots and a little turnip may be added to the pot, also herbs and spices, e.g., clove, peppercorns and mace, according to taste.

The liquor in which the meat is boiled should never be thrown away, as it contains nourishment and flavour. Some of it can be used to make the sauce to accompany the meat, and any remaining should be used for soup.

STEAMING

Prepare the meat as for boiling, but allow double the cooking time. Meat cooked in this way is particularly suitable for invalids. (See the chapter on Invalid Cookery.)

GRILLING

Grilling is a quick method of cooking, so only tender and juicy cuts of meat are suitable. Steak for grilling must be well hung; fresh, unhung meat never grills satisfactorily but is tough and stringy when cooked. Rump and fillet steak, chops, cutlets, tender liver and kidneys all make delicious grills. Sausages, bacon, mushrooms and tomatoes can also be included, to complete the dish.

Preparation of the Meat

Wipe steak with a damp cloth and cut it into portions if necessary, leaving, where possible, a rim of fat. Have it no more than 1½ inches thick and beat it well with a rolling pin (this breaks down some of the fibres and makes the meat more tender).

Remove the skin and spinal cord from chops and trim them neatly. If unshapely, tie with string or fix with a skewer. Chops can also be boned and then tied or skewered into a good shape.

Wash and wipe liver and cut into slices ½ inch in thickness.

Wash and skin kidneys and cut in half, removing the core.

Season all meats on both sides with salt and pepper, and if liked, sprinkle a little lemon juice over. Brush all over with oil or melted butter or dripping. The grid also should be brushed with fat.

Cooking

The heat should be intense to begin with, so pre-heat the grill. Place the meat under the grill and heat quickly so that the surface juices coagulate, keeping in the flavour and goodness. Allow about 2 minutes for heating, then turn and heat on the other side. Turn frequently during cooking, using tongs or 2 spoons, taking care not to pierce the flesh, or the juice will run out. When it is cooked (see below), remove it from the pan, dish, and serve at once with maître d'hôtel butter and chipped potatoes, and garnish with watercress and grilled tomatoes.

Time for Grilling

Steak, 1½ inches thick	12–15 minutes
Lamb or mutton chops, about 1 inch thick	8–10 minutes
Pork chops	15–20 minutes
Veal cutlets	15–20 minutes
Liver	10 minutes
Kidneys	10 minutes
Sausages	10–15 minutes

MIXED GRILL

A mixed grill consists of a variety of the meats mentioned above. Start with those which require longest cooking, so that all are ready together. Serve with mushrooms, tomatoes, chipped potatoes and watercress, with pats of maître d'hôtel butter. Tomatoes are cut in half and grilled for 2–3 minutes, and the mushrooms grilled for 5 minutes, or they can be fried.

FRYING

Any meat that is suitable for grilling may also be fried.

The Preparation and Cooking

Prepare the meat in the same way as for grilling, except that pieces of liver, kidneys and sausages may, if desired, be rolled in seasoned flour before cooking.

Heat a little dripping, cooking fat or lard in a frying pan and when it is hot, add the meat and cook quickly on both sides, so that the surface is sealed and the juices retained. Lower the heat and cook more gently, turning the food occasionally, until it is done. The time required will be approximately the same as for grilling.

BEEF

The flesh of beef should be firm and a deep red, the fat soft and cream-coloured.

CUTS OF BEEF AND HOW TO TREAT THEM

Sirloin (can be boned and rolled)	Roast
Fillet steak (the under-cut of the sirloin)	Fry or grill
Ribs (can be boned and rolled)	Roast
Round	Roast
Topside	Roast
Topside (if pickled)	Boil
Silverside (usually pickled)	Boil
Rump steak	Fry or grill
Top rump	Roast
Aitch-bone	Roast
Aitch-bone (if pickled)	Boil
Brisket	Stew or braise
Brisket (if pickled)	Boil
Flank	Stew or braise
Flank (if pickled)	Boil
Shin (gravy beef) Top rib Neck or sticking Clod Blade or chuck	Stews, soup, stock, etc.

Beef for Roasting

The best joints for roasting are the sirloin and the ribs. *The sirloin* comes from the lower part of the back of the animal next to the rump, and has a short bone in it corresponding in shape to a mutton chop, though, of course, much larger. The meat on top of the bone is called the upper-cut and that under the bone, the under-cut or fillet. *The ribs*, on the other hand, have a long bone and are similar in shape to a mutton cutlet, though again, of course, much larger in size. The meat is all on top of the bone—there is no fillet or under-cut. Both sirloin and ribs can be purchased either with the bone or boned and rolled.

The rump, which comes from the tail end of the animal, though usually cut for steaks, may also be roasted. As there are no bones or excessive fat, it is an economical joint.

The aitch-bone, which is the lower part of the rump, is sometimes roasted, but more usually pickled and boiled.

The round of beef, which comes from the top part of the leg, is divided into topside and silverside. Both these joints may be roasted, but silverside is more suitable for salting and boiling.

The brisket, which comes from the belly, is very good pickled, boiled and braised, but may also be used fresh for boiling or braising.

Roast beef should be served slightly underdone, as it is more succulent, especially when cold. It is usually accompanied by Yorkshire pudding, horseradish cream, and a thin brown gravy.

Beef for Grilling or Frying

The fillet (the under-cut from the sirloin) is the best part for grilling or frying. It is cut across the grain in ½–1 inch slices, forming fillets of beef and tournedos of beef, used for many entrées. They can also be served as plain grilled steak, fried steak and onions, mixed grill and so on. The only other cut suitable for grilling or frying is well-hung *rump steak*.

The other parts of beef, which are unsuitable for roasting, grilling or frying, are excellent for stews, meat pies, puddings, soups, broths, mince or casserole dishes.

BAKED MEAT SHAPE

2 rashers of bacon	Seasoning
1 onion	1 cupful mashed potato
1–2 stalks of celery	Tomatoes or mushrooms for garnish
½ lb. sausage-meat	
½ lb. minced raw beef	½ pint brown sauce

Chop or mince the bacon and fry lightly, to extract the fat. Chop or mince the onion and celery finely, and fry with the bacon. Mix well with the sausage-meat and minced beef, and season thoroughly. Bake in a greased loaf tin in a moderately hot oven (400° F., mark 6) about 1 hour—until mixture is cooked and shrinks slightly from the sides. Turn on to a hot dish and cover the top with mashed potato, piped or forked on neatly. Brown under the grill, and cook the tomatoes or mushrooms under the grill too. Pour the sauce round the shape and garnish with tomatoes or mushrooms.

BAKED STEAK WITH BANANAS

½–¾ lb. beefsteak	1 tsp. sugar
Seasoning	2–3 slices bacon
Nutmeg	A little water
2 bananas	Parsley or watercress

Choose a tender piece of steak 1 inch in thickness, wipe it and split it open, leaving one end uncut, like an open book. Season with pepper, salt and grated nutmeg. Cut the bananas in pieces, lay them on one side of the steak, sprinkle with sugar and cover with the other. Place thin slices of bacon on the top and fasten together with a small skewer. Place in a baking dish with a little water and bake in a moderately hot oven (400° F., mark 6) ½–1 hour, basting occasionally. Garnish with parsley or watercress.

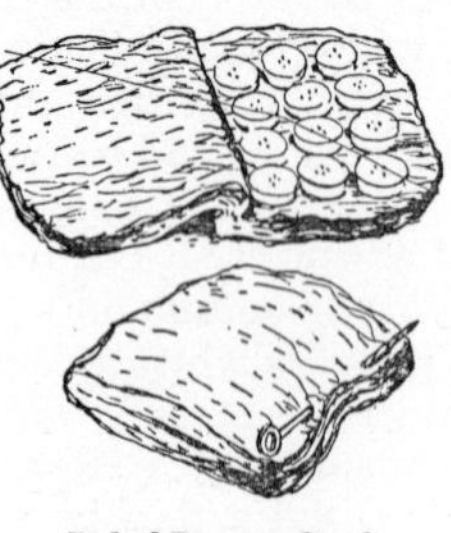

Baked Banana Steak

BEEF AND LENTIL STEW

¼ lb. lentils	¼ lb. onions
¼ lb. stewing steak	1 lb. potatoes
½ lb. mixed root vegetables	Water as required
	Seasoning

Soak the lentils overnight, washing them thoroughly first. Using the liquor in which they were soaked, bring to the boil and simmer gently for 5 minutes. Wipe the meat and cut into neat pieces. Prepare and dice all the vegetables, except the potatoes ; well grease a large casserole. Arrange meat at the bottom, cover with the lentils and water, add the root vegetables and season carefully. Cut the potatoes in slices and arrange on the top, then sprinkle with salt. The water should come quite half-way up the casserole. Cover with a tight-fitting lid, and bake in a moderate oven (350° F., mark 3) for 2–3 hours, or until tender.

BEEF LOAF (HOT)

1 lb. beef	2 tbsps. chopped pickles
¼ lb. fat bacon	Seasoning
1 onion	1 egg or some gravy
1 cupful breadcrumbs	2 dessertsps. flour
2 tbsps. parsley	1 cupful stock or gravy

Mince the beef with half the bacon and put it into a basin. Add the onion, finely chopped, the breadcrumbs, chopped parsley and pickles. Season well with pepper and salt, mix thoroughly and moisten with a beaten egg, or some good gravy. Form the mixture into a round or oblong and place it on a greased baking dish. Cover with greased paper and bake in a hot oven (450° F., mark 8) for ½ hour. Lay the remaining pieces of bacon on the top and continue the cooking until the bacon is brown and crisp. Remove the meat and bacon to a hot dish and keep it in a warm place while making the gravy Add 1 dessertsp. of flour to the fat in the tin and brown it over the fire. Pour in a cupful of stock or gravy, and stir until boiling. Skim if necessary, season to taste, and strain round the meat. The flavour is improved by the addition of 1–2 tbsps. tomato pulp. Serve the beef loaf with mashed or sauté potatoes. The following day, if there is any remaining, it may be cut in thin slices and served cold with a good salad.

GLAZED BEEF LOAF (COLD)

2 lb. beef	Grated nutmeg
1 small onion	½ tsp. allspice or Jamaica pepper
Chopped parsley	
¼ lb. fat bacon	2 eggs
6 oz. breadcrumbs	A little stock
Seasoning	Glaze

Choose lean, juicy beef, and wipe it with a clean, damp cloth. Cut it in pieces, removing any skin and gristle, and put it through the mincing machine. Chop the onion and the parsley and add them to the beef; also the bacon, cut in small pieces, and the breadcrumbs. Season well with pepper, salt, a little grated nutmeg and the allspice or Jamaica pepper. Moisten with the well-beaten eggs and a little stock, and knead the mixture with the hands until all the ingredients are thoroughly blended. Then grease an oblong bread-tin or fireproof dish and press the meat mixture into it. If you want a more decorative loaf, place 1 or 2 hard-boiled eggs in the centre, covering them with meat mixture. Cover with greased paper and bake in a hot oven (450° F., mark 8) about 1½ hours, or until the meat is thoroughly cooked : the time will depend somewhat on the depth of the dish used. When ready, lift out, put in a dish or tin with a weight on the top, and leave until cold.

Turn out next day and brush over with a little glaze. This can be made simply and quickly by dissolving a meat-cube and 1 tsp. of powdered gelatine in 2 tbsps. cold water : let them soak in the cold water first, then place over the heat.

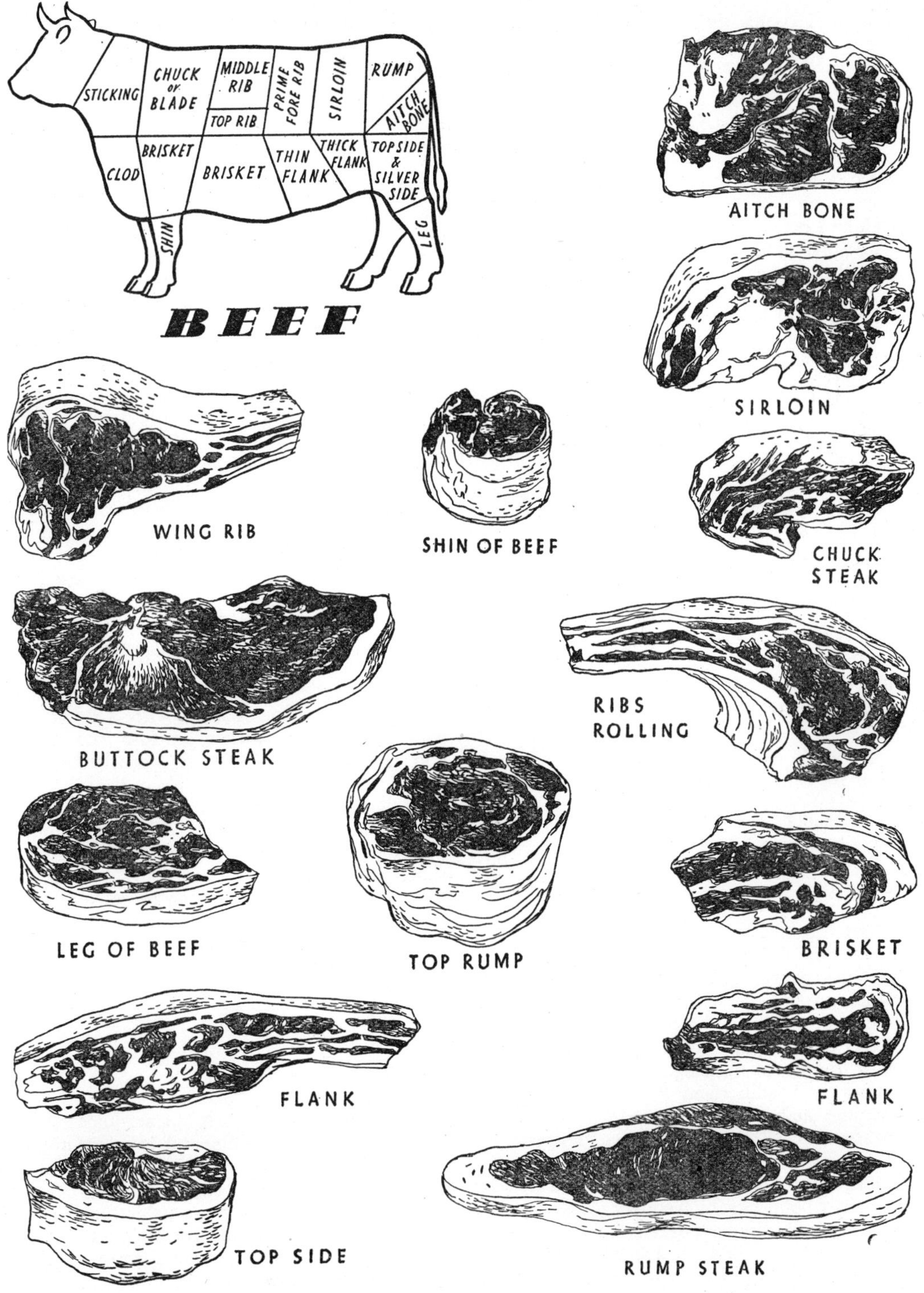
STICKING
CHUCK or BLADE
MIDDLE RIB
TOP RIB
PRIME FORE RIB
SIRLOIN
RUMP
AITCH BONE
CLOD
BRISKET
BRISKET
THIN FLANK
THICK FLANK
TOP SIDE & SILVER SIDE
SHIN
LEG
BEEF
AITCH BONE
SIRLOIN
WING RIB
SHIN OF BEEF
CHUCK STEAK
BUTTOCK STEAK
RIBS ROLLING
LEG OF BEEF
TOP RUMP
BRISKET
FLANK
FLANK
TOP SIDE
RUMP STEAK

This loaf is a good cold dish, which is easily served, and comes in handy for luncheons or making sandwiches. It should be made one day at least before it is required.

BEEF OLIVES

1 lb. thick steak	1 diced carrot
2 oz. veal forcemeat	1 sliced onion
1 oz. flour	A piece of celery
Salt and pepper	A piece of turnip
$1\frac{1}{2}$ oz. dripping	1 pint stock

Cut the meat into thin slices, beat well, then cut into oblongs about 2 by 3 inches. Spread each piece with forcemeat, roll up and tie with string or fix with tiny meat skewers. Toss in the seasoned flour and fry lightly in the hot dripping. Add the vegetables, seasoning and the stock, cover and stew gently for about $1\frac{1}{2}$ hours. Lift out the olives, remove string and skewer, and dish them on a bed of creamed spinach or mashed swedes or turnips. Skim the gravy in which they have been cooked (thickening it if necessary with 1 tsp. or so of flour blended with 1 tbsp. stock), boil up, season well and strain some of this sauce over the olives. Serve the remainder separately.

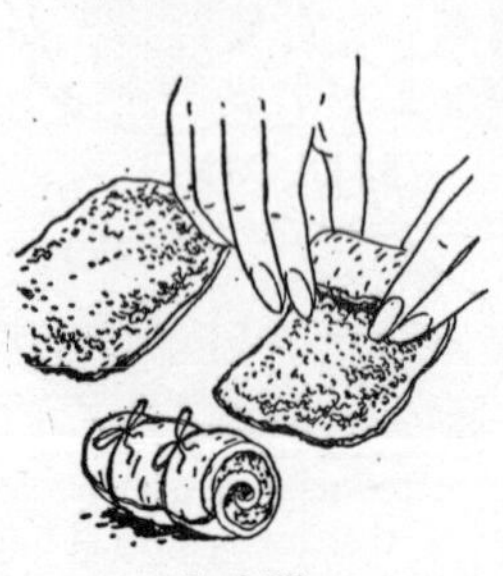
Beef Olives

If preferred, the piece of steak may be cut transversely in half, stuffed, tied into shape and cooked as one large beef olive. In this case, allow 2 hours' cooking time.

BEEF ROLL

1 lb. stewing steak	1 egg
$\frac{1}{4}$ lb. fat bacon	Flour and dripping
3–4 cooked potatoes	Brown or tomato sauce
Seasoning	Cooked vegetable or bacon
Chutney or pickles	rolls to garnish

Cut the meat and bacon in pieces and put them through the mincing machine. Chop the potatoes and add them to the mince, add seasonings and chutney or pickles to taste, and bind together with the beaten egg. Form into a roll, using a little flour, and place it in a baking tin with some hot dripping. Bake in a hot oven for about 1 hour, basting frequently. Serve with brown or tomato sauce poured round. Garnish with a cooked vegetable or a few rolls of bacon. This roll is also good cold, served with salad.

BROWN STEW

$\frac{3}{4}$–1 lb. stewing steak	1 pint stock or water
1 onion or leek	Seasoning
2–3 carrots	2–3 mushrooms
A piece of turnip	Tomatoes
A stalk of celery	1 cupful of cooked beans
2 tbsps. dripping	Bouquet garni
1 oz. flour	

Wipe the meat and cut into neat pieces. Peel the onion and cut into thin rings. Prepare the other vegetables and cut into rings or dice. Melt the dripping in a pan, place half the meat in the fat and fry quickly until it is lightly brown, then turn and fry on the other side. Do not put all the meat in the pan at once, as it will cool down the fat and the frying will be very slow. Remove from the pan and brown the remaining meat. Lift the meat out on to a plate, reheat the fat and add the onion or leek. Fry for a few minutes, until lightly coloured. Remove from the fat, then add the flour and fry until browned. Add the stock gradually, season and bring to the boil. Put in the meat, vegetables and bouquet garni, cover and simmer gently for $2–2\frac{1}{2}$ hours. Alternatively, turn contents of pan into a casserole and cook gently in a slow oven (300°–325° F., mark 1–2) 3–4 hours. Then, remove the bouquet garni, reseason and, if necessary, add a few drops of gravy browning to colour. If fat meat is used, the gravy sometimes becomes greasy; this can easily be rectified by blending 1 tsp. of flour with a little cold water in a cup, stirring it into the gravy, and reboiling; the flour will absorb the extra fat.

Brown stew can be varied by (1) adding potato dumplings; (2) by cooking with a cabbage leaf placed over the top, or by adding 1 tbsp. piquant sauce and a clove of garlic to sharpen the flavour. If liked, potatoes can be cooked in the same pot as the stew. They should be peeled and placed whole on top of the stew for at least 1 hour.

FILLETS OF BEEF MADEIRA

$\frac{3}{4}$ lb. lean beef	Flour
1 tsp. finely chopped parsley	1 egg
	2 bananas
Pepper and salt	$\frac{1}{4}$ tsp. lemon juice
Dripping or olive oil for frying	Egg and breadcrumbs for coating the bananas
1 small onion	$\frac{1}{2}$ pint thin gravy

Mince the beef, add the parsley, pepper and salt. Heat a little dripping or olive oil. Meanwhile, chop the onion finely and fry it in the hot fat to a golden-brown. Stir in $\frac{1}{2}$ oz. flour, brown slightly, add the minced meat, then stir in sufficient beaten egg to make the mixture bind. Spread on a cold plate, divide evenly, shape into round cakes, dredge with flour and fry in hot dripping or olive oil in a shallow frying pan. Split the bananas in half lengthwise and across, dip into lemon juice and sprinkle with pepper and salt. Dip in egg, coat with breadcrumbs and fry lightly. Serve the fillets on a hot dish, placing the bananas between, and serve with a thin gravy.

FILLETS OF BEEF WITH BANANAS

Cut 4–5 round fillets of beef, sauté them in butter for 6 minutes, or until sufficiently cooked, and season with pepper and salt. Place them on potato cakes of the same size, and on the top lay a small section of banana that has been sautéed in butter. Add 2–3 tbsps. water and 1 tsp. meat extract to the pan in which the meat was cooked; stir until boiling, and pour round the dish. Garnish with finely shredded horseradish.

FRIED MINCE STEAKS

1 lb. minced beef	Pepper and salt
2 oz. chopped suet	A little flour for coating
1 tbsp. grated onion	Fat for frying
A pinch of allspice.	

Mix all the ingredients together and form into cakes 3 inches in diameter and about 1 inch in thickness. Dip them very lightly into flour, using only enough to give a thin film over the surface of the meat. In a frying pan, melt a little fat, and when smoking hot, put in the meat cakes and seal them quickly on both sides. Then cover the pan and finish the cooking at a lower temperature: from 10–12 minutes should be sufficient. When the steaks are ready, remove them to a hot dish and serve them with a brown and thickened gravy as directed for Beef Loaf. A small cake of mashed and browned potatoes may be put on the top of each steak, or served separately. A little grated horseradish and small baked tomatoes would make another suitable garnish.

GOULASH

2 onions	A bunch of herbs, tied in muslin
2 oz. butter or dripping	Paprika pepper
1½ lb. good beef steak	Salt and pepper
1½ oz. flour	¼ pint red wine
1 pint stock	Lemon juice
2 tomatoes or a little tomato sauce	Dumplings or noodles

Slice the onions finely and fry them in the butter or dripping. Fry also the meat, cut into dice, then add the flour, and brown slightly. Add the stock, the tomatoes cut up (or tomato sauce), the herbs, and enough paprika pepper to flavour—about ½ tsp. Add salt, and a little white or black pepper also, if liked, cover and simmer gently until tender—about 2 hours. When half cooked, stir in the wine and a squeeze of lemon juice. Serve with dumplings or noodles.

GRILLED STEAK

Choose well-hung fillet or rump steak, 1–1½ inches thick. Beat rump steak on a board with a rolling pin—this breaks down some of the fibres and helps to make the meat tender. Fillet steak may also be beaten, but being very fine in texture does not usually require it. Season on both sides with salt and pepper and, if liked, a squeeze of lemon juice also, then brush all over with olive oil or melted butter or dripping. Grease the grid also, lay the meat on it and place under the hot grill. Cook for about 2 minutes until the outside is browned, then turn and cook for about 2 minutes on the other side. Then reduce the heat and continue cooking, turning frequently, until sufficiently cooked—12–15 minutes in all. Use blunt utensils for turning the meat (cooking tongs, spoons, round-ended knife, etc.), so as not to pierce the flesh, or the juices will run out. Dish at once on a hot dish, place small pats of maître d'hôtel butter on the meat and garnish with watercress. Serve with chipped potatoes and baked or grilled tomatoes.

ROLLS OF BEEF IN LETTUCE

Prepare the same mixture as required for Fried Mince Steaks (above). Divide it into pieces the size of an egg and shape them lightly into rolls, using a very little flour. Wrap each of these in a tender lettuce leaf from which any hard stalk has been removed. Or, the leaves of a young cabbage may be substituted for the lettuce, but these should first be scalded in boiling water to soften them, and then drained. Make the rolls as compact as possible and pack them in a single layer in a greased stewpan. Pour in enough stock

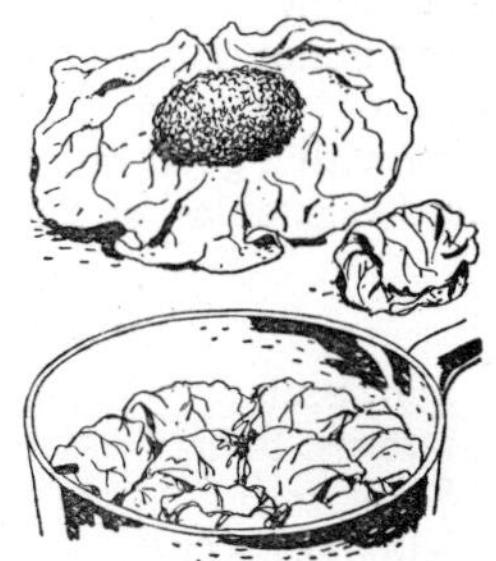

Rolls of Beef in Lettuce

or gravy barely to cover them, lay a round of greased paper on the top and put on the lid. Simmer gently for 20–30 minutes, then arrange the rolls neatly on a hot dish and pour any gravy over the top. A few sauté potatoes or baked tomatoes may be used as a garnish.

HAMBURG STEAK

1 small onion	3 tbsps. breadcrumbs
Dripping	Salt and pepper
½ lb. rump steak, minced raw	1 egg
	Mustard sauce

Chop the onion finely and fry it lightly in a little dripping. Mix the steak, breadcrumbs, salt and pepper and onion in a basin and bind with the beaten egg. Form with the hands into a steak about 2 inches thick. Place on a greased tin with a little dripping, and cook in a hot oven (450° F., mark 8) for 20–30 minutes. Serve with mustard sauce, chipped potatoes and baked tomatoes, and fried onion rings.

MEAT AND POTATO LOAF

Use the recipe given for making Hamburg Steak (above). When the steak is lightly baked, remove from the oven, and cover with a thick coating of well-flavoured, creamy mashed potatoes. Fork the surface, and return to the oven to brown. Serve with brown sauce.

BAKED STEAK LOAF

1 tbsp. chopped onion	Pepper and salt
½ oz. dripping	1 tbsp. tomato or mushroom ketchup
½ lb. minced raw steak	Brown sauce to serve
1 oz. seed tapioca or sago	Diced vegetables or salad to garnish
¼ pint stock	

Fry the onion in the dripping until lightly browned. Combine all the ingredients, mixing them together very thoroughly. Turn into a greased and crumbed bread tin. Cover and bake for 45 minutes in a moderately hot oven (400° F., mark 6), or steam for 1 hour. Turn out and serve with a good brown sauce and garnish with diced vegetables, or serve cold with salad.

JUGGED BEEF

2 lb. beef	2 small onions
2 tbsps. flour	4 cloves
Seasoning	Stock or water
¼ lb. fat bacon	1–2 glasses port
A bunch of herbs	Forcemeat balls
½ lemon	2 tbsps. red-currant jelly
1 in. cinnamon stick	

Choose a nice, thick piece of stewing steak, wipe it with a damp cloth and cut it in small cubes: the pieces must be very neat and not ragged-looking. Coat them with flour, seasoned with pepper and salt. Cut the bacon into dice, put it into a saucepan and fry it for a few minutes. Add the meat, the herbs, lemon rind and cinnamon tied in muslin, and the onions stuck with the cloves. Cover, and cook slowly for 20 minutes, shaking the pan occasionally. Then mix any remaining flour with a little water and add it to the saucepan with enough stock or water to cover the meat. Add also the juice of ½ lemon and half the wine. Stir over the heat until the liquid reaches boiling point; then turn contents of saucepan into a casserole, cover, and cook in moderate oven (350° F., mark 4) until the meat is tender—about 2 hours. It is a good plan to place the casserole in a tin with a little water round it. Half an hour before serving, drop in some forcemeat balls, and a few minutes before the dish is required, remove the herbs and add the red-currant jelly and the rest of the wine. Serve in the casserole.

Note: If no casserole is available, this may be cooked in the saucepan and then served in any deep meat dish.

LANCASHIRE HOT-POT

12 oz. lean beef or steak	¾ pint water
1 tbsp. seasoned flour	A few pieces of fat beef or about ½ oz. dripping
1½ lb. potatoes	
4 medium-sized onions	

Cut the meat into pieces about ½ inch square and coat these with the seasoned flour. Peel the potatoes and cut into quarters, or if very large, into eighths. Slice the onions and put a layer in the bottom of a casserole or pie dish. Place the meat on top of the onions and top with the potatoes. Pour over the water and place a few small pieces of fat meat or dripping on top of all. If a casserole is used, put on the lid, or if a pie dish, cover tightly with greased paper. Bake in a moderate oven (350° F., mark 4) for 2 hours. About 20 minutes before serving, remove the lid or paper and brown the potatoes.

POT ROAST WITH VEGETABLES

Salt and pepper	1 cupful of water
Flour	Carrots, turnips and potatoes
A joint of beef weighing about 3 lb.	Gravy browning, if desired
3 tbsps. fat	

Mix the salt, pepper and 1 tsp. or so of flour and rub on the meat. Brown the meat in the hot fat, then slip a low trivet under it. Add the water, cover tightly, and cook gently until tender—about 1½–2 hours—turning occasionally. One hour before serving, add the vegetables.

Dish the meat and vegetables on a hot dish and make the gravy. For this, add 2 tsps. of flour made into a smooth paste with a little water, and mix into the meat and vegetable juices; stir until well cooked, adding a little gravy browning if desired; season well.

Other meat may be cooked in the same way.

SPICY MEAT CASSEROLE WITH DUMPLINGS

1 lb. stewing beef	A bunch of herbs with 1 clove, piece of bay leaf, 2 peppercorns, and 2 allspice berries, tied in muslin
A piece of onion or leek	Flour to thicken
2–3 large carrots	Gravy browning
1 small turnip	Dumplings
1 stalk celery	
Salt	
1 tbsp. ketchup	
Cold water	

Cut the meat into neat pieces, prepare and slice the vegetables and shred the celery. Put the meat and vegetables into a casserole, add salt, ketchup, and herbs tied in muslin, and cover with cold water. Put on lid and bake in moderate oven (350° F., mark 4) about 2 hours, till meat is nearly tender. Remove from the oven, take out the herbs, and thicken the stew, allowing 2 tbsps. flour blended with 2 tbsps. water to each ½ pint liquid. Stir until boiling, reseason if necessary and colour with gravy browning. Add the dumplings, put on the lid and cook for 25 minutes. Serve in the casserole.

ROLLED STEAK

8 oz. piece of steak (cut in one thin slice)	½ oz. dripping
1 stalk of celery, minced	3 tbsps. breadcrumbs
1 onion, minced	Salt and pepper
1 carrot, minced	4 oz. pastry (shortcrust, if roll is to be baked, suetcrust if it is to boiled)
Fresh herbs (parsley, thyme, etc.)	

Lay the piece of steak on a board and beat, with a rolling pin, to a thickness of about ¼ inch. To make the stuffing, sauté the minced celery, onion and carrot in the dripping for about 5 minutes, then add a good sprinkling of chopped fresh herbs. Add the breadcrumbs and seasoning and mix well. Place this stuffing in the centre of the piece of steak, then roll the meat over it and, if it is to be cooked without pastry, tie it up securely with string or thread, like a parcel.

The roll may be cooked in four ways:

1. Roast for ¾ hour in a strong, covered saucepan with a little dripping, turning it at frequent intervals. Serve with plenty of vegetables (which may be cooked in the pan with the meat, if liked) and a rich gravy made from the dripping in the saucepan.

2. Stew for about 1½ hours, in a good, brown sauce with mixed vegetables, frying the roll to a golden-brown in dripping before making the sauce.

3. Steam the roll, first encasing it in pastry crust. Make 4 oz. suetcrust pastry in the usual way, roll it out about ½ inch thick, and wrap the meat roll in it, moistening the edges of the pastry where it joins (do not string the meat roll first). Wrap in greased paper, tie in a cloth, and steam for about 3 hours. Serve with vegetables and a sauce or gravy.

4. Bake the roll in the oven. For this 4 oz. shortcrust pastry is needed, rolled into an oblong, about ¼ inch in thickness, and wrapped round the meat roll (again, do not tie the meat first with string or thread). Place on a greased baking sheet and bake in a hot oven (450° F., mark 8) until lightly browned, reducing to moderate (375° F., mark 5) until cooked through —about 1 hour in all. Serve with vegetables and a sauce or gravy.

SCOTCH COLLOPS

1 lb. minced beef	Pepper and salt
2 tbsps. dripping or butter	A pinch of nutmeg
1 onion	1 tbsp. ketchup
1 cupful stock (or a meat cube dissolved in water)	1 teacupful breadcrumbs
	Toast, baked tomatoes, rice or spaghetti

The beef should be carefully minced, with a small proportion of fat. Melt the dripping in a strong stewpan and when it is smoking hot, put in the minced beef and the onion, finely chopped. Pound these with a wooden spoon until the meat has lost its red appearance and is nicely browned. Pour in the stock or add a meat cube, dissolved in a cupful of water. Season to taste, put on the lid and simmer slowly for ½ hour. Then add the ketchup and the breadcrumbs, which will absorb any liquid fat, and cook for a few minutes longer. Garnish with small pieces of toast, with baked tomatoes, or with a border of rice or spaghetti.

SCOTCH MEAT MOULD

2 lb. shin or other stewing beef	18 black peppercorns
1 cow heel	A blade of mace
Salt	2 allspice berries
	A bunch of herbs

Wipe the shin of beef and cut in small pieces. Saw the bones in pieces. Cut up the cow heel, wash and scrape until thoroughly clean.

Put the meat and bones into a large saucepan, cover with cold water, add 1 level tbsp. salt and bring slowly to the boil. Add herbs and spices, and simmer slowly for several hours until the meat is really tender and soft. Strain into a basin and leave overnight. Next day, remove all bone, skin and gristle from the meat, pass through a mincing machine, and put in a saucepan. Add the jellied stock, having scraped off any fat, reheat and season. Pour into a mould. Turn out when set.

PRESSED BEEF—I

4–5 lb. pickled brisket or beef	A bouquet garni
2 onions	Water
2 carrots	Glaze
1 small turnip	Mustard and cress

Wash the meat, trim if very fat, and put into a
30 pan with vegetables, herbs and water, cover and
simmer gently until tender—about 4 hours. Lift the meat from the pan and drain, then remove any bones or gristle and form into a good shape. Pack into a cake tin or basin, cover with a plate or saucer and weight down, or tie in a cloth placed between two boards or tins and press with weights. Leave until cold, then turn out or unwrap if tied, glaze and serve garnished with mustard and cress.

PRESSED BEEF—II

Flank of beef	Water
Flavouring vegetables and herbs	Glaze

For the Pickle

6 oz. salt	$\frac{1}{2}$ oz. saltpetre
4 oz. brown sugar	$\frac{1}{2}$ oz. basalt
$\frac{1}{2}$ tsp. mustard	$\frac{1}{2}$ tsp. ground cloves
$\frac{1}{2}$ tsp. allspice	1 tsp. black pepper

Take several lbs. of flank of beef, remove the inside skin and rub daily with the pickle for 8–10 days. Then rinse thoroughly in cold water. Form into a roll, tie into shape and put in a pan with flavouring vegetables and herbs, and cover with boiling water. Bring to the boil, remove any scum that rises, then cover and simmer gently until tender—about 3 hours. Take out the meat, pack into a mould and weight down, or tie in a cloth and press between boards. When cold, trim, glaze and garnish.

RAGOÛT OF BEEF

$1\frac{1}{2}$ oz. dripping	Pepper and salt
2 onions	A bunch of herbs
$1\frac{1}{2}$ lb. stewing steak	2 carrots
$1\frac{1}{2}$ oz. flour	1 small turnip
1 pint stock	

Melt the fat, chop the onions finely, and fry golden-brown. Remove the onion from the saucepan, then cut the meat into pieces of equal size, and fry. Remove from the saucepan, add
the flour to the fat in the saucepan and cook 31
over a gentle heat until brown in colour, then add the stock and stir until it comes to the boil. Add the meat, onion, seasoning and herbs, and allow to simmer gently for 1 hour. Slice and cut the carrots and turnip into dice, add these to the stew, and continue to cook for about another hour. Arrange the meat and vegetables on a hot dish, pouring the gravy over. If liked, dice of carrot, which have been boiled in salted water, may be used for a garnish.

CORNED BEEF

Corned beef is a very useful stand-by and can be served in a variety of ways. Here are some suggestions :—

Cold

Slice thinly and arrange the slices on a dish or platter with a garnish of parsley, watercress, tomatoes, etc. Serve with a sweet chutney and creamed or fried potatoes.

As an Open Sandwich

For a snack meal, lay thin slices of corned beef on pieces of bread and butter, and place sliced pickled gherkins, stuffed olives, etc., on the meat. Arrange on a platter and garnish with cress.

As a Brown Stew

Make a good, well-flavoured brown sauce, strain and add the corned beef, cut into neat dice. Heat through, then dish with a garnish of diced carrots, green peas or other vegetable, and served with boiled potatoes.

As a Meat Pie

Dice the corned beef, toss in seasoned flour and place in a shallow pie dish with a sprinkling of very finely chopped onion and a few tbsps. of stock. Cover with a lid of shortcrust or flaky pastry, glaze with egg or milk, and bake in a hot oven (450° F., mark 8) until the pastry is browned and cooked through—20–30 minutes, according to the thickness.

As a Fricassee

Make a creamy white sauce, and add sliced cooked vegetables and diced corned beef. Heat through, then serve garnished with croûtons of fried bread, bacon rolls and chopped parsley.

As a Curry

Make a good curry sauce and strain over diced corned beef. Reheat, without boiling, and serve with dry boiled rice.

Au Gratin

Dice the corned beef, lay it in an au gratin dish and warm in the oven. Cover with a creamy white sauce, sprinkle with breadcrumbs and grated cheese, and brown under the grill.

Fritters

Cut the corned beef neatly in slices, dip in coating batter and fry in hot fat. Serve with a piquant sauce.

As a Risotto

Add diced corned beef to some risotto, when the rice is nearly cooked. Before dishing, mix the meat in lightly with a fork or skewer.

In Scrambled Egg

Diced corned beef added to scrambled egg turns it into a rather more substantial snack.

In Réchauffés

Include left-overs of corned beef in shepherd's pie, mince, hash and other meat réchauffés.

CORNED BEEF HASH

$\frac{1}{2}$ lb. corned beef	Pepper and salt
2 lb. cooked potatoes	Piquant table sauce
1 onion	Parsley
2 oz. dripping	

Cut the corned beef into small cubes, mash the cooked potatoes, and chop or slice the prepared onion very thinly. Heat the dripping in the frying pan and fry the onion until golden-brown. Add the meat and potatoes, season with pepper, salt and table sauce. Mix well, then smooth out the mixture, and cook very slowly until piping hot and nicely browned underneath —about $\frac{1}{2}$ hour. Turn on to a hot dish, browned side uppermost, garnish with parsley and serve immediately.

VEAL

Veal is the flesh of young calves. The lean should be very pale in colour and what little fat there is should be perfectly white.

The best joints for roasting are the top of the leg (called the fillet), the loin, and the best end of the neck. The shoulder of veal is next in quality for roasting, and then the breast. The other parts of veal, which are not suitable for roasting, make excellent stews and pies. The top of the leg or fillet, if sliced, is very good egg-and-crumbed and fried (see Escalopes of Veal). The loin and best end can be cut into chops or cutlets, and fried, grilled, braised and so on.

As veal is deficient in fat, it is usually combined with bacon or ham, which may be either cooked with it (as in Veal and Ham Pie), or served as a garnish of bacon rolls (as in Veal Fricassee).

Roasting Veal

Veal joints are usually stuffed with veal forcemeat, and may be covered with strips of bacon while roasting; bacon rolls may be served as a garnish. Veal is always served well done and accompanied with a thick gravy. For details of roasting meat and making gravy, see the beginning of this chapter.

CUTS OF VEAL AND HOW TO TREAT THEM

Shoulder (bladebone)	Roast or stew
Loin	Roast
Loin (when cut into chops)	Fry or grill
Neck (scrag)	Stew
Best end of neck	Roast
Best end of neck (when cut into cutlets)	Fry or grill
Fillet (i.e., top of leg) in the piece	Roast
Fillet (i.e., top of leg) if sliced	Fry or fricassee
Knuckle	Stew or boil
Breast	Stew or braise
Breast (if boned, stuffed and rolled)	Roast, stew or braise

BLANQUETTE OF VEAL

1 lb. veal (neatly cut up)	2 egg yolks
2 onions	2 tbsps. cream
A bouquet garni	Juice of 1 lemon
White stock or water	Chopped ham, lemon and parsley to garnish
$2\frac{1}{2}$ oz. butter	
2 oz. flour	

Put the veal, onions and herbs in a stewpan with enough white stock or water to cover.

Simmer very gently until tender—1½ hours. Strain and keep the meat hot. Make a sauce with the butter, flour and 1 pint of the stock. Cook well, then add the egg yolks, beaten with cream and lemon juice, and reheat carefully, but do not re-boil. Pour over the veal and garnish with chopped ham, lemon fans and chopped parsley.

BRAISED VEAL

1 lb. fillet or loin of veal	A small bouquet of herbs
6 oz. bacon	A little lemon juice
1 carrot	Pepper and salt
1 turnip	½ pint veal stock or water
1 onion	Mashed potatoes
3 stalks of celery	Green peas
1 oz. butter	

Cut the veal into fillets or cutlets and lay a small piece of bacon on each. Prepare the vegetables, cut into quarters and steam them in the butter. Add the bouquet of herbs, the lemon juice and seasoning, and just cover with stock or water. Place the fillets on top of the vegetables, cover with greased paper and the pan lid and braise for 30 minutes, basting occasionally. Remove the fillets and keep hot. Strain the stock, then return it to the pan and boil rapidly until it is reduced considerably. Dish the fillets on a border of mashed potatoes, pour over the reduced stock and serve with the green peas in the centre of the dish.

BREAST OF VEAL STUFFED AND ROASTED

3–4 lb. breast of veal	A little flour
Lemon juice	Dripping
Seasoning	Brown or tomato sauce

For the Stuffing

1 large cupful bread-crumbs	1 tbsp. parsley
	Grated rind of ½ lemon
4 tbsps. chopped suet	Seasoning
4 tbsps. cooked and chopped ham	1 egg yolk and milk

Wipe the veal on both sides with a cloth wrung out of cold water, and then with a sharp-pointed knife remove all the bones and gristle. Spread the meat out with the skin side underneath and trim it into an oblong shape, laying the trimmings on the part that is thinnest. Rub all over with lemon juice and season with pepper and salt.

Then prepare the stuffing: Mix together in a basin the breadcrumbs, suet, ham, parlsey and the grated rind of ½ lemon. Season with pepper and salt and moisten with the egg yolk and a little milk. Lay this stuffing in the centre of the veal, make into a neat roll, and sew up with a needle and fine string. Flour the roll on all sides, put it in a roasting tin with some good dripping, and roast it for about 1½ hours, basting it frequently with the fat. When ready, place on a hot dish, remove the string, and pour brown or tomato sauce round. A piece of boiled ham and baked tomatoes or green peas would be good accompaniments.

BREAST OF VEAL STEWED

1½ lb. breast of veal	½–1 pint coating sauce (made with half milk and half veal liquor, with the addition of 1–2 tbsps. finely chopped parsley)
2 oz. veal forcemeat	
Salt	
1 onion	
1 carrot	
A piece of turnip	
Bacon rolls	Rounds of cooked carrot

Wipe the veal, bone the meat and stuff with the forcemeat, roll and fasten into shape with small skewers and sew where necessary. Put into a pan with the bones, barely cover it with cold water and add salt. Bring to boiling point, skim well and add the prepared vegetables, in large dice. Stew gently for 2 hours with the bones. Place the meat on a hot dish and coat it with the parsley sauce. Garnish with neat pieces of carrot and bacon rolls.

FRICASSEE OF VEAL (WITH RAW VEAL)

1 lb. uncooked stewing veal	4 peppercorns
	A small blade of mace
1 onion	A strip of lemon rind
1 piece of turnip	White stock or water
1–2 carrots	Salt and pepper
1–2 stalks of celery	Bacon rolls and parsley to garnish
A bunch of herbs	
1 clove	

For the Sauce

1 pint veal stock	Juice of ½ lemon
2 oz. butter	1 egg yolk
2 oz. flour	2–3 tbsps. cream

Cut the meat into cubes, removing any skin or gristle. Prepare and slice the vegetables or cut into dice. Put the meat and vegetables into a stewpan, together with the bag of herbs and spices (tied in muslin), and just cover with hot white stock or water. Add salt, put on the lid and simmer very gently until the meat is tender, about 1½ hours. Turn into a bowl, strain off the stock and measure 1 pint, making it up to this amount with milk if necessary. Melt the butter in the saucepan, stir in the flour to make a roux and gradually add the veal liquor, stirring

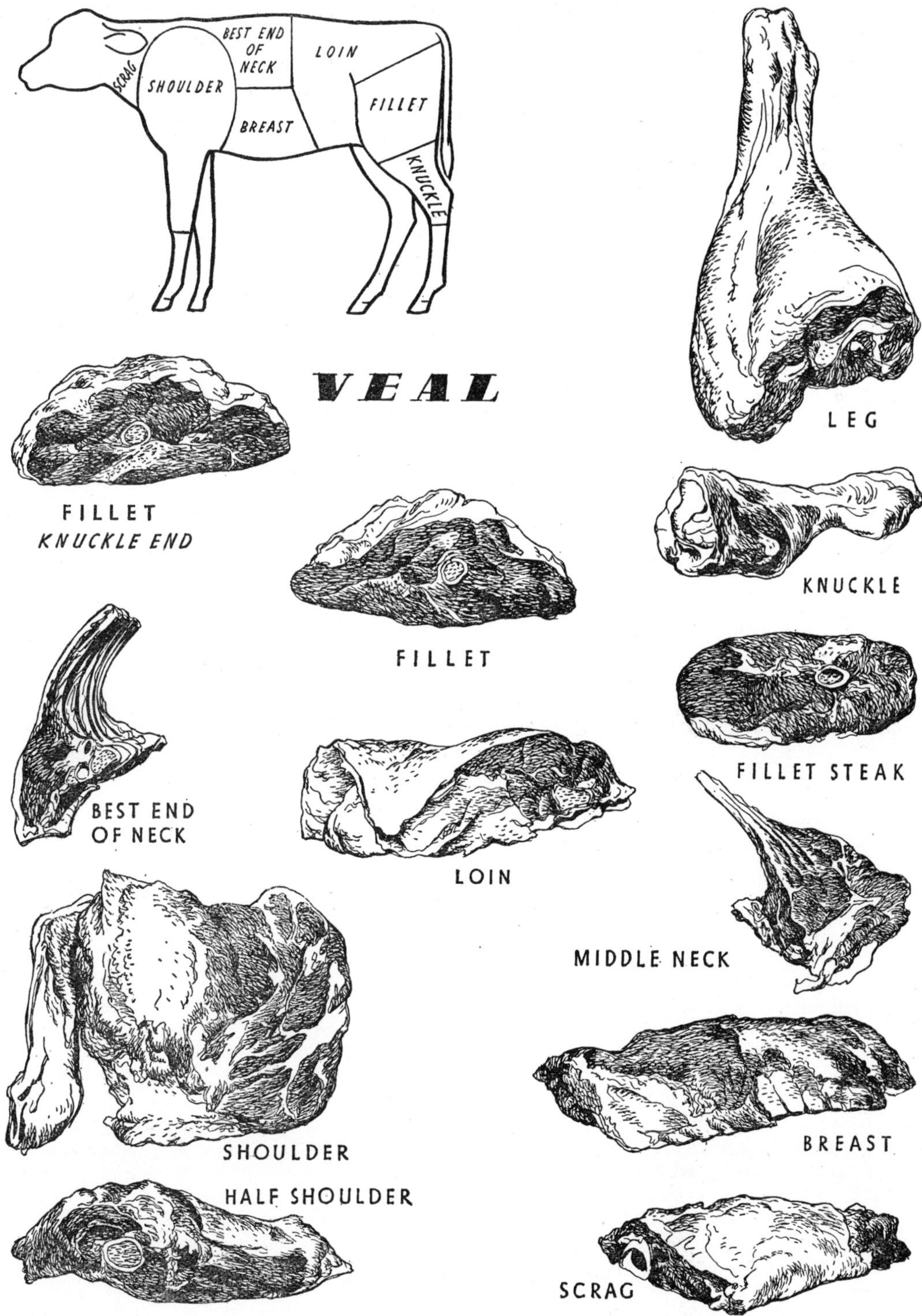
SCRAG
SHOULDER
BEST END OF NECK
LOIN
BREAST
FILLET
KNUCKLE
VEAL
LEG
FILLET
KNUCKLE END
FILLET
KNUCKLE
FILLET STEAK
BEST END OF NECK
LOIN
MIDDLE NECK
SHOULDER
BREAST
HALF SHOULDER
SCRAG

thoroughly. Bring to the boil and cook for 2–3 minutes. Add salt and pepper if necessary, then remove from the heat and stir in the lemon juice and the egg yolk, beaten with the cream. Reheat carefully without allowing the mixture to boil. Replace the meat and vegetables, and when hot through arrange on a hot dish and pour the sauce over. Garnish with bacon rolls and a little chopped parsley.

FRICASSEE OF VEAL (WITH COOKED MEAT)

¾ lb. cooked veal	1 tbsp. parsley
1 oz. butter	1–2 egg yolks
1 oz. flour	A squeeze of lemon juice
½ pint veal stock	Bacon rolls, croûtons and baked tomatoes to garnish
Seasoning	
A pinch of nutmeg	

This is a very good way of using up the remains of cooked veal. Remove all skin and gristle and cut the meat into small, neat pieces. Make a sauce with the butter, flour and stock, and season it with white pepper, salt and a pinch of nutmeg. Put in the veal and let it warm through, but without boiling. Just before serving, stir in the parsley, finely chopped, and the egg yolk, beaten with a little lemon juice. Serve in a hot dish and garnish with rolls of bacon, croûtons of toast or pastry, and, if liked, a few small, baked tomatoes. A few button mushrooms, cut in halves, or some cooked green peas, may be added to the fricassee to give flavour.

GALANTINE OF VEAL

3 lb. breast of veal	¼ lb. cooked ham or tongue
Carrot, turnip and onion	3 hard-boiled eggs
Lemon	Glaze
Seasoning	Parsley or salad to garnish
1 lb. pork sausage-meat	

Remove the bones and gristle from the veal and trim away any parts that are not eatable. Wash and break up the bones, and put them into a large saucepan or fish-kettle with cold water to cover them, and a small quantity of cut-up vegetables. Let these cook while you are preparing the meat. Wipe it first on both sides with a damp cloth, and rub it over with a cut lemon. Sprinkle it with white pepper, salt and a little grated lemon rind. Then spread over the sausage-meat in an even layer and lay on the ham, cut in very thin slices. Place the 3 eggs in a row across the centre, and roll up. Sew together with a needle and fine string; then wrap in a pudding cloth, tying the galantine at both ends in the form of a bolster. Place it in the saucepan with the bones and vegetables, and simmer slowly for 3 hours, or until tender. Then press it until cold between two tins or dishes with a weight (about 4 lb.) on the top. Next day, remove the cloth, draw out the string, and brush over the top and sides with liquid glaze. When dry, garnish with parsley or salad.

JELLIED VEAL AND HAM

1 lb. fleshy veal	Chopped parsley
6 oz. fat ham or bacon	2 hard-boiled eggs
	Some jelly stock
Seasoning	Parsley or green salad to garnish
½ a lemon	

This makes a very good cold dish for luncheon or supper. Wipe the veal with a damp cloth, remove all skin and bone, then weigh it and cut it in small pieces. Trim the ham and cut that also in small pieces. Mix together and season with pepper, salt, grated lemon rind and juice, and a little chopped parsley. Cut the eggs in slices, use some of the pieces for decorating a plain mould, and mix the remainder with the meat, etc. Fill up the mould with the meat mixture, melt the stock and pour it over. (Should the stock used not be sufficiently stiff, melt a little gelatine in it.) Cover with greased paper and bake in a slow oven (325° F., mark 2) about 2 hours, or until the veal feels tender when tested with a skewer. If necessary, fill the mould up with more stock and set it aside to cool and stiffen. Turn out of the mould when required and serve garnished with parsley or some green salad.

STEWED KNUCKLE OF VEAL

3 lb. knuckle of veal	A small piece of turnip
1 onion	Sprigs of thyme and parsley
1 carrot	
1 stalk of celery	Salt and pepper

For the Sauce

2 oz. butter	¾ pint veal liquor from the knuckle
2 oz. flour	
¼ pint milk	A little chopped parsley

Have the knuckle cut up into convenient-sized pieces and put it into a pan with just enough boiling water to cover. Boil gently for 2–3 minutes, removing any scum that rises, then add the cut-up vegetables, the herbs and seasoning, cover and simmer gently until the meat is tender —2–3 hours. A few minutes before serving, make a sauce with the butter, flour, milk and the liquor from the knuckle, season well and add some chopped parsley. Lift the knuckle from the pan, drain well and place on a hot dish. Coat with the sauce and garnish with the cooked carrot.

Note : The remainder of the liquor from the knuckle should be reserved for making soup, etc.

VEAL CAKE

1 hard-boiled egg	6 oz. lean cooked ham
Pepper and salt	1 tsp. gelatine
½ tsp. grated lemon rind	A little stock
1 tsp. chopped parsley	Parsley
¾ lb. lean veal	

Slice the egg and decorate the bottom of a plain, round mould or tin with some of the slices. Mix the pepper, salt, grated lemon rind and parsley together. Cut the veal into small pieces of equal size, about ½ inch square, and cut the ham into thin slices. Arrange the veal, ham and the rest of the sliced egg in layers, sprinkling each with the mixed seasoning. Add the gelatine to just sufficient stock to cover the meat. Pour over the meat, cover with a piece of greased paper, and cook in a slow oven (325° F., mark 2) for 2½ hours. If the stock has evaporated, fill up the mould at once with more stock to which a little gelatine has been added. Place a plate on top and weight down. When cold, turn out and garnish with a little parsley.

VEAL CUTLETS (OR ESCALOPES)

1 lb. fillet of veal	½ pint brown or tomato sauce
Lemon	Rolls of bacon or green peas to garnish
Seasoning	2 oz. butter or dripping
Egg and breadcrumbs to coat escalopes	
Mashed potatoes	

The meat should be cut in slices about ¼ inch in thickness. Trim it and cut it in neat rounds or oval-shaped pieces, beating it out if too thick in parts. Rub each piece over with a cut lemon and sprinkle lightly with pepper and salt. Then egg-and-breadcrumb the cutlets, pressing the crumbs well on with a broad-bladed knife, and re-shaping the cutlets neatly in a board. Lay them on a tin or dish, with a double fold of kitchen paper under them, and let them rest for a short time to dry.

Meanwhile, prepare ½ pint of brown or tomato sauce and some nicely mashed potatoes. Also, make ready a few little rolls of thinly sliced bacon, fix these on a skewer, and cook them in the oven or under the grill for a few minutes.

To cook the cutlets, melt the fat in a frying pan. When smoking hot, place in the cutlets. Fry them rather slowly, first on one side and then on the other, until they are well browned. Allow from 10–12 minutes for the cooking, as veal must not be underdone; lift out and drain on paper. Arrange mashed potato in a circle on a hot dish, and place the cutlets along the top, one leaning against the other. Fill up the centre with the rolls of bacon, or with nicely cooked peas if preferred, and pour the sauce round. Serve cut lemon separately.

MINCED VEAL WITH SPINACH

Left-over cooked veal (½–¾ lb.)	Salt and pepper
1 oz. butter	1–2 tbsps. cream
2 tbsps. flour	Freshly cooked spinach
¼ pint stock or gravy	Sippets of toast
¼ pint milk	Bacon rolls

Mince the veal finely, removing any skin or gristle. Melt the butter and add the flour, then stir in the liquid by degrees and bring to the boil, stirring; cook 2 or 3 minutes, then remove from the heat and stir in the veal. Season with salt and pepper and make thoroughly hot. Just before serving, stir in the cream. Arrange the spinach round a hot dish, pour the veal in the centre and garnish with sippets of toast and bacon rolls.

STEAMED VEAL AND CAULIFLOWER

Choose a nice fleshy piece of veal about 2–2½ lb. in weight. Wipe it carefully with a damp cloth and tie it in shape with string, or wrap it in a piece of muslin, if necessary. Prepare some vegetables—about a cupful each of carrot, turnip, onion and celery cut in slices—and put them into a stewpan. Barely cover with cold water, bring to the boil, and lay the veal on the top. The meat must not sink into the liquid, but be cooked with the steam only. Cover it with greased paper, put on a tight-fitting lid, and cook slowly by the side of the stove until tender: about 2 hours should be allowed. When required, lift the veal on to a hot dish, remove the fastening, and coat with tomato sauce. Garnish with cauliflower. and serve mashed potatoes separately.

MUTTON AND LAMB

The flesh of mutton and lamb should be light red in colour and firm in texture. The fat should be white and firm and there should be a fair proportion, though not an excessive amount.

Most joints of lamb or mutton may be roasted, the most suitable being leg, shoulder, loin and best end of neck. Middle neck and scrag end of the neck are suitable only for stewing, braising and casseroles. The breast (boned, stuffed and rolled) may also be roasted, but is more usually stewed or braised. Saddle of mutton or lamb, which is perhaps the choicest joint for roasting, consists of the whole of the back, from the beginning of the best end of the neck to the end of the loin.

Roast mutton and lamb are not served underdone, but at the same time care should be taken not to overcook them, or the flesh will be dry. The accompaniments for roast lamb are mint sauce or mint jelly, and for mutton red-currant jelly and onion sauce. Joints of mutton, such as shoulder, leg or loin, are sometimes boned and stuffed, in which case sage and onion stuffing is generally used, though veal forcemeat is also suitable.

A thickened brown gravy is served with roast lamb and mutton.

Chops and cutlets are the only suitable joints of mutton and lamb for grilling and frying. The chops come from the loin and the cutlets from the best end of the neck.

CUTS OF MUTTON OR LAMB AND HOW TO TREAT THEM

Scrag end of neck	Stew or braise
Middle neck	Stew or braise
Best end of neck—in the piece	Roast or braise
Best end of neck—when cut into cutlets	Fry or grill
Loin—in the piece	Roast
Loin—cut into chops	Fry or grill
Leg	Roast or boil
Shoulder	Roast—can be boned and stuffed
Breast	Stew
Breast—if boned	Can be stuffed and roasted, or braised
Sheep's head	Stew or broth
Trotters	Stew

BOILED LEG OF MUTTON AND CAPER SAUCE

½ leg of mutton	4 carrots, turnips and onions of medium size
Boiling water	
Salt and pepper	Caper sauce

Wipe the meat. Have ready sufficient fast-boiling water to cover completely the joint to be cooked. Place the joint in this, and when the water again reaches boiling point, allow it to boil foı a few minutes. Then add sufficient salt and pepper to flavour, and the vegetables cut into quarters. Allow to simmer gently until the joint is cooked: the normal time to allow is 20 minutes to the lb. and 20 minutes over. When cooking is almost complete, prepare the caper sauce, using the liquid from the pot. Serve the meat on a hot dish, put the vegetables round and pour over the caper sauce.

Neck of mutton may be treated in the same way.

BRAISED LAMB CUTLETS AND GREEN PEAS

1 onion	1 lump sugar
4 lamb cutlets	A little water
2–3 young turnips	1 cupful green peas
Seasoning	Chopped parsley

Slice the onion very thinly and put it into an earthenware casserole. Wipe and trim the cutlets and lay them on the top. Add the turnips, cut in dice, the seasoning and sugar. Pour in water, nearly covering the contents, put the lid on, and stew very gently for ¼ hour. Then add the peas, freshly shelled, and cook for 20–30 minutes longer. Serve very hot with a little finely-chopped parsley sprinkled over the top.

Note: Mutton cutlets or a piece of fillet of veal could be cooked in the same way, allowing rather longer time. The cooking may be done either in the oven or on top of the stove. The vegetables may be varied, and young carrots, tomato, French beans, shredded celery, etc., used instead of green peas.

GOLDEN STEW OF MUTTON

1 lb. breast of mutton	A piece of bay leaf
1½ oz. flour	½ tsp. thyme
1 tsp. curry powder	2 peppercorns
1 onion or leek	Salt
1 cupful diced celery	1½ lb. potatoes
¾ pint stock or water	

Wipe the meat and cut into neat pieces, removing the excess fat. Mix the flour and curry powder and toss the meat in this. Cut up some of the fatty pieces, put in a saucepan and heat gently to extract the fat. When melted and smoking hot, add half the meat and fry until browned on all sides, remove from the pan and brown the remaining meat. Add the onion cut in slices, the celery and the excess flour and curry powder, and fry together for several minutes. Stir in the liquid and bring to the boil. Add the herbs tied (in muslin), salt and meat, cover and simmer gently until the meat is nearly

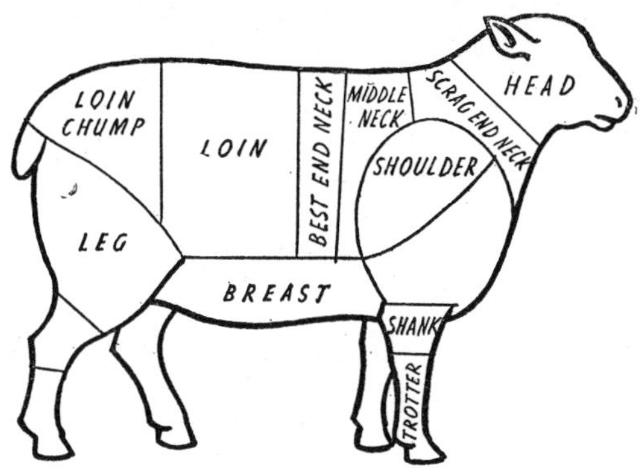

SHOULDER

HALF SHOULDER (*Blade End*)

MUTTON

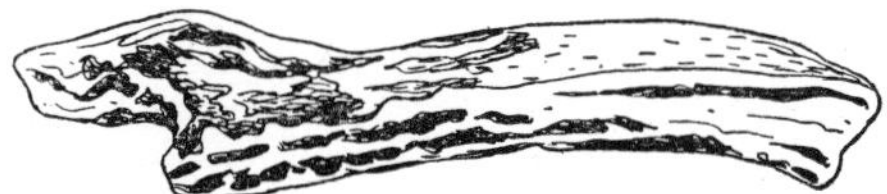
BREAST

HALF SHOULDER (*Knuckle End*)

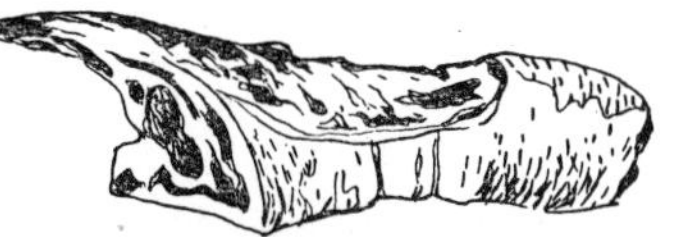
SCRAG END OF NECK

BEST END OF NECK

CUTLET

LEG

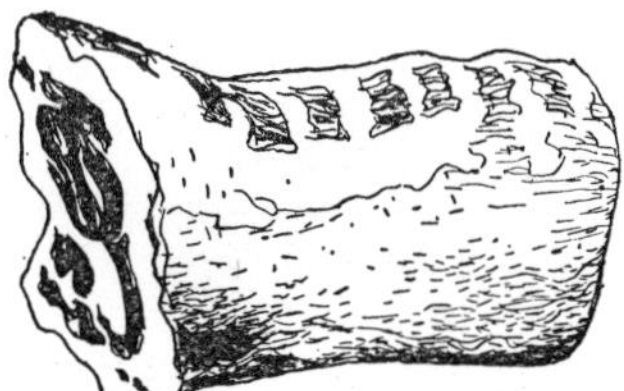
LOIN

HALF LEG (*Fillet End*)

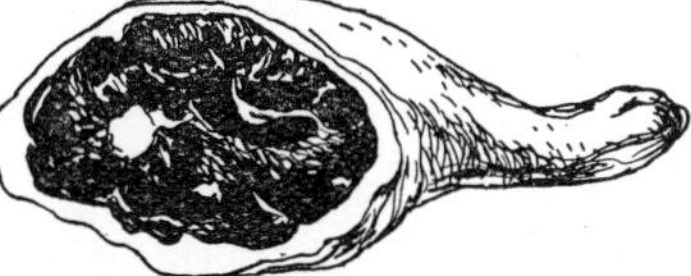
HALF LEG (*Knuckle End*)

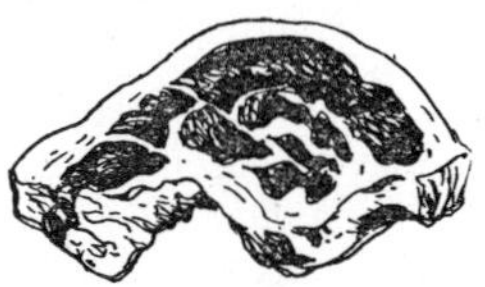
CHOP

HIND QUARTER

tender—1½–2 hours. Remove the herbs and add 5–6 medium-sized potatoes cut in half. Simmer for a further ¾–1 hour, or until the potatoes are tender. Reseason if necessary and serve hot.

GRILLED LAMB OR MUTTON CHOPS

(*See colour picture facing page* 129.)

Remove the skin and trim off some of the fat from the chops, wipe them with a damp cloth, then brush over with salad oil or butter. Heat and grease the grill, place the chops in position over a clear, bright fire or under a glowing red gas or electric grill. Cook on one side for about 2–3 minutes, until the outside is browned, then turn and cook on the other side. Continue to cook, turning frequently, until the meat is just cooked through—8–10 minutes. Use two spoons or tongs for turning, to obviate piercing the meat. Place the chops on a hot dish, with fried potatoes arranged around. This dish is much improved if a small pat of maître d'hôtel butter is placed on each chop.

HARICOT MUTTON

1½ lb. best end neck of mutton
2 onions
1–2 carrots
½ a turnip
2 tbsps. flour
1 pint stock or water
Salt and pepper
A little ketchup or sharp sauce

Have the meat chined and divide it into cutlets. Trim off some of the fat and put the trimmings into a pan over gentle heat to extract the fat, then fry the mutton lightly in it. When lightly browned on both sides, remove the meat and sauté the cut-up vegetables for a few moments. Sprinkle in the flour, then add the stock gradually and bring to the boil, stirring. Season with salt and pepper. Put the meat and vegetables in a casserole or stewpan, pour the gravy over, cover and simmer gently until tender —1½–2 hours. When cooked, arrange the meat and vegetables in a deep dish, carefully skim all the fat from the top of the gravy, reseason if necessary, and add a little ketchup or sharp sauce, then pour over the meat. If liked, the dish may be garnished with diced vegetables that have been cooked separately, or with cooked haricot beans tossed in chopped parsley.

IRISH STEW

1 lb. middle neck of mutton
2 lb. potatoes
2 large onions
Salt and pepper
Chopped parsley

Prepare the meat by wiping thoroughly, removing the marrow and cutting into neat joints. Cut the potatoes and onions into rings and place alternate layers of the vegetables and meat in a pan, finishing with a layer of potatoes. Add salt and pepper, and sufficient water to half-cover. Bring to the boil and simmer gently for about 2 hours, or until the meat and potatoes are tender.

Pile the meat, gravy and some of the potatoes in the centre of a hot dish. Place the rest of the potatoes at either end of the dish and sprinkle a little chopped parsley over them.

MUTTON AND LAMB CUTLETS, FRIED

Buy small, lean cutlets cut from the best end of the neck, remove the skin and any unnecessary fat, and scrape the bone for at least 1 inch, giving the cutlets a good shape and a neat appearance. Prepare some breadcrumbs. Beat an egg on a plate. Season each cutlet, brush over with egg and cover it with crumbs. Wipe all crumbs off the exposed bone and fry the cutlets in smoking-hot fat for 10 minutes, turning them once or twice. When golden-brown, drain on soft paper and dish with a cutlet frill on the end of each cutlet. Brown or tomato sauce should be poured round and the dish garnished with green peas or young carrots.

SPICED LAMB ROLL

1 breast of lamb
1 pint of water (or more)
1 onion
Salt and pepper
2 cloves
6 peppercorns
A blade of mace
A pinch of mixed herbs
Bay leaf

With a sharp knife cut out all the bones from both pieces of breast. Put these bones in a pan with the water, onion, seasonings and spices (tied in muslin), cover and bring to the boil. Meanwhile, skin the breasts and cut away any excess fat from the thicker ends (rendering it down for dripping). Lay the breasts on a board, flatten them, roll up as evenly as possible, and tie with a fine string, like a parcel. Add them to the pan, season and simmer until tender—2 hours or longer, according to the coarseness of the meat.

There are several ways of serving this dish :—

One way is to take the meat (removing the string) and tie in a pudding cloth, then squeeze well to remove the excess fat. Press, and when cold remove the cloth and serve, garnished with parsley and accompanied by vegetables or a good salad.

A second way is to pack the meat into a cake tin or tongue glass (first removing the string), cover with a saucer and weight down. When cold, turn out, garnish with parsley or watercress, and serve with vegetables or a salad.

If a hot dish is required, make a piquant white sauce, using some of the stock in which the meat was cooked and some milk. The stock will be fatty, so skim it well before using it (the fat skimmed off will be useful for dripping). Season the sauce with salt and pepper, and flavour with vinegar and lemon juice. Cut the rolled breast neatly in slices ½ inch thick, coat with the sauce, garnish with chopped parsley, and serve at once.

PILAU OF MUTTON

1–1½ lb. mutton	A pinch of ground cloves
1½ pints light stock	Salt
3 oz. rice	1–2 oz. butter
A pinch of ground cinnamon	1–2 tomatoes

Choose a piece from the loin or neck of mutton, wipe it carefully and trim off the fat. Put the meat into a saucepan with the stock and stew it until tender, then lift it out and put it to one side. Wash the rice in several waters, and sprinkle it into the stock in which the mutton was cooked, add the spices and salt, and let it simmer very slowly till the rice is cooked and the liquid absorbed. Add the butter in small pieces, allowing it to soak into the rice. Brown the meat in the oven, or, if preferred, cut it in pieces and fry it brown in a little of the butter. Serve it embedded in the rice and garnish with small pieces of baked tomato.

There are many different ways of preparing a pilau: the kind of meat may be varied, and also the garnish and seasoning. Seeded raisins or sultanas are sometimes added to the rice, and fried onions, hard-boiled eggs or forcemeat balls might be used as a garnish.

ROAST CROWN OF MUTTON

Buy two pieces of the best end of the neck, each with six or seven cutlets (and taken if possible from the opposite sides of the animal, though this is not essential). They should be chopped—not chined—and sliced between the bones to about half-way down, the ends of the bones being scraped clean. Trim neatly and bend round to form a crown, securing it with skewers and string. Stuff the centre with sausage-meat or sage and onion stuffing, and twist some pieces of buttered paper round each of the exposed bones, to prevent them burning.

Roast in the usual way (allowing 25 minutes to the lb. and 25 minutes over), and before dishing decorate with potato balls stuck on to the ends of the bones to form "jewels." Serve with gravy made from the dripping and roast potatoes. A little red-currant or other sharp jelly goes very well with it. If onions have not been used in the stuffing, a little onion sauce will be a pleasant addition.

STUFFED BREAST OF MUTTON OR LAMB

1 breast of mutton or lamb

For the Stuffing

4 oz. breadcrumbs	½ tsp. grated lemon rind
2 tsps. chopped parsley	Salt and pepper
A good pinch of mixed herbs	Beaten egg and milk

For the Sauce

1 oz. butter	3 tsps. finely chopped parsley
1 oz. flour	1 tsp. lemon juice
½ pint milk or milk and stock	1 tsp. vinegar
Salt and pepper	

Bone the breast of mutton or lamb (or ask your butcher to do this for you), and trim off any excess fat. Reserve the bones for making fresh vegetable broth or other soup, and the fat to render down for dripping.

To make the stuffing, mix together all the dry ingredients, season well and moisten with beaten

Stuffed Breast of Lamb

34

egg and milk. Spread the stuffing on the breast, roll up neatly and tie with fine string. Wrap in greaseproof paper and steam for 2½–3 hours, About ¾–1 hour before it is cooked, vegetables such as carrots, turnips, etc., to serve with it, also potatoes, may be placed in the steamer to cook.

To make the sauce, melt the fat, stir in the flour and add the milk or milk and stock by degrees. Bring to the boil, stirring, and cook for 2–3 minutes, beating well with a wooden spoon, then season with salt and pepper, and lastly, add the finely chopped parsley, the lemon juice and vinegar.

Dish the meat on a hot dish, removing the string, coat with the sauce, and serve with the vegetables.

SUMMER STEW

- 1 lb. middle neck of mutton
- ½ lb. small turnips
- ½ a bunch of young carrots
- 2 onions
- 1 lb. peas
- Salt and pepper
- 1 lb. small new potatoes
- 2 tbsps. chopped mint
- 2 tbsps. chopped parsley

Wipe the meat, remove the narrow and cut the mutton into neat pieces. Prepare the vegetables, leaving them whole.

Place the meat, turnips, carrots and onions in a saucepan, and barely cover with water. Add seasoning, bring to the boil, and simmer gently for ½–¾ hour. Add the potatoes, peas, mint and parsley and continue simmering for a further hour, or until the meat and vegetables are tender. Taste, and reseason if necessary. Turn into a hot dish and serve immediately.

PORK

In the past, pork was considered out of season in the summer. With modern cold storage methods, however, pork is now sold at any time of the year, but being very rich, it is not really acceptable in the hot weather.

Pork should never be served in the least underdone but always very thoroughly cooked. To counteract the richness of the fat, something sweet and tart is usually served with pork: apple sauce with roast pork or pork chops; sweet chutney with cold pickled pork or cold roast pork, and tomatoes, prunes, apples, etc., in casserole of pork, and so on.

Suitable joints of pork for roasting are leg, shoulder (blade-bone), loin and spare rib. Usual accompaniments are apple sauce, sage and onion stuffing, and thickened brown gravy. If there is no place in the joint for the stuffing, it is baked separately in a fireproof dish.

Belly of pork, which is always rather fat, is usually pickled, and when boiled is very good as an accompaniment for meat lacking in fat, such as veal or chicken, and is excellent cold with chutney, salad, and so on.

"Pork pieces" and joints not suitable for roasting can be braised, casseroled, or made into pork pie.

Pork chops may be grilled, fried, or stuffed and baked. They may also be braised

CUTS OF PORK AND HOW TO TREAT THEM

Leg	Roast
Shoulder (blade-bone)	Roast
Loin—in the piece	Roast
Loin—when cut into chops	Fry, grill, or bake
Spare rib	Roast
Belly (usually pickled)	Boil or stew
Hand (usually salted)	Boil
Pork pieces	Pork pie or stew

BAKED STUFFED PORK CHOPS

Flatten the chops and trim them if necessary, lay them on a baking dish and cover the lean part of each chop with a layer of sage and onion stuffing. Cover with greased paper and bake in a moderately hot oven (400° F., mark 6) until the lean is well cooked and the fat crisp and brown—about ½ hour. Serve with baked tomatoes and apple sauce.

BOSTON CASSEROLE (PORK AND BEANS)

- 6 oz. haricot beans
- ¾–1 lb. salt pork
- 2 stalks celery, sliced
- 1 large carrot, sliced
- 2 tbsps. sugar
- 2 tbsps. syrup or treacle
- ½ tsp. mustard
- Pepper
- Water

Soak the haricot beans overnight, then drain them. Place the pork in a casserole, surround with the beans, then add the other ingredients and enough water barely to cover. Cover with the lid and bake in a slow oven (300° F., mark 1) or about 4 hours, adding more water as and when this appears necessary. About an hour before the casserole is ready to be served, remove the lid and bring the piece of pork above the surface of the other ingredients. Return to the oven and continue cooking for a further hour, until the pork is crisped on the outside, then serve at once.

Note: The celery and carrot can be omitted if preferred.

CASSEROLE OF PORK

- 1½ lb. loin of pork
- 1 oz. dripping
- 2 small onions
- ¾ lb. apples
- 1 oz. flour
- ¾ pint stock
- Pepper and salt
- A little made mustard
- 4 cloves

Divide the meat into chops. Melt the dripping in a frying pan; peel and slice the onions and apples to form rings, and fry until golden-brown. Remove the onions and apples and fry the chops. Remove them from the pan and stir in the flour, adding a little more dripping

Steak and Mushroom I

if necessary. Cook the flour until it is nicely browned, stir in the stock, bring to boiling point, and add the seasonings. Place the chops in a casserole, cover with the fried apples and onions and pour on the prepared gravy. Cover with a lid and cook in a slow oven (325° F., mark 2) for about 1½ hours.

FILLETS OF PORK AND TOMATOES

1 lb. sharp apples	4 tomatoes
Sugar if necessary	1 lb. fillet of pork
1½ oz. butter	Pepper and salt

Peel and core the apples and put into a saucepan. Add 2 tbsps. water and cook until tender; then beat until creamy, adding a little sugar if the apples are very sour. Lastly, add a small piece of butter, about the size of a hazelnut. Meanwhile, choose 4 very firm tomatoes of equal size, and dip for a moment into boiling water: this allows the skins to be removed easily. Cut into slices ¼ inch thick. Place on a greased baking sheet and cook for 15–20 minutes in a moderate oven (350° F., mark 4). Cut the pork into neat rounds about ¾ inch thick. Season with pepper and salt, and fry in a little butter, turning them from side to side to ensure thorough cooking. Arrange the fillets around the dish, placing a slice of tomato on top of each fillet and the apple purée in the centre.

FRIED PORK CHOPS

If the meat is really young and tender, this is a very satisfactory way of cooking pork chops. Fry them slowly in plenty of fat, either butter or good lard, until well cooked—15–20 minutes, turning them frequently while cooking. Serve with fried onions and apple sauce. Alternatively, they may first be egg-and-breadcrumbed, then fried and served with tomato sauce.

BRAISED PORK CHOPS WITH APPLES

Put 4 thick pork chops in a lightly greased casserole, brown on both sides, then sprinkle with salt, 1 oz. washed sultanas and 1 tsp. chopped sage. Arrange 2 cored and sliced apples on top, add ½ pint water, and cook in a moderate oven (350° F., mark 4) for ¾–1 hour, or until chops are tender.

FRIKADELLER (DANISH)

¾–1 lb. fresh pork	Fat for frying
2 tbsps. flour	Purée of potatoes or spinach
1 egg	Brown or tomato sauce
A little milk	Dressed cucumber, etc.
Seasoning	

A piece of lean pork should be chosen. Cut it in small pieces, and then pass it through the mincing machine two or three times—more if you like. Put the mince into a basin with the flour, beaten egg, a little milk and seasoning to taste. The mixture should be of a consistency that will keep its shape in a spoon. Cover the basin and let it stand for 1–2 hours or until it is time to do the cooking. Melt some fat in a shallow pan, and when smoking hot drop in the pork mixture in spoonfuls, keeping it as much in the shape of the spoon as possible. Fry until brown on all sides and well cooked. Drain free from fat, and dish up on a purée of potatoes or spinach. Serve with a good brown or tomato sauce, also with dressed cucumber or beetroot, or some pickled damsons or peaches.

ROAST CROWN OF PORK

Six ribs from each side of a loin of pork are required for this handsome dish, and each rib should be trimmed in the same way that a cutlet is prepared, only they must not be separated. The sections of meat are turned, so that the bones are on the outside, and fastened together in a circle with a piece of string or tape.

Place some veal forcemeat in the centre of the meat, and cover the ends of the bones with greased paper cones, to prevent their browning too quickly. The joint is now ready for cooking. Roast in a moderately hot oven (400° F., mark 6), allowing 25–30 minutes to each lb. plus 25–30 minutes —2 hours will probably be required for a crown roast, perhaps a little longer if it is very meaty, because it must be well done. During the roasting, it must be basted frequently with the dripping in the pan, to which a cupful of boiling water may be added after the meat is brown. Season the meat with salt a short time before serving.

Roast Crown of Pork

A few minutes before serving, remove the paper from the rib bones and place small white onions, parboiled in slightly salted water, one on the end of each rib bone.

To accompany the pork, a piquant gravy should be made after the roast is lifted from the pan. Make a thick gravy in the usual way, season with salt, pepper and paprika, and skim carefully. Strain and stir in 2 tbsps. finely chopped pickles before serving. Finally, reheat the gravy.

rilled Lamb Chops

tuffed Roast Hearts

PORK AND PRUNE HOT-POT

¼ lb. prunes	1 oz. flour
1 lemon	Salt and pepper
1 lb. pork	½ oz. dripping.

Cover the prunes with cold water, soak for a few hours, then stew them with the rind of a lemon until tender. Strain off the juice and keep it. Remove the stones from the prunes. Wipe the pork, cut it into neat pieces, and pass these through the seasoned flour. Melt the dripping in a frying pan and fry the pork until brown. Place the pork and prunes in alternate layers in a casserole. Make some brown gravy with the remaining fat, flour and about ½ pint of the prune juice. Pour this over the pork. Add to the hot-pot the juice of the lemon. Cover with the casserole lid or greased paper and stew in a moderate oven (350° F., mark 3) for about 1 hour. Serve in the casserole.

GRILLED PORK CHOPS

Flatten the chops with a wetted rolling pin or special cutlet beater, trim and season. Brush with oil, grill quickly on both sides, then reduce the heat of the grill and cook slowly, until the chops are well cooked—15–20 minutes. Garnish with grilled mushrooms or tomatoes, or fried onions, and serve with apple sauce or brown sauce.

BACON

The fat should be firm and free from any yellow marks, the lean should be a deep pink colour, and the rind should be thin, smooth and elastic.

Bacon Rashers

The choicest for grilling or frying are the back rashers. They are easily recognised, as the fat and lean are not intermixed. Next in popularity are streaky rashers—narrow rashers with alternate streaks of lean and fat. Collar gives a wider rasher with more lean than fat, and is sometimes rather coarse for grilling and frying, but is suitable for using in pies and other made-up meat dishes. Gammon rashers have considerably more lean than fat, but are good fried or grilled. All rashers, except gammon, should be cut fairly thin for frying or grilling. Gammon rashers are usually preferred thicker.

To Prepare Bacon for Frying or Grilling

Cut off the rind thinly with a pair of scissors or a very sharp knife. Trim off any "rusty" or discoloured parts on the under edge and cut out any bones or gristle. If liked, snip the fat at intervals with the scissors to prevent the rashers curling up.

To Fry Bacon

Put it into the frying pan without added fat, except in the case of collar and gammon, which are best cooked in fat. Heat gently until the fat becomes transparent, turning the bacon frequently to ensure even cooking. When it is thoroughly cooked, lift out on to a hot dish, then use the bacon fat in the pan for frying bread, mushrooms, tomatoes, eggs or other accompaniment.

To Grill Bacon

Lay the bacon in the grill pan under a hot grill and cook until the fat loses its transparency, turning frequently. Lean bacon, such as collar or gammon, should be brushed over with fat before placing it under the grill, otherwise it tends to dry up during the cooking. Serve with grilled tomatoes, mushrooms, fried bread, and fried eggs, which can be cooked in the fat from the bacon.

To Boil Bacon

Choose bacon in the piece for boiling and soak it in tepid water for 1–2 hours: then scrape the underside as clean as possible. Put it into a saucepan of cold water and bring it gradually to the boil, removing any scum that rises. Simmer very gently, allowing 20 minutes to the lb. and 20 minutes over. When cooked, remove from the water, carefully strip off the rind and sprinkle with fine bread raspings. Serve hot with parsley sauce, young broad beans or peas, and boiled potatoes, or serve cold with salad.

BACON AND EGG PIE

8–10 oz. shortcrust pastry	1 tsp. chopped parsley
2 gammon rashers	Salt and pepper
3 eggs	

Make the pastry, cut 2 pieces and roll out each piece to fit an 8-inch pie plate. Line the plate with one piece. Prepare the filling by cutting up the bacon into small pieces, mixing it with the beaten egg and chopped parsley, with seasoning of pepper and a little salt added. (If bacon is very salt, omit the salt altogether.) Pour this filling into the lined plate, damp round the edge of the pastry and cover with the other piece. Bake in a moderately hot oven (400° F., mark 6) until nicely crisp and brown—30–40 minutes.

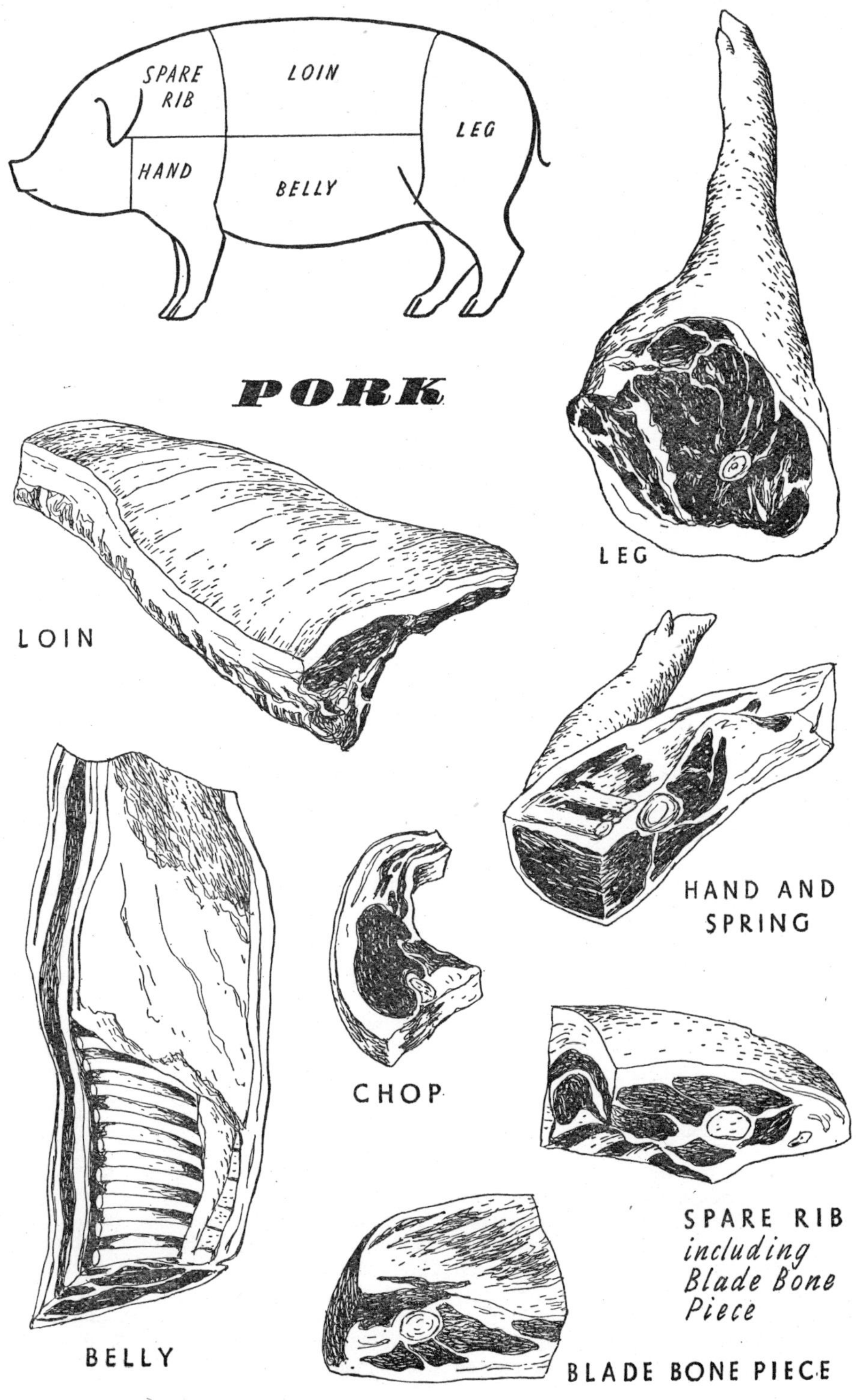
SPARE RIB
LOIN
LEG
HAND
BELLY
PORK
LEG
LOIN
HAND AND SPRING
CHOP
BELLY
SPARE RIB including Blade Bone Piece
BLADE BONE PIECE

SAVOURY BACON ROLLS

4 rashers streaky bacon | Spinach purée
4 oz. veal forcemeat

Rind and trim the rashers and cut them in half. Make the forcemeat and divide it into eight. Lay one portion of stuffing on each piece of bacon, roll up and lay side by side in a fireproof baking dish. Bake in a moderate oven (375° F., mark 5) for about 40 minutes, until the bacon is crisp and brown, turning the rolls once during the cooking to crisp undersides. Dish on a bed of spinach, garnish with baked tomatoes and serve with brown or tomato sauce.

HAM

When selecting a ham, the weight is important, and if the size of the family permits, a large ham,

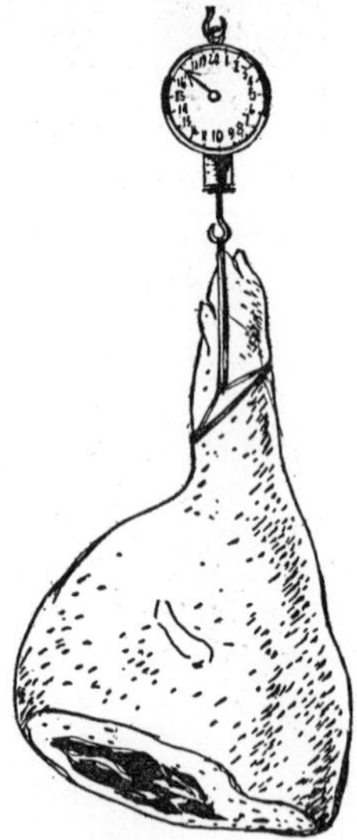

Weighing a Ham

weighing, say, 17–20 lb., should be chosen in preference to one weighing 12–14 lb., for the loss in weight during cooking is proportionately less in large than in small hams. If, however, some members of the family do not care for the fat, a small and lean ham should be selected.

The method of curing is also worthy of consideration, for hams can be disappointing with regard to flavour when cooked. If cured carelessly or not matured sufficiently long, the flavour is likely to be poor, but if well cured and properly matured, the flavour will be good, and such hams can be kept in excellent condition for many months, stored in a cool, dry, airy place.

A ham may be cooked whole, or if divided into 2 or 3 sections, each piece may be cooked by a different process, and thus greater variety is introduced. The first cut should be slanting and parallel with the shank bone : this cuts off the knuckle. The other piece can be divided into 2 joints, the cushion and the butt. It is not usual further to divide the knuckle, but if liked, slices suitable for grilling can be taken from its cut end.

York Hams

These are dry salt-cured and have general popularity, being mild-flavoured and firm in texture ; the lean is of an attractive pink colour.

Suffolk Hams

When fully mature, these hams are of characteristic sweetness (being sweet-cured), and of delicious flavour.

Wiltshire Hams

These are cured on the carcase and are more correctly termed gammon. They are mild-cured and do not therefore keep very well.

Home-Cured Hams

These vary very much according to the recipe used, but are generally mild and very delicate in flavour.

Irish Hams

These may be dry salt-cured (as in Belfast) or pickle-cured and boned before being smoked.

Danish Hams

These are usually small and mild-cured.

BOILING A HAM : FIRST METHOD

Weigh the ham and calculate the length of time for cooking, allowing for small hams, and for cuts of bacon and ham, 20 minutes to the lb. and 20 minutes over, after they have come to the boil ; for example, a ham weighing 10 lb. before soaking would require 200 plus 20 minutes, making a total of 220 minutes, or 3 hours and 40 minutes' cooking. For whole hams weighing from 12 lb. upwards, allow 15 minutes to the lb. plus 15 minutes, after boiling point is reached. Soak the ham for 12 hours in cold water, and, when ready for cooking, wash to remove the " bloom " or green mould, put into cold water and bring quickly to the boil. Then simmer slowly for the required length of time.

When cooking is completed, allow the ham to remain in the water for about 30 minutes then place it on a meat stand to drain. When almost cold, remove the brown skin, sprinkle with golden-brown breadcrumbs and place a frill round the knuckle bone.

Hams that are to be served hot as an accompaniment to roast turkey or chicken would, of course, be removed from the water immediately boiling is completed.

In large households, or when a large ham is required for a party, it is quite possible that the joint will be too large to be accommodated in an ordinary pan. A clothes boiler or gas copper can be utilised for the purpose. It is hardly necessary to mention that the copper must be scrupulously clean and all trace of soap or curd removed before it is used for cooking purposes: it is also equally important to remove all trace of grease after use.

BOILING A HAM: SECOND METHOD

Omit the soaking and when ready to cook, wash the ham, cover completely with cold water and bring very slowly to boiling point, taking at least 1½–2 hours. When boiling point has been reached, the ham should simmer slowly for the required length of time.

Leave the ham in the water in which it has been cooked for about 30 minutes after cooking, then finish as above.

HOW TO USE A HAM PRESS

For schools and institutions, also in kitchens where a large quantity of cold meat is required, a ham press will be found invaluable.

To remove the bone, take a sharp-pointed knife and cut round the bone as far as the leg socket. Then begin to loosen the meat from the other end of the bone, working gradually to the middle. In order to avoid waste, it is necessary to keep the knife close to the bone during the process. Although awkward at first, with a little practice, boning is not difficult.

After removing the bone, put the meat into the press with a quart of water and place the whole press in a covered pan containing sufficient boiling water to reach half-way up the press. Better results are obtained if the ham and press are allowed to remain in the saucepan of water until cold. The method of pressing meat whilst cooking is particularly economical, as carving is simplified and no waste occurs.

STEAMING A HAM

This is a method of cooking particularly suitable for hams of mild cure, for if it is not covered with boiling water, there is less opportunity for the salt, etc., to escape. Weigh the ham, calculate the time required for cooking, allowing 20 minutes over, and then soak for 12 hours. If a large steamer is not available, place the ham on a meat stand in a fish-kettle or boiler containing at least 2 inches of water. Have a supply of boiling water available for replenishing the water in the steamer as it boils away.

BAKING A HAM

This is an excellent way of cooking by which the maximum amount of goodness is conserved. Although the ham is actually baked, it is necessary partly to cook it by boiling before putting in the oven, otherwise the flavour is apt to be strong. The method is as follows :—

Weigh the ham, wash and soak. Calculate the cooking period, allowing 20 minutes to the lb. plus 20 minutes for small hams weighing up to 12 lb. and 15 minutes to the lb. plus 15 minutes for large hams. Boil the ham for half this period. Meanwhile, prepare a paste of flour and water, the amount depending entirely on the size of the ham and whether a whole, half, or quarter ham is used. Mix the flour and water together to a soft dough, as when making pastry, flour a board and roll it out until it is about ½ inch thick. The pastry should be mixed fairly stiffly, otherwise difficulty is experienced in rolling it out and also in covering the ham.

When the boiling period is completed, remove the ham, allow it to cool for about ½ hour, then cover tightly with the flour and water paste and tie in position with string, or wrap round tighly with muslin. If the ham has been cut, care should be taken that the cut end is covered completely.

If your oven is not big enough to accommodate a large ham without difficulty, it is advisable to divide it as shown before baking. Remove the grid shelves and see that the dripping pan is in position. then suspend the ham from the hook in the crown plate. If no hook is available, place it on a meat stand in a baking tin. As the ham is covered with paste, no basting is required and there is little risk of the meat becoming dry. Bake in a moderately hot oven (400° F., mark 6) for the remainder of the calculated cooking time.

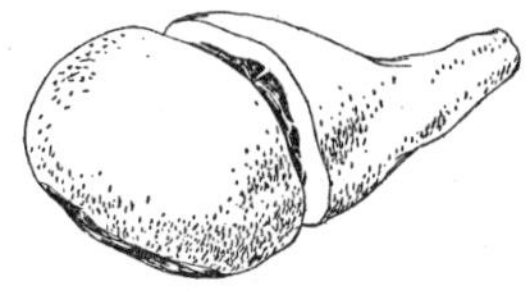

Dividing a Ham

About 20 minutes before baking is completed, remove the pastry, and return the ham to the oven. When cooked, brush over with glaze and serve with cider sauce. Alternately, finish in the American way, as follows :—

Remove the skin and while hot score the fat in squares or diamonds, then cover the surface
35 with about 6 oz. brown sugar, and stud the squares with cloves. Return the ham to a moderately hot oven (400° F., mark 6) and cook until golden-brown—about 15 minutes.

GRILLED HAM

Slices from the knuckle or butt end are excellent grilled. If the ham is very salt, the slices of meat may be soaked for 1 hour before grilling. After soaking, dry with a cloth, brush over with a little melted butter, and grill fairly slowly. The time required depends on the thickness of the ham—about 10–15 minutes.

BRAISED HAM

½ a ham, either bottom or knuckle end	A bouquet garni
½ a carrot	1 quart stock
1 turnip	3 sliced tomatoes
1 onion	Mushrooms, if liked
	½ pint rich brown sauce

Soak the ham for 12 hours at least, longer if possible. Place in a large pan with the carrot, turnip, onion and herbs. Add just sufficient water to cover and simmer for 2½–3 hours, according to the size of the joint, then remove from the saucepan and peel off the brown skin. Place the meat in a braising pan or strong, deep saucepan, add the stock, tomatoes and mushrooms, if used. Place in a moderate oven (375° F., mark 5), put on the lid, which should be tight-fitting, and cook for 1–1½ hours, according to size of the ham. Dish up, strain the stock, and reduce it to a half-glaze by boiling, then brush over the top. Add the brown sauce to the remainder, boil up and serve as gravy.

DEVILLED HAM

1½ oz. butter	½ tsp. curry powder
½ tsp. cayenne pepper	1 tsp. piquant sauce
1 tsp. ground ginger	Slices of ham
A good pinch black pepper	Parsley to garnish

Make the devilled butter by pounding or blending the butter, cayenne, ginger, black pepper, curry powder and sauce together. Spread the slices of ham fairly generously with the mixture, place under a hot grill, and cook until nicely browned. Serve immediately.

HAM CROQUETTES

1 cupful cooked ham	Nutmeg
2 cupfuls cooked potatoes	A little milk
1 tsp. chopped parsley	A little flour
2 tbsps. butter or dripping	Egg and breadcrumbs
Seasoning	Fat for frying
	Parsley

Any scraps of ham may be used ; put them through the mincer and then measure. Sieve the potatoes and chop the parsley finely. Put all into a saucepan with about 2 tbsps. melted butter or dripping, season with pepper and a little nutmeg. Moisten with milk if necessary, and make the mixture thoroughly hot. Then turn on to a floured board to cool, and form into croquettes, using a little flour. Dip into beaten egg and then roll in breadcrumbs. Fry until brown in hot fat, drain on paper and serve garnished with parsley.

HAM TOAST WITH MUSHROOMS

1 teacupful cooked ham	Rounds of toast or fried bread
½ oz. butter	Grilled or fried mushrooms
Mustard and cayenne	
2 eggs	
Salt if necessary	

Chop finely 1 teacupful of cooked ham, using a fair proportion of fat. Put it into a saucepan with the butter and season with mustard and cayenne. Add the eggs, well beaten, and a little salt if necessary. Stir over the heat until thick. Serve on rounds of toast or fried bread, and garnish with grilled or fried mushrooms.

HAMPTON PIE

½ lb. cooked ham	2–3 tbsps. stock or milk
¼ lb. tongue	1–2 hard-boiled eggs
1 tbsp. finely chopped parsley	1 onion, sliced and fried
2 tbsps. tomato ketchup	Mashed potatoes or pastry to cover
1 tbsp. made mustard	

Mince the ham and tongue and mix with the parsley, ketchup, mustard and stock or milk. Butter a pie dish and arrange the meat, sliced eggs and fried onion rings in layers. Cover with mashed potatoes or flaky pastry. Bake in a hot oven (450° F., mark 8) for 10–15 minutes, to brown potatoes, or 20–30 minutes to cook pastry.

POT-ROASTED HAM

1 slice of ham (about 1 lb.)	3 apples
4 tbsps. brown sugar	½ cupful water
6 potatoes	1 meat cube
	Seasoning, if desired

Select a slice of ham about 1 inch thick and

weighing about 1 lb. It must be mild-cured and tender; if inclined to be salt, soak it first in cold water. Trim off the fat, cut this into small pieces and sprinkle it over the bottom of a baking dish. Lay the ham in the dish and sprinkle the sugar over. Peel the potatoes, and halve and core the apples without paring. Arrange them round the ham, add the water, cover closely, and bake in a moderately hot oven (400° F., mark 6) for about 1 hour. Baste occasionally, adding more water if necessary. Make a gravy of the juice in the dish by mixing it with a meat cube and other seasoning, if desired.

SCALLOPED HAM AND POTATOES

½ lb. uncooked ham	½ pint milk
1 lb. potatoes	Pepper
2 small onions	2–3 cloves
2 tbsps. butter	Salt, if necessary
2 tbsps. flour	

Have the ham cut in thin slices and cut these across into small pieces. Slice the raw potatoes, let them soak in cold water for 1 hour, then drain and dry them in a towel. Slice also the onions, and make a white sauce with the butter, flour and milk. Grease a fireproof dish, arrange in it the ham, potato and onion in layers, sprinkling with pepper, the cloves and a little salt if necessary. Pour the white sauce over all and bake for 1 hour in a moderate oven (375° F., mark 5), keeping dish covered for first half of time.

STUFFED HAM

3–4 slices of ham	1 egg
1 apple	Flour
1 cupful breadcrumbs	1 cupful milk
Seasoning	½ cupful water
Nutmeg	3–4 potatoes

Choose a mild-cured ham, have the slices cut rather thinly, and cut each slice in two. Peel, core, and chop the apple, mix it with the breadcrumbs, season with a little pepper and nutmeg, and moisten with beaten egg. Put a layer of this mixture between 2 pieces of ham, making meat sandwiches. Coat these lightly with flour and lay them in a greased baking dish. Pour the milk and water over, and bake for about ½ hour in a moderate oven (375° F., mark 5), basting occasionally. Parboil the potatoes, place them round the dish and finish cooking in the oven.

BATH CHAPS

A Bath chap is prepared from the pig's cheek, cured and smoked as for a ham. To cook it, soak for a few hours and then simmer in fresh water for about 2 hours. Remove the skin, cover with raspings and serve cold. As there is in some cases a rather high proportion of fat, Bath chap is often served with tongue or some other lean type of meat.

SAUSAGES

Sausages may be made from pork or beef, pork sausages being rather more expensive and usually more popular than beef sausages; they require longer cooking than beef sausages.

When buying sausages, be sure that they look and smell fresh, and use them as soon as possible after purchasing. Put them in a cool place meanwhile—either hang them in a cold larder, or wrap them in greaseproof paper and place in the refrigerator.

One pound of sausages serves 3–4 people.

Sausage-meat is more convenient for certain made-up dishes, and also for stuffings.

In addition to the recipes given here, see also Toad-in-the-Hole, Scotch Eggs, Baked Meat Shape, Sausage Rolls and Sausage Stuffing.

TO BAKE SAUSAGES

Prick the sausages, place on a greased baking tin and cook in a moderately hot oven (400° F., mark 6) until browned—about 20 minutes. Serve on fried bread with gravy.

TO FRY SAUSAGES—I

Prick the sausages, flour them lightly and cook in a little hot fat until evenly browned—10–20 minutes. Fry gently or the skins will burst. Serve on toast or fried bread or mashed potato.

TO FRY SAUSAGES—II

Parboil the sausages, skin them, coat them with egg and crumbs and fry in hot deep fat.

TO GRILL SAUSAGES

Prick well, place under the hot grill and cook until well browned all over, turning them frequently—15–20 minutes in all. Serve with mashed potatoes, grilled tomatoes, bacon, etc.

CHIPOLATA SAUSAGES

Grill, fry or bake as above; being smaller, they require rather less cooking time.

APPLES STUFFED WITH SAUSAGE

6 tart cooking apples	¾ lb. cooked sausage-meat

Wipe the apples, remove the core, then scoop

out a good part of the apple, but leave a thick shell. Chop the apple, mix with the sausage-meat, adding a little additional seasoning if liked; this naturally depends on the flavour of the sausage-meat—a very little powdered ginger, chopped parsley, powdered mace or black pepper can be added. Refill the apples with this mixture, piling up the filling, put in a buttered pie dish or meat tin, and bake in a moderate oven (375° F., mark 5) until the sausage-meat is cooked—about ½–¾ hour. Serve with chipped potatoes.

LUNCHEON SAUSAGE

1 lb. beef sausage-meat	1 tbsp. chopped pickles
1 lb. pork sausage-meat	2 tbsps. sauce or ketchup
¼ lb. breadcrumbs	Glaze
¼ lb. ham or tongue	
Pepper and salt	
2 tsps. mixed spice	

Put the two kinds of sausage-meat into a basin, add the breadcrumbs and the ham or tongue, cut in small pieces. Season lightly with pepper and salt, spice, chopped pickles and the sauce or ketchup. Then mix together until all the ingredients are thoroughly blended. Make into a roll, tie in a pudding cloth, and cook slowly in stock for 1½–2 hours. Lift out when ready and press between 2 dishes with a weight on top, until cold. Next day, remove cloth, and glaze.

SAUSAGE CROQUETTES

4 oz. rice	½ lb. small sausages
Pepper and salt	Breadcrumbs for coating
Cayenne pepper	Fat for frying
A little made mustard	Tomato sauce or egg sauce or puréed spinach
1 egg	

Put the rice into boiling salted water and boil until tender. Strain, then pour cold water through to separate the grains. Add pepper, salt, cayenne and a little mustard. Add half a beaten egg, and put on to a plate to cool, then divide equally into the same number of portions as there are small sausages. Remove the skin from the sausages, form each into a ball or flat cake, and coat with the rice. Brush over with the remainder of beaten egg, coat with bread-crumbs, and fry in a pan of deep fat from which a faint, blue smoke is rising. Serve with home-made tomato sauce, egg sauce or puréed spinach.

SAUSAGE, BACON AND CORN PIE

Grill 1 lb. pork sausages and ½ lb. streaky bacon, and cook a packet of quick-frozen sweet corn. Make ½ pint well-seasoned tomato sauce, add the corn and the cut-up sausages and bacon and put in a pie dish. Cover with puff pastry and cook for 15–20 minutes in a hot oven (450° F., mark 8) until well-risen and golden, then cook for a further 5 minutes at a lower heat.

SAUSAGE AND TOMATO PIE

1 small onion	¼ pint stock
1 lb. pork sausages	1 lb. cooked potatoes
2 large tomatoes	A little butter
Salt and pepper	

Peel, slice and fry the onion. Grill or fry the sausages, cut each of them into halves length-wise, and lay half of them in a pie dish. Cover with the onion rings and peeled and sliced tomatoes. Add salt and pepper, then place the remaining sausages and the stock in the dish and cover with a thick layer of mashed potatoes. Smooth this with a knife and then decorate with fork markings. Place small pieces of butter on top and brown in a hot oven, or under the grill.

SAVOURY SAUSAGE FLAN

¾ lb. sausage-meat	2 tbsps. chopped parsley
2 eggs	2 tbsps. chopped onion
½ pint milk	Salt and pepper

Line a sandwich tin or flan ring with the 3
sausage-meat, about ½ inch thick. Beat the eggs and stir in the milk, then add the parsley, onion and seasoning. Pour into the sausage case and bake in a moderately hot oven (400° F., mark 6) until the custard is set and the sausage-meat cooked—about ½ hour. Serve hot or cold.

SAUSAGE LOAF WITH POTATO CRUST

1 onion	1 lb. sausage-meat
2–3 stalks of celery	Seasoning
½ oz. dripping	Creamy mashed potato

Chop or mince the onion and celery, fry gently in the fat, then stir into the sausage-meat, adding seasoning to taste. Place in a greased loaf tin, and bake in a moderate oven (375° F., mark 5) for ¾–1 hour. Turn out on to a fireproof dish, cover the surface thickly with mashed potato, and return it to the oven for about 10 minutes to brown. Serve with a good brown sauce.

SAUSAGE PANCAKES

4 oz. flour	Salt and pepper
1 egg	1 lb. sausages
½ pint milk	Fried tomatoes

Mix the flour to a smooth batter with the egg and half of the milk. Beat well for about 5 minutes, stir in the rest of the milk, season, and set aside. Fry the sausages until golden-brown, remove from the pan and keep hot. Pour off the fat, leaving just enough in the pan to fry a pancake. When browned on both sides, roll up with a sausage inside and lay on a hot dish. Add a little more of the sausage fat to the pan, fry a second pancake and fill again with a sausage. Repeat until all the batter and sausages are used. Serve very hot with fried tomatoes.

SMOTHERED SAUSAGES

1 lb. mashed potato	Chopped parsley or thyme
1 teacupful cooked chopped celery	1 egg
½ lb. cooked sausage-meat	Breadcrumbs
	2 tbsps. tomato sauce
Seasoning	Parsley to garnish

Put the mashed potatoes into a basin, add the chopped celery and chopped sausage-meat; add additional seasoning of pepper and salt, if necessary, and chopped parsley or thyme, if liked. Blend well, and add sufficient beaten egg to bind, but reserve a little for brushing over the roll. Form the mixture into a thick roll, put into a buttered fireproof baking dish, brush the roll over with the beaten egg, and coat with breadcrumbs. Bake in a moderate oven (375° F., mark 5) until golden-brown. Put on to a hot dish, or if suitable serve in the dish in which it has been cooked. Pour tomato sauce round, and garnish.

SUNDAY NIGHT SUPPER SAUSAGE

Make up some sausage-meat into 6 round cakes and fry them until crisp and brown. Poach the same number of eggs. Lay each slice of sausage on a round of toast and place a poached egg on the top. Serve with tomato sauce poured round and garnish with parsley.

MADE-UP MEAT DISHES

BEDFORDSHIRE ROLL

2 onions	Rasher of fat bacon
¼ lb. raw minced meat	

For the Roll

8 oz. flour	3–4 oz. suet
2 tsps. baking powder	Cold water
1 tsp. salt	Salt and black pepper

Parboil the onions and chop roughly. Mince the meat and fat bacon. Make the suet pastry and roll out in an oblong. Spread with onions and meat and season with salt and black pepper. Damp edges, roll up, and tie in a floured cloth. Boil for 2 hours. To dish, remove the cloth from the roll. Turn on to a hot dish and pour the sauce over (see this page).

For the Sauce

4 onions	Seasoning
A stalk of celery	Stock
1 carrot	1 oz. dripping
Parsley stalks	1 oz. flour

Peel the onions and put in a saucepan with the celery, carrot, and parsley. Season and cover with stock. Cook until the onions are tender; then strain off the liquid and measure ¾ pint. Chop the onions finely. Melt the dripping, add the flour, and fry until brown. Add the stock by degrees and boil up, stirring. Season, and add the chopped onions.

BEEF À LA MAÎTRE D'HÔTEL

¾ lb. cooked beef	1 dessertsp. lemon juice
2 oz. butter	¼ pint stock or gravy
Chopped parsley	½ cupful breadcrumbs
Pepper and salt	

Cut the meat in very thin slices. Work the butter to a cream with a wooden spoon, add a little parsley and seasoning, and then the lemon juice by degrees. Spread a little of this mixture on each slice of meat and arrange in a greased baking dish. Heat the stock or gravy and pour it over. Sprinkle the breadcrumbs on the top. Bake in a hot oven (450° F., mark 8) for 10 minutes—no longer, or the meat will dry and toughen. Serve with baked potatoes.

Thinly sliced corned beef is delicious preared in this way—omit the salt in this case.

CROQUETTES

½ lb. minced cooked beef or other meat	Pepper and salt
½ oz. dripping	A little grated nutmeg
½ small onion	A few drops of piquant sauce
1 tbsp. flour	Egg and breadcrumbs
¼ pint stock or gravy	Fat for frying
1 tsp. finely chopped parsley	Parsley to garnish

Mince the meat finely, removing the skin and gristle. Melt the dripping in a saucepan, add the chopped onion and fry until golden-brown. Remove the fried onion from the pan, stir in the flour, and cook until brown in colour. Gradually add the stock, bring to the boil, and cook for 5 minutes, stirring. Stir in the fried onion and minced meat, pepper, salt, parsley, a little grated nutmeg, and a few drops of piquant sauce. When cold, divide into 6–8 pieces, according to the size required. Flour the hands and shape the mixture into balls or flat cakes, brush over with beaten egg and coat with dry breadcrumbs. Have ready a pan of deep fat from which a faint, blue smoke is rising. Place the balls in a frying basket and lower into the fat. Fry until golden-brown, drain well, then arrange on a hot dish and garnish with parsley. Serve with a good sauce or gravy.

RISSOLES

Rissoles are made from the same mixture as croquettes, the only difference being that instead of being coated with breadcrumbs, the mixture is enclosed in pastry and cooked. Trimmings and pieces of pastry that are left over from making pies and tarts can be used. Roll out the pastry very thinly and cut into rounds about
37 $2\frac{1}{2}$–3 inches in diameter, moisten the edges with cold water, place some of the mixture on each round of pastry and fold to form half circles. Press the edges together, brush over with beaten egg and sprinkle with crushed vermicelli or toss in breadcrumbs. Fry until golden-brown in a pan of deep fat from which a faint, blue smoke is rising, then drain on kitchen paper and serve immediately, with brown gravy or tomato sauce.

HASH

1 lb. cooked mutton or beef	1 pint water, stock or gravy
A bunch of herbs (bay leaf, parsley and thyme)	1 oz. flour
1 onion	Pepper and salt
1 carrot	2 tsps. mushroom ketchup or piquant sauce
1 turnip	Toast
$1\frac{1}{2}$ oz. dripping	

Cut the meat into thin slices of even size, removing gristle and fat, and set aside. Put any bones into cold water with the herbs, half the onion, sliced carrot and turnip, then bring to the boil and simmer gently for 1–$1\frac{1}{2}$ hours. Strain and make up to 1 pint with stock or gravy. Meanwhile, chop the remaining half onion finely, and fry it in the dripping until golden-brown. Remove the onion from the pan, stir the flour into the fat and continue to cook over a low heat until it is deep golden-brown in colour, then stir in the onion and gradually add the stock, stirring to prevent lumps forming. Bring to the boil and cook for 10 minutes, adding pepper and salt, if required, and the mushroom ketchup or piquant sauce. Place the meat in the gravy and reheat for 5 minutes, but do not allow the hash to boil after the meat has been added. Place the meat in the centre of the dish and pour the gravy round. Decorate with sippets of toast.

To make sippets of toast, cut thin slices of bread and toast evenly. Cut into strips 1 inch wide and then into 1-inch squares by cutting the strips at right angles. Divide each square in half to form triangles.

MINCE
(using cooked meat)

Mince is prepared in exactly the same way as hash, except that the meat is minced after the gristle and fat are removed, instead of being sliced. The minced meat is added to the gravy after it is cooked, and is reheated without boiling.

A mince of cold meat can be made very attractive if served with a border of mashed potatoes, spinach, rice or savoury macaroni, and variety can be introduced by different flavourings, for example, celery seed or fresh celery can be cooked with the stock for the gravy, and the addition of a few stewed mushrooms to the mince just before serving improves the flavour considerably. If liked, the mince may be served on slices of toast.

LAMB RING MOULD

$\frac{3}{4}$ pint aspic jelly	Salt and pepper
Stuffed olives (or radishes)	Potato salad
1 small onion, chopped	Watercress
12 oz. cold lamb, minced	Tomatoes

Prepare the aspic jelly. Decorate the border
mould with slices of stuffed olives (or sliced 38
radishes). This is done by lining the mould with a little aspic jelly and placing the decorations in position with more of the aspic. Add the very finely chopped onion, minced lamb and seasoning to the remainder of the jelly, and when beginning to set, pour it into the mould. When quite set, turn out on to a glass or silver dish, fill the centre of the ring with potato salad, and garnish with the watercress and slices of tomato.

MEAT-CAKES WITH POACHED EGGS

2 cupfuls cooked meat	1 egg
2 oz. butter	2 tbsps. flour
2 shallots or onions	A few breadcrumbs
2 cupfuls cooked potatoes	Brown or tomato sauce
2 tsps. chopped parsley	Poached eggs
Seasoning	
2 tsps. ketchup	

Any remains of tender, cooked meat may be used—beef, mutton, veal, or a mixture of meats with a little tongue or ham to give flavour. Remove any skin and gristle from the meat and chop it finely, or put it through the mincing machine. Melt the butter in a saucepan, add the shallot, finely chopped, or 2 tsps. of chopped onion, and cook it for a few minutes. Sieve the potatoes and put them into the saucepan with the prepared meat, the parsley, finely chopped, and a seasoning of pepper, salt and 1 tsp. of ketchup. Mix well and moisten with about half the egg, well beaten. Form this mixture into flat cakes, using a little flour. Dip them into the remainder of the beaten egg and coat with breadcrumbs. Place the meat-cakes on a greased tin, and bake them in a hot oven (450° F., mark 8) until brown and thoroughly hot—about 15 minutes. Meanwhile, prepare a little brown or tomato sauce, and poach an egg for each cake. Arrange the meat-cakes on a hot dish, place a poached egg on top of each cake and then pour the sauce round.

MEAT LOAF

1½ lb. raw lean meat (beef, veal, rabbit, mutton or a mixture of any of these)	Salt and pepper
	Nutmeg
	1 tsp. mixed spice
3 oz. fat bacon	2 eggs
2 tbsps. chopped onion	Stock
6 oz. breadcrumbs	Brown crumbs

Cut the meat into small pieces and pass it, with the bacon, twice through the mincing machine. Chop the onion and add to the meat, with the breadcrumbs and the seasonings. Add the beaten eggs and sufficient stock to moisten. Press tightly into a greased bread tin, cover with greased paper and steam for about 2 hours. Take off the paper, press the meat mixture down with weights and leave until cold. Turn out, toss in brown crumbs, and serve cut in thin slices.

SAVOURY MINCE WITH CHESTNUTS

1 lb. chestnuts	1 lb. Brussels sprouts
1 onion	1 oz. dripping
2 cloves	1 oz. flour
A blade of mace	8 oz. minced cooked meat or game
Stock	
1 oz. butter	Salt and pepper

Nick a piece of skin off each chestnut. Put in cold water, bring to the boil and cook for 2–3 minutes. Skin and place in a pan with onion, cloves, mace, and stock to cover. Simmer gently until tender (½–¾ hour), then strain, reserving the liquid. Toss the chestnuts in ½ oz. butter and keep hot. Wash the sprouts, cook in boiling salted water, then strain and toss in butter. Meanwhile, measure ½ pint of liquid from the chestnuts. Melt the dripping, add the flour and fry until brown, then stir in the liquid and boil. Add the meat, reheat and season. Dish the mince with a border of chestnuts and sprouts.

SHEPHERD'S PIE

1 lb. potatoes	Dripping
2 tbsps. milk	½ lb. minced cold meat
½ oz. butter	Stock
Pepper and salt	1 tsp. chopped parsley
1 onion	¼ tsp. mixed herbs

Boil the potatoes and when thoroughly cooked, strain off the water. Mash, then stir in the milk, butter, pepper and salt, and beat well. Chop or slice the onion, fry in a little dripping and mix in the minced meat with a little stock, pepper, salt, parsley and herbs. Half-fill the dish with the prepared meat mixture. Cover the top with mashed potato, piling it up in the centre, and mark with a fork or whisk. Bake in a moderately hot oven (425° F., mark 7) for 20–30 minutes. If necessary the pie can be put under a slow grill to brown the top.

BEEF RÉCHAUFFÉ WITH CREAMED POTATOES

2 slices of bacon	¾ lb. cooked beef
2 small onions	¼ pint stock or gravy
1 tbsp. chopped parsley	1 tbsp. vinegar
Pepper and salt	Creamed potatoes

Cut the bacon in dice and fry it with the finely chopped onion. When lightly browned, add the parsley and seasoning. Cut the beef in wafer-thin slices and arrange in a greased baking dish, alternating a layer of beef with a layer of the onion mixture. Heat the stock and vinegar and pour them into the dish. Cover the meat and bake in a hot oven (450° F., mark 8) for 10–15 minutes. Garnish with creamed potatoes.

MEAT PIES

Shortcrust, flaky pastry and hot-water crust can all be combined with various kinds of meat fillings to make delicious main dishes or snacks. (For instruction for the various types of pastry, see chapter on Pastry Making.)

Preparation of Filling

Almost any kind of meat may be used—beef, mutton, veal, pork, chicken, pigeon, rabbit, or game, or a mixture of two or three kinds together. All meat should be carefully wiped with a clean, damp cloth, or washed if necessary, then trimmed and cut up in the form suited to its kind. Solid meat should be cut up in small pieces, or in thin slices and rolled; game, poultry and rabbit are cut into small joints and the larger bones removed. There should be nothing uneatable in the form of skin, gristle, or superfluous fat, although a little bone is sometimes permissible.

The meat should then be carefully seasoned with pepper and salt and other flavouring added, according to the kind of meat used and to suit individual taste. A little grated lemon rind and juice with finely chopped parsley is suitable for white meat, some chopped onion or shallot and a sprinkling of Jamaica pepper for the darker kinds. Onion must, however, be added with caution, as it is not agreeable to every palate. Sometimes the meat is browned in a little fat before it is put into the pie dish; this makes it richer, and gives a darker-coloured gravy. If a slightly thickened gravy is required, the meat should be coated with flour.

Whenever possible, good and tender meat should be used for making a pie, but if a tough and inferior kind has to be used, it should be partially cooked before the pastry cover is put on. This should be done in such a way as to lose none of the flavour of the meat. The best method is to cover the pie dish of meat with another dish, and to place it in a moderate oven for 1 hour or longer; or the meat may be stewed in a pan or double cooker to make it tender. It must, of course, be allowed to cool again before the pastry is laid over it. The prepared meat should be packed into the pie dish rather loosely, and the dish should be sufficiently small to allow the contents to be well raised in the centre, and thus give the pie a plump appearance. In a large dish, a pie funnel is advisable.

It is very important that every pie should have some good gravy. The dish should be half-filled with stock or water before covering, and additional liquid poured in when the pie is cooked. If any bones and trimmings have been taken from the meat, these might be used for making a little stock while the pie is cooking. If the pie is to be served cold, a little gelatine should be dissolved in the stock, so as to form a jelly.

Beefsteak and Kidney: Cut 1 lb. beef in thin strips and dip them in flour seasoned with pepper, salt and a little cayenne pepper. Skin, core and wash 2–3 sheep's kidneys and cut them in small pieces. Roll up the beef with a small piece of fat and a little kidney inside each piece. A little finely chopped onion may also be added. Then pack the rolls in a pie dish with a little ketchup and stock or water. A few mushrooms, peeled and cut in pieces, may also be included. If necessary, pre-cook the meat as described above.

Chicken: Cut 1 tender fowl into neat joints, removing the skin and all the larger bones. Season carefully with pepper, salt and a little powdered mace, and mix with ¼ lb. ham cut in small pieces, grated lemon rind and juice, and some chopped parsley. Add some forcemeat balls and hard-boiled eggs, cut in pieces, also some stock made from the bones of the fowl. If a cold pie is wanted, it should be filled up with good jelly stock when it has been cooked. A few slices of hard-boiled egg may be included.

Rabbit: Wash 1 young rabbit carefully, letting it lie in salt and water for 1 hour or so. Then put it into a saucepan with cold water to cover it, bring to the boil and throw the water away. Rinse and dry the rabbit and cut it in small, neat joints. Dip these in flour and season with pepper and salt. Mix with 4–6 oz. ham or bacon, cut in strips, and sprinkle with finely chopped parsley and a little grated lemon rind. Pack into a pie dish and pour round a little stock or water. 1 or 2 hard-boiled eggs, cut in pieces may be added, or a few forcemeat balls, made as for Jugged Hare. Salt pork, cut in small pieces, may be used instead of ham or bacon.

Veal and Ham: Cut 1 lb. fleshy veal in small pieces, free from skin. Trim ¼ lb. ham or bacon and cut it in thin strips. Mix them together with some finely chopped parsley, the grated rind of ½ lemon and a very little lemon juice. Season with pepper and salt. Pack into the pie dish with 1–2 hard-boiled eggs cut in pieces, and add a little water. A few veal forcemeat balls may be added.

Pigeon: Cut 4 pigeons in half and wash them thoroughly. Put them in a saucepan with ½ lb. sliced streaky bacon, ½ lb. cut-up steak and ¼ lb. sliced mushrooms; cover with stock, add seasoning and simmer gently for 2 hours. Cool before putting into the pie dish.

To Cover a Meat Pie

Various kinds of pastry may be used for covering a meat pie, though flaky pastry is the most usual. The proportion of ½ lb. of flour and 4–6 oz. of fat will be quite sufficient to cover the quantities of filling given, and this size of pie will serve from 4–6 persons.

The pastry, when made, should be rolled out to the shape of the dish, about ¼ inch thick and 1 inch wider all the way round. Cut off the extra inch, wet the rim of the pie dish and lay this strip round. If a join in the pastry is necessary, seal the pieces together with a little cold water, but do not overlap, or the covering of the pie will be uneven in thickness. When the rim of the dish is neatly covered, damp it over slightly with cold water, using a brush or wisp of paper. Then lay on the larger piece of pastry to cover.

Press this on round the edges, easing it over the meat. Care should be taken not to stretch the pastry in any way, or it will shrink away from the dish in baking and spoil the appearance of the pie. Now take a sharp knife, hold up the dish in the left hand, and with the right trim neatly round the edges, cutting in short, quick strokes and keeping the knife blade inclining outwards, so that the pastry lies slightly over the rim. When it is neatly trimmed, knock up the extreme edge of the pastry with the back of a knife, making it look like the leaves of a book. Then scallop round the edge at intervals of about $\frac{3}{4}$ inch. To do this, draw the back of the knife upwards and inwards over the edge of the pastry with the right hand, while pressing the pastry, which lies at the side of the knife, outwards with the thumb of the left hand. Make a hole or slit in the top of the pie, to allow the steam to escape while cooking, and brush over the pastry with beaten egg, or with egg and milk, to give it a gloss. Then roll out the trimmings of pastry very thinly, cut out some leaves and make a rose or tassel to ornament the pie : see detailed instructions below.

The Ornamentation

To make leaves, cut a strip of the pastry $1\frac{1}{2}$ inches wide, and cut as shown below into diamond-shaped pieces, then mark each of these with the back of the knife to represent the veins of a leaf; from 5–7 leaves will be required for an average-sized pie.

To make a rose, take a small piece of pastry about the size of a thimble, and work into it as much dry flour as it will take up; then roll it

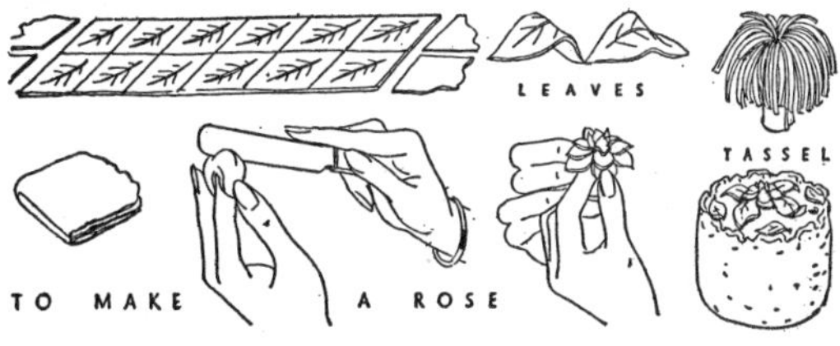

out as thin as a sheet of paper. Cut a square, and fold in four, making a smaller square. Lay this folded piece of pastry over the point of the finger and fold the edges downwards over the finger. Then with a sharp knife make a cross on the top, cutting neatly, but not quite, through all the pastry folds. Remove from the finger, squeeze the edges together, and the top will expand, the cut pieces opening out like the petals of a rose.

To make a tassel, cut a strip of pastry 2 inches in width, and score it across like a fringe to about half its width, then roll up to form a tassel, as seen in the illustration.

Arrange the leaves in a circle on the top of the pie, and put a rose or tassel in the centre, taking care that the ventilation hole is not closed up. Brush over the decoration with beaten egg, and the pie is ready for baking. It will not spoil if allowed to stand in a cool place for a short time before being placed in the oven.

The Baking

Put the pie on a baking tin and place it in a hot oven (450° F., mark 8) until the pastry is set and beginning to brown, then lower heat in order that the meat may cook more slowly. As soon as the pastry is sufficiently browned, it should be covered with a double fold of kitchen paper, sprinkled with water, to prevent it becoming too brown. The time for cooking the pie will depend very much on the kind of meat being used—from $1\frac{1}{2}$–2 hours is an average time. The meat may be tested by running a skewer into it through the hole in the top. When the pie is sufficiently cooked, remove it from the oven. Heat some stock or gravy and pour it in through a funnel placed in the hole, or by means of a small jug. Wipe the pie dish with a wet cloth, place it on a dish, and garnish the top of the pie with a good sprig of parsley.

STEAK AND KIDNEY PIE

1 lb. beefsteak	A little stock or water
3–4 oz. kidney	6 oz. flaky pastry
1 tbsp. seasoned flour	Beaten egg

Wipe the meat and cut into slices 1–2 inches by 3 inches and about $\frac{1}{4}$ inch thick, then beat them with the rolling pin. Prepare and cut up the kidney. Dip the meat in the seasoned flour and roll up with a piece of kidney inside each roll. Place in a pie dish, with a pie funnel if necessary, and add stock or water to come about half-way up. Roll out the pastry about $\frac{1}{4}$ inch thick and about 1 inch larger all round than the pie dish. Cut off strips of pastry 1 inch wide. Moisten the edge of the dish with water and lay the pastry strips on the edge of the dish, pressing lightly in place. Moisten the pastry strip with water. Lift the remaining pastry on the rolling pin and lay it over the pie dish. Seal and trim the edges and decorate by knocking up the edge with a knife. Make a ventilating hole in the centre and decorate with pastry leaves. Brush the pastry with beaten egg. Bake in a hot oven (450° F., mark 8) until well risen and just beginning to brown—about 20 minutes—then reduce the heat to moderate (350° F., mark 4) and continue cooking for about 2 hours, until the meat is tender and the pastry well browned and crisp.

If the meat is not very tender, pre-cook it as described on page 140.

STEAK AND MUSHROOM PIE

(*See colour picture facing page* 128.)

Make as for Steak and Kidney Pie, but replace the kidney by cut-up mushrooms, and add 1–2 sliced skinned tomatoes, also a sliced onion, if desired.

CORNISH PASTIES

6 oz. raw potato	Salt and pepper
¾ lb. lean raw steak or mutton	2–3 tbsps. cold water
	1 lb. shortcrust pastry
1 tbsp. chopped onion	Egg yolk or milk

Wash and pare the potatoes and cut into dice. Mix with the meat (cut up very small or minced), the finely chopped or minced onion, seasoning and water. Roll out the pastry thinly and cut into rounds about the size of a saucer. Wet the edges of the pastry and put 1 tbsp. of the meat mixture on each round. Fold over, press the edges of the pastry well together and flute it with the fingers. Stand the pasties upright on a baking sheet, brush over with a little beaten egg or milk and bake in a hot oven (450° F., mark 8) till the pastry begins to brown, then reduce to a moderate heat 350° F., mark 4) and continue cooking until meat is tender—about 1 hour in all.

SAUSAGE ROLLS

To prepare the sausages, remove the skin and cut into three (or into 1-oz. pieces, if using sausage-meat); and roll into sausages, using a little flour. Roll out some flaky or puff pastry to about ⅛ inch in thickness and cut into 4-inch squares—if required for light refreshments, 2½-inch squares will be large enough. Brush the bottom edge of the pastry with water and place the sausage-meat on the top half of the squares. Fold the pastry over on to the damped pastry edge. Place on a baking sheet, brush over with beaten egg, and set aside in the cool for ½ hour. Bake in a hot oven (450° F., mark 8) until well browned—about 20 minutes, and serve either hot or cold. Garnish with small pieces of parsley.

RAISED PIES

There are two different ways of making raised pies with hot-water crust pastry. By the first method the pie case is moulded by hand. (This special pastry is flexible while warm, but hardens and retains its shape as it cools.) By the second method a special raised pie mould is used. This opens at the side, and can be easily removed when the pie is cooked; see sketch on next page. These moulds can be obtained in many different sizes.

Raised pies are generally served cold, and as a rule, are somewhat solid in texture. There must be no bones nor gristle, and a delicious meat jelly should fill up all the crannies. A tasty force- or sausage-meat is sometimes used to line the pie and act as a padding for the pieces of meat. Lard or lard and butter is generally used in the making of the crust, as butter alone is apt to render it too soft.

LITTLE MUTTON PIES

For the Crust

½ lb. flour	2 oz. lard
¼ tsp. salt	4 tbsps. milk and water

For the Filling

¾ lb. lean good-quality mutton	A pinch of grated nutmeg
	A pinch of powdered mace
Pepper and salt	
2 tsps. finely chopped onion	Stock

Mix the flour and salt in a basin, bring the lard, milk and water just to boiling point, pour into the middle of the flour, and mix to a soft dough, adding extra water if necessary. Knead until smooth, and leave to stand in a warm place while preparing the meat. Cut the meat into small pieces, mix with the seasonings, and moisten with stock.

Keep one-third of the paste for the pie lids and divide the rest into 3–4 pieces. Roll into smooth balls and then form into little cases with the finger and thumb or round the base of a tumbler. Work quickly, and remember to keep pastry warm. Fill with meat, raise the sides again with the hands, and roll out lids from the remaining dough. Damp the edges of the pies and press in the lids. Decorate the edges with the back of a knife and make a small hole in the top. Place on a greased baking sheet and bake in a hot oven (450° F., mark 8) until the pastry is lightly browned and set, then reduce the heat to moderately hot (400° F., mark 6). Continue cooking for about 40 minutes in all. Fill the pies up with hot gravy or stock.

PORK PIE

1 lb. lean pork pieces	Pepper and salt
1 apple	1 lb. hot-water crust
A pinch of powdered cloves	Egg yolk
	Stock

Wipe the meat and cut it into small pieces. Peel, core and slice the apple and mix it with the meat, together with the cloves and seasoning. Sprinkle with 1 tbsp. of water. Wash any bones, cover these with cold water in a saucepan and allow to simmer gently, to make stock for a pie.

Make the pastry, cut off one-quarter of it and leave it in a warm place. Mould the remainder of the paste to line the raised pie mould, or raise it by hand into an oval or round pastry case, then fill up with the prepared meat mixture. Roll the reserved piece of pastry to form a lid for the pie. Make a hole to allow the steam to escape; trim the edges and decorate according to taste. Brush the top with egg yolk, and if no mould is used, pin a band of stiff greased paper round the pie. Bake in a moderately hot oven (400° F., mark 6) for about 1 hour, then reduce to moderate (350° F., mark 4) and cook until tender. When ready, fill up with well-seasoned stock and serve hot or cold.

RAISED PIGEON OR GAME PIE

For the Pastry

1 lb. flour	4 oz. butter
1 tsp. salt	1 egg yolk
¼ lb. lard	Cold water

For the Filling

3 pigeons	Nutmeg
½ lb. veal	Cayenne
½ lb. ham	Lemon rind
¼ lb. breadcrumbs	2–3 eggs
Seasoning	Jelly stock

To Make the Pastry

Do this first, as it will improve by lying for a while before it is used.

Sieve the flour and salt into a basin and rub in the two kinds of fat until as fine as breadcrumbs. Then mix into a firm paste, using the egg yolk, beaten with a little water. Turn this on to a floured board, and knead lightly with the hands until smooth and free from cracks. Cover the pastry over and lay it aside whilst preparing the filling.

To Prepare the Filling

Bone the pigeons and cut the flesh in small pieces. Trim the veal and ham, cut them also in pieces and put them through the mincing machine. Add the breadcrumbs to this mince, season rather highly with pepper, salt, a pinch of nutmeg, a good dash of cayenne and a little grated lemon rind, and mix all together into a smooth paste or farce. Hard-boil the eggs and cut them in pieces.

Alternatively, replace the pigeons by game, e.g., 1 good-sized partridge or 2 grouse.

To Finish the Pie

Grease a raised pie mould and line it with the pastry rolled out to about ¼ inch in thickness. Be careful to press the pastry into any moulds

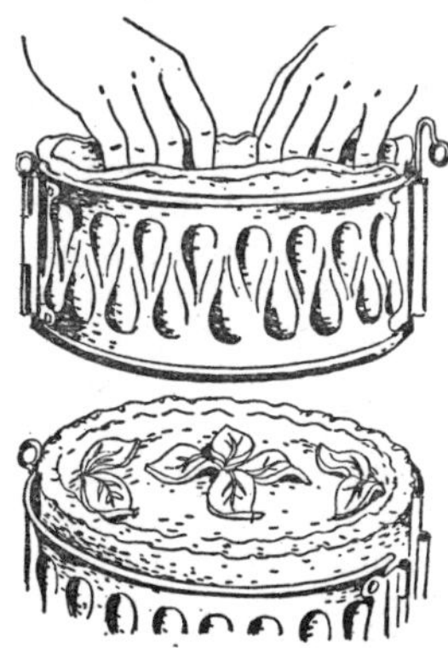

Filling a Pie Mould

and to keep it of an even thickness all over. Trim off the edges with a pair of scissors. Then line the mould with the farce mixture, fill up the centre with the pieces of pigeon and egg, adding more seasoning, and cover with more of the farce. Wet the inner edge of the pastry lining the mould, and roll out the trimmings of pastry to form a lid. Lay this on, pressing the two edges together, and trim round with a pair of scissors. Make a hole in the centre, brush over with beaten egg, and decorate with leaves made out of the remaining scraps of pastry.

Place the pie on a baking tin and bake in a hot oven (450° F., mark 8) until the top crust is cooked and brown. Then cover with paper, reduce the heat, and cook about 2 hours longer, until the meat feels tender. Lift the pie from the oven and when slightly cooled remove the tin. Fill up the pie with jelly stock made from the bones and trimmings of the pigeons, with a little gelatine added. When quite cold, serve garnished with parsley or watercress, or with chopped aspic jelly and salad.

Note: Game may be used instead of the

pigeons, and sausage-meat instead of the veal and ham farce given in this recipe.

RAISED VEAL AND HAM PIE

For the Filling

$\frac{3}{4}$ lb. veal	Pepper and salt
$\frac{1}{4}$ lb. ham	2 eggs
Parsley	Some jelly stock
Lemon	

For the Pastry

1 lb. flour	$\frac{1}{4}$ lb. lard
1 tsp. salt	$\frac{1}{3}$ pint milk or water

First prepare the filling. Weigh the veal, free from skin and bone, wipe it with a damp cloth and cut it in small pieces. Add to it the ham, cut in small pieces, season with chopped parsley, a little grated lemon rind and juice, pepper and salt. Mix well together and just moisten with a little cold water. Hard-boil the eggs, and cut them in 6–8 pieces.

Make the pie crust as described under Hot-water Crust, page 271. Fill the case with the meat mixture and eggs, and shape it up again if necessary. Roll out the remaining piece of pastry, wet the inside edge of the pie crust, and lay on the cover. Press the two edges together and trim round neatly with a pair of scissors, leaving a ridge about $\frac{1}{2}$ inch in height standing straight up round the pie. Snip this ridge with the scissors at a distance of about $\frac{1}{2}$ inch apart. Then, with the fingers, bend the fringe-like pieces outwards and inwards alternately to make a pretty edge. Make a good hole in the centre of the pie and brush all over with egg yolk, beaten with a little water. Roll out any remaining scraps of pastry and cut out leaves and narrow strips for decoration. Fix these on to the sides and top of the pie and give them also a coating of egg. Pin or clip a double piece of stiff kitchen paper (greased on the inside) round the outside of the pie to keep it in position. Lift the pie with a fish-slice or broad knife and place it on a greased baking tin.

Bake in a hot oven (450° F., mark 8) 15–20 minutes, and then in a cooler one for $1\frac{1}{2}$ hours or until meat feels quite tender when tested with a skewer and pastry is golden-brown. Have ready some well-seasoned stock that will jelly when cold. This may be made from the bones and trimmings of the veal, with a little gelatine added if necessary. Fill up the pie with this by means of a funnel, and set it aside until cold. Serve with a salad.

MEAT PUDDINGS

BEEFSTEAK AND KIDNEY PUDDING

1 lb. stewing steak	$\frac{1}{4}$ tsp. pepper
2 sheep's kidneys or $\frac{1}{4}$ lb. ox kidney	$\frac{1}{2}$ lb. suetcrust pastry
1 tbsp. flour	2 tsps. finely chopped onion (optional)
$\frac{1}{2}$ tsp. salt	Stock or water

Grease a 6-inch pudding basin and a piece of greaseproof paper. Wipe the meat, cut it into slices about $\frac{1}{4}$ inch thick and beat them with a rolling pin to make the meat tender. Cut the core from the kidney, remove the skin (if sheep's kidney), wash well and cut into small pieces. Toss the meat and kidney in the seasoned flour and roll up each slice of meat with a piece of kidney in the centre.

Make the suetcrust pastry, cut off one quarter of the dough for the lid, roll out the remaining dough to about twice the size of the top of the basin and lower carefully into the basin, taking care not to stretch or tear it and avoiding big creases. Fill with the prepared meat, add the finely chopped onion, if liked, and 2–3 tbsps. stock (or water). Roll out the pastry lid, moisten the pastry round the edge of the basin and place the lid on the top. Cover with greased paper, folding the edge under and finally twisting the end of the paper to hold it securely. Steam for at least 3 hours, or even longer if coarse meat is used. If more convenient, the pudding may be boiled, in which case a cloth should be tied over the paper. When cooked, remove the paper (and cloth) and serve in the bowl with a folded table napkin tied round it. Garnish with parsley, and serve a small jug of boiling stock or water separately to add to the pudding on opening it.

LUNCHEON MEAT ROLY-POLY

8 oz. self-raising flour	Tinned spiced luncheon meat
A pinch of salt	2 tbsps. chopped celery
3 oz. lard	1 tbsp. chopped onion
Cold water to mix	Parsley sauce

Mix together the flour and salt. Cut and rub in the fat very thoroughly with the finger-tips, and mix to a soft dough with cold water. Roll into an oblong. Cover with thin slices of luncheon meat and sprinkle with the chopped celery and onion; there is no need to add extra seasoning. Roll up like a roly-poly, wrap in greased paper, and tie in a cloth. Steam for about $1\frac{1}{2}$ hours, and serve with a good parsley sauce, or bake it in a moderate oven (350° F., mark 3) for 1 hour.

MEAT AND BACON ROLY-POLY

4 oz. minced raw meat
2 oz. minced bacon
2 oz. minced onion
½ tsp. mixed herbs
2 tsps. chopped parsley
Salt and pepper
A little stock or gravy
8 oz. suetcrust pastry

Mix together the minced raw meat, bacon and onion. Add the herbs and season well with salt and pepper, then moisten with a few tbsps. of stock or gravy.

Make the pastry in the usual way. Roll into an oblong about ¼ inch in thickness and spread to within ½ inch of the edge with the prepared filling. Moisten the edges and roll up as for jam roly-poly. Roll in greased paper. Tie in a cloth and steam for 2–3 hours. Serve with gravy or a good sauce

MEAT AND VEGETABLE ROLY-POLY

4–6 oz. fresh minced meat
1 onion
1 carrot
Seasoning
Stock or gravy
8 oz. suetcrust pastry
Brown sauce

Mince the meat, peel and chop the onion, wash and grate the carrot. Mix the meat and vegetables together, season, and add stock or gravy to moisten.

Roll out the pastry and spread on the filling, then damp the edges and roll up like a roly-poly. Wrap in greased paper, tie in a cloth and boil for about 2 hours, or steam for 2½–3 hours. Turn out, and serve with a well-flavoured brown sauce.

SEA PIE

4 oz. haricot beans or split peas
½–1 lb. stewing steak or neck of mutton
1 onion (or 1 leek, if preferred)
2–3 carrots
1 turnip
A stalk of celery
1 oz flour
Salt
Freshly ground black pepper
About 1 pint stock or water

For the Crust

8 oz. flour
Salt and pepper
1 tsp. baking powder
2 oz. shredded suet
Cold water

Soak the beans or peas overnight, with a pinch of bicarbonate of soda added to the water. Cut the meat in neat pieces, and mix with fresh vegetables, cut into dice or sliced. Mix the 1 oz. flour with the salt and black pepper. Fill a casserole or saucepan with layers of meat, diced vegetables and beans, sprinkle with the seasoned flour, then pour on liquid till the mixture is barely covered. Make the crust by mixing the flour, seasoning, baking powder and suet, and adding enough water to make a light dough. Roll out 1 inch smaller than the size of the casserole or saucepan. Bring the meat and vegetables to the boil, then place the crust on top, cover with a close-fitting lid and simmer for 2½ hours. When ready, cut the crust in triangular slices like a cake, and serve the stew in the casserole, with the pastry on top.

HEADS, TAILS AND OFFAL

BRAINS

The brains of the calf, sheep, and lamb are usually sold with the head, or they may be purchased separately. Brains are considered a delicacy, especially those from young animals, and being nourishing and easily digested are often given to invalids and convalescents. Calves' brains are probably the most widely used, but these recipes for cooking them can be followed also for lambs' and sheep's brains. Allow 1 set of small brains per person.

TO COOK CALF'S BRAINS

1 set of brains	Lemon juice
Seasoning	A bunch of herbs

The brains must be very fresh. Wash them in cold salted water, removing the loose skin and any clots of blood, then let them lie in fresh cold water for 1 hour at least. When thoroughly cleansed, put the brains into a small saucepan with cold water to cover them, a pinch of salt, and a good squeeze of lemon juice. Add a small bunch of herbs (parsley, thyme, and bay leaf), and simmer slowly for ¼ hour. Then strain and keep the brains hot. Serve in one of the following ways :—

CALF'S BRAINS ON TOAST

Cook the brains as above. Make a good white sauce (see chapter on Sauces) and add to it the yolk of an egg and a good squeeze of lemon juice. Place the brains on 2 rounds of toast, strain the sauce over, and garnish with lemon, a few potato balls or green peas.

FRIED CALF'S BRAINS

Cook the brains as above and let them cool. When firm, cut them in slices and coat them lightly with flour. Then egg-and-breadcrumb them and fry in boiling fat until a light brown colour. Serve with cut lemon.

SAUTÉED CALF'S BRAINS

Prepare and cook the brains as above, then sauté them in butter for a few minutes and lift them on to a hot dish. Allow the butter to brown. Add chopped parsley and capers and a dash of vinegar, pour over the brains and serve at once.

SCALLOPED CALF'S BRAINS

Cook as above, then arrange the brains in scallop shells, cover with white sauce and sprinkle breadcrumbs and grated cheese on the top. Put in the oven or under the grill for a few minutes to brown the top.

BRAIN CAKES

1 calf's brain	1 egg yolk
1 oz. butter or margarine	Egg and breadcrumbs for coating
1 oz. flour	Fat for frying
¼ pint milk	Parsley to garnish
1 tsp. chopped parsley	White sauce
2 oz. breadcrumbs	
Salt, pepper and nutmeg	

Cover the brain with cold water, add 1 tsp. of salt and bring to the boil. Skim, then boil gently for 10 minutes. Strain, leave to get cold, and then cut into small pieces. Melt the butter, stir in the flour, gradually add the milk, then stir until the mixture boils and thickens. Add the brain, parsley, breadcrumbs, salt and pepper, and a very little nutmeg. Add the egg yolk and stir for a few minutes over a low heat without boiling. Let the mixture get cold, then divide it into little cakes : sprinkle these with flour, brush with beaten egg, and toss in breadcrumbs. Fry in smoking-hot fat until crisp and golden-brown, garnish with parsley and serve with white sauce or other good sauce.

CALF'S HEAD

Remove the brains and wash the head thoroughly, paying particular attention to nostrils and ears. Soak in cold water for 2 hours. Dry, and rub over with a cut lemon to whiten it.

The brains may be served separately as described above, or used for a sauce or garnish.

BOILED CALF'S HEAD

1 calf's head	1½ oz. butter
2 carrots	1½ oz. flour
2 stalks of celery	½ pint milk
1 turnip	½ pint calf's head stock
Salt and pepper	1 tbsp. chopped parsley
12 peppercorns	1 lemon
Mixed herbs	A little sherry

Cover the cleaned head with cold water, bring to the boil, and skim. Add the vegetables and seasoning, with a little mixed herbs, and simmer for 2 hours. Prepare the brains; put them in a muslin bag 1 hour before the head is ready and boil them with it. Remove the brains after ½ hour's boiling and leave to cool. While the head is simmering make a sauce: melt the butter in a separate pan, add the flour, and cook for several minutes. Then add the milk, with ½ pint of liquor from the head, stir together until boiling, and simmer for 10 minutes. Chop the brains finely and add them to the sauce, with a little chopped parsley, the juice of a lemon, seasoning, and sherry. The head may be served as it comes from the stewpan, with the sauce served separately, or it may be coated with egg and breadcrumbs and baked in a moderately hot oven (400° F., mark 6) for 20 minutes. In this case baste frequently while baking. Serve with a garnish of thin slices of the tongue and lemon.

CALF'S HEAD WITH MAÎTRE D'HÔTEL SAUCE

Remains of a cooked calf's head	1 tbsp. chopped parsley
1 tbsp. lemon juice	

For the Sauce

1 oz. butter	2–3 tbsps. clear stock
1 oz. flour	Bay leaf
½ pint milk	Salt and pepper

To prepare the sauce, melt the butter, stir in the flour, and cook gently, but do not let the flour brown. Add the milk gradually and stir until the sauce boils. Add the stock and the bay leaf, simmer for 10 minutes, remove the bay leaf, season and strain. Heat the meat in the sauce, adding the lemon juice and parsley, and serve.

CALF'S HEAD ROLLED AND STUFFED

½ a calf's head	1 lemon
3 oz. suet	Seasoning
7 oz. breadcrumbs	1 egg
1 tbsp. mixed herbs	Salt

Remove the tongue and brains from the head after cleaning and then roll off the flesh in one piece, starting at the lip. Mix the suet with 6 oz. of breadcrumbs, the herbs, and 1 tsp. of grated lemon rind, season, and then mix the whole with the egg, reserving a little. Lay this forcemeat in the centre of the head, roll up and fasten with string. Cover bones and tongue with cold water, add 1 tbsp. of salt and bring to the boil. Skim, add the stuffed head, and simmer for 2 hours. Half an hour before the head is ready, put the washed and skinned brains into a muslin bag and cook for 15 minutes with the head. Take out the tongue and brains and chop them into small pieces. Brown the remaining breadcrumbs. Remove the head from the pan, brush it with lightly beaten egg, cover with the breadcrumbs, and serve with the chopped tongue and brain as a garnish.

ROAST CALF'S HEAD

1 calf's head	1 lemon
1 oz. butter	Bacon rolls
Dripping	Brown gravy
Salt and pepper	

Skin the head, wash it well, rub it lightly with the butter, place in a baking tin with dripping, season with salt and pepper, and roast in a moderately hot oven (400° F., mark 6) until tender—1–1½ hours. While roasting, the head should be sprinkled from time to time with lemon juice and basted thoroughly. Garnish with bacon rolls. Serve with brown gravy and potatoes.

PIG'S HEAD

Scald in boiling water, then scrape the skin well to get rid of the hairs, split head open, remove the brains, eyes and snout. Cleanse thoroughly. Soak overnight in strong salt and water. Rinse in fresh water and drain.

PIG'S HEAD—TO PICKLE

For Dry Pickle

1 lb. common salt	1½ oz. saltpetre

Mix the salts together, rub the mixture into every part of the head, let it lie for 5–6 days, turning and basting every day, then drain and wash again.

For Wet Pickle

1 lb. block salt	1 oz. saltpetre
6 oz. brown sugar	1 gallon water

Boil for 5 minutes, keeping the surface skimmed, then drain into a large basin and leave until cold. Lay the pig's head in the pickle for 3–4 days, turning every day. Wash thoroughly in running cold water before use.

BOILED PIG'S HEAD WITH ONION SAUCE

1 pig's head	Brown crumbs

For the Sauce

5 large onions	1 pint milk and stock
1½ oz. flour	Salt and pepper
1½ oz. butter	

Put the head and tongue into a large saucepan, cover with cold water, bring to the boil, and skim. Simmer very gently until tender; this will take 3–4 hours. Boil 5 onions with the head until soft, then remove and chop finely. Make a sauce with the flour, butter, milk and stock. Add the onions and seasoning. To dish, lift out the head, sprinkle with brown crumbs, garnish with the tongue cut in slices, and hand the onion sauce separately.

BRAWN

1 pickled pig's head	Pieces of carrot and turnip
Peppercorns	1 large onion
Salt	1 hard-boiled egg
Bunch of herbs	

Cut off the ears, remove the brains and all gristle from the head. Place head in a pan with the peppercorns, salt, bunch of herbs, carrot, turnip, and onion, cover with water, and bring to the boil Skim carefully and allow it to cook until the meat is quite tender—about 3 hours is
40 usually sufficient. Strain off the liquid, remove the meat from the bones and cut into small pieces, being careful to remove any fat or gristle. Skim off the fat and boil the remaining liquid until reduced to half. Garnish the bottom of a brawn mould or cake tin with chopped white of egg. Pack the meat in tightly and pour over some of the liquid. Put a saucer and weight on it, leave until quite cold and set. The ears should be scalded, scraped free from hair, washed well, and boiled until tender with the head, then cut into strips and mixed with the head meat.

When required for use, dip the mould into hot water and turn the brawn out on to a dish.

COLLARED PIG'S HEAD

1 pig's head (salted)	1 onion
Root vegetables (carrots, turnip, celery, etc.)	2 cloves
Seasoning	Finely grated lemon rind
Peppercorns	Nutmeg

Wash the pig's head in cold water, put it into a saucepan with the tongue, vegetables, salt, and peppercorns, and an onion stuck with the cloves. Cover with cold water, bring slowly to boiling point and simmer for several hours until tender. Lift out the head, cut in half and take out the bones. Skin the tongue and cut in slices. Season the head with pepper, grated lemon rind and grated nutmeg, and sandwich the tongue between the two sides of the head. Roll up and tie firmly in a cloth in a sausage shape. Cook in the stock for another 2 hours. Then press the roll between two dishes with a weight on top until cold. Remove the cloth and cut in slices as required.

PHILADELPHIA SCRAPPLE

½ a pig's head	Salt, pepper, paprika
2 pig's feet	Stock
1 onion	Maize meal
1 carrot	Coarse oatmeal
¼ of a turnip	Sugar

Prepare the head and feet. Cover with cold water, add vegetables, salt and peppers, and boil until tender. Remove meat and put through a mincing machine. To each 1 lb. of meat allow 1 pint of stock, 4 oz. maize meal, and 4 oz. oatmeal. Mix together and cook in a double saucepan for 1–2 hours, until the meal is cooked. Add seasoning and sugar to taste. Put into wet moulds and set to cool. To serve the scrapple, cut in slices, toss in breadcrumbs, and fry until golden-brown.

SHEEP'S HEAD

DRESSED SHEEP'S HEAD

1 sheep's head, prepared as for calf's head	1 oz. flour
Boiling water	1 oz. butter
Salt	¼ pint milk
Flavouring vegetables	Bacon rolls
A bunch of herbs	2 tsps. grated lemon rind
2 cloves	1 tbsp. chopped parsley
6 peppercorns	

Put the head with the tongue in a saucepan with boiling water, add salt, flavouring vegetables, herbs, and spices. Simmer until the meat will slip away from the bones—about 2 hours.

Wash and soak the brains, tie in muslin and cook with the head for 10–15 minutes. Drain and chop. Make a sauce with the flour, butter, milk, and sufficient of the broth (strained) to make it the consistency of thick cream. Add the chopped brains and season.

Lift the head from the liquid, cut off all the meat and arrange on a hot dish. Coat with the brain sauce and garnish with the sliced, skinned tongue and grilled bacon rolls. Sprinkle the whole dish with the grated lemon rind mixed with the parsley.

For SHEEP'S HEAD BROTH see chapter on Soups.

SHEEP'S HEAD PIE

1 sheep's head	¼ lb. lentils
1 small piece celery	4 rashers cold fried bacon
1 small onion	Salt and pepper
2 carrots	1 tsp. mixed herbs

For the Pastry

8 oz. flour	¼ tsp. salt
4 oz. dripping	Cold water to mix

Prepare the head as for Sheep's Head Broth, half cover it with cold water and bring to the boil. Skim the broth and add the sliced vegetables, lentils, and brains. Simmer steadily for 2 hours, turning the head occasionally. Remove the head from the pan and reduce the liquor to ½ pint. Meanwhile, cut the meat off the head, skin and slice the tongue, chop the brains. Put in a pie dish, together with the bacon, seasoning, and herbs. Add the reduced liquid. Cover with a shortcrust made from the flour, dripping, salt, and water, and bake in a moderately hot oven (400° F., mark 6) for ½–¾ hour.

HEARTS

All hearts need long, slow cooking to make them tender. Ox heart, being larger than calves', sheep's or lambs', requires longer cooking. An ox heart will serve 5–6, a calf's or sheep's 1–2, and a lamb's 1 person.

Wash the hearts thoroughly in several changes of cold water. Cut off the flaps and lobes and remove all pieces of gristle. Cut away the membrane which divides the two cavities, and see that the inside is quite free from blood. Soak in cold water for at least ½ hour.

BOILED HEART

1 calf's heart	½ pint good brown sauce
Flavouring vegetables	Diamonds of toast
Salt	Chopped parsley

Prepare the heart, cover with cold water, add flavouring vegetables and salt, and simmer very gently for 1½–2 hours. Remove the heart and cut in dice. Make the brown sauce with the stock. Reheat the heart in the sauce, serve garnished with toast and sprinkled with freshly chopped parsley.

CALF'S HEART, STUFFED AND STEWED

1 calf's heart	Flour
6 tbsps. breadcrumbs	Dripping
Chopped parsley	1 cupful water or stock
Grated lemon rind	Tomato sauce (see below)
1 tbsp. chopped ham	Lemon
Seasoning	Roast or sauté potatoes
1 tbsp. melted butter or margarine	
Egg or milk	

Wash the heart thoroughly and remove the large veins and arteries. Soak it for ½ hour or longer in cold water to which a little salt has been added. Then blanch it, i.e. put it into a saucepan with cold water to cover, bring to the boil, throw the water away, and rinse the heart. It should now be clean and ready for stuffing. Mix all the dry ingredients in a basin and add the chopped ham, season carefully, and bind together with the melted butter and a little egg or milk. Put this stuffing into the heart and sew it up, or tie a piece of greased paper over the top. Then roll in flour to make it thoroughly dry. Melt a small quantity of dripping in a stewpan, put in the heart and brown it on all sides. Pour in a cupful of water or stock and stew slowly until the heart is tender—1½–2 hours. When ready, lift it on to a hot dish and remove the string or paper. To make a sauce prepare 1 cupful of tomato purée by rubbing some fresh or tinned tomatoes through a sieve. Mix this with 2 tbsps. flour and add to the liquid left in the saucepan. Stir until boiling, season to taste, and when thoroughly cooked strain over the heart. Garnish with lemon and roast or sauté potatoes.

SCALLOPED SHEEP'S HEARTS

2 sheep's hearts	1 oz. flour
½ pint stock or water	Mashed potatoes
Flavouring vegetables (carrot, onion, etc.)	1 oz. browned breadcrumbs
A bouquet garni	2 tsps. chopped parsley
Salt and pepper	

Wash the hearts thoroughly in several changes of cold water and cut off the flaps, lobes, and all pieces of gristle, taking care to wash the blood away from the inside. Cut in neat slices or dice and put into a pan with ½ pint stock, flavouring vegetables, cut into small pieces, and bouquet garni tied in muslin. Add salt, cover closely, and stew gently until quite tender (about 2 hours). Remove the bag of herbs.

Blend the flour with a little stock and add it to the saucepan, stirring while it comes to the boil. Add more seasoning if necessary, and cook for 2–3 minutes. Arrange the slices of heart and vegetables in scallop shells and coat with the sauce. Pipe a border of mashed potatoes round the edge, sprinkle with browned crumbs, reheat if necessary, and decorate with parsley.

STEWED OX-HEART

2 oz. fat	Carrot and turnip
1 ox-heart	A bouquet garni
1 oz. flour	Salt and pepper
1 pint stock	6 oz. macaroni
2 onions	4 tbsps. tomato sauce

Melt the fat, slice the heart, toss in flour and fry in the hot fat. Add stock, vegetables, herbs and seasonings, and simmer gently until tender —2–3 hours. Boil the macaroni in salted water until tender. Reheat in tomato sauce (or, alternatively, toss in melted butter and sprinkle with chopped parsley). Serve the heart in the centre of a hot dish, strain the gravy over and place the macaroni round.

STUFFED ROAST HEARTS

Fill the heart with veal forcemeat or sage and onion stuffing. Sew up with fine string and place in a baking tin with dripping. Bake in a moderate oven (350° F., mark 4), basting frequently, and turning the heart several times. Great care must be taken to cook heart gently, otherwise it may be tough. Cook until tender, allowing about 2–3 hours for a bullock's heart, 1–1½ hours for a calf's heart, and ¾–1 hour for a sheep's heart. Serve with thickened gravy, and have red-currant jelly with bullock's heart.

Small hearts may be arranged as seen in the colour picture opposite page 129, with alternate rows of cauliflower sprigs, sprouts and piped mashed potato.

KIDNEYS

Ox kidney is inexpensive but somewhat strong in flavour, and requires long cooking to make it tender. Sheep's and pigs' kidneys are delicate in flavour and cook comparatively quickly. Allow 1½–2 sheep's or pigs' kidneys, or 4 oz. ox kidney per person.

Skin the kidney if necessary. Cut out the core with sharp scissors and wash thoroughly in tepid water. Dry before using.

CURRIED KIDNEY EN COCOTTE

½ lb. ox kidney	3 oz. rice
Seasoned flour	Chopped parsley

For the Sauce

1 small onion	1 tsp. curry paste
1 oz. dripping	½ pint stock
2 tsps. curry powder	1 tsp. lemon juice
1 small apple	2 tsps. chutney
1 tomato	

Soak the kidney in warm water, cut into small pieces, discarding the core, and toss in seasoned flour. Make the sauce as follows: chop the onion finely and fry it in the dripping until golden-brown. Add the kidney and curry powder and fry for a few moments. Stir in the chopped apple, sliced tomato, and curry paste. Then add the stock and bring to the boil, stirring continuously. Add the lemon juice and chutney, and simmer gently for about 2 hours, until the kidney is tender, taking care that the sauce does not stick or burn.

Cook the rice in boiling salted water, then drain, rinse, and dry it. Dish the kidney in cocotte dishes, arranging the rice in a border round the kidney, and garnish with a little parsley.

DEVILLED KIDNEYS

1 calf's or 2 sheep's kidneys	1 carrot, diced
	1 bay leaf
½ pint stock	Salt, paprika, cayenne
1 small onion, minced or chopped	4 tbsps. breadcrumbs
	½ cup thick tomato sauce
1 stalk of celery, minced or chopped	Parsley

Cook the kidneys in the stock until tender, with the onion, celery, carrot, and bay leaf. Remove the kidney, drain, and chop into small pieces. Season highly with salt, paprika, and a few grains of cayenne. Mix with the breadcrumbs and tomato sauce. Pour into individual dishes and bake in a moderately hot oven (400° F., mark 6) for ¼ hour. Garnish with parsley.

GRILLED KIDNEYS

2 sheep's or pigs' kidneys	Salt and pepper
Salad oil	Maître d'hôtel butter

Split the kidneys, take out the core and open back the two halves. Skin and skewer them to keep them flat. Brush with oil, sprinkle with salt and pepper and grill until brown on both sides, then reduce the heat and continue cooking until tender—about 10 minutes. Serve on toast with a pat of maître d'hôtel butter.

KIDNEY HOT-POT

3–4 sheep's kidneys
1 tbsp. flour
Seasoning
1 oz. butter or bacon fat
A little stock or water
1 onion
½ lb. potatoes

Split the kidneys, remove the skin and white core, and cut into pieces. Put the flour on to a plate with some pepper and salt, and toss the pieces of kidney in it until they are well coated. Now melt the fat in a small saucepan and cook the kidney in it until browned on all sides. Pour in the stock or water and stir until boiling. Slice the onion very thinly, and cut the potatoes in ¼-inch slices, and lay them on the top. Sprinkle with more pepper and salt, put the lid on the pan and cook very slowly for ½ hour. Shake the pan occasionally to prevent the contents sticking.

The addition of a few fresh mushrooms, peeled and cut in slices, would be an improvement to the hot-pot.

MADRAS KIDNEYS

2 sheep's kidneys
Salt and pepper
Cayenne
½ tsp. grated lemon rind
Beaten egg
Breadcrumbs
Frying fat
Rounds of buttered toast
Curry paste

Skin the kidneys and cut them into halves lengthwise. Season with salt and pepper and a very little cayenne. Mix the lemon rind with the egg and dip the kidneys in the mixture. Roll in breadcrumbs and fry lightly in hot fat. Serve on small rounds of buttered toast spread lightly with curry paste.

KIDNEYS AND MUSHROOMS

3–4 sheep's kidneys
1 tbsp. flour
1 oz. butter or bacon fat
Seasoning
A little stock or water
½ lb. mushrooms
Fried or toasted bread rounds
Watercress or bacon rolls to garnish

Skin and core the kidneys, cutting them in halves. Wash them in salt and water, dry in a cloth and coat with flour. Melt half the fat in a frying pan, and, when hot, cook the pieces of kidney until well browned. Then put them into a small saucepan, add seasoning and a very little stock or water, cover, and simmer slowly for 20 minutes. Meanwhile, prepare the mushrooms: peel them and remove the stalks, wash them if necessary in a little salt and water and then dry. Melt the remainder of the fat in the same frying pan, put in the mushrooms and fry them for a few minutes. When the kidneys are tender add the mushrooms and cook together for about 5 minutes. Serve the kidneys on fried or toasted rounds of bread, and place the mushrooms in the centre. Garnish with watercress or small rolls of fried bacon.

A calf's kidney or a piece of calf's liver may be cooked in the same way.

A little finely-chopped onion or shallot may be added to the kidney. Small red tomatoes may be used in place of mushrooms. Chestnuts are also very good combined with kidney. They should be parboiled and peeled, then cooked along with the kidney.

STEWED OX KIDNEY

1 lb. ox kidney
4 tbsps. flour
Seasoning
2 oz. dripping
1 onion
1 pint stock
1 carrot
Green peas to garnish

Prepare the kidney and cut in neat pieces. Toss in the seasoned flour. Make the dripping smoking hot, slice the onion and fry until golden-brown. Remove from the pan, reheat the fat and fry the kidney lightly. Stir in any remaining flour, and brown. Add stock, bring to boiling point, season, put in the fried onion and sliced carrot, cover with a lid, and simmer very gently for about 2 hours. Serve in a hot dish garnished with green peas.

For KIDNEY SOUP see chapter on Soups.

LIVER

Ox liver is the cheapest obtainable, but is coarse in texture and needs careful cooking to make it palatable. Calf's liver is delicately flavoured and is most generally used. Pig's liver and sheep's liver are also good to use. Allow 4 oz. of liver per head.

Wash liver thoroughly in tepid water. Cut out any tubes and dry the liver.

CALF'S LIVER WITH PIQUANT SAUCE

1 lb. calf's liver
Flour
Salt and pepper
4 finely chopped shallots
2 chopped gherkins
3 tbsps. vinegar
Fat for frying
1 oz. butter
½ pint water

Slice the liver and dip it into 1 tbsp. of flour seasoned with salt and pepper. Bring the shallots, gherkins, and vinegar to the boil and boil rapidly for a few minutes; keep hot. Fry the liver in hot fat until brown and tender, remove and keep hot. Pour off the fat from the pan in which the liver was fried, but retain the brown sediment. Add the butter to this and when hot, sprinkle with flour and cook until brown. Add ½ pint of water gradually and stir until boiling. Simmer for 5 minutes. Strain and mix with the shallots, etc., season, and serve poured round the liver.

FRIED LIVER AND BACON

1 lb. calf's liver	4 rashers bacon
4 tbsps. flour	2 tbsps. dripping
Salt and pepper	½ pint stock

Cut the liver into slices ½ inch thick, and dip in the seasoned flour. Fry the bacon lightly and keep hot. Add the dripping to the bacon fat and heat; when smoking lightly, add the liver and fry on both sides. Reduce the heat and fry gently until tender. Arrange on a hot dish, placing the bacon on top. Strain off any surplus fat from the pan, add a sprinkling of flour, stir in the stock, boil up, season, and strain this gravy round the liver.

LIVER À LA CRÈME

1 lb. calf's liver	A pinch of thyme
1 onion	1 bay leaf
2 carrots	Salt
1 stalk of celery	1 wineglassful vinegar
1 oz. fat	1 cupful sour cream
2 tbsps. chopped parsley	4 tbsps. breadcrumbs
	Stock if necessary

Prepare the liver and cut it into slices ¼ inch thick. Slice the onion, carrots, and celery into the melted fat with the parsley, thyme, and bay leaf. Add the sliced liver and salt, and stew gently for 10 minutes. Add the vinegar, cream, and breadcrumbs, and continue to keep the whole slowly cooking until the liver is tender, adding stock if necessary to thin the sauce.

LIVER CASSEROLE

½ lb. ox liver	1 oz. breadcrumbs
1 carrot	2 tsps. chopped parsley
1 oz. dripping	A good pinch of mixed herbs
1 onion	Salt and pepper
½ oz. flour	1 lb. potatoes
½ pint stock	

Cut up the liver, removing the pipes. Scrape the carrot, then mince the liver and carrot finely. Melt the dripping in a saucepan, add the chopped onion and fry until golden-brown. Mix in the flour, add the minced liver and carrot and the stock, and bring to the boil, stirring. Remove from the heat, add the breadcrumbs, parsley, and herbs, and season well with salt and pepper. Pour into a large fireproof dish and cover completely with a layer of sliced potatoes. Cover with the lid and bake in a moderately hot oven (400° F., mark 6) about ¾ hour, removing lid when potatoes are half-cooked to allow them to brown.

RICE CROWN WITH LIVER

½ lb. calf's liver	½ pint stock
1 oz. flour	Tomato sauce
Seasoning	½ lb. rice, cooked
1 oz. dripping	Parsley

Cut the liver into neat slices, dip in seasoned flour, and fry in the smoking-hot dripping. When lightly browned on both sides, reduce the heat and fry very gently until tender. Remove from the pan and keep hot. Add the remaining flour to the fat, stir until brown, then add the stock and boil until the sauce thickens. Stir in a little tomato sauce or purée and reseason. Reheat the cooked rice with some sauce or purée and a little finely chopped parsley. Pack loosely into a border mould and turn on to a hot dish. Place the liver in the centre and pour the sauce round.

LIVER À LA FRANÇAISE

½ lb. calf's liver	4 rashers bacon
4 oz. veal forcemeat	Stock

Prepare the liver and cut in slices ½ inch thick. Lay in a fireproof dish, spread a thick layer of well-seasoned veal forcemeat on each slice and cover with a thin rasher of bacon. Pour a little stock round the liver, cover the dish with greased paper and bake in a moderate oven (375° F., mark 5) ¾ hour.

LIVER DUMPLINGS

½ lb. calf's liver	2 tbsps. flour
Slice of bread soaked in milk	Salt and pepper
	Grated rind of ½ lemon
1 chopped onion	1 egg
1 heaped tsp. chopped parsley	Stock or salted water
	2 oz. butter

Chop the liver very finely. Squeeze the bread dry and mix into a paste with the liver, onion, parsley, and flour. Season with salt and pepper and add the lemon rind. Moisten with beaten egg and make into small balls. The egg should be added very cautiously, and it is advisable to test the consistency of the mixture by dropping small pieces into boiling water before rolling the balls. Boil in stock or salted water for 15–20 minutes and serve with melted butter poured over. Serve dry boiled rice separately.

POOR MAN'S GOOSE

1 lb. ox liver	1 tbsp. chopped sage
2 large onions	2 lb. potatoes
4 oz. fat bacon	Dripping
2 tbsps. seasoned flour	

Prepare the liver and cut in slices ¼ inch thick. Slice the onions and cut the bacon in 1-inch squares. Toss the liver in the seasoned flour and fill a pie dish with alternate layers of liver, bacon, onions, and sage. Cover with a thick layer of potatoes, add water to come just below the potatoes, and put some small pieces of dripping on top. Cover the pie dish with greased paper and bake in a moderate oven (350° F., mark 4) for 1½–2 hours. Twenty minutes before serving, take off paper to allow potatoes to brown.

LIVER AND ONIONS

3 sliced onions	2 cloves
2 oz. butter	2 peppercorns
1 lb. calf's liver	Bay leaf
Salt	Stock
Flour	Lemon rind

Fry the sliced onions in butter to a light yellow. Add the liver, sliced, salted, and dredged with flour. Add herbs (tied in muslin) and seasoning and stock to cover. Cover the pan tightly and stew until tender—about 1 hour—turning the liver from time to time. Remove bag of herbs and serve sprinkled with grated lemon rind.

SPANISH LIVER

½ lb. calf's liver	Cinnamon
1 cup white breadcrumbs	Tabasco sauce
1 tbsp. chopped parsley	1 cup stock
1 chopped onion, fried in butter	1 tbsp. salad oil
Mint	Cooked rice

Stew the liver until tender, drain, and cut in cubes. Mix the breadcrumbs, parsley, and onion, and season with a little finely chopped mint, a pinch of cinnamon, and a few drops of tabasco sauce. Put into a saucepan, add the liver, stock to moisten, and then the salad oil. Stir until boiling and serve on a bed of dry boiled rice.

SWEETBREADS

The most delicate sweetbreads are lambs', but these are rather more expensive than the other kinds. Bullocks' sweetbreads are cheap, but inclined to be coarse, and require long, slow cooking, about 3–4 hours, to make them really tender. Between the two extremes are calves' sweetbreads, which are very good. Both heart and throat sweetbreads can be bought, the heart sweetbread being the better, as it has fewer membranes and is a nicer shape.

Allow 1 small sweetbread per person.

To Prepare Sweetbreads

Use very fresh; wash and soak in cold water for several hours. Blanch by covering with cold water with a few drops of lemon juice added, bring slowly to boiling point and boil for 5 minutes. Throw into cold water and pull off any fat and skin that will come away easily. Use as required.

SWEETBREADS SUPRÊME

2 calves' sweetbreads	½ a bay leaf
1 onion, sliced	Pepper and salt
1 carrot, sliced	1 tbsp. cream
1¾ pints white stock	1 egg
2 oz. butter	Juice of ½ lemon
1 oz. flour	Slice of bread
1 onion	Frying fat
1 clove	

Put the sweetbreads into a pan with the sliced onion and carrot and 1 pint of stock, cover, and simmer until tender. Meanwhile, make a sauce as follows :—

Melt 1 oz. of the butter in a pan, add the flour but do not brown. Add ¾ pint stock, the onion, clove, bay leaf, pepper and salt, and cook for 5–10 minutes, stirring. Cool slightly and add the rest of the butter, cream, and egg yolk by degrees. Cook for a further few minutes but do not let boil. Add the lemon juice and strain. Fry the slice of bread in hot fat until golden-brown. Dish the sweetbreads on the fried bread and coat with the sauce.

SWEETBREADS WITH BROWN SAUCE

2 calves' sweetbreads	1 oz. butter
2 onions	Brown gravy
4 small mushrooms	Salt and pepper
2 tbsps. chopped parsley	½ lemon

Prepare the sweetbreads and cook them for 2 hours. Peel and mince or chop the onions, chop the mushrooms and the parsley and mix together. Slice the sweetbreads thinly and fry them on both sides in the butter. Add the chopped mixture with 2 cupfuls of hot brown gravy, and stew together 30 minutes. Remove sweetbreads, skim any fat from the sauce, season and squeeze in the juice of ½ a lemon. Serve this sauce over the sweetbreads.

LAMBS' SWEETBREADS À LA BOURGEOISE

1 lb. lambs' sweetbreads	4 tbsps. cooked turnip
1 oz. butter	½ pint brown sauce
Stock	1 tbsp. mushroom ketchup
Salt and pepper	1 tbsp. tomato sauce
4 tbsps. cooked peas	
4 tbsps. cooked carrot	

Prepare the sweetbreads and toss them in a pan with the butter until they are lightly fried. Barely cover with stock, season, cook gently for 1 hour. Drain and dry. Boil the vegetables separately. Make ½ pint good brown sauce with the stock from the sweetbreads, and add 1 tbsp. each of mushroom ketchup and tomato sauce. Put the vegetables and sauce into a casserole with the sweetbreads and cook in a moderately hot oven (425° F., mark 7) for about 15 minutes.

SWEETBREADS WITH SAUCE JARDINIÈRE AND MACARONI

1 calf's sweetbreads	2 tsps. flour
1 onion	1 tbsp. milk or cream
2 oz. butter	1 cupful cooked runner beans or green peas, or diced mixed vegetables
Salt and pepper	
2 tomatoes	
½ pint stock	4 oz. macaroni

Prepare the sweetbreads. Fry the onion lightly in the butter, season with salt and pepper and add the sweetbreads and sliced tomatoes. Add the stock, cover the pan and simmer slowly, turning the sweetbreads from time to time, if necessary adding more stock. Simmer until really tender—2–3 hours. Thicken the sauce with 2 tsps. flour blended with 1 tbsp. of milk or cream and stirred carefully in. Cook for 2–3 minutes and add the vegetables. Meanwhile, put the macaroni into fast-boiling salted water and boil briskly for 20–30 minutes, until tender, then strain. Dish the sweetbreads in the sauce, surrounded by the macaroni.

BRAISED SWEETBREADS

Bed of vegetables (carrot, onion, turnip, celery)	Stock
	2 calves' sweetbreads
2 oz. dripping	2 rashers bacon
Seasoning, peppercorns	½ pint tomato sauce
A bouquet garni, tied in muslin	Green peas or diced cooked carrots

To prepare the bed of vegetables, slice the vegetables thickly and sauté them in dripping for a few minutes. Add seasonings and bouquet garni. Cover with stock, lay the prepared sweetbreads on top and cover with bacon and greased paper. Cover the pan and cook gently until tender—about 2 hours. Remove the bag of herbs. Dish, coat with some hot tomato sauce and garnish with peas or carrots.

FRICASSEE OF SWEETBREADS

2 tbsps. butter	½ pint stock
1 grated onion	½ tsp. lemon juice
Chopped parsley	2 calves' sweetbreads, cooked
Salt	
Lemon rind, grated	Sippets of fried bread
2 tbsps. flour	

Melt half the butter, add the onion, a pinch of parsley, salt, and lemon rind, and cook gently for about 10 minutes. Add the rest of the butter, stir in the flour and gradually add the stock. Simmer, stirring until smooth. Add the lemon juice and the sweetbreads, cut into quarters. Simmer for 15 minutes. Serve garnished with sippets of fried bread.

FRIED SAVOURY SWEETBREADS

Prepare and parboil a pair of sweetbreads in the ordinary way, drain, and press them until cold. Slice them about ½ inch thick, and coat each piece with egg and breadcrumbs. Cut 2 rashers of bacon in small pieces, fry slowly in a chafing dish until crisp, then keep hot. Fry the sliced sweetbread in the bacon fat until golden-brown. Serve very hot, sprinkled with paprika pepper.

SWEETBREADS TARTARE

½ lb. cooked sweetbreads	2 tsps. chopped parsley
2 tbsps. mayonnaise	1–2 tomatoes
½ tsp. chopped chives	¼ pint cooked green peas
2 tsps. chopped capers	

Cook the sweetbreads as described on page 153. Mix the mayonnaise with the chopped herbs. Cut up the sweetbreads and toss them in the mayonnaise. Slice the tomatoes very thinly and line several scallop shells with the slices. Put 2 tbsps. of sweetbread into each shell and garnish with a few green peas. Chill the sweetbreads before serving.

SWEETBREADS WITH MAYONNAISE

1 lb. calves' sweetbreads	Mayonnaise
Stock	6 olives
2 oz. cooked tongue	Coralline pepper
1 hard-boiled egg	Chervil or small cress
Seasoning	

Prepare the sweetbreads and stew in stock for 2 hours, until very tender. Lift out and leave to cool. Break into small pieces, and mix with tongue, cut in dice, chopped hard-boiled egg, and a little seasoning. Add mayonnaise to moisten. Place 1 tbsp. of the mixture into each individual dish, put a good tsp. of mayonnaise on top and garnish with a ring of chopped olives, coralline pepper, and chervil. Serve cold.

OX-TAILS AND CALF-TAILS

DRESSED OX-TAIL

1 ox-tail	A bouquet garni, tied in muslin
Seasoning	2 tsps. lemon juice
2 oz. flour	Cooked spaghetti, tossed in a little melted butter and sprinkled with chopped parsley
2 oz. dripping	
Flavouring vegetables (onions, carrots, etc.)	
1 pint good brown stock	

Wash the tail, cut up at the joints and trim off excess fat. Put in cold water to cover, add salt, bring to the boil, and boil for 15 minutes. Strain, dry the ox-tail and toss in flour. Make the dripping smoking hot, fry the ox-tail in this and fry one sliced onion and the remaining flour until brown. Cover with the stock, add flavouring vegetables, bouquet garni, and seasonings; simmer very gently for about 3 hours, until the meat is tender. Lift the pieces on to a hot dish, remove the bag of herbs, thicken the sauce if necessary, then boil up and skim, reseason, and flavour with lemon juice. Strain over the tail and make a border of the prepared spaghetti.

FRIED OX-TAIL

1 ox-tail	Breadcrumbs
$1\frac{1}{2}$ pints stock	Salad oil
Salt and pepper	Brown gravy
1 egg	

Wash and dry the tail and divide it at the joints. Put in a pan with the stock, season, and simmer for 2–3 hours. Drain and leave until cold. Coat with egg and breadcrumbs, and fry in hot oil until golden-brown. Serve with brown gravy.

STEWED OX-TAIL OR CALF-TAIL

1 ox- or calf-tail	1 meat cube
1 oz. dripping	About 1 quart stock or water
Flour	Salt and pepper
Flavouring vegetables (onion, carrot, celery, turnip)	A few drops of lemon juice or vinegar
Herbs, cloves, peppercorns, etc.	Diced carrot and turnips to garnish (optional)

Cut the tail into pieces and trim off any excess fat. Melt the dripping, lightly dredge the pieces of tail in flour and fry them and the onion until golden-brown. Add the flavouring vegetables, cut into small pieces, the herbs and spices tied in muslin, the meat cube, and stock or water to cover. Season, cover closely, and simmer gently until tender (about 3–4 hours, or longer if necessary). Remove the bag of herbs. Skim off all fat; if liked, leave to stand overnight, and remove fat when cold.

Blend 2 oz. flour with a little stock and add it to the stew, stirring while it comes to the boil. Add more seasoning, if necessary, and a few drops of lemon juice or vinegar. Arrange the meat and vegetables on a hot dish and strain the sauce over, garnishing if liked with diced carrot and turnip, cooked separately.

OX-TONGUES AND CALF-TONGUES

These need long cooking to make them tender, but if properly prepared and cooked they make very delicious dishes. Choose an ox-tongue with a smooth skin, which indicates that it comes from a young animal.

Allow 4 oz. tongue per person.

To Prepare and Pickle

Wash and scrape the tongue thoroughly until all slimy substance is removed. Rinse in cold water and dry. Cut off some of the gristle and root part. Rub all over with coarse salt and leave overnight to drain. Prepare a wet pickle as for pig's head. When cool, strain over the tongue, completely covering it with the liquid. Allow to soak for at least a week.

BOILED OX-TONGUE

Soak the pickled tongue in cold water for several hours. (If a smoked tongue is used it will need 12 hours' soaking.) Wash the tongue, skewer into shape, put into lukewarm water,
bring slowly to the boil, and skim. Add flavour- 41
ing vegetables and peppercorns, and simmer the tongue very gently until tender: a 6 lb. tongue will need to simmer for 3–4 hours. When tender, take out the tongue, plunge into cold water so that the skin will come off easily, and skin it very carefully. Slip out any bones in the root and cut off remaining gristle.

To Serve Cold

Roll the tongue into a round shape while still hot and put it into a tongue press or pack it tightly into a round cake tin, fill up with some jellied stock, weight down, and leave to set. Turn out and garnish with watercress or other salad. It is very good with cold ham.

Alternative Method

Truss into shape on a board by fastening the root and tip with skewers. When cold, trim and glaze (page 189) and garnish with parsley and piped butter.

To Serve Hot

Omit the process of plunging into cold water. Skin the hot tongue and glaze or sprinkle with breadcrumbs. Garnish with slices of lemon and parsley and serve with a good sauce.

Note : When preparing ox-tongue for a small family, the cooked tongue can be cut in half, one half served hot and the remaining half pressed and served cold later in the week.

RÉCHAUFFÉ OF TONGUE

Cut slices of cold tongue and spread lightly with a little freshly made mustard. Dip in pure salad oil, and drain well. Melt a knob of butter in the blazer of a chafing dish, and when it is hot lay the tongues in. Fry till golden-brown, turn, and fry on the second side. Remove from the pan, add a few slices of thinly cut skinned tomato, and cook rapidly to a pulp, season, and add a few drops of piquant table sauce, then return the tongue to the pan and serve very hot, with toast.

OX-TONGUE WITH HORSERADISH SAUCE

½ an ox-tongue	2 tbsps. grated horseradish
1 oz. flour	½ tsp. sugar
1 oz. butter	Salt
¾ pint milk	1 tsp. vinegar

Prepare and boil the tongue as described on page 155. Meanwhile, make the sauce as follows :—

Blend the flour and butter and gradually add the milk ; keep stirring while boiling for 5 minutes. Add the horseradish, sugar, salt, and vinegar, and mix well together. Cut the hot tongue into long slices and arrange on a dish. Serve with the hot sauce.

FRIED CALF'S TONGUE CUTLETS

1 boiled calf's tongue	¼ tsp. lemon juice
1 egg	Breadcrumbs
1 tbsp. water	Fat for frying
Grated nutmeg	White sauce
Salt and pepper	

Cut the boiled tongue into slices ½ inch thick. Beat up the egg with 1 tbsp. of water, a grating of nutmeg, salt, pepper, and the lemon juice. Dip the tongue into the egg mixture, then into the breadcrumbs, and fry to a golden-brown. Drain, and serve hot with a good sauce.

SHEEPS' TONGUES

To Prepare

Soak the tongues in salted water for 2–3 hours and rinse before use. The tongues may, if desired, be blanched before cooking : place them in a pan of cold water, bring to the boil, then remove and rinse in fresh cold water.

To Cook

Place in a saucepan with stock to cover, and add flavouring vegetables and seasonings. Simmer gently until tender—about 3 hours. Sheep's tongues require long, slow cooking to make them really tender. Skin the tongues, remove any bones and cut off any gristle from the roots.

BOILED TONGUES WITH CHUTNEY SAUCE

4 sheep's tongues or 1 calf's tongue	2 doz. seeded raisins
	1 tsp. cinnamon
1 onion	4 cloves
1 tbsp. melted butter	4 oz. brown sugar
2 tbsps. flour	1 tbsp. treacle
1 sliced lemon	2 tbsps. vinegar

Boil the tongues till tender in salted water, pare off the skins, and slice. Cut up the onion into the melted butter, stir in the flour, and gradually add 1 pint of the tongue liquor. Add the lemon, with seeds removed, the raisins, cinnamon, cloves, sugar, treacle, and vinegar. Bring to the boil and simmer gently for about ½ hour. Lay the slices of tongue in the mixture and reheat.

BRAISED SHEEP'S TONGUES

4 sheep's tongues	6 peppercorns
Mixed vegetables (onion, carrot, turnip, celery)	A bouquet garni
	2 rashers bacon
1 oz. dripping	Glaze
Stock	Mashed potatoes
Seasoning	½ pint brown sauce

Parboil the tongues, then trim the root ends and take off the skin. Slice the vegetables thickly into a pan, add the dripping, and cook for 10 minutes. Add sufficient stock barely to cover the vegetables. Add seasonings and bouquet garni. Place the tongues on the bed of vegetables, cover with the rashers of bacon and with greased paper. Put the lid on the pan and cook gently for 2–3 hours, until the tongues are tender.

Add more stock if necessary. Serve the tongues, brushed with glaze, on a bed of mashed potatoes. Pour the brown sauce round.

FRIED SHEEP'S TONGUES

4 sheep's tongues	3 oz. breadcrumbs
1 oz. butter	Fat for frying

Braise the tongues as in previous recipe, then dip each half-tongue in melted butter, coat with breadcrumbs and fry till brown. Serve hot with tomato sauce.

SHEEP'S TONGUES WITH LEMON SAUCE

4 sheep's tongues	1 oz. butter
1 stalk celery	2 tbsps. flour
1 tsp. chopped parsley	2 tsps. sugar
1 carrot	1 tsp. grated lemon rind
½ an onion	juice of 1 lemon

Prepare the tongues and stew them until tender with celery, parsley, carrot, and onion. Skin them and cut lengthwise. Melt the butter, stir in the flour, and gradually add the sugar, lemon rind and juice, with ½ pint of the tongue broth. Bring to the boil, stirring, then put in the tongues and simmer gently for several minutes. Serve in the sauce.

SHEEP'S TONGUES WITH PARSLEY SAUCE

Prepare 4 tongues according to directions on page 156. Cut in 3 lengthwise and keep hot. Prepare a sauce from the following ingredients:—

1 oz. butter	Salt and pepper
1 oz. flour	2 tbsps. finely chopped parsley
½ pint tongue stock	
¼ pint milk	

Melt the fat, stir in the flour, add the stock and milk gradually, and stir until boiling. Season, add the parsley and the sheep's tongues and reheat. Serve with mashed potatoes.

CROUSTADE OF SHEEP'S TONGUES

3–4 sheep's tongues	½ pint parsley sauce
Light stock (or water)	Seasoning
Flavouring vegetables	½ a lemon
Herbs	1 hard-boiled egg

For the Croustade

Mashed potatoes	½ an egg
A little butter	Salt and pepper

First blanch the tongues, that is, put into a saucepan with cold water to cover, bring to the boil, then strain and rinse in fresh cold water. Cook them until tender (about 3 hours) in light stock (or water) with flavouring vegetables and herbs. When the tongues are tender, remove them from the saucepan, skin and trim them, and then cut in thin slices. Make a parsley sauce with ½ oz. of butter, ½ oz. flour, ½ pint of the liquid in which the tongues were cooked, and 1 tbsp. of finely chopped parsley. Season with pepper and salt, a little grated lemon rind, and a good squeeze of lemon juice. Put the pieces of tongue into this, with the white of egg cut in shreds, and make all thoroughly hot over gentle heat. Dish in a potato croustade (see below), sprinkle the sieved egg yolk over the top, and garnish with sections of lemon.

A Croustade of Potato

Take about 2 cupfuls of smoothly mashed potato, add a little melted butter and half a beaten egg, and season with salt and pepper. Grease a cake tin, measuring about 6 inches across (one with a loose bottom is best), and line the bottom and sides of the tin with a thick layer of the prepared potato. Bake in a moderately hot oven (425° F., mark 7) for about 20 minutes, until brown and crisp, then remove carefully, place on a hot dish, and it is ready for filling.

SMOTHERED TONGUES

4 sheep's tongues or 1 calf's tongue	2 onions
Salt and pepper	Butter

Scald and skin the tongues and season well with salt and pepper. Slice the onions over the tongue and leave standing overnight. Melt a little butter in a pan and put into it the sliced tongues, together with the juice drawn out by the seasoning. Cover the pan and cook very gently for 3–4 hours. Great care must be taken to prevent the tongues sticking; cook preferably in a double saucepan or in a basin in a steamer, adding a little stock if necessary.

JELLIED SHEEP'S TONGUES

3 sheep's tongues	Flavouring vegetables (carrot, turnip, celery, onion, etc.)
Stock	
Seasoning	½ oz. gelatine

Soak the tongues in salt water for several hours. Rinse and put in a saucepan with stock or water, seasoning, and flavouring vegetables. Stew for 3–4 hours, until really tender. When ready, remove the skin and the root of the tongues. Pack the tongues neatly inside a small cake tin, rolling them round so that they fit tightly into the tin. Melt ½ oz. gelatine in ½ pint of the stock and fill the mould with this. Cover with a saucer and a weight and leave to set. Turn out and serve with salad.

TRIPE

Tripe is the lining of the stomach of the ox. When properly prepared, it is very appetising and is suitable for serving at luncheons or hot suppers. It is also considered to be very light and nourishing, and is frequently ordered for people of weak digestion.

There are several different kinds of tripe, according to the part of the animal from which it is taken; thus there are the blanket, honeycomb, book, monk's hood, and reed. The first two are the most commonly used. When cooking tripe, there are three special points which should always be borne in mind: (1) It must be carefully dressed or prepared; (2) it must be well seasoned; and (3) it must be served piping hot.

How to Prepare Tripe

All tripe requires a certain amount of treatment and cooking before it can be said to be "prepared." The amount of preparation it receives before being sold varies considerably in different parts of the country. As a rule, it has had several hours' cooking by the tripe-dressers before it is sold, and when this is the case, the following amount of preparation will be sufficient :—

Wash it well, put it into a saucepan with cold water to cover it, bring to the boil, pour off the water, and cover again with fresh cold water. Then simmer slowly for 2–3 hours, or until the tripe is tender.

If the tripe is bought in a rougher state, it will require to be washed and scraped in several waters and blanched several times before it is ready for boiling, and then in the final boiling longer time must be allowed. After boiling, the tripe is ready to make up in different ways. If not required at once, it should be covered with its liquid and left to stand in a cool place. The liquid in which tripe is cooked should always be kept for sauce or stock.

TRIPE AND ONIONS

2 Spanish onions — ½ pint milk
1½ lb. prepared tripe — Seasoning
1 oz. butter — A pinch of nutmeg
1 oz. flour — Toast
½ pint tripe liquor

Peel the onions and cook them together with the tripe, until both are tender. Then drain, reserving the liquor. Cut the tripe in pieces and chop the onions. Melt the butter in a fireproof casserole, mix in the flour, and then add the tripe liquor, a little at a time. Stir until boiling, add milk, seasoning, onions, and tripe, and simmer all together for about 15 minutes, stirring occasionally. Serve in the casserole, garnished with toast cut in pieces.

TRIPE WITH LEEKS

A few leeks — A bunch of herbs
1 lb. tripe — Salt and pepper
½ pint stock — 1½ oz. flour
½ pint milk — Parsley

Wash the leeks carefully, removing all sand and grit, slice them in half lengthwise, and then cut into 2-inch lengths. Prepare the tripe and cut it up into small pieces. Put it with the leeks into a saucepan, add ¾ pint of the liquid, and the herbs tied in muslin, and season with salt and pepper. Cover, and allow to simmer gently for 2 hours, or until the tripe is very soft and tender. Remove the bag of herbs.

Blend the flour with the remaining ¼ pint of liquid and add it to the tripe, stirring well. Cook for 2–3 minutes, reseason if necessary, and serve in a deep dish or platter, garnished with a little chopped parsley.

TRIPE PIE

1 lb. tripe — ¼ pint tripe liquor
1 Spanish onion — ¼ pint milk
1 oz. butter — Seasoning
1 tbsp. flour — Mashed potatoes

Cook the tripe and onion until tender. When it is ready, strain it, keeping the liquor. Cut the tripe in thin shreds and chop the onion. Now make a sauce: melt the butter in a saucepan, stir in 1 tbsp. flour, and add gradually ¼ pint liquor from the tripe and ¼ pint milk. Stir until boiling; add the onion and tripe and season to taste. Stew all together for a few minutes. This may now be served as simple stewed tripe; or, to make a pie, turn the tripe into a greased pie dish, top it with mashed potatoes, and bake in a hot oven (450° F., mark 8) until golden-brown—about 20 minutes.

FRIED TRIPE

Choose a thick piece of well-cooked tripe and cut it in pieces. Soak these for a short time in equal parts of oil and vinegar, drain, and coat lightly with flour. Then either egg-and-breadcrumb the tripe, or dip it in a good frying batter. Fry in deep fat to a golden-brown, drain on paper, and serve garnished with parsley. Serve separately a sharp sauce, such as Tartare (page 203).

RAGOÛT OF TRIPE

1 lb. tripe	Salt
1 oz. dripping	2 cloves
1 onion	6 peppercorns
1 oz. flour	1 blade of mace
¾ pint stock	A pinch of mixed herbs
1 carrot	1 bay leaf
2 tomatoes or 1 tbsp. tomato sauce	2–3 tbsps. vinegar
	Gravy browning

Wash the tripe and cut it into neat pieces. Melt the dripping, fry the chopped onion lightly, mix in the flour, and add the stock by degrees. Bring to the boil, stirring continuously, then add the sliced carrot, tomatoes and salt, spices and herbs (tied in muslin). Lastly, add the tripe and the vinegar, cover, and simmer very gently for about 2 hours, or until the tripe is thoroughly tender, taking care not to let the sauce stick or burn, and removing the bag of herbs after about 1 hour. Before serving, reseason and add a little gravy browning, if necessary, to give a rich brown colour.

TRIPE ROLL

1–2 lb. tripe	Nutmeg
4 large potatoes	A little milk if necessary
2 tbsps. chopped parsley	A little flour
1 onion	Salad oil
2 cupfuls breadcrumbs	3–4 slices fat bacon
2 oz. cooked ham	Well seasoned tomato sauce
Seasoning	

Choose the tripe in one piece and of a shape suitable for rolling. Boil it according to directions given on page 158. Boil and mash the potatoes, add to them the parsley, chopped onion, breadcrumbs, and finely chopped ham, and season to taste with pepper, salt, and a good pinch of nutmeg. If too dry, add enough milk to bind together. Lay the tripe on a board and spread it with the mixture. Roll tightly and tie with string. Roll in flour, then in oil, and again in flour. Lay strips of bacon over the top, and place in a baking tin on a trivet. Bake for 1 hour in a moderately hot oven (400° F., mark 6). Cut the roll in slices, and cover with hot tomato sauce.

TRIPE WIGGLE

1 lb. tripe	A squeeze of lemon juice
½ pint white sauce	Parsley and lemon to garnish
1 cupful picked shrimps	
Seasoning	
A pinch of mace	

Cut the tripe into small pieces: it must be very tender and well cooked. Make a good white sauce, using 1 oz. butter, 1 oz. flour, and ½ pint milk and tripe liquor mixed. When cooked, add the tripe and shrimps, and season carefully with pepper, salt, mace, and lemon juice. Cook all together for a few minutes. Serve garnished with parsley and slices of lemon. This dish is very good; it may be varied by using oysters instead of shrimps.

TRIPE AND MUSHROOMS EN CASSEROLE

1 lb. tripe	1 shallot
2 tbsps. vinegar	1 oz. flour
2 tbsps. salad oil	2 cupfuls tinned tomatoes
½ lb. mushrooms	Seasoning
2 oz. butter	1 cupful breadcrumbs

The tripe must be well cooked. Cut it into narrow strips about 2 inches in length and place them to soak in the vinegar and oil for ½ hour. In the meantime, clean the mushrooms and cut them into rather thin slices. Heat 1½ oz. butter in a saucepan, add the shallot, finely chopped, and brown it slightly. Then add the mushrooms, cook for 3–4 minutes, and lift them out with a draining spoon. Add the flour to the fat left in the pan and mix until smooth, add the tomatoes and cook until the sauce thickens. Season to taste and strain before using. Grease a fireproof casserole, place in it a layer of the tripe, and cover lightly with the tomato sauce. Then add the mushrooms, another thin layer of sauce, and half the breadcrumbs. Over this place another layer of tripe and the remainder of the sauce. Sprinkle the rest of the breadcrumbs over the top, dot with ½ oz. butter, and bake uncovered for ¼ hour in a hot oven (450° F., mark 8).

MISCELLANEOUS RECIPES

SCOTCH HAGGIS

A sheep's paunch	½ lb. oatmeal
The liver, heart, and tongue of a sheep	Seasoning
	Grated nutmeg
½ lb. suet	2 tbsps. ketchup
2 large onions	Some stock

The paunch—the bag in which the haggis is cooked—should lie in clean, cold water until wanted. Wash the liver, heart, and tongue, simmer them slowly for about 1 hour, and drain. Then cut them in pieces, removing any skin and gristle, and put them through the mincing machine. Mince also the suet and onions, and toast the oatmeal to a golden-brown. Mix all together, season rather highly, add the ketchup, and moisten with stock. Unless a very large haggis is wanted, cut the paunch into two or three bags, sewing them up where necessary with a needle and cotton. Fill them three-parts full with the mixture, sew up the opening, and prick all over with a darning needle to prevent bursting. Plunge them into a saucepan of boiling water with a plate at the bottom, and simmer slowly for 1½–2 hours, pricking occasionally. Drain, and serve on a folded serviette. A small hole is cut in the skin, and the contents scooped out. The usual accompaniments are creamed potatoes and mashed swedes.

These haggis will keep for several days, and can be reboiled for a short time when wanted. As the mixture is rich, and only a small quantity can be eaten, it is a mistake to make them large.

CHITTERLINGS

These are the intestines of ox, calf, and pig—pig's chitterlings being probably the most popular. They are cleaned and usually boiled before being sold, and if fresh should have no unpleasant smell. If the chitterlings have not been boiled, wash them very thoroughly, and simmer gently for about 2–3 hours, until tender.

Chitterlings may be used in a number of ways, the most usual being to fry or bake them until crisp and golden. They may be stewed in a little milk or stock with onions and other vegetables, and are delicious if stuffed with a well-seasoned sage and onion stuffing, then baked. They may also be used as a filling for pies, patties, and turnovers.

FRIED PETTITOES

4–6 sucking pig's feet | Batter
Stock | Frying fat

Wash the feet, bring them to the boil in the stock, and simmer for ½ hour. Take the feet, drain, split them open, dip in batter, and fry in hot fat till brown. Drain and serve garnished with fried parsley.

JELLIED PIGS' FEET

Wash and blanch the feet and put into a saucepan with salt and a bunch of herbs, a blade of mace, a slice of onion, and a small carrot. Just cover with cold water and simmer gently until the meat is tender. Strain the liquid into a basin. Cut the meat from the bones, dice, and add to the stock with 1 dessertsp. of chopped parsley. Turn into a wet mould and set.

For CALF'S FOOT JELLY see chapter on Invalid Cookery.

PIG'S CHEEK

If a long-cured cheek is used, it must first be soaked for 6 hours, but one fresh from the pickle need only be washed in 2 or 3 waters (see Pig's Head). Bring it to the boil in warm water, simmer for 2½ hours, skin, cover with browned breadcrumbs, and bake in a moderately hot oven (425° F., mark 7) for about ½ hour. Serve the pig's cheek either hot or cold.

Braised Duck with Pineapp

POULTRY

Poultry, which comprises fowls, guinea fowls, ducks, geese, and turkeys, is usually sold dressed ready for cooking (i.e., cleaned, plucked, and frequently also trussed), and this saves much time and trouble for the housewife. You need not be appalled, however, if you find yourself faced with the job of preparing a bird, for it is not very difficult, and is fully described in these pages.

Choosing Poultry

When buying a chicken, feel the end of the breast-bone with the thumb and finger. In a young bird the end of this bone is soft and flexible. If it is hard and rigid, the bird is probably too old to roast satisfactorily and will have to be steamed or boiled (or it can be steamed first for, say, 2 hours, to make it tender, and then finished off in the oven for $\frac{1}{2}$–$\frac{3}{4}$ hour to make it crisp and brown). Look at the feet, too. In young birds they are smooth, with small—not coarse—scales, and with short spurs.

Turkeys should be plump and white-fleshed—birds weighing 14 lb. or over are generally best; under this weight they tend to be scraggy. Short spurs and smooth black legs are indications that the turkey is young.

Geese and ducks should have soft and pliable feet, yellow in colour, and yellow bills.

Hanging Poultry

Poultry should be hung for two or three days after killing, before it is cooked. In cold weather it can, if necessary, be hung for about a week, but it must never be kept until it is " high," as in the case of game birds, for instead of its ripening and developing flavour, putrefactive changes take place in the poultry on long keeping, making it unwholesome for food. Hang poultry by the feet in a cool, airy larder. Whether the bird is plucked before or after hanging is immaterial, but it is important that the inside should be left in: once drawn, the bird should not be kept for more than a few hours in hot weather or a day in cold weather. Protect it from flies while hanging, using muslin if the larder is not fly-proof. Never leave birds wrapped in paper or even lying on a dish or plate—always hang them.

Plucking and Singeing

The feathers are much easier to remove while the bird is still warm; for this reason, poultry is usually plucked, or at least rough-plucked, immediately after killing. If many feathers remain, spread a piece of old sheeting or a large piece of paper on the floor or table and pluck on to this. Hold the bird firmly, take two or three feathers at a time and pull them sharply towards the head—i.e., in the opposite direction to that in which they lie. Do not attempt to pluck handfuls of feathers at a time, or you may tear the skin. Large wing feathers are firmly attached and must be plucked singly, with pliers if necessary. All feathers must be plucked out, but down (such as that on a goose), and any hairs, can be singed off.

To singe, hold the bird over an open flame—a gas burner, lighted taper, or piece of burning paper—turning it quickly so that the hairs and down are all singed off.

Drawing

Except in the case of a very young bird, it is advisable to draw the sinews in the leg. To do this, first cut a small slit with a sharp-pointed knife in the leg just above the claw and in the direction of the leg bone, thus exposing the sinews. Slip a skewer underneath one of the sinews, and, holding the foot firmly, pull on the skewer. This will draw out the sinew from the flesh of the leg. There are four or five sinews in each leg, and they should be taken singly—do not try to draw them all at once.

Unless the bird is very young, it is usual to cut off the feet. As it is difficult to cut through the bone, you will probably find it easier to sever the leg at the joint. Bend the foot back, insert the knife in the joint, and cut through. (Keep the feet for the giblet stock. First wash

ff Pastries

and scald them, then remove the scales, nip off the claws and add the feet to the giblets.)

To cut off the head, first cut through the skin of the neck about 2 inches from the body. Slip back the skin and cut off the neck close to the trunk. Keep the neck for stock; discard the head.

Before drawing the bird, slit the skin of the neck a little way down the back of the bird—far enough to enable you to get your fingers inside to loosen the windpipe and gullet: this greatly simplifies the process.

Now, cut round the vent at the tail end with scissors or a sharp knife, taking care to avoid puncturing the entrails. The hole should be large enough to slip your fingers inside the body; then, taking hold of the gizzard, you can draw out all the entrails, including the lungs, windpipe, and gullet. Reserve the giblets (liver, gizzard, and heart) and any fat (there is always plenty in a goose); the rest of the entrails should be burnt. Wipe out the inside of the bird with a clean, damp cloth.

Boning

To bone a chicken, first cut off the neck, the end joints of the wing pinions, and also the feet, severing at the first joint of the leg. Commence boning at the neck. Using a small, sharp knife, and keeping it close to the bone, separate the flesh from the bone. To bone the wings, cut through from inside where the wing joins the body, then work down the bone, scraping the flesh from it and turning the wing inside out; repeat with the other wing. Continue to work down the body, boning the legs in the same manner as the wing. Finally, turn right side out.

The Giblets

Cut out the gall-bladder from the liver, keeping it intact, and discard it; discard also the flesh on which the gall-bladder rests, as this may have a bitter flavour. Carefully cut through the flesh of the gizzard up to, but not through, the crop; then peel off the flesh and discard the crop. Wash the liver, gizzard, and heart, and put them (with neck and prepared feet) into a pan, cover with water, and stew gently for $\frac{3}{4}$–1 hour to make stock for the gravy.

Stuffing

Fowls and turkeys are stuffed at the breast end. Loosen the skin, pack the stuffing firmly and evenly over the breast, and tuck the flap of skin under. Any stuffing that remains can be put into the tail end, or rolled into balls and cooked in the dripping in the roasting tin. It is not usual to stuff very young chickens.

Ducks and geese are stuffed at the tail end.

Trussing

The object of trussing is to keep the bird a good shape so that it will be easy to carve. A trussing needle (a long needle with an eye large enough to take fine string) is useful for the job, but if you have not one of these, an alternative way is to use a skewer and a length of fine string.

Place the tips of the pinions towards the backbone so that they hold the neck skin in position; then set the bird on its back and press the legs well into the side, thus raising the breast. Slit the skin of the vent and put the tail (the "parson's nose") through this.

Thread the trussing needle with string and insert it close to the second wing joint on the right side, passing it out so as to catch the corresponding joint on the left side. Insert the needle again in the first joint of the same wing (i.e., the left side), pass it through the flesh at the back, catch the tips of the pinions and the neck skin and pass it out near the first joint of the wing on the right side. Tie the two ends of the string into a bow. To truss the legs, re-thread the needle and insert it through the gristle at the right side of the "parson's nose." Pass the string over the right leg, through the skin at the base of the breast-bone, over the left leg, through the gristle at the left side of the "parson's nose," then carry it behind the legs and tie firmly to keep it in position.

To truss without a trussing needle, insert the skewer right through the bird just below the thigh bone, and turn the bird on its breast. First, catching in the wing pinions, pass the string under the ends of the skewer and cross it over the back. Turn the bird over, and tie the ends of the string together round the tail, at the same time securing the drumsticks.

Roasting

The various type of poultry require their special stuffings and accompaniments when roasted—see table below.

Chickens and turkeys, since they lack fat, should be covered with a piece of fat bacon and basted frequently with dripping during cooking. They are usually served with boiled ham or bacon rolls as an accompaniment.

Ducks and geese on the other hand are rich in fat and are therefore served with a sharp sauce

—usually one made of apple—to take off the richness. There is generally a good deal of fat inside a goose—place some of this over the bird; any that remains should be rendered down for dripping.

TABLE FOR ROASTING POULTRY

Bird	*Time*	*Stuffing and Accompaniments*
Chicken	1 hour (1¼–1½ hours, if very large)	Any good forcemeat. Serve with gravy, bread sauce, sausages, fried crumbs, bacon rolls
Duck	1–1¼ hours	Sage and onion stuffing, gravy, and apple sauce
Goose	1½ hours or longer	As for duck
Guinea Fowl	30–45 minutes	Watercress, gravy, and orange salad
Pigeon	20–30 minutes	Watercress, gravy; special stuffing given under Pigeon
Turkey	15 minutes per lb. (weight after dressing) up to 14 lb.; 10 minutes per lb. for larger birds	Sausage, celery, chestnut or other forcemeat. Serve with gravy, bread sauce, sausages, bacon rolls

(See individual recipes for oven temperatures.)

ROAST CHICKEN

Prepare the bird as already described. Stuff with veal forcemeat and truss neatly, lay a rasher of fat bacon over the breast of the bird, and place it on a trivet in a roasting tin containing some dripping. Parboil some potatoes, and while still hot place them round the bird, then cook in a moderately hot oven (400° F., mark 6), basting occasionally. (See table for time.)

Forcemeat balls, sausages, and bacon rolls may be added to the tin about ½ hour before the chicken is ready, or may be cooked separately. Fifteen minutes before cooking is completed, take off the piece of bacon to allow the breast to brown. The breast may be "frothed"—i.e., dredged with flour and basted, when the bacon is removed.

Meanwhile, prepare the bread sauce (see chapter on Sauces), cover, and keep it hot. Place the cooked bird on a hot dish, arrange the accompaniments round and keep hot while making the gravy. To do this, pour off all but 1 tbsp. of the fat in the tin, sprinkle in 4 tbsps. flour, and stir in about ½ pint giblet stock. Bring to the boil, stirring, then add salt, pepper, and a touch of gravy browning if necessary. The chicken's liver, mashed, may be added to the gravy to enrich it.

Just before serving, garnish the chicken with a bunch of watercress or parsley. Serve with the bread sauce and gravy handed separately, roast potatoes, and a green salad or other vegetable.

BOILED FOWL

Draw the fowl in the usual way, wipe the inside with a cloth wrung out in hot water, or allow cold water to run through the bird; then proceed to truss it. Pull out the sinews and cut off the legs at the knee joints. Loosen the skin from the thighs by inserting the fingers into the bird and working between the flesh and skin. Then press the leg joints upwards and against the side of the fowl, so that instead of the legs being on the outside as when roasting, they are now pushed inside, and although hardly visible, their shape can be seen through the skin. Well wash the liver and gizzard, and remove the yellow inside skin from the latter. Make a small slit in the skin of each wing, place the liver through one and the gizzard through the other. Pull the skin tightly over the neck to close the opening. Then fold the ends of the wings over the back, holding the neck skin down tightly with them. Hold firmly in position with skewers. Secure the legs thus: thread a trussing needle with string and pass it through the side of the fowl close to the second wing joint, over the legs and through the body, catching the leg and wing at the other side and tying securely. The bird is now ready for boiling.

In order to keep the flesh a good colour, rub the bird over with lemon juice. Place in just sufficient fast-boiling water to cover it; add sufficient salt to season (1 tsp. to the quart) and allow the water to boil for the first 8 minutes, then simmer slowly until cooked. If liked, flavouring vegetables (onion, carrot, etc.) and a bunch of herbs may be added to the pan with the bird. The time required depends on both the age and size of the bird, but roughly, a small and young bird could be sufficiently cooked after it has been boiling for 1 hour, but an old bird might require as long as 3½–4½ hours' slow boiling. Remove the chicken, drain, and place on a hot dish. Serve with parsley, egg, or white sauce. It is customary also to serve boiled ham with boiled chicken.

CHICKEN BREASTS IN PORT WINE

1 clove of garlic	¼ pint port wine
2 small onions	¼ lb. mushrooms
2 oz. butter	Seasoning
1 jar of chicken breasts	Chopped parsley
½ pint chicken stock	

Cut the garlic clove and rub it round the inside of a chafing dish. Peel the onions and slice them finely, melt the butter in the chafing dish and fry the onion slices, stirring occasionally, until they are golden-brown and just tender. Fry the chicken breasts lightly with the onions and add the chicken stock, port wine, and sliced mushrooms; bring to the boil, and simmer for 15 minutes, season, and garnish with the parsley.

CHICKEN À LA MARENGO

1 chicken	A few mushrooms
2 tbsps. olive oil	2 or 3 truffles
½ pint good tomato sauce	Crescents of puff pastry for garnishing
½ pint Espagnole sauce	
½ gill sherry	

Clean the chicken and cut it into joints, removing the skin. Fry to a golden-brown colour in the hot oil, drain, and place in a casserole or saucepan. Add the sauces, sherry, and the neatly sliced mushrooms and truffles. Cover, and simmer gently, until tender—about 1 hour. Arrange the chicken on a dish, skim the sauce if necessary and pour over, garnish with the sliced truffles and mushrooms and pastry crescents.

CHICKEN AND MUSHROOM VOL-AU-VENT

½ lb. puff pastry	½ pint Béchamel sauce
Egg to glaze	½ lb. small mushrooms
6–8 oz. diced cooked chicken	Cress and parsley

Roll out pastry to about 1 inch in thickness, and cut through, using a large, round cutter or cutting round a saucer. (Try not to cut nearer than ½ inch to the edge of the pastry.) With a smaller cutter or knife, mark a circle inside the larger one, to form a lid, cutting about half-way through the pastry. Make cuts round the edges of the top of the pastry and brush the top with egg. Bake in a hot oven (450° F., mark 8) for about 30–35 minutes, covering the pastry with greaseproof paper when it is sufficiently brown. Avoid opening the oven door more than necessary. When the pastry is cooked, remove the lid and take out any soft pastry inside. Heat the diced chicken in the sauce and fill the vol-au-vent with it. Put on the lid, and serve with grilled mushrooms, cress and parsley.

Other savoury fillings may be used, for example, diced or minced cooked rabbit, ham, tongue, or any game or poultry. Vol-au-vents may be served cold, in which case the main filling ingredient should be added to a cold sauce and the filling put into cold pastry cases.

Sweet vol-au-vents may be filled with fruit and cream or a good sweet custard filling.

CHICKEN EN CASSEROLE

1 chicken	2 stalks of celery
Seasoning	2 or 3 carrots
A little flour	½ pint tomato purée
Fat	1 oz. butter or margarine
1 doz. small onions	Boiled rice

Select a tender fowl or chicken and cut it into neat pieces, making about 10 joints. Dredge these with well-seasoned flour, and sauté them in hot fat or dripping until well browned on all sides. Then lay the pieces in a deep casserole, with the onions, the celery, cut in small pieces, and the sliced carrots. Sprinkle with salt and pepper and pour in ½ pint sieved tomato purée, or enough to cover the chicken. Dot the surface with a few small pieces of butter, cover with the casserole lid, and cook in a moderate oven (350° F., mark 4) until the chicken and vegetables are tender, the time required being 2½–3 hours. Remove any grease that is present on top of the sauce, stir the contents of the casserole, and serve hot. A dish of carefully boiled rice may be handed separately.

CHICKEN RISOTTO

Remains of boiled chicken	Salt
	4 peppercorns
1 pint stock	A blade of mace
1 onion	A parsley stalk
A few mushrooms	Chicken liver and gizzard
1½ oz. dripping	
½ lb. rice	

Cut the cold chicken into neat joints, and cut the giblets into small pieces. Boil the remaining chicken bones with some of the first chicken stock to give 1 pint of good stock. Peel and slice the onion and mushrooms, and fry in the hot dripping until lightly browned. Add the rice, and fry gently for 4–5 minutes. Pour on the boiling stock, add the seasoning, the spices and parsley (tied in muslin), and the liver and gizzard. Stir well, then cover closely and cook very gently until all the liquor is absorbed and the rice tender (about 30–40 minutes). Do not stir the rice during cooking, but fork it gently once or twice if necessary, and when it is nearly cooked, remove the bag of herbs.

Lay the chicken on the top of the rice for 10 minutes to heat before serving. Serve piled on a hot dish or in the dish in which it is cooked, with grated cheese and a green salad as accompaniments.

POULET À L'INSTITUT

1 spring chicken	1 oz. fat (butter if possible)
1 lemon	6 gulls' eggs
4 tbsps. seasoned flour	

For the Sauce

1 carrot	½ pint giblet stock
1 turnip	1 sprig of parsley
1 onion	1 bay leaf
1 stalk of celery	2 blades mace
1 oz. butter	

Prepare the sauce first: cut up the vegetables in small pieces and fry them for a few minutes in the fat. Meanwhile, cut the chicken into quarters, wash, and wipe it perfectly dry, rub liberally all over with cut lemon, and afterwards coat with seasoned flour; then fry for 20 minutes in the fat. During this process continue making the sauce. Place the vegetables on a plate, straining off as much fat as possible. Fry the rest of the seasoned flour in it until a rich golden-brown. Add the stock, vegetables, parsley, and spices (tied in muslin), stir until all is boiling, and simmer for 15 minutes. Arrange the chicken in the centre of a hot dish; strain the sauce round, and finally garnish with the cooked and shelled gulls' eggs.

DEVILLED CHICKEN

Cold chicken	1 tsp. made mustard
A dash of cayenne pepper	1 tsp. vinegar
1 tsp. black pepper	2 dessertsps. salad oil
1 tsp. piquant sauce	

Cut the chicken into neat pieces, removing any skin and surplus fat. Blend all the remaining ingredients for the dressing, and when smooth brush over the pieces of chicken to be grilled. Place under a glowing grill and cook quickly, turning the pieces until they are all nicely browned. Serve immediately.

FRIED CHICKEN

Young and tender chickens can be fried raw, but older birds are best partly cooked before being fried. Prepare the bird by plucking, drawing, and singeing in the usual way. Cut a small bird in halves or quarters, or a larger one into neat joints. Season with salt and pepper and coat all over with flour. Then fry in hot fat, turning them so that they brown on all sides—10–15 minutes. Serve with brown gravy.

An alternative way is to season the joints, then dip in egg and coat with soft breadcrumbs and fry in deep fat. Serve with fried parsley and, if liked, a cream sauce or gravy.

GRILLED CHICKEN

Young and tender chickens are very suitable for cooking in this way. Pluck, draw, and singe the bird, remove the head and neck and the feet at the first joint. Split the bird down the back but without cutting through the skin of the breast, and flatten the bird out, removing the breast-bone and breaking the joints where necessary. Skewer the legs and wings closely to the body, keeping it flat. Brush over with olive oil or melted butter, sprinkle with salt and pepper and place on a greased grid, skin side up. Grill under moderate heat for about 10 minutes, then turn and grill on the underside a further 10 minutes, or longer if necessary. Serve plain with clear gravy made from the giblets and garnish with watercress.

An alternative method is to sprinkle with a mixture of finely chopped onion, parsley, and breadcrumbs, after brushing with the oil or butter, and when cooked to garnish with watercress and serve with brown or tomato sauce.

MARYLAND CHICKEN

2½–3 lb. chicken	Béchamel sauce
Seasoned flour	Sweet corn fritters (see below)
Beaten egg	Bacon rashers
Breadcrumbs	
Fat for frying	

For the Corn Fritters

5 oz. flour	1 tbsp. melted fat
3 tsps. baking powder	6 tbsps. milk
1 tsp. salt	1 small tin of sweet corn
½ tsp. sugar	Deep fat for frying
2 eggs	

Clean and joint the chicken, then roll the pieces in the seasoned flour, dip in beaten egg, and coat with breadcrumbs. Melt the fat in a frying pan (using enough to cover the bottom of the pan), and when it is hot fry the chicken till golden-brown—15–20 minutes; turn it often, and do not let the pieces touch each other. Serve with the sauce, sweet corn fritters and crisp bacon rashers.

To make the corn fritters, sieve the dry ingredients, then add the remaining ingredients. Drop tablespoonfuls of the mixture into the hot fat and fry for 3–4 minutes; alternatively, sauté in butter in a frying pan. Drain well.

FRICASSEE OF CHICKEN

1 young chicken	1 tbsp. melted butter
2 oz. butter	A pinch of cayenne pepper
2 oz. flour	1 tsp. lemon juice
1 pint chicken stock	Cooked rice
2 egg yolks	Cooked mushrooms to garnish (optional)
3 tbsps. cream	

Simmer the chicken for about ¾ hour, then cut it into neat joints. Make a sauce with the butter, flour, and chicken stock, and cook for about 10 minutes. Put the egg yolks in a basin, mix with the cream, butter and pepper, and add to the slightly cooled sauce. Reheat, without boiling, then add the lemon juice. Serve the chicken on a bed of cooked rice, pour the sauce over it, and if desired garnish with mushrooms.

CASSEROLED POUSSINS

4 poussins	2 oz. butter
8 rashers of streaky bacon	¼ pint chicken stock
	1 lemon
Seasoning	2–3 tbsps. gravy
1 onion	Potato straws and cress to garnish
1 bay leaf	

Cover the breast of each poussin with a thin slice of bacon, sprinkle with salt and pepper, and place in a roasting tin on a bed of the bacon and sliced onion, with the bay leaf. Put a little butter over each bird, brown quickly in a hot oven (475° F., mark 9), then untruss the poussins. Put the butter, stock, and lemon juice in a casserole and add the birds, cover, and cook for a further 45 minutes in a moderate oven (350° F., mark 4). Serve on a hot dish with the liquor, enriched with the gravy; garnish with potato straws and cress.

CHAUDFROID OF CHICKEN

Cold boiled chicken — Beetroot
43 1 pint chaudfroid sauce — Aspic jelly
A few slices of tomato — Lettuce or endive
Truffles — Salad

Skin the chicken and chop off the end of the leg bones. Prepare the chaudfroid sauce, and, when cold and nearly set, coat the chicken with it, being careful to cover it completely. Cut up the tomato, truffles, and beetroot into small rounds, diamonds, triangles, etc., dip in aspic, and arrange in a fancy pattern on the breast of the chicken. Pour a little cold liquid jelly very carefully over the chicken, taking care not to disarrange the decoration. Dish the chicken on salad and garnish with chopped aspic jelly.

If preferred, the chicken may be jointed, each joint being coated separately. Serve in the same way as above.

GALANTINE OF CHICKEN

1 chicken	Pepper and salt
12 oz. sausage-meat	Spice
Slices of ham and tongue	Glaze
2 hard-boiled eggs	A little butter
Truffles and pistachio nuts	Aspic jelly

Draw and clean the chicken; draw the sinews, and bone (see page 168). Cut down middle of back, spread some of the sausage-meat thickly over the chicken, and arrange the ham, tongue,
slices of egg, and truffles and pistachio nuts on 4
top of the sausage-meat. Sprinkle with pepper and salt and a very little powdered spice. Cover with a layer of sausage-meat. Fold in both ends and roll up tightly. Tie in a clean cloth, putting the fold of the cloth on the fold of the galantine. Simmer it in good stock for about 2 hours, then take out and re-tie the cloth, to get it as tight as possible. Place it on a dish and place a weighted dish on top to press it firmly. (If a tongue-press is available, this could be used.) When cold, brush over with glaze, decorate with a little piped butter and chopped aspic jelly.

JELLIED CHICKEN AND GRAPE SALAD

½ oz. gelatine	5–6 tbsps. mayonnaise or salad cream
3 tbsps. cold water	
3 tbsps. boiling water	3 tbsps. green peas or diced celery
2 oz. sugar	
1 tsp. salt	1 small shallot, chopped
3 tbsps. lemon juice	8 oz. diced cooked chicken
2 tbsps. vinegar	
½ lb. grapes	

Soak the gelatine in the cold water and add the boiling water, sugar, and salt. When dissolved, add the lemon juice, vinegar, and mayonnaise. As it begins to thicken, add the grapes, from which the stones have been removed, the peas or diced celery, the chopped shallot, and the diced chicken. Blend all thoroughly and put into a wetted round or square mould (a perfectly clean cake tin would serve the purpose). Put into a refrigerator, and when thoroughly set, turn on to a dish and garnish with crisp lettuce leaves.

CREAM OF CHICKEN MOULDS

1½ oz. rice	Pepper and salt
1 pint milk	2 tsps. chopped parsley
½ lb. cold cooked chicken	Paprika and parsley to garnish

Use a double saucepan and cook the rice

in the milk until all the latter is absorbed. Cut the chicken into neat, small pieces, removing all the skin, and add it to the rice with the seasoning and parsley. Stir well together and fill small ramekin cases, then garnish.

Alternatively, the mixture can be moulded into small cones, which should be egged, crumbed, and fried. When cold, decorate the top of each cone with paprika and chopped parsley, and garnish with mustard and cress.

MAYONNAISE OF CHICKEN

When well prepared and daintily served, this is an ideal luncheon dish. A cooked chicken, mayonnaise sauce, garnish, and some fresh green salad are required for its preparation, while the addition of some sparkling aspic jelly adds to its attractiveness. A steamed chicken is best, as it is generally more juicy and whiter in appearance than one that has been roasted. Cut it into joints, making in all about 9 small portions, thus: cut off the wings with a small slice from the breast attached (2); remove the legs and cut them in two by the joint (4); then cut off the wish-bone, removing with it a piece of the breast (1); and, finally, raise the breast from the back of the carcase and cut it in two crosswise (2). Remove as much skin as possible from these pieces and cut away any unsightly pieces of bone. Lay them with the best side uppermost on a wire stand, and coat them with the sauce.

The mayonnaise sauce should have been made the previous day, as it improves and thickens if allowed to stand for a short time. It will also be improved for coating purposes if 2–3 tbsps. liquid aspic can be added to it a few minutes before being used. Coat the pieces of chicken evenly with the sauce and let them set. To give them a brighter appearance, a little liquid aspic may be run over the surface. Then decorate according to fancy, with small pieces of truffle, pickled gherkin, leaves of small cress or chervil, etc., using a garnish that will make a pretty contrast in colour to the yellow of the mayonnaise sauce. Let the sauce and decoration become thoroughly set before dishing. Then arrange in the centre of the serving dish some carefully prepared green salad tossed in French dressing. Stand the pieces of chicken round this and garnish with more salad and chopped aspic jelly.

ROAST DUCK

Ducks have more fat than chickens, and the meat is all dark, but there is very little flesh on the bones, so allow at least ¾ lb. of dressed duck per person, or the portions will be meagre.

Pluck, draw, and singe the bird. A young duckling does not require stuffing, but it is usual to stuff an older duck with sage and onion 45
stuffing at the tail end. Then truss the bird for roasting and sprinkle the breast with pepper and salt. Roast in a hot oven (450° F., mark 8), basting frequently. The average time for roasting is 1 hour (approximately 15 minutes per lb. of the trussed bird's weight). Serve garnished with watercress.

A young duckling is best served simply with fresh green peas and potatoes, but if stuffed with sage and onion stuffing, serve with fried or roast potatoes, gravy, and apple sauce.

BRAISED DUCK WITH PINEAPPLE

(*See colour picture facing page* 160.)

1 small pineapple	½ pint good brown sauce
½ bottle of white wine	1 tsp. tomato ketchup
1 duck	
Dripping	

Cut up the pineapple and leave it to soak overnight in the wine. Put the duck in a roasting tin with the dripping, and brown in a very hot oven (475° F., mark 9) for about 30 minutes. Drain off all the fat, and put the duck in a double roaster. Strain the wine and add to the brown sauce and tomato ketchup. Pour this over the duck, put on the lid of the roaster and cook in a moderate oven (350° F., mark 4) for a further 1–1½ hours, according to the size of the duck; when it is cooked put it on a dish and keep hot. Skim all the fat off the sauce, using blotting paper to remove the last of it. Put the cut-up pineapple into the sauce and heat it for about 5 minutes. Arrange the pineapple round the duck and pour the sauce over the whole. Serve with Parisian potatoes and runner or French beans.

DUCK WITH ORANGE SAUCE

1 duck	Stock
Seasoning	1 orange
3 tbsps. dripping	2 tbsps. cornflour
3 tbsps. chopped onion	Potato purée

Cut an uncooked duck into neat joints and season each piece with pepper and salt. Melt the dripping in a saucepan, and fry the joints in this together with the onion. When brown, lift out the pieces and place them in a large saucepan 46
or stewpan with the carcase, any trimmings, and enough stock to cover. Cook until tender, then lift out the joints and strain the liquid. Put the latter into a saucepan, add the grated rind of an orange and the juice mixed with the cornflour. Stir until boiling, and skim if necessary. Reheat

the pieces of duck in the sauce, then dish them up on a bed of potato purée and pour the sauce over. Garnish with more of the purée, put through a forcing bag, and with sections of orange, which have been heated over steam.

DUCK WITH RISOTTO

2 tbsps. olive oil	½ pint tomato purée
1 duck	¼ pint stock or water
1 rasher of bacon	Seasoning
1 clove of garlic	4–6 oz. mushrooms
1 small onion	Risotto
1 carrot	Orange slices
A few sticks of celery	

Heat the oil in a large stewpan or heatproof casserole, and add the duck; turn it to brown it all over, and then remove it. Add the bacon and the cut-up garlic and vegetables, and cook these in the oil. Put in the duck and then the tomato purée, stock, and seasoning. Cover, and simmer gently for about an hour, then add the thickly sliced mushrooms and cook for a further 15 minutes, or until the duck is tender. The bird can be dished up either whole or jointed. Serve with a simple risotto, either placing the whole bird on it or, if the duck is jointed, combining it with the risotto, mixed with the mushrooms and the strained liquor; garnish with orange.

ROAST DUCK WITH WALNUT STUFFING

1 duck and giblets	Flour
Salt	1 tbsp. flour
Walnut stuffing (see below)	½ pint stock from the giblets
Butter or dripping	Watercress

Wash the giblets very thoroughly, put into a pan and cover with water, add salt, and simmer gently to make stock for the gravy. Fill the body of the duck with the walnut stuffing (see below) and neatly sew up the opening. Truss the bird. Cover the breast with greased paper, and roast in butter or dripping, basting frequently—see recipe on page 167. Towards the end of the cooking time, remove the paper, dredge the breast of the bird with flour and allow it to brown. Dish up the bird, removing any trussing string or thread, and keep it hot while the gravy is made. Pour away most of the fat from the tin, leaving any juices, then add the flour and stir this well in, then cook it until it colours. Add the stock, boil for a few minutes, and adjust the seasoning as required. Serve the duck garnished with watercress.

To make the Walnut Stuffing, sieve 1 lb. cooked potatoes, and add 2 oz. melted butter, seasonings, beaten egg to bird and 6 oz. finely chopped shelled nuts. Mix all ingredients well.

DUCK À LA MODE

1 cooked duck	1 tbsp. ketchup
Seasoning	1 tbsp. red-currant jelly
Grated lemon rind	1 glass port
2 chopped onions	Potato balls and small baked tomatoes to garnish
A little fat	
2 tbsps. flour	
¾ pint stock or gravy	

Cut the duck into joints and season each piece with pepper, salt, and grated lemon rind. Fry the chopped onion in a little fat until brown, sprinkle in the flour, and brown that also. Then add gradually the stock or gravy and stir until boiling; add the ketchup, the red-currant jelly and port wine. Place the pieces of duck in the sauce and leave by the side of the heat until thoroughly hot, then dish up and garnish with potato balls and small baked tomatoes. This dish is very suitable for serving "en casserole."

BRAISED DUCK WITH VEGETABLES

1 duck	2 turnips
Sliced onion and carrot	2 carrots
Rashers of bacon	A little butter
A bouquet garni	A pinch of sugar
Salt and pepper	Green peas and diced bacon to garnish
½ pint rich brown stock	
¼ pint brown sauce	

Put the trussed duck into a casserole on a bed of the sliced onion, carrot, bacon, and bouquet garni. Season with salt and pepper, and fry or bake until the duck has a good colour. Pour off the fat, and add the stock and sauce. Lid the casserole and continue cooking in a moderately hot oven (425° F., mark 7) till the duck is quite done, basting occasionally. Meanwhile peel the 2 turnips and carrots and cut into fancy shapes with a Parisian cutter. Toss them in a stewpan with some butter, add salt and the sugar, and continue cooking them in the oven with the duck. Joint the bird, dish up, place the vegetables round, and keep hot. Skim the sauce, reduce it, and then strain it over the duck. Garnish with the peas and bacon.

DUCK À LA PORTUGAISE

1 large duck	1 small glass of sherry
Seasoning	4 small tomatoes
Butter	3 thin slices of tongue
1 pint brown stock	1 truffle (if available)
A bouquet garni	6–8 mushrooms
½ pint Espagnole sauce	Grated nutmeg
½ pint tomato sauce	Mashed potatoes

Wipe the duck with a damp cloth and then joint it neatly. Put the carcase in a casserole, sprinkle with salt, place wings, legs, etc., on top, spread a small piece of butter on each, and put in a hot oven (450° F., mark 8) for 10 minutes. Take out the duck, put the carcase in a stewpan with the stock and bouquet garni, and stew for ½ hour. Add the sauces, skim off the fat, and add the sherry, then reduce a little. Slice the tomatoes coarsely and fry lightly in some butter. Cut the tongue in thin strips, and slice the truffle. Rub the sauce through a tammy cloth. Put the pieces of duck in a stewpan with the sauce, truffle, and mushrooms, and stew gently for about ½ hour. Toss the tongue in a little butter over a quick heat for a few minutes. Season the duck with a pinch of pepper and a little grated nutmeg, dish up on a bed of mashed potatoes, and garnish with the tomatoes, tongue, and mushrooms. Pour the sauce over it.

ROAST GOOSE

Roast goose is served with apple or gooseberry sauce, sage and onion stuffing, and gravy. The tart sauce helps to counteract the richness.

Pluck, draw, and singe the bird, as described at the beginning of this chapter. Cut off the neck close to the body, leaving a good piece of skin for folding under. Cut off the under pinions of the wings, so that there is one joint left on each wing, and cut off the legs at the first joint. The bird is then ready to be stuffed. Prepare some sage and onion stuffing and stuff the goose at the tail end.

To truss the goose, use metal skewers if possible, as these are easily removed before sending the bird to the table. Work with the breast side uppermost and tail end away from you. Pass a skewer through one wing, then through the body and out through the other wing. Pass a second skewer through the end of the wing joint on one side, through the thick part of the leg and out on the other side in the same way. Pass a third skewer through the loose skin near the end of the leg, through the body and through to the other side in the same way. Enlarge the vent, pass the tail through it, and fix with a small skewer. Wind the string round the skewers, in a similar way to that used for lacing a boot, keeping the limbs firmly in position, but avoid passing the string over the breast of the goose. Tuck in the neck under the string, sprinkle the bird with salt, put in the roasting tin and cover with the fat taken from inside the bird, then with greased paper.

For a large goose allow 2½ hours; for a small one 1½ hours is sufficient. The oven should be hot (450° F., mark 8) for the first ¼ hour, then reduced to moderate (350° F., mark 4) until the goose is cooked. Baste every 20 minutes. Half an hour before the bird is cooked, remove the paper, to brown the breast, and baste well. If the goose is very fat, pour off some of the fat that collects in the tin during the roasting process.

Gravy : Wash the giblets, cover with water, add a small onion, and salt and pepper. Simmer gently for 1½ hours. When the goose is dished, strain the fat from the baking tin, pour in the giblet stock, boil, strain a little from the baking tin round the bird, and serve the rest separately.

The goose's liver is considered a great delicacy and is the basis of Pâté de Foie Gras.

RAGOÛT OF GOOSE WITH CHESTNUTS

1 small goose	2 tbsps. tomato purée
1 onion	A bouquet garni
3 tbsps. dripping or margarine	Salt and pepper
	1 lb. chestnuts
1½ oz. flour	1 cupful green peas
½ pint stock	Creamed potatoes

Cut the goose into pieces, chop the onion, and fry both in the hot dripping until brown. Add the flour and cook this until it browns, stirring it constantly and adding a little more dripping if needed. Add the stock, tomato purée, bouquet garni, salt and pepper, and cover the pan closely. Stew gently till tender (about 1½ hours), stirring occasionally and adding more stock if needed. Meanwhile, slit the chestnut skins and boil the nuts for 10 minutes, then peel them and shell the peas, and add both to the ragoût, after skimming away any fat which is on the surface. Serve with a border of creamed potatoes or boiled rice.

BRAISED GOOSE WITH CELERY SAUCE

1 goose	1 oz. butter
Carrot, onion, celery	1 small glass of port wine (optional)
2 rashers of bacon	
1 bay leaf	2 tsps. red-currant jelly
Salt and pepper	¼ pint rich brown sauce

For the Sauce

1 head of celery	¾ pint white stock or milk and water
1 oz. butter	
1 oz. flour	Seasoning

Put the trussed goose on a bed of cut-up vegetables, bacon and bay leaf in a baking tin, season with salt and pepper, and spread the butter over the top of the bird. Cook first in a hot oven (450° F., mark 8) to brown the surface nicely, then reduce the heat to moderate (350° F., mark 4), and cook for about 1½ hours, basting frequently. When the goose is almost done, cut it into convenient-sized pieces. Add the port wine and red-currant jelly to the brown sauce, then place the pieces of goose in this, and cook gently till quite tender.

To make the celery sauce, mince or chop the celery and fry it for a few minutes in the butter. Add the flour and cook for a few minutes, stirring all the time, then slowly add the liquid. Bring to the boil, still stirring continuously, then simmer gently for 20 minutes. Sieve, reheat, season, and serve with the goose.

ROAST TURKEY

There are several different ways of serving roast turkey, but perhaps it is never better than when simply roasted with a few prepared chestnuts put inside, garnished with watercress, with no other sauce than its own gravy. Many people, however, prefer something more elaborate, and would not consider the dish complete unless one, or even two kinds of stuffing were used in its preparation. Chestnut and sausage stuffings are perhaps the two favourites, and, in the case of a large turkey, it is quite usual to put one kind in the neck, and another kind in the body of the bird. A simple veal stuffing could also be used, or a truffle stuffing. Sew the stuffing in, and truss the turkey for roasting, making it as plump and even in shape as possible.

Roast in a moderate oven (350° F., mark 4) for 1½–2½ hours, according to size. A small turkey of 7–8 lb. will take 1½ hours, 10–12 lb. about 2 hours, and of 12–14 lb. about 2½ hours. Baste frequently with some good dripping or bacon fat. If no bacon fat is available, it is a good plan to lay some slices of fat bacon over the breast of the bird; to prevent the skin from becoming too brown, a covering of paper may be used.

Serve with brown gravy and bread sauce. Cranberry or some other sharp sauce may also be served. The gravy should be handed separately, but small fried sausages, forcemeat balls, or rolls of bacon and cut lemon may be used to garnish the turkey. Smoked tongue or ham is also a favourite accompaniment.

BOILED TURKEY

When the bird is small this is a very good way of cooking it. It may be stuffed with a sausage-meat stuffing or with a forcemeat flavoured with oysters or mushrooms. Allow about 2½ hours to cook a 10-lb. bird, and more or less time according to size.

Rub the turkey over with lemon juice, to whiten the flesh, and wrap it up in greased cooking paper. Plunge it into boiling water or light stock, to which a few vegetables and especially celery have been added. Cook slowly for the required time, skimming when necessary.

Boiled turkey may be served with any of the following sauces—celery, egg, parsley, oyster or Béchamel; in addition a special sauce for it is given on page 203. The bird is usually masked with the sauce, and then garnished with rolls of bacon, or balls of sausage-meat and cut lemon.

BLANQUETTE OF TURKEY

½ lb. cold turkey	Pepper and salt
1½ oz. butter or margarine	A pinch of mace
1 oz. flour	1 egg yolk
¾ pint light stock	2 tbsps. cream

This can be made when there are quite small pieces of turkey to be used up. Remove all skin and bone from the turkey, cut it in small, neat pieces, and then weigh it. Make a sauce with the butter, flour, and stock, and cook it thoroughly. Season with white pepper, salt, and a pinch of mace, and then remove the saucepan from the heat. Add the egg yolk and cream and mix them in quickly. Reheat the turkey in this without allowing it to boil—a double cooker or bainmarie is best to use for the purpose. Serve with a suitable garnish, such as rolls of bacon, grilled tomatoes, small forcemeat balls, or croûtons of toast or pastry.

DEVILLED TURKEY LEGS

These are always appreciated by those who like something tasty. Chop off any unsightly length of bone and score the fleshy parts of the leg with a sharp knife. Make deep, even ridges both round and across, and then brush over with melted butter.

To prepare the devilled mixture, mix on a plate 1 tsp. each of French and English mustard, 2 tsps. finely chopped chutney, a pinch of ground ginger, pepper, salt, a little cayenne, and a few browned breadcrumbs. Spread this mixture over and into the cuts, and let the turkey legs stand for 1 hour or longer. Then cook them on a greased grid under a hot grill until crisp and brown. Serve quickly, garnished with watercress. Small pats of butter and some piquant sauce may be served separately.

TURKEY SOUFFLÉ PIE

¾ lb. shortcrust or flaky pastry	A squeeze of lemon juice
	2 tsps. chopped parsley
¾ lb. cold turkey	2 large or 3 small eggs
½ pint white sauce	Salt and pepper

Choose a pie dish about 2 inches deep and line it with the pastry, then decorate the edges. Chop the turkey very small and mix with the sauce, lemon juice, and parsley. Separate the eggs, beat the yolks and stir into the turkey mixture, then fold in the egg whites, beaten to a stiff foam. Season to taste with salt and pepper and pour the mixture into the pastry shell. Bake in a moderate oven (350° F., mark 4) for 40–50 minutes

Chicken or other poultry or white meat may be used in the same way.

TURKEY À LA TOSCANE

1 breakfastcupful breadcrumbs	1 tbsp. salad oil
4 tbsps. chopped ham	Seasoning
2 tsps. chopped onion	Slices of cold turkey
1 tbsp. chopped parsley	Frying fat
1 tsp. curry powder	Mashed potatoes
Grated lemon rind	Tomato sauce
1 egg	Cranberry or redcurrant jelly

This dish can be made when there are some good slices of turkey to be reheated. Mix together the breadcrumbs, ham, onion, parsley, curry powder, and grated lemon rind, and spread them on a sheet of paper. Beat up the egg on a plate, and add to it the salad oil and a pinch of salt. Trim the slices of turkey, making them as equal in size as possible, brush them over with the egg, then toss them in the breadcrumb mixture, pressing the latter on to the pieces. When ready for serving, fry the slices in hot fat until a rich brown colour. Drain, and serve on a bed of nicely mashed potatoes with thin tomato sauce poured round. Cranberry or redcurrant jelly may be served separately.

GUINEA FOWL

This bird belongs to the same family as the pheasant and is not unlike it in taste, being very savoury and easily digested. It has slate-coloured plumage speckled with white spots and is about the same size as the pheasant. When choosing a guinea fowl, the same points should be borne in mind as when choosing a chicken. They are in season all the year round, but are at their best from February to June, and are very welcome when game is scarce.

Guinea fowl can be cooked in any way suitable for the ordinary fowl or chicken. When roasting guinea fowl, larding and frequent basting with plenty of fat are absolutely necessary, for the flesh of this bird is naturally dry and without fat, and if not carefully cooked, is dry and uninteresting to eat.

When guinea fowl is boiled or steamed, an oyster or celery sauce is a good accompaniment.

ROAST GUINEA FOWL

Singe, draw, and wipe the bird, and truss for roasting, tying a piece of fat bacon over the breast. Then roast in a moderately hot oven (400° F., mark 6) for ½ hour or longer according to size, basting frequently with butter or dripping. Garnish with watercress, and serve gravy and orange or other salad separately.

GAME

This is the name given to birds and animals hunted and killed for food, which are protected by law at certain times of the year. The birds (" feathered " game) are fairly numerous, but in this country the animals (" ground " game) are chiefly deer and hares; rabbits are also dealt with here, for convenience' sake, and so are pigeons, although strictly speaking only wild pigeons count as game.

FEATHERED GAME

When buying game from a poulterer, you should be able to judge its age and quality. Game birds are sold unplucked, and the plumage is a guide to age, as all young birds have soft, even feathers. With pheasant and partridge, the long wing feathers are " V "-shaped in a young bird, as distinct from the rounded ones of an older bird. Smooth, pliable legs, short spurs and firm, plump breasts are other points to look for. Game is generally very expensive when it first comes into season, but is often not at its best until later, when it is also cheaper. For game seasons, also cooking times, etc., see table on next page.

Hanging

Game birds require to be hung before being cooked, otherwise their flesh is tough and tasteless. The exact time for hanging depends on the weather and on individual taste, varying from a week in " muggy " weather to as long as 2–3 weeks in frosty weather. The birds should be hung by the neck in a cold, dry, airy place without being plucked or drawn. They should be examined from time to time, especially any that have been shattered when shot, or have got wet, or been packed up for any length of time before hanging, as such birds do not keep so well. For most people the bird is sufficiently mature when the tail or breast feathers will pluck out easily. With a pheasant, the flesh on the breast begins to change colour and the bird smells " gamey." Snipe, woodcock, ortolans and quail, which are cooked with the inside—the " trail "—left in, should not be allowed to get too high before cooking. Wild duck and other water fowl should be hung for a few days only—the flesh tends to turn rank if kept long.

Preparation

When the bird is ready for cooking, pluck, draw and truss it as for poultry, except that the feet are left on and it is not usual to draw the sinews. Snipe, woodcock, ortolans and quail are merely plucked and trussed but not drawn, the " trail " being cooked inside the bird, as mentioned above. Place the bird on a piece of toast for roasting, and serve on this.

Cooking

Generally speaking, the more simply the game is cooked, the better. For a young bird, there is no better way than roasting, but older birds, which are likely to be tough if plainly roasted, can be braised, casseroled or stewed.

Game birds lack fat, so it is usual to cover the

breast before roasting with pieces of fat bacon (this is called barding), and to baste frequently with butter or margarine during the cooking. When the bird is half cooked, the bacon can be removed; the breast is then dredged with flour and basted (this is called "frothing," and is done to brown the breast). Sometimes a knob of butter or a piece of juicy steak is put inside the bird before roasting.

Accompaniments

A thin gravy is handed with roast game, and as a rule fried crumbs and game chips are served. Bread sauce and green salad are served with pheasant, partridge, grouse, ptarmigan and capercailzie. Orange salad is served with wild duck, widgeon and teal.

Bird	*Season*	*Roasting times (in minutes)*	*No. of servings per bird*
Black Cock	Aug. 20–Dec. 10	50	2
Capercailzie	Aug.–Dec.	30–60	4–5
Curlew	Aug.–Mar.	15	2
Grouse	Aug. 12–Dec. 15	30–45	3
Hazel Hen	Dec.–June	20	1
Landrail	Aug.–Sept.	12–20	1
Ortolan	May–Aug.	15–25	1
Partridge	Sept. 1–Feb. 1	30–45	4
Pheasant	Oct. 1–Feb. 1	30–60	4–5
Plover	Aug.–Mar. 1	15–25	2
Ptarmigan	Aug.–Dec.	30–45	3
Quail	May–Sept.	12–20	1
Ruff and Reeve	Aug.–Sept.	10–15	2
Snipe	Aug. 15–Mar. 15	15–25	1
Teal	Oct.–Feb.	20–25	2
Widgeon	Aug.–Mar. 15	20–25	2–3
Wild Duck	Aug.–Mar.	20–35	3–4
Wild Geese	Aug.–Mar. 15	60–80	4–5
Wood Pigeon	All the year	15–20	2
Woodcock	Aug.–Mar. 15	15–25	1

Nowadays, supplies of these birds are imported, and the seasons are not so restricted.

CAPERCAILZIE

For roasting, choose a hen bird, and be sure it is very young. Hang well, then pluck, draw and truss Cook and serve as for grouse, below, barding with bacon and basting well.

Capercailzie can also be boiled or stewed, stuffed with either chestnut or sausage stuffing and served with celery sauce.

ROAST GROUSE

Grouse has a very distinctive flavour and is claimed by many gastronomes to be the finest of the game birds. After hanging, pluck, draw and truss the grouse, and bard it. Put a knob of seasoned butter inside the bird and place on a slice of toast. If liked, the bird may be wrapped in a vine leaf. Roast in a moderately hot oven (425° F., mark 7) for $\frac{1}{2}$–$\frac{3}{4}$ hour, basting frequently When half cooked, remove the vine leaf and bacon and "froth" the bird.

Dish on the toast on which it is baked, and garnish with watercress. Serve with thin gravy, bread sauce, fried crumbs and straw potatoes. A lettuce or watercress salad may also be served.

ROAST PARTRIDGE

Select a young bird and pluck and clean it, season the inside with pepper and salt, and replace the liver. Stuffing may be put in if desired—either a simple stuffing made of bread-crumbs, parsley, etc., or a more elaborate one with chopped mushrooms or truffles. Then truss the partridge in the same way as a chicken is trussed, pressing up the breast to give it a plump, rounded appearance. The breast may be waistcoated with a vine leaf and bacon to shield it from drying, while the legs (which the heat takes much longer to penetrate), are cooking. For this, a fine vine leaf should be trimmed in rectangular form, spread lightly with butter, and laid on the breast with a thin slice of bacon of the same size on the top: these should be fixed in place with a piece of string, and removed before the bird is sent to table. With adequate basting with good butter, however, the breast may be kept from dryness without this extra precaution. The average time for roasting a partridge is 30 minutes in a moderately hot oven (425° F., mark 7); it must not be sent to table underdone, but at the same time over-cooking must be avoided.

Remove the trussing strings and serve at once with a good brown gravy made in the roasting tin, thus: add a small quantity of water, or meat stock that is not flavoured with vegetables, and with a spoon rub down any juice that adheres to the sides of the tin. Boil 2–3 minutes, remove all grease from the surface, season to taste and strain.

The method of garnishing and choice of accompaniments is very much a matter of taste and of fashion. A garnish of watercress—seasoned and sprinkled with a few drops of vinegar—and quarters of lemon are often served. Bread sauce and browned crumbs are liked by some, while potato chips and a salad are indispensable additions. A crisp lettuce salad, with a suspicion of tarragon added, is a favourite; a fruit salad or fruit sauce makes a good accompaniment to roast game.

COLD PARTRIDGE

Partridge to be eaten cold should be cooked in the following way, rather than roasted. Prepare the bird, then wrap it in slices of fat bacon and put into a pan with enough boiling salted water just to cover. Simmer gently until tender —30–40 minutes according to age and size. When cooked, lift it from the pan and immerse it in cold water for a few minutes, then remove the bacon, and when cold serve with lettuce.

PARTRIDGES EN CASSEROLE À LA CRÈME

Take 2 young partridges, season them and truss neatly. Put them into a deep earthenware dish or casserole with some hot butter, and cook them in a moderately hot oven (425° F., mark 7) for about 25 minutes, basting occasionally. Just before serving the birds, pour in 2–3 tbsps. cream and baste the birds with this. Serve in the casserole. Fry some fingers of bread in butter, spread them with a farce made of the pounded liver of the partridges, and serve separately.

PARTRIDGE WITH CABBAGE

2 partridges	Carrot and onion
Butter or bacon fat	2–3 cloves
1 cabbage	A bouquet garni
Thin slices of bacon	Stock
Seasoning	Smoked sausages

This is one of the best ways of serving partridges when they are no longer in their first youth; the red-legged partridge can be cooked very well in this manner.

Draw, clean and singe the partridges and truss them into shape, then brown them in a saucepan with a little butter or bacon fat. Cut a fine cabbage in quarters, removing the outside leaves and any hard pieces of stalk. Wash it well, parboil it for ½ hour, then strain. Line a saucepan or earthenware casserole with thin slices of bacon, and lay in half of the cabbage, with seasoning to taste. Place the partridges on the top with a few small pieces of carrot, 1 onion stuck with 2–3 cloves and a bouquet garni, then cover with the rest of the cabbage and more seasoning. Moisten with stock, cover closely and cook in a moderately hot oven (400° F., mark 6) for 1½ hours, or until the birds are tender. One or two smoked sausages, lightly fried, are sometimes added.

To serve, remove the partridges, bacon and sausage from the casserole, and cut the partridges into neat joints and the sausage in pieces, remove the carrot, onion and bunch of herbs, and cut the cabbage in shreds with a sharp knife. Arrange the cabbage neatly on a hot dish with the pieces of partridge on the top and the bacon and sausage round.

A SALMI OF PARTRIDGE

Partridges	A little white wine
A little butter	Stock
Carrot	1 tomato
Onion	A few mushrooms
1–2 shallots	Croûtons of fried bread
2 tbsps. flour	

This can be made with either cooked or uncooked birds. If the latter, they should be roasted and left rather underdone, as they will finish cooking in the sauce. Cut each partridge into 5–6 pieces, according to its size. Remove the skin and the larger bones of the carcase, arrange the pieces in a casserole and cover whilst making the sauce. Chop up the scraps, put them into a frying pan with a little butter, a few small pieces of carrot and onion and 1–2 shallots. Fry until brown, then sprinkle with about 1 tbsp. flour and brown that also. Moisten with a little white wine and stock, and add a tomato, cut in pieces; cover and cook slowly for 1 hour. Meanwhile, cook a few fresh mushrooms, putting the trimmings in the sauce. When the sauce is ready, strain it over the pieces of partridge and let them heat thoroughly, but without boiling. In a salmi the sauce should be thick and velvety and the joints of game should seem to have been cooked with it, and must not appear to be swimming in gravy. Garnish with the mushrooms and some croûtons of fried bread.

ROAST PHEASANT

Pheasant requires to be well hung, otherwise the flesh is dry and tasteless; it needs on an average from 10–11 days—rather less should the weather be "muggy," up to 3 weeks if frosty.

Pluck, draw and truss the bird, bard it with bacon and, if liked, place a piece of juicy rump steak inside the body. Cook in a moderately hot oven (400°–425° F., marks 6–7) for about ¾ hour, basting frequently with butter. Shortly before cooking is completed, remove the bacon, dredge the breast with flour and baste well. Place on a hot dish and garnish with watercress and some of the tail feathers. Serve with thin gravy, bread sauce, fried crumbs and chipped potatoes, and if desired with a green salad.

PIGEONS

Pigeons are not strictly speaking game, and there is no closed season for them. Choose young birds with plenty of flesh and smooth, supple feet, avoiding those with rough, dry legs, which are a sign of age. Pigeons are not hung, but are eaten quite fresh. These birds may be roasted if wished, but they are sometimes inclined to be tough when cooked in this way, so unless very young, it is perhaps better to stew them or cook them in a casserole (see recipes below). The flesh, which is dark in colour, tends to be rather close and dry, and there is no fat on the pigeons, so the breasts are always larded for roasting, and fat bacon or ham is included in stews and casseroles made of these birds.

CASSEROLE OF PIGEONS

2 pigeons	A piece of turnip, sliced
2 tbsps. flour	1 stalk of celery, sliced
Pepper and salt	1 onion, sliced
A piece of ham or bacon	¾ pint stock or water
1 oz. dripping	A bunch of herbs
1 carrot, sliced	Mashed potatoes

Prepare the pigeons, cut in halves and toss in seasoned flour. Dice the ham or bacon and fry until lightly browned, then remove it from the pan. Add the dripping to the pan and fry the pigeons in this until lightly browned, and then remove from the pan. Add the vegetables and sauté for several minutes, then add the flour, stir in the stock and bring to the boil, stirring. Return pigeons and bacon to pan, and add the bunch of herbs. Cover, and simmer gently until the pigeons are tender (about 2 hours), or put into a casserole and cook in a slow oven. Remove the herbs and add more seasoning if necessary. Place a border of mashed potatoes round a hot dish, arrange the pigeons and vegetables in the centre and pour the sauce over, or serve in the casserole.

ROAST PIGEON

Pluck and draw the pigeons, singe them if necessary and truss them, tying a piece of fat bacon over the breast. Spread with some softened butter and roast in a hot oven (450° F., mark 8) for 15–20 minutes, according to size, basting well and removing the bacon slowly before cooking is completed, to allow the breast to brown. Dish with a garnish of watercress and serve gravy or a sauce separately. If liked, the pigeons may be halved before dishing.

PIGEON PIE : See Raised Pies in Meat chapter.

QUAIL AND ORTOLANS

Pluck and singe the birds, but leave the trail inside. The crop may be drawn from a hole made in the back of the neck, and the head and neck removed. For roasting, the breasts should be covered with vine leaves and wrapped in thin rashers of fat bacon. Roast in a hot oven (450° F., mark 8) for 12–25 minutes, basting with butter. To dish, the vine leaves and bacon should be left on, and each bird placed on a croûton of fried bread or buttered toast. Serve with thin gravy, fried crumbs and chipped potatoes.

QUAIL CASSEROLE

2 quails	2 oz. rice
Flour	6–8 oz. diced carrots
1 onion	Salt and pepper
½ oz. dripping	Water

Clean the quails and dust with flour. Wash and slice the onion. Melt the dripping in a casserole and, when smoking hot, put in the onion and the quails. Put on the lid and cook gently for about 10–15 minutes, until lightly coloured, stirring occasionally. Stir in the rice, diced carrot, seasonings, and enough water barely to cover the ingredients. Put on the lid and cook very gently for about 1½ hours, until the vegetables and quails are tender. Serve in the casserole.

WILD DUCK, TEAL AND WIDGEON

Hang for a short time only, then pluck, draw and truss like a duck. Spread with softened butter and roast in a hot oven (450° F., mark 8) for 20–25 minutes, basting frequently: they should on no account be overcooked. Garnish with watercress and serve with thin gravy and orange salad, or with Bigarade sauce.

WOODCOCK AND SNIPE

Pluck but do not draw the birds. Truss and cover the breast with fat bacon and spread with softened butter. Place each bird on a piece of toast or bread to catch the drippings, and roast in a hot oven (450° F., mark 8) for 15–20 minutes. Dish on the toast or bread and garnish with lemon and watercress. Serve with thin gravy, fried crumbs and chipped potatoes, and if liked, a salad.

LITTLE GAME SALADS

6 oz. cooked game	1 hard-boiled egg
2 oz. cooked ham	Stuffed olives
Beetroot	Watercress
Potatoes	Dressing (see below)

Mince the game and ham, moisten with 1 tbsp. dressing, turn into small moulds or patty tins and press down. Dice the beetroot, potatoes and egg white. Toss in the dressing and arrange on individual dishes. Turn each game mould carefully on to a bed of vegetables. Garnish each with a slice of olive and arrange watercress round the edge.

For the Dressing

Yolk of 1 hard-boiled egg	2 tbsps. olive oil
Black pepper and salt	1 tbsp. white vinegar
$\frac{1}{2}$ tsp. made mustard	

To make the dressing, remove the yolk from the hard-boiled egg, and beat it in a basin with the seasonings; then stir in the oil and the vinegar.

SALMI OF GAME

Portions of game, turkey or duck ($1\frac{1}{2}$ lb. approximately)	A sprig of thyme 6 peppercorns A sprig of parsley
1 oz. butter or dripping	A small piece of mace
2 small onions	A small piece of lemon rind
$\frac{1}{2}$ oz. flour	
$\frac{1}{2}$ pint thin gravy or stock	1 tbsp. red-currant jelly
Juice of 1 lemon	

Divide the game into tidy joints. Melt the butter or dripping, and when smoking hot fry the joints lightly, then remove from the pan. Chop the onions finely and fry until golden-brown, remove, and stir the flour into the remaining fat. (If necessary, a little more dripping or butter may be added.) Stir until thoroughly blended and cook slowly over a low heat, until golden-brown in colour. Strain in the gravy and lemon juice and bring to the boil. Tie the thyme, peppercorns, parsley, mace and lemon rind in a small piece of muslin, add to the gravy and simmer slowly for 40 minutes. Add the red-currant jelly and stir until it is blended. Remove the muslin containing the herbs, put in the joints of game and reheat for 5–10 minutes. When thoroughly heated, place the joints on a dish, pour the gravy over and serve immediately.

GROUND GAME

VENISON

Buck Venison is in season from June till the end of September, and Doe Venison from October till December. The flesh of the buck is considered to be finer than that of the doe, but in either case the deer should not be more than 3 years old, being at its best from $1\frac{1}{2}$–2 years. The lean should be very dark and the fat white; if there is plenty of fat it shows that the venison is in good condition. As the flesh is inclined to be tough, venison should be hung, for 2–3 weeks according to the weather, in a cool, airy place, wiped daily with a cloth to remove moisture, and dusted with pepper and ginger.

Test it at intervals by running a skewer through the haunch; as long as the skewer, when withdrawn, has no unpleasant smell, the meat is in good condition.

Venison is cut into 4 parts; the haunch, neck, shoulder and breast. Slow methods of cooking are better for the breast, but the other joints roast or fry well, the haunch being the prime cut. When frying venison, treat it like beefsteak, but allow more fat.

ROAST VENISON

The best joint for roasting is the haunch, but the loin, neck and fillet may also be cooked this way. It is best to cover the joint with a paste made by mixing flour and water to a stiff dough (allowing about 3 lb. flour to a haunch), and rolling it out to $\frac{1}{2}$ inch in thickness. Venison requires a good deal of fat in the cooking. Roast in a slow oven (325° F., mark 2), allowing 25 minutes to the lb. Twenty minutes before the cooking is completed, remove the paste, dredge the joint with flour and return it to the oven to brown.

Serve venison very hot, otherwise the fat is spoilt. It should be accompanied by a good gravy and by gooseberry, red-currant, cranberry or raspberry jelly.

STEWED VENISON

1 lb. venison	Stock
$1\frac{1}{2}$ oz. flour	A bunch of herbs, tied in muslin
Salt, pepper, nutmeg	
1 onion	1 dessertsp. vinegar
$1\frac{1}{2}$ oz. dripping	

Use the shoulder, breast and neck. Cut the venison in joints and toss in the seasoned flour. Slice the onion. Fry the meat and onion in the hot fat until lightly browned, then stir in any remaining flour, and brown, before adding the stock, bunch of herbs and vinegar. Cover, and stew in a slow oven (325° F., mark 2) or on top of the stove until tender—2–3 hours. Serve with stewed celery or a green vegetable.

HARES AND RABBITS

Hares, like game, should be hung for about a week, or longer in very cold weather, to improve the flavour and texture of the flesh. They are suspended by the hind feet, without being paunched. Since hare's blood is rich and of good flavour, a pot is hung under the head to catch it, and the blood is used in the gravy. Rabbits (which are now scarce in this country) should be eaten fresh—the fresher the better. They should be paunched as soon as possible after killing; this is usually done in the field, while they are still warm.

Hares and rabbits are usually prepared by the poulterer, but occasionally it falls to the housewife's lot to do this.

Paunching, Skinning and Jointing

With a pair of scissors, snip the skin at the fork and cut it up to the breast-bone, taking care to cut the pelt only. Ease the pelt away from the skin on each side of the stomach. Place the animal on newspaper and open the paunch by cutting the inside skin in the same direction as the pelt was cut. Draw out the entrails and burn them. Remove the kidneys and reserve them. Detach the liver, taking care not to
8 puncture the gall-bladder. Cut out the gall-bladder from the liver, keeping it intact, and discard it; cut away also the flesh on which the gall-bladder rests, as this may have a bitter flavour. Draw out the lungs and heart and discard the lungs. If the hare is to be jugged, the blood should be saved from the heart area.

Cut off the feet at the first joint. Loosen the skin around the back legs, then, holding the end of the leg, bend it at the joint; the flesh can then be grasped and the skin pulled off. Do the same with the front legs. Then draw the skin off the head, cutting it through at the ears and the mouth. Cut out the eyes with a sharp knife.

Wash rabbits well and soak for a while. Wipe hares with a clean, damp cloth.

To joint a rabbit or hare, first remove the legs. Cut the back into several pieces, giving the back of the knife a sharp tap with a hammer or weight to cut through the bone. Cut off the head and cut the ribs in two, lengthwise. The head, split in two, may be included in the stew or casserole, but is not served.

ROAST STUFFED HARE OR RABBIT

1 young hare or rabbit	$\frac{1}{4}$ oz. flour
Fat bacon	$\frac{1}{2}$ pint water or stock
Dripping for basting	Bread sauce

For the Stuffing

4 oz. breadcrumbs	1 tsp. thyme 49
2 oz. finely chopped suet	A squeeze of lemon juice Salt and pepper
2 tsps. chopped parsley	A few drops of piquant sauce
A little grated lemon rind	Beaten egg or milk to mix

Prepare the hare or rabbit in the usual way. Wash the heart, liver and kidneys thoroughly, put into cold water and bring to boiling point. Strain, discarding the water, chop finely and put into a large basin with the other stuffing ingredients. Mix thoroughly and stir in sufficient beaten egg or milk to blend. Stuff the cavity with this forcemeat and sew up, leaving a fairly long thread at each end so that the string can be removed easily when cooking is completed. Cut the sinews in the hind legs at the thigh, bring legs forward and press closely against the body: the forelegs must be bent back in the same way. Two fine metal skewers are required for keeping them in position, or if preferred, a trussing needle and string may be used. The head must be raised; in order to keep it in position, put a skewer through the mouth and fix down on to the back. The hare or rabbit is much improved in appearance and flavour if fat bacon is tied on the back and the whole covered with greased paper during the cooking.

The average time taken to cook in a moderate oven (325° F., mark 4) is $1\frac{1}{2}$–2 hours for a hare, 1–$1\frac{1}{2}$ hours for a rabbit, and it should be basted every 15 minutes. Fifteen minutes before it is ready, remove paper and bacon, baste and allow to brown, then lift on to a hot dish and take out the skewers and string. Drain away surplus fat and add $\frac{1}{4}$ oz. flour, brown it, then add about $\frac{1}{2}$ pint stock or water to make a thick gravy; boil 5 minutes, and strain this round the hare or rabbit. Serve with bread sauce.

JUGGED HARE

1 hare	A bunch of herbs
1–2 oz. dripping	A small bay leaf
1 rasher of bacon	4 peppercorns
$1\frac{1}{2}$ pints stock or water	A small blade of mace 50
$1\frac{1}{2}$ oz. flour, blended with a little stock	2 tsps. red-currant or other sharp jelly
1 onion stuck with 2 cloves	1 glass of port or other red wine
Seasonings	Forcemeat balls

Skin and paunch the hare, reserving the blood and saving the liver, heart and kidneys. Wipe the hare and cut into joints. Heat the dripping in a casserole and fry the joints in it with the bacon. When the meat is lightly browned, add stock to cover, and stir in the blended flour, the onion, seasonings and herbs, tied in muslin.

Cover and cook very gently in a moderate oven (350° F., mark 3) or on top of the stove, until tender (about 3 hours).

A few minutes before serving, remove the onion and herbs. Stir in the strained blood, red-currant jelly and wine, and reheat without boiling. Garnish with forcemeat balls.

To make the forcemeat balls, use the recipe for Stuffing for Hare on page 187. Form the forcemeat into balls, toss in flour, and fry in hot fat until lightly browned, or if more convenient, place on a baking tin with a spoonful or so of hot dripping and bake in a moderately hot oven (425° F., mark 7) for about 15 minutes, basting now and then.

ROAST SADDLE OR BARON OF HARE

The body of the hare alone is used, being cut off close to the shoulders. (The legs, neck and head can be jugged, or converted into soup.) Prepare a savoury stuffing, place this into the saddle, fold the skin over it, and secure it well at the ends. The flesh of the back may either be larded or have slices of fat bacon laid over it. Cover with greased paper, place on a roasting tin with some dripping and milk, and roast in a hot oven (450° F., mark 8) for 30–40 minutes, according to size. Baste frequently, as the flesh of a hare is very apt to taste dry. Serve with brown gravy and hand red-currant or guava jelly separately.

TERRINE OF HARE OR RABBIT

½ lb. liver
¼ lb. fat bacon
Seasoning
1 onion
1 hare or rabbit
1 tsp. mixed herbs
A little butter

Soak the liver in cold water for ½ hour, and then dry it in a cloth. Cut both liver and bacon into small dice, and fry them together until cooked, adding a little more fat if necessary. Season well, and sprinkle in the onion, finely chopped. Then strain off the fat and put the mixture through a mincing machine, in order to make a smooth farce. Mince also the hare or rabbit liver and any trimmings, and add these.

Wash the hare or rabbit and cut in in small joints, or, better still, in small pieces free from bone. Season with pepper, salt and finely powdered herbs, then fry the pieces for a few minutes in the fat left from the above mixture. Now take a strong terrine or fireproof dish, grease it, and put in a layer of the liver farce. On this put a layer of hare, and continue putting in alternate layers until the dish is full: the last layer should be one of farce. Smooth over the top with a knife, cover with greased paper, stand the terrine in a tin with hot water coming halfway up the sides, and cook in a moderate oven (375° F., mark 5) for 1½ hours. When ready, run a little liquid butter over the top; serve cold.

BROWN CASSEROLE OF RABBIT

1 large rabbit
2 oz. seasoned flour
2 oz. dripping
1 sliced onion or leek
1 meat cube, or 1 tbsp. meat extract
1½ pints stock or water
2 carrots, diced
1 turnip, diced
A stalk of celery
A bunch of herbs, tied in muslin
1 tbsp. tomato ketchup
A pinch of nutmeg
Forcemeat balls or fried croûtons

Wash and joint the rabbit and soak in cold water. Dry the joints and toss in seasoned flour. Heat the fat until smoking hot. Fry the joints of rabbit, several at a time, until lightly browned, then remove from the pan. Add the onion and the remaining flour and fry until lightly browned. Add the meat cube and stock or water, and stir until boiling. Put the rabbit, the diced vegetables and the celery, cut in small pieces, into a casserole, and pour the sauce over them. Add the bunch of herbs, tomato ketchup and a little grated nutmeg. Cover, and cook in a moderate oven (350° F., mark 4) for about 2 hours. Remove the herbs and serve garnished with forcemeat balls or croûtons of fried bread.

RABBIT HOT-POT

1 rabbit
Seasoned flour
2–3 onions
1½ lb. potatoes
Chopped parsley
Stock or water

Wash and cut the rabbit into joints, dry them, then toss in seasoned flour. Slice the onions and cut the potatoes into quarters or eighths, according to their size. Place a layer of onion in the bottom of a large casserole, put the seasoned joints of rabbit on the top, sprinkle liberally with finely chopped parsley, and cover with onion and potato. Add sufficient water or stock to nearly cover the rabbit, and cook in a slow oven (325° F., mark 2) for 2–2½ hours. The casserole should be covered with a lid or greased paper, which should be removed a short time before serving, to enable the potatoes to brown.

CURRY MAKING

A curry is a savoury dish, highly flavoured with a mixture of condiments and spices, many of which are grown in India. Although British housewives can hardly expect to compete with Indians in the making of their native dish, there are many very good curries which can be made from ingredients obtainable in this country.

The condiments used in curries have, in addition to their fragrant and aromatic properties, the power of stimulating digestion by increasing the secretion of the gastric juices; thus curry is especially welcome when the appetite is poor.

CURRY POWDER AND PASTE

Curry is obtainable in powder form and may be either pale or dark in colour. For white meat, poultry and eggs, light curry powder is preferable, but for game, beef and so on, a dark curry is more suitable. Curry is also available in paste form, the paste often containing, in addition to the usual spices, ingredients which cannot be preserved so well in powder form. Though a good curry can be made by using curry powder only, some people prefer to use a mixture of both powder and paste.

The following condiments, all of them very finely ground, are usually contained in curry powder, but of course different makers have their own recipes and use the spices in varying proportions: cayenne, allspice, cinnamon, ginger, turmeric, coriander, fenugreek, mustard.

It is possible to prepare curry powder at home by drying, grinding and mixing the various condiments to suit individual taste (a recipe is given at the end of this chapter). There are, however, good brands of powder on the market to suit all palates, so home preparation is seldom worth while.

FLAVOURINGS FOR CURRIES

The recipes that follow may be varied in flavour by slightly modifying the ingredients to taste. For example, by the addition of, say, a saltspoonful of powdered mixed spice, mace, cinnamon or allspice, the curry powder may be altered to suit individual palates. A very little garlic vinegar (that is, vinegar in which a few chopped cloves of garlic have been steeped), or the addition of 1 tbsp. of preserved tamarinds, instead of lemon juice, gives variety. Freshly grated coconut and a little coconut milk, or grated almonds, walnuts or Brazil nuts, all help to give a soft, mellow flavour if added in small quantities. Whatever ingredients are used to flavour a curry, they should be so well blended that no individual flavour predominates in the finished dish.

RICE FOR CURRIES

Carefully boiled dry rice goes with all curries. This is usually served separately, though some of it may be placed on the dish around the curry.

The aim in cooking rice for currying is to boil it so that each grain is completely cooked but separate one from the other. There are different ways of doing this, but the following method always gives a satisfactory result.

Use the best quality rice (Patna whole, or unpolished, for preference, owing to its Vitamin B content). Wash it well and have ready a large pan of fast-boiling water containing just sufficient salt and lemon juice to impart a good flavour. Sprinkle in the rice and allow it to boil vigorously so that the grains revolve rapidly in the water whilst they are cooking. Stir occasionally to prevent the rice from sticking, and take care not to overcook, but when it has boiled for about 10 minutes, remove one or two grains and break them in half. If sufficiently cooked, they will be semi-transparent throughout and soft through. If still hard in the centre, continue boiling, testing at intervals, until tender—this may take up to 18 minutes, according to the variety of rice. Strain the rice through a strainer or sieve. Place under the cold water tap and allow plenty of water to run through, thus removing any loose starch and separating the grains. Then place the rice on a clean baking sheet, colander or sieve, cover and reheat in a slow oven or above the stove. If time does not allow for reheating the rice, use boiling water instead of cold to rinse it, then dry in a warm place for a few minutes.

In the East, various appetisers such as mint sauce made with garlic vinegar, tomato chutney or a sweet mango chutney, red or green chillies served with oil or vinegar, and preserved fish (such as Bombay Duck), are also served. *Chapattis* and *Pappadum* are types of Indian breads often served with curries. (See recipes for accompaniments at the end of this chapter.)

WET CURRY

2 oz. butter or fat	2 tbsps. chopped coconut
¼ lb. onions	About ½ pint light stock or coconut milk
1 lb. uncooked meat	Juice of ½ lemon
1 tbsp. curry powder	Boiled rice
2 tsps. curry paste	Chutney
2 tbsps. sultanas	
1 tbsp. rice flour	
Salt to taste	

Melt the fat in a saucepan, add the onions, finely chopped, and cook for a few minutes. Then add the meat, cut in small pieces, the curry powder, curry paste, sultanas, rice flour and coconut, and stir over the heat a few minutes longer. Now add gradually enough light stock or coconut milk to make the curry soft, but not sloppy. Season with salt to taste. Cover and cook slowly by the side of the heat or in a slow oven (325° F., mark 2) until tender—from 1–2 hours, according to the kind of meat used. Add lemon juice, and serve with rice and chutney.

DRY CURRY

1 oz. dripping	A pickled gherkin
2 small onions	1 clove of garlic
1 lb. lean beef	1 tbsp. chutney
2 tsps. curry paste	Juice of ½ lemon
1 tbsp. curry powder	Salt
1 tsp. piquant sauce	Boiled rice

Melt the dripping, fry the onions, add the meat and cook until nicely browned. Add the curry paste and powder and continue to cook. Then add the piquant sauce, pickled gherkin, garlic and chutney, and cook slowly for about 1–2 hours over a very gentle heat. Add the lemon juice and salt, and serve with boiled rice.

Note : Special care is required in the cooking of dry curry, to prevent the contents of the pan burning. When possible, it should be cooked in a double saucepan

CURRY OF COLD MEAT

2 oz. dripping	A little lemon juice
1 onion, chopped	2 tsps. red-currant jelly
1 tbsp. curry powder	A few raisins or sultanas
1 oz. flour	Seasoning to taste
1 apple, chopped	Cold cooked meat, as available
¾ pint stock	

Melt the fat and fry the onion lightly. Add the curry powder and fry this. Stir in the flour, and add the apple and stock. Cover, and simmer gently for ½ hour, then add the rest of the flavourings, and season. Add the cooked meat and thoroughly reheat it in the sauce.

CURRIED FOWL

(Made with raw fowl)

1 small fowl	½ an apple
1 tbsp. curry powder	1 pint white stock or water
1 oz. seasoned flour	2 tsps. curry paste
2 oz. butter	Lemon juice
2 onions	2 tbsps. cream

Prepare the fowl and cut it into neat joints, removing the skin. Mix together the curry powder and seasoned flour and coat the joints of fowl with it. Melt the butter in a stewpan and sauté the sliced onions in it for a few minutes, until pale yellow. Remove the onions and fry the joints in the butter to a light brown. Add the chopped apple and try this also, then pour in the stock, and bring to the boil, stirring. Return the onions to the pan, together with the curry paste, cover and simmer gently until tender—1 hour or longer, according to the age of the fowl. Shortly before serving, stir in the lemon juice and cream and add more seasoning

5

if necessary. Arrange on a hot dish with a border of boiled rice, and garnish with lemon fans, chopped parsley and paprika pepper.

CURRIED CHICKEN

(Made with cooked chicken)

1 onion
½ an apple
1 oz. butter
2–3 tsps. curry powder
1 tbsp. flour
½ pint stock
Seasoning
Cold roast chicken
A squeeze of lemon juice
A little cream, if liked

Slice the onion and chop the apple, and fry these to a golden-brown in the hot butter. Stir in the curry powder and flour, then add the stock gradually and bring to the boil, stirring. Season with salt, cover and simmer gently for about ½ hour. Add the chicken, cut into neat pieces, to the pan and heat gently for a few minutes, but without boiling, until the meat is thoroughly hot. Stir in the lemon juice and cream, if used, and add more seasoning if necessary. Dish with a border of boiled rice and garnish with lemon fans, chopped parsley and paprika pepper.

CURRIED VEAL

Follow the recipe for Curried Fowl (above), if the meat is raw. For Curried Veal made with cold cooked meat, see Curried Chicken above.

DRY VEAL CURRY

1 lb. lean veal
2 medium-sized onions
1 clove of garlic
1 oz. fat
1 tbsp. curry powder
2 tsps. curry paste
Salt to taste
A few pickled gherkins
1 tbsp. chutney
Juice of ½ a lemon

Cut the meat into small pieces. Chop the onions and garlic very finely and fry them lightly in the hot fat. Add the curry powder and paste, and cook thoroughly for 3–4 minutes. Add the meat, season to taste with salt, and cook until nicely browned. Add the gherkins, chutney, and lemon juice, and cook slowly for 2–2½ hours. Serve garnished with cut lemon and accompanied by boiled rice.

CURRIED MINCED MUTTON

Prepare in the same way as for curry sauce, but vary by adding 2 medium-sized tomatoes, 2 tbsps. freshly grated coconut and a few sultanas or raisins; when these are cooked, add the minced cooked mutton. Heat gently for a few minutes until well heated, but do not boil.

CURRY OF MINCED BEEF

2 oz. fat
1 large onion
2 cloves of garlic
2 tbsps. curry powder
1 tsp. tomato purée
1 lb. minced beef
Salt to taste

Melt the fat, fry the chopped onion and garlic lightly, add the curry powder, and cook for a further 3–4 minutes. Stir in the tomato purée and minced meat, and season to taste with salt. Simmer for ½–¾ hour. Serve with boiled rice and chutney.

CURRIED PORK

1 lb. pork
1 oz. dripping (if lean pork is used)
2 onions
1 tbsp. curry powder
1 large tart apple
2 small cloves of garlic
½ pint coconut milk or stock
2 tbsps. freshly grated coconut
Juice of 1 lemon
Boiled rice
Mixed diced vegetables (optional)

Cut the meat into pieces about ½ inch square and fry: if fairly fat, it can be cooked without the addition of dripping. When cooked, remove from the pan, add the sliced onions and fry. Add the curry powder and chopped apple to the pan, and cook dry over a low heat for about 10 minutes. Add the meat, the chopped garlic and sufficient coconut milk or stock to cover the meat, then the grated coconut, and simmer very slowly until the meat and vegetables are cooked. Add the lemon juice and serve with dry boiled rice.

Note: Mixed diced vegetables, as available, may be added and cooked with the other ingredients.

CURRIED TRIPE, MALAY STYLE

1 lb. tripe
1 tbsp. vinegar
2 tbsps. coriander seed
2 tsps. turmeric powder
A pinch of cumin
1 tsp. ground mustard
1 tsp. pepper
1 oz. fat
1 onion
1 clove of garlic
2 oz. coconut infused in boiling water for 15 minutes
2 tbsps. mango chutney
A little stock
Salt to taste

Wash the tripe and cut it into small, neat pieces. Cover it with cold water and simmer it until tender. Make a paste with the vinegar, coriander seeds, turmeric, cumin, mustard, and pepper. Melt the fat and fry the chopped onion and garlic. Add the paste, mix thoroughly, and cook for 3–4 minutes. Add the strained coconut milk, the chutney, the tripe, and enough stock to make a thick gravy. Season with salt, heat through thoroughly and serve.

BENGAL CURRY

4 oz. butter, margarine, or dripping	1–1½ lb. tender meat or parboiled chicken, cut in pieces
5–6 oz. thinly sliced onion	2 tsps. salt
1 clove of garlic	¾ pint stock
4 tbsps. curry powder	1 tbsp. lemon juice
1 tbsp. mixed spice	Boiled rice
A good pinch of saffron	

Heat the fat, fry the onion and crushed garlic until well browned, then add the curry powder, spice and saffron, and fry again for 5–10 minutes. Add the meat or chicken, salt, stock and lemon juice, and cook, stirring intermittently, for about ½ hour, or until the stock is partly absorbed and the curry thick. Serve with boiled rice.

If the meat is not very tender, cook it first and fry it until lightly browned before adding it to the curry.

CEYLON CURRY

(Made with cold meat)

¾ lb. cold mutton	½ pint stock or gravy
1 onion	1 tbsp. coconut milk, if obtainable
1½ oz. butter or dripping	1 dessertsp. lemon juice
½ oz. flour	A pinch of salt
2 tsps. curry powder	½ tsp. piquant sauce
2 tsps. curry paste	Boiled rice
2 tbsps. sultanas	
1 apple	

Cut the mutton into small dice. Chop the onion finely, melt the butter or dripping and fry the onion golden-brown, then stir in the flour, curry powder, paste, sultanas and chopped apple. Add the cold stock or gravy, and coconut milk if obtainable, then bring to the boil, add the lemon juice and salt, and simmer gently for ¾ hour. Add the meat and piquant sauce, then heat through and serve with a border of rice.

MADRAS CURRY (HOT)

2 oz. almonds	A very small piece of cinnamon stick
2 oz. margarine or fat	1 tsp. ground cloves
2 onions	1 tbsp. flour
1 clove of garlic	1 pint stock
2 tsps. ground coriander seed	1 lb. meat
2 tsps. black pepper	1 tbsp. turmeric powder
1 tsp. ground chillies	2 tsps. sugar
1 tsp. ground cumin seed	Salt to taste
1 tsp. ground cardomom	Juice of 1 lemon

Chop the almonds and cover them with boiling water, allow to stand for 15 minutes, then strain them. Meanwhile melt the margarine or fat and fry the chopped onions and garlic lightly. Add the spices and flavourings (except the turmeric), and the flour, cook for 5 minutes, then stir in the stock and add the meat, cut into neat pieces. Simmer until the meat is tender—1½–2 hours. Add the infusion of almonds, the turmeric powder and the sugar, season to taste with salt, and simmer for a further 15 minutes. Add the lemon juice, and serve with rice.

QUICK CURRY

1 tin of stewed steak	Meat stock
1 oz. dripping	Salt
1 onion	A squeeze of lemon juice
1 oz. flour	
1 tbsp. curry powder	Boiled rice

Open the tin of steak. Melt the dripping and fry the chopped onion until lightly coloured. Stir in the flour and curry powder and mix thoroughly, then add ½ pint stock (including the gravy from the tin), and a little salt and lemon juice. Simmer for a few minutes and then add the meat, heat thoroughly, and serve with a border of boiled rice.

FISH CURRY

2 small onions (sliced)	1 tomato, skinned
2 oz. butter	1 lb. uncooked fish
1 tbsp. curry powder	A little garlic
Salt to taste	Water

Fry the sliced onions in the butter. Put in the curry powder and salt and stir to mix. Add the tomato, quartered, then the pieces of fish, seasoned with curry powder and salt, and fry them brown. Add the chopped garlic, pour in a teacupful of warm water and let the curry cook in the pan with the lid on till the fish is tender when tested—15–20 minutes; take care not to let the fish get mashed.

CURRIED COOKED FISH

Use any cold cooked fish. Prepare it by removing the skin and bones and cutting into small pieces. Warm some curry sauce and add the fish, then reheat and serve with boiled rice.

CURRIED CRAB

1 onion	1 tin of crab
2 oz. dripping	½ pint stock or water
1 small apple	Seasoning
1 tbsp. curry powder	4 oz. rice
2 tbsps. flour	Lemon and parsley to garnish

Slice the onion and fry in the melted fat, then

fry the chopped apple. Add the curry powder and cook for several minutes. Add the flour, the liquid drained from the tin of crab, and the stock or water. Season well, put in the cut-up crab and heat. Meanwhile cook the rice in boiling salted water, drain and rinse well, then dry thoroughly. Dish up the curry in a border of rice. Garnish with lemon and parsley.

SCRAMBLED CURRIED CRAB

Hot buttered toast	4 eggs
2 oz. butter or margarine	4 tbsps. cream or milk
2–3 tsps. curry powder	Celery salt or salt
1 tin flaked crab	A little black pepper

Have ready hot buttered toast cut into rounds or triangles. Melt the fat and stir in the curry powder and the flaked crab. When thoroughly hot, pour in the beaten eggs, to which the cream or milk has been added. Add the seasonings. Cook quickly, scrambling the eggs in the usual way. Serve piled on to the buttered toast.

CURRIED CRAWFISH TAILS

2 crawfish tails	Lemon slices
½ pint curry sauce	Boiled rice
Chopped parsley	

Remove the flesh from the tails, cut it up roughly and wash the shells. Prepare a good curry sauce and add the fish to it. Heat the mixture through and place it in the warmed shells. Garnish with chopped parsley and lemon, and serve at once with carefully boiled rice. If preferred, the curried fish may be served in a dish, instead of in the shells.

CURRIED PRAWNS

Prepare some prawns by skinning and cutting into small pieces, then add, with the juice of ½ a lemon, to some curry sauce. Cook for about 8 minutes, serve on a hot dish with a border of rice, and garnish with a few whole prawns. If liked, the curry sauce can be strained before using, to remove the onion, etc.

VEGETABLE CURRY—I

1 oz. dripping	2 tbsps. sultanas or raisins
2 onions	A few mushrooms
2 lb. prepared vegetables, according to taste	Stock
	Lemon juice
1 tbsp. curry powder	Pepper and salt
2 tsps. curry paste	Cayenne
2 small cloves of garlic	Boiled rice

Melt the dripping and fry the sliced onions with the other vegetables, which should be cut into convenient sizes, adding a little more dripping if necessary. Then add the curry powder and paste and fry gently for about 10 minutes. Add chopped garlic, the sultanas or raisins, a few mushrooms and just sufficient stock to cover the vegetables. Simmer until tender, and then add lemon juice, pepper, salt and a little cayenne. Serve with boiled rice.

Vegetable curry may be made from almost any vegetables, but judgment and personal taste will decide which types combine well together. The following are a few examples of palatable mixtures :—

Green peas, cucumber, new potatoes, runner or French beans.

French beans, cauliflower, tomatoes.

French beans, root artichokes, green peas.

Carrots, green peas, French beans.

Carrots, turnips, tomatoes, French beans.

Small button mushrooms improve any curry.

VEGETABLE CURRY—II

1 lb. onions	½ pint stock or water
1 lb. tomatoes	Salt and pepper
½ lb. cooking apples	2 bananas
2 oz. dripping	3 eggs
2–3 tbsps. curry powder	

Slice the onions, tomatoes and peeled apples, then fry them in the dripping until the onions are brown. Add the curry powder and fry for a few minutes. Add the liquid and seasoning and simmer for 1½ hours, stirring from time to time. Add the sliced bananas, and when they are tender, cool a little, stir in the beaten eggs and serve at once.

CEYLON CURRY OF TOMATOES

6 firm tomatoes	Pepper and salt
1 oz. butter	2 tbsps. coconut
1 apple	1 lump of sugar
1 medium-sized onion	1 teacupful rice
2 tsps. curry powder	Slices of lemon to garnish
1 tsp. curry paste	
1 tbsp. rice flour	Parsley to garnish
½ pint water	

Peel the tomatoes and leave them whole. Melt the butter in a saucepan, put in the apple and onion, finely chopped, and cook for a few minutes without browning. Add the curry powder, curry paste and rice flour, and mix them well in. Pour on the water and stir until boiling. Season to taste and put in the coconut and lump of sugar. Lay in the tomatoes, cover closely, and cook over gentle heat until the tomatoes are tender but not broken: baste them occasionally with the sauce. Wash and boil the rice, then drain and let it dry, keeping it hot. Press it into a basin or plain mould and let it take the shape, then turn out in the centre of a hot dish and serve the tomatoes and sauce neatly round. Garnish with slices of lemon and a little parsley.

LENTIL CURRY

1 pint lentils	Juice of ½ lemon
1 quart water	Pepper and salt
1½ oz. dripping	A little cayenne
3 medium-sized onions	Boiled rice
¾–1½ oz. curry powder, according to strength	¼ lb. pickled pork, if liked
2 cloves of garlic	

Wash the lentils well, and put on to boil in the water. When boiling, reduce the heat, and simmer for 30 minutes. Melt the dripping in the saucepan, slice the onions, and fry until golden-brown in the dripping. When cooked, add the curry powder and fry, stirring constantly so as not to allow it to burn. Add the lentils, and the liquid in which they have been cooked, to the fried onions and curry powder, also the garlic, finely chopped, and continue to cook until the onions and garlic are quite tender and the liquid sufficiently reduced. Lastly, add the lemon juice and seasoning. Serve with rice.

The flavour is improved if a small piece (about ¼ lb.) of pickled pork is cooked with the lentils.

NUT CURRY

4 oz. mixed nuts	2 tsps. curry paste
1 oz. dripping	Seasoning
½ an apple	¾ pint milk
2 tsps. chopped onion	1 oz. sultanas
1 small potato	1 tbsp. flour
2 tsps. curry powder	Boiled rice

Roast the nuts in a hot oven for a few minutes to enhance their flavour. Melt the dripping in a saucepan, and fry the chopped apple, the chopped onion, the chopped nuts, and the potato cut in small dice. Add the curry powder, the curry paste and the seasoning. When thoroughly blended, stir in the milk, add the sultanas, and simmer very gently for ½ hour, or until the potato is cooked. Add the blended flour and boil for a further 5 minutes. Dish with a border of boiled rice.

CURRIED ONIONS AND RICE

4 large onions	Salt
2 tsps. curry powder	A little powdered mace
2 oz. butter or margarine	4 oz. cooked rice

Choose onions of the same size and slice them evenly. Cook in a little water until tender and then drain well. Add the curry powder, fat and seasonings and continue to cook for a few minutes. The onions can be served on a hot dish with a border of hot rice, or if preferred, the rice can be added to the onions, reheated and served together.

PUMPKIN CURRY

1 lb. pumpkin	Salt to taste
2 small onions, sliced	½ lb. tomatoes
2 oz. butter	Stock
1 tsp. curry powder	

Peel the pumpkin and cut it into thick pieces. Fry the sliced onions in the butter till brown. Add the curry powder and salt and mix well. Add the tomatoes, cut into pieces, pour in a little stock and stir to form a thick, rich paste. Throw in the pumpkin pieces and add a very little or no water, as pumpkin is very watery. Let the curry simmer over a very gentle heat, stirring occasionally, but taking care not to mash the pumpkin pieces. Remove from the heat when the gravy becomes thick.

CURRIED EGGS: See chapter on Eggs.

CURRY SAUCE

2 medium-sized onions	⅓ pint stock or coconut milk
1 oz. dripping or butter	Salt
1 tbsp. curry powder	A little cayenne
1 tsp. curry paste	2 tbsps. chutney
1 tbsp. of rice flour or ordinary flour	1 tbsp. cream (optional)
A clove of garlic	

Slice the onions and chop finely. Melt the fat, fry the onions golden-brown and add the curry powder, paste and rice (or ordinary flour). Cook for 5 minutes, then add the garlic, pour in the coconut milk or stock and bring to the boil. Add the seasonings and chutney, then simmer for 30–40 minutes. This sauce is much improved by the addition of 1 tbsp. cream immediately before use, and less curry powder may be used for those who prefer a "mild" dish.

Note: The rice flour and ordinary flour can be omitted, for a curry is thickened by reduction of the liquid and by long, slow simmering.

CURRY POWDER

1 oz. turmeric	2 oz. cumin seed
4 oz. coriander seed	1½ oz. fenugreek
½ oz. red chillies	½ oz. powdered ginger
½ oz. black pepper	¼ oz. poppy seed

The strength of curry powder is a matter of individual taste and it is often more satisfactory to mix your own rather than to use the bought variety.

If not already powdered, crush the ingredients in a pestle and mortar and mix them all well together. Sieve to remove any imperfectly crushed seeds and pound these again, then add to the mixture. Stored in an airtight jar, curry powder will keep quite satisfactorily. This recipe is for a powder of medium strength; a hotter one can be made by increasing the quantity of chillies.

ACCOMPANIMENTS FOR CURRIES

Besides rice, accompaniments for curries include chapattis, pappadums, Bombay ducks, sambals, pickles, and chutneys. Some of these are usually bought ready prepared; others can be made at home and a few recipes are given here.

PAPPADUMS

These should be fried in oil or hot fat for a minute. Press the pappadum down for a second so that it will puff up evenly and not curl. Turn after a few seconds. Drain on a cloth or paper.

CHAPATTIS

This is an unleavened Indian bread eaten with curry. It is made from wholemeal flour and water mixed to a soft dough. Roll the dough out thinly, cut into 4–5 inch rounds, and fry in smoking hot oil until well puffed up and brown. Drain well and serve at once.

POTATO SAMBAL

Cut several cold potatoes in cubes and blend lightly with chopped green chillies, a little finely chopped spring onion and olive oil. Season and add lemon juice.

COCONUT MILK

Coconut and infusions of coconut are used in a number of Indian recipes, both as an ingredient and as an accompanying side dish.

Fresh coconut gives a more mellow and richer result when used for coconut milk, although desiccated coconut is quite satisfactory. To prepare the milk, grate the coconut flesh and pour over enough boiling water to cover the nut. Leave to stand for 20–30 minutes to make an infusion, then squeeze the liquid out through a fine strainer. A thinner milk can be obtained by using the grated coconut a second time.

The coconut may be dried slowly and used as a separate accompaniment, or may be added to a curry.

BOMBAY DUCK

This is a popular sambal to accompany any curry. The smell when the duck is baked or fried is rather unpleasant, but it is a good appetiser, either served broken in small pieces or crumbled and sprinkled over the curry.

Bake the pieces of duck in a hot oven until crisp and brown. If necessary flatten them during cooking. The duck may also be fried in hot fat and then drained before serving. Bombay duck is also used as an ingredient in recipes for some sambals.

STUFFINGS, ACCOMPANIMENTS AND GARNISHES

STUFFINGS

SAGE AND ONION STUFFING

2 large onions	4–5 sage leaves or 2 tsps. dried sage
Boiling water	
½–1 oz. butter	1 tsp. salt
4 oz. breadcrumbs	½ tsp. pepper

Prepare the onions, put them into a pan of cold water, bring to the boil and cook for about 5 minutes. Strain off the water, cover with fresh boiling water and cook until tender. Drain well and chop finely, then add the butter, breadcrumbs, chopped sage and seasoning, and mix well together.

Use for stuffing goose and duck. This stuffing is served also with pork and sometimes with mutton; if the meat is boned, it may be stuffed, otherwise cook the mixture in a separate dish and serve it with the meat.

VEAL FORCEMEAT AND FORCEMEAT BALLS

2 oz. suet	½ tsp. mixed herbs
1–2 oz. ham or bacon	Rind of ½ lemon
4 oz. breadcrumbs	Salt and pepper
1 tbsp. chopped parsley	Beaten egg

Chop the suet and the ham or bacon finely and mix with the breadcrumbs. Add the chopped parsley, mixed herbs and grated lemon rind. Season well with salt and pepper and add enough beaten egg (or egg and milk) to bind.

Use for stuffing veal, chicken, rabbit, hearts, fish and so on. Alternatively, roll into small balls, using a little flour for coating, then fry or bake until brown, and serve with the above.

SAUSAGE STUFFING—I

Follow the recipe for Veal Forcemeat, adding ¾–1 lb. of sausage-meat.

SAUSAGE STUFFING—II

1 oz. dripping	6 tbsps. fresh breadcrumbs
1 large onion	
1 lb. pork sausage-meat	2 tsps. chopped parsley
Seasoning	1 tsp. mixed herbs

Melt the dripping, chop the onion and mix with the sausage-meat. Lightly sauté the sausage-meat and onion in the dripping for a few minutes, to give it a good flavour. Mix in the other ingredients and use as required.

CHESTNUT STUFFING

1 lb. chestnuts	1 oz. butter
About ½ pint stock or milk	A little grated lemon rind
2 oz. ham or bacon	Salt and pepper
3–4 oz. breadcrumbs	Sugar
2 tsps. chopped parsley	1 egg

Make a slit in both ends of the chestnuts (this facilitates the removal of the skin) and boil them in water for about 10 minutes. Then, taking a few at a time from the water, skin them. Put the shelled nuts into a pan with enough stock or milk just to cover and simmer gently until tender, then mash the chestnuts or rub through a sieve. Pound with the finely chopped ham or bacon, then add the breadcrumbs, finely chopped parsley, melted butter and grated lemon rind; season with salt, pepper and sugar, and bind with the beaten egg.

Use for stuffing turkey, chicken, etc.

HAM STUFFING FOR VEGETABLES

½ oz. butter	Salt, pepper and mustard
1 tsp. finely chopped onion	A few drops of piquant sauce
2 oz. ham	Beaten egg or milk
1 oz. breadcrumbs	

Melt the butter and fry the finely chopped onion gently until golden-brown and tender. Remove from the heat and stir in the chopped ham and breadcrumbs. Season with salt, pepper and mustard and a few drops of piquant sauce, and bind with beaten egg or milk.

MUSHROOM STUFFING

3–4 oz. mushrooms	Seasoning
1–2 shallots	2 oz. breadcrumbs
1 oz. butter	Sauce, cream or beaten egg to bind
2 tbsps. chopped parsley	

Prepare the mushrooms and shallots and chop

or mince them finely, then fry in the hot butter for a few minutes. Add the chopped parsley, seasoning and breadcrumbs, and mix well, then moisten with a little sauce, cream or beaten egg.

Use to stuff vegetables (tomatoes, aubergines, marrow, etc.), or birds such as pigeons, quail and so on.

NUT FORCEMEAT

4 oz. breadcrumbs
2 oz. ground or finely minced nuts
¼ tsp. salt
⅛ tsp. pepper
A good pinch of mixed herbs
Beaten egg or milk to mix

Mix together the breadcrumbs and nuts (walnuts, hazel nuts and pine kernels are suitable for this), add the salt, pepper and herbs and enough beaten egg or milk to moisten.

Use for chicken, turkey, etc.

OYSTER STUFFING

1½ doz. sauce oysters
6 oz. breadcrumbs
2 oz. suet or 1½ oz. butter
Grated rind of ½ lemon
1 tbsp. parsley
A pinch of mace
Salt and cayenne
1 egg

Beard the oysters and cut them in pieces. Simmer the beards in the oyster liquor to extract the flavour, and then strain. Mix all the dry ingredients in a basin, add the oysters, the lightly beaten egg and enough oyster liquor to moisten.

Use this stuffing for the breast of a boiled turkey.

CELERY STUFFING

Make in the same way as Oyster Stuffing (above), using cooked celery, finely chopped, instead of the oysters, and a little milk with the beaten egg to moisten. Use for stuffing fish.

SHRIMP STUFFING

Make in the same way as Oyster Stuffing, substituting ½ pint picked shrimps for the oysters, and adding a little milk to the beaten egg for moistening. Use for stuffing fish.

TOMATO STUFFING

½ lb. fresh tomatoes or ¼ pint bottled tomato pulp
1 small onion
½ oz. butter
3–4 oz. breadcrumbs
1 egg
Seasoning

If fresh tomatoes are being used, stew gently without any water until soft and fairly thick, and rub through a sieve, so making about ¼ pint of tomato pulp. Chop the onion finely and fry it lightly in the melted butter. Add the tomato pulp, breadcrumbs and beaten egg, season to taste and mix thoroughly.

STUFFING FOR HARE OR RABBIT

Heart, liver and kidneys of a rabbit or hare
4 oz. breadcrumbs
2 oz. finely chopped suet
2 tbsps. chopped parsley
1 tsp. thyme
Salt and pepper
A little grated lemon rind
A squeeze of lemon juice
A few drops of piquant sauce
Beaten egg or milk to mix

Put the heart, liver and kidneys, after preparing and washing thoroughly, into cold water, bring to boiling point, and cook for 2–3 minutes. Strain and throw the water away. Chop finely and put into a large basin, with the other stuffing ingredients. Mix throughly, and stir in sufficient beaten egg or milk to bind.

ACCOMPANIMENTS

BACON ROLLS

These are small rolls of crisply cooked bacon used to garnish meats that lack fat, e.g., veal, rabbit and chicken.

Bacon Rolls

Choose thinly sliced streaky bacon. Cut it into strips about 2 inches long, roll up and stick on to a skewer; cook until crisp, either on a tin in the oven (about 20 minutes) or under a slow grill (5–10 minutes), turning at intervals to prevent uneven cooking.

FRIED CRUMBS

These are fresh breadcrumbs fried until crisp and brown, for serving with game.

Allow ½ oz. of butter or margarine to 2 oz. of fresh breadcrumbs. Melt the fat, add the crumbs, and mix well together. Fry over gentle heat until golden-brown, stirring constantly, otherwise they will brown unevenly and burn.

MAÎTRE D'HÔTEL BUTTER

1 oz. butter
2 tsps. very finely chopped parsley
1 tsp. lemon juice
Salt and pepper

Mix all the ingredients thoroughly into a creamy paste, using a fork or wooden spoon.

Shape into pats and make very cold. Serve with grills, etc.

WATERCRESS BUTTER

Make as above, using chopped watercress in place of parsley. This is a useful alternative to maître d'hôtel butter when for any reason parsley is unobtainable.

PULLED BREAD

Pull pieces of bread about the size of a large walnut from a fresh loaf. Dip these in milk and place on a baking sheet, then bake in a moderately hot oven (400° F., mark 6) until golden-brown. Dish on a folded napkin, and serve in place of bread or rolls at dinner.

DRY TOAST

Cut the bread in slices ¼–½ inch thick and cook until brown on both sides before a clear red fire or under a hot grill. Cut off the crusts, if wished, and place slices at once in a toast rack; this allows the steam to escape and keeps the toast crisp—if it is laid flat, the steam condenses in the toast, making it soggy. If the toast is required very dry, cook the bread more slowly.

Dry toast should be served while crisp and fresh—it soon becomes tough on standing.

BUTTERED TOAST

Make as above, but as soon as the bread is toasted, remove the crusts, if liked, place on a hot plate or muffin dish and spread with softened butter. Lay the pieces of toast one on top of the other, spreading each layer with butter, then cut in convenient-sized pieces; serve at once.

FAIRY TOAST

Cut wafer-thin slices of bread (this is more easily done if the crust is cut off the bread before slicing) and lay on baking sheets. Bake in a slow oven (325° F., mark 2) until they curl up and become crisp and a pale golden-yellow. Air on a cake rack and serve at once in toast racks or piled on a platter or in a bowl, or store in an airtight tin.

MELBA TOAST

Cut stale bread into very thin slices, lay on baking sheets and dry off in the bottom of a very slow oven. Before serving, brown them lightly in a moderate oven (350° F., mark 3) or under a very slow grill. Air on a rack.

DUMPLINGS, ETC.

DUMPLINGS TO SERVE WITH STEW

6 oz. flour
1½ tsps. baking powder
½ tsp. salt
A pinch of mixed spice
Pepper
1½ oz. fat
Cold water

Mix the dry ingredients and rub in the fat with the tips of the fingers. Mix to a firm, light dough with cold water. Divide into 10 or 12 equal-sized portions and roll into balls. Place on top of the meat in the hot stew, cover and cook for 25 minutes.

POTATO DUMPLINGS

(To serve with Meat or Vegetable Casserole)

2 oz. flour
2 tsps. baking powder
Salt and pepper
1 oz. fat (lard or butter)
6 oz. dry mashed potato

Mix together the flour, baking powder and seasoning and rub in the fat very thoroughly with the finger-tips, until the mixture resembles fine breadcrumbs. Add the sieved cooked potatoes and mix lightly to form a soft dough (it is not usually necessary to add any liquid). Roll into dumplings, about the size of a walnut, and place on the top of the meat and vegetables in the casserole, about 20 minutes before the cooking is completed. Increase the oven heat to moderately hot (425° F., mark 7), and cook for a further 15–20 minutes, until the dumplings are well risen and brown. (If it is not convenient to raise the temperature of the oven, keep the casserole covered so that the dumplings cook in the steam; in this case they will not, of course, brown.)

HERB PUDDING

(To serve with Meat)

4 oz. flour
2 tsps. baking powder
2 oz. fine breadcrumbs
1½–2 oz. suet
1 tsp. salt
½ tsp. pepper
1 tbsp. chopped parsley
3 tsps. chopped fresh herbs (thyme, marjoram, etc.), or 1 tsp. mixed dried herbs
1 egg (optional)
Milk

Mix together the flour, baking powder and breadcrumbs and add the very finely chopped suet. Season with salt and pepper, add the chopped parsley and other herbs, and stir in the beaten egg and enough milk to make of a soft, dropping consistency, taking it is usually con-mixture lightly.

To serve with roast meat, it is usually convenient to cook the pudding in the oven, in which case pour it into a greased shallow tin or oven dish and bake in moderate oven (350° F., mark 4) until well risen and firm—about 1 hour. If preferred, the pudding may be steamed; for this, put the mixture into a greased basin, cover with greased paper and steam for 2½–3 hours.

HERB DUMPLINGS

(To serve with Stewed Meat or Soup)

Use the above recipe but add only enough liquid to mix to a soft dough. Form into small dumplings, flour lightly and add to the boiling stew or soup about 30–40 minutes before it is required.

MARROW DUMPLINGS

1 oz. beef marrow
½ oz. butter
2 tsps. chopped parsley
½ tsp. finely chopped onion
1 egg
2 oz. breadcrumbs
Salt and pepper
A little milk

Work the marrow and butter together until smooth and creamy, then add the chopped parsley and onion, beaten egg, breadcrumbs and seasoning. Moisten with a little milk and form into round dumplings about the size of a walnut. Flour lightly, then put into boiling stock and simmer for 20–30 minutes. Serve with roast meat, or in soups or stews.

CHEESE PINWHEELS

4 oz. flour
3 tsps. baking powder
1 tsp. salt
2 oz. butter or margarine
4 oz. dry mashed potatoes
3–4 oz. grated cheese

Mix together the flour, baking powder and salt and rub in the fat very thoroughly with the finger-tips, until the mixture resembles fine breadcrumbs. Add the sieved potatoes and knead lightly on a floured board. Roll out to an oblong ½ inch thick and sprinkle with the grated cheese. Roll up like a Swiss roll and cut off slices about ⅓ inch thick. Use this mixture as a crust over a meat or vegetable casserole: 15–20 minutes before the casserole is cooked, take from the oven, remove the lid and place the cheese pinwheels (raw) on top. Bake for 15–20 minutes on the top shelf of a hot oven (450° F., mark 8) to cook the pinwheel crust.

Alternatively, serve the cheese pinwheels hot or cold as a savoury snack. Place the (raw) pinwheels flat on a greased tin and bake in a hot oven (450° F., mark 8) for about 15 minutes.

GARNISHES

MEAT GLAZE

Boil 4 quarts of good first stock (made from meat and bones) in a strong saucepan, first removing any grease that may be on the stock. Bring to the boil and continue to boil for several hours, until the stock is reduced and is of the consistency of glaze. It is then ready to use for brushing over hot or cold joints, galantines and so on. The amount of glaze obtained from this quantity of stock should be about ¼ pint. After use, any remaining glaze should be tied down in small pots, and when required the pot should be stood in a pan of boiling water until sufficiently melted to brush over the joint.

ECONOMICAL MEAT GLAZE

2 meat cubes
½ oz. gelantine
¼ pint water

Dissolve the meat cubes and gelatine in the water and stir until they are dissolved. Use within 2–3 days, as this glaze will not keep.

FRIED PARSLEY

(To garnish Fried Fish, Croquettes, etc.)

Choose good-sized pieces of well-curled parsley. If necessary to wash them, shake them well to remove the water, then dry thoroughly in a cloth. After frying the food to be garnished, draw the pan of fat from the fire and allow it to cool for 2–3 minutes. Then put in the parsley carefully and a little at a time, as the fat tends to spit, especially if the parsley is at all wet. Cook for 1 minute or so, until the parsley is crisp, then remove with a frying spoon, drain well and use at once.

ROSE RADISHES

Choose round radishes and wash them well, removing any root, but leaving 1 inch or so of the stalk. With a small, sharp knife (or potato peeler) peel the coloured skin down in sections to look like petals, starting at the root end and continuing nearly as far as the stalk; do this all round, leaving the middle of the radish as the flower centre. Soak in water for a short time to make the petals open out. Before using, shake well to remove water; use to garnish salads, hors d'œuvre and so on.

Rose Radish

LILY RADISHES

(*For decorating Hors d'Oeuvre and Salads*)

Select round radishes, trim them, and with a small sharp-pointed knife make V-shaped incisions around each, finally just cutting through the centre of the radish, when the two halves will come apart attractively notched.

Lily Radish

CURLED CELERY

(*To garnish Salads, Hors d'Oeuvre, etc.*)

Cut very thin shreds lengthwise from a stalk of celery. Soak in cold or iced water until curled—about an hour. Drain well before using.

CUCUMBER CONES

(*To garnish Salmon Mayonnaise, Salads, etc.*)

Make a cut in a thin slice of cucumber from

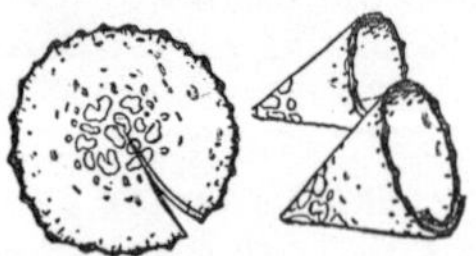

Cucumber Cones

the centre to the outer edge. Wrap one cut edge over the other to form a cone.

CRIMPED CUCUMBER

(*To garnish Salads, Hors d'Oeuvre, etc.*)

Working lengthwise, remove strips of the cucumber skin about $\frac{1}{8}$ inch wide at intervals of about $\frac{1}{8}$ inch. Then cut the cucumber crosswise in thin slices.

GHERKIN FANS

Use whole gherkins, choosing long, thin ones. Cut each gherkin lengthwise into thin slices, but leave them joined at one end. Fan out the gherkins, so that the slices overlap each other. A most attractive garnish can be made by combining gherkin fans and radish roses.

RED AND GREEN PEPPERS

These make a good garnish for galantines and other cold meats. Cut the skin of the uncooked peppers into fancy shapes with small cutters, or trim into julienne strips. Dip the pieces into glaze or aspic jelly, and place in position.

LEMON FANS

(*To garnish Fish, Veal, etc.*)

Cut $\frac{1}{8}$-inch thick slices of lemon in half, to form half circles. Cut the rind again in half, but leave the centre membranes attached, then open out to form fans.

Lemon Fans

POTATO BALLS

Peel 1 or 2 large potatoes and with a Parisian potato cutter scoop out rounds from all over the surface of the potato. Press the cutter well into the potato when scooping, to make sure the balls are well shaped. Put at once into cold water and when all are ready, cook gently in boiling salted water until tender but not broken—about 10 minutes. Drain well and, if liked, toss in a little butter and finely chopped parsley. Use to garnish entrées, fish dishes and so on.

VEGETABLE BALLS

Other vegetables besides potatoes, such as carrots, turnips, cucumber, vegetable marrow, etc., can be cut into balls to use as a garnish, and often a mixture of vegetables is used.

Prepare and cook the balls as described above. If a smaller garnish is required, use a pea cutter instead of a Parisian potato cutter. In this case, a few fresh green peas can be included in the garnish.

PARISIAN POTATOES

Scoop out the potato balls with a Parisian potato cutter as described above. When all are

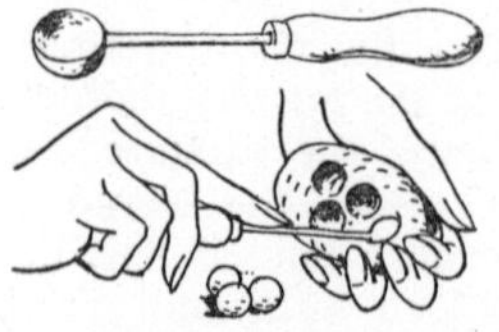

Parisian Potatoes

ready, remove from the cold water and dry thoroughly in a cloth, then fry in deep fat until golden-brown and tender—10–15 minutes. Drain on crumpled kitchen paper and use at once to garnish entrées, fish dishes and so on.

CROÛTONS

For croûtons to garnish entrées (such as fricassee of veal, chicken or rabbit, creamed sweetbreads, veal or chicken Marengo and so on), cut slices of bread ¼ inch in thickness and cut these into fancy shapes, such as rounds, squares, fingers, crescents, heart shapes or diamonds. Fry in hot butter until golden-brown on both sides, or cook in deep fat if preferred. Drain well on crumpled kitchen paper and use at once.

For croûtons to serve with soup, make some toast just beforehand, and cut this into small, neat dice. If desired, bread may be lightly buttered before being toasted. As an alternative to toasting, brown the bread dice in a moderate oven.

PROFITEROLES

Tiny rounds of choux pastry, like miniature cream buns, used for garnishing elaborate cold sweets and gateaux. For the recipe for choux pastry, see the chapter on Meringues, Éclairs and Cream Buns.

FLEURONS OF PASTRY

Roll the pastry (usually puff, flaky or rough puff) to ¼ inch in thickness, then stamp into crescents with a small round cutter. To do this, place the cutter about ½ inch on to the edge of the pastry for the first cut, then move the cutter a further ½ inch inwards and cut again, thus forming a crescent. Continue the length of the pastry, moving cutter ½ inch each time. Put on a baking sheet, brush tops lightly with beaten egg and bake in a hot oven (450° F., mark 8) until well risen, golden and firm—7–10 minutes. Use with entrées.

Fleurons of Pastry

HERBS AND SPICES

Herbs are invaluable for adding interest and savour to home cooking—they so greatly improve the flavour of soups, stews and other savoury dishes that a supply should be available in every kitchen. When in season, herbs are best used fresh, but for winter use they may be dried and then stored—see below. Most herbs are fairly strong in flavour, so they should be used in moderation, and when mixed herbs are used, no one flavour should predominate unduly.

The following is a list of the herbs, etc., most commonly used in cookery. See also the illustrations on opposite page.

Balm : A fragrant herb, the leaves of which have a lemon flavour and scent. It is milder than most herbs, and therefore used in larger quantities, as a flavouring for soups, stews, fruit and claret cups.

Basil : Rather strong, with a perfume resembling cloves. Used sparingly in soups and stuffings.

Bay Leaf : Used in small amounts for flavouring custards and milk puddings, also for soups and stews; combined with other herbs to make a bouquet garni.

Borage : Flavour resembles cucumber; used in flavouring cider and claret cup, and as an addition to salads.

Chervil : A plant with the aroma of aniseed; chervil improves the flavour of any herbs with which it is mixed, hence its value in a bouquet garni. Finely chopped, it can be used in small amounts in salads, especially with cucumber, and in egg dishes. It is not usually dried.

Chive : Has a mild onion flavour, and when used in salads, omelettes and vegetable dishes is more agreeable to most people than ordinary onions, as it is not so rich in sulphur, and is therefore more digestible.

Dandelion : Young leaves from specially cultivated plants may be included in salads.

Dill : A rather bitter-flavoured herb, used for the preparation of dill vinegar, and in a sauce to serve with fish. A little finely chopped dill may be included in salads, soups, stews and savoury dishes—use it sparingly, as it is strong in flavour.

Fennel : Mainly used in fish dishes and sauces, fennel sauce being particularly good with mackerel.

Garlic : Though very popular on the Continent, this is not widely used in this country, as it is rather strong. To obtain a delicate garlic flavour, rub the inside of the salad bowl with the cut edge of a clove of garlic; for stews, curry, sauces, etc., crush the clove.

Horseradish : Used freshly grated in sauces and in a cream served with roast beef and some meat entrées. A little may be added to sandwich fillings.

Horseradish

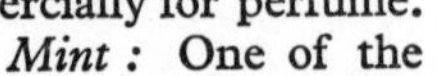

Marjoram : An ingredient of mixed herbs; also used commercially for perfume.

Mint : One of the most widely used herbs, useful for flavouring new potatoes and peas during the cooking, and as an addition to salads, etc. Mint sauce and mint jelly are popular accompaniments.

In the North of England a very good mint pasty is eaten, with a filling made of equal quantities of chopped mint, brown sugar and currants pounded together.

Nasturtium : The seeds may be pickled and used as a substitute for capers. The young leaves make an excellent addition to a salad.

Parsley : This well-known herb is rich in iron and vitamin content; it should be chopped just before use, and not too finely, except for special garnishes. Add it to salads, sandwich fillings, soups, etc.

Rosemary : Used chiefly for stuffings, meat, soups and stews, especially kidney and tripe dishes. Needs to be used sparingly, as it is very strong.

Sage : Included with onions in a stuffing for pork, duck and goose. (See recipe in chapter on Stuffings.) Used also to flavour savoury dishes and salads.

Savory : Used in small quantities for

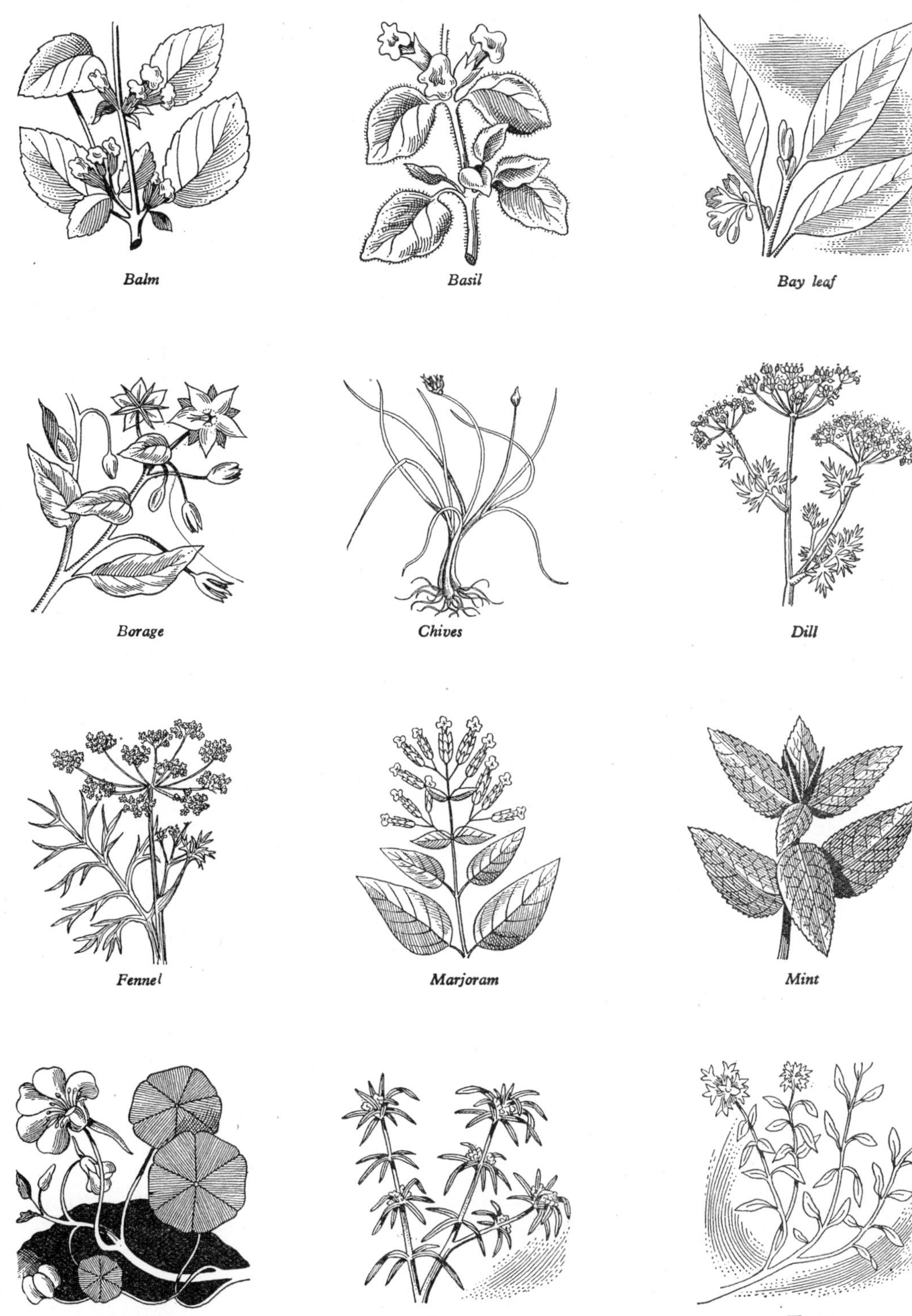

Balm *Basil* *Bay leaf*

Borage *Chives* *Dill*

Fennel *Marjoram* *Mint*

Nasturtium *Rosemary* *Thyme*

flavouring sausages, for cooking with broad beans and in tomato sauce.

Shallot : Often pickled; otherwise used in the same way as onions.

Tarragon : Used for flavouring the white vinegar to be used for Tartare sauce, etc., also for French mustard. Use it fresh, if possible, as it loses its essential oil when dried. (For recipe for Tarragon Vinegar, see chapter on Pickles and Chutneys.)

Thyme : Can be rubbed into the flesh of meat and poultry before cooking; also used for stuffings, lemon thyme being excellent in veal stuffing.

BOUQUET GARNI

This is a bunch of herbs used in soups, stews, sauces, and so on, to give flavour. It usually consists of a sprig each of parsley, thyme and marjoram, and a bay leaf is often included. Other herbs, such as balm, savory and lemon-scented thyme, may also be used, if available. Bind them together in a faggot, or better still, tie them in a piece of muslin, and cook them in the pot with the liquid and other ingredients. When sufficient flavour has been extracted, the bouquet garni may be lifted out. If the soup or sauce is to be sieved, there is no need to tie the herbs in muslin.

When fresh herbs are not available, a pinch or so of mixed dried herbs may be used instead. If the dish calls for spices such as cloves, peppercorns and mace, these are usually included in the bag of herbs.

FINES HERBES

The mixture of herbs known by this name, and use for flavouring omelettes, etc., is usually composed of equal quantities of chopped parsley, chervil, chives and tarragon.

DRYING HERBS

Herbs should be picked when fully grown, but not yet in flower—June and July are usually the best months. Gather them early on a dry day, after the dew has gone, but before the sun robs them of their volatile oils.

Spread the leaves on shallow trays with a base of muslin or perforated wood or metal, and place these in a warm room where the air can circulate around them, but away from strong light. Turn the herbs daily until they are brittle and dry, then they should be snipped from the stems and stored in clean, dry bottles.

Parsley needs different treatment. Pick it early in the day, wash it, put it on a clean baking tray and leave it in a hot oven for about 1 minute, until it is crisp and dry. Powder it up, and put it into jars when cold.

SPICES

This term covers a wide variety of vegetable seasonings, pungent and aromatic in both taste and odour, which are used to flavour savoury and sweet dishes. They are obtainable either singly or in combination (e.g., as mixed spice and curry powder). The best flavour is obtained from freshly ground spices, so they should be bought in small quantities.

The following is a list of the most commonly used spices:

Allspice : The dried and ground berries of the pimento tree, which grows in South America and the West Indies. Allspice is said to combine the flavours of cinnamon, cloves and nutmeg, hence its name. It is employed in pickling and in preparing spiced meats, and is also used in gingerbread and fruit puddings, etc.

Aniseed : The seeds of a plant of the fennel family, cultivated in Europe and the Far East. The volatile oil expressed from them is used as a flavouring for liqueurs, cordials and confectionery, and also medicinally.

Cardamoms : The spicy, bitter seeds of a reed-like plant grown largely in India and the Far East. They are used in the preparation of sauces, curry powder and cordials, and in spicing cakes. As they lose their flavour quickly when ground, they should be bought in the pod.

Carraway : A plant of the parsley family, which grows in various parts of Europe; the seeds have a warm, pungent taste, and can be used either whole or ground, for flavouring liqueurs, bread, confectionery, etc.

Cassia : The inner bark of a tree grown in the Far East and similar regions. It resembles cinnamon in appearance, aroma and taste (though it is somewhat coarser) and it is used in the same way.

Chillies : The name given to various small species of bright red capsicums, grown in Africa, South America, and the Far East. They are used in flavouring chutneys, etc. to which they impart a hot taste. When ground, they become cayenne pepper, which is used for flavouring cheese dishes, stews, etc.

Cinnamon : The bark of a species of laurel, widely grown in India, the West Indies, etc.;

the best type comes from Ceylon. Stick cinnamon should be light yellow in colour, thin, closely rolled and aromatic. For flavouring cakes, biscuits, etc., the ground form is generally used. Oil of cinnamon is included in liqueurs, and has medicinal uses.

Cloves : The dried unopened buds of an evergreen shrub which grows in hot, moist climates such as the Moluccas. They have a strong, hot, spicy taste and smell, and are used for flavouring both sweet and savoury dishes, being particularly good with apples. Ground cloves are sometimes used in biscuits and so on.

Coriander : The seeds of a plant similar to parsley, grown in Europe, North Africa, and other regions. When dried, they have a mild aromatic taste and smell, and are used for flavouring gin, and in cordials, confectionery, medicines and pickles. Coriander is also an important ingredient in curry powder.

Cumin : A plant of the parsley family, and related to carraway ; its aromatic seeds are used on the Continent to flavour liqueurs, cordials, cheese and breads.

Fenugreek : A plant of the clover family, the ground seeds of which are used in curry powder ; its flavour somewhat resembles that of celery.

Ginger : A reed-like plant grown in Africa, Asia, and the West Indies. Both the stems and the fibrous roots have a characteristic hot flavour, and are used in various forms in cookery and also in medicine. The dried roots, when finely ground, are used to flavour cakes, puddings, etc., or they may be used whole in jam and pickle making. Jamaica ginger is considered the best type.

Mace : The husk of the nutmeg, which is used in both " blade " and ground form, to improve the flavour of sauces, stews, pickles, cakes, puddings, etc. It is usually included in curry powder.

Mustard : There are three types of mustard seed—white, brown and black. The brown and black seeds contain myronic oil, which gives the true piquant flavour, but makes them of poor keeping quality ; the white seeds, though inferior in flavour, keep better. Manufactured mustard powder is usually a mixture of one or more varieties, finely ground and with a cereal (e.g. wheat flour) added to absorb oil and retard fermentation.

Nutmeg : The kernel of the fruit borne by an evergreen tree grown in various tropical countries. Nutmegs are usually bought whole, and grated as required ; the flavour is agreeable but strong, and the spice should be used with care. It is good in various types of cakes, puddings, milk puddings, etc.

Paprika : The red fruit of a capsicum grown in Hungary, dried and ground. The characteristic sweet, aromatic taste, devoid of pungency, makes it a good addition to many savoury dishes, especially those containing tomato, and it also serves as a garnish.

Pepper : There are several varieties of pepper, most of which are obtained by grinding the fruits of certain plants which have a hot, pungent taste. The whole peppercorns are sometimes used for flavouring soups, etc., and in pickles.

Black and white pepper are both made from the berries of the *Piper nigrum*, which grows in hot countries. The black variety is made from the unripe berries, and the white type is produced by grinding the ripe berries after the outer dark husk has been removed. Black pepper is more pungent and has a better aroma, though it does not look so attractive when sprinkled over food.

Cayenne pepper is made from capsicums—see Chillies.

Paprika pepper : see separate entry.

Pimento or Jamaica pepper is another name for Allspice, which see.

Coralline pepper is a fancy name given to bright red ground chillies.

Turmeric : The dried and ground roots of a plant of the ginger family. It has a distinctive aromatic odour and taste, and is yellow in colour. Turmeric is used to flavour and colour curry powder.

Vanilla : This flavouring is made from the seed pods of a climbing plant of the orchid family, grown in Mexico, etc. Whole pods may be used to flavour the milk used in puddings, etc., or sugar may be flavoured by mixing ground or whole pods with it in the proportion of 4 pods to 1 lb. Store in a jar with a well-fitting lid, and use as required for cakes, etc. Vanilla essence, which is made from the pods, is a convenient form for domestic use. Like most essences it is strong in flavour and should be used sparingly.

SAUCES

A well-made sauce, however simple, will often give just the right finish to a dish, improving both flavour and appearance, so that a little time and trouble spent in preparing it are well worth while. It need not be a complicated process: many sauces can be made in a few minutes from quite simple ingredients. They can, if necessary, be made early in the day, and reheated in a double saucepan, or kept hot by being covered and stood in a meat tin containing hot water—an improvised "bain marie." In this way the sauces keep hot without a skin forming on the surface and without going lumpy. The flavouring and colouring are added at the last minute.

The liquid used is of great importance, as it affects the flavour of the sauce. For sauces accompanying fish, the fish bones may be used to make stock, half fish stock and half milk being used for the sauce. Vegetable water or stock made from bones should be used for gravies and brown sauces; milk, or milk and white stock for white sauces.

The foundation of all brown and white sauces in which flour is the thickening agent is the roux, formed by cooking the butter and flour together. For white sauces the butter should be melted, the flour added and the two stirred and cooked together until well incorporated. The liquid should then be added by degrees, the sauce being stirred and cooked after each addition, until the right consistency is obtained. Brown sauces are made in the same way as white sauces, except that the dripping or butter is melted, the flour added and the roux cooked slowly until it acquires an even golden-brown colour. Well-flavoured stock is then added and the cooking finished as above.

It is most important that the liquid should be added gradually, as the starch grains must be thoroughly separated, otherwise the flour forms lumps. In order to complete the cooking of the starch grains in the flour, it is essential that the sauce should be stirred and boiled for 3–5 minutes. During this time the starch grains absorb the liquid, swell, burst and thicken the sauce. If by any chance the sauce turns lumpy, strain it; and if it is too thin, add to it a little flour blended with additional liquid; stir and boil for another 5 minutes.

A well-made and well-beaten sauce is usually sufficiently smooth and glossy for ordinary domestic purposes, but if a specially glossy and smooth textured sauce is required it can be squeezed through a tammy cloth—made of a special woollen material of very fine texture.

Any special flavouring or colouring should be added just before the sauce is served.

MEAT STOCK FOR SAUCES: See recipes in the Soups chapter.

FISH STOCK FOR SAUCES

For a sauce to serve with fish, there is no comparison between one made with a well-flavoured fish stock and one in which milk or water forms the liquid part—the latter is entirely lacking in character. Wash the trimmings of fish, breaking up the bones and discarding the black skin. Put them into a saucepan with equal parts of milk and water to cover them, and add a few parsley stalks, a small piece of onion, a blade of mace, ½ dozen white peppercorns, 1–2 cloves and a bay leaf. Simmer for about ½ hour to extract the flavour, then strain and use as required. A little white wine can be used instead of milk and gives a delicious flavour.

SEASONED MILK FOR SAUCES

Put as much milk as required into a saucepan, and add to it a small quantity of carrot, turnip, onion and celery, a few parsley stalks, 1–2 cloves, a small blade of mace and a few peppercorns. Stand this in a warm place to infuse, then strain, and cool before using.

BASIC RECIPES FOR WHITE AND BROWN SAVOURY SAUCES

WHITE SAUCE

1 oz. butter or margarine
1 oz. flour
¾ pint milk, or milk and stock
Salt and pepper

Melt the butter, stir in the flour, then add the liquid gradually, stirring well during the process. Continue to stir until the liquid comes to the boil, then boil slowly for 3–5 minutes. Add seasonings.

For a coating sauce, use only ½ pint liquid.

PANADA OR BINDING SAUCE

2 oz. butter or margarine
2 oz. flour
½ pint milk or other liquid
Seasoning

Melt the butter, stir in the flour, then add the liquid gradually, stirring well during the process. Continue to stir well until the liquid thickens, then boil slowly for 3–5 minutes, beating hard. Add seasonings, and use to bind a mixture, as in meat or fish croquettes.

BÉCHAMEL SAUCE (SAVOURY WHITE SAUCE)

1 pint milk
1 shallot
A piece of carrot
1 stalk of celery
1 clove of garlic
1 bay leaf
8 peppercorns
2 oz. flour
2 oz. butter
¼ pint cream (optional)
Salt and pepper

Put the milk, vegetables, garlic, bay leaf and peppercorns into a pan and bring slowly to the boil. Cover and leave in a warm place for a few minutes to infuse. Strain and make a sauce, using the flour and butter in the usual way. When cooked allow to cool slightly, then add the cream and seasoning, reheat, but do not boil.

VELOUTÉ SAUCE (RICH WHITE SAUCE)

6 peppercorns
A few parsley stalks
4 chopped button mushrooms
1 oz. butter
1 oz. flour
½ pint white stock (veal or chicken)
Lemon juice
Pepper and salt
2 tbsps. cream

Fry the peppercorns, parsley stalks and mushrooms in the butter without browning, stir in the flour and add the stock. Simmer 1 hour, strain or pass through a tammy cloth, add the other ingredients and reheat.

BROWN SAUCE (PLAIN)

1 small onion
1 small carrot
1 oz. butter or dripping
1 oz. flour
¾ pint brown stock
Seasoning
Gravy browning, meat cube or glaze, if liked

Chop the onion and carrot into small pieces, melt the butter and fry the vegetables until deep brown in colour, but do not allow them to burn. Stir in the flour, blend with the vegetables and continue to cook until the flour is also golden-brown. Gradually add the stock, bring to the boil, stirring meanwhile, and simmer gently for 15–20 minutes, and then strain. Season to taste.

If the sauce is not deep enough in colour, a few drops of gravy browning may be added, or a meat cube may be used to improve the flavour.

ESPAGNOLE SAUCE (RICH BROWN SAUCE)

2 oz. butter or dripping
2 oz. bacon
1 shallot
1 large tomato
1 small carrot
2 oz. flour
1 pint brown stock
1 dessertsp. mushroom ketchup
A bouquet garni
Pepper and salt

Melt the butter and fry the chopped bacon in it, then fry the sliced vegetables until lightly browned. Add the flour and fry all to a rich golden-brown. Add the rest of the ingredients and simmer for 40 minutes, then skim and sieve. Reheat the sauce and season it.

1 tbsp. or so of sherry may be added to the sauce just before serving.

GRAVY

See recipe under ROAST MEAT in the Meat chapter. Gravy served with game is improved by the addition of a little red wine.

VARIATIONS OF BASIC SAVOURY SAUCES

ALLEMANDE SAUCE

½ pint Velouté sauce (see recipe in this chapter)
2 egg yolks
1 oz. butter or 2 tbsps. cream
Lemon juice

Heat the Velouté sauce gently until somewhat reduced, then remove from the heat and add the beaten egg yolks gradually, stirring well. Add the butter or cream and a squeeze of lemon juice, and cook over boiling water until thick and creamy.

ANCHOVY SAUCE

1 oz. butter or margarine
1 oz. flour
¼ pint milk
¼ pint fish stock or water
Anchovy essence

Melt the butter or margarine, stir in the flour and add the milk and fish stock gradually. Bring to the boil, stirring meanwhile to prevent lumps forming. When it reaches boiling point, add sufficient anchovy essence to produce an attractive colour and a decided flavour. Continue to cook, stirring for 3–5 minutes.

AURORE SAUCE—I

Make Béchamel sauce and add enough paprika pepper to give the sauce a good pink colour.

AURORE SAUCE—II

Make a Velouté sauce and colour it pink with tomato purée.

BÉARNAISE SAUCE

2 shallots or 1 onion
2 tbsps. tarragon vinegar
2 tbsps. malt vinegar
½ pint Béchamel sauce
2 egg yolks
½ tsp. chopped parsley

Simmer the shallots in the vinegars until reduced to 1 tbsp. Strain and add to the Béchamel sauce, together with the egg yolks. Reheat without boiling, using a double saucepan if possible. Add the parsley and serve.

BIGARADE SAUCE

1 Seville orange
¼ pint Espagnole sauce
¼ pint good gravy
Lemon juice
1 glass port
Seasoning

Cut the peel of half the orange into thin "julienne" strips. Just cover them with water, boil for 5 minutes and drain. Boil the Espagnole sauce, gravy and half the juice of the orange till reduced to half. Add the orange peel, 1 tsp. lemon juice and the port and season well. Serve with roast wild duck and game.

CAPER SAUCE

1 oz. butter or margarine
1 oz. flour
¼ pint stock
½ pint milk
A little vinegar
Pepper and salt
1½ tbsps. capers

Melt the butter, stir in the flour, add the stock and milk gradually, bring to the boil, stirring meanwhile, and cook for 3–5 minutes. Add the vinegar, pepper, salt and chopped capers. Continue to cook, stirring meanwhile, for 3–4 minutes.

CARDINAL SAUCE

½ pint Béchamel sauce
Salt and pepper
Grated nutmeg
A little lemon juice
Lobster butter (see page 447)
2 tbsps. cream

Make a Béchamel sauce, following the recipe on page 197, cook and beat it well. Season with salt and pepper, a little grated nutmeg and a squeeze of lemon juice. Beat in the lobster butter, and lastly add the cream. Then pass through a tammy cloth and reheat, but do not boil.

CELERY SAUCE

½ a head of celery
1 oz. butter or margarine
1 oz. flour
¾ pint milk and celery liquor
Seasoning
Celery salt

Wash the celery well and cut into small pieces, barely cover with cold water and simmer until tender. Melt the butter or margarine, then add the flour, and stir well. Strain the celery, saving the liquid. Make up to ¾ pint with milk and add gradually to the butter and flour, stirring well all the time. Boil for 5 minutes, stirring, then add the seasonings, and the sauce is ready for use.

CHASSEUR SAUCE

2 tsps. home-made glaze
1 tsp. lemon juice
Seasoning
Cayenne pepper
½ pint Espagnole sauce
A little red-currant jelly
¼ pint port wine

Add the glaze, lemon juice and seasonings to the Espagnole sauce. Reheat and allow to reduce for about 10 minutes. Add the jelly and port wine, reheat and serve. Use to accompany venison.

1 tbsp. chopped mushrooms, lightly fried in a little butter, may be added to the Espagnole sauce, with glaze, lemon juice and seasoning.

CHAUDFROID SAUCE (WHITE)

¼ pint aspic jelly	1 tsp. lemon juice
¼ oz. gelatine	¼ pint cream or unsweetened evaporated milk
½ pint good white sauce (see Béchamel sauce)	

Melt the aspic jelly in a pan, add the gelatine, and stir over a low heat until it is dissolved. Warm the sauce and stir in the melted aspic and gelatine. Beat hard, add the lemon juice, cook for 5 minutes, strain, and when almost cold add the cream or evaporated milk. This sauce is used for coating cold cooked foods.

A simpler method is to use equal quantities of aspic jelly and Béchamel or other light sauce. Melt the jelly and add to the warm sauce. Mix well and pass through a tammy cloth. When just on the point of setting, use at once for coating galantine, cold chicken and so on.

CHAUDFROID SAUCE (BROWN)

½ pint aspic jelly	Seasoning
½ pint Espagnole sauce	A little cream

Heat the aspic jelly and add to the hot sauce. Bring to the boil, season and pass through a tammy cloth. Add the cream, and when just beginning to set, use for coating purposes.

CHEESE SAUCE

1 oz. butter or margarine	2 tbsps. grated cheese (Parmesan for preference)
1 oz. flour	Salt, pepper and mustard
¾ pint milk	

Melt the butter, stir in the flour, then add the milk gradually, and bring to the boil, stirring meanwhile. When it reaches boiling point, simmer for 3–5 minutes. Add the grated cheese and stir well. Season to taste.

CHESTNUT SAUCE

½ lb. chestnuts	1 oz. flour
½ pint white stock or water	Salt and pepper
1½ oz. butter	2–3 tbsps. cream

Make a slit in the chestnuts, boil them for 2–3 minutes in water, then, taking them from the water a few at a time, remove the skins. Put the shelled nuts into a pan with the stock, cover and simmer until tender, then mash or pass them through a fine sieve. Melt the butter and stir in the flour to form a roux, then add the chestnut purée and bring to the boil, stirring—the sauce should be thick, but it may be necessary at this point to add a little milk or extra stock. Season well with salt and pepper, remove from the heat and stir in the cream. Reheat without boiling, and serve at once with boiled turkey or other poultry.

CIDER SAUCE

½ pint cider	1 bay leaf
¾ pint thick brown sauce	2 cloves
Salt and pepper	

Mix the cider and sauce thoroughly together, add the seasoning and flavourings. Simmer steadily, stirring occasionally, until the sauce is reduced to the desired consistency. Strain and serve with ham dishes.

CUCUMBER SAUCE

Cook a small cucumber, sieve, and add to ½ pint hot Béchamel sauce. For added flavour and depth of colour, pound 2 tbsps. spinach and sieve it with the cucumber purée; 1 tbsp. cream may also be added.

An alternative method is to use raw cucumber, which gives a stronger-flavoured sauce. Chill the cucumber, then grate it, and mix with an equal quantity of whipped chilled cream. Season with salt, pepper and vinegar, and serve at once.

CURRY SAUCE

See chapter on Curry Making.

DEMI-GLACE

Mix ½ pint Espagnole sauce with ¼ pint good beef gravy and a little meat glaze.

EGG SAUCE

½ oz. butter or margarine	1 hard-boiled egg
½ oz. flour	Pepper and salt
½ pint milk	

Melt the butter, stir in the flour and blend thoroughly, cooking meanwhile over gentle heat. Add the milk gradually, stirring, until the liquid comes to the boil, then boil slowly for 3–5 minutes. Chop the egg, stir into the cooked sauce and season with pepper and salt. If preferred, chopped hard-boiled egg can be added to ½ pint Béchamel sauce; for use with fish, it is a good plan to use fish stock.

FENNEL SAUCE

½ oz. butter or margarine	1 dessertsp. finely chopped fennel
½ oz. flour	
½ pint milk or other liquid	Salt and pepper

Make a white sauce in the usual way, and just before serving add the finely chopped fennel, salt and pepper, and blend for 1 minute.

FISH SAUCE

1 oz. butter or margarine	Salt
1 oz. flour	White pepper
½ pint fish stock	A squeeze of lemon juice

Melt the butter in a saucepan and stir in the flour until smooth. Then add the stock gradually and stir until boiling. Season to taste, simmer for 2–3 minutes in order to cook the flour thoroughly and add the lemon juice. An extra piece of butter or 1 tbsp. of cream stirred in just before serving will improve the sauce. Or, it can be made richer by adding 1–2 egg yolks, but the sauce must not boil after these are in.

This white sauce forms the foundation of many other fish sauces, e.g., Mussel and Oyster Sauces.

HOLLANDAISE SAUCE

2 tbsps. water or fish stock	2 oz. butter
1 dessertsp. tarragon vinegar	Salt and cayenne
2 egg yolks	1 dessertsp. lemon juice

Put the water or stock, vinegar and egg yolks into a basin and stand the basin in a saucepan of hot water. Whisk over heat until the sauce thickens, then draw the saucepan to one side and add the butter in small pieces, stirring well. Season to taste and add the lemon juice. The sauce must not boil or it will curdle.

MOCK HOLLANDAISE SAUCE

2 egg yolks	A little lemon juice or vinegar
2 tbsps. cream	
½ pint Béchamel sauce	

Beat together the egg yolks and cream and add to the Béchamel sauce. Heat carefully in a double saucepan to cook the eggs, but on no account allow to boil. Using a teaspoon, add a very little lemon juice or vinegar, drop by drop, to give a slightly sharp taste to the sauce.

HORSERADISH SAUCE (HOT)

1 tbsp. grated horseradish	1 tsp. cream
½ tsp. vinegar	½ pint Béchamel sauce
2 tsps. caster sugar	

Moisten the horseradish with vinegar. Add sugar and cream to the Béchamel sauce. Heat up, add horseradish and season well.

HORSERADISH CREAM (COLD)

2 oz. horseradish	A little salt and pepper
¼ pint cream	2 tsps. lemon juice

Wash and scrape the horseradish and grate into very fine flakes. Partly whip the cream, stir in the seasoning, and lastly, the lemon juice and grated horseradish. Blend thoroughly, and chill before serving.

HUNGARIAN SAUCE

2 tbsps. chopped onion	¼ pint white wine
2 oz. butter	A bunch of herbs
Salt	1 pint white sauce
Paprika pepper	

Fry the onion in half the butter without allowing it to colour, add the salt and pepper. Moisten with the wine, add the herbs and reduce to half quantity. Mix in white sauce; simmer for 5 minutes, add the remainder of the butter, beat it and pass the mixture through a tammy cloth. This sauce should be a delicate pink colour.

ITALIAN SAUCE

1 oz. butter or margarine	1 glass white wine
1 tbsp. each of chopped onion, carrot and lean raw ham	Seasoning
1 oz. flour	1 dessertsp. chopped parsley
½ pint stock	Chopped mushroom (optional)

Melt the butter in a saucepan, put in the onion, carrot and ham, and fry them for a few minutes until lightly browned. Then add the flour and brown that also. Add the stock and wine gradually and stir until boiling. Season to taste, simmer for 15 minutes and strain. Reheat, and add parsley at the last moment. A few chopped mushrooms may also be added.

MADEIRA SAUCE

½ pint Espagnole sauce	¼ pint Madeira
1 tsp. home-made glaze	Seasoning

Add all the ingredients to the Espagnole sauce, reheat and serve.

MAYONNAISE: See chapter on Salads and Salad Dressings.

MEAT SAUCE

1 oz. dripping	1 tsp. piquant sauce
1 tbsp. chopped onion	¼ tsp. mixed herbs
¾ oz. flour	Salt and pepper
½ pint stock	4 oz. minced cooked meat
1 tbsp. tomato purée	

Melt the dripping and fry the onion till golden-brown. Add the flour and stir in the stock by degrees. Bring to the boil, stirring, and add the tomato purée, piquant sauce and herbs.

Season well, cover, and simmer gently for 10 minutes. Lastly, add the finely minced meat, reheat, and serve with noodles, savoury rice, etc.

MELTED BUTTER

(*To serve with asparagus, globe artichokes, etc.*)

Melt 2 oz. butter gently, preferably over hot water, so that it does not brown at all. Add salt and pepper and strain before serving.

MELTED BUTTER SAUCE

2 oz. butter	½ pint cold water
¾ oz. flour	Pepper and salt

Melt the butter, stir in the flour and blend thoroughly, cooking meanwhile over gentle heat. Add the cold water gradually, bring to the boil and allow to cook slowly for 5–7 minutes, stirring occasionally. Season with pepper and salt.

Stock, or a mixture of stock and milk, may be used instead of water, if preferred.

An alternative method is to make ordinary white sauce, and, just before serving, to whisk in extra butter, a little at a time, in the proportion of 1 oz. of butter to ½ pint white sauce.

MORNAY SAUCE

Make Béchamel sauce, and just before serving add grated Parmesan cheese and cayenne pepper to taste.

MUSHROOM SAUCE

½ lb. mushrooms	1 oz. flour
½ pint stock	¼ pint milk
1 small onion	Pepper and salt
1 oz. butter	1 egg yolk

Wash and peel the mushrooms, chop finely and cook for ½ hour in the stock with the onion. When cooked, rub through a sieve. Melt the butter in a saucepan, stir in the flour, and add the milk gradually. Bring to the boil, stirring meanwhile, add the mushroom purée and seasoning, and simmer for ¼ hour. Remove from the stove, allow to cool slightly, then stir in the beaten egg yolk. Cook for a few minutes, but do not boil, as the egg is liable to curdle.

MUSSEL SAUCE

Add prepared mussels to ½ pint fish sauce.

MUSTARD SAUCE

1 oz. butter or margarine	¼ pint water
½ oz. flour	2 tbsp. vinegar
½ tsp. dry mustard	Pepper and salt

Melt the butter, fry the flour and mustard lightly, add the water gradually, then the vinegar, pepper and salt. Stir and boil gently for 3–5 minutes.

NORMANDY SAUCE

½ pint white sauce made with fish liquor	½ oz. butter Lemon juice
1 egg yolk	

Make a white sauce in the usual way, but using a fish liquor; cook and beat well. Cool slightly, beat in the egg yolk and reheat carefully without boiling. Stir in the butter a little at a time and add lemon juice to taste.

ONION SAUCE—I

½ oz. butter or margarine	3 tbsps. chopped cooked onion
½ oz. flour	
½ pint milk or stock	Salt and pepper

Melt the butter, stir in the flour, then add the liquid gradually, stirring well during the process. Continue to stir until the liquid comes to the boil, then boil slowly for 3–5 minutes. Add the chopped onion, salt and pepper and blend thoroughly.

ONION SAUCE—II

1 medium-sized onion	¼ pint milk
¼ pint water (approx.)	A knob of butter
1 oz. flour	Salt and pepper

Slice or chop the onion and stew in the water until tender—10–15 minutes. Do not strain. Blend the flour to a smooth cream with the milk and stir into the cooked onion. Bring to the boil and cook for 2–3 minutes, stirring the while. If necessary, thin down with a little water. Beat in a knob of butter and season well.

ORANGE SAUCE (SAVOURY)—I

1 oz. butter	Juice of 2 oranges
1 oz. flour	1 egg yolk
½ pint light stock	Salt to taste
Grated rind of 1 orange	

Melt the butter, mix in the flour and add the stock gradually. Stir until boiling. Add the orange rind and juice and simmer for 10 minutes. Stir in the egg yolk, season, and strain.

ORANGE SAUCE (SAVOURY)—II

(*To serve with duck*)

½ pint Espagnole sauce	Cayenne pepper
1 Seville orange	¼ pint port wine
Juice of ½ a lemon	

Pass the Espagnole sauce through a tammy cloth and add the very finely shredded orange rind. Cook gently until tender. Add the orange and lemon juice and the cayenne pepper. Cook for a further 10 minutes, add the port wine, reheat and serve.

OYSTER SAUCE

Open 12 oysters, then remove the beards. Put them with their liquor in a small pan, together with 1–2 oz. butter; cover, and cook gently for 4 minutes. Add to $\frac{1}{2}$ pint white or Béchamel sauce, and flavour with a little lemon juice.

PARSLEY SAUCE

$\frac{1}{2}$ oz. butter or margarine	1 tbsp. freshly chopped parsley
$\frac{1}{2}$ oz. flour	A pinch of salt
$\frac{1}{2}$ pint milk or other liquid	Pepper

Melt the butter, stir in the flour, then add the liquid gradually, stirring well during the process. Continue to stir until the liquid boils, then boil slowly for 3–5 minutes. Just before serving, add the parsley, salt and pepper, stir in and blend for 1 minute.

PEPPER SAUCE

$\frac{1}{2}$ a rasher of bacon	A small piece of mace
$\frac{1}{2}$ oz. butter	A small piece of bay leaf
A small piece of onion and carrot	$\frac{1}{2}$ pint rich brown sauce (see Espagnole sauce)
12 peppercorns	

Fry the half rasher of bacon and add the butter. Chop the onions and the carrot and fry in the bacon fat and butter until just golden-brown. Crush the peppercorns and add to the pan with the herbs. Add the brown sauce, boil gently for 10–15 minutes, stirring occasionally, and then strain and serve.

PIQUANTE SAUCE

12 peppercorns	1 tsp. chopped capers
2 tbsps. vinegar	1 tsp. chopped gherkin
$\frac{1}{2}$ pint Espagnole sauce	1 tsp. chopped parsley

Simmer the peppercorns in the vinegar until the vinegar is reduced to half. Strain and add to the hot sauce, together with the capers, gherkins and chopped parsley.

PIQUANT PARSLEY SAUCE

1 oz. butter	Salt and pepper
1 oz. flour	1 tbsp. chopped parsley
$\frac{1}{4}$ pint milk	$\frac{1}{2}$–1 tbsp. tarragon vinegar
$\frac{1}{4}$ pint stock	

Melt the butter, stir in the flour and cook gently without browning. Add the milk and stock gradually and bring to the boil, stirring. Boil for 2–3 minutes, beating well to make it smooth and glossy, then season with salt and pepper. Just before serving, add the finely chopped parsley and vinegar to taste.

PIQUANT ANCHOVY SAUCE

Follow the directions for Piquant Parsley Sauce, adding about 1 tsp. of anchovy essence and omitting any extra salt. Instead of 1 tbsp. chopped parsley, add 1 small tsp.

RÉFORME SAUCE

A few peppercorns	$\frac{1}{4}$ pint port wine
$\frac{1}{2}$ pint Espagnole sauce	A little lemon juice
2 tsps. red-currant jelly	Seasoning

Add the peppercorns to the sauce and boil for a few minutes. Pass through a tammy cloth. Add the other ingredients, reheat and serve.

ROBERT SAUCE

2 oz. butter	A few peppercorns
2 onions	Salt and pepper
1 oz. flour	$\frac{1}{4}$ tsp. mustard
$\frac{1}{2}$ pint brown stock	4 tbsps. white wine
A bunch of herbs	A little lemon juice
A bay leaf	1 tsp. caster sugar

Melt the butter and fry the sliced onions in it over gentle heat until golden-brown—about 10 minutes. Stir in the flour to form a roux, then gradually add the stock and bring to the boil, stirring. Add the herbs, bay leaf and peppercorns, tied in muslin, and season with salt. Cover and simmer for about $\frac{1}{2}$ hour, then remove the bag of herbs and stir in the mustard, wine, lemon juice and sugar; reseason if necessary and strain before serving with goose, pork, veal or steaks.

SHRIMP SAUCE

2 tbsps. picked shrimps	1 oz. butter or margarine
$\frac{1}{4}$ pint water	1 oz. flour
1 tbsp. vinegar	$\frac{1}{4}$ pint milk
A small blade of mace	A little anchovy essence
A small piece of bay leaf	

Make fish stock by boiling the shells and heads of the shrimps with $\frac{1}{4}$ pint water and the vinegar, mace and bay leaf slowly for 10 minutes in a covered pan: strain. Melt the butter, stir in the flour, and add the milk and fish stock gradually, then bring to the boil, stirring meanwhile. Cook for 3–5 minutes. Add the shrimps and continue to boil for another 3–5 minutes. Add anchovy essence to give a pink tint.

SOUBISE SAUCE

2–3 onions
½ pint Béchamel sauce
Seasoning
Nutmeg and 1 tbsp. cream (optional)

Cook the onions in a little water, sieve and add to the hot Béchamel sauce. Season and serve at once. A little grated nutmeg and 1 tbsp. cream may be added to the sauce before serving, if desired.

SUPRÊME SAUCE

Make as for Velouté sauce, but add up to ¼ pint of cream.

TARTARE SAUCE (COLD)

½ pint mayonnaise
½ tsp. chopped tarragon
3 tsps. chopped capers
1 tbsp. chopped gherkins
1 tsp. chopped chervil
1 tbsp. chopped parsley

Add all the other ingredients, finely chopped, to the mayonnaise sauce, and mix thoroughly. Set aside for a short time before using, to allow the flavours to blend.

TARTARE SAUCE (HOT)

½ pint Béchamel sauce
2 egg yolks
1 tsp. chopped gherkins
1 tsp. chopped parsley
2–3 drops of lemon juice
Cayenne
Salt

Have the Béchamel sauce hot but not boiling, and add the egg yolks to it. Mix well and heat gently without boiling. Add the gherkins, parsley and lemon juice and seasoning to taste.

TOMATO SAUCE

1 lb. tomatoes
2 onions
1 rasher of bacon
2 oz. butter
A bunch of herbs
1 pint stock
Salt and pepper
2 tsps. sugar
1 oz. cornflour
Milk to mix

Wash and cut up the tomatoes, peel and slice onions, chop the bacon and put all into a pan with the melted butter; cook with the lid on for 10 minutes, shaking frequently. Add the herbs, stock, seasoning and sugar, and simmer gently for 30 minutes. Strain and sieve the mixture, return it to the pan and bring to the boil. Blend the cornflour with a little cold milk, add to the pan and bring to the boil, stirring constantly. Cook for 5 minutes, reseason, and serve.

WATERCRESS SAUCE

1 oz. butter
1 oz. flour
¾ pint milk
1 dessertsp. finely chopped watercress
Salt and pepper

Melt the butter, stir in the flour and add the liquid gradually, stirring well all the time. Continue to stir until the mixture boils, and then boil gently for 3–5 minutes. Add the chopped watercress, salt and pepper, stir and blend well for 1 minute.

WHITE WINE SAUCE

¼ pint white sauce
3 tbsps. white wine
½ oz. butter
1 egg yolk
A squeeze of lemon juice

Make the white sauce rather thick, and add to it the white wine. When boiling draw to the side of the heat and stir in the butter and egg yolk. Season to taste and add the lemon juice, but do not boil again.

SAUCE FOR BOILED TURKEY

2 oz. butter
2 oz. flour
½ pint milk
1 pint turkey stock
White pepper and salt
1 tbsp. chopped parsley or 2 hard-boiled eggs

Melt the butter in a saucepan without allowing it to brown, stir in the flour and cook it for a minute. Then add the milk gradually, and 1 pint light stock from the boiled turkey. Stir until boiling, simmer for a few minutes and season to taste with white pepper and salt. Add the parsley or the finely chopped eggs at the last.

MISCELLANEOUS SAVOURY SAUCES

APPLE SAUCE

2 lb. apples
1–2 oz. butter or margarine
Sugar or lemon juice, if required

Choose good cooking apples, peel and slice with a stainless steel knife, then cook gently to a pulp in a covered pan. Beat with a wooden spoon until smooth, and add the butter. Sugar may be added if liked, but a tart apple sauce is just the right accompaniment to goose or duck. On the other hand, if the apples are sweet, a little lemon juice may be added.

BARBECUE SAUCE—I

1 oz. butter or margarine
4 oz. chopped onion
1 tsp. salt
1 tsp. granulated sugar
2 tbsps. lemon juice
1 tbsp. hot water
1 tsp. thick bottled meat sauce

Melt the butter, add the onion and simmer until tender. Add the remaining ingredients, and heat. Use for meat or poultry.

BARBECUE SAUCE—II

A few bacon rinds	½–1 tsp. paprika
2 tsps. mustard	4 tbsps. vinegar
1 tbsp. sugar	2 tsps. cornflour
1 tbsp. red jelly or jam	3 tbsps. stock

Fry bacon rinds lightly to extract fat, then remove rinds from pan. Mix in the mustard, sugar, jelly or jam and pepper, and stir in the vinegar. Add the cornflour, blended with the stock, bring to the boil and simmer for about 5 minutes. Serve with savoury meat dishes such as spiced tinned meat, sausages, etc.

BLACK BUTTER SAUCE

2 oz. butter	Salt and pepper
2–3 tbsps. vinegar	

Melt the butter in a pan and heat it gently until brown but not burnt. Remove from the heat, stir in the vinegar and seasoning, and reheat before serving.

BREAD SAUCE

1 medium-sized onion	A few peppercorns
2 cloves	¾ oz. butter
¾ pint milk	3 oz. breadcrumbs
Salt	

Peel the onion and stick the cloves into it, place in a saucepan with the milk, salt and peppercorns, bring almost to boiling point and leave in a warm place for about 20 minutes, in order to extract the flavour from the onion. Remove the peppercorns, and add the butter and breadcrumbs. Mix well and allow to cook very slowly for about 15 minutes, then remove the onion.

If liked, the onion may be removed before adding the breadcrumbs, but a better flavour is obtained by allowing the flavour of the onion to penetrate the breadcrumbs by cooking them together.

CRANBERRY SAUCE

Pick and wash 1 lb. cranberries and put them into a stewpan with 1 teacupful water. Stew until reduced to a pulp, bruising them well with the back of a wooden spoon. Then add ¼ lb. sugar, and a little port wine if desired.

CUMBERLAND SAUCE

Rind and juice of 2 oranges and 2 lemons	½ tsp. mixed mustard
	1 glassful of port wine
1 pint red-currant jelly	2 tbsps. piquant sauce

Remove the white pith from the oranges and lemons. Cut the rind into very firm small strips and simmer for 5 minutes in the fruit juice and melted jelly. Add mustard, cool, then add the wine and piquant sauce.

Use when cold. This will keep for some time if tied down or kept in a cool place. It is excellent served with ham, braised tongue or cold beef.

To give alternative flavours, add 1 dessertsp. grated horseradish or ½ tsp. ground ginger or 6 chopped glacé cherries.

GOOSEBERRY SAUCE

1 lb. gooseberries	2–3 oz. sugar
¼ pint water	½–1 oz. butter or margarine

Place the gooseberries, water and sugar in a pan and cook gently until the gooseberries are soft and the mixture has formed a thickish pulp. Alternatively, use bottled gooseberries, using only ¼ pint of the liquid, adding sugar only if they were bottled without any. Pass the mixture through a sieve, return the pulp to the pan, reheat and put in the butter at the last moment. This is delicious with goose or duck.

MAÎTRE D'HÔTEL BUTTER

See chapter on Stuffings, Accompaniments and Garnishes.

MINT SAUCE

2 tbsps. chopped mint	1 tbsp. boiling water
2 tsps. sugar	1½ tbsps. vinegar

Strip the mint from the stalks and chop it finely. Put the sugar and boiling water in a sauce-boat and stir until dissolved, add the mint and stir in vinegar to taste. This sauce should be left to stand for 1 hour before serving, to improve the flavour.

RAISIN SAUCE

4 oz. brown sugar	1½ tsps. piquant sauce
4 tbsps. hot water	1 tsp. salt
6 oz. seedless raisins	1 tsp. pepper
2 tbsps. butter or salad oil	½ tsp. powdered cloves
	A few grains of mace
4 tbsps. vinegar	4 tbsps. red-currant jelly

Simmer the brown sugar and water together for 5 minutes, stirring until the sugar is dissolved. Add all the remaining ingredients, and cook until the jelly dissolves. Serve with baked ham or similar meats.

VINAIGRETTE SAUCE

Make French Dressing and to it add equal quantities of chopped parsley, chopped gherkins and chopped chives.

BASIC RECIPES FOR SWEET WHITE SAUCES

SWEET WHITE SAUCE

1 oz. butter or margarine	Sugar to sweeten
1 oz. flour	1 tbsp. cream or evaporated milk
$\frac{3}{4}$ pint milk or milk and water	

Melt the butter, stir in the flour and blend thoroughly; then add the cold milk gradually and bring to the boil. Add the sugar and boil for 5 minutes, stirring meanwhile. Lastly, stir in the cream or evaporated milk.

CORNFLOUR SAUCE

2 tsps. cornflour	A strip of lemon rind
$\frac{1}{2}$ pint milk	2 tsps. sugar

Blend the cornflour to a smooth cream with a little of the milk. Heat the remainder of the milk with the lemon rind, and when boiling pour on to the blended cornflour, stirring. Return it to the pan, bring to the boil and cook about 5 minutes, stirring continuously. Take off the heat, remove the lemon rind and sweeten to taste. Serve hot with steamed or baked puddings. If preferred, use a flavouring essence such as vanilla, in place of the lemon rind, adding it as the last.

CUSTARD SAUCE—I

$\frac{1}{2}$ pint milk	1 egg or 2 yolks
A strip of lemon rind	1 oz. sugar

Heat the milk and lemon rind together, but do not boil. Pour on to the well-beaten egg, stirring. Return to the pan and cook over hot water until the sauce coats the back of the spoon thinly. Add the sugar. Strain and cool, stirring occasionally, or serve hot if liked.

Note : For details of cooking egg custard, see the chapter on Milk Puddings and Custards.

CUSTARD SAUCE—II

1 tbsp. custard powder	Vanilla or other flavouring (optional)
$\frac{1}{2}$ pint milk	
1 tbsp. sugar	

Blend the custard powder to a smooth cream with a little of the milk. Heat the remainder of the milk, and when boiling pour on to the blended custard powder, stirring. Return it to the saucepan, bring to the boil and cook for 3–4 minutes, stirring continuously. Remove from the heat and sweeten to taste, adding flavouring such as vanilla essence, coffee essence, etc. Serve hot or cold. If to be served cold, cover with a lid or stir occasionally during the cooling, to prevent a skin forming. This gives a thin sauce; if a thicker custard is required, use 3 tsps. custard powder.

SWEET SAUCES

APRICOT SAUCE

$\frac{1}{2}$ lb. fresh apricots	Sugar to taste
A little water	$\frac{1}{2}$ glass Madeira

Halve and stone the apricots and place them in a pan with a very little water. Crack the stones to obtain the kernels, skin and crush these and add them to the apricots. Cook gently until soft, then pass through a sieve. Return the purée to the pan, sweeten to taste and stir in the Madeira. If too thin, reduce the sauce by boiling for a few minutes.

Note : When fresh apricots are not available, follow recipe for Jam Sauce, using apricot jam.

BRANDY SAUCE

2 tsps. cornflour	1 egg yolk
$\frac{1}{2}$ pint milk	2–3 tbsps. brandy
$1\frac{1}{2}$ oz. sugar	

Blend the cornflour with a little of the milk. Boil the remainder of the milk and pour on to the cornflour, then return to the pan and boil for 5 minutes, stirring all the time. Add the sugar, cool slightly, then stir in the egg and brandy. Serve at once.

BUTTERSCOTCH SAUCE

2 oz. granulated sugar	$\frac{1}{4}$ pint milk
3 tbsps. boiling water	$\frac{1}{4}$ oz. butter
2 tsps. cornflour	

Put the sugar into a thick saucepan and heat gently until it caramelises. Shake the pan a little during the cooking, to prevent uneven browning, but do not stir. When quite liquid and a good brown colour, remove from the heat, cool slightly, and add the boiling water by degrees. Return to the heat and simmer until the caramel is dissolved, then set aside. Blend the cornflour with 2 tbsps. of the milk; bring the rest to the boil, and pour on to the cornflour. Bring back to the boil, add the butter and cook for 2 minutes. Serve hot or cold.

CHOCOLATE SAUCE—I

$1\frac{1}{2}$ oz. unsweetened chocolate	A pinch of salt
	$\frac{1}{2}$ oz. butter
$\frac{1}{3}$ pint water	2 oz. sugar
2 tsps. cornflour	Vanilla essence

Break up the chocolate, add half of the water and dissolve over gentle heat. Mix the cornflour and salt to a smooth cream with a little of the remaining cold water, heat the remainder and when boiling pour on to the blended cornflour, stirring. Return to the saucepan and bring to the boil, stirring. Add the dissolved chocolate, butter and sugar and cook for 4 or 5 minutes, stirring and beating well. Lastly, add the vanilla essence.

CHOCOLATE SAUCE—II

½ oz. butter
½ oz. flour
2 oz. plain chocolate
1 oz. sugar
A pinch of salt
½ pint water
1 egg
A few drops of vanilla essence

Melt the butter and stir in the flour to form a roux. Dissolve the chocolate, sugar and salt in the water over gentle heat and add this mixture by degrees to the roux, stirring. Bring to the boil and cook gently for about 5 minutes, stirring all the time. Cool slightly, add the egg yolk and vanilla essence, beating well, and reheat without boiling. Just before serving, fold in the stiffly beaten egg white.

COFFEE SAUCE

1 oz. butter or margarine
½ oz. flour
½ pint black coffee or diluted Café Vierge
1 oz. sugar
Vanilla
1 egg yolk

Melt the butter in a small saucepan and mix in the flour, then add the coffee gradually and stir until boiling. Simmer slowly for 5 minutes, add the sugar and flavouring, and, just before serving, stir in the egg yolk. Do not allow the sauce to boil again.

COFFEE CUSTARD SAUCE

¼ pint strong black coffee or diluted Café Vierge
¼ pint milk
1 egg
1 oz. sugar
A pinch of salt

Heat the coffee and milk, pour on to the beaten egg, and cook as for custard sauce. Add sugar and a pinch of salt. Strain and cool, or serve hot.

CREAM SAUCE

¼ pint cream
1 tbsp. caster sugar
Vanilla
A few grains of salt

Whip the cream slightly, and add the sugar gradually while beating. Flavour with vanilla, add a very little salt, and serve the sauce quite cold, piled up in a crystal or china dish.

HARD SAUCE (BRANDY BUTTER)

2 oz. fresh butter
4 oz. caster sugar
1 tbsp. brandy

Cream the butter and sugar until light-coloured and frothy. Keep cool until required, and just before serving add the brandy a little at a time. Hand the sauce separately with Christmas or plum pudding.

JAM OR MARMALADE SAUCE—I

1 tsp. jam or marmalade
2 tsps. caster sugar
¼ pint water
1 tsp. cornflour
A little lemon juice
Colouring (optional)

Place the jam or marmalade, sugar and water in a saucepan and bring to the boil. Add the cornflour, mixed with a little cold water, and boil up until the sauce is clear and the cornflour cooked—about 5 minutes. Add the lemon juice, and a little colouring to improve the colour of the sauce, if necessary.

JAM OR MARMALADE SAUCE—II

2 oz. sugar
2 tbsps. jam or marmalade
½ pint water
A few drops of lemon juice

Boil the sugar, jam or marmalade and water together until syrupy. Add the lemon juice and strain. Serve hot.

LEMON OR ORANGE SAUCE

1 large lemon or orange
1–2 oz. sugar
1 oz. butter
½ oz. flour
½ pint water
1–2 egg yolks

Wipe the lemon or orange, grate the rind and rub it into the sugar. Melt the butter in a saucepan and add the flour, stirring it in well, then add the water gradually and stir until boiling. Simmer slowly for 2–3 minutes and add the sugar and strained lemon or orange juice. Then remove the saucepan from the heat, and quickly stir in the egg yolks. Pour at once into a sauce-boat.

LEMON SAUCE

Rind and juice of 1 lemon
6 oz. loaf sugar
½ pint water

Peel the lemon very thinly and cut the rind into thin shreds. Boil the sugar and water gently with the lemon rind until reduced by half, then add the strained juice. Boil up the sauce, and serve with steamed lemon, marmalade or ginger pudding, etc.

LOGANBERRY SAUCE

½ lb. loganberries — 1 tsp. cornflour
2 oz. sugar — 2–3 tbsps. water

Stew the loganberries and sugar together for 10–15 minutes. Strain and measure, and if necessary make up to ¼ pint with water. Add the cornflour blended to a cream with the water, bring to the boil and boil for 5 minutes.

MOUSSELINE SAUCE

2 oz. caster sugar
¼ pint cream
2 egg yolks
2–3 tbsps. Madeira or other wine, or fruit syrup

Whisk together the sugar, cream (or top of the milk) and egg yolks over warm water, until the mixture is light and frothy. Add the wine, and whisk until the sauce thickens.

Serve immediately, with Christmas Pudding and other hot sweets.

NUTMEG CREAM

½ pint thin cream — ¼ tsp. vanilla essence
2 tsps. sugar — 1 tsp. grated nutmeg

Combine the ingredients and stir until the sugar is dissolved. Serve cold with baked apples or pears, fruit dumplings, etc.

PEACH SAUCE

½ oz. cornflour — 1 oz. sugar
¼ pint water — A strip of lemon rind
½ pint peach syrup — Cochineal

Blend the cornflour with a little of the cold water. Simmer the water, syrup, sugar and lemon rind for 5 minutes, then strain on to the cornflour. Return to the pan, bring to the boil and cook for 5 minutes, stirring. Colour a faint pink.

PRUNE SAUCE

½ pint prune purée — A pinch of salt
Juice of 1 lemon — ½ tsp. ground cinnamon
Sugar to taste — ¼ pint Moselle or sherry

Put all the ingredients together in a saucepan and simmer gently for about 10 minutes, stirring frequently. Serve with plain steamed puddings.

RUM SAUCE

½ oz. cornflour
½ pint water
1 tbsp. sugar
1 tbsp. rum
1–2 drops essence of cinnamon
1 oz. butter

Mix the cornflour with a little cold water. Boil the remainder of the water and pour it on to the cornflour, mixing well. Pour into a saucepan and stir until boiling. Add the sugar, flavouring and rum, and last of all the butter, broken in small pieces.

RUM SYRUP

¼ lb. sugar
¼ pint water
A small piece of lemon rind
A squeeze of lemon juice
Rum to flavour

Dissolve the sugar in the water, add the strip of lemon rind and boil for about 5 minutes. Add the lemon juice and rum. Serve with Babas or Savarins.

SABAYON SAUCE

1 egg yolk — ¼ pint sherry
2 tsps. caster sugar

Whisk all the ingredients together over a gentle heat or over hot water: excessive heat must be avoided or the egg will curdle. Whisk until frothy and lightly set, and pour round the pudding just before serving.

SWEET CHAUDFROID SAUCE

Equal quantities of stiff lemon jelly and thick cream
Sugar to taste
Flavouring and colouring if required

Melt the jelly and half whip the cream, then combine the two ingredients. Sweeten to taste and add any colouring or flavouring. Use when just on the point of setting to coat half pears, peaches and so on, for cold sweets.

SYRUP SAUCE

4 tbsps. water — Juice of ½ lemon
2 tbsps. golden syrup

Mix all the ingredients together and boil rapidly for a few minutes.

WHIPPED SAUCE

2 oz. fresh butter — ¼ pint boiling water
2 oz. caster sugar — 3 tbsps. sherry
2 egg whites

Beat the butter and sugar to a cream. Add one egg white; beat for a few minutes with a small whisk, then add the second egg white and beat again. Just before serving, stir in the boiling water and sherry, stand the basin over a saucepan of hot water and whisk until frothy. Serve at once.

WINE SAUCE

1 oz. butter — 1 oz. sugar
½ oz. flour — 3 tbsps. sherry
¼ pint water

Melt the butter in a saucepan and stir in the flour. Then add the water gradually and stir until boiling. Cook for 3–5 minutes and add the sugar and wine at the last.

SAUCES FOR ICED SUNDAES

STRAWBERRY SAUCE

Boil 2 oz. sugar with ¼ pint water until they form a syrup. Add ½ lb. strawberries, which have been crushed with a silver fork. Remove from the heat and chill the sauce thoroughly before using.

RASPBERRY SAUCE

Make as for Strawberry Sauce above.

Alternatively use tinned fruit instead of the fresh, in which case substitute the liquid from the tin for the water, and use sugar only if necessary. If the seeds are objected to, the sauce may be rubbed through a fine hair sieve. The sauce should be made well before it is to be used, so that it may be served very cold.

MELBA SAUCE

4 tbsps. red-currant jelly
3 oz. sugar
¼ pint raspberry purée
2 tsps. arrowroot or cornflour
1 tbsp. cold water

Mix together the jelly, sugar and the raspberry purée, and heat until boiling. Blend the arrowroot or cornflour with the cold water and add to the raspberry mixture. Continue cooking until the mixture becomes thick and clear, stirring all the time with a wooden spoon. Strain and cool.

Serve with Peach Melba and other sundaes.

MARSHMALLOW SAUCE

4 oz. granulated sugar
3 tbsps. water
8 marshmallows
1 egg white
A few drops of vanilla essence
Colouring

Dissolve the sugar in the water, then boil together for about 15 minutes. Add the marshmallows, cut into small pieces with scissors. Beat the egg white very stiffly, then gradually fold in the marshmallow mixture. Add vanilla and enough carmine or cochineal to tint pale pink. Serve with ice cream.

Peppermint may be used instead of vanilla to flavour: in this case colour the sauce pale green.

PEPPERMINT CREAM SAUCE

1 oz. sugar
½ teacupful water
2–3 marshmallows
1 egg white
2–3 drops of essence of peppermint

Put the sugar and water into a saucepan and make a syrup. Add the marshmallows, cut in pieces, and stir carefully until dissolved. Whip up the white of egg in a basin and pour the marshmallow mixture gradually on to it, stirring all the time. Flavour with peppermint, and set aside until quite cold.

CARAMEL SAUCE

Melt a cupful of granulated sugar in a strong pan and heat until it becomes a clear and amber-coloured syrup. Then add 1 cupful of boiling water gradually and simmer for 15 minutes. Use either hot or cold. The addition of a few chopped walnuts will give a delicious flavour to the sauce.

CHOCOLATE SAUCE

Melt 1 oz. of good chocolate in a small saucepan over hot water. Add ½ oz. butter and pour on gradually 1 teacupful of boiling water. Bring to the boil, flavour with vanilla, and sweeten to taste. Simmer 10 minutes longer, strain and use either hot or icy cold.

FOAMY ORANGE SAUCE

Beat the whites of 2 eggs until very stiff. Add gradually 1 tbsp. caster sugar finely sifted, and ½ teacupful of orange juice, beating constantly. Just before serving mix in 1 tsp. finely grated orange rind and pour this over the ice cream. A dash of colour may be added by putting a few thin slices of candied peel over the top of the sauce.

CREAM FILLINGS, ETC.: See the chapter on Cake Decorating.

VEGETABLES

Vegetables, especially greens, should be used as soon as possible after gathering, for their food value is then at its highest. If storage for a short time is unavoidable, keep them in a cool, airy place—for example, in a vegetable rack placed in a cold larder, or in the vegetable compartment of the refrigerator.

PREPARATION OF VEGETABLES

Ideally, vegetables should be prepared immediately prior to cooking. Wash green vegetables quickly, separating the leaves but not cutting them up. Scrub roots and peel or scrape them. Cook at once, doing any necessary cutting with a sharp knife. Do not leave them to soak, as this causes the minerals and the water-soluble vitamins to dissolve out, and thus lessens the food value. If for any reason the cut vegetables cannot be cooked immediately, put them in a bowl without water, cover them, and put in a cool place until required. Alternatively, barely cover them with water and use this water for cooking the vegetables.

METHODS OF COOKING VEGETABLES

Boiling

Use as little water as possible. Put the water into a pan and heat to boiling point, put the prepared vegetables into the boiling water, and bring back to the boil as quickly as possible. Cook with the lid on.

The time for cooking varies with individual vegetables, from 10 minutes for young green vegetables to 1 hour or even longer for some roots, the average being about 20 minutes.

Salt: The flavour of boiled vegetables is improved by cooking with salt. Use approximately 1 small tsp. salt to 1 pint of water.

Bicarbonate of Soda: It should not be necessary to use bicarbonate of soda if greens are properly boiled, but some people consider that a small quantity (a pinch to 2 lb. of greens) is justified, since it improves the colour.

Steaming

This method is mainly suitable for root vegetables. Prepare them as described above, cover the steamer, keep the water boiling rapidly, and allow about half as long again as for boiling.

Conservative Method

This is a very good method, since the liquor is served with the vegetables and the flavour is conserved. Suitable vegetables are celery, onions, and roots such as carrots and turnips, either alone or mixed. Some people like green vegetables cooked by the conservative method, but many others find them indigestible when so cooked.

Prepare the vegetables in the usual way, leaving whole if young and small, or cutting into dice or slices. Place in a strong saucepan or casserole with a very little water (or stock), a knob of butter, and seasoning of salt and pepper. Cover and cook over a low heat or in a slow oven until tender, 20–30 minutes for very young vegetables or from 1–1½ hours if old, adding more liquid if necessary—there should not be more than 1–2 tbsps. liquor left at the end of cooking. Just before serving, add a good sprinkling of freshly chopped parsley, and serve in the casserole or in a heated vegetable dish.

Baking

Vegetable marrow, parsnips, Jerusalem artichokes, and carrots are excellent baked in dripping, as for roast potatoes. Prepare as usual, cut into even-sized pieces, and place in a tin or fireproof dish with some hot dripping (or round the meat while it is roasting). Cook in a moderately hot oven (400° F., mark 6) until tender and browned—¾–1 hour.

Braising

Vegetables such as onions, leeks, celery, and many root vegetables are very good braised.

Prepare as usual, then fry in a little hot dripping until lightly browned. Add salt and pepper and enough stock to half-cover. Cover with a lid and cook gently until tender. Lift the vegetables into a hot dish, boil up the liquor until reduced to a glazing consistency and pour over. Sprinkle the vegetables with a little chopped parsley before serving them.

Pressure Cooking

A pressure saucepan is excellent for cooking vegetables. The cooking times are considerably shorter when such a pan is used—exact times being given in the manufacturer's handbook. See the chapter on Pressure Cookery for fuller details.

SERVING VEGETABLES

Drain carefully, pressing green vegetables lightly—they are unappetising if left wet. (The liquid can often be used for soups and gravies.) If further cutting or chopping is necessary, do this at the last possible moment.

The addition of a sprinkling of salt and pepper and a knob of butter to the cooked vegetables is an improvement in nearly all cases. Small quantities of chopped herbs can be added just before serving.

To give variety, vegetables may be served in one of these ways :—

Glazed

Drain the boiled or steamed vegetables carefully, then shake with a knob of butter over low heat before serving. A little finely chopped parsley or onion may be added to vary the flavour.

Creamed

All root vegetables, with the exception of potatoes, may be served coated with a creamy white sauce. This is a good method to use when serving a mixture of vegetables. If liked, the sauce may be covered with grated cheese and the dish browned under the grill.

Scalloped

Prepare as for creamed vegetables, place in scallop shells or a shallow fireproof dish, sprinkle with a few breadcrumbs and a little grated cheese, heat through, and brown in the oven or under the grill.

VEGETABLE ENTRÉES

Although vegetables are most often served as an accompaniment to a main course, when suitably " dressed " they can be served by themselves to make an excellent entrée.

The vegetables should be easy to serve and attractively garnished. A good casserole—earthenware, fireproof glass or metal—is essential for cooking many of these dishes, for in this way all the flavour is retained, and the food remains pleasantly crisp, instead of becoming watery, as so often occurs if the vegetables are boiled. Individual earthenware or fireproof porcelain cassolettes are also useful, as the vegetables can easily be kept hot in them until required, and are then quickly served. Natural scallop shells (obtainable from the fishmonger) or shell-shaped dishes in fireproof glass are invaluable for various quickly prepared vegetable entrées, such as those given in the au gratin section.

Sauces play an important part in the preparation of these dishes, and they should be as rich and smooth-textured as possible—a flavourless, gluey sauce can completely spoil the entrée.

Suitable vegetable dishes for serving in this way include the following, recipes for which appear in this chapter :—

Aubergines with Ham Filling
Celery au Gratin
Chicory Soufflé
Cucumber à la Poulette
Dressed Cauliflower
Fried Marrow and Mushrooms
Mushrooms à la Pompadour
Scalloped Onions
Stuffed Tomatoes
Sweet Peppers, au Gratin or Fried

A B C OF VEGETABLES

ARTICHOKES (JERUSALEM)

First scrub them, then peel them quickly into clean cold water, using a stainless knife or peeler and keeping them under the water as much as possible, to prevent discoloration. A little salt and a squeeze of lemon juice (or a few drops of vinegar) added to the water help to keep them a good colour. Cook in boiling salted water, to which a little lemon juice (or vinegar) has been added to preserve their white colour. Cook until tender (about 30 minutes), drain them very well before dishing and garnish with finely chopped parsley. If liked, serve with a white sauce.

Artichokes are also very good baked in dripping to serve with roast meat.

ARTICHOKES (GLOBE)

The artichokes should be of a good green colour, with tightly clinging, fleshy leaves: spreading leaves or fuzzy, purplish centres indicate over-maturity.

Cut off the stem close to the base of the leaves. Take off the outside layer of leaves and any others which are dry or discoloured. Remove the choke (that is, the feathery part which is the potential flower) from the centre. Wash carefully, and if liked tie the tops of the leaves neatly together. Cook in boiling salted water until tender, that is until the leaves pull out easily—anything from 20–40 minutes. Drain upside down, untying the tops, and serve on a folded napkin. Hand melted butter sauce, or Hollandaise sauce, separately.

Globe artichokes may also be served cold, with a vinaigrette dressing.

It may be as well to add that the leaves should be pulled out with the fingers, dipped in the sauce, and the soft end sucked. When the centre is reached, the choke, or soft flowery part, if not already taken out, is removed, and the bottom, which is the chief delicacy, is eaten with a knife and fork.

ASPARAGUS

Cut off the woody end of the stalks and scrape the white part lightly, removing any coarse spines. Tie in bundles, and place upright in a saucepan of boiling salted water. Boil for 10 minutes, then lay flat, and continue cooking until tender—a further 10–15 minutes. Drain very well and untie the bundles before dishing. Serve with melted butter or Hollandaise sauce.

Asparagus may also be served cold, with a vinaigrette dressing or with mayonnaise.

ASPARAGUS À LA VINAIGRETTE

Asparagus
3 tbsps. olive oil
1 tbsp. chilli vinegar
1 tbsp. tarragon vinegar
1 tbsp. finely chopped parsley, tarragon, and chervil

This is a particularly good dish for lunch on hot days, either alone or with other salads. Cook the asparagus in the usual way, and strain quite free of moisture. Cut off the tough part of the stalks, allow to cool, and place the asparagus in a small salad bowl. Prepare the vinaigrette sauce by mixing the remaining ingredients, and pour it over the asparagus tips.

If preferred, the asparagus can be served whole, and the vinaigrette sauce handed in a sauce-boat, the vegetable being eaten in the same way as when it is served with oiled butter.

ASPARAGUS WITH CHEESE DRESSING

Cook the asparagus in the usual way, and cut off the inedible part of the stalk. Place in a vegetable dish, sprinkle with finely grated Parmesan cheese, and pour over oiled butter, to which pepper and salt have been added, and 1 tsp. lemon juice to every 2 tbsps. oiled butter. An even better flavour can be obtained if a mixture of half Gruyère and half Parmesan cheese is used: both must be dry and finely grated.

AUBERGINE OR EGG PLANT

Aubergines should be of uniform purple colour, firm, smooth, and free from blemishes. To prepare them, cut off the stem and calyx and wipe over. For some dishes, the aubergines are required to be peeled; for others, the skin is left on. They are usually stuffed and baked, sautéed, or fried.

FRIED AUBERGINES

Peel the aubergines and cut into thick slices, removing any coarse seeds. Coat with seasoned flour and fry in butter or olive oil.

Alternatively, the sliced aubergines may be egg-and-crumbed, or dipped in batter and fried in deep fat.

STUFFED AUBERGINES

Do not peel the aubergines but steam or boil hem for about ½ hour. Then cut in half lengthwise and scoop out the pulp. Season the pulp and add to it some butter and chopped hard-boiled egg, or, if preferred, some fried tomato. Mix well, adding a few breadcrumbs if too slack, and pile into the cases. Sprinkle with breadcrumbs, dot with small pieces of butter, and bake in a moderate oven (375° F., mark 5) for about ½ hour. Serve hot.

BAKED AUBERGINES

Do not peel the aubergines but cut into slices about ½ inch thick. Lay them on a folded cloth, sprinkle lightly with salt and leave for ½ hour. Gently wipe the slices to remove as much moisture as possible. Lay the prepared slices in a buttered shallow fireproof dish. Sprinkle them thickly with seasoned white breadcrumbs, pour over a little melted butter and bake in a moderately hot oven (400° F., mark 6) for 15 minutes. Garnish with fried mushrooms and baked tomato halves. Serve with tomato sauce.

SAUTÉED AUBERGINES

Cut a large aubergine into ¼-inch crosswise slices. Sprinkle the slices with salt and pepper, and a little flour, or dip into beaten egg, then into breadcrumbs, and sauté in a little hot fat until golden-brown and tender on both sides. Or, serve thick sautéed slices of aubergine on toast on which a thin slice of boiled ham has been laid.

AUBERGINES À LA PROVENÇALE

2 aubergines	1 oz. butter
Seasoning	A little chopped onion
½ lb. tomatoes	3 tbsps. breadcrumbs

Wipe the aubergines and cut them in half lengthwise. Scoop out the seeds and pulp, sprinkle the halves well with salt, and let them lie upside down for ½ hour. (This is not absolutely essential, but it drains away the water from the plant.) Skin and slice the tomatoes and fry lightly in the butter, together with the chopped onion and seeds and pulp from the aubergines. Add 2 tbsps. of the breadcrumbs and season well. Drain and wipe the pieces of aubergine and fill them with stuffing, piling it high. Sprinkle with breadcrumbs and place on a greased baking sheet. Bake in moderate oven (375° F., mark 5) for 30–40 minutes. Serve at once.

AUBERGINES WITH HAM FILLING

2 aubergines	1 tbsp. chopped mushrooms
2 oz. chopped ham or tongue	Seasoning
2 tsps. chopped onion	Egg to bind
2 tsps. chopped parsley	2 tbsps. breadcrumbs
Grated lemon rind	1 oz. butter

Prepare the shells as in the previous recipe. Put all the chopped ingredients into a basin with the pulp ; season well and bind with beaten egg. Pile into the prepared cases, sprinkle with breadcrumbs, place a few knobs of butter on top, and bake in a moderate oven (375° F., mark 5) for 30–40 minutes.

BEANS (BROAD)

Shell, and cook in boiling salted water until tender—20–30 minutes. If liked, serve with parsley sauce.

When very young and tender, that is, when the pods are only a few inches long and the beans inside very small, the whole pods may be cooked and served, and these make a very delicious dish.

Towards the end of the season the skins of the beans may be very thick and tough—in this case it is well worth removing them before cooking.

BEANS (FRENCH AND RUNNER)

Head, tail, and string the beans, and slice them diagonally. Cook in boiling salted water until tender—15–20 minutes, skimming if necessary. Drain well, then toss with salt and pepper and a knob of butter before dishing.

Cold cooked French or runner beans are a useful ingredient in salads and hors d'œuvre (see chapters on Hors d'Oeuvre and on Salads and Salad Dressings).

CASSEROLE OF STRING BEANS

1 lb. French or runner beans	1 cupful stewed tomatoes or tomato sauce
1½ oz. butter or margarine	Salt and pepper
2–3 tsps. finely chopped onion	

String and cut up the beans and cook until tender in boiling salted water, then strain and put into a casserole. Melt the butter or margarine in the saucepan, add the chopped onion and sauté for a few minutes without browning. Add the stewed tomatoes or tomato sauce, and season to taste. Pour over the beans in the casserole, cover, and cook in a moderate oven (375° F., mark 6) for 20–30 minutes.

FRENCH BEANS WITH SPAGHETTI

½ lb. French beans	2 oz. grated cheese
3 oz. spaghetti	Seasoning
2 oz. butter	A red pepper, if liked

The beans should be young and fresh. Wash and string them, cut into thin strips with a sharp knife, and throw them again into cold water. Then drain, put them into a saucepan with boiling salted water, and boil quickly with the lid off the saucepan for about 20 minutes, or until the beans are tender : remove any scum that rises. Meanwhile, break the spaghetti in pieces, put it into a saucepan with warm water to cover it and add 1 oz. of the butter. Simmer slowly until tender and the water is all absorbed. Add the cheese and seasoning and toss over the heat for a few minutes longer. Drain the beans when ready, return them to the pan, and toss over the heat for a minute or two to dry. Add the remaining butter and some seasoning, and toss lightly until thoroughly mixed. Arrange the spaghetti in a border on a hot dish and pile the beans in the centre. A red pepper, chopped and heated in butter, makes a pretty garnish.

RUNNER BEANS WITH CARROTS

½ lb. young carrots — Seasoning
1 lb. runner beans — 2 tbsps. salad oil

Scrape the carrots and slice in very thin rounds. String and slice the beans thinly. Put 1 inch of water in a strong saucepan, add the carrots, salt and pepper, and cook for 10 minutes with the lid on. Add the beans and oil, and continue cooking for a further 20 minutes, or until tender. Taste, reseason if necessary, and serve.

SPANISH BEANS

1 large onion — 1 dessertsp. flour
1 tomato — 1–1½ pints stock or water
1 chilli — 1 lb. scarlet runners
Pepper — 1 tsp. salt
1 oz. butter or margarine

Slice the vegetables thinly. Cook the onion, tomato, chilli, and pepper together in the fat until well done and golden-brown. Then stir in the flour and brown it, add hot stock or water, stir until boiling, then add the beans and salt, and cook for about 1 hour. Serve hot in a fireproof dish as an accompaniment to meat, or as a vegetarian savoury.

BEETROOT

Cut off the stalks 1 inch or so above the root, then wash the beetroots, taking care not to damage the skin, or they will " bleed " when boiled. Boil in salted water until tender, or wrap in greased paper and bake in a moderate oven (375° F., mark 6). The time depends on the age and freshness—2 hours is the average. When cooked, peel off the skin, and cut into cubes or slices. Serve hot, coated with a creamy white sauce, or cold, sliced, in vinegar.

Beetroots can be cooked in a much shorter time if peeled and sliced when raw and cooked in a small amount of liquid in a covered saucepan until tender. Again, the time taken varies, the average being ½ hour. Serve in the liquor in which the beetroots were cooked, or use the liquor to make a sauce, instead of the milk suggested in the recipe below.

CREAMED BEETROOT

1 large or 2 small beetroot — Salt and pepper
1 oz. butter — 2 tsps. vinegar
1 oz. flour — Grated horseradish (optional)
½ pint milk

Cook the beetroot very carefully, preserving its red colour. Skin, and cut into dice. Melt the butter in a pan, and mix in the flour. Add the milk by degrees, and bring to the boil, stirring continuously. Boil for 2–3 minutes and then add the seasoning and vinegar. Add the cubes of beetroot to the sauce, and heat until the beet is hot through and the sauce coloured pink. Dish, and serve at once, sprinkled, if liked, with a little grated horseradish.

BROCCOLI

There are several varieties of broccoli. The white broccoli, with a fairly large flower head similar to cauliflower, is cooked and served in the same way as cauliflower.

Purple broccoli is also cooked like cauliflower, but, as it has a more delicate flavour, is generally served plain or buttered.

Purple sprouting broccoli and calabrese (which is a green sprouting broccoli) are cooked as asparagus.

BRUSSELS SPROUTS

Wash well, removing any discoloured leaves, and cut a little cross in the stalk. Cook in boiling salted water until tender (10–20 minutes). Drain very thoroughly, then return to the pan and reheat with salt and pepper and a knob of butter.

BRUSSELS SPROUTS AND CHESTNUTS

Although a rather unusual combination in this country, Brussels sprouts are frequently cooked with chestnuts in Holland. The sprouts should be prepared in the usual way and the shell removed from the chestnuts. Put both in boiling water and boil hard for 10 minutes, then strain both free from moisture, and remove the thin brown skin from the chestnuts. Melt 2 oz. of butter to about 1 lb. of chestnuts and Brussels sprouts, and stew them in the butter until both are thoroughly tender—about 15 minutes. Serve very hot.

CABBAGE, AND OTHER SIMILAR GREENS

(Savoy, Curly Kale, Spring Greens, Sprout Tops and Turnip Tops)

Wash thoroughly, then shred coarsely, removing very thick stalks. Cook in boiling salted water, boiling quickly until just tender (15–20 minutes, or less if very young and tender). Drain thoroughly, press lightly, and toss with a knob of butter and a sprinkling of salt and pepper. Make very hot before dishing.

CABBAGE À LA BAVAROISE

1 red or white cabbage	3 large apples
3 oz. fat bacon	1 raw grated potato
1 finely chopped onion	½ pint stock
2 oz. sugar	1 glass port or Madeira wine (optional)
5 tbsps. vinegar	
2 tbsps. salt	A little gravy
2 tsps. carraway seed	

A cabbage of about 3 lb. in weight is needed for this dish. Remove the outer leaves and stump, wash it well, and cut into thin slices. Chop the bacon finely, fry it in a saucepan until well browned, then add the onion and sugar. Put the cabbage in the pan with the vinegar, salt, carraway seed, finely sliced apples, potato, and stock. Cover the pan and cook the cabbage slowly for about 2 hours, until there is no liquid left. Take it off the heat and taste; it should have a pleasant sour-sweet taste. If necessary, add some sugar, vinegar or salt, the wine, if used, and a little gravy. Serve very hot.

SCALLOPED CABBAGE

1 quart shredded cabbage	4 oz. diced or shredded cheese
½ pint well-seasoned white sauce	1 tbsp. grated cheese

Shred a fine white cabbage into ribbons, making 1 quart. Cook until tender in boiling salted water, drain well, and put in a greased baking dish. To some white sauce, made with ½ milk and ½ liquor from the cabbage, add the diced or shredded cheese, cook gently until the cheese is melted, and whip together until smooth. Pour the sauce over the cabbage, stir together lightly, sprinkle with the grated cheese, and brown in a very hot oven or under the grill.

SHREDDED CABBAGE

1 young cabbage	A little sugar
Salt	½ oz. butter
A blade of mace	Black pepper

Wash the cabbage well and shred it finely. Put it in a saucepan containing 2 tbsps. slightly salted water and a blade of mace. Sprinkle a little salt and sugar over the layers of shredded cabbage as it is put into the saucepan, and cook gently until the cabbage is tender but still crisp. Strain off the surplus moisture, then add the butter and a little coarsely ground black pepper. Blend thoroughly, and serve on a hot dish.

SHREDDED CABBAGE WITH TOMATO SAUCE

Choose a fresh cabbage with a firm heart. Cut it in two or four, and remove the hard stalk, together with any coarse and discoloured leaves. Wash the halves or quarters in plenty of water until quite free from any grit, and drain well. Then, with a sharp knife, cut the cabbage across into shreds. Throw at once into boiling salted water and cook quickly until tender. Drain it very thoroughly in a colander. Reheat the cabbage with a little good white sauce, adding enough to moisten and bind the shreds together. Add pepper, a little nutmeg, and more salt if necessary. Pile up in the centre of a hot vegetable dish, and pour a little tomato sauce round the base. Decorate with croûtons of fried or toasted bread.

Cabbage prepared in this way is very tender and delicious, and makes quite a good dish served with poached egg or fried tomatoes on the top. A little chopped red pepper may be added to the mixture; or, used as a garnish, it will make a pretty contrast in colour.

STUFFED CABBAGE

1 firm round cabbage	2 tsps. chopped parsley
1 doz. chestnuts	1 oz. melted butter
2 oz. minced beef or sausage-meat	1 beaten egg
	Seasoning
2 oz. cooked rice	1 pint stock
2 tsps. chopped onion	

Wash the cabbage, keeping it whole, and boil in salted water for 15 minutes. Drain well. Cook and skin the chestnuts, chop and mix with remainder of the ingredients, except the stock. Season well. Open out the cabbage leaves, put a spoonful of stuffing in the centre, and the rest between the leaves, reforming into a firm, round shape. Wrap in well-greased paper, place in a baking tin with stock poured round and bake in a moderate oven (375° F., mark 6) for 1 hour.

STUFFED CABBAGE LEAVES

1 oz. butter	A pinch of mixed spice
1 lb. lean minced meat	A little water, stock, or brown gravy—approx. 4 tbsps.
1 tsp. parsley	
Mint, if liked	10–12 medium-sized cabbage leaves
2 oz. cooked rice	
Salt and pepper	1 egg
1 sieved boiled onion	½ a lemon

Melt the butter in the pan, add the minced meat and cook slowly until the meat is brown. Add the chopped parsley, a little chopped mint, rice, salt and pepper, boiled onion, and spice. Add the liquid, and continue to cook for another 5 minutes. Whilst the mixture is cooling, blanch the cabbage leaves, which should be of as even a size as possible, by dipping them into fast-boiling water for 2 minutes, and drain them. Place equal quantities of the mixture inside each cabbage leaf and roll them up, tucking the ends in to form a neat "package." Place them as closely together as possible in a saucepan, add sufficient seasoned stock to cover, and cook slowly for ½–¾ hour. When they are cooked lift out of the stock, place on a hot dish and pour over them an egg and lemon sauce. To make this, whisk the egg until frothy, then add gradually the juice of the half-lemon and slowly pour in ⅓ pint of the hot liquid from the saucepan, whisking all the time. Cook over a low heat, stirring all the time, until the mixture thickens, but take care the sauce does not boil, or it will curdle.

CARROTS

Scrub them and scrape lightly. Large, old carrots may require peeling thinly and cutting into strips or rounds. Cook in boiling salted water until tender—this may take anything from 20 minutes for young carrots to 1 hour or more if old or coarse. Glaze with butter and toss in chopped parsley or coat with a creamy-white sauce. Alternatively, mash with a potato masher, and reheat with salt, pepper, and a knob of butter.

Carrots are particularly suitable for cooking by the conservative method, or they can be braised.

CARROTS AND CAPER SAUCE

1 lb. carrots	1 oz. butter
1 shallot	1 oz. flour
Salt and pepper	1 tbsp. capers
Stock or water	1 tsp. caper vinegar
About ½ pint milk	

Scrape the carrots, slice them thinly, and put into a saucepan together with the finely chopped shallot and seasoning. Barely cover with stock or water. Cook steadily until tender, then strain off the liquor and measure it. Make up to ½ pint with milk. Make a sauce with the butter, flour, and liquid. Cook for 5 minutes, add the capers and vinegar and coat the cooked carrots with this sauce.

BRAISED CARROTS

1 lb. carrots	A pinch of caster sugar
1½ oz. butter	Salt and pepper
½–¾ pint brown stock	Chopped parsley

Wash and scrape the carrots and cut lengthwise into neat, even slices. Put into a pan, cover with cold water, bring to the boil, and strain. Heat the butter, drop in the carrots, and fry until a golden-brown. Add half the stock, the sugar and seasoning, and cook gently for ½ hour. Baste the carrots occasionally and add the rest of the stock if required. When the carrots are tender, serve on a hot dish, pour a little of the liquor round, and sprinkle finely chopped parsley over.

CARROT SAVOURY TOASTS

1 lb. thinly sliced carrots	½ tsp. salt
	Cayenne
1 tsp. sugar	Paprika
1 onion	2 oz. grated cheese
1 oz. butter	Strips of buttered toast
½ oz. flour	
1 cupful stock	

Cook the carrots until tender in boiling salted water to which the sugar has been added. Chop the onion finely and sauté in the fat until light brown. Stir in flour, cook until blended, and add the stock. Add the seasonings and grated cheese, boil up, stirring continually, and pour over the carrots, which have been drained and laid on strips of buttered toast.

CAULIFLOWER

Wash well, and cut a cross in the stalk. Cook in boiling salted water until tender (20–30 minutes). Since the stalk takes longer to cook, it is best to place the cauliflower stalk downwards in the pan. Remove any scum, to prevent it settling on the top of the flower. Drain carefully and, if liked, coat the cauliflower with a white or cheese sauce.

An alternative method is to divide the cauliflower into florets before cooking—it cooks more evenly in this way and is easier to dish.

CAULIFLOWER AU GRATIN

1 cauliflower	½ pint milk
1½ oz. butter	3 oz. grated cheese
1 oz. flour	Pepper and salt

Choose a good, firm cauliflower, and cook it in plenty of fast-boiling water to which salt has been added. When cooked, strain, and place in an au gratin dish. Melt the butter and stir in the flour. Add the milk, then bring to the boil, and continue to boil for about 5 minutes, stirring all the time. Add the cheese, season with pepper and salt, and pour over the cauliflower, sprinkling a little grated cheese on top. Brown in the oven or under the grill for a minute or two.

CAULIFLOWER CHEESE TARTLETS

6 oz. shortcrust pastry — ½ pint thick white sauce
1 good-sized cauliflower — 3 oz. grated cheese
Seasoning

Roll out the shortcrust pastry to about ¼ inch in thickness, and with it line 6–8 patty tins. Prick well, or line with paper, and weight down with baking beans, and bake in a hot oven (450° F., mark 8) until cooked and lightly browned—about 15 minutes—then remove beans and paper.

Meanwhile, cook the cauliflower in boiling salted water until tender, then drain and divide into florets. Pack these tightly into the pastry cases, so that they look like miniature cauliflowers. Well season the white sauce and add half the grated cheese, coat the cauliflower tartlets with the sauce, sprinkle the rest of the grated cheese on top and brown in the oven or under the grill.

CAULIFLOWER SAVOURIES

Cooked cauliflower — 1 dessertsp. chopped parsley
1 egg — 2 oz. cheese
½ pint milk
Salt and pepper

Separate the cauliflower into florets and put these in small ramekin cases. Beat the egg, then add the milk, the seasonings, parsley, and cheese. Pour over the cauliflower in the ramekin cases, and bake in a moderate oven (375° F., mark 5) for 20 minutes, or until lightly set.

DRESSED CAULIFLOWER

1 cauliflower — ½ pint hot white sauce
2 hard-boiled eggs (hot) — Chopped parsley

Break the cauliflower into florets, cook in salted water until tender, then drain well. Arrange the florets and the sliced hard-boiled eggs on a hot dish, reserving a little yolk for garnishing. Pour the well-seasoned sauce over and garnish with very finely chopped parsley and sieved egg yolk.

CELERIAC

(*The root of Turnip-rooted Celery*)

Peel the celeriac fairly thickly: the small roots may be cooked whole, but larger ones should be sliced thickly or cut into dice. Cook in boiling salted water or stock until tender—1 hour or even longer. Drain well, and serve with melted butter, or a good white sauce such as Béchamel or Hollandaise sauce.

Celeriac may also be braised, or served au gratin. Celeriac fritters are good; for these, the celeriac should be cut into strips or slices, cooked until tender, drained and dried, then coated in batter, fried in deep fat, and served with fried parsley.

CELERY

Wash, cut into even lengths, and tie in bundles. Cook in boiling salted water until tender (½–1 hour, depending on the coarseness of the celery). Drain carefully, and, if liked, serve coated with a white, brown, or cheese sauce.

Celery may also be cooked by the conservative method, and is very good braised.

CELERY AU GRATIN

1 head of celery — ¼ pint milk
1 oz. butter — 2 oz. grated cheese
1 oz. flour — Salt and cayenne pepper
¼ pint celery water — Browned breadcrumbs

Prepare the celery and cut it into dice. Cook in a small amount of boiling salted water until tender, and drain well. Make a white sauce with the butter, flour, and liquid. Add half the cheese to the sauce and season to taste. Fill the dish with alternate layers of sauce and celery. Sprinkle the top with the remaining cheese and a few browned crumbs. Reheat in the oven for 10–12 minutes, or put under a slow grill until hot through and browned.

BELTED CELERY

4 celery hearts — 1 oz. flour
4 rashers of streaky bacon — ½ pint milk or milk and celery stock
1 oz. margarine — Salt and pepper

Parboil the celery, if necessary tying the hearts 5
to keep them together. Drain well, and wrap a piece of bacon round the middle of each celery heart, then lay them in a fireproof dish. Melt the margarine and add the flour, gradually stir in the liquid, season well, and pour over the celery. If liked, grated cheese or finely chopped parsley may be added to the sauce. Bake in a moderate oven (375° F., mark 5) 20–30 minutes.

CHICORY

(*Also called Succory*)

These plants are grown in the dark, to preserve their delicate flavour and prevent them from becoming too bitter, hence the long, thin leaves are practically white, or if coloured at all, are only pale yellowy-green at the tip. In this country they are generally eaten raw as a salad plant, but may also be cooked as for lettuce.

Note : The French call this vegetable "Endive Belge," and our "Endive" they call "Chicorée,b which can lead to confusion in following French recipes.

CHICORY SOUFFLÉ

6–8 heads of chicory	Salt, pepper, and nutmeg to season
½ pint Béchamel sauce	Grated cheese
3 eggs	

Wash the chicory and remove the outside leaves, and cook for 20 minutes in boiling salted water. Drain, chop finely, and add the sauce, 3 egg yolks, and seasoning of salt, pepper, and nutmeg. Fold in the stiffly beaten egg whites and bake in a buttered soufflé dish for 20 minutes in a moderate oven (375° F., mark 5). Serve with a sprinkling of grated cheese.

CORN ON THE COB

Pick the cobs when they are plump and well formed, and of a pale golden-yellow colour. Cook as soon after picking as possible.

Remove the outside leaves and silky threads. Put into boiling water, and cook 10–12 minutes for fresh young cobs—overcooking makes them tough. Drain, and serve on a folded table napkin. Serve melted butter or pats of butter separately.

CUCUMBER

Cucumbers are usually eaten raw as a salad vegetable, but they may also be cooked. To do this, peel the cucumber, cut in half lengthwise, and then into pieces about 2 inches long, removing the seeds. Boil in salted water, or steam, until tender—20–30 minutes. Drain very carefully, place on a hot dish, and coat with white sauce or melted butter.

Cucumbers may also be stuffed (see below), or can be braised.

CUCUMBER À LA POULETTE

1 large cucumber	A pinch of nutmeg
½ tsp. sugar	1 dessertsp. chopped parsley
Seasoning	1 dessertsp. lemon juice
1 oz. butter	1 egg yolk
1 dessertsp. flour	

Trim a small piece off each end of the cucumber, peel, and cut in slices ½ inch in thickness then stamp out the seedy part in the centre with a small round cutter, in order to form rings. Place these in a fireproof casserole with the sugar, a little salt, and boiling water to cover. Put on the lid, and simmer gently until the cucumber is tender but not broken. Then drain, reserving the water to make the sauce, and arrange the cucumber neatly in a hot dish.

Melt the butter in the casserole, put in the flour, and mix until smooth. Then pour in a cupful of the water from the cucumber, and stir until boiling. Add some pepper, nutmeg, parsley, and lemon juice, and simmer a minute or two. Remove from the heat and quickly stir in the egg yolk. Pour the sauce over the cucumber and serve at once.

A little chopped hard-boiled egg white is sometimes added to the sauce.

STUFFED CUCUMBER

1 large, straight cucumber	½ pint Espagnole sauce
¼ lb. chopped ham	Croûtons of fried bread
Seasoning	Rounds of ham and truffle

Skin the cucumber, cut in 2-inch pieces, and take out the seeds with a round cutter or smal vegetable knife. Season the meat, add 1 tbsp sauce, pile into the prepared rounds, and bake slowly in a moderate oven (350° F., mark 4) for about 20 minutes. Dish on croûtons of fried bread, put on rounds of ham and truffle as a lid, and pour Espagnole sauce round.

STUFFED CUCUMBER WITH CHICKEN

1 large cucumber	A little grated lemon rind
2 tbsps. chopped cooked chicken	Seasoning
2 tbsps. breadcrumbs	A little white sauce
1 tsp. chopped parsley	Brown or tomato sauce

Choose a firm, straight cucumber, remove the ends, and cut in pieces about 2 inches long. To give these a striped appearance, remove small wedges from the outside of the cucumber, leaving alternate strips of the peel. Scald the cucumber in boiling salted water for 5 minutes, rinse in cold water, and drain well. Scoop out the centres and place the rings on a greased baking sheet. Chop the chicken, mix with the other ingredients, and pile into the prepared rings. Sprinkle with browned breadcrumbs. Cover with greased paper and bake in a moderate oven (375° F., mark 5) until tender—½ hour. Serve with brown or tomato sauce poured round.

ENDIVE

There are two types of endive, the "Curly Endive," which has very crinkly leaves, and the "Batavian Endive," with much smoother leaves. Both are very pale green in colour—almost white in the heart—and of somewhat bitter flavour. In this country they are generally eaten raw as salad plants, but in France (where they are called Chicorée) they are often served stewed, braised, and so on, in the same way as lettuce.

KOHL RABI

These should be eaten while they are small and young. Cut off the leaves and peel thickly. If small, leave whole, otherwise cut into thick slices. Cook in boiling salted water until tender (½–1 hour, according to size). Serve coated with a white sauce or glaze with butter and toss in chopped parsley.

LEEKS

Remove the coarse outside leaves, and cut off the tops and roots. Wash very thoroughly, splitting them down to within 1 inch or so of the bottom, to ensure removing all grit—if necessary cut them through completely to achieve this. Tie in a bundle and cook in boiling salted water until tender (30–40 minutes). Drain very thoroughly, then place on a piece of toast to absorb any remaining liquor. Serve coated with a white or cheese sauce.

LETTUCE

Lettuces, both the cabbage and the cos varieties, are used chiefly as salad vegetables. They can, however, also be cooked in various ways, for example stewed or braised.

BRAISED LETTUCE

Wash the lettuces carefully to remove all grit and any insects. Take off the outer leaves, then put into a saucepan of boiling water and cook for about 5 minutes. Lift out the lettuces and place at once into cold water, then drain them very thoroughly, pressing lightly to remove the water. Put them into a stewpan with salt and pepper, a little chopped onion, a good knob of butter, and enough stock just to cover. Cover, and simmer gently for about 1 hour. Lift out the lettuces, drain carefully, and place on a hot dish. Thicken the liquor in which they cooked and pour this sauce over the lettuces. Sprinkle with a little chopped parsley before serving.

For MARROW, see Vegetable Marrow.

MUSHROOMS

Both field and cultivated mushrooms are treated in the same way. Skin the mushrooms and remove the stalks. If at all muddy or gritty, wash them and drain thoroughly. Young, freshly picked mushrooms need not be skinned, but in this case the cap should always be washed. Cut off and discard the earthy end of the stalks; the rest of the stalk can be included in the dish or as an ingredient in the stuffing and so on.

BAKED MUSHROOMS

Prepare the mushrooms and place them, stalks uppermost, in a greased baking dish. Place a small pat of butter on each mushroom, season with salt and pepper, and cover with greased paper. Bake in a moderate oven (375° F., mark 5) for about 20 minutes, or until tender. Serve in the dish in which they were cooked.

GRILLED MUSHROOMS

Prepare the mushrooms, then brush them all over with olive oil or melted butter. Oil or butter the grill, place the mushrooms on it, and cook under a hot grill for 2–3 minutes, turning when half cooked. Dust with salt and pepper and serve very hot.

FRIED MUSHROOMS

Prepare the mushrooms in the usual way and season with salt and pepper. Melt some butter (or bacon fat if the mushrooms are to be served with bacon) in a frying pan and fry the mushrooms gently for about 5 minutes, or until tender, turning them when half cooked. Serve very hot on buttered toast or fried bread.

MUSHROOMS À LA POMPADOUR

Potato balls	2 oz. butter
5 even-sized mushrooms	Maître d'hôtel butter
5 croûtons of bread	½ pint brown sauce
2 tomatoes	

Prepare some potato balls (see Accompaniments), cook in boiling salted water, drain, and then keep hot. Peel the mushrooms, remove the stalks, and trim to an even size. Cut out thin rounds of stale bread, a little smaller than the mushrooms, as these will shrink during the cooking. Skin the tomatoes and cut into slices to fit bread. Bake tomato slices on greased tin in a moderate oven (375° F., mark 5). Fry the croûtons of bread in hot fat and keep them hot. Fry the mushrooms in the butter and drain well. Place a slice of tomato on each croûton of bread and a mushroom on each tomato. Arrange down the centre of an entrée dish, put a small round of maître d'hôtel butter on each mushroom, pour the brown sauce around, and put a few potato balls at each end or at the sides of the dish.

CASSEROLE OF MUSHROOMS

¾ lb. mushrooms
3 tomatoes
1 onion
1 oz. butter or margarine
1 sheep's kidney
Salt and pepper
1 tbsp. chopped parsley
A little stock or water

Grease a casserole or pie dish. Wash and peel the mushrooms and remove the stalks, which may be used if liked. Skin and slice the tomatoes. Cut the onion into rings and fry in the fat to a golden-brown. Cut the kidney into small pieces and fill up the dish with alternate layers of the ingredients. Season each layer well, sprinkle on a little parsley, and finish with a layer of mushrooms on the top. Add a little water or stock, cover, and cook gently until the mushrooms are tender: this will take 30 minutes in a moderate oven (375° F., mark 5). The dish may be made in individual casseroles if preferred.

MUSHROOM SAVOURY

1 lb. mushrooms
4 tomatoes
1 onion
Butter or dripping
4 heaped tbsps. breadcrumbs
Salt and pepper
1 tsp. grated lemon rind
Croûtons of fried bread

Prepare the mushrooms and skin and slice the tomatoes. Fry the sliced onion in a little butter or dripping. Butter an au gratin dish and arrange the mushrooms, tomatoes, crumbs, and onion in it in layers. Season each layer and sprinkle with the lemon rind. Cover with greased paper and bake in a moderate oven (375° F., mark 5) for ¾ hour, or until the mushrooms are tender. Garnish with croûtons of fried bread.

SCALLOPED MUSHROOMS

½ lb. mushrooms
1 oz. flour
1 oz. fat
¾ pint milk
Salt and pepper
Grating of nutmeg
4 hard-boiled eggs
2 tomatoes
Browned crumbs
Chopped parsley
Coralline pepper

Prepare the mushrooms and cut them and the stalks into pieces, roughly ½ inch square. Make a white sauce with the flour, fat, and milk. Put in the mushrooms, seasoning, and nutmeg, and simmer gently for about 10 minutes, or until the mushrooms are tender. Stir occasionally, and a few minutes before the mixture is ready add the eggs and the tomatoes. Have ready hot, greased scallop shells or a pie dish, pour the mixture in, sprinkle with hot brown crumbs, and garnish with chopped parsley and coralline pepper.

MUSHROOM STEW

1 lb. mushrooms
¾ pint milk
1 oz. butter
1 oz. flour
Powdered mace
Pepper and salt

Peel the mushrooms and cut them up, add to the milk, and bring to boiling point. Melt the butter, add the flour and seasonings, and make into a sauce with the milk from the mushrooms. Pour this sauce over the mushrooms and allow to cook for 15 minutes, stirring frequently. Serve with toast.

STUFFED MUSHROOMS

6 large mushrooms
A small clove of garlic
½ oz. butter
1 heaped tbsp. breadcrumbs
1 heaped tsp. grated cheese
1 tsp. chopped parsley
Salt and pepper
A few drops of piquant sauce
A little milk or stock
Browned crumbs
6 croûtons fried bread
Fried parsley

Prepare the mushrooms, which should be of good shape and trimmed to an even size. Chop the stalks and trimmings finely. Cut the garlic and rub round the pan to be used for making the stuffing. Melt the butter in the pan and add the chopped stalks and trimmings, crumbs, cheese, chopped parsley, seasoning, and sauce, using sufficient milk or stock to make the mixture bind; it must not be wet. Cook slowly until the breadcrumbs are well swollen. Put the mushrooms on a greased tin, pile stuffing on each one, and sprinkle with browned breadcrumbs. Cover the tin with greased paper and bake in a moderate oven (375° F., mark 5) for about 15 minutes. Have ready the croûtons of bread, which should be slightly smaller than the mushrooms. Serve the mushrooms on the croûtons, garnished with fried parsley.

Chopped ham or lean bacon may be used instead of cheese.

STEWED MUSHROOMS AND CHESTNUTS

Boil ½ lb. of chestnuts in their skins until they are soft—about 20 minutes. Then skin them and simmer the nuts in good beef stock for 15 minutes. Fry ½ lb. mushrooms in butter until they are brown. Add to the stock containing the chestnuts and simmer for ½ hour. Prepare some brown roux by heating 1 oz. butter until it froths, adding an equal amount of flour, and cooking to a rich brown colour. Pour the liquor from the chestnuts and mushrooms gradually into the roux, stirring until it thickens, add the chestnuts and mushrooms and simmer in a saucepan with the lid off for 15 minutes. Serve very hot.

NETTLES

Young nettles are cooked in the same way as spinach. When old, the nettles have an unpleasant flavour, and are not worth cooking.

ONIONS

Cut off the roots, and remove the papery outside skin. Cook in boiling salted water until tender (30–45 minutes—according to size). Drain carefully, and coat with a white or brown sauce.

Onions are good cooked by the conservative method, or braised.

BAKED ONIONS À LA FRANÇAISE

1 lb. small white onions	½ pint stock or gravy
Seasoning	Butter or dripping
2 oz. brown sugar	

Peel the onions and cook them in boiling salted water for ¼ hour. Then drain and dry them, grease a shallow earthenware dish, put in the onions and sprinkle them with pepper, salt, and the sugar. Pour round ½ pint of good stock or gravy and place some small pieces of fat on the top. Bake in a moderate oven (375° F., mark 5) until the onions are tender, basting them occasionally with the stock.

STUFFED ONIONS

4 large Spanish onions	Salt and pepper
2 sheep's kidneys	¾ pint brown stock
¼ tsp. mixed herbs	

Peel the onions, scoop out the centres and fill with the chopped kidneys, herbs and seasoning. Place in a casserole, add the stock and cook in a moderate oven (375° F., mark 5) for about 2½–3 hours. Serve on a hot dish with the gravy.

BAKED STUFFED ONIONS

4 medium-sized onions	A little white sauce
2 tbsps. breadcrumbs	A little dripping
Salt and pepper	Mashed potatoes
2 oz. grated cheese	White sauce (see below)

Peel and parboil the onions in salted water,
55 removing them before they are soft. Drain and cool, then scoop out the centres very carefully, using a pointed knife to cut the onion top and a small teaspoon to remove the centre. Chop the centres finely, mix with the crumbs, seasoning, and 1 oz. of the grated cheese, and moisten with a little white sauce if necessary. Fill the onions, and place them in a greased fireproof dish. Put the shavings of dripping on top, and sprinkle with the remaining grated cheese. Bake in a moderately hot oven (400° F., mark 6) for about ½ hour, until tender and nicely browned. Dish on a bed of creamy mashed potatoes, and serve with a white sauce made with equal quantities of milk and onion liquor, well seasoned and flavoured with grated cheese.

ONION AND CHEESE PASTY

¾ lb. onions	2 tbsps. stock
3 oz. cheese	8 oz. shortcrust pastry
Salt and pepper	Egg

Prepare the filling by mincing, grating, or chopping the onion very finely. Add the cheese, seasoning, and stock. Mix well and allow to stand whilst the pastry is being prepared. Make the pastry and roll out into a neat, long oblong about ¼ inch thick. Moisten the edges with water or egg and put the filling on half the pastry to within ½ inch of the edge. Fold the other half of the pastry over and mark into squares or fingers with a knife, pressing the edges together. Glaze with beaten egg and bake in a moderately hot oven (400° F., mark 6) for ½ hour, or until the onion is tender. Serve hot or cold.

ONION CRISP

12 small onions	2 oz. flour
½ pint milk	Seasoning
4 tbsps. cooked green peas	2 oz. breadcrumbs
2½ oz. butter	2 tbsps. minced nuts

Peel the onions, boil them in the milk and a little water until tender, then remove them whole and place in a greased dish with the peas. Make a thick sauce with the milk in which the onions were cooked, 2 oz. butter and flour. Season well. Pour over the onions, sprinkle with breadcrumbs and nuts, and put a few knobs of butter on top. Put in a hot oven or under a red-hot grill for a minute or two to crisp the top.

ONIONS WITH BACON

4 onions	Salt and pepper
2 oz. bacon	3 tbsps. hot water
1 oz. white breadcrumbs	Bacon fat

Peel the onions and boil them until tender. Drain, and scoop out a small section from the top of each. Place them in a baking dish and fill the cavities with chopped uncooked bacon. Cover top with the rest of the bacon, sprinkle with breadcrumbs and seasoning, then pour the hot water, to which some bacon fat has been added, around the onions. Bake with occasional basting in a moderately hot oven (400° F., mark 6) until lightly browned—20–30 minutes.

SCALLOPED ONIONS (ITALIAN STYLE)

2 lb. white onions	Pepper, salt and cayenne
2 oz. butter or margarine	1 cupful cooked ham
2 oz. flour	Gruyère or Parmesan cheese
½ pint stock	Parsley
¼ pint milk	

Peel the onions, cut them in quarters, and cook them in boiling salted water until tender. Meanwhile, make a sauce with the butter, flour, stock, and milk. Cook it well and season with pepper, salt, and a little cayenne. Also chop finely the cooked ham, and grate a little Gruyère or Parmesan cheese. Drain the onions and put half of them in a well-greased baking dish. Pour over them half the sauce and then put on a layer of chopped ham. Cover with the remainder of the onions and the sauce, and sprinkle the top with a light coating of grated cheese. Place the dish in a hot oven (450° F., mark 8) until a rich brown colour—about 20 minutes. Serve garnished with a little parsley.

PARSNIPS

Scrub and peel thinly, and cut into even-sized pieces. Cook in boiling salted water until tender—this may take anything from ½–1 hour. Drain, glaze with butter, and toss in chopped parsley. Alternatively, mash the parsnips and reheat them with salt, pepper, and a knob of butter before dishing.

Parsnips are also very good baked in dripping with roast meat.

PARSNIP AND WALNUT CROQUETTES

1 lb. parsnips	2 oz. chopped walnuts
1 oz. butter	Egg and breadcrumbs
1 oz. flour	Fat for frying
¼ pint milk	Parsley
Pepper and salt	

Cook the parsnips until quite tender, then rub them through a sieve. Melt the butter in a small saucepan and stir in the flour, then add the milk and bring to the boil, stirring all the time. Season to taste. To this sauce, add the sieved parsnips and the chopped walnuts; stir them well in, then turn the mixture on to a plate, and spread into a flat cake. When this is cold, form into balls, egg-and-crumb them, and fry in hot fat. Serve on a hot dish, garnished with parsley.

PARSNIP SOUFFLÉ

4 parsnips	A pinch of nutmeg
½ pint white sauce	Pepper and salt
2–3 eggs	2 tbsps. chopped nuts

Choose parsnips of medium size. Clean them, cut in pieces, and boil in salted water until tender. Then drain off all the water, and rub the parsnips through a sieve or put them through a vegetable presser. Put the purée into a basin, and add some good white sauce of a fairly thick consistency. Add also the egg yolks and seasoning to taste. Mix well, and lastly stir in the egg whites, which have been beaten to a stiff froth. Turn into a greased soufflé dish, sprinkle the nuts over the top, and bake in a moderately hot oven (425° F., mark 7) for 20–30 minutes. Serve immediately.

PEAS (GREEN)

After shelling, cook in boiling salted water, with a pinch of sugar and a sprig of mint, until tender—10–20 minutes. Drain, removing the mint, and toss with a knob of butter before dishing. Old peas may be cooked by the conservative method.

SAUTÉ OF PEAS

2 lb. peas	Salt and pepper
2 small onions	About ½ pint water or stock
1 oz. butter	1 tsp. chopped parsley

Shell the peas, and peel and slice the onions. Melt the butter in a saucepan, add the peas, and sauté for about 2 minutes. Add the onions, salt and pepper, and the water or stock—the liquid should only just cover the peas. Cover, and cook gently until tender—about 20–30 minutes. Do not strain, but serve the liquid with the peas. If liked, the lid can be removed about 10 minutes before cooking is completed, so that some of the water evaporates. Sprinkle in the chopped parsley just before serving.

POTATOES

Wash or scrub the potatoes; scrape if new, or peel thinly if old. Keep them under water, or they will discolour.

Boiling

Potatoes should be put into boiling salted water, and the pan should be covered. Boil gently until tender—about 20 minutes. Drain carefully (the water may be reserved for soup or gravy), dry over a gentle heat, and add a little chopped parsley before dishing.

Add a sprig of mint to new potatoes while cooking, and serve them glazed with a little butter or margarine.

Some varieties of potato boil very unevenly, disintegrating on the outside while still hard in the middle. The following method of boiling is good in this case: put them into boiling salted water and boil gently for 10–15 minutes. Then drain off the water, cover with a folded cloth and the pan lid, and keep them warm at the side of the stove for a further 10–15 minutes. They will continue to cook in their own steam without breaking up.

Potatoes are delicious boiled in their skins, and in addition waste is considerably smaller, and the loss of vitamins and mineral salts reduced to a minimum. They may be served in their skins, but if you have time to skin them before they go to the table, so much the better.

Steaming

Steaming is an excellent way of cooking potatoes. Allow rather longer time than when boiling—that is, about 30–40 minutes—then serve glazed or mashed. Or, cook and serve the potatoes in their skins, as follows :—

Choose fairly large potatoes of even size, scrub them well, then cut a little cross in the skin—about an inch or so each way. Steam until they feel tender when tested with a skewer. You will find the skin will have opened at the cross—fork up the potato a little inside the opening, then add a knob of butter, a sprinkling of salt and pepper, and a little sprig of parsley. Pile on a hot dish and serve at once.

Creaming

This method of serving is particularly useful when the potatoes are old and of poor texture, or when they tend to discolour on boiling. To be really delicious, creamed potatoes must be very smooth and creamy in texture, and served very hot. First, boil or steam the potatoes until perfectly tender, but not overcooked, and drain. Then remove the skins (if not already done) and either press through a coarse wire sieve or beat up well with a fork or whisk. When quite smooth return to the pan and add salt, pepper, a knob of butter, and a little hot milk. Beat well until light and fluffy, and make thoroughly hot before dishing. For a change, add a little finely chopped raw onion or freshly chopped parsley or watercress before serving.

If you have to keep potatoes hot, and wish to serve them mashed, leave them whole in the water in which they are cooked, then strain and mash them when required.

Dry-Mashing

Cooked potato for adding to pastry, cakes, and puddings needs to be "dry mashed," as distinct from creamed.

First boil or steam the potatoes until tender, then rub while still hot through a wire sieve or strainer. If left until cold before mashing they will be sticky and glutinous, instead of fluffy.

Baking

"Jacket potatoes" are popular and very easy to prepare. Choose even-sized potatoes. Scrub and dry them, and bake in a moderately hot oven (400° F., mark 6) until they feel soft when pinched—½–¾ hour for small potatoes and about 1 hour if large.

Roasting

Potatoes roasted in the dripping round the meat are always delicious. They are usually peeled, but some people prefer to leave the skins on when cooking them in this way. Wash and peel the potatoes and cook in boiling salted water for 5–10 minutes. Drain, and put them in the roasting tin with the melted dripping. Sprinkle with salt, and cook in a moderate oven (375° F., mark 5) for ¾–1 hour, basting occasionally, and turning them so that they brown evenly. (If liked, the potatoes may be rolled in seasoned flour before being put in the tin.)

Frying

Chipped potatoes are a national favourite—directions for making them are given under "To Fry" in the chapter in Cookery Processes and Terms.

Sautéing

The potatoes are first boiled before being sautéed. Be sure not to overcook them in the preliminary boiling, or the resulting dish will be rather greasy.

Cut the cooked potatoes into thick slices and fry in a little hot dripping until brown and crisp. Serve very hot, sprinkled with salt. If liked, mix a little chopped onion and freshly chopped parsley with them before dishing.

GOLDEN SCALLOP

Make a cheese sauce by adding 1 teacupful of grated cheese to ½ pint well-seasoned white sauce. Select a yellow cheese, in order to give the sauce a golden colour. Cut cooked potatoes in slices, and arrange them in layers with the sauce in a greased baking dish. Sprinkle more cheese over the top and brown under the grill or in a hot oven. This may be served with a green vegetable, such as spinach, or with a pretty green salad.

MAÎTRE D'HÔTEL POTATOES

Boil the potatoes in their skins. Peel them, and cut into slices about ¼ inch thick. Put into a clean frying pan 2 tbsps. best olive oil, pepper, salt, chopped parsley, and ½ tsp. vinegar. Toss the potatoes in this mixture till they are thoroughly well heated, and serve them at once.

CARAMELLED POTATOES

1½ oz. sugar	1 lb. small evenly shaped,
1 oz. butter	boiled potatoes
1 tbsp. hot water	

Heat the sugar gently in a strong frying pan until it becomes a golden-brown syrup. Add the margarine and water and stir. Put in the potatoes and shake over the heat until they are evenly browned. Serve very hot.

If small potatoes are unobtainable, potato balls can be cut from jarge raw potatoes with a Parisian potato cutter; boil these and allow to cool before caramelling them.

DUCHESSE POTATOES

1 lb. cooked potatoes	1 tbsp. cream
1 oz. butter	Salt and pepper
1 egg	

Rub the potatoes through a sieve. Melt the butter in a saucepan, add the potatoes and, when warm, the beaten yolk of egg and the cream. Season the mixture well, and thoroughly mix together. Turn out on to a floured board, and divide into small squares. Place these on to a greased baking tin and brush over with beaten egg. Mark into lines with the back of a knife. Brown in a hot oven (450° F., mark 8) and pile neatly in a hot vegetable dish.

If preferred, this mixture may be forced on to the baking tin in rosettes, by means of a large star pipe. Glaze and bake as above.

SCALLOPED POTATOES

4 medium-sized potatoes	1 oz. flour
½ tsp. salt	1 oz. butter
¼ tsp. pepper	About ¾ pint milk

Wash and peel the potatoes and cut in slices. Put a layer in a buttered baking dish and sprinkle with salt and pepper. Dredge with flour and spread with butter. Repeat, and add milk until it may be seen through the top layer. Bake 1¼ hours in a moderate oven (375° F., mark 5) until the potato is soft and the top golden-brown.

POTATO AND BACON CASSEROLE

2 lb. potatoes	Salt and pepper
2 onions	Milk
2–4 oz. bacon	Butter
Chopped parsley	

Peel the potatoes and cut in thin slices. Peel the onions and cut in thin rings. Cut the bacon into small pieces. Fill a casserole with alternate layers of potatoes, onion rings, bacon, chopped parsley, and seasonings. Then three-parts fill with milk and place some small pieces of butter on top. Cover, and cook over very gentle heat, until the vegetables are tender, or, alternatively, bake in a moderate oven (375° F., mark 5) for about 1 hour. If the casserole is cooked in the oven, remove the lid 20 minutes before serving, to brown the potatoes on top.

POTATO CROQUETTES

½ lb. cooked potatoes	Pepper and salt
½ oz. butter	Brown crumbs
1 tsp. chopped parsley	Frying fat
1 egg	Fried parsley

Sieve the potatoes, or mash them thoroughly with a fork until they are quite free from lumps; melt the butter in a saucepan, add the potatoes, chopped parsley, and a little of the beaten egg, season well, and beat until the mixture is creamy. Turn the mixture on to a lightly floured board and form into a roll, taking care not to allow any of the flour to enter the mixture. Divide the roll into even-sized pieces and form these into balls. Coat with the remainder of the egg, cover with crumbs, and then re-coat with egg and crumbs again, to prevent the balls from bursting on cooking. Fry in hot fat until they are light golden-brown. Garnish with fried parsley and serve very hot.

POTATO GALANTINE

4 medium-sized boiled potatoes	2 oz. grated cheese	
Butter or margarine	1 tbsp. tomato ketchup	
Salt and pepper	1 egg yolk	
½ tsp. made mustard	Breadcrumbs for coating	56
	Tomato sauce	

Mash the potatoes whilst hot, adding a little butter. Season, and add the grated cheese and ketchup. Bind with an egg yolk, then turn on to a floured board and shape into a roll. Brush with egg or milk and sprinkle the top with breadcrumbs. Place in a tin, cover with greased paper, and bake in a moderate oven (375° F., mark 5) for ½ hour. Lift on to a hot dish, using a fish slice, and serve with tomato sauce.

SAVOURY BAKED POTATOES

6 large potatoes	A little butter or margarine
6 tbsps. hot milk	Paprika
3 oz. finely grated cheese	Parsley
Seasoning	

Wash and scrub the potatoes, prick them several times with a fork, and bake in a moderately hot oven (400° F., mark 6) until well cooked. Then cut the potatoes in halves lengthwise and scoop out the centre, being careful to keep the skins intact. Put the potato into a basin and mix it with a fork until free from lumps. Add the hot milk, most of the cheese, and seasoning to taste. Stir until blended, and then fill up the potato shells with the mixture. Sprinkle the rest of the cheese on the top, brush over lightly with a little melted butter and brown in the oven. Sprinkle with a little paprika before serving, and garnish with parsley.

STUFFED CHEESE POTATOES

4 large potatoes	A little milk
1 oz. butter, margarine or dripping	2 oz. breadcrumbs
	3 oz. grated cheese
1 tsp. chopped onion	Seasoning
1 ripe tomato	Brown gravy
1 egg	

Cut the potatoes in half lengthwise and scoop out part of the centres. Meanwhile, melt half the fat in a pan and add to it the chopped onion and the skinned tomato, cut in small pieces. Cook gently, with frequent shaking of the saucepan, for 10–15 minutes. Blend thoroughly, add the well-beaten egg, a little milk, the breadcrumbs, and the cheese, season, and place a portion of the mixture in each of the potato cases. Finish by baking in a little hot dripping in a moderate oven (350° F., mark 4) for ½ hour. Serve with brown gravy.

SWEET POTATOES

Sweet potatoes are not much eaten in this country. They may be cooked and served in any of the ways suitable for ordinary potatoes. In America, where they are very popular, they are also served as a sweet, cooked with sugar or molasses and flavoured with cinnamon, etc.

PULSES

Dried peas, split peas, and haricot and butter beans require to be soaked overnight in cold water. A pinch of bicarbonate of soda added to the soaking water helps to soften them, especially in hard-water districts. To cook, put into fresh, cold water, bring to the boil, and boil gently until tender; the time varies considerably, some taking up to 2½ hours. They may be served glazed, or with a good sauce—white, cheese, or tomato.

Lentils may be soaked overnight, though this is not essential. To cook, cover with cold water, bring to the boil, and simmer very gently until tender and the liquid absorbed, adding more liquid if necessary. (Time about ½ hour.)

BEANS AND BACON

½ lb. haricot beans	A small stick of celery, or ¼ tsp. celery seed tied in muslin
A pinch of bicarbonate of soda	
¼ lb. streaky bacon	Salt and pepper
1 small onion	½ pint water or stock
½ lb. tomatoes	½ oz. flour

Wash the beans, cover with cold water, add a pinch of bicarbonate of soda, and soak for 24 hours. Trim the bacon and fry it in a saucepan, remove it, and fry the sliced onion and then the tomatoes in the bacon fat. Rinse the beans in clean water and add them to the fried vegetables, together with the celery, salt and pepper, and the liquid. Simmer steadily until the beans are tender—about 1½–2 hours. Then blend the flour with a little water, pour on some of the gravy, return to the pan, stir, and boil. Add the bacon and allow it to reheat on the top of the beans. Serve the beans on a hot dish and garnish with the bacon.

CASSEROLE OF BEANS WITH SAUSAGES

½ lb. haricot beans	1–2 bacon rashers
1 clove of garlic or 1 onion	Seasoning
	Water
6 bottled tomatoes, or 2 tbsps. tomato sauce	1 lb. small sausages

Soak the beans overnight. Put in a casserole with the crushed clove of garlic or the sliced onion, the tomatoes, bacon (cut up), and seasoning. Add sufficient water to cover. Put on the lid, and cook in a slow oven (325° F., mark 2) until very soft, adding extra water if necessary. If the oven is not available, cook the beans in a saucepan. Grill or fry the sausages, and add to the beans a few minutes before serving. Serve in the casserole in which they were cooked.

HARICOT BEANS IN SAUCE

½ lb. haricot beans
½ oz. butter
½ oz. flour
½ pint bean liquor
Seasoning
½ tsp. vegetable extract
2 tbsps. tomato sauce or ketchup
Gravy browning, if necessary

Soak the beans overnight in cold water. Cook in salt water until tender, strain, and reserve some of the liquor. Melt the butter and add the flour. Cook for 2–3 minutes on a low heat. Remove from the heat and add the bean liquor, a little at a time, beating well. Bring to the boil, stirring; season, and add the vegetable extract and tomato sauce. If necessary, add a little gravy browning to give a rich reddish-brown colour. Pour this sauce over the haricot beans and serve piping hot.

LENTIL AND TOMATO RISSOLES

¼ lb. lentils, cooked in ½ pint water
1 small onion
1 oz. butter
1 oz. flour
¼ pint water
Salt and pepper
1 tsp. vegetable extract
2 tbsps. tinned tomato pulp
Egg and breadcrumbs
Fat for frying
Brown or tomato sauce

Wash the lentils, cover with the water, bring to the boil, and cook until thick. Fry the onion in the butter, remove, add the flour, and cook until brown, stir in the water, bring to the boil, season, and add the vegetable extract and fried onion. Put the cooked lentils and tomato pulp into the sauce, cook for a few minutes, turn on to a floured plate, and cool. Shape into rissoles, coat with egg and breadcrumbs, and fry in smoking-hot fat. Drain well, and serve with brown or tomato sauce.

PEASE PUDDING

½ lb. split peas
Pepper and salt
1 oz. butter
1 egg
A pinch of sugar

Wash the peas well, removing any discoloured ones, and soak overnight in cold water. Tie loosely in a cloth and place in a saucepan with a pinch of salt and boiling water to cover. Boil for 2–2½ hours, or until soft. Sieve, and add the butter, well-beaten egg, pepper, salt, and pinch of sugar. Beat together until thoroughly mixed, and then tie up tightly in a floured cloth. Boil for another ½ hour, turn out on to a hot dish and serve.

If preferred, the second boiling may be dispensed with and the mixture piled up on a hot dish: the egg then would be omitted.

PUMPKIN

Pumpkin is good made into soup or pumpkin pie. It may also be served as a vegetable, cooked and mashed as are turnips or swedes.

SALSIFY

Scrub the roots and scrape them quickly, placing them at once into cold water with a few drops of lemon juice or vinegar added; this helps to keep them a good colour. Cut into short lengths, and cook in boiling salted water until tender (about 2 hours). Serve with a white sauce.

SEAKALE

Wash well, cut off the ends, and tie into neat bundles. Cook in boiling salted water, to which a squeeze of lemon juice has been added (this is to preserve the white colour), until tender—20–30 minutes. Drain well, remove the string, and serve on toast, coated with a good white or Béchamel sauce. Seakale may also be braised or served au gratin. Cold, it may be served with a vinaigrette dressing, or added to a salad.

SPINACH

Wash well in several waters to remove all grit, and strip off any coarse stalks. Pack into a saucepan with only the water that clings to it. Heat gently, turning it occasionally, then bring to the boil and cook gently until tender—about 15 minutes. Drain thoroughly, and reheat with a knob of butter and a sprinkling of salt and pepper. If liked, the spinach may be sieved and 1–2 tbsps. white sauce, "top of milk," or sour cream added to it. Reheat before serving.

SPINACH AND EGGS WITH TOMATO SAUCE

2 lb. spinach
1 cupful white sauce
½ tsp. sugar
Seasoning
2–3 hard-boiled eggs
Tomato sauce
Croûtons of fried bread

Pick and wash the spinach, removing all the hard stalks. Put it into a saucepan with only the water that hangs on the leaves and cook it until tender, stirring occasionally. When ready, drain, and press out all the water. Turn the spinach on to a board and chop it with a knife. Then reheat with the white sauce, sugar, and seasoning to taste. Arrange it on a hot dish, piling it high in the centre with a flat ridge at the base. Cut the eggs in slices and place them in a circle on the top of the ridge. Heat for a minute or two in the oven, then serve with tomato sauce poured round, and garnish with croûtons of fried bread.

SPINACH AND MUSHROOM CREAM

2 lb. spinach	Nutmeg
¼ lb. mushrooms	Salt and pepper
1 oz. butter	1 hard-boiled egg
¼ pint white sauce	

Prepare and boil the spinach as usual. Drain, then mash finely and keep hot. Skin and chop the mushrooms, then sauté them in the butter. Add them to the white sauce, together with a grating of nutmeg and seasoning. Reserve the yolk of egg for garnishing and add the chopped white to the sauce. Arrange the spinach in a neat border on a hot dish. Reheat the sauce and pour in the centre of the spinach border, then sieve the yolk of egg over.

SQUASH

Cook as for marrow, turnips, or swedes.

STACHYS

(Called also Japanese Artichokes or Chinese Artichokes)

Wash the tubers and trim off the ends. Plunge for a minute into boiling water, then rub off the skins in a clean cloth. Put at once into cold water to which a little salt and a squeeze of lemon juice have been added—this is to preserve their colour. Cook in boiling salted water until tender—15–20 minutes. Drain well, then return to the pan and toss with a piece of butter, a sprinkling of salt and pepper, and a little chopped parsley. Serve very hot.

Stachys can also be served creamed or au gratin, and are very good cold, in a salad.

SWEDES

Scrub, peel thickly, then cut into even-sized pieces. Cook in boiling salted water until tender (½–1 hour according to size and age). Drain, then mash well, and reheat with a knob of butter and a sprinkling of salt and pepper. If liked, add a little chopped parsley before dishing.

SWEET PEPPERS

Sweet peppers, both red and green, can be eaten raw as a salad vegetable. Being very pungent in flavour, they should be sliced or chopped and only a small quantity added to the
57 salad. Small amounts of the peppers, again sliced or chopped, may be included in savoury dishes made with rice and macaroni and so on.

Peppers may be fried, or stuffed and baked.

To prepare them, cut off the stalks, cut in half lengthwise, and remove the seeds and any stringy membrane. If required for flavouring, they may then be sliced or chopped. For frying, parboil in boiling salted water for about 5 minutes, then drain, dip in egg and breadcrumbs, and fry in deep fat.

For stuffed peppers, parboil in boiling salted water for a few minutes, then stuff with any savoury mixture of meat, fish, cheese, or vegetables. Cover with breadcrumbs, dot with pieces of butter, and bake in a moderately hot oven (425° F., mark 7) for 15–20 minutes or longer, according to the nature of the stuffing which is used. Serve with a good sauce.

SWISS CHARD

(Also known as Spinach Beet or Seakale Beet)

This is really two vegetables in one, the green part of the leaves being prepared and cooked as for spinach, and the mid-ribs treated in the same way as for seakale.

TOMATOES

Although strictly speaking a fruit, the tomato is nearly always used as a vegetable and has come to be classed as such. It can be used either raw or cooked. Perhaps it is never better than when eaten in its natural state, especially if it is the home-grown variety that has been ripened in the sun. The small, bright red tomatoes are particularly delicious in flavour, and it would be a mistake to cook these; the simple accompaniment of oil and vinegar, with a seasoning of pepper and salt, is all that they require. Or, if preferred, the raw tomatoes may be peeled and sliced and mixed with a light dressing.

When it is necessary to remove the skin from tomatoes, plunge them for a minute into boiling water, then lift out, put immediately into cold water, and, when cool, the skin will peel off quite easily with a knife.

BAKED TOMATOES

Halve and put on a greased baking sheet with a piece of butter on each and a sprinkling of salt and pepper. Cover with greased paper and bake in a moderate oven (375° F., mark 5) until they are tender, but not broken—about 15 minutes.

They may also be cooked whole; in this case do not season or cover them.

STEWED TOMATOES

Place the whole tomatoes in a stewpan with a very little stock. Add salt and pepper, then cover and simmer very gently until tender but not broken—15–20 minutes.

TOMATOES EN SURPRISE

4 even-sized tomatoes	Table sauce
1 small onion or 2 medium-sized mushrooms	4 eggs
	Seasoning
1 oz. butter	

Cut off the stalk end of the tomatoes and scoop out the pulp. Fry the chopped onion or mushrooms in the butter and put a little at the bottom of each tomato. Add ½ tsp. of the table sauce. Break each egg separately and pour one carefully into each tomato. Season, and bake in a moderately hot oven (400° F., mark 6) until the egg is lightly set.

TOMATOES STUFFED WITH ASPARAGUS

4 large, firm tomatoes	1 small gherkin
¼ pint green asparagus tips	Mayonnaise
Salt	Lettuce
A grating of nutmeg	

Wipe the tomatoes, removing the centre with the handle of a teaspoon and rejecting the core. Cook the asparagus tips until tender and drain well. Season and flavour the tomato pulp, add the asparagus and the chopped gherkin, and fill the tomato shells with the mixture. Mask with thick mayonnaise and garnish with fancy shapes of gherkin. Serve at once on lettuce.

TOMATOES WITH CHEESE STUFFING

6 firm tomatoes	Seasoning
2 tbsps. breadcrumbs	½ oz. butter
2 tbsps. Parmesan cheese	6 rounds of toast

Choose tomatoes of equal size. Cut a small round from the top of each and scoop out the pulp. Mix the crumbs and cheese, moisten with tomato pulp, and season well. Refill the tomato cases, sprinkle over crumbs or grated cheese and place a piece of butter on each. Bake on a greased tin in a moderately hot oven (400° F., mark 6) for 15–20 minutes. Serve on rounds of buttered toast and garnish with parsley.

STUFFED TOMATOES

4 even-sized tomatoes	½ tsp. chopped parsley
1 oz. chopped ham	½ tsp. salt
1 tsp. chopped onion	1 pinch of pepper
½ oz. butter	½ a cucumber
2 tbsps. fresh breadcrumbs	Croûtons of fried bread
	Sprigs of parsley

Wash and dry the tomatoes. Cut a small round from each tomato at the end opposite the stalk, leaving it attached at one side. Scoop out the centre with a teaspoon handle. Sauté the ham and onion in the butter for about 3 minutes. Add the crumbs, parsley, seasonings, and pulp removed from the tomatoes. Fill the tomatoes with this mixture and pile neatly on top. Place the lids over and bake in a moderately hot oven (400° F., mark 6) for about 15 minutes. The cucumber garnish can be cooked in the same dish. Wipe the piece of cucumber and cut down in four strips. Wrap these in a buttered paper and bake for 15 minutes. Place the tomatoes on the croûtons of fried bread and garnish with parsley and the cucumber.

TURNIPS

Turnips require to be peeled thickly. Cook in boiling salted water until tender; the time depends on the age and size, and may vary from 15 minutes to 1 hour. Drain, then mash or chop, and reheat with a knob of butter, salt, and pepper. If preferred, serve coated with a good white sauce.

Young turnips may be cooked by the conservative method.

VEGETABLE MARROW

Marrows should be eaten when very young. When very small they can be cooked, whole and without peeling, in boiling salted water until tender (about 15 minutes). Drain carefully, and serve with melted butter or Hollandaise sauce.

Large marrows must be peeled, the seeds removed, and the flesh cut into even-sized pieces. Cook in boiling salted water until tender (about 30 minutes), and drain very thoroughly. Serve with a white or cheese sauce.

Vegetable marrow is very good roasted in the dripping round the meat.

STUFFED MARROW—I

3 oz. minced bacon or ham	1 beaten egg
	A little stock
1 oz. minced onion	A vegetable marrow
3 oz. minced liver	A little butter or dripping
4 oz. breadcrumbs	
Mixed herbs or finely chopped parsley	Garnish of baked tomatoes, bacon rolls and parsley
Pepper and salt	

Put the bacon and onion in a good-sized saucepan and fry lightly. Add the liver and fry this also. Add the breadcrumbs and seasonings and herbs. Cool slightly and stir in the beaten egg, then add sufficient stock or water to moisten thoroughly. Do not peel the marrow, but lay it flat and with a sharp knife remove an oval-shaped wedge from the top, then scrape out all the seeds. Fill with the prepared stuffing and replace the lid.

To bake, place on a greased roasting tin with some pieces of butter or good dripping on it, and cover with a piece of well-greased paper. Bake in a moderate oven (350° F., mark 4) for about 1 hour, or until quite tender. Place on a hot dish and garnish with baked tomatoes, bacon rolls, and parsley. Gravy may be handed separately.

STUFFED MARROW—II

1 small vegetable marrow	Seasoning
3 tbsps. minced cooked meat or sausage-meat	1 tbsp. sauce or beaten egg
3 tbsps. breadcrumbs	½ pint thick gravy or tomato sauce
1 tsp. chopped parsley	
Grated lemon rind	

Wash and peel the marrow, keeping it whole, Cut a wedge out lengthwise and scoop out the seeds and soft pulp. Mix the minced meat. breadcrumbs, parsley, and lemon rind. Season well, and bind with a little sauce or beaten egg. Put this stuffing in the marrow and fit the wedge in again. Wrap in well-greased paper and place on a greased baking tin. Bake in a moderate oven (350° F., mark 4) for 30–45 minutes, or until tender. Remove the paper, place the marrow on a hot dish and pour the gravy or sauce round.

STUFFED MARROWS WITH RICE AND CREAM SAUCE

3 lb. marrow	1 tsp. chopped parsley
6 oz. rice	Salt and pepper
2 Spanish onions	5 heaped tbsps. crumbs
3 oz. butter	1 egg and 1 egg white

For the Sauce

58

2 oz. butter	1 egg yolk
3 oz. flour	½ a lemon, if liked
¾ pint milk	Seasoning
½ pint marrow liquor	

Choose small marrows: peel them, cut out a wedge, and scoop out the seeds carefully. Boil the rice in ½ pint water. Fry the sliced onions in some of the butter, add ¼ pint water, the rice, parsley, and seasoning. Cook until the rice has absorbed all the water. Add the breadcrumbs and beaten eggs and mix thoroughly. Fill the marrows with this stuffing. Put them in a wide, shallow saucepan with 1 tbsp. butter and enough boiling water just to cover. Simmer until tender, lift out the marrows, drain well, and keep hot on a dish.

To make the sauce, melt the butter, add the flour, stir well, then add the milk and marrow liquor by degrees. Stir and boil for 3 minutes, cool a little, add the egg yolk, lemon juice, and seasoning. Reheat, but do not boil, and pour the sauce over the marrows.

STUFFED MARROW AU GRATIN

1 young marrow	2 oz. sweet almonds
3 tbsps. breadcrumbs	Seasoning
1–2 tbsps. milk	A pinch of grated nutmeg
2 hard-boiled eggs	
2 oz. grated Parmesan cheese	Egg yolk to bind

Wash and peel the marrow and cut in rings about 1 inch thick. Arrange in a buttered fire-proof dish. Soak the breadcrumbs in the milk. Add chopped hard-boiled egg, grated cheese, chopped almonds, seasoning, and nutmeg. Bind with egg, and pile into prepared rings of marrow. Sprinkle with cheese, and bake in a moderate oven (375° F., mark 5) until nicely browned and the marrow tender—about ½ hour.

FRIED MARROW AND MUSHROOMS

Choose a small, young marrow, peel, and cut into slices ¼–½ inch thick, but do not remove the seeds. Peel about ¼ lb. mushrooms. Melt a little margarine or dripping in a pan, and fry the slices of marrow on both sides until golden-brown, sprinkling them with salt and pepper while in the frying pan. Dish and keep hot. Melt a little more fat, if necessary, and fry the mushrooms for 2–3 minutes. Arrange on the marrow and garnish with parsley.

WATERCRESS

Watercress is usually eaten raw as a salad plant or used as a garnish, but may also be cooked as for spinach, and makes a good soup.

MIXED VEGETABLE DISHES

BROAD BEANS AND SPRING ONIONS

1 lb. broad beans	1 doz. spring onions
Parsley	2 oz. bacon
2 oz. margarine	1 egg yolk

Cook the beans in salted water with a little parsley. Melt the margarine, add the sliced spring onions, and fry until soft and golden-brown. Add the chopped bacon and the egg yolk, blended with 4 tbsps. of the bean water. Add the drained beans, heat through for a few minutes without boiling, season, and serve with chopped parsley sprinkled over the top.

VEGETABLE RING

1 lb. potatoes, mashed	Seasoning
2 lb. of a variety of cooked diced vegetables	Grated cheese
	½ pint cheese sauce

Form a ring of hot mashed potato on a fire-proof platter or shallow dish. Fill the centre with the hot seasoned vegetables and some of the grated cheese. Pour the cheese sauce over the centre and allow some to coat the potato ring. Sprinkle the top with the rest of the grated cheese. Reheat, and brown in hot oven (450° F., mark 8) or under grill, for 10–15 minutes.

CASSEROLE OF VEGETABLES WITH CHEESE DUMPLINGS

¼ pint haricot beans	2 tomatoes
2 onions	½ pint stock or gravy
2 oz. dripping	2 tsps. chopped parsley
2 carrots	Salt and pepper
2 stalks of celery	

For the Dumplings

3 oz. flour	Powdered herbs
½ tsp. baking powder	Seasoning
1 oz. grated cheese	Milk and water to mix

Soak the beans for 24 hours, boil until tender, then drain. Cut the onions into rings, fry in the dripping until golden-brown, add the sliced carrots and celery, and stir until all the fat is absorbed. Place in a casserole, add the sliced tomatoes, the liquid, the chopped parsley, and, lastly, the beans, seasoning each layer; cover, and cook gently for 40 minutes.

Make the dumplings by combining all the dry ingredients and mixing to a soft dough with milk and water. Divide into small portions, place on top of the vegetables, and cook for a further 20 minutes.

TOMATO AND CARROT BORDER

½ lb. tomatoes	Cayenne pepper and salt
¼ lb. young carrots	Macedoine of vegetables
½ oz. gelatine	Mayonnaise
4 tbsps. water	Lettuce

Cook the tomatoes and carrots until tender, then rub through a fine sieve. Add the gelatine, dissolved in the water, and season to taste with cayenne and salt. Pour into a border mould and allow to set. When the jelly is set, turn on to a glass dish and fill the centre with a mixture of diced cooked vegetables and mayonnaise. Decorate with crisp lettuce leaves. If liked, a few drops of carmine may be added to the jelly to improve the appearance, and a few drops of brandy to bring out the flavour.

SALADS AND SALAD DRESSINGS

SALADS

The name " Salad," as one epicure has pointed out, is practically the same in most European languages. Its common origin is the Latin *Sal*—salt—since a salad, in its simplest form, is something dipped in salt. The summer is perhaps the happiest time for salad enthusiasts, but even the winter offers ample opportunity for salads, for there are so many vegetables that can be used, either raw or cooked, in this type of dish. Probably the most popular kind of salad is that made of uncooked green plants; however, a complete meal from a salad bowl can be very enjoyable and satisfying, for salad plants combine delightfully with all kinds of shell fish, with salted and pickled fish, with cold salmon, or even with the more ordinary white fish, and are equally good with cheese, eggs, cold meat and so on.

Most of us eat salads because we like their crisp freshness. At the same time, we fully realise that we count on raw salad vegetables for supplying us with some of our daily quota of Vitamins A and C, and with mineral salts. Vitamin C is somewhat fugitive, so the vegetables must be carefully prepared, or a good deal of this vitamin will have vanished before the salad is eaten. The vitamin content is highest when the vegetables are fresh from the ground—with each day that the plants are out of the earth, their value is considerably lessened, until eventually they have little of the virtue of fresh food. If you are not able to take salad plants straight from the garden, you can at least choose the freshest the shops have to offer and use them at once.

Preparing Salad Plants

The old method of soaking greenstuffs in large quantities of cold water has been superseded—this process causes loss of water-soluble vitamins and mineral salts, especially if the leaves are sliced or chopped before soaking.

To clean the vegetables, wash them quickly but thoroughly in running cold water, and shake them well over the sink. Then place in a salad basket or clean tea towel and shake (out of doors for preference, and using a smooth, swinging movement) to remove the rest of the moisture. This is very important; so many people spoil a salad by leaving the vegetables wet.

In the hot weather salad plants wither soon after they are picked, unless they can be placed in the covered vegetable drawer of a refrigerator. A withered lettuce can, however, be revived quite quickly as follows: wash in running cold water, then shake the leaves slightly but leave some of the moisture on them. Place in a polythene bag or a bowl covered with a plate, and put it in the coldest place you have—a refrigerator for preference, a cold larder, a shady place in the garden. In an hour or so the leaves will have crisped up—but don't forget to shake off the rest of the water before serving.

Freshly cut vegetables rapidly lose vitamin value. However, an acid dressing helps to reduce loss of vitamin C; if such a dressing is not available, it is wise to leave the salad uncut. The large leaves, with their attractive curly shapes, will provide a salad as good to look at as it is to eat.

Dressing the Salad

The dressing can make or mar a salad. The mistake often made is to use too much dressing, with the result that it swamps the salad instead of making it appetising. If correctly mixed, no surplus dressing should be seen at the bottom of the salad bowl after the salad is thoroughly mixed—there should be just sufficient dressing to flavour the plants and not to soak them.

Herbs in Salads

Parsley is an addition to any salad. Do not chop it very finely, but tear it with the fingers (or snip with scissors) straight on to the salad just before serving. A few leaves of fresh mint, sage, thyme, dill or tarragon can be used as flavouring (one at a time, not all together), chopped and sprinkled over the salad. Some people like verbena, too, or rosemary, but these have slightly scented flavours, so do not be too liberal with them unless you know the tastes of the people you are serving.

Garlic

Many of those who say they dislike garlic don't really know how to use it. Garlic is pungent and needs using with discretion, so you will find one small " clove " ample for a good-sized bowl of salad. There are several ways of using it, depending on how much you like the flavour. First, remove the papery outside skin of the clove. If you like a very subtle flavour, cut the clove across and rub the cut surface thoroughly all over the inside of the bowl just before making the salad. If you like a stronger flavour, crush the garlic with a broad-bladed knife (do this on a plate, unless you have a board that you keep specially for onion-chopping) and scrape into the salad bowl.

When to Serve Salads

Some salads may be served as an accompaniment to another dish, while others form a course in themselves. A dinner salad, to accompany a main dish of meat and so on, should be a very simple affair, with a French dressing. More substantial salads with mayonnaise or other rich dressing should be served at luncheon or supper or at a small dinner where the meat course is scanty. In such cases the richer dressing plays its part in adding extra nourishment.

APPLE SALAD

2 dessert apples	6 pickled walnuts
1 medium-sized carrot	Salad dressing
1 celery heart	Watercress

Slice the apple without peeling, grate the prepared carrot, chop celery and walnuts. Mix with the salad dressing, pile in a salad bowl and garnish with the watercress.

ASPARAGUS AND CORN SALAD

1 bundle cooked asparagus	¼ pint mayonnaise
1 small tin of sweet corn	Lettuce
2 tbsps. chopped capers or 1 tsp. finely grated horseradish	1 hard-boiled egg
	2 tomatoes

Cut the asparagus heads off to a depth of 2 inches, keep a few for garnishing and put the remainder in a basin with the corn and capers. Add the mayonnaise and blend well. Serve in individual salad dishes, garnished with lettuce, sliced egg and tomato.

BANANA MAYONNAISE

2 bananas	1 oz. chopped walnuts
1 lettuce	1 orange
Mayonnaise	

Slice the bananas lengthwise and arrange them on a bed of lettuce, coat with the mayonnaise, and sprinkle the walnuts over. Peel the orange, divide into quarters and arrange these in between the banana slices.

BANANA AND MINT SALAD

Remove the skins from the required number of bananas and cut them in halves lengthwise. Place them on leaves of crisp lettuce, and sprinkle them with lemon juice and some finely chopped mint. Serve with mayonnaise or salad dressing to which have been added some chopped nuts.

BEETROOT AND CAPER SALAD

Peel the cooked beetroot and cut into slices approximately 1 inch thick. Scoop out the centre, and chop the part scooped out, together with a few capers and gherkins. Mix with a little mayonnaise and place the mixture in the beetroot " baskets." Serve on a bed of watercress.

BEETROOT AND CHICORY SALAD

1 beetroot	2–3 cooked potatoes
Chicory	1 lettuce
French dressing	Egg

Cut the beetroot into neat dice. Take the inside stalks of the raw chicory, slice them and add to the beetroot. Mix with the dressing and leave for a few minutes. Put on a dish with the sliced potatoes as a border, garnish with lettuce and sieved yolk and chopped white of egg.

BEETROOT CUPS WITH SALAD

The small, round and ruby-red beetroots are the best to use. Wash them to get rid of the earth, being very careful not to break the skin, cook them in boiling water until tender, then immerse them in cold water and remove the skins. If it is desired to have the beetroots very decorative, they may be cut with a round fluted cutter such as is used for cutting out biscuits, or they may remain round and smooth. Scoop out the centres of the beetroots and place the cups to marinate for ½ hour in a dressing of salad oil and tarragon vinegar. Meantime, prepare a filling in the following manner : chop some of the white inside stalks of crisp celery and mix it with some salad dressing. Drain the beetroot cups and fill them with the mixture. Serve on lettuce leaves sprinkled with a little more of the dressing.

The pulp from the inside of the beetroot may be chopped up and put at the foot of the salad dish.

BIRD'S NEST SALAD

Cut some fine tomatoes in halves and remove the seeds and soft insides. Make some soft cheese into balls, using the butter pats, and flavour them with a little finely powdered sage. Put three balls into each tomato half, arrange the tomatoes on some crisp lettuce leaves, and surround with the delicate leaves of watercress. Serve with mayonnaise or other suitable salad dressing.

BUTTERFLY SALADS

4 large, firm tomatoes
2 hard-boiled eggs
A little mustard and cress
A few celery tops, if available
Salad dressing

Wipe the tomatoes and place them stem side down; with a sharp knife cut the tomato almost in half and then in half again. Slice the eggs thinly and put 4 slices very carefully between the four quarters of the tomato. Arrange in the centre either a little mustard and cress or a few tops from the heart leaves of celery, and place on a small salad plate. Garnish with mustard and cress and hand salad dressing separately.

CABBAGE AND CELERY SLAW

2 cupfuls shredded raw cabbage heart
1 cupful shredded raw celery
1 cupful sliced cooked potatoes
1 tbsp. minced onion
Mayonnaise

Put the prepared vegetables and onion in a basin and add enough mayonnaise to moisten, tossing lightly with a spoon and fork. Pile in a salad bowl and serve.

CABBAGE OR BRUSSELS SPROUTS SALAD

¼ firm cabbage or savoy heart, or 12 large sprouts
2 oz. walnuts
1 sour dessert apple
1 celery heart
1 slice onion
Salad dressing
2 tomatoes

Prepare the cabbage or sprouts and shred very finely. Chop the nuts, the unpeeled apple and the celery, chop the onion very finely and add these ingredients to the raw cabbage. Blend slightly with salad dressing and pile in a salad bowl. Garnish with small sections of tomatoes.

CABBAGE SLAW

1 head of young cabbage
Mayonnaise
Chopped herbs
Chopped onion
Sugar
Vinegar

Wash and shred the cabbage and mix with the mayonnaise, a sprinkling of chopped herbs and chopped onion. Add a pinch of sugar and a little vinegar to sharpen the flavour, if required. Serve very cold.

CALIFORNIA SALAD

Cucumber
Celery
2 apples
2 bananas
4 tomatoes
Salt and pepper
Lemon juice
Salad dressing
Lettuce

Cut the cucumber and celery into dice. Slice the apples, bananas and tomatoes thinly. Sprinkle the tomatoes and cucumber with salt and pepper. Squeeze the juice of half a lemon over the apples and bananas. Mix all the ingredients, mask lightly with salad dressing, and arrange on a bed of lettuce.

CARLTON SALAD

1 ripe pear
Lettuce
6 black or white grapes
1 tomato
Mayonnaise

Peel and core the pear and cut it into wedge-shaped pieces; put these on the lettuce leaves, arrange in a salad bowl, add the skinned grapes and put the skinned tomato in the centre. Mask with mayonnaise.

CARROT SALAD

1 lettuce
6 young carrots
6 spring onions
French dressing
6 radishes

Prepare the lettuce and arrange a few well-curled heart leaves in a flat salad bowl. Shred the rest of the heart finely and put it into a basin. Grate the carrots on to the lettuce, then add the finely sliced onions. Blend all together with a little French dressing and pile on the prepared lettuce. Garnish with "lily" radishes. (To prepare "lily" radishes, see section on Garnishes.)

CAULIFLOWER AND BEAN SALAD

1 young cauliflower
2 cupfuls cooked kidney or haricot beans
2 tsps. finely grated onion
Mayonnaise
1 tsp. finely grated horseradish
Small cress

Wash the cauliflower and divide the head into florets. Rinse well in cold water, and mix with the beans and grated onion. Measure about ½ gill mayonnaise into a bowl and stir in sufficient horseradish to give a sharp flavour. Toss the vegetables in the mayonnaise, pile in a bowl and garnish with small cress.

CAULIFLOWER SALAD

1 cooked cauliflower
1 small onion
1 small cooked beetroot
A few green cabbage leaves (heart)
French dressing

Divide the cauliflower into florets and cut the stalks into neat pieces. Then chop the onion very finely, cut the beetroot into neat dice and shred the cabbage leaves finely. Add these ingredients to the cauliflower, pour the French dressing over and blend lightly with a spoon and fork. Serve in a salad bowl, as an accompaniment to cold meats.

CELERY AND CREAM CHEESE SALAD

Celery
Lettuce
3 oz. cream cheese
2 tbsps. salad oil
1 tbsp. vinegar
Salt and pepper

Wash the celery well and cut it into thin strips about 1 inch long. Arrange some fresh lettuce leaves in a salad bowl, pile the celery in the centre and pour over a cream-cheese dressing made as follows: mix the cream cheese with the salad oil and vinegar and add pepper and salt to taste. If the dressing is too thick to pour evenly, it may be thinned with a little milk.

CHEESE AND TOMATO SALAD

4 large tomatoes
4 heaped tbsps. finely grated cheese
French dressing
Mustard and cress

Wash the tomatoes, dry them well and cut into thin slices with a sharp or saw-edged knife. Arrange the tomatoes in layers in a flat salad dish, sprinkling cheese between the layers. Pour French dressing over and garnish with mustard and cress.

COLD MEAT SALAD

¼ lb. cold meat
1 cooked beetroot
A few spring onions
1 lettuce
Salad dressing
4 tomatoes

Cut the meat and beetroot into neat dice and add the thinly sliced onions. Arrange the best leaves of the lettuce in a salad bowl, shred the rest and add to the meat. Blend all lightly together with salad dressing and pile in the salad bowl. Decorate with the thinly sliced tomatoes.

CRAB AND TOMATO SALAD

4 cooked new potatoes
1 fresh crab or small tin of crab
Mayonnaise
½ lb. small, firm tomatoes
Lettuce and watercress

Dice the potatoes, add the crab meat and blend with the mayonnaise. Slice the tomatoes thinly, put the lettuce and watercress in a salad bowl, add the tomatoes, then pile the crab and potatoes on the top.

EGG SALAD

4 hard-boiled eggs
3 firm tomatoes of medium size
1 small shallot
Tarragon
A small bunch of mustard and cress
French dressing

Cut the hard-boiled eggs in thin slices. 60
Remove the skin from the tomatoes and slice them. Chop the shallot and tarragon as finely as possible; wash and dry the mustard and cress, and arrange neatly in a shallow salad bowl. Put the egg and tomato slices in alternate layers, sprinkling each layer with the chopped shallot and tarragon. Pour over some French dressing.

EGG AND POTATO SALAD

2 potatoes, boiled in their skins
Salad dressing
1 small raw beetroot
1 small onion
2 hard-boiled eggs
Mustard and cress
6 pickled damsons

Peel the potatoes and cut them into neat dice, add a little salad dressing and mix lightly. Grate the beetroot on a suet grater and blend with a little salad dressing. Chop the onion finely and add half to the potato and half to the beetroot. Select a shallow salad bowl, pile the potatoes in the centre and cover with the beetroot, forming a smooth mound. Shell the eggs, cut in half lengthwise, remove and reserve the yolks. Now cut each half-white into four lengthwise, select the best-shaped pieces and arrange them on the top of the beetroot to resemble a flower. Sieve the yolks and put some in the centre of the "petals." Garnish with mustard and cress and place the damsons around the dish.

EGG AND TOMATO SALAD

3 tomatoes
3 eggs, hard-boiled
1 large gherkin
Salt and pepper
Cayenne pepper
2 tbsps. cream cheese
Mayonnaise
Lettuce

Cut the tomatoes in half, scoop out the centre of each and halve the eggs. Blend the finely chopped egg yolks and gherkin, seasoning and cream cheese. Stuff the whites of egg and tomatoes with this filling, coat with mayonnaise and serve on a bed of lettuce.

FISH SALAD

Lettuce
1 lb. cold cooked fish
Mayonnaise
Capers
2 tomatoes
2 hard-boiled eggs
4 anchovies

Prepare the lettuce and make a bed of it in a flat dish. Divide the fish into neat pieces, removing any skin or bone, and arrange it neatly on the lettuce. Coat each piece with thick mayonnaise and garnish with capers. Cut the tomatoes and hard-boiled eggs in half, cutting a little off each half egg so that it will stand upright; put these alternately around the dish. Bone the anchovies, cut them in half, then roll up and put one on each piece of egg and tomato.

GRAPEFRUIT BASKET SALAD

1 small bunch of mustard and cress
2 grapefruits
2 bananas
Salad dressing

Prepare the mustard and cress, draining well, and reserve a little for garnishing, cut off the stalks of the rest and chop. Cut the grapefruit in half, scoop out the fruit and cut it into neat pieces, then wipe the skins thoroughly. Add the thinly sliced bananas and chopped cress to the fruit. Blend with a little salad dressing and fill the grapefruit halves with this mixture. Garnish with the mustard and cress.

GRAPEFRUIT AND SHRIMP SALAD

Lettuce
1 grapefruit
½ a cucumber
1 pint picked shrimps
French dressing

Prepare the lettuce and arrange a neat bed of the heart leaves in a shallow salad bowl. Peel the grapefruit, remove the pith, and divide it into sections; cut each section into three and put the juice and grapefruit into a basin. Peel the cucumber, cut it into small dice and add it and the shrimps to the grapefruit. Pour on French dressing and mix lightly with a spoon and fork. Pile the mixture on the lettuce leaves and garnish with a few of the shrimp heads if they are available.

GREEN SALADS

Use a combination of two or more green salad plants, such as lettuce, cress, watercress, endive, chicory, spinach, sorrel and the cabbage family. Wash the salad plants quickly in fresh, cold water. If necessary, place in a covered bowl and crisp up in a refrigerator or cold larder. Meanwhile, take a large bowl and make some French dressing, adding a little finely chopped onion or crushed garlic. Dry the salad plants very thoroughly by shaking in a salad basket or clean tea towel. Add to the prepared dressing and toss lightly with two spoons, so as to coat the leaves without bruising them. Sprinkle, if liked, with a little chopped parsley or other herbs.

HARICOT BEAN SALAD

1–2 onions
1 small carrot
Mayonnaise
1 tbsp. chopped parsley
2 cupfuls cooked haricot beans
Watercress or endive to garnish

Prepare the onion and carrot and mince or grate. Measure about ½ gill mayonnaise into a bowl and stir in the onion to flavour. Toss the haricot beans in the mayonnaise, and sprinkle in the carrot and chopped parsley. Pile in a bowl and garnish with watercress or endive.

ITALIAN SALADS

Use individual salad plates for this.

Place on a few crisp lettuce leaves a round slice of a sweet orange from which the pith has been carefully removed. In the centre of it place a maraschino cherry, and around the slice place a few asparagus tips. Pour a little French dressing over the whole.

LEMON SALAD

1 orange
2 lemons
2 tbsps. caster sugar
1 tsp. chopped tarragon
French dressing
Lettuce

Dip the fruit into boiling water, peel it, removing the pith, and slice thinly. Arrange in a salad dish in layers, sprinkling sugar and tarragon between the layers. Pour the dressing over and garnish with small, crisp lettuce leaves.

LETTUCE AND TOMATO SALAD

Firm even-sized tomatoes
Shallot
Small cabbage lettuce
Tarragon
Salad dressing

Skin the tomatoes and cut them into slices. Rub the cut shallot round the inside of the salad bowl. Arrange the lettuce (retaining the heart for garnish) and the tomatoes in layers, adding a sprinkling of chopped tarragon on each layer. Top the salad with the heart of the lettuce and arrange a few slices of tomato around. Hand salad dressing separately.

LOBSTER MAYONNAISE

1 medium-sized lobster
1 hard-boiled egg
2 lettuces
¼ pint mayonnaise

Remove the meat from the lobster, retaining any coral for garnish. Flake the flesh with a fork, or divide into neat pieces. Slice the hard-boiled egg and prepare the lettuces. Arrange some of the lettuce in a salad bowl. Mix the lobster meat with the mayonnaise sauce and the remainder of the lettuce, torn into small pieces. Pile lightly on the lettuce leaves in the bowl, garnish with slices of hard-boiled egg, the lettuce hearts, and head and claws of the lobster and the coral.

LOBSTER AND CUCUMBER SALAD

½ pint cleared and well-jellied white stock
1 tsp. vinegar
Salt and pepper
1 small tin peas or 2 cupfuls cooked peas
2 oz. capers (or pickled nasturtium seeds)
½ a small cucumber
1 lobster
1 lettuce

Line a border mould with jellied stock flavoured with vinegar, salt and pepper (in hot weather it will generally be found necessary to add a little gelatine), and then add layers of peas, capers and diced cucumber, with jellied stock between the layers. When set, turn out. Fill the centre with cooked lobster. Decorate with lettuce and some of the cucumber.

LUNCHEON SALAD

1 lb. cooked potatoes
2 spring onions
½ tsp. chopped parsley
Salad dressing
1 head of lettuce
¼ lb. cooked tongue
Endive
½ lb. tomatoes
2 hard-boiled eggs
A few anchovies

Cut the potatoes into neat dice, add the thinly sliced onions and parsley and toss lightly in salad dressing. Pile in the centre of the dish and arrange a bed of lettuce around. Roll the thinly cut tongue into cornet shapes, put a few sprigs of endive in each and place neatly at even intervals around the dish. Halve the tomatoes and place a slice of hard-boiled egg and then a curled anchovy on each. Arrange between the cornets of tongue.

MACARONI SALAD

Mince finely 1 small onion and 1 green pepper, if procurable. Cut into dice about ½ a small cucumber, or prepare 1 cupful of finely sliced white celery. Mix these together, and add a large cupful of cooked macaroni cut into small pieces. Prepare 2–3 tbsps. mayonnaise or other salad dressing, seasoning it to taste. Mix this lightly with the other ingredients, being careful not to break the macaroni. Serve the salad with a surround of crisp lettuce leaves, or a little watercress. Small pieces of tomatoes may also be used as a garnish; they make a pretty contrast in colour.

MINT AND ONION SALAD

1 bunch spring onions
1 doz. mint leaves
1 tbsp. caster sugar
Vinegar

Slice the onions thinly and chop the mint finely. Arrange in layers in a small glass dish, sprinkling sugar between the layers. Cover with vinegar and let stand for ½ hour before serving. This is especially delicious with cold lamb.

MUSHROOM SALAD

½ lb. cooked mushrooms
French dressing
Watercress
2 tomatoes

Cut up the mushrooms into neat pieces, sprinkle liberally with French dressing and soak for half an hour. Arrange a bed of watercress in a salad bowl, lift the mushrooms on to it and pour over any remaining liquor. Garnish with thinly sliced tomatoes.

ORANGE SALAD

2 oranges
Tarragon and chervil
1 tbsp. salad oil
1 dessertsp. vinegar
1 tsp. lemon juice

Choose sweet oranges and peel them, removing all the white pith. Then cut the oranges in thin slices, removing the seeds. Put the pieces in a salad dish and sprinkle with a little chopped tarragon and chervil if obtainable. Mix the oil, vinegar and lemon juice, add to the salad and let it stand for a short time.

ORANGE AND MINT SALAD

Endive
2 oranges
1 dessertsp. caster sugar
1 tbsp. finely chopped mint
French dressing

Prepare the endive and drain well. Peel the oranges, removing the pith, and cut into thin slices. Put the orange in layers in a salad bowl, sprinkling each layer with sugar and mint. Pour dressing over and garnish with endive.

PEPPER SALAD

Pickled red and green peppers make a good piquant salad. To pickle them, wash and dry them, but leave the stalks on, then put them in a jar and fill this up with vinegar; put a saucer on the top to prevent the peppers floating, and leave for a fortnight.

To make the salad, take out an equal quantity of green and red peppers, cut off the stalks, slit and remove the seeds. Wash them in warm water and cut into strips. Season with salt, pour 2 tbsps. olive oil over and 1 tbsp. chopped parsley. Mix well and arrange on a plate.

POTATO SALAD—I

1 lb. cooked potatoes	1 tbsp. mayonnaise
Salt and pepper	1 tbsp. white vinegar
2 tbsps. cooked celery	Parsley

Cut the potatoes into dice or small slices, place in a basin with the salt, pepper and chopped celery. Mix the mayonnaise and vinegar together and pour over, mixing all thoroughly together. Pile up in a salad bowl and decorate with chopped parsley.

POTATO SALAD—II

3 large cooked potatoes (very firm)	Thick salad cream
	Finely chopped parsley
2 spring onions	Watercress

Cut the potatoes into neat dice, slice the white part of the onion finely and add it to the potatoes. Blend the vegetables with a thick salad cream, pile lightly on a dish, sprinkle with parsley and garnish with watercress.

RAISIN AND NUT SALAD

Watercress	2 oz. walnuts
2 sharp dessert apples	Salad dressing
4 oz. seeded raisins	

Wash and pick the watercress and leave it draining whilst the rest of the ingredients are being prepared. Wipe the apples; do not peel them, but grate them on a clean suet grater into a basin. Add the chopped raisins and nuts and a little salad dressing and mix lightly. Pile on individual glass plates and garnish with sprigs of watercress.

RAVIGOTE SALAD

1 head of lettuce	French dressing
4 large tomatoes	1 teacupful diced celery
¼ lb. ham	1 teacupful tinned or cooked peas
¼ lb. tongue	

Prepare the lettuce and reserve the best pieces for garnishing the salad, breaking up the rest of the leaves with the fingers. Slice the tomatoes and cut them into small pieces; cut the ham and tongue into neat dice. Blend all the ingredients lightly with French dressing, using a fork and spoon for this purpose. Line the salad bowl with lettuce and arrange the salad mixture in it.

RUSSIAN SALAD

Carrots	Capers
Turnips	Parsley
Oil and vinegar	¼ pint cooked green peas
½ pint thick mayonnaise	
Cayenne, salt and pepper	Aspic jelly
6 anchovies (filleted)	12 prawns
A few slices of smoked salmon (optional)	A few pickled walnuts
	Hard-boiled egg
Gherkins	

Cut the carrots and turnips into fancy shapes and cook separately in boiling salted water. When cold mix with a little oil, vinegar and mayonnaise. Season with cayenne, salt and pepper. Cut the anchovies, salmon and gherkins into dice, then add a few capers and chopped parsley, together with the vegetables. Stir in sufficient aspic jelly to bind. Prepare a border mould of aspic jelly garnished with prawns, pickled walnuts, hard-boiled egg, etc. Mask a medium-sized *bombe* mould with aspic and garnish with fancy shapes of salmon, gherkins and prawns. Fill up the centre with alternate layers of the salad mixture and aspic jelly. When set turn out and place the *bombe* shape in the border mould.

RUSSIAN SALAD (ECONOMICAL)

Cooked mixed vegetables, such as carrots, peas, beans, potatoes, asparagus, turnips, etc.	2 anchovies
	A little cold fish
	2–3 tbsps. mayonnaise
A few gherkins, capers and olives	Aspic jelly (if available) to garnish

Cut the vegetables into small dice or rounds, chop the gherkins, capers and olives, fillet and shred the anchovies and flake the cooked fish. Mix all the ingredients with some mayonnaise, and serve in small individual dishes or in a large bowl. If aspic jelly is available, cut into fancy shapes or chop and use for garnishing.

SALAD IN ASPIC

½ pint aspic jelly	¼ lb. carrots, cooked
½ lb. new potatoes, cooked	¼ small cauliflower, cooked
¼ lb. shelled green peas, cooked	1 lettuce
3 tbsps. mayonnaise	Mustard and cress

Prepare the aspic jelly as described in the Jellies chapter. Set a thin layer in the bottom of some small dariole moulds, and then place a layer of potatoes, cut in small circles. Cover this with aspic and allow to set. Add a layer of peas. Cover with aspic and allow to set as before. Mix 3 tbsps. mayonnaise with 3 tbsps. aspic and add the remainder of vegetables, cut into small dice. Fill up the moulds with this, allow to set, turn out and arrange on a bed of lettuce. Garnish with mustard and cress.

SALAD VIRGILE

Take 2 teacupfuls of boiled rice, dry as for curry, add to it 1 tbsp. purée of tomatoes, and 6–8 tbsps. cooked beef cut in thin, fine shreds, also 1 tbsp. finely chopped onion. Season with French salad dressing to which a little mustard has been added. Mix well, arrange neatly in a salad dish, and surround with a border of chopped hard-boiled egg, and sprinkle with parsley. This makes a good luncheon salad.

Thin slices of tomato may be used instead of the purée.

SALMON MOULDED SALAD

1 pint aspic jelly	4 oz. peas, cooked
1 hard-boiled egg	Lettuce
1 small tin salmon	Salad dressing

Prepare the jelly and pour sufficient into a loaf-shaped mould to cover the bottom. When this has set, decorate with slices of hard-boiled egg, cover with jelly and leave to set. Put in a layer of salmon and jelly, leave to set, then a layer of peas and jelly. Repeat until all are used. When set, turn out and serve on a bed of lettuce and hand salad dressing separately.

SHRIMP SALAD

3 tbsps. mayonnaise	Sliced cucumber
1 pint shrimps, picked	Tomato
Shredded lettuce	

Stir the mayonnaise into the shrimps, pile the mixture in a salad bowl, garnish with lettuce, cucumber and sliced tomato.

SARDINE SALAD

Put lettuce or endive and chopped onions in a salad bowl and place sardines on top of the pile. If olives stuffed with pimentos can be obtained, one may be placed on each of the sardines. Serve with French dressing.

3

SPINACH SALAD—I

6 tbsps. cooked spinach	Lettuce
Mayonnaise	4 olives
A little cinnamon	2 hard-boiled eggs

Combine the spinach, mayonnaise and cinnamon, pile on crisp lettuce leaves, garnish with olives and slices of hard-boiled eggs.

SPINACH SALAD—II

¼ lb. spinach	Thin salad dressing
2 spring onions	1 small beetroot

Wash the spinach very thoroughly, dry well, then strip the leaves from the stalks and veins. Cut it up into thin shreds with a sharp knife; add the thinly sliced onions and blend with a salad dressing. Put into a salad bowl and garnish with the beetroot, cut into small rounds.

STUFFED APPLE SALAD

Lettuce	Salt and pepper
4 dessert apples	2 tbsps. lemon juice
2 tbsps. seeded raisins	1 tbsp. cream or condensed milk
2 tbsps. chopped hazelnuts	

Prepare the lettuce and arrange the heart
leaves on individual dishes. Select rosy apples 64
if possible, wash and wipe them thoroughly, then remove the core with a corer. Cut the raisins into four, add them to the hazelnuts and season lightly. Stir the lemon juice gradually into the cream or milk and add this dressing to the nuts and raisins. Mix well and stuff the apples with the mixture. Put an apple on each bed of lettuce.

STUFFED CELERY

Celery heart	Salt and pepper
Cream cheese	Coralline pepper

Split the celery heart in half lengthwise, spread thickly with seasoned cream cheese and garnish with coralline pepper. If time permits, the tender stalks can be filled individually with the cheese and served as cocktail snacks.

STUFFED TOMATO SALAD—I

Cut slices from the top of as many tomatoes as are required. Remove pulp and invert tomatoes to drain. Make a mixture of the following ingredients: cucumber, cut in cubes, and tomato pulp, previously drained and then cut in pieces, capers, peas and chopped pickles. Mix with salad dressing and pile into the tomato cups. Serve on lettuce leaves.

STUFFED TOMATO SALAD—II

8 firm tomatoes (about 1 lb.)	1 tbsp. thick mayonnaise
2 hard-boiled eggs	Lettuce
4 tbsps. cooked peas	

Cut a slice from the top of the tomatoes, remove the pulp and turn upside down to drain. Chop one of the eggs and mix with peas and mayonnaise. Pile into the tomatoes and place them on lettuce leaves; garnish with the other egg, which should be cut into long, wedge-shaped slices.

SUMMER VEGETABLE SALAD

Cooked new potatoes	Salad dressing
Cooked French beans	Lettuce
Cooked asparagus tips, if available	Mustard and cress

Dice the potatoes and cut the beans into small pieces. Blend all the ingredients with salad dressing, and serve on a bed of lettuce, garnished with mustard and cress.

"TOADSTOOL" SALAD

5 hard-boiled eggs	Mustard and cress
½ oz. melted butter	3 very small red tomatoes
Seasoning	
5 olives	Thick mayonnaise

Shell the eggs and cut off a small slice from one end so that they will stand up. Scoop out the yolks carefully, sieve them, add the butter and seasoning. Stone the olives and fill them with the yolk mixture, cover the outside with the rest of the mixture and stuff the eggs with them. Arrange the eggs on a bed of mustard and cress, cut the tomatoes in half and scoop out the pulp, put a half on each egg to resemble a toadstool and "spot" with a skewer dipped in mayonnaise

TOMATO SALAD

4 tomatoes	2 tbsps. salad oil
A small piece of onion	1 dessertsp. vinegar
½ an apple	1 tbsp. chopped parsley, if desired
Salt and pepper	

65 Remove the stalks from the tomatoes; if desired, the skin also may be removed by immersing in boiling water. Cut the tomatoes in slices, arrange neatly in a shallow dish, and sprinkle on the chopped onion, chopped apple, salt and pepper. Mix the oil and vinegar, and pour over the salad. Decorate with the chopped parsley.

TOMATO ROSETTE SALAD

Place firm tomatoes in boiling water for ½ minute, cool in cold water, scoop out the stem end and remove the skin. Cut into eighths, not quite through to the bottom, so that when placed on a lettuce leaf each tomato will fall open like a flower. Moisten some cream cheese with salad dressing and push through a wire strainer into the centre of the tomato, for stamens.

VEGETABLE MAYONNAISE

½ a cooked cauliflower	¼ pint cooked haricot beans
4 gherkins	
4 cooked potatoes	2 hard-boiled eggs
2 cooked carrots	Salad cream or mayonnaise
2 cooked beetroots	
Celery	Watercress

Divide the cauliflower into small heads. Cut the gherkins and vegetables into neat dice, and slice the eggs. Bind all lightly with a little salad cream or mayonnaise. Pile in a salad bowl and garnish with watercress.

When time permits, the salad can be garnished attractively as follows: cut out thin rounds of carrot, potato and beetroot, using fluted cutters of varying sizes, and cut circles of gherkins, using a very small cutter. These rounds, together with the sliced egg, can be arranged neatly on the piled salad, each ring of garnish consisting of rounds decreasing in size.

WALDORF SALAD

Put a few crisp lettuce leaves on a plate and on them place thin slices of a sweet apple. If preferred, the apple can be cut into small dice. Over this sprinkle some chopped nuts, and serve with French dressing.

WELLINGTON SALAD

Place a slice of tinned pineapple on a few lettuce leaves, and over this sprinkle some chopped celery. Serve with mayonnaise. Endive, in place of lettuce, gives this salad a very pleasant taste.

WINTER SALAD

2 apples	¼ of an onion
A heart of celery	French salad dressing
¼ lb. cooked beetroot	Chopped parsley

Cut the apple, celery and beetroot into very small dice, add the chopped onion and toss in the French salad dressing. Strain off any salad dressing that has not been absorbed. Pile up the salad in a small crystal bowl and sprinkle a little chopped parsley on top.

SALAD DRESSINGS

The success of a salad dressing depends very much on the quality of the ingredients. Use pure, fresh olive oil, bright and golden in colour and delicate in taste, for an inferior oil can spoil the flavour of the whole salad. When buying oil for salad dressing, choose for preference a brand clearly marked "Olive Oil"; those marked "Salad Oil" may be of any composition, but usually consist of cotton seed or other such oils. While these are perfectly wholesome and can be used effectively for making dressings, naturally the flavour is not so good as that of pure olive oil. When oil is subjected to warmth and light it tends to go rancid; for this reason, it is advisable to buy it a small quantity at a time and store it in a cool, dark place. Oil is sometimes packed and sold in tins and, of course, this method of packing protects it from the light.

Use the finest malt vinegar, mild in flavour, or better still, a good French wine vinegar. Avoid crude or strongly flavoured brands, which are likely to make the dressing less palatable. Lemon juice can be used in place of some or all of the vinegar if desired, and is preferred by some people. Herb-flavoured vinegars, such as tarragon vinegar, may be included, but only in small quantities, otherwise the flavour of the herb may predominate.

Seasonings, such as salt and peppers, should be measured carefully; their presence should not be accentuated in the finished dressing.

There are many recipes for salad dressings, but strictly speaking, only two standard ones—French dressing and mayonnaise.

The French dressing, consisting of oil and vinegar with seasoning, is the simplest of all, and is usually preferred by the true connoisseur. It may be varied by adding flavouring ingredients such as chopped chives or herbs, or piquant ingredients such as relish or chopped pickles, olives and so on.

Mayonnaise is essentially an emulsion of oil and raw egg yolk, with seasonings and vinegar to give piquancy. The oil must be added very gradually, otherwise it is liable to separate out. This dressing may be made in sufficient quantities to last for a few days, but it should not be kept longer than this. Store it in bottles with a cork or glass stopper, and keep it in a cool, dark place, or better still, in a refrigerator.

There are other fancy varieties of salad dressings, which may include such ingredients as curry powder, chutney, tomato ketchup, grated horseradish, whipped white of egg and so on, and some of which, containing flour, require to be boiled: the following recipes offer a good variety to choose from. Generally speaking, these fancy salad dressings should be made as required and used up within 2–3 days, unless otherwise stated in the recipe.

SIMPLE DRESSINGS

FRENCH SALAD DRESSING

¼ tsp. salt
⅛ tsp. pepper
¼ tsp. mustard
A pinch of sugar
1 tbsp. vinegar
2 tbsps. olive or salad oil

Put the salt, pepper, mustard and sugar in a bowl, add the vinegar, and mix well. Beat in the oil with a fork, and when it thickens use at once. The oil separates out on standing, so if it is necessary to mix the ingredients beforehand, beat up again immediately before use. A good plan is to mix the dressing in a salad-cream bottle, then shake up vigorously just before serving.

A little tarragon vinegar is sometimes added. The proportion of oil to vinegar varies with individual taste; the French would use rather a larger quantity of oil than we should. Use the vinegar sparingly.

VARIATIONS OF FRENCH SALAD DRESSING

With Chives

Mix 2 tbsps. French dressing with 1 tbsp. chopped chives. Good with vegetable salads.

With Herbs

Mix 2 tbsps. French dressing with 1 tbsp. chopped parsley, ½ tsp. powdered marjoram, and a pinch of powdered thyme. Good with vegetable or meat salads.

With Pickles

Mix 2 tbsps. French dressing with 2 tbsps. pickle relish, or 2 tbsps. chopped dill pickle. Good with vegetable, meat or fish salads.

With Olives

Mix 2 tbsps. French dressing with a few sliced stuffed olives or a few chopped ripe olives. Good with vegetables, fruit, or fish salads.

FRENCH DRESSING WITH LEMON

2–3 tbsps. olive oil
1 tbsp. lemon juice
Pepper and salt

Add the oil gradually to the condiments, and when salt is dissolved, pour in the lemon juice.

HONEY DRESSING

1 tbsp. olive oil
1½ tsps. lemon juice
1 tsp. clear honey

Put all the ingredients into a basin, whisk well and use at once—or whisk before serving.

VINAIGRETTE DRESSING

Add a little chopped parsley, chopped gherkin or capers and chives to a French dressing.

MAYONNAISE DRESSINGS

MAYONNAISE

2 egg yolks
½ tsp. made mustard
Pepper and salt to season
¼ pint (approx.) olive oil
1 dessertsp. white vinegar or strained lemon juice
1 tsp. tarragon vinegar
1 tsp. chilli vinegar

Put the egg yolks into a basin with the mustard, pepper and salt. Mix thoroughly, then add the oil, drop by drop, stirring hard with a wooden spoon or a whisk the whole time, until the sauce is thick and smooth. Add the vinegars gradually and mix thoroughly. If liked, lemon juice may be used instead of the vinegars or it may replace the white vinegar only.

Mayonnaise Dressing

Note : To keep the basin firmly in position whilst making the sauce, twist a damp cloth tightly round the bottom. This prevents the basin from slipping on the table. In order that the oil may be added one drop at a time, put in the bottle-neck a cork from which a small wedge has been cut. Should the sauce curdle during the process of making, put another egg yolk into a basin and add the curdled sauce very gradually in the same way as the oil is added to the original egg yolks.

VARIATIONS OF MAYONNAISE

Caper Mayonnaise

Mix 2 tbsps. mayonnaise with 1 tsp. capers, 1 tsp. chopped pimento and ½ tsp. tarragon vinegar. This is good with fish and vegetable salads.

Cream Mayonnaise

Mix 2 tbsps. mayonnaise and ¼ pint light or heavy whipped cream. Good with salads containing fruit.

Cucumber Mayonnaise

Mix 2 tbsps. mayonnaise with ½ a small cucumber, which has been pared, chopped and drained. Good with fish salads, particularly those which are made with crab, lobster and salmon.

Herb Mayonnaise

Mix 2 tbsps. mayonnaise with 2 tsps. chopped chives and 1 tbsp. chopped parsley. Good with meat or fish salads.

FOAMY MAYONNAISE

2 egg yolks
Salt and pepper
Salad oil (about ¼ pint)
2 small tbsps. lemon juice
1 egg white

Cream the yolks and seasonings and add the oil, drop by drop, stirring hard all the time until the mayonnaise is thick and smooth. Stir in the lemon juice. Put in a cool place until required, and just before serving, fold in the stiffly whisked egg white.

PIQUANTE DRESSING

¼ pint thick mayonnaise
Paprika pepper
1 tbsp. tomato ketchup
1 tbsp. chopped olives

Make the mayonnaise, add a dash of paprika pepper, the ketchup and olives, and mix well.

COOKED SALAD DRESSINGS

COOKED SALAD DRESSING

4 egg yolks
1 tsp. salt
1 tsp. sugar
¼ pint milk
¼ pint salad oil
4–5 tbsps. vinegar

Beat the yolks, salt and sugar together, until creamy. Add the milk and oil gradually, stirring well all the time. Lastly, add the vinegar gradually. Cook in a double pan, stirring constantly until thick. Cool and bottle. Shake well before using.

BOILED SALAD DRESSING—I

1 oz. flour
1 tbsp. sugar
2 tsps. dry mustard
1 tbsp. salt
¼ pint milk
2 eggs
2 oz. butter
¼ pint vinegar
¼ pint sour cream or salad oil

Mix all the dry ingredients and blend with the milk. Bring to the boil, stirring continuously, and boil for 5 minutes. Cool a little, add the beaten eggs and butter, beat well and cook until thick, but do not boil. Now add the vinegar gradually, beat well, then stir in the cream or oil, and bottle. Shake well before using.

BOILED SALAD DRESSING—II

1 oz. butter
1 oz. flour
½ pint milk
1 egg
2–3 tbsps. malt vinegar
1–2 tbsps. tarragon vinegar (optional)
Salt, pepper, sugar and mustard
1–2 tbsps. tomato purée (optional)

Melt the butter and add the flour to make a roux. Stir in the milk by degrees, bring to the boil and cook for 2 minutes, stirring continuously. Remove from the heat and cool slightly. Add the beaten egg and cook for a further few minutes, taking care not to curdle the egg. Add the vinegars and salt, pepper, sugar and mustard, to taste. Lastly, add a little tomato purée, if liked, and allow to cool, beating occasionally.

BOILED SALAD DRESSING—III

1 tbsp. flour	½ tsp. salt
Cayenne pepper	¼ pint milk
1½ tbsps. sugar	2 egg yolks
2 tsps. mustard	4 tbsps. vinegar

Mix the dry ingredients to a smooth cream with a little of the cold milk. Heat the remainder of the milk and when boiling, stir it in, then allow to boil, stirring. Cook slightly, then add the beaten egg yolk, and heat sufficiently to thicken without boiling. When cold, stir in the vinegar.

Note : This dressing may be kept for a short time if ¼ pint water is used instead of the milk. A little whipped cream may be stirred in before serving.

MOCK MAYONNAISE DRESSING

4 eggs	Salt and pepper
3 tbsps. milk	Mustard
⅛ pint vinegar	Sugar

Beat the eggs well, then mix in the milk and the vinegar. Season well with salt, pepper, mustard and sugar. Cook over gentle heat until thick, stirring frequently. Allow to cool, adding more seasoning, if necessary.

Note : This mayonnaise will keep for several weeks. Bottle and store in a cool place.

ONE-EGG SALAD DRESSING

½ oz. sugar	1 egg
½ tsp. made mustard	¼ pint milk
½ tsp. salt	¾ oz. butter
¼ tsp. pepper	2 tbsps. vinegar

Mix the sugar, mustard, salt and pepper with the beaten egg, and add the milk. Cook over gentle heat until the dressing thickens, add the butter and the vinegar. Cool and bottle.

MISCELLANEOUS SALAD DRESSINGS

ASPIC DRESSING

1 tsp. castor sugar	3 tbsps. vinegar (preferably ½ tarragon, ½ white)
Salt and pepper	
½ tsp. dry mustard	
2 hard-boiled eggs	2 tbsps. cream
¼ pint olive oil	½ pint aspic jelly

Put the sugar, seasonings and egg yolks in a mortar, pound well, and add the oil drop by drop, beating well, then stir in the vinegar and cream. Dissolve the jelly, and when it is cold and at the point of setting, stir in the prepared dressing and use at once for coating vegetable salads, etc.

BLOATER PASTE DRESSING

Work together 1 tsp. bloater paste, ¼ tsp. mustard, a pinch of salt and pepper, and ¼ tsp. paprika. Add a few drops of piquant sauce, 3 tbsps. salad oil and 1 tbsp. vinegar. Mix thoroughly, then add 1 tbsp. capers, ½ tsp. chopped chives and ½ tsp. chopped parsley. Pour over the salad. A salad finished with this dressing is excellent with cold fish.

CREAM DRESSING

Salt and cayenne	2 tbsps. vinegar
¼ pint cream	

Add seasoning to cream and whip it until thick. Then add vinegar (French wine, for preference) very gradually. Chill and use as required.

HORSERADISH DRESSING

½ cupful sour cream	1 tsp. lemon juice
3 tbsps. grated horseradish	1 tsp. vinegar
	Salt and cayenne
A pinch of sugar	

Whip the cream until thick and add the horseradish, which has been carefully cleaned and then grated. Add sugar, lemon juice and vinegar. Season to taste. This is very good served with roast beef.

LEMON PEANUT DRESSING

4 tbsps. peanut butter	½ tsp. sugar
2 tbsps. milk	¼ tsp. paprika
2 tbsps. lemon juice	¼ tsp. salt
¾ tsp. grated horseradish	

Cream the peanut butter and add the milk, a little at a time, together with the other ingredients. Serve with salad.

LOBSTER SALAD DRESSING

3 hard-boiled egg yolks	1 tsp. anchovy essence
1 tbsp. made mustard	¼ pint vinegar
2 tsps. salt	3 dessertsps. salad oil
4 dessertsps. mushroom ketchup	

Sieve or pound the egg yolks and add the mustard and salt. Stir in the ketchup, anchovy essence and vinegar. Beat well, then add the oil drop by drop, stirring all the time, and bottle. Shake before using.

POTATO DRESSING

1 baked potato	1 tsp. sugar
1 tsp. salt	2 tbsps. vinegar
2 tsps. mustard	4 tbsps. oil

Remove the mealy part from a baked potato and rub it through a sieve. Add salt, mustard and sugar, then half the vinegar. Mix well, add the oil slowly, and then the rest of the vinegar. This makes a delicious creamy sauce if properly prepared.

CONDENSED MILK SALAD DRESSING

1 egg	¼ pint sweetened or unsweetened condensed milk
1 tsp. made mustard	
½ tsp. salt	
¼ pint vinegar	

Beat the egg and seasoning very thoroughly, add the vinegar by degrees and beat well; lastly, stir in the milk, using the kind desired, according to taste. Correct the seasoning if necessary, and use at once, or keep in a stoppered bottle until required.

SAVOURY SALAD DRESSING

4 tbsps. salad oil	1½ tbsps. tomato ketchup
1 tbsp. tarragon vinegar	Black pepper and salt
2 tsps. piquant sauce	A pinch of cayenne

Mix together the first four ingredients, and then season to taste. Beat well together until thoroughly blended, and serve at once on a green salad.

SOUR CREAM DRESSING

¼ pint thick sour cream	½ tsp. sugar
2 tbsps. white vinegar	1 tsp. salt
2 tbsps. chopped onion	A little pepper

Mix all the ingredients thoroughly.

SOUR MILK DRESSING

A simple dressing, which is practical in the summer-time, is made from sour milk. Allow the milk to become solid, then beat up with salt, pepper and sugar to taste. It is particularly good with green salads.

SPANISH SALAD DRESSING

2 tsps. caster sugar	1 tbsp. cold water
1 tsp. salt	1 tsp. piquant sauce
1 tsp. made mustard	1 tbsp. tomato ketchup
A pinch of paprika	5 tbsps. salad oil
1 tbsp. lemon juice	

Mix together in a basin the sugar, salt, mustard and paprika. Moisten these with the other ingredients, beat thoroughly, and serve on any plain salad.

WHITE SALAD CREAM

¼ pint cream	2 tsps. lemon juice
2 tbsps. tarragon vinegar	2 egg whites

Beat the cream until fairly stiff, then stir in the vinegar gradually. Season to taste, add lemon juice, fold in stiffly beaten egg whites

EGG COOKERY

Eggs are valuable, not only for their excellent protein but also because they contribute useful minerals, especially iron, and vitamins A, B_1 and B_2. The egg yolk also contains fat. When possible, serve 4–5 eggs per person a week in your family meals, either as egg dishes or in custards, puddings, cakes and so on.

Buying Eggs

The peak of egg production is in the spring and early summer. At this time, when they are most cheap and plentiful, it is advisable to preserve some of them for the winter months. For directions for preserving eggs see page 491. The shell colour of eggs varies with the breed of chicken and does not affect the flavour or nutritional value of the contents. In fact, the appearance of eggs is of little guidance when purchasing them, so buy them from a reliable dealer to be sure of their quality and freshness.

To Test for Freshness of Eggs

There is always a small air space inside the egg, and this increases as the egg ages. The fresher the egg, therefore, the fuller it is. There are two ways of testing this. One is to hold the egg vertically between your eye and a strong light. You can then see if there is a void at the top end and how great it is. The other way is to place the egg in a tumbler of cold water. It lies flat if fresh and full. If it tilts slightly, it is probably not fresh enough to boil but will fry or scramble satisfactorily. If it floats it is very likely to be quite bad.

Storing Eggs

Eggs deteriorate very rapidly. They should be kept in a cool, airy place (preferably not in a refrigerator). If they are shop bought, they are best used immediately, as there is every likelihood that they are several days old. When using eggs that have been stored in a refrigerator, leave them at room temperature a short while before using, or run warm water over them.

Ducks' Eggs

Ducks' eggs are larger and richer than hens' eggs. To ensure that they are wholesome, they should be very thoroughly cooked, at least 10 minutes being allowed for boiling. They can be included in cakes (except sponge mixtures) and puddings, but they should not be used for making meringues or any sweet which is cooked for only a short time or at a low temperature, nor should they be preserved or stored.

Turkey and Goose Eggs

Turkey eggs are as delicate in flavour as hens' eggs, but are, of course, larger. They can be cooked by any of the methods given for hens' eggs and can be used for all cakes and puddings. Longer time should be allowed for boiling—to soft-boil, allow about 7 minutes. Goose eggs can be used similarly.

Gull, Plover, Pheasant and Guinea Fowl Eggs

These are usually served hard-boiled. Cook for 10–15 minutes.

Using Eggs in Cookery

Eggs are used in cookery for three chief purposes: for emulsifying, for thickening and binding, and for raising or "foaming."

The yolk only is used as an emulsifying agent (in mayonnaise, for instance). Beaten eggs are utilised for thickening sauces and custards, for binding such things as fish cakes, and for coating foods likely to disintegrate during cooking, such as fried fish, fritters, croquettes, etc.

Eggs are widely used as a raising agent for cakes and batters; where an extra light mixture is required the egg whites are whisked separately before being added. Whisked egg whites are also used for making meringues, soufflé omelettes, soufflés and light, foamy sweets and icings.

Except in the case of hard-boiled eggs, the more lightly egg dishes are cooked, the better. This applies particularly to fried and baked egg dishes and omelettes—too long cooking over-hardens the albumen and makes the dish tough. Custards and similar dishes containing eggs should be cooked over hot water, i.e., in a double boiler, rather than over direct heat, to prevent the eggs from curdling.

To Separate an Egg

Give the egg a sharp knock against the side of a basin or cup, and break it in half; tapping it lightly two or three times is liable to crush the shell instead of breaking it cleanly, and may cause the yolk to mix into the white. Having broken the shell, pass the yolk back and forth from one half of the shell to the other, until all the white has dropped into the basin. Lest accidents should happen, treat each egg separately.

BOILED EGGS

Choose a small saucepan and put in it enough water to just cover the eggs. Bring the water to the boil, then add the eggs and boil for 3–4 minutes. Fresh eggs take a little longer to cook than those which are a few days old. The water should boil gently—if it boils too rapidly the eggs are liable to crack.

CODDLED EGGS

Bring the water to the boil in a small saucepan as for ordinary boiled eggs. Put in the eggs and place a lid on the pan. Remove the saucepan from the heat, but put in a warm place where the water will not boil but will still keep hot. Leave the eggs in the water for 10 minutes, when the white should be just set, and the yolk creamy.

POACHED EGGS

Eggs for poaching are at their best when about 2 days old—very fresh eggs or staler ones are difficult to keep whole. If you are going to poach a number of eggs at a time, you will need a wide pan such as a deep frying pan or fish-kettle or a specially constructed egg poacher. Alternatively, muffin rings, or even pastry cutters, can be placed in the water to hold the eggs. Pour in enough water to cover the eggs completely, add salt to flavour and bring to the boil. Break the first egg into a cup and drop it gently into the boiling water. When just set, drop in the next egg, and so on until all the eggs, or as many as the pan will take, are cooking. Cook gently, and remove the eggs from the pan in turn when they have cooked for 2–3 minutes—they should be just set but not hard. A fish slice or a perforated spoon will be found best for removing the eggs. Drain, and then serve as desired—on hot buttered toast, or on spinach, etc., garnished with small sprigs of parsley.

Milk may be used in place of water—it is then served with the eggs.

FRIED EGGS

If the eggs are to be served with bacon, cook the bacon first, then remove it and keep hot. Break each egg separately into a cup and drop carefully into the hot fat. Cook gently, basting with hot fat so that the eggs cook evenly on top and underneath. When just set, remove from the pan with a fish slice or broad palette knife, and serve with the bacon.

HARD-BOILED EGGS

Put into a pan of cold water, bring to the boil and boil for about 10 minutes. Then place at once under running cold water until cold; this prevents the yolk from discolouring on the outside, and enables the shell to be removed quite easily. To remove the shell, tap all round the egg with the back of a knife, and shell.

SCRAMBLED EGGS

2 tbsps. milk	Salt and pepper
½ oz. butter	Buttered toast
2 eggs	

Heat the milk and the butter in a strong saucepan, but do not boil. Beat the eggs, add salt and pepper and pour into the saucepan. Stir over a gentle heat until the mixture begins to thicken, then remove from the heat and stir until creamy. Pile on to hot buttered toast and serve immediately.

BAKED EGGS (OEUFS SUR LE PLAT)

Use individual oven-proof dishes of glass or china (ramekin cases) for this dish. Place them on a baking sheet with a knob of butter in each dish and put in a moderately hot oven (400° F., mark 6) for a minute or two. When the butter is melted, break a fresh egg into each dish, season with salt and pepper and return to the oven until just set—5–8 minutes. Serve at once.

OMELETTES

With care and attention to instructions, anyone can master the art of omelette making. A certain amount of knack and delicate handling are necessary, and one must not be discouraged if the first two or three omelettes are not altogether successful: proficiency will come with practice.

An omelette is nourishing and quickly made, and can be a convenient dish to serve in an emergency. It is also the means of using up odds and ends—the remains of cooked meat, fish, vegetables and sauces can all be utilised, either in the omelette itself or served as a separate filling or accompaniment.

Have everything in readiness before beginning to make an omelette, and a dish heating on which to serve it. It must be served at once—an omelette must never wait, but rather be waited for.

The eggs used should be very fresh, and good butter is best for the cooking.

Special little omelette pans are obtainable and should be kept for this purpose only. In the absence of such a pan, however, a good quality frying pan can be used with success. Whether of cast iron, copper, enamelled iron or aluminium, the pan should be thick, so that when heated it will hold sufficient heat to cook the eggs as soon as they are put into it. Thus, the omelette can be in and out of the pan in a few seconds—one of the essentials for success; slow cooking and overcooking both make an omelette tough.

To season a new omelette pan, heat it slowly, then melt a knob of butter in it and rub it well in with a piece of soft paper.

To clean the pan after use, do not wash it, but rub it over first with some soft paper, then with a clean cloth.

Basically, there are only two different kinds of omelettes: the plain omelette, in which the white and yolk of egg are beaten together, and the soufflé omelette, in which the egg whites are whisked separately and folded into the mixture, giving it a fluffy texture. There are, of course, many different recipes, the variations being supplied by the different ingredients added to the eggs or used in the filling.

To Prepare the Omelette Pan

Place the pan over gentle heat, sprinkle in a little salt and rub round vigorously with a small pad of kitchen paper. The salt, being gritty, ensures that the surface of the pan is perfectly clean and smooth, and having done its work, can be dusted out with a clean, dry cloth, whereas washing (which is undesirable with omelette pans) would be necessary if a scouring powder had been used.

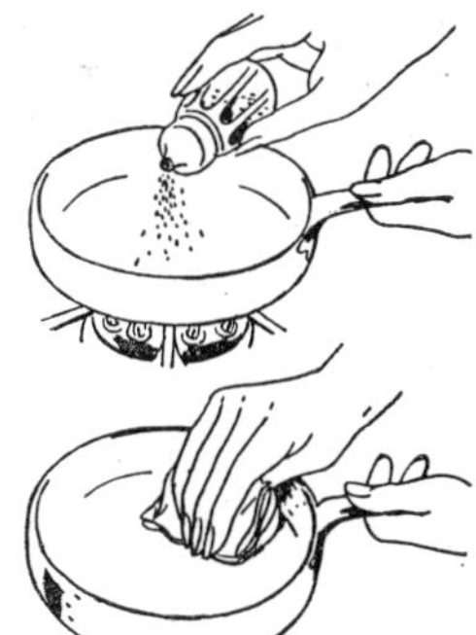

Preparing the Pan

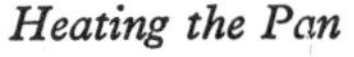

Heating the Pan

It is important that the pan should be thoroughly and evenly heated through, so, a few minutes before the omelette is to be cooked, place the pan on a very gentle heat. When ready for the mixture it should feel comfortably hot to the back of the hand held about an inch away from the surface. The heating should be very gentle, to ensure that the pan is evenly heated right to the sides; a fierce heat will cause the pan to heat unevenly.

Fat for Greasing

Undoubtedly butter gives the best flavour. However, as it usually contains water and salt, which are apt to make the omelette stick, it should first be clarified, i.e., melted and heated gently to drive off the water, then poured off the sediment. Unsalted margarine (or clarified if salted) can be used as a substitute for butter. Bacon fat may also be used, and as a rule this does not require clarifying.

SIMPLE OMELETTE

First prepare the pan, set it to warm and make everything ready for serving the omelette. If
the flavour of garlic is liked, rub a small piece 66
over the inside of the basin before beginning. Break the eggs (allowing two per person) into a basin and beat them just enough to blend the yolks and whites. Then add 1 tsp. water (or milk) per egg, salt and pepper and mix these in; 1 tsp. chopped parsley and a pinch (not more) of

finely powdered herbs may also be added to the beaten eggs if desired. Now put some butter in the hot pan and tilt the pan so that the whole surface is evenly greased. Pour in the mixture and immediately stir it round with a fork until no liquid egg is left; when the eggs are delicately set, but still creamy on top, roll the omelette over, starting at the handle end of the pan, and turn at once on to the hot dish. An omelette thus cooked will be barely coloured on the outside, somewhat creamy inside and without a hint of toughness. Some people prefer to continue cooking until the omelette is brown on the outside, but the result will be somewhat tough.

STUFFED OMELETTE

Prepare the filling, make it hot and have it handy, then cook the omelette as described above. Put the filling on to the omelette just before folding it and turn it quickly on to the hot dish.

SOUFFLÉ OMELETTE

3 eggs — 3 tbsps. water or milk
Seasoning — ½ oz. butter

Divide the yolks from the whites of the eggs, putting them in separate bowls. Beat the yolks with a wooden spoon until creamy and lemon-coloured. Add the seasoning and water or milk, and beat again. Whisk the whites as stiffly as possible. At this point place the pan with the butter over a low heat, and let the butter melt without browning. Turn the whites into the yolk mixture, and with a spoon fold them in carefully, but not over-much. Grease the sides of the pan with the butter and pour in the mixture. Cook over a moderate heat until it is a golden-brown on the underside. Then place the pan in a moderate oven or under the grill, until the omelette is browned on the top. Remove at once when ready, as overcooking will tend to make it tough. Run a spatula gently round the edge and underneath the omelette to loosen it, then make a mark across the middle at right angles to the handle and double it over. Turn gently on to a hot plate, garnish, serve at once.

CHEESE OMELETTE

Make a simple omelette, and sprinkle it with grated cheese when nearly cooked. Finish under the grill, browning the cheese.

FISH OMELETTE

3 eggs — 2–3 tbsps. cooked white fish
1 tsp. chopped parsley — 1 oz. butter
Seasoning

This is a good way of using up small quantities of fish. Separate the yolks from the whites of the eggs, putting the yolks into a basin and the whites on to a large plate. Add the chopped parsley and seasoning to the yolks, and beat them with a wooden spoon until soft and creamy. Then add the fish, broken up finely with a fork. Beat the egg whites until they are really stiff, and melt the butter in an omelette pan. Fold the whites into the creamy mixture and pour all into the melted butter. Stir the mixture over the heat until it begins to set. Then slip the palette knife underneath and fold over, first from one side and then from the other, making the omelette oval in shape. If not cooked sufficiently in the centre, hold under the grill or in front of the fire for a minute or two. Then turn the omelette on to a hot dish and serve at once.

HAM OR TONGUE OMELETTE

Make a soufflé omelette and add 2 tbsps. cooked and minced ham or tongue to the creamed yolks of eggs before mixing in the beaten whites.

KIDNEY OMELETTE

Skin 2 sheep's kidneys and cut them in small pieces, removing the hard core from the centre. Melt ½ oz. butter in a small pan, put in the kidney with 1 tsp. finely chopped onion, and fry a little. Add seasoning and 1 tsp. chopped parsley. Put the lid on the pan and cook slowly for about 10 minutes. Place this mixture in the centre of a plain omelette. A little gravy may be served round the omelette.

MUSHROOM OMELETTE

Prepare some fresh mushrooms, cut them in thin slices, cook them in a little butter, and season to taste. Put them in the centre of the omelette before folding it over.

TOMATO OMELETTE

2–3 ripe tomatoes — Pepper and salt
A little butter (approx. 1½ oz.) — 2–3 eggs
1 tsp. chopped shallot — 1 tsp. chopped parsley
1 tbsp. warm water

Peel the tomatoes, cut them in pieces and cook them for a few minutes in a small quantity of butter, with the chopped shallot and seasoning. Keep this mixture hot whilst making the omelette. Beat up the eggs with pepper and salt, the chopped parsley and warm water. Melt 1 oz. butter in an omelette pan, and as soon as it begins to frizzle, pour in the egg mixture. Stir lightly with a fork until it begins to set. While still soft, put some of the tomato mixture in the centre and fold over. Turn on to a hot dish, and pour the rest of the tomato mixture round the sides.

SWEET OMELETTE

This may be made by either of the recipes
37 given for a savoury omelette, but the soufflé omelette is perhaps the more suitable. Sugar takes the place of the seasoning, and a suitable flavouring is added. Warmed jam or stewed fruit is generally put in the centre before folding it over, and the omelette is dusted with caster sugar before being sent to table.

BAKED OMELETTE SOUFFLÉ

4 eggs	A pinch of salt
2 tbsps. caster sugar	Sugar for dredging
6 almonds, blanched and chopped	Jam or stewed fruit (optional)
2 tbsps. milk or cream	

Separate the yolks from the whites of eggs, and beat the yolks with the sugar thoroughly. Add the almonds, blanched and finely chopped, and the milk or cream. Beat the whites to a stiff froth with a pinch of salt, and add them to the yolks, etc. Butter a flat dish, and on it pile up the omelette mixture. Bake in a moderate oven (350° F., mark 4) for 15–20 minutes. Sprinkle with sugar and serve at once. A little jam or some pieces of stewed fruit may be put at the bottom of the dish.

SURPRISE SOUFFLÉ OMELETTE : see page 338.

OTHER EGG DISHES

BLANQUETTE D'OEUFS

4 fresh eggs	1 tsp. anchovy essence
1 oz. margarine	Seasoning
1 oz. flour	1 tsp. chopped parsley
½ pint milk	

First put the eggs into boiling water and cook for 4–5 minutes: they should not be hard-boiled, but just firmly set, so that they can easily be removed from their shells. Meanwhile, prepare the sauce: melt the margarine and stir in the flour, then heat gently for a few minutes, stirring all the time—care must be taken not to brown the flour. Now add the milk a little at a time, stirring all the while, then bring to the boil. Add the essence and seasoning, and simmer gently for 5 minutes. Arrange the shelled eggs, which should be hot, down the centre of the dish, coat each and the dish with the sauce, and garnish each egg straight down the centre with a line of parsley. This is quite easily accomplished if the finely chopped parsley is placed straight down the edge of a knife, and pushed carefully off on to the egg with another knife.

CELERY AND EGG CROQUETTES

¼ pint celery purée	1 egg yolk
4 hard-boiled eggs	Egg and crumbs for coating
1 oz. butter	Fat for frying
1 oz. flour	Fried parsley
Pepper and salt	

Stew some celery in a little milk for about 1 hour, then sieve it. Roughly chop the hard-boiled egg. Melt the butter, add the flour and cook thoroughly without browning. To this add the celery purée and bring slowly to the boil. Add the egg and seasonings and, when cool, the egg yolk. Turn the mixture on to a plate. Shape into croquettes, coat with egg and bread-crumbs and fry in deep fat to a golden-brown colour. Drain the croquettes well, and serve garnished with fried parsley.

BAKED EGGS IN SAUSAGE

½ lb. sausage-meat	1 oz. butter
4 eggs	1 tsp. chopped parsley
Pepper and salt	

Butter four small china dishes and line with sausage-meat. Put in a moderate oven (350° F., mark 4) to bake for about 15–20 minutes, then remove from the oven. Break the eggs carefully, and place one in each of the sausage-lined dishes. Sprinkle with pepper and salt, and top each with a little butter. Cover with greased paper, and return to the oven for 15 minutes, or until the eggs are set. Just before serving, sprinkle with fresh, finely chopped parsley.

EGGS IN ASPIC

¾ pint aspic jelly	4 hard-boiled eggs
Truffle, tomato, etc., to garnish	Salad

Make some aspic jelly, or, if packet aspic is used, dissolve this according to the instructions on the packet. When cold, but still liquid, line some dariole moulds with the jelly, then decorate with small pieces of truffle, white of egg, tomato, etc. (For masking and decorating a mould, see chapter on Jellies.) Pack the prepared moulds with sliced hard-boiled eggs and fill up with liquid aspic jelly. Leave to set, then turn out on to a bed of salad.

EGGS BAKED IN CREAM

Butter as many small fireproof dishes or cocottes as required. Put 1 tsp. cream in the bottom of each and add a light sprinkling of salt and pepper. Break 1 new-laid egg into each,
68 sprinkle more pepper and salt on top, and cover
with more cream. Place the dishes in a meat tin containing sufficient water to come half-way up the sides, cook in a moderate oven (350° F., mark 4) until the eggs are just set—about 15 minutes—and serve at once.

CURRIED EGGS

4 hard-boiled eggs	½ pint stock or water
1 onion	Salt
½ an apple	2 tsps. lemon juice
2 oz. butter	4 oz. cooked rice
2 tsps. curry powder	Chopped parsley
1 oz. flour	Paprika pepper

69 Boil the eggs hard and put into cold water. Remove the shell and cut the eggs into halves. Chop the onion and apple finely, then melt the butter in a saucepan and fry the onion lightly. Add the apple, curry powder and flour, and cook for a few minutes. Add the stock gradually and season with salt and lemon juice. Boil up and skim, then cover and simmer for about 30 minutes. Put the eggs into the sauce, and when thoroughly heated, place in a hot dish, surround with rice, and decorate with finely chopped parsley and paprika pepper.

EGG CUTLETS

4 tbsps. thick white sauce	Pepper and salt
	A little flour
4 tbsps. white bread-crumbs	Beaten egg and bread-crumbs for coating
4 hard-boiled eggs	Fat for frying
1 tsp. lemon juice	Parsley to garnish
A pinch of powdered mace	Macaroni or spaghetti for " bones "

Warm the sauce, add the breadcrumbs and chopped eggs, lemon juice and seasonings. Blend thoroughly, spread on a plate to cool, and divide into four or six portions of equal size. When cold and firm, shape into small cutlets, using a little flour. Brush each over with beaten egg and coat with breadcrumbs, then fry in deep fat until golden-brown. Drain off all surplus fat, serve on a paper d'oyley, and garnish with parsley. If liked, a small piece of raw macaroni or spaghetti, according to the size of the cutlets, can be put into the narrow end of each cutlet to imitate the bone.

EGGS BONNE FEMME

4 hard-boiled eggs	Seasoning
1 tsp. chopped tarragon	A few slices of beetroot
1 oz. butter	Mustard and cress

Cut the eggs in halves and remove the yolks. Cut a very small slice from the bottom of each egg (and put it inside); this is to enable it to stand firmly. Pound the yolks with the chopped tarragon, butter, and a little pepper and salt, if necessary, depending on the saltness of the butter. Pipe this filling into the white of egg cases, piling it up. Place each half-egg on a slice of beetroot, decorate the top with a few small pieces of mustard and cress, and serve on a dish surrounded by cress.

Note: This savoury should not be prepared until it is required to be served, because the colour from the beetroot is liable to spread into the whites of the egg.

EGG AND BACON PIE

1 lb. streaky bacon	4 eggs
Pepper	Beaten egg to glaze

For the Pastry

10 oz. flour	5 oz. lard or margarine
A good pinch of salt	Cold water

Make a shortcrust pastry from the above ingredients. Cut in half, roll out and line a pie plate with one piece. Cut up the bacon finely and season with pepper. Arrange it on the plate to form a cross. Break the eggs separately, pour one into each " compartment " and season. Moisten the edges of the pastry, roll out the remaining pastry and cover the pie. Glaze with beaten egg, and bake in a moderately hot oven (425° F., mark 6) about ¾ hour. Serve hot or cold.

EGG AND HAM CUTLETS

3 oz. cooked ham	2 tsps. finely chopped parsley
3 hard-boiled eggs	
1 oz. butter	Egg, breadcrumbs and fat for frying
1 oz. flour	
¼ pint milk	Macaroni for " bones "
Seasoning	Parsley to garnish

Chop the ham and eggs as finely as possible. Melt the butter, stir in the flour, add the milk and bring to the boil, stirring. Season with pepper and salt and cook for 5 minutes. Add the chopped ham and eggs; mix well, and add the chopped parsley. Turn on to a plate, smooth top, then mark into equal-sized pieces and put aside to cool. When cold, shape into cutlets with a palette knife. Brush over with beaten egg, coat with fine white breadcrumbs and fry in deep fat until golden-brown. Serve on a dish-paper, placing a small piece of raw macaroni in each cutlet to represent bone. Garnish with parsley.

EGG AND HAM CROÛTES

Croûtes of bread	Finely chopped parsley
4 hard-boiled eggs	½ oz. butter
3 oz. cooked ham	Salt
Piquant sauce	

Toast the bread and cut into rounds, or fry croûtes of bread. Moisten a knife and cut the eggs in halves, removing the yolk with a teaspoon. Chop the ham finely, and pound it with the yolks of egg, a little piquant sauce, 1 tsp. of the chopped parsley, butter and salt. When thoroughly well blended, fill the egg whites, heaping the mixture well in the centre. Garnish with a little chopped parsley. Place each half-egg on a croûte of fried bread or toast.

EGG FLAN

For the Cheese Pastry

6 oz. flour	Egg yolk and cold water to mix
3 oz. margarine	Salt and cayenne
3 oz. cheese	

For the Filling

¼ pint aspic jelly	3 hard-boiled eggs
3 small, firm tomatoes	

For the Garnish

Stiff mayonnaise	Watercress
Curled anchovies	

Prepare a pastry from the first group of ingredients, line a flan ring with this, bake " blind," and allow to become quite cold. Dissolve the aspic jelly and cool until just at the point of setting. Meanwhile, skin the tomatoes and slice thinly, slice the eggs, and arrange both of these in the flan case. Pour on the aspic jelly and allow to set. Garnish with mayonnaise, curled anchovies and watercress.

EGG FRICASSEE

4 hard-boiled eggs	1 tsp. chopped parsley
Pepper and salt	Croûtons of fried bread and small baked tomatoes or green peas, for garnish
A little nutmeg	
½ pint white sauce	

Cut the hard-boiled eggs into four; add the pepper, salt and nutmeg to the sauce, and reheat the eggs in the sauce, but do not reboil them. Remove from the heat and add the finely chopped parsley. Serve in small, individual glass casseroles or on one large dish, garnished with croûtons or triangles of fried bread and small baked tomatoes or green peas.

EGG AND CHEESE FRICASSEE

This is prepared in exactly the same way as an Egg Fricassee (this page), except that to each egg at least 1 tbsp. of finely grated cheese should be allowed. Slice the egg or cut into eight sections, put on a buttered pie dish and pour over the sauce, to which the cheese has been added. Sprinkle the top very liberally with more grated cheese, and a light sprinkling of breadcrumbs. Brown in a hot oven (450° F., mark 8) or under the grill, and serve in the cooking dish.

EGGS IN SPINACH CASES

1 breakfastcupful spinach purée	1 oz. butter or a little cream
4 new-laid eggs	Finely chopped parsley or tomato sauce or mushroom ketchup
Pepper and salt	

Butter four individual glass or china casseroles, and line with the spinach, previously cooked and chopped very finely or rubbed through a sieve. Break a new-laid egg into each dish, sprinkle with pepper and salt, put a little butter or cream on the top of each, place the small dishes on a baking sheet or in a meat tin, cover with buttered paper, and bake in a moderate oven (350° F., mark 4) until the eggs are lightly set—15–20 minutes. Sprinkle finely chopped parsley on top of each, or if preferred, 1 tsp. of tomato sauce or mushroom ketchup.

PARMESAN BALLS

½ pint cold water	2 oz. Parmesan cheese, grated
1 oz. butter	1 oz. Cheddar cheese, grated
2½ oz. flour	Fat for frying
1½ oz. cornflour	
3 eggs	
Seasoning	

Put the water and butter on to boil, and when boiling, sprinkle in the flour and cornflour (previously sieved) and cook, stirring vigorously, until the mixture leaves the sides of the pan. Remove from the heat, allow to cool slightly, and add the eggs, one by one, beating each in thoroughly. Add the seasoning and grated cheese; turn on to a plate, spread into a flat cake, and put to cool. When cool, take teaspoonfuls of the mixture and drop into hot fat, when the merest trace of blue smoke is rising from it. As these balls take from 10–15 minutes to cook, the fat must not be too hot when they are put in, otherwise they will become over-browned before they are cooked through.

SAVOURY HAM CUSTARD

¼ lb. ham	Salt and pepper
3 eggs	Mashed potatoes
¾ oz. cornflour	Mushrooms for garnish
¾ pint milk	Brown or tomato sauce

Line a greased cake tin with slices of ham. Separate the whites and yolks of the eggs. Mix the cornflour to a smooth paste with a little of the milk, boil the remainder of the milk, then pour on to the cornflour, stirring; return to the pan and cook for 5 minutes. Then add the salt and pepper and the well-beaten egg yolks. Whip the whites very stiffly and fold into the custard. Pour into the prepared tin, and steam for 20–30 minutes. Turn out, and serve with a border of mashed potatoes, garnished with fried mushrooms. A brown or tomato sauce is a good accompaniment to this dish.

HAM EN PANIER

6 small rolls	1 tsp. chopped parsley
½ lb. cooked ham	Pepper, salt and made mustard
3 hard-boiled eggs	
½ pint white sauce	Watercress

Cut a slice from each roll and scoop out the soft centre. Dry out the shells in a slow oven (325° F., mark 2), browning slightly. Mince ham and 2 eggs and heat them in the sauce, adding the chopped parsley and a seasoning of pepper, salt and made mustard. Fill up the bread cases with this mixture, and garnish with slices of the remaining egg and sprigs of watercress.

POACHED EGGS AND CREAMED SPINACH

2 lb. spinach	4 rounds of toast or fried bread
¼ pint cream or unsweetened tinned milk	4 eggs
Seasoning	Parsley
2 oz. streaky bacon	

Pick over and wash the spinach and cook until tender. Drain, sieve, add the cream and seasoning and keep hot. Cut the bacon into neat lengths, roll up, put on skewers and grill them until crisp. Fry or toast the bread and keep hot. Poach the eggs and place them on the bread. Put the spinach into an entrée dish, arrange the eggs down the centre, sprinkle with finely chopped parsley, and garnish the dish with the bacon rolls. Serve at once.

SAUSAGE CAKES

½ lb. sausage-meat	4 eggs
A little powdered mace	1 tsp. chopped parsley
Black pepper, if liked	Tomato sauce

Blend the sausage with the mace and, if liked, a little black pepper. Shape into four flat cakes, about the size of water biscuits. Fry until well browned on both sides, then put on to a hot dish. Fry or poach the new-laid eggs and place one egg on the top of each sausage cake. Garnish with parsley, and serve with tomato sauce.

SAUSAGE SCRAMBLE

4 sausages (beef or pork)	Pepper, salt and a little made mustard
4 eggs	4 rounds of buttered toast
4 dessertsps. water	

Remove the skin from the sausages and cut them into small pieces. Put them into a small frying pan, and cook gently at first until sufficient fat has come from the sausages to fry them. When nicely browned, pour off any surplus fat. Break the eggs into a basin, add the water and seasonings, and beat lightly. Pour the beaten eggs into the pan containing the cooked sausage-meat, and scramble. When the eggs are lightly cooked, pile up the sausage scramble on the rounds of buttered toast.

SCALLOPED EGGS

4 hard-boiled eggs (hot)	½ pint white sauce
4 anchovies	Brown crumbs
1 tbsp. capers	Parsley

Butter four scallop shells and put a sliced egg in each. Add the chopped anchovies and capers to the sauce, pour the sauce on the eggs and sprinkle lightly with brown crumbs. Reheat in a moderate oven (350° F., mark 4) for 10 minutes. Garnish with parsley.

SCOTCH EGGS—I

½ lb. sausages or sausage-meat	Breadcrumbs
	Fat for frying
4–5 hard-boiled eggs	Parsley
2 tsps. seasoned flour	Tomato sauce
A little piquant sauce	Croûtons of fried bread
Beaten egg	

Remove the sausage-meat from the skins and shell the eggs. Pass the eggs through the seasoned flour. Add a few drops of piquant sauce to the sausage-meat and divide equally into four or five pieces, according to the number of eggs. Cover each egg with the sausage-meat, doing this as evenly as possible to keep the egg a good shape. Brush over with beaten egg, toss in breadcrumbs and fry in deep fat, from which a very faint blue smoke is rising. As the sausage-meat is raw, it is essential that the frying should not be hurried unduly, and for this reason the fat must not be too hot. When golden-brown in colour, remove from the fat and drain. Cut in half widthways, garnish with a small piece of parsley, and serve with tomato sauce.

The eggs may be placed on croûtons or rounds of fried bread. To do this, cut slices of bread about $\frac{3}{4}$ inch thick, and cut into rounds with a 2-inch pastry cutter. Fry in deep fat; as the bread does not require cooking but only browning, the fat may be considerably hotter than when frying the eggs.

SCOTCH EGGS—II

$\frac{3}{4}$ lb. boiled potatoes	Flour
Salt	Fat for frying
Cayenne	Breadcrumbs
3 oz. grated cheese	Rounds of fried bread
1 beaten egg	Tomato sauce
3 hard-boiled eggs	

Mash the potatoes and season with salt and cayenne. Add the grated cheese and sufficient beaten egg to produce a fairly stiff paste. Beat very thoroughly, until smooth. Shell the hard-boiled eggs and flour them slightly, turn the potato mixture on to a floured board, divide into three. Flatten out each piece, put one of the eggs on each and fold around. Roll and shape neatly. Coat with beaten egg, then toss in the breadcrumbs. Fry in fat from which a faint blue smoke is rising, until golden-brown. Cut in half widthways. Serve hot on rounds of fried bread with tomato sauce.

SCRAMBLED EGGS AND FISH

$\frac{1}{4}$ lb. cooked fish	2 dessertsps. water
3 eggs	4 rounds of buttered toast
A little mustard	Chopped tarragon or parsley
Pepper and salt	
1 oz. butter	

Any white fish can be used, or if preferred, cooked kipper. Flake the fish finely. Put the eggs and seasonings into a basin, and whisk until they are well mixed. Stir in the fish. Melt the butter in a saucepan, and immediately it is hot, pour in the egg and fish mixture and the water. Scramble this in the same way as when scrambling eggs, taking care not to overcook the mixture. Pile equal quantities on the rounds of buttered toast, sprinkle with chopped tarragon or parsley, and serve immediately.

SCRAMBLED EGGS WITH SWEET CORN

1 small tin of corn	Salt and pepper
4 eggs	Buttered toast or curried rice (see below)
$\frac{1}{2}$ oz. butter	

Strain the corn to remove as much moisture as possible. Scramble the eggs in the usual way, and when almost cooked, add the sweet corn and cook all together. This dish can be served on buttered toast in the same way as ordinary scrambled eggs, or with a border of curried rice. For this, cook the rice as for curry, then make a very good, thick curry sauce, mix with the rice and form into a border on the dish.

SCRAMBLED EGGS (ITALIAN)

2 oz. spaghetti	A piece of butter the size of a walnut
2 eggs	
Salt and pepper to taste	Spinach and tomato for garnish
2 tbsps. unsweetened evaporated milk	

Break the spaghetti into short pieces and cook in fast-boiling salted water until tender, then strain. Beat the eggs and add the salt, pepper, evaporated milk and cooked spaghetti. Mix well together and scramble in the melted butter in the usual way. Serve on a bed of cooked, sieved spinach, garnished with slices of tomato.

SCRAMBLED EGGS AND NOODLES

3 oz. noodles or macaroni	Pepper and salt
4 eggs	1 oz. butter
4 tbsps. milk	$2\frac{1}{2}$ oz. grated cheese
A little made mustard	

Heat two pints of water, add $\frac{1}{2}$ oz. salt, and when boiling, add the noodles and cook until tender. When the noodles are nearly cooked, prepare the eggs. Break separately into a basin, beat thoroughly, stir in the milk, add $\frac{1}{4}$ tsp. made mustard with pepper and salt to season. Melt the butter in the saucepan, pour in the seasoned eggs and the milk, and scramble lightly in the usual way. Strain the noodles free from moisture, sprinkle in the grated cheese, and toss over low heat.

An attractive dish is made by serving the noodles either as a border with the scrambled eggs in the middle, or as a bed on which the eggs rest. To make a more substantial dish, increase the proportion of noodles, and serve with a green vegetable or a salad.

STUFFED CHEESE EGGS

2 hard-boiled eggs	Beaten egg and bread-crumbs
$\frac{1}{2}$ oz. butter	
$\frac{1}{2}$ oz. flour	Fat for frying
3 tbsps. milk	Fried parsley
$\frac{3}{4}$ oz. grated cheese	Cheese sauce
Salt and pepper	

Split the eggs lengthwise and remove the

yolks. Make a panada thus: melt the butter, add the flour, then the milk and cook until the mixture leaves the sides of the pan. Add the grated cheese, seasoning and sieved yolks of egg, and mix all well together. Fill the whites of egg with this mixture and join the halves together again. Coat each egg with beaten egg and breadcrumbs, fry in hot fat, garnish with fried parsley and serve with cheese sauce.

STUFFED EGGS TARTARE (COLD)

¼ pint Tartare sauce Watercress for garnish
3 hard-boiled eggs

Make the sauce as described on page 203, and set aside for a short time to allow the flavours to blend. Cut the hard-boiled eggs in half lengthwise, remove the yolks and mix with some of the Tartare sauce. Fill the whites with this mixture and coat with the Tartare sauce. Serve garnished with watercress.

TONGUE AND EGGS TARTARE

Prepare some hard-boiled eggs and cut them into halves. Cut the cold tongue into the required number of rounds, 2½ inches in diameter. On the top of each round of tongue, place a slice of firm red tomato, cut ¼ inch in thickness, and over these put a half-egg with the yolk side down. Coat with cold Tartare sauce, and garnish with watercress or small leaves of lettuce.

CHEESE

All cheese is made from milk curds, separated from the whey (usually by the action of rennet) and suitably ripened.

The quality and source of the milk (whether cow's, goat's or ewe's), and the particular processes used in the making, give rise to an almost endless variety of cheeses. Local conditions of climate and vegetation and, of course, seasonal changes, also influence the finished product, which explains why some varieties are essentially local and cannot be produced in large quantities under factory conditions.

BRITISH CHEESES

The following list includes well-known British cheeses and some of the more unusual ones.

Blue Vinney

Blue Vinney is a hard cheese made in Dorsetshire from skimmed cows' milk and sometimes called Blue Dorset. It is white in colour with a blue vein, hard in texture and of a rather strong flavour.

Caerphilly

Originally a Welsh cheese, this is now made also in Somerset, Wiltshire, Devon and Dorset. It is a whole milk cheese, pressed only lightly and eaten in its "green" state—about ten days old. Each cheese weighs about 8–9 lb.

Cheddar

Cheddar is perhaps the best known and most widely used of the English hard cheeses, and one of the oldest. Made originally in Somerset —where the best Cheddar cheese is still to be obtained—it is now produced in various other parts of the country and also in Scotland, Canada, Australia, New Zealand and so on; in fact the name "Cheddar" is given to any cheese which undergoes the "cheddaring" process, regardless of where it is made. The original farmhouse Cheddar is still the best, but the factory-produced varieties are wholesome, nourishing and cheap, and provide an excellent everyday food and a useful cooking cheese.

Cheshire

Cheshire is also well known and widely enjoyed, and is the oldest English cheese. Like Cheddar, it is a hard cheese, but rather more crumbly in texture. There are two varieties of Cheshire cheese, the red, which is artificially coloured, and the white. The red is usually rather milder than the white. Occasionally, more by accident than design, a red Cheshire cheese will turn blue, that is to say, will develop a system of blue veins which spread all over the cheese and give it a very fine, rich texture and flavour.

Cheshire cheese, like Cheddar, can also be imitated, but not successfully, the genuine cheese from Cheshire being far superior.

Dunlop

Dunlop is a Scottish cheese made originally in Dunlop, Ayrshire, but now fairly general throughout Scotland. It is not unlike Cheddar, but moister and of a closer texture.

Gloucester

There are two varieties of this cheese, the Double Gloucester and Single Gloucester. Both are round and flat, but the Double Gloucester is thicker and somewhat bigger than the Single.

Double Gloucester is close and crumbly in texture, somewhat similar to Cheshire, but in most connoisseurs' opinion, very superior to it in flavour. Unfortunately, it is difficult to obtain except in the district in which it is made.

Single Gloucester is more open and soft in texture than the Double, and the flavour, though good, does not compare with that of Double Gloucester.

Leicester

Leicester cheese is made in the same manner as Cheddar, but is usually harder.

Slipcote

Slipcote is a soft cheese produced at Wissenden. It is made up into little cheeses which are placed between cabbage leaves for a week or two to ripen. When ripe, its skin or coat becomes loose and slips off—hence the name.

Stilton

Stilton is in Huntingdonshire, but genuine Stilton cheese is made also in Leicestershire and Rutland. It is a double-cream cheese, that is, made from the richest milk (to which the cream of other milk may also be added), and is made only from May to September. It is semi-hard, and has a blue veining caused by a mould which is inoculated into the cheese. The cheese itself is white in colour, and the veins of blue mould should be evenly distributed throughout. The rind, of a dull, drab colour, should be well crinkled and regular, and free from cracks. Stilton is at its best when fully ripe, that is, from 6–9 months after it has been made. A good Stilton needs no port or anything else added to it; only when it has gone dry through exposure to air is this necessary.

Wensleydale

There are two distinct types of cheese made in the vale of Wensleydale in Yorkshire. The best known is the double-cream cheese, cylindrical in shape and similar to Stilton, growing blue when ripe, but of smaller dimensions. The other variety is a flat-shaped white cheese which is eaten fresh.

Cream Cheese

Cream cheese is made in Devonshire and Cornwall and many other parts of the country, and can in fact be made at home by the housewife. The whey is allowed to drain from the cream and when sufficiently firm—after 3–4 days—it is ready for use. It is always very mild in flavour and must of course be eaten fresh, as it will not keep.

Home-Made Sour Milk Cheese

Milk that has soured reasonably quickly may be used to make a palatable "cream" cheese. Put it in a scalded muslin cloth (e.g., a flour bag) and hang it up till the whey ceases to drip. Remove curds, and if desired add salt and pepper and a knob of butter or margarine, then beat. Flavouring such as chopped chives or paprika may be added.

Sour milk cheese should be made carefully under hygienic conditions, or there may be some risk of contamination. To accelerate souring, it is advisable to use a preparation known as a "starter."

Packet and Processed Cheese

These cheeses are commercially prepared by patent processes by which the development of the cheese is arrested at a selected stage, so that further ripening is prevented. They are generally mild in flavour and soft and crumbly in texture. Such cheeses do not develop a rind and are usually wrapped in tinfoil or otherwise protected from the air.

CONTINENTAL CHEESES

There are very many different cheeses made on the Continent, and the following are merely a few of the better-known ones generally obtainable in this country.

Bel Paese

A rich, creamy cheese of mild flavour, made in various parts of Italy, and usually from October to June. The cheeses weigh about 5 lb. each.

Brie

A French farm cheese, made in the north of

France. It is made from whole milk, is mould-inoculated and soft in texture. It is flat and round, usually 14 inches across, 1–1½ inches thick and about 6 lb. in weight.

The best Brie is made in the autumn, and is obtainable from November to May. Those made in the spring and summer are inferior.

Camembert

A French soft cheese made of cows' milk, the curd being inoculated with a white fungus. The cheese is at its best when it begins to get soft. If allowed to over-ripen, it becomes too soft and gases are generated, giving it a smell which many people find unpleasant. Camembert was made originally at Camembert, but is now made also in other parts of Normandy. The best is made from the richest milk during the summer months.

Danish Blue

A soft white cheese with a blue mould veining, made in Denmark in imitation of Roquefort.

Edam

A Dutch cheese, round in shape like a ball, bright red outside and dark yellow inside, and about 5 lb. in weight. It is not milled but pressed in round moulds which give it its shape. Imitations of this cheese are made in Germany, Belgium, and Jugoslavia.

Fontainebleau

A French cheese of the cream type, soft and fresh, made in the country round Fontainebleau, mostly in the summer.

Fromage à la Crème

This is sour milk cheese, made in the same way as the Home-Made Sour Milk Cheese described on page 254, but without the addition of salt. When drained, it is softened with a little milk and served with fine sugar and cream.

Gorgonzola

A semi-hard, blue-veined cheese, made in Italy in the district round Milan. It is sharp in flavour, and very popular in this country.

Gouda

A Dutch cheese not unlike the Edam in taste and texture, but flatter in shape and very much larger. There are also small Gouda, about 1 lb. in weight, known as Little Dutch.

Gruyère

A hard cheese usually about 2 feet in diameter and 6 inches thick, and weighing anything from 100–200 lb. Originally it came exclusively from Switzerland, but is now made also in France, Italy and so on. It is pale yellow in colour and is honeycombed with "eyes" or holes, caused by the rapid fermentation of the curd. It has an excellent flavour and is useful for cooking.

Limburger

A semi-hard, whole-milk cheese made in Belgium (and also in Germany and Alsace), from December to May. It is full-flavoured and strong-smelling.

Parmesan

This Italian cheese is the hardest cheese of all. After a special process the curd is broken up, heated, packed into a mould the shape of a millstone and matured for at least two and usually three years. When ripe the crust is mostly black, but the cheese should be a pale straw colour and full of tiny holes like pinpricks. It is almost invariably used, finely grated, for cooking.

Petit Gruyère

An imitation Gruyère made in Denmark. It is pasteurised and sold packaged, the portions being wrapped in tinfoil.

Petit Suisse

An unsalted cream cheese, cylindrical in shape, made in France. It is very mild in flavour.

Pommel

A double-cream cheese, unsalted, made in France all the year round and not unlike Petit Suisse.

Pont L'Évêque

A French semi-hard cheese, about 4 inches square and 1½ inches thick. It is made practically all the year round in the Pont L'Évêque district of Normandy. It is coloured yellow and is salted repeatedly while maturing.

Port-Salut

A French semi-hard cheese, round in shape, from 7–10 inches across and from 1½–3 inches thick. It was made originally by the monks of

Port du Salut, and is now made in various other parts of France and also in Belgium. It has a very mild and delicious flavour, and should be eaten while still slightly soft.

Roquefort

This is the only ewes' milk cheese which has obtained a world-wide reputation. It is made in the village of Roquefort in the Cevennes mountains of France during the lambing season. It can only be made in this district, partly because the sheep-grazing land here is particularly suitable, but also because of the limestone caverns of Roquefort itself, which play a very important part in the maturing of the Roquefort cheese. Mouldy breadcrumbs (containing the same mould as that used in the making of Stilton) are introduced into the curd as a maturing agent.

THE CHEESE COURSE

When serving cheese as a course, choose varieties which differ in style, flavour and consistency and arrange them attractively on a board or platter. To accompany them, serve any of the following: plain bread, biscuits (plain or very slightly sweetened), hot rolls, toast, rye bread and French bread. Celery, radishes, and watercress are also welcome accompaniments.

Cream cheese may be served with biscuits and red-currant jelly, or crab-apple jelly. Alternatively, paprika, carraway seeds or chopped chives may be added to the cheese if these flavours are popular; and some people like chopped pineapple mixed with cream cheese, especially when served in a salad.

When serving Edam cheese, slice off the top, use this as a cover and serve the cheese whole, the cheese being scooped out with a spoon or cheese scoop.

Stilton cheese is also served whole. A table napkin is wrapped round it and the cheese is scooped out.

To Keep Cheese

Though cheese often requires months—sometimes years—to bring it to full maturity, once ripe it deteriorates comparatively rapidly. So buy only enough to last a few days to a week and store it in a cool place, such as a cold larder; cover it loosely to protect it from the air, but do not make it air-tight. If entirely exposed to the air the cheese will become hard and dry, and if tightly covered it is likely to mould. A cheese dish with a ventilated cover is good for the purpose, but failing this, cover with an upturned bowl.

A refrigerator is not ideal for storing cheese, but if it must be used, the cheese should first be wrapped in waxed paper or tightly covered, otherwise it dries too rapidly.

CHEESE IN COOKING

To Dry Cheese for Grating

If you want cheese to become hard and dry, leave it exposed to the air in a dry, though cool, place. It is best to hang it in a muslin bag, as then the air can circulate completely. If left on a plate or board to dry, stand the cheese on its rind; cheese that has no rind should be turned occasionally, otherwise the underside will remain soft and will very likely mould. Cheese that has formed mould on the surface is not necessarily spoiled. The mould should be scraped off and the cheese either used up quickly or dried for grating.

To Grate Cheese

If the cheese is dry, use a fine grater. A soft or processed cheese, however, should be shredded rather than grated. Very soft cheeses can be sliced and added to sauces and so on, without grating or shredding.

To Cook Cheese

The less cooking cheese has, the better. Over-heating tends to make it tough and indigestible, so when making a dish such as Welsh Rarebit or Cheese Sauce, always heat the cheese very gently and do not cook the mixture more than necessary once the cheese is added.

CHEESE OMELETTE: See Egg Cookery chapter.

MACARONI CHEESE

2 oz. macaroni	Piquant sauce
1 oz. butter	A little made mustard
1 oz. flour	Salt
$\frac{3}{4}$ pint milk	4 oz. grated cheese

Break up the macaroni into pieces of equal length, and cook in fast-boiling salted water. Meanwhile, prepare the sauce: melt the butter in a saucepan, stir in the flour and add the milk;

bring to the boil, add 1 tsp. or so of piquant sauce, if liked, and a little made mustard and salt, and simmer for 10 minutes. Stir in the grated cheese, reserving some for sprinkling over the top, stir in the well-drained macaroni, and blend well. Put the mixture into a pie dish, sprinkle the top with grated cheese, and brown under the grill or in a hot oven.

WELSH RAREBIT

½ lb. fresh Cheddar or Cheshire cheese	A few grains of cayenne
	Salt
½ tsp. dry mustard	A little beer or stout
A little paprika	Hot buttered toast

Shred the cheese, put it into a double boiler and let it melt slowly over hot water; keep the water beneath the cheese just under the boiling point, so that the cheese may melt slowly. Add the mustard, paprika, cayenne and salt, according to the needs of the cheese. Then stir in very gradually as much beer or stout as the cheese will take up. When finished, the mixture should be smooth, velvety and very tender. Serve on hot buttered toast, or on hot toasted biscuits.

Milk or meat gravy with a little piquant sauce may take the place of the beer or stout in making this mixture.

See also the recipes in the chapter on Economical Cookery.

TOMATO RAREBIT

1 oz. butter	3 oz. grated cheese
1 tbsp. flour	Cayenne pepper
¼ pint milk	1 egg
¼ pint tomato purée	Buttered toast
A pinch of sugar	Parsley

Melt the butter in a saucepan and stir in the flour, mixing until smooth. Add gradually the milk and tomato purée (made by rubbing fresh or tinned tomatoes through a sieve), add the sugar and stir until boiling. Mix together the grated cheese and a good pinch of cayenne. Add these to the sauce in the pan, together with the well-beaten egg. Stir carefully over the heat until thoroughly hot, but do not boil again. Pour over neat pieces of buttered toast, sprinkle with chopped parsley, and serve very hot.

BUCK RAREBIT

Prepare a mixture as for Welsh Rarebit and serve on hot buttered toast, with a poached egg on top. This makes an excellent dish when something more substantial is required.

CHEESE SOUFFLÉ (HOT)

3 eggs	¼ pint milk
1 oz. butter	3 oz. grated cheese
½ oz. flour	Salt and pepper

Separate the yolks from the whites of the eggs. Melt the butter and stir in the flour. Gradually add the milk and bring to the boil, stirring. Cool slightly; add cheese, seasoning and egg yolks, one by one, beating well. Fold in the very stiffly beaten egg whites and put the mixture into a prepared soufflé case (see chapter on Soufflés). Bake in a moderately hot oven for about 30 minutes, until well risen and brown. Serve at once.

A simpler version of Cheese Soufflé appears in the chapter on Economical Cookery.

CHEESE PUDDING

6–8 thin slices bread and butter	2 tsps. piquant sauce
	4 oz. grated Cheddar cheese
2 eggs	
A little made mustard	1 pint milk
Salt and pepper	1 oz. breadcrumbs
1 onion	

Cut the slices of bread into neat pieces and arrange in a pie dish. Break the eggs into a basin, and add the seasonings, finely chopped onion and the sauce. Beat well, and add the cheese, reserving about a quarter for the top. Stir in the milk, and pour this mixture over the bread and butter in the pie dish. Allow to soak for about 15 minutes before baking. Mix the remaining cheese and breadcrumbs together, sprinkle over the top of the pudding, and bake in a moderate oven until set—about ¾ hour.

This is a useful way of utilising left-over bread and butter.

CHEESE CHARLOTTE

6 oz. breadcrumbs	Celery salt
1 lb. apples	1½ oz. butter or margarine
1½ oz. sugar	
Salt	3 tbsps. water or milk
4 oz. grated Parmesan	Chopped parsley

Grease a round tin and dust well with bread-crumbs. Put in a layer of thinly sliced apples, and sprinkle with sugar and salt. Sprinkle some of the cheese over and season with celery salt. Cover thinly with crumbs and small pats of butter. Repeat until the tin is filled (reserving a little cheese), then add the water or milk. Cover finally with crumbs and butter. Put a small plate or saucer on top of the mixture and bake in a moderately hot oven until the apples are cooked and the charlotte brown—from 30–45 minutes. Turn on to a hot dish and sprinkle with cheese and a little parsley.

CHEESE DREAMS

Make some sandwiches with buttered bread and slices of cheese: the bread should be about ¼ inch and the cheese ⅛ inch thick. Trim off the crusts and cut the sandwiches into convenient-sized pieces. Then melt some butter in a frying pan, put in the sandwiches and fry them until brown and crisp on both sides. Serve very hot with a little highly seasoned sauce over each.

CHEESE EGG

1 egg	1 heaped tbsp. grated cheese
Salt	½ oz. butter
Cayenne pepper	A square of hot, buttered toast
3 tbsps. milk	Ham or beetroot to garnish

Beat the egg and seasonings together, then stir in the milk and mix thoroughly. Add the grated cheese and mix well. Melt the butter, add the mixture, and stir over a gentle heat until lightly set. Arrange on the hot buttered toast and garnish with strips of ham or beetroot.

CHEESE FRITTERS

4 oz. flour	½ tsp. cayenne pepper
1 tbsp. very finely chopped onion	1 egg Milk
1 clove of garlic, very finely chopped or crushed	2 oz. grated cheese (preferably Parmesan) 2 tsps. baking powder
1 tsp. salt	Fat for frying

Mix all the dry ingredients, except the cheese and baking powder. Add the egg, and gradually stir in sufficient milk to make a stiff batter. Beat well. Have ready a little smoking-hot fat. Just before frying, add the cheese (reserving a little) and baking powder to the batter. Drop teaspoonfuls of the mixture into the fat and fry until they are a golden-brown. Drain, toss in the remaining cheese and serve very hot.

PIMIENTO AND CHEESE FRITTERS

Use tinned red peppers, drain them from their liquid and leave them wrapped in a cloth to dry. Meanwhile. prepare some slices of Cheddar cheese, cut about ⅛ inch in thickness and slightly smaller in size than the peppers. Season the pieces with pepper and salt and slip one inside each of the red peppers. Then coat the peppers lightly with flour on both sides; put them into a little hot butter in a frying pan, and cook them slowly until the cheese has melted, turning them once. Place them on rounds or squares of toast, and serve them very hot, garnished with parsley.

MACARONI AND CHEESE RISSOLES

2 oz. macaroni	1 egg yolk
1 oz. butter	Egg and breadcrumbs
1 oz. flour	Fat for frying
¼ pint milk	Parsley or celery to garnish
2–3 oz. grated cheese	
Seasoning	

Cook and drain the macaroni, let it dry, and then chop it finely. Melt the butter in a saucepan, add the flour and stir until blended. Then beat in the milk gradually, and stir until the mixture holds together. Now remove the saucepan from the heat, and stir in the macaroni, cheese, seasoning and egg yolk. Mix thoroughly and turn the mixture on to a plate to cool. When firm and set, divide it into 10–12 equal-sized pieces and form each portion into a roll, or any other shape preferred, using a very little flour. Then egg-and-breadcrumb the rolls, and fry them in hot fat until a golden-brown. Drain on paper and serve garnished with parsley or curled celery.

CELERY AND CHEESE AU GRATIN

1 head of celery	1 tsp. lemon juice
½ pint good white sauce	Chopped parsley
1 oz. butter	Pimiento or tomato to garnish
3 oz. grated cheese	

Cut the celery into small pieces of even size, cook in boiling salted water until tender, then drain. Make the sauce, add the butter, celery, most of the grated cheese and the lemon juice. Blend all together, then put into a well-buttered gratin dish or pie dish, sprinkle the top with the rest of the cheese and brown under a red-hot grill or in a very hot oven. Decorate with a ring of chopped parsley and a few pieces of either pimiento or tomato.

POTATO AND CHEESE GALANTINE

6 medium-sized potatoes	Pepper and salt
½ oz. butter	Beaten egg
1 tsp. made mustard	Breadcrumbs for coating
3 oz. grated cheese	
Tomato sauce or ketchup to mix	Tomato sauce

Boil the potatoes and mash while still hot, adding the butter and the rest of the ingredients, with 1 tbsp. tomato sauce or ketchup and egg to bind. Turn on to a floured board, and shape into a roll. Brush over with a little beaten egg and roll in breadcrumbs. Bake in a slow oven, covered with greased paper, for about 30–40 minutes. Serve on a hot dish and pour tomato sauce around it.

GNOCCHI ALLA ROMANA

½ pint milk or white stock	1 egg yolk
A knob of butter	1 small cupful white sauce
2 oz. semolina	1 cupful grated cheese
Seasoning	

Heat the milk or white stock in a saucepan together with a small piece of butter. Sprinkle into it the semolina and let it simmer very slowly, stirring occasionally, until thoroughly cooked and thick. Then remove it from the heat, season with white pepper and salt and stir in the egg yolk. Turn the mixture on to a plate, spread it out smoothly and let it cool. Meanwhile, prepare a small cupful of good white sauce, well seasoned, and grate a cupful of cheese. When the semolina is set, cut it into small square pieces and lay them in a well-greased dish. Sprinkle them liberally with cheese, coat with the sauce, and put more cheese on the top. Place the gnocchi in a hot oven for a few minutes, until thoroughly hot and nicely browned.

GNOCCHI EN CASSEROLE

¾ pint milk	¼ pint stock or water
2 oz. semolina	1 oz. butter
4 oz. grated cheese	1 tbsp. sharp jelly (red-currant, apple, etc.)
Salt, pepper and mustard	½ oz. flour
1 red cabbage (medium-sized)	

To make the gnocchi, heat the milk and sprinkle in the semolina, stirring well. Cook gently until the mixture thickens and the grains soften (about 20 minutes), stirring frequently. Then add 3 oz. of the grated cheese, and season well with the salt, pepper and mustard. Spread on a wetted plate to set.

Meanwhile, wash and chop the cabbage finely and put it into a casserole with the stock or water, butter, some seasoning and the jelly. Cook gently for about ½ hour, then stir in the flour, and place the gnocchi (cut into squares), on top of the cabbage. Sprinkle with the remaining 1 oz. grated cheese and cook for a further 15 minutes. If liked, brown under the grill.

CUCUMBER AU GRATIN

1 large cucumber	2 oz. grated cheese
Salt	Butter
½ pint white sauce	Parsley

Peel a large cucumber and cut it in ½-inch slices. Sprinkle these with salt, and either steam or boil them until tender, but not broken. Make ½ pint of good white sauce, fairly thick and well seasoned, and add most of the cheese. Grease a shallow fireproof dish, put into it a little of the sauce, and lay the cucumber on the top. Pour the rest of the sauce over and sprinkle with more cheese. Lay a few small pieces of butter on the top and place in a hot oven until nicely browned. Serve hot, garnished with parsley.

CREAM CHEESE SAVOURIES

Small savouries, served on breakfast biscuits, crackers, toast or fried bread, can be made in great variety from cream cheese and any scraps of tasty food.

Mix the cheese with mustard and vinegar to taste. Add chopped ham, pineapple, chicken, tomato, pickled mushrooms, cucumber, sardines, nuts, or pickled onions, as taste dictates. The biscuits, etc., should be hot, and having been spread with the mixture, they should be put under the grill for a few seconds just before serving.

Note : For recipes for other dishes containing cheese, see chapter on After Dinner and Cocktail Savouries.

CEREALS

ARROWROOT

A pure starch powder obtained from a plant grown in the West Indies. As purchased in this country, it is a light, white, odourless powder.

Arrowroot is an easily digested and pure form of starch, and is invaluable for invalid dietary. When mixed with boiling water, it forms a clear jelly, and can be used for thickening sauces, and also fruit juices which are used for covering flans and similar dishes—see FRUIT FLAN in Pastry Making chapter. Mixed with milk it may be used for puddings, and it also makes a popular thin, crisp biscuit (see Biscuits chapter).

BARLEY

Barley is a cereal grown in Great Britain and in many other countries. Pot barley, Scotch barley, or hulled barley, which have the outer husk of the grain removed, are used in soups, stews, etc.; they require 2–3 hours' cooking to make them digestible. Pearl barley, which is steamed, rounded, and polished in a mill, is also used in soups and stews, but requires rather less cooking—$1\frac{1}{2}$–2 hours.

Barley

Barley is also ground into a meal, which is sometimes used for porridge and gruel and as an ingredient in bread.

In addition to the above, there are also patent preparations of barley obtainable, either as ground barley or as partially cooked flaked barley. They are useful for making milk puddings, gruel, and so on. With these preparations, the makers' directions should be closely followed.

An infusion of barley—barley water—makes a soothing invalid drink.

MAIZE (INDIAN CORN)

A cereal which is grown in enormous quantities in the Americas, and also in many other parts of the world. Maize is used to produce corn syrup, alcoholic beverages, corn oil, etc., to cook as a vegetable (see Corn on the Cob), and to grind into meal and flour, of various degrees of fineness, for use in the production of cornflour, custard powder, starch, and cereal preparations of different types. Maize porridge, corn bread, hominy and corn mush in the U.S.A., polenta in Italy, and stirabout in Ireland, are some of the best-known dishes made with corn meal. As it does not keep well, it should be bought in small quantities.

CORNFLOUR

Cornflour, the very finely ground inner part of the Indian corn, consists mainly of starch, and is therefore useful for making milk puddings and cornflour moulds (see chapters on Milk Puddings and Invalid Cooking), also for thickening soups, sauces, and stews.

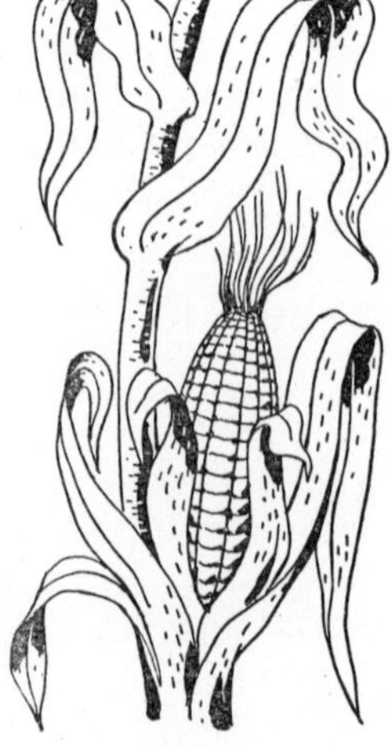

Maize

Cornflour should never be added dry to a hot or liquid mixture, but should always be blended to a smooth cream with a small amount of cold liquid (milk, stock, or water, according to the recipe). The remainder of the liquid may then be added hot, the whole returned to the pan, and the mixture brought to the boil, stirring. Once it is boiling, a mixture containing cornflour should be boiled for 8–10 minutes, to make sure that all the starch grains are thoroughly cooked, otherwise the dish will have a raw taste. During this cooking the mixture must be stirred almost continuously, as otherwise the starch is likely to form lumps, or the mixture to stick and burn.

HOMINY PORRIDGE

2 oz. hominy Salt
1 pint water

Wash the hominy and soak overnight in the water. Then put into a saucepan, bring to the boil, and cook gently until swollen and tender—$\frac{1}{2}$–1 hour—stirring frequently. If more convenient, cook in a double saucepan, allowing rather longer time for cooking. Add salt to taste, and serve as for oatmeal porridge.

OATS

Oats are generally used in the form of oatmeal, that is, the hulled, ground oats. There are different varieties, according to the grade of grinding.

1. Coarse oatmeal, suitable for porridge, haggis, soups, and stews, requiring 1–2 hours' cooking.

2. Medium oatmeal, suitable for porridge, requiring 20–30 minutes' cooking, and also used for general cooking purposes such as for oatmeal biscuits, scones, oatcakes, parkin, and so on.

Oats

3. Fine oatmeal or oatmeal flour, used for porridge or gruel, requiring about 5 minutes' cooking, and also for general cookery, though less frequently used than medium oatmeal.

4. Rolled oats are another form of oatmeal. The grain is passed through hot rollers which crush it, and at the same time partially cook it. It is used for porridge, requiring only about 5 minutes' cooking, and also in general cookery for flapjacks, flakemeal cookies, and so on. (See Biscuits chapter.)

Coarse, medium, or fine oatmeal or rolled oats may be used for porridge, according to individual taste and the time available. Accompaniments for porridge are also a matter of individual choice, some people liking to sprinkle it with white or brown sugar or treacle, while others prefer salt. It is usually served with hot or cold milk, or with cream.

PORRIDGE WITH COARSE OR MEDIUM OATMEAL

4 tbsps. oatmeal Salt (approx. 1 tsp.)
1 pint water

Heat the water in a thick saucepan, and when boiling sprinkle in the oatmeal, stirring well with a wooden spoon. Continue to stir and boil for a few minutes, then allow to simmer until the meal is well swollen and quite tender. This will take 20–30 minutes for medium oatmeal, and up to 2 hours for coarse; in the latter case it is advisable to cook over hot water after the initial boiling, or in the simmering oven of a solid fuel cooker, otherwise the meal is likely to stick and burn.

The texture of the finished porridge is again very much a matter of taste. More boiling water may be stirred in before serving if a thin porridge is preferred. The salt is usually added when the porridge is half cooked.

PORRIDGE WITH FINE OATMEAL

4 tbsps. fine oatmeal Salt
1 pint water

Blend the oatmeal to a smooth cream with a little of the water. Heat the remainder of the water and, when boiling, pour it on to the blended meal, stirring. Return to the saucepan, bring to the boil, and cook for about 5 minutes, stirring continuously. Add salt to taste and serve hot.

PORRIDGE WITH ROLLED OATS

2 oz. rolled oats Salt
1 pint water

Heat the water and when boiling sprinkle in the oatmeal, stirring vigorously with a wooden spoon. Continue to stir and boil for about 5 minutes, then add salt to taste, and serve very hot.

When using special brands of flaked oats, the manufacturers' directions printed on the packet should be carefully followed.

MEALY PUDDING WITH SAUSAGES

1 lb. oatmeal	2 onions
½ lb. beef suet	Salt and pepper

Choose medium or coarse oatmeal. Toast it in the oven, turning it over frequently until it is golden-brown all over. Shred the suet finely and chop the onions very finely. Mix oatmeal, onions, and suet together and season highly with salt and pepper. Tie in a cloth and boil for about 1 hour. Turn out, and serve with sausages, fried bacon, grilled herrings, etc.

Note: If pudding skins are obtainable, this mixture can be tied in the skins to make sausages. Cook the sausages in gently boiling water for ½ hour and serve as above.

RICE

The vitamins in rice are concentrated in the husk and germ of the grain, and these are removed in the process of milling. Milled rice is a dull fawn colour and is termed "unpolished" or "natural." The ordinary white rice with which we are most familiar is subjected to a further process of polishing. The natural rice has rather more flavour and food value than polished rice, but is not so easy to obtain. The same applies to the unrefined grain or brown rice: this has only the hull removed, and the coating of bran which it retains gives it a pleasant, nutty flavour, and contains mineral salts and some members of the Vitamin B complex. It requires rather longer cooking than white, or polished, rice.

For plain boiled rice, curries, risotto, and such dishes, in which the aim is to keep the grains separate, the Indian varieties of rice, such as Patna and Burma, are best. For rice puddings, creams, etc., where a softer, creamier texture is required, the varieties of rice from Carolina, Java, and so on, are more suitable. The different types have similar food value.

Rice, like other cereals, is a good source of starch, though it contains less protein than most cereals. Unpolished and brown rice supply valuable B vitamins and minerals.

Rice can be used as a garnish or accompaniment in place of a starchy vegetable such as potatoes, or may form the basis of lunch or supper dishes in combination with meat, fish, eggs, cheese, and so on. It is also used to make sweet dishes such as rice pudding, rice cream, etc. When used as a main ingredient, other starchy foods should be avoided.

To Cook Rice

When cooking rice to use as a main dish, accompaniment or garnish, the aim is to soften the grains sufficiently to make them digestible, but to avoid cooking so much that they disintegrate and clog together. This may be done in two ways, either by cooking for a short time in plenty of rapidly boiling water (Method 1), or cooking more slowly in a measured amount of liquid in a covered vessel (Method 2—see below).

When cooking rice for a pudding or cream, the aim is to soften the grain so completely that the mixture becomes of an even texture throughout. To achieve this, the grain is cooked very gently in a measured amount of milk, either in a slow oven (325° F., mark 2) or over hot water, for 2 or even 3 hours. (See recipes in Milk Puddings chapter.)

BOILED RICE—METHOD I

Have ready a good saucepan of boiling water and add salt in the proportion of 1 tsp. to 1 quart of water. A squeeze of lemon juice helps to keep the rice a good colour, but is not essential. Wash the rice (Patna if possible) in cold water and add it to the pan of fast-boiling water. Boil rapidly, stirring occasionally to prevent the rice from sticking. After about 10 minutes' cooking, remove one or two grains and break them in half. If still hard in the centre, continue cooking, testing at intervals, until tender throughout. This may take anything up to 18 minutes, according to the variety of rice. Turn into a colander or inverted sieve (reserving the rice water for soups or sauces), and pour boiling water through it to remove any loose starch and separate the grains. Cover with a cloth, and allow to dry for some minutes in a warm place, then dish and serve. Garnish with paprika pepper, chopped parsley, and so on, as desired.

BOILED RICE—METHOD II

For this method use a thick pan with a well-fitting lid. Wash the rice thoroughly in cold water, drain, and place it in a thick saucepan with cold water in the proportion of ½ pint of water to ¼ lb. of rice. Then add a sprinkling of salt and cover with a tightly fitting lid. Bring slowly to the boil and continue cooking over very gentle heat for 25–30 minutes (the exact time for cooking varies with the type of rice), by which time the grain should be quite tender, having swelled and absorbed the water.

It is important to keep the pan covered so that the steam cannot escape, and also to cook over very gentle heat, otherwise the rice is likely to stick and burn. Avoid stirring the rice during cooking, but if stirring is necessary, use a fork or skewer rather than a spoon. If the rice appears to need a further small amount of water during cooking, shake a few drops carefully into the pan. When completely tender, the rice is ready to dish and serve—no straining is necessary.

PILAU OF CHICKEN LIVERS

5–6 chicken livers
2 oz. butter or margarine
⅓ pint chicken broth or water
Pepper and salt
1 medium-sized onion
6 oz. rice
Powdered mace
½ tsp. curry powder
A pinch of saffron (optional)
1 tbsp. sultanas
Paprika pepper

Well wash the chicken livers, cut them into small pieces and fry in a little of the fat until well browned. Then cover with the stock, season well, and simmer until tender. Meanwhile, put the remainder of the fat into a saucepan, add the chopped onion, and fry until golden-brown. Add the washed and well-drained rice and seasonings, and cook slowly until the grains are very lightly browned; if necessary, add a little more butter or margarine. Add the chicken liver stock and cook until the rice has absorbed the liquid, but do not overcook it; the rice grains should remain separate. Add the livers and sultanas and blend well. Serve on a hot dish, garnished with a little paprika.

RICE AND STEAK BALLS

½ lb. sieved tomatoes
1 pint stock
½ lb. rump steak
2 oz. suet
2 tbsps. raw rice
2 tbsps. sieved boiled onion
1 beaten egg to bind
Flour

Make tomato stock by boiling the stock with the sieved tomatoes; if fresh tomatoes are not available, tomato purée or tomato sauce may be used instead. Mince the steak, chop the suet finely and mix with all the remaining ingredients. Flour the hands, form mixture into balls the size of walnuts, and flour the outside of each lightly. Put into fast-boiling tomato stock, reduce the heat, and simmer slowly for 2 hours. Serve in the stock in which the balls have been cooked or, if preferred, they can be served separately and the stock handed as a sauce.

RISOTTO

1 rasher of bacon
2 oz. dripping or butter
1 onion
½ lb. rice
A few mushrooms, neatly sliced
2 tomatoes
Salt and pepper
A bunch of herbs
1 pint stock or water
Grated cheese

Rind and dice the bacon and fry it lightly to extract the fat, then remove it from the pan. Add the dripping or butter and when hot, fry the sliced onion in it until a light brown. Add the rice (dry) and continue frying gently until the rice becomes opaque—4–5 minutes—stirring frequently. Add the sliced mushrooms, the tomatoes, cut in quarters, and the bacon. Add a good sprinkling of salt and pepper and a bunch of fresh herbs. Have the stock or water boiling and pour it on to the rice in the pan. Stir well, then cover closely and cook over a very gentle heat until all the liquid is absorbed, the rice soft, and each grain separate—30–40 minutes. It is best to leave the risotto undisturbed during the cooking. If it is found necessary to stir it, use a fork or skewer in preference to a spoon. Remove herbs and serve the risotto piled on a hot dish with grated cheese sprinkled over or handed separately.

To make a more nourishing dish, remains of cooked meat or sausages can be included. These should be placed on top of the rice in the pan 10 minutes or so before cooking is completed to heat through, and can then be either mixed into the risotto or arranged round it when dishing.

SAVOURY RICE AND BANANAS

¼ lb. rice (Patna, if available)
2 oz. butter
2–3 bananas
1 onion
Seasoning
2 tsps. curry powder

Wash the rice in several waters, then drain and cook quickly in boiling salted water until tender. Drain again, and run some hot water through the rice to separate the grains. Now melt the butter in a frying pan, put in the bananas, cut in quarters, fry them for a minute or two, and then keep them hot. Add the finely chopped onion to the butter left in the frying pan, and cook it slowly until tender and golden-brown. Then put in the rice, sprinkle with pepper, salt, and curry powder, and stir with a fork until thoroughly hot. Dish neatly and garnish with the fried bananas.

To make a more substantial dish, two or three fried eggs may be placed on the rice.

RYE

A hardy cereal which will grow in cold climates and in poor soil. The grain, which is brown and hard, with a slightly sour taste, is often mixed with other flours in bread making, and is used on the Continent for making black bread. It makes a damp, heavy bread, however, unless some other flour is mixed with it. It is also used for making thin, dry, crisp biscuits.

SAGO

This pearly grain, which is used in a similar way to true cereals, is obtained from the powdered pith of a type of palm-tree. It is used for milk puddings and fruit moulds (see chapter on Milk Puddings), in invalid dishes and for thickening soups ($\frac{1}{2}$ oz. per pint of liquid).

TAPIOCA

This is obtained from the roots of the cassava plant, which grows in hot countries. Tapioca is sold in different forms, the flake and pearl types being the most common; the flakes are large, irregularly shaped pieces, while the pearls are small, seed-like shapes which cook more quickly.

Tapioca contains very little protein, and consists almost entirely of starch. Its chief uses are for making milk puddings and moulds (see Milk Puddings) and for thickening soups: allow $1\frac{1}{2}$–2 oz. pearl tapioca to 1 pint of liquid.

WHEAT

This is the grain that is grown in most parts of the world to provide the flour used in making bread, cakes, biscuits, puddings, etc. (See the appropriate chapters for recipes.)

Wheat

The nutritional value of wheat is similar to that of barley, oats, and rye, though it varies somewhat with different varieties and in different climates. Though the protein of wheat is not so valuable as animal protein, it is nevertheless a body-building food, and 1 lb. of bread contains about a third of the daily protein requirement; wheat products also contain varying amounts of B vitamins, calcium, and iron.

ITALIAN PASTES

One special class of products made from wheat is known as the Italian pastes, and includes macaroni, spaghetti and vermicelli. They are made from a special white flour of high gluten content, such as is produced in Italy, where these pastes are much eaten, though they are also made and enjoyed in other countries.

Macaroni is the largest of these pastes, and is generally seen in tubular form, but can also be made into shells, fluted ribbons, tiny letters, and so on. Spaghetti is smaller than macaroni, usually in long lengths, and solid. Vermicelli is finer still and also solid. It is not practical to make these pastes at home, but they are easily obtainable, and since they are dried, they can be stored for long periods.

Noodles is another paste made from flour and usually contains also egg, which gives it a yellow colour and, of course, greater food value. It is generally rolled very thinly and cut into ribbons. A recipe for Home-made Noodles is given in this chapter.

These Italian pastes are good sources of starch. They are easy to prepare and cook, and are very useful for lunch or supper dishes, in combination with meat, fish, eggs, cheese, etc. If using them in a main dish, avoid serving other starchy items such as pastry, or vegetables which are rich in starch (such as potatoes or beans) in the same course.

Macaroni, spaghetti, and noodles are used as a garnish for entrées, stews, soups, and so on, or may serve as a vegetable in place of potatoes. Macaroni and noodles are also used to make puddings (see Caramelled Noodles in this chapter, and Macaroni Pudding in the section on Milk Puddings). Vermicelli is used mainly as a garnish for soups and savoury dishes.

Ravioli is a savoury dish made from a flour paste similar to noodles. The raw paste (which is used freshly made in this case, and not dried) is rolled very thinly, and small amounts of a tasty mixture, such as cooked chicken or other meat moistened with a sauce, or a vegetable filling of spinach purée or creamed mushrooms, are enclosed in it, the paste completely enveloping the filling, like miniature jam puffs. The ravioli is not dried, but merely "rested" for a few hours and is then ready for cooking. A recipe for Ravioli is given in this chapter.

Cooking Italian Pastes

For use as a main dish, accompaniment or garnish, these pastes are usually cooked in boiling salted water until tender, the time depending on the thickness :—

Macaroni requires	20–30 minutes
Spaghetti, Noodles, Ravioli	15–20 minutes
Vermicelli	7–10 minutes

When used as an ingredient in soups and stews, they are often added raw a short time before the dish is ready to serve.

In some cases, these pastes are cooked in stock or milk in place of water.

ITALIAN-STYLE MACARONI

½ lb. macaroni
2½ pints water
Salt and pepper
1½ oz. butter
3 oz. grated Parmesan or Cheddar cheese

The macaroni can either be cooked whole or broken into 2- or 3-inch lengths, or the cut variety can be used. When the water is boiling, drop in the macaroni, add the salt and cook until most of the liquid is absorbed and the macaroni tender. The length of time required for cooking varies according to the size and variety of the macaroni or other paste (see directions given above). When tender, strain free from moisture, return to the saucepan and place over a low heat for a few minutes to remove any moisture remaining. Add the butter and cheese, pepper and salt, blend with the macaroni, then reheat, and serve immediately with more grated cheese, if liked.

ITALIAN MACARONI WITH TOMATO

½ lb. Italian macaroni
1 quart boiling salted water
1–2 oz. butter
2 tbsps. tomato purée
2 tbsps. water
Seasoning
Parmesan cheese

Break ½ lb. of good Italian macaroni into pieces, wash it and throw it into the boiling salted water. Cook until just tender, strain through a colander, and place on a hot dish. Meanwhile, prepare the following sauce : heat the butter in a small saucepan until it is a golden-brown, being careful that it does not burn, then add the tomato purée, together with 2 tbsps. water and seasoning to taste. Bring to the boil and pour over the macaroni. Sprinkle with grated Parmesan cheese and serve at once.

MACARONI PIE

½ lb. macaroni
½ lb. minced meat
½ onion, sliced
Pepper and salt
A pinch of ground cinnamon
¼ lb. butter
2 tbsps. flour
¼ pint milk
2 egg yolks
Parsley to garnish

Cook the macaroni in boiling salted water for about 20 minutes. When tender, strain and rinse with cold water. Cook the meat with the finely sliced onion, pepper, salt, cinnamon powder, and a little butter over gentle heat for about 10 minutes. Melt half the butter and add the flour, stirring vigorously. Add the milk gradually, stirring all the time. Cook, stirring, for about 5 minutes, then add the egg yolks, and continue stirring until it thickens. Season with salt and pepper. Melt the remainder of the butter and put in a deep plate, add half the macaroni, then put on the meat and cover with the rest of the macaroni. Pour on the egg mixture and bake in a moderately hot oven (425° F., mark 7) for 10–15 minutes, taking care it does not burn. Garnish with parsley and serve hot.

MACARONI WITH CHESTNUTS

4 oz. macaroni
¾ lb. chestnuts
1 onion
¼ pint milk
2 oz. butter
Pepper and salt
2 tsps. chopped parsley
2 oz. grated cheese

Boil the macaroni until tender, drain, and cut into short lengths. Boil the chestnuts for 15 minutes, drain them and remove the skins. Stew the chestnuts and sliced onion in the milk until tender, and then rub them through a sieve. Melt the butter in a saucepan, add the macaroni and chestnut purée and cook for a few minutes, adding a little extra milk if the mixture is too thick. Season well and add the chopped parsley. Pour the mixture into a buttered fireproof dish, sprinkle the cheese on top and brown in a hot oven or under the grill.

SCRAMBLED EGG AND MACARONI

4 oz. macaroni
2 oz. butter
2 oz. grated cheese
3 eggs
2 tsps. parsley
1 tbsp. water
Pepper and salt

Cook the macaroni in salted water until tender, then strain, add 1 oz. butter and the finely grated cheese. Toss the macaroni to mix well, and place on a hot dish. To scramble the eggs, beat them lightly, add 2 tsps. of finely chopped parsley, 1 tbsp. water, pepper, and salt. Melt the remaining 1 oz. of butter in a saucepan, put in the beaten egg, scramble lightly, and serve on the top of the macaroni.

NOODLES (NOUILLES)

8 oz. flour
1 tsp. salt
1 oz. butter or lard
1 egg
Milk and water or water

Mix together the flour and salt and rub in the fat very thoroughly. Add the beaten egg and enough milk and water, or water only, to make a very stiff dough, and knead until smooth. Divide into two portions and roll out very thinly. Flour the surface, fold each piece up into a long roll and cut off pieces about ¼ inch wide with a sharp knife. Toss in a floured cloth to unroll the strips and leave to rest in the floured cloth for ½–1 hour before cooking. Any not required to be cooked immediately should be dried until crisp by hanging in a warm dry place—near the stove, or before the fire. These can then be stored for a short period.

To cook, put into boiling salted water and boil gently until tender—about 15 minutes—then strain and use as required.

CARAMELLED NOODLES

Noodles, made with ¼ lb. flour, etc. (see above)
1 oz. butter
½ tsp. ground cinnamon
Butterscotch sauce

Make the noodle paste as described above, cutting into ½-inch strips and then into squares or short lengths. Cook in boiling salted water for about 15 minutes, then drain well. Add the butter and cinnamon. Reheat, and serve with hot butterscotch sauce poured over.

NOODLES WITH TOMATO PURÉE

Noodles made with ¼ lb. flour, etc.
1 oz. butter
2 tbsps. chopped parsley
4 tbsps. tomato purée
1 clove of garlic
2 oz. grated cheese

Make the noodle paste as described above, cutting the strips as thinly as possible. Cook in boiling salted water for 15 minutes, then strain off the water. Add the butter, chopped parsley, tomato purée, and the garlic cut up finely (or crushed). Reheat, then pile on a hot dish, sprinkle with the grated cheese and serve with a green salad.

SPAGHETTI EN CASSEROLE

Stew ¼ lb. spaghetti in ¾ pint of chicken or veal stock until it is tender and the liquid absorbed. Add 1 oz. butter, the sieved pulp of 1 or 2 tomatoes, pepper, and salt. Make all thoroughly hot, and serve in the casserole with poached or scrambled eggs on the top. A little grated cheese may also be added.

SPAGHETTI IN MUSHROOM SAUCE

¾ lb. mushrooms
1 moderately large onion
4–5 tomatoes
2 tbsps. olive oil or 2 oz. butter
1 oz. flour
½ pint stock or milk
A bunch of herbs
½ tsp. parsley
Pepper and salt
4–6 oz. spaghetti
Grated cheese

Chop the mushrooms and onion finely, and slice the tomatoes. Put the oil or butter in a saucepan and heat gently. First cook the mushrooms for about 5 minutes, until evenly browned, remove them from the saucepan, and add the chopped onion. Fry this, then remove and cook the tomatoes, adding a little more fat if necessary. Remove the tomatoes from the pan and stir the flour into the remaining oil or butter. Cook the flour slowly for a few minutes, add the ½ pint of milk or stock, and bring to the boil, stirring constantly. Return the onions, tomatoes, and mushrooms to the pan, add the bunch of herbs, the parsley, pepper, and salt. Simmer very gently for 15 minutes. Remove the herbs, then add the cooked spaghetti and blend it with the sauce. Serve in a hot vegetable dish, sprinkling the top generously with grated cheese, or hand the cheese separately.

SPAGHETTI AND TOMATO SAUCE

4 oz. spaghetti
½ oz. butter
3 oz. cheese

For the Sauce

Rasher of fat bacon or pieces of ham
1 small onion
Small tin of tomatoes or ¾ lb. fresh tomatoes
4 tbsps. stock or water
Small sprigs of parsley, thyme, and ½ a bay leaf, tied together
Seasoning

Make the tomato sauce as follows: cut the bacon into pieces and fry gently in a saucepan; when cooked, remove from the pan and fry the chopped onion in the bacon fat. Add a small tin of tomatoes or sliced fresh tomatoes, stock, herbs, and seasoning. Simmer for 40 minutes, then rub through a fine sieve.

While the sauce is being made, put the spaghetti on to cook in about 2½ pints of boiling salted water. Allow the spaghetti 10–15 minutes for cooking; when tender, strain, add ½ oz. butter, heat very gently to remove any surplus moisture, add the tomato sauce and grated cheese, and reheat.

ITALIAN RAGOÛT

1 medium-sized onion
1 lb. tomatoes
3 oz. spaghetti
¼ lb. cheese
Celery or celery salt
Pepper
1 pint stock or water

Slice the onion very thinly. Wash the tomatoes and cut them into slices. Break up the spaghetti into short lengths to fit the casserole. Grate the cheese. Arrange the prepared ingredients in layers in the casserole, seasoning fairly liberally with finely chopped celery, or celery salt, and pepper; add the stock or water. Cook either in a moderate oven (375° F., mark 5) or on the top of the stove, allowing it to simmer gently for ¾ hour after it comes to the boil.

MUSHROOMS AND SPAGHETTI

¼ lb. spaghetti
1 onion
4 tbsps. chopped red pepper
2 oz. butter
¼ pint stock
1 lb. mushrooms
Seasoning
2 tbsps. chopped parsley

Cook the spaghetti in boiling salted water until tender. Then drain, run some hot water over it, and keep it hot. Meanwhile, chop the onion and the red pepper. Melt the butter in a saucepan, add the onion and red pepper, and cook for a minute or two. Then add the stock, the mushrooms, prepared and cut in halves, and seasoning; cover and simmer for 10 minutes, or until the mushrooms are tender. Put the spaghetti in a hot dish, sprinkle the parsley over, and pour the mushroom mixture on the top. Serve with a green salad for luncheon or supper.

POACHED EGGS AND SPAGHETTI EN CASSEROLE

Cook ¼ lb. spaghetti in salted water, stock, or milk and water until tender. When cooked, strain off the liquid and stir in 1 tbsp. tomato paste or purée or 2 tbsps. tomato sauce. Put into a hot casserole. Meanwhile, poach 2 or 3 eggs, drain well, and serve on top of the spaghetti. Serve with grated Parmesan cheese.

SCALLOPED CABBAGE AND SPAGHETTI

4 oz. cooked spaghetti
1 young cabbage
½ pint well-seasoned white sauce
4 oz. grated cheese
Pepper and salt
A little made mustard
Breadcrumbs

Cook the spaghetti in salted water until tender. Shred the cabbage and cook quickly in boiling, salted water. Prepare the white sauce, add the cheese (reserving some for the top of the dish), pepper, salt, and a little mustard. Arrange the cooked cabbage and spaghetti in layers in an au gratin dish, pouring a little sauce over each layer and finishing with sauce on top. Sprinkle very generously with grated cheese and breadcrumbs. Bake in a hot oven (450° F., mark 8) for about 20 minutes.

RAVIOLI

Noodle paste, made with ¼ lb. flour, etc.
A little gravy or sauce
Grated cheese and sauce
2 oz. minced cooked meat, or bacon, ham, rabbit, etc.
Salt and pepper

Make the noodle paste as directed opposite, divide in half, and roll each piece very thinly into a large square. Add enough gravy or sauce to the minced meat to bind it, season well, and place teaspoonfuls of it on to one of the squares of paste, spacing them out evenly, about ½ inch apart. Moisten the spaces between the meat with a little cold water, brush over the other square of paste with cold water and

RAVIOLI

place it (wet side down) on top, pressing well down between and all round the little heaps of meat to enclose them in the paste. Then with a sharp knife (or pastry cutter), cut down between them to form little cushions. Press the edges of the ravioli well together, expelling any air bubbles, then spread on a rack and leave in a cool, dry place for several hours. Cook for 15–20 minutes in boiling salted water. Drain, and serve with grated cheese and a good sauce.

BRAISED RAVIOLI

Make the ravioli as above and place on a bed of vegetables in a pan or casserole. Just cover with stock, add salt and pepper, and braise until tender—30–40 minutes. Drain the ravioli and vegetables from the stock, and pile on a hot dish. Sprinkle with grated cheese and serve with a sauce made by thickening the liquor which was used for braising the ravioli.

SEMOLINA

Semolina is made from the same part of the wheat grain as is used for making flour. In the case of semolina, however, the grain is ground, more or less coarsely according to the grade, and not finely milled as is flour. The coarser grades require 15–20 minutes' cooking; the finer grades 7–10 minutes. Semolina is chiefly made into milk puddings, but is also used for savoury dishes such as gnocchi, and to thicken some soups and stews.

To cook semolina, sprinkle the grain into the boiling liquid, and continue cooking (stirring meanwhile) until the grain is swollen and tender and the mixture thick.

A basic recipe for making Gnocchi is given below, and some ways of using them are suggested in the Cheese chapter. For sweet dishes made with semolina, see the Milk Puddings chapter.

GNOCCHI

½ oz. butter	1 egg yolk
½ pint milk	4 tbsps. thick white sauce
2 oz. semolina	3 oz. grated cheese
Pepper and salt	

Put the butter in the milk and allow mixture to come to the boil, then sprinkle in the semolina, stirring well. Simmer, still stirring, until the grain is thoroughly cooked, and the mixture thick—about 10 minutes. Remove from the heat, add pepper, salt, and egg yolk. Beat all together, to blend the ingredients thoroughly. Turn the mixture on to a plate, smooth it well, and when cold cut into even-sized squares. Heat the sauce and add most of the grated cheese to it. Place the squares of gnocchi in the bottom of an au gratin dish or pie dish, coat with the sauce, sprinkle with the remainder of the grated cheese, and cook in a hot oven (450° F., mark 8) until hot and browned—about ¼ hour.

PREPARED BREAKFAST CEREALS

There is a number of patent breakfast cereals on the market such as flaked and "puffed" wheat, corn (maize), rice, etc., which receive the necessary cooking at the factory before being packaged.

These ready-prepared cereals may be served as they come from the package, but are often improved by being warmed through in the oven or under a slow grill, to make sure that they are perfectly crisp. Serve with sugar (white, brown, or Demerara), syrup or treacle and milk (hot or cold) or cream. For a change, serve sliced raw or tinned fruits with these cereals, or dried fruits such as stoned dates, raisins, cooked prunes, or apricots. Some of these cereals may also be used in puddings.

CANADIAN APPLE CHARLOTTE

3 oz. wheat flakes	½ lb. peeled and sliced apples
2 oz. butter	Powdered cloves
1½ oz. sugar	Sugar
1 tsp. lemon juice	

Crush the wheat flakes. Melt the butter and the sugar in a saucepan, and stir in the flakes and lemon juice. Mix well, and use part of the mixture to line a fireproof dish. Place in the centre the apples, cloves, and sugar, and cover with the remainder of the wheat flake mixture. Bake in a moderate oven (375° F., mark 5) for about 30 minutes.

FLUFFY FRUIT CUPS

1 oz. butter (melted)	2 tbsps. sugar
2 heaped tbsps. cornflakes	½ pint milk
½ lb. cooking apples	A few drops of vanilla essence
2 eggs	

Run a little melted butter round 4 or 5 ramekin cases and line them with the cornflakes, making certain that the flakes adhere to the sides of the cups. Peel and core the apples, cut into halves and place one half, round side down, in each cup. Combine the eggs and sugar and add the milk, a little at a time, then the vanilla essence. Pour this custard over the apples and bake in a moderate oven (375° F., mark 5) for 30–40 minutes, until the custard is set and the apples tender. Serve at once while the apples are fluffy and risen above the custard.

ROLLED OATS PUDDING

2 oz. rolled oats	1 pint milk
1 oz. sugar	1 oz. butter
3 oz. currants	

Grease a pie dish. Put in the oats, sugar, and currants, pour the milk over, then add the butter, cut in small pieces. Bake in a moderate oven (350° F., mark 3) for 1½–2 hours, stirring occasionally. Serve with stewed fruit.

PASTRY MAKING

There are seven main types of pastry—shortcrust (both flour and potato), suetcrust, rough puff, flaky, puff, hot-water crust and choux. The chief difference between them is the method of introducing the fat: in the short pastries it is rubbed into the flour, in suetcrust the chopped suet is simply mixed in, without further manipulation, and in the puff and flaky types the fat is rolled into the dough; in hot-water crust and choux pastry the fat is melted in hot liquid before being added to the flour.

In addition to the above types, there is a variety of pastry made from a yeast dough.

INGREDIENTS

Flour

Plain flour is recommended for pastry-making in general. Self-raising flour gives good results with the plainer pastries, though the texture is slightly different. In suet pastry, where a raising agent is needed, self-raising flour may be used instead of plain flour and baking powder.

Raising Agent

Baking powder may be used in suet pastry in the proportion of 1 tbsp. to every lb. of plain flour. If, for economy reasons, shortcrust pastry is made with less than half fat to flour, baking powder should be used, in the proportion of 2 tsps. to 8 oz. flour. No chemical raising agent is used in the richer types of pastry such as puff and flaky pastry, the raising agent in this case being air, enclosed between the layers.

Fat

Butter, lard, white vegetable fats, margarine or dripping may all be used for pastry. Butter gives the best flavour and should always be used for puff pastry. Margarine is best mixed with butter or lard. Lard is suitable for shortcrust and flaky pastry, used either alone or combined with margarine. Either fresh or packaged suet is used for suetcrust pastry.

GENERAL HINTS ON PASTRY MAKING

1. Coolness is the keynote to good results. Handle the pastry as little as possible, and always use the finger-tips for rubbing in the fat. Rich pastries are improved by being cooled on a cold slab or in a refrigerator between rollings.

2. Always sieve the flour and salt together into the mixing bowl, as this helps to lighten the mixture. Additional air may be incorporated by lifting the flour from the bowl with the finger-tips when rubbing in.

3. Add liquid carefully; an excess causes a sticky, unmanageable dough, and any extra flour then added will alter the proportions of the ingredients and cause the pastry to be tough.

4. Rolling out must be done lightly but firmly; do not roll more than necessary.

5. Pastry requires a hot oven—too slow an oven causes pale, hard pastry. Generally speaking, the richer the pastry, the hotter the oven. (For table of oven temperatures see page 51.)

SUETCRUST PASTRY

This may be used for both sweet and savoury dishes, and can be baked, steamed or boiled. Steaming and boiling are the most satisfactory methods—baked suetcrust is inclined to be hard. In this type of pastry a raising agent is always added; the proportion is usually 1 tbsp. to every lb. of flour, but in certain pudding recipes the amount of baking powder is reduced if breadcrumbs are mixed with the flour.

6–8 oz. suet
1 lb. flour
1 tbsp. baking powder
2 tsps. salt
Cold water to mix

If necessary, prepare the suet by removing any skin and chopping very finely. Mix together the flour, baking powder, salt and suet. Stir in enough cold water to form a light, elastic dough, which will leave the basin clean. Turn on to a floured board, knead very lightly and roll out, usually to a thickness of ½ inch, handling as little as possible. Use as required, for roly-poly, boiled or steamed fruit pudding, beefsteak pudding, and so on.

SHORTCRUST PASTRY

1 lb. flour	8 oz. fat
1 tsp. salt	Cold water to mix

Sieve together the flour and salt. Add the fat (lard and margarine mixed), and rub it very lightly with the finger-tips until the mixture resembles fine breadcrumbs. Mix to a stiff paste with a very little cold water, then turn on to a floured board, roll out lightly, handling as little as possible. Use as required—see recipes. Shortcrust pastry is baked in a hot oven, except when it is combined with ingredients which would be spoiled if cooked at so high a temperature—as in custard tart.

Note: For a more economical shortcrust pastry, use only 5–6 oz. fat, and add 1 tbsp. baking powder to 1 lb. flour.

RICH SHORTCRUST OR FLAN PASTRY

8 oz. flour	2 tsps. caster sugar
1 tsp. salt	1 egg yolk
5 oz. butter (or margarine and butter mixed)	Cold water

Sieve the flour and salt into a basin. Rub in the fat with the tips of the fingers until the mixture resembles fine breadcrumbs—do this very lightly, or the mixture will become greasy and heavy. Add the sugar. Beat the egg yolk and add 1–2 tbsps. cold water. Add just sufficient egg and water to the dry ingredients to mix to a firm dough. Turn on to a floured board, knead or pat lightly into a round, roll out and use as required for flans, tartlets, etc.

CHEESE SHORTCRUST PASTRY

3 oz. flour	2 oz. grated cheese
Salt and cayenne	1 egg yolk
1½ oz. butter	A little water

Sieve the flour, salt and cayenne, and rub in the butter very lightly with the tips of the fingers. Add the grated cheese and mix well. Beat up the egg yolk with about 1 tbsp. water and mix the dry ingredients with this until a stiffish paste is formed. Knead lightly until free from cracks, then turn on to a floured board, roll out and use as required.

POTATO SHORTCRUST PASTRY

8 oz. flour	4 oz. fat
1 tsp. salt	8 oz. sieved cooked potatoes
1 tbsp. baking powder	

Sieve together the flour, salt and baking powder. Rub in the fat with the tips of the fingers until the mixture resembles fine breadcrumbs. Add the sieved potatoes and rub well in. Knead into a dough, if possible without the addition of extra water, but if the potatoes are very dry, add a little cold water. Turn on to a floured board, roll out lightly, handling as little as possible, and use as required for meat and other savoury pies.

ROUGH PUFF PASTRY

Rough puff is a rich pastry similar in type to flaky and puff pastry, but more quickly made, and for this reason it is often preferred by the busy housewife. It may be used for any dishes for which either puff or flaky pastry is suitable—meat pies, patties, sausage rolls, jam puffs, and so on.

8 oz. flour	A squeeze of lemon juice
1 tsp. salt	Water to mix
4–6 oz. fat	

Sieve together the flour and the salt. Cut the fat into small pieces and drop it into the flour. Add a squeeze of lemon juice and sufficient water to make a stiff dough. Turn on to a floured board and roll into an oblong. Fold in three by bringing the top one-third down over the centre and folding the bottom one-third up over it. Give the pastry a half-turn so that the folds are to the sides and allow to stand in the cool for a few minutes. Repeat this rolling and folding three or four times, in order thoroughly to incorporate the fat and the flour. Roll out and use as required. This pastry requires to be cooked in a very hot oven.

FLAKY PASTRY

This pastry is very popular for meat pies, mince pies, jam puffs, Eccles cakes, etc. Good flaky pastry can always be judged by the evenness of the flakes and the crispness of texture when it is cooked. Important points are: mixing the dough to the correct consistency; even rolling; equal distribution of the fat; and quick cooking.

10–12 oz. fat	Cold water to mix (approx. ½ pint)
1 lb. flour	
1 tsp. salt	Lemon juice

First work the fat with a palette knife until it is of a firm but pliable consistency.

Sieve the flour and salt together. Divide the fat into four. Rub one quarter of it into the flour until no lumps can be felt. Mix to an elastic dough with the water, adding a squeeze of lemon juice. Turn on to a floured pastry board and knead lightly, if necessary, to remove the creases.

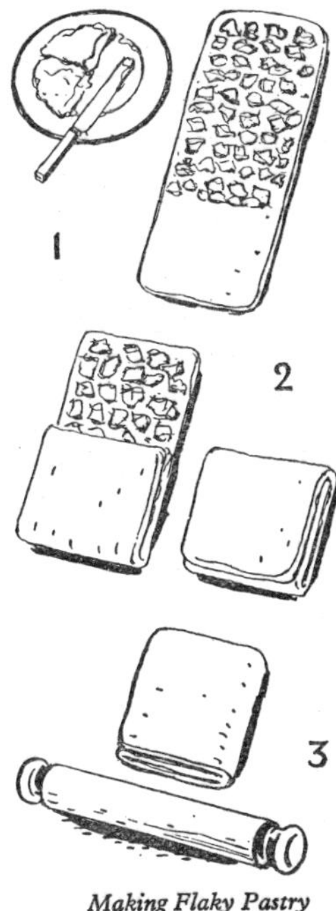

Making Flaky Pastry

Roll out to a long strip about 6–7 inches wide; distribute one quarter of the fat in small pieces evenly over the top two-thirds of the pastry, taking care not to place it too near the edges. Fold into three, i.e. place the bottom edge (which is free of fat) two-thirds up the strip of pastry and bring the top edge over so that it lies along the folded edge (there should then be alternate layers of pastry and fat). Give the pastry a half-turn, so that the folds are to the sides. Press the open edges together lightly with the rolling pin.

Dredge the board and rolling pin sparingly with flour and roll out the pastry again into a strip. Spread with another portion of fat. Repeat the process again, using the remaining portion of fat. Repeat the rolling and folding once more, this time without adding any fat. Roll out and use as desired. This pastry requires to be baked in a hot oven.

PUFF PASTRY

This is the richest type of pastry, and when well made is superior to any other in appearance and taste. It is used for any dish requiring a very light pastry, such as vol-au-vents, patties, French pastries, mince pies, and so on. (See colour picture facing page 161.)

Use a fine flour and good butter to give the best results, and take great care when folding and rolling the pastry: uneven rolling and careless folding will cause the pastry to rise crookedly in the oven and it may even topple over. Cool and rest the dough between rollings.

The baking of this pastry also requires much care and judgment. The secret of success lies in having the pastry cold and the oven hot; when the pastry has risen to its full height the heat may be reduced slightly to allow it to finish cooking.

½ lb. flour	A squeeze of lemon juice
A pinch of salt	Cold water to mix
½ lb. butter	

First wash the butter to remove all salt and buttermilk: put it into a basin under cold running water and squeeze it in the water until of a waxy consistency and easy to handle. Then dry it in a lightly floured cloth and pat it until every drop of water has been expelled. Whatever fat is used, it must be of about the same consistency as the dough, so if necessary, work it until it is soft enough.

Sieve the flour and salt into a basin and rub in a piece of the butter about the size of a walnut. Add the lemon juice and sufficient cold water to form an elastic dough. Turn on to a lightly floured board, and knead vigorously for a few minutes until it is smooth and velvety and no longer sticks to the fingers. Roll it out into a round. Shape the remainder of the butter into a flat cake, half the size of the round of dough, and place it in the centre. Fold over the sides of the dough to enclose the butter completely, and pat down with rolling pin.

Roll out into a long, narrow strip. Fold the pastry in three, folding the first lap away from you and the second one towards you. Then turn the pastry half-way round, bringing the folds to the side. Press the edges firmly with a rolling pin to enclose all the air possible; 71
this completes what is called one turn in making puff pastry. Repeat the rolling and folding seven times in all, putting the pastry aside, covered with greaseproof paper, in a cool place for at least ¼ hour after each rolling. Use for Cream Horns, Patty Cases, Vol-au-Vents, etc.

HOT-WATER CRUST

This pastry is used for making raised pies such as veal and ham pie, pork pie, game pie, and so on. It is mixed, as it name implies, with hot water. While warm, the pastry is flexible, but as it cools it hardens, retaining its shape. While still warm and pliable, the pastry is moulded into the shape of the pie, either with the hands or by using a special pie mould. Such moulds open at the side and can therefore be removed with ease when the pie is cooked; they are usually rather elaborate in design—see the sketch in the Meat Cookery chapter.

1 lb. flour	$\frac{1}{3}$ pint milk or milk and water
2 tsps. salt	
$\frac{1}{4}$ lb. lard	

Sieve the flour and salt into a warm basin. Melt the lard in a small saucepan, add the milk or milk and water, and bring just to boiling point. Pour this mixture into the centre of the flour and mix up quickly into a paste. Turn out on to a floured board and knead with the hands until the dough is smooth and free from cracks.

Cut off about a quarter of the quantity and keep it warm for making the lid and decorations later on. Mould the larger piece at once, while still warm, into an oval or round pie case, making it the desired height, and with the walls and bottom of an equal thickness. Detailed instructions for moulding and shaping the pies are given in the Meat chapter, together with various recipes for fillings, times of baking, and so on.

CHOUX PASTRY

Proportions and method of making choux pastry, with recipes, are given in the chapter on Éclairs and Cream Buns.

YEAST PASTRY

$\frac{1}{2}$ oz. yeast	1 oz. margarine
About $\frac{1}{2}$ pint tepid milk	1 oz. lard
	1 oz. sugar
$\frac{1}{2}$ lb. plain flour	1 egg

Cream the yeast with a little of the milk, sprinkle with a little flour, and set aside for 5 minutes to rise. Cream the fats and sugar until light, and beat in the egg, adding a little of the flour to make a smooth cream. Add the yeast and the remaining flour, with enough milk to make a soft dough. Beat well, cover with a cloth, and set aside for about $\frac{3}{4}$ hour. Turn on to a board and knead, then roll out and use as required. Bake for 20–30 minutes in a moderately hot oven (425° F., mark 7).

A richer type of yeast mixture is used for the Danish pastries in the Cake Making chapter.

TARTS, PIES, FLANS, ETC.

MAKING A FRUIT PIE

8 oz. shortcrust pastry	Sugar to sweeten
2 lb. fruit (approx.)	Cold water

Make the shortcrust pastry. Prepare fruit according to kind. Half-fill a pie dish with the fruit, add sugar to sweeten, and fill the dish up with the rest of the fruit. (If the dish is not well filled, place a pie funnel or upturned egg cup in the centre.) Add sufficient water to cover the bottom of the dish.

Roll the pastry about $\frac{1}{4}$ inch thick and to the shape of the pie dish, but about 1 inch larger all round. Cut off a strip of pastry wide enough to cover the rim of the pie dish. Wet the rim
and press on the strip without stretching it, 7
damping the edges where they join. Moisten the strip with water, then lift the piece of pastry on the rolling pin and lay over the fruit, taking care not to stretch it. Press lightly on to the pastry rim and trim off any rough edges with a sharp knife. Knock up the edges of the pastry with the back of the knife and decorate with tiny flutes. Glaze with milk or egg white, if liked, and make two small holes with a skewer to allow steam to escape. Bake near the top of a hot oven (450° F., mark 8) for 15–20 minutes, until the pastry is set and lightly browned. Then reduce the heat, or move to a lower shelf, and continue to cook until the fruit is tender (this can be tested with a skewer) and the pastry well browned and crisp. Dust with caster sugar and serve hot or cold.

A well-made pie crust is crisp throughout and nicely rounded on the pie dish. If the pastry is mixed too soft, rolled too thinly, or put into too cool an oven, the crust is likely to sink into the fruit and be soggy when baked.

MAKING AN OPEN TART

Make some shortcrust pastry, turn it on to a floured board and form into a ball. Roll out into a round $\frac{1}{4}$–$\frac{1}{8}$ inch thick and about 3 inches larger than the plate in diameter.

For a Flat Tart

Cut off a rim of pastry wide enough to fit the edge of the plate. Place the strip in position, without stretching it, then damp lightly. Fit the round of pastry evenly and neatly on the plate, taking care not to pull or stretch it. Press the pastry lightly on to the plate, and on to the damped pastry rim, making sure that there are no air bubbles under the crust. Trim round

the plate with a sharp knife, knock up the pastry edge with the back of the knife and decorate
3 with tiny flutes or other edging. Place filling in the centre and bake in a hot oven (450° F., mark 8) at first, then lower heat according to the kind of filling.

For a Tart with a Raised Rim

A raised rim is useful if you want the tart to hold plenty of filling, or if you are using a meringue top.

Roll as above and place the round of pastry neatly and evenly on a flat pie plate, taking great care not to pull or stretch it. Press lightly on to the plate, making sure that there is no air enclosed under the crust. Trim evenly with a pair of scissors, leaving $1\frac{1}{2}$ inches overhanging all round the edge. Fold this overhanging pastry up underneath between the pastry and the rim of the plate all the way round. Bring this double fold to an upright position. Now flute this rim by placing the point of the forefinger of the left hand against the inside of the pastry rim and pinching the outside fold of pastry at this point with the tips of the right thumb and forefinger: press the pastry on to the pie plate as you make each flute. Repeat at $\frac{1}{2}$-inch intervals until the entire rim is fluted. The pastry case is now ready for the filling, if an unbaked pastry case is called for in the recipe.

If the pastry is to be baked "blind," prick the centre with a fork to remove any air bubbles, place a round of greased paper greased side down on the centre of the pastry and weight down with baking rice. Bake in a hot oven (450° F., mark 8) for 15–20 minutes, until the pastry is set and almost cooked. Then remove filling and return the tart to the oven for about 5 minutes to complete baking and to dry off the centre.

If time permits, put the tart in a cool place for a short time before baking, to allow the pastry to become firm.

MAKING A COVERED PLATE PIE

Make the pastry in the usual way, then turn it on to a lightly floured board and form into a ball. Cut in two, having one piece slightly larger than the other. Roll out the smaller piece to an even round, slightly larger than the plate, to allow for the depth, and about $\frac{1}{8}$ inch thick. Lay this round of pastry evenly on the plate, pressing it on lightly and taking care not to stretch or pull it. Fill the centre with the fruit or filling. Roll the second piece of pastry to an even round to fit the top of the pie, keeping it rather thicker than the bottom piece (between $\frac{1}{8}$ and $\frac{1}{4}$ inch thick). Damp the edges of the crust with cold water and lay the pastry lid in position, pressing it lightly on to the pastry rim. Trim the edges with a sharp knife. Knock up the pastry edges with the back of a knife and decorate with tiny flutes. Make several parallel slits in the lid to permit steam to escape, or cut out 2 or 3 tiny rounds with a cutter $\frac{1}{2}$ inch in diameter. Glaze the surface with slightly beaten egg white or with a sugar and water syrup. Bake as directed.

LINING A PIE DISH WITH PASTRY

It is usual to line only the sides of a pie dish—there is then no risk of having sodden pastry in the bottom of the dish if a moist filling is used.

Roll the pastry (about $\frac{1}{4}$ inch thick) into a long strip, then cut across in half. Damp the edges of the dish, then line the sides with the pieces of pastry, overlapping the joins to make the pastry fit neatly. Trim off rough edges. Damp the pastry rim, and decorate with tiny rounds of pastry overlapping each other.

MAKING A FLAN CASE

Flan cases are usually made with rich shortcrust or flan pastry. Plain shortcrust pastry may be used, however, or rough puff or flaky, if this is preferred.

Grease a piece of paper, lay it on a baking sheet, greased side uppermost, and place the flan ring on it. Grease another piece of soft paper to hold the baking rice, beans or other filling. If you have no flan ring use a well-greased shallow sandwich tin with a round of greased paper in the bottom, placing a strip of paper under the round and up the sides to 74
facilitate removing the case when baked.

Make the pastry in the usual way. Place it on a floured board and form into a ball. Roll out into a round $\frac{1}{4}$–$\frac{1}{8}$ inch thick and about an inch larger all round than the flan ring. Place the round inside the flan ring and press into position, taking care not to stretch or pull the pastry. See that the pastry is pressed flat at the base and that it is of equal thickness all over, so that it forms a well-shaped case. Trim the edges with a sharp knife, or by pressing the rolling pin sharply over the edge of the rim to cut the pastry clear. Prick the bottom lightly.

If the flan is to be baked "blind," place the piece of soft greased paper, greased side down, inside the case and half-fill with baking beans.

If possible let the flan stand in a cool place for half an hour before baking. This makes the pastry firm and helps to give the flan a good shape. Bake in a hot oven (450° F., mark 8) until pastry is almost cooked and edges lightly browned—about 15 minutes. Remove filling and paper, and return case to oven for a few minutes to dry off and complete cooking. Remove the flan ring and lift on to a rack to cool. A well-made flan case should be nicely shaped and evenly coloured, with a very short crust. The pastry is best eaten the day it is cooked, but flan cases can be made the day before and crisped through in the oven before filling.

MAKING TARTLET CASES

Make the pastry in the usual way, turn on to a floured board and form into a ball. Roll out about ⅛ inch thick and cut in rounds with a floured cutter, a size larger than the patty tins to be used, to allow for the depth of the tin. Line the tins evenly and neatly with the pastry, pressing it gently with the thumbs against the sides and bottom of each tin so that no air is enclosed under the crust. The tartlet cases are now ready to be filled.

If they are to be baked before filling, i.e. baked " blind," prick the bottom of the cases with a fork, then place in each a piece of soft greased paper, greased side down, and half-fill with baking rice. If possible, leave for half an hour in a cool place before baking, to firm the pastry. Bake in a hot oven (450° F., mark 8) for about 10 minutes, until the pastry is almost cooked and the edges are lightly browned. Remove filling and return to the oven for a few minutes to dry off and complete cooking.

MAKING TINY TARTLET CASES, BOAT-SHAPED CASES, ETC.

Use shortcrust, flan, or cheese pastry. Roll out the pastry twice as thick as the cases are required. Invert the tins on the pastry and press down, thus cutting out rounds, oblongs or boat shapes. Fit the pastry into the tin and press it gently with the thumbs until it covers the whole of the inside of the tin with an even layer, taking care to press out any air bubbles. Trim the edges with a sharp knife. Fill with greased paper and baking rice and bake " blind."

RECIPES FOR SWEET PASTRY DISHES

Recipes for sweet dishes only are given here; savoury dishes using pastry will be found in the chapters on Meat, Cheese, Eggs, etc., and in " After-dinner and Cocktail Savouries."

ALMOND MACAROON TART

6 oz. shortcrust pastry	3 egg yolks
Red-currant or other jelly	6 oz. caster sugar
8 medium-sized macaroons	1 orange
	2 egg whites

Make a flan case with the pastry and bake " blind." Spread the inside of the case with a layer of the jelly. Crush the macaroons with a rolling pin, beat the egg yolks and sugar together until creamy, add the macaroons and orange juice and mix well. Fold in the stiffly beaten whites of egg and put into the prepared case. Bake in a moderately hot oven (425° F., mark 7) for about 20 minutes. Serve hot or cold.

ALMOND TARTLETS

4 oz. shortcrust pastry	2 oz. sugar
Apricot jam	1 egg
4 oz. whole almonds	A squeeze of lemon juice
2 oz. margarine	

Line 8–10 patty tins with the pastry. Roll the pastry trimmings and cut narrow strips for decoration. Put 1 tsp. jam in the bottom of each pastry case. Blanch the almonds, then chop them fairly finely. Cream the margarine and sugar, beat in the egg, then the almonds and the lemon juice. Half-fill the pastry cases with the mixture and place two narrow strips of pastry crosswise on the top. Bake in a hot oven (450° F., mark 8) for about 7 minutes until the pastry is set, then reduce the heat. Continue cooking until the tartlets are nicely risen and a pale golden-brown—about 30 minutes in all. Be careful not to cook the tartlets too quickly, as the rich filling scorches easily. Dust the top of the tartlets with caster sugar and serve hot or cold.

APPLE AMBER

4 oz. shortcrust pastry	1 lemon
1 lb. apples	2 eggs
2 oz. butter	2 oz. sugar (for meringue)
Sugar to taste (for apples)	

Peel, core, and slice the apples. Put them with the butter and a very little (if any) water into a saucepan and cook until tender. Sweeten to taste and rub through a sieve or beat until smooth. Add the grated lemon rind, the lemon juice and the egg yolks to the apple mixture. Line a pie dish with pastry. Pour the apple mixture into the dish. Bake in a moderately hot oven (425° F., mark 7) for about 30 minutes, until the pastry is browned and the filling set. Whisk the whites of eggs very stiffly and fold in the 2 oz. sugar. Pile lightly on top of the apple filling and dredge with caster sugar. Bake in a cool oven (250° F., marks ¼–½) for 20–30 minutes, until the meringue is crisp to the touch and lightly coloured. Serve hot or cold.

APPLE CAKE

½ lb. shortcrust pastry
1 lb. cooking apples
3 oz. sugar
1 tbsp. water
Egg white for glazing

Cut the pastry in half and roll out into two rounds the size of a dinner plate. Put one round on a greased baking sheet. Peel the apples, slice thinly, and lay them on the round of pastry to within an inch of the edge. Sprinkle with sugar, add the water, moisten the edges of the pastry with water, and cover with the second round of pastry. Press the edges together and pinch into flutes. Brush over with egg white and sprinkle with sugar. Bake in a hot oven (450° F., mark 8) until the apples are tender—for about 25 minutes.

APPLE DUMPLINGS

6 oz. shortcrust pastry
4 good-sized cooking apples
Demerara sugar
Egg white for glazing

Make the pastry. Peel and core the apples. Divide the pastry into four and roll each piece into a round large enough to enclose an apple. Put an apple on each piece of pastry and fill the centre with brown sugar. Damp the edge of the pastry with water, gather the pastry round the apple, pressing lightly, and turn the dumpling over. Place on a greased baking sheet. Glaze with white of egg, if liked. Bake in a hot oven (450° F., mark 8) until the pastry is golden-brown. Reduce heat and continue to cook until the apples are tender when tested with a skewer. Serve hot with custard sauce.

Flaky pastry may be used if preferred.

SPANISH APPLE FLAN

6 oz. shortcrust pastry
½ lb. caster sugar
¼ pint water
A few drops of vanilla essence
6 small cooking apples of equal size
½ pint packet vanilla jelly
A little apricot jam
6 crystallised cherries
Whipped cream and angelica

Line a flan ring or deep sandwich tin with pastry and bake "blind" in hot oven (450° F., mark 8). Meanwhile, boil sugar and water a few minutes, flavour with vanilla and cook the peeled and cored apples carefully in this syrup. Drain the apples well, boil the syrup rapidly until reduced by half, pour it on to the jelly square and leave to cool. Cover the inside of the pastry with warm apricot jam, put the apples in the case with a cherry in each hole, pour the half-set jelly over and leave to set. Decorate with piped cream and angelica.

BROWN SUGAR APPLE TART

6 oz. shortcrust pastry
1 lb. good cooking apples (approx.)
4 oz. brown sugar
1 oz. butter or margarine

Line a pie plate with pastry as directed for Flat Tart. Core and peel the apples, cut in quarters and then slice fairly thickly. Arrange the slices overlapping regularly on the pastry. Sprinkle with a layer of brown sugar, completely covering the apples. Put on the butter in small dabs. Bake in a hot oven (450° F., mark 8) for about 10 minutes, until the pastry is set and lightly coloured, then reduce the heat and cook more slowly until the apples are tender and the whole tart is coloured an attractive golden-brown. Serve hot or cold.

This tart makes an excellent sweet for a buffet supper if baked on an oblong baking tray and cut in fingers when cold.

SPICED APPLE TART

For the Pastry

6 oz. flour
1 tsp. ground cinnamon or mixed spice
4 oz. margarine
1 oz. sugar
Egg yolk and water to mix

For the Filling

2 lb. cooking apples
4 oz. dates, sultanas, or raisins
Sugar to taste
A pinch of mixed spice

Peel and core the apples and stew to a pulp with a very little water. Add the dates (cut up) or cleaned fruit, sugar to taste, and spice. Allow to cool. Make the pastry as for rich shortcrust pastry, and line a flan ring with it, reserving a piece for the lid. Fill with the cooled apple mixture. Moisten the edges of the pastry and cover with the lid. Bake in a moderately hot oven (400° F., mark 6) at first, then reduce heat and cook until firm and well browned—about ¾–1 hour. Remove the flan ring and lift carefully on to a warm plate. Dredge with caster sugar and serve either hot or cold.

APPLE AND PUMPKIN TART

8 oz. shortcrust pastry
A thick slice of ripe pumpkin
1 lb. apples
Brown sugar
½ tsp. mixed spice
Powdered cloves
A little grated nutmeg

Peel the pumpkin, remove seeds and pithy part, and cut the flesh into thin slices. Core, peel and slice the apples ¼ inch thick. Half-fill the pie dish with the apple and pumpkin, then sprinkle thickly with sugar and add a dusting of the spices. Fill the dish with remaining fruit, sugar and spices. Add a very little water. Roll out the pastry and cover as for fruit tart. Bake in a hot oven (450° F., mark 8) for about 15–20 minutes, until the pastry is set and lightly browned. Reduce heat and cook until the fruit is tender.

APPLE AND QUINCE TART—I

8 oz. shortcrust pastry
2 lb. apples
1 quince
Sugar

Core, peel, and slice the apples ¼ inch thick. Core and peel the quince and cut into thin slices. Mix the apple and quince together, half-fill the pie dish, add sugar to sweeten, and fill the dish piled high with the rest of the fruit. Add a very little water. Roll out the pastry and cover as for Fruit Tart. Bake in a hot oven (450° F., mark 8) for 15–20 minutes, until the pastry is set and lightly browned, then reduce the heat and cook until the fruit is tender.

APPLE AND QUINCE TART—II

8 oz. shortcrust pastry
2 lb. apples
6 tbsps. quince jelly
1 oz. butter or margarine
Sugar
Sugar and water syrup for glazing

Peel, core, and slice the apples ¼ inch thick. Arrange half the fruit in a rather deep plate, cover with half the quince jelly and half the butter flaked in small pieces. Add a sprinkling of sugar to sweeten. Top with the rest of the apples, jelly, and butter. Roll out the pastry into a round and cover the dish as for Fruit Tart. Glaze with sugar and water syrup. Make 2 or 3 parallel slits in the top. Bake in a hot oven (450° F., mark 8) for 15–20 minutes, until the pastry is set and lightly browned. Reduce the heat and cook until the fruit is tender.

APPLE TURNOVERS

8 oz. shortcrust or flaky pastry
Sliced apple
Brown sugar
A pinch of powdered cloves
Egg white and sugar for glazing

Roll the pastry into a square or oblong ⅛ inch thick and cut into 4 or 6 squares. Brush with water and place some sliced apple, brown sugar and a pinch of powdered cloves on each square. Damp the pastry edge, then fold over to form a triangle and press the edges well together, to seal them, otherwise the filling is likely to ooze out during cooking and burn.

Place on a greased baking sheet. Brush with egg white and sprinkle with sugar. Bake in a hot oven (450° F., mark 8) for 15–20 minutes, until the pastry is golden-brown, then reduce heat and cook until the apples are tender.

BANANA AND RHUBARB PLATE PIE

8 oz. shortcrust pastry
1 lb. young rhubarb
2 bananas
Brown sugar
Sugar and water syrup for glazing

Line a plate with pastry. Wash the rhubarb, cut into 1-inch lengths, and cut the bananas into thick slices. Fill the plate with layers of fruit and a liberal sprinkling of brown sugar, packing the fruit tightly, as it will shrink considerably in cooking. Cover as for Plate Pie, and glaze with sugar and water syrup. Bake in a moderately hot oven (425° F., mark 7) until the crust is nicely browned, then reduce heat and cook until the fruit is tender. Serve hot with cream or custard.

BAKEWELL TART

4 oz. shortcrust pastry
Raspberry jam
2 oz. butter
2 oz. sugar
1 egg
2 oz. ground almonds
1–2 drops almond essence

Line a flan ring or sandwich tin with the pastry and spread with a layer of raspberry jam. Beat the butter and sugar together until soft and creamy. Add the beaten egg by degrees, beating very thoroughly. Stir in the ground almonds and almond essence, and spread over the jam in the pastry case. Bake in a moderately hot oven (400° F., mark 6) for 30–40 minutes, until the tart is well risen and brown, and the filling is set. Dredge with icing sugar.

BAKEWELL TART (RICH)

6 oz. flaky pastry
Raspberry jam
Lemon curd
2 oz. butter
Grated rind of ½ a lemon
2 oz. sugar
2 small eggs (or one large)
5 oz. ground almonds
3 oz. cake crumbs
A squeeze of lemon juice
Milk if required

Line a plate with the pastry as directed for Flat Tart, keeping the pastry thin in the centre of the plate, with a fairly thick border. Spread a layer of raspberry jam on the bottom of the pastry and cover with a layer of lemon curd. Cream the butter, grated lemon rind and sugar very thoroughly. Beat the eggs in a basin, and add the beaten egg by degrees to the creamed mixture, beating all well together. Then lightly stir in the ground almonds and the cake crumbs, with a squeeze of lemon juice. Add 1 tbsp. of milk, if required, to give a soft dropping consistency. Spread the mixture over the lemon curd. Bake in a hot oven (450° F., mark 8) for about 10 minutes to set the pastry, then reduce the heat and cook for about 50–60 minutes in all, until the filling is set, risen, and golden.

BANBURY PUFFS

6 oz. puff or flaky pastry	Sugar
Egg white to glaze	

For the Filling

2 oz. raisins, stoned and chopped	1 oz. melted butter
	1 tbsp. brandy
2 oz. currants, cleaned	1 tbsp. cake crumbs
1 oz. candied peel, chopped	Nutmeg and mixed spice
2 oz. Demerara sugar	

Roll out the pastry thinly and divide into 2 pieces. Mix together all the filling ingredients and spread the mixture over one piece of pastry. Brush the second piece with egg white, place over the filling, and press lightly. Brush the surface with egg white, dust with sugar, mark in sections, and lay on a tin. Bake in a hot oven (450° F., mark 8) for about 25 minutes, until pastry is crisp and golden. Cut in pieces.

Another method is to roll out the pastry thinly and cut into 5-inch rounds. Put 1 dessertsp. of the mixture on each round, draw edges together and seal. Turn over and roll out lightly into boat shapes. Bake the puffs as above.

BELGIAN TART

4½ oz. flour	Cold water
2½ oz. cornflour	1 egg yolk (optional)
oz. butter or margarine	

For the Filling

1 lb. apples	1 egg yolk
Sugar	Grated rind of 1 lemon

For the Meringue

1 egg white	1½ oz. sugar

Sieve the flour and cornflour, rub in the fat and mix with cold water and egg yolk to a stiff dough. Roll out and line a greased sandwich tin with the pastry, keeping sufficient for a lid.

Stew the apples with a very little water and sweeten to taste. Sieve or beat with a fork until smooth, then cool. Stir in egg yolk and lemon rind.

Turn into the pastry case, damp the edges, and cover with a pastry lid. Bake in a moderately hot oven (400° F., mark 6) until the pastry is cooked and lightly browned—about 30 minutes. Turn the tart carefully on to a baking sheet. Whip the egg white stiffly, fold in 2 tbsps. sugar, and spread over the top of the tart. Rough up with a fork, sprinkle with the remaining sugar and crisp off in a cool oven (250° F., mark ¼). Dish and serve cold.

CHERRY PLATE PIE

8 oz. rich shortcrust pastry	A squeeze of lemon juice
	1 tbsp. sharp jelly or jam
2 lb. jar of bottled cherries	2 tsps. cornflour or arrowroot
¼ pint cherry juice	Sugar and water syrup to glaze
Sugar to sweeten	

Line a plate with pastry. Drain and stone the cherries. Put the cherry juice, sugar, lemon juice and jelly into a saucepan. Add the cornflour or arrowroot, blended with a spoonful of juice. Cook, stirring, until the mixture boils and thickens. Add the cherries and set aside to cool. Then pour into the lined pie plate and cover with pastry. Glaze with syrup. Bake in a moderately hot oven (425° F., mark 7) for about 30 minutes, until nicely browned.

If fresh cherries are used, cook as for Gooseberry Plate Pie (see page 280).

CREAM CRISPS (PALMIERS)

Puff pastry	Whipped cream or jam
Caster sugar	Sieved icing sugar

Roll the pastry out evenly until it is ¼ inch thick and about 20 inches long, then sprinkle it thoroughly with caster sugar. Fold the ends over to the centre until they meet and press
with the rolling pin. Sprinkle thoroughly with 71
sugar and fold the sides to the centre again. Press and sprinkle with sugar. Place the two folded portions together and press, then with a sharp knife cut into ¼-inch slices. Place cut edge down on a baking sheet, allowing room to spread, sprinkle with caster sugar and bake in a hot oven (450° F., mark 8) until golden-brown. Cool on a rack, and just before serving, pipe

sweetened cream on to half of the slices, sandwich with the remaining ones, and dredge with icing sugar. Jam may be used in place of cream.

CREAM HORNS

Roll out thinly some puff or flaky pastry into an oblong about 12 inches long, and cut into 1-inch strips. Moisten one edge of each strip and roll round a cream horn tin, starting at the
71 pointed end of the tin and overlapping the pastry very slightly. Bake in a hot oven (450° F., mark 8) until crisp—10–15 minutes. Slip them off the tins, and when cold, fill with a spoonful of jam or fruit, top with whipped cream and dredge with icing sugar.

CREAM SLICES

6 oz. flaky pastry
2 oz. butter or margarine
2 oz. caster sugar
2 tbsps. boiling water
2 tbsps. cold milk
A few drops of vanilla essence
Apricot jam
White glacé icing

Roll out the pastry into an oblong about 3–4 inches wide and ¼ inch thick. Cut crosswise into fingers about 1½ inches wide, place these on a greased baking tray and bake in a hot oven (450° F., mark 8) for 10 minutes, then slice each strip through the middle and allow to cool.

To make the filling, cream the butter and sugar until really white and fluffy, add the boiling water, 1 tsp. at a time, beating well all the time, and then mix in the cold milk equally slowly and continue beating until all is absorbed; flavour with vanilla essence. Sandwich the pastry slices together with jam and vanilla cream, and ice the top with glacé icing.

When fresh cream is available, prepare it as follows: whisk it well, fold in caster sugar to sweeten, and continue to whisk until the cream is firm and thick. Use with jam to fill the slices.

CURD CHEESE CAKES

Curd from 1 pint junket
6 oz. shortcrust pastry
1 large or 2 small eggs
2 oz. butter
¼ tsp. salt
4 oz. sugar
1 oz. currants
A little grated nutmeg
2 tsps. baking powder

Prepare the junket with 1 pint milk. When set, cut it up, tie in muslin, and allow to drip. Let it drain well, then beat up the curds with a fork. Line some patty tins with shortcrust pastry. Beat the eggs, melt the butter and combine all the ingredients, adding the baking powder at the last. Three-parts fill the patty cases with the curd mixture and bake in a moderately hot oven (425° F., mark 7) for 24–30 minutes, or until the pastry is attractively browned and the curd is lightly set.

CUSTARD TART

4 oz. shortcrust pastry
1 egg
½ oz. sugar
½ pint milk (short measure)
Nutmeg

Line a deep pie plate with the pastry. Beat the egg and sugar together and pour on the hot milk, stirring meanwhile. Strain into the prepared pastry case and grate a little nutmeg over. Bake in a hot oven (450° F., mark 8) for about 10 minutes until the pastry is set, and then reduce the heat and continue to bake in a moderate oven (350° F., mark 3) until the custard is set—about 30 minutes in all. An extra egg yolk added before baking is an improvement.

DATE TART

4–6 oz. shortcrust pastry
¼ lb. large dates
A little rum or cognac
3 egg whites
2 oz. ground almonds
4 oz. caster sugar

Line a shallow plate or sandwich tin with pastry as for Flat Tart. Stone the dates, cut them into 4 and soak them in the rum for about 20 minutes. Beat the whites of egg to a stiff froth, add the almonds, sugar and drained dates. Fill the pastry shell with the mixture, and bake in a moderately hot oven (425° F., mark 7) for about ½ hour. Sprinkle with caster sugar.

ECCLES CAKES

6 oz. flaky pastry
Egg white to glaze
Caster sugar

For the Filling

1 oz. butter
4 oz. currants
1–2 oz. mixed peel
Grated nutmeg and spice to taste
1 oz. sugar

To make the filling, melt the butter and add the cleaned currants, chopped peel, spices, and sugar. Roll out the pastry ¼ inch thick, and cut in large rounds with a plain cutter. Place a spoonful of the filling on each round. Damp the edges of each pastry round and draw them together to enclose the filling. Turn smooth side up, mark across with 3 cuts to show the currants, then flatten with a rolling pin, so that the currants just show through the pastry. Place on a flat baking tin, brush with beaten egg white, and dredge with caster sugar. Bake in a hot oven (450° F., mark 8) for about 15 minutes, until pastry is golden-brown and crisp.

FRANGIPAN FLAN

6 oz. flan pastry — Fruit

For the Frangipan Cream

$\frac{1}{2}$ oz. custard powder (light weight)
$\frac{1}{4}$ pint milk
1 egg yolk
1 oz. ground almonds
$\frac{1}{2}$ oz. sugar
$\frac{1}{2}$ oz. shredded browned almonds
Caster sugar

6 Bake a flan case, and fill with the prepared fruit (banana, orange, grapes, a few tinned apricots, etc.). Make a custard from the custard powder and milk and cook well, then cool slightly and add the egg yolk, ground almonds, and sugar. Spread the custard on the fruit, sprinkle the almonds and caster sugar on the top, and brown under a grill. Serve this flan either hot or cold.

FLORENTINE PIE

5 apples
Grated rind of $\frac{1}{2}$ lemon
A little grated nutmeg
2 oz. sugar
Angelica
6–8 oz. shortcrust pastry
2 egg whites
3 oz. caster sugar

Peel and slice the apples and cook them to a mash with a very little water (2–3 tbsps.), the lemon rind and grated nutmeg. When mashed, add the sugar and as much angelica cut into small pieces as there is apple. Cook until thick. Meanwhile, line a pie plate with the pastry and bake "blind" in a hot oven (450° F., mark 8) for about 15 minutes. Then remove the baking rice or beans and pour in the apple mixture. Whisk the egg whites stiffly, fold in the caster sugar, and pile this meringue on the top of the pie. Bake in a moderate oven (350° F., mark 3) until the meringue is firm and lightly coloured—about $\frac{1}{2}$ hour. Serve this pie hot or cold.

FRUIT FLAN

4 oz. rich shortcrust pastry
Fruit—tinned, bottled, or fresh

For the Glazing Syrup

2 tsps. powdered
7 arrowroot
$\frac{1}{4}$ pint fruit juice
1–2 oz. sugar
A squeeze of lemon juice
1 tbsp. red-currant jelly or apricot jam
Colouring if required

Make a 6-inch flan case, bake "blind," and cool on a rack. If tinned or bottled fruit is used, drain it well, so that it will not make the pastry sodden, then cut into pieces and arrange neatly in the flan case, filling it well. If fresh fruit is used, put some extra fruit in a saucepan with $\frac{1}{4}$ pint of water and sugar to sweeten, and stew this to give fruit juice for the glazing syrup.

Blend the arrowroot with a little of the fruit juice. Put the rest of the juice and the sugar into a saucepan and boil for a minute or two. Add the lemon juice, jelly or jam, and the blended arrowroot, and stir and boil until the syrup is quite clear and of a coating consistency when tested over the back of a wooden spoon. It is important that the syrup should be well flavoured and of a thick glazing consistency; if too thin, it will soak into the pastry and make it sodden. Add a few drops of colouring if required. Quickly strain over the fruit in the flan case, filling it to the top. Put aside for a little while to set the glaze. Serve cold.

JELLIED FRUIT FLAN

Prepare and bake the flan case and fill with
fruit as directed for Fruit Flan. Make a jelly 78
glaze from :—

$\frac{1}{4}$ pint fruit juice
Sugar to sweeten
2 tsps. powdered gelatine

Put the fruit juice in a saucepan with the sugar and gelatine. Stir over gentle heat until dissolved. Cool, and when just commencing to set, pour over the fruit in the case. Leave aside for a little while for the glaze to set.

FRUIT TARTLETS

These are made in the same way as Fruit Flan. Make rich shortcrust pastry and with it line 8 or 10 tartlet cases. Bake "blind" and cool on a rack, then fill and glaze the tartlets as for fruit flan.

Fruit tartlets make a pretty sweet if two or three kinds of fruit are used for filling e.g. apricots, red cherries, and greengages.

CINNAMON CHERRY TARTLETS

4 oz. cinnamon pastry (see below)
Red or black cherries—tinned, stewed, or bottled

For the Syrup

$\frac{1}{4}$ pint fruit juice
1–2 oz. sugar
A tiny piece of stick cinnamon
A squeeze of lemon juice
2 tsps. arrowroot
1 tbsp. red-currant jelly

Make rich shortcrust pastry, adding $\frac{1}{2}$ tsp. ground cinnamon to 4 oz. flour. Use the same method as for fruit tartlets (above). When making the glazing syrup, boil the fruit juice, sugar, and cinnamon together for a few minutes before adding the other ingredients.

GOOSEBERRY PLATE PIE

8 oz. flaky pastry	2 tsps. cornflour or arrowroot
1 lb. gooseberries	Egg white
¼ pint water	Caster sugar
2–4 oz. sugar	

Line a pie plate with pastry. Top and tail the gooseberries, rinse, then place in a saucepan with about ¼ pint water. Cover and cook very gently until tender, taking care to keep the berries whole; drain in a colander. Measure ¼ pint of the juice, put this back in the saucepan with the sugar, or add the cornflour or arrowroot, blended with a spoonful of cold water. Cook, stirring, until the mixture boils and thickens, add the gooseberries and set aside to cool, then pour into the lined pie plate. Cover as for plate pie. Glaze with beaten egg white and dust with caster sugar. Bake in a hot oven (450° F., mark 8) for about 10 minutes, then reduce the heat somewhat and cook for about 30 minutes, until the pie is well risen and nicely browned. Serve hot with cream.

JAM PUFFS

8 oz. puff or flaky pastry	Egg white
Jam	Caster sugar

Roll out the pastry into a square about ⅛ inch thick, cut across into 8 small squares, brush over with water and place 2 tsps. jam on each square. Fold the pastry over to form a triangle and press edges well together to seal them,
71 otherwise the jam is likely to ooze out during cooking and burn. Place on a baking sheet, brush with beaten egg white, and sprinkle with caster sugar. Bake in a hot oven (450° F., mark 8) for 15–20 minutes, until well risen, golden-brown, and firm underneath.

JAM ROLY-POLY

Make 6–8 oz. suetcrust pastry in the usual way and turn on to a lightly floured board. Roll out into a strip 6–8 inches wide and ¼ inch thick. Moisten the edges with water and spread with jam to within ½ inch of the edge. Roll up, pressing the edges together lightly. Wrap round with greaseproof paper and roll in a pudding cloth, rolling fairly loosely to allow for
79 swelling. Tie each end firmly and fasten the middle of the cloth with a safety pin. Steam steadily for 2–2½ hours or boil for about 1½ hours. Lift out, remove the cloth and paper, and serve the roly-poly on a hot dish, accompanied by custard or jam sauce.

JAM TARTLETS

Roll out 6 oz. shortcrust pastry to rather less than ¼ inch thick. Cut with a fluted pastry 8
cutter to fit about 12 shallow patty tins. Place 2 tsps. jam in the centre of each. Bake in a hot oven (450° F., mark 8) for about 15 minutes.

LATTICED JAM TART

Line a pie plate with pastry as directed for a flat tart, but do not put the underneath strip of pastry round the edge of the plate—this goes on later. Reserve a small piece of the pastry dough for decorating. Pour enough jam into the pastry case to fill the centre. Decorate with strips of pastry (¼ inch wide), arranged lattice fashion on top of the jam. Moisten the edge of the tart with water, then lay on a strip of pastry the width of the rim, all the way round, covering the ends of the criss-cross strips. Press down with the prongs of a fork and glaze with sugar and water, or egg white. Bake in a moderately hot oven (425° F., mark 7) for 20–30 minutes, until pastry is nicely browned. (An 8-inch plate requires about 8 oz. pastry.

LEMON CURD TARTLETS

4 oz. shortcrust pastry	1 oz. whole almonds
Lemon curd	Whipped cream

Line some small patty tins with the pastry and bake "blind." Make the lemon curd, cool, and fill the tartlet cases two-thirds full. Blanch the almonds, shred finely, and toast in a cool oven. Whip the cream and spread a thin layer neatly over the lemon curd in each tartlet. Sprinkle with the cooled toasted almonds.

LEMON MERINGUE PIE

6 oz. shortcrust pastry	4 oz. sugar
1 oz. cornflour	½ oz. butter
½ pint water	2 egg yolks
1 lemon	

For the Meringue Top

2 egg whites	Cherries and angelica to decorate
4 oz. sugar	

Line a plate with the pastry, finishing with a raised fluted rim, and bake "blind," as directed. Mix the cornflour to a thin cream with some of the water. Heat the rest of the water and, when boiling, pour on to the cornflour, stirring. Return to the saucepan, add the lemon juice, and boil for 4–5 minutes, stirring constantly. Add the sugar, butter, and grated rind, cool slightly and beat in the egg yolks one by one. Pour into the pastry case.

Whisk the egg whites very stiffly. Whisk in 1 teaspoonful of sugar, then fold in the remaining sugar. Pile on top of the lemon mixture. Bake in a slow oven (325° F., mark 2) for about ½ hour, until the filling is set and the meringue crisp, and pale fawn. Decorate and serve cold.

LEMON OR ORANGE OPEN TART

4 oz. shortcrust pastry — 1 egg
1½ oz. butter — 1 oz. cake crumbs
1 oz. sugar — 1 lemon (or orange)

Line a plate or shallow dish with pastry. Cream the butter and sugar, add the egg and crumbs, beat well, then add the lemon rind and juice. Spread this on the pastry and bake in a moderately hot oven (425° F., mark 7) until the pastry is cooked and the mixture golden-brown—about ½ hour.

MINCE PIES

8 oz. flaky or puff pastry — Egg white and sugar to glaze
Mincemeat

Place the piece of pastry dough on a floured board and roll out to ⅛-inch thickness. Cut the required number of rounds to make lids for the patty tins to be used. Fold up the trimmings, roll out ⅛ inch thick and cut out rounds to line the tins, making the rounds a size larger than the tins to allow for the depth. Line the tins, fill with mincemeat, damp the edges and put on the pastry lids. Decorate the edges with tiny flutes and make a hole with a skewer in the top of each. Glaze and bake in a moderately hot oven (425° F., mark 7) for 20–30 minutes.

PINEAPPLE CREAM CAKES

3 oz. shortcrust pastry — Glacé icing, made with pineapple juice
3 tbsps. cream — Yellow colouring
2 tbsps. pineapple

Make the pastry and with it line 6 or 8 small patty tins. Bake them "blind" and allow to cool. Whip the cream and add the well-drained, chopped pineapple; fill the pastry cases.

Make the glacé icing, using the pineapple juice instead of water; colour it pale yellow and ice the tartlets very carefully, so as to cover the cream filling completely. If liked, decorate with a slice of pineapple.

PUMPKIN PIE

8 oz. flaky pastry — A pinch of ginger
2 eggs, beaten — 2 tsps. cinnamon
4 oz. sugar — ½ tsp. salt
8–12 oz. steamed pumpkin — ¼ pint milk
A little grated nutmeg — Whipped cream

Line a pie plate with the pastry, doubling the edge and fluting it with the fingers. Mix together the filling ingredients, put into the pastry case and bake in a moderately hot oven (400° F., mark 6) for about 40 minutes, until the pastry is brown and the filling set. Serve topped with whipped cream.

RED-CURRANT LATTICE PIE

(*See colour picture facing page* 288)

8 oz. shortcrust pastry — 1 lb. red-currants
Egg for glazing — 2–3 oz. sugar

Line a fireproof plate with pastry, trim the edges and keep the trimmings to make the lattice. Flute the edges of the pastry and brush with a little egg. Prepare and wash the red-currants and fill the dish, sprinkling sugar between the layers of fruit. Roll out the rest of the pastry and cut into strips. Damp the inner side of the pastry rim and place the strips in a lattice on top of the fruit. Brush the lattice with egg, and bake in a moderately hot oven (400° F., mark 6) until pastry is brown and crisp. Sprinkle with sugar, and serve with cream.

RHUBARB AND CINNAMON PLATE PIE

For the Pastry

10 oz. flour — 1½ tsps. ground cinnamon
6 oz. margarine — Egg yolk
1–1½ oz. sugar — Water to mix

For the Filling

1½ lb. rhubarb — Sugar and water syrup to glaze
Brown sugar
Ground cinnamon

Make the pastry as for rich shortcrust, and line a pie plate with it.

Wash the rhubarb and cut in 1-inch lengths. Fill the plate with layers of fruit and a liberal sprinkling of brown sugar, dust each layer with ground cinnamon, cover as for plate pie and glaze with sugar and water syrup. Bake in a moderately hot oven (425° F., mark 7) for about 30 minutes, until crust is nicely browned and fruit tender. Serve hot or cold, with cream.

RHUBARB SHEAVES

6 oz. shortcrust pastry — 4 sticks young rhubarb
Egg white — 2 oz. caster sugar

Prepare the pastry, roll out into strips 4 inches long and 2½ inches wide, and brush with egg white. Skin each stick of rhubarb and cut into 3½-inch lengths, roll in the caster sugar and wrap in the pastry, sealing the edges well. Bake in a moderately hot oven (425° F., mark 7) for about 20 minutes. Dredge with caster sugar and tie into sheaves with the rhubarb skin.

STRAWBERRY BOATS

4 oz. rich shortcrust pastry
About 1 lb. ripe strawberries

For the Glazing Syrup

¼ pint fruit juice
1–2 oz. sugar
2 tsps. powdered arrowroot
A squeeze of lemon juice
1 tbsp. red-currant or gooseberry jelly

Make the required number of boat-shaped cases with the pastry and bake "blind." Cool on a rack. Pick over the strawberries. Keep back some of the less well-shaped ones and put in a saucepan with ¼ pint water and sugar, and stew to give fruit juice for the glazing syrup. Make the glazing syrup as described under Fruit Flan. Fill the pastry cases with ripe, even-sized strawberries. Glaze with a spoonful of syrup and leave to set. Arrange attractively on a flat dish and decorate with strawberry leaves.

Loganberries, raspberries, or blackberries may be used in the same way.

STEAMED FRUIT PUDDING

½ lb. suetcrust pastry
1 lb. fruit (apples, damsons, etc.)
4 oz. sugar
A little water

Make the pastry in the usual way and line a greased basin with two-thirds of it. Place half of the prepared fruit in the basin, add the sugar and the remaining fruit, with about 2 tbsps. water. Roll out the rest of the pastry into a round, wet the edges and place on top of the pudding. Press the edges lightly to seal them, cover with greased paper and steam for 2½–3 hours. Turn out on to a hot dish and serve with cream or custard sauce.

SYRUP LAYER PUDDING

8 oz. suetcrust pastry
Rind and juice of ½ a lemon
1 oz. breadcrumbs
4–6 oz. golden syrup or black treacle

Make the pastry, adding the grated lemon rind to the flour. Mix the breadcrumbs and lemon juice with the syrup. Divide the pastry into six pieces graduating in size. Put 1 tbsp. of the syrup mixture into the bottom of a greased basin. Roll the smallest piece of pastry into a round and place on top of the syrup. Cover with another tbsp. of syrup and then the next largest piece of pastry, rolled to a round, repeating until the pastry is used up and the basin two-thirds full. Cover with greased paper and steam 2½–3 hours. Turn on to a hot dish.

APPLE AND COCONUT PUDDING

(*See colour picture facing page* 289)

Roll the suetcrust pastry into rounds, as for Syrup Layer Pudding above. Put a little golden syrup and desiccated coconut at the bottom of the basin, then a layer of pastry, a layer of sliced apple and some more syrup and coconut; continue in this way, finishing with a pastry layer, and steam as above.

SYRUP TART

6 oz. shortcrust pastry
3–4 tbsps. syrup
2 oz. breadcrumbs
Juice of ½ a lemon

Line a plate with pastry as directed for a Flat Tart. Mix the syrup, breadcrumbs and lemon juice together, and pour this mixture into the pastry. Bake in a moderately hot oven (425° F., mark 7) for 20–30 minutes, until the pastry is cooked and the filling golden-brown. Cool and serve. Top with whipped cream if liked.

SWISS TART

4 oz. shortcrust pastry
½ lb. plums
A little sugar
¼ oz. margarine

Line a pie plate with shortcrust pastry and decorate the edge. Cut the plums in half, remove the stones and then cut in quarters. Arrange the quarters in overlapping circles on the pastry. Sprinkle with sugar and some fine shavings of margarine. Bake in a hot oven (450° F., mark 8) until pastry is lightly browned, then cook more slowly until fruit is tender.

Sliced apples or damsons (halved and stoned), may also be used for this tart.

MIXED FRUIT TART (WINTER)

8 oz. cinnamon shortcrust pastry (see below)
½ lb. prunes
1 lb. cranberries
1 lb. apples
½ pint water
6 oz. sugar (approx.)
Caster sugar

Wash the prunes and soak in the ½ pint water overnight, if possible. Pick over the cranberries. Core, peel, and slice the apples. Put the three kinds of fruit into a saucepan with the water, cover and stew for about ½ hour. Then add 6 oz. sugar and stew a little longer, until all the fruit is tender. Remove the prune stones and pour the fruit into a deep plate. Make the pastry as for rich shortcrust, adding 1 tsp. ground cinnamon to the flour. Roll out the pastry and cover as for Fruit Tart. Bake in a moderately hot oven (425° F., mark 7) for about 30 minutes until the pastry is crisp and nicely brown. Dust with caster sugar and serve hot or cold with cream.

MIXED FRUIT TART (SUMMER)

8 oz. rich shortcrust pastry	4 oz. sugar
2 lb. mixed soft fruit	Egg white
	Caster sugar

Make the pastry. Pick over the fruit carefully and half-fill a pie dish. (Raspberries, redcurrants, and strawberries make a good mixture.) Add a good sprinkling of sugar and cover with the rest of the fruit and sugar, piling the fruit high on the dish. Roll out the pastry and cover as for Fruit Tart. Glaze with beaten egg white and dredge with caster sugar. Bake in a moderately hot oven (425° F., mark 7) for about 30 minutes, until pastry is golden-brown and fruit tender. Dredge with caster sugar. Serve hot or cold with cream or custard.

WELSH CHEESE CAKES

Shortcrust or flan pastry	4 oz. butter
Raspberry jam	4 oz. caster sugar
3 oz. flour	2 eggs
A pinch of salt	A little milk if necessary
2 tsps. baking powder	Icing sugar
3 oz. ground rice	

Line some deep patty tins with the pastry, but do not cook. Put 2 tsps. raspberry jam in each. Sieve together the flour, salt, and baking powder and mix in the ground rice. Cream the butter and sugar thoroughly. Add the beaten egg, beating in a little at a time so that the mixture does not curdle; sprinkle in a little of the flour if any signs of curdling appear. With a metal spoon stir in the flour and ground rice, adding a little milk as required to give a dropping consistency. Half-fill the patty tins with the mixture. Bake in a moderately hot oven (400° F., mark 6) for about 20 minutes, until pastry is crisp and cake mixture well risen and golden. Dredge with sugar before serving.

HOT PUDDINGS

Most of the hot sweets served in the average household fall into one of about half a dozen main categories, as listed below. The majority are dealt with in special chapters in this book, while in this section will be found the recipes for suet and sponge puddings, and for some miscellaneous baked puddings.

Pastry

Pastry is the basis of many hot sweets. Shortcrust is perhaps the most widely used ; for pies, flans, tarts, and tartlets and such favourites as apple turnover and lemon meringue pie, it is eminently suitable. Flaky pastry is occasionally used for sweet dishes such as jam puffs, Eccles cakes, mince pies, and so on. Suetcrust pastry makes good cold-weather sweets such as steamed fruit puddings. (See the chapter on Pastry.)

Milk Puddings

Milk, cooked together with a cereal, provides another group of hot puddings, and is an excellent means of using some of the daily quota of milk, especially in the children's menus.

Custard is used to give the finishing touch to many hot puddings, while steamed and baked custards (and variations of them, such as Cabinet Pudding and Bread and Butter Pudding) make very nourishing dishes in themselves. (See chapter on Milk Puddings and Custards.)

Batters

Essentially a mixture of flour, milk, and eggs, but often combined with other ingredients, batters make excellent baked and steamed puddings and may also be fried, to make pancakes and all kinds of fritters. (See the chapter on Batters.)

Soufflés

Steamed and baked soufflés are very light and delicious hot puddings, and nourishing too, since they contain a high proportion of eggs. (See the chapter on Soufflés.)

Steamed Puddings

This large group includes suet puddings and sponge puddings (or cake mixture puddings).

Suet Puddings : Suet puddings (that is, puddings steamed in a basin or mould, as distinct from suetcrust pastry) contain chopped or shredded suet and, as a rule, breadcrumbs. The secret of making them light is to make the mixture slack (soft dropping consistency) and cook them steadily and thoroughly—at least 2 hours for an average-sized pudding. When suet is not available, cooking fat, lard, or margarine (or a mixture) may be substituted, in which case the fat is rubbed into the flour and baking powder. Puddings thus made can be cooked for rather shorter time than those in which suet is used, though long cooking does them no harm.

Sponge or Cake Mixture Puddings : These are made by the creaming method, that is to say, the fat and sugar are creamed together, the eggs beaten in and the flour folded in. These puddings should be very light and spongy. Success depends on the thorough creaming together of the fat and sugar, light handling of the mixture once the dry ingredients are added, making the mixture of a soft, light consistency, and steady cooking.

The general rules for steaming puddings are as follows :

1. Grease the basin thoroughly to prevent the pudding sticking.
2. Have ready greased a piece of greaseproof paper large enough to cover the top of the basin, with enough to twist under the edge.
3. Have the steamer ready boiling before moistening the pudding mixture.
4. Have the pudding mixture of a soft consistency.
5. Fill the basin only two-thirds full, to allow for the pudding to rise. Cover closely with the greased paper. A cloth may be tied over the paper, but it is not really necessary when steaming.
6. Keep the pan or steamer boiling vigorously all the time the pudding is in. Replenish when necessary, using boiling water.
7. Cook thoroughly, that is, allow the full cooking time given in the recipe.

Boiled Puddings

Suet mixtures are sometimes boiled instead of being steamed. After preparing the mixture, tie a roll or dumpling in a floured cloth, or, if the mixture is being cooked in a basin, cover it closely with a greased paper and a floured cloth. Boiled puddings require slightly less time to cook.

Baked Puddings

Apart from such things as pastry, pies, and tarts, baked puddings include a number of fruit dishes, e.g., Apple Amber, recipes for which are given in this chapter.

STEAMED SUET PUDDINGS

BASIC RECIPE FOR STEAMED SUET PUDDING

4 oz. flour and 4 oz. fresh breadcrumbs	1 tsp. salt
or	4 oz. suet, chopped or shredded
6 oz. flour and 2 oz. fresh breadcrumbs	2 oz. sugar
2 tsps. baking powder	Milk to mix (about $\frac{1}{4}$ pint)

Sieve the flour, baking powder, and salt into a basin. If fresh suet is used, shred or chop very finely, adding a little of the measured flour to facilitate the chopping. Mix all dry ingredients together in the basin. Make a well in the centre of the dry ingredients and add sufficient milk to give a soft dropping consistency. Turn into a greased basin, filling it two-thirds full. Cover with greased paper. Steam steadily for 2 hours, or longer. Turn out on a hot dish and serve with syrup or a sweet sauce.

This recipe may be varied in a number of ways, as follows :

JAM (OR MARMALADE) PUDDING

Put 2 tbsps. of jam (or marmalade) in the bottom of the basin. Serve with jam or marmalade sauce.

FRUIT PUDDING

Add 4–6 oz. dried fruit (sultanas, currants, 82
or raisins) and 2 tsps. mixed spice to the dry ingredients. Serve with custard or white sauce.

ORANGE (OR LEMON) PUDDING

Add the grated rind of an orange (or lemon) and $\frac{1}{2}$ oz. chopped candied orange (or lemon) peel to the dry ingredients. Serve with a sauce made from the orange (or lemon) juice.

AUSTRALIAN PUDDING

3 oz. flour	2 oz. sultanas
1 tsp. baking powder	2 oz. currants
A pinch of salt	1 oz. peel
1 tsp. mixed spice	3 oz. sugar
$2\frac{1}{2}$ oz. suet	2 tsps. grated lemon rind
2 oz. breadcrumbs	1 egg
2 oz. raisins	Milk to mix

Sieve the flour, baking powder, salt, and spice into a basin. Shred or chop the suet very finely and add with the breadcrumbs to the flour. Add the prepared fruit, chopped peel, sugar, and lemon rind, and mix well. Make a well in the centre of the dry ingredients, add the beaten egg, and sufficient milk to give a soft dropping consistency. Turn into a greased basin, filling it two-thirds full, cover with greased paper, and steam steadily for 2 hours. Turn out on a hot dish and serve with sweet white sauce.

BROWN ALMOND PUDDING

3 oz. wholemeal breadcrumbs	3 oz. honey
	1 egg
3 oz. flour	Milk to mix
$\frac{1}{2}$ tsp. baking powder	Almond essence
$2\frac{1}{2}$ oz. suet	A few almonds for decoration
2 oz. chopped nuts	

Mix the dry ingredients in a basin, add the honey and beaten egg, and sufficient milk to give a soft dropping consistency. Flavour with a few drops of almond essence. Turn into a greased basin, or small dariole moulds, decorated with a few split almonds. Cover with greased paper, and steam steadily for 2½ hours, or 1½ hours if small moulds are used.

Turn out and serve with a sweet white sauce flavoured with almond essence.

CARROT PUDDING

¾ lb. carrots	4 oz. suet
¼ lb. stoned raisins	1 tsp. baking powder
¼ lb. currants	3 oz. sugar
2 oz. flour	3 eggs
6 oz. breadcrumbs	Grated nutmeg
½ tsp. salt	A little milk

Cook the carrots until tender and mash them. Prepare the fruit, add it and the rest of the dry ingredients to the carrots and mix well. Add the beaten eggs, a little grated nutmeg, and sufficient milk to bring to a soft dropping consistency. Put the mixture into a greased basin, cover with greased paper, and steam for 2½ hours. Turn out and serve with custard sauce.

DATE PUDDING

2 oz. flour	2½ oz. suet
½ tsp. mixed spice	2 oz. sugar
A good pinch of salt	1 tbsp. treacle
1 tsp. baking powder	1 egg
4 oz. dates	Milk to mix
3 oz. breadcrumbs	

Sieve the flour, spice, salt, and baking powder together. Cut up the dates, add them with the breadcrumbs, the finely chopped or shredded suet, the sugar and treacle to the sieved ingredients, and mix well. Stir in the beaten egg and sufficient milk to bring to a soft dropping consistency. Put the mixture into a greased basin and steam for 2 hours. Turn out and serve with lemon sauce.

GLOUCESTER PUDDING

6 oz. flour	4 oz. apple, finely chopped
1½–2 tsps. baking powder	2 oz. mixed peel
3 oz. suet	1 egg
3 oz. sugar	About 4 tbsps. milk

Sieve together the flour and baking powder. Add the finely chopped or shredded suet and the sugar. Chop the apple and the candied peel and add them to the dry ingredients. Make a well in the centre, add the beaten egg and sufficient milk to give a soft dropping consistency. Turn into a greased basin, filling it two-thirds full, cover with greased paper, and steam steadily for about 2 hours. Turn out and serve with custard sauce.

HONEY CAP PUDDINGS

2 tbsps. honey	½ tsp. salt
3 oz. stoned dates	1 oz. bran
2½ oz. suet	2 oz. sugar
6 oz. flour	Milk to mix
2 tsps. baking powder	

Grease some small dariole moulds and put a little honey at the bottom of each. Cut the dates into small pieces. Shred and chop the suet very finely. Sieve together the flour, baking powder, and salt, then add the bran, dates, sugar, and suet, together with sufficient milk to mix to a soft dropping consistency. Three-quarters fill the dariole moulds and cover each with greased greaseproof paper. Steam for 1½ hours. Turn out on a hot dish.

MARMALADE PUDDING

4 oz. flour	4 oz. breadcrumbs
½ tsp. salt	1 egg
2 tsps. baking powder	4 tbsps. marmalade
3–4 oz. suet, finely chopped or shredded	Milk to mix

Sieve the flour, salt, and baking powder together. Add the suet and crumbs and mix well. Add the beaten egg, the marmalade, and sufficient milk to give a soft dropping consistency. Put the mixture into a greased basin, two-thirds filling it, cover with greased paper, and steam steadily for at least 2 hours. Turn out and serve with marmalade sauce.

RICH FIG PUDDING

5 oz. figs	4 oz. breadcrumbs
2 oz. almonds	4 oz. sugar
4 oz. flour	Grated rind of 1 lemon
½ tsp. salt	2 eggs
2 tsps. baking powder	Sherry or milk to mix
4 oz. suet	

Chop the figs and blanched almonds. Sieve the flour, salt, and baking powder together. Add the finely chopped suet, breadcrumbs, sugar, figs, almonds, and lemon rind to the sieved ingredients. Mix with the beaten eggs and sherry or milk to a soft dropping consistency. Put the mixture into a greased basin, two-thirds filling it, cover with greased paper, and steam for 2½ hours. Turn out and serve with marmalade sauce or custard sauce.

SCOTCH DUMPLING

(An alternative to Christmas Pudding)

¼ lb. currants
¼ lb. sultanas
2 oz. raisins
2 oz. mixed peel
½ lb. plain flour
¼ lb. minced suet
1 teacupful breadcrumbs
1 teacupful brown sugar
A pinch of salt
1 tsp. bicarbonate of soda
1 tsp. cream of tartar
1 tsp. mixed spice
About ½ pint sour milk or buttermilk

Prepare the fruits in the usual way, chopping the raisins and peel. Mix all dry ingredients together, and add enough sour milk or buttermilk to make a soft dropping consistency. Put into a greased basin or mould, two-thirds filling it, cover with greased paper, and steam for 3 hours. Turn on to a hot dish and decorate with a sprig of holly.

Though this pudding does not need to mature, as does a Christmas pudding, it can, if wished, be kept for as long as 1–2 weeks after the first cooking. It will then need to be reheated in the steamer for 2–3 hours before serving.

SPOTTED DICK

4 oz. flour
A pinch of salt
2 tsps. baking powder
4 oz. breadcrumbs
3–4 oz. suet
3 oz. currants
Milk or water to mix

Sift together the flour, salt, and baking powder. Add the breadcrumbs, the finely chopped or shredded suet, and the prepared currants. Mix to a soft dropping consistency with milk or water. Turn into a greased basin, two-thirds filling it. Cover with greased paper and steam steadily for 2–3 hours. Turn out on to a hot dish and serve with custard or a sweet white sauce.

SYRUP SPONGE PUDDING

4 oz. flour
1 tsp. bicarbonate of soda
½ tsp. salt
2 tsps. ground ginger
4 oz. suet
4 oz. breadcrumbs
2 oz. sugar
¼ pint syrup or treacle
1 egg
¼ pint milk (approx.)

Sieve the flour, bicarbonate of soda, salt, and ginger into a basin. Shred or chop the suet very finely. Add it, with the breadcrumbs and sugar, to the flour. Make a well in the centre of the dry ingredients. Add the syrup and the beaten egg, with enough milk to give a soft dropping consistency, and mix very thoroughly. Turn into a greased basin, filling it two-thirds full. Cover with greased paper. Steam steadily for at least 2 hours. Turn on to a hot dish and serve with syrup sauce.

CURRANT DUMPLINGS

½ lb. flour
A pinch of salt
2 tsps. baking powder
4 oz. suet
3 oz. currants
2 tbsps. sugar
Grated rind lemon
Water to mix

Sieve together the flour, salt and baking powder. Add the chopped suet, currants, sugar and lemon rind, and mix to a soft dough with the water. Roll the dough into 12 balls, drop these into fast-boiling water and boil for 20 minutes in a covered pan. Drain well, and serve with butter and brown sugar or with sweet white sauce.

APPLE PUDDINGS

4 oz. self-raising flour
4 oz. breadcrumbs
4 oz. chopped suet
2 oz. sugar
½ lb. cooking apples (Bramley if possible)
1 egg
Milk to mix

Mix together the flour, breadcrumbs, suet and sugar. Chop the apples finely and add these to the mixture. Make a well in the centre, add the egg, then mix to a soft consistency with the milk. Put into small greased moulds and steam for 1½ hours. Serve with custard.

PRUNE-CAPPED PUDDING

4 oz. breadcrumbs
4 oz. flour
2 tsps. baking powder
4 oz. sugar
4 oz. suet
1 lemon
1 egg
Milk
½ lb. stewed prunes
Blanched almonds

Mix together the dry ingredients and add the finely grated lemon rind, then mix to a soft dough with the lemon juice, egg and milk. Stone the prunes and put the fruit at the bottom of a greased basin, with the almonds, then put the mixture on top and steam for 3 hours. Turn out, and serve with custard sauce.

SIX-CUP PUDDING

1 teacup breadcrumbs
1 teacup flour
1 teacup chopped suet
1 teacup jam
1 teacup raisins
1 tbsp. sugar
1 tsp. bicarbonate of soda
1 teacup milk

Put the breadcrumbs, flour, jam, suet, fruit, and sugar into a basin. Dissolve the bicarbonate of soda in 1 tbsp. of the milk, mix the pudding to a soft dropping consistency with the rest of the milk, then add the dissolved soda and mix thoroughly. Put into a well greased basin and steam for 2½ hours, turn out, and serve with custard or jam sauce.

MAKING CHRISTMAS PUDDINGS

Whatever the ingredients called for in the particular recipe, the general method is much the same.

Preparation and Cooking

Stone the raisins, unless seeded ones are used. Wash, dry, and pick sultanas, currants, and raisins. Remove sugar from peel and shred the peel finely. Blanch and chop the almonds. Grate or chop the suet finely. Make the breadcrumbs. Grate the apple, carrot, and lemon rind (when included in recipe).

Sieve the flour, salt, and spices into a basin large enough to hold all the ingredients. Put all the prepared ingredients and sugar into the basin and mix thoroughly. Beat up the eggs; squeeze the lemon; measure the milk. Add these to the dry ingredients and mix to a soft dropping consistency. If time permits, leave for several hours and mix again.

Put pan or steamer on to boil. Grease basin and covering paper and prepare cloths. Fill basin to the top, cover with paper, tie on pudding cloth securely, pinning or tying up the corners. Boil for 5 hours, replenishing the water as required, or steam for 7½ hours. Remove and allow to cool. Take off the pudding cloth, wipe the basin, then re-cover it with a clean, dry cloth. Hang in the larder or put in a cool place.

Serving the Pudding

Tie on a greased paper and a cloth and boil for a further 4 hours, or cover with greased paper only and steam for 6 hours. Turn out on a hot dish, and put a sprig of holly in the centre. Serve accompanied by caster sugar with brandy sauce, cream or custard sauce.

To fire a Christmas pudding, dish the pudding, and just before serving pour a little warmed brandy (or whisky) over it and set it alight. Send to table while still burning.

OLD ENGLISH PLUM PUDDING

½ lb. raisins	2 oz. Barbados sugar
¼ lb. currants	1 tsp. salt
½ lb. suet	1 tsp. grated nutmeg
¼ lb. brown breadcrumbs	3 eggs
1½ oz. flour	¼ pint milk

Follow method already given. Makes 1 pudding weighing about 2¼ lb.

GOOD HOUSEKEEPING CHRISTMAS PUDDING

2½ lb. raisins	1 lb. flour
1½ lb. sultanas	½ tsp. grated nutmeg
1½ lb. currants	1 tsp. cinnamon
¾ lb. peel	2 tsps. salt
2 oz. sweet almonds	1 lb. Barbados sugar
2 oz. bitter almonds	6 eggs
1 lb. suet	1 pint milk
½ lb. breadcrumbs	

Follow method already given. Makes 5 puddings 2 lb. 5 oz. each.

CHRISTMAS PUDDING (ECONOMICAL)

4 oz. sultanas	2 eggs
2 oz. currants	1 oz. syrup
2 oz. seedless raisins	1 tsp. orange marmalade
2 oz. Valencia raisins	A little milk or water
5 oz. flour	A few drops of vanilla essence
½ tsp. salt	A few drops of almond essence
3 oz. fine breadcrumbs	A little browning
3 oz. suet or cooking fat	
3 oz. sugar	
A small tsp. mixed spice	
A little grated nutmeg	

Wash and pick over the dried fruit. Stone and chop the Valencia raisins. Put the flour, salt, and breadcrumbs into a bowl. If suet is used, add this finely chopped or shredded; if cooking fat is used, rub it lightly and thoroughly into the flour and breadcrumbs. Add the sugar and spices and mix well. Add also the prepared dried fruits. Now add the beaten eggs, the syrup and the marmalade, and enough milk or water to give a soft dropping consistency. Stir in the vanilla and almond essences, and enough browning to colour it lightly. When thoroughly mixed put into 1 medium-sized or 2 small greased basins, nearly filling them, cover with greased paper, and, if liked, a cloth, and steam for about 6 hours.

When the pudding is cooked, remove the cloth and paper, and as soon as it is cold cover with clean paper and a cloth before storing.

These puddings will keep for quite 3–4 weeks. If, however, a plainer mixture is required, reduce fruit or sugar by one-third, but do not make the puddings until a day or so beforehand.

STEAMED SPONGE PUDDINGS

CANARY PUDDING (STANDARD RECIPE)

4 oz. flour	2 eggs
A pinch of salt	2 tbsps. milk
1 tsp. baking powder	A few drops of vanilla essence
4 oz. butter	Sauce as desired
4 oz. caster sugar	

Red-Currant Lattice

Fruit Bun Pu

Sieve together the flour, salt, and baking powder. Cream the butter and sugar until soft and white. Beat in the eggs separately, with a sprinkling of flour. Stir in the remaining flour lightly, and the milk and vanilla. Put into a greased basin, two-thirds filling it, cover with greased greaseproof paper and steam for 1½ hours. Turn out and serve with jam sauce.

A variety of puddings can be made by decorating the basin with tinned pineapple, apricots, raisins, cherries, etc., before putting the mixture into it. By varying the flavouring ingredient and accompanying sauce, many different sponge puddings can be made, using the Canary Pudding mixture as a basis.

CANARY PUDDING (ECONOMICAL RECIPE)

3 oz. butter or margarine
3 oz. sugar
1 egg
A few drops of vanilla essence
5 oz. flour
2 tsps. baking powder
2–3 tbsps. milk or milk and water

Cream the fat and sugar together until light and creamy. Add the beaten egg by degrees with the vanilla, and beat thoroughly. Stir in the flour and baking powder, adding enough milk to make a soft dropping consistency. Put into a greased basin, cover with greased paper, and steam 2 hours or longer. Turn out and serve with jam sauce.

CHOCOLATE SPONGE PUDDING—I

Add 1 oz. of chocolate to Canary Pudding mixture. Grate or cut up the chocolate and dissolve it in the milk over gentle heat. Beat into the creamed mixture after adding the eggs. Serve with chocolate sauce.

CHOCOLATE SPONGE PUDDING—II

Add 1 oz. of cocoa and a few drops of vanilla essence to the Canary Pudding mixture. Add the cocoa to the flour and use extra milk, if necessary, to bring the mixture to a soft dropping consistency. Add the vanilla essence to the creamed mixture before incorporating the dry ingredients. Serve with chocolate sauce or custard sauce.

CHERRY SPONGE PUDDING

Add 2 oz. glacé cherries to Canary Pudding mixture, cutting up the cherries and adding them with the dry ingredients. Serve with custard sauce or sweet white sauce flavoured to taste with a little sherry.

K

ponge Pudding

and Coconut Pudding

COFFEE SPONGE PUDDING

Add 2 tbsps. coffee essence and a drop or two of vanilla essence to Canary Pudding mixture, adding the essences to the creamed mixture after beating in the eggs, and reducing the quantity of milk if necessary. Serve with coffee custard.

JAM SPONGE PUDDING

(*See colour picture opposite*)

Place 2 tbsps. jam in the basin before putting in the Canary Pudding mixture. Serve with custard sauce.

JAMAICA PUDDING

Dice 2–4 oz. preserved ginger and add it to the standard mixture. Serve with some hot golden syrup or a white sauce flavoured with preserved ginger.

LEMON OR ORANGE SPONGE PUDDING

Add the grated rind of 1 lemon to Canary Pudding mixture, putting it into the creamed mixture after adding the eggs. Serve with lemon or orange sauce.

CASTLE PUDDINGS (STEAMED)

Prepare a mixture as for Canary Pudding. Two-thirds fill greased dariole moulds with the mixture, cover with greased paper, and steam from 20–30 minutes. Turn out and serve with jam sauce poured round.

CASTLE PUDDINGS (BAKED)

Two-thirds fill the greased dariole moulds with the mixture and bake in a moderately hot oven for about 30 minutes, until well risen, golden-brown, and firm to the touch. Turn on to a hot dish and serve with jam sauce poured round.

RASPBERRY PUDDING

4 oz. flour
A pinch of salt
1 tsp. baking powder
3 oz. butter
2 oz. caster sugar
2 eggs
2 tbsps. raspberry jam

Sieve together the flour, salt, and baking powder. Beat the butter and sugar to a cream. Add the eggs separately with a little of the flour and beat well. Stir in the remaining flour and the jam and mix thoroughly. Put the mixture into a greased basin, cover with greased paper, and steam for 1½ hours. Turn out and serve with custard sauce or jam sauce, made with raspberry jam.

STEAMED CHOCOLATE PUDDING

1½ oz. butter or margarine	¼ pint milk
1½ oz. sugar	½ tsp. baking powder
1 egg	1 oz. cocoa
4 oz. soft white breadcrumbs	Vanilla essence

Cream the fat and sugar. Add the egg yolk and a few crumbs to the creamed mixture and beat together. Add the milk and the remaining crumbs; mix lightly together. Add the baking powder, cocoa, and vanilla essence to the mixture and fold in the stiffly beaten egg white. Pour the mixture into a greased mould, cover with greased paper, and steam steadily for about 1 hour, until well risen and firm. Turn on to a hot dish and coat with chocolate sauce.

DUCHESS PUDDING

4 oz. flour	1 oz. shelled walnuts
A pinch of salt	4 oz. butter
1 tsp. baking powder	4 oz. sugar
1 oz. raisins	2 eggs
1 oz. glacé cherries	Milk if necessary
1 oz. candied peel	

Sieve together the flour, salt, and baking powder. Stone and cut up the raisins, cut up the cherries, and chop the peel and nuts. Cream the butter and sugar together until soft and light in colour and texture. Add the beaten eggs by degrees, together with a little of the flour if the mixture shows signs of curdling, and beat very thoroughly. Stir in the flour and baking powder lightly, adding a little milk, if necessary, to give a soft dropping consistency. Add the prepared fruit and nuts. Put into a greased basin, two-thirds filling it, cover with greased paper, and steam for about 1½ hours. Turn on to a hot dish and coat with jam sauce made from greengage or apricot jam.

CARAMEL PUDDING

1½ oz. loaf sugar	2 eggs
¼ pint milk	6 oz. flour
4 oz. butter	Salt
4 oz. caster sugar	1 tsp. baking powder

Dissolve the sugar over gentle heat in 1 tbsp. water, then boil until it turns caramel colour. Add the hot milk carefully and dissolve the caramel, then cool. Beat the butter and sugar to a cream and add the egg yolks. Stir in the flour, salt, and baking powder and the caramelled milk alternately. Fold in the stiffly whipped whites of egg. Put the mixture into a greased basin, cover with greased paper, and steam for 2 hours. Turn out and serve with coffee custard sauce.

STEAMED PRUNE PUDDING

4 oz. flour	10 prunes (soaked)
1 tsp. baking powder	½ tsp. grated lemon rind
2 oz. butter	1 oz. breadcrumbs
2 oz. sugar	A little milk, if necessary
2 eggs	

Sieve together the flour and baking powder. Beat the butter and sugar to a cream. Add the eggs one at a time, together with a little of the flour; beat well. Drain and cut up the prunes and add them, together with the lemon rind, breadcrumbs, and flour to the creamed mixture. Stir thoroughly, adding a little milk, if necessary, to bring to a soft dropping consistency. Put into a greased basin, cover with greased paper and steam for 1½ hours. Turn out and serve with lemon sauce or custard sauce.

CHOCOLATE LEMON LAYER PUDDING

3 oz. butter or margarine	Grated rind of ½ a lemon
3 oz. sugar	½ oz. cocoa
2 eggs	Lemon curd
4 oz. self-raising flour	

Cream the butter and sugar and add alternately the beaten eggs and the sieved flour, mixing well. To half the mixture add the grated lemon rind, and to the remainder add the sieved cocoa. Place a little lemon curd in the base of a greased pudding basin, put in alternate layers of the chocolate and lemon mixture, cover with greased paper and steam for 1½ hours. Turn out, and serve if liked with lemon sauce.

To make a lemon sauce, use the juice and grated rind of 1 lemon, made up to ½ pint with water; bring to the boil. Blend 2 tsps. arrowroot with a little water and add this, together with 3–4 tbsps. sugar. Continue to cook until the sauce becomes clear.

LAFAYETTE PUDDING

4 oz. butter or margarine	2 oz. fine breadcrumbs
4 oz. sugar	1 tsp. baking powder
2 eggs	2 oz. glacé cherries
4 oz. flour	3 tbsps. milk
3 oz. ground almonds	

Cream together the fat and the sugar, and then beat in the eggs separately. Mix together the dry ingredients and add the cut-up cherries. Fold the dry ingredients into the first mixture, alternately with the milk. Put into a greased basin and steam gently for 2 hours. Serve with almond-flavoured sauce or custard.

DATE CAP PUDDING

4 oz. dates	3 oz. sugar
Juice and grated rind of 1 lemon	2 eggs
	6 oz. flour
1–2 tsps. water	1 tsp. baking powder
3 oz. butter or margarine	Milk to mix

Chop the dates, simmer with the lemon juice and cold water, then put them into a greased basin. Cream together the fat and sugar, beat in the eggs, and lastly, fold in the sieved flour, grated lemon rind and baking powder. Add sufficient milk to give a soft dropping consistency, put into a prepared basin and cover. Steam for 1½ hours, and serve with custard sauce.

BAKED PUDDINGS

ADAM AND EVE PUDDING

1 lb. good cooking apples	2 oz. sugar
3 oz. Demerara sugar	1 egg
Grated rind of 1 lemon	4 oz. flour
2 oz. butter	½ tsp. baking powder

Peel, core, and slice the apples; add Demerara sugar and lemon rind and put them into a fireproof dish or pie dish with 1 tbsp. of water. Cream the butter and sugar thoroughly, add the egg and beat well, then stir in the flour and baking powder, and spread on the top of the apples. Bake in a moderate oven (375° F., mark 5) for about 1 hour, or until the apples are tender and the cake mixture well risen and firm.

APPLE AMBER (WITH BREAD)

4 oz. butter	Sugar to sweeten apples
Stale bread	2 eggs
1½ lb. apples	2 oz. sugar for meringue

Melt the butter, cut the bread into thin slices, and draw these through the melted butter, then line a pie dish with them. Peel and core the apples and stew them with a little water. When soft, sweeten, and rub through a sieve or mash well. Separate the whites and yolks of the eggs, add the yolks to the fruit and fill up the pie dish with the mixture. Bake in a moderately hot oven (400° F., mark 6) for 15 minutes. Whip the egg whites until stiff, fold in 1½ oz. of the sugar, and pile on the top of the dish. Sprinkle with the remaining sugar and bake in a slow oven (300° F., mark 1) until the meringue is crisp and lightly coloured.

For APPLE AMBER made with pastry, see the Pastry chapter.

APPLE CHARLOTTE

2 lb. apples	¼ pint water
Grated lemon rind (or ½ tsp. ground ginger)	3 tbsps. Demerara sugar
	Bread and butter
	3 tbsps. syrup

Stew the apples with the lemon rind or ginger, and water and mash them; add 2 tbsps. sugar. Line the sides of a greased dish with bread and butter—buttered side inwards. Pour in apple pulp and cover with buttered bread, buttered side uppermost. Cover the bread with 1 tbsp. sugar, then the syrup. Bake in a moderately hot oven (400° F., mark 6) for ½ hour, until a crisp crust is formed on the top.

APPLE CHARLOTTE DE LUXE

2 oz. butter, melted	¼ tsp. cinnamon
Slices of stale bread	6–8 oz. sugar
2 lb. cooking apples	2 egg yolks
½ a lemon	Fruit syrup (see below)
3 tbsps. water	

Grease a Charlotte mould with clarified butter. Cut the bread into strips ¼ inch thick, about 1½ inches wide, and long enough to reach from top to bottom of the Charlotte mould. Cut a round piece the same size as the bottom of the mould. Dip the circle in the melted butter and put on the bottom of the mould. Dip the strips in the butter and arrange closely against the side of the mould, overlapping each other. Fill the mould with apple purée (which is prepared by stewing the apples, lemon rind and juice, water and cinnamon together), adding the sugar and the beaten egg yolks. Trim off the edges of the strips of bread and cover with a piece of bread the size of the top of the mould. Bake in a moderate oven (375° F., mark 5) for about 40 minutes. Turn on to a hot dish and serve with hot fruit syrup. To make this, heat ¼ pint syrup —obtained either by boiling the parings and cores of the apples in water to which sugar has been added, or from bottled or tinned fruit if available—and colouring it slightly with cochineal.

APPLE AND PRUNE CHARLOTTE

Bread and butter	Grated rind of 1 lemon
Demerara sugar	2 tbsps. water
½ lb. apples	A few prune kernels
¼ lb. prunes (soaked)	

Line a pie dish with bread and butter and sprinkle with Demerara sugar. Fill up the dish with alternate layers of sliced apples and stoned prunes, grated lemon rind and sugar. Add the water and cover the top with slices of bread and butter, sprinkling the chopped kernels from the prune stones on the top. Bake in a moderate oven (375° F., mark 5) for ¾-1 hour.

APPLE AND CRANBERRY SPONGE

2 oz. sponge cakes	2 eggs
1 pint stewed apples and cranberries, sweetened	2 oz. caster sugar for meringue

Crumble the sponge cakes, add the stewed fruit, and beat well. Leave for about 1 hour to soak. Add the beaten yolks and mix thoroughly. Bake in a moderate oven (375° F., mark 5) for 20–30 minutes. Whisk up the whites of egg very stiffly, fold in 1½ tbsps. of the caster sugar, pile on top of the sponge, and sprinkle with the remaining caster sugar. Return to the oven to brown and set—about 20 minutes.

APPLE STRUDEL

10 oz. flour	6 tbsps. breadcrumbs
½ tsp. salt	6 oz. currants and sultanas
1 beaten egg	
2–3 tbsps. warm water	3 tsps. cinnamon
3–4 lb. cooking apples	Grated rind of 1 orange and 1 lemon
3 oz. brown sugar	
3 oz. finely chopped blanched almonds	1 oz. butter
	2 oz. white sugar

Sieve the flour and salt into a basin and mix to a soft dough with the beaten egg and a little warm water. Knead or beat until it is elastic and no longer sticks to the board—about 15 minutes. Roll the dough out slightly, place it on a well-floured cloth which has been pinned out over a table, and leave for 10 minutes. Meanwhile, prepare the apples, cutting them in thin slices; add the sugar, almonds, breadcrumbs, dried fruit, cinnamon, and lemon and orange rind, and mix well together. Gently pull and stretch the dough out, placing both hands underneath it until it is paper-thin, but take care not to tear it. (Strudel dough can be stretched out to an enormous size with careful manipulation.)

Pile the apple mixture at one end of the dough, then lift up one end of the cloth, roll the apple and paste up, and slide on to a well-buttered baking sheet. Pour a little melted butter over. Bake in a moderately hot oven (400° F., mark 6) for 20 minutes, then reduce to moderate, and continue to bake until crisp and light golden-brown, brushing over occasionally with the melted butter. Remove from the oven, dust heavily with white sugar, and serve warm on a wooden platter, accompanied, if possible, by a bowl of whipped cream.

BAKED APPLES

6 cooking apples	Demerara sugar
4 tbsps. water	Butter

Wipe the apples thoroughly and cut through the skin around the centre of the apples. Remove the core with an apple corer and stand the apples in a fireproof dish or baking tin. Pour the water around and fill up the centre of each apple with Demerara sugar and top with a knob of butter. Bake in a moderately hot oven (400° F., mark 6) until tender—¾-1 hour. Serve hot or cold.

BAKED STUFFED APPLES—I

2 lb. large apples	2 oz. sugar
½ lb. dates	Water
1 oz. nuts	Butter

Prepare the apples as for baked apples. Stone the dates and cut them up finely, add the chopped nuts and sugar and mix well. Fill each apple with the stuffing and place in a fireproof dish or baking tin, adding sufficient water to come ¼ inch up the side. Place shavings of butter on the apples and bake in a moderately hot oven (400° F., mark 6) until tender—about 1 hour.

BAKED STUFFED APPLES—II

12 prunes or dates	4 large cooking apples
1 tbsp. syrup or honey	1 oz. butter
Squeeze of lemon juice	Water

Stone the prunes or dates and chop finely, then mix with the syrup and lemon juice.

Wipe the apples and carefully remove the core with an apple corer. Cut them in half crosswise, place in a baking tin and arrange the stuffing so that it fills the hole and is sandwiched between the halves of the apple. Place a good knob of butter on each apple. Pour in enough water just to cover the bottom of the tin, and bake in a moderately hot oven (400° F., mark 6) for about 1 hour.

CANADIAN FRUIT PIE

1 lb. fruit, e.g., apples, plums, etc.	2 oz. butter
	5 oz. flour
3 oz. sugar	A pinch of salt

Slice the fruit, lay it in a pie dish, and sprinkle with 1 oz. sugar and a very little water. Rub the fat very finely into the flour, until the mixture resembles breadcrumbs. Add 2 oz. sugar and a pinch of salt and mix well. Sprinkle thickly over the surface of the fruit. Bake in a moderately hot oven (400° F., mark 6) until the crust is golden-brown, and the fruit tender—20–30 minutes. Serve with cream or custard.

FRUIT BUN PUDDING

(*See colour picture facing page* 288)

6 oz. flour	2 tsps. ground cinnamon
¼ oz. yeast	Stewed damsons, plums or apricots
4 oz. sugar	
¼ pint milk	Beaten egg
3 oz. fat	Sugar glaze

Put the flour into a bowl and warm slightly. Cream the yeast with 1 tsp. sugar and add the warmed milk. Melt 2 oz. of the fat and add to the flour, with the yeast and the milk. Using the hand, beat thoroughly to form a soft dough, then put aside in a warm place. When it has doubled its bulk, remove from the bowl and knead thoroughly, then roll out into an oblong. Brush it with the remaining melted fat, sprinkle liberally with sugar and cinnamon, roll up and cut into slices. Put the fruit in a dish, place the buns on top (cut side up), and set aside to prove. Brush over with a little egg and bake in a moderately hot oven (425° F., mark 6) until golden-brown and well risen—about 15–20 minutes. Glaze with a little sugar and water, and return it to the oven for 2–3 minutes.

PINEAPPLE BETTY

1 large tin of pineapple (slices or chunks)	3 tbsps. brown sugar
	1 orange
2 teacupfuls soft white breadcrumbs	1–2 oz. melted butter

Shred or chop the pineapple. Put alternate layers of breadcrumbs, sugar, grated orange rind, melted butter, and pineapple in a pie dish, and sprinkle each layer with orange juice and pineapple juice. Finish with a layer of crumbs. Bake in a moderately hot oven (400° F., mark 6) for about 40 minutes. Dust with fine sugar and serve with pineapple juice, reduced to a thick consistency, or with cream or custard.

WEST INDIAN PUDDING

2 oz. breadcrumbs	A little cinnamon (optional)
4 large bananas	
2 oz. sugar	1½ oz. butter or suet
Grated rind of ½ lemon	Banana and crystallised cherry to decorate
Juice of 1 lemon	

Butter a pie dish or some individual cups and coat well with fine breadcrumbs—for preference these should be freshly made and not dry. Remove the skins from the bananas and mash them with the sugar, lemon rind and juice and a little cinnamon, if liked. Put a layer of the mashed fruit into the pie dish and cover with breadcrumbs, on top of which either put small pieces of butter or sprinkle with finely chopped suet. Continue the layers until the dish is full and all the ingredients used up. Breadcrumbs should form the top layer, and they should be well buttered to prevent scorching. Bake in a moderate oven (375° F., mark 5) for 30–40 minutes; when almost cooked, decorate with slices of banana and a few crystallised cherries.

APPLE GINGER CAKE

1 lb. apples	2 tsps. ginger
4 oz. margarine	½ tsp. allspice
4 oz. sugar	1 tsp. cinnamon
1 egg	1 tsp. bicarbonate of soda
4 oz. treacle	1½ gills sour milk
6 oz. flour	

Wash, peel, and core the apples and cook them with very little water until they form a thick pulp. Cream the fat and sugar until light and fluffy; beat in the egg and the treacle. Sieve the flour and ginger, allspice and cinnamon. Dissolve the bicarbonate of soda in the sour milk. Fold the milk and the dry ingredients alternately into the creamed mixture. Bake in a ring mould in a moderate oven (375° F., mark 5) for about 1 hour, or until firm to the touch. Turn out, fill the centre with the apple and serve hot.

DUTCH APPLE PUDDING

½ lb. self-raising flour	3 oz. sugar
A pinch of salt	2 tsps. cinnamon
3 oz. suet	1 tbsp. lemon juice
Water to mix	2 tbsps. syrup
1½ lb. apples	

Sieve the flour and salt, stir in the chopped suet, add a little water and mix to a dough with a round-bladed knife. Knead on a board and cut into two. Grease and line a small Yorkshire pudding tin with this mixture. Cover with a layer of sliced apples, sprinkle with sugar, cinnamon and lemon juice. Add a second layer of apples. Roll out the second piece of pastry, damp the edges and cover the pie. Spread the syrup over the pastry, and bake for 1½ hours in a moderate oven (350° F., mark 4).

BANANA BREAD PUDDING

Slices of bread and butter	2 eggs
	4 oz. sugar
4 bananas	1 pint milk
Juice of 1 lemon	

Grease a pie dish and fill it with alternate layers of bread and butter and sliced bananas. Sprinkle with the lemon juice. Beat the eggs well, add sugar and milk and pour over bread and bananas. Bake in a moderate oven (350° F., mark 4) for 1 hour, until firm when tested.

BAKED ORANGE PUDDING

4 oz. butter or margarine	5 oz. flour
4 oz. sugar	½ tsp. baking powder
3 eggs	Orange curd
Grated rind and juice of 1 orange	4 oz. caster sugar for meringue topping

Cream the fat and sugar until light and creamy. Beat in 2 of the egg yolks and one whole egg, the orange rind and the juice, then fold in the flour and baking powder. Put into a greased dish and bake in a moderate oven (375° F., mark 5) until well risen and firm—about ½ hour. Remove from the oven and spread the top with a little orange curd. Whisk the remaining egg white until stiff, fold in the caster sugar, and whisk well. Pile on top of the pudding, and bake in a slow oven (325° F., mark 2) until golden-brown.

RAILWAY PUDDING

8 oz. flour	Milk to mix
2 tsps. baking powder	Finely grated rind of 1 lemon
4 oz. margarine and lard mixed	Jam
3 oz. sugar	Caster sugar
1 egg	

Sieve the flour and baking powder together and rub in the fat. Add the sugar, and mix to a dropping consistency with the beaten egg and the milk; flavour with the lemon rind. Put into a greased shallow cake tin and bake in a moderate oven (375° F., mark 5) until golden-brown—about 30–40 minutes. Turn out, split in half and spread with the warmed jam; put together again, cut into squares and sprinkle liberally with caster sugar.

MIXED FRUIT COBBLER

8 oz. self-raising flour	Sweetened cooked fruit (apples, cherries, blackcurrants, bananas, gooseberries, apricots)
1 oz. sugar	
2 oz. butter or margarine	
1 egg	Egg and sugar to glaze
Milk to mix	

86 Mix together the dry ingredients and rub in the fat, then mix to a soft scone dough with the egg and milk. Knead lightly on a floured board and cut into rounds or rings ½ inch thick. Heat the fruit in a pan, and when it boils pour it into a pie dish. Place the scones on top, brush lightly with egg and sprinkle with sugar. Bake in a moderately hot oven (425° F., mark 7) for 5–10 minutes, until the scones are well-risen and brown.

MINCEMEAT SLICES

6 oz. plain flour	2 oz. sugar
4 oz. butter or margarine	Mincemeat

Sieve the flour, rub in the fat and add the sugar. Place half this mixture in a greased tin and cover with mincemeat. Place the remainder of the flour mixture on top and press down firmly. Bake in a moderate oven (350° F., mark 4) for about ½ hour. Serve cut in squares or triangles and accompanied by hard sauce or custard.

PEACH MERINGUE PUDDING

6 small sponge cakes	4 oz. sugar
2 large yellow peaches	Sieved apricot jam
½ pint milk	Blanched almonds (optional)
2 eggs	

Break the cakes in small pieces, and put at the bottom of a fireproof dish. Skin the peaches, first plunging them into boiling water. Heat the milk and pour it on to the egg yolks, mix thoroughly and add half of the sugar. Pour over the cakes and place over it one peach, thinly sliced. Whip the egg whites, add the remaining sugar and whisk again, then pile the mixture over the sliced peach. Cut the remaining peach in four and arrange on top, adding the nuts, if used; brush the peaches with apricot jam. Place in a slow oven (300° F., mark 1) for about ½ hour, or until the meringue is crisp and the custard set.

BLACKBERRY CRUMBLE

½ lb. blackberries	4 oz. flour
½ lb. apples	3–4 oz. sugar
4 oz. margarine	

Rinse the blackberries; peel the apples and slice them thinly. Rub the margarine into the flour, add 2 oz. sugar and mix well. Boil the fruit in a very little water for a few minutes, to soften it, sweeten to taste and place it in a fireproof dish. Sprinkle the flour mixture over, and bake in a moderately hot oven (425° F., mark 7) until golden-brown—about 20 minutes.

PEACH PUDDING

1 small tin of halved peaches	6 oz. flour
	1 tsp. baking powder
3 oz. margarine	Water to mix
3 oz. sugar	Raspberry jam
1 egg	2 tsps. lemon juice

Grease a fireproof dish and put in some of the peaches. Cream the fat and sugar and beat in the egg. Sieve in the flour and baking powder, add just sufficient water to give a soft dropping consistency, and mix well. Put the mixture over the peaches and bake in a moderate oven (350° F., mark 4) for 1 hour, or until the mixture has shrunk away from the sides of the dish. Turn out on a hot dish and put 1 small tsp. jam in the centre of each peach. Serve with a sauce made from peaches and lemon juice, and decorate with the rest of the fruit.

CHOCOLATE PEAR PUDDING

Make and cook as for Peach Pudding, using fresh, canned or bottled pears, and adding 1 tbsp. cocoa and a few drops of vanilla essence to the pudding mixture. Turn out carefully, decorate, and serve with chocolate sauce.

BAKED PRUNE PUDDING

½ lb. prunes	3 oz. brown sugar
¾ pint stale breadcrumbs	1½ oz. margarine
¼ pint water	1 oz. bread raspings
½ a lemon	

Grease a two-pint pie dish. Soak the prunes in the water and boil them until soft, then stone and halve them. Cut the lemon in thin slices. Place half of the crumbs in a pudding dish, cover with half of the prunes, the lemon slices and the sugar, and dot with 1 oz. of the margarine. Repeat the first four layers, but top with bread raspings, dotting with the remainder of the margarine. Add the water or prune juice, and bake in a moderately hot oven (425° F., mark 7) for 30 minutes.

COTTAGE PUDDING

4 oz. margarine and lard mixed	Almond essence
4 oz. sugar	3 oz. raisins
1 egg	2 oz. chopped glacé cherries
7 oz. self-raising flour	1–2 oz. chopped almonds
1 tsp. mixed spice	Water to mix

Cream together the fat and sugar until soft and white, add the egg and beat well. Sieve in the flour and spice, add a few drops of almond essence, most of the fruit and nuts, and mix to a soft dropping consistency, with a little water. Turn into a greased oven-glass dish, decorate with nuts and cherries, dredge with sugar and cover with the lid. Bake in a moderately hot oven (425° F., mark 7) for 1½ hours, then remove the lid and continue to cook until top is golden—about 30 minutes. Serve with a sauce.

PEACH UPSIDE-DOWN PUDDING

2 tbsps. golden syrup	2 eggs
½–¾ lb. sliced peaches	1 tsp. baking powder
4 oz. butter or margarine	6 oz. flour
4 oz. caster sugar	Milk to mix

Well grease a 6-inch cake tin and put a round of greased paper at the bottom. Coat the base with golden syrup and arrange the sliced peaches decoratively over this. Cream the fat and sugar and beat in the eggs. Sieve together the baking powder and flour and fold into the mixture, with a little milk to give a soft dropping consistency. Put the mixture into the tin and bake in a moderately hot oven (400° F., mark 6) until well risen and brown—about 35–40 minutes. Turn the pudding out upside-down and serve with syrup sauce—see page 207.

Upside-down Pudding can be varied by using other fruits—fresh, bottled or tinned—or the mixture can be flavoured with ginger, chocolate, lemon, etc. Serve with a suitable sauce.

PINEAPPLE GINGER PUDDING

5–6 tbsps. golden syrup	2 tsps. ground ginger
A 12-oz. tin of crushed pineapple	1 tsp. bicarbonate of soda
	Milk for mixing
12 oz. flour	4 oz. butter or margarine
2 oz. sugar	1 egg

Grease a 7-inch square cake tin and place a piece of greased paper on the bottom. Put 2–3 tbsps. of the syrup in the tin and place half the drained pineapple on top of it. Mix together the flour, sugar, and ginger, and dissolve the bicarbonate of soda in 1 tbsp. of the milk. Melt the butter, and add the remaining syrup and the rest of the pineapple to it. Make a well in the centre of the dry ingredients and add the syrup mixture, with the egg and enough milk to give a thick pouring consistency. Lastly, add the dissolved bicarbonate and beat well, then put the mixture into the prepared tin. Bake in a slow oven (325° F., mark 2) for 1 hour, until well-risen and firm. Turn out upside-down and serve with more syrup.

RHUBARB CHARLOTTE

1½ lb. rhubarb	1 lemon
3 oz. breadcrumbs	4 oz. sugar
2 oz. grated suet	A little butter or margarine

Prepare and cut the rhubarb. Mix the breadcrumbs, suet, grated lemon rind, lemon juice and sugar. Put a layer of rhubarb in a pie dish, then a layer of the breadcrumb mixture, and add a few shavings of butter. Repeat until the dish is full, finishing with a layer of breadcrumbs and a little butter. Bake in a moderate oven (350° F., mark 4) for ¾–1 hour.

RAISIN SCONE PUDDING

6 oz. raisins	8 oz. flour
¼ pint water	3 tsps. baking powder
2 oz. sugar	A pinch of salt
½ tsp. lemon juice	1½ oz. butter or margarine
2 oz. nuts	Milk and water to mix

Put the stoned raisins in a saucepan with the

water, 1 oz. sugar, lemon juice and nuts, and simmer slowly until the raisins are soft and tender, and the mixture becomes a thick paste. Sieve the flour, remaining sugar, baking powder and salt into a basin. Rub in the fat and mix with the liquid to form a soft dough. Divide the dough into two parts, roll out each portion to the size of a fireproof plate, and line this with one piece. Spread the raisin filling on the bottom, damp the edges and cover with the second piece. Bake in a moderately hot oven (425° F., mark 7) until brown and cooked thoroughly—about 30 minutes; it may be necessary to cook for a further 10 minutes at a lower temperature.

MISCELLANEOUS PUDDINGS

SAXON PUDDING

4 oz. sponge cake crumbs — 2 oz. sugar
2 oz. ground almonds — 2 eggs
2 tbsps. cream or top of the milk — 2 oz. shredded or diced pineapple
2 tbsps. milk — Grated rind of 1 lemon
2 oz. butter or margarine

Grease a plain mould thoroughly. Put the crumbs and ground almonds into a basin, pour on the cream and milk and leave to soak for about 30 minutes. Cream together the fat and sugar and beat in the egg yolks alternately with the soaked mixture and the drained pineapple. Beat in the lemon rind, and lastly, fold in the stiffly beaten egg whites. Steam carefully for 1½–2 hours, turn out, and serve with a pineapple flavoured sauce.

RICH CHOCOLATE PUDDING

2 oz. plain chocolate — 1½ oz. sugar
¼ pint milk — 1 egg
4 oz. fine white bread-crumbs — Vanilla essence
1½ oz. butter or margarine — ½ tsp. baking powder
Almonds

Break the chocolate into small pieces, melt it in the milk and pour on to the crumbs. Leave
87 to soak for 15–20 minutes. Cream together the fat and sugar until soft and light, beat in the egg yolk, then beat in the soaked crumbs. Add a few drops of vanilla essence and the stiffly beaten egg white. Lastly, fold in the baking powder, put the mixture into a greased mould and steam gently for 1 hour, until well-risen and firm. Turn it out on to a hot dish, decorate with a few blanched almonds and serve with chocolate sauce—see page 205.

CAKE CRUMB PUDDING

1½ cupfuls stale cake crumbs — 3 oz. flour
½ pint hot milk — 1 tbsp. baking powder
4 oz. sugar — A pinch of salt
1 egg — ½ cupful chopped figs
½ cupful chopped walnuts

Soak the cake crumbs in the hot milk for 10 minutes; add the sugar and beaten egg. Mix and sift together the flour, baking powder and salt. Add the figs and walnuts, then add the crumb and milk mixture slowly, stirring all the time. Pour into a greased mould, cover tightly and steam for 2½ hours.

RASPBERRY MERINGUE PIE

1 small Swiss roll — 2 egg whites
1 large tin of raspberries — 4 oz. sugar

Cut the Swiss roll in slices and use to line a fireproof dish. Drain the raspberries from the tin and arrange them on the sliced Swiss roll. Whisk the egg whites until stiff, then whisk in half the sugar and fold in the rest of it. Pile on the fruit and sprinkle with a little caster sugar. Bake in a slow oven (325° F., mark 2) for 10–15 minutes, until the meringue is crisp.

APPLE CORNFLAKE CRUNCH

1 lb. apples — 2 oz. brown sugar
2 cups cornflakes — 2 oz. butter or margarine

Peel and slice the apples. Put a layer of apples in a fireproof dish, then a layer of cornflakes, sprinkle liberally with sugar and put a few knobs of margarine on top. Continue until all the flakes and apples have been used up. Bake in a moderately hot oven (425° F., mark 7) until the apple has cooked and the mixture is crisp.

APRICOT LAYER PUDDING

1 tbsp. golden syrup — 3 oz. sugar
1 jar or tin of apricots or peaches in syrup — 1 egg
8 oz. self-raising flour — Milk to mix
4 oz. margarine — Arrowroot or cornflour to thicken sauce

Grease a basin, put the golden syrup at the bottom and over this arrange a circle of apricots or sliced peaches. Sieve the flour and rub in the fat, then add the sugar and mix with the beaten egg and milk to a soft dropping consistency. Put a layer of this pudding mixture in the basin, then another layer of fruit, and cover with the remainder of the pudding mixture. Cover with greased paper or a pudding cloth, and steam for 2 hours. Make the fruit syrup up to ½ pint with water, and thicken it with 1 tsp. arrowroot or cornflour. Add any remaining fruit, cut into pieces, and serve this sauce with the pudding.

MILK PUDDINGS AND CUSTARDS

MILK PUDDINGS

Milk puddings are easy to make and provide an excellent means of introducing plenty of milk into the family meals. You can use full cream milk, diluted tinned milk, or skimmed milk. If skimmed milk is used you should add extra fat—butter, margarine or even finely chopped suet—to make up for the lack of cream.

Milk puddings can be enriched by the addition of beaten eggs or by stirring in a little cream or undiluted evaporated milk, or by putting shavings of butter or margarine on top of the pudding before baking. If eggs or cream are included they should be added towards the end of the cooking, and care should be taken not to overheat the mixture after the eggs have been added or they are likely to curdle.

If you tire of plain milk puddings (and children, particularly, often do), you can vary them in a great many ways, as you will see from these recipes. Some simple variations are to add dried fruits (such as raisins or sultanas), grated lemon or orange rind, or chocolate or caramel flavouring, or to cover baked puddings with jam and a meringue topping.

Proportions to Use

For Milk Puddings, allow :—

- 1½ oz. whole or small grain to 1 pint milk.
- 1 oz. ground grain to 1 pint milk.

For Milk Moulds, allow :—

- 2 oz. whole or small grain to 1 pint milk.
- 1½ oz. ground or powdered grain to 1 pint milk.

Directions for Making

Whole Grain

Rice, tapioca, etc. Add the whole grain to the cold milk and cook very slowly in the oven or in a double saucepan until the grain softens and absorbs the milk—about 2 hours, or even longer. It saves cooking time to soak the grain in the milk for a while prior to cooking. If you have a pressure cooker, the time will be appreciably shortened. (See chapter on Pressure Cookery.)

Small Grain, Crushed Grain

Fine sago, semolina, seed tapioca. Bring milk to boiling-point, then sprinkle in the grain, stir and simmer it until it thickens (10–15 minutes). Cook for a further ½ hour in the oven (or in the saucepan).

Ground Grain, Powdered Grain

Ground rice, cornflour. Mix the grain with a little cold milk, bring the rest of the milk to boiling-point, then stir in the blended grain. Stir and simmer until the mixture thickens and the grain is cooked (5–7 minutes).

RICE PUDDING

1½ oz. rice	A knob of butter
1 pint milk	Grated nutmeg
½–1 oz. sugar	

Wash the rice and put it into a pie dish with the milk and sugar. Put shavings of butter and a little grated nutmeg on top. Bake in a slow oven for 2–3 hours. Stir once or twice during the first hour.

It is the long, slow baking that gives the delicious creamy texture, pinkish colour and crisp brown skin to a baked milk pudding. If, however, it is inconvenient to use the oven, the pudding may be cooked in a double boiler, until the grain is tender and the mixture thick—about 2 hours.

To make the pudding richer, 1 tbsp. evaporated milk may be added.

FRUIT RICE PUDDING

Make as for Rice Pudding, adding 1–2 oz. of dried fruit before cooking.

CHOCOLATE RICE PUDDING

Make, as for Rice Pudding, dissolving 2 oz. grated chocolate in the milk before adding to the rice, and omitting the butter; a few drops of vanilla essence may also be added.

CREAMED RICE

1½ oz. rice	Vanilla to flavour
1 pint milk	¼ pint cream
Sugar to sweeten	Fresh fruit if liked

Wash the rice and put in a double saucepan with the milk. Cook gently until the grain is tender and the mixture soft and creamy—about 2 hours. Set aside to cool, then sweeten and flavour to taste. Half-whip the cream, and fold lightly into the rice. Pile in a glass dish or in individual glasses, and top with extra cream or with fresh raspberries or strawberries.

APRICOT RICE PUDDING

2 oz. dried apricots or a small tin of apricots	1 pint milk
	1 oz. sugar
1½ oz. rice	2 eggs

Wash the dried apricots and put to soak overnight. Cook in a little water with sugar to taste. (If preferred, a small tin of apricots can be used.) Cook the rice in the milk and when cooked add the 1 oz. sugar. Beat the eggs into the cooked rice. Put the drained apricots into the bottom of a pie dish. Pour the rice mixture on top and bake in a moderately hot oven (400° F., mark 6) for about 15 minutes, to heat through and to brown the top. Serve with the apricot juice, boiled until syrupy.

LEMON MERINGUE RICE PUDDING

1½ oz. rice	1 or 2 eggs
1 pint milk	Sugar
Juice and rind of 1 lemon	Jam

Wash the rice and put into a double saucepan with the milk and thinly peeled lemon rind. Cook gently until the rice is tender and the mixture thick and creamy—about 2 hours. Remove the lemon rind and stir in the lemon juice. Slightly cool the mixture and beat in the egg yolks and a little sugar to sweeten. Put a layer of jam on the bottom of a pie dish and pour on the rice mixture. Whisk the egg whites very stiffly, then add 1 tbsp. sugar for each egg white and whisk again. Pile on top of the pudding and sprinkle thickly with sugar. Bake in a moderate oven (350° F., mark 4) for 20–30 minutes, until the meringue top is lightly coloured and crisp to the touch. Serve hot.

DANISH SPONGE

2 oz. rice	¼ oz. gelatine
1 pint milk	2 tbsps. water
1 oz. sugar	2 egg whites
Flavouring	Fruit and fruit syrup to serve
Colouring	

Wash the rice thoroughly, then cook it slowly in the milk until soft and creamy. Sweeten, flavour and colour to taste. Dissolve the gelatine in the water over gentle heat and add it to the rice, then cool. Beat the egg whites very stiffly and fold into the cold rice mixture. Turn into a wetted mould and allow to set. After turning out, place small pieces of fruit (stewed fruit, or fresh fruit salad) at each end of the dish and pour fruit syrup around.

GLAZED PINEAPPLE RICE PUDDING

1½ oz. rice	Sugar to taste
1 pint milk	1 small tin of pineapple
1 egg	

Wash the rice and put it in a double saucepan with the milk. Cook gently until the grain is tender and the mixture thick and creamy—about 2 hours. Cool slightly, add the beaten egg and sugar to taste, and reheat, without boiling, to cook the eggs. Pour into a fireproof glass dish or a pie dish.

Drain the pineapple and arrange the pieces on top of the pudding. Meanwhile, put the juice into a saucepan, add a little sugar and boil for about 5 minutes, or until it has reduced to a glazing consistency; pour over the pineapple.

GROUND RICE PUDDING

1½ oz. ground rice	½ oz. butter
1 pint milk	1 egg, if liked
½ oz. sugar	Flavouring if desired

Mix the ground rice to a thin creamy consistency with some of the measured milk. Heat the rest of the milk in a saucepan, and when almost boiling, stir into the ground rice. Return to the pan and boil, stirring, for several minutes, until thick and creamy. Sweeten and pour into a greased pie dish, put shavings of butter on top, and bake in a moderate oven (350° F., mark 4) for about 30 minutes, until lightly browned. Serve with jam or stewed fruit.

If desired, an egg may be added to enrich the pudding. Add the beaten egg to the slightly cooled mixture with the sugar, and cook in a moderate oven for ½–¾ hour. If flavouring is liked, add a few drops of vanilla or other essence, or cook a piece of lemon rind in the mixture, removing it before pouring into the pie dish.

SEMOLINA PUDDING

1 pint milk	½ oz. sugar
1½ oz. semolina	1 egg

Heat the milk, and when almost boiling, sprinkle in the semolina, stirring all the time.

Stir until boiling, then simmer for 10–15 minutes, until the grain is soft, stirring frequently. Remove from the heat, add sugar and cool slightly. Separate the yolk and white of the egg. Beat the yolk into the semolina and mix well. Whisk the white stiffly, and fold into the semolina mixture. Pour into a greased pie dish, and bake in a moderate oven (350° F., mark 4) for about 30 minutes, until the pudding is lightly browned.

SEMOLINA ORANGE (OR LEMON) PUDDING

1 pint milk
1½ oz. semolina
1 orange or lemon
2–3 oz. caster sugar
1 egg

Bring the milk to the boil, stir in the semolina and grated rind. Stir and boil for 15 minutes. Add the sugar, fruit juice and egg yolk. Beat well and pour into a pie dish. Whip up the egg white stiffly, pile on the top, sprinkle with sugar. Bake in a moderate oven (350° F., mark 4) for 20 minutes.

CHOCOLATE SEMOLINA WHIP

2 oz. grated chocolate
1 pint milk
1½ oz. fine semolina
½ oz. sugar
A few drops of vanilla essence

Dissolve the chocolate in the milk and bring to the boil. Sprinkle in the semolina and cook, stirring well, for 7–10 minutes, until thick. Remove from the heat, add sugar to sweeten and a little vanilla essence. Turn into a basin and whisk until cold. Serve in individual glass dishes, topped with whipped cream.

CHOCOLATE TAPIOCA PUDDING

1 pint milk
1½ oz. seed-pearl tapioca
1½ oz. sugar
2 oz. chocolate
2 egg yolks

For the Meringue

2 egg whites
2 oz. caster sugar

Heat the milk, and when almost boiling, sprinkle in the seed-pearl tapioca. Simmer for 15–20 minutes, or until the tapioca is cooked, stirring frequently. Stir in the sugar, grated chocolate and egg yolks. Mix well and pour the mixture into a pie dish. Whip up the egg whites stiffly. Fold in 1½ tbsps. of the sugar to form a meringue and pile this in peaks on top of the pudding. Dredge with the remaining sugar. Bake in moderate oven (350° F., mark 3) for 20–30 minutes, or until the meringue is crisp to the touch and lightly coloured.

TAPIOCA SPONGE PUDDING

1 oz. seed-pearl tapioca
A pinch of salt
¾ pint milk
1 oz. caster sugar
1 egg
Lemon or vanilla flavouring

Wash the tapioca and soak it in a little water for ½ hour. Then strain and put with the salt and milk into a saucepan and bring to the boil. Simmer, stirring occasionally, until the tapioca is cooked. Cool a little, add the sugar, egg yolk and flavouring. Whip the egg white stiffly and fold it into the mixture. Put into a greased pie dish and bake in a moderately hot oven (400° F., mark 6) for about 20 minutes.

MACARONI PUDDING

2 oz. macaroni
1 pint milk
1 oz. sugar
1 egg

Break the macaroni into small pieces, and put into a saucepan with the milk. Simmer very gently until tender—about 30 minutes. Remove from the heat, sweeten and cool slightly. Stir in the beaten egg, and pour into a buttered pie dish. Bake in a moderately hot oven (400° F., mark 6) about 30 minutes, until lightly browned.

If desired, add 1–2 oz. dried fruit before cooking, or flavour with vanilla, etc.

CORNFLOUR MOULD

1 pint milk
Lemon rind or other flavouring
1½ oz. cornflour
1 oz. sugar

Take three-quarters of the milk, add a thin strip of lemon rind and bring slowly to the boil. Mix the cornflour to a smooth paste with the remaining cold milk. Strain the hot milk on to the cornflour, stirring well. Return to the saucepan, stir, and boil for 5 minutes. Add the sugar and pour into a wetted mould. When set, turn out and serve with fruit or jam, and cream.

CHOCOLATE MOULD

2 oz. chocolate
2 tbsps. milk
1½ oz. cornflour
1 pint milk
1 oz. sugar
Vanilla essence

Cut up the chocolate, add the 2 tbsps. milk, and dissolve over gentle heat. Mix the cornflour to a smooth paste with ¼ pint of the milk. Heat the rest of the milk and pour on to the blended cornflour, stirring well. Add the dissolved chocolate, return to the pan, stir and boil for 5 minutes. Add the sugar and vanilla essence and pour into a wetted mould. When set, turn out and serve with cream.

QUEEN OF PUDDINGS

$\frac{1}{2}$ pint milk	$\frac{1}{2}$ oz. sugar
$\frac{1}{4}$ pint breadcrumbs	2 egg yolks
Grated rind of 1 lemon	2 tbsps. raspberry or other jam
$\frac{1}{2}$ oz. butter	

For the Meringue

2 eggs whites   2 oz. sugar

Heat the milk and pour it on to the breadcrumbs; add the lemon rind, butter and sugar and leave aside for about $\frac{1}{2}$ hour, for the bread to swell. Beat in the egg yolks, and pour into a greased pie dish. Bake in a moderately hot oven (400° F., mark 6) for about $\frac{1}{2}$ hour, until set.

Spread a thick layer of jam on the top, heating the jam if necessary, so that it will spread easily. Whisk the egg whites very stiffly, then fold in $1\frac{1}{2}$ tbsps. ($1\frac{1}{2}$ oz.) of the sugar. Pile on top of the pudding and dredge with the remaining sugar. Return to a moderate oven (350° F., mark 4) for 20–30 minutes, until the meringue is lightly coloured and crisp to the touch.

JUNKETS

Junket is made by adding rennet to new milk. Rennet is prepared from the digestive juice of the calf and contains an enzyme which acts on the protein in the milk and sets it, forming junket—or "curds and whey." The enzyme is most active at blood heat, so the milk must be warmed to this temperature before the rennet is added. Care must be taken (1) not to overheat the milk, or the enzyme will be destroyed and (2) not to chill too rapidly, or the enzyme may become inactive and prevent the junket setting. Junket should not be disturbed until it is served; once cut, the whey tends to run out and separate from the curds, spoiling the texture of the junket. Left-over junket that has separated out can be used to make Curd Cheese Cakes (see recipe in Pastry chapter).

Rennet is usually sold in the form of a liquid without added colouring or flavouring. There are also commercial preparations of rennet in powder, tablet and liquid form, which are already coloured and flavoured. When using these, any special directions supplied by the manufacturer should be carefully followed. Rennet should be kept in a cool, dry place.

JUNKET

1 pint new milk	Nutmeg or other flavouring
Rennet essence	

Heat the milk to blood heat. Stir in the required amount of rennet essence according to the directions on the bottle (this varies with the different makes). Pour at once into a glass dish or into individual glasses and put in a warm place to set. Chill before serving. Just before serving, grate a little nutmeg over.

Variations

Flavour the milk with any of the following:—

1–2 tbsps. brandy or rum.

$1\frac{1}{2}$ oz. of chocolate dissolved in 3 tbsps. of the milk.

Vanilla, almond or fruit essence, and appropriate colouring.

DEVONSHIRE JUNKET

Make the junket in the usual way. When set, cover with a layer of Devonshire cream flavoured with brandy, and, if liked, sprinkle with grated nutmeg or a dusting of sugar and cinnamon.

COFFEE JUNKET

Make the junket in the usual way, adding sufficient coffee essence to flavour the milk. Just before serving, cover the surface of the junket with grated chocolate and chopped nuts.

If preferred, brewed coffee may be used instead of essence, but this should be very strong, otherwise the milk will become too much diluted and the junket will not set.

CUSTARDS

Custards, which are essentially a mixture of egg and milk, depend for their texture on the thickening properties of the eggs. When heated gently, the egg coagulates and the mixture thickens, but if overheated, the egg hardens and tends to separate out from the liquid, causing the mixture to curdle; so when cooking egg custards, heat the mixture only sufficiently to cook the egg, i.e., to just under boiling point.

Custard powders consist essentially of starch, and do not of course contain eggs. They should be prepared according to directions supplied with them.

Baked Custards

See that the oven is at moderate heat only (350° F., mark 3). The custard may be stood in a tin containing water, to prevent it becoming overheated and consequently curdling.

Steamed Custards

See that the water in the steamer simmers only

—do not let it boil vigorously or the custard will very likely curdle. Draw the steamer to the side of the heat so that water is bubbling only on one side of the pan, and place the custard on the side away from the heat.

Cup Custard or Custard Sauce

Use a double saucepan, or a thick saucepan over very gentle heat, and stir all the time. Test the consistency over the back of the spoon, and as soon as the custard thickens, remove from the heat and pour into a jug or dish—do not leave it in the pan, or it may curdle.

Proportions for Custards

For Baked Custards:
1 egg to ½ pint milk.

For Steamed Custards:
1 egg to ¼ pint milk.

For Cup Custard and Custard Sauce:
Thin: 2 yolks (or 1 whole egg) to ½ pint milk.
Thick: 3–4 yolks (or 1½–2 whole eggs) to ½ pint milk.

BAKED CUSTARD (BASIC RECIPE)

1 pint milk	1 oz. sugar
2 eggs	Nutmeg

Heat the milk, but do not boil it. Beat the eggs and the sugar, then add the hot milk, stirring. Strain into a greased pie dish and grate a little nutmeg on the top. Bake in a slow oven (325° F., mark 2) for about 40 minutes, until the custard is set. On no account allow the mixture to boil, or the eggs will curdle.

STEAMED CUSTARD

2 eggs	½ pint milk
½ oz. sugar	Flavouring, e.g., vanilla

Beat the eggs and sugar. Heat the milk and pour it on the beaten eggs. Add flavouring, strain into a buttered mould and cover with buttered paper. Steam very gently for ½ hour, or until firm. On no account allow the water in the steamer to boil vigorously, or the custard will curdle. Turn out, and serve hot or cold.

CARAMEL CUSTARD

4 oz. sugar	4 eggs
¼ pint water	½ oz. sugar
1 pint milk	

Put the 4 oz. sugar and water into a small pan, dissolve, then heat without stirring until a rich brown colour. Do not make the caramel too dark, or it will taste bitter. Pour quickly into a clean hot soufflé tin, and holding the tin with a cloth, coat the inside well all over. Leave to set. Heat the milk. Beat the eggs and ½ oz. sugar, and pour on the hot milk. Strain into the tin, and cover with greased paper. Steam very gently until set—about 1–1¼ hours. Turn out carefully into a warm dish. Serve hot or cold.

If preferred, the custard may be baked instead of steamed. Prepare as above and cook in a slow oven (325° F., mark 2) until set—about 40 minutes. Turn out, and serve hot or cold.

CUP CUSTARD

2 egg yolks (or 1 whole egg)	½ pint milk
	Vanilla essence
½ oz. sugar	Ratafia biscuits

Beat the egg yolks and the sugar together. Heat the milk, and when hot, but not boiling, pour on to the eggs, stirring. Strain into a saucepan, and stir with a wooden spoon over gentle heat, until the custard thickens and coats the back of the spoon. Stir all the time, and do not allow the custard to boil, or it will curdle. Add the vanilla essence and pour the custard into a jug. Stir occasionally while cooling, and when cold pour into individual custard cups.

Decorate each cup with a ratafia biscuit, if available.

Whole eggs may be used for Cup Custard, but yolks only are preferable, since they make a custard of a decidedly smoother and more velvety texture.

BREAD AND BUTTER PUDDING

2–3 slices thin bread and butter	½ oz. sugar
	½ pint milk
1–2 oz. currants or sultanas	1 egg
	Nutmeg

Cut the bread and butter into neat strips, and lay in a buttered pie dish, buttered side up, sprinkling each layer with fruit and sugar (but omitting fruit in the top layer). Heat the milk and pour on to the beaten egg. Strain into the pie dish, grate nutmeg on top and let stand for ½ hour, to let the bread swell. Bake in a moderate oven (350° F., mark 3) for about ½ hour, until set and lightly browned.

NEWMARKET PUDDING

Follow the recipe for making Bread and Butter Pudding, but flavour the milk with cinnamon and bay leaf. To do this, add 1 inch of stick cinnamon and 1 bay leaf to the milk; infuse for 10 minutes, strain and use.

OSBORNE PUDDING

1 egg
1 oz. sugar
½ pint milk
A pinch of salt
4 thin slices brown bread and butter
Marmalade

Beat the egg and sugar, beat in the milk, add the salt. Spread the bread and butter with marmalade and lay in a buttered pie dish. Strain the egg and milk over. Bake in a moderate oven (350° F., mark 4) for about 1 hour, or until the custard is set.

LOGANBERRY MERINGUE

1 tin loganberries, or 1 lb. stewed loganberries
Sponge cake
2 eggs
4 oz. caster sugar
½ pint milk (short measure)

Drain the loganberries, reserving the juice, and place in the bottom of a fireproof dish. Cover with thin slices of sponge cake. Beat up the egg yolks with 1 oz. sugar. Heat the milk slightly, pour over the beaten yolks, then return to the saucepan and cook, stirring, over gentle heat until the custard thickens, taking care not to let the mixture boil, or it will curdle. Pour over the sponge cake. Beat up the egg whites stiffly, then fold in the remaining sugar, and pile over the pudding. Place in a slow oven (325° F., mark 2) for 30–40 minutes, until meringue is crisp and very lightly coloured. Boil the fruit syrup until reduced by half, and serve with pudding.

PINEAPPLE AND BANANA MERINGUE

6 bananas
1 small tin pineapple
2 eggs
4 oz. sugar
½ pint milk

Slice the bananas and place in a shallow fireproof dish. Arrange the sliced pineapple on top. Make a custard by beating the egg yolks and 2 oz. of sugar together and pouring the heated milk over, beating while doing so. Strain back into a pan and cook until thick. Pour over the bananas and pineapple in the dish. Make the meringue by beating the egg whites stiffly and folding in the remaining 2 oz. of sugar. Pile on top of the custard. Put into a moderate oven (350° F., mark 3) for about ½ hour, to set the meringue. Decorate with banana and pineapple.

CABINET PUDDING (PLAIN)

2 oz. stoned raisins
4 oz. bread
2 eggs
½ pint milk
1 oz. sugar
Vanilla essence

Grease a basin and decorate it with some of the raisins. Cut the bread into ½-inch dice. Beat the eggs, add the milk, sugar and vanilla essence and the rest of the raisins. Pour over the bread and soak for ½ hour. Pour into the prepared basin, cover with greased paper and steam gently for about 1 hour, until set. Turn out, and serve with jam sauce.

CABINET PUDDING (RICH)

Glacé cherries
3 eggs
1½ oz. caster sugar
¾ pint milk
Vanilla essence
4 small sponge cakes

Grease a plain tin mould and line the bottom with a round of greased paper. Decorate with halved cherries. Beat the eggs and sugar, add the milk and vanilla essence and beat well. Cut the sponge cakes into small dice and put them in the tin, strain the eggs and milk over and soak for 20 minutes. Cover with greased paper and steam gently for about 1 hour, until set. Turn out, and serve with Sabayon sauce.

VIENNOISE PUDDING

½ oz. loaf sugar
¼ pint milk
2½ oz. sponge cake or bread
1½ oz. sultanas
½ oz. candied peel, chopped
1 tsp. grated lemon rind
1 oz. glacé cherries, chopped
1½ oz. caster sugar
1 egg
2 tbsps. sherry

Put the loaf sugar into a pan and heat very slowly until it is light brown in colour, shaking the pan frequently—do not stir. Draw the pan to one side and add the hot milk carefully, then dissolve the caramel over gentle heat. Cut the sponge cake or bread into dice, add the sultanas, peel, lemon rind, chopped cherries and sugar. Beat the egg and pour on the caramelled milk and sherry. Strain over the other ingredients and soak for ½ hour. Pour into a greased basin, cover with greased paper, and steam gently for about 1 hour, until set. Turn out, and serve with Sabayon sauce.

ZABAGLIONE

4 egg yolks
2 oz. caster sugar
¼ pint sherry or Marsala

Beat the egg yolks and sugar together until the mixture is light and almost white. Add the wine and blend well. Cook over boiling water, beating constantly and taking care not to allow the mixture to curdle. As soon as it begins to rise, pour it into glasses and serve hot.

BATTERS AND WAFFLES

Batters, which are a mixture of milk, eggs and flour, are very easy to make. The baked batter puddings (including Yorkshire Pudding) and pancakes are all made from a simple basic mixture, while only slight modification of this recipe is required to make a coating for fruit fritters and such-like dishes. Waffle batters are similar, but include a raising agent.

It is a custom to make batters at least an hour before they are to be cooked. Recent experiments, however, show that equally light dishes result when the batter does not stand before cooking. The mixture, therefore, may be made whenever most convenient and either used at once or allowed to stand in a cool place. Waffle batters should not be allowed to stand.

BASIC RECIPE FOR BATTER

(For Pancakes, Baked and Steamed Batters)

4 oz. flour
A pinch of salt
1 egg
About $\frac{1}{2}$ pint milk (or milk and water)

Sieve the flour and salt into a bowl. Make a well in the centre. Drop in the egg, add half the liquid by degrees, and mix to a smooth batter, using a wooden spoon and gradually drawing in the flour from the sides. Now beat the batter until thoroughly aerated, for 5–10 minutes. This is best done with the back of the spoon, the spoon being held like a pencil and the movement being made with the wrist. When it is thoroughly beaten (i.e., when the surface of the batter is covered with bubbles), stir in the remainder of the liquid to give the consistency of thin cream.

PLAIN COATING (OR FRITTER) BATTER

4 oz. flour
A pinch of salt
1 egg
About $\frac{1}{4}$ pint milk (or milk and water)

Sieve the flour and salt into a basin. Make a well in the centre, drop in the egg and gradually add the liquid, drawing in the flour from the sides, mixing and beating thoroughly; add sufficient liquid to bring to a coating consistency Beat well and use as required.

RICH COATING (OR FRITTER) BATTER

4 oz. flour
A pinch of salt
1 tbsp. olive oil
About $\frac{1}{4}$ pint tepid water
2 egg whites

Sieve the flour and salt into a basin. Make a well in the centre, add the oil and half the water. Draw in the flour from the sides, mix and beat well. Add sufficient water to bring to a coating consistency. Just before using, fold in the stiffly beaten egg whites.

BATTER CASES

These are made by means of a special basket-shaped iron, which is heated by dipping into hot fat; it is then dipped into pancake batter, plunged into hot deep fat and left for a few minutes, until the batter is golden-brown. The batter case is then slipped off the iron and returned to the fat to finish cooking inside. The cases are filled with a savoury mixture, and served as an entrée or as a hot smörgasbörd dish.

BAKED BATTER PUDDING

Prepare the batter as in the basic recipe. Heat about $\frac{1}{2}$ oz. butter in a baking tin or shallow fireproof dish. When smoking hot, pour in the batter and bake in a hot oven (450° F., mark 8) for about 40 minutes, until well risen, crisp and brown. Serve at once with butter and syrup or jam.

LITTLE BATTER PUDDINGS

The batter mixture may be cooked in individual ramekin cases, instead of in a large dish; proceed as above, but cook for only about 20 minutes. 88

YORKSHIRE PUDDING

Prepare the batter as in the basic recipe. Put 1 tbsp. dripping from the roast meat into a Yorkshire Pudding tin or shallow fireproof dish. When smoking hot, pour in the batter and bake in a hot oven (450° F., mark 8) for about 40 minutes. Serve cut in squares, as an accompaniment to roast beef, etc.

If desired, the roast meat may be placed on a trivet directly over the Yorkshire Pudding : the juices of the meat will drip down on to the pudding and give it a delicious flavour.

TOAD-IN-THE-HOLE

The method of making is exactly the same as for Yorkshire Pudding, except that ½ lb. of
89 sausages, or some small squares of meat, are placed in the tin or dish with the fat and heated through before the batter is poured on.

RAISIN BATTER

Make as for Baked Batter Pudding, adding 2 oz. of cleaned and stoned raisins to the batter. Dredge with caster sugar before serving.

BAKED APPLE BATTER

4 oz. flour	1 lb. apples
½ pint milk	1 oz. butter
1 egg	½ tsp. grated lemon rind
A pinch of salt	4 oz. sugar

Prepare the batter as in the basic recipe. Peel and core the apples and cut into slices. Heat the butter in a pie dish, add the apples, sprinkle the lemon rind and sugar over and pour on the batter. Bake in a moderately hot oven (400° F., mark 6) for about ¾–1 hour.

LARGE OVEN PANCAKE

1½ oz. butter	A pinch of salt
1½ oz. caster sugar	Grated rind of ½ lemon
2 eggs	¾ pint milk
2 oz. flour	Butter for frying

Cream the butter and sugar, add 1 egg and half the flour and salt. Beat well, add the second egg and the remaining flour and lemon rind, then stir in the milk and leave 1 hour. (A curdled appearance at this stage makes no difference to the finished dish.) Melt a little butter in a flat fireproof dish and heat until smoking hot. Pour in the batter and bake in a moderately hot oven (400° F., mark 6) for 30–40 minutes, or until set. Serve with stewed fruit or jam.

SAUCER PANCAKES

Make the mixture as above, but put into six buttered saucers and bake in a hot oven (450° F., mark 8) for about 15 minutes. Put a spoonful of hot jam in the centre of each, fold in half and dredge with caster sugar. Serve at once.

STEAMED BATTER

Make the batter according to the basic recipe. Pour into a greased basin and steam for 1 hour. If liked, a few currants may be sprinkled at the bottom of the basin before putting in the batter.

PANCAKES

Make the batter as described in the basic recipe. Heat a little lard in a frying pan until it is smoking hot, run it around the sides of the pan, and pour off any surplus. Pour in sufficient batter to cover the pan thinly (a jug will be
found best for the purpose), and cook quickly 90
until the pancake is golden-brown underneath, then turn or toss and cook the second side. Turn out on to sugared paper, sprinkle with sugar, and squeeze lemon juice over. Roll up, and serve at once.

CRÊPES SUZETTE

4 oz. flour	4 tbsps. sugar
A pinch of salt	2 oz. butter
1 egg	Juice of 2 oranges
3 egg yolks	1 tbsp. Curaçao, Grand Marnier or other liqueur
½ pint milk	
1½ oz. melted butter	3 tbsps. brandy

Sieve the flour and salt; beat the egg and egg yolks with a little of the milk and mix them into the dry ingredients, with the 1½ oz. melted butter and the rest of the milk. Beat the mixture
until smooth, then use it to make some small 9
pancakes, which should be kept flat and hot. Put the sugar into a clean frying pan and heat it gently, shaking the pan occasionally, until it is golden-brown. Remove the pan from the heat, add the 2 oz. butter and the orange juice and heat gently, taking care that the caramel does not turn to toffee. Put one pancake into the pan, heat it gently in the sauce, fold into four, remove and keep hot. Continue until all the crêpes have been treated in the same way. Add the liqueur and brandy to the sauce, and replace the folded crêpes in the pan. Reheat, set light to the sauce, and serve immediately. If necessary, light some additional warmed brandy and pour it over the crêpes.

FRUIT FRITTERS

Prepare the fruit as required. Peel apples and cut into slices ¼ inch thick, then fold these in a clean cloth until required, to prevent discoloration. Peel bananas, cut in half lengthwise and cut
each piece in half. Peel oranges and tangerines, 9
remove pith and divide into sections.

Prepare a fritter batter and have ready a deep pan of clean fat, heated until a faint smoke appears on the surface. Lift the fruit with a skewer, dip it into the batter, drain well and lower carefully into the fat, removing the skewer by twisting it. Turn the fritters, and when both sides are golden-brown, lift out, drain well, and put on crumpled kitchen paper to drain well. Sprinkle with caster sugar and serve at once.

SPICED APPLE FRITTERS

4 oz. flour	4 oz. chopped apple (1 good-sized apple)
1 tsp. baking powder	1 oz. sugar
A good pinch of mixed spice	1 egg
A good pinch of ground cinnamon	About 4 tbsps. milk
A good pinch of ground cloves	Lard for frying
	Caster sugar

Mix together the flour, baking powder and spices. Add the finely chopped apple and the sugar. Make a well in the centre and stir in the beaten egg and enough milk to make a batter of a thick creamy consistency. Do not let this batter stand, but place spoonfuls at once into a frying pan containing a little hot lard, and fry till golden-brown on both sides. Serve at once with syrup or a sweet sauce, or dredged with caster sugar.

FIVE-MINUTE FRITTERS

4 oz. flour	1 dessertsp. olive oil
1 tsp. baking powder	About 4 tbsps. milk
1–2 oz. currants	Lard for frying

Mix together the flour, baking powder and cleaned currants. Stir in the oil and enough milk to make a batter the consistency of thick cream. Place the batter in tablespoonfuls in the hot fat and fry quickly until golden-brown on both sides. Serve at once with jam or sugar.

Note : This batter should be fried as soon as it is mixed.

WAFFLES

Waffles are crisp, light wafers made from a batter and cooked in a special waffle iron. There are two types—those made for use over a coal fire or gas ring and those which are electrically heated. The electrically heated iron, though rather more expensive, is more convenient to use ; both grids are heated by the electric current so that the waffle is cooked on both sides at the same time, and no turning is required. Waffle irons, like omelette pans, should never be washed, otherwise the batter is liable to stick. The directions supplied with some irons also state that greasing is not necessary, but if any trouble is experienced with the batter sticking, the iron may be brushed over with a little lard or clarified butter. A steel-bristled brush is excellent for removing crumbs in the crevices, and the iron should always be cleaned in this way.

Unless the manufacturer advises to the contrary, it is always wise to season the grid of a new waffle iron before you use it, as this helps to prevent the waffle sticking. To season, brush the grids of the cold waffle iron thoroughly with an unsalted melted fat, such as cooking fat or salad oil. Heat to baking temperature, and allow to cool.

The cooking time for waffles varies with different irons, but as a rule, 2–3 minutes is sufficient, and second waffle may be made as soon as the first one is cooked. Waffles are always better when served immediately, but if they must be kept for a few minutes, place them on a wire rack or grid in the oven or under a slow grill. If they are piled on a plate and allowed to stand, the steam will soften them and make them sodden.

Maple syrup is the correct accompaniment for waffles, and this should be served cold. Fruit syrups or golden syrup are good substitutes, or waffles may be served with melted butter. Waffles sandwiched with layers of red-currant jelly or with jam look very attractive and are delicious as an alternative to cake for tea. The top may be sprinkled with icing sugar. Another filling is whipped cream, sweetened and flavoured with vanilla.

Savoury waffles (unsweetened and salted) are becoming increasingly popular. Creamed chicken or creamed veal make good fillings, or the waffles may be used as an accompaniment to dishes such as fried chicken or grilled sausages. Savouries such as mushrooms or kidneys and other small delicacies used for snacks, can be pleasantly varied by being served on waffles.

There are many recipes for waffle mixtures, some of which are given here. A standard recipe may be varied by using a different kind of flour or any of the commercial pancake flours, and by adding a flavouring ingredient, and also by serving with different syrups. Either sweet or sour milk may be used.

To Make Waffles

See that the waffle iron is clean, then heat it through evenly. Prepare the batter just before 93
it is required for cooking, following the particular recipe : it should be of the consistency of thick

cream. Pour enough batter into the iron just to run over the surface (a measure is usually supplied with electric waffle irons). Do not over-fill, or the mixture will not be able to rise properly and will ooze out of the iron. Close the iron over the mixture and leave 2–3 minutes to cook, turning the iron, if using one of the non-electric type. When cooked, the waffle should be golden-brown and crisp and easily removed from the iron. If it sticks, cook for a minute longer.

PLAIN WAFFLES

4 oz. flour	1 egg
2 tsps. baking powder	2 tbsps. melted butter
A pinch of salt	About ¼ pint milk
1 oz. sugar	½ tsp. vanilla essence

Sieve the dry ingredients into a basin and make a well in the centre. Drop in the egg yolk and melted butter, and then add the milk gradually. Beat well, add the vanilla essence, and lastly, fold in the stiffly beaten egg white. Cook as above, and serve immediately.

AMERICAN WAFFLES

6 oz. flour	½ pint milk
A pinch of salt	2 oz. melted butter or margarine
3 tsps. baking powder	Vanilla essence
1 oz. caster sugar	
2 eggs	

Sieve the flour, salt and baking powder into a basin, and stir in the sugar. Make a well in the centre of the dry ingredients and add the egg yolks. Mix these in, adding the milk and melted butter alternately. Lastly, stir in the vanilla essence. Whip up the egg whites very stiffly and fold in lightly. Pour the batter into the heated waffle iron and cook according to the directions given above. Serve immediately with butter and golden or maple syrup.

CHEESE WAFFLES

Make the batter as for Plain Waffles, omitting the sugar and vanilla, and adding 2 oz. finely grated cheese just before folding in the egg white. Serve with creamed ham or any creamed vegetable.

PINEAPPLE WAFFLES

Add 4 oz. drained, crushed pineapple to the mixture for Plain Waffles. Serve with pineapple sauce made by boiling ¼ pint of the syrup from the pineapple with 2 oz. sugar.

SAVOURY SANDWICH WAFFLES

½ lb. flour	2 eggs
½ tsp. salt	2 oz. melted butter
1 tsp. bicarbonate of soda	About ¾ pint milk
2 tsps. cream of tartar	Tomato and watercress to garnish

For the Filling

½ oz. butter	¼ lb. minced ham
½ oz. flour	A pinch of cayenne pepper
¼ pint stock	1 tbsp. chutney

Sieve the flour, salt and raising agents together. Add the egg yolks and melted butter, together with sufficient milk to mix to a fairly thin batter. Lastly, fold in the stiffly beaten egg whites. Heat the waffle iron. Cook as usual. While the waffles are cooking, prepare the hot filling as follows: melt the butter and add the flour, then stir in the stock by degrees and boil for a few minutes, stirring. Add the minced ham, pepper and chutney. Spread the filling thinly on a waffle and put another waffle on the top. Garnish with sliced tomato and a sprig of watercress.

SOUR MILK WAFFLES

4 oz. flour	1 egg
1 tsp. bicarbonate of soda	1 tbsp. melted butter
2 tsps. baking powder	1 breakfastcupful sour milk or buttermilk
Salt	

Proceed as for Plain Waffles, but do not separate the yolk from the white of the egg. These waffles are very good served with butter instead of syrup.

SPICED WAFFLES

½ lb. flour	2 eggs
½ tsp. salt	3 oz. butter
1 tbsp. baking powder	About ¾ pint milk
½ tsp. mixed spice	

Sieve together the flour, salt, baking powder and mixed spice. Stir in the egg yolks and melted butter, together with sufficient milk to mix to a fairly thin batter. Lastly, fold in the beaten egg whites. Cook as usual, serve with maple syrup.

SOUFFLÉS—HOT AND COLD

HOT SOUFFLÉS

These are made from a panada mixture which is lightened by the addition of stiffly beaten egg whites. Its success depends largely on the adequate whisking of the egg whites, their very light but thorough incorporation into the mixture, and careful cooking.

Hot soufflés can be either steamed or baked. These soufflés, consisting as they do very largely of tiny air bubbles, sink rapidly when removed from the oven or steamer, so they should be served only on occasions when they can be eaten immediately they are cooked. In the case of a steamed soufflé, have the sauce made in readiness before the soufflé is quite cooked.

Whether baking or steaming, cook the soufflé immediately the mixture has been prepared, in moderate and steady heat. If too fierce heat is used, the mixture is liable to rise too rapidly and will sink later.

To Prepare a Tin for a Steamed Soufflé

For steaming, a round or oval soufflé tin, with smooth, slightly sloping sides, is required. The soufflé is turned out before being served.

To prepare the tin, well grease it with clarified butter, melted lard, or olive oil. Cut a round of greaseproof paper to fit the bottom of the tin exactly, place in position, and grease it well. Take a band of strong greased paper consisting of three thicknesses, long enough to reach round the tin and wide enough to extend from the middle to 3 inches above the top. Place this tightly round the outside of the tin and tie it firmly in position. The object of the paper is to support the sides of the soufflé as it rises, so it must be sufficiently firm to withstand steam, and for this reason it must be well greased. Finally, cut a round of paper large enough to fit on top of the paper band and well grease it. This is to cover the soufflé and prevent condensed steam from coming into contact with the mixture.

Soufflé Tin

To Prepare a Case for a Baked Soufflé

For baking, a special china soufflé dish, fairly shallow in depth, smooth inside and fluted outside, is used. These are usually of plain white china, but they are also obtainable in fireproof glass and in coloured chinaware. To prepare the dish, tie a paper band, 3 inches taller than the dish, around the outside, then grease dish and inside of band thoroughly.

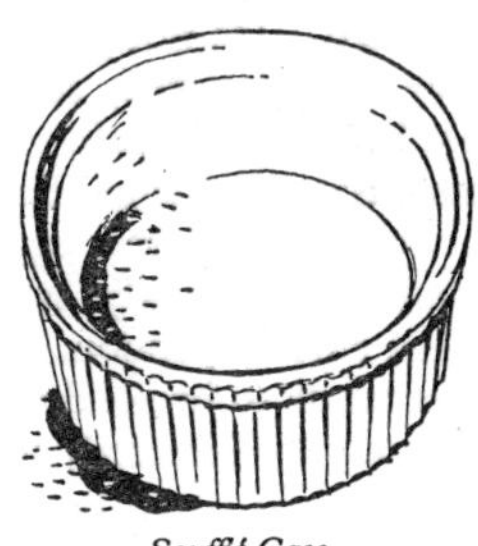

Soufflé Case

To Prepare the Soufflé Mixture

The preparation of the basic mixture is the same whether the soufflé is steamed or baked. It can, of course, be varied by the introduction of additional ingredients and flavourings.

The foundation, or panada, consists of flour, butter, and milk, in the proportions of 1 oz. flour and 1 oz. butter to ¼ pint milk. The egg yolks are always separated from the whites and are beaten into the panada. The stiffly beaten whites are folded in as the last step. The preparation of the panada is important, for unless it is smoothly blended and thoroughly amalgamated with the egg yolks, the texture of the soufflé is likely to be leathery.

When making the panada, choose a rather large saucepan—large enough not only to beat the egg yolks in, but also to fold in the whites.

VANILLA SOUFFLÉ (STANDARD RECIPE)

(For Soufflé Case approx. 6 inches by 2¼ inches)

1 oz. butter	1 tbsp. caster sugar
1 oz. flour	Vanilla essence
¼ pint milk	4 egg whites
3 egg yolks	

Put on the steamer or heat the oven. Prepare the soufflé tin or case as described. Weigh out all ingredients carefully. Melt the butter in a fairly large pan over a low heat, and stir in the flour with a wooden spoon. Add the hot milk gradually and stir over the heat until the mixture thickens, then beat hard until it leaves the sides of the pan. Be sure it is quite smooth.

Remove from the heat and add the egg yolks, one at a time. Beat in each yolk thoroughly, and blend all the ingredients so that no unmixed panada remains around the sides of the pan. Add the sugar and vanilla essence (or other flavouring when used) and leave aside while preparing the egg whites.

Beat the egg whites to a stiff froth—it is essential that they should be very thoroughly whisked. Do not prepare them until just before they are required, so that the air bubbles will not break down before the eggs are incorporated with the other ingredients.

Fold the beaten egg whites into the panada mixture as lightly as possible, using a metal, not a wooden, spoon. Do not stir the mixture, as this tends to break down the air bubbles. When thoroughly blended, steam or bake as described below.

To Steam the Soufflé

Pour the mixture into the prepared tin, half-filling it, to allow for rising. Place the round of greased paper on the top of the paper band and put into the steamer. (If a steamer is not available, place in a deep saucepan containing about 2 inches of boiling water, slipping a pastry cutter under the soufflé case to raise it slightly.) Allow the water in the steamer, or saucepan, to boil only gently; avoid moving it about while the cooking is in progress. Continue to steam for 40 minutes, or until it feels firm when lightly pressed in the centre. Have ready custard, jam, or sweet white sauce.

To dish the soufflé, remove the paper band and gently reverse the tin on to a hot dish, then remove the tin and the round of paper from the bottom. Coat with the sauce, and serve immediately.

To Bake the Soufflé

Put the mixture into the prepared soufflé case, half-filling it, place a round of greased paper on top of the paper band, and bake in a moderately hot oven (400° F., mark 6) for about 30 minutes, or until well risen, golden-brown, and firm in centre. Remove paper, and serve at once.

CHOCOLATE SOUFFLÉ

Use the same recipe and method as for Vanilla Soufflé, but dissolve 1½ oz. chocolate in the milk before using it for making the panada. Serve with chocolate sauce.

CHERRY SOUFFLÉ

Follow the recipe for Vanilla Soufflé, adding 2 oz. glacé cherries, each cut in four. Bake or steam. If steamed, serve with a sweet white sauce flavoured with vanilla or sherry.

COFFEE SOUFFLÉ

Follow the recipe for Vanilla Soufflé, but in place of ¼ pint milk, use half milk and half coffee for making the panada. Bake or steam. If steamed, serve with coffee sauce.

PINEAPPLE SOUFFLÉ

Cut out a few pieces of angelica to form diamond-shaped leaves. Decorate the bottom of the buttered soufflé tin with these. Well drain 2 oz. chopped pineapple and fold it into the mixture after the yolks of egg have been added. Steam as for Vanilla Soufflé. Serve with a sauce made from the pineapple juice. (This mixture may also be baked.)

ORANGE SOUFFLE

A little butter and caster sugar to prepare the soufflé case	1½ oz. butter
2 oranges	2 oz. flour
½ pint milk	3 egg yolks
½ oz. caster sugar	4 egg whites
	Icing sugar

Butter and dredge with caster sugar a china soufflé case, measuring approximately 6 inches by 2¼ inches. Grate the orange rind and boil up in the milk with the sugar; strain and reboil the milk. Melt the butter in a fairly large saucepan, stir in the flour, mix well, add the boiling milk, and whisk until smooth. Beat in the 2 egg yolks separately and allow the mixture to cool. Meanwhile, whisk up the 3 egg whites stiffly and fold them lightly into the mixture. Half-fill a prepared soufflé case with the mixture. Bake in a moderately hot oven (400° F., mark 6) for 35–40 minutes, till risen well above the case. Remove from the oven, sprinkle with icing sugar and serve immediately with or without a sauce. A simple orange sauce is made by boiling ¼ pint of orange juice with loaf sugar to form a syrup, adding 1 or 2 small pieces of orange rind before serving.

COLD SOUFFLÉS OR MOUSSES

Cold soufflés also contain beaten egg whites, and they are set with gelatine. The usual method is to whisk together the egg yolks, sugar, and flavouring (fruit juice, coffee, chocolate, etc.) over hot water until thick and creamy. The dissolved gelatine is then added and the mixture allowed to cool somewhat. The whipped cream, if used, is then folded in, and lastly, the stiffly beaten egg whites. This produces a very light and fluffy mixture, attractive in appearance and very delicious to taste. Savoury cold soufflés may also be made.

To Prepare and Fill a Dish for a Cold Soufflé

Cold soufflés should be prepared so that they appear to have risen like a hot soufflé. A china or glass soufflé case is used, similar to those in which soufflés are baked. It is prepared as follows :—

Cut a strip of firm paper long enough to go round the case, overlapping slightly, and deep enough to reach from the bottom of the dish to about 2 inches above the top. Place it round the outside of the dish so that it fits exactly and pin it firmly in position or tie it with string. Take care to see that the paper forms a true circle, not an oval, otherwise the soufflé will not have a smart appearance when finished.

Prepare the mixture according to the recipe and pour it at once into the soufflé case, filling it 1–2 inches above the rim. Put in a refrigerator or cold larder to set.

The quantities given below are suitable for a soufflé dish measuring 2–3 inches deep and 6 inches across.

Dishing the Soufflé

When quite firm, remove the string or the pins very carefully and take off the paper. To do this, hold a knife which has been dipped in boiling water against the paper. This will melt the mixture slightly and enable the paper to be removed easily, leaving a smooth and not jagged edge. Decorate the top with some suitable decoration, such as piped cream, cherries, angelica, almonds, pistachios, etc.

The side of the soufflé mixture which stands above the dish may be decorated with chopped pistachio nuts, ratafia crumbs, and so on. Press the finely chopped nuts or crumbs on to the mixture with a broad-bladed knife, letting any loose crumbs fall away. Repeat the process until the side is covered evenly all over.

CARAMEL SOUFFLÉ

1½ oz. loaf sugar	4 tbsps. water
1 tbsp. water	1½ oz. crushed almond rock or ratafia biscuits
¼ pint milk	½ pint cream or evaporated milk
6 egg yolks	4 egg whites
2 oz. caster sugar	Whipped cream
¼–½ oz. gelatine (short weight)	

Prepare a soufflé case. Put the loaf sugar and water into a saucepan and cook to caramel colour. Add the hot milk to the caramel, re-dissolve, and pour on to the beaten yolks and caster sugar. Cook gently until thick. Dissolve the gelatine in the water over gentle heat, add it to the custard, and cool. Stir in the almond rock or ratafias and the half-whipped cream or milk. Whip the egg whites very stiffly and fold into the mixture. Put into the prepared case and allow to set. Before serving, decorate with cream, sweetened and flavoured to taste.

This mixture may also be set in a deep glass bowl—see colour picture facing page 321.

CHOCOLATE SOUFFLÉ

1 oz. almonds	Vanilla essence
3 eggs	⅓ pint cream or evaporated milk
2 oz. caster sugar	Pistachio nuts
2 oz. chocolate	Whipped cream
2 tbsps. water	
¼–½ oz. gelatine	

Prepare a soufflé case. Blanch the almonds, shred them, and brown lightly in the oven. Whisk the egg yolks and sugar over a pan of very hot water until thick and creamy, then remove from the heat. Melt the chocolate in the water over a gentle heat, add the gelatine, and continue heating until dissolved, then stir into the whisked mixture, together with the chopped almonds and vanilla essence. Fold in the whipped cream lightly. Whip up the egg whites very stiffly and fold them into the mixture. Pour into the prepared soufflé case and leave to set. Before serving, decorate with pistachio nuts and sweetened and flavoured cream.

MILANESE SOUFFLÉ

3 lemons	2 tbsps. water
4 eggs	¼ pint cream
4–6 oz. caster sugar	Crystallised violets and angelica
¼–½ oz. gelatine	

Prepare a soufflé case as directed. Wipe the
lemons and grate their rind lightly. Add the 95
egg yolks, sugar, and lemon juice to the grated rind, and whisk over a pan of hot water until thick and creamy. Add the gelatine, dissolved over gentle heat in the water, and allow to become

cool but not set. Stir in the cream lightly, and lastly, fold in the stiffly beaten egg whites. Pour the mixture into the prepared case and allow to set. Remove the paper, and decorate with crystallised violets and angelica.

ORANGE SOUFFLÉ

2 large oranges	2 tbsps. water
$\frac{1}{2}$ lemon	$\frac{1}{4}$ pint evaporated milk or cream
3 eggs	
2–3 oz. caster sugar	Crystallised orange and angelica
$\frac{1}{4}$–$\frac{1}{2}$ oz. gelatine	

Prepare a soufflé case. Wipe the oranges and grate the rind into a basin. Strain the orange and the lemon juice. Add the egg yolks, sugar, orange and lemon juice, and whisk over a pan of hot water until the mixture is thick and creamy. Dissolve the gelatine in the water over gentle heat, add to the orange mixture, and cool. Whip the evaporated milk or cream and stir it lightly into the mixture. Lastly, fold in the stiffly beaten egg whites. Pour into the prepared case and leave to set. Decorate with slices of crystallised orange and angelica.

Note: A Cheese Soufflé recipe is given in the Cheese chapter; other savoury soufflés can be made in a similar way.

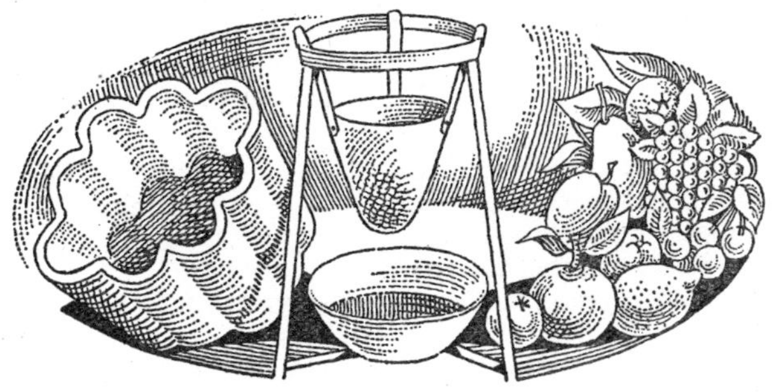

JELLIES AND CREAMS

Any number of pleasing and attractive cold sweets may be made by using gelatine for setting. Here are given proportions and general rules for making jellies and creams, and many suggestions for jellied sweets.

JELLIES

With most powdered gelatine ½–¾ oz. is usually needed to set 1 pint liquid into a jelly that will mould but not be too stiff. (The larger quantity of gelatine may be used in warm weather.) It has been found that most cold sweets set more firmly in a refrigerator than when merely left in a cool place; therefore use the minimum quantity of gelatine, if the sweet is to be set in the refrigerator. Whatever brand is used, the manufacturer's instructions should be carefully followed.

Packet jellies, which are already flavoured and sweetened, may be used for many cold sweets, though powdered gelatine, if correctly used, is probably more economical.

To Make a Jelly

1. Measure the gelatine very accurately. Some brands of gelatine are sold with a special measuring cup holding, say, ½ oz. If your kitchen scales will not weigh quantities less than 1 oz. and you have no special gelatine measure, use a tablespoon—1 small rounded tbsp. powdered gelatine is approximately ¾ oz. If you use sheet gelatine and want to estimate how much to use, count the number of sheets in the packet as it comes from the grocer and calculate how many sheets to the oz. (usually 5 sheets per ½ oz.).
2. Have the necessary amount of liquid (fruit juice, milk, wine, etc.) ready warmed, and see that it has a good flavour, appropriate colour and is sufficiently sweet.
3. Put the gelatine in a small basin and add a little cold fruit juice or water (not milk)—1 oz. gelatine requires ¼ pint liquid to dissolve it—and heat over a pan of hot water until dissolved.
4. When thoroughly dissolved, combine with the measured liquid and pour into a wetted mould.

When using packet jellies, follow the manufacturer's directions.

Points about Making Jellies

1. Sheet gelatine dissolves more easily if it is first soaked for a short while in a little cold water before being heated. Flake or strip gelatine should also be soaked for 2–3 hours. It is not necessary to soak powdered gelatine.
2. If a jelly is wanted quickly, heat only a small amount of the measured liquid to dissolve the gelatine and add the remainder of the liquid cold.
3. Use small individual moulds if you want jellies in a hurry. If ice is available, stand the moulds in a dish and surround with chopped ice.
4. For milk jellies, the milk should be absolutely fresh, and must be only lukewarm when added to the jelly, otherwise it is likely to curdle.
5. When solid ingredients (such as fruit and nuts) are included, they should be stirred in

when the jelly is just beginning to set. In this way, they can be distributed evenly throughout.

6. When making a jelly from fresh pineapple juice, boil the juice for 2–3 minutes first; this is to kill an enzyme contained in the juice which breaks down gelatine, destroying its setting properties.

To Unmould a Jelly

Prepare a bowl of water just hot enough to "sting" the hand slightly. If a metal mould is used, pass the mould quickly right through the water, wipe with a clean cloth, dabbing the top of the jelly to dry it, then invert on to the hand and give a good shake. As the jelly loosens, place it over the dish, slip the hand away, then lift off the mould.

If a china mould is used, stand or hold the mould in the hot water (the water should come just to the top of the mould) for a minute or two, according to the thickness of the mould. Then loosen round the edge with the fingers and turn out as above.

Decorate with chopped jelly, whipped cream or fruit, etc.

To Mask or Line a Mould

Added interest is given to jellies or creams if the mould is masked and decorated—i.e. lined with a coating of jelly and decorated with fruit or nuts, etc.

These directions should be followed when masking a mould:

Fill a large basin with small pieces of ice and nest the mould in it. Pour about 2–3 tbsps. cold but liquid jelly into the wetted mould, and rotate it slowly until the inside is evenly coated. Continue pouring in and setting cold liquid jelly until the whole surface is lined with about ⅛ inch of the jelly. Dip the decoration (slices of pistachio nuts, cherries, angelica, etc.) in liquid jelly and, by means of 2 skewers (or hatpins), place in position in the mould, allowing each piece to set firmly. Finally, pour a thin coating of jelly over. Allow to set.

ORANGE JELLY

3 oz. loaf sugar
3 oranges
1 lemon
½ oz. gelatine
½ pint cold water

Rub the loaf sugar on the rind of 1 orange and the lemon. Soak the gelatine in the water, add the sugar, and dissolve over moderate heat. Add the strained orange and lemon juice and bring just to the boil. Strain through a piece of muslin into a wetted mould.

Note: There should be ¼ pint of fruit juice; if not, make up with water.

MILK JELLY

2 oz. caster sugar
3 thin strips of lemon rind
1 pint milk
½–¾ oz. gelatine
3 tbsps. water

Add the sugar and lemon rind to the milk and allow to infuse for 10 minutes over gentle heat. Dissolve the gelatine in the water over gentle heat and add the cooled milk. Strain into a wetted mould and leave to set.

LEMON MILK JELLY

½ oz. gelatine
¼ pint water
¼ lb. sugar
½ pint milk
Rind and juice of 2 lemons

Heat the gelatine, water, lemon rind, juice and sugar, but do not boil. Pour on to half of the milk and cool. Put the rest of the milk into a wetted mould and strain the gelatine mixture into the mould. Set without stirring.

LEMON EGG JELLY

2 lemons
½ lb. loaf sugar
½ oz. gelatine
2 eggs
1 pint water and lemon juice

Wipe the lemons and peel them thinly, then put the peel into a saucepan with the sugar, and the lemon juice made up to 1 pint with water. Simmer gently for 10 minutes, then add the gelatine, and when dissolved, allow to cool a little. Strain through a fine strainer on to the beaten eggs. Cook gently until the mixture thickens, but do not allow to boil. Cool and pour into a wetted mould.

Note: If liked, the eggs may be separated, the yolks being added to the strained lemon mixture and the stiffly whisked whites being folded in when the mixture is cold, but not set.

HONEYCOMB MOULD

2 large eggs	Vanilla essence
1 pint milk	½ oz. powdered gelatine
1½ oz. sugar	2 tbsps. water

Separate the yolks and whites of the eggs. Make a custard with the yolks, milk and sugar, and flavour with vanilla. Dissolve the gelatine in the water and add it to the custard. Whisk
6 the egg whites very stiffly and fold lightly into the cool custard mixture. Pour into a glass dish or mould, and turn out when set. Serve with chocolate sauce or with stewed fruit or jam and cream.

BANANA JELLY

1 pint packet of lemon jelly	Crystallised cherries and pistachio nuts
2–3 small bananas	

Dissolve the jelly in ¾ pint hot water. Cut the bananas into slices. Decorate a fancy mould by putting 1 tbsp. of the jelly into a wet mould and running it slowly all over the inside, so that a thin coat of jelly sets evenly. This should be done in a cold room, or the mould should be placed over a bowl of chipped ice. Dip several half cherries and slices of pistachio nuts into a little jelly and place in position in the bottom of the mould; (shamrock leaves made from three slices of pistachio nuts are very effective). When the decorations are firm, pour in about 1 tbsp. jelly and allow to set, then add alternately the slices of banana and a layer of jelly. It is essential to allow each layer of jelly to set before adding more, otherwise the banana will not be suspended throughout the jelly. When the mould is full, put in a cool place to set. Turn out and serve.

CLEAR LEMON JELLY

4 lemons	6 oz. loaf sugar
Whites and shells of 2 eggs	1½ pints cold water
	3 cloves
1–1½ oz. gelatine	½ inch of stick cinnamon

Wash the lemons and the eggs. Peel the rind in thin strips from 3 of the lemons and squeeze the juice of 4, adding water if necessary to make up to ½ pint. Put the lemon rind, the lemon juice, gelatine, sugar and water together with the cloves and cinnamon into a large, clean, lined saucepan. Lastly, add the egg whites and the crushed egg shells, place over gentle heat and commence at once to whisk. Continue to whisk the mixture until nearly boiling, by which time there should be a thick froth on the surface. Stop whisking and allow the froth to rise and crack, then reduce the heat and simmer gently for 5 minutes. Before straining the jelly, pour boiling water through a tammy cloth or jelly-bag into a basin below, to warm the cloth and basin. This prevents the setting of the jelly before straining is complete. Empty the water from the basin, then carefully pour the jelly through the cloth, allowing it to drip into the basin below. The whites and shells of the eggs, as well as the cloth, serve to filter the jelly, and for this reason it is better to have a second warm basin ready to place under the jelly-bag, as the first jelly to come through should be refiltered to make it crystal clear. Avoid shaking the jelly.

When nearly cold, pour into a wetted mould, and leave to set, then turn out. Alternatively, use for Macédoine of Fruit (below), Sweet Chaudfroid Sauce, and so on.

MACÉDOINE OF FRUIT

Make some lemon jelly (see above), prepare a variety of fresh fruits such as black grapes, bananas, cherries, sections of orange, raspberries and pieces of pineapple. Place about 1 inch of jelly in the mould and arrange a few fruits in this.
Allow the jelly to set. Add more jelly and fruit, 96
and again allow to set. Continue until the mould is completely filled.

It is essential that each portion of jelly poured into the mould be allowed to set before more is added, otherwise the fruit will move and the finished appearance be spoilt.

CLARET JELLY

½ pint water	Rind and juice of ½ lemon
½ pint claret	½ oz. gelatine
2 oz. sugar	Cochineal

Put all the ingredients into a saucepan and slowly bring to simmering point. Strain through muslin, add a little cochineal to improve the colour and pour into a wetted mould. When set, turn out and serve with cream.

Claret and other wine jellies may be cleared, if desired, with egg whites and shells as for Clear Lemon Jelly.

ORANGE SNOW

¾ oz. gelatine	3 tbsps. lemon juice
4 tbsps. cold water	¼ pint orange juice
½ pint boiling water	3 egg whites, stiffly whisked
3 oz. sugar	

Soak the gelatine in the cold water, add the boiling water and sugar, and dissolve over gentle heat. Add the fruit juices and put in a cold place until cold but not set. Whisk until light and frothy. Fold in the stiffly whipped egg whites and put into a wetted mould.

Note : ¾ pint of any fruit juice from tinned or fresh fruit may be used in place of the boiling water and orange juice.

LEMON SNOW

¾ oz. gelatine	4–6 oz. sugar
4 tbsps. cold water	¼ pint lemon juice
½ pint boiling water	3 egg whites

Follow the method for Orange Snow (above).

LEMON SPONGE

Rind and juice of 2 lemons	½ oz. gelatine
	½ pint cold water
4 oz. caster sugar	3 egg whites

Put the thinly peeled lemon rind, lemon juice, sugar, gelatine and water into a saucepan. Bring slowly to the boil, stirring now and again. Strain and cool. Whisk the egg whites stiffly and add the lemon mixture when it is cold, but not set. Whisk to a stiff froth and put into a wetted mould or pile in a glass dish.

PRUNE MOULD

½ lb. prunes	½ oz. gelatine
¾ pint water	¼ pint claret
2 oz. sugar	Whipped cream
Rind of 1 lemon	Chopped almonds

Wash the prunes, cover with the water and soak overnight. Stew gently with the sugar and lemon rind, then lift out the prunes and sieve them. Dissolve the gelatine in the prune juice over gentle heat and add it, with the wine, to the sieved prunes, mixing well. Pour into a wetted border mould and leave to cool. When set, turn out and fill the centre with sweetened whipped cream and chopped almonds.

Sherry may be used as an alternative to claret.

ASPIC JELLY

Rind of 1 lemon	2–3 tbsps. sherry
1 carrot	6 peppercorns
1 turnip	½ tsp. salt
1 onion	1½ oz. gelatine
A little celery	1½ pints good stock
2–3 tbsps. lemon juice	Whites and shells of 2 eggs
2–3 tbsps. tarragon or chilli vinegar	

Wipe the lemon and peel or grate the rind. Prepare the vegetables, cutting them into four, then place in a large, lined saucepan with the lemon rind and juice, the vinegar, sherry, peppercorns, seasoning, gelatine and stock. Wash and crush the egg shells and add them to the pan, also the egg whites. Put over a low heat and begin to whisk vigorously. Bring nearly to boiling point, whisking meanwhile, stop whisking and allow the froth to rise to the top of the pan, then draw aside and leave in the warm for five minutes. Strain through a clean scalded cloth or jelly-bag, passing it a second time through the cloth if not absolutely clear.

Use for such dishes as Eggs in Aspic, Aspic Dressing, Chaudfroid Sauce, and so on, or as a garnish to cold savoury dishes.

CALF'S FOOT JELLY : see Invalid Cookery.

CREAMS

There are three kinds of creams :

1. Whole creams, in which cream is the main ingredient.
2. Custard creams, which are made from a combination of cream and custard.
3. Fruit creams, which are made from fruit purée and cream ; custard may also be included.

General Proportions for Making Creams

The general proportion of gelatine to use for creams is ¼–½ oz. gelatine to 1 pint of the mixture. Use slightly more gelatine if the mixture is very thin, and slightly less in the case of a very thick mixture.

A TYPICAL WHOLE CREAM

¼–½ oz. gelatine	3 oz. sugar
2 tbsps. water	Flavouring
1 pint cream	

Prepare the mould and mask and decorate it if desired. Dissolve the gelatine in the water over gentle heat. Half-whip the cream, fold in the sugar and flavouring (vanilla, almond, coffee, melted chocolate, etc.) and lastly, add the hot dissolved gelatine, pouring it in a thin stream and stirring well to prevent it setting in lumps (i.e., "roping"). When just on the point of setting, pour quickly into the mould and leave to set.

A TYPICAL CUSTARD CREAM

½ pint custard (2 eggs, ½ pint milk, 2 oz. sugar, few drops vanilla)	¼–½ oz. gelatine
	2 tbsps. water
	½ pint cream, half-whipped
Flavouring ingredient	

Prepare a mould. Make the custard in the usual way, add the flavouring ingredient and stir occasionally as it cools. Meanwhile, dissolve the gelatine in the water over gentle heat, then add to the lukewarm custard. Fold in the half-whipped cream and when just on the point of setting, pour into the mould.

A TYPICAL FRUIT CREAM

$\frac{1}{2}$ pint fruit purée from raw, stewed or tinned fruit	$\frac{1}{4}$–$\frac{1}{2}$ oz. gelatine
Sugar to taste	2 tbsps. water
Colouring if required	$\frac{1}{2}$ pint cream (or $\frac{1}{4}$ pint cream and $\frac{1}{4}$ pint custard)

Prepare the mould. Drain the fruit if tinned or stewed, rub through a fine sieve and measure the purée. Add sugar and colouring. Dissolve the gelatine in the water over gentle heat and while still hot, pour it in a thin stream into the fruit purée, stirring well. Fold in the half-whipped cream (and custard if used) and pour into the mould.

APPLE CREAM

2 lb. apples	$\frac{1}{4}$ tsp. ginger essence
Juice and rind of 1 lemon	$\frac{1}{2}$ oz. powdered gelatine dissolved in 2 tbsps. water
$\frac{1}{4}$ pint water	
4 oz. caster sugar	
2 oz. crystallised ginger	$\frac{1}{4}$ pint cream

Stew the apples, lemon rind, juice and $\frac{1}{4}$ pint water to a pulp. Add the sugar, sieve and measure the purée—it should be 1 pint. When nearly cold, add the chopped ginger and essence and the gelatine, dissolved in water over gentle heat. When cold, but not set, fold in the half-whipped cream, and pour into a wetted mould.

CANTON CREAM

3 egg yolks	$\frac{1}{4}$–$\frac{1}{2}$ oz. gelatine
$1\frac{1}{2}$ oz. sugar	$\frac{1}{2}$ pint cream
$\frac{1}{4}$ pint milk	Ginger in syrup

Whisk the egg yolks and sugar together, pour on the hot milk and cook until thick. Melt the gelatine in 2 tbsps. ginger syrup or water over gentle heat. Add to the custard mixture and cool. Fold in the half-whipped cream and 1 tbsp. finely cut ginger. Set as usual.

CHARLOTTE RUSSE

$\frac{1}{3}$ pint lemon jelly	2 tbsps. water
Cherries and pistachio nuts, or angelica to decorate	2 tbsps. milk
	$\frac{1}{2}$ pint cream
8–10 Savoy fingers	1 tbsp. brandy or $\frac{1}{2}$–1 tsps. vanilla essence
$\frac{1}{4}$ oz. gelatine	$1\frac{1}{2}$ oz. caster sugar

Pour a thin layer of jelly into the bottom of a plain 1-pint soufflé tin, and allow to set. Decorate with cherries and pistachio nuts, pour over a thin layer of jelly, and allow to set. Line the sides of the mould with Savoy finger biscuits, trimming them at the sides and ends and dipping the ends in the jelly before putting them into position. Allow to set. Pour in a thin layer of jelly. Dissolve the gelatine in the water over gentle heat and add the milk. Whip the cream until fairly stiff, stir in the gelatine, flavouring and sugar. Put into the prepared mould and allow to set. When quite set, turn out carefully on to a glass or silver dish.

CHARTREUSE OF BANANAS

$\frac{1}{2}$ pint lemon jelly	1–2 oz. caster sugar
4 bananas	$\frac{1}{2}$ a lemon
$\frac{1}{4}$ oz. pistachio nuts	$\frac{1}{4}$–$\frac{1}{2}$ oz. gelatine
$\frac{1}{2}$ pint cream	2 tbsps. cold water

Line a plain 1-pint soufflé tin or cake tin with a thin layer of lemon jelly. Cut 1 or 2 of the bananas into thin slices, dip each slice in a little cold jelly, and entirely line the mould with them. Fill in the spaces with very finely
chopped pistachio nuts. Coat the inside with 96
another thin layer of jelly. Pass the remaining bananas through a sieve and add to the half-whipped cream, together with the sugar and lemon juice. Dissolve the gelatine in the water over gentle heat and add to the cream mixture. Pour into the prepared mould and allow to set. When quite set, turn out carefully on to a glass dish, and decorate with any remaining jelly, chopped fairly small.

COFFEE CREAMS

$\frac{1}{2}$ pint milk	1 dessertsp. coffee essence
2 eggs	$\frac{1}{4}$ pint cream
$1\frac{1}{2}$ oz. sugar	Chopped pistachio nuts or glacé cherries to decorate
$\frac{1}{4}$ oz. gelatine	
2 tbsps. water	
Vanilla essence	

Heat the milk and pour on to the beaten eggs and sugar, stirring meanwhile. Cook in a double
saucepan until thick, then cool. Dissolve the 96
gelatine in the water over gentle heat, and add it with vanilla and coffee essence to the custard. Half whip the cream and fold into the cooled mixture, pour into individual glasses, and leave to set. Decorate with pistachio nuts or glacé cherries.

If preferred, this mixture may be moulded, and when set, turned out, in which case increase the amount of gelatine to $\frac{1}{2}$ oz.

DOLCE ALLA CIOCCOLATA

2 eggs
½ pint milk
1 oz. caster sugar
Vanilla essence
¼ lb. Savoy fingers or sponge cakes
4 oz. chocolate melted in 2 tbsps. water or milk

Prepare a custard from the eggs, milk and sugar, Cool, and add the vanilla essence. Line a glass dish with sponge fingers or sponge cakes. Pour a little of the custard into the dish and crumble the remaining sponge cakes on to it. Pour on half the melted chocolate, then the rest of the custard, lastly, the rest of the chocolate. Put aside until cold.

HUNGARIAN CHOCOLATE

2½ oz. plain chocolate
4 tbsps. strong coffee
4 egg whites
2 oz. caster sugar
Grated sweet chocolate or pistachio nuts

Cut up the chocolate finely, add the coffee, and dissolve over gentle heat. Beat until smooth and put into a basin to cool. When the chocolate is cool, whip up the egg whites very stiffly and gradually whisk in the sugar. Add 2 tbsps. of the egg white mixture to the chocolate and stir in thoroughly. Fold the rest of the beaten egg white into the chocolate mixture and pile in small glasses. Sprinkle with either grated sweet chocolate or finely chopped pistachio nuts

NURSERY CREAM

½ pint boiling water
½ pint packet raspberry jelly
½ pint packet raspberry blancmange powder
½ pint milk
2 oz. desiccated coconut
Sugar to taste

Pour the boiling water over the jelly and stir well until dissolved. Blend the blancmange powder with a little of the milk. Infuse 1 oz. of the coconut with the remainder of the milk for a few minutes. Pour the infused milk on to the blended blancmange powder, stirring well. Return to the saucepan, and cook for 2–3 minutes, stirring. Add the jelly and sugar, pour into a wetted mould and leave to cool. When set, turn out and sprinkle with the remainder of the coconut.

PINEAPPLE CREAM

1 pint packet pineapple jelly
½ pint hot water
1 egg
½ pint milk
1 tbsp. sugar

Dissolve the jelly in the hot water, and set aside to cool. Break the egg into a basin, beat it, and add the milk. Strain this into a saucepan and stir over a gentle heat until the custard thickens—do not let it boil or it will curdle—add the sugar, and cool. When the jelly and custard are cool, add the jelly gradually to the custard, stirring all the time. Pour into a wet pint mould, allow to set, and turn out when required.

Creams of all flavours may be made in this way by using different jellies in their preparation.

RASPBERRY AND RED-CURRANT CREAM

1½ lb. raspberries and red-currants
4 oz. caster sugar
½ pint cream
½ oz. gelatine
2 tbsps. water

Sieve the fruit and measure out ½ pint purée, put it into a basin with the sugar and fold in the lightly whipped cream. Dissolve the gelatine in the water over gentle heat and stir lightly into the prepared mixture. Pour into a wetted mould, leave to set, and turn out.

STRAWBERRY CREAM

1 pint packet strawberry jelly
½ pint boiling water
¼ pint strawberry purée and juice
¼ pint cream
A little sugar
Whipped cream and chopped jelly to decorate

Dissolve the jelly in ½ pint of boiling water and cool. Sieve the strawberries, adding juice to make a ¼ pint. Stir the purée into the jelly, and lastly, add the half-whipped cream, sweetening if necessary. Pour into a wetted mould. Turn out, decorate with whipped cream and chopped jelly.

STRAWBERRY SPONGE

1 pint packet strawberry jelly
Boiling water
1 egg white
2–3 tbsps. cream
1 small tin strawberries
Small pieces of angelica

Make the jelly, using the juice from the strawberries made up to 1 pint with water. Allow to get cold, but not set, add the egg white and whisk until creamy and thick. Whisk in the cream. Arrange the strawberries in individual glasses and pile the sponge mixture on the top. Decorate with strawberries and small leaves of angelica.

WHIPPED CREAM, DEVONSHIRE CREAM, etc.: see Cake Fillings.

FRUITS AND FRUIT DISHES

All fruits, whether fresh, tinned or dried, are important for their vitamin and mineral content; they also provide necessary roughage. Being refreshing and of delicious flavour, fruit adds interest to everyday meals and in one form or another is popular with most people.

The citrus fruits (oranges, grapefruits, lemons and tangerines) and others, notably strawberries, black-currants and tomatoes, are particularly valuable sources of Vitamin C, so try to serve at least one of these daily. Any one of the following contains the day's quota of Vitamin C for one person:

1 medium-sized orange
½ medium-sized grapefruit
3 tbsps. orange or lemon juice
4 tbsps. grapefruit juice
⅓ pint tomato juice or stewed tomatoes
2 medium-sized raw tomatoes
½ lb. raw strawberries

If ripe fruits have to be stored for a short time before serving, they should be kept in a covered container in the refrigerator (except bananas), or in a cold larder. If slightly under-ripe, keep them in a warm room until fully ripe.

A bowl or basket of assorted fresh fruits contrasting in flavour, shape and colour, is a welcome addition to almost any meal, and adds colour and interest to the table. They should be washed before serving. For formal occasions, dessert plates, fruit knives and forks and finger bowls are necessary.

A CONCISE DICTIONARY OF FRUITS

(Including the main English and imported varieties.)

APPLE

There is a large variety of English apples, both cooking and eating; in addition, Commonwealth and foreign apples, particularly eating varieties, are imported to this country.

A good cooking apple is generally large and green, juicy, and with a high acid content; such apples become soft and fluffy on cooking. Some of the best cooking apples are:

Bramley Seedling
Dunn's Seedling
Edward VII
Lane's Prince Albert
Lord Derby
Monarch
Newton Wonder
Sturmer Pippin
Victoria

Sometimes windfalls of a mixed variety of apples are sold for cooking purposes, but such a "mixed bag" is often not very satisfactory, as some apples remain tough on cooking.

A good dessert apple is usually smaller and often very prettily coloured. As a rule, they are sweet, crisp and juicy, with a characteristic aromatic flavour and fragrance. Some of the most popular varieties are:

Beauty of Bath
Blenheim Orange
Cox's Orange Pippin
Ellison's Orange Pippin
Golden Delicious
Granny Smith
James Grieve
Jonathan
Laxton's Superb
Ribston Pippin
Sturmer Pippin
Worcester Pearmain

Apples have perhaps more uses than any other fruit, and owing to supplies from abroad, good varieties are obtainable all the year round.

Storage of Apples

Many varieties of apples will keep for months if properly stored and, in fact, some do not reach their full flavour and fragrance until they have been kept for some weeks, or even months, according to the variety. Apples bought from a shop do not as a rule keep well, since they are bound to become somewhat bruised by the time they reach the purchaser. For storing, apples must be free from all bruises, grubs and blemishes so, if they are not home-gathered, they should be purchased direct from the grower; in either case they should be carefully picked over. There are two methods of storing them :

1. By placing them out on shelves; in shallow boxes; or directly on the floor; in such a way that no two apples touch, and where they can easily be examined from time to time. Should any signs of mould appear, the affected apples should be removed at once, otherwise the infection is liable to spread. On no account should the apples touch—mould is more likely to develop if the apples are in close contact, and, of course, spreads more quickly.
2. Where space does not allow for the apples to be spread out, they may be wrapped individually in apple wrapping papers (specially prepared oiled tissue paper); they may then be stored compactly in boxes, baskets and so on. Should mould develop in any of the apples, the paper will prevent it spreading.

Only apples that are proved to be good keepers are worth storing; many varieties deteriorate on storing, becoming withered and shrivelled, or soft and woolly.

APRICOT

This stone fruit, when fully ripe, is delicious eaten raw, though if at all under-ripe, it is sour and uninteresting, and quickly becomes woolly when over-ripe. Apricots are also very good cooked, as in apricot pie, and make delicious jam.

The kernels of fresh apricots have an almond taste which goes well with the flavour of the fruit, so it is well worth cracking the stones to obtain the kernels for fresh apricot jam, compote of apricots and so on, or a few fresh almonds may be included instead.

Apricots may also be dried and are very useful, especially when fresh fruit is scarce. They may be stewed, used as a filling for a boiled pudding with suetcrust, or made into jam.

Tinned apricots are popular, and are useful for flans, fruit salads and other cold sweets.

AVOCADO PEAR

A pear-shaped dark green fruit, very popular in America. It is best if eaten when the flesh has softened to the consistency of butter. When ready for eating, it should yield to a gentle pressure of the whole hand. If slightly under-ripe, the softening can be hastened by keeping in a warm room. They should not be put into the refrigerator until shortly before serving.

To prepare, first make a deep cut through the flesh, up to but not through the seed, entirely encircling the fruit. Now separate by holding the fruit between the palms of the hands and revolving the hands in opposite directions. This loosens the seed, which is discarded. Pare or not, according to how it is to be used.

Serve half an unpared avocado per person with salt, pepper and a wedge of lemon, as a first course to be eaten with a spoon. Alternatively, serve with French dressing in the centre as a salad, or pare the halves, slice them into crescent-shaped strips and serve in salads.

BANANA

There are two chief varieties of banana :

1. The Jamaica or Plantain Banana, which is long and fairly large. The flesh is of a creamy colour and somewhat insipid in flavour.
2. The Canary or Dwarf Banana, which is smaller and shorter, the flesh being more pink in colour, with a very aromatic flavour, considered by most people to be far superior.

Bananas are delicious eaten raw, particularly if served with sugar and cream, with a little lemon juice to bring out their flavour, and are useful for jellies, trifles, creams, and so on. They may also be cooked (baked or fried), but many people consider this spoils their flavour.

If bananas are slightly under-ripe when purchased (i.e. greenish at the tip), keep them in a warm atmosphere until a deep yellow all over, or even slightly speckled with brown.

BLACKBERRY

Blackberries, both wild and cultivated, grow extensively in this country and are very popular. The cultivated varieties are often larger and more juicy than the wild, and are usually rather different in flavour.

Ripe blackberries are very good eaten raw (carefully picked over and washed) and served with sugar and cream. When cooked, they are often combined with apples, as the flavours of these two fruits go very well together, and the apples, being fleshy, help to give substance to the dish, blackberries alone being somewhat watery. In the making of blackberry jam and jelly, apples are included to supply the acid and the pectin which is lacking in the blackberries, and thus help the preserve to set. As blackberry seeds are very hard, many people prefer to sieve the fruit when it is cooked, as in blackberry fool, blackberry and apple conserve, or bramble jelly.

BLACK-CURRANT

Black-currants are grown widely in this country and are very popular. They are a rich source of Vitamin C, and a purée made from them can be given to infants and small children. Black-currant tea is a soothing drink much appreciated by those with coughs and chest colds. When fully ripe, black-currants may be served as dessert; they are also very good cooked in pies and tarts, and can be used to flavour ices.

BLAEBERRY (BILBERRY)

(Also called Whortleberry, Whinberry, etc.)

Bilberry

These little dark blue berries ripen in August and September on the Welsh mountains and on the English moors. They have a distinctive and delicious flavour, and are usually served cooked, in pies and tarts, though they may be eaten raw if very ripe. They make a jam of excellent flavour.

CAPE GOOSEBERRY

These are the berries of the Cape Gooseberry, commonly called " Chinese Lantern," which is grown in this country more for decoration than for the fruit, as this does not often ripen well in this climate. When fully ripe, the berries, each enclosed in the lantern-shaped calyx, are of a pretty orange-yellow colour. They may be eaten raw as dessert or made into jam or jelly. They look very attractive and are very delicious to eat if the calyx is bent back and the berry dipped into fondant, dished in tiny paper sweet cases and served with petits fours. These berries are also imported in tins (usually under the name of Golden Berries), and are useful for fruit salads and fruit cocktails.

Cape Gooseberry

CHERRY

There are several varieties of cherry grown and marketed in this country, the best-known eating cherries being the Black Heart and the White Heart, which ripen in June and July. These are delicious raw—either for dessert, or in fruit cocktails, fruit salad and other cold sweets—and are also very good cooked, in cherry pie, or as stewed cherries. They may also be bottled or tinned, the red or black varieties being rather more suitable for this purpose, as the white cherries turn a somewhat unappetising fawnish colour on bottling.

Cooking cherries, of which the Morello and the Mayduke are the best-known varieties, ripen later in the season—about August. Being very sharp, these are not suitable for eating raw but are delicious cooked, if well sweetened. For preserves, the cooking varieties should be chosen; dessert cherries have insufficient acid and pectin to make them suitable for this purpose.

CHERRY PLUM

These are small round fruits of a pretty red and yellow colour, like large cherries, which are grown in this country, and ripen in July and August. They are mealy and uninteresting eaten raw, but are excellent stewed and are good for bottling. The skins are tough, but can be slipped off quite easily from the cooked plum.

CRANBERRY

These are small crimson berries about the size of currants, grown in this country, where they ripen in the autumn, and also imported from France and America. They are too hard and acid to be eaten raw, but are useful in cooking, for mixing with apples as in cranberry and apple pie, or for making cranberry sauce to serve with turkey and game. They are also used for making preserves.

DAMSON

This very small, dark-blue plum ripens late in the season, usually August. If absolutely ripe, damsons can be eaten raw, but are not very enjoyable, and are much better when cooked, in such dishes as pies, suetcrust puddings, fools, and so on. They also make delicious jam, jelly and cheese; having a high acid and pectin content, they give a very good set in these preserves.

The true damson is very small, slightly pointed at one end, with a smooth, pointed stone. There is another small blue plum called the Damson Plum (or Damasine), slightly larger than the damson, not so pointed and with a rounder, rougher stone. These sometimes pass for damsons, but are generally considered inferior in flavour.

DATE

This is the fruit of the date palm tree, cultivated in Northern Africa, Western Asia and Southern California. Dates are popular in this country for dessert and in making sweetmeats, and also for use in cooking, in cakes, steamed pudding, baked stuffed apples, and so on. The dessert dates are rather expensive, generally loosely packed (often " on the stem "), and not stoned, but a cheaper variety can be bought which is quite suitable for cooking, solid packed, in bulk, and frequently stoned; it is as well to wash these before using.

FIG

There are two chief varieties of figs grown in this country: the Green Fig, which is green or greenish-yellow inside, even when fully ripe, and the Purple Fig, which ripens to a deep reddish purple in the centre. A fully ripe fig, freshly gathered, is one of the most delicious dessert fruits, but unfortunately in this climate they seldom ripen fully out of doors, so to be certain of them they must be grown in a hothouse, which makes them somewhat rare and usually rather expensive.

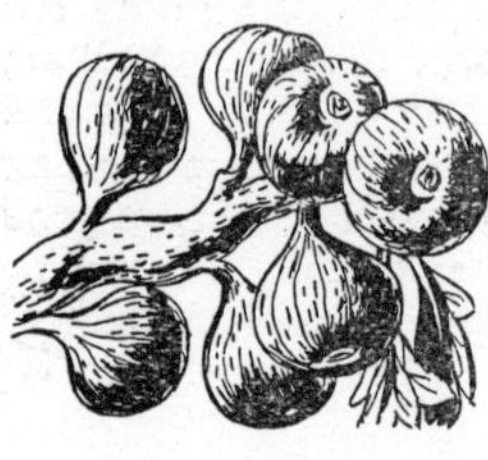

Fig

The imported dried figs are widely used, for dessert and also for cooking, as in steamed fig pudding, stewed figs, as an ingredient in dried fruit salad and so on.

GOOSEBERRY

There are many different varieties of gooseberries, round or long, hairy or smooth, cooking or dessert. The early varieties are usually ready in May and are very welcome, being among the first of the English fruits. When very young and small, they make very delicious pies and puddings, the seeds being small then and the skins tender, but if allowed to get big before cooking, the skins become tough and sour and the seeds large and hard.

For dessert, gooseberries should be fully mature, otherwise they taste sour. Dessert gooseberries may be green, red, yellow or white, according to the variety.

To prepare gooseberries for cooking, the stalk and calyx should be either pinched or cut off (called " topping and tailing "), and they should be thoroughly washed.

Having a high acid and pectin content, gooseberries make good preserves that set well. They are also very suitable for bottling, particularly when very young and small.

GRAPE

The climate in this country is not suitable for growing grapes out of doors, but there are many varieties of English hothouse grapes, both black and green, which are very luscious, though rather expensive. We also import a large quantity of grapes from North Africa, America, and other countries, and some of these are much less expensive.

Grapes are used chiefly for dessert and (with the tough skin removed) are included in fruit salads, fruit cocktails, and macedoine of fruit. It is not usual to cook them, but the grape thinnings and any bunches of grapes which have failed to ripen by the end of the season can be added to preserves, or the juice extracted from them, and used in making fruit drinks or jellies.

Dried grapes (i.e., raisins) are very useful in the kitchen for cakes and puddings.

GRAPEFRUIT

Cultivated widely in Trinidad, Palestine, Florida, and California, etc., grapefruit, both fresh and tinned, is imported to this country, where it is popular for breakfast, as hors d'œuvre, in fruit cocktails and fruit salads. Fresh grapefruit is generally served in halves, with sugar.

GREENGAGE

A small green plum which ripens to a yellowish green, usually in September. To many people's taste, they are the most delicious of all dessert plums. They also make excellent tarts, puddings, and preserves.

The Golden Gage is larger than the greengage, yellower in colour and of less distinctive flavour. This fruit cooks and bottles well, and it also makes a very good type of jam.

Strawberry Cream P

JAPONICA

Japonica apples, the fruit of the ornamental Japonica tree, though edible, are of little value as a culinary fruit. They have a very distinctive, somewhat scented, flavour, and small quantities, peeled and sliced, are sometimes included with apple pie and similar dishes, to give variety. They can also be used in jams or jellies.

LEMON

This is perhaps the most useful fruit in the kitchen. The rind and juice are used, in small quantities, to flavour all manner of mixtures and also to make such dishes as lemon meringue pie.

Lemon juice contains appreciable quantities of Vitamin C. It is also rich in acid and pectin, which makes it a very useful addition to fruits of poor setting quality when making preserves from them. On account of its acidity, it is often used in place of vinegar, e.g., for salad dressings.

The oil which is contained in the skin is extracted to make a flavouring essence which is useful in cooking, or it may be obtained from the fresh lemon by rubbing lump sugar over the surface of the (washed) lemon.

LIME

A citrus fruit, like a small green lemon. It is too acid to eat raw, but makes a good cordial and delicious marmalade. The rind and juice can be used in small quantities for flavouring in the same way as lemon is used, but being of a very distinctive flavour it is not so useful as is lemon.

LOGANBERRY

Loganberries are not unlike raspberries, but are larger and rather more acid, with a hardish hull in the centre. When fully ripe they are of a dark purplish red. They are suitable for dessert if ripe, and make good tarts, preserves, etc.

MEDLAR

The medlar is not unlike the rose hip in shape, but larger (about the size of a walnut) and of a golden-brown colour. Medlars should not be eaten until quite soft and mealy, and even then they are not always very interesting when eaten raw. They make good preserves, however, especially if mixed with lemon juice to bring out their flavour and aid in the setting.

Medlar

MELON

There are many varieties of melon, which include the following :

Cantaloup Melon : The exterior is segmented and the flesh of a pinky-yellow colour with a delicious flavour. When ripe it should have the characteristic melon fragrance and the blossom end should yield to slight pressure.

Tiger Melon : This is also segmented, and striped green and yellow in colour.

Honeydew Melon : When ripe, honeydews have a creamy yellow, smooth skin and the blossom end yields to slight pressure. They are usually oval in shape and the flesh is greenish in colour, sweet and fragrant.

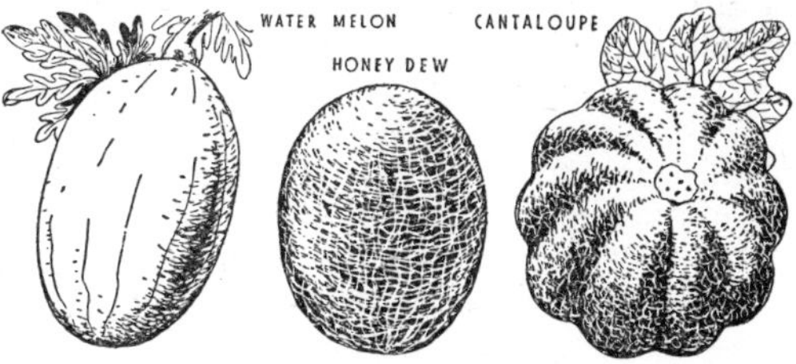

Water Melon : These melons, imported from the Continent and North Africa, have a somewhat insipid flavour, but are cool and refreshing. The colour varies considerably.

A slice of ripe melon makes a good hors d'œuvre. Small cubes or balls scooped out of a ripe melon may be added to fruit cocktails and fruit salad.

MULBERRY

Mulberry trees occur occasionally in various parts of the country. The berries are red, ripening to a deep purplish colour, not unlike the loganberry. They have a very distinctive flavour, and when fully ripe, are delicious as a dessert fruit, served with sugar if necessary. They may also be cooked, with or without other fruits, in pies, puddings and tarts.

Having a low pectin content, they do not make satisfactory preserves used alone, but combine well with apple for jam and jelly.

NECTARINE

This is a variety of peach, but generally smaller and with a smooth skin. The flesh is firmer and richer in flavour than the peach. It is an excellent dessert fruit, undoubtedly best eaten raw, but may also be cooked if wished.

ORANGE

There are many different varieties of orange, both sweet and bitter.

Sweet oranges are used as dessert fruit, also for fruit salads, fruit cocktails and in jellies and cold sweets. The juice is rich in Vitamin C and is consumed widely on this account.

Bitter oranges (Seville oranges and other bitter varieties) are not suitable for eating raw, but make excellent preserves and marmalade. They are also used for orange sauce and orange salad to serve with wild duck, etc.

PEACH

A stone fruit, very juicy and of excellent flavour and fragrance. The skin is rough and not pleasant to eat. As the English climate is not particularly suitable for ripening peaches out of doors, they are generally grown in hothouses. A fully ripe, freshly gathered English peach is one of the most delicious dessert fruits, and indeed they are best eaten this way, though some people also cook them and make them into preserves.

Peaches imported from South Africa are excellent and moderately priced during the period from December to March. Italian peaches, available approximately from May to September, are large and have very yellow flesh; they can be used for cooking or as dessert.

Peaches are also dried, and may then be used in any way suitable for dried apricots.

PEAR

There are many different varieties of pear grown and marketed in this country; we also import quite a large number.

They vary considerably in shape, flavour, and texture, Many varieties are very juicy and sweet and, when absolutely ripe, are an excellent dessert fruit, but when over-ripe they soon become woolly and uninteresting. The English dessert pears, which are ready in late August, September, and early October (such as the William, Conference, Doyenne du Comice), must be very carefully watched so that they may be eaten as soon as they are fully ripe, as, once ripe, they are very soon past perfection, often in a few hours in hot weather. Later varieties, which can be kept until Christmas or longer, and most of the imported pears also, are not so "difficult," remaining in a ripe state for several days before they begin to deteriorate. When ready to eat, a dessert pear should yield to slight pressure at the stalk end.

Other varieties are only suitable for cooking, and even the best of these usually require an additional flavouring such as clove, lemon, ginger or cinnamon.

Pears are not particularly suitable for preserving, since they lack acid and pectin and are somewhat poor in flavour, but they may be bottled with success, and are also very good pickled.

PERSIMMON

An orange-yellow fruit with a smooth, shiny skin, and about the size of a large dessert apple, which is imported to this country from America. They should not be eaten until they are very soft (by which time they usually darken in colour), and even then they are not very delicious eaten raw, being sweet yet at the same time somewhat acid and bitter. Persimmons are used for flavouring ices and jellies, and for making preserves.

PINEAPPLE

Pineapples, both fresh and tinned, are imported into this country, where they are very popular. The best come from Hawaii. When ripe, the pointed spikes or leaves at the top of a fresh pineapple loosen easily when pulled: also the flesh should be of a deep yellow colour with a noticeable fragrance. Fresh pineapple is very good for dessert, cut in slices across and served with sugar; small cubes or sections (and also tinned pineapple) may be included in fruit cocktails, fruit salads and other cold sweets.

PLUM

There are many varieties of plums, both dessert and cooking, grown and marketed in this country. We also import dessert plums from Africa, America, and other places.

Among the early varieties of the home-grown plum are the small purple variety, such as Rivers Early, which are juicy and of good flavour and useful for cooking and preserving. The best-known and probably the most popular English plum is the Victoria, which ripens in August. When fully ripe, it is an excellent dessert plum, and is also very good for cooking and preserving. There are also the Yellow Egg Plum, suitable both for cooking and preserving, and the Purple Egg Plum, dark purple in colour and a better quality than the yellow. Amongst the later varieties, the Monarch is perhaps the best known; ripening in September, this very large, dark purple plum is good eaten raw, and is excellent for cooking and preserving.

POMEGRANATE

A pomegranate resembles a large orange in size, but with a red-brown, firm, leathery rind.

Pomegranate

It has many seeds and a crimson juicy pulp. It is used in fruit salads, fruit cocktails and for flavouring ices and fruit drinks.

PRUNE

Prunes are dried plums of varieties particularly suitable for this treatment. Some kinds (such as Bordeaux Plums and other French plums) are very good eaten as dessert, in their dry form, and may be stuffed with marzipan, nuts, fondant and so on, to make sweetmeat. Usually, however, prunes are stewed and served as a sweet with cream or custard, or made into moulds and other puddings.

QUINCE

The quince is a fruit not unlike an apple in appearance, but with a golden-yellow skin and tough yellow flesh which turns pink on cooking. It has a very distinctive flavour, which goes well with apple; a small amount of quince (peeled and sliced) is often included in dishes such as apple pie, for variety. Quince have high acid and pectin content, and so make good setting preserves, of characteristic flavour.

Quince

RASPBERRY

Raspberries are one of the most delicious of the English soft fruits. They are usually red, but may also be yellow or white, and while they mostly ripen in June and July, there are some varieties which are not ready until October or November.

They are most popular as a dessert fruit, served with sugar and cream, usually alone, though they are sometimes mixed with strawberries or with red-currants. They are used to make fruit drinks or syrups, for flavouring ices and for including in fruit salads and fruit cocktails. They are also good cooked in pies and tarts, and make excellent preserves. Raspberry vinegar is a popular country beverage, often taken for sore throats.

RED-CURRANT

Red-currants are widely grown in this country, and when fully ripe may be eaten as dessert, served in their clusters, which are dipped in fine sugar before eating. Frosted red-currants are also delicious as dessert; the clusters, carefully washed and dried, are coated with lightly beaten egg white, then dipped in fine caster sugar and allowed to dry, in the sun or in a warm atmosphere, before serving.

Red-currants are also useful in cooking, making an excellent jelly to serve with mutton and other meat, and are also combined with fruits which lack acid and pectin, such as strawberries, cherries and also raspberries, when making preserves of these fruits.

White-currants are an albino strain of red-currants.

RHUBARB

(Though not strictly speaking a fruit, this is usually classed as such.)

The early spring rhubarb, which is forced, has light pink, tender stems and pale yellow leaves. It is particularly welcome, being the first home-grown fruit to appear on the market, often as early as January. The garden rhubarb, which comes later, has reddish green stalks and large, dark green leaves.

Rhubarb is not eaten raw but is usually served stewed, with cream or custard, or made into such dishes as rhubarb pie, boiled rhubarb pudding and rhubarb fool. Being very acid, it requires much sweetening.

ROSE HIP

The fruit of the English wild rose, though not particularly interesting in flavour or texture, is valuable on account of its high Vitamin C content. Rose hips are not suitable to eat raw, being somewhat sour and containing, in addition to hard seeds, many fine silky-looking hairs, which are unpleasant to eat and inclined to be irritating to the digestive tract. Hips are best made into a purée or a syrup, and these, if carefully prepared so that all the hairs are removed, can be given to infants and children. A jam of rather unusual flavour can be made from rose hip purée.

Rose hips should not be picked until after the first frost, as their vitamin content is not at its highest until they have been touched with frost.

ROWANBERRY

The fruit of the mountain ash or rowan tree, the berries ripening to a brilliant orange. They are too bitter to eat raw, and are only suitable for making into jelly, and even this is too bitter for many people's tastes, but is enjoyed by some when served with meat, like red-currant jelly.

Rowanberry

SLOE

These attractive-looking, dark-blue fruits, like very tiny damsons, are found in the English hedgerow, but being exceedingly acid and bitter, they are of little culinary use. They are, however, used to make Sloe Gin—the sloes when steeped in the gin impart to it a delicious and unusual flavour.

Sloe

STRAWBERRY

Strawberries are a very delicious and popular English soft fruit, ripening in June.

Large, perfect strawberries may be washed, left unhulled, and served with fine sugar, when they are eaten in the fingers after dipping in the sugar. Alternatively, they may be hulled and washed and served with sugar and cream. The raw berries are also included in fruit salad and fruit cocktails, and puréed they make delicious creams and ices.

They are not particularly nice cooked, nor do they bottle very successfully, losing shape, texture, and colour in the process. They do, however, make luscious jam.

TANGERINE

Tangerines belong to the mandarin orange family and are at their best from November to January. They are delicious in flavour, small in size and deep orange in colour, and the skin, which is loose and puffy, peels off very easily; generally there is a large number of seeds. They are eaten as dessert, included in fruit salads, ices, and so on. They do not lend themselves to cooking, but can, if liked, be included in marmalade, though rather sweet for this purpose.

STEWED FRUIT AND FRUIT SALADS

When the aim is to keep the individual pieces of fruit whole and of good shape (e.g., to serve as stewed fruit, for fruit in jelly, fruit trifle, and so on), the prepared fruit should be put into a syrup made from sugar and water and stewed gently until tender. The amount of water and the proportion of sugar for the syrup will naturally vary with the juiciness and sweetness of the fruit, but the recipe opposite will act as a guide.

If, on the other hand, the fruit is required stewed to a mash to make into a purée (for fruit fools, creams, and so on), it is better to cook it without sugar and in the minimum of water until tender, and then sweeten it, since the addition of sugar to the raw fruit toughens it and prevents it mashing properly.

Apples and Pears: Peel thinly, core and cut into quarters or eighths. Place at once in the prepared syrup to prevent the fruit from discolouring.

For fruit salads, the apples and pears, if very crisp, may be softened by stewing for 2–3 minutes in the syrup. Alternatively, raw fruit may be shredded coarsely into the fruit salad just before serving.

Bananas : Prepare these at the last moment, as they discolour quickly when exposed to the air. Peel, cut into slices about $\frac{1}{8}$ inch thick and place immediately in the syrup.

Oranges, Tangerines, Grapefruit : Peel, and remove all the white pith. Then either divide into segments, removing the skin if liked, or cut the whole orange into slices $\frac{1}{8}$–$\frac{1}{4}$ inch thick, using a very sharp knife. In either case, remove any pips. Prepare these fruits over a plate so that any juice can be collected and added to the syrup.

Grapes : It is usual to peel grapes for a fruit salad, though some people prefer them unskinned. Remove grapes carefully from the stalk and peel with a small silver or stainless knife. Make a slit down the side of the grape and remove the pips.

Cherries : Take the cherries off the stalks and wash them carefully. Remove the stones, either with a cherry stoner or by making a slit down one side of the cherry and removing the stone with a pointed knife.

Stone Fruit (e.g., Plums, Greengages, etc.) : Pick over the fruit, removing the stalks, and wash thoroughly. Very large plums may be halved and the stones removed before stewing. For fruit salad, use dessert plums, and peel, stone and slice them. If cooking plums are included in the fruit salad, they should first be stewed until tender but not broken.

Soft Fruits (e.g., Strawberries and Raspberries) : Pick over the fruit, removing any stalks. Strawberries usually require washing. When ready, place in the prepared syrup.

Dried Fruit (e.g., Prunes, Apricots, Figs) : Wash well. Just cover with cold water and allow to soak overnight. Cook slowly in the water in which they were soaked (see recipe), and use as stewed fruit or for fruit salad.

STEWED FRESH FRUIT

1 lb. fresh fruit
3–4 oz. sugar
$\frac{1}{4}$ pint water ($\frac{1}{2}$ pint for hard fruits)

Prepare the fruit. Bring the sugar and water to the boil. Add the fruit, simmer gently until tender. Lift out the fruit, simmer the juice until slightly syrupy and pour over the fruit.

Some fruits are improved with additional flavouring, for example :

Stewed apples : Flavour with lemon juice, grated lemon rind, cloves, cinnamon stick or marmalade. Remove cloves, etc., before serving.

Stewed pears : Flavour with cloves or cinnamon stick. Remove before serving.

Stewed plums : Add the plum kernels or a few sweet almonds.

Stewed rhubarb : Flavour with root ginger, cinnamon stick or strip of lemon rind. Remove before serving.

STEWED DRIED FRUIT

1 lb. dried fruit
1 pint water
$\frac{1}{4}$ lb. Demerara sugar

Wash the fruit very thoroughly, add the water and soak for 12 hours. Put into a saucepan, with the sugar, bring to the boil and simmer gently until tender. Remove the fruit, boil the juice for a few minutes until syrupy, then pour over the fruit.

STEAMED DRIED FRUIT

1 lb. dried fruit
Sugar if required

Wash the fruit thoroughly, cover with water and soak for 12 hours. Drain well and steam for 20–30 minutes, until tender.

Note : Fruit cooked in this way has a very good flavour. Sugar may be sprinkled over before serving.

FRUIT SALAD

1 lb. sugar
$\frac{1}{2}$ pint cold water
2 lemons
A selection of fruits in season

Bring the sugar, water and thinly peeled lemon rind to the boil. Boil for 5 minutes. Put the prepared fruit into a basin, add the lemon juice and strain over it the boiling syrup. Allow to get cold.

This salad may be served in various ways, and looks attractive if put in half-orange or grapefruit skins, with a notched edge, as seen in the colour picture opposite page 64.

WINTER FRUIT SALAD

$\frac{1}{4}$ lb. prunes
$\frac{1}{4}$ lb. dried apricots
1 banana
2 oranges
1 grapefruit
$\frac{1}{4}$ lb. sugar
$\frac{1}{2}$ pint water
1 lemon

Wash the dried fruits, cover with the water and soak for 12 hours. The next day cook the fruits in the water in which they have been soaking. Drain them and add the sliced banana, the oranges and grapefruit divided into sections. Put the sugar, water and thinly peeled lemon rind into a saucepan, bring to the boil, and boil for 5 minutes. Strain over the prepared fruit, add the lemon juice, and leave to cool.

COMPOTE OF PEARS

2 lb. pears	2–3 cloves
6 oz. sugar	1 inch of cinnamon stick
½ pint water	A little red wine
Juice of ½ lemon	(optional)

Make a syrup of the sugar and water, putting them with all the flavouring ingredients into a saucepan, bring slowly to the boil, and boil for 10 minutes.

Choose good stewing pears, peel them with a silver knife, and cut them in halves. Remove the cores, being careful not to break the pieces, and put them into cold water to prevent discoloration. Strain the pears and stew them slowly in the syrup, until tender, then lift them out carefully with a spoon. Continue to boil the juice until syrupy, allow it to cool slightly, and then strain. If liked, a little red wine may be added to the syrup when stewing the pears. Apples may be cooked in the same way.

MELON WITH FRUIT SALAD

1 melon	Sugar if required
1 small tin of fruit salad	1 glass red wine
1½ tsps. powdered gelatine	A few drops of carmine
	Vine leaves or fern to
The juice of ½ lemon	garnish

Choose a ripe hothouse or cantaloup melon of medium size. Cut a slice off the top, scoop out the seeds, then scoop out the inside without making the walls too thin. Discard the seeds and cut the pulp of the melon into small pieces. Turn the melon itself upside-down to drain whilst preparing the filling. Drain the syrup from the fruit salad. Put the fruit into a basin and add to it the cut melon. Pour the syrup into a small saucepan, add the gelatine and lemon juice, and dissolve over gentle heat. A little sugar may also be added if necessary. Strain into a basin, add the wine and a few drops of colouring. Cool and pour over the fruit. A short time before the melon has to be served, fill it with the fruit salad and replace the lid. Place the melon on a pretty dish and garnish it with vine leaves or sprigs of fern.

ORANGE BASKETS

6 large oranges	A few tinned apricots
¼ lb. grapes	A few tinned or glacé
2 bananas	cherries
1 dessert pear	Angelica

97 Wipe the oranges and cut off the tops. Remove the pulp carefully without piercing the skin, and squeeze it in muslin to obtain the juice. Stone the grapes, slice the bananas and the pear, cut up the apricots and add the cherries. Pour the orange juice over. Notch the edges of the oranges with a pair of scissors and fill them with the prepared fruit. Soak the angelica and cut in narrow strips to form handles to the baskets. Chill and serve.

FRUIT DISHES

APPLE SNOW

4 sponge cakes	Juice of ½ a lemon
½ pint cup custard	2 egg whites
½ pint sieved stewed apples	Colouring, if liked
	Cherries and angelica
6 oz. caster sugar	to decorate

Cut the sponge cakes into thin slices, lay in a glass dish and pour the custard over; allow to soak. Put the apple pulp in a basin, and add the sugar and lemon juice. Whisk the egg whites until stiff, add to the apple mixture, add colouring if liked, and continue whisking until stiff and very fluffy. Pile on to the custard in the dish and serve at once, decorated with cherries, angelica, etc.

APPLE SWEET

1 lb. cooking apples	Red jelly or apricot jam
Sugar	½ pint sponge cake crumbs
Butter	Chopped pistachio nuts

Peel, core and slice the apples, and stew with a very little water, adding sugar to sweeten. Mash, and beat over gentle heat for a few minutes adding a knob of butter and a spoonful of red jelly or sieved apricot jam, and mix well. Put a layer of jelly or sieved jam in a deep dish and sprinkle with half the cake crumbs. Put the apple purée in the dish and smooth on top. Cover with a layer of jelly or jam and sprinkle with the rest of the cake crumbs. Decorate with chopped pistachio nuts. Chill, and serve with cream, if desired.

APRICOT FOOL

Rub some tinned apricots through a sieve, adding a small proportion of the syrup. To one cupful of the purée add one cupful of custard, sweeten to taste, and flavour with 1–2 drops essence of almonds. Keep in a cool place until wanted, then serve in custard glasses, with a little whipped sweetened cream on the top. Garnish with a piece of apricot, or some crystallised fruit or flowers.

Note: Other tinned fruits, including raspberries, etc., may be used in the same way.

BANANA MADELEINES

- 4 bananas
- 2 tbsps. raspberry jam
- 1½ tbsps. desiccated coconut
- Whipped cream

Cut the bananas in half slantwise, removing the tips to make them look like logs; brush with the jam and roll in the coconut. Serve with whipped cream.

BANANA TRIFLE

- 1 pint custard
- 3–4 sponge cakes
- Apricot jam
- 5 bananas
- 2 egg whites
- 2 oz. sugar
- ¼ pint cream
- Cherries, angelica or pistachio nuts

Make the custard. Split the sponge cakes in two, spread thickly with apricot jam, and arrange with the sliced bananas in layers in a dish. Pour on the hot custard and leave until cold. Immediately before serving, whip up the egg white as stiffly as possible, and fold in the sugar and the whipped cream. Pile in peaks on the top of the trifle and decorate with cherries, small pieces of angelica or chopped pistachio nuts.

If liked, sweetened whipped cream can be used alone, without the addition of the egg white.

BORDER OF PEARS

- 3 oz. rice
- 1 pint milk
- 1 oz. butter
- 3 oz. caster sugar
- Vanilla essence
- Pears
- 2 tbsps. whipped cream

First wash the rice, boil it, and when half cooked strain off the water and add the milk. Add the butter, and continue to cook until the rice is tender and has absorbed the milk. Add the sugar and the vanilla flavouring. Pour into a wet mould and set aside to get quite cold. When cold, turn out into the centre of a glass dish, border with pears, and garnish with cream. A border of apricots can be prepared in the same way.

CARAMELLED BANANAS

- 3 tbsps. sugar
- 2 tbsps. water
- 4 ripe bananas

Make a caramel by heating the sugar and water until just golden-brown. Arrange the bananas in the blazer of a chafing dish over hot water, and pour the caramel sauce over them. Cook slowly for about 10–15 minutes, basting them constantly with the caramel. Serve on a dish, with the remainder of the caramel poured over. Sponge fingers make an excellent accompaniment for this banana sweet.

CHERRY TRIFLE

- 6 oz. sugar
- 1 lb. cherries
- Sponge cakes or cake crumbs
- ½ pint custard
- Cherry jam or red-currant jelly
- 2 oz. sweet almonds
- ¼ pint cream
- Pistachio nuts

Make a syrup with the sugar and just sufficient water to cover the fruit; wash the cherries and stew them in the syrup. Split the sponge cakes 96
and spread them with cherry jam or red-currant jelly; if cake crumbs are used, a thin layer of jam may be spread on top of them. Pour the stewed cherries over and leave for about ½ hour for the sponge cakes to soak, then cover with the custard. Blanch the almonds and shred each into about three; sprinkle these on top of the custard, reserving a few for decoration. Whip the cream stiffly with a little castor sugar; pile in rocky heaps on top of the almonds. Sprinkle with chopped pistachio nuts, and stick a few almonds into the cream.

CHOCOLATE BANANAS

- ½ lb. couverture (covering) chocolate
- 6 bananas
- Walnuts and pistachio nuts
- Whipped cream

Cut up the chocolate finely and melt over gentle heat. Peel the bananas, slice them in half lengthwise and lay on a wire tray. Coat with the melted chocolate, and sprinkle with chopped walnuts and pistachio nuts. Serve with whipped cream.

CINNAMON APPLES

Peel some good eating apples and cut them in quarters. Melt some margarine in a chafing dish, and when it is foaming, put in the apple pieces, laying them flat over the bottom of the dish, not piled on each other, so that each piece may be turned. Cook them slowly, turning them with a fork so that they are done on all sides, until they are attractively browned and quite soft. Finally, sprinkle a little brown sugar and ground cinnamon over them, and cook for a few seconds longer.

CRÈME WAFLEN

- 1 large tin of strawberries or fresh strawberries
- ¼ lb. ratafias
- 2 oz. sugar
- Lemon juice
- Strawberry juice or sherry
- 1 large, flat, round sponge cake
- Apricot jam
- 9–10 wafer biscuits (or enough to put round the sponge) 98
- Some royal icing
- 1 pint cream

Put the strawberries (without the juice) into a basin with the ratafias, sugar and a good squeeze of lemon juice. Add sufficient juice or sherry to moisten and leave for 1 hour. Spread the side of the sponge cake with apricot jam and stand the wafer biscuits on end round the cake, joining them with a "rope" of icing. Tie a ribbon around the centre of the biscuits, allow the icing to harden. Whisk the cream, add the prepared fruit, etc., and fill the case with the mixture. Decorate to taste, and serve at once.

GOOSEBERRY FOOL

2 lb. gooseberries
¼ pint water
Sugar to taste
¼ pint custard
¼ pint cream

Top and tail the gooseberries, wash them and stew them in a saucepan with the water. Cook them gently until tender, then rub them through a fine sieve and add the sugar. Allow this purée to cool; add to it the custard and cream, and beat with a wire whisk for a few minutes. Serve in a glass or china bowl, or in small custard glasses, with a spoonful of whipped cream on the top.

Cream may replace all the custard, if available.

Other fruit fools—rhubarb, raspberry, blackberry, etc.—may be made in a similar way.

NOUGAT PUDDING

1 pint packet lemon jelly
¾ pint water
16 glacé cherries
10 marshmallows
6 ratafias
1 oz. almonds
½ oz. pistachio nuts
Juice of ½ lemon
½ pint cream
2 tbsps. sugar

99 Dissolve the jelly in the boiling water and allow to cool. Cut up the cherries, marshmallows, ratafias and the blanched almonds and pistachio nuts. When the jelly is cool, whisk until frothy, then stir in the prepared ingredients, lemon juice, half-whipped cream and sugar. Put the mixture into a wetted oblong tin; when set, slice with a knife dipped in hot water.

PEAR CONDÉ

4 medium-sized cooking pears (peeled)
2 oz. rice
1 pint milk
1 tbsp. sugar
1 tsp. gelatine
2 tbsps. water
4 tbsps. raspberry or other red jam

Cut the pears in half and remove the cores, then stew them until tender. Cook the rice in a double saucepan with the milk and sugar until it is creamy—about 1½–2 hours. Soak the gelatine in 2 tsps. of the water, and boil the jam with the remainder of the water, then add the soaked gelatine. Place a spoonful of rice in the bottom of each individual dish and arrange 2 pear halves on top. When the jam mixture is cool and of a syrupy consistency, pour it over the pears.

Apricot or Peach Condé may be made in the same way with fresh, bottled or canned fruit.

RASPBERRY FOOL

½ oz. arrowroot
½ pint milk
4½ oz. sugar, approx.
1 egg yolk
1 lb. raspberries

Blend the arrowroot with a little of the cold milk, boil the rest and pour on to the blended arrowroot, return to the saucepan, bring to the boil and simmer for 5 minutes. Cool a little and add ½ oz. sugar and the egg yolk. Prepare the fruit, put with the remaining sugar into a saucepan and cook over low heat, until mashed. Sieve and add to the custard, adding more sugar if required. Serve in glass dishes with whipped cream and decorate with blanched almonds, if desired.

STRAWBERRY GÂTEAU

Bake 2 sponge cakes in either square or round tins; alternatively, use 2 bought cakes. Spread the bottom cake with crushed strawberries and cream or mock cream. Using a large pastry cutter, cut a circle out of the centre of the second cake, and place the resulting "frame" on the bottom cake. Pile more crushed strawberries and cream in the centre, decorate with a few choice berries, and serve at once. The cream may be replaced by ice cream, if required.

SUMMER PUDDING

2 tbsps. water
5 oz. sugar
1 lb. raspberries and red-currants
4 oz. bread
Whipped cream or cold custard sauce

Put the water and sugar together and bring to the boil, add the fruit, and stew carefully, until tender. Line a pudding basin with bread, cut into thin slices, pour in the stewed fruit and cover with thin slices of bread: the basin should be full. Place a saucer with a weight on it on top of the pudding. Leave for several hours. Turn out, and serve with cream or custard sauce.

TIPSY CAKE

1 large sponge cake (baked in a fancy mould)
Sherry
Juice of 1 lemon
1 pint custard
Ratafia essence
2 oz. sweet almonds
Pistachio nuts or crystallised fruits

Place the sponge cake in a glass dish and soak

with sherry and the lemon juice. Make the custard, flavour it with ratafia essence and pour over the cake. Blanch the almonds, cut into spikes and stick these into the cake to resemble a porcupine's quills. Sprinkle with chopped pistachio nuts or decorate with crystallised fruits.

TRIFLE

8 small sponge cakes	$\frac{3}{4}$ pint good custard
Jam	$\frac{1}{2}$ pint cream
2–3 glasses of sherry (or fruit juice)	Sugar and flavouring
	2 oz. ratafias
6 macaroons	1 oz. shredded almonds

Split the sponge cakes and spread them with jam. Arrange them in a glass dish, pour the sherry or fruit juice over and soak for $\frac{1}{2}$ hour. Sprinkle the crushed macaroons over these and pour on the custard. Whip the cream, sweeten and flavour it, and spread or pipe it over the custard. Decorate with ratafias and almonds.

APRICOTS WITH BRANDY

Use a tin of apricots, or cook some fresh apricots in syrup, allowing them to cool in the latter case. Place the drained apricot halves in a shallow serving dish, cut side uppermost. To $\frac{1}{2}$ pint of the syrup add 3 tbsps. brandy. Fill the centres of the apricots with sweetened whipped cream, topped with glacé or cocktail cherries, and pour the brandy syrup round.

PEACHES IN LIQUEUR

Choose peaches which are not too ripe, plunge them into boiling water and leave for 3 minutes, then peel. Place the peaches in a serving bowl and cover with a light sugar syrup (see below), pouring it over whilst still hot; flavour with liqueur and leave to cool. Serve very cold, with fresh cream.

To make the light syrup, boil 1 pint water and 6 oz. sugar for 5 minutes, then skim. If using it with pears, etc., cook them in the syrup until soft. If desired, the syrup may be flavoured by adding a piece of vanilla pod while it is being boiled.

FLAMED PEARS IN PORT WINE

Carefully stew some prepared pears in a light syrup flavoured with port (to $\frac{1}{2}$ pint syrup allow $\frac{1}{4}$ pint port). Thicken the syrup with arrowroot (1 tsp. to $\frac{1}{4}$ pint), pour it over the pears, and just before serving, sprinkle with a little warmed brandy and ignite this.

PEARS IN RUM

Prepare this at least 1 hour before it is required. Peel some really ripe dessert pears and cut them in thin slices, place them neatly in a dish and sprinkle with caster sugar, ground cinnamon and rum. Keep in a cold place until required.

ICES AND ICED PUDDINGS

These are favourites with most people, and provide an easy way of lending a festive touch to a meal. The cook-hostess finds them particularly useful, for they can be prepared beforehand and kept in the refrigerator till the last minute.

Nowadays ice cream in a wide variety of flavours can be bought almost everywhere at reasonable cost, so recipes for quickly made and delicious sweets using block ice cream are given in this chapter. However, there are limits to the adaptations possible, and anyone possessing a refrigerator who cares to make her own ice cream can, by varying the basic recipes, achieve a much wider range of colourings and flavourings.

TYPES OF ICES

Broadly speaking, there are two main varieties of ices—Cream Ices and Water Ices—but these can be made up and served in a number of different ways, as described below.

Cream Ices

The word " cream " is often a misnomer, as it is rarely possible nowadays to serve an ice made entirely of cream—in most cases the cream is considerably thinned down with other ingredients, or a substitute is used. A very good mixture can be made with equal parts of cream and custard (egg custard, made with the yolks only, is the best), or a combination of cream and fruit purée. If necessary, the cream may be entirely omitted and replaced by unsweetened evaporated milk, home-made cream substitute, or a commercial preparation. Commercially prepared ice cream mixtures are also available, and these are quite satisfactory if used according to the manufacturer's instructions.

Although pure cream ices can be very simply flavoured, the economical mixtures require a rather more distinctive flavouring to make them interesting. The addition of about 1 tsp. gelatine to 1 pint mixture helps to prevent a granular consistency when the ice cream is made in a refrigerator; another method of improving the texture of refrigerator ice creams is to whip or stir the mixture during the freezing.

Water Ices

The foundation of these is a syrup made from sugar and water, to which is usually added some fruit juice or purée to give flavour; wine or liqueur is also frequently added. Water ices, including sherbets (see below) may be served alone or combined with cream ices, fresh fruits, fruit salad, etc.

Sherbets

A sherbet is a water ice in which whipped egg white is included, giving a fluffy texture.

Sorbets

A sorbet is a semi-frozen water ice, flavoured with liqueur; it is not moulded, but is served in a tall goblet or glass. Strictly speaking, it should precede the roast in a full dinner, the idea being that it clears the palate and prepares one for the courses to follow. Nowadays it is quite usual for a sorbet to be served as part of the sweet course, often combined with diced fruit or fruit salad.

Mousses

These are made from a very light frozen mixture—custard, cream, fruit purée or a combination of these. They usually contain stiffly beaten egg whites, which give them their lightness and fluffy texture. If a mixture containing gelatine is used, it may be chilled, instead of being frozen. Serve in individual glasses, or in dishes.

Parfaits

A parfait is usually understood to be a rather rich form of mousse—light because it contains whipped egg whites. Cream and fruit syrups are also included in the ingredients. Parfaits can be prepared quite well without being agitated during the freezing process, and for this reason they can be made successfully in the drawers of a refrigerator.

Sundaes

These are made from a combination of ice cream, fruit syrup, fruit, and often nuts, the ice cream being prepared in the usual way and the other ingredients added in the serving glass.

Bombes

This is the name given to an iced pudding, which is frozen in a bombe-shaped mould. Any ice cream mixture can be used, or a combination of several. The half-frozen mixture is packed into the mould and the lid secured; it is then buried in a mixture of ice and salt, or placed in a refrigerator. See recipe for full details. The bombe is usually dished on a round of sponge cake and decorated, more or less elaborately, with fruits, nuts, wafers, whipped cream, and spun sugar.

Iced puddings other than bombes can be made by using fancy moulds, similar to jelly moulds, but with tight-fitting lids, or the mixture may be moulded in small individual moulds made in the shape of fruits.

MAKING ICE CREAM

To obtain the best results, the mixture should be a reasonably rich one. It should be well sweetened—that is to say, it should taste slightly over-sweet at room temperature, otherwise it will be tasteless when frozen. Take care, however, not to add too much sugar, which would not only make the ices sickly, but would also prevent the mixture from freezing satisfactorily. The flavouring also is less pronounced when the ice is frozen, so the mixture should taste really well flavoured at room temperature. Any colouring required should be added sparingly, for pale and delicate shades are always the most attractive.

The most usual method of freezing home-made ice cream is in the refrigerator, though pail and other types of freezers are available. See below.

Using a Refrigerator

Set the dial at "maximum" or "quick freeze" about 1 hour before the mixture is ready, and prepare the mixture from a reliable recipe. For refrigerator freezing you will require a rich mixture containing cream and eggs, or else, if a plainer mixture is used, it will be necessary to include some gelatine, to help prevent the formation of ice crystals. Place the mixture in the ice trays and put these in the freezing compartment of the refrigerator. Stir the mixture at intervals of 20 minutes until it is half-frozen, then leave it undisturbed until it is sufficiently stiff. Alternatively—and this is the better method—allow it to semi-freeze, remove it to a cool bowl, and whisk it thoroughly with a rotary whisk; replace the mixture in the freezing compartment in the trays, and leave for 2–3 hours, until frozen hard. (The time required varies greatly according to the type of refrigerator and the mixture used.) Once the mixture is frozen sufficiently it can be left in the trays until required, but the temperature control can be turned to a less cold setting, to prevent over-freezing the ice and cooling the food compartment more than necessary.

Using a Pail-type Freezer

These freezers are still available, and make excellent ice cream, from both rich and economical recipes, since the continual rotation of the mixture will automatically break up any ice particles and give a very smooth texture. The initial cost of this type of freezer makes it less used to-day; it is, however, especially suitable for large-scale catering in hotels and guest houses, etc., for households which entertain frequently, and, of course, for those who do not possess a refrigerator.

Briefly, the pail freezer consists of a wooden bucket in which is placed a metal cylinder to hold the ice cream mixture. This cylinder is packed round with a freezing mixture, according to the manufacturer's instructions, and paddles are then inserted in the ice cream mixture and turned by hand for about 15–20 minutes. After "ripening" for 1–2 hours, the ice cream is ready to serve.

Other Freezers

There is now available a smaller edition of the above type of freezer, designed particularly for home use.

MOULDING AND SERVING ICES

To Mould Bombes and other Iced Puddings

Plain mixtures should be half-frozen, i.e., frozen to a mushy consistency, before being moulded. (Mousse and Parfait mixtures, being fluffy in texture, can be moulded when cold and then frozen—see below.) The preliminary freezing may be carried out in a refrigerator or bucket freezer; avoid freezing the mixture too hard, or it will not mould satisfactorily. Now, pack the half-frozen mixture into the chilled mould, filling this to the brim and taking care to leave no air spaces, and press on the lid.

(*a*) *To freeze in a refrigerator*, place the filled and covered mould in the coldest part of the freezing unit and leave undisturbed with the temperature control set to "coldest" for about 2 hours, or longer.

(*b*) *To freeze by burying in ice and salt*, either wind a piece of adhesive tape round the join of the lid or wrap the whole mould tightly in greased grease-proof paper; this is to prevent the salt seeping through to the mixture and spoiling the flavour. Bury the mould in a bowl or bucket of crushed ice and freezing salt, using four parts of ice to one part of salt. Cover with a sack or piece of old blanket and stand in a cool place for at least 2 hours, draining off the melted ice from time to time and adding more ice and salt if necessary.

To unmould the pudding, chill the serving dish and have ready any rounds of sponge cake, garnishes, and decorations required. If the mould has been buried in ice and salt, rinse it in cold water. Dip in tepid water for a few seconds, then remove any adhesive tape and the lid, and invert on to the serving dish or sponge cake base. Garnish, decorate, and serve at once.

Making Bombes with Two Mixtures

Iced puddings, such as Bombes, may be made with two mixtures—one as the lining and the other as the filling. Chill the mould, then line it to a thickness of ¾–1 inch with one of the frozen mixtures. Put the other frozen mixture in the centre and fill up with the first mixture. Cover, and freeze as for a plain Bombe. Good combinations of ice creams are: vanilla and raspberry, coffee and vanilla, chocolate and orange, and so on.

Neapolitan Ice Cream

This is made with three kinds of ice cream, usually white (vanilla), brown (chocolate), and pink (raspberry). Use a square or oblong mould and pack in the half-frozen mixtures in layers. Cover, and freeze as above.

Moulding Mousse or Parfait Mixtures

Make the mixture and, when cold, pour it into the mould. Cover with waxed paper, put on the lid, and freeze as above. If freezing in the refrigerator, leave 4 hours or even longer, according to the refrigerator. If the mould is to be buried, use a mixture of one part ice to one part freezing salt, and leave in this for a least 4 hours.

To Serve Ice Creams

Use an ice cream scoop to dish the ices, or, failing that, a soup spoon, dipping it in tepid water before scooping up the ice cream. Serve in any of the following ways:

1. On chilled ice cream plates (of glass or silver) or on saucers, with wafer biscuits.
2. In paper or china soufflé cases decorated with fresh or preserved fruits (cherries, angelica, etc.).
3. In silver sundae cups or stem glasses, topped with whipped cream and wafers.
4. As a sundae, with fruit, fruit syrup, nuts, etc.
5. As an iced meringue, putting a spoonful of ice cream between two meringue cases on a small plate. Pipe with whipped cream and decorate with fruits or nuts. If vanilla ice is used, a hot chocolate sauce is a good accompaniment.

ICE CREAMS

VANILLA ICE CREAM

½ pint milk
3 oz. sugar
2 egg yolks and 1 whole egg (or 2 whole eggs)
1 tsp. vanilla essence
½ pint cream

Heat the milk and sugar, and pour on to the beaten eggs, stirring. Return to the saucepan and cook over gentle heat, stirring continuously until the custard thickens. Remove from the heat, add vanilla essence, and allow to become cold. Fold in the half-whipped cream, and freeze.

APRICOT ICE CREAM

¼ pint apricot purée
2 tbsps. lemon juice
½ pint vanilla custard
Sugar to sweeten
½ pint cream

Stir the apricot purée and lemon juice into the custard and sweeten to taste. Fold the lightly-whipped cream into the mixture. Freeze.

BANANA ICE CREAM

¾ pint vanilla custard
3 bananas
Juice of 1 lemon
Sugar to sweeten
½ tsp. gelatine
1 tbsp. water
¼ pint cream

Make the custard in the usual way. Mash the

bananas and pass through a sieve. Add the lemon juice and banana purée to the custard, and sweeten to taste. Stir in the gelatine, dissolved in the water, then the half-whipped cream. When quite cold, freeze.

BURNT ALMOND FROZEN CREAM

4 oz. sugar	1 tsp. gelatine and 1 tbsp. cold water
¼ pint boiling water	¼ pint cream
½ pint unsweetened evaporated milk	2 oz. chopped roasted almonds
A pinch of salt	1 tsp. vanilla essence
1 egg	

Put 2 oz. of the sugar into a strong pan and heat very gently until golden-brown, then add the boiling water gradually and re-dissolve. Stir in the evaporated milk, salt, beaten egg, and remainder of the sugar. Cook in a double saucepan until thick, then add the gelatine dissolved in the 1 tbsp. water. When the mixture is quite cold, fold in the half-whipped cream, the nuts, and vanilla essence. Freeze.

CHOCOLATE ICE CREAM

2 oz. margarine	2 eggs
3 oz. caster sugar	½ pint evaporated milk (previously scalded) or cream
3 oz. chocolate	
Vanilla essence	

Cream together the margarine and sugar. Melt the chocolate and cool it slightly before adding it to the creamed mixture, together with essence to flavour and the beaten egg yolks. Whisk the evaporated milk until thick and creamy, fold it into the chocolate mixture and place in the freezing tray. Freeze to a mush, then take it out of the tray, beat well, and add the whisked egg whites. Freeze again until firm. Serve with ice cream wafers.

COFFEE ICE CREAM

¼ tsp. gelatine	¼ pint milk
1 pint strong coffee	Vanilla essence
4–5 oz. sugar	¼ pint cream

Dissolve the gelatine in a little of the coffee. Put the sugar, milk, and remaining coffee on to warm, add the dissolved gelatine, and vanilla essence to flavour, and allow to become cold. Fold in the half-whipped cream and freeze to a mush (coffee ice should not be frozen stiffly) and serve in cups.

GINGER ICE CREAM

¼ pint milk	1½ oz. preserved ginger
1 egg	1 tbsp. ginger syrup
2 oz. sugar	¼ pint cream

Make a custard from the milk, egg yolk, and sugar; cool. Add the ginger, cut into small pieces, the ginger syrup, whipped cream, and stiffly beaten egg white. Freeze.

GOOSEBERRY ICE CREAM

½ lb. gooseberries	½ pint custard
2 tbsps. water	¼ pint cream
3–4 oz. sugar	

Stew the gooseberries in the water until tender, then sieve, and add the sugar. Stir in the custard and, when the mixture is cold, fold in the half-whipped cream. Freeze.

ICED FRUIT PUDDING

3 egg yolks	½ pint fruit purée
4 oz. caster sugar	¼ pint cream
Juice of ½ lemon	1 egg white
1 tsp. gelatine	Fruit for garnishing
2 tbsps. water	1 oz. chopped browned almonds
A few drops of almond essence	1 oz. chopped angelica

Put the egg yolks and sugar into a saucepan and whisk over hot water until thick. Add the lemon juice and the gelatine, dissolved in the water over gentle heat. Stir in the almond essence, the fruit purée, the half-whipped cream, and, lastly, the stiffly beaten egg white. Freeze until nearly stiff, pack into a bombe mould, and bury in ice and salt for 3 hours. Turn out, garnish with fresh or tinned fruit, and sprinkle the almonds and angelica over the top of the pudding.

ICED PUDDING

4 oz. crystallised fruit	A round of Genoese sponge
1 tbsp. Maraschino	Jam
½ pint cream	Pistachio nuts
1 pint rich custard	Ice wafers
2–3 oz. sugar	Spun sugar (optional)
A squeeze of lemon juice	

Cut the crystallised fruits into small pieces (reserving a few for decoration) and soak in the Maraschino. Fold the half-whipped cream into the cold custard, sweeten, and add the lemon juice. Freeze, and when mushy, stir in the prepared fruit. Decorate an ice or bombe mould with the remaining fruit and fill up with the frozen mixture. Cover, and embed in a bucket of ice and freezing salt; leave for 3–4 hours. Unmould on to a round of Genoese sponge, the sides of which have been brushed with jam and rolled in chopped pistachio nuts. Put ice wafers around the sides, and decorate with spun sugar if desired.

LEMON ICE CREAM

½ pint milk
2 level tbsps. cornflour
Juice of 2 lemons
Grated rind of 1 lemon
4 oz. sugar
2 eggs
¼ pint cream

Warm the milk, and meanwhile blend the cornflour with the lemon juice and rind. Add the blended cornflour to the milk, and cook until thick; should the mixture curdle, just continue to cook it—as the milk thickens, the curdling will be rectified. Add the sugar and egg yolks, and leave to cool. Combine this mixture with the whipped cream, and freeze to a mush. Beat thoroughly, then add the whipped egg whites, and freeze till firm.

MACAROON ICE CREAM

8 macaroons
½ pint egg custard
2 oz. caster sugar
Vanilla essence
½ pint cream

Crush the macaroons and add to the custard, together with the sugar and vanilla essence, and fold in the half-whipped cream. Freeze.

PEACH CREAM SHERBET

Measure 2 cupfuls of mashed fresh peaches and cover with 1 cupful of sugar. Let stand for 3 hours, then fold in 1 cupful of cream, whipped stiff, and freeze. If tinned peaches are used, the amount of sugar should be reduced, and the syrup in the tin omitted.

PINEAPPLE EN SURPRISE

Choose a ripe pineapple with a pretty green top. Cut off the top and carefully scoop out the inside without destroying the skin. Chill the case. Sieve the pulp and add to it an equal amount of cream and custard, mixed with sugar to taste, and the strained juice of ½ a lemon. Freeze in the usual manner until the right consistency is obtained.

Stand the pineapple case in a round of sponge, and when it is time for serving fill up with the frozen mixture and replace the top. Decorate round the base with some glacé fruits or with small sprays of maidenhair fern.

PRALINE BOMBE

4 oz. loaf sugar
¼ pint hot water
4 egg yolks
4 oz. almond toffee
1 tsp. vanilla essence
A pinch of salt
½ pint cream
1 pint vanilla ice cream

Put the sugar into a saucepan and heat very gently until coffee-coloured, add the hot water, re-dissolve the caramel, and cool. Pour the dissolved caramel on to the beaten egg yolks, and cook in a double saucepan until thick. Cool, add the crushed toffee, the vanilla essence, and salt, and fold in the half-whipped cream. Freeze. Line a mould, or bombe mould, with the vanilla ice cream, fill with the praline ice cream, and pack in ice and salt. Leave for 3 hours.

PRALINE ICE CREAM

1 pint milk
4 egg yolks
3–4 oz. caster sugar
¼ pint cream
2 oz. French almond rock
A little almond essence

Heat the milk and pour on to the beaten egg yolks and sugar, stirring. Cook over gentle heat until the custard thickens, stirring continuously. Allow to become cold, add the half-whipped cream, crushed rock, and flavouring. Freeze.

STRAWBERRY CREAM SHERBET

To 2 cupfuls crushed strawberries, allow 1 cupful sugar and 1 cupful cream. Pick the strawberries and crush them uniformly with a stainless fork. Add sugar and stand the mixture in a cool place, or on ice, for at least 3 hours. Then whip the cream and fold it into the crushed fruit carefully. Pour into the freezer, and freeze in the usual manner until stiff enough to serve.

STRAWBERRY ICE CREAM

1 pint crushed strawberries
½ pint vanilla custard
2 oz. sugar
½ pint cream
Cochineal
A few strawberries to decorate

Add the strawberry pulp to the custard, then the sugar. Fold in the half-whipped cream and add a few drops of cochineal. Freeze, and serve with fresh strawberries to decorate.

PARFAITS AND MOUSSES

BUTTERSCOTCH PARFAIT

1 oz. butter
3 oz. Demerara sugar
¼ pint water
4 egg yolks
½ pint thick cream or unsweetened evaporated milk
Vanilla essence

Melt the butter and sugar in a saucepan, and boil for 1 minute. Add the water and heat until the butterscotch is dissolved. Put the egg yolks into a basin and whisk them until they are light and frothy. Add to the butterscotch mixture gradually and continue to cook lightly for about

5 minutes. Allow to cool, then fold in the whipped cream or whipped evaporated milk and vanilla essence. Freeze.

COFFEE PARFAIT

¼ lb. loaf sugar	½ pint cream
2 tbsps. water	¼ pint pineapple juice
1 egg white	Vanilla essence
¼ pint very strong coffee	A round of pineapple

Boil the sugar and water to 230° F., or to the thread stage (see chapter on Sweets). Pour in a thin stream on to the stiffly beaten egg white, beating all the time until thick. Cool, then stir in the coffee and the whipped cream. Freeze. Simmer the pineapple juice until reduced by half, add vanilla essence, cool, and pour a little over each serving of ice cream. Decorate with pieces of pineapple.

FRUIT PARFAIT

¼ lb. sugar	A few drops of lemon or other flavouring essence
2 tbsps. water	Fruit salad and whipped cream to serve
1 egg white	
½ pint cream	

Boil the sugar and water to 230° F. or until it makes a thread (see Sweet Making chapter). Pour in a thin stream on to the stiffly whisked egg white, beating meanwhile, and beat until thick. Cool, add the flavouring essence and the whipped cream, and freeze.

Meanwhile, prepare some fruit salad, then chill it. Divide over each serving of parfait, and top with whipped cream.

RASPBERRY PARFAIT

1 lb. fresh raspberries or 1 tin of raspberries	2 egg whites
	A pinch of salt
4 oz. sugar	Juice of ½ a lemon
4 tbsps. water	⅛ pint cream

If fresh raspberries are used, sprinkle over them about 1 dessertsp. caster sugar (this is in addition to the 4 oz. mentioned in the recipe); mash them with the sugar, leave for about ¼ hour, then rub through a sieve. If tinned raspberries are used, strain off the syrup and rub through a sieve; if necessary, add a little water or syrup to make up to ½ pint. Boil the sugar and water to 230° F., or until it makes a thread (see Sweet Making chapter). Beat the egg whites with a pinch of salt until they stand in peaks. Pour the hot syrup in a thin stream on to the egg whites, whisking, and continue to whisk until thick. Then allow to cool, stirring the mixture from time to time whilst it is cooling. When cold, fold in the raspberry purée, lemon juice, and whipped cream. Freeze in the usual way.

STRAWBERRY PARFAIT

¼ pint water	½ pint evaporated milk
¼ lb. strawberry jam	
1 egg white	Cochineal

Boil water and jam to 217° F., pour on to the stiffly beaten egg white, and beat well. When the mixture is cold, add the evaporated milk and a few drops of colouring, then freeze. Serve with fresh strawberries and fresh or synthetic whipped cream, if available.

BANANA AND MACAROON MOUSSE

4 bananas	1½ oz. macaroon crumbs
A pinch of salt	½ pint cream or evaporated milk
3–4 oz. caster sugar	
1½ tbsps. lemon juice	

Sieve the bananas, then add the salt, sugar, lemon juice, and macaroon crumbs, and mix thoroughly. Fold in the half-whipped cream (or evaporated milk), and freeze the mixture in the usual way.

BANANA AND PINEAPPLE MOUSSE

4 bananas	¼ pint custard
2–3 oz. caster sugar	¼ pint cream
¼ pint crushed pineapple	2 egg whites
Juice of 1 orange	

Mash the bananas with the sugar, mix with the pineapple and orange juice, and chill. Stir the fruit mixture into the custard, then fold in the half-whipped cream and stiffly beaten egg whites. Freeze.

CHESTNUT MOUSSE

½ lb. chestnuts	A few drops of vanilla essence
⅓ pint milk	
1 packet vanilla jelly	¼ pint cream
½ pint hot water	1 egg white
1 oz. sugar	Pistachio nuts

Blanch and peel the chestnuts, and cook in the milk until tender, if necessary adding a little water. Rub through a sieve. Dissolve the packet of jelly in the ½ pint of water and add to it the chestnut purée, with the sugar and essence. Stir occasionally until almost cold, fold in the lightly whipped cream and the stiffly whipped egg white. Put the mixture into a dish, and leave in a cold place to set. Decorate with slices of pistachio nut arranged in the form of shamrocks, and press chopped pistachio nuts against the sides.

RASPBERRY MOUSSE

1 large tin of raspberries
1 oz. caster sugar
¼ pint cream or evaporated milk
½ oz. gelatine
2 tbsps. water or raspberry juice
2 egg whites
Whipped cream to decorate

Strain the raspberries and sieve them, then add the sugar and whipped cream. Dissolve the gelatine in the water over gentle heat and add to the raspberry mixture. Whip the egg whites very stiffly and fold into the prepared mixture. Pour into a dish, and leave in a cold place to set. Pipe with whipped cream.

STRAWBERRY MOUSSE

⅓ pint strawberry purée
Juice of ½ a lemon
½ pint cream
2 egg whites
2 oz. caster sugar
A pinch of salt

Use fresh or tinned strawberries and rub through a sieve to make the purée. Add the lemon juice. Whip the cream (for economy, use evaporated milk instead of cream, or a half-and-half mixture if preferred) and whip up the egg whites stiffly. Blend all the ingredients together. Freeze.

WATER ICES AND FRUIT SHERBETS

(*Recipes marked * are not suitable for preparing in a refrigerator*)

SYRUP FOR WATER ICES

½ lb. loaf sugar
1 pint water
Juice of ½ lemon

Put the sugar and water into a lined saucepan, bring them slowly to the boil, and then boil gently for 10 minutes without stirring. Add the lemon juice, and strain through muslin before use.

ORANGE WATER ICE

Rind of 2 oranges
Rind of 2 lemons
1 pint syrup for ices (see above)
¾ pint orange juice
¼ pint lemon juice
2 egg whites
Glacé orange to decorate

Grate the rind of the oranges and lemons, put into a basin, pour the boiling hot syrup over it, and leave until cold. Add the fruit juice, and strain. Half freeze the mixture, then fold in the egg whites, beaten to a stiff froth, and continue the freezing until stiff. Serve in cups or in paper soufflé cases, and decorate with small slices of glacé orange.

Other kinds of fruit juice can also be used.

LEMON WATER ICE *

4 lemons
1 lb. loaf sugar
2 pints water

Wash the lemons and pare off the rind. Put the sugar, lemon rind, and water into a saucepan, bring to the boil, and boil for 10 minutes. Cool, add the lemon juice, and freeze.

RASPBERRY WATER ICE *

1 pint raspberry purée
1 pint syrup for ices (see above)
Juice of 1 lemon
A few drops of carmine
Fresh raspberries, if obtainable

Use either fresh or tinned raspberries to make the purée. Add to it the syrup, the strained lemon juice, and, if necessary, a few drops of carmine to improve the colour. Freeze until sufficiently stiff, then serve in small glasses, and decorate with some of the fresh fruit if possible. Or, a glass may be half-filled with raspberries and then filled up with the raspberry ice.

RASPBERRY AND RED-CURRANT WATER ICE *

½ lb. loaf sugar
1 pint water
Juice of ½ lemon
½ pint raspberry purée
½ pint red-currant purée
Fresh raspberries

Bring the sugar and water to the boil, and boil for 10 minutes. Add the lemon juice, and strain. Prepare the purées by cooking the fruits for a short time with a very little water, and then rubbing through a hair sieve. Combine the purée and syrup. Allow to become quite cold; freeze. Serve in ice cups and decorate with fresh raspberries.

APPLE SHERBET

½ lb. stewed apples
¼ pint water
3 oz. sugar
Cochineal
1 wineglassful cherry brandy
1 egg white
Sweetened cranberry juice

Sieve the apples, add the water, sugar, brandy, and sufficient cochineal to make a pale pink. Fold in the stiffly beaten egg white, then freeze, and serve in glasses with 1 tbsp. of cranberry juice over each portion.

APRICOT AND GRAPEFRUIT SHERBET

½ pint water
½ lb. sugar
¾ pint grapefruit juice
1 dessertsp. lemon juice
½ pint apricot purée
1 egg white
2 tbsps. sugar
Fruit to garnish

Put the water and ½ lb. sugar into a perfectly clean saucepan, dissolve slowly, then boil for 5 minutes. Cool thoroughly. Meanwhile, extract the required quantity of juice from fresh grapefruit and add it to the lemon juice and apricot purée, which has been made by rubbing cooked or tinned apricots through a sieve. Mix all with the syrup, pour into the freezer and partially freeze. When the sherbet is of the consistency of a soft cream, open the freezer and fold into the mixture the egg white, beaten to a stiff froth, with the sugar added. Then continue the freezing until stiff enough to serve. Small pieces of brightly-coloured fruit may be used as a garnish.

Note : As the acidity of fruit varies, it is better to taste a sherbet before freezing, to make sure that it is of the proper sweetness to suit individual taste.

ORANGE FRUIT SHERBET

½ lb. sugar	2 tbsps. lemon juice
¾ pint water	¼ pint cream
1 pint orange pulp and juice	1 egg white

Boil the sugar and water for 10 minutes, skim, and cool. Cut some oranges in halves crosswise and carefully remove the pulp and juice, discarding the seeds and hard centres. Measure the quantity required, add the lemon juice and combine with the cold syrup. Freeze the mixture until it is of a soft creamy consistency. Whip the cream and whip also the egg white until stiff, and fold both into the sherbet. Freeze until stiff enough to serve.

STRAWBERRY SHERBET

¾ lb. sugar	½ pint orange juice
1 pint water	Juice of ½ a lemon
1 tsp. powdered gelatine	1 egg white
1 pint strawberry purée	2 tbsps. sugar

Boil ¾ lb. of sugar and the water 10 minutes, and skim if necessary. Dissolve the gelatine in a very little water, stir it into the hot syrup, and set aside to cool.

To make the strawberry purée, pick over the berries and press through a sieve, and then measure. Add the cold syrup to the fruit purée, together with the orange and lemon juice. Half freeze, then add the whipped egg white and the sugar. Freeze until stiff enough, then serve garnished with fresh strawberries.

Raspberry Fruit Sherbet may be prepared in the same way.

SUNDAES AND FROZEN DESSERTS

A block of bought ice cream can be " dressed up " in many ways, as suggested in the recipes below. Buy the ice cream only a short time before it is to be used : if you have no refrigerator, it can be kept for an hour or two by wrapping it in layers of newspaper immediately it is purchased, and putting it in the coolest place available.

The special sauces given at the end of the Sauces chapter can be used with many of these ice cream sweets.

BANANA SPLIT

Vanilla ice cream	1 oz. chopped blanched nuts
4 bananas	Sponge fingers or wafer biscuits
4 tbsps. Melba sauce or raspberry purée	

Put a spoonful of ice cream in the bottom of each dish or saucer. Split the bananas in half lengthwise and place two halves in each dish. Put another spoonful of ice cream on top, pour 1 tbsp. Melba sauce (see Peach Melba) or raspberry purée over, and sprinkle with chopped nuts. Serve immediately, with the sponge fingers or wafer biscuits.

FRUIT AND NUT SUNDAE

Put a spoonful of any ice cream mixture into a sundae glass. Pour over some flavoured fruit syrup, cover with whipped cream, and sprinkle with chopped nuts.

Sundaes may be made in a variety of ways by 101
changing either the frozen mixture or the sauce that is poured round. A strawberry, caramel, or chocolate sauce may be used instead of fruit syrup. Marshmallow cream may be substituted for real cream.

PEACH MELBA

½ pint peach syrup	Carmine colouring
8 round sponge cakes	A block of ice cream
2–3 tbsps. raspberry jam	8 half-peaches
1 tsp. gelatine	Whipped cream
1 tsp. lemon juice	Chopped nuts

Boil the peach syrup for a few minutes, and 102
pour a little over each sponge cake. Put the jam, gelatine, and lemon juice into a basin with the remaining syrup, heat gently over a pan of hot water to dissolve the gelatine, then strain the mixture and tint it with carmine. Put a round of cake in each sundae dish, cover with a spoonful of ice cream, then add a half-peach, and pour some of the Melba sauce over. Top with whipped cream and chopped nuts.

PEAR MELBA

This may be made with tinned pears in a similar way to Peach Melba, or as follows :

put a spoonful of vanilla ice cream into each glass or cup and lay half a tinned pear on top; pour over 2 tbsps. strawberry or raspberry purée, and cap with whipped cream.

BAKED ALASKA

1 sponge cake	¼ tsp. cream of tartar
Ice cream	4 oz. caster sugar
2 egg whites	

Scoop out the centre of the sponge cake, leaving the base about ½–1 inch thick, and pile
103 some stiffly frozen ice cream in the centre. Whisk the egg whites with the cream of tartar until stiff, and fold in the sugar. Place the cake on some greaseproof paper laid on a baking sheet, or put it in a fireproof dish. Coat the outside of the cake and the ice cream with the meringue mixture, making sure that there is no cake or ice cream showing. Now put the sweet into a very hot oven and leave for 4–5 minutes, until the meringue is lightly coloured.

SURPRISE SOUFFLÉ OMELETTE

2 eggs	½ pint stiffly frozen ice cream
3 oz. caster sugar	
1 round of sponge cake	Sugar for dredging

Separate the eggs. Beat the yolks and sugar together, then whisk the whites very stiffly, and stir lightly into the yolks. Hollow the centre of the cake, and pile up the ice cream in this. Cover with the omelette mixture, dredge thickly with sugar, and place in a very hot oven for a few minutes, until lightly set and browned, then serve at once.

CHOCOLATE REFRIGERATOR CAKE

1 sponge cake	1 tsp. vanilla essence
4 oz. sweetened chocolate	¼ tsp. salt
4 tbsps. milk	½ pint cream or mock cream
104 4 oz. sugar	
4 egg yolks	Chocolate vermicelli

Line a 6-inch cake tin with greaseproof or waxed paper, and cover the sides and bottom with thin slices of sponge cake. Melt the chocolate over hot water and add the milk. Blend 3½ oz. of the sugar with the egg yolks and beat gently over hot water until creamy; add the chocolate mixture, and cook together. When the mixture is thickening, add the vanilla essence and salt. Fill the tin with layers of the chocolate mixture and slices of the sponge cake, covering the top with cake. Chill for 12 hours. Turn out, and mask with the cream, whipped with the remaining ½ oz. sugar. Sprinkle the top and sides of the cake with chocolate vermicelli.

ICE CREAM CAKE

Line a refrigerator tray with waxed paper. Place thin slices of sponge cake over the bottom of the tray, spread with sieved apricot jam and then cover with a slice cut from a block of ice cream. Add two more layers of cake, jam, and ice cream, finishing with a layer of cake. Cover with waxed paper, put the tray into the ice compartment, and leave until the "cake" is firm—about 1–2 hours. Turn out, and serve with whipped cream.

LEMON REFRIGERATOR CAKE

Sponge cakes	¼ pint water
Sherry	1 egg
Juice of 2 lemons	¼ oz. gelatine
4 oz. sugar	2–4 oz. cream
Rind of 1 lemon	

Cover the bottom of an oblong tin with halved sponge cakes, and sprinkle with a little sherry. Heat together the lemon juice, sugar, grated lemon rind, and water. Stir in the beaten egg yolk, and cook for a few minutes without boiling. Dissolve the gelatine in a little water and add to the lemon mixture, then leave until just setting. Fold in the stiffly beaten egg white and the unwhipped cream, and pour half the mixture over the sponge cakes. Arrange another layer of sponge cake on top and cover with the remaining lemon mixture; leave to set.

AFTER-DINNER AND COCKTAIL SAVOURIES

SAVOURIES

A savoury to be served as the final course of a dinner or lunch should be little and good—a tasty morsel to round off the meal and leave a good impression on those who have partaken of it. So it should be small, well-flavoured and daintily garnished and, if it is to be a hot savoury, it must be served piping hot.

Savoury dishes intended to form the main course at lunch or supper, or to serve at dinner in place of the sweet course, can afford to be more substantial. For these occasions, many of the dishes described in this section are suitable (larger portions being served, of course), while there are many others given in the chapters on Cheese, Eggs, and so on.

Cheese is a favourite ingredient for the savoury. Where it is the principal ingredient, and a good "cheesy" flavour is required (in such dishes as Welsh rarebit, cheese fondue, and so on), an ordinary cooking cheese, such as Cheddar, can be used. Parmesan cheese, being very tasty (and incidentally very hard) is particularly suitable when a small amount of concentrated flavour is required—for making cheese pastry, flavouring a filling, or sprinkling on the top of savouries. On the other hand, a mild cream cheese forms a good basis for a savoury filling, and can be varied by flavouring with ingredients such as chopped chives or celery, paprika and so on.

Good savouries can be made from chicken, veal, sweetbreads, etc., but being very delicate in flavour, these should not be mixed with highly flavoured ingredients, which are likely to overpower them.

Foie gras, tongue, chicken livers, and smoked meats such as bacon and ham, make very tasty savouries.

Shell fish, smoked fish (kipper, bloater, haddock), and preserved fish such as sardines and anchovies, being very well-flavoured, are also useful ingredients for savouries.

Olives, capers, gherkins, chutney, and the like are often added to give piquancy, where flavour is lacking.

Serving Savouries

There are many ways of presenting these small savouries, according to the particular occasion.

Pastry Biscuit Savouries: Pastry (cheese, shortcrust, or puff are all suitable), rolled thinly, then stamped into rounds or cut into fingers or other fancy shapes, pricked and baked, makes a useful foundation. When cold, the biscuits may be spread with a suitable mixture and decorated, or sandwiched together with a savoury filling. When making pastry, it is a good idea to bake a few such biscuits to have in readiness for an emergency. Keep them in an airtight tin and warm through to crisp them before filling and decorating. When time is short, water biscuits or small plain or cheese biscuits can take the place of pastry for this type of savoury—keep a supply in reserve.

Bouchées, Boats, Tartlets, etc.: Pastry is also used for making bouchées and similar savouries. The cases should be very thin and the filling very tasty. The cases may be made in advance, but should not be filled until shortly before they are to be served, as once moistened, the pastry soon becomes soggy.

Many delicious savouries can be made in a few moments with trimmings of pastry: the Anchovy Puffs and Twists given in this chapter are good examples.

Canapés and Croûtes: Savouries served on rounds or fingers of buttered toast or fried bread form another large group. The bread should be thinly cut and should be fried in butter rather than in frying fat, especially if the canapés are to be served cold.

Savouries with Choux Pastry: Choux pastry is used to make savoury éclairs. These are rather smaller than the sweet variety, and if very light and crisp, and filled with a well-flavoured cream filling, they form a delicious savoury. They can also be made in the form of miniature cream buns. Another popular choux pastry savoury is cheese aigrettes, which are served hot; the pastry is flavoured with cheese and is fried instead of being baked.

Cassolettes: Butter cassolettes make excellent cases for a savoury filling and are particularly suitable for those who do not like pastry. They are made by coating butter balls with egg and breadcrumbs, frying them, then removing the excess butter from the centre and filling with a savoury mixture: see the recipes in this chapter.

COCKTAIL SNACKS

Savouries to serve with cocktails are intended to stimulate and not to cloy the appetite, so they should be piquant rather than satisfying. Since they are to be eaten in the fingers, they should be small and confined to varieties that can be taken without messing the hands or that are suitable to serve on cocktail sticks.

Many of the most popular cocktail savouries are served cold, but it is a good idea to offer at least one hot savoury—Chipolata sausages, served piping hot on cocktail sticks, are always welcome, and such savouries as haddock balls (also served on sticks) or some well-flavoured canapés, are other suggestions. A list of appetisers and savouries to serve with cocktails is given below: the detailed recipes are given in this chapter, or elsewhere in the book.

Cheese Straws: They will keep in good condition for several days, so you can make a supply of them and keep them handy for emergencies. Store them in a tin and warm through to crisp them before serving.

Cheese Biscuits: These may be varied almost endlessly by cutting them in different shapes and sizes, and either spreading them or sandwiching them together with various fillings. Recipes are given in this section.

Savoury Rolls: Split very tiny finger rolls, such as bridge rolls, and spread with a savoury filling. Failing rolls, you can cut fingers or fancy rounds of bread and butter and spread these with the filling.

Savoury Boats or Bouchées: Use very tiny boat-shaped tins or bouchée tins to make the cases, and fill with a good savoury filling. Garnish attractively, and serve either hot or cold. See recipes in this section.

Canapés, to serve as cocktail savouries, should be very small and dainty, and may be served hot or cold. If hot, the croûtes may be fried, but for cold canapés, toast is perhaps more suitable. See recipes in this section.

Chipolata Sausages: Grill, fry, or bake them, place a cocktail stick in each sausage and serve very hot. If you like, you can spread them with a little made mustard before serving, or hand mustard with them.

Popcorn provides a tasty accompaniment to cocktails. The popcorn seeds are obtainable in packets or tins and are very quick and easy to prepare according to the directions given.

Savoury Balls: Haddock balls or similar fried savouries are usually enjoyed. Make them small and serve very hot on cocktail sticks. Garnish the dish with parsley or watercress.

Radishes: Wash carefully and cut off any roots, but leave about an inch of the stems to hold them by. Or you can cut the radishes into "rosettes" or "lilies." See that salt is handy—you can arrange the radishes on a dish or platter with a salt cellar in the centre.

Celery goes well with cocktails. Serve it plain, with salt handy, or cut the stalks into lengths and fill with a savoury cream cheese.

Stuffed Prunes: Stone the prunes (or French plums) and stuff them with salted nuts or other savoury filling. As they tend to be sticky, serve them on cocktail sticks.

Olives: Both Spanish and French olives are suitable for serving with cocktails, so are stuffed olives. The latter may be bought ready prepared, or you can stone the olives yourself and fill with a good savoury filling.

Salted Almonds or Brazil Nuts are good as cocktail savouries and are very simply prepared.

Potato Crisps are always popular. Heat them through to make sure they are really crisp, and sprinkle liberally with salt before serving.

SAVOURIES MADE WITH PASTRY OR BISCUITS

ANCHOVY PUFFS

6 anchovies	1 dessertsp. grated Parmesan cheese
Puff pastry trimmings	A little watercress
Egg for glazing	

Skin and fillet the anchovies. Roll the pastry out thinly and cut into 12 circles with a plain 1½-inch cutter. Glaze half of each circle with egg and lay half an anchovy, folded, on each circle. Fold the pastry over and press the edges firmly together. Place on a slightly damped baking tray, glaze with egg and sprinkle with grated cheese. Bake in a hot oven (450° F., mark 8) for 10–15 minutes, until well-risen and golden-brown. Serve hot on a dish paper, garnished with watercress.

ANCHOVY TWISTS

Make some cheese pastry and roll it out until it is about ⅛ inch thick, then cut in strips 2½ inches long by ½ inch wide. Prepare thin fillets of anchovy of the same length and place one on each strip of pastry, pinching the two together at the top tightly (a little beaten egg can be used, if necessary, to make them stick), then twist them several times. Squeeze the two ends tightly together at the other end. Brush each over with a little beaten egg, and cook in a moderately hot oven (425° F., mark 7) until crisp and golden-brown—10–15 minutes.

ASPARAGUS BISCUITS

On small rounds of cheese pastry, spread some cream cheese softened with a little cream. On each lay three asparagus tips and dust with coralline pepper.

CELERY CREAMS

¼ pint cream	Cheese pastry biscuits —about 1 dozen
2 tbsps. chopped celery	Paprika pepper
Salt	Celery heart leaves
Cayenne pepper	

Whip the cream fairly stiffly and stir in the chopped celery and seasoning to taste. Pile on to the savoury biscuits, garnish with paprika pepper and decorate with tiny sprigs of the celery heart leaves. Serve these creams very cold.

Chopped walnuts may be used in place of celery for a change.

CHEESE AIGRETTES

1 oz. butter	2 egg yolks
¼ pint water	1 egg white
2 oz. flour	Cayenne and salt
2 oz. grated cheese	

Put the butter and water into a small saucepan and bring them to the boil. Add the flour and beat until the mixture draws away cleanly from the sides of the pan. Then draw the saucepan to the side of the stove, and add the cheese, egg, and seasoning to taste. Beat thoroughly and turn on to a plate to cool. When required, drop small pieces into a saucepan of hot fat and fry to a golden-brown. Drain on paper, and serve hot, sprinkled with more cheese if liked.

CHEESE AND BACON SAVOURY

6 rashers bacon	Seasoning
3 oz. cream cheese	Shortcrust pastry

Trim each rasher and cut in half. Cream the cheese until it is quite soft, add salt and pepper to taste, then spread the bacon with the mixture and roll it up. Roll out some shortcrust pastry 106
very thinly and enclose each roll of bacon in pastry, pressing the edges well together. Bake these in a hot oven (450° F., mark 8) for 15–20 minutes, and serve at once.

If a cold dish is preferred, slices of cold ham should be substituted for the bacon.

CHEESE AND CELERY STRAWS

2 oz. butter or margarine	Salt and cayenne pepper
2 oz. flour	1 large tbsp. finely chopped celery heart
2 oz. breadcrumbs	A little egg yolk
2 oz. finely grated cheese	

Rub the fat into the flour and breadcrumbs. Add the cheese, pinch of salt and a few grains of cayenne pepper. Mix with the finely chopped celery and egg yolk (if necessary) to make a stiff paste. Roll out ¼ inch thick and cut into fingers or straws. Place on a greased baking sheet, and bake in a moderately hot oven (425° F., mark 7) until crisp—that is, for 10–15 minutes. Serve either hot or cold.

CHEESE STRAWS

Make 3 oz. cheese pastry and roll out into a 105
strip about 4 inches in width, trim the edges, and cut across into narrow straws. Place on a

greased tin, and out of the scraps cut a few rings. Bake in a moderately hot oven (425° F., mark 7) until golden-brown and firm to the touch. Place a few straws through each ring, and serve them either hot or cold.

CHEESE D'ARTOIS

$\frac{1}{4}$ lb. puff pastry	Salt, pepper, and cayenne
1 egg	1 oz. butter
2 oz. Parmesan cheese	Watercress

Roll the pastry thinly and divide equally into two. Beat the egg and add to the grated
105 cheese, salt, pepper, and cayenne. Add the butter (melted). Spread this mixture on one half of the pastry. Wet the edges and place the other half over it. Press the edges together, brush over with a little beaten egg and mark across in fingers. Bake in a hot oven (450° F., mark 8) for about 15 minutes, until golden-brown on top and underneath, then divide up. Serve hot or cold, garnished with watercress.

CHEESE AND OTHER SAVOURY ÉCLAIRS

Choux pastry	Anchovy paste
Cream cheese	

Make the choux pastry, put it into a bag with a small, plain, round pipe ($\frac{1}{4}$ inch diameter), and force on to a greased and paper-lined baking sheet; only about $1\frac{1}{2}$ inches should be piped out, and all should be of uniform size. Bake in a hot oven (450° F., mark 8) until the éclairs are light, well puffed out, and golden-brown.

When cold, fill with cream cheese to which a little anchovy paste has been blended. If preferred, a rich cheese sauce can be used, made with 1 oz. butter, 1 oz. flour, $\frac{1}{4}$ pint milk, $1\frac{1}{2}$ oz. grated cheese, salt, pepper, and made mustard. Alternatively, fill with cream, whipped and with grated Parmesan folded into it.

Other suggestions for fillings are caviare, with a squeeze of lemon juice; hard-boiled egg yolk, pounded with a little anchovy paste; pounded kippers, blended with butter and seasonings; pounded game, chicken, or veal with butter; rich savoury sauce containing chopped ham and chicken, oysters, etc.

CHOPPED TONGUE AND TOMATO SAVOURY

6 tbsps. chopped tongue	Cheese biscuits
Pepper and salt	Cocktail onions
2 tbsps. tomato ketchup	

Season the chopped tongue with pepper and salt and add the tomato ketchup. Pile on cheese biscuits, and decorate each with a cocktail onion.

CRAB FINGERS

On small fingers of pastry or toast (or cheese biscuits), spread flaked crab mixed with salad dressing, and garnish with finely chopped parsley.

CREAM CHEESE PATTIES

Rich flaky or shortcrust pastry	Seasonings
Cream cheese	Paprika pepper

Roll the pastry to about $\frac{1}{8}$ inch in thickness, and cut into circles, using a small round cutter. Remove the centres from half of the circles, forming rings. Bake in a hot oven (450° F., mark 8) from 6–10 minutes, until golden-brown, then cool. Beat the cream cheese until it is easy to spread, and season to taste. Spread the rounds of pastry with the cheese and place a pastry ring on top, sprinkled with paprika pepper.

CREAM CHEESE TARTLETS

3–4 oz. shortcrust pastry	1 egg
1 oz. cream cheese	Pepper and salt
$\frac{1}{4}$ pint thick white sauce	1 oz. Parmesan cheese
$\frac{1}{2}$ tsp. piquant sauce	Paprika pepper

Line a number of small tartlet tins with the shortcrust pastry. Beat the cream cheese to a creamy consistency with a fork, and add the white sauce, piquant sauce, yolk of egg, and a little pepper and salt. Beat the white of egg until stiff, and fold gently into the mixture. Three-parts fill the lined tartlet tins with the mixture, and bake in a moderately hot oven (425° F., mark 7) for about 15–20 minutes. Before serving, sprinkle a little grated Parmesan cheese on top and dust with paprika pepper.

HAM ROLLS

Spread some thin slices of ham with cream cheese and roll each round a strip of gherkin. Serve on pastry fingers, finger biscuits or strips of bread and butter.

NUT AND OLIVE PATTIES

$\frac{1}{2}$ lb. puff pastry	$\frac{1}{4}$ tsp. vegetable extract
Beaten egg	Salt and pepper
$\frac{3}{4}$ oz. butter	2 oz. walnuts
$\frac{1}{2}$ pint milk	6 olives
$\frac{3}{4}$ oz. flour	

Roll out the pastry $\frac{1}{2}$ inch thick and stamp out patty cases with a 2-inch cutter. Stamp out lids with a 1-inch cutter. Brush lightly with beaten egg and bake in a hot oven (450° F., mark 8) for 15 minutes. Scoop out the uncooked paste and put the patties into the oven to dry off. Meanwhile, make a sauce from the butter, milk, and flour, flavour with vegetable extract, then season and add the chopped nuts and chopped olives. Reheat. Fill the patty cases with the mixture and serve the patties hot or cold, as preferred.

PRAWN BOUCHÉES

¼ lb. rich shortcrust pastry
¼ pint prawns
4 olives
¼ pint aspic jelly
Parsley

Roll out the pastry thinly, line small bouchée tins with it, and bake "blind." Pick the prawns, reserving the heads, chop them up, and stone and chop the olives. When the tartlets are cold, put a little chopped olive and prawn at
5 the bottom of each, and cover with a layer of aspic jelly when it is very cold, and just starting to set. Place a prawn head in the centre of each before the jelly has quite set. Garnish with a little chopped parsley or tiny sprigs of parsley.

Savoury tarts of this kind should be prepared only just before they are to be eaten, so that the pastry is crisp and fresh.

SALMON SLICES

Shortcrust pastry or cheese pastry
2 oz. cooked salmon
Pepper and a little salt if required
Mayonnaise

Roll out the pastry thinly, cut into fingers about 3 inches long and ½ inch wide, and bake in a moderately hot oven (400° F., mark 6) until golden-brown. Flake the salmon, add the pepper, salt, and mayonnaise and blend well. Spread on the fingers of pastry and serve cold.

TOMATO BONNE-BOUCHES

2 oz. butter
1 hard-boiled egg
1 tbsp. chutney
Cayenne pepper
Salt
8–9 rounds of pastry or small biscuits
3–4 firm, red tomatoes
Watercress or chervil to garnish

First prepare the savoury butter by pounding together the butter, chopped hard-boiled egg, chopped chutney, cayenne, and a little salt. When thoroughly mixed, rub through a fine sieve. Spread rounds of cheese pastry or small biscuits with this butter, and put the remainder into a forcing bag with a fancy pipe. For each biscuit, prepare a section of bright red tomato free from skin. Fix it on to the biscuit with some of the butter and pipe round in a pretty design. Garnish with leaves of watercress or sprigs of chervil, and serve very cold.

YORK FINGERS

Cheese
Trimmings of puff or shortcrust pastry
Beaten egg
A little grated cheese
2 oz. minced ham
Horseradish sauce
Coralline pepper

Cut the cheese in very thin flakes and roll out the pastry very thinly. Put the flakes of cheese on top of the pastry, fold it over, and roll out again. Cut into oblongs or fingers, about ½ inch wide and 3 inches long, brush with beaten egg, sprinkle with a little finely grated cheese, and bake in a hot oven (450° F., mark 8) until golden-brown. When cold, mix the ham with the horseradish sauce and place on the fingers. Sprinkle with coralline pepper.

CROÛTES AND CANAPÉS

ANCHOVY TOASTS

4–5 fillets of anchovy
½ oz. butter
Pepper
Ground mace and nutmeg
Toast

Shred the fillets as finely as possible; melt the butter and add the shredded fish, pepper, powdered mace and nutmeg to it. Pound well and rub through a sieve. Cut fingers of toast and spread the anchovy paste on them.

ANCHOVY AND EGG TOASTS

3–4 anchovies
2 hard-boiled eggs
Buttered toast
Egg white or parsley

Pound the anchovies with the yolks of the hard-boiled eggs; if preferred, anchovy paste can be used instead of the fillets. Have ready thin, even-sized fingers or croûtes of hot buttered toast, spread with the anchovy butter, and garnish with chopped egg white or parsley.

ANGELS ON HORSEBACK

8 croûtons of bread, about 2 inches in diameter
4 rashers of streaky bacon
8 oysters
A little cayenne pepper
Lemon juice
Watercress

Fry the croûtons until pale golden-brown in deep fat or butter. Cut each rasher in half, put an oyster in the middle of each, and sprinkle with cayenne pepper and a squeeze of lemon juice. Roll the bacon round the oyster; if necessary, spike each with a cocktail stick or small wooden skewer, to keep rolled. Place one roll on top of each croûton, put in a moderately hot oven (400° F., mark 6) until the bacon is lightly cooked—about 15 minutes. Garnish with a little watercress.

BANANA BONNE-BOUCHES

106 2 bananas
8 fingers of thin toast
Cayenne and salt
Parsley
Lemon fans

For the Devilled Butter

⅛ tsp. cayenne pepper
A pinch of ground ginger
A pinch of curry powder
1 oz. butter

Cut the bananas in half, then split them. Trim to even lengths, and prepare slices of thin bread long enough and wide enough for the bananas. Toast these and spread with the devilled butter, which is prepared by beating the pepper, ginger, and curry powder into the butter. Spread the bananas with the devilled butter and grill them, then lift on to the toast and sprinkle a little cayenne and salt on top. Garnish the dish with parsley and lemon fans. Serve hot.

BANANAS ON HORSEBACK

4 pieces of bread
1 egg
1 teacupful milk
Pepper
Salt
Nutmeg
4 small bananas
Fat for frying

Cut half a slice of bread ¼ inch in thickness for each banana and trim off the crusts. Lay the pieces in a deep plate, pour over them the well-beaten egg and the milk. Season with pepper, salt, and a very little grated nutmeg. Let the bread soak until the liquid is absorbed. Meanwhile, peel the bananas and fry them in hot butter or good frying fat. Keep them warm and next fry the bread, browning the pieces on both sides. Dish up, placing a fried banana on the top of each piece of bread. Serve very hot.

CAMEMBERT CANAPÉS

Cut long, narrow fingers of toast—about 3 inches by ½ inch—and butter them. Cut Camembert cheese of the same shape, but very slightly smaller. Place the cheese on top of
106 the fingers of toast, then put under a red-hot grill until toasted: this should be done very quickly. Sprinkle the top with coralline or paprika pepper, and serve immediately.

CHEESE CANAPÉS

3 filleted anchovies
6 rounds of fried bread (1½ inches across)
1 oz. grated cheese
Coralline pepper
Very finely chopped parsley

Chop the anchovies very finely and spread thinly over the croûtes of fried bread. Sprinkle with grated cheese, and place under the grill or at the top of a hot oven (450° F., mark 8) until the cheese is melted. Garnish with coralline pepper and chopped parsley.

CHEESE FONDUE

1 oz. butter
1 teacupful milk
½ teacupful breadcrumbs
1 teacupful grated cheese
Seasoning
1 egg
Fingers of toasted bread or biscuits

Put the butter and milk into a saucepan and bring them to the boil. Add the breadcrumbs and grated cheese and season to taste. Stir all over gentle heat until the cheese is melted, add the beaten egg and mix well until thoroughly hot. Serve on fingers of toasted bread or biscuits.

CHICKEN LIVER CROÛTES

3–4 chicken livers
1 oz. butter, melted
Salt
A squeeze of lemon juice
Cayenne pepper
8 croûtes of fried bread
2 hard-boiled eggs
Finely chopped parsley

Cook the chicken livers, then chop and pound them into a paste with a little of the melted butter. Season with salt, a squeeze of lemon juice and a dash of cayenne. Spread this mixture fairly thickly on rounds of fried bread. Cut the hard-boiled eggs in quarters, dip each section in melted butter, then sprinkle with salt and finely chopped parsley. Place one section of egg on each croûte. Serve hot or cold.

CHICKEN LIVERS ON TOAST

3–4 chicken livers
2 tsps. flour
Salt and pepper
1 oz. butter
A little stock (about ¼ pint)
½ glass sherry or Madeira
Croûtes of toast
A few mushrooms (optional)

Wash and dry the chicken livers, cut them in small pieces and toss them in the flour with a seasoning of salt and pepper. Melt the butter in a frying pan, put in the prepared livers and stir them over the heat until nicely browned. Add a little stock and ½ glass sherry or Madeira, and mix well. Cook slowly for 10–15 minutes. Serve on pieces of toast. A few mushrooms, if available, may be added.

CREAM CHEESE CANAPÉS

1 packet cream cheese
A little mushroom ketchup
1 tsp. chopped chives
Paprika pepper
Shortcrust pastry biscuits, or croûtes of toast

Cream the cheese by working it with a palette knife, add the mushroom ketchup and sufficient chives and paprika pepper to suit the palate. Spread on to small pastry biscuits, or croûtes of freshly made toast.

CREAM CHEESE AND CELERY CANAPÉS

Plain round cheese biscuits or pastry	A few drops of tomato ketchup
Butter	1 tbsp. finely chopped celery
1 small cream cheese	Celery tops to garnish
Cayenne pepper	

Spread the biscuits thinly with a little butter. Beat the cheese, seasoning, ketchup, and celery together. Pile up neatly on the biscuits, and garnish each with a small piece of celery top.

CROÛTES ALMIRA

Croûtes of fried bread	2 tbsps. white sauce
	Seasoning
2 ripe tomatoes	Butter
2 tbsps. grated cheese	Chopped parsley

Cut six or seven rounds of bread $\frac{1}{4}$ inch in thickness, and the same number of rings of bread two sizes smaller. Fry these until brown, drain on paper, and keep them warm. Wipe the tomatoes, cut them in pieces, and rub through a sieve. Add the grated cheese to the tomato purée, and then the white sauce, which should be thick enough to bind all together. Season to taste and pile the mixture on the top of the rounds of fried bread, in the shape of a dome. Place in a moderate oven (350° F., mark 4) until thoroughly hot, spread the rings of bread with a little butter, dip them in finely chopped parsley and lay them on the top.

CROÛTES OF FRIED CHEESE

6 Petit Suisse cheese or $\frac{1}{4}$ lb. Gruyère	Croûtes of bread
	1 oz. butter
1 beaten egg	Watercress
2 oz. breadcrumbs	

Divide the small cheeses into half, or cut rounds of cheese. Brush over with beaten egg, coat with breadcrumbs, and repeat this process twice to make a firm covering. Fry the croûtes golden-brown in butter, then fry the cheese. Place the cheese on the croûtes, and garnish with watercress.

DEVILS ON HORSEBACK

6 blanched almonds	3 thin rashers of streaky bacon
Olive oil	
Salt	6 small croûtes of fried bread
Cayenne pepper	
6 French plums	Watercress

Sauté the almonds in a little olive oil until they are golden-brown. Then toss them in a little salt and cayenne pepper. Remove the stones from the plums and insert the almonds in their place. Cut the rind off the bacon, flatten the rashers with a knife blade, cut in half and roll around the plums. Pass a fine skewer through the rolls, and grill, turning until all the sides of the bacon are a golden-brown. Meanwhile, fry small crescents of bread in smoking-hot fat, drain them well and keep hot. Place a plum on each croûte. Garnish with watercress and serve very hot.

FISH CANAPÉS

Use smoked fish, or a mixture of smoked and fresh fish. Flake the cooked fish finely and season with pepper, salt, and cayenne. Flavour with a few drops of lemon juice, some chopped pickles, or a little anchovy or shrimp paste. Heat in a saucepan with a little butter and enough fish sauce to moisten. Spread the mixture on neat strips of hot buttered toast, and decorate with a sprinkling of paprika or strips of red pimiento.

FOIE GRAS CANAPÉS

Cut croûtes or rounds of bread about $1\frac{1}{2}$ inches in diameter, and fry until golden-brown. Spread with foie gras, and on top of each place one or two slices of stuffed olives and add a squeeze of lemon juice.

HAM TOAST

3 oz. cooked ham	A little milk or stock
2 eggs	6 rounds of buttered toast
Seasoning	

Mince the ham finely, including a little of the fat. Put it into a small saucepan with the eggs, well beaten, season to taste, and moisten with a little milk or stock. Heat gently to cook the egg, stirring slowly, then spread neatly on pieces of hot buttered toast.

LOBSTER CANAPÉS

1 tbsp. chopped onion	1 teacupful milk or cream
1 oz. butter	1 cupful lobster meat (tinned or fresh)
2 tbsps. chopped water-cress	Seasoning
1 tbsp. flour	Rounds of fried bread
A pinch of curry powder	Paprika
	Parsley and lemon

Fry the chopped onion in the butter until it is a golden-brown. Add the watercress, flour, a pinch of curry powder, and the milk or cream. Stir until boiling, then add the cooked lobster, season to taste, and heat thoroughly. Heap the mixture on rounds of bread which have been fried brown in hot butter. Sprinkle with paprika and heat through in a moderately hot oven (425° F., mark 6) or under the grill for a few minutes. Serve hot, garnished with parsley and lemon.

MUSHROOM CROÛTES

½ lb. mushrooms	Pepper and salt
1 oz. butter	6 croûtes of fried bread
2 tbsps. thick white sauce	

Select 6 small mushrooms of even size, fry these in the butter and reserve them for garnish. Chop the remainder of the mushrooms finely and fry them in the butter. Mix them with the white sauce and season well with pepper and salt. Pile this mixture on the croûtes of bread and on each serve one small fried mushroom.

NEAPOLITAN CROÛTES

4 oz. cooked haddock	6 slices tomato
A little cream	6 slices pickled walnut
6 croûtes of fried bread	6 slices gherkin

Heat the flaked haddock, moistened with a little cream, and spread this over the croûtes of bread, completely covering the top. Lay on each a thin slice of tomato, then a slice of pickled walnut and a thin slice of gherkin. Reheat for a few minutes in the oven, and serve very hot.

PRUNES À L'INDIENNE

6–8 prunes	6–8 sweet almonds
1 hard-boiled egg	Biscuits or croûtons of fried bread
Chutney	
Seasoning	Butter

The best quality prunes or French plums should be used. Soak or cook them until they are soft enough to remove the stones. Make one slit in them to do this, otherwise keep them as whole as possible. Put the yolk of the hard-boiled egg into a basin, add to it a large teaspoonful of chutney, finely chopped, and other seasoning to taste, and mix well. Also blanch and toast the sweet almonds. Line the inside of the prunes with the chutney mixture, lay an almond in the centre of each, and fold over, bringing back the prunes to their original shape. Place the prunes on a greased dish, cover with greased paper, and put in a moderately hot oven (400° F., mark 6) until hot—about ¼ hour. Take an equal number of small oval biscuits or croûtons of fried bread, spread them with a little butter, and toast them in the oven for a few minutes. Then sprinkle them with the white of the egg, finely chopped, place a prune on the top of each, and garnish with a few shreds of toasted almonds.

SARDINES À LA TARTARE

Skin the required number of sardines and carefully remove the heads and backbones. Cut strips of bread, the same size as the sardines, and fry them a golden-brown. When cool, arrange the fish on these croûtons, coat them with Tartare sauce, and garnish with capers and thin strips of red pepper.

SARDINES PIÊMONTAISES

6–8 croûtes of bread	Paprika pepper
6–8 sardines	Parsley
Fat for frying	

For the Sauce

4 egg yolks	1 tsp. tarragon vinegar
½ oz. butter	
1 tsp. vinegar (cider or malt)	Made mustard
	Salt and pepper

Cut the croûtes of bread very slightly larger than sardines, and fry them in hot fat until golden-brown. Place the sardines on greaseproof paper in a tin, and put into a moderate oven (375° F., mark 5) until hot through—about 10 minutes. Meanwhile, prepare a sauce with the egg yolks, butter, vinegars, a little made mustard, salt, and pepper. Put these ingredients into the inner container of a double saucepan and whisk hard over hot water until the sauce thickens; it must not boil, or it will curdle. Place the sardines on the croûtes of bread, and coat each one neatly with the sauce. Garnish with paprika and tiny sprigs of parsley.

SARDINE SNACKS

12 medium-sized sardines	Butter
Tomato ketchup	Fried breadcrumbs
A good squeeze of lemon juice	Curled celery
	Lemon fans
6 strips toast	

Heat the sardines in a little tomato ketchup, to which has been added a good squeeze of lemon juice. Butter half a dozen strips of toast, each large enough to hold two sardines. When the fish are thoroughly heated, remove them from the sauce, coat them with fried breadcrumbs, and lay them on the toast. Pour a little of the sauce over each portion, and garnish with curled celery and lemon fans.

SARDINE STRIPS

1 tin sardines
Pepper and salt
Cayenne pepper
Pieces of buttered toast
Egg yolk
Chopped parsley

Pound the sardines and season well. Spread on strips of buttered toast, and decorate with sieved hard-boiled egg yolk and a little finely chopped parsley.

SAUSAGE CANAPÉS

6 croûtes of fried bread or toast
Butter
French mustard
Pepper
6 slices of breakfast sausage
Gherkin
Radishes

Prepare the croûtes of bread and then spread them with butter, which has been mixed with French mustard and pepper. Lay on each a slice of breakfast sausage, and then decorate with thin slices of gherkin and radish, neatly arranged.

SAVOURY MUSHROOMS

6 mushrooms of equal size
2 tbsps. chopped ham
Chopped onions to taste
$\frac{1}{2}$ oz. butter
2 tbsps. breadcrumbs
2 tsps. chopped parsley
Grated lemon rind
Seasoning
1 tbsp. stock or gravy
6 rounds of fried bread
Parsley and red pepper for garnish

Peel the mushrooms and cut off the stalks, wash them quickly in salt water and dry in a cloth. Arrange with the gills uppermost on a greased baking tin. Fry the ham, chopped onion, and mushroom trimmings in butter. Add breadcrumbs, chopped parsley, lemon rind, seasoning and stock, and heat through. Pile stuffing on to each mushroom, cover, and bake in a moderate oven (375° F., mark 5) for 15–20 minutes. Have ready a hot dish. Stand the mushrooms on rounds of hot fried bread, and garnish with parsley and red pepper.

SHRIMP TOASTS

Spread pounded shrimps and butter on small rounds of toast, garnish with shelled shrimps and put a caper in the centre of each.

SCOTCH WOODCOCK

Triangles of buttered toast
Pounded anchovies or anchovy paste
2–3 tbsps. milk
$\frac{1}{2}$ oz. butter
2 egg yolks
Pepper and salt
Anchovy fillets
Pieces of red pepper or paprika pepper to garnish

Spread the buttered toast with pounded anchovies or anchovy paste. Beat together the milk, butter, and egg yolks, and cook over a slow heat till thick and creamy. Season, without adding too much salt, pour the mixture over the toast, and garnish with crossed pieces of anchovy fillet and pieces of red pepper or some paprika pepper.

TOMATO CANAPÉS

3–4 firm tomatoes
Salt and pepper
A little fine sugar
1 shallot
$\frac{1}{4}$ oz. butter
Croûtes of bread
Butter or oil for frying
1 oz. cream cheese
A little grated cheese

Allow a slice of tomato, cut $\frac{1}{2}$ inch thick, for each canapé. Place them in a shallow buttered baking dish and sprinkle with salt, pepper, a little fine sugar, and the finely chopped shallot. Put a few small pieces of butter on the top, and bake in a moderate oven (350° F., mark 4) until the tomatoes are cooked, but not broken—about 15 minutes. Cut as many rounds of bread as may be required, and fry them in butter or oil until brown on both sides. Lay a slice of the prepared tomato on each round, and garnish with small balls of cream cheese rolled in grated Cheddar or Parmesan cheese.

WELSH RAREBIT: see Cheese chapter.

WOODCOCK TOASTS

2 cooked chickens' livers
1 tsp. anchovy essence
1 oz. butter or margarine
1 egg yolk
2–3 tbsps. cream
6 fingers of buttered toast
Parsley

Pound the chickens' livers with the anchovy essence, butter, and egg yolk, and sieve the mixture. Add the cream to the paste and warm it slowly, stirring well until it thickens. Spread this paste on to the buttered fingers of toast and serve very hot, garnished with a little finely chopped parsley.

SAVOURY CASSOLETTES

For those persons who do not, or cannot, enjoy pastry, cassolettes make excellent cases for any of the savoury fillings suggested here. They are crisp and delicious, and very much easier to make than one would imagine from a cursory glance at the recipe. For after-dinner savouries, they must be small in size.

CASSOLETTES OF HAM

¼ lb. fresh butter
Egg and crumbs for coating
1 tbsp. cream cheese
2 oz. finely chopped lean ham
Mustard

Divide the butter into pieces of even size—¼ lb. would make about 8 small cassolettes—and shape them into balls with butter pats or with the hands. Place in a refrigerator or cold larder until very firm, brush over with beaten egg, then coat with breadcrumbs, pressing the crumbs well into the butter. Repeat three or four times until a thick, substantial coating is made. Using a very small round cutter, cut half-way into the coated ball, but do not remove the cut portion. Put the balls into a frying basket and fry until the breadcrumbs are golden-brown, in deep fat from which a faint blue smoke is rising. Drain off surplus fat. Remove the lid of each cassolette, and pour out the melted butter from inside. Beat the cream cheese until it is stiff, stir in the ham and a little mustard, and fill the cassolettes with this mixture, handling them gently, as they are fragile.

Alternatively, use a cheese, meat, game, poultry, or fish filling.

BREAD CASSOLETTES

When time is short, cassolettes can be cut from bread. The bread should be at least 2 days old, and the pieces should measure about 2½ inches long by 1 inch wide. Cut out the middle, and fry till golden-brown. If preferred, rounds of bread can be cut from thick slices of bread and the centre cut out as when making vol-au-vents. Any savoury filling can be used.

MISCELLANEOUS SAVOURIES

ASPARAGUS CRISPS

Thin bread and butter
Grated Parmesan cheese
Asparagus tips
Beaten egg
Watercress
Coralline pepper

Cut the bread and butter in half, and sandwich two pieces together with grated Parmesan cheese and the asparagus tips. Brush the top with egg, sprinkle with grated Parmesan cheese and bake in a hot oven (450° F., mark 8) until crisp and brown—about 10 minutes. Serve garnished with watercress and a little coralline pepper.

CHEESE BALLS

Shape cream cheese into little balls, placing a salted almond in the centre of each, and roll in tiny sprigs of parsley.

CHEESE MERINGUES

2 egg whites
2 tbsps. grated Parmesan cheese
Salt and cayenne pepper
Fat for frying
Parsley or watercress

Whisk the egg whites very stiffly. Fold in the cheese and seasoning carefully. Have ready a pan of hot fat, from which a faint blue smoke is rising. Drop 1 tbsp. of the mixture at a time carefully into the fat, and cook until golden-brown — 2–3 minutes. Drain well on soft paper. Serve very hot, garnished with watercress or parsley.

CHEESE SOUFFLÉS (COLD)

Parmesan cheese
1 oz. cream cheese
Mustard and cayenne
¼ pint aspic jelly
Paprika

Prepare some small ramekin cases by folding a double piece of strong white paper round the outside of each, allowing it to extend 1½–2 inches above the top of the case. Grate the Parmesan cheese very finely; beat the cream cheese until it is quite soft, and add the seasoning. Prepare the aspic jelly (ready-made aspic jelly can be used), and when it is cold, but not quite set, whisk it until it is light and spongy. Then whisk in the creamed cheese and continue to beat lightly. Carefully stir in 1 oz. of the grated Parmesan cheese, pour at once into the cases and allow to set. Run a layer of the jelly on top of each soufflé, or decorate with a little chopped jelly. Remove the paper bands and garnish with grated cheese and paprika.

CHEESE AND TOMATO SOUFFLÉS (HOT)

6 small tomatoes
Pepper and salt
Sugar
1 teacupful fine breadcrumbs
¼ oz. butter
1 teacupful hot milk
Cayenne
½ tsp. made mustard
2–3 tbsps. grated cheese
2 eggs

Peel the tomatoes, season them with pepper, salt, and a light sprinkling of sugar, and place each one in a small greased soufflé dish. Then make a cheese soufflé mixture. Put the breadcrumbs and butter into a basin, pour over the hot milk and soak for a few minutes. Season with pepper, salt, a dash of cayenne, and the made mustard, and mix thoroughly. Add the grated cheese and the yolks of eggs, and lastly, stir in the whites of the eggs, which have been beaten to a stiff froth. Pour some of this mixture round each tomato and bake in a hot oven (450° F., mark 8) from 10–15 minutes. Serve immediately.

CORNED BEEF AND ONION STICKS

Cut the corned beef into small cubes. Thread each cube, with a cocktail onion, on a cocktail stick. These can be presented attractively by sticking them in a large red apple.

CREAMED SHRIMPS

1 oz. butter
1 oz. flour
A little cream
½ pint milk
½ pint picked shrimps
1 oz. grated cheese
Pepper and salt
A few breadcrumbs
Parsley
Toast fingers

Make a white sauce with the butter, flour, cream, and milk. Add the lightly boiled shrimps and half of the cheese, and season to taste. Simmer for 5 minutes. Put the mixture into individual ramekin dishes, sprinkle the top with cheese and a few crumbs, and reheat in a hot oven (450° F., mark 8) 5–10 minutes. Garnish with parsley, and serve with toast.

As an alternative, creamed lobster or crab could be offered. The method of preparation is exactly the same, except that the flaked tinned lobster or crab takes the place of the shrimps.

DEVILLED ALMONDS

1 oz. sweet almonds
1 tbsp. of olive oil
  or 1 oz. butter
1 tsp. piquant sauce
1 tbsp. chutney
Cayenne pepper and salt

Blanch and dry the almonds. Put the oil in the saucepan, or melt the butter, and fry the almonds in the fat till nicely browned. Add the piquant sauce, chutney, and the seasonings, stir into the almonds and cook slowly for about 4 minutes. Serve on hot toast or biscuits.

HADDOCK BALLS

Cook some smoked haddock, flake it thoroughly and mix to a fairly stiff paste with a little white sauce. Season well and leave to cool. Form paste into balls, egg and crumb them and fry them in smoking-hot fat. Serve hot on cocktail sticks.

HAM SAVOURIES

6 rounds bread
4 tbsps. melted butter
4 tbsps. grated cheese
3 slices cooked ham

For each savoury, dip a round of bread in melted butter and then in the grated cheese. Place the bread, plain side down, on a buttered baking dish. Prepare another round of bread in the same way, and place it on the first, plain side up, and with a thin slice of cooked ham between them. Brush the top with melted butter and bake in a hot oven (450° F., mark 8) until a delicate brown—about 10 minutes. Tomato sauce may be served separately, if desired.

HERRING ROE SAVOURY

6 soft herring roes
About ¼ pint milk
Cayenne pepper
Salt
Lemon juice
½ oz. melted butter
2 tbsps. breadcrumbs
2 scrambled eggs
2 tsps. chopped capers
  or gherkins
Lemon and parsley

Poach the roes in a little milk, drain and season with Cayenne, salt, and lemon juice. Cut them into convenient-sized pieces, brush over with a little melted butter, sprinkle with breadcrumbs, and brown in a hot oven (450° F., mark 8) for a few minutes, or under the grill. Prepare some scrambled egg, add to it a few chopped capers or pickled gherkins, and season rather highly. Fill small ramekin cases with the mixture, lay one or two pieces of roe on the top of each, and serve hot, garnished with lemon and parsley.

PARMESAN WAFERS

Ice cream wafers
Parmesan cheese
Little pieces of butter
Seasoning
Watercress
Coralline pepper

Cut the wafers in half and sandwich two pieces together with grated cheese, seasoning, and a few small pieces of butter. Cover the top with grated Parmesan cheese, and bake in a hot oven (450° F., mark 8) until crisp and brown—5–10 minutes. Serve garnished with watercress and sprinkled with a little coralline pepper.

PRAWN FRITTERS

2 oz. flour
Seasoning
1 dessertsp. salad oil
2 tbsps. warm water
1 egg white
¼ pint large shelled
  prawns
Deep fat for frying

Sieve the flour and seasoning, make a well in the centre, and stir in the salad oil and sufficient water to make a thick coating batter. Fold in the stiffly beaten egg white. Dip the prawns in the batter and drop into smoking fat. Fry until crisp and golden-brown. Drain well and serve, piled on a paper d'oyley on a hot dish. Garnish with heads of prawns.

SALTED NUTS

Almonds are the nuts most commonly selected for salting, but walnuts, peanuts, pecans, cashew nuts, etc., can also be used, and a mixture of nuts prepared in this way makes an interesting dish.

Almonds and other nuts with a brown underskin require to be blanched before they can be salted. Place the nuts in a small saucepan, pour warm water over them, and bring it to the boil, then drain off the boiling water and run cold water over the nuts until they are cool enough to handle. The skin can then be readily slipped off with the fingers. After removing the brown skin, dry the nuts carefully in a towel.

For each cupful of blanched nuts place about 1 tbsp. fresh butter or oil in a frying pan and make it hot. Then distribute the nuts in a thin, even layer over the surface of the pan. Fry slowly, stirring continuously, until the nuts are a uniform, delicate brown. Remove them from the pan and drain. Then sprinkle the nuts generously with fine table salt, using a sprinkler, or toss them in salt in a paper or old cloth. Spread out to cool and become crisp before serving; or dry off in a cool oven. A little paprika pepper may also be sprinkled over the nuts, if desired, and the flavour may be varied by adding 1 tsp. each of onion and celery salt to the table salt.

If liked, the nuts may be browned in the oven. Use the same proportion of nuts and fat. Heat the fat in a shallow tin, put in the nuts in a single layer, and place them in a moderate oven. Let them roast until sufficiently brown, stirring and turning them over frequently. Then drain carefully and salt them as above.

SPICED NUTS

Follow the same procedure as for salted nuts as far as the browning stage, then for each cupful of nuts mix ¾ tsp. salt and ¼ tsp. mixed spice, and sprinkle freely over the browned nuts. Allow them to become cool and crisp before serving.

STUFFED PRUNES

Stone the prunes and fill with a mixture of chopped ham, chopped gherkin, and mayonnaise. Serve on thin slices of tomato, and garnish with parsley or watercress.

SURPRISE PLUMS

4 cooked French plums
1 cream cheese
Cochineal (optional)
Lettuce, cress, or celery

Remove the stones from the plums very carefully by splitting each plum half-way down into four "petals." Roll the cheese into smooth fingers and put one into each plum, arranging the four points neatly against the cheese. The appearance is improved if the cheese is beaten with a little cochineal to produce a delicate pink tinge. Serve on a bed of lettuce or cress, or celery stalks can be used as a garnish if preferred.

TOMATO CREAM SAVOURY

¼ pint tomato purée
½ oz. gelatine
4 tbsps. Parmesan cheese
Seasoning
3 tbsps. thick cream
Some plain biscuits
Butter
Parsley

Make the purée by rubbing some fresh red tomatoes through a hair sieve. It should not be too thin. Put it into a saucepan with the gelatine and stir over the heat until dissolved. Then turn into a basin to cool. Add the grated Parmesan cheese, season with cayenne and a little salt, and lastly, stir in the cream, slightly whipped. When the mixture is beginning to set, pour it into small moulds which have been rinsed out with cold water. Set aside until firm. When required, turn out, and serve on plain thin biscuits that have been buttered and sprinkled with chopped parsley. Garnish with parsley or watercress, or as desired.

WINE AND WINE IN COOKERY

WHAT IS WINE?

Wine is the fermented juice of freshly gathered grapes. When ripe, the grapes are gathered and crushed to extract their sweet juice, which is then suitably fermented. The process of fermentation is natural and inevitable. It transforms the grape sugar into alcohol, and the grape juice becomes wine. Thus alcohol is an integral part of wine—present in the proportion of rarely less than 9% or more than 15%. Incidentally, the alcohol acts as a preservative, preventing the growth of yeasts, moulds, enzymes and bacteria; that is why wine is pure and why it keeps so well. Sometimes additional alcohol is put into wine, and such wine is then termed "fortified."

There are many different species of vines grown in many different parts of the world, and there are great differences between the soil, aspect and climate of the various vineyards. There are also differences between the methods of vine growing and wine making. Thus there are many different kinds of wines. Also, the quality of the grape juice varies from year to year according to the weather that prevails during the growth and ripening of the grapes, so even the same wines vary from vintage to vintage.

HOW TO BUY WINE

If you are not conversant with the different brands of wine, or what it is reasonable to have to pay for them, you will be wise to go to a reliable wine merchant with a reputation to lose, and let him advise you. If you buy from a wine merchant and his wine fails to satisfy you, he will put the matter right, for his responsibility lasts as long as the wine he sells.

The best wine for you to buy is the wine which best suits your own taste, and in time you will train your palate so that you may trust your own judgment. Whatever wine you buy, see that it is sound, that is, clear and pleasant to look at, sweet-smelling and clean on the palate.

HOW TO KEEP WINE

Wine should be kept in a cool, dark cellar. The cellar should be underground but well ventilated. It should be cool in summer and winter alike, and, of course, clean.

When wine is delivered to you, remove the straw envelopes and paper wrappings and examine every bottle before storing it away. A cellar intended for storing wine is fitted with bins (compartments, like deep shelves), which enable the bottles to be stored in a horizontal position. This is to ensure that the whole of the inside face of the cork is constantly in contact with the liquid. If bottles are stored upright or at an angle, the corks are likely to shrink and air will then find its way into the bottle and will spoil the flavour of the wine.

If you are short of cellar space and cannot bin away cased wines as soon as they arrive, see that the cases are placed so that the bottles lie in a horizontal position.

Wine Bins

When binning port, see that the white "splash" on the bottles is uppermost. It will then be in exactly the same position as before it reached your cellar, and the crust, which is bound to be disturbed by the moving, will settle better if the bottle is in its original position.

Never bin a bottle of wine which shows signs of "ullage," that is, if the wine is beginning to ooze out through the cork. Watch your wine once it is binned so as to remove and use quickly any bottles that begin to "weep."

HOW TO SERVE WINE

Decanting

Wines should always be served brilliantly clear. All those which throw a sediment (principally red wines) should be carefully decanted. Such sediment fouls the wine if it passes from the bottle to the glass. Even slight movements will disturb the sediment, so whenever possible decant wine in the cellar, straight from the bin. Take the bottle very gently from the bin and lay it in a cradle. Then remove the metal cap or wax protecting the outside face of the cork. Wipe the upper lip of the bottle thoroughly with a clean cloth, then drive in the corkscrew slowly and draw the cork steadily, without jerking the bottle. Now wipe the inside lip of the bottle clean and holding the bottle firmly, slowly pour the contents into the decanter held in your left hand. Place a light behind the shoulder of the bottle and watch the wine as it passes through the neck. At the first sign of loose sediment in the neck of the bottle, stop decanting, even though there may still be some wine left in the bottle. It is better to lose a little wine than to spoil a decanter of good wine with a little sediment.

Temperature

The temperature at which to serve wines is of great importance. Extremes must be avoided—if the wine is to be warmed or cooled, it must be done gradually, as shocks are bad for wine.

White wines should be served cold. They may be iced by standing the bottle in water containing ice—no ice should ever be put into the wine itself.

Red wines should be at the temperature of the room in which they are to be served. Do not attempt to warm them up quickly, but decant them an hour or so before the meal and let them stand in the dining-room, but away from the fire, so that they can take the temperature of the room.

Glasses for Wine

Fine glasses add to the enjoyment of fine wine, for they enable one to appreciate its colour.

Both decanters and glasses should, of course, be perfectly clean. After careful washing and drying, they should be polished with a clean glass cloth. Though different-shaped glasses are made for serving different wines, a fairly large goblet or stem glass can be used for almost any wine. The important point is that the glass should not be too small, nor should it be filled to the brim (except with Champagne). If the glass is too full or too small, the subtle "bouquet" of the wine—its greatest charm—cannot be appreciated.

When to Serve Wines

The order in which wines should be served varies according to individual tastes and the food served. The classical order, however, is as follows:

With oysters: Chablis or Dry Champagne.
With soup: Pale Sherry or Dry Madeira.
With fish: Champagne or Dry White Wines.
With entrées: Claret.
With roast or game: Burgundy.
With sweets: Sauternes.
With cheese: Port, Brown Sherry or Madeira.

For informal meals, when one wine is served throughout, it should be chosen to harmonise with the main course.

NOTES ABOUT WINES

Port

Port is a fortified wine made from grapes grown in the Upper Valley of the Douro River in Portugal, and shipped from Oporto. It is fortified by brandy added at the time of the pressing of the grapes. There are a number of different types of port: red, white or tawny in colour, and different in style, age, strength and sweetness. A Vintage Port is the best, that is to say, Red Port, made from the grapes of one year (a "vintage" year, which means a good and sunny year) and from grapes which are perfectly sound and perfectly ripe when picked; the wine being shipped from Oporto eighteen months to two years after the vintage and bottled in England soon after landing. Then it must be given time, twelve to fifteen years or longer, to mature.

Sherry

Sherry is a wine made from white grapes grown in the South of Spain, in the Jerez district. It is usually fortified but not necessarily. Sherry is allowed to ferment in its own way and is fortified, if at all, by the addition of brandy at a much later stage of its existence. The vintage of sherry does not count for much, nor does any individual vineyard, but what does matter is the shipper. Sherry is a blend of wines similar in style but made from the grapes of different vineyards and of wines of different years, blended together so as to maintain the standard associated with certain marks or brands registered by the different sherry shippers.

Madeira

Madeira is a fortified wine made and matured in the island of Madeira. It is fortified and matured in a different way from port and sherry. The fermented grape juice, or new wine, is subjected to heat and is then racked and rested, after which it is fortified by the addition of cane spirit. At this stage the wines are blended together and left for some years to mature.

Claret

Claret is the red wine of Bordeaux. In colour it should be a brilliant ruby red, never black or pink. It differs very much in bouquet and flavour according to the species of grapes, the soil and aspect of the vineyard, the method of pressing the juice and the length of time it has been kept.

White Bordeaux (Graves and Sauternes)

Graves and Sauternes are white wines coming from Bordeaux. Graves are fairly dry and Sauternes rather sweet.

Burgundy

There are many wines, red and white, still and sparkling, known as Burgundy. They are made in three Départements of France, formerly part of the old province of Burgundy and now known by the names of Côte d'Or, Saône-et-Loire and Rhône. The Côte d'Or produces the best and dearest red Burgundies, particularly in the northern part. To the south, the Saône-et-Loire district, and further south still, the Rhône, produce lighter, though nevertheless pleasing, and much less expensive wines.

The best-known White Burgundy is Chablis. The white wines of the Côte d'Or Département are finer but they are also more expensive.

Champagne

Champagne is a sparkling wine made from grapes grown within the former boundaries of the ancient province of Champagne. Champagne is always blended, and this is for two reasons, the first being that the wines from different vineyards, although similar in type, are different in style, and it is only by judicious blending that the individual wines are improved, their special qualities being merged into a harmonious whole. The second reason is that the quantity of wine made each year from individual vineyards is so small that shippers must blend the wine of a number of vineyards in order to have sufficient Champagne uniform in style to meet the demands of their customers. A Vintage Champagne is a Champagne bearing the date of the particular year when the grapes were gathered, from which it was mainly, if not entirely, made.

Alsace Wines

The white wines from the vineyards on the left bank of the Rhine, from Mulhouse to Strasbourg.

Hocks

Hocks are Rhenish white wines, deriving their name from Hochheim on the Main River, close to where it joins the Rhine.

Moselles

Moselles come from the vineyards of the Moselle River which runs from France into Germany, meeting the Rhine at Coblenz.

Brandy

Brandy is a spirit distilled from wine. The quality of the brandy depends upon the suitability of the wine distilled, the manner of distillation, and how and for how long the brandy has been kept. The most suitable wines are the white wines of the Charentes, two of the western Départements of France, below Nantes and above Bordeaux, with the town of Cognac at their centre.

OTHER WINES

Chianti : The best-known Italian red wine ; light and fairly dry. There is also a little White Chianti of good quality.

Malaga : Malaga is one of the best sweet wines of Spain.

Marsala : The best and best-known fortified dessert wine of Italy. It is made from grapes grown in Sicily.

Muscatel : A sweet wine made in Spain and Italy from Muscat grapes.

Tokay : The best and best-known wine of Hungary.

Vermouth : A white wine in which aromatic herbs and other ingredients have been cooked. The Italian Vermouth is darker in colour and sweeter than the French.

LIQUEURS AND SPIRITS

Absinthe: A highly concentrated wormwood distillate.

Advocaat : A Dutch liqueur, yellow in colour, with a flavour of eggs and brandy.

Bénédictine : One of the most popular of all liqueurs, distilled in France.

Brandy : A spirit distilled from wine (see this page). Also :

Apricot Brandy : Flavoured with apricot.

Cherry Brandy : Flavoured with Morello cherries.

Chartreuse : One of the most famous French liqueurs. There are two chief types : the yellow, which is sweeter, and the green, which is stronger.

Cointreau : A French Curaçao, used as an after-dinner cordial, and to flavour punches, cocktails, etc.

Crème de Cacao : A French liqueur, chocolate in colour, with the flavour of cocoa ; very sweet.

Crème de Menthe : A very popular liqueur possessing valuable digestive properties. It is made of wine or grain spirit flavoured with peppermint and sweetened.

Curaçao : A sweet digestive liqueur made of spirit—wine or grain—sugar and orange pulp.

Drambuie : A Scotch liqueur, golden in colour, with the flavour of whisky and heather honey.

Grand Marnier : A French liqueur, light brown in colour and with the flavour of orange.

Kirsch (or Kirschwasser) : An Alsatian spirit distilled from cherries, white in colour, and with a strong flavour of bitter almond from the kernels within the cherry stones.

Kümmel : A Baltic liqueur, colourless, and with the flavour of carraway or cummin. It is now distilled in England as well as in France and Holland.

Mandarine : A French liqueur, red in colour, and with the flavour of tangerine oranges.

Maraschino : A Dalmatian liqueur, white, with a very distinctive flavour of the bitter cherry from which it is distilled.

Monastine : A French liqueur, lemon-yellow in colour, and somewhat similar in flavour to Yellow Chartreuse.

Noyau : A French liqueur (now also produced

in London, Amsterdam and elsewhere) made from the kernels of cherry stones. It has a nutty flavour of bitter almonds, and is rather sweet. There are two sorts, white and pink.

Prunelle : A French liqueur, pale green in colour, and with the flavour of sloes.

Punch : A drink made from hot water or milk and a mixture of ingredients, one of which is usually a spirit; sugar and various flavouring herbs and spices are added. Rum, brandy, whisky, champagne, sherry, white wine, cider, and ale may each serve as a basis for punch. Cold punches, which often contain fruit juices, ginger ale or soda water, usually count as a type of soft drink. A toddy is a hot punch made by the glass rather than in a punch bowl.

Quetsch : An Alsatian spirit, white in colour, and with the flavour of the Quetsch, a purple plum much grown in Alsace.

Raspail : A French liqueur possessing valuable digestive properties.

Sloe Gin : One of the most popular of all English-made liqueurs and cordials.

Triple-Sec : The name of white Curaçao liqueur, used for a number of different brands.

Van der Hum : The best liqueur made in South Africa, its chief flavour being derived from the Nartje, or South African tangerine.

La Vieille Cure : A French liqueur, brown in colour, of high alcoholic strength, and with a very aromatic and quite distinctive flavour.

Vodka : A colourless and tasteless spirit made by distilling grain or inverted and fermented starch obtained chiefly from the potato; the national spirit of Russia.

WINE IN COOKERY

Wine can be very useful in the kitchen, but it must be used both with discretion—the right wine being chosen for the dish—and with restraint, for while a small amount of wine will often make a dish, adding too much may easily ruin it.

When the wine is actually cooked with the food, most of the alcohol, of course, evaporates during the process, but the flavour of the wine remains, becoming mellower as the cooking proceeds.

Sherry

Sherry is perhaps the most generally useful wine in cookery. It may be added to soups, particularly turtle soup, tomato soup and meat soups, such as game, giblet, kidney and oxtail soup, but in very small quantities—only a few drops per serving—as the flavour of the sherry should not predominate.

It goes particularly well with ham and bacon. Slices of ham baked in sherry are delicious, or it may be added to the sauce, such as Espagnole sauce, to serve with ham dishes or meat entrées. Calf's head, too, is improved with the addition of sherry, both to the sauce to serve with the meat and to calf's head soup.

Sherry is used in many sweet dishes. It is the classic wine for trifle and tipsy cake, and may be used instead of water for dissolving the gelatine in soufflés and creams. It goes into Viennoise pudding and the Sabayon sauce that is served with it. Other sweet sauces, such as prune and whipped egg sauces, may include sherry.

Port

In the kitchen, port is associated with game dishes. It invariably goes into jugged hare (or rabbit) and into hare soup, and in either of the sauces that accompany duck, viz., Bigarade sauce and orange sauce. It may always be added to the gravy for game, especially when stewed, as in a salmi. Cumberland sauce to serve with cold game and Réforme sauce for meat entrées may both include port.

Red Wine

A glass of red wine added to beef or mutton while braising or roasting improves both the meat and gravy. It goes well with other meat dishes too, such as salmi of game, and venison, also in meat soups and Bordeaux sauce to serve with meat or game. In wine jelly it helps both the colour and flavour.

White Wine

Dry white wine can be used instead of vinegar in salad dressings, and a few drops may be added to clear soup or to the sauces to go with white meats, such as veal and chicken. White wine sauce is a favourite French accompaniment to fish dishes, notably Sole au Vin Blanc, and white wine is an essential ingredient in Sole Véronique.

Two other sauces which include white wine are Italian sauce and Hungarian sauce.

Sweet white wine adds a finishing touch to many sweet dishes or their sauces, particularly those made of fruit.

Madeira

Madeira may take the place of sherry in turtle

soup, and is an improvement to compote of pigeons. It is, of course, an essential ingredient of Madeira sauce.

Brandy

Brandy goes particularly well with dried fruit, and so is found in recipes for wedding cakes, Christmas cakes and mincement, and it may be added to the fruity filling for Eccles cakes and Banbury puffs. It is used to make brandy sauce or butter for the Christmas pudding.

Liqueurs

A very small amount of a sweet liqueur such as Maraschino or Kirsch makes all the difference to a fruit salad or fruit compote. Liqueurs are also used to flavour ices and iced puddings or the sauces to serve with them.

Rum

Rum is an alternative to brandy in Christmas dishes, and makes a delicious syrup to serve with Babas and Savarins; see recipes in this book.

TYPICAL RECIPES USING WINE

PIQUANT HARE OR RABBIT

1 hare or rabbit leg per person	Sprigs of thyme
Bacon for larding	Tarragon leaves
1 half-bottle white wine	Coarsely ground pepper
1 glassful wine vinegar	Olive oil
2–3 carrots	1 tbsp. dry mustard
2–3 small onions	1 dessertsp. tomato sauce
1 bay leaf	A little flour
Sprigs of parsley	Some fresh cream or top of the milk

Wipe the hare or rabbit legs and lard them with the bacon. Prepare a marinade with the wine, vinegar, sliced carrots and onions, herbs and pepper, let the meat stand in this for 2 hours, then drain it well. Heat the oil and brown the meat on all sides. Add about half the marinade liquor, the mustard and the tomato sauce, and cook for 1 hour. When the meat is well cooked, remove it and keep it hot. Add the blended flour to the gravy and boil for a few minutes, then remove the pan from the heat, add the cream and strain this gravy over the hare or rabbit.

KIDNEYS WITH WHITE WINE

Skin the kidneys and cut them into very thin slices. Melt a little butter, and sauté the kidney slices in the hot fat. When the meat is tender, drain, and pile on a hot dish. Add a little white wine to the pan, also a little finely chopped shallot. Continue to heat the wine until it is reduced by a half, and add some meat glaze, a knob of butter and some sliced cooked mushrooms. Boil this sauce for a few minutes, then pour it over the kidneys. Sprinkle with finely chopped parsley and some small croûtons of fried bread.

STUFFED PHEASANT

1 pheasant	1 egg yolk
Pork sausage-meat	Bacon for barding
A few chicken livers	1 glassful Madeira or sherry
Salt and pepper	1 tsp. tomato purée
A little chopped parsley	Nutmeg
A little cream or top of the milk	Fried croûtons

Prepare the bird in the usual way, then make a stuffing with the sausage-meat, chicken livers, seasoning, parsley, cream (or top of the milk) and egg yolk—the mixture should be fairly stiff. Stuff the bird with this filling, cover it with bacon and roast it in the usual way in a moderate oven (375° F., mark 5) for about 45 minutes. When the bird is three-parts cooked, add the wine, tomato purée, more seasoning if required, and a little grated nutmeg, with a little hot water, if required. Finish the cooking, basting frequently with the sauce. To serve, remove bacon, place pheasant on a dish, garnish with croûtons, and pour the sauce over all.

FILLETS OF SOLE IN CHAMPAGNE

Place the folded fillets in a fireproof dish, season with salt and pepper and cover with thinly sliced mushrooms. Put a glass of champagne in a pan with the fish bones, and cook for about 10–15 minutes. Remove the bones, add 1 tbsp. tomato purée, and continue to heat until the sauce is somewhat reduced. Add ½ lb. tomatoes, peeled, seeded and cut in quarters, and cook the sauce until it is of a creamy consistency, then add a knob of butter and season with paprika pepper. Cover the fillets with the sauce and bake in a moderate oven (350° F., mark 4) for ½ hour. Serve sprinkled with finely chopped parsley.

GRAVY MADE WITH WINE

A very delicious gravy to serve with roast meat may be made with red wine. Drain off the fat from the baking tin into the dripping pot, then pour in half a glass of wine. Scrape round the edges of the tin to include and dissolve the browned meat juices, and boil the gravy for 2 minutes. Add a little stock or water, and seasoning to taste, cook for another 2 minutes, and the gravy is ready.

NEUCHÂTEL FONDUE

A little butter and garlic	2 tsps. cornflour
$1\frac{3}{4}$ lb. Emmenthal cheese	1 glass Kirsch
$\frac{1}{4}$ pint good white wine	Pepper

Grease an earthenware pan with butter and rub it round with a small piece of cut garlic. Cut the cheese in thin slices and place it with the wine in the prepared dish. Put over a spirit stove, heat gently until the cheese is melted, stirring slowly until it becomes a thick cream. Just before it is cooked add the cornflour, blended with the Kirsch and pepper. Lower the heat so that the mixture cooks slowly, with an occasional bubble. The dish is placed on the table and each person puts cubes of bread on the end of a fork, and dips these into the fondue, twisting the cubes to prevent strings of the mixture hanging down. A white wine is the best accompaniment.

BRANDIED MELON

Cantaloupe melon	3 tbsps. water
3 oz. sugar	$\frac{1}{4}$ pint brandy

Cut a thin slice from the stem end of the melon and remove all the seeds. Dissolve the sugar in the water, stir in the brandy, and pour into the melon. Replace the lid, secure it with cocktail sticks or tooth-picks, and stand the melon upright; chill it in a refrigerator for several hours, preferably overnight. To serve, drain off the liquid, and peel and dice the melon flesh; put in a bowl, cover with the liquid and serve with cream.

WINE CUSTARDS

$\frac{3}{4}$ pint dry white wine	A pinch of cinnamon
2 oz. sugar	4 egg yolks

Bring the wine, sugar, and cinnamon slowly to boiling point. Meanwhile, beat the egg yolks until light and foamy, and pour into the wine, stirring constantly. Strain the mixture through a fine sieve and pour it into some earthenware or heatproof custard cups. Place these in a pan of hot water, and cook in a moderate oven (350° F., mark 3) for 45 minutes.

BANANA CREAM

$\frac{1}{2}$ pint milk	2 wineglassfuls sweet white wine
6 oz. sugar	$\frac{1}{2}$ pint lightly whipped cream or evaporated milk
6 egg yolks	Glacé cherries
1 tsp. vanilla essence	
$\frac{3}{4}$ oz. gelatine	
6 bananas	

Heat the milk, and beat together the sugar and egg yolks. Add the milk and vanilla to the eggs, return the mixture to the pan and cook very slowly until it is thick. Dissolve the gelatine in a little hot water. Mash the bananas with the wine and fold in the cream, then add the cool egg mixture, and lastly, the dissolved gelatine. Pour into sundae glasses, and decorate with cherries.

PEACH COMPOTE

4 medium-sized peaches	$\frac{1}{4}$ pint white wine
Juice of $\frac{1}{2}$ a lemon	4 oz. sugar
$\frac{1}{4}$ pint water	Whipped cream

Skin the peaches by scalding them in boiling water. Cut each in half and sprinkle with lemon juice. Mix together the water, wine and sugar and bring to the boil. Put the peach halves into this syrup and poach them for 10 minutes, drain the peaches and place in a serving dish. Reduce the liquid until it is thick and syrupy, pour it over the fruit and top with whipped cream.

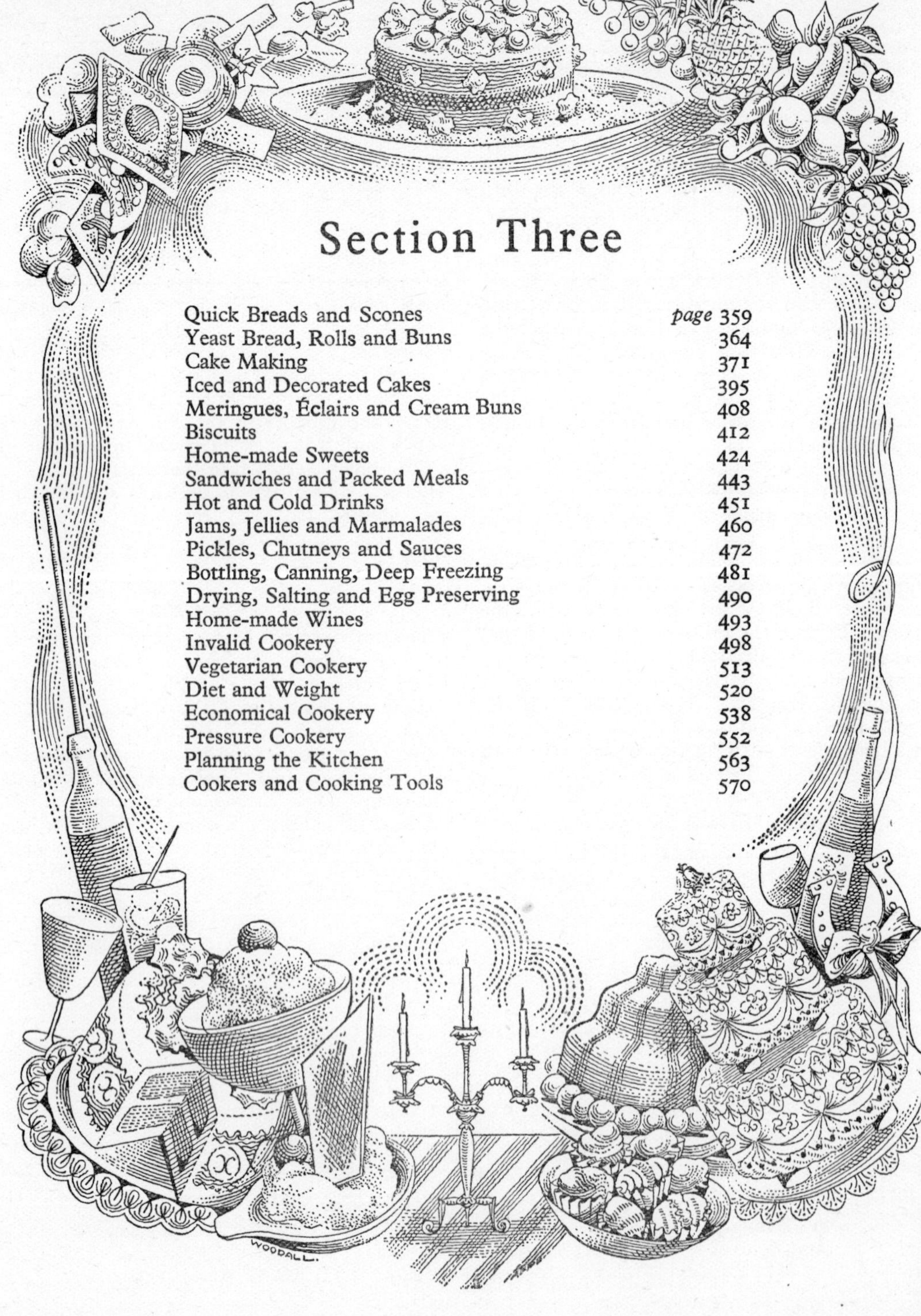

Section Three

QUICK BREADS AND SCONES

Home-made bread and rolls raised with baking powder, or similar raising agents, are quick and easy to make, and are excellent plain fare for tea-time, picnics and so on. A number of basic recipes are given here: these may be varied by using different kinds of flour, and by adding fruit or spices. Wholemeal flour is suitable for scones and breads, and the occasional use of a proportion of oatmeal, barley meal or corn meal with white flour gives interest and variety.

Raising Agents for Quick Breads

Baking powder or bicarbonate of soda, used in conjunction with cream of tartar or with sour milk or buttermilk, is used for scones and quick breads. The proportions are as follows:

2 tbsps. baking powder to 1 lb. of plain flour.

2 tsps. bicarbonate of soda and 4 tsps. cream of tartar, to 1 lb. plain flour, when using sweet milk.

2 tsps. bicarbonate of soda and 2 tsps. cream of tartar to 1 lb. of plain flour, when using sour milk or buttermilk. If the milk is very sour, omit the cream of tartar altogether.

When using self-raising flour, follow any directions given on the package—additional raising agent is not as a rule necessary.

Points about Making Quick Breads

1. Always sieve the raising agents carefully with the flour before rubbing in the fat, to remove lumps and ensure even distribution of the raising agent.

2. Mix all scone and quick bread mixtures to a soft, spongy dough, just dry enough to handle without its sticking to the basin or board. If the dough is stiff the mixture will not rise well and the result will be heavy.

3. Roll out or pat the dough into shape very lightly, and handle as little as possible once it is mixed. Too much handling (a common fault) presses out the bubbles and gives a heavy dough.

4. Form very quickly and lightly into the required shapes. Place rolls 1 inch apart if they are liked crusty on all sides, and almost touching each other if soft edges are preferred.

5. If there is a delay in getting baking powder rolls into the oven, put them in the refrigerator until they can be baked.

6. In making a batch of buns, sometimes bake half of them plain to be served hot, and add chopped raisins, dates or nuts to the other half; these can then be served toasted the next day.

7. To make hot rolls for breakfast, mix and sift the dry ingredients, measure the fat and grease the tins overnight, and the rolls can be in the oven in no time.

8. Left-over baking powder rolls may be reheated by arranging them in a covered casserole, sprinkling with a little water and heating them about 10 minutes in a hot oven (450° F., mark 8). Alternatively, split left-over baking powder rolls, butter them and toast under the grill. A sprinkle of grated cheese adds a good flavour.

BAKING POWDER BREAD

1 lb. flour	Milk or water to mix
2 tbsps. baking powder	(about $\frac{1}{2}$ pint)
2 tsps. salt	

Sieve the flour, baking powder and salt into a basin, make a well in the centre and stir in enough liquid to make a soft, spongy dough. Turn on to a floured board, knead very lightly, and form into 2 flat loaves. Cut 3 marks on each with a knife. Put on a floured baking sheet and bake in a moderately hot oven (425° F., mark 7) for about 45 minutes, or until well risen, nicely browned and firm underneath.

BAKING POWDER ROLLS

$\frac{1}{2}$ lb. flour	1 oz. fat
1 tbsp. baking powder	About $\frac{1}{4}$ pint milk or
1 tsp. salt	water

Sieve the dry ingredients into a basin and rub in the fat. Make a well in the centre of the ingredients, and stir in enough liquid to give a light, spongy dough. Turn on to a floured board, cut into 8 pieces and form very quickly into twists or rolls. Place on a floured baking sheet. Glaze with beaten egg and milk, if liked. Bake in a hot oven (450° F., mark 8) for 15–20 minutes, until they are well risen and browned and sound hollow when tapped on the underside.

CHEESE POTATO BREAD

4 oz. flour	2 oz. sieved cooked potatoes
1 tsp. salt	2 oz. grated cheese
3 tsps. baking powder	
Milk and water to mix	

Sieve the flour, salt and baking powder, add the sieved potatoes and grated cheese, and rub lightly together with the finger-tips. Make into a soft dough with liquid and form quickly into small rolls. Bake in a hot oven (450° F., mark 8) about 15 minutes, until well risen and browned.

IRISH BROWN BREAD

8 oz. flour	1 oz. cooking fat
1 tsp. salt	4 tbsps. medium or coarse oatmeal
1 tsp. bicarbonate of soda	Thick sour milk to mix

Sieve the flour, salt and bicarbonate of soda together and rub in the fat with the finger-tips until no lumps can be felt. Mix in the oatmeal, make a well in the centre of the dry ingredients and add sufficient thick sour milk to make a soft, light dough. Turn out on a floured board, form into a round flat cake, place on a floured baking sheet and mark in four. Bake in a moderately hot oven (425° F., mark 7) for about 30 minutes, until firm and lightly browned. Wrap in a tea towel, and place on a rack to cool.

MALT LOAF

3 tbsps. malt	3 oz. chopped dates
3 tbsps. golden syrup	1 egg
$\frac{1}{3}$ pint milk	1 tsp. bicarbonate of soda
8 oz. self-raising flour	

Place the malt, syrup, and milk in a saucepan and beat until well blended. Sieve the flour and
107 add the chopped dates. Beat the egg and add to the flour, together with the malt mixture, stirring all the time. Dissolve the bicarbonate of soda in a little water and add it to the mixture, then pour this into a bread tin and bake in a moderate oven (375° F., mark 5) for about 1 hour, or until firm.

NUT AND DATE BREAD

6 oz. flour	1 oz. chopped nuts
2 oz. wholemeal flour	$\frac{1}{2}$ tsp. bicarbonate of soda
A pinch of salt	Milk
$1\frac{1}{2}$ oz. fat	4 oz. syrup
3 oz. stoned chopped dates	

Mix flours and salt in a bowl and rub in the fat. Add the stoned, chopped dates and the chopped nuts. Dissolve the bicarbonate of soda in a little milk; slightly warm the syrup. Make a well in the centre of the dry ingredients and add the syrup and the bicarbonate of soda, with sufficient extra milk to give a light, sticky dough. Turn into a greased and floured bread tin, and bake in a moderately hot oven (400° F., mark 6) for about 50 minutes, until well risen and browned and firm underneath.

SODA BREAD

1 lb. flour (white, or white and wholemeal mixed)	2 tsps. cream of tartar
2 tsps. salt	1 oz. fat
2 tsps. bicarbonate of soda	About $\frac{1}{2}$ pint sour milk, buttermilk or sweet milk

(If sweet milk is used, increase the cream of tartar to 2 tsps.).

Sieve the flour, salt, bicarbonate of soda and cream of tartar into a basin and rub in the fat. Make a well in the centre of the ingredients and mix in enough liquid to make a soft, spongy dough. Turn on to a lightly floured board and shape quickly into 1 or 2 round cakes. Place on a floured baking sheet or tin and score 3 marks on each with a knife. Bake in a moderately hot oven (425° F., mark 7) 30–40 minutes, until well risen and lightly browned, and firm underneath.

OVEN SCONES (BASIC RECIPE)

$\frac{1}{2}$ lb. flour	1 tsp. cream of tartar
$\frac{1}{2}$ tsp. salt	1–2 oz. fat
1 tsp. bicarbonate of soda	Milk to mix (about $\frac{1}{4}$ pint)

(If sour milk is used to mix, reduce the cream of tartar to $\frac{1}{2}$ tsp.).

Sieve the flour, salt, bicarbonate of soda and
cream of tartar into a basin and rub in the fat. 1
Make a well in the centre and stir in enough milk to make a light, spongy dough, just firm enough to handle. Turn on to a floured board, knead very lightly, if necessary, to remove any cracks, then roll out lightly to 1 inch thick, or pat out with the hand. Cut in rounds with a sharp cutter dipped in flour or cut into triangles with a sharp knife. Place on a floured baking sheet, glaze if liked with beaten egg or milk, and bake near the top of a hot oven (450° F., mark 8) for 7–10 minutes, until well risen and nicely browned. Cool on a rack.

FRUIT SCONES

Follow above recipe, adding 2 oz. currants, sultanas or raisins to the dry ingredients. Chopped dates may be used if preferred.

OATMEAL SCONES

Follow scone recipe, substituting 2 oz. of oatmeal for 2 oz. of the flour.

RICH AFTERNOON TEA SCONES

Follow the recipe for scones, adding 2–3 tbsps. caster sugar to the dry ingredients, and use 1 beaten egg with 1–2 tbsps. water or milk to mix.

If liked, 2 oz. dried fruit (sultanas, raisins, etc.) may be included, in which case rather less sugar is needed.

CHEESE SCONES

8 oz. flour
2 tsps. cream of tartar
1 tsp. bicarbonate of soda
2 oz. butter
3–4 oz. grated cheese
Salt and pepper
1 tsp. dry mustard
About ¼ pint milk

Sieve together the flour, cream of tartar and bicarbonate of soda and rub in the fat thoroughly. Add the finely grated cheese, a sprinkling of salt and pepper and the mustard, and mix to a soft dough with the milk. Turn on to a floured board, knead lightly if necessary to remove any cracks, and roll or pat out about 1 inch thick. Cut into rounds, triangles or finger shapes, place on a greased baking sheet, glaze with beaten egg and milk, and bake in a hot oven (450° F., mark 8) for about 10 minutes.

WHOLEMEAL SCONES

1 lb. wholemeal
1 tsp. salt
2 tsps. bicarbonate of soda
1 tbsp. cream of tartar
2 oz. lard
2 oz. granulated sugar
2 tbsps. black treacle
About ½ pint milk

Add the sieved salt, bicarbonate and cream of tartar to the wholemeal, rub in the lard, and add the sugar and treacle. Mix to a soft dough with the milk. Roll out ½–¾ inch thick, cut into rounds and bake in a hot oven (450° F., mark 8) for 15–20 minutes. Brush over with sugar and milk.

MAKING GIRDLE SCONES

A girdle is a circular piece of iron, slightly convex and with a half-hoop handle. In the absence of a girdle, these scones and cakes may be cooked in a thick, strong frying pan, or they may be placed directly on the hot plate of an electric cooker.

To prepare the girdle, rub over with a small pad of kitchen paper and a little salt (or with fine steel wool), to ensure that it is smooth and clean, then dust with a dry cloth. The girdle (or frying pan or hot plate), should then be evenly heated throughout before the scones or cakes are placed on it, and it is important that an even heat be maintained throughout the cooking. The convex shape of the girdle helps to ensure even heating—if a frying pan is used, an asbestos mat placed underneath it helps to spread the heat evenly. Judging the heat of the girdle or hot plate is largely a matter of experience. It is tested by holding the back of the hand about an inch from the surface: a steady but not fierce heat should be felt, similar to the heat of an iron used when ironing cotton material. Another test is to sprinkle dry flour on the girdle—if it is sufficiently hot the flour will brown lightly in about 2 minutes.

For scones, it is enough to flour the hot girdle lightly before cooking them, but for batters, the girdle requires to be greased. A piece of suet held on the end of a fork or wrapped in a piece of paper and rubbed over the hot girdle is a convenient way of greasing it; if no suet is to hand, lard (wrapped in paper or muslin) may be used instead. Do not have the fat running on the girdle, but use only sufficient to grease the surface lightly.

The exact time required for cooking scones, etc., on a girdle, depends on the thickness of the mixture and the temperature of the girdle. Girdle scones should not be made more than ¾ inch in thickness, and the heat should be slow enough to cook them through without scorching them, generally about 5 minutes on each side. When cooked on one side they should be turned carefully with a flat, broad knife, to cook the other side. With a little experience, it is easy to tell by the touch whether the scone is cooked through, but if in doubt, just break open the edge with the point of a knife—if ready it will be light and spongy inside.

GIRDLE SCONES

8 oz. flour
1 tsp. bicarbonate of soda
2 tsps. cream of tartar
A pinch of salt
1½ oz. butter or margarine
½–1 oz. sugar
2 oz. sultanas (optional)
¼ pint milk or milk and water

Sieve the flour, bicarbonate of soda, and cream
of tartar with a pinch of salt. Rub in the butter 107
and add the sugar and cleaned sultanas, if used. Mix to a fairly soft dough with the milk. Turn on to a floured board and knead very lightly, if necessary, to remove any cracks. Roll out ½ inch thick and cut in triangles or rounds. Place on a hot floured girdle. Cook steadily until well risen and pale brown underneath. Turn over gently

and cook until the other side is browned and the centre is dry.

For OAT CAKES, see chapter on Biscuits.

OATMEAL BANNOCKS

6 oz. flour	2 oz. medium oatmeal
1 tbsp. baking powder	1 tbsp. sugar
1 tsp. salt	Approx. ¼ pint milk and water
1 oz. margarine	

Mix together the flour, baking powder, and salt, and rub in the fat very thoroughly with the finger-tips. Add the oatmeal and sugar, and mix well. Make a well in the centre of the mixture and add enough liquid to form a soft, light dough. Form into flat, round cakes or bannocks, about ½ inch thick. Cook on a hot girdle or electric hot plate until well risen and brown, turning the cakes when cooked on the under-side.

To vary the bannocks, add 1 oz. sultanas and ½ oz. candied peel.

POTATO CAKES

1 lb. potatoes	1 oz. butter
2 tsps. salt	3–4 oz. flour

Boil the potatoes, then drain and sieve them. Add the salt and butter and work in as much flour as the potatoes will easily absorb. Turn on to a floured board and knead lightly.

For Thin Potato Cakes : Roll out ¼ inch thick and cut into rounds or triangles. Cook on a hot greased girdle or in a thick frying pan until golden-brown on both sides—about 8–10 minutes. Spread with butter and serve hot.

For Thick Potato Cakes : Form the dough into a roll about as thick as a rolling pin, cut off slices about ½ inch thick, dust with flour and cook on a hot greased girdle or in a thick frying pan until golden-brown on both sides—about 10–15 minutes. Serve hot with butter.

Cold cooked potatoes can be used, but the cakes will not be so light as when freshly boiled hot potatoes are used. A little grated cheese may be included if liked.

SCOTCH PANCAKES OR DROP SCONES

8 oz. flour	1–4 oz. granulated sugar
1 tsp. bicarbonate of soda	2 eggs
1 tsp. cream of tartar	½ pint milk (buttermilk for preference)

107 (If fresh milk is used, add another 1 tsp. cream of tartar.)

Sieve the flour, bicarbonate of soda and cream of tartar together, and add the granulated sugar. Whisk the eggs and stir them into the dry ingredients with enough of the milk to make a batter of the consistency of thick cream. The mixing should be done as quickly and lightly as possible, using a large metal spoon. Do not beat. If a thin pancake is wanted, add rather more milk.

Place the mixture in spoonfuls on a hot, lightly greased girdle ; for round pancakes drop it from the point of the spoon, for oval ones, from the side. Keep the girdle at a steady heat, and when bubbles rise to the surface of the pancakes and burst, turn the cakes over, using a knife, and continue cooking until golden-brown on the other side—4–6 minutes in all. Place on a clean linen cloth, cover with another, and place on a rack to cool. This keeps in the steam and the pancakes do not become dry. Serve with fresh butter or with whipped cream and jam.

For richer drop scones, add a little fat (about 1 oz.), either rubbing it into the flour or adding it melted with the eggs and milk. If liked, 2 oz. sultanas may be added.

The quantity of sugar varies considerably according to taste. Many people like pancakes only slightly sweetened, in which case 1 oz. sugar would be sufficient. It is not advisable, however, to add more than 4 oz. of sugar to the ½ lb. flour, as the pancakes tend to stick to the girdle and break when being turned if more is used.

SULTANA GIRDLE CAKES

8 oz. flour	2 oz. sultanas
2 tsps. cream of tartar	1 oz. sugar
1 tsp. bicarbonate of soda	1 egg
2 oz. butter	Milk to mix

Sieve together the flour, cream of tartar and bicarbonate of soda, then rub in the butter thoroughly. Add the cleaned sultanas and sugar and mix with the beaten egg and sufficient milk to make a soft dough. Roll out about ¼ inch thick, cut into rounds or triangles, and cook on a hot girdle as for girdle scones.

Other dried fruit may be substituted for the sultanas, if preferred, or a mixture may be used. Raisins should be stoned and cut up.

TREACLE SCONES

8 oz. flour	A pinch of salt
1 tsp. cream of tartar	1 oz. butter
1 tsp. bicarbonate of soda	2 oz. treacle or syrup
	Milk

Sieve together the dry ingredients and rub in the butter. Warm the syrup slightly, add a little milk and mix the whole to a fairly soft dough. Turn on to a floured board, and cut as for plain girdle scones, i.e., ½ inch thick. Place on a hot greased girdle and cook steadily, but rather slowly, until well risen and lightly coloured underneath. Turn over gently and cook slowly until the scones are browned underneath and dry in the centre. Be very careful when cooking these scones not to let them scorch, as scones with treacle or syrup in them are inclined to do so. Serve either hot or cold with fresh butter.

Treacle scones may also be baked in the oven. Make as above but cut 1 inch thick. Bake in a moderately hot oven (400° F., mark 6).

WHOLEMEAL GIRDLE SCONES

4 oz. wholemeal	½ tsp. salt
4 oz. plain flour	2 tbsps. sugar
1 tsp. bicarbonate of soda	1 oz. butter
2 tsps. cream of tartar	Milk to mix

Sieve together the dry ingredients. Rub in the butter as for plain girdle scones, and mix to a slightly softer dough with the milk. Roll out ½–¾ inch thick and bake in the same way as plain girdle scones.

SIMPLE DOUGHNUTS

½ lb. flour	2 oz. sugar
½ tsp. bicarbonate of soda	1 oz. butter
½ tsp. cream of tartar	1 egg
A pinch of nutmeg	Sour milk
A pinch of cinnamon	Fat for frying

Sieve all the dry ingredients into a basin and rub in the butter. Make a well in the centre and pour in the well-beaten egg and enough sour milk to make a softish dough. Drop in small spoonfuls into hot fat, and fry until a delicate brown colour, turning them frequently. Lift out, and drain on paper sprinkled with sugar.

Alternatively, the dough may be made stiffer, turned out on a floured board and lightly kneaded until free from cracks, then rolled out to ¼ inch in thickness, cut out in rings with two round cutters, and fried as before. The flavouring, too, may be changed at will.

If sour milk is not available, use sweet milk and add an extra 1 tsp. of cream of tartar.

For DOUGHNUTS made with yeast, see chapter on Yeast Mixtures.

YEAST BREAD, ROLLS AND BUNS

The special quality and flavour of home-made bread is always appreciated, and buns and cakes made with yeast as a raising agent are a welcome change from those made with baking powder.

Some beginners are afraid to tackle yeast mixtures, but these are not really difficult as long as it is realised that yeast, unlike other raising agents, is a living plant, requiring gentle warmth in order to grow. Like any other plant, yeast also requires food, and this it obtains from the carbohydrates in the flour and from the moisture used in making the dough. Under these conditions, yeast grows rapidly, and as it grows a harmless and tasteless gas—carbon dioxide—is formed. The bubbles of this gas are responsible for the sponginess of the mixture; the growing yeast also produces alcohol, which gives the characteristic "yeasty" smell and taste to freshly baked bread.

The yeast used for home baking is compressed, or baker's, yeast. It is obtained from the grocer, baker, or flour dealer, and it must be bought fresh, when it will be rather like a piece of putty, cool and moist to the touch, with a fresh yeasty smell. Stale yeast is dry and crumbly. It is best to buy just enough yeast for immediate needs, but if it has to be kept for a few days, store it covered in a refrigerator or other cold place.

Various brands of dried yeast can be bought when fresh yeast is unobtainable. When using these, follow the manufacturers' instructions carefully to ensure good results.

PROCESSES IN BREAD MAKING

These are clearly defined, and, generally speaking, they hold good for most yeast mixtures. As already mentioned, warmth is an essential, so throughout the bread-making processes, up to the baking, warm utensils and liquid, and a warm place for rising and proving, must be supplied.

Warming: Warm both the bowl of flour and the liquid (water, or a mixture of milk and water) used for mixing the dough. The temperature of the liquid should be lukewarm or blood heat (i.e., about 98° F.)—not hot—or the yeast will be destroyed. Add salt to the flour in the proportion of approx. 2 tsps. salt to 1 lb. flour.

Adding the Fat: If any fat is to be used in the bread, rub it into the warm flour. Though not essential in bread, the addition of a small amount of fat improves the flavour and helps to keep the bread moist. It is specially recommended when using wholemeal, to combat the tendency of brown bread to become dry. (In richer yeast mixtures, in which a fair proportion of fat is used, this is generally melted and added along with the liquid ingredients.)

Creaming the Yeast: Put the yeast, with or without the addition of a very little sugar, into a basin and work it with a teaspoon for a minute or two—until it liquefies. At this stage add half the tepid liquid to the creamed yeast.

Setting the Sponge: Make a well in the flour and pour the creamed yeast and liquid into the middle. Then sprinkle a little of the flour from the sides over the surface of the liquid, cover the basin, and stand it in a warm place for about 20 minutes to start the yeast working. This process is not essential, and is omitted in many recipes. When the setting is omitted, mixing is proceeded with immediately, and a rather longer time may be needed for the bread to rise.

Mixing the Dough : It is very important to mix the dough to the right consistency, which should be soft and elastic—almost sticky. On no account allow it to become stiff or hard, as the bubbles of carbon dioxide are unable to work their way through a tough, close dough, and heavy bread results. The amount of liquid absorbed by different flours varies, but as a general guide, 1 lb. of flour of average moisture content requires ½ pint liquid to make a dough of good consistency.

Kneading : The object of kneading is to distribute the yeast evenly throughout the dough, and this process must therefore be done thoroughly. Insufficient kneading results in an unevenly risen dough with large holes. To knead, hold the bowl with the left hand and with the right hand take hold of the outer edge of the dough, pull this to the middle, and push it with the knuckles. Work all round the dough and continue until it is firm, smooth, and elastic. The easiest way is to turn the bowl a little each time with the left hand, kneading in the same place with the right. If more convenient, the dough may be kneaded on a floured board, turning the dough with the left hand and kneading with the right. At least 10 minutes' kneading is required for 3½ lb. flour.

Rising : Put the dough into a lightly floured bowl, and cut it across with a sharp knife to facilitate rising. Cover the bowl with a damp cloth (to prevent a crust forming), and leave in a warm place to rise. Suitable places are on the rack over the stove, if a pan or steamer is boiling below; in the grill compartment of the cooker if the oven is alight; before an open fire; at the side of a range or boiler; near a radiator; or even in the airing cupboard. The important point is that the dough should be gently and evenly warmed to approximately blood heat, for at this temperature the yeast works rapidly —if overheated it is destroyed and the bread will not then rise, and if too cold the yeast will be inactive. Leave the dough to rise until it has doubled its size. From time to time feel the basin, which should be warm but not hot. The time depends on the temperature and the amount of dough, but 3½ lb. flour usually takes about 1 hour.

Moulding : Have ready some warm bread tins or baking sheets, greased and, if liked, lightly floured. Turn the dough on to a floured board and re-knead it for two or three minutes. Then cut into pieces large enough to make the tins ½ to ¾ full. Knead each piece lightly until smooth and put into the tin, smooth side uppermost; with the knuckles, lightly press the dough into the corners of the tin.

When using baking sheets, cut the dough into equal-sized pieces, shape into rounds or ovals, and place directly on the sheet; or make cottage loaves by cutting one-third from each and shaping the two pieces into rounds, smoothing out the creases. Place the larger round on the tin and the smaller round on top. Flour the little finger and press it through the centre of both pieces.

Proving : During the re-kneading, some of the bubbles of carbon dioxide are expelled and thus the dough shrinks in size; it also cools slightly, so time must be allowed for the dough to rise again. This process is termed "proving." Return the tins to a warm place for 10–20 minutes, according to the size or until the dough reaches the top of the tin.

Baking : Place the loaves in a hot oven (450° F., mark 8) for the first 15 minutes. During this time the yeast is "killed," the bubbles of gas expand, the gluten in the flour sets, and the shape of the loaves is defined. The heat can then be reduced to moderate. The cooking time depends on the size—a 2-lb. loaf will take about 45 minutes. When ready, the loaves should be well risen and golden-brown, and when taken from the tin and tapped underneath with the knuckles they should sound hollow.

Cooling : Remove the loaves from the tins and place on a rack to allow the steam to escape. When cold, store in a bread tin.

Glazing : Buns, yeast cakes, and fruit loaves, etc., may be coated with a sweet glaze, which is brushed on as soon as they come from the oven.

To make this, dissolve 2 oz. sugar in 2–3 tbsps. water, bring to the boil, and boil for 3–4 minutes without stirring, until syrupy; use hot.

HOME-MADE BREADS

WHITE BREAD

3½ lb. white flour   1 oz. yeast   108
½ oz. salt   1¾ pints tepid water

Warm the sieved flour and salt and make a well in the middle. Cream the yeast with a little of the water, add the remainder, and pour into the centre of the flour. Sprinkle with a little of the flour and stand covered in a warm place to "set the sponge" for about 20–30 minutes. Mix the dough, adding more liquid if required, and knead well until smooth and elastic. Cover, and put to rise until double the size (about 1 hour). Re-knead the dough, cut into pieces, and shape each piece, kneading until free from cracks. Put into warmed greased tins and prove for 20 minutes. Bake in a hot oven (450° F., mark 8) for 15 minutes. Then reduce the heat to moderate (350° F., mark 4) and bake until the bread is cooked. Turn out and cool.

WHOLEMEAL BREAD

3 lb. wholemeal flour	2 tsps. sugar
1½ oz. salt	1¾ pints water (approx.)
2 oz. lard	
1 oz. yeast	

Add the salt to the wholemeal, rub in the lard, and stand the bowl in a warm place. Cream the yeast and sugar, and add half the tepid liquid. Make a well in the centre of the flour, and add the yeast and enough of the remaining liquid to make a rather soft dough. Knead thoroughly, then put to rise until double the size. Re-knead, shape, and put into tins (which have been greased and dusted with wholemeal flour), half-filling them. Prove for about 20 minutes, and bake in a hot oven (450° F., mark 8) for 15 minutes, then reduce to moderate (350° F., mark 4), and bake until the loaves are brown and sound hollow when tapped underneath. Wholemeal takes longer to cook than white bread, and generally requires more moisture to mix.

QUICK WHOLEMEAL BREAD

1 lb. wholemeal flour	1 oz. yeast
¼ oz. salt	2 tsps. sugar
1 oz. lard	½ pint warm water

In this modern method of bread-making, setting the sponge and kneading are omitted, and rising and proving are telescoped, so the process is much quicker. The texture of the bread is close, and the top somewhat uneven.

Put the flour and salt to warm in a bowl, then rub in the lard. Cream together the yeast and sugar, and add the warm water. Make a well in the centre of the flour, and gradually add the liquid; when this is all mixed in, put the dough into a greased and floured 2 lb. size tin and leave it in a warm place for about ¾ hour, until it is well risen. Then bake in a moderately hot oven (425° F., mark 7) for 45 minutes.

CURRANT BREAD

1¼ lb. flour	1 oz. candied peel
2 tsps. salt	½ oz. yeast
1 oz. melted butter or lard	2 tsps. caster sugar
½ lb. currants	½ pint tepid milk (approx.)

Sieve the warmed flour and salt into a basin and rub in the fat. Add the cleaned currants and chopped peel, and mix well. Cream the yeast with the sugar and add the tepid milk. Make a well in the flour, add liquid, sprinkle a little of the flour from the sides on top, cover with a clean cloth, and put in a warm place to "set the sponge" for about ½ hour. Then mix to a soft dough, knead thoroughly on a floured board, and leave in a warm place to rise for about 1 hour, or until double its size. Divide in 2 or 3 pieces and knead each into a smooth ball. Press lightly into greased and floured bread tins, filling the tins just over half-full. Prove in a warm place for 30–40 minutes, until the dough has risen to the top of the tin. Bake in a hot oven (450° F., mark 8) for 15 minutes, then reduce the heat to moderate (350° F., mark 4) and bake until cooked through—¾-1 hour in all. They should be nicely browned and sound hollow when tapped underneath. Glaze with sugar and water on taking from oven.

BUNS AND ROLLS

BATH BUNS

1 lb. flour	3 oz. sultanas
6 oz. butter	2 oz. candied peel
1 oz. yeast	Grated rind of ½ lemon
1–2 oz. loaf sugar	5 oz. caster sugar
¼ pint milk	Egg and milk to glaze
2 eggs	Crushed loaf sugar

Warm and sieve the flour and rub in the butter thoroughly. Cream the yeast with 1 tsp. sugar and add the lukewarm milk. Beat the eggs, mix with the yeast and milk, and pour into a well made in the centre of the flour. Mix, and beat well, adding a little more milk if required, to make a soft, sticky mixture, then cover the basin with a clean, damp cloth, and put to rise in a warm place for about 1 hour, or until the mixture has doubled its size. Mix the sultanas, chopped peel, lemon rind, and caster sugar together, and put to warm slightly. Turn the dough on to a floured board and mix the fruit roughly with it—do not knead it in, or you will not obtain the required result. Divide into 12 or 14 roughly shaped buns and place on a greased baking sheet. Prove for 5–10 minutes, then brush with egg and milk, and sprinkle with crushed loaf sugar. Bake in a hot oven (450° F., mark 8) for about 20 minutes.

BRIDGE OR SANDWICH ROLLS

½ lb. flour	4 tbsps. tepid milk
A pinch of salt	1 egg
½ oz. yeast	2 oz. butter
1 tsp. caster sugar	

Sieve the flour and salt into a basin and make a well in the centre. Cream the yeast with the caster sugar, add half the liquid and pour into the flour. Beat the egg with the remainder of the milk and stir it into the flour with the melted butter, mixing to a soft, smooth dough. Stand the dough in a warm place until it has doubled its size. Turn on to a board and cut into narrow strips the size of bridge rolls—about 3 inches in length is suitable. Roll in the hands, place them on greased baking tins, and prove for a few minutes. Brush with beaten egg, and bake in a hot oven (450° F., mark 8) for about 15 minutes.

BRIOCHES

1 lb. fine flour	4 whole eggs and 4 yolks
1 tsp. salt	4–6 oz. melted butter
½ oz. yeast	1 oz. caster sugar
2–3 tbsps. warm water	Beaten egg to glaze

Sieve the flour and salt together and make two wells in the flour. Cream the yeast with a little of the warm water and pour into one well. Put the beaten eggs and yolks, melted butter, and sugar into the other well. Beat well with the hand, adding more water if required, to make a soft, sticky mixture. Cover, and allow to rise in a warm place for 1 hour. Brush about 24 deep patty pans with melted butter. Shape the dough into an even number of large and small balls. Put a large ball at the bottom of each patty pan, make a hole in the centre and put in a small ball. Prove for 20 minutes, brush with beaten egg, and bake in a hot oven (450° F., mark 8) for 5–10 minutes.

CHELSEA BUNS

4 oz. butter	2 eggs
¼ pint milk	1 lb. flour
4 oz. caster sugar	A little melted lard
½ oz. yeast	3 oz. currants

Melt the butter, add most of the milk, and 3 oz. of the sugar, and warm together. Cream the yeast with the rest of the milk; beat the eggs. Sieve the flour, add the warmed ingredients and the creamed yeast to the flour, together with the beaten eggs, and mix thoroughly. Put to rise, covered with a clean, damp cloth, in a warm place until the dough has doubled its size. Flour a pastry board, roll the dough into a long oblong strip as evenly as possible, and about ½ inch in thickness. Brush with melted lard, sprinkle with the remaining 1 oz. sugar and the cleaned currants. Roll up, then cut off slices about 1 inch thick. Pack these fairly close together, with the cut edge uppermost, in a greased oblong or square tin. Allow to prove in a warm place for 30 minutes, then bake in a moderately hot oven (425° F., mark 7) for 20–30 minutes.

When the buns are almost baked, brush over with a mixture of sugar and water in the proportion of 4 tbsps. sugar to 1 of water, boiled together; return them to the oven for a moment or two. Turn on to a rack to cool.

CROISSANTS

1¼ lb. flour	1 oz. yeast
¼ oz. salt	½ oz. sugar
1½ oz. melted butter	4–6 oz. butter
½ pint milk and water	Egg and milk to glaze

Warm the flour in a basin and add the salt. Add the melted butter to the milk and water, and warm together. Cream the yeast and sugar. Make a well in the centre of the flour and mix to a light dough with the yeast and milk. Knead lightly and set to rise for about 30 minutes. Turn on to a floured board, knead lightly, and roll out to an oblong. Weigh out the remaining butter and divide it into three. Place one portion
of the butter in small heaps over the top two- 111
thirds of the dough, then fold in three, turning the bottom third up first and bringing the top third over it. Seal the ends with the rolling pin and give one half turn. Roll again into an oblong, spread with the second portion of butter, fold, and turn, as before. Repeat this once more with the remaining portion of fat.

Roll out the dough very thinly, cut into squares and then into triangles. Roll each triangle into a crescent, starting to roll at the longest side and finishing with the point, curling the ends round to form a crescent. Place on a greased tin and prove about 10 minutes. Then brush over very gently with beaten egg and milk, and bake in a hot oven (450° F., mark 8) until well risen, golden-brown, and hollow-sounding when tapped—10–15 minutes.

CRUMPETS

½ oz. yeast	A pinch of bicarbonate of soda
1 pint milk and water	2 tsps. salt
1 lb. flour	

Cream the yeast with a little of the tepid liquid, add the rest, and pour into the flour. Beat very thoroughly with the hand for 5 minutes. Stand it covered in a warm place for
108 1 hour. Dissolve the bicarbonate of soda and salt in a little warm water and add to the sponged mixture. Beat up and put to rise again for ¾ hour. Have ready a greased girdle, moderately hot. Grease some crumpet rings and let them heat on the girdle. Pour in enough batter to cover the bottom thoroughly. Allow to cook gently until the top is set. Remove the rings, turn the crumpets over, and allow to dry for a few minutes on the underside.

DOUGH CAKE

½ lb. flour	1 egg
A pinch of salt	A little grated nutmeg
1 oz. butter or margarine	½ oz. chopped peel
½ oz. yeast	1 oz. sugar
Milk and water to mix	2 oz. currants

Sieve the flour and salt into a basin, and rub in the fat. Mix the yeast with a little of the warm milk and water, add to the flour, together with the rest of the ingredients, and mix to a soft dough with the milk and water. The dough should be slightly softer than is required for bread. Beat very thoroughly with the hand, put into a greased and warmed loaf tin, half-filling it, and allow to rise in a warm place until the dough reaches the top of the tin. Then bake in a moderately hot oven (425° F., mark 7) for about 30 minutes.

DOUGHNUTS

½ lb. flour	3–4 tbsps. warm milk
A pinch of salt	1 egg
2 oz. butter	Jam
½ oz. yeast	Fat for frying
Caster sugar	Cinnamon (optional)

Warm the sieved flour and salt in a basin and rub in the butter. Cream the yeast with 1 tsp. caster sugar and add to it the tepid milk and beaten egg. Pour into the centre of the flour and mix to a soft dough. Beat well with a wooden spoon or the hand, and leave to rise until the dough becomes twice the original size; then knead lightly. Divide into 10–12 pieces. Shape each into a ball—flatten a little and place about ¼ tsp. of jam in the centre of each piece. Gather the edges together over the jam, forming balls. Place on a greased and floured tin, and leave in a warm place for a few minutes to prove. Heat some deep fat until smoking faintly but not too hot, and fry the doughnuts in it until golden-brown and cooked through (about 5 minutes). Drain, then turn out on to a paper and dredge with caster sugar. If preferred, sprinkle with a little ground cinnamon mixed with sugar. Serve very fresh.

For doughnuts made without yeast, see next chapter.

HOT CROSS BUNS

1¾ lb. flour	½ tsp. grated nutmeg
1 oz. yeast	4–6 oz. currants
4 oz. caster sugar	1 oz. candied peel
¾ pint milk or milk and water	4 oz. butter
¼ tsp. salt	2 eggs
½ tsp. cinnamon	Milk and sugar to glaze

Sieve ½ lb. of the flour into a basin. Cream the yeast with 1 tsp. of the sugar and stir in the tepid milk. Strain into the sieved flour and mix well together. Cover with a cloth, and put in a warm place to set the sponge for about 20 minutes. Meanwhile, sieve the remainder of the flour with sugar, salt, cinnamon, and nutmeg, and stir in the currants and chopped peel. Melt the butter and beat the eggs. When the mixture has well "sponged" in the first basin, stir in all the dry ingredients, pour in the melted butter and the beaten eggs and mix thoroughly, beating with the hand. When well mixed and beaten, cover the basin with a cloth and put aside in a warm place to rise for about 1 hour, or until the dough has almost doubled its size. Flour the hands, take small portions of the dough and shape into round buns. Place on a well-greased and floured baking tin, allowing room for the buns to spread. Cut a cross on the top and again put in a warm place to prove for about 20–30 minutes. If necessary, re-mark the cross before putting into a very hot oven (475° F., mark 9). When golden-brown and almost cooked, glaze the buns by brushing them with a little milk and sugar. Cool on a rack.

LARDY CAKE

2 lb. white bread dough	½–1 oz. carraway seeds or 4 oz. currants (optional)
6 oz. lard or butter	Sugar and water to glaze
7 oz. sugar	

Roll out the dough into an oblong and spread on it half the lard or butter and half the sugar, covering only the top two-thirds of the dough. (If carraway seeds or currants are added, they should be sprinkled over the lard and sugar when these are spread on the dough.) Fold the dough into three, bringing the bottom third up first and folding the top third over it. Seal the ends by pressing them with the rolling pin and give one half turn. Roll again into an oblong, spread the top two-thirds with the remaining fat and sugar, fold and turn as before, then roll out to fit a Yorkshire pudding tin, having the dough 1–1½ inches thick. Allow to rise in a warm place, and bake in a moderately hot oven (425° F., mark 7) for ¾–1 hour. When half cooked, the cake may be brushed over with a thick sugar and water syrup, if liked.

MILK ROLLS

1 lb. flour
½ tsp. salt
2 oz. lard
½ oz. yeast
About ½ pint milk
Egg to glaze

Warm the flour, add the salt, and rub in the lard. Cream the yeast and add most of the tepid milk to it. Add this to the flour and mix to a soft, elastic dough, adding more milk if required. Knead well. Put to rise for 1 hour, or until double the size. Turn on to a floured board and knead well. Shape into rolls, dinner buns, or twists. Put on to a warmed greased tin and prove for 10–20 minutes, until they have risen well, but avoid overproving. Glaze with beaten egg and bake in a hot oven (450° F., mark 8) for 15–30 minutes, according to size, until well risen, golden-brown, and hollow-sounding when tapped underneath.

MUFFINS

1 oz. yeast
1 pint water
3 tsps. salt
1½ lb. flour

Mix the yeast with the warm water, add the salt to the sieved flour, and add the liquid and yeast by degrees. Beat well with the hand for 15 minutes: thorough beating at this stage is most essential. Stand the batter in a warm place for 5 hours, and cover with a cloth. Beat up again and stand for a further ½ hour. Meanwhile, take a deep baking tin, dust very liberally with flour and put in a warm place. When the muffin mixture is ready, turn on to a floured board and cut into even-sized pieces. Although the mixture is very soft, only sufficient flour should be used to make handling easy. Roll the portions of dough into flat cakes rather smaller than the muffin rings and put them in the floured tin. Allow to prove for 20 minutes. Have ready a moderately hot floured girdle or hot plate, grease some muffin rings, and heat them. Drop the muffins in the rings and cook for 5 minutes; turn completely over, and cook for another 5 minutes. Remove the rings and press the sides of the muffins to see if they are quite cooked.

SALLY LUNN TEACAKES

¾ lb. flour
½ tsp. salt
½ oz. yeast
2 tsps. sugar
⅓ pint milk and water
1 egg
1 oz. lard or margarine
Egg or milk and sugar to glaze

Sieve the flour and salt into a basin. Cream the yeast with the sugar, stir in the tepid liquid, and pour into the centre of the flour. Add the beaten egg and melted fat, and mix to a light, soft
dough. Knead well. Divide into 2 or 3 pieces, 108
shape into rounds, and put into small greased and floured cake tins, half-filling them. Set in a warm place until the dough rises to the top of the tins, then bake in a hot oven (450° F., mark 8) for 15–20 minutes. Brush over with a little beaten egg, or milk and sugar, a few minutes before finally removing from the oven.

YORKSHIRE TEACAKES

Follow the recipe for Sally Lunn Teacakes, adding 2 oz. fruit (currants or sultanas) and omitting the egg, if liked. Allow the dough to rise in the bowl, then knead again, shape into flat round cakes, and prove in a warm place for a few minutes. Bake in a hot oven (450° F., mark 8) about 15 minutes. Glaze and cool.

SAVARIN

½ oz. yeast
1 tsp. caster sugar
¼ pint milk
½ lb. flour
½ tsp. salt
4 eggs
5 oz. butter
Shredded almonds or desiccated coconut
Fruit syrup to coat
Glacé or crystallised fruits

Cream the yeast and sugar together and add the tepid milk. Sieve the flour and salt and
pour the yeast and milk into the centre, sprinkling 110
a little flour over. Put to rise for ½ hour, then beat in the eggs and melted butter with the hand very thoroughly. Brush out a border mould with melted butter, sprinkle in shredded almonds or desiccated coconut, and pour in the mixture until the mould is half-full. Cover, and put to rise in a warm place until the mixture rises to the top of the mould. Bake for ¾ hour in a moderate oven (375° F., mark 5). Turn out, and when cold pour a well-flavoured fruit syrup over, then fill the centre with glacé or crystallised fruits.

BABA AU RHUM

Prepare a mixture as for Savarin. Butter one large or several small baba moulds and sprinkle a few currants at the bottom. Proceed as for a Savarin. When the Baba is turned out, prick, baste well with hot rum syrup (see Sauces chapter), and serve hot or cold.

YEAST CURRANT BUNS

1¾ lb. flour	1 egg
4 oz. caster sugar	1 tsp. salt
1½ oz. yeast	4 oz. currants
¾ pint milk or milk and water	1 oz. candied peel
4 oz. butter	Milk and sugar to glaze

Sieve ½ lb. of the flour into a basin. Cream 1 tsp. of the sugar with the yeast and stir in the lukewarm liquid. Then strain into the sieved ½ lb. of flour, and mix well together. Cover with a cloth and put in a warm place to set the sponge for ¾ hour. When the mixture is well risen, stir in the remainder of the flour, and beat in the butter, beaten egg, salt, sugar, currants, and chopped peel. Mix and beat thoroughly, using the hand. When thoroughly mixed and well beaten, cover, and put to rise for about 1 hour, until the dough has almost doubled its size. Flour the hands well, take small portions of the dough and shape into buns; put well apart on a greased baking sheet, put in a warm place to prove for 20–30 minutes, and bake in a hot oven (450° F., mark 8). When golden-brown and almost cooked, glaze by brushing over with milk and sugar. Cool on a rack.

YEAST FRUIT LOAF

1 lb. flour	½ pint tepid milk and water
4 oz. butter	4 oz. sultanas
4 oz. sugar	2 oz. currants
1 tsp. salt	½ tsp. grated nutmeg
¾ oz. yeast	
1 egg	

Warm the flour, rub in the butter, and add the sugar and salt. Cream the yeast. Beat the egg, pour on the warm milk and add it, together with the creamed yeast, to the flour. Mix and beat thoroughly, then cover and allow to rise for about 1¼ hours. Beat in the fruit and nutmeg very thoroughly, and put into two greased loaf tins (6 by 4 by 3 inches). Prove for about 30 minutes. Bake in a moderately hot oven (425° F., mark 7) for 15 minutes, and then reduce the heat to moderate (350° F., mark 4) for 30 minutes, or until well risen and brown and firm underneath. Remove from the tins and cool on a rack.

YEAST RIBBON CAKE

12 oz. flour	1 egg
½ tsp. salt	2 oz. glacé cherries
2 oz. margarine	2 oz. candied peel
3 oz. sugar	2 oz. dried fruit
½ oz. yeast	4 tbsps. icing sugar
½ pint warm milk and water	A little water

Sieve the flour and salt into a bowl, rub in the fat, and add the sugar (reserving 1 tsp.). Cream the yeast with this sugar and add ¼ pint of the warm liquid. Mix into the dry ingredients, together with the beaten egg and enough of the remaining liquid to mix to a soft but not sticky dough. Add the sliced cherries, chopped peel, and dried fruit. Knead until smooth, then leave in a warm place for about 45 minutes, or until it has doubled its bulk. Turn the dough out on to a floured board, knead well, and form into a ball. Using a piece of linen tape or a narrow strip of cloth, tie the ball as if it were a parcel, putting the knot at the top. Place on a greased tin, cover, and allow to rise until it is double the size. Bake in a hot oven (450° F., mark 8) for about 15 minutes, then lower the temperature and continue to cook for a total of 45 minutes, or until done. Cut the tape and allow the cake to cool. When it is quite cold, mix the sieved icing sugar with water and decorate the top. When the icing is dry, tie the cake up with red ribbon.

CAKE MAKING

Cake making is a big subject, but not nearly so complicated as it appears at first sight, for though there are very many different cakes, basically the methods of making are few. So it is not necessary to learn a great many recipes, but rather to try to master the method of making and baking each type of cake; then you will be able to attempt any cake recipe you come across, and feel confident of success.

Cakes are classified as "Plain," "Rich," or "Sponge" according to the proportion of fat, sugar, and eggs which they contain and the method by which they are made. Gingerbreads form a small subsidiary group of plain cakes.

Plain Cake mixtures contain up to one half fat and sugar to flour (i.e., a cake made with 1 lb. flour may contain up to ½ lb. each of fat and sugar), and the fat is rubbed into the flour—this is called the Rubbing-in Method.

Rich Cake mixtures contain higher proportions of fat and sugar. This necessitates a different method of making; the fat and sugar are creamed together, the egg beaten in, and the flour folded into the mixture. This is called the Creaming Method.

Sponge Cake mixtures usually contain no fat but a high proportion of eggs and sugar. The eggs and sugar are whisked together and the flour folded in very lightly—this being known as the Whisking Method.

(For fuller descriptions of the method of rubbing in, creaming, and whisking, see the chapter on Cookery Processes and Terms.)

CAKE INGREDIENTS

Flour

Use good quality flour and keep it dry. Self-raising flour may be used for plain cakes, but for richer cakes and sponges, where varying quantities of raising agent are required, it is better to use plain flour and a reliable raising agent. As flour "settles down" on standing in the bin, it should be sieved before use to aerate it,

Fats

Butter is the ideal fat to use for cake making—its flavour is good and cakes made with butter keep well. Margarine, which is usually made from a mixture of fats, is the best substitute; choose a good brand of margarine for cake making. Lard is pure fat, but its flavour is not very good in cakes, so it is best used in conjunction with margarine or butter. White vegetable cooking fats are useful, but have little flavour, so are best combined with butter or margarine. Dripping, if mild in flavour and well clarified, is suitable for plain cakes.

See page 44 for the method of clarifying dripping and other fats.

Sugar

Granulated sugar is satisfactory for plain cakes, but it is better to use fine caster sugar for creamed and sponge mixtures. Moist brown and Demerara sugar are good for gingerbreads, as they help to give a treacly flavour.

Raising Agents

Use a reliable brand of baking powder (or make your own according to the recipe below) and measure it very accurately. Baking powder usually consists of bicarbonate of soda and an acid-reacting chemical, such as cream of tartar; when moistened, these react together to give a gas—carbon dioxide. Flour contains a sticky, rubber-like substance called gluten, which, when wet, is capable of holding the gas made by the raising agent in the form of tiny bubbles. Since all gases expand when heated, the tiny bubbles formed through the mixture become larger during the baking, and the cake rises, Cake mixtures are capable of holding only a certain amount of gas, and if too much raising agent is used the cake rises very well at first but then collapses, and a heavy, close texture is the final result.

Bicarbonate of soda and cream of tartar, or bicarbonate of soda and vinegar, are sometimes used in place of baking powder.

Sour milk is used in some cakes; as it contains an acid, the cream of tartar should be reduced.

Home-Made Baking Powder

2 oz. cream of tartar 3 oz. ground rice
1 oz. bicarbonate of soda

Be sure that the sieve and bowl are perfectly dry, as the mixture must not be allowed to get damp. Sieve the ingredients together two or three times to ensure thorough mixing. Put at once into a tin or storage jar with an airtight cover, and keep tighly covered when not in use.

Eggs

By incorporating whisked egg in a cake mixture, air may be used as a raising agent instead of carbon dioxide. Thus, when a high proportion of egg is used and the mixture is whisked, as in sponge cakes, very little, if any, extra raising agent is needed. In creamed mixtures also the eggs are beaten in, and so long as the correct proportion of egg is used, and the mixture is well beaten, little additional raising agent is required. In plain cakes, where beaten egg is added together with the liquid, egg helps to bind the mixture, but it does not act as a raising agent.

Fruit and Nuts

Fruit must be carefully picked over and cleaned before using, unless cleaned packaged fruit is bought.

To clean currants and sultanas, wash in several cold waters and drain. Dry in a cloth, then spread out on a flat tin or sieve and dry off very slowly in a warm place. For quick cleaning, rub on a wire sieve or in a tea towel with a little flour, then pick over to remove stalks.

To prepare raisins: Wash, remove the stalks, and take out the stones with a small knife or with the fingers. Keep dipping the knife (or fingers) in a basin of warm water to prevent the stones from sticking.

To shred peel: Remove the sugar, and if the peel is very hard, soak it for a minute or two in boiling water. Then dry, and cut into fine shreds or chop with a very sharp knife.

To blanch almonds: Put in a saucepan with cold water to cover, bring just to the boil, strain, and run cold water over them. Then remove the skins, which will slip off quite easily.

To skin hazelnuts: Heat through in the oven or under a slow grill, shaking them occasionally to turn them. Then rub them in a clean cloth, and the papery skins will powder off.

THE CAKE TINS

Sizes of Cake Tins

When stocking your kitchen choose good strong cake tins, and include one or two shallow ones for cakes you intend to make and use straight away—a shallow cake bakes quickly and is convenient to cut. Use deep tins for cakes made to keep (Fruit Cakes, Rich Seed Cake, etc.).

Here are some useful sizes:—

Type of Tin	*Diameter*	*Depth*
Round tin:		
For Madeira or Fruit Cake (8 oz flour)	7″–8″	3″
For fatless Sponge (3 eggs; for 5 eggs use 2 tins)	7″	2″
For large Fruit Cake (1 lb. flour)	9″–10″	3″
Sandwich tins: for Victoria Sandwich (2 eggs), use 2 tins	7″	1″ or 1½″
Square tin: for Gingerbread (1 lb. flour)	8″ × 8″	2″
Oblong loaf tin: for Plain Cake or Loaf (¾ lb. flour)	8″ × 4″ (base)	3″
Flat oblong tin: for Swiss Rolls (3 eggs)	9″ × 12″	½″
Patty tins: for Queen Cakes, etc. (4 oz. flour, 12 cakes)	2″	¾″

Preparation of Cake Tins

Grease all cake tins lightly with unsalted or clarified fat, or oil. The quickest way of greasing them is to brush over with a pastry brush dipped in the melted fat. They may also be dredged with flour as an additional precaution against sticking: sprinkle a little flour in the tin and shake until coated, then shake out any surplus flour.

For sponge cake, first grease the tins, then dust them with 1 tsp. flour mixed with 1 tsp. caster sugar. For sponge sandwiches, line the bottom of the tins with a round of greaseproof paper; for rich mixtures and fruit cakes, line the whole tin.

Greaseproof paper is the best to use for lining tins, but white kitchen paper may be used; in either case the paper should be greased.

To Line a Cake Tin

Cut a piece of strong greaseproof paper long enough to reach round the tin and high enough to extend about 2 inches above the top edge.

Cut another piece to fit the bottom of the tin. Fold up the bottom edge of the long strip about 1 inch, creasing it firmly, and snip this folded portion with a pair of scissors; this enables the paper band to fit a square, round, or oval tin neatly. Brush both pieces of paper with melted fat and place the strip in position first: the bottom piece keeps the snipped edge of the band in position and makes a neat lining.

To Line Sandwich Tins

Lining Cake Tins

Cut a round of grease-proof paper to fit the bottom of the tin exactly. A "tail" of paper may be left on each side to facilitate turning out the cake.

To Line a Swiss Roll Tin

Cut a piece of paper about 2 inches larger all round than the tin. Place the tin on it, and in each corner make a cut from the corner of the paper as far as the corner of the tin. Grease both paper and tin, and put in the paper so that it fits closely, overlapping it at the corners.

Paper and Foil Baking Cases

These baking cases may be used in place of tins for small cakes, sponge cakes, and so on. They require no preparation. The aluminium foil ones have the advantage that they may be used again.

BAKING CAKES

Managing the Oven

Before starting to make cakes, arrange that the oven will be at the correct temperature by the time it is required.

With a heat-controlled oven, all that is necessary is to set the thermostatic control to the temperature required and to put on the heat. If the oven is not heat-controlled, it is advisable to use a thermometer, unless you are very experienced at gauging the temperature by some other simple means. Place the thermometer on the shelf you propose to use, put on the heat, then regulate it to maintain the required temperature. Before heating the oven, adjust the shelves to the position you will require.

Position of Cakes in the Oven

Small plain cakes, scones, and Swiss rolls (all baked at a high temperature) are placed at the top of the oven, directly underneath the browning sheet, or just below the roof of the oven.

Small rich cakes, sandwich cakes, and biscuits, which require more moderate temperatures, are placed just above the centre of the oven.

Larger cakes are placed in the centre of the oven, where the heat is even and steady.

Very large, rich mixtures, such as Christmas cakes, are placed towards the bottom of the oven, where there is little chance of their becoming over-browned on the top surface.

Oven Temperatures

It is difficult to generalise about the different oven-heats for baking cakes, but, obviously, the larger and deeper the cake, the longer it will take to cook, and the cooler the oven will have to be to avoid over-cooking the outside before the cake has completely cooked through. In addition, rich mixtures need to be cooked at lower temperatures than plainer ones. The following chart will act as a general guide:—

Plain Cakes	*Oven*	*Time*
Small (e.g., Rock Cakes)	Hot	15–20 minutes
Large	Moderately hot lowering to moderate	Approx. 1 hour per lb. of mixture (varying with depth tin)
Rich Cakes		
Small (e.g., Queen Cakes)	Moderately hot	15–20 minutes
Sandwich Cake	Moderate to moderately hot	15–35 minutes (depending on depth)
Large (e.g., Madeira)	Moderate	Approx. 1 hour per lb. (varying with depth of tin)
Large (e.g., Fruit)	Moderate	1–1¼ hours per lb. of mixture (according to richness
Sponge Cakes		
Large	Moderate	Depending on size and depth
Swiss Roll	Very hot	7–9 minutes
Sponge Sandwich	Hot	9–12 minutes
Gingerbread	Moderate	Depending on size and depth
Scones	Very hot	8–10 minutes
Biscuits	Moderate to moderately hot	15–20 minutes

The following table indicates the oven temperatures corresponding to the above descriptions, and also the settings for the standard thermostats fitted to modern cookers.

Oven description	*Approx. temp. and electric setting*	*Standard gas thermostat*
Very slow	250° F., 275° F.	¼, ½
Slow	300° F., 325° F.	1, 2
Moderate	350° F.	3, 4
	375° F.	5
Moderately hot	400° F., 425° F.	6, 7
Hot to very hot	450° F., 475° F.	8, 9

To Test when a Cake is Cooked

With a little practice, it is easy to judge whether or not small cakes are sufficiently cooked. They should be well risen, golden-brown in colour, and firm to the touch, both on top and underneath, and they should begin to shrink from the sides of the tin on being taken out of the oven.

Larger cakes present more difficulty, especially for beginners, although the oven-heat and time of cooking give a reliable indication. The following tests are a guide :—

(*a*) Press the centre of the top of the cake very lightly with the finger-tip. The cake should be spongy and it should give only very slightly to the pressure, then rise again immediately, leaving no impression.

(*b*) Fruit cake : lift gently from the oven and " listen " to it, putting it fairly close to the ear. A continued sizzling sound indicates that the cake is not cooked through.

(*c*) Insert a hot skewer or knitting needle (never a cold knife) in the centre of the cake. It should come out perfectly clean. If any mixture is sticking to it, the cake requires longer cooking.

Cooling

Allow the cake a few minutes to cool before turning out of the tin ; during this time it will shrink away from the sides and is more easily removed. Turn out very gently, remove any paper and place, right side up, on a cake rack. Leave until quite cold before putting in a tin.

Storing Cakes

Store cakes in a tightly covered tin or in a crock covered closely with a lid. Most cakes are nicest eaten quite fresh, but fruit cakes and gingerbreads improve with keeping, and should be kept at least 24 hours before being cut, and even longer if rich.

Fruit cakes which are to be kept for any length of time should be wrapped in greaseproof paper before putting in the tin.

Never store both cakes and biscuits in the same tin ; the biscuits will absorb moisture from the cakes and lose their crispness.

CAKE-MAKING FAULTS

1. *If your cake sinks in the middle*, it may be for any of the following reasons :

(*a*) The cake is not cooked through. Check up on the baking time and temperature, and be sure that the cake responds to the test before removing it from the oven.

(*b*) A sudden drop in the oven temperature at a critical stage of the cooking. Avoid opening the oven door too often or too suddenly, and do not alter the position of the cake while it is still soft. See that no draught blows directly on to the oven from the kitchen door or window.

(*c*) Too much raising agent, causing the mixture to " over-work " itself.

(*d*) Mixture made too wet. Test the consistency of the cake mixture carefully before putting it in the tin.

(*e*) Too much sugar in proportion to the other ingredients.

2. *Fruit sinks to the bottom* of a cake either because :

(*a*) The mixture is too slack to support the fruit, or

(*b*) The fruit is not properly dried after washing.

(*c*) The baking temperature is too low.

(*d*) The fruit is in too large pieces.

3. *A cake that boils out through a crack in the top* was put into too hot an oven. If the initial temperature is too high, the outside of the cake sets and forms a crust before the cake starts to cook in the centre ; then, instead of rising evenly, the mixture has to force its way out of the top.

4. *If your cake is heavy and sticky inside* it may be due to any of the following :

(*a*) Baking at too high a temperature and for too short a time, so that the outside cooks too quickly, leaving the centre slightly raw. Reduce the heat next time you use the recipe or place the cake lower in the oven. Be sure to allow the full baking time.

(*b*) Making the mixture too wet, so that the cake does not dry out in the centre.

(*c*) Cooling too suddenly. See that the cake is not put in a draughty place when first taken from the oven.

(*d*) Packing away while still warm. Make sure the cake is absolutely cold before putting it away in the cake tin.

5. *A close or heavy texture* may be caused by any of the following:

(*a*) Not enough raising agent. Check up on the recipe, and measure baking powder accurately. If the cake is raised by air beaten into the mixture, perhaps you are not beating sufficiently thoroughly.

(*b*) Heavy handling. Cakes require a very light touch, especially when mixing in the dry ingredients.

(*c*) Too dry a mixture. If not moistened enough, the cake is likely to be close and dry when baked.

(*d*) Too wet a mixture. Too much liquid when mixing causes the cake to have a close, heavy texture.

6. *If your cake tastes dry* it was probably too long in the oven, or perhaps the oven was too slow. Both over-cooking and baking at too low a temperature will cause a cake to dry unduly.

7. *If the texture is coarse and open* you have probably used too much raising agent.

LARGE CAKES MADE BY RUBBING-IN METHOD

PLAIN CAKES (BASIC RECIPE)

1 lb. flour
$\frac{1}{2}$ tsp. salt
1–2 tbsps. baking powder (according to the amount of fat and eggs used)
4–8 oz. fat
4–8 oz. sugar
4–8 oz. fruit
Up to 4 eggs
Milk to mix

Sieve the flour, salt, and baking powder together. This removes any lumps that may be in the flour, aerates it, and at the same time thoroughly mixes the dry ingredients.

Rub in the fat lightly, using the tips of the fingers. Continue until the mixture resembles fine breadcrumbs or until no lumps of fat remain. Lift the mixture up while doing this, to aerate it. Add sugar and prepared fruit.

Beat the eggs and add to the dry ingredients with some of the milk or water, mixing quickly and lightly with a wooden spoon and adding more liquid as required, to give a stiff dropping consistency. To test this take a good spoonful of the mixture, and, holding the spoon on its side over the bowl, count slowly. The mixture should drop from the spoon by the time 4 or 5 is reached. If the mixture is too stiff the resulting cake will be dry, crumbly, and close in texture—if too slack, the cake will be heavy and sodden.

Turn the mixture into the prepared tin or tins, three-quarters filling them.

For Baking Temperatures, see recipes, also the Charts on pages 373 and 374.

BATCH CAKE

8 oz. flour
$\frac{1}{2}$ tsp. salt
1 tbsp. baking powder
1 tsp. mixed spice
3 oz. lard or dripping
3 oz. sugar
3 oz. mixed currants and sultanas (or other fruit)
$\frac{1}{2}$ oz. candied peel
Approx. $\frac{1}{4}$ pint milk

Sieve together the flour, salt, baking powder, and spice, and rub in the lard or dripping very 112
thoroughly with the finger-tips. Add the sugar, fruit, and chopped peel, and mix very lightly to a soft "tacky" dough with the milk. Turn out at once on to a greased baking sheet. Pat down a little with the spoon into a round about $1\frac{1}{2}$ inches thick, and bake in a hot oven (450° F., mark 8) for 20–30 minutes, until well risen and browned and firm to the touch. Turn on to a rack to cool. This cake may be served while still warm, if desired.

PLAIN CHERRY CAKE

12 oz. flour
A pinch of salt
3 tsps. baking powder
6 oz. butter or margarine
4 oz. glacé cherries
6 oz. sugar
1 egg
Milk (3–5 tbsps.)
$\frac{1}{2}$ tsp. vanilla essence

Prepare a 6-inch cake tin. Sieve the flour, salt, and baking powder into a basin. Rub in the fat with the tips of the fingers until it resembles fine breadcrumbs. Cut the cherries into quarters and add, with the sugar, to the dry ingredients, and mix well. Make a well in the centre, stir in the beaten egg and add sufficient milk to give a dropping consistency. Lastly, stir in the vanilla essence. Put into the prepared tin, and bake in a moderate oven (350° F., mark 4) for about $1\frac{1}{4}$ hours.

For RICH CHERRY CAKE see recipe under Creaming Method.

CHOCOLATE CAKE (ECONOMICAL)

6 oz. flour
1 oz. cocoa
2 tsps. baking powder
A pinch of salt
$3\frac{1}{2}$ oz. butter or margarine
2 oz. desiccated coconut
4 oz. sugar
1 egg
Vanilla essence
Milk to mix

Sieve the flour, cocoa, baking powder, and

salt into a basin. Rub the butter into the flour, add the coconut and sugar, and stir in the beaten egg. Lightly mix in the vanilla essence with sufficient milk to produce a fairly moist mixture. Put into a prepared tin, and bake in a moderate oven (350° F., mark 4) for about ¾ hour.

For RICH CHOCOLATE CAKE see recipe under Creaming Method.

EGGLESS CAKE

6 oz. flour	Grated rind of ½ a lemon
A pinch of salt	Milk to mix
3 tsps. baking powder	A few drops of lemon essence
2½ oz. butter or margarine	
3 oz. sugar	
2 oz. currants	

Grease and flour a small cake tin. Sieve the flour, salt, and baking powder into a basin. Rub in the butter with the tips of the fingers, add the sugar and currants and grated lemon rind, and mix to a fairly stiff consistency with the cold milk. Add a few drops of lemon essence before the mixing is completed. Put into the tin, and bake in a moderate oven (375° F., mark 5) for about 1 hour until firm to the touch.

FARMHOUSE CAKE

½ lb. wholemeal flour	½ lb. sugar
½ lb. white flour	¼ lb. sultanas
1 tsp. spice	¼ lb. raisins
1 tsp. bicarbonate of soda	1 oz. candied peel
	1 egg
112 6 oz. butter or dripping	Milk to mix

Sieve together the flours, spice, and bicarbonate of soda. Rub in the fat with the tips of the fingers until like fine breadcrumbs, then add the sugar, fruit, and chopped peel. Mix with the egg and milk to a fairly soft consistency, and put the mixture into a greased tin (8 inches in diameter). Bake in a moderately hot oven (400° F., mark 6) for about 2 hours.

PLAIN FRUIT CAKE

6 oz. flour	3 oz. sugar
2 oz. ground rice	2 oz. currants
2 tsps. baking powder	2 eggs
3 oz. butter or margarine	2–4 tbsps. milk
1 oz. desiccated coconut	

Place flour, ground rice, and baking powder in a bowl, and rub in the fat. Add the coconut, sugar, and prepared currants, mix with the beaten eggs and milk until of a dropping consistency. Put in a greased lined tin, and bake in moderate oven (375° F., mark 5) about 1 hour.

HOLIDAY CAKE

1 lb. flour	8–12 oz. mixed fruit (raisins, currants, sultanas)
2 tsps. baking powder	2 oz. chopped dates
1 tsp. grated nutmeg	Grated rind of 1 lemon
1 tsp. mixed spice	3 eggs
8 oz. fat (dripping or lard and margarine mixed)	Milk to mix
7 oz. sugar	

Sieve the flour, baking powder, and spices. Rub in the fat with the tips of the fingers until like fine breadcrumbs. Add the sugar, prepared fruit, and lemon rind. Beat the eggs and add to the dry ingredients, with sufficient milk to give a dropping consistency. Turn into a greased cake tin, 7 inches in diameter, and bake in a moderately hot oven (425° F., mark 7), lowering to moderate (350° F., mark 4), about 2 hours.

LEMON CAKE

8 oz. flour	1 egg
A pinch of salt	1 dessertsp. lemon juice
2 tsps. baking powder	A little milk if necessary
4 oz. butter or margarine	2–3 drops lemon essence (optional) 11
4 oz. sugar	
Grated rind of 1 small lemon	

Prepare a 5-inch cake tin by greasing well with melted lard. Sieve the flour, salt, and baking powder into a basin. Rub in the fat with the tips of the fingers, stir in the sugar and grated lemon rind. Mix well, make a well in the centre, and stir in the beaten egg, lemon juice, and a little milk. If liked, two or three drops of essence may be added with the final mixing. Put into the prepared tin, and bake in a moderate oven (375° F., mark 5) for about 1 hour.

PLAIN SEED CAKE

8 oz. flour	1 oz. carraway seeds
A pinch of salt	1 egg
2 tsps. baking powder	A little milk (about 3–4 tbsps.)
4 oz. butter or margarine	
4 oz. sugar	

Prepare a 5-inch cake tin. Sieve the flour, salt, and baking powder into a basin. Rub in the fat with the tips of the fingers until it resembles fine breadcrumbs. Add the sugar and carraway seeds, and mix well. Make a well in the centre, stir in the beaten egg and just sufficient milk to mix. Put into the prepared tin, and bake in a moderate oven (375° F., mark 5) for about 1hour.

For RICH SEED CAKE see the recipe given under the heading Creaming Method.

RAISIN CAKE

1 lb. flour
2 tsps. baking powder
6 oz. butter or dripping
6 oz. seeded raisins
$\frac{1}{4}$ lb. currants
Rind of $\frac{1}{2}$ lemon
$\frac{1}{2}$ lb. sugar
2 eggs
Milk to mix

Sieve the flour and baking powder into a large basin and rub in the fat until free from lumps. Add the raisins and currants, carefully prepared, the grated lemon rind, and the sugar. Mix all together, and make a well in the centre. Add the eggs, well beaten, and enough milk to give a dropping consistency. Put into a tin that has been greased and lined with paper, and bake $1\frac{1}{2}$ hours in a moderate oven (350° F., mark 4).

SODA CAKE

8 oz. flour
A pinch of salt
1 tsp. bicarbonate of soda
1 tsp. cream of tartar
A little grated nutmeg
4–5 oz. butter or margarine
4–5 oz. sugar
6 oz. currants
1 egg
About $\frac{1}{4}$ pint of sour milk to mix

Prepare a 6-inch cake tin. Sieve the flour, salt, bicarbonate of soda, cream of tartar, and nutmeg into a basin. Rub in the fat with the tips of the fingers until it resembles fine breadcrumbs, then add the sugar and currants, and mix well. Stir in the beaten egg and sufficient milk to form a fairly soft mixture. Put into tin, and bake in moderately hot oven (400° F., mark 6) for 1 hour.

SULTANA CAKE

12 oz. flour
A pinch of salt
3 tsps. baking powder
6 oz. butter or margarine
4–6 oz. sultanas
6 oz. sugar
1–2 eggs
Flavouring, e.g., vanilla, lemon
A little milk to mix

Prepare a $6\frac{1}{2}$-inch tin. Sieve the flour, salt, and baking powder into a basin. Rub in the fat until the mixture resembles fine breadcrumbs, then add the sultanas and sugar, and mix well. Make a well in the centre and stir in the beaten egg and flavouring ingredient, with just sufficient milk to make it moist enough to drop from the spoon. Put into the cake tin, and bake in a moderately hot oven (425° F., mark 7), lowering to moderate (350° F., mark 4), for about $1\frac{1}{2}$ hours.

TYROL CAKE

8 oz. flour
1 tsp. ground cinnamon
$3\frac{1}{2}$ oz. fat
2 oz. caster sugar
2 oz. currants
2 oz. sultanas
1 tsp. bicarbonate of soda
$\frac{1}{4}$ pint milk
3 tbsps. honey

Sieve the flour and ground cinnamon into a basin, and rub in the fat with the tips of the fingers. Add the sugar and prepared fruit, then make a well in the centre. Dissolve the bicarbonate of soda in the milk, add to the honey, and pour into the centre of the dry ingredients, mixing thoroughly. Put into a prepared cake tin, and bake in a moderate oven (350° F., mark 5) for 20 minutes, reducing the heat when the cake begins to brown, and continue cooking for 50–60 minutes, till it is golden-brown and firm to the touch.

WHOLEMEAL LUNCH CAKE

1 lb. wholemeal
A pinch of salt
$1\frac{1}{2}$ tbsps. baking powder
8 oz. margarine
8 oz. sugar
3 oz. currants
3 oz. sultanas
2 tsps. mixed spice
1 tsp. cinnamon
2 eggs
A little milk to mix

Put the wholemeal, salt, and baking powder into a basin. Rub the fat into it with the tips of the fingers, then stir in the sugar and prepared fruit and spices. Mix thoroughly, make a well in the centre, stir in the beaten eggs, and mix to a dropping consistency, adding milk as required. Pour into a well-greased 8-inch cake tin, and bake in a moderate oven (350° F., mark 4) for $1\frac{1}{2}$–2 hours.

SMALL CAKES MADE BY RUBBING-IN METHOD

COCONUT CAKES

8 oz. flour
A pinch of salt
2 tsps. baking powder
4 oz. butter
4 oz. sugar
4 oz. desiccated coconut
1 egg
A little milk to mix

Grease a baking sheet and dredge with flour. Sieve the flour, salt, and baking powder into a basin. Rub in the fat until it resembles fine breadcrumbs. Add the sugar and coconut, and mix well. Make a well in the centre, stir in the beaten egg, and add just sufficient milk to make a stiff mixture. With a teaspoon and fork, place the mixture in rocky heaps on the baking sheet, and bake in a hot oven (450° F., mark 8) for 15–20 minutes according to size.

COFFEE CAKES

7 oz. flour
1 oz. cornflour
1 tbsp. baking powder
4 oz. butter or margarine
4 oz. caster sugar
1 large egg
Milk
3 tsps. coffee essence 113
Coffee butter icing
Icing sugar

Sieve flour, cornflour, and baking powder. Rub in fat lightly with the tips of the fingers until the mixture is like fine breadcrumbs. Add the sugar. Beat the egg, and add a little milk and the coffee essence. Add gradually to the dry ingredients, mixing to a stiff consistency. Pile in rocky heaps on a greased baking sheet. Bake in a hot oven (450° F., mark 8) for 15 minutes. Cool on a rack. When cold, split in half, and fill each cake with 1 tsp. of coffee butter icing. Dredge liberally with icing sugar.

LEMON CHERRY BUNS

8 oz. flour	2 tsps. grated lemon rind
½ tsp. salt	2 tsps. lemon juice
4 oz. ground rice	2 eggs
1 tbsp. baking powder	Milk to mix
6 oz. butter	Glacé cherries
113 6 oz. caster sugar	

Sieve the flour and salt, add the ground rice and baking powder. Rub the butter into the flour, add the sugar, lemon rind, lemon juice, and the well-beaten eggs, together with sufficient milk to mix to a dropping consistency. Blend thoroughly, and put into paper baking cases or greased tins, put half a cherry on top. Bake in a moderately hot oven (425° F., mark 7) for about 20 minutes, or until well risen and brown.

ORANGE CAKES

Follow the recipe for Coffee Cakes, adding the grated rind of 1 orange to the dry ingredients and omitting coffee essence; use orange icing.

PEANUT BUTTER COOKIES

6 oz. self-raising flour	2 oz. peanut butter
½ tsp. salt	1 oz. cooking fat
½ tsp. powdered cinnamon	1–2 oz. sugar
A good pinch of powdered cloves or spice	1 egg
	Milk to mix

Sieve the flour, salt, and spices together in a basin. Add peanut butter and cooking fat, and rub in with the finger-tips until no lumps can be felt. Stir in the sugar, then add the beaten egg and enough milk to make a soft, dropping consistency. Half-fill greased patty tins with the mixture and sprinkle the top with a little sugar. Bake in a moderately hot oven (425° F., mark 7) for about 15 minutes, until well risen, golden, and firm to the touch. Cool on a rack.

RASPBERRY BUNS

8 oz. flour	4 oz. caster sugar
113 3 tsps. baking powder	Milk to mix
A pinch of salt	A little raspberry jam
3 oz. butter or margarine	

Put the flour, baking powder, and salt into a basin. Rub in the fat with the tips of the fingers, stir in the sugar, and mix to a stiff dough with milk. Flour a board, turn the mixture on to it, and knead up lightly with floured hands until it is smooth. Roll out to a thickness of about ¾ inch. Cut into rounds with a fairly large cutter, place 1 tsp. of raspberry jam in the centre of each, moisten the edges of the pastry lightly, gather up tightly, enclosing the jam. Place on a greased and floured baking sheet with the smooth side uppermost. With a knife, cut a cross on each, place in a hot oven (450° F., mark 8) and bake for 20 minutes, or until they are firm to the touch and golden in colour.

ROCK CAKES

8 oz. flour	4 oz. sugar
A pinch of salt	2 oz. currants
2 tsps. baking powder	1 oz. finely chopped peel
½ tsp. grated nutmeg	1 egg
½ tsp. mixed spice	A little milk to mix
4 oz. butter or margarine	

Grease a baking sheet and dredge lightly with flour. Sieve the flour, salt, baking powder, grated nutmeg, and mixed spice into a basin. Rub in the fat with the tips of the fingers until the mixture resembles fine breadcrumbs. Stir in the sugar, currants, and chopped peel, and mix well. Make a well in the centre, and stir in the beaten egg and just sufficient milk to make a stiff mixture. With a teaspoon and fork, place the mixture in rocky heaps on the baking sheet, and bake in a hot oven (450° F., mark 8) for 15–20 minutes, according to size of cakes.

SPICY SQUARES

4 oz. margarine	2 oz. sugar
8 oz. flour	2 tsps. baking powder
A pinch of salt	1 egg

For the Filling

2 oz. currants	3 oz. flour
2 oz. chopped candied peel	2 tsps. mixed spice
2 oz. chopped blanched almonds	2 tsps. baking powder
3 oz. sugar	3 oz. melted margarine
	2 eggs

Rub the margarine into the flour, add the salt, sugar, and sieved baking powder, and bind to a stiff dough with the egg. For the filling, mix together the fruit and all the dry ingredients, then add the melted fat and the eggs to bind, making the mixture of a fairly soft consistency. Divide the dough into two, and roll out half of it to fit the bottom of a tin about 9 by 7 inches. Cover with the filling and put on the remaining dough. Mark the surface with a fork, bake for 30–40 minutes in a moderate oven (350° F., mark 4), and cool. Cut into even-sized squares.

LARGE CAKES MADE BY CREAMING METHOD

RICH CAKES (BASIC RECIPE)

1 lb. flour	8 oz.–3 lb. fruit
8–16 oz. fat	Milk to mix, if necessary (according to the amount of fat and eggs)
8–16 oz. sugar	
4–8 eggs	
Up to 2 tsps. baking powder	

Cream the fat and sugar together in a large basin, using the back of a wooden spoon, and working the ingredients until they resemble whipped cream in appearance and texture. If the fat is very hard, let it stand at room temperature or warm it very slightly before use, but on no account allow it to become oily through overheating or the mixture will be heavy and close in texture. If by any mischance the fat has become too soft, stand the basin in a bowl of cold water or in a cold place for a short while for the fat to solidify somewhat, then continue the creaming operation.

Break the eggs one at a time into a small basin, add gradually to the creamed fat and sugar, and beat vigorously, keeping the mixture smooth and creamy. The addition of too much egg at a time or insufficient heating may result in the curdling of the mixture. In this case, sprinkle in about 1 tbsp. of the measured flour before continuing to add the eggs.

[When using an electric mixer for creaming a cake mixture, first soften the fat at room temperature before putting it into the basin. Then switch on the current at the speed recommended, and beat the fat until soft; add the sugar and beat for the required time. Now add the eggs (whole), one at a time, and allow about 1 minute's beating for each egg. Mix in the flour by hand with a metal spoon.]

Using a metal spoon, gradually mix in the sieved flour and baking powder very lightly, together with the prepared fruit (if used), and add any necessary liquid alternately with the flour to give a soft dropping consistency, i.e., the mixture should just drop from the spoon without shaking. While creaming the fat and sugar and beating in the eggs, beat as vigorously as you like, but once you have started to add the flour, handle the mixture *as lightly* as possible, folding or stirring it—never beating.

Three-quarters fill prepared tin or tins, and bake. For Baking Temperatures see recipes and the Charts on pages 373 and 374.

For ICINGS, FILLINGS, ETC., see chapter on Iced and Decorated Cakes.

BANANA CAKE

8 oz. flour	2 eggs
2 tsps. baking powder	4 tbsps. milk
3 oz. butter	Banana filling (see recipe on page 398)
7 oz. caster sugar	

Sieve flour and baking powder. Cream the butter and sugar together. Separate the whites from the yolks of the eggs, add the yolks and a little of the flour to the creamed mixture, and beat well. Then add the milk and the rest of the flour, and blend thoroughly. Whip up the egg whites very stiffly and fold into the cake mixture. Pour into an 8- or 9-inch sandwich tin, previously lined with greased paper, and bake in a moderately hot oven (425° F., mark 7) for about 30 minutes, or until the cake is pale brown and firm in the centre. When cold, split, and spread with banana filling.

BATTENBERG CAKE

8 oz. butter	Vanilla essence
8 oz. sugar	Carmine
4 eggs	½ lb. almond paste
8 oz. flour	Raspberry jam
1 tsp. baking powder	

Prepare two oblong tins measuring 9 by 5 inches and at least 1 inch deep. Grease these lightly and line with greaseproof paper. Cream the butter and sugar very thoroughly, add 1 egg and beat thoroughly, sprinkling in a little of the flour if mixture is inclined to curdle. Repeat until all the eggs have been incorporated, then fold in the remainder of the flour, the baking powder, and the vanilla essence. Put half the mixture into one of the tins, colour the other half pink, and put in the second tin. Hollow out the centres slightly, so that the cakes will be flat and even when cooked. Bake in a moderately hot oven (425° F., mark 7) for 25 minutes, or until firm and pale brown. Turn out and cool.

Meanwhile, prepare some almond paste, and warm some raspberry jam in a saucepan. When the cakes are cold, cut off the outside edges and then cut into even lengths, as broad as the cake is deep. Nine of these strips will be required. Brush over entirely with the warmed jam, using a pastry brush, and arrange the strips with the colours alternately, pressing very well together.

Lay a piece of greaseproof paper on the table, sprinkle with caster sugar, and roll out the almond paste on it to an oblong about 9 inches wide by 12 inches long and a quarter of an inch in thickness. Brush lightly with jam just where the prepared cake is to be put. Lift the cake on to the almond paste and press the paste very firmly against the sides and along the top edges, leaving the ends uncovered. Trim off the surplus paste. Turn the cake right over so that the underside is now the top, mark across diagonally with the back of a knife, then cross in the opposite direction. Crimp the edges of the almond paste between the finger and thumb to form a neat edge. Allow to stand for several hours wrapped in greaseproof paper, then trim off the ends and serve.

CARAMEL SPONGE SANDWICH

6 oz. flour
A pinch of salt
1 tsp. baking powder
4 oz. butter
4 oz. caster sugar
2 eggs
Apricot and walnut filling

For the Caramel

16 lumps of sugar (2 oz.)
$\frac{1}{4}$ pint hot milk

Sieve the flour, salt, and baking powder. Cream the butter and sugar and beat in the egg yolks. Make the caramel by melting the loaf sugar in a saucepan and heating it until it is a light coffee colour. Cool a little, add the hot milk, and dissolve the caramel in it. When the caramel is lukewarm, beat up with the creamed ingredients. Stir in the dry ingredients and mix well, adding more milk if required. Fold in the stiffly beaten egg whites, turn into a greased, deep sandwich tin, and bake in a moderate oven (350° F., mark 4) for $\frac{3}{4}$ hour, or until it feels firm. Cool, split, spread with walnut and apricot filling, and sprinkle with sieved icing sugar.

CHERRY CAKE (RICH)

8 oz. flour
$\frac{1}{2}$ tsp. salt
1 tsp. baking powder
3 oz. glacé cherries
6 oz. butter or margarine
6 oz. caster sugar
2 eggs
Milk to mix
Vanilla essence

Prepare a cake tin. Sieve the flour, salt, and baking powder into a basin. Cut the cherries into four and add to the flour. Cream the butter and sugar, beat in each egg separately, then stir in the dry ingredients lightly, adding a little milk to mix, and lastly, the vanilla essence. Blend thoroughly, put into the tin, and bake in a moderate oven (350° F., mark 4) about 1 hour.

CHOCOLATE CAKE (RICH)

3 oz. flour
1 tsp. baking powder
1 oz. ground rice
4 oz. grated chocolate
4 oz. butter
3 oz. caster sugar
2 eggs
Vanilla essence
Chocolate butter icing
Chocolate glacé icing
Crystallised violets and mint leaves

Sieve the flour and baking powder and mix in the ground rice very thoroughly. Put the grated chocolate into a small basin and place over a saucepan of hot water to melt. Cream the butter and sugar. Add the melted chocolate, which should only be just warm, to the creamed mixture, and mix lightly together. Beat the eggs in a basin, then add to the creamed mixture, beating in about $\frac{1}{3}$ of the egg at a time. Mix in the flour, stirring lightly. Lastly, add vanilla essence. Turn into a greased and lined 6-inch cake tin, and bake in a moderate oven (350° F., mark 4) for $\frac{3}{4}$–1 hour. When cold, split in half and fill with butter icing. Ice with glacé icing, and decorate with violets and mint leaves.

Alternatively, fill and decorate with coffee butter icing, as in the colour picture facing page 384.

DIVORCE CAKE

Follow the recipe for Rich Chocolate Cake (above).

When cool, split the cake in half. Sandwich together with rum butter, and dust the top with fine sugar.

CHRISTMAS CAKE

12 oz. flour
A good pinch of salt
1 tbsp. mixed spice
$1\frac{1}{2}$ lb. currants
1 lb. sultanas
6 oz. mixed peel
$\frac{1}{4}$ lb. sweet almonds
Grated rind of 1 lemon
$\frac{1}{4}$ lb. glacé cherries
10 oz. butter
10 oz. caster sugar
6–8 eggs, according to size
A little lemon juice
Almond icing
Royal icing

Select a thick substantial tin, about 8 inches in diameter, and line with two thicknesses of greased paper. Weigh all the ingredients. Sieve the flour, salt, and spice together. Prepare the fruit, chop the peel and almonds, grate the lemon rind, and cut the glacé cherries into three or four pieces. Add the prepared fruit, peel, and almonds to the flour and spice. Put the butter and sugar into a large basin, and beat them together until they are thoroughly blended and resemble stiffly whipped cream in appearance. Beat in each egg separately. Lastly, stir in the dry ingredients and then the lemon juice, adding a little milk if necessary. When thoroughly blended, turn the cake mixture into the prepared tin and place in a slow oven (325° F., mark 2), reducing to very slow (275° F., mark ½) after the first 1½ hours, or when the cake begins to brown. The length of time required for baking depends on the size and depth of the cake. If the quantities given be baked in one large tin, allow from 4–5 hours. When cold, ice with almond and royal icings.

CHRISTMAS CAKE (ECONOMICAL)

8 oz. sultanas
4 oz. currants
4 oz. seedless raisins
4 oz. Valencia raisins
8 oz. margarine
8 oz. fine sugar
4 eggs
1 tbsp. marmalade
A little grated lemon rind
A few drops of vanilla essence
A few drops of almond essence
10 oz. flour
1 tsp. mixed spice
A little grated nutmeg
½ tsp. bicarbonate of soda (dissolved in 2 tbsps. milk or water)
A few drops of gravy browning

Prepare an 8-inch cake tin. Wash and pick over the dried fruit, and stone and chop the Valencia raisins.

Cream the fat and sugar together very thoroughly until soft and light in texture and colour; add the beaten eggs, a spoonful at a time, beating well; add the marmalade, grated lemon rind, and vanilla and almond essences, and mix thoroughly; then stir in the prepared fruits. Gradually add the flour and spices, together with the bicarbonate of soda dissolved in milk or water, and a few drops of gravy browning. The mixture should be of a soft dropping consistency. Mix thoroughly and put into the prepared tin, then bake in a slow oven (300–325° F., marks 1–2) for about 4 hours.

RICH ALMOND CAKE

14 oz. flour
A pinch of salt
2 oz. ground rice
2 oz. ground almonds
1 lb. butter
1 lb. sugar
7–8 eggs
2 tbsps. sherry
Ratafia essence
Almond icing
Royal or American icing

Grease and line an 8-inch cake tin. Sieve the flour and pinch of salt, add ground rice and ground almonds, and mix thoroughly. Cream the butter and sugar. When pale in colour and of whipped cream consistency, beat in the eggs one at a time, adding a little of the flour if the mixture shows signs of curdling. Stir in the flour lightly with the other ingredients, adding lastly, the sherry and a few drops of ratafia essence. Put into a tin and bake in a moderate oven (350° F., mark 4) about 40 minutes, then in a slow oven (325° F., mark 2) about 1½ hours. Ice with almond and royal or American icing.

DEVIL'S FOOD CAKE

8 oz. flour
¼ tsp. salt
1 tsp. bicarbonate of soda
3 oz. grated chocolate
¼ pint milk
¼ lb. butter
2 eggs
10 oz. light brown or caster sugar
A few drops of vanilla
Chocolate butter icing
American icing
Chocolate to decorate

Line two 7-inch sandwich tins and grease them. Sieve the flour with the salt and bicarbonate of soda on to a piece of kitchen paper. Warm the grated chocolate in the milk until it has dissolved. Cream the butter in a basin, and beat in the sugar gradually until the mixture is soft and creamy. Add the eggs one at a time and beat the mixture again thoroughly. Stir in the sieved dry ingredients alternately with the milk containing the dissolved chocolate. Add the vanilla essence. Bake in the two prepared tins for 35 minutes in a moderate oven (350° F., mark 4).

When cooked, turn out on to a wire cake tray. sandwich with chocolate butter icing, and ice with American icing. Decorate with spikes of curled chocolate, placed on the icing when it is cold, but just before it sets.

DREAM CAKE

8 oz. flour
1 tsp. baking powder
A pinch of salt
3 oz. chopped walnuts
3 oz. glacé cherries
6 oz. butter
6 oz. sugar
3 eggs
½ tsp. vanilla essence
A little milk
American icing (optional)

Sieve the flour, baking powder, and salt together. Chop the walnuts and cut the cherries into quarters, then add to the flour. Cream the butter and sugar, add the eggs one at a time, beating well, then sprinkle in the flour, and fold in lightly. Add the vanilla essence, and a little milk if necessary. Put into a prepared cake tin and bake in a moderate oven (350° F., mark 4) for 1¼–1½ hours. When cold the cake can be coated with American icing if liked.

DUNDEE CAKE

4 oz. currants
4 oz. raisins
4 oz. sultanas
4 oz. candied peel
2 oz. whole almonds
1 lemon
1 orange
10 oz. flour
8 oz. butter
8 oz. soft brown sugar
4 eggs

Grease and line an 8-inch tin. Prepare fruit, chop peel and nuts (leaving a few nuts for decorating cake top) and grate orange and lemon peel. Mix dry ingredients. Cream the butter and sugar until light and creamy, then beat in eggs, one at a time, and lastly fold in dry ingredients. Put mixture into tin, and arrange almonds on top. Bake in a slow oven (325° F., mark 2) for 2½–3 hours. When quite firm to the touch, remove from tin, and cool on rack.

GENOA CAKE

8 oz. sultanas	A pinch of salt
8 oz. currants	Grated lemon rind
4 oz. candied peel	7 oz. butter or margarine
1½ oz. sweet almonds	6 oz. caster sugar
8 oz. flour	3 eggs

Clean the sultanas and currants. Chop the peel, and blanch and chop the almonds, reserving some split almonds for the top. Sieve the flour, salt, and baking powder together. Add a little
114 grated lemon rind and the fruit, etc. Cream the butter and sugar, add eggs one at a time, and beat hard. Should any signs of curdling appear, sprinkle in a little flour before adding more egg. Stir in the dry ingredients lightly with a metal spoon, adding a little milk if necessary to give a dropping consistency. Put the mixture into a greased and lined tin (8-inch diameter), place almonds on top, and bake in a moderate oven (350° F., mark 3) for 30 minutes, then in a slow oven (325° F., mark 2) until golden-brown and thoroughly cooked—about 2 hours.

GINGER CAKE

6 oz. flour	2 eggs
1½ tsps. baking powder	1–2 tbsps. milk
4–6 oz. preserved ginger	Glacé icing
3½ oz. butter	Slices of ginger
3½ oz. sugar	

Sieve flour and baking powder. Chop the ginger in small pieces and mix with 1 tbsp. of the sieved flour. Cream the butter and sugar. Beat in the eggs whole, adding one at a time,
114 and beat very thoroughly, adding a sprinkling of flour if the mixture appears curdled. Mix in the flour lightly, adding about one-third at a time. Add milk, if required, to give a dropping consistency. Lastly, stir in the ginger. Turn into a greased and lined tin 6 inches in diameter. Bake in a moderate oven (350° F., mark 4) for about 1 hour. Ice when cold.

To ice the top of the cake, pin a double band of greaseproof paper firmly round the cake, having the paper 1 inch higher than the cake top. Make some glacé icing, pour on to top of cake and, when partially set, place slices of ginger overlapping round the edge of the cake just inside the paper band. When the icing is set, gently pull off the band of paper.

ICED GINGER SPONGE CAKE

4 oz. butter	2 tsps. baking powder
2 oz. sugar	1 tbsp. ground ginger
4 oz. syrup	Milk to mix
1 egg	Glacé icing
8 oz. plain flour	Preserved ginger

Cream the fat and sugar very thoroughly, beat in the syrup, and add the beaten egg by degrees. Mix the flour, baking powder, and ground ginger, and add it gradually, together with enough milk to make a soft, light mixture. Put into a greased and lined tin, and bake in a moderate oven (350° F., mark 4) for about 1 hour. Place on a rack, and when cold, ice with thin glacé icing, and if liked, decorate with preserved ginger.

MADEIRA CAKE

8 oz. flour	5 oz. butter or margarine
A pinch of salt	3 eggs
2 tsps. baking powder	Lemon essence
Grated lemon rind	Milk to mix
5 oz. caster sugar	Slice of citron

Prepare a cake tin. Sieve the flour, salt, and baking powder together, and add the very finely grated lemon rind. Put the sugar and butter into a basin and work together until they are of a creamy consistency. Beat in the eggs, adding a little at a time to prevent curdling. Fold in the dry ingredients, and lastly, add a little lemon essence, and milk if required. Put into the prepared tin, place in a moderate oven (375° F., mark 5), and bake for 1–1¼ hours. The slice of citron should be put on top of the cake as soon as it is set; if put on before the cake is put into the oven, it is inclined to sink.

Alternatively, bake in a square tin and top with nuts, as in the colour picture facing page 384.

ORANGE CAKE—I

2 oz. butter	2 eggs
2 oz. margarine	4 oz. flour
4 oz. sugar	1 tsp. baking powder
Grated rind of 1 orange	Icing sugar

For the Filling

3 oz. cake crumbs	Juice of 1 orange
1 oz. butter	3 oz. sugar
1 grated orange rind	1 egg yolk

Cream the fats and sugar, add the grated

orange peel and eggs, beating well, then stir in the sieved flour gradually, adding baking powder with the last portion. Place in two greased sandwich tins, and bake in moderate oven (375° F., mark 5) 25–30 minutes. Turn out and cool.

Put all the filling ingredients, except the egg, into a saucepan. Heat for 5 minutes, stirring all the time. Allow to cool slightly, add the egg, and stir over a low heat. Spread on one of the cakes, and sandwich together. Dredge liberally with icing sugar.

ORANGE CAKE—II

Follow the recipe for Madeira Cake, adding the grated rind of 2 oranges in place of the lemon rind. Put the cake in a rather shallow round tin about 8 or 10 inches in diameter, and bake in a moderate oven (375° F., mark 5) 40–50 minutes.

When cold, split in half, fill with orange filling, and ice with orange glacé icing.

ORANGE LAYER CAKE

3 oz. flour	2 medium-sized eggs
¼ tsp. baking powder	Milk to mix
1 oz. cornflour	Orange butter icing or orange filling
Rind of 1 orange	Orange glacé icing
4 oz. butter	
¼ lb. caster sugar	

Prepare a sandwich cake tin. Sieve the flour, baking powder, and cornflour together, and add the finely grated orange rind. Cream the butter and sugar together, beat in each egg separately, and fold in the dry ingredients, adding a little milk if necessary. Pour the mixture into a prepared sandwich tin and cook for about ½ hour in a moderate oven (375° F., mark 5). When quite cold, split, spread with butter icing or orange filling, and coat with orange glacé icing.

PINEAPPLE AND WALNUT CAKE

¼ lb. shelled walnuts	5 eggs
½ lb. glacé pineapple	1 tsp. pineapple essence
¾ lb. flour	A little milk
Grated nutmeg	Glacé icing
½ lb. butter	Glacé pineapple to decorate
½ lb. caster sugar	

Toast the walnuts a few minutes in the oven, rub off as much of the brown skin as possible, and then chop them, but not too finely. Cut the glacé pineapple into small pieces. Sieve the flour with a little grated nutmeg. Cream the butter, add the sieved sugar, then the beaten eggs, and mix them in thoroughly. When the mixture has been well beaten, flavour with pineapple essence and stir in the flour, etc., very lightly. Mix carefully, adding a little milk if necessary to bring it to the right consistency. Add the prepared walnuts and pineapple, and turn the mixture into a cake tin that has been greased and lined with paper. Bake in a moderate oven (350° F., mark 4) for 1½–2 hours, according to size.

This cake may either be left plain or coated with glacé icing, with thickly cut glacé pineapple on top.

PLUM CAKE

½ lb. currants	½ lb. flour
¼ lb. sultanas	½ lb. butter
½ lb. raisins	½ lb. sugar
3 oz. glacé cherries	4 eggs (½ lb.)
3 oz. French plums	Milk if necessary
3 oz. almonds	2 tbsps. brandy
6 oz. citron peel	

To prepare the fruit, wash and dry the currants and sultanas; stone the raisins; cut the cherries into two and the plums into four; shred almonds; chop peel. Mix together with the flour. Cream the butter and sugar thoroughly, and beat in the eggs one at a time, adding a little flour should the mixture show signs of curdling. Stir in the prepared fruit and flour, with 1 tbsp. or so of milk if necessary, to give a soft dropping consistency. Put into a cake tin, 8 inches in diameter, greased and lined with two thicknesses of paper. Bake in a slow oven (325° F., mark 2) for 3½–4 hours.

Next day, sprinkle the brandy over the top of the cake, using a teaspoon. Wrap the cake in greaseproof paper, and store for several weeks before cutting.

RICH SEED CAKE

(*See colour picture facing page* 384)

6 oz. flour	4 oz. butter
½ tsp. baking powder	4 oz. sugar
A pinch of salt	2 eggs
2 tsps. carraway seeds	A little milk

Sieve the flour, baking powder, and salt together, and add the carraway seeds. Put the butter and sugar into a basin, and cream until pale in colour, then beat in each egg separately; stir in the sieved flour, adding a little milk to make the mixture of a dropping consistency. Put into a prepared tin, and bake in a moderately hot oven (400° F., mark 6) about 1 hour.

SAND CAKE

2 oz. butter or margarine	1 oz. plain flour
4 oz. caster sugar	4 oz. cornflour
2 eggs	2 tsps. baking powder
	Grated lemon rind

Grease and line a 1-lb. loaf tin. Cream together the fat and sugar, beat in the eggs one at a time, then lastly fold in the sieved flour, cornflour, baking powder and lemon rind. Put into the prepared tin and bake in a moderately hot oven (400° F., mark 6) for 1 hour, until it is a light golden-brown, and firm to the touch. Allow it to cool slightly before turning out on to a rack.

SILVER CAKE

¼ lb. butter	2 tsps. baking powder
¼ lb. caster sugar	4–5 egg whites
¼ lb. flour	½ tsp. essence of almonds
2 oz. cornflour	

This is a good cake to make when there are egg whites left over from other cooking. Put the butter into a warm basin with the sugar, and beat them together with a wooden spoon until of a soft, creamy consistency. Sieve the flour, cornflour, and baking powder, and add them alternately with the egg whites, which have been beaten to a stiff froth. Mix very lightly, and flavour to taste. Have ready a cake tin which has been greased and dusted out with flour and sugar mixed, half-fill it with the mixture, and bake in a moderate oven (375° F., mark 5) until well risen and firm to the touch—about 1 hour. Alternatively, the mixture may be baked in small tins, if preferred, in which case bake in a slightly hotter oven for 20–30 minutes.

SIMNEL CAKE

8 oz. flour	3 oz. mixed candied peel
A pinch of salt	6 oz. butter
1 tsp. grated nutmeg	6 oz. caster sugar
1 tsp. cinnamon	3 eggs
12 oz. currants	Milk to mix
4 oz. sultanas	Glacé icing (optional)

For the Almond Paste

12 oz. caster sugar	1 egg
8 oz. ground almonds	Lemon juice

To prepare the Almond Paste: Mix the sugar and ground almonds together, and add sufficient beaten egg and a squeeze of lemon juice to make a pliable paste. Turn on to a board dredged with castor sugar and knead to mix thoroughly. Take about a third of the paste and roll to a round the size of the cake tin. Put aside while preparing the cake mixture.

To make the Cake: Sieve together the flour, salt, and spices, add the clean and picked currants and sultanas and the chopped peel. Cream the butter and sugar together very thoroughly. Beat in each egg separately, adding a sprinkling of the sieved flour if the mixture shows signs of curdling. Stir the remainder of the flour, etc., into the creamed mixture, adding a little milk if required, to give a dropping consistency. Put half the mixture into the greased and lined cake tin, smooth the top carefully, and cover with the round of almond paste. Put the remainder of the cake mixture on top, and bake in a moderate oven (350° F., mark 3). The time depends on the thickness of the cake, but about 3 hours should be sufficient. Place on a rack to cool.

To finish the Cake: Cover the top of the cake with a round of the almond paste, and decorate with small balls of paste placed round the edge (eleven is the traditional number). Brush the paste with the remaining beaten egg, and brown in a quick oven or under the grill. A little glacé icing can be run into the centre of the cake when it is cool, or the word "Easter" may be piped in white glacé icing. A fluffy chick makes a pleasant decoration, and a band of yellow ribbon is often tied round the cake.

VICTORIA SANDWICH CAKE (STANDARD RECIPE)

4 oz. fat	½ tsp. baking powder
4 oz. sugar	A little milk, if necessary
2 eggs	Jam
4 oz. flour	Caster sugar

Cream the fat and sugar together until light and creamy, then beat in the eggs, adding a little at a time so that the mixture does not curdle. Sieve the flour and baking powder together and fold very lightly into the mixture, together with a little milk, if necessary, to give a soft dropping consistency. Put into two greased sandwich tins, and bake in a moderate oven (375° F., mark 5) for 25–30 minutes. Cool on a cake rack and, when cold, sandwich together with jam. Dust lightly with caster sugar.

VICTORIA SANDWICH CAKE (ECONOMICAL RECIPE)

2 oz. fat	4 oz. flour
2 oz. sugar	2 tsps. baking powder
1 egg	2–3 tbsps. milk or water
A few drops of vanilla essence	Jam
	Caster sugar

Cream the fat and sugar together until light and creamy, add the beaten egg by degrees, and the vanilla essence. Sieve the flour and baking powder together, and mix very lightly into the creamed mixture, together with the milk or water. Turn into a greased sandwich tin, and bake in a moderate oven (375° F., mark 5) about ½ hour. Turn on to a rack and, when cool, split and fill with jam. Dust with caster sugar.

WALNUT CAKE

- 8 oz. flour
- A pinch of salt
- 3 oz. chopped walnuts
- 6 oz. butter
- 6 oz. sugar
- 3 eggs
- ½ tsp. vanilla essence
- American icing
- Walnuts to decorate

Prepare a 7-inch cake tin. Sieve the flour, salt, and baking powder, and add the chopped walnuts. Cream the butter and sugar together until they are white, then stir in each egg separately and beat hard. Fold in the dry ingredients, add the essence, and blend well. Put into tin, and bake in a moderate oven (350° F., mark 4) about 1½ hours. When cold, coat with American icing and decorate with walnuts.

SINGLE-TIER WEDDING CAKE

- 1¼ lb. flour
- A pinch of salt
- ½ tsp. ground cloves
- ½ tsp. ground cinnamon
- ½ tsp. mixed spice
- 4–8 oz. chopped nuts
- 2 lb. sultanas
- 1 lb. raisins
- 1½ lb. currants
- 8 oz. shredded candied peel
- 8 oz. glacé cherries
- Grated rind and juice of 1 lemon
- 1 lb. butter or margarine
- 1 lb. sugar
- 10 eggs
- A few drops of vanilla essence
- 2 tsps. caramel or gravy browning
- Milk or brandy to mix

Sieve the dry ingredients into a bowl and add nuts, prepared fruit, peel, and lemon rind. Cream the fat and sugar until light, and beat in the eggs one at a time. Add the essence and caramel. Lightly stir in the dry ingredients, adding the lemon juice and a little liquid to give a stiff, dropping consistency. Put the mixture into a lined 11-inch cake tin, and bake in a moderate oven (350° F., mark 3) for 1 hour. Reduce the oven to "slow" (300° F., mark 1) and bake for a further 3½–4 hours, or until cooked. When the top is sufficiently brown, cover with a double sheet of greaseproof paper. If preferred, brandy may be poured over the cake when it is cold; small holes made in the top and bottom of the cake with a darning needle or skewer will help the brandy to penetrate.

When the cakes are cold, wrap them in greaseproof paper and store for at least 2–3 weeks, to allow them to mature slightly before covering them with almond paste and royal icing. About 2 lb. almond paste and 3–4 lb. icing sugar for the royal icing will be required. For directions for icing formal cakes, see the chapter on Iced and Decorated Cakes.

Caramel

Put ½ lb. sugar and a few drops of water in a strong saucepan, heat slowly, and allow it to become brown. When a blue smoke commences to rise from the sugar, add ¼ pint of water. Allow this to boil up again, then leave it to cool, and bottle what is not used immediately.

TWO-TIER WEDDING CAKE

- 2 lb. butter or margarine
- 2 lb. caster sugar
- 18 eggs
- ½ lb. sweet almonds
- ½ lb. glacé cherries
- ½ lb. candied peel
- 8–10 lb. mixed dried fruit
- ½ tsp. bicarbonate of soda
- 1 tsp. ground cinnamon
- ½ a grated nutmeg
- 1 tsp. mixed spices
- ½ tsp. ground cloves
- 2½ lb. flour
- Caramel, browning or coffee extract

Prepare a 12-inch and a 7-inch cake tin. Cream the fat and sugar and beat in the eggs one at a time. Add the chopped nuts, sliced cherries, chopped peel, cleaned fruit, bicarbonate of soda, and spices to the flour. Add to the creamed mixture, together with the caramel or other darkening agent. Put the mixture into the tins and flatten the top with a palette knife. Bake in a moderate oven (350° F., mark 3), reducing the heat to "slow" (300° F., mark 1) after about 3 hours. Bake the small cake for about 5 hours in all, and the large one about 8 hours.

Store as above, before icing. About 3 lb. almond paste and 6 lb. icing sugar will be required —more if the cake is given an extra coat of royal icing, which is advisable, as the lower cake has to support the weight of the top tier.

THREE-TIER WEDDING CAKE

- 5½ lb. currants
- 2 lb. sultanas
- 2 lb. stoned raisins
- 1 lb. sweet almonds
- 1½ lb. glacé cherries
- 1 lb. mixed peel
- 1 lemon
- 3 lb. flour
- 3 tsps. ground cinnamon
- 1½ tsps. ground mace
- A pinch of salt
- 3 lb. butter
- 3 lb. sugar
- 24 large eggs
- ⅓ pint rum or brandy
- A little caramel or browning

Prepare three tins, measuring 12 inches, 9 inches and 5 inches in diameter.

Wash and pick the dried fruit, stone the raisins, blanch and chop the almonds, cut the glacé cherries in half, chop the mixed peel, and grate the lemon rind and strain the juice. Sieve the flour, cinnamon, mace, and salt into a large mixing basin. Stir in the prepared fruit, almonds, etc. Cream the butter and sugar until pale in colour. Add the eggs to the creamed

is Iced Cake

ery Dice Cakes

butter and sugar, beating each one in separately. Should the mixture curdle, mix in a little flour. Fold in the dry ingredients, adding the brandy or rum and lemon juice gradually. Add sufficient caramel (see above) to give the mixture a good brown colour. Pour into paper-lined and well-greased tins, and bake in a slow oven (325° F., mark 2) for 4½–6½ hours, according to size.

Store as above before icing. About 6 lb. almond paste and 10 lb. icing sugar will be needed—more if an extra coat of icing is given—see last paragraph in previous recipe.

SMALL CAKES MADE BY CREAMING METHOD

APPLE MUFFINS

2 oz. butter
3 oz. sugar
1 egg
4 oz. flour
3 tsps. baking powder
½ tsp. salt
½ tsp. cinnamon
½ tsp. nutmeg
½ cupful milk and water
2 oz. finely chopped apples
A little cinnamon and nutmeg to dust top (optional)

Cream the fat with 2 oz. of the sugar and beat in the egg. Mix all the dry ingredients and add gradually, with the milk, to the creamed butter and sugar. Fold in the apples, and fill greased muffin rings or round tins with the mixture. Sprinkle the remaining sugar, mixed, if liked, with a little cinnamon and nutmeg, over the top. Bake in a hot oven (450° F., mark 8) for 20–25 minutes.

CHERRY AND ALMOND CAKES

1 oz. chopped almonds
2 oz. glacé cherries
3 oz. flour
1 oz. cornflour
1 tsp. baking powder
4 oz. butter or margarine
4 oz. caster sugar
2 eggs
A little milk
White glacé icing
Glacé cherries to decorate

Chop almonds and cherries, dusting the latter with a little of the measured flour to prevent their sticking together. Sift together the flour, cornflour, and baking powder, and add to it the chopped cherries and almonds. Cream the fat and sugar thoroughly and beat in the eggs, adding a little at a time so that the mixture does not curdle. Lightly fold in the flour mixture together with a little milk, if necessary, to give a soft dropping consistency. Place in spoonfuls in greased patty tins, and bake in a moderate oven (375° F., mark 5) for about 20 minutes. When cold, ice, and decorate with cherries.

CHERRY AND LEMON SLICES

6 oz. butter
6 oz. sugar
2 eggs
10 oz. self-raising flour
2 oz. glacé cherries
A little milk to mix
Lemon glacé icing
Cherries and angelica to decorate

Work the butter and sugar together until they are of a soft, creamy consistency. Add the eggs and a sprinkling of flour alternately to the creamed mixture. Beat thoroughly, and stir in remaining flour and chopped cherries, together with sufficient milk to give a soft consistency. Blend well, put into a lined, greased oblong cake tin, and bake for 35 minutes in a moderately hot oven (400° F., mark 6). Cool on a rack. Trim the edges and cut into oblongs. Coat with icing, and decorate.

CHOCOLATE CAKES

3½ oz. flour
1 oz. cocoa
1 tsp. baking powder
4 oz. butter
4 oz. caster sugar
2 eggs
A little vanilla essence
A little milk
Chocolate glacé icing

Sift together the flour, cocoa, and baking powder. Cream the fat and sugar thoroughly, and beat in the eggs a little at a time. Add the vanilla essence and stir in the dry ingredients, together with sufficient milk to give a soft, dropping consistency. Place in teaspoonfuls into greased patty tins, and bake in a moderate oven (350° F., mark 4) for 15–20 minutes. When cold, coat with chocolate glacé icing.

CHOCOLATE GEMS

1½ oz. grated chocolate
4 oz. self-raising flour
A pinch of salt
2 oz. butter
1½ oz. sugar
1 egg
Vanilla essence
Chocolate glacé icing
"Hundreds and thousands"

Grate the chocolate finely, and sieve it with the flour and salt into a basin. Cream the butter and sugar, stir in the beaten egg and fold in the dry ingredients, adding sufficient vanilla essence to flavour. Cover a baking sheet with rice paper and drop the mixture in spoonfuls on to it. Cook in a moderately hot oven (425° F., mark 7) for about 10 minutes, or according to size. When cold, ice, and sprinkle with "hundreds and thousands."

CHRISTMAS SNOWBALLS

Any white cake mixture (such as Victoria Sandwich mixture) can be used for these.

Have ready some small, round-bottomed

patty tins, greased, and dusted out with a mixture of flour and sugar. Half-fill them with the mixture and bake in a moderately hot oven (400° F., mark 6) about 15 minutes, or until lightly browned and firm to the touch. Turn out the of the tins to cool. If necessary, cut a slice off the top of the cakes to make them level, and put together with some tart jelly between, thus forming a ball.

Alternatively, the little cakes may be slightly hollowed out, and the cavity filled with some rich custard or thick cream before they are put together.

Cover the balls with some plain white icing, holding them on a fork or skewer while doing so. Then roll in desiccated coconut and caster sugar mixed. Allow the snowballs to dry and serve them garnished with sprigs of holly.

COBURG CAKES

6 oz. flour	3 oz. butter
½ tsp. bicarbonate of soda	3 oz. sugar
	2 eggs
½ tsp. allspice	1 tbsp. warm water
½ tsp. ground ginger	2 dessertsps. syrup
½ tsp. cinnamon	

Sieve the flour, bicarbonate of soda, and spices. Cream the butter and sugar, then add the eggs one at a time, beating thoroughly. Add the water and syrup mixed together, alternately with the flour, stirring in lightly. Place the mixture into two small, greased sandwich tins, or, if small cakes are required, three-quarters fill small, greased patty tins. If sandwich tins are used, bake in a moderately hot oven (400° F., mark 6) for about 30 minutes—if patty tins, bake in a rather hotter oven for about 20 minutes.

SMALL ICED FANCY CAKES

The basis of these is a Victoria Sandwich mixture or a Genoese Sponge mixture. Make the cake mixture in the usual way, but bake it in a flat tin so that it will be about 1½ inches thick when cooked. Leave to stand overnight or for several hours before icing—it is difficult to cut neatly if fresh from the oven. Either glacé or fondant icing is suitable, and it may be used in either of the following ways:

1. Cover the slab with a layer of the icing of suitable colour and flavour, and when set, lift carefully on to a board and cut with a sharp knife into fingers, squares, triangles, or diamonds, decorating with cherries, angelica, etc.

2. Cut the cake into fancy shapes before icing, shake off loose crumbs, and coat each cake with icing. Place the cake on the end of a broad-bladed knife to do this, hold it over the bowl and pour the icing over. Allow excess icing to drip off, then transfer carefully to the cake rack and decorate at once.

GOLDEN BUNS

1½ oz. butter	3 oz. flour
1½ oz. sugar	1 oz. custard powder
2 egg yolks	A pinch of salt
A few drops of almond essence	1 tsp. baking powder
	Milk

Cream the fat and sugar together until light and creamy, beat in the egg yolks, and add a few drops of almond essence. Sieve together the flour, custard powder, salt, and baking powder, and stir them a little at a time into the creamed mixture, together with enough milk to make a soft, dropping consistency. Three-quarters fill greased patty tins, and bake in a moderately hot oven (400° F., mark 6) for about 15 minutes.

MADELEINES

4 oz. butter	Red jam
4 oz. sugar	Desiccated coconut
2 eggs	Glacé cherries and
4 oz. flour	angelica

Beat the butter and sugar to a white cream and add gradually the eggs and a little of the flour, beating thoroughly. Stir in the remaining
flour. Grease a dozen small dariole moulds 115
and three-parts fill with the prepared mixture. Bake in a moderately hot oven (400° F., mark 6) for about 20 minutes, or until firm and browned. Turn out, and trim off the bottoms so that the cakes stand firmly and are of even height. When nearly cold, brush with the melted jam, holding the cakes on a skewer. Roll in the desiccated coconut. Dip a cherry in a little jam, place on top of each madeleine, and put on 2 leaves of angelica.

MARZIPAN SQUARES

2 oz. caster sugar	2 oz. ground almonds
4 oz. butter	Raspberry jam
1 egg yolk	Royal icing
4 oz. flour	1 oz. chopped almonds

Work the sugar into the butter until it is of a creamy consistency, then add egg yolk, flour, and ground almonds. Set in a cool place for 1 hour. Divide into two, roll out one half, lay on a clean baking tray, and spread nearly to the edge with raspberry jam. Roll out the second piece of paste and press it gently on the other to form a sandwich. Bake in a moderate oven (375° F., mark 4) until nearly cooked. Pipe royal icing across the top of the marzipan in each direction, to form small squares. Cut it into squares or oblongs with a sharp knife, and return to the oven. Leave until the icing turns pale fawn. Decorate with chopped almonds.

QUEEN CAKES

4 oz. butter or margarine	1 tsp. baking powder
4 oz. caster sugar	A little milk, if necessary
2 eggs	
4 oz. flour	2 oz. sultanas

Thoroughly cream together the fat and the sugar; add the eggs a little at a time, beating
115 well. Sift in the flour and baking powder and fold into the mixture, together with a little milk, if necessary, to give a soft, dropping consistency. Add the prepared fruit and place in spoonfuls in greased patty tins. Bake in a moderate oven (375° F., mark 5) for about 15–20 minutes, until firm to the touch and a golden-brown colour.

For an economical version, halve the quantities of fat, sugar and eggs, but otherwise follow the recipe above.

RECIPES FOR SPONGE MIXTURE

SPONGE CAKES (BASIC RECIPE)

To each shell egg allow: $1–1\frac{1}{2}$ oz. sugar
1 oz. flour

Put the measured flour on a sheet of kitchen paper and stand it in a warm place to dry it.

Put the eggs and sugar together into a large basin. Stand the basin over a saucepan half-filled with hot water; place the pan over gentle heat and begin at once to whisk the eggs and sugar very briskly. Continue whisking until the mixture is thick and fluffy, and stiff enough to retain the impression of the whisk for a few seconds. The lightness of the cake depends largely on beating the eggs and sugar really stiffly, and this process takes 15–20 minutes. Remove the basin from the heat as soon as the mixture is whisked sufficiently.

When using an electric mixer, put the eggs and sugar into the basin, and whisk at the recommended speed until of the required texture.

Sift in one-third of the flour over the mixture and fold in very lightly with a large metal spoon. Add the remaining flour in the same way. If the recipe calls for any water, it is added at this stage. It is important to agitate the mixture as little as possible when incorporating the flour, so choose a large spoon and fold very lightly with bold strokes. Stirring or beating at this stage will break down the air bubbles and thus spoil the texture of the cake, making it close and tough. Do not use an electric mixer.

This is the true sponge mixture, but a little melted fat is sometimes added to prevent the cake going dry. When a larger proportion of fat is included, the mixture is known as a Genoese Sponge—see recipe opposite.

Pour mixture into prepared tins, three-quarter filling them, and bake. For Baking Temperatures see recipes, also Chart on page 373.

PLAIN SPONGE CAKE

4 eggs	4 oz. flour
6 oz. caster sugar	

Mix as above, and pour the mixture into a cake tin 7 inches in diameter, greased and dusted with sugar and flour. Bake in a moderate oven (350° F., mark 4) for about 1 hour.

SPONGE LAYER CAKE

4 eggs	1 oz. melted butter
4 oz. sugar	Butter cream or jam
$3\frac{1}{2}$ oz. flour	and whipped cream

Put the eggs and sugar into a large basin. Stand the basin over a saucepan of hot water and whisk the eggs and sugar, beating briskly until light and thick, the mixture being stiff enough to retain the impression of the whisk for several seconds. Remove basin from heat. Sift one-third of the flour over the surface of the mixture and fold in very lightly, using a large metal spoon. Add the remaining flour in the same way, and lastly, fold in the melted butter, which must not be too hot. Pour into a greased cake tin, 7 inches in diameter. Bake in a moderate oven (350° F., mark 4) for about 1 hour. When cold, split in half with a sharp knife, and fill with butter cream or with a layer of jam and cream.

COFFEE LAYER CAKE

Follow the recipe for Sponge Layer Cake, adding 2 tsps. of coffee essence with the melted butter. When cold, cut in half with a sharp knife, and fill with a layer of coffee butter icing. Ice with coffee or chocolate glacé icing.

LEMON LAYER CAKE

Follow the recipe for Sponge Layer Cake, but adding the grated rind of 1 lemon to the mixture. Grate the rind lightly over the surface of the whisked mixture and fold in with the flour. When cold, cut in half with a sharp knife. Fill with lemon curd or butter icing, and ice with lemon glacé icing.

FUDGE CAKE

5 oz. shelled walnuts
5 oz. caster sugar
4 eggs
¾ oz. fresh white breadcrumbs

To Serve

Fresh cream
Sugar
Vanilla essence
6 walnut halves

Mince or chop the nuts. Put the caster sugar and egg yolks into a large basin and beat over a pan of hot water until light and creamy, then remove from the heat. Beat the egg whites very stiffly. Fold the minced nuts into the yolks and sugar, folding in a little of the beaten egg whites with them. Fold in the remaining beaten whites with the breadcrumbs.

Turn into two greased sandwich tins, about 6 inches in diameter, and bake in a moderate oven (375° F., mark 5) for about 30 minutes. Remove carefully from tins and cool on rack. Next day, sandwich together with sweetened and flavoured whipped cream, spread a layer of cream on top, and decorate with walnuts.

GENOESE SPONGE (BASIC RECIPE)

3 oz. butter
2½ oz. flour
½ oz. cornflour
3 large eggs
4 oz. caster sugar

Clarify the butter and sieve the flour and cornflour. Put the eggs and sugar into a large basin, stand over a saucepan of hot water, and whisk briskly until light and thick, the mixture being stiff enough to retain the impression of the whisk for a few seconds. Remove basin from the heat. Sift about half of the flour over the surface of the mixture and fold in very lightly. Add the remaining flour in the same way, alternately with the cooled clarified butter. Genoese sponge must be very lightly mixed or the fat will sink to the bottom and cause a heavy cake. Pour into a shallow greased and lined tin. Bake in a moderate oven (375° F., mark 5) until golden-brown and firm to the touch, the time depending on the depth of the cake—about ¾ hour.

This mixture may be used as a foundation for layer cakes, iced cakes, and petits fours, etc.

CHOCOLATE GENOESE

Follow the recipe for Genoese Sponge, adding 2 oz. chocolate and 1 tsp. baking powder. Sieve the baking powder with the flour. Melt the chocolate in a basin placed over the water; when quite soft, whisk into the thick egg and sugar mixture just before folding in the flour.

CHOCOLATE BOXES

½ lb. coating chocolate
Genoese sponge slab, 1 inch thick
Apricot jam
¼ pint sweetened whipped cream
1 oz. crystallised ginger
1 oz. crystallised cherries

First prepare some chocolate squares: melt the chocolate to blood heat in a basin over hot water and beat well; spread evenly on waxed paper and as it begins to set, mark into squares 2 by 2 inches. When set remove from the paper.

Cut the Genoese slab into 2-inch squares. Coat the sides with jam and press the chocolate squares into position round the sides to form a box, with the cake as a base. Fill each box with a spoonful of sweetened whipped cream, to which the chopped ginger and cherries have been added. Serve in paper cases.

MOCHA CAKE

4 eggs
4 oz. flour
½ tsp. baking powder
4 oz. caster sugar
Vanilla essence
2 oz. sweet almonds
Coffee glacé icing
Crystallised violets or mimosa flowers to decorate

Grease a round 8-inch cake tin, and coat with a mixture of sieved flour and caster sugar. Separate the yolks from the egg whites and put into two medium-sized basins. Sieve the flour with the baking powder and put into a warm place until required. Sieve the sugar and add it to the egg yolks, together with a few drops of vanilla essence, and beat with a wire whisk for 10–15 minutes, or until pale in colour and light in texture. Then whip up the egg whites to a very stiff froth and add them to the first mixture alternately with a little flour. Fold the mixture over and over, mixing as lightly as possible, put it into the tin, and bake in a moderate oven (350° F., mark 4) until well risen, lightly browned, and firm to the touch—about 1 hour. Cool for a few minutes, then turn out on to a sieve and leave until cold. Meanwhile, blanch and shred the almonds and brown them lightly in a cool oven (325° F., mark 2); also prepare the coffee icing.

Split the cake once or twice, according to its height, spread with coffee icing, and place the pieces together again. Then coat the sides lightly with icing and roll them in the toasted almonds. Decorate the top of the cake with the remainder of the icing, put through a forcing bag with a fancy pipe. Further decoration may be added in the form of crystallised flowers.

PERFECTION SPONGE

5 oz. sugar	2 egg whites
¼ pint cold water	4 oz. flour
3 egg yolks	

Put the sugar into a clean saucepan with the cold water. Bring to the boil and boil hard for 5 minutes, then cool for 5 minutes. Meanwhile, put the yolks and egg whites into a large basin and whisk thoroughly, pour on the syrup gradually, and continue whisking for 15 minutes, or until the mixture thickens. Sift one-third of the flour over the mixture and fold in very lightly with a large metal spoon. Add the remaining flour in the same way. Pour into the prepared tin, and bake in a moderate oven (375° F., mark 5) for about 1 hour.

This recipe produces a deliciously light sponge, but it is a little more difficult to make than the standard sponge mixtures ; it is therefore advisable to postpone trying it till after the others have been made successfully.

SWISS ROLL

3 eggs	1 tbsp. hot water
4 oz. caster sugar	Caster sugar to dredge
4 oz. flour	Warm jam

Put the eggs and sugar together into a large basin and stand this over a saucepan of hot water. Whisk the eggs and sugar very briskly until light and thick, the mixture being firm enough to retain the impression of the whisk for a few seconds. Remove basin from heat. Sieve about one-third of the flour over the surface of the mixture and fold in very lightly, using a large metal spoon. Add the remaining flour in the same way, and lightly stir in the hot water.

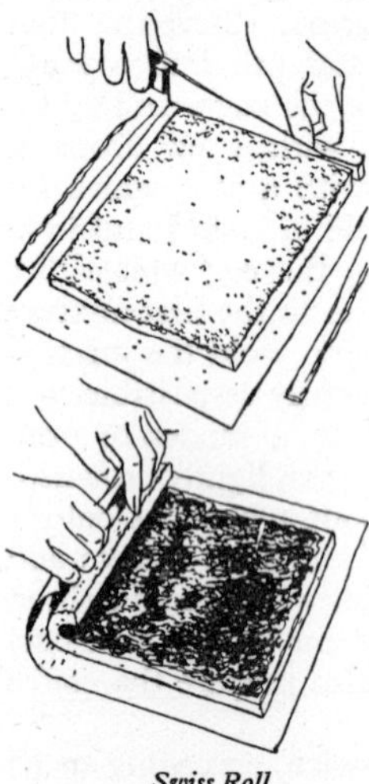
Swiss Roll

Pour the mixture into a prepared Swiss roll tin, 9 by 12 inches. Allow the mixture to run over the whole surface before putting into the oven. Bake in a hot oven (450° F., mark 8) for 7-9 minutes, until golden-brown, well risen, and firm.

Meanwhile, have ready a sheet of greaseproof paper (a tea towel lightly wrung out of hot water may be placed under the paper). Sprinkle liberally with caster sugar. Turn the cake quickly on to the paper. Trim off the edges with a sharp knife, and spread with warm jam. Roll up with the aid of the paper, making the first turn firmly, so that the whole cake rolls evenly and is a good shape when finished. Roll the cake lightly after the first turn. Dredge with sugar and cool on a cake rack.

CHOCOLATE LOG

3 oz. flour	3 eggs
1 tsp. baking powder	3 oz. caster sugar
2 oz. grated chocolate, dissolved in 1 tbsp. water	Butter icing Chocolate butter icing Angelica to decorate
About 1 tbsp. milk	

Prepare a Swiss roll tin. Sift together the flour and baking powder. Dissolve the chocolate in the water and add to it a little milk. Whisk the eggs and sugar over hot water until thick and frothy, pour in the dissolved chocolate and milk, and lightly stir in the flour. Pour into the prepared tin, and bake in a hot oven (450° F., mark 8) for 7–10 minutes. Turn out on to a sugared cloth or sugared paper, and roll. When cold, unroll, spread with icing, and re-roll. Pipe on chocolate butter icing, and decorate.

RECIPES FOR GINGERBREADS

GINGERBREAD (BASIC RECIPE)

1 lb. flour	½ lb. brown sugar
1 tsp. salt	6 oz. butter
1 tbsp. ground ginger	¾ lb. treacle or syrup
1 tbsp. baking powder	½ pint milk
1 tsp. bicarbonate of soda	1 egg

Sieve together the flour, salt, ginger, baking powder, and bicarbonate of soda. Warm the sugar, butter, and treacle, but do not allow to get hot. Warm the milk and beat the egg. Combine all the ingredients, mixing very thoroughly. Pour into a greased and lined tin, and bake in a moderate oven (350° F., mark 4) for about 1½ hours, or until firm to the touch.

DARK GINGERBREAD

3 oz. fat	2 tsps. ground ginger
3 oz. brown sugar	1 tsp. bicarbonate of soda dissolved in a little milk and water
3 oz. treacle	
8 oz. flour	

Put the fat, sugar, and treacle in a basin, and beat together until light and creamy. Stir in the flour and ginger lightly, adding the dissolved bicarbonate of soda by degrees. Mix to a soft, dropping consistency, adding more liquid if necessary, put into a greased tin about 6 inches square, and bake in a moderate oven (350° F., mark 3) for 1¼–1½ hours. Cool, then store in an airtight tin for at least 24 hours before cutting.

OLD-TIME GINGERBREAD

7 oz. flour
1 tsp. cinnamon
2 tsps. ground ginger
A pinch of salt
3 oz. chopped dates
5 oz. treacle or syrup
2 oz. lard
1 egg
3 oz. brown sugar
4 tbsps. milk
1 tsp. bicarbonate of soda dissolved in a little milk

Sieve the flour, cinnamon, ground ginger, and salt. Add the chopped dates. Warm the treacle and lard together until both are melted, then beat the egg and sugar together, and add the two mixtures to the flour alternately. Stir in the milk and, lastly, add the bicarbonate of soda dissolved in milk. Mix thoroughly, and pour into a fairly shallow greased tin. Bake in a moderate oven (350° F., mark 3) for ¾–1 hour, depending on the depth of the tin.

ORANGE GINGERBREAD

1½ lb. flour
½ lb. sugar
2 tsps. cinnamon
2 tsps. bicarbonate of soda
1 tbsp. ginger
A pinch of salt
A pinch of cayenne
½ lb. butter, dripping, or margarine
6 oz. candied orange peel
1 orange
½ lb. treacle or syrup
3 eggs

Sieve all the dry ingredients into a large basin, and rub in the fat with the tips of the fingers until quite free from lumps. Add the candied orange peel, cut in fine shreds, and the grated rind of the fresh orange. Make a well in the centre and pour in the treacle or syrup, previously warmed, the eggs, well beaten, and the strained juice of the orange. With a large wooden spoon, mix gradually from the centre outwards, until all the ingredients are thoroughly blended. The addition of a little milk or water may be necessary if the eggs are small, for the mixture should be of a consistency that will just drop from the spoon. Beat well, then pour into a well-greased Yorkshire pudding tin, or into several small cake tins, not more than three-parts filling them. Bake the gingerbread in a moderate oven (350° F., mark 4) for 1½ hours or longer, according to size, or until it is well risen and feels firm to the touch. Turn out on a sieve or wire stand and leave until quite cold. This gingerbread will keep well if stored in an airtight tin.

SCOTCH GINGER CAKE

¾ lb. flour
½ tsp. salt
2 tsps. bicarbonate of soda
3 tsps. ground ginger
2 oz. sultanas
4 oz. peel
1½ oz. preserved ginger
¾ lb. black treacle
6 oz. butter or margarine
3 oz. brown sugar
3 eggs
2 tbsps. milk

Sieve the flour, salt, bicarbonate of soda, and ground ginger into a basin, and add the sultanas, the chopped peel, and the preserved ginger, cut into small pieces. Put the treacle, fat, and sugar in a saucepan and warm gently until melted. Beat the eggs and milk. Combine all the ingredients, beat very thoroughly, and pour into a greased and lined tin—7 inches square. Bake in a moderate oven (350° F., mark 3) for about 2 hours, or until the centre is firm to the touch. Cool a little before turning out of the tin.

GINGER PARKIN

6 oz. wholemeal flour
6 oz. fine oatmeal
2 tsps. mixed spice
2 tsps. ground ginger
2 tsps. cinnamon
1 tsp. bicarbonate of soda
2 tsps. cream of tartar
4 oz. margarine or lard
3 oz. brown sugar
¾ teacupful syrup
1 egg

Put the wholemeal flour, oatmeal, spices, bicarbonate of soda, and cream of tartar into a basin. Mix well, and rub in the fat until it resembles fine breadcrumbs. Put the sugar and syrup into a saucepan, and warm, but do not allow them to become hot. Stir into the dry ingredients, then add the beaten egg and mix well. Pour into a well-greased Yorkshire pudding tin and bake in a slow oven (325° F., mark 2) for about 1–1¼ hours.

MISCELLANEOUS CAKE RECIPES

STRAWBERRY SHORTCAKE—I

8 oz. flour
A good pinch of salt
1 tbsp. baking powder
2 oz. butter
1 egg (optional)
Cold milk
Caster sugar

For the Filling

Butter or cream to spread
Strawberries
Cream

Butter two sandwich tins of medium size, Sieve the flour, salt, and baking powder into a basin, and rub the butter into the flour until it is finely divided. Then mix to a soft dough with the egg and milk. Turn the mixture on to a board, divide in half, knead it up lightly, and then flatten it so that two rounds fit the sandwich tins: the dough should be slightly less than $\frac{1}{2}$ inch deep. Brush each round with a little butter, and bake in a hot oven (450° F., mark 8). When cooked, remove from the tins and spread liberally with butter or whipped cream, and fill with fresh strawberries and cream. Large berries should be cut in halves or quarters, piled up lavishly on top of one of the buttered or creamed cakes, and topped with cream, then covered with the second cake, which in turn is buttered, and topped generously with fruit and cream. Dredge with sugar.

STRAWBERRY SHORTCAKE—II

$\frac{1}{4}$ lb. butter	1 tsp. salt
$\frac{1}{4}$ lb. caster sugar	$\frac{1}{2}$ teacupful milk
2 eggs	Flavouring
6 oz. flour	Fruit filling
$\frac{1}{2}$ tsp. baking powder	

Put the butter and sugar into a basin and beat them well with a wooden spoon, until they are of a light and creamy consistency. Add the yolks of the eggs and beat again. Sieve the flour, baking powder, and salt, and add them to the mixture alternately with the milk, mixing as lightly as possible. Beat the whites of the eggs to a very stiff froth and fold them into the other ingredients, together with a little flavouring. Bake in two greased sandwich tins for 30 minutes in a moderate oven (375° F., mark 5). When ready, put the cakes together with fruit filling.

FILLINGS FOR SHORTCAKES

Strawberry: About 1–1$\frac{1}{2}$ lb. strawberries will be sufficient for six or eight servings. Wash and hull the strawberries, then set some aside to decorate the top of the cake. Mash the remainder with a stainless fork, and add caster sugar to taste. Let the mixture stand until the sugar is dissolved. Place part of this filling on one of the cake layers, then cover with the other layer. Place more filling on the top layer of the cake, cover with whipped cream, and decorate with the whole strawberries. Pour the juice from the fruit round the cake, and it is ready to serve immediately.

Raspberries, loganberries, peaches, apricots, and pineapple are prepared in the same manner. When tinned fruits are used they should be drained from the syrup and cut in pieces. The syrup may be reduced by boiling, and sugar added if necessary, also a little lemon juice and a drop or two of pink colouring. Strain it and use as a sauce when cold.

RICH STRAWBERRY GÂTEAU

4 oz. flour	1 egg yolk
2 oz. rice flour	1 tbsp. cream
4 oz. butter	Strawberries
2 oz. ground almonds	Sugar
3 oz. caster sugar	Whipped cream

Put the flour and rice flour into a basin. Add the butter and rub in with the tips of the fingers, handling very lightly. Add the ground almonds and sugar. Mix to a firm dough with the egg yolk, beaten with cream. Turn on to a lightly floured board and divide into two portions. Roll each into a round about $\frac{1}{2}$ inch thick and fit into greased sandwich tins lined with greased paper. Prick all over. Bake in a moderately hot oven (400° F., mark 6) for 30–40 minutes, until firm and lightly coloured. Cool on a rack.

Prepare and crush the strawberries, leaving a few whole for decoration. Whip and sweeten the cream. Just before serving, sandwich the shortbreads together with layers of cream and crushed strawberries. Decorate the top with cream and whole strawberries.

ANGEL CAKE—I

1$\frac{1}{2}$ oz. flour	1 tsp. cream of tartar
1$\frac{1}{2}$ oz. cornflour	5 egg whites
A pinch of salt	5 oz. caster sugar
1 tsp. baking powder	A little vanilla essence

Sieve the flours, salt, baking powder, and cream of tartar into a basin. Whisk the egg whites to a stiff froth, fold in the sugar and the dry ingredients very lightly, adding a few drops of essence at the last. When thoroughly combined, pour into an ungreased border cake tin and bake in a moderate oven (350° F., mark 4) for about 45 minutes. When well risen, cover with greaseproof paper to prevent the top from browning. Remove from oven when cooked, and invert the tin on a wire rack until cool; the cake should then fall out.

ANGEL CAKE—II

4$\frac{1}{2}$ oz. flour	$\frac{1}{2}$ tsp. vanilla essence
7$\frac{1}{2}$ oz. granulated sugar	$\frac{1}{4}$ tsp. almond essence
8–10 egg whites	Blanched almonds (optional)
$\frac{1}{2}$ tsp. salt	
2 tsps. cream of tartar	

Sift the flour and a quarter of the sugar together. Beat the egg whites and salt together until foamy, then add the cream of tartar and beat until stiff enough to stand in peaks, but not dry. Add the remaining sugar, 2 tbsps. at a time, beating after each addition, until the sugar is just blended. Fold in flavourings. Sift about

2 tbsps. of the flour and sugar over the mixture, and fold in very lightly. Repeat until all is used. Turn into an ungreased border mould and cut gently with a knife to remove any large air bubbles. Bake in a moderate oven (350° F., mark 4) for about 1 hour.

Invert the cake in the tin on a cake rack until cold, then remove the tin. If preferred, the cake can be baked in two 9-inch layer cake tins in a moderate oven for about 30 minutes.

After the first 10 minutes of baking, blanched almonds can, if liked, be sprinkled carefully over the top of the mixture without disturbing it in the oven.

DANISH PASTRIES

1 oz. yeast	Macaroon mixture or almond paste for filling
¼ pint milk	Egg to glaze
A pinch of salt	Glacé icing
11 oz. plain bread flour	Roasted, flaked, or chopped almonds to decorate
2 eggs	
1 oz. sugar	
6 oz. butter or margarine	

Break down the yeast with a little tepid milk. Add the salt to the flour and make a well in the centre. Beat the eggs, and put them with the yeast and sugar into the centre of the flour. Gradually mix in the flour, and beat the dough well, then leave in a warm place for 15 minutes, covered with a cloth. Roll out the dough fairly thinly on a floured board, and place the butter or margarine in the centre. Fold the dough over the butter and give two "turns," as for puff pastry. Allow to stand for 10–15 minutes, then give two further turns followed by another rest in a cool place. Roll out the pastry ¼ inch thick and cut it into triangles, with bases measuring about 6½ inches. Roll a little of the filling into a sausage shape and place it near the base of one of the triangles. Commencing with the base of the triangle, roll it up, bend it round to form a crescent, and place on a greased baking sheet. Prove the crescents at a temperature of 85° F. for 20 minutes. Brush them with egg, and bake in a hot oven (450° F., mark 8) for 15–20 minutes, until golden-brown. Whilst they are still hot, brush them over with glacé icing and sprinkle with the nuts.

Danish Custard Buns are made as follows: Roll the dough out ¼ inch thick and cut it into strips 10–12 inches long and ½ inch wide. Twist the ends of each strip in opposite directions. Lay them on a baking sheet, forming each into a spiral, starting at the centre, press the centre down to leave a hollow, and prove as above. Brush over with beaten egg, and place a small portion of cold thick custard in the centre of each bun. Bake in a hot oven (450° F., mark 8) for 10–15 minutes, until golden-brown, then brush over the outer ring of each bun with glacé icing while still hot, and sprinkle with roasted, flaked, or chopped almonds.

EASTERN CAKES

3 egg whites	Coffee butter icing
6 oz. caster sugar	Glacé icing, coloured pink
6 oz. ground almonds	

Line a shallow baking tin with greased paper. Whisk the egg whites until very stiff, and fold in the sugar and almonds lightly. Spread the mixture on a prepared tin, and bake in a moderate oven (350° F., mark 4) until just set—about ½ hour. Stamp into rounds with a small cutter, and return to oven to continue cooking until lightly browned and quite set. Remove the rounds, and cool on a rack. Allow the trimmings to continue cooking until crisp and a rich golden-brown colour, then crush them with a rolling pin or pound them in a mortar. Sandwich the rounds together in pairs with coffee butter icing, spread a little of the icing round the edge, and roll in the cake crumbs. Decorate the top of each cake with pink glacé icing.

HAZELNUT CAKE

2½ oz. hazelnuts	Hazelnuts to decorate
3 egg whites	Icing sugar
2 oz. fine sugar	

For the Filling

3 egg yolks	⅓ pint milk
2 oz. sugar or honey	Vanilla essence
1 oz. flour	

Skin the hazelnuts by heating through in the oven and rubbing in a cloth. Grind or mince them finely. Whisk the egg whites very stiffly, and fold in the nuts and sugar as lightly as possible. Grease three small sandwich tins and place rounds of greased paper in the bottoms. Spread a layer of mixture in each and bake in a moderate oven (350° F., mark 4) about ½ hour. Remove from the tins carefully, pull off the paper, and place the cakes on a rack to cool.

Meanwhile, make the filling. Mix the yolks and sugar, stir in the flour, and add the milk by degrees. Bring to the boil, stirring continuously, and cook for a minute. Add the vanilla essence, and allow to cool. Sandwich the cakes together with the filling, spreading some on the top also. If liked, it can be piped on top with a writing pipe. Decorate with whole or ground hazelnuts and dust with icing sugar.

EGGLESS FRUIT CAKE (BOILED)

6 oz. mixed dried fruits	½ tsp. salt
3 oz. fat	2 tsps. baking powder
4–5 oz. sugar (brown if possible)	½ tsp. mixed spice
¼ pint water	A little grated nutmeg
8 oz. flour	1 tsp. bicarbonate of soda

Prepare the fruits according to kind, and chop if necessary. Put them with the fat, sugar, and water into a saucepan, bring to the boil, simmer for 10 minutes, and allow to cool. Meanwhile, sieve together the flour, salt, baking powder, and spices. Dissolve the bicarbonate of soda in a very little water. Combine all ingredients together and stir thoroughly, but do not beat. Pour quickly into a greased cake tin, about 6 inches in diameter, and bake in a moderately hot oven (400° F., mark 6) for 1½–2 hours.

COCONUT PYRAMIDS I

2 egg whites	5 oz. desiccated coconut
5 oz. sugar	

Whisk egg whites stiffly and fold in sugar and coconut. Pile on a greased tin, covered with rice paper, press into shape, and bake in a slow oven (300° F., mark 1) until pale fawn in colour—about ¾–1 hour. The mixture may be tinted pink or green before shaping.

COCONUT PYRAMIDS II

½ tin condensed milk	8 oz. desiccated coconut
1 tsp. vanilla essence	

Mix, then drop in dessertspoonfuls (1 inch apart) on to rice paper laid on a greased baking sheet. Bake in a moderate oven (350° F., mark 3) for 10 minutes, until lightly tinted.

MAIDS OF HONOUR

1 pint milk	1 tbsp. brandy
A pinch of salt	1 oz. blanched almonds
1 tsp. rennet	A little sugar
3 oz. butter	Puff pastry
2 eggs	A few currants

Warm the milk to blood heat, add salt and rennet, and leave to set until firm. Leave it to drain through fine muslin overnight, then rub the curds through a sieve with the softened butter. Whisk the eggs and brandy together and add to the curds, together with the finely chopped almonds and sugar. Line some deep patty tins with the puff pastry, fill with the mixture, and sprinkle with currants; bake in a moderately hot oven (425° F., mark 7) 20 minutes.

FLORENTINES

3¾ oz. butter	1 oz. cherries
4 oz. caster sugar	1 oz. candied peel
4 oz. broken walnuts and almonds (mixed)	½ egg-cupful of cream
1 oz. sultanas	4 oz. block chocolate to coat

Melt the butter, add the sugar and boil together for 1 minute. Stir in all the other ingredients, lastly folding in the whipped cream.

Drop in small, well-spaced heaps on greased and floured trays. Bake in a moderate oven (375° F., mark 5). When golden-brown, remove from the oven and cool slightly; press edges to a neat shape. Remove from tray and cool on a rack. Spread with melted chocolate and mark with a fork or decorating comb.

ICED AND DECORATED CAKES

Although there are innumerable cakes which look tempting and attractive just as they come from the oven, there are occasions when an iced cake seems more appropriate. Many people, too, find genuine creative pleasure in decorating cakes and biscuits, and welcome a chance to try their skill.

Types of decoration range from nuts, crystallised fruits and flowers, etc., through the simpler glacé and fondant icings, right up to the professional-looking piped royal icing used on wedding, birthday, and Christmas cakes. Recipes for the various icings and fillings are given in this chapter, together with directions for making some novelty cakes, etc.

EQUIPMENT FOR ICING

The equipment needed varies according to the work you wish to attempt. For glacé and fondant icings, you will probably need nothing extra, for most kitchens will already have the necessary wire rack and palette knife, etc. Feather-icing and piped butter icing require the use of a paper forcing bag (see this page) and a few simple nozzles. For the more elaborate types of royal icing decorations found in a classic wedding cake, some extra equipment is needed, as described below.

Icing Pipes and Bags

The most satisfactory kind of icing pipes are made of hand-cut brass without screws, designed to use in conjunction with a piping bag. The amateur does not require a large number of these pipes : one or two plain ones useful for a number of purposes (such as dots, lines, scrolls, network, writing, and for the centre of flowers) ; two or three star pipes of different sizes ; a medium and a small leaf pipe and a rose, would be a good assortment to start with. The illustrations of cakes suggest the results that can be achieved with different pipes.

To make forcing bags : Strong but pliable 118
greaseproof paper is required. Take a piece of paper 8–9 inches square and fold it in half diagonally, creasing the fold very firmly. Hold in the left hand with the thumb pointing towards the centre, and fold into a cone shape by bringing the right-hand corner up to the centre corner and wrapping the left-hand corner round to the back of the centre (see plate 118b). Arrange the paper so that the three corners are on top of each other, and the bottom of the cone has a very sharp point. Continuing to hold the three corners firmly, fold them over together two or three times to prevent their uncurling.

Cut off a very small piece from the point of the paper cone, just sufficient to enable the pipe to project about half-way through the bag, and insert the pipe. The bag is then ready.

Palette Knife

A long-bladed, firm palette knife, such as is used for general cooking purposes, is necessary for spreading and smoothing the icing.

Icing Table

Although not absolutely essential, a strong, steady, heavy metal cake-icing table, adjustable as to height and angle, will simplify the work considerably. Icing tables made of thin tinned iron can also be procured and are much less expensive, though not quite so convenient to use. If a special stand is not available, use an upturned plate placed on top of a basin. Since this does not revolve, it is necessary to turn the plate continuously during the process of decoration or, if more convenient, for the worker to move round the cake.

Icing Nails

For elaborate flower-making and for raised network, icing nails, shaped like large household nails, are necessary. The icing is piped on to the head of the nail, the nail being held in the hand and revolved as necessary. A mesh stand is used for holding the nails while the icing dries.

Dividing Rings

A set of flat, concentric metal dividing rings, graduated in size and marked in eight equal sections, will help the amateur to space the decoration evenly, but are by no means essential.

Sugar-boiling Thermometer

A thermometer (see Sweet Making chapter) is useful for icings made with a sugar syrup—American icing, fondant icing, and so on. In boiled icing recipes the sugar is dissolved in the water before boiling. Once the syrup comes to the boil, put in the thermometer and leave it in the syrup until the required temperature is reached.

If you have no sugar thermometer, use the tests given in the Sugar-boiling Chart in the Sweet Making chapter.

RECIPES FOR CAKE ICINGS, GLAZE, ETC.

ALMOND ICING—I

1 lb. ground almonds
1 lb. icing sugar
2 eggs
1 tsp. vanilla essence
½ tsp. orange flower water
Juice of 1 lemon

Mix the ground almonds and sugar together. Beat the eggs lightly and add them, with the flavouring essences and lemon juice, to the dry ingredients. Mix to a paste, and knead thoroughly, then use as required.

ALMOND ICING—II

½ lb. icing sugar
½ lb. caster sugar
1 lb. ground almonds
2 tsps. lemon juice
A few drops of vanilla essence
Egg to mix

Sieve the two sugars and mix them with the ground almonds. Add flavourings and enough beaten egg to bind all together, then turn the paste on to a sugared board or slab, work with the hands until smooth, and roll out.

ALMOND ICING—III

1 lb. loaf sugar
¼ pint water
A pinch of cream of tartar
12 oz. ground almonds
2 egg whites
3 oz. icing sugar

Put the loaf sugar and water into a pan and dissolve slowly. When it boils, add the cream of tartar, then bring to a temperature of 240°F. Remove from the heat and stir rapidly until the syrup becomes cloudy. Stir in the ground almonds and egg whites and cook for a few minutes over a gentle heat, stirring well. Pour on to an oiled slab of marble or of enamelled iron, add the sieved icing sugar, and work well with a palette knife, lifting the edges of the mixture with the knife and pressing them into the centre. As soon as the mixture is sufficiently cool, knead with the hands until smooth. Additional sieved icing sugar may be kneaded in if required.

AMERICAN ICING

A special feature of American icing is that, whilst it forms a crust on the outside, it never becomes really hard and rocky as does royal icing. Though it is mostly used on sponge mixtures, walnut, and cherry cakes, it can be applied to any cake, either rich plum or plain sponge. The decorations must be ready to be put on immediately the icing is poured over the cake and before it has time to set.

2 egg whites
¼ pint water
1 lb. loaf sugar

Whisk the eggs to a stiff froth and heat the water and sugar to a temperature of 240° F. Pour the syrup in a thin stream on to the egg whites and whisk until the mixture thickens and is almost cold; then pour the icing quickly over the cake.

The secret of success is to see that the syrup reaches the required temperature, and that the eggs and syrup are beaten hard the whole time the icing is cooling. Judgment must also be exercised in determining when the icing has reached the correct consistency, for if too liquid, a thin coating only remains on the cake.

Suitable decorations are walnuts, cherries, and other crystallised fruit, or flowers and fern leaves, either bought or home-made out of royal icing.

BUTTER ICING

4 oz. fresh butter — Vanilla essence
6 oz. sieved icing sugar — Colouring, if required

Cream the butter, add the sugar by degrees, beating until smooth and creamy, then add the essence and colouring, if required.

Chocolate Butter Icing: Add 1–2 oz. plain chocolate, melted.

Coffee Butter Icing: Add 1–2 tsps. coffee essence.

Hungarian Icing: Add 2 oz. melted chocolate, 2 tsps. coffee essence, and 2 tbsps. chopped walnuts.

Orange or Lemon Butter Icing: Add 1 tsp. of the grated rind and 1 tbsp. of the juice: omit the vanilla essence.

FONDANT ICING

Make the fondant according to the directions given in the chapter on Sweet Making, and thin with sugar syrup until it is of such a consistency that it will coat the back of a spoon well.

GLACÉ ICING

$\frac{1}{2}$ lb. sieved icing sugar — 2–3 tbsps. warm water
A few drops flavouring essence — Colouring, if required

Put the sieved icing sugar and flavouring in an enamelled saucepan, and add the water very gradually over a gentle heat. Stir till warm. Do not let the icing get too hot or it will become crystallised. It should be thick enough to coat the back of a spoon. If too thin, more sugar should be added, or more water if too thick. Add colouring last of all, and use at once.

CHOCOLATE GLACÉ ICING

1 oz. grated chocolate — 4 oz. icing sugar
1 tbsp. water, approx. — 1 tsp. vanilla essence

Put the chocolate into a saucepan, add the water, allow it to melt, let it boil for 2 minutes, then cool. Rub the icing sugar through a hair sieve and add it to the chocolate, together with the vanilla essence. Mix all together and allow the icing sugar to dissolve, but on no account allow it to get hot or it will become dull on cooling. Use while still warm.

Alternatively, use $\frac{1}{2}$ oz. of cocoa powder instead of the chocolate. Blend this with the water, cook for 2 minutes, and allow to cool. Add a knob of butter to keep icing glossy.

COFFEE GLACÉ ICING

1 lb. icing sugar — Coffee essence
5 tbsps. water, approx.

Place the sugar in a saucepan and add the
water and coffee essence gradually, stirring all 120
the time. Heat gently, but do not let the icing get very hot, otherwise it will have a dull appearance when cold. The icing is of the right consistency when it is just thick enough to coat the back of a spoon.

ORANGE OR LEMON GLACÉ ICING

$\frac{1}{2}$ lb. sieved icing sugar — 2 tbsps. orange or lemon juice, approx.
A few drops of colouring

The method is exactly as for ordinary glacé icing, with the use of fruit juice instead of water.

GLAZE FOR MARZIPAN

2 oz. gum arabic — $\frac{1}{3}$ pint water (for sugar)
$\frac{1}{3}$ pint water (for gum) — 1–2 oz. spirits of wine
1 oz. granulated sugar

Crush the gum arabic and dissolve in the water. Dissolve the sugar in water and boil to 228° F. Remove from heat. When stiff, add the spirits of wine. Leave to cool, then strain through muslin, and bottle. Apply the glaze with a small brush.

ROYAL ICING

2 egg whites — 1 lb. icing sugar, approx.
1 dessertsp. glycerine

Put the egg whites into a bowl, add the glycerine (this prevents the icing from becoming too hard with keeping), and beat slightly. Sieve the sugar and gradually beat it into the egg whites. The mixture should be soft, but stiff enough to stand up in $\frac{1}{2}$-inch peaks. Icing used for a second coat should be runny, but thick enough to coat the back of a spoon.

TRANSPARENT ICING

1 lb. loaf sugar — A little lemon juice
$\frac{1}{2}$ pint water

Boil the sugar and water together and continue heating until the temperature reaches 229° F. Whilst boiling, remove any scum that rises on the sugar and brush the sides of the pan with a little cold water. When 229° F. is reached, pour the sugar into a clean basin, stir in a little lemon juice, and beat until it thickens and becomes opaque; then pour over the cake. This icing gives an excellent finishing coat to a cake which has been iced with royal icing, and is recommended for Christmas, christening, and bride cakes, when a specially attractive and professional-looking background is desired.

CAKE FILLINGS

ALMOND AND WALNUT FILLING

4 tbsps. ground almonds	4 tbsps. sieved apricot jam
2 tbsps. finely chopped walnuts	1 tsp. vanilla essence

Mix all the ingredients thoroughly together; use as required.

APRICOT AND WALNUT FILLING

4 tbsps. apricot jam	$1\frac{1}{2}$ oz. walnuts
A squeeze of lemon juice	

Rub the apricot jam through a sieve, then stir in the lemon juice and chopped nuts.

BANANA FILLING

2 bananas	$\frac{1}{4}$ tsp. grated lemon rind
2 oz. caster sugar	
A little lemon juice	2 tbsps. cream

Sieve the bananas, add the sugar, lemon rind, and juice, and finally, add the stiffly whisked cream. Whisk the whole together for 10 minutes, then spread between the cake. The top of the cake should be sprinkled with icing sugar, or if preferred, glacé icing may be put on, although this makes it rather sweet, with the rich banana filling.

CONFECTIONER'S CUSTARD

$1\frac{1}{2}$ tbsps. cornflour	1 oz. caster sugar
$\frac{1}{2}$ pint milk	$\frac{1}{2}$ tsp. vanilla essence
2 egg yolks	

Blend the cornflour with the milk, stir and boil until it thickens. Simmer, stirring all the while for about 5 minutes. Add the egg yolks, sugar, and flavouring. Cook over a moderate heat for a few minutes, stirring. Use cold.

ORANGE FILLING—I

Juice of 2 oranges	2 oz. sugar
2 tbsps. lemon juice	2 oz. cornflour
Water	2 egg yolks
Rind of 1 orange	1 oz. fresh butter

Make the fruit juices up to $\frac{3}{4}$ pint with water. Add the grated rind and sugar. Mix the cornflour to a smooth paste with a little of the liquid. Boil the rest, pour on to the cornflour, return to the pan and boil for a few minutes. Add the egg yolks and butter, cool and use.

ORANGE FILLING—II

3 oz. cake crumbs	Juice of 1 orange
1 oz. butter	3 oz. sugar
The grated rind of 2 oranges	1 egg yolk

Put all the filling ingredients, except egg yolk, into a saucepan. Heat for 5 minutes, stirring all the time. Allow to cool slightly, add the egg and stir over a low heat. Allow to cool and use as required.

RICH BUTTER CREAM

6 oz. granulated sugar	3 oz. fresh butter
2 tbsps. water	Flavouring
2 egg yolks	

Put the sugar and water in a small saucepan, place over heat and dissolve the sugar. When the syrup is perfectly clear bring to the boil, and boil without stirring until the syrup makes a good thread on the end of a skewer. Stand aside for a few minutes. Beat the yolks in a basin. Pour on syrup in a thin stream, whisking all the time: if the syrup is added too quickly or too hot, the eggs will curdle. Beat until cool. Cream the butter and whisk a little at a time into the egg mixture. Flavour as desired. Use very cold.

RUM BUTTER

$\frac{1}{4}$ lb. butter	2 tbsps. rum
$\frac{3}{4}$ lb. soft brown sugar	A little caster sugar
$\frac{1}{2}$ large nutmeg, grated	

Melt the butter very slowly. Mix the sugar and nutmeg in a bowl, first crushing out any large lumps of sugar with a rolling pin on a board. Add the rum and then the melted butter. Stir well until the mixture thickens. Dredge lightly with caster sugar, and leave to get quite cold.

CREAM AND MOCK CREAM

WHIPPED CREAM

Have the cream, also the utensils to be used, as cool as possible, and work in a cool place. Whisk the cream with a fork, whisk, or a rotary beater, until it begins to thicken, and then add any flavouring and sugar to taste. Continue to whisk until the cream will cling firmly to the whisk or fork, but beware of over-whisking, which will cause the cream to curdle.

DEVONSHIRE CREAM

For this you require really fresh milk, straight from the cow—not bottled. Pour it into a shallow pan and leave to stand for about 12 hours (in hot weather, 6 hours) for the cream to rise to the surface. Now heat the milk very slowly, until the surface begins to wrinkle; on no account allow it to boil—the more slowly the heating is done, the better the result. The time required depends on the size and shape of the pan and the amount of heat applied, but about 1 hour is usually necessary. Transfer the pan at once to a cool place, and leave until next day before skimming off the cream.

WHIPPED EVAPORATED MILK

When evaporated milk is to be whisked, it is best to scald it first (though this is not necessary if the milk is already homogenised). Put the unopened tin in a pan of water, bring to the boil and let it boil for about 15–20 minutes, keeping the tin fully immersed. Allow it to become quite cold before opening it. Milk scalded in this way will keep as long as untreated milk, provided the tin is not opened. When it is required for use, whisk it in the usual way.

MOCK CREAM—I

2 oz. butter or margarine
2 oz. caster sugar
2 tbsps. boiling water
1 tbsp. cold milk
Vanilla essence

Cream together the fat and sugar until very soft and light. Beat in the boiling water a very little at a time, and then add the milk in the same way. Flavour with a few drops of vanilla essence. If made of suitable consistency, this " cream " can be piped.

MOCK CREAM—II

1 egg white
1 tbsp. golden syrup

Whisk the egg white until stiff. Pour in the slightly warmed syrup, beating at the same time, until the mixture resembles a thick cream. Use with fruit salad and similar dishes.

SYNTHETIC CREAM

Various proprietary preparations are made as a substitute for cream, and these should be used as directed by the manufacturers.

GENERAL HINTS ON CAKE ICING

1. Choose the type of icing most suitable for the cake you wish to decorate. Glacé, fondant, and American frosting are good for sponge, sandwich, and Madeira cakes. For fruit cakes, use almond paste covered with royal icing, American frosting, or fondant icing.

2. Allow the cake to become quite cold before icing. If iced while warm, it will become soggy and the icing will not stick so well.

3. See that the surface is free from crumbs and that the cake is a good shape. If it has risen with a crack across the top, cut off the cracked part, using a sharp knife, then trim if necessary, to make a rounder surface.

4. Put ready any decoration before beginning to ice the cake.

5. If the cake is to be a layer or sandwich cake, spread the layers with filling and fit them neatly together, avoiding gaps: this is easy to do when using one deep cake cut across, but if the layers have been baked in separate tins you may need to trim the edges to give a neat, even surface for icing.

TO COAT A CAKE WITH GLACÉ OR FONDANT ICING

Place the cake on an inverted plate, or on a wire rack placed over a basin; any surplus icing running off the cake can then be collected with a palette knife and used again. Have the icing of exactly the right consistency (test this on the back of the spoon), and pour it quickly from the saucepan or basin on to the centre of the cake, letting it overflow down the sides. If any gaps are left, take up some icing with a palette knife and gently apply it where it is needed. Try to ice the cake without using a knife, if you can, as " doctoring up " the sides may give an untidy effect. Put any decorations in position before the icing has set, but leave the icing to dry before applying a piped decoration.

To ice the top only: Pin a double band of greaseproof paper tightly round the cake, about 1 inch higher than the top. Pour on sufficient icing to give a thickish coating. When it is nearly set place any decorations in position, and when quite set, gently pull off the paper, if necessary using a knife dipped in hot water to loosen it. ½ lb. icing sugar will ice a 6-inch cake.

To Ice Small Cakes

See the cakes are free from crumbs, then ice by one of these methods :—

1. Place the cakes in position on a wire cake rack, with a dish underneath to catch drops of

icing. Take a good tablespoonful of icing and pour it on to the top of a cake from the front of the spoon, allowing sufficient icing to flow evenly down the sides and entirely coat the cake.

2. If you prefer, you can balance the cake on the end of a palette knife, hold it over the pan or basin of icing and ice with a spoon, as above.

3. Dip the cakes one at a time in the icing. Hold each cake upside down between your thumb and finger, dip the top of the cake into the prepared icing.

For a richer effect, brush the cakes over with melted jam, and cover with thin almond paste before icing them. For additional decoration, mount balls or other fancy-shaped pieces of almond paste on top of the cakes, before coating with icing.

TO COAT A CAKE WITH ALMOND ICING

When a wedding or similar cake is to be covered with royal icing, it is customary to coat it first with almond icing, which gives a smooth surface and prevents cake crumbs working into the icing.

For preference, cover the whole of the cake, both sides and top, with almond paste, but if cost must be considered, the paste may be applied to the top only.

Before commencing to ice the cake, see that it is a good shape. If it has risen unevenly, trim it somewhat, but there is no need to make it perfectly flat, as slight unevenness can be rectified when the almond icing is put on the top.

Cut off about one-third of the almond paste and roll out on a sugared board to a round the size of the top of the cake. Roll out the remaining paste and cut a strip the width and length of the sides of the cake. Use the trimmings of the paste to fill in any cracks or to level the top of the cake. Brush over the surface with slightly beaten egg white, melted sieved jam or golden syrup, place the round of paste on the top, and press evenly. Then put the strip round the sides of the cake, moistening the edges with the beaten egg white, and joining them neatly.

Place the cake, upside down, on a sugared board, pressing it lightly to make the top perfectly flat (or you can roll the top with a rolling pin). Then press the sides straight with a broad-bladed knife so that the cake is a good shape, or use a jam jar to roll the sides. Turn right side up, and set aside for several days in a warm dry place, before applying the royal icing. This gives the outside time to dry slightly, so that there is less likelihood of the oil from the almonds working through the white icing and discolouring it.

TO COAT AND DECORATE A CAKE WITH ROYAL ICING

Beat the royal icing well for at least 10 minutes, and see that it is of the correct consistency, i.e., thick enough just to stand in points when tested. Keep the basin covered with a piece of damp muslin or a damp cloth, as the icing quickly hardens when exposed to the air.

Place the cake on a revolving icing table, if you have one, or on an inverted cake tin or an upturned plate over a basin. Use a palette knife or a long broad-bladed knife to spread the icing on the cake, and have a jug of hot water handy to dip the knife into. Spread the icing evenly over the cake, and smooth the top by drawing the knife evenly across it. Smooth the sides by holding the knife upright and drawing it evenly and firmly round the cake. Dip the knife in hot water when necessary, but shake off excess drops so as not to make the icing really wet.

Leave the cake to stand for several days, to dry off the icing, but see that it is protected from dust. When the icing is perfectly dry, level the surface with a sharp knife.

Finish the cake by applying a second coat in the same way, or, if preferred, thin some royal icing to a pouring consistency with lightly beaten egg whites and pour over the cake, pricking out any bubbles with a needle or skewer.

Wedding cakes may be finished with a third coating of transparent icing. This gives them a specially attractive and professional appearance.

If only one coat of royal icing is used, make it slightly thinner (i.e., so that it will coat the back of a wooden spoon), pour it on to the centre of the cake, and gradually work it over the surface with a palette knife.

When the top coat of icing is perfectly dry, the cake is ready for decorating with piping, etc.

Planning the Design

The design may be very simple or really elaborate, according to taste. The inexperienced are advised to choose a simple pattern, and

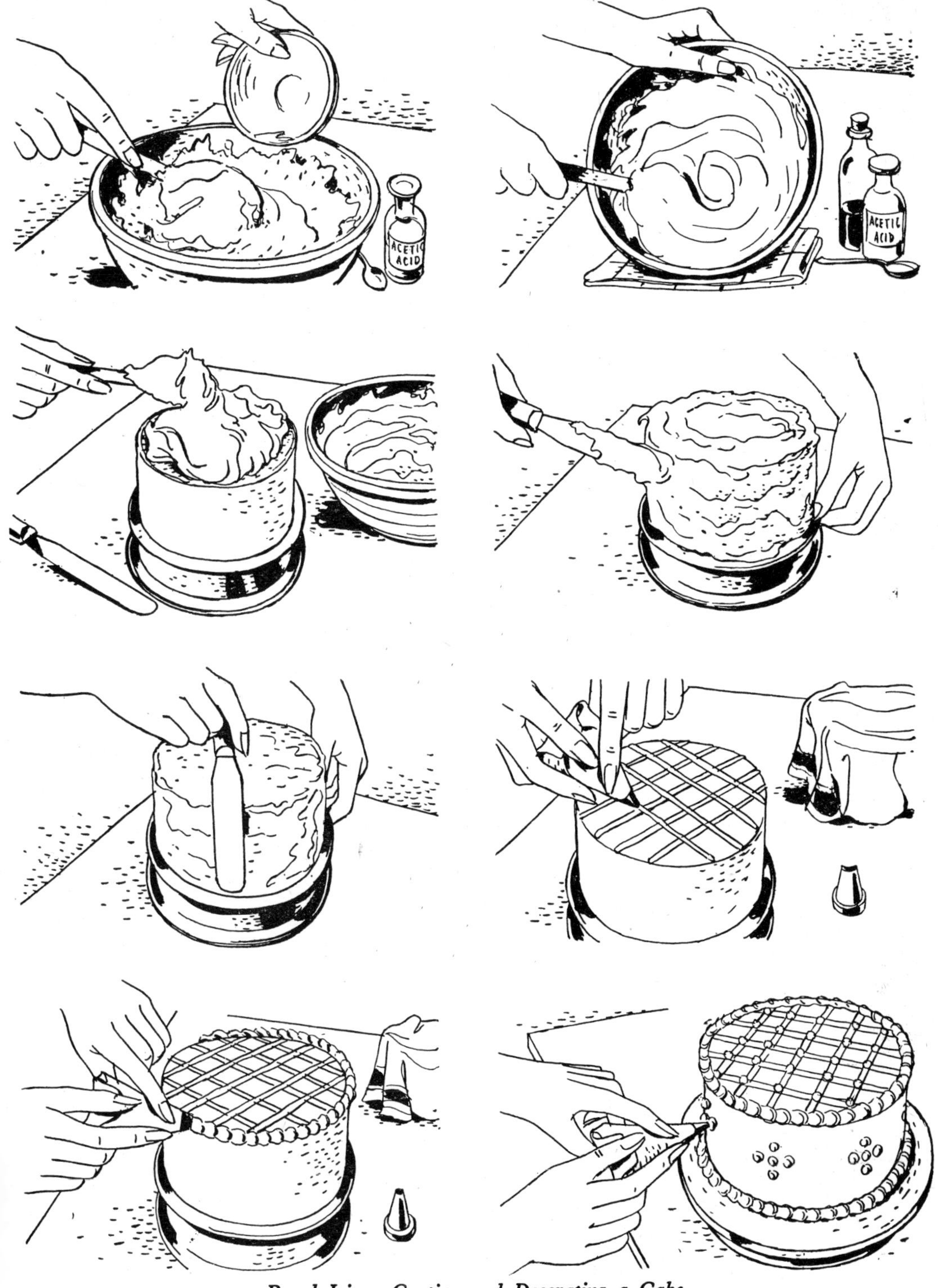

Royal Icing—Coating and Decorating a Cake

should there be any small irregularities on the background icing, the pattern should be arranged so that the defects are minimised. In any case, it is important to plan the design before starting to execute it. Dividing rings help in planning out a formal pattern. If no metal dividing rings are available, cut them out of strong paper or cardboard.

If you have artistic ability, you can sketch the design lightly in pencil directly on to the cake, but those less skilled will need to outline it on paper first. Cut a piece of white paper the exact size of the top of the cake, divide it into equal-sized sections, either by creasing it or with pencil, ruler, or compasses; then sketch the design on to it. Place the paper on top of the cake and transfer the pattern by pricking through the paper with a pin. In a simple, bold design, it is only necessary to make the pinholes here and there, at the key points; then, on removing the paper, these points can be joined with a light pencil line if necessary, before the piping is begun.

Piping

Piping is the term used for all kinds of ornamentation made with a forcing bag and pipe. The choice of pipes and the method of making a greaseproof paper forcing bag are discussed at the beginning of this chapter. Make some royal icing and beat it well, making it just stiff enough to stand in points when tested in a basin; colour it if desired. Keep the basin covered with a piece of damp muslin or damp cloth—once a crust forms on the icing, it cannot be smoothed out completely, and small pieces of it will stick in the nozzle of the pipe.

To Use a Forcing Bag and Pipe

Prepare the bag, cut a small piece off the bottom of the cone and insert the pipe. With a teaspoon, shake a spoonful or so of the icing into the centre of the bag, keeping the top and outside of the bag, and the hands, free of icing. To close the bag, press the top edges together and ease the icing downwards, taking care not to allow any of it to work up on the sides. Fold in the sides, and lastly bring the top down, folding it over twice to form a tightly fitting cover. Hold the bag with the nozzle projecting through the first and second fingers of the working hand and the top held down with the thumb.

If you have not done any piping before, practise forcing designs on to an upturned plate before attempting to decorate the cake itself. Once you have mastered the use of a forcing pipe, you can force the decoration straight on to the cake, but be sure that the final coating of icing on the cake is set firmly—however proficient you are, you will want to be able to scrape off any icing if you should make a mistake.

Piped Sugar Roses

Stick a small square of greaseproof paper on an icing nail with a dab of icing. Using royal icing of ordinary stiffness and a petal nozzle, pipe a knob in the middle to form the flower centre, and allow this to dry for a minute or two. Pipe the first and second petals, holding the nozzle as upright as possible and with the thick side of the nozzle at the base. Turn the nail round very slowly as you pipe the successive rose petals. Continue piping the petals, but do not make too many, which gives a shapeless, crowded effect. When you come to the final ring of petals, work the top edge of each outwards in a pleasing natural curve.

When the rose is finished, carefully remove it from the icing nail, together with its paper, and leave it on a tray or flat surface for 24 hours, until set. Attach each rose to the cake with a little freshly made icing.

Leaves can be piped in a similar way with a leaf nozzle.

Pansies, Narcissi and other Flowers

Use the same petal nozzle as for the rose, and hold it with the thick edge to the centre of the icing nail and the thin edge outwards. Pipe several petals flat on to the paper, gradually turning the nail as you work. The exact number of petals will depend on the particular flower you are making, but five is probably the most common number.

Carefully remove the paper from the nail and let the flower dry. When it is hard, pipe a dark yellow spot into the little hole left in the centre of the petals.

Flat Trellis

When working trellis straight on to the cake, first prick out the pattern, then pipe the icing through a writing pipe, holding this about 1 inch above the cake. If the icing is allowed to fall in this way, it will form really straight lines. Allow the first set of lines to dry a little, then pipe across them to give the trellis effect. If you wish to make the trellis stand out well, you can pipe a third set of lines over the second, after allowing these to dry slightly: this gives a slightly raised effect.

Raised Trellis

To make a raised trellis shape, the lines must be piped over an icing nail or a round or boat-shaped patty tin. First grease the nail or tin, then pipe the lines as described above. Leave the trellis to set hard (preferably for 24 hours) before removing it. Warm the patty tin or icing nail slightly, and carefully remove the trellis. This can then be fixed to the cake, a little wet icing being used to hold it firmly in position.

Trellis and piped designs are generally used for celebration cakes as shown in the photographs and in colour plate facing page 385. (For Wedding Cake recipes, see Cake Making chapter.)

Cutting a Wedge from an Iced Cake

Sometimes a wedge is cut from a wedding or birthday cake before it is decorated, to facilitate cutting at the actual party. When the design is marked out, decide where a wedge can be cut without spoiling the decoration, make two neat cuts through the sugar coating from edge to centre of the cake, and with a sharp knife cut right through the almond paste and cake, completely severing the wedge.

The wedge is then usually encircled with white satin ribbon. To protect this from grease stains, cut a strip of thick greaseproof paper slightly more than twice the width of the ribbon and long enough to go round the two cut surfaces of the wedge. Crease it lengthwise along the middle, slip the ribbon in between and tie it round the wedge. Replace the wedge in the cake, and complete the decoration.

SIMPLE CAKE DECORATIONS

Nuts, Fruit, Frosting, etc.

Almonds : Blanch and dry the nuts, and either use them plain, as on the top of a Dundee cake, or brown them by putting whole, split, or chopped nuts on a piece of paper on a baking sheet, and heating them in a moderate oven until they are the desired colour ; shake them frequently to ensure even browning.

Chopped almonds are often used to decorate the sides of large or small cakes, which have either been coated with butter icing or brushed over with a little melted jam or marmalade. Split browned almonds can be used for the same purpose, and should be arranged neatly so that they completely cover the surface.

Walnuts : Halved walnuts are a favourite decoration for iced cakes, particularly those flavoured with coffee or chocolate, or coated with American icing. Walnuts may be chopped, blanched, and browned in the same way as almonds, to decorate or to add to cake fillings.

Crystallised Fruits, etc. : Angelica makes a colourful decoration for small and large cakes, and is usually used with glacé cherries, crystallised violets, mimosa balls, rose petals, etc. Cut into narrow strips, it can be shaped to resemble small leaves.

Chocolate Vermicelli and Chocolate Shot : These can be used on small cakes, which should first be dipped in melted couverture chocolate or glacé icing, or brushed over with melted jam or marmalade.

Coloured Sugar or Desiccated Coconut : Put a small quantity of the sugar or coconut on a piece of paper or saucer, add a few drops of colouring, and work it in with the fingertips or a spoon until the sugar or coconut is evenly coloured, then leave to dry. Sprinkle over small cakes or round the edge of a larger one.

Edible Frosting : Put 2 oz. white gum arabic crystals with 2–3 tbsps. hot water into a small pan. Stand the pan in another saucepan containing boiling water or use a double saucepan, and stir until all the gum is dissolved. Have ready a glass pastry board or a clean sheet of glass. Take a perfectly clean pastry brush (it is essential that no trace of grease or flour remain in the bristles), dip it into the gum and coat the surface of the glass. A fairly large area of glass should be coated if much frost is required. Place the glass in a warm room to dry, and the next day, with a sharp knife, scrape off the gum, which will have formed in a thin film : if small flakes are preferred, they can be further crushed with a rolling-pin. The frost thus obtained makes an attractive last-minute decoration to all kinds of iced cakes, particularly at Christmas.

Sugar " Lace " Pattern

Brush the top of a flat gingerbread or sandwich cake with a little golden syrup or melted honey. Place a doily on the surface and sprinkle well with sieved icing sugar, then remove the doily carefully, leaving the pattern in sugar on the cake. (If the actual cake surface is sticky, there is no need to brush it with honey or syrup.)

Feather-icing

Ice a sandwich cake with glacé icing of coating consistency, and while still wet, pipe across it lines of fairly stiff chocolate glacé icing, about ½ inch apart, using a writing nozzle or a paper forcing bag with a small piece cut away from the tip. Now, quickly run a skewer or sharp-pointed knife across the lines and back again, at 1-inch intervals, to produce the "feathered" effect; leave to dry.

For a "spider" cake, pipe the stiff icing in equidistant circles, and draw the skewer through these towards the centre of the cake, then in the opposite direction.

If you wish to decorate the sides of the cake (e.g. with butter cream and chopped nuts, jam and cake crumbs or crushed breakfast cereals, etc.), do this before icing the top.

Piped Butter Icing

Apply a coat of glacé icing, and when this has become sufficiently firm, decorate with butter icing. This is usually applied by means of a piping bag, with either a rose or plain
128 nozzle. Bold or delicate effects may be obtained by varying the size of the nozzle: for petits fours and small cakes, a fine nozzle giving a delicate tracery is the usual choice. Cakes decorated in this way should be used fairly soon after they are iced.

Outline and Stencil Designs

For these a smooth, firm surface is essential, so royal icing or American frosting is especially suitable, but glacé icing can be used, providing it has set firmly and is not at all tacky.

If you have not sufficient skill to produce an attractive freehand drawing with the forcing bag and nozzle, try using a needlework transfer with a clear, definite outline. Place it in position and pin it carefully. Now, using another pin, prick all along the lines of the transfer. Remove the paper, then, using butter or royal icing in a shade contrasting with the
129 background, outline the pattern. Add any necessary finishing touches, and leave to set.

A stencil provides another easy way of decorating a cake. Any simple design will do, provided the cardboard is fairly stiff; you can cut out your own pattern if you cannot buy a suitable one. Place the stencil firmly in position on the cake, and spread the cut-out part with suitably coloured icing as evenly as possible. Then remove the stencil carefully, so as not to damage the design. When the icing is set, the raised part can, if desired, be coloured with a paint brush and edible colouring.

RECIPES FOR DECORATED CAKES AND GÂTEAUX

NINE SQUARES CAKE

Bake a cake about 6 inches square, and mark the surface with a knife into 2-inch squares. Cover the sides with butter cream, roughing it up with a fork. Make up some stiff glacé icing in 2 colours, e.g., white and chocolate. Pipe straight lines over the markings with butter cream, then fill in, alternating the colours, using a pointed knife to get into the corners.

FRESH FRUIT GÂTEAU

Prepare an 8-inch sandwich cake in two tins, and spread cream or butter icing on one half of the cake. Cut six rounds out of the surface of the second cake, then sandwich the two cakes together and dust the top liberally with icing sugar. Fill the round holes with raspberries, which have been sweetened with sugar and left for a while. The sides of the cake may be coated with cream, smoothed over and marked out with a knife. Serve this cake as soon as possible.

RUSSIAN CAKE

For this, use left-over sandwich or sponge cake, or cake trimmings, and if necessary augment them with about 4 oz. of other plain cake. Pack the pieces in a greased tin of suitable size, using sufficient red or yellow jam to stick them together. Bake in a moderate oven (350° F., mark 4) for 10 minutes, then leave in tin to cool. Cover with a thin layer of almond paste.

The "feather" icing is made as follows: coat the cake with pink glacé icing and while this is still wet, pipe lines of white and chocolate icing across; now draw a skewer rapidly lengthwise through the icing, to give the feathered effect.

CHRISTMAS CAKE FOR CHILDREN

Bake a Madeira or sandwich cake in an oblong tin, and fill it with one of the suggested fillings. Coat the top and sides with green glacé icing, and leave to set. Arrange nine chocolate drops across the top from corner to corner, placing them in position when the icing is still slightly soft, or use a little soft icing for fixing; on each write one letter of the word "Christmas" in stiff green icing. Cut some more chocolate drops in half and place along the base and round the top edge of the cake. Finish with a narrow ribbon and two sprigs of green or silver holly.

COFFEE YULE LOG

Prepare a chocolate Swiss roll, and when it is cold, fill the roll with coffee butter cream. Remove a piece from the end of the log, cutting at a slight angle, and put this piece in position at the side of the roll to form a branch, fixing it with the butter cream. Cover the outside of the log with butter icing, either piped or roughed up with a fork to represent the tree bark. Dust lightly with icing sugar, and decorate with robins and holly. Leave to set before serving.

CHRISTMAS CAKE

For a quick finish to a Christmas cake, cover it with almond paste and coat with well-beaten royal icing. Flatten the top surface of the cake, but draw the icing round the sides into peaks, using the handle of a teaspoon or a knife. Leave to dry, then decorate the top with piped lattice icing, leaving a round in the centre. Place a small red ribbon bow or a sprig of holly in the circle. Arrange the cake on a silver board, cover the edge with rough icing, and pipe a red shell edging round the base of the cake.

STORK CHRISTENING CAKE

Coat the cake with almond paste and royal icing in the usual way. Using a writing nozzle, pipe across the cake two bands of trellis (about 2 inches wide, or to suit the size of the cake); these should cross at right angles at the centre. Outline the bands with small dots set closely together. In each of the blank quarters thus formed, place a sugar rose and leaves. Continue each of the trellis bands down the sides of the cake with a "fringe" made by piping straight lines, each terminating in a dot of icing. Pipe small roses all round the bottom edge of the cake, and place a model stork at the centre top.

NOVELTY CAKES

Given the necessary imagination, skill, and patience, cakes can be contrived to represent almost anything from a basket of fruit to a cottage or engine. The foundation of most of these novelty cakes is a plain sponge or Madeira cake mixture; when cooked this can be cut and built up to the shape required.

Do not be too ambitious for a first attempt at one of these cakes, and if possible begin by making a sketch, however rough; this will help you to work out the shape and size of cake required, and the way in which it should be cut and reassembled to form the main structure. For a Cartwheel, Mushroom, Basket, or Clock Cake use a round sandwich tin, and a square or rectangular tin for a Letter, Parcel, or Book cake. A Snowman, Guy Fawkes or Crinoline Lady cake can quite easily be made by baking the cake mixture in a pudding basin and finishing it as required. A china head and shoulders can be obtained for the Crinoline Lady cake, while for the Snowman or Guy Fawkes, a head can be made of the cake mixture, baked in a deep bun tin.

HEDGEHOG CAKE

Bake an oval cake, split it in half, fill with coffee butter cream, and trim to a hedgehog shape. Pipe stars all over the surface, using chocolate butter cream, then place the cake on an oval dish, and pipe in the head and tail. Add halved glacé cherries for the eyes. Shred some blanched almonds and use to represent the "prickles," making sure that they all slant away from the head.

Alternatively, bake a fruit cake mixture in the usual way in a round tin. When the cake is cold, coat the top and sides with almond paste. Have ready some blanched and lightly baked almonds. Dip the pointed end of each almond into a little egg white, and stick them into the almond paste; continue until the whole of the cake is neatly covered. As the almond paste hardens on exposure to the air, the almonds must be placed in position as soon as the cake is covered.

"PUFFING PETER" TRAIN CAKE

Make a sponge cake mixture, using 12 oz. flour, etc., and bake it in a greased and lined Swiss roll tin (12 by 8 inches) and in a greased ½-lb. cocoa tin (for the engine boiler). Make

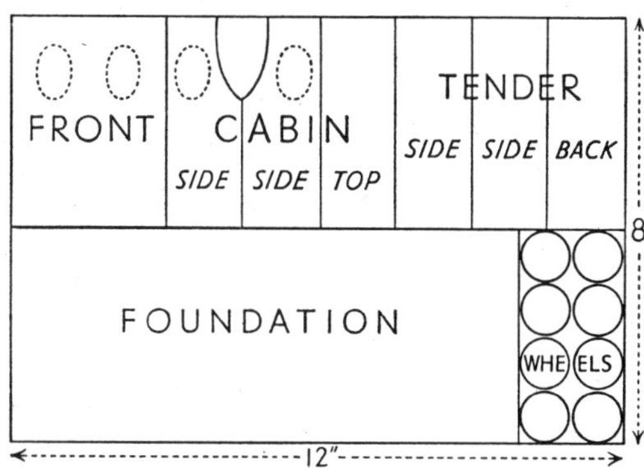

some chocolate glacé icing, using 12 oz. sugar, a little white royal or butter icing and some chocolate butter icing.

Divide the cake as shown in the diagram, and piece the engine together with chocolate butter icing. Trim the foundation close to the boiler and tender, and stick the wheels well into the sides; use the trimmings for the funnel. Put in a cool place for the icing to harden, then coat the engine with chocolate glacé icing and leave to set firmly. Next, using a little white royal or butter icing and a writing pipe, outline the edges of the engine and windows, and write the name on the boiler. Use chocolate icing for the wheel spokes. Fill the tender with sweets or chocolates and make a flag with rice paper. Add a few blobs of icing for the smoke coming out of the funnel.

PARCEL CAKE

Bake a sponge mixture in an oblong tin, and when it is cool, turn it upside down and coat with chocolate icing. When this is set make up a little white icing and write the name and address of the child for whom the cake is intended. Then add a few drops of yellow colouring, and pipe lines to represent string. A drop or two of red colouring may be used to make sealing wax, and some stamps should be stuck on with icing sugar.

BIRTHDAY BOOK

Make a sponge cake mixture, using 6 oz. flour, etc., and bake it in an oblong tin measuring 6 by 8 inches. Allow it to cool, and meanwhile make some vanilla butter icing, using 3 oz. icing sugar. Make also some chocolate glacé icing, using about 6 oz. icing sugar. When the cake is cool, cut it in half and spread it with vanilla butter icing, reserving some for piping. Trim the cake to the shape of a book, and use a little almond paste to make the rounded back. Coat the top surface and rounded back of the book, taking care not to let any icing run down the other edges. When this icing has set, use the remaining butter icing and a star nozzle to pipe lines round the edges representing the leaves of the book. Now, using a writing nozzle, outline the edge of the book, decorate the back and write the title. A piece of rice paper may be cut to represent a book-mark and pushed into the "leaves."

MUSIC CAKE

Make a two- or three-layer sandwich cake, and fill with mock cream or other suitable filling. Coat it with white glacé icing, and when this is set, use a writing nozzle and chocolate glacé icing to pipe on a few bars of appropriate music—e.g., "Happy Birthday to You." Silver balls may be used to represent the notes, if desired.

MUSHROOM CAKE

Sandwich two sponge cakes together with coffee or chocolate butter icing, and when they are cool, cover the bottom and sides with almond paste. Either cover the top of the cake with coffee butter icing, and then mark this with a fork to represent the underside of a mushroom, or else pipe the icing on, using a fluted nozzle. Add a short "stalk" of almond paste, which may first be lightly dipped in cocoa or chopped nuts.

SMALL DECORATED CAKES

PETAL CAKES

Cut 2-inch rounds of Genoese sponge or sandwich cake. Spread the sides of each with butter cream and roll them in desiccated coconut. Brush the top of each cake with warm sieved apricot jam. Make petals from rounds of thinly rolled pink almond paste, and put five petals on each cake. Finish with a mimosa ball in the centre.

CHOCOLATE WALNUT RINGS

Using a chocolate sandwich mixture, make some small ring cakes. Pipe small stars of chocolate butter cream round the top of each, and inside the ring. Put a walnut in the centre.

NURSERY DICE OR DOMINOES

(*See colour picture facing page* 385)

Using a plain writing nozzle, pipe spots of stiff glacé icing on to small cakes which have been coated with chocolate or coloured glacé icing.

TOFFEE CAKES

Cut 2-inch rounds of Genoese sponge or sandwich cake. Dissolve 4 oz. granulated sugar in ¼ pint water, then heat without stirring until it is a rich brown colour. Pour a little in the centre of each cake, and smooth it out to the edges; as the toffee begins to set, mark the top of each cake in four sections with a knife, and decorate with split blanched almonds. Pour any remaining caramel on to a greased plate, and when it is set break it into small pieces. Spread coffee butter cream thinly round the sides of each cake, and roll it in the crushed caramel.

PARTI-COLOURED TARTS

These striking-looking fancy cakes are very easy to make. Line some patty tins with pastry, place a little jam at the bottom, fill with sponge sandwich mixture and bake in the usual way. When the tarts are cold, cover half of each top with chocolate glacé icing, and the other half with white icing. When this is set, pipe a dividing line of butter icing down the centre.

TEATIME DELIGHTS

Cut some Genoese sponge or sandwich cake into fancy shapes, and remove any loose crumbs with a pastry brush; alternatively, brush the cakes over with warmed sieved jam and coat with thin almond paste. Coat with glacé icing, tinted and flavoured to taste. When the icing is nearly dry, decorate the cakes with angelica, silver balls, crystallised rose petals, nuts, marzipan fruits or piped butter cream. Place in paper cases.

MACARONI CAKES

Bake some sandwich cake mixture in wide-based patty tins. Put the cakes upside down, spread butter cream thinly round the sides, and toss them in finely chopped browned almonds. Brush the tops with a little melted apricot jam, then, using a large writing nozzle, pipe them with irregular lengths of butter cream to represent cooked macaroni. Dust lightly with a few more chopped browned almonds.

BUTTERFLY CAKES

Bake a sandwich cake mixture in patty tins and leave to cool. Prepare some butter icing, using the same flavouring as was added to the cake mixture, e.g., coffee, cocoa, vanilla essence, etc.

Cut a round from the top of each cake, and cut this into two "wings." Pile or pipe some butter icing in the centre of the cake, and place the wings in the icing at an angle. Dredge the cakes lightly with icing sugar before serving.

APRICOT AND COFFEE CAKES

From a slab of sandwich or Genoese sponge cake cut rounds 2 inches in diameter. Coat the sides with well-creamed coffee butter icing, and dip them into finely chopped toasted almonds. With a rose nozzle, pipe a circle of icing round the top edge of each cake, and fill the centre with sieved apricot jam; place small pieces of pistachio nut in the butter icing ring. Serve the cakes in paper cases.

ICED BOATS

Bake some sandwich or sponge cake mixture in large boat-shaped tins, and leave to cool. Coat either the whole cakes or just the tops with glacé icing, and leave to set. Make two rice-paper sails for each cake, and place in position with the help of a little glacé or butter icing. If desired, details such as port-holes may be piped on the sides of the cakes.

QUICKLY DECORATED CAKES FOR A CROWD

When catering for large numbers it is easier to bake oblong slabs of cake or flat, round sandwich cakes, which can be easily and quickly decorated then cut up.

For icing a slab of cake measuring 11 by 8 inches (which will cut into 40 pieces), use 1 lb. icing sugar and flavourings, etc., in proportion.

COFFEE DIAGONALS

Coat a slab of sandwich cake with coffee glacé
icing, and when this is nearly set, pipe double
lines of slightly stiffer coffee icing across the 131
cake; in between sprinkle grated chocolate.
Trim the cake with a knife dipped in hot water,
then cut it diagonally into slices.

FEATHERED SLICES

Ice a slab of cake with glacé icing, and while this is still wet, pipe lengthwise lines of fairly stiff chocolate glacé icing about $\frac{1}{2}$ inch apart, using a writing nozzle or a paper forcing bag with a small piece cut away at the tip. Now quickly run a skewer or sharp-pointed knife across the lines and back again, 1 inch apart, producing the "feathered" effect. Leave to dry, trim the edges of the slab and cut into fingers.

ICED SANDWICH FINGERS

Coat one thin sandwich cake with green glacé icing, and another with vanilla butter icing. Pipe lines of slightly darker green icing across the first cake, dividing the top into 12 sections, and finish with pieces of walnut and toasted split almonds. Score the top of the second cake with a fork, and mark the top into 12 sections; decorate with violets, silver balls and angelica.

GALA SQUARES

Make a shallow oblong or square slab cake and brush it with apricot jam. Using a small vegetable nozzle, pipe thick lines of butter icing diagonally across slab, about $1\frac{1}{2}$ inches apart. Fill alternate spaces with apricot jam and green-tinted coconut. Cut the cake into $1\frac{1}{2}$-inch squares, so that each piece has one half covered with jam and the other with coconut.

PETITS FOURS

Cut long strips of cake (plain sponge, sandwich cake, Battenberg, etc.) and cover some with almond paste, scoring it with a knife and crimping edges. Put long rolls or triangular pieces of paste along other cakes, then coat with coloured glacé icing. Piped butter cream may be used on some strips instead of almond paste; leave to stiffen before coating with glacé icing. Finish the cakes with piped butter cream, glacé cherries, etc., repeating the decoration down each strip. Cut into various shapes, using a knife dipped in hot water.

MERINGUES, ÉCLAIRS AND CREAM BUNS

Although these types of cakes have little in common, they are all firm favourites for party occasions, and will repay the extra time and trouble spent in making them.

MERINGUES

These are a confection made from egg white and sugar; they are usually plain (i.e., made from these two ingredients only), but sometimes a flavouring ingredient, such as coffee or chocolate, chopped almonds or pistachio nuts, or grated lemon rind, is included by way of a change. Filled with whipped cream, ice cream, marshmallow, fruit or other filling, meringues make a delicious dinner sweet and are very popular for afternoon tea.

Provided they have been dried completely and are stored in an airtight tin, meringue cases will keep in good condition for several weeks, so it is a good plan to keep a small supply in readiness to make an attractive sweet or cake for the unexpected guests.

Success in making meringues depends very largely on incorporating air into the egg white, so be sure that the eggs are fresh and take care when separating the whites that none of the yolk gets into them (see the Egg chapter); if any yolk is mixed with the whites, or if the eggs are stale, they will not whip successfully.

Before beginning to whip the egg whites, make all necessary preparations of the boards, tins or apparatus for shaping and the oven for baking, so that, once whipped, the mixture does not have to stand, as this is likely to spoil it.

Equipment

Ideally, meringues should be baked on a board made of hard wood, such as birch, though tins can be used with success. Wood, being a bad conductor of heat, keeps the meringues at a much more steady temperature than tin, which is a good conductor of heat. The boards are about 1½ inches thick, and are either smooth, or have meringue-shaped hollows in the surface. When new they must be well oiled with olive oil, and should always be brushed lightly with the oil before use.

If you use a tin, see that the surface is very smooth and absolutely free from grease and dirt. A shallow baking sheet is suitable (use the under side, as this facilitates the removal of the meringues should they be inclined to stick), and to make sure that it is perfectly smooth, rub over with a little soap on a ball of steel wool, rinse and dry thoroughly, then oil very lightly with olive oil. (Do not brush the oil on but spread it very sparingly with the finger-tips; if too much oil is used, it soaks into the meringues, giving them an unpleasant flavour and appearance.) Alternatively, cover the baking sheet with greased greaseproof paper.

To shape oval meringues all that is needed is a jug of cold water, two tablespoons and a knife. Fancy shapes, pyramids, baskets, etc., are made by forcing the mixture through a bag and a plain "meringue pipe." These are made in several sizes, ¼ inch, ½ inch, etc., the measurements referring to the diameter of the tube. Bags may be of fabric or can be made of greaseproof paper. To do this, cut a piece of greaseproof paper about 14 inches square, fold into a triangle, and make into a cornet shape, securing it by turning the top corners over several times. Cut 1–1½ inches off the point and insert the pipe.

Proportions and Mixing

To each egg white allow 2 oz. sugar; the nicest texture is obtained by using caster sugar and granulated sugar in equal quantities.

Put the egg whites into a mixing bowl (it is advisable in very hot weather or in a warm kitchen to chill them slightly), whisk them *very* stiffly (using a hand wire whisk for preference) and continue to whip for a further 4–5 minutes, until they are whisked "dry." It is important that this process be done very thoroughly, for if the eggs are not whipped sufficiently they will not be able to support the sugar.

Add the granulated sugar (1 oz. per egg white) and whisk again briskly until the mixture regains its former stiffness. Then fold in the caster sugar (1 oz. per egg white) very lightly, using a large metal spoon, and agitating the mixture as little as possible, to preserve the lightness. The mixture is now ready for shaping.

To Shape the Meringues

With Spoons : Dip one of the spoons into the jug of cold water, shake off excess drops and fill with the meringue mixture. Using a knife, smooth the mixture along the sides of the spoon until it resembles the shape of a finished meringue case, with a definite ridge along the top. Take the second wet spoon, half lift the mixture out of the first spoon and, carefully preserving its shape and keeping the ridge on the top, allow it to slide out on to the prepared tin or board, using the first spoon just to free it from the second spoon.

With Forcing Bag and Pipe : Fill the prepared bag and pipe, and squeeze out into the tin or board, in pyramids, rounds or ovals.

If a hollowed-out board is used, fill the holes with the mixture and smooth flat along the top with a knife.

Cooking

The heat of the oven is a very important factor; the temperature must be very low (200° F.) and maintained so for several hours, in order to dry the meringues without colouring them. Too hot an oven not only browns the meringues, but causes syrup to ooze out from under them, spoiling the appearance and making them tough in texture.

It is usually convenient to bake meringues after the oven has been heated for some other purpose. In using a solid fuel stove the best plan is to wait until the fire is dying down, put the meringues into the coolest part of the oven, and leave them in until the stove is cold—overnight if convenient. An electric oven usually retains sufficient heat to cook the meringues without actually having the current on, or, at the most, it need only be switched on intermittently, provided that the oven has previously been used and that the whole framework is heated through. With a gas stove it is usually sufficient to have the smallest possible flame; the thermostatic control should be turned to the lowest setting, and then the gas turned as low as it will stay alight. In all cases the meringues should be put near the oven bottom, to avoid browning.

Dredge the meringues lightly with caster sugar, place in the cool oven and leave until they are firm and crisp on top and underneath, and slide easily off the tin. This may take 4–5 hours, and they should remain perfectly white in colour.

MERINGUE À LA CHANTILLY

To 12 meringue cases (6 whole meringues) allow ¼ pint double cream. Sweeten and flavour the cream with a pinch of sugar and a drop of vanilla essence, and whip it. Put the meringue cases together in pairs with the cream between, either spreading it with a knife or forcing it, and place in paper cases.

If the cream is forced, use a star pipe and finish with a row of stars where the meringues join. Sprinkle the cream with chopped pistachio nuts, or crushed violet or rose petals.

MERINGUES WITH CHOCOLATE SAUCE

Chocolate sauce is a great improvement to meringues when they are served as the sweet course for lunch or dinner. Prepare 6 meringues, filled with cream (as for Meringues à la Chantilly). Just before the meal make a sauce with :—

1 tbsp. cornflour	½ pint milk
2 tsps. cocoa	Vanilla essence to flavour
2 tsps. sugar	

Mix the cornflour, cocoa and sugar to a cream with a little of the milk. Heat the rest of the milk and pour on to the cornflour, stirring well. Return all to the saucepan and bring to the boil, stirring continuously. Boil for 2–3 minutes, still stirring. Add vanilla essence, pour into a sauceboat or jug, and serve hot with the meringues.

COFFEE MERINGUES

Coffee essence can be added to the meringue mixture when the caster sugar is folded in (1 small tsp. coffee essence to each egg white); a good effect is also obtained by making meringues as for Meringue à la Chantilly and adding 1 tsp. coffee essence to the ¼ pint of cream for filling them.

CHOCOLATE MERINGUES

To each egg white allow 1 tsp. cocoa. Add the cocoa to the caster sugar, and sieve them together before filling into the mixture. Fill as for Meringue à la Chantilly.

COLOURED MERINGUES

Meringue mixture can be coloured pale pink, green, etc., by adding one or two drops of colouring when the caster sugar is folded in. Cream for filling can also be coloured.

MERINGUES WITH STRAWBERRY ICE CREAM

A very delicious sweet can be made by filling meringue cases with an ice cream mixture, and decorating with cream, etc. In the following recipe a strawberry ice is suggested, but any flavour and garnish may be used.

Have ready 8 pairs of meringue cases. Make 1 pint of strawberry ice cream from fresh or tinned strawberries. Freeze until just firm. Whip 3 tbsps. sweetened cream, and prepare a
132 bag and star pipe. Scoop out the centre of the meringue cases from the bottom and fill with the strawberry ice, putting them together in pairs. Place each in a sundae glass, decorate the join with a line of whole strawberries and stars of the whipped cream, and sprinkle lightly with chopped pistachio nuts.

If preferred, this can be served as a complete dish. Chill a round glass dish and pile the ice cream in it in a mound. Arrange the meringue cases all over the ice and place the whole strawberries in the gaps, finishing with stars of cream and nuts. Genoese sponge may be put under the ice cream.

MERINGUE BASKETS

Small baskets can be piped straight on to the tin and baked in the usual way. For larger baskets the meringues are made about the size of a halfpenny, and when baked, are built up on to a base of Genoese sponge; the meringues are held together with small stars of royal icing, white or coloured. When set, the baskets are filled with an ice cream mixture of fruit and cream, and decorated with piped cream, pieces of fruit, cherries and angelica, etc., and chopped nuts. Angelica can be used to make the handles for the baskets.

ALMOND MERINGUE FINGERS

2 egg whites	$1\frac{1}{4}$ oz. split burnt almonds
$\frac{1}{2}$ tsp. almond essence	
4 oz. caster sugar	Butter cream

Whisk the egg whites stiffly until they are
132 firm, then add the almond essence and whisk for another 3 minutes. Fold in the sugar very carefully. Pipe the mixture on to a baking tin, lined with clean white paper. Sprinkle each finger with the split almonds. Bake in a slow oven (300° F., mark 1) till firm and dry. When cold, sandwich together with butter cream.

MERINGUE TOPPING

Allow up to 2 oz. caster sugar to each egg white. Whisk the egg white until very stiff, then fold in the sugar lightly. Pile on top of the cooked tart or pudding and put in a slow oven (300° F., mark 1) for 20–30 minutes, until the meringue is crisp and very lightly coloured.

This topping is particularly good on fruit tarts, puddings, etc.

ÉCLAIRS AND CREAM BUNS

Éclairs, cream buns and profiteroles are made from choux pastry, which has a characteristic light and airy texture, due in part to the precooking of the paste in the saucepan and also to the thorough beating while incorporating the eggs. Baking is also important. To make cream buns or puffs of the characteristic "choux" (literally, cabbage) shape, and with a hollow centre, the paste must be baked in its own steam, i.e., in a covered container. If an ordinary round shape is desired, the buns may be baked on an open tin as are éclairs. In all cases, careful timing of the cooking and regulation of the oven temperature are necessary.

CHOUX PASTRY

$1\frac{1}{2}$ oz. margarine	$2\frac{1}{2}$ oz. plain flour
$\frac{1}{4}$ pint water	2 eggs

Place the margarine and water in a pan, and bring to the boil. Remove the pan from the heat, fold in the flour, then beat until the paste forms into a ball in the middle of the pan. Leave to cool very slightly, whilst beating the eggs. Add these gradually to the mixture, beating lightly after each addition. Use sufficient egg to give a mixture of piping consistency which will just hold its shape. The paste is now ready for shaping.

ÉCLAIRS

Put the paste into a forcing bag with a plain round pipe of $\frac{1}{2}$-inch diameter, and force in finger lengths ($3\frac{1}{2}$–4 inches long) on to a greased baking sheet, keeping the lengths very even. Bake in a moderately hot oven (400° F., mark 6) for about 35 minutes, until well risen, crisp and of a golden-brown colour. Remove from the tin, slit down the sides with a sharp-pointed knife to allow the steam to escape, and leave on a cake rack to cool. When cold, fill with whipped cream, or flavoured custard, and ice the tops with a little chocolate or coffee glacé icing.

CREAM BUNS

To make cream buns of the characteristic
light, crisp texture, which is obtained by baking
the pastry in its own steam, you require a large,
shallow tin (such as a toffee tin) with a tight-
fitting lid. Make the choux paste in the usual
way, put into a bag with a ½-inch pipe, and force
out in small balls on to the greased tin. Leave
plenty of space between the buns, as they expand
3 very considerably during cooking. Cover with
the lid, and bake undisturbed in a moderately hot
oven (400° F., mark 6) for 45–50 minutes. On no
account open the tin during the cooking, or the
steam will escape and the buns will collapse.

The beginner will find it a help when baking cream buns to place one bun outside the tin as a guide; unless this is cooked, those inside cannot be done. When the test bun is cooked, allow those in the tin a good five minutes longer.

When it is estimated that the buns are ready, shake the tin gently—if cooked the buns will rattle. Then remove them carefully from the tin, slit to allow the steam to escape and leave on a rack to cool. When quite cold, fill with whipped cream, sweetened and flavoured, or with confectioner's custard, and dredge with icing sugar. For a sweet, they may be served with chocolate sauce.

If you have no tin suitable for the purpose, use a flat baking sheet and invert a roasting tin over it, sealing down the edges with a thick paste of flour and water, so that the steam is kept in during cooking.

CREAM PUFFS

Fill the choux paste into a bag with a ½-inch plain pipe, and force in balls on to a baking sheet. Bake in a moderately hot oven (400° F., mark 6) until well risen and golden—30–35 minutes. Split and cool on a rack. When cold, fill with whipped cream and dredge with icing sugar.

PROFITEROLES

With a ¼-inch plain pipe, force the paste in very small balls on to a baking sheet. Bake in a moderately hot oven (400° F., mark 6) until well risen, crisp and golden—20–25 minutes. Split and cool on a rack. When cold, fill with cream and ice the tops with glacé icing, or glaze with sieved warmed apricot jam, and sprinkle with chopped pistachio nuts. Alternatively, fill with ice cream and serve with hot chocolate sauce.

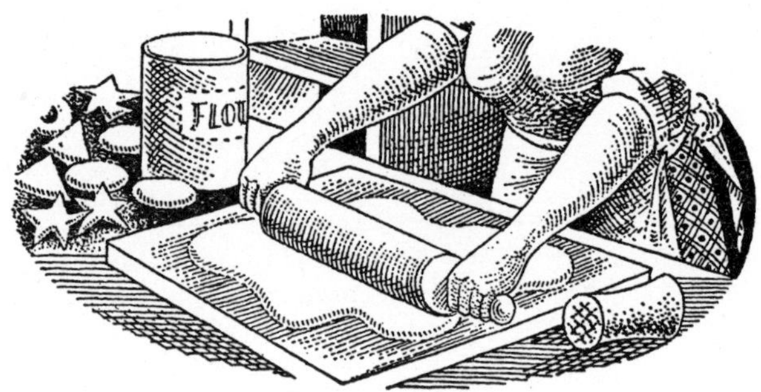

BISCUITS

Home-made biscuits are always popular, and a well-filled biscuit tin is a good standby for elevenses and other snacks, and for when you have unexpected guests to tea.

EQUIPMENT

1. An even surface for rolling out the dough. Use your pastry board if it is large enough and quite smooth, or the top of an enamelled table.
2. Sharp biscuit cutters.
3. A broad-bladed palette knife or spatula to lift the biscuits on and off the baking sheets.
4. Baking sheets. These should fit conveniently into the oven, leaving a space of 2 or 3 inches all round so that the air can circulate. If too little space is allowed the hot air collects under the sheet and the biscuits brown on the bottom. Have at least two sheets, so that you can fill one while the other is in the oven.
5. A large cork, the same size as your biscuit cutter, with criss-cross runnels cut across it will give a professional touch to biscuits. Dip the cork in castor sugar and press on to the stamped-out biscuits, after they have been put on the baking sheet. The pressure makes the biscuits thinner, and the pattern shows after baking.

BISCUIT MAKING HINTS

Roll biscuit dough thinly and very evenly, so
134 that the biscuits are the same thickness through-
out, otherwise they will not brown evenly when baking. Even pricking with a fork or pressing with a cork will keep the biscuits flat. Get as many biscuits as you can out of the first rolling, as the re-rolled scraps are never quite as "short."

Some biscuit mixtures can be forced into fancy shapes by means of a piece of apparatus specially designed for the purpose, and known usually as a "cookie press." It consists of a hand syringe through which the mixture is pressed on to the baking sheet, different nozzles being used for different shapes. It is only suitable for fairly soft, rich mixtures.

When baking biscuits, use a moderately hot oven. Rich mixtures require a lower temperature.

Place the baking sheets on the top shelves of the oven, directly below the browning sheet, if there is one. Keep a watchful eye on them during baking, removing any biscuits from the sheet as soon as they are evenly coloured. To cool the biscuits, lay them flat on a wire rack.

Pack away the biscuits in a tightly covered tin as soon as they are cold. Never leave them out, as they quickly absorb moisture from the air and become soft, and never put them in a tin with cakes. To crisp soft biscuits, place in a moderately hot oven for several minutes, then cool on a rack.

SWEET BISCUITS (FOUNDATION RECIPE)

4 oz. butter
4 oz. sugar
1 egg
8 oz. flour
2 tsps. baking powder
A few drops of vanilla essence
Milk
Caster sugar to dredge

Cream the fat and sugar together, until soft and light in colour and texture. Add the beaten egg a little at a time, and beat well. Stir in the flour and baking powder, and add the vanilla essence, together with a little milk, if necessary, to make a firm dough. Roll out $\frac{1}{8}$ inch thick, stamp out with a fancy cutter and place on a greased tin. Bake in a moderately hot oven (400° F., mark 6) for about 10–15 minutes, or until evenly browned. Dredge with caster sugar and cool on a rack.

Spice Biscuits : Add 1 tsp. mixed spice and 1 tsp. ground cinnamon to the flour.

Fruit Biscuits : Add to the creamed mixture 2 oz. dried fruit (currants, raisins, peel, etc.), chopped, if necessary.

Lemon Biscuits : Add the grated rind of 1 lemon to the mixture, and omit the vanilla.

CHERRY RINGS

Add $1\frac{1}{2}$ oz. chopped glacé cherries to above mixture, and keep $\frac{1}{2}$ oz. for decoration. Roll out dough as above, then, using a round fluted cutter, cut it into rounds and remove centres with a small cutter. Bake as above.

CHOCOLATE CREAM SANDWICHES

Follow Sweet Biscuit recipe, but substitute 1 oz. cocoa for 1 oz. of the flour. Roll dough out, prick, cut into fingers about $1\frac{1}{2}$ by 3 inches, and put on a greased baking tray. Bake as above for 10–12 minutes. When the biscuits are cool, sandwich together with vanilla butter cream.

CHOCOLATE CRESCENTS

Cut out crescents of the Sweet Biscuit dough and bake as above. When the biscuits are cool, ice them with coffee glacé icing and sprinkle with finely grated chocolate.

SILVER STARS

Roll out some Sweet Biscuit dough, cut it with a star-shaped cutter, place on a baking tray and decorate with silver balls at the points of each star, or with a ring in centre. Bake as above.

SULTANA PINWHEELS

Cut some Sweet Biscuit dough into 2-inch diamonds. Fold over one point of each diamond, then put three diamonds together, pinwheel fashion, damping the joins to make them hold, and press a few sultanas into the centre. Bake as above. Cool on a rack.

SUGAR PRESS COOKIES

8 oz. self-raising flour
A pinch of salt
1 tsp. ground cinnamon
4 oz. margarine
4 oz. caster sugar
Vanilla essence
1 egg
Milk to mix
Glacé cherries and angelica, or royal icing to decorate

Sieve the dry ingredients. Cream the fat, add
the sugar gradually, cream well and add a few 136
drops of essence. Beat in the egg, then add the dry ingredients and stir till the mixture binds together, adding a little milk if required. Put the mixture into a cookie press and force on to a greased baking sheet. Bake in a moderately hot oven (425° F., mark 7) for 7–10 minutes. Decorate with glacé cherries and angelica before baking, or decorate after baking with royal icing.

ALMOND FINGERS

$\frac{1}{2}$ lb. flour
2 tsps. baking powder
4 oz. butter
2 oz. caster sugar
1 egg yolk

For the Icing

$\frac{1}{4}$ lb. Valencia almonds
1 egg white
$\frac{1}{4}$ lb. icing sugar

Sieve the flour and baking powder and rub in the butter with the tips of the fingers. Add the sugar and knead into a stiff paste with the egg yolk. Continue to knead well until all the paste will form into one piece, then roll or press out into a rectangle about 10 by 6 inches. Place this on a flat tin, previously covered with greased paper.

Blanch and chop the almonds; whip the egg white until it is frothy, but not stiff, and add the sieved icing sugar to it. Spread this mixture all over the pastry rectangle and sprinkle it with the chopped almonds. Bake in a moderate oven (350° F., mark 4) until it is a light golden-brown. Remove from the oven, cut into fingers with a sharp knife and leave these on a wire tray to cool.

ARROWROOT BISCUITS (MILK BISCUITS)

4 oz. arrowroot
2 oz. flour
1 oz. margarine
$\frac{1}{2}$–1 tbsp. sugar
Vanilla essence
Milk

Mix the arrowroot and flour and rub in the margarine with the tips of the fingers. Add the sugar and a drop of vanilla essence and mix to a stiff paste with a little milk. Knead lightly, and roll out very thinly on to a floured board. Prick and cut in rounds with a fluted $2\frac{1}{2}$-inch cutter. Place on a greased tin, and bake in a moderately hot oven (425° F., mark 7) for 10–15 minutes, until crisp and very lightly coloured.

BOURBON BISCUITS

6 oz. flour	A little water
2 tbsps. cocoa	A few drops of vanilla essence
4 oz. margarine	
4 oz. caster sugar	Melted chocolate for filling
1 egg yolk	

Sieve together the flour and cocoa and rub in the fat very thoroughly, until the mixture resembles fine breadcrumbs. Stir in the caster sugar and mix well. Mix to a firm dough with the egg, water and essence. Roll the dough out thinly on a floured board and mark in oblongs about 3 by ¾ inch, using a pastry wheel if available. Place on a greased baking tin and cook in a moderately hot oven (425° F., mark 7) for 10–15 minutes. When cold, sandwich together, and if desired, dust with sugar.

BRANDY SNAPS

(*See colour picture facing page* 384)

3 oz. syrup	1 tsp. ground ginger or grated lemon rind
2 oz. sugar	
3 oz. butter	1 tsp. brandy (optional)
2 oz. flour	

Melt the syrup, sugar and butter and allow to cool slightly, then add the flour and ground ginger or grated lemon rind, mixing well. Stir in the brandy and put in small teaspoonfuls, 3–4 inches apart, on a well-greased tin. Bake in a moderate oven (375° F., mark 5) until well spread and just golden-brown. Allow to cool for a moment, then lift off with a palette knife and quickly roll over the greased handle of a wooden spoon. Slip off carefully. If the biscuits cool too much, and are too brittle to roll, return them to the oven for a moment to soften.

CHOCOLATE BISCUITS

6 oz. self-raising flour	4 oz. caster sugar
2 tbsps. cocoa	A little water
4 oz. butter	Vanilla essence

Sieve together the flour and cocoa and rub in the fat very thoroughly, until the mixture resembles fine breadcrumbs. Add the caster sugar and mix well. Mix to a very firm dough with a tbsp. or so of cold water to which 1 or 2 drops of vanilla essence have been added. Turn on to a floured board, roll out ¼ inch thick and stamp into rounds or fancy shapes. Put on a greased baking sheet and cook in a moderately hot oven (425° F., mark 7) about 10–15 minutes. To finish, dust with caster sugar.

As an alternative, make the biscuits thinner, then sandwich together with chocolate butter and ice with chocolate (or white) glacé icing.

CHOCOLATE CORN ROUGHS

Crisp up 1 oz. cornflakes in a slow oven (300° F., mark 1), then allow them to cool. Break up ¼ lb. block chocolate into a basin, and stand it over a saucepan containing hot water, but do not allow it to get too hot. When just melted and soft, stir in the cornflakes lightly, in order not to break them. Place in heaps, using two forks, on waxed greaseproof paper and leave until they are quite set.

CHOCOLATE REFRIGERATOR COOKIES

5 oz. margarine	1 tsp. baking powder
6 oz. caster sugar	½ tsp. salt
1 egg	1½ oz. cocoa
1 tsp. vanilla essence	1 oz. melted chocolate
12 oz. flour	Milk to mix, if required

Place the margarine in a bowl and soften it by beating. Add the sugar, and continue beating until light and fluffy. Beat in the egg, adding a little at a time, and then the essence. Sieve the dry ingredients and add with the melted chocolate. Stir the mixture until it binds together—it may be necessary to add a little milk. Turn the dough on to a board, form into an oblong, wrap in synthetic skin or waxed paper, put in the refrigerator or on a cold slab in the larder, and leave overnight. The next day, slice thinly and bake on a greased tray in a moderately hot oven (425° F., mark 7) for 5–7 minutes.

DATE REFRIGERATOR COOKIES

5 oz. margarine	8 oz. flour
4 oz. brown sugar	A pinch of salt
1 egg	1 tsp. bicarbonate of soda
1 tsp. vanilla essence	
5 oz. chopped nuts	

Cream the fat and sugar till the mixture is soft and creamy, then beat in the egg slowly, with the essence. Stir in the dates and the sieved dry ingredients. Mix till the dough binds together, then put it on a lightly floured board and form it into an oblong. Wrap and chill as directed above; the next day, slice thinly and bake as above.

WALNUT REFRIGERATOR COOKIES

4½ oz. flour	3½ oz. brown sugar
1 tsp. baking powder	½ an egg
A pinch of salt	1 tsp. vanilla essence
1 oz. margarine	2–3 oz. chopped walnuts
1 oz. lard	

Sieve the flour, baking powder and salt together. Cream the fats and sugar until fluffy and add the egg and essence, mixing well, then stir in the dry ingredients and nuts. Shape into a roll, wrap and chill. The next day, slice thinly and bake in a moderately hot oven (400° F., mark 6) for 10–12 minutes.

CHOCOLATE RIBBONS

4 oz. margarine	A pinch of salt
4 oz. caster sugar	2 tbsps. cocoa
1 egg	A few drops of vanilla essence
$7\frac{1}{2}$ oz. self-raising flour	A little milk to mix

Cream the fat and sugar till light and fluffy. Whisk the egg lightly, then beat slowly into the mixture. Sieve the dry ingredients and stir in lightly, adding the essence and a little milk if necessary to give a piping consistency. Using the smallest éclair nozzle, force the biscuits on a baking tin, piping four lines, $3\frac{1}{2}$ inches long and touching each other. Bake in a moderately hot oven (400° F., mark 6) for 10–15 minutes.

CHOCOLATE WALNUTS

5 oz. flour	Apricot jam
$1\frac{1}{2}$ oz. sugar	Almond paste
$2\frac{1}{2}$ oz. butter	Chocolate glacé icing
A little beaten egg	Walnuts
1–2 tsps. water	

Sieve the flour and sugar and rub in the butter until it is very finely divided. Add the egg and a very little water and mix to a smooth paste. Roll out until it is $\frac{1}{4}$ inch thick, then cut out rounds with a small fluted cutter. Place on a tin lined with paper, and bake in a moderate oven (375° F., mark 5) for 15–20 minutes. When cool, spread a little jam on each. Cut rounds of almond paste the same size as the biscuits and press these on the biscuits. Coat with chocolate icing and place a walnut on top of each.

CINNAMON BARS

4 oz. fat	1 tbsp. ground cinnamon
3 oz. sugar	A pinch of salt
$\frac{1}{2}$ an egg	Chopped nuts
5 oz. plain flour	

Cream the fat and sugar together until white and soft, and beat in the egg, reserving a little of the white for glazing the biscuits. Sieve the dry ingredients together and gradually add to the creamed mixture. Press the dough into an oblong tin (about 8 by 6 inches), brush the surface with egg white and sprinkle with chopped nuts. Bake in a slow oven (325° F., mark 2) for 1 hour, then slice and allow to cool in the tin. When the biscuits are cold, place on a wire tray.

CINNAMON SLICES

6 oz. ground almonds	$\frac{1}{2}$ tsp. cinnamon
6 oz. icing sugar	Egg white

For the Icing

2 oz. icing sugar	Egg white
2 tsps. flour	

Sieve the dry ingredients into a basin, and make into a fairly stiff paste with egg white. Knead with the hand until smooth, then roll out on a slightly floured board into a long narrow strip, about $\frac{1}{8}$ inch in thickness. Prepare the icing by mixing the sugar and flour together and moistening with egg white. Spread this smoothly over the paste with a wetted palette knife, and then cut into fingers. Place these on a greased and floured tin, and bake in a moderate oven (375° F., mark 5) until a light brown colour and firm and crisp to the touch—about 20 minutes.

CLOVER LEAF COOKIES

2 oz. margarine	A few carraway seeds
2 oz. caster sugar	$\frac{1}{2}$ tsp. ground ginger
$\frac{1}{2}$ an egg	1 tsp. grated lemon rind
4 oz. plain flour	

Cream the margarine and sugar together and beat in the egg. Gradually add the sieved flour and knead well. Divide into three portions, and work a different flavouring into each. Divide the three mixtures into small even-sized pieces and roll these into balls. Group one ball of each flavour together, placing them on a greased baking tray, and press flat with a palette knife, forming the clover leaf shape. Bake in a moderately hot oven (400° F., mark 6) for 10–15 minutes. Cool on a wire tray.

COCONUT CREAMS

$\frac{1}{2}$ a small tin of condensed milk	1 tsp. lemon juice
	4 oz. desiccated coconut

Stir the ingredients together, then drop mixture in teaspoonfuls on to rice paper or on to an oiled baking tray, placing them about 1 inch apart. Bake in a moderately hot oven (400° F., mark 6) for 10–12 minutes, until firm and lightly browned.

COCONUT MACAROONS

4 oz. lump or granulated sugar	1 egg white
	4 oz. desiccated coconut
Cream of tartar	Rice paper

Dissolve the sugar in 2 tbsps. water and boil to 225° F., then add a pinch of cream of tartar, dissolved in 1 tsp. water. Whip the egg white with a pinch of cream of tartar till stiff. Heat the sugar and water to 250° F., then gradually pour into the egg white, beating well. Add the coconut and mix well. Place in heaps on a baking tray lined with rice paper, and bake in moderate oven (350° F., mark 3) until light golden-brown and crisp.

COFFEE KISSES

2 egg whites
4 oz. caster sugar
4 oz. ground almonds
Coffee glacé icing

For the Filling

2 oz. butter
3 oz. icing sugar
Coffee essence

Beat the egg whites stiffly, then very lightly fold in the caster sugar and the ground almonds. Put in teaspoonfuls on a flat greased tin. Bake in a moderate oven (375° F., mark 5) until biscuits are pale brown in colour, about 10–15 minutes. Lift gently from the tins and place on a sieve, round side up, to cool. When cold, ice half the biscuits, spread the remainder with the filling made as for coffee butter icing, then sandwich the biscuits together. Alternatively, sandwich the biscuits together with coffee butter icing, and toss in icing sugar. Serve in little paper cases.

CRACKER BISCUITS

$\frac{1}{2}$ lb. self-raising flour
1 tsp. salt
1–2 oz. butter
Cold water

Sieve together the flour and salt and rub in the fat very thoroughly, then mix to a pliable paste with cold water. Turn on to a floured board, knead lightly for a few minutes, then roll out very thinly into an oblong. Mark lightly into
138 three. Fold up the bottom third, bring down the top third over it, seal the edges and give the pastry a half turn. Repeat this rolling and folding twice. Finally, roll out the pastry very thinly and evenly. Trim off the edges with a sharp knife and cut into 3-inch squares. Put on to greased baking sheets, prick well, and bake in a moderate oven (375° F., mark 5) for about 20 minutes, until golden-brown on top and underneath.

CHEESE CRACKER BISCUITS

Follow recipe as for plain Cracker Biscuits, but include 3 oz. grated cheese, sprinkling 1 oz. of the cheese over the dough before folding it each time.

CUSTARD CREAM BISCUITS

4 oz. butter
4 oz. sugar
1 egg yolk
4 oz. self-raising flour
4 oz. custard powder
Milk to mix
Butter cream filling

Cream the fat and sugar very thoroughly, beat in the egg yolk, then mix in the flour and custard powder with sufficient milk to make a fairly stiff dough. Turn out on to a floured board, knead lightly, and roll thinly. Cut into fingers or rounds and place on greased tins. Prick them and bake in a moderately hot oven (425° F., mark 7) till golden-brown—about 15 minutes. Sandwich together with butter cream filling.

"DIGESTIVE" BISCUITS

6 oz. flour
1 tsp. salt
$1\frac{1}{2}$ oz. coarse oatmeal
$\frac{1}{2}$–1 oz. sugar
2 tsps. baking powder
3 oz. lard or cooking fat
Milk to mix

Mix the dry ingredients together and rub in the fat very thoroughly with the tips of the fingers. Mix in enough milk to give a firm dough. Turn on to a floured board, knead lightly and roll out rather thinly, then cut in rounds. Place on a greased baking sheet, prick, and bake in a moderately hot oven (425° F., mark 7) until lightly coloured—about 15 minutes.

EASTER BISCUITS

12 oz. flour
A pinch of salt
6 oz. butter
5 oz. caster sugar
1 egg
3 oz. currants
1 oz. peel
A pinch of saffron steeped overnight in 1 tbsp. milk or brandy
Egg white
A little caster sugar

Sieve the flour and salt. Cream the butter and sugar. Add the beaten egg to the creamed mixture with a little of the sieved flour. Stir in remaining flour, currants and finely chopped peel, and mix in the saffron-flavoured milk or brandy. The dough should be softer than pastry but stiff enough to roll out. Roll out $\frac{1}{8}$ inch thick and cut into large rounds. Place on a greased baking sheet and bake in a moderately hot oven (400° F., mark 6) for about 20 minutes, until lightly coloured. After 10 minutes' baking, brush with beaten egg white and dredge with caster sugar.

FAIRY WAFERS

1 egg white
1 oz. fine sugar
1 oz. flour

Beat the egg white very stiffly; fold in the sugar and the sifted flour alternately. Put teaspoonfuls of the mixture well apart on a greased baking sheet, and spread out very thinly into rounds. Bake in a hot oven (450° F., mark 8) until the biscuits colour lightly, about 5–7

minutes. Remove from the tin, curl round a rolling pin, and cool on a sieve.

These biscuits are excellent to serve as an accompaniment to ice cream, fruit fools and other cold sweets.

NUT FAIRY WAFERS

Make as above, but sprinkle with 1 oz. chopped nuts before baking.

FLAKE-MEAL MACAROONS

3 oz. lard or margarine	3 oz. rolled oats
1½ oz. sugar	3 oz. flour
2 tbsps. syrup	A good pinch of salt
Almond essence	¼ tsp. baking powder

Cream the fat and sugar together until light, then work in the syrup and a few drops of the almond essence. Mix together the rolled oats, flour, salt and baking powder and work them by degrees into the creamed mixture. Divide into pieces about the size of a walnut. Roll each into a ball and place on a greased baking sheet, flattening them into rounds. Bake in a moderately hot oven (400° F., mark 6) until golden-brown—about 15 minutes.

FLAPJACKS

2 oz. sugar	2 tsps. water
2 oz. butter or margarine	5 oz. rolled oats

Warm together the sugar, fat and water until dissolved. Cool slightly, then stir in the oats. Pack into two greased 6-inch sandwich tins and bake in a moderate oven (350° F., mark 4) until golden-brown—½–¾ hour. Cut into triangles while still in the tin. Leave the flapjacks in the tin a short while before turning out.

GINGER FLAPJACKS

Make as above, adding ½ tsp. ground ginger to the mixture together with the oats.

SYRUP FLAPJACKS

¼ lb. butter	½ lb. rolled oats
1 oz. sugar	¼ tsp. salt
4 tbsps. syrup	

Beat the butter and sugar together until of a creamy consistency, stir in the warmed syrup and work in the oats and salt until well blended. Put the mixture into a small greased Yorkshire pudding tin, pressing it into position. Bake in a moderately hot oven (400° F., mark 6) for ½–¾ hour, until golden-brown. Cut into strips and leave in the tin until cold. If removed whilst hot, the flapjacks are liable to crumble.

O

ature Kebabs

ury Snack Rolls

GARIBALDI BISCUITS

2 oz. currants or other dried fruit	1 oz. butter
	1 oz. sugar
4 oz. self-raising flour	Milk to mix
A pinch of salt	

Chop the dried fruit—currants, raisins, sultanas, or a mixture. Put the flour and salt into a bowl and rub in the butter lightly with the finger-tips, until no lumps remain. Then stir in the sugar. Add enough milk (1–2 tbsps.) to make a stiff dough. Turn the dough on to a floured board. Pat lightly into shape and roll until ⅛ inch in thickness. Roll very evenly, keeping the dough regular in shape, then cut in half. Sprinkle one half evenly with the chopped fruit. Cover with the other piece of dough. Lightly flour the board and roll the mixture again until ⅛ inch thick, keeping it as a square as possible. Trim the edges, then mark into squares or fingers. Place on a greased tin and bake in a moderately hot oven (400° F., mark 6) until golden—about 15 minutes. Lift on to a rack to cool, then separate the biscuits.

GINGER BISCUITS

4 oz. butter or lard	3 tsps. ground ginger
4–5 tbsps. golden syrup	1 tsp. bicarbonate of soda
4 oz. sugar	
10 oz. flour	

Warm the butter, syrup and sugar slightly, and beat to a cream. Add the flour, ginger and bicarbonate of soda, and mix to a stiff dough. Roll out very thinly and cut into rounds. Place on a greased tin, and bake in a moderate oven (375° F., mark 5) for 15–20 minutes. Allow the biscuits to cool before lifting off the tin.

GINGER CRISPIES

3 oz. butter	4 oz. flour
3 oz. caster sugar	2 tsps. ground ginger
1 egg yolk	Milk, if needed
1 oz. chopped crystallised ginger	½ cup cornflakes

Cream the butter and sugar together, then beat in the egg yolk and the chopped ginger. Lightly stir in the flour and ground ginger, sieved together, adding a spoonful of milk if necessary, but keeping the consistency stiff. Form into small balls and roll in the cornflakes, pressing them into the mixture. Place on greased baking sheets, allowing room for spreading. Bake in a moderately hot oven (400° F., mark 6) until the biscuits are lightly browned—about 20 minutes.

GINGER NUTS

6 oz. flour
A pinch of salt
1 tbsp. ground ginger
1 tsp. mixed spice
1 tsp. cinnamon
2 oz. butter
4 oz. brown sugar
Syrup to mix (approx. 1 tbsp.)

Sieve the flour, salt and spices together. Cream the butter and sugar, and stir in the dry ingredients alternately with the syrup (which may be warmed very slightly in order to make the mixing easier) to make a fairly stiff paste. Roll into balls about the size of a walnut, place on a greased baking tin, and flatten slightly. Bake in a moderate oven (375° F., mark 5) until browned and crisp—about 20 minutes.

GINGER PARKINS

2 oz. lard or cooking fat
4 oz. flour
4 oz. medium oatmeal
2 oz. sugar
137 1 tsp. ground ginger
1 tsp. cinnamon
2 tsps. bicarbonate of soda
1 egg
2 oz. syrup

Rub the fat into the flour thoroughly, then add the rest of the dry ingredients. Beat up the egg, and add it, together with the syrup, kneading with the hand. Form into small balls and place well apart on a greased baking sheet. Bake in a moderate oven (375° F., mark 5) for 20–30 minutes.

GOLF BISCUITS

½ lb. fine oatmeal
½ lb. wholemeal flour
4–6 oz. dripping or butter
¼ lb. brown sugar
A pinch of salt
1 tsp. cinnamon
2 tsps. cream of tartar
½ tsp. bicarbonate of soda
1–2 eggs
A little milk

Put both kinds of meal into a basin and rub in the fat lightly, until free from lumps. Add the other dry ingredients and mix thoroughly. Then form into a paste with the beaten egg and a little milk. Knead until smooth and roll out fairly thinly. Cut into rounds, place them on a greased tin and prick the biscuits with a fork. Bake in a moderately hot oven (400° F., mark 6) for 15–20 minutes, or until crisp and brown.

GRANTHAMS

½ lb. butter or margarine
½ lb. caster sugar
1 small egg
½ lb. flour
1 tsp. bicarbonate of soda
2 oz. coconut
Either 2 tbsps. cocoa or 1 tbsp. ground ginger

Cream the butter and sugar together and beat in the egg. Add the sieved flour and bicarbonate of soda, then add the coconut and other flavouring. Knead well and roll the mixture into balls. Put on to a greased baking sheet, and bake in a slow oven (300° F., mark 1) for about ¾ hour.

HONEY GINGER NUTS

6 oz. flour
1 tsp. ground ginger
2 oz. margarine
2–3 tbsps. honey

Mix the flour and ginger and rub in the fat very thoroughly. Add enough honey to make a stiff dough. Roll into little balls about the size of a walnut, place on a greased baking sheet and flatten slightly with the hand. Bake in a moderate oven (375° F., mark 5) for about 15 minutes.

JAMMY FACES

3 oz. margarine
2 oz. sugar
1 egg
A few drops of vanilla essence
6 oz. flour
1 tsp. baking powder
A pinch of salt
Milk or water to bind
Jam for filling

Cream together the fat and sugar until soft and creamy. Gradually beat in the egg and the vanilla essence. Sieve in the flour, baking powder and salt, and sufficient milk or water to make a stiff dough. Roll out to ⅛ inch thick, and stamp out into rounds with a 2-inch cutter. Then place half the biscuits on a greased baking sheet ready for the oven; from the other half stamp out, with a very small cutter, two rounds to represent eyes and a slit for the mouth. Place on a greased baking tray, and bake in a moderately hot oven (400° F., mark 6) about 20 minutes, until evenly brown. Cool, then spread the plain biscuits with jam and cover with the "faces."

JIFFY COOKIES

2 heaped tbsps. peanut butter
½ large tin sweetened condensed milk
2 oz. cornflakes
1–2 oz. cleaned raisins or sultanas

Cream the peanut butter and the condensed milk well together. Stir in the cornflakes and dried fruit. Place the mixture in small spoonfuls on a well-greased tin fairly well apart. Bake in a moderate oven (350° F., mark 4) for 15–20 minutes, until golden-brown and firm. Remove from the tin at once and cool on a rack.

JUMBLES

5 oz. butter
5 oz. sugar
1 egg
10 oz. self-raising flour
2 tsps. grated lemon rind
2 oz. ground almonds

Cream the butter and sugar together, add the beaten egg gradually, then stir in the flour, lemon rind and almonds. Form, a portion at a time, into a roll ½–¾ inch in diameter, cut off lengths, and form into " S " shapes. Place on a greased baking sheet, and bake in a moderately hot oven (400° F., mark 6) about 10 minutes.

LEMON WAFERS

8 oz. flour	3 oz. granulated sugar
3 tsps. baking powder	2 tsps. grated lemon rind
1 tsp. ground ginger	2 tbsps. lemon juice
A pinch of salt	3 tbsps. golden syrup
4 oz. margarine	

Sieve the dry ingredients together, rub in the fat and add the sugar. Stir in the lemon rind and juice with the syrup and mix well. Turn the dough on to a floured board and knead before rolling out very thinly. Cut in rounds with a 2-inch fancy cutter, and place on a greased baking tray. Bake in a moderately hot oven (425° F., mark 7) for 10–12 minutes.

LUNCHEON CELERY BISCUITS

2 oz. margarine	3–4 tsps. celery seeds
8 oz. flour	Cream or " top-of-milk " to mix
A pinch of salt	

Rub the fat into the sieved flour and salt. Add the celery seeds, and mix to a stiff, pliable dough with cream or milk. Knead the mixture, and beat it with a rolling pin, then roll out very thinly and cut into 2½-inch rounds; bake on a greased tray in a hot oven (450° F., mark 8) for 10–15 minutes.

MACAROONS

(*See colour picture facing page* 384)

2 egg whites	1 oz. ground rice (good measure)
4 oz. ground almonds	
8 oz. caster sugar	1 tsp. orange flower water

To Decorate

Split almonds	A little egg white

Whisk the egg whites fairly stiffly. Stir in the almonds, sugar, ground rice and flavouring, and mix thoroughly. Cover a greased baking sheet with rice paper and place the mixture in small heaps on the rice paper, or pipe, using a calico forcing bag and large plain pipe, leaving room for spreading. Place a split almond on each biscuit, brush with egg white and bake in a moderate oven (350° F., mark 3) for about 20–25 minutes, until pale golden-brown. It is important to cook macaroons slowly, to allow them to colour evenly and to get a good texture.

CHOCOLATE MACAROONS

3 small egg whites	1 oz. finely grated chocolate
5 oz. ground almonds	
5 oz. caster sugar	A few blanched almonds or glacé cherries
¾ oz. ground rice	
½ tsp. vanilla essence	

Whip the whites to a light froth. Mix the dry ingredients and add the egg whites and essence, reserving a little if necessary, to avoid making the mixture too moist. Mix thoroughly and shape into small balls of even size, then place on a tin covered with rice paper, and put half a blanched almond or glacé cherry on each. Bake in a moderate oven (350° F., mark 3) for 25 minutes, until firm and cooked through. Large macaroons will take longer to cook and must be baked in a slow oven.

MARSHMALLOW CREAMS

6 oz. flour	Milk to mix
A pinch of salt	1 tbsp. golden syrup
3 oz. margarine	Colouring and flavouring
3 oz. caster sugar	Jam
1 egg (separated)	Nuts or glacé cherries

Sieve the flour and salt, and cream the fat and sugar until light and fluffy. Beat in the egg yolk, and add the dry ingredients and stir in enough milk to give a soft dough. Turn out on to a floured board, roll out and cut into 1½-inch rounds with a scone cutter. Place on a greased baking tray, prick, and bake in a moderate oven (375° F., mark 5) for 10–15 minutes. Allow to cool, and meanwhile make a mock marshmallow cream: Whisk up the egg white and syrup over hot water until thick, fluffy and quite stiff; colour and flavour if desired (e.g., with ¼–½ tsp. coffee essence). Sandwich the biscuits together with jam and coat the tops with the marshmallow, roughing it up if desired. Decorate, using, for example, halved walnuts on biscuits topped with coffee-flavoured marshmallow.

MERINGUE TOPS

2 oz. margarine	3 oz. flour
4 oz. caster sugar	1 oz. chocolate powder
A few drops of vanilla essence	A pinch of salt
	Butter cream or apricot jam
1 egg (separated)	

Cream the fat and 2 oz. of the sugar with the essence until quite soft. Whisk the egg yolk and lightly beat it into the creamed mixture. Sieve the flour, chocolate powder and salt, add, and stir till the mixture binds together; knead on a lightly floured board and roll out to ¼ inch thick. Cut with a small fancy cutter, put on a greased baking tray and bake in a moderately hot oven (400° F., mark 6) for 5–7 minutes. Whisk the egg white and 1 oz. sugar until very stiff, then fold in the remaining sugar. Put the meringue mixture into a forcing bag fitted with a star pipe, and pipe in rosettes on to an oiled baking tray. Bake in a slow oven (300° F., mark 1) for 40–60 minutes, or until firm but not coloured. When biscuits and meringues are cold, join a meringue to each biscuit with butter cream or jam.

NEGRESS BISCUITS

3 oz. chocolate	1 egg yolk
2 tbsps. milk	½ tsp. vanilla essence
4 oz. butter	Butter icing
8 oz. flour	Glacé or fondant icing
2 oz. sugar	

Boil the chocolate in the milk for 2 minutes. Rub the fat into the flour and add the sugar. Add the egg yolk and the vanilla essence to the slightly cooled chocolate, beat well together and add to the flour, etc. Knead well until the paste becomes smooth. Allow to cool, turn on to a floured board and roll out fairly thinly. Cut into rounds with a floured cutter, and bake in a moderate oven (350° F., mark 4) for about 20 minutes. When cold, sandwich the biscuits together with butter icing and pour a little glacé or fondant icing on the top.

NEVA BISCUITS

¼ lb. caster sugar	½ lb. flour
A pinch of cream of tartar	Flavouring
2 eggs	Carmine

Sieve the sugar and cream of tartar into a basin and add the eggs. Stand the basin over a saucepan of hot water, and beat the mixture with a small wire whisk until light and frothy. Then remove it to the table and sift in the flour very lightly. Add flavouring to taste, and colour pink with carmine. Have ready some fancy-shaped moulds, greased and dusted out with flour and sugar mixed. Half-fill these with the mixture, and bake in a moderate oven (375° F., mark 5) until well risen and firm to the touch.

When cool, these biscuits may be finished off in many different ways: they may be coated lightly with jam and sprinkled with coconut or other chopped nuts, or coated with any simple icing and decorated with crystallised flowers. They are also very good served plain.

NURSERY WHEELS

137

6 oz. flour	3 oz. sugar
½ tsp. baking powder	Vanilla essence
A pinch of salt	Milk to mix
3 oz. butter	2 tsps. cocoa

Sift together the flour, baking powder and salt. Cream the butter and sugar together very thoroughly. Add the flour, vanilla essence and sufficient milk to mix to a stiff paste. Divide the mixture in half. Blend the cocoa powder thoroughly into one half. Roll out both halves thinly into equal-sized pieces. Place the chocolate piece on top of the white one, and roll up tightly like a Swiss roll. Allow to stand in a cool place ½ hour to become firm. Cut in slices ¼ inch thick, place on a greased baking sheet, and cook in a moderate oven (350° F., mark 4) for 15–20 minutes. Dust with caster sugar.

NUT ROCKS

4½ oz. sieved icing sugar	2 egg whites
Almond or vanilla flavouring	3 oz. shredded almonds or shredded walnuts

Put the icing sugar with the unwhisked egg whites into a mixing bowl. Stand the bowl over a saucepan half-filled with boiling water, and whisk the mixture until it clings stiffly to the whisk. Add the flavouring and nuts, and put in teaspoonfuls on a greased and floured tin. Bake in a slow oven (325° F., mark 2) for 20–30 minutes, until crisp outside and soft inside. The rocks should hardly colour.

OAT CAKES

4 oz. medium oatmeal or 3 oz. oatmeal and 1 oz. flour	¼ tsp. salt
A pinch of bicarbonate of soda	1 level tbsp. bacon fat or dripping
	Boiling water

Mix the oatmeal, flour (if used), bicarbonate of soda and salt. Melt the fat with 1 tbsp. water and pour into the centre of the dry ingredients. Mix to a soft consistency, adding boiling water as required. Turn out on to a floured board, knead lightly and roll out very thinly. Cut across in 8 triangles, place on a floured tin, and bake in a moderately hot oven (400° F., mark 6) until the edges curl up and the oat cakes are crisp—20–30 minutes. Alternatively, cook on a hot girdle until the edges curl, then toast in the oven until lightly browned.

OAT CRUNCHIES

1 oz. margarine	2 oz. flour
1 oz. sugar	2 oz. rolled oats
1 egg white or ½ an egg	½ tsp. baking powder
Vanilla or other flavouring	

Cream the fat and the sugar. Add the egg white by degrees, beating well. Add the vanilla, and stir in the flour, oats and baking powder. Using a teaspoon and fork, put out in little heaps on a greased baking sheet as for rock cakes. Bake in a moderate oven (350° F., mark 4) for 15–20 minutes.

OATMEAL BISCUITS (SAVOURY)

3 oz. flour	1 tsp. salt
4 oz. medium oatmeal	2½ oz. good dripping
½ tsp. baking powder	Cold water

Mix the flour, oatmeal, baking powder and salt. Rub in the dripping with the tips of the fingers, until the mixture is crumbly. Mix with cold water to a stiff dough. Roll out ¼ inch thick, and cut in rounds with a large cutter. Place on a greased tin, and bake in a moderately hot oven (400° F., mark 6) for about 20 minutes.

These biscuits are excellent to serve for breakfast or to eat with cheese.

ORANGE OATMEAL CRESCENTS

4 oz. lard or margarine	1 tsp. baking powder
4 oz. brown sugar	A pinch of salt
4 oz. oatmeal	Rind and juice of 1 orange
4 oz. flour	3–4 tbsps. milk

Cream the fat and sugar till fluffy, and stir in the oatmeal. Sieve the dry ingredients and add, with the orange rind and juice. Mix well, adding milk to bind to a stiff paste. Roll out on a floured board, prick, cut in crescents, using a round cutter, and put on a greased baking tin. Bake in moderately hot oven (425° F., mark 7) for about 10 minutes till golden-brown. Leave the biscuits in the tin to crisp before putting them on a rack to cool.

PEANUT BISCUIT RUFFLES

4 oz. peanut butter	1 tsp. baking powder
1½ oz. margarine	½ tsp. mixed spice
3 oz. sugar	½ tsp. ground cinnamon
1 egg	½ tsp. vanilla essence
4½ oz. flour	A little water

Thoroughly cream the fats and sugar together, add the beaten egg a little at a time, beating well, then stir in the flour, baking powder and flavourings. A very dry mixture is required, and water should be added only if the dry ingredients cannot be combined without. Use the hands for the last stages of mixing, as it is easier to judge the consistency and to combine the ingredients in this way. Roll out fairly thinly and ruffle the surface with a fork. Cut into fingers or stamp with cutters, and place on a greased tin. Bake in a moderately hot oven (425° F., mark 7) for 10–15 minutes, until brown and crisp.

PEANUT MACAROONS

4 oz. peanuts	5 oz. brown sugar
½ tsp. salt	½ tsp. vanilla essence
1 egg white	

Toast the peanuts in the oven for a few minutes, then chop them or put them through a rather coarse mincing machine, and sprinkle them with salt. Put the egg white on a large plate and beat it to a very stiff froth. Add the sugar gradually, continuing the beating, flavour with vanilla, and finally, fold in the prepared nuts. Arrange teaspoonfuls of the mixture on a greased tin about 1 inch apart, and bake in a slow oven (325° F., mark 2) until lightly browned and firm to the touch—about 20 minutes.

ALMOND PETITS FOURS

1½ egg whites	½ tsp. orange flower water
4 oz. ground almonds	½–1 whole egg
2 oz. caster sugar	Cherries or angelica
½ tsp. ratafia essence	A little egg white

Beat the egg whites until frothy. Add the
ground almonds, sugar and flavourings. Beat 137
the whole egg, and add sufficient to the mixture to make a soft paste. Put into a calico forcing bag with a large star pipe. Pipe stars on to a greased baking sheet, lined with rice paper. Decorate with tiny pieces of cherries or angelica. Brush with egg white. Bake in a moderate oven (350° F., mark 4) for about 15–20 minutes, until lightly coloured.

MARZIPAN PETITS FOURS

4 oz. ground almonds	2 egg yolks
4 oz. caster sugar	Cherries and angelica to decorate
Almond essence	

Mix ground almonds and sugar and add the flavouring, and sufficient well-beaten egg yolk to make a stiff paste. Form with the hand into fancy shapes, or roll out with caster sugar and cut in squares, diamonds, etc. Decorate with cherries and angelica, cut in small pieces. Lay on rice paper on a greased baking sheet, and bake in a moderate oven (350° F., mark 4) until firm and very lightly coloured—15–20 minutes. Glaze, if liked.

PINEAPPLE FINGERS

4 oz. margarine	2 oz. custard powder
4 oz. sugar	7–8 squares of glacé pineapple
1 egg yolk	
6 oz. flour	White glacé icing

Cream the margarine and sugar very thoroughly, beat in the egg yolk, then stir in the flour and custard powder. Chop 4–5 squares of pineapple into small pieces and add to the other ingredients, mixing well together. Turn on to a lightly floured board, roll out ¼ inch thick, cut into fingers and place on a greased baking tray. Bake in a moderately hot oven (425° F., mark 7) for 10–12 minutes, cool, then ice. Slice remaining pineapple and decorate the biscuits with it.

RASPBERRY RINGS

3 oz. self-raising flour — Cold water
1 oz. cornflour — Jam
1½ oz. fat — Glacé icing
1 oz. sugar

Mix together the flours, and rub in the fat very thoroughly. Add the sugar and mix to a stiff dough with cold water. Roll out thinly and cut in small rounds, then cut out rings to match the rounds. Place in a greased tin, and bake in a moderately hot oven (400° F., mark 6) until lightly browned. Cool on a rack. Spread the rounds with jam, and dip the rings in glacé icing. Place the rings on top of the rounds so that the jam shows through in the centre.

SHORTBREAD

5 oz. flour — 2 oz. caster sugar
1 oz. rice flour — 4 oz. butter

Line a baking tin with a piece of greased kitchen paper. Sieve the flour into a bowl, add the rice flour and sugar, and knead the butter into the dry ingredients, using the hand. When the mixture binds together, pack into a shortbread mould or turn on to a lightly floured board, press into a round cake, then prick a design on the shortcake, using a fork, and crimp up the edges, using a finger and thumb. Place on the prepared tin, and bake in a moderate oven (350° F., mark 3) until firm and lightly browned (1–1½ hours). Lift carefully on to a wire tray and dredge with caster sugar. When cold, cut into wedge-shaped pieces or fingers.

ALMOND SHORTBREAD

4 oz. butter — 3 oz. ground almonds
6 oz. flour — ¼ tsp. salt
3 oz. caster sugar

Beat the butter with a spoon until it is soft. Rub it into the dry ingredients and work with the hands until it is pliable. In cold weather the butter may be slightly warmed, but should on no account be allowed to oil. Butter a sandwich tin or a shallow oblong tin, put the shortbread into the middle and knead out with the knuckles until it is even and flat. Prick all over with a fork, and bake in a moderate oven (350° F., mark 3) for about ¾ hour, or until pale brown in colour and firm to the touch. While it is still warm, cut into pieces of even shape, but do not remove from tin until it is nearly cold.

CHOCOLATE SHORTBREAD BISCUITS

4 oz. flour — 2 tbsps. cocoa
1 oz. ground rice — 4 oz. butter
3 oz. sugar — Water to mix

Mix the dry ingredients together and rub in the butter very thoroughly. Knead all together to a smooth, firm dough, adding a very little water if necessary. Roll out and cut into neat fingers. Place on a baking sheet, prick well, and bake in a moderately hot oven (400° F., mark 6) for 15–20 minutes. Dredge with caster sugar.

In hot weather, if the butter is very soft, cream the butter and sugar and then stir in the dry ingredients to form a smooth, firm dough.

GINGER SHORTBREAD

6 oz. flour — 1 tsp. ground ginger
2 oz. caster sugar — 4 oz. butter
1 oz. chopped ginger

Put all the dry ingredients into a basin, and rub in the butter until the mixture is like crumbs. Knead together, then pack (about ½ inch thick) into a thick greased baking tin, and press flat with the hand. Bake in a moderate oven (350° F., mark 3) until golden-brown and firm—about 1 hour. Cut into neat pieces. Remove from the tin when cold.

SHREWSBURY BISCUITS

4 oz. butter — ½ lb. flour
4 oz. caster sugar — 2 tsps. grated lemon rind
1 egg

Cream the butter and sugar together very thoroughly, add the beaten egg by degrees and beat well. Add the sieved flour and grated lemon rind, mix to a stiff paste, and turn out on to a floured board. Knead lightly and roll out thinly Cut into rounds with a fancy cutter, place on the baking sheet, and bake in a moderate oven (350° F., mark 4) until pale brown (about 15 minutes). Allow to cool on a wire tray.

SOUVENOFFS

3 oz. flour — 1 drop of lemon essence
1 oz. sugar — Red-currant jelly
2 oz. butter — Icing sugar

Mix the flour and sugar, and work in the fat and lemon essence with the fingers until the mixture binds together. Knead until smooth, then roll out very thinly—this requires some care, but if the mixture breaks, the dough requires more kneading. Cut into rounds, place on a greased tin, and press with a runnelled cork dipped in caster sugar. Bake in a moderate oven

(350° F., mark 3) until cooked but barely coloured. Lift carefully on to a rack and leave to cool. When cold, sandwich together with red-currant jelly and dust with icing sugar. The finished biscuits should be very thin.

ACORN COOKIES

2 oz. margarine	A pinch of salt
2 oz. caster sugar	A few drops of ratafia essence
1 small egg	Chocolate glacé icing
3 oz. flour	Chocolate vermicelli
1 oz. cornflour	

Cream the margarine and sugar until soft and fluffy, then beat in the egg slowly. Sieve in the dry ingredients and flavour with the essence. Put the mixture into a forcing bag fitted with a small éclair nozzle and pipe it on to a greased baking tray, making one end of each cookie slightly thicker, to give the acorn shape. Bake in a hot oven (450° F., mark 8) for 5–7 minutes, and cool on a wire tray. Coat the thick end of each cookie with chocolate glacé icing and sprinkle with the chocolate vermicelli, for the " cup " of the acorn.

POPCORN BALLS

4 oz. granulated sugar	1 oz. butter or margarine
2 tbsps. golden syrup	1 pint popped corn
¼ cup water	

Dissolve the sugar with the syrup and water, then bring to the boil and add the fat; bring up to 260° F., then pour over the popcorn. Stir till it is cool enough to handle, then mould into balls with your hands, and put on a greased tray to harden.

SUNSHINE BISCUITS

6 oz. flour	2 oz. butter
A pinch of salt	2 oz. sugar
1 tsp. baking powder	1 egg
	Yellow royal icing

Sieve together the flour, salt, and baking powder. Cream the butter and sugar thoroughly, and beat in the egg. Stir in the dry ingredients to make a firm dough. Roll out thinly, cut into rounds with a crinkled cutter, and bake in a moderate oven (350° F., mark 4) until firm and lightly coloured. When cold, spread one with royal icing coloured yellow, place a second biscuit on top and coat with more of the icing. (Glacé icing may be used instead of royal icing, if preferred.)

TIGER BISCUITS

3 oz. butter	Butter icing
4 oz. flour	Sieved apricot jam
1–2 oz. sugar	Chopped walnuts
A very little water	

Rub the butter into the flour and sugar, and mix to a stiff paste with a very little water if needed. Roll out, cut into rounds and lay on a greased baking sheet. Bake in a slow oven (325° F., mark 2) for about 30 minutes. Sandwich biscuits together with butter icing or coffee butter icing, brush with sieved apricot jam and roll in finely chopped walnuts.

VANILLA BISCUITS

¼ lb. flour	1 egg yolk
¼ lb. rice flour	½ tsp. vanilla essence
3½ oz. caster sugar	A little water
3½ oz. butter or margarine	

Mix the dry ingredients in a basin, and rub in the fat with the tips of the fingers. Beat up the egg yolk with the flavouring and a very little water, add this to the dry ingredients, and knead until free from cracks. Turn the dough on to a floured board and roll out thinly. Cut into fancy shapes, place them on a greased and floured tin, and bake in a moderate oven (350° F., mark 4) for about 20 minutes, until a golden-brown colour. Sprinkle with sugar, and cool on rack.

WATER BISCUITS

¼ lb. self-raising flour	2 tbsps. water
A pinch of salt	½ oz. margarine

Sieve the flour and salt into a basin, put the water and margarine into a pan, heat gently, and when the margarine has melted, pour it into the flour, and mix to a smooth paste. Turn on to a floured board, roll out thinly and stamp into rounds. Bake in a moderately hot oven (425° F., mark 7) for 15–20 minutes, until golden-brown on top and underneath. Cool on a rack, then toss in salt and keep in a tin. Serve with cheese.

WHOLEMEAL BISCUITS

1 oz. lard	½ tsp. baking powder
¼ lb. wholemeal flour	A good pinch of salt
2 tsps. sugar	Milk to mix

Rub fat into flour very thoroughly, then add remaining ingredients and mix to fairly stiff paste with milk. Roll out thinly and stamp into rounds. Place on a greased tin, prick well, and bake in a moderate oven (350° F., mark 4) until pale brown and firm—10–15 minutes.

HOME-MADE SWEETS

Sooner or later most cooks want to try their hand at home-made sweets, even if only a simple toffee or fudge. Indeed, sweet making is a fascinating art, and once the simple rules are grasped, a variety of sweets can be made. If prettily packed (see colour picture facing page 416), they make very acceptable gifts.

It is important to realise that sweet making cannot easily be fitted in with other cooking; firstly, it needs undivided attention and great accuracy, and secondly, a damp atmosphere can often spoil the results. A warm, dry atmosphere is ideal, and although one cannot control the weather, at least matters need not be made more difficult by having a steamy kitchen.

SWEET MAKING EQUIPMENT

While it is not necessary to have a large amount of expensive apparatus, certain utensils are really essential. Expense will be saved in the long run if these are purchased at the start, so that waste of time and ingredients may be avoided.

It is a good idea to keep the utensils all together and to use them solely for their own purpose, for scrupulous cleanliness and freedom from grease and smell are essential to success.

Sugar-boiling Thermometer

This is not absolutely essential, but without it only approximate temperatures can be measured, which limits the number of recipes and makes success more a matter of luck than a certainty.

Sugar-boiling thermometers are usually mounted on brass with a brass or wooden handle, and are graduated from 60° F. to 360° F., or in some cases as high as 450° F. When buying a thermometer, choose one which is clearly graduated and easy to read, and which has a sliding clip for slipping over the edge of the saucepan to hold the thermometer firmly.

Before using a new thermometer, it should be placed in a pan of cold water, brought slowly to the boil and then allowed to remain in the water till cold again. This is to "season" it.

A sugar-boiling thermometer will measure more accurately and wear longer if it is always boiled in water before being plunged into boiling sugar syrup. If this is not done, there is a danger of its cracking when placed in the syrup.

Always shake the thermometer before use, so that the mercury thread is unbroken. Once the syrup comes to the boil, put in the thermometer and leave it until the required temperature is reached. The thermometer must be placed upright in the pan with the bulb completely covered by

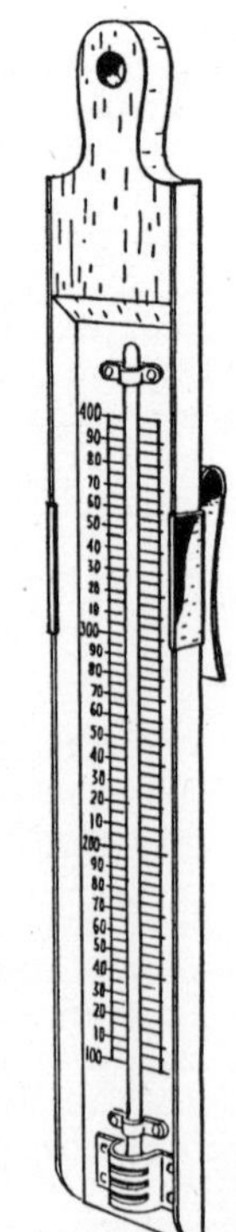

Sugar Thermometer

the syrup; be sure to read it at eye level. Remove the pan from the heat immediately the required temperature is reached. Take out the thermometer and replace it in hot water until convenient to wash it. See that it is perfectly clean and free from sugar crystals, before putting it away in a safe place—any sugar left from the previous boiling might easily cause a fresh boiling to crystallise.

Saucepans

Saucepans for sweet making should be strong and thick (preferably of lined copper or cast aluminium), otherwise a high temperature sweet mixture may stick or burn. Enamel pans are unsuitable, as the very high temperatures may crack the enamel lining. The inside of the pan must be absolutely smooth and free from pits or chips. The pan must be large enough to allow the mixture to boil rapidly—for toffee and caramel mixtures, which are very liable to froth up and boil over, it should not be filled more than half full. A 4-pint saucepan is a convenient size for average batches, and another smaller one also will be found useful, as some recipes require two syrups to be made simultaneously.

The inside of the pan must be scrupulously clean. As even a thick pan will sometimes burn, it is a good plan to rub the inside surface with a little olive oil or butter before putting in the mixture. This will tend to lessen the possibility of sticking.

Caramel Bars

Though they are not essential, these are very useful in sweet making. They are made of ½–¾-inch square steel, and vary in length from 10–16 inches, 4 bars constituting a set. When arranged in rectangular formation on a marble slab or enamel-topped table, they take the place of a tin to pour the mixture into, and have the advantage that they can be adjusted to the required size in a few seconds. When the mixture is set, it is an easy matter to remove the bars and cut the sweets neatly without any waste.

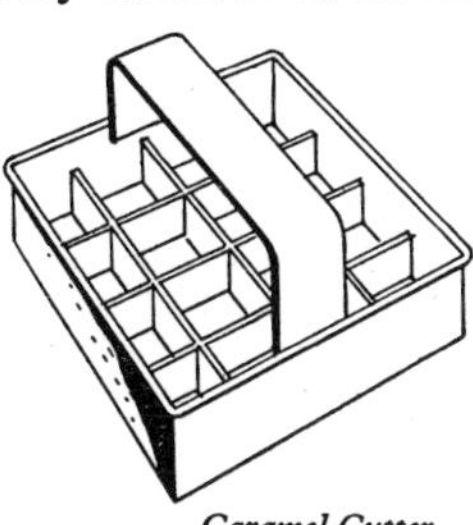
Caramel Cutter

Caramel Cutter

This again is by no means essential, but is useful for marking caramels into squares, so that the shapes can be cut quickly and evenly. It consists of a metal framework with cutting bars equally spaced at right angles to each other.

Marble Slab

This sweet making aid is rather expensive to buy and is not absolutely necessary. An old-fashioned washstand top is a cheaper substitute, or an enamelled surface, such as an enamel-topped table, can be used instead of marble. Certain plastic surfaces can be used for heats up to 280° F., but preferably not beyond this.

Spatula and Palette Knife

A special spatula made of hard wood is helpful for tapping down the crystals of sugar when making a syrup, for working fondant mixtures, beating fudges and so on. A palette knife (preferably of stainless steel) with flexible blade is useful for shaping sweets, etc.

EQUIPMENT FOR ADVANCED SWEET MAKING

For more advanced sweet making, such as fondant centres for chocolates, chocolate dipping, crystallising and so on, the following additional apparatus is necessary:

Starch Tray (for making chocolate centres): This is a box, usually made of wood, 2–3 inches deep and anything from 12–20 inches square. Small plaster of Paris moulds, glued on to strips of wood slightly longer than the box is wide, are also required. To use the tray, it is filled evenly with confectioner's starch, previously well dried and carefully sifted. Impressions are made in the surface of the starch with the plaster of Paris moulds, and the liquid mixture (fondant, jelly, etc.) is poured into these impressions through a funnel and allowed to set. They are then removed and brushed free from starch. These shapes are used for centres for chocolates, etc.; they can be coated at once, or may be kept stored in a dry place until required.

Rubber Fondant Mat: This consists of a sheet of rubber about 1 inch thick, with fancy-shaped impressions into which liquid fondant, jelly or chocolate is run, and allowed to set. When the shapes are firm, they can be removed easily by bending back the rubber.

Funnel and Plug: A metal funnel, with a wooden plug shaped somewhat like a wooden meat skewer. This is used for filling into the impressions in a starch tray or rubber mat or into peppermint cream rings.

Cream Rings : Round metal rings, useful for moulding peppermint creams and similar sweets.

Dipping Forks : Small forks with two or three wire prongs or with a loop at the end. They are used for lifting sweets out of coating fondant or chocolate, the prongs or loop being used to make a raised design on the top of the sweets.

Marzipan Moulds : Moulds made of pewter or plaster of Paris in the form of fruit, leaves, nuts, shells, etc., for shaping marzipan.

Hydrometer : This is an instrument for measuring the density of syrups used for crystallising. The type which is most commonly used for crystallising, etc., is known as the Beaumé hydrometer.

Boiling Tube : This is used in conjunction with a hydrometer for testing the density of a syrup. It is so designed that very little syrup is required for the test, and as the glass is heat-resisting, there is little risk of the hot syrup breaking the glass.

Crystallising Tray : A small square or oblong tin, into which is fitted a wire tray on small feet. The tin has a small screw cap near the bottom of one corner, to enable the syrup to be drained off when required.

Chocolate-dipping Pan : A double saucepan, usually of copper, tin-lined, specially designed for melting the chocolate used for coating chocolate centres.

SUGAR BOILING

This process is the basis of most sweet making, and is also employed in some icing. The sugar is first dissolved in water and brought to the boil. At this stage the thermometer will register 212° F., and the mixture will remain at this temperature until enough water has been evaporated to produce a syrup consistency. Then the temperature will start to rise, continuing as more water evaporates. The syrup first becomes very thick but pale, darkening gradually, until finally, at 350° F., it becomes dark brown. (At this stage it is known as burnt sugar, and being no longer sweet, it can be used for darkening gravy.)

A sugar-boiling thermometer, and if possible a saccharometer, are desirable for this work, but for simple sweets it is possible to use instead the homely tests described below. The list gives the various stages between boiling point and caramel, with their special names and the method of testing the stages. Although definite temperatures are quoted for the different stages, the sugar passes almost imperceptibly from one stage to the next.

Smooth (215°–220° F.) : The mixture begins to look syrupy. To test, dip the fingers in water, then in the syrup ; the thumb slides smoothly over the fingers, but the sugar clings to the finger. Used for crystallising purposes.

Thread (230° F.–234° F.) : Boil the solution for 2–3 minutes. Dip the fingers into cold water, dip them in the syrup, then back again into cold water ; press the finger and thumb together, pull them apart and a fine thread will be observed.

Used for making liqueurs.

Soft Ball (235° F.–245° F.) : When a drop of the syrup is put into very cold water, it forms a soft ball ; at 235° F. the soft ball flattens on removal from water, but the higher the temperature, the firmer the ball, till it reaches the Firm Ball stage.

Used for making fondants and fudge.

Hard Ball (245° F.–265° F.) : The syrup, when dropped into cold water, forms a ball which is hard enough to hold its shape, but is still plastic.

Used for making caramels and marshmallow.

Soft Crack (270° F.–290° F.) : The syrup, when dropped into cold water, separates into threads which are hard but not brittle.

Used for toffees.

Hard Crack (300° F.–310° F.) : When a drop of the syrup is put into cold water, it separates into threads which are hard and brittle.

Used for hard toffees and rocks.

Caramel (310° F.) : Shown by the syrup becoming golden-brown. Used for making praline and caramels, also for flavouring caramel custard, etc.

CRYSTALLISATION

The technique of dissolving and boiling sugar needs great care, as the syrup has a tendency to re-crystallise if not handled correctly.

The chief causes are : (1) the agitation of the mixture by stirring or beating, and (2) the presence of any solid particles such as sugar crystals, grit, etc., in the syrup while it is boiling.

To obtain a clear syrup, therefore, the pan must be perfectly clean and the sugar must be completely dissolved before the mixture is allowed to boil. Should any crystals form on the sides of the pan after the boiling has begun, they should be brushed down with a clean pastry brush dipped in cold water. Also, there must be no stirring or agitation of the mixture, but a wooden spatula can be used to tap the grains of sugar on to the bottom of the pan while dissolving, to hasten the process. Once the sugar is dissolved and the syrup has been brought to the boil, it can be heated rapidly to

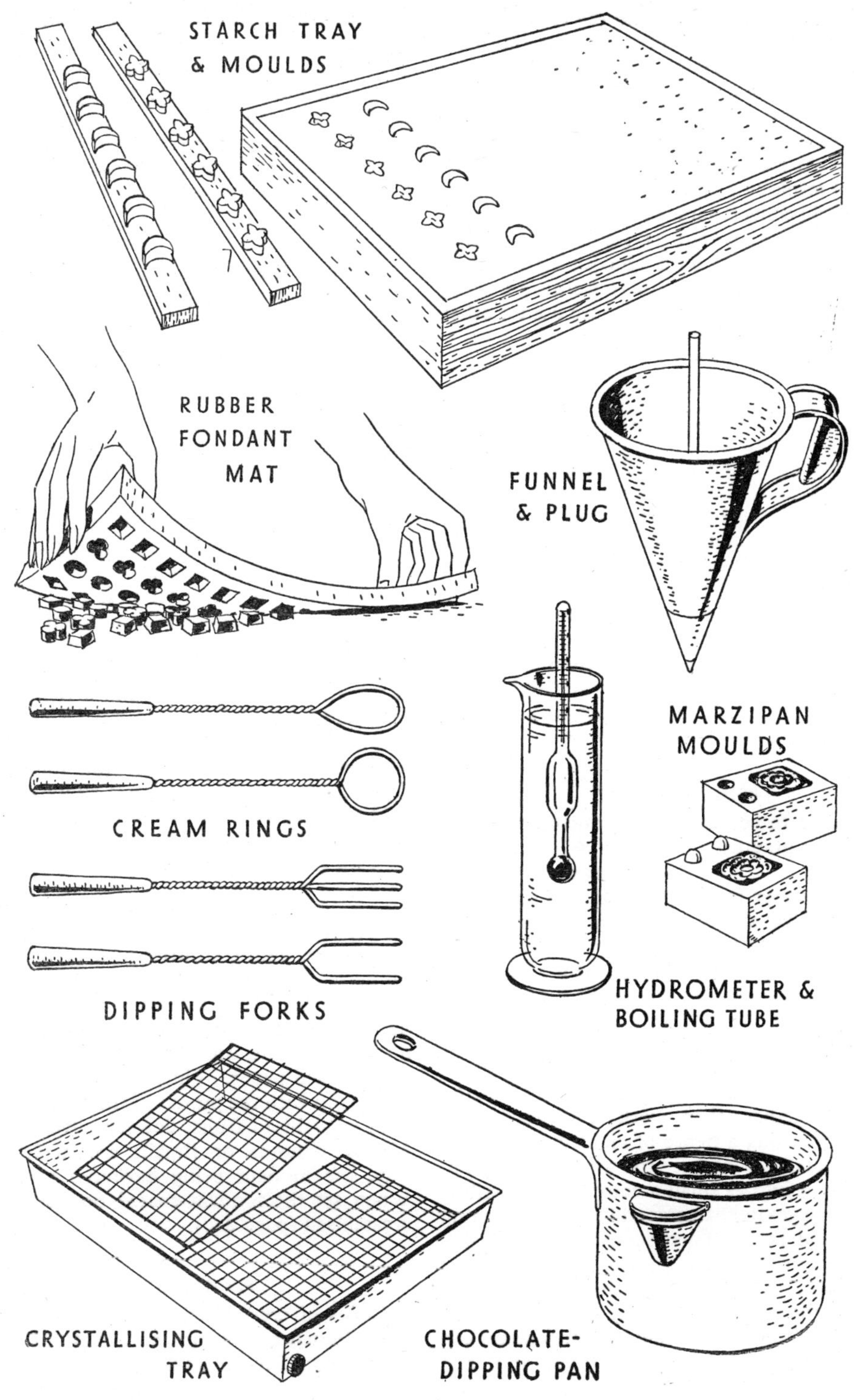
STARCH TRAY
& MOULDS
RUBBER
FONDANT
MAT
FUNNEL
& PLUG
MARZIPAN
MOULDS
CREAM RINGS
DIPPING FORKS
HYDROMETER &
BOILING TUBE
CRYSTALLISING
TRAY
CHOCOLATE-
DIPPING PAN

the exact temperature stated in the recipe and at once removed from the heat, so that the temperature does not rise any higher.

Another way of preventing crystallising during the boiling is to add a small amount of glucose, golden syrup or honey (¼ lb. glucose to 1½ lb. sugar). Alternatively, add a small pinch of cream of tartar or a squeeze of lemon juice. Any of these will convert some of the sugar into invert sugar, which does not crystallise so readily. Sweets made partly with glucose soften more quickly, so that while glucose is useful in making fondants, cream of tartar is of more use for other types of sweet making.

FONDANTS

Fondant forms the basis of a large number of sweets, and it is also used for chocolate centres and for icing cakes, etc. It is produced by boiling syrup—in the proportion of 1 lb. loaf sugar and ¼ pint water—to a temperature of 240°–245° F., following all the directions for sugar boiling. The fondant is then cooled on a marble slab and worked until it becomes opaque and firm. It is then ready for use and can be thinned by the addition of syrup, or enriched by the addition of cream or evaporated milk. Store in a covered jar or tin.

BOILED FONDANT

¼ pint water, full measure
1 lb. loaf or granulated sugar
1 oz. glucose or a good pinch of cream of tartar

Put the water into a pan, add the sugar and let it dissolve slowly, following the rules for sugar boiling. When the sugar has dissolved, bring the syrup to the boil, add the glucose or cream of tartar and boil to 240° F.

Have ready the marble slab sprinkled with
139 water, pour on the syrup and leave for a few minutes to cool. When a skin starts to form round the edges, take the spatula and collect the mixture together, then work it forwards and backwards, using a figure of eight movement of the spatula. Continue to work the syrup, collecting it into as small a compass as possible, until it changes its character and grains, becoming opaque and firm. Then scrape it off the slab and knead in the hands until of an even texture throughout. The fondant is then ready to use, or it may be stored in a covered jar or tin until required. (If no slab is available, the fondant can be "turned" in a bowl until thick, and then kneaded on greaseproof paper; when a bowl is used, let the syrup cool for 15 minutes before "turning" is commenced.)

Fondant required for icing cakes or coating sweets should be put into the upper part of a double saucepan and melted over very gentle heat, sugar syrup (or a few drops of water) being added to thin it down if required. Do not overheat fondant, as this makes it rough and destroys the gloss.

FONDANT CREAMS AND CHOCOLATE CENTRES

Make some fondant as above, and knead it well (particularly if it has been stored for some time). To improve the texture and flavour, add a little cream, evaporated milk or melted butter. (If using fondant already made, add the cream, milk or butter when it is melted.) Now divide the mixture into portions and flavour and colour them appropriately to make lemon, raspberry, rose, violet, orange and coffee creams, etc. Roll the fondant out on a slab, using icing sugar for dredging, and either cut into the required shapes, or model by hand.

To obtain fancy shapes, or to make chocolate centres, melt the fondant in a double saucepan over very gentle heat, using a little sugar syrup (or a few drops of water) to help to liquefy it. When it is liquid, pour it into a funnel with a plug and run it out into cream rings, a starch mould or rubber moulds. For chocolate centres, a starch tray is best, but for fondants for crystallising it is better to use a rubber mat.

Directions for chocolate dipping and crystallising are given at the end of this chapter.

FONDANT-COATED BONBONS

Prepare the fondant as above and melt over gentle heat, adding a little sugar syrup or a few drops of water to give the correct consistency for coating. Add colouring or flavouring if desired, dip the sweets or nuts one at a time into the fondant, using a dipping fork, and drop on to waxed paper. Finish by marking a design on the top with the prongs of the fork or decorate with crystallised fruits, flowers, silver balls, etc. Mocha Walnuts or Brazils are made in this way, the fondant being flavoured with coffee. When set the fondant-coated bonbons may be crystallised (page 440).

FRUIT FONDANTS

Cubes of crystallised ginger, glacé pineapple, small bunches of raisins and many other fruits can be dipped in the liquid fondant cream, which may be tastefully coloured if desired. After dipping, lift on to wax paper and dry. Serve within the next two or three hours if the fruit is fresh and juicy.

HARLEQUIN CREAMS

Use any trimmings left after making coloured fondants, and work into balls.

HAZEL CREAMS

Colour the fondant a pale green, flavour with vanilla, shape into small oval sweets and press a hazelnut in the centre of each.

OPERA CREAMS

1 lb. loaf sugar
¼ pint water
2 oz. glucose
A few drops of Maraschino
1 tbsp. cream
Sieved icing sugar

Put the sugar, water and glucose into a saucepan and heat slowly, stirring all the time, until the sugar is dissolved. Skim when necessary, and brush any scum or crystals from the sides of the pan with a brush dipped in cold water. Boil without stirring to 240° F. and pour on to a wetted slab or large dish. Work until it is opaque, using first a wooden spoon or spatula, then the hands. Hollow out slightly and add the Maraschino and the cream, together, with sufficient icing sugar to make it of the right consistency for shaping. Form a neat square and roll out 1 inch thick, using a little icing sugar to prevent it sticking. When the mixture is smooth and even, leave it until cold, then cut in neat squares with a sharp knife or caramel cutter. This mixture may be made up in different colours and flavours.

PEPPERMINT CREAMS

2 lb. loaf sugar
2 oz. glucose or ¼ tsp. cream of tartar
½ pint cold water
Oil of peppermint

Heat the sugar, glucose or cream of tartar and water in a strong saucepan until the sugar is dissolved, and then raise to 240° F. As soon as this temperature is reached, pour the fondant on to a wet enamelled table or slab, sprinkle with cold water on the top and allow to cool. Work with a spatula until it becomes a creamy and thick paste, then knead with the hands until smooth and firm. Add a few drops of oil of peppermint. (Oil of peppermint is considerably stronger than essence of peppermint and should be used sparingly.) Roll out and cut into rounds.

A quicker version of Peppermint Creams is made by using stiff royal icing, to which have been added a few drops of peppermint essence. Roll out, and cut into small rounds with a cutter.

RAINBOW CREAMS

Roll out a layer of violet cream fondant ¼ inch thick, moisten with egg white and place a layer of plain marzipan on top. Moisten again with egg white and cover with a layer of rose fondant cream. Each layer should be very flat and ¼ inch thick. Roll slightly, cut into small squares, rounds or diamonds. Leave to dry for 24 hours.

MARZIPAN

Marzipan requires comparatively few ingredients and is not difficult to make. By using different colourings and moulding the paste into fruit, flowers or conventional shapes, you can make a wide variety of sweetmeats which will be very popular and will certainly add colour and interest to a box of home-made candies.

There are two types—boiled and unboiled. Unboiled marzipan is quick to make; it should be handled as little as possible, as heat makes it oily, so that it cracks badly in moulding and shaping. For marzipan fruits and flowers, therefore, and other sweetmeats which need a good deal of handling when shaping, it is better to use boiled marzipan.

Shaping the Marzipan

Oranges, apples, pears, peaches, bananas, etc., may all be modelled from marzipan.

Different coloured marzipans are blended in layers and cut out for chocolate centres, or shaped in fancy moulds or blended with fruits and nuts. Neapolitan desserts are made by rolling out lengths of the paste in contrasting colours, enclosing them in a thin sheet of plain marzipan and shaping the whole into a square of about an inch, like a miniature Battenberg cake. A little syrup, or better still, dissolved gum arabic, is brushed over the sections to make them adhere firmly. Small pieces are cut off with a sharp knife, and can be wholly or partly dipped in chocolate, or they may be crystallised.

BOILED MARZIPAN—I

1 lb. loaf sugar
¼ pint water
A pinch of cream of tartar
¾ lb. ground almonds
2 egg whites
3 oz. icing sugar (more if required)

Put the loaf sugar and water into a pan and dissolve slowly. When it boils add the cream of tartar, then bring to a temperature of 240° F. Remove from the heat and stir rapidly until the syrup grains. Stir in the ground almonds and egg whites and cook for a few minutes over a gentle heat, stirring well. Pour on to an oiled slab of marble or enamelled iron, add the sieved icing sugar, and work well with a palette knife, lifting the edges of the mixture with the knife and pressing them into the centre. As soon as the mixture is sufficiently cool, knead until smooth. Additional sieved icing sugar may be kneaded in if required. Divide into portions and add colouring and flavouring according to requirements. Marzipan will keep excellently for 2–3 weeks, if wrapped in greaseproof paper and stored in a cool place.

BOILED MARZIPAN—II

1 lb. loaf sugar	¾ lb. ground almonds
¼ pint water	Orange flower water
4 oz. glucose	2 egg yolks

Dissolve the sugar in the water, bring to the boil, add the glucose and raise the temperature to 242° F. Mix in the ground almonds, 1 tsp. of orange flower water and the beaten egg yolks, and place the mixture on a cool slab, working it up until it is cool.

UNBOILED MARZIPAN

1½ lb. ground almonds	1½ tsps. vanilla essence
10 oz. fine caster sugar	1½ tsps. orange flower water
10 oz. sieved icing sugar	
Juice of a small lemon	Egg white

Mix the dry ingredients, make a well in the centre, add the flavourings and use sufficient egg white to make the mixture bind to a soft but dry paste. Colour, and after forming into fruit or other desired shapes, leave these on a rack to dry.

CHOCOLATE MARZIPAN

6 oz. grated chocolate	6 oz. sieved icing sugar
2 tbsps. water	1 egg
¾ lb. ground almonds	2 tsps. lemon juice
6 oz. caster sugar	1 tsp. vanilla essence

Melt the chocolate in the water and add to the ground almonds and sugars, which should be thoroughly mixed together. Beat the egg, add the lemon juice and essence to it, and add them to the chocolate mixture. Knead well, adding extra lemon juice if required. Shape into mushrooms or potatoes, or into even-shaped bars. Roll in caster sugar and allow to dry.

MARZIPAN APRICOTS

Colour the paste as nearly as possible the shade of an apricot. Roll into a ball and shape each piece like an apricot, marking a dent down the side. A few splashes or dots to imitate the brown specks found on an apricot should be made on one side, with either melted chocolate or chocolate colouring.

MARZIPAN DATES

Only the best dessert dates should be used. Remove the stones and fill the cavities with marzipan. The stuffed dates may be rolled in caster sugar and placed in fancy paper cases.

MARZIPAN DICE

Trimmings of coloured marzipan or almond paste can be used up in the following way: roll out the pieces of marzipan separately into oblongs of even size and thickness. Brush lightly with egg white and lay on top of one another. Roll lightly with a rolling pin and press the layers together. Cut into small blocks of even size, roll in caster sugar and dry.

MARZIPAN LOGS

Make a thin roll of pink marzipan and roll out a strip of green marzipan wide enough to cover it. Brush lightly with egg white and cover the pink roll with the green paste. Cut into small logs, coat with chocolate and roll in desiccated coconut which has been coloured pale green.

MARZIPAN WALNUTS

Roll the marzipan into small balls and press a half-walnut into the top surface. If preferred, two half-walnuts can be used, with the marzipan as a centre.

STUFFED FRENCH PLUMS

¼ lb. ground almonds	½ a beaten egg or egg yolk
¼ lb. icing sugar	
½ tsp. lemon juice	Green, mauve and pink colouring
¼ tsp. orange flower water	French plums
¼ tsp. vanilla essence	

Mix the ground almonds and sugar, add the flavourings, mix to a stiff paste with the egg, and knead well. Divide into three and colour the portions green, mauve and pink, by working a few drops of vegetable colouring into each. Select good quality French plums, as ordinary prunes which require soaking are not very suitable. Remove the stones and replace with a small roll of the almond mixture. Roll the stuffed fruit in granulated or caster sugar and place in fancy cases.

FUDGES

The chief ingredients of fudge are sugar in some form, butter and milk or cream, in varying proportions; by adding flavourings such as chocolate, fruits, honey, etc., a large number of very delicious candies may be obtained.

The mixture is heated to a temperature of between 235° F. and 240° F. and then it is "grained"—that is, stirred until crystals are formed. As soon as this change takes place, but while it is still liquid, the fudge is poured into an oiled tin or caramel bars and cut up as soon as it is firm. Care must be taken not to let it set in the saucepan.

These mixtures have to be stirred occasionally during cooking, which is contrary to sugar-boiling rules, but they are not likely to crystallise during boiling and, being rather rich, they are very apt to stick and burn if left unstirred.

CHOCOLATE FUDGE—I

1 lb. granulated sugar	1 tsp. glucose
¼ pint fresh milk	2 tbsps. cream
2 oz. grated unsweetened chocolate	2 oz. butter
	½ tsp. vanilla essence

Put the sugar, milk and chocolate into a pan, heat and tap gently with a wooden spatula until the sugar is dissolved. Add the glucose, cream and butter, then insert the thermometer, previously heated in hot water, and continue to boil the fudge, stirring occasionally, until the thermometer registers 238° F. If a thermometer is not available, drop a small piece of fudge into a cup of cold water: if it forms a soft ball that will hold together and can be handled, remove the saucepan from the heat and add the vanilla essence. Beat the mixture, pushing the spoon forward, lifting up the mass, turning it over and bringing it back, until the whole becomes creamy and thick. Turn the mixture into an oiled tin, or on to an oiled slab between oiled bars, smooth it down with the spatula, and when cold, cut in neat pieces of even size with a heavy knife.

CHOCOLATE FUDGE—II

½ pint fresh milk	2 oz. unsweetened chocolate
1 lb. granulated sugar	2 oz. sweetened chocolate
5 oz. butter	2 oz. honey

Stir all together in a thick saucepan until a temperature of 238° F. is reached. Remove from the heat and leave for 15 minutes. Then beat with a wooden spoon until very thick. Press firmly into a buttered tin. When set, cut into neat squares.

CREAMY CHOCOLATE FUDGE

2 oz. unsweetened chocolate	3 oz. Demerara sugar
	2 oz. butter
4 tbsps. evaporated milk	2 oz. walnuts
4 tbsps. water	Vanilla essence
¼ lb. granulated sugar	

Put the chocolate, milk and water into a thick saucepan, and stir gently over moderate heat until the chocolate is dissolved, add the sugars and stir until a temperature of 235° F. is reached. Add the butter, chopped walnuts and vanilla essence. Beat to a thick cream, then pour into an oiled tin. Mark when half set into squares. Cut through and turn out when quite cold.

CHOCOLATE GINGER FUDGE

1 lb. granulated sugar	1 oz. butter
½ pint milk	2 oz. preserved ginger
4 oz. unsweetened chocolate	1 tsp. vanilla essence

Dissolve the sugar in the milk, add grated chocolate and butter and boil to 238° F., stirring all the time. Remove from the heat, add the finely chopped ginger and the vanilla essence, beat until creamy, turn into a buttered or oiled tin, press with a spatula, and cut up when cold.

DATE FUDGE

¼ pint milk	A good pinch cream of tartar
1 lb. brown sugar	2 oz. butter
3 oz. unsweetened grated chocolate	2 tsps. lemon juice
	4 oz. dates

Put the milk, sugar, chocolate, cream of tartar and butter into a pan and bring to a temperature of 238° F., stirring frequently, as the mixture is very apt to burn. Remove from the heat. Add the lemon juice and finely chopped dates, and beat until thick and creamy. Pour into a greased tin and cut into squares when cold.

RAISIN FUDGE

Use the same ingredients as for Date Fudge, omitting the dates and lemon juice. When the fudge has reached a temperature of 240° F., add 3 oz. chopped, seeded raisins and a few drops of vanilla essence. Proceed with the beating as before. Pour into an oiled tin and cut into cubes when the fudge is nearly cold.

GINGER FUDGE

A variation of the above may be made by adding 2 oz. of finely chopped crystallised ginger and a few drops of ginger essence in place of the dates and lemon juice.

HONEY FUDGE

4 oz. honey
1 lb. granulated sugar
3 tbsps. water
⅛ tsp. cream of tartar
2 egg whites
½ tsp. vanilla essence
1 tsp. desiccated coconut

Put the honey, sugar, water and cream of tartar into a saucepan, bring slowly to the boil, and cook gently until a temperature of 260° F. is reached. Have ready the stiffly beaten egg whites; pour the boiling syrup slowly on to them, beating vigorously. Add the vanilla essence and desiccated coconut. Beat until thick and creamy, pour into a buttered pan and leave overnight. Next day, cut into squares. Turn out and leave in the air for a day or so, until they are firm and dry.

MARSHMALLOW FUDGE

1 lb. granulated sugar
¼ pint evaporated milk
¼ pint fresh milk
1 oz. butter
A pinch of cream of tartar
½ lb. marshmallows
2 oz. chopped walnuts

Put the sugar, evaporated and fresh milk, butter and cream of tartar into a strong saucepan. Dissolve slowly and boil to 240° F., stirring all the time with a wooden spoon.

Remove from the heat, add the marshmallows, cut into small pieces, and the chopped walnuts. Beat until the mixture begins to stiffen. Pour into an oiled tin and mark into squares when cold.

NUT AND CHERRY FUDGE

1 lb. granulated sugar
½ pint evaporated or ordinary fresh milk
2 oz. butter
¼ lb. chopped, browned almonds
2 oz. glacé cherries, roughly chopped

Dissolve the sugar in the milk, bring to the boil, add the butter and boil to 238° F., stirring slowly all the time. Remove from the heat, add the nuts and fruit, beat till creamy, turn into a buttered or oiled tin, press down with a spatula, and when the fudge is cold, cut it into neat squares of even size.

NUT AND RAISIN FUDGE

2 oz. butter
1 lb. Demerara sugar
½ pint evaporated milk
2 oz. blanched almonds, browned and chopped
2 oz. seedless raisins

Put the butter, sugar and milk into a thick saucepan, and stir over moderate heat until the sugar is thoroughly dissolved. Increase the heat and, stirring, bring to a temperature of 238° F. Remove from the heat and add the almonds and raisins. Beat to a thick cream and pour into an oiled tin. Mark into squares and cut up when cold.

A few drops of almond essence may be added, if liked.

ORANGE FUDGE—I

1¼ lb. caster sugar
⅓ pint milk
4 oz. butter or 3 oz. margarine
2 tbsps. orange juice
3 tsps. grated orange rind
4 oz. candied orange peel

Dissolve the sugar in the milk, boil for 5 minutes, then add the butter, orange juice and grated rind. Stir occasionally and boil to 240° F., then remove from the heat, add the finely chopped peel, and beat until smooth and creamy. Pour into an oiled tin and when nearly cold, cut into squares.

ORANGE FUDGE—II

1¼ lb. caster sugar
¼ pint evaporated milk
2 oz. butter
2 tsps. grated orange rind
2 tbsps. orange juice

Put the sugar and milk into a thick saucepan over moderate heat, stir occasionally until dissolved. Add the butter, grated orange rind and juice and, stirring gently, bring to a temperature of 238° F. Remove from the heat, beat until it is the consistency of a thick cream and pour into an oiled tin. When nearly cold, cut into squares.

LEMON FUDGE

This can be prepared in exactly the same way as Orange Fudge, above, lemon juice and rind being substituted for the orange.

WALNUT FUDGE

1 lb. granulated sugar
½ pint evaporated milk
1 oz. plain chocolate
4 tbsps. cocoa
1 oz. butter
A pinch of salt
¼ lb. walnuts
1 tsp. vanilla essence

Put all the ingredients, except the walnuts and essence, into a pan and bring to a temperature of 238° F., stirring continuously to prevent burning. Remove from the heat. Have the nuts ready chopped, and add them with the essence to contents of the saucepan, beating well until thick and creamy. Pour into a greased tin, and cut into squares when cold.

TOFFEES AND BUTTERSCOTCH

Toffees are simple mixtures, requiring to be boiled to a high temperature, from 280° to 310° F. The majority of toffees contain butter, but some are made merely from sugar, water and flavouring.

The following rules for toffee making should be observed very carefully:

1. Use a large pan and oil the sides, as toffee is inclined to boil over.
2. Do not stir unless the recipe specially states that stirring is necessary.
3. Rich mixtures containing cream require gentle stirring. This is best done with the sugar-boiling thermometer.
4. Move the position of the thermometer from time to time, as toffee may stick to the bulb and give an inaccurate reading.
5. Keep the heat very low after the toffee has reached a temperature of 260° F.
6. Always warm any nuts, and see that they are warm when added to the toffee.
7. When the required temperature is reached, pour the mixture out briskly; do not use a spoon.
8. Cool toffee at an even temperature. Mark out when lukewarm, using a buttered or oiled knife; press the knife downwards, drawing it straight through with a sawing movement—it should not be dragged heavily or drawn across the surface. If toffee is cut when hot it loses its shape, and if too cold it is impossible to cut straight.
9. Rub the toffees in absorbent paper such as kitchen paper; this removes the surplus oil—then wrap in waxed papers.

To Pull Toffee

Certain toffees (Toffee Cushions and the like) are "pulled," which gives them a satiny, silvery look, and attractive effects are achieved by combining pulled and unpulled toffee before cutting it into cushions.

The toffee should be pulled immediately it is cool enough to handle, as it soon loses its pliability. Oil the hands and throw the toffee over a large, cleaned, oiled hook fixed at a convenient height; catch it and pull, repeating until the desired colour is obtained. For Toffee Cushions, finally pull out the toffee into an even roll about 1 inch in diameter and cut off inch-long pieces with oiled scissors, turning the roll so that each cut is at right angles to the previous one. To obtain a striped effect, pull half (or a smaller or larger proportion of the toffee) and keep the remainder warm meanwhile; then form both pulled and unpulled toffees into a roll, pressing them together, and pull out to the desired thickness, twisting the roll if liked, then cut into squares, cushions, oblongs, etc. (See recipe for Striped Peppermint Humbugs.)

It is essential to handle the toffee quickly and efficiently when pulling, so the amateur would be wise to try simple Toffee Cushions before attempting striped effects, especially if working single-handed.

ALMOND BRITTLE

¾ lb. loaf sugar
¼ pint water
½ lb. golden syrup
2 tsps. glucose
1 oz. butter
3 oz. browned almonds
½ tsp. lemon essence
1 good tsp. bicarbonate of soda

Dissolve the sugar in the water with the golden syrup and glucose, stirring occasionally, and boil to 300° F. Add the butter, browned almonds and essence and reheat to melt the butter. Stir in the bicarbonate of soda and pour on to a well-oiled slab in a very thin sheet. Roll out immediately with an oiled rolling pin and break up when firm and brittle.

COCONUT BRITTLE

Make as for Almond Brittle, substituting 3–4 oz. desiccated or strip coconut for the almonds.

ALMOND TOFFEE

1 lb. Demerara sugar
¼ pint water
1 oz. butter
½ tsp. cream of tartar
2–3 drops acetic acid
2 tbsps. golden syrup
3 oz. chopped almonds

Put the sugar and water into a thick pan, cover, dissolve quickly and bring to the boil. Remove the lid, add the butter, cream of tartar, acetic acid and golden syrup. Cover and boil again for a few minutes. Remove the lid and heat to 300° F. Pour on to a greased tin, sprinkle chopped nuts over and turn the sides to the middle. When cold enough to handle, pull lightly with oiled fingers. When nearly set, cut into cushions or squares. Wrap in waxed paper or Cellophane when cold. Store in an airtight tin.

ALMOND TOFFEE SQUARES

1 lb. Demerara sugar
¼ pint water
Almond essence
3 oz. blanched split almonds

Put the sugar and water into a strong pan, and boil without stirring till a temperature of 310° F.

is reached. The temperature must be watched carefully, as it rises rapidly and the flavour will be spoilt if it is allowed to go higher than this. Add a few drops of essence. Spread the almonds on an oiled tin and pour the toffee on to them to form a thin sheet. When sufficiently cool, mark into squares. Break the toffee when cold.

BARCELONA TOFFEE

3 oz. shelled Barcelona nuts	1 dessertsp. vinegar
1 lb. granulated sugar	2 tbsps. water
1 oz. butter	A pinch of salt
	1 tsp. vanilla essence

Put the nuts on a tin in the oven, toast for a few minutes and then chop them roughly and keep hot. Put all the ingredients, except the nuts and vanilla essence, into a saucepan, stirring until
141 dissolved. Remove the spoon and boil the toffee with the thermometer in, and without stirring, until it reaches 300° F., or until the toffee will break off crisply when tested in cold water; add the vanilla. Pour half on to an oiled slab between oiled bars; sprinkle the hot nuts and vanilla essence on top. Then pour over the remainder of the toffee. When set, mark with the back of a knife and when cold break in pieces. Wrap in waxed paper or Cellophane. Store in an airtight tin.

BARLEY SUGAR—I

1 lb. loaf sugar	A pinch of cream of tartar
$\frac{1}{4}$ pint water	
1 lemon	

Put the sugar and water into a saucepan and when the sugar has dissolved, add strips of
141 lemon rind and the cream of tartar. Boil the mixture to 240° F. Remove from the heat and add the lemon juice. Boil to 310° F., remove the rind and pour on to a lightly oiled slab. Cool slightly, and fold sides to middle. Cut into strips with oiled scissors, and twist. Store in airtight jars.

BARLEY SUGAR—II

$\frac{1}{2}$ lb. loaf sugar	Rind of $\frac{1}{2}$ a lemon
$\frac{1}{4}$ pint water	Lemon essence
$\frac{1}{2}$ lb. glucose	

Put the sugar and water into a saucepan and dissolve slowly. Add the glucose and lemon rind. Boil to 312° F. Remove the rind, add a few drops of lemon essence, pour on to an oiled slab, and, when cooled slightly, fold the sides to the centre. Rub the fingers with salad oil and pull out the sweetmeat. Quickly divide into pieces with an oiled knife, pull and twist.

BUTTERED ALMONDS

1 lb. sugar	$\frac{1}{2}$ lb. Valencia almonds (blanched and well dried in the oven)
3 oz. butter	
2 tbsps. glucose	
$\frac{1}{4}$ pint water	

Put all the ingredients, except the almonds, into a covered pan. Bring to the boil, stirring until the sugar is dissolved. Boil for a few minutes, remove the lid, and without stirring bring the syrup to a temperature of 300° F., or until the mixture becomes brittle when dropped in cold water. Drop the toffee in small rounds on to an oiled or buttered slab or tin, or else into oiled sweet rings. Place an almond at once on each and cover with a little more toffee.

Note: If margarine is substituted for butter, use only $1\frac{1}{2}$ oz.

BUTTERSCOTCH

1 lb. Demerara sugar	2–4 oz. fresh butter
$\frac{1}{4}$ pint water	

Put the sugar and water into a saucepan, dissolve slowly, and boil to 280° F., wiping down the sides of the pan with a brush dipped in water during the process. Add the butter a little at a time, pour into an oiled tin or on to an oiled slab between oiled bars, and when half set, mark into squares. Store in an airtight tin.

Note: Margarine does not give as satisfactory a result as butter in this recipe.

CREAMY TOFFEE

1 lb. sugar	1 tsp. cream of tartar
$\frac{1}{4}$ pint water	4 tbsps. thick fresh cream
2 oz. glucose	

Put the sugar and water into a thick pan and heat very gently, to dissolve the sugar. Bring to the boil, add the glucose and cream of tartar, and heat to 250° F. Warm the cream separately, then add it very slowly to the boiling mixture, stirring occasionally, until it has all been added. Stand the pan on an asbestos mat and very slowly bring the mixture to 270° F. Have a greased tin ready, pour the mixture into the tin and leave to set. When half-set, mark into squares; break it into pieces when it is quite cold. Wrap and store as usual.

GOLDEN TOFFEE

2 lb. loaf sugar	6 oz. butter
$\frac{1}{2}$ pint water	4 tbsps. glucose

Put all the ingredients into a covered saucepan and bring to the boil. Boil for a few minutes, remove the lid, and without stirring bring the syrup to a temperature of 300° F. or until the mixture becomes brittle when a little is dropped into cold water. Pour into oiled tins or on to an oiled slab between oiled bars, and cool. When cool, mark into squares with a greased knife or caramel cutter, taking care that the toffee is sufficiently cold to keep the impression of the knife or cutter. If it is not cool enough the marks will not be retained, and if too cold the toffee will have to be broken up into uneven pieces. If marked at the right stage, however, the toffee can be broken when cold into neat squares or oblongs. Wrap in waxed paper or Cellophane. Store in an airtight tin.

HONEYCOMB TOFFEE

¼ pint cold water	3 tbsps. golden syrup
1 lb. loaf sugar	1 tsp. bicarbonate of soda
A pinch of cream of tartar	1 dessertsp. warm water

Put the cold water, sugar, cream of tartar and golden syrup into a strong saucepan and put on a low gas. Stir occasionally with the thermometer until the sugar has dissolved. Boil without stirring until the mixture reaches 310° F. Remove the saucepan from the heat, mix the bicarbonate of soda in the dessertsp. of warm water and add to the boiling toffee. Stir gently and pour at once into a greased tin or on an oiled slab between oiled bars. Mark when half-set.

PEPPERMINT HUMBUGS

½ pint water	3 oz. butter or 2 oz. margarine
2 lb. Demerara sugar	Oil of peppermint
4 tbsps. golden syrup	
½ tsp. cream of tartar	

Put the water, sugar, syrup, cream of tartar and butter into a strong pan, dissolve quickly, then cover, bring to the boil, and boil rapidly for a few minutes without stirring. Then remove the lid and wash down the sides of the pan with a brush dipped in cold water, repeating this process if necessary until the syrup reaches a temperature of 290° F. Pour on to an oiled marble slab or an oiled tin, and leave to cool for a short time. Pour 1 tsp. of the oil of peppermint on to the toffee. Oil the hands slightly and fold the sides into the centre, pulling until the desired shade is reached. This process can be carried out more readily by throwing the toffee over a hook fixed at a convenient height in the wall. Finally, pull the toffee into an even roll about 1 inch in diameter, cut into cushions, and allow to cool on an oiled enamel table or tin. When cold, wrap in Cellophane and keep in an airtight jar or tin, if possible.

STRIPED PEPPERMINT HUMBUGS

2 lb. Demerara sugar	½ tsp. cream of tartar
3 oz. butter or 2 oz. margarine	3 tbsps. golden syrup
½ pint water	Oil of peppermint

Put all the ingredients, except the oil of peppermint, into the saucepan. Dissolve the sugar thoroughly over moderate heat and then bring to a temperature of 290° F. Pour on to a greased slab or tin, and allow to cool a little. With a greased palette knife, fold the sides into the centre, adding the peppermint. When cool enough to handle, cut off one-third and pull until pale in colour, but still soft. Meanwhile, gently fold the larger amount sides to middle and form into a thick roll without pulling more than can be helped. When the light-coloured strip is ready, divide quickly into four and press on to the outside of the roll. Pull out evenly and gently to the required size. Cut into cushions with oiled scissors.

It is essential to handle the toffee quickly and, until experience is gained, two people should work together.

TOFFEE CUSHIONS

1 lb. loaf sugar	3 tbsps. golden syrup
¼ pint water	2 oz. butter
1 tsp. vinegar	

Put all the ingredients in a strong, unlined pan. Dissolve quickly and bring to the boil with the lid on. After boiling for a few minutes, remove the lid, wipe down the sides of the pan with a brush dipped in water, and boil the syrup to 290° F., or until the toffee becomes brittle when a little is dropped into cold water. Do not stir while heating or the toffee may become sugary. Pour into an oiled tin and allow to cool, but not to set. As soon as it begins to set, oil
the hands and remove the soft toffee from the 141
tin. Pull between the hands or throw over a greased hook fixed at a convenient height in a wall. The pulling and folding should be continued either with the hands or over the hook until the toffee becomes silvery. Then pull into a roll about 1 inch in diameter. Cut into pieces with a pair of oiled scissors and allow to fall on to a greased tin or enamelled table top, keeping each piece separate. When cold, roll in waxed paper or Cellophane. Store the sweets in an airtight tin.

Coloured cushions are quite easily obtained by colouring the hot toffee before pulling it. Pale pinks, greens and mauves are particularly attractive in these pulled toffees.

POPCORN TOFFEE SQUARES

1 lb. granulated sugar
¼ pint water
1 quart popped corn (2 oz. corn)

First of all pop the corn according to the directions on the tin or packet, and spread it in a greased tin. Dissolve the sugar in the water, bring to the boil, and heat till it is golden-brown (310° F.), then pour it over the popcorn. When the toffee is half set, mark it into squares; when cold, break into pieces and put into a tin with an airtight lid.

TREACLE TOFFEE

1½ lb. brown sugar
8 oz. butter
1 lb. treacle
⅓ pint water
A pinch of cream of tartar

Put all the ingredients, except the cream of tartar, into a pan, cover and bring to the boil rapidly. When the toffee boils, add the cream of tartar dissolved in a little cold water. Replace the lid, continue boiling for a few minutes longer, remove the lid, wash down the sides of the pan with a brush dipped in cold water, then boil to 260° F. (or until a drop of the mixture forms a hard ball in cold water). Pour into oiled tins or on to an oiled slab between oiled bars to cool, mark with a knife, break into squares when cold, and wrap and store as usual.

CARAMELS, TABLETS AND NOUGATS

Caramel mixtures are basically very similar to fudges, except that they are not grained but are heated to a temperature of between 245° and 255° F. With caramels it is easier to test by dropping a little of the mixture in cold water rather than by the thermometer—a soft ball will give a soft caramel and a firm ball a hard caramel. The general rules for sugar boiling should be observed, but since the mixtures are generally rich, containing butter, cream, evaporated milk and so on, they need to be stirred occasionally during cooking. When ready the mixture should be turned out on to an oiled slab between oiled bars and when nearly set, should be marked with a caramel cutter or a knife. Later, the caramels should be divided and wrapped in waxed or Cellophane paper.

Nougat is a white (or pink) type of toffee, containing a generous proportion of nuts, etc. Egg whites are usually included.

PLAIN CARAMELS

1 lb loaf sugar
1 lb. glucose
4 oz. butter
⅓ pint water
Colouring
Flavouring

Place the first four ingredients in a pan and heat rapidly to 250° F., stirring continuously. Colouring and flavouring such as nuts or essences may now be added if desired. Pour into an oiled tin or caramel bars and when set, but not quite cold, turn out, cut into strips, then into squares, with sharp oiled scissors or a caramel cutter. Allow to cool on a greased slab, then wrap neatly in waxed paper and store in tins. If preferred the caramels may be left unwrapped: in which case, the mixture should be raised to 255° F. and the cut caramels should be left to cool on a wire tray, care being taken that they do not touch one another and so stick together.

CREAM CARAMELS

8 oz. soft brown sugar
2 tbsps. water
4 oz. butter
Vanilla essence
3 tbsps. cream

Dissolve the sugar and water. Add the butter, vanilla and cream, and boil to the "ball" degree (about 250° F.). Pour into oiled caramel bars, and when cold mark into squares with a caramel marker or a knife. Cut with a sharp knife and wrap neatly in waxed paper.

CARAMELLED ALMONDS

7 oz. loaf sugar
1 dessertsp. water
2 oz. blanched and split almonds

Dissolve the sugar and water in a strong pan, preferably of copper, and heat gently until it becomes a light coffee colour. Care must be taken, or the caramel will quickly turn colour and burn. Stir in the split almonds, pour into an oiled tin and spread with a spoon until it is ¼ inch thick. When nearly set, mark into small squares, and when cold wrap in waxed paper or Cellophane. Store in an airtight tin. Caramelled almonds do not keep crisp for any length of time, so it is advisable to make small quantities as required.

COCONUT TABLET

½ pint milk and water
1 oz. butter
2 lb. loaf sugar
½ tsp. cream of tartar
¼ lb. desiccated coconut

Put the milk and water, butter and sugar into the pan and dissolve, stirring frequently. Add the cream of tartar and stir occasionally. Boil to a temperature of 245° F., then stir in the coconut and boil again to 245° F., stirring occasionally after adding the coconut. Cool a little and then stir with either a wooden spoon or spatula until creamy and white. Pour into an oiled tin and cut into bars when cool.

FIG TABLET

This is made as above, 4 oz. finely chopped figs being substituted for the coconut.

HAZEL TABLET

2 lb. Demerara sugar
½ pint cold water
1 tsp. vanilla essence
3 oz. chopped hazelnuts

Dissolve the sugar in the water quickly, bring to the boil and continue boiling until a temperature of 245° F. is reached. Add the vanilla essence and nuts, and boil until a temperature of 245° F. has again been reached. Allow to cool a little, then beat until well grained but liquid. Pour into a greased tin, and when nearly set, cut into neat pieces.

GINGER TABLET

Use the same ingredients as for Hazel Tablet, but omit the nuts and vanilla essence and add ½ oz. of ground ginger. This must be measured very carefully, or the tablet will be too hot in flavour. There is no need to boil a second time; just cool a little and beat after adding ginger.

WALNUT TABLET

¼ pint milk
1 lb. loaf sugar
2 oz. golden syrup
1 oz. butter
2 oz. chopped walnuts
1 tsp. vanilla essence

Heat the milk, sugar, syrup and butter slowly, stirring occasionally until the sugar mixture boils. Boil to 245° F., then stir in the walnuts and essence. Stir with a wooden spoon or spatula until thick and creamy. Pour into an oiled tin: cut into bars when nearly cold.

NOUGAT—I

1 lb. honey or golden syrup
4 egg whites
Rice paper
4 oz. whole glacé cherries
½ lb. whole blanched almonds
1 oz. whole blanched pistachios
½ lb. whole hazelnuts (skinned)

For the Syrup

1 lb. loaf sugar
¼ pint water
Vanilla essence

Put the honey into a basin and melt over a pan of water. Add the stiffly beaten egg whites and stir well over a pan of gently boiling water until the mixture will form a hard ball. Avoid overheating, and stir continually to hasten the reducing (this will take about 1½ hours). Meanwhile, line a tin with rice paper, moistening the edges with water to make the side strips stick. When the honey mixture is nearly ready, heat the sugar and water and cook to 280°–285° F. (the "crack"), adding the vanilla essence when the syrup is nearly cooked. Heat the fruit and nuts on a tray in the oven. Pour the sugar mixture on to the honey by degrees and beat. Then add the prepared fruits and nuts. Turn on to marble, well sprinkled with icing sugar, and press well together to make it compact. Press into the tin, cover with rice paper, put a weight on it and stand for 24 hours. When cold, cut with a sharp, hot knife.

NOUGAT—II

3 oz. golden syrup or honey
3 egg whites
¾ lb. loaf sugar
¼ pint water
2 oz. glucose
2 oz. glacé cherries
Vanilla essence
3 oz. blanched and chopped almonds
1 doz. blanched pistachio nuts

Melt the honey or syrup in a basin over a pan of hot water, add the stiffly beaten egg whites and beat occasionally until thick and white. Meanwhile, make a syrup in the usual way, adding the glucose when the sugar has dissolved. Boil to 265° F., then add the syrup to the honey mixture, whisking steadily. Add the vanilla essence, fruit and nuts. Pour on to rice paper between bars, put a second sheet of rice paper on top, and when set, cut into bars or small cubes.

RUSSIAN CARAMELS

3–4 oz. butter
3 oz. caster sugar
3 oz. golden syrup
2 large tins sweetened condensed milk
1 tsp. vanilla essence

Oil the butter in a saucepan, stir in the sugar, golden syrup and milk. Cook, stirring continuously and very thoroughly round the bottom and sides of the pan, until thick and lightly browned (238°–240° F.). The caramel may be tested in cold water, and if a soft ball is formed it is ready. (If a firmer caramel is preferred, continue cooking until a harder ball is formed or a temperature of 245°–250° F. is reached.) Add the vanilla essence and turn on to an oiled slab or tin. When firm, mark with an oiled roller, stamp lightly with an oiled marker, and cut up into squares. Rub off the oil with absorbent paper and wrap in waxed tissue.

SOFT VANILLA CARAMELS

1 lb. sugar
¼ pint milk
4 oz. liquid glucose
8 oz. unsweetened condensed milk
2 oz. cocoa butter (melted)
Vanilla essence
4 oz. fine coconut (optional)

Place the sugar and milk in a large pan and heat slowly until dissolved, then bring to the boil, add the liquid glucose and boil to 250° F. Now add the condensed milk slowly, keeping the boiling mixture gently stirred. When the milk is all used, add the cocoa butter, previously melted, and the coconut, if used. Boil up to 255° F., add flavouring and pour into oiled caramel bars ready for cutting when partly set.

MISCELLANEOUS RECIPES

AMERICAN RAISIN CANDY

6 oz. loaf sugar	1 oz. almonds, blanched, chopped and browned
2–3 tsps. water	
3 oz. chopped raisins	

Put the sugar and water into a thick pan and heat gently, tapping the lumps with a spatula but without stirring, until it becomes a golden-brown syrup. Stir in the raisins and nuts, and turn out at once on to an oiled tin. When setting, mark and cut into squares.

CHOCOLATE TRUFFLES

3 oz. chocolate	1 tsp. rum
1 egg yolk	Granular chocolate or chocolate powder
½ oz. butter	
1 tsp. whipped cream	

Just melt the chocolate over hot water, without allowing it to become hot. Add egg yolk, butter, cream and rum. Beat till thick and pasty. Using two teaspoons, form into balls and roll in granular chocolate or chocolate powder.

If they are to be kept for any length of time, roll into balls and leave to dry. Then dip in melted chocolate and roll in chocolate vermicelli or finely chopped nuts.

COCONUT ICE

3 lb. loaf sugar	1 lb. desiccated coconut
¾ pint milk	Colouring

Dissolve the sugar in the milk, then boil for about 10 minutes or until a temperature of 240° F.
142 is reached. Remove the pan from the heat and stir in the coconut. Pour half the mixture into an oiled tin, colour the remainder in the saucepan and pour quickly on to the first half. Mark into bars when half-set.

EDINBURGH ROCK

1½ lb. loaf sugar	Colourings and flavourings
¾ pint water	
Cream of tartar	Icing sugar

Put the sugar and water into a saucepan and dissolve carefully, stirring gently from time to time. Next, add a good pinch of the cream of tartar and bring to a temperature of 258° F. Pour on to a greased slab and allow to cool for a few minutes. Using a fondant scraper, gently lift the sides to the centre and, when cool enough to handle, divide into two. Add colouring and flavouring to each portion. Dip the fingers in icing sugar and gently pull without twisting until the mixture becomes dull. Pull to an even shape and lay on waxed paper. When nearly set, cut into even strips.

If the help of a second worker is available, the mixture may be divided into four—it is inadvisable to attempt to handle more than two portions single-handed.

MARSHMALLOWS

10 oz. granulated sugar	1 egg white
1 dessertsp. glucose	1–2 tbsps. orange flower water
½ pint water	
¾ oz. powdered gelatine	

Dissolve the sugar and glucose in ¼ pint water and boil to 260° F.

Meanwhile, dissolve the gelatine in another ¼ pint water and keep warm. Whisk the egg white stiffly. Pour the gelatine on to the boiling syrup, whisking all the time. Add the orange flower water, and then the egg white, still whisking, and continue whisking until thick and stiff—it may take 20 minutes. While still liquid, pour into a tin lined with greaseproof paper and dredged with icing sugar. When set, cut up with scissors, roll in icing sugar and leave to dry for about 24 hours.

Marshmallow Delight : 1 oz. chopped brown almonds and 1 oz. chopped cherries can be added during the beating.

Lemon Marshmallows : Add a little lemon essence instead of orange flower water, and colour pale yellow.

Peppermint Marshmallows : Add peppermint essence and colour pale green.

PEPPERMINT ICE

1 lb. granulated sugar	Essence of peppermint
¼ pint milk	

Put the sugar and milk into a saucepan and stir until they come to the boil. Stir occasionally until a temperature of 245° F. is reached, or when a little dropped in cold water will form into a soft ball. Remove the mixture from the heat, add 1 tsp. of essence of peppermint and stir evenly until it begins to turn thick. Have ready a wet tin and pour the mixture into this, letting it remain until nearly cold. Cut into neat pieces of equal size. Another way of shaping the ice is to use oiled caramel bars arranged on an oiled slab.

If liked, Peppermint Ice may be coloured green.

RASPBERRY JELLIES

1 lb. loaf sugar	Raspberry essence
½ pint cold water	A few drops of carmine
1 oz. powdered gelatine	Icing sugar

Put the sugar and water into a saucepan and dissolve slowly. Bring to the boil, and boil to 240° F. Soak the gelatine in half a gill of water, dissolve and bring to the boil. Add to the syrup, together with the raspberry flavouring, colour with a few drops of carmine, strain through muslin and pour into wet plates or tins. The liquid should not be more than about 1 inch in thickness. Stand in a cool place to set, then cut into cubes and roll in sieved icing sugar.

CRÈME DE MENTHE JELLIES

Use the same basic ingredients as above, but substitute essence of peppermint and green colouring for raspberry essence and carmine.

TURKISH DELIGHT

1 lb. granulated sugar	2 oz. honey
1½ pints of water	A few drops of lemon extract
½ tsp. tartaric acid	A few drops of rose water
3 oz. cornflour	Pink colouring
7 oz. icing sugar	

Put the sugar and ¼ pint of water into a saucepan and bring to a temperature of 240° F. Add the tartaric acid and stand aside for the short time required to blend the cornflour. Mix the cornflour and icing sugar with a little of the remaining cold water. Boil the rest of the water and when boiling, pour on to the blended cornflour and sugar, stirring hard to prevent lumps forming. Return to the saucepan, boil, and beat vigorously until clear and thick. Then add the syrup gradually, beating meanwhile over the heat. Continue to boil for 20–30 minutes: the time of boiling must not be shortened, as it is essential that the character of the starch be changed, and the prolonged boiling with acid brings about this necessary change. At the end of 30 minutes the mixture should be of a very pale straw colour and transparent. Add the honey and flavourings and blend thoroughly. Pour half the contents of the pan into a buttered tin, colour the remainder pale rose pink and pour it on top of the mixture already in the tin. Stand it aside until quite cold. Dip a sharp knife into icing sugar, cut the mixture into neat pieces and toss in icing sugar. Protect from the dust, and stand aside in the sugar for at least 24 hours before packing. It should be packed in a generous quantity of icing sugar and in boxes.

This recipe produces a Turkish Delight very similar to the genuine oriental variety, but as the latter is made with Turkish wheat, it is impossible to get absolutely identical results.

QUICK TURKISH DELIGHT

1 lb. loaf sugar	Colouring and flavouring essence
¼ pint water	2 oz. icing sugar
1 oz. powdered gelatine	1 oz. cornflour
A few chopped nuts	

Put the sugar and water into a pan, dissolve slowly and boil until a temperature of 240° F. is reached. Soak the gelatine in a little water, dissolve, and bring to the boil. Add to the syrup, with the nuts, colouring and a few drops of orange flower water or other flavouring. Pour into a level tin about 6 inches square and allow to cool and set. When set, dip the tin quickly into hot water. Turn the Turkish Delight out on to a paper spread thickly with 2 oz. sieved icing sugar and 1 oz. cornflour mixed. Coat with this and cut into squares with a knife which has been dipped into hot water. Roll each square very thoroughly in the sugar and cornflour. Pack in tins.

CARAMELLISED FRUITS

½ lb. loaf sugar	A large pinch of cream of tartar
4 tbsps. water	Prepared fruit
1 tsp. glucose	

Make a syrup of the sugar and water in a small, deep saucepan. When the sugar has quite dissolved, add the glucose and cream of tartar. Boil gently until it is golden-brown and a temperature of 290° F. is reached.

Dip the prepared fruit, one piece at a time, into the syrup. Drain well by tapping the dipping fork on the edge of the saucepan and place neatly on an oiled slab until quite dry. Then place in paper cups and serve.

CRYSTALLISED SWEETS

Crystallising, though usually regarded as a somewhat difficult branch of confectionery, is really quite a simple operation if a few elementary but important principles are first grasped.

The utensils already in use for chocolate and general sweetmeat making will serve for practically every purpose, the only essential addition being a crystallising tin—a small square or oblong tin, into which a wire tray with small feet fits easily; the tin has a small screw cap at one corner near the bottom, to enable the syrup to be drained off. Some people like to work with a saccharometer—an instrument for testing the density of syrup—but with ordinary care the sugar thermometer will answer the purpose.

Making the Syrup

Prepare some syrup in the proportion of 2 lb. of loaf sugar to 1 pint water. Dissolve gradually, and when it boils, skim carefully to remove any impurities or, better still, strain through a hair sieve as soon as reduced to syrup. Neither glucose nor cream of tartar is required, and the sugar should be quickly boiled up to 220°–225° F. according to whether a large or a small crystal is desired in the finished sweets: the higher degree results in the larger crystals.

Lift the pan on to a firm, level table and leave the syrup to cool. Cover with a piece of paper which has a small hole cut from the middle. (The paper should rest on the syrup itself, not just over the pan.) On no account must the pan be disturbed, or the syrup will become grainy. It is not necessary for the syrup to be quite cold before being used, but if it is used too hot, it may grain, or in the case of fondant bonbons, the latter will be likely to melt. This method of preparing syrup is suitable for all crystallising work.

Crystallising Bonbons

Prepare the fondants as described on page 428. If rich bonbons are required, use a proportion of cream or full-cream condensed milk with the fondant. Use delicate shades, and flavours and colours which harmonise.

When the fondants are cast and removed from the moulds, pack them quite closely, but not touching, on the wire crystallising tray. Lay another wire tray on top to keep them in the syrup, and set the tin in a warm place, then pour in the cooled syrup at one side of the tin, so as to cover the fondants completely. Cover with a damp cloth, and after about 12 hours, draw off the syrup by removing the small cap at the corner of the tin. (This syrup must not be used again for crystallising, but may be used for various other purposes when syrup is required as an additional ingredient.) The tin is then set in a warm cupboard until the bonbons are covered with a surface of fine sparkling crystals. If a specially thick coating of crystals is required, the fondants may be left in the syrup a few hours longer, or the process may be repeated with fresh syrup.

CANDYING FRUIT

This somewhat resembles candied orange and lemon peel, but has a glossy surface, and is preserved in a sugar syrup so that it remains moist and sticky on the outside. Glacé fruits are used in cakes and sweets, as decorations on sweet dishes and as dessert, particularly at Christmas time. Glacé cherries are the best-known type, but almost any good-quality fruit can be treated in this way.

To Prepare the Fruits

Tinned or fresh fruit may be used: fresh fruit should first be stewed gently with a little water until tender. Make up the syrup from the fruit to 1 pint by adding water; add ¾ lb. sugar and stir gently over a very low heat until the sugar has dissolved. If a hydrometer is available, test the strength of the syrup, which should register 25° Beaumé scale. If the reading is below the right degree, add more sugar—if above, more water. Re-boil and re-adjust until the correct degree is attained. Place the fruit in a bowl, pour the syrup over it, keep the fruit under the syrup with a big saucer or a plate and leave for 24 hours. The process then consists of re-boiling the syrup at intervals, the strength being gradually increased, as shown in the table below.

Day	*Sugar to add (for ½ lb. fruit)*	*Beaumé Reading*	*Soak for:*
1st	½ lb. to ½ pint syrup or water	25°	24 hrs.
2nd	2 oz. dissolved in syrup and reboiled	26°	24 hrs.
3rd	Ditto	27°	24 hrs.
4th	Ditto	29°	24 hrs.
5th	3 oz. dissolved in syrup. Add fruit and reboil 3–4 minutes	33°	48 hrs.
7th	Ditto	35°	3–4 days
10th–11th	Drain fruit from syrup, put on a rack and dry slowly in a warm place or very cool oven.		

After the final drying the fruit is ready, but a more professional result is obtained by giving a glacé or a crystallised finish as described below.

Glacé Finish

Dissolve 1 lb. sugar in ¼ pint water and stir carefully over a low heat. (The syrup remaining after the candying process must not be used for this purpose.) When the sugar is dissolved, bring to the boil undisturbed, and test the strength of the syrup with a hydrometer : it should register 35° Beaumé. If necessary, add a little more water or sugar to bring to the correct strength. Have ready a clean cake rack over a tin. Pour a little syrup into a cup, dip the pieces of fruit in one at a time, using a skewer or dipping fork, and put on the rack to dry. Keep the syrup in the pan warm and covered with a damp cloth (a double pan will be found convenient for the purpose). As the syrup in the cup gets cloudy, replace it with fresh. After dipping, dry the fruit as before, turning from time to time.

This process can also be applied to candied fruits.

Crystallised Finish

Prepare some crystallising syrup as described on page 440. Arrange the glacé or candied fruit on a cake tray or rack and place in a deep tin. Put a second rack firmly on top of the fruit and pour the syrup over gently. If necessary a clean weight should be put on the rack to keep it in position over the fruit. Cover with a damp cloth and leave for 12–18 hours, when crystals will be seen on the surface. Remove the top rack and lift out the one containing the fruit. Allow to drain, then dry in a warm place.

TO CANDY ANGELICA

Pick the green shoots in April or May, drop them straight into brine (¼ oz. salt to 4 pints water), and leave to soak for 10 minutes to preserve the green colour. Rinse in cold water.

Cook the angelica in boiling water until quite tender—about 5–7 minutes. Drain, and scrape to remove outer skin.

Using the water the angelica was boiled in, make a syrup of 6 oz. sugar to ½ pint of the juice ; place the angelica in a bowl, add the syrup, cover and leave for 24 hours.

Drain off the syrup, add 2 oz. of sugar to every ½ pint of the original juice and bring to the boil ; pour back into the bowl over the angelica, cover and leave for 24 hours.

Repeat the process described in the last paragraph a further five times, until the syrup is of the consistency of running honey. Boil the angelica for 2–3 minutes at the last addition of the sugar, then leave for 2 days. Dry off on a hot rack or in a very cool oven (150° F.). Store in screw-top jars.

The following alternative method is simpler and quicker :

Choose tender stalks and cut them in pieces 3–4 inches long. Place in a pan with sufficient water to cover, bring to the boil, simmer until tender and bright green, then dry in a cloth. Put in a pan with 1 lb. sugar to each lb. of stalks, cover, and leave to stand for 2 days. Bring slowly to the boil, continue to boil until the angelica is clear and green, then put in a colander to drain. Toss the stalks in fine sugar, and let them dry off in a cool oven before storing.

MARRONS GLACÉS

2 lb. Italian chestnuts	Vanilla essence
Lemon juice	A pinch of cream of tartar
1 pint water	
2 lb. sugar	Glacéing syrup (see below)
2 tsps. glucose	

Score the chestnuts, put into boiling water and boil for 5 minutes. Skin, and place in warm water to which a squeeze of lemon juice has been added. Boil very gently until tender. Lift out carefully and dry well. Boil ½ pint of water, 1 lb. sugar and 1 tsp. of glucose to a temperature of 218° F. Add vanilla essence and pour this over the chestnuts, cover and leave in a warm place for two days. On the third day drain the chestnuts well and prepare a syrup consisting of the remaining 1 lb. sugar, ½ pint of water and a pinch of cream of tartar. Boil these ingredients to 230° F., and when the syrup is ready, put in the nuts and just bring to the boil. Lift out the nuts and drain well. Put on a rack to dry in a warm place. When quite dry, prepare the glacéing syrup, boiling together 1 lb. sugar, ¼ pint water and 1 tsp. glucose until the syrup reaches 225° F. Add the nuts, bring to the boil again and stir the syrup until it grains slightly. Lift out the nuts and place on an oiled tin

CHOCOLATE MAKING

Anyone who wishes to become really expert at this very specialised branch of sweet making, must be prepared to study the subject thoroughly and to devote a considerable amount of time to practising it. Special equipment also is necessary. However, if you want to try your hand at chocolate making, you can do so using ordinary kitchen equipment, and will probably be quite pleased with the results.

HOME-MADE CHOCOLATES

The centres can be made of marzipan, toffee, caramel, fudge, fondant, nuts, etc. For chocolate dipping, you will need couverture chocolate (i.e., covering chocolate, which is good quality plain block chocolate, containing an adequate proportion of cocoa butter). A dry warm day must be chosen; success depends on melting the chocolate so gently that it is never hotter than blood heat (using a special chocolate-dipping pan, with water jacket, or failing that an ordinary double boiler), and on not allowing any moisture (either steam or splashes of water) to reach the chocolate. The most even temperature is obtained by melting the chocolate (previously finely cut up or shredded) very gently until liquid; beating it until cold and of a jelly consistency; then remelting it. It is then ready for dipping.

The temperature is all-important. The most practical method of testing it is by tasting the chocolate; it should feel slightly cool on the tongue. If it is too warm, the chocolate will dry cloudy and white; if too cool, it will coat the centres too thickly. The chocolates are dipped one at a time, using a fork, and dropped on to waxed paper. They can be finished by marking with the prongs of the dipping fork or by decorating with nuts, fruits, silver balls, etc.

CHOCOLATE EASTER EGGS

Use good quality couverture chocolate and prepare it as for chocolate dipping, first melting it to a jelly consistency, then beating until cold before remelting. Rub out the inside of the Easter egg moulds with cotton wool, half-fill with the chocolate and tilt so as to run the couverture to the edge of the mould quite evenly all round. Do this two or three times, then pour the surplus back into the chocolate pan. Run the finger round the edge of the mould, then turn upside down on a cool flat surface. As the shells cool, they will contract slightly and may be removed by pressing gently at one end. The outer glazed surface caused by the contact with the bright tin must not be handled more than can be helped. The shells can be joined by lightly touching the two halves on to a warm, flat tin, so that just sufficient chocolate melts to enable them to set firmly together.

Wrap the eggs in tinfoil, or decorate them with ribbon, sugar or chocolate piping and so on.

SANDWICHES AND PACKED MEALS

Sandwiches may be cut in numerous varieties of shapes and sizes to suit different occasions, ranging from a snack meal to afternoon tea. They can be made open or covered, they may be served either hot or cold, and the base may be cold and the filling hot, or vice versa. Rolls, etc., may be used as alternatives to bread, and toast, hot rolls, scones, or Scotch pancakes and waffles are all excellent for sandwiches which are to be served hot; buns and cakes, provided they are not too sweet, may be cut in thin slices and used for sweet sandwiches.

If you make sandwiches frequently, you will be wise to invest in a knife specially designed for slicing bread, i.e., with a saw or serrated edge, or if you prefer to use an ordinary blade, you need a good knife sharpener, so that you can keep it well sharpened. A pastry board is good for cutting the bread and laying out the slices ready for spreading. Fancy cutters may be used for making dainty novelty tea-time and bridge party sandwiches.

MAKING SANDWICHES

When making sandwiches, complete each of the following operations in turn, so far as possible.

Preparing the Filling

Meat should be minced or cut small, and vegetables, apples, nuts, herbs, etc., should be chopped, shredded, or grated. On occasions when sandwiches have to be made in advance, avoid very moist fillings, which soak into the bread or biscuits.

Cutting

If possible, use bread which is 24 hours old (except for rolled sandwiches, which require very fresh bread, otherwise they break in rolling). If you have to use very fresh bread, chill it well in the refrigerator before attempting to slice it, and see that the knife is very sharp. (It sometimes helps to dip the knife in hot water from time to time when slicing fresh bread.)

The thickness of the slices depends on their use; they should be very thin for afternoon tea sandwiches, and up to ¼ inch thick for sandwiches to serve as a snack meal. A small loaf (approximately 1 lb.) cuts 20–25 slices and requires about ¼ lb. butter; a large loaf (approximately 2 lb.) cuts 50–60 slices and requires about ½ lb. butter; a 3-lb. sandwich loaf cuts 70–80 slices and requires approximately ¾ lb. butter.

It is usually possible to buy sandwich loaves already sliced, which is very useful when a large number of sandwiches have to be made in a short time.

Whether the crusts are removed or not is a matter of taste, and also depends on when the sandwiches are to be served. Tea and party sandwiches are usually served without them, but for snacks, lunch boxes, and picnics, the crusts are generally left on. Cut off crusts at the last possible moment, to prevent the edges of the sandwiches from drying. Use the crusts for puddings made with bread, or dry them to make raspings.

Spreading and Filling

The butter (or margarine) for sandwiches should be worked with a spoon or knife until soft and creamy; in cold weather it may be warmed slightly to help to soften it, but it must not be oiled. When softened, it is easier to spread without tearing the bread; also it spreads more evenly, which is important, especially when sandwiches must be made in advance (for picnics or lunch boxes), since the butter helps to prevent the filling from soaking into the bread. The sandwiches are always nicer if both slices of bread are buttered; if, for the sake of economy, only one side of the sandwich is to be buttered, choose a filling that is not very moist, such as meat or fish pastes, cheese spread, and so on. Mixing the softened butter with the filling, or with part of it (e.g., paste, chopped or grated fillings, white sauce, mayonnaise, etc.), saves time when there are many sandwiches to spread.

For very thin sandwiches, spreading the butter on to the bread before slicing helps in cutting the bread thinly without tearing it, but for thicker sandwiches it is quicker to slice the bread and spread it afterwards: take the slices of bread in pairs, as they come from the loaf, and lay them out on the board ready for spreading, so that adjacent slices can be paired and will fit neatly.

There is an almost endless variety of ingredients suitable for sandwich fillings, and many suggestions and recipes are given here. In addition, one can buy meat and fish pastes, mayonnaise sandwich spreads, cheese spreads, relishes, and so on, which are useful to have as a stand-by. The fillings should be spread thinly for tea sandwiches, and more generously for lunch or picnic sandwiches. If the crusts are to be removed, avoid spreading the filling to the outer edge, where it will be cut off with the crusts.

Serving Sandwiches

Sandwiches for picnics, lunches, or suppers are easily eaten if cut diagonally in halves or quarters. Dainty sandwiches for teas or parties may be cut with fancy cutters, though this is rather extravagant, leaving many trimmings to be used up. An alternative is to cut with a knife into tiny squares, strips, fingers, diamonds, etc. It is a good idea to cut the slices lengthwise for this purpose.

To keep the sandwiches fresh, cover them with a basin or a damp cloth until required. When several varieties of filling are used, the type should be indicated by the garnish or by a sandwich flag.

When making sandwiches in advance of serving them, wrap them in waxed paper, parchment paper, or Cellophane, then in a damp towel, and put them in the refrigerator or cold larder. An alternative method is to keep the sandwiches in the covered rectangular container (i.e., the vegetable crisper), with which most refrigerators are equipped.

To keep open sandwiches, line a shallow tin with waxed paper and lay the sandwiches close together, but without stacking them. Cover first with a sheet of waxed paper, then with a damp towel, and place immediately in the refrigerator or cold larder. Alternatively, open sandwiches can be glazed thinly with liquid aspic jelly over the filling; this gives them an attractive appearance and prevents them drying. In either case, leave the final touches of decorating and garnishing until dishing the sandwiches.

Wrap sandwiches for the picnic basket or lunch box in waxed paper. If there are many different kinds, some sweet and some savoury, it is as well to label the packets.

Collapsible sandwich tins are ideal for walkers, since they can be folded flat and carried home in the pocket.

Left-Over Sandwiches

If there are a few sandwiches left over, wrap them in waxed paper and place in the refrigerator or larder until later, when they can be served fried, or may be spread on the outside with butter or margarine and toasted under the grill. An alternative is to make left-over sandwiches into Snippet Pie: a basic recipe is given in the Economical Cookery chapter.

TYPES OF SANDWICH

ROLLED SANDWICHES

The bread must be very fresh, and it will be found easier to cut if the crust is cut off before slicing. Slice the bread as thinly as possible, spreading on the butter before slicing. Spread with filling and roll up neatly. For decoration, the ends may be dipped in finely chopped parsley, sieved egg yolk, coralline pepper, and so on.

Asparagus Tips Rolls: Have the asparagus tips slightly longer than the bread is wide. Roll up each asparagus tip in a piece of bread and butter so that the tip projects slightly. Dip the other end in mayonnaise and chopped parsley.

Sausage and Gherkin Rolls: Grill or fry some small chipolata sausages and allow them to cool. Roll up a sausage and a little chopped gherkin into each piece of bread and butter.

Prawn Cream Rolls: Chop some prawns roughly and mix with a little whipped cream or mayonnaise, and season well. Put about 1 tsp. of the mixture on each piece of bread and butter, roll up, and decorate with a prawn head peeping out of the end of the roll.

Rolled Bread and Butter: Buttered bread may be rolled without any filling and served in place of ordinary bread and butter, the idea being that the rolls can be eaten easily without the fingers becoming buttery.

PINWHEEL SANDWICHES

Make large rolled sandwiches with slices cut

lengthwise off the loaf, and then cut them across to give a " Swiss roll " effect.

BREAD BARS

Cut ½-inch slices of bread into bars and spread the whole outside surface with the sandwich mixture. Roll the bars in chopped parsley, chopped nuts, or sieved egg yolks, etc.

NEAPOLITAN SANDWICHES

Prepare thin bread and butter, both brown and white, and three or four savoury fillings of contrasting colours, for example, tomato, liver pâté, watercress, and egg. Spread a piece of the bread and butter with one of the fillings and cover with a second piece of bread, buttered side down. Now butter the top, spread with one of the other fillings and cover with a third piece of bread and butter. Continue in this way, building up a large block of alternate layers of bread and butter and filling, working the different colours in rotation. Cut off the crust and press well. Wrap the whole block in waxed paper and leave it in a cool place for some hours, weighted slightly. When required, cut into slices across the filling, making sandwiches of many coloured stripes. Arrange the sandwiches on a plate to show the striped effect.

HARLEQUIN SANDWICHES

These are made by using two kinds of bread in each sandwich—white bread for one side, with brown or wholemeal bread the other, or, for sweet sandwiches, white or milk bread on one side and malt bread or other sweet brown bread on the other. Any kind of filling can be used for these sandwiches, which may be cut into shapes with fancy cutters.

THREE-DECKER SANDWICHES

These are made with three slices of bread and butter and two different fillings. They are suitable for a snack lunch or supper.

Spread one piece of the bread and butter with one of the fillings and cover with a second piece of bread and butter, buttered side down. Butter the top of this piece, spread with the second filling, and cover with the remaining piece of bread and butter.

Good combinations for these sandwiches are :

Chopped cooked ham or bacon, with well-seasoned scrambled egg.

Flaked salmon moistened with mayonnaise or whipped seasoned cream, with thinly sliced cucumber seasoned with salt, pepper, and vinegar.

Chopped grilled ham or sausages, with sweet chutney.

Cream cheese, with chopped celery or finely grated young carrot seasoned with salt and pepper.

TOASTED SANDWICHES

The ingredients to fill these sandwiches must be already cooked and the bread must not be so thick as to prevent the heat penetrating through to the filling. Make the sandwich in the ordinary way, then toast under a hot grill until well browned, turning to cook the underside.

Any variety of savoury filling can be used : shredded cheese, thin slices of cooked meat, flaked fish, etc. The sandwiches can vary in size from small cocktail fingers to substantial snack-meal sandwiches. The following fillings are particularly good : bacon and mushrooms, prawns and curry butter ; sausage and tomato.

Other hot sandwiches may be made with rolls baked in the oven, with bread that has been toasted on one side, or with hot waffles, pancakes, or drop scones.

OPEN SANDWICHES

If bread is used, it is best cut in fancy shapes. Halved scones and crispbread are attractive if surmounted by coloured foodstuffs, held in position by the butter spread. Unsweetened biscuits are another useful stand-by as a base for open sandwiches. They are particularly good for " spread-your-own " parties, when guests are given a choice of several sandwich fillings in bowls, with an assortment of biscuits, which they spread for themselves : in this way the biscuits keep crisp. If preferred, they may, of course, be served already spread, in which case they should not be prepared until the last possible moment ; the biscuits soon become soggy when spread, particularly if the filling is a moist one.

SMŒRREBRŒD

This is one of the most important features in the Scandinavian catering world. It has no English equivalent, though the open sandwich is the nearest approach. The word " smœrrebrœd " means literally " smeared bread," or pieces of bread with something laid on.

The foundation of " smœrrebrœd " is bread, evenly cut and spread with plenty of good butter. Different kinds of bread can be used according to individual taste, rye bread being the prime favourite, and the shape of the pieces can also be varied. On the top of the bread can be arranged almost any kind of dainty morsel. An assortment of different kinds of " smœrrebrœd " can be made to look very attractive. They also make a very handy and tasty meal, which is easily served and eaten and entails very little washing up.

Suggestions for Smœrrebrœd

Delicately cut slices of cold meat—ham, veal, tongue, roast or spiced beef, sausages, etc., garnished with strips of green or red pepper or grated horseradish.

Small pieces or slices of cooked fish with a garnish of cucumber, or a little mayonnaise salad.

A mixed salad, made of different kinds of vegetables, cut small and blended with mayonnaise.

Picked shrimps or prawns, sardines or anchovies with appropriate seasoning.

Slices of radish, tomato, cucumber or beetroot, seasoned and suitably garnished.

Thin slices of cheese.

Hard-boiled egg, cut in thin slices and garnished with strips of anchovy or marinaded herring.

Slices of cold game garnished with tart red jelly.

Slices of roast goose or duck with pieces of stewed apple, stoned prunes or pickled red cabbage.

SUGGESTIONS FOR SANDWICH FILLINGS

In addition to a single filling such as meat, egg, cheese, etc., many unusual and interesting fillings may be achieved by combining two, three or even more ingredients, as in the examples given below. All ingredients such as gherkins, celery, olives, etc., should be chopped small.

Meat and Poultry

Minced mutton and mint sauce.

Minced beef and horseradish sauce.

Beef with horseradish sauce and onion, or gherkins and French mustard.

Fried bacon and chopped pickled onions.

Minced cooked liver and bacon with mustard.

Chicken or other white meat with celery and mayonnaise, or olives and tomato sauce.

Minced chicken and ham.

Tongue and chopped olives.

Fish

Cooked smoked haddock and parsley sauce.

Flaked crab and capers.

Kipper and mustard.

Any cooked white fish and chopped pickled walnuts.

Fish with tomato sauce and onion (or pickle), shredded cabbage and mayonnaise.

Salmon, mashed potato, and cucumber.

Salmon, or smoked salmon with lettuce and lemon juice, or cucumber and tomato sauce.

Finely chopped shrimps, mayonnaise, and lettuce.

Oysters with cress and cream cheese.

Crab, lobster, and other shellfish with cress and cucumber, or tomato and mayonnaise.

Caviare with olives.

Smoked cod's roe with tomato, lettuce, and lemon juice.

Egg

Scrambled egg, well seasoned, with chopped chives or parsley.

Scrambled egg, well seasoned, with small cress.

Chopped hard-boiled eggs mixed with melted butter, with French dressing and piquant sauce to flavour.

Chopped hard-boiled eggs with lemon juice, chopped parsley and mayonnaise.

Scrambled egg with anchovy essence and chopped watercress.

Egg (hard-boiled, scrambled or fried) with cream cheese and chives, or capers and tomato sauce.

Cheese

Grated cheese with made mustard and sharp table sauce.

Grated cheese with melted butter and chopped capers.

Grated cheese with vegetable extract, butter, and chopped parsley.

Cream cheese with chopped nuts, lemon juice, and chopped parsley.

Cream cheese with chopped green peppers and chopped onion.

Various kinds of cheese with celery and pickles, chives and parsley, or apple and chutney.

Salad and Vegetable

Finely shredded raw cabbage, mayonnaise, and a little grated horseradish.

Grated raw carrot, shredded celery, and mayonnaise.

Grated raw carrot and chutney.

Tomato and chopped watercress with mayonnaise.

Lettuce and chopped chives and mayonnaise.

Butter, creamed with anchovy paste, and chopped watercress.

Raw grated carrot, peanut butter, and mayonnaise.

Chopped pickled onions and grated cheese.

Fried mushrooms, tomato, and parsley.

Cooked peas, mint, and mayonnaise.

Onions, lettuce, and vinegar.

Pickled onion, cucumber, and piquant sauce.

Apple, grated onion, and mayonnaise.

Sweet Mixtures

Minced stoned dates and minced walnuts blended with cream.

Chocolate spread with chopped sultanas or raisins and chopped apple.

Mashed bananas with lemon juice, sugar, and grated chocolate.

Peanut butter with chopped dates and honey.

Cream cheese with grated orange rind and orange juice.

Chopped olives with chopped seedless raisins.

Chopped crystallised ginger with whipped cream, lemon juice, and sugar.

Apple, nutmeg, and brown sugar.

Mashed banana and chopped raisins and orange juice.

Dried fruit, peanut butter, and sliced orange.

Dates, ginger, and chopped apple.

Chopped nuts, honey, and orange or lemon juice.

SANDWICH BUTTERS

ANCHOVY BUTTER

5 anchovies — Lemon juice
2 oz. butter — Pink colouring

Wash the anchovies, remove all bones, and dry. Pound them with the butter and add a squeeze of lemon. Rub through a very fine sieve. Colour if necessary. Use for savoury biscuits, sandwiches, and so on.

CHUTNEY BUTTER

2 oz. smooth-textured chutney, such as apple, or tomato — 2 oz. butter — ¼ tsp. lemon or lime juice

Put all the ingredients into a basin and work with a wooden spoon until well blended. Keep in a jar or basin.

Savoury butters of this type will be found delicious if used in place of plain butter and served either alone or with other fillings.

DEVILLED BUTTER

2 oz. butter — A little cayenne
A squeeze of lemon juice — ½ tsp. curry powder
A pinch of pepper

Blend thoroughly with a wooden spoon.

GREEN BUTTER

½ oz. watercress — Salt and cayenne
2 oz. butter — Green colouring

Wash the watercress, pound in a mortar, and press through a hair sieve. Cream the butter, add the sieved cress and seasoning, and colour if necessary. Use as a spread for biscuit or pastry savouries, for sandwiches and so on.

LOBSTER BUTTER

Pound ½ oz. lobster coral with 1 oz. butter, and pass the mixture through a sieve.

HOME-MADE PASTES, ETC

BLOATER PASTE

2 bloaters — Salt and pepper
Butter — Melted butter to cover

Cook the bloaters either by baking in a moderate oven or by poaching in water. Remove the skin and bones whilst the fish is still hot and rub the flesh through a sieve. Weigh the sieved fish and add to it an equal weight of butter. Pound both well together, or, if a pestle and mortar are not available, cream the butter and work in the fish gradually but thoroughly. Season to taste and press tightly into small glass jars. Cover with melted butter and store in a cold place. Keep for a few days only.

CHEESE AND TOMATO PASTE

2 large tomatoes — 4 oz. breadcrumbs
1 oz. butter — Seasoning
2–4 oz. grated cheese — 1 tsp. mustard
1 egg — Clarified fat to cover

Peel the tomatoes and cook in butter for 5 minutes. Then add the cheese, egg, crumbs, and seasoning, and heat through carefully. Pound mixture well, pack into pots, and cover with clarified fat. Keep cool, and use within 3–4 days.

COD'S ROE PASTE

Wash the roe well, tie in muslin, and cook

gently in boiling salted water for ½–1 hour, according to size. Drain. Melt 2–3 oz. butter in a pan. Add the roe and seasoning, and stir over gentle heat for 5 minutes, then pound and sieve the mixture. Use as required, for croûtes, canapés, savoury biscuits, and so on, or as a sandwich spread.

LIVER PASTE

¾ lb. liver	½ pint stock or water
1 oz. flour	Salt and pepper
1 oz. dripping	A bouquet garni
1 onion	A little melted butter

Cut the liver into slices, removing the pipes, and coat with the flour. Melt the dripping in a saucepan or casserole, and fry the liver lightly. Add the sliced onion, sauté for a few minutes, then stir in the remainder of the flour. Add the stock and seasoning, and bring to the boil, stirring. Add a bunch of herbs and a bay leaf tied in muslin, cover, and simmer gently until very tender—¾–1 hour. Remove the bag of herbs, lift the liver from the sauce and pass it through a fine mincer, then sieve. Add more seasoning if necessary, and enough of the gravy to make of a soft paste consistency. Pack into small pots, cover at once with a little melted butter, and leave to cool.

Keep in a cold place, and use within a few days (or less in hot weather). Served with freshly made toast and fresh butter, this makes an excellent breakfast dish or hors d'œuvre, and is very good as a sandwich spread, combined with watercress.

PÂTÉ DE FOIE

Calf's tongue (about ½ lb.)	Cayenne pepper
Calf's liver (about ½ lb.)	A pinch of ground cloves
1 oz. butter, melted	1 tsp. piquant sauce
Salt and pepper	A few truffles
½ tsp. made mustard	Melted butter to cover

Boil the tongue and liver in salted water in separate pans until tender. Drain, and when cold, pound in a mortar (reserving a little of the tongue), and add melted butter gradually to form a smooth paste. Season with salt and pepper, mustard, and a little cayenne, then add the ground cloves and sauce to taste. Add small dice of the remaining tongue and the cut truffles. Put into an earthenware pot or a basin or small jars, cover with a little melted butter, and put in a cool place until required.

This pâté will not keep for more than a few days, especially in warm weather.

POTTED MEAT

1 lb. lean beef	Mace
¼ pint stock	Pepper and salt
1 clove	2 oz. butter

Cut off the gristle and fat from the meat. Cook slowly with the stock, clove, mace, and seasoning in a casserole or earthenware pot in a moderate oven or in a steamer for about 2½ hours, or until very tender. Pass through a mincer or pound in a mortar. Mix in 1 oz. melted butter and a little stock to moisten, if necessary, and press into glass dishes. Cover with the remaining 1 oz. melted butter.

Home-made potted meat should be prepared as required. Containing no preservative, it will not keep for more than a few days.

POTTED MEAT

(using cooked meat)

½ lb. cooked beef	½ tsp. mixed spices
2–3 oz. fat ham or bacon (cooked)	2 tsps. made mustard
Pepper and salt	2 oz. butter

Trim the meat and fat ham, removing all skin, gristle, and sinew. Cut them in pieces and put them twice through the mincing machine. Put the minced meat into a mortar or strong basin and add seasoning according to individual taste. Melt the butter and add most of it to the meat. Then pound all well together, pack into pots, and run the remainder of the butter over the top. Use while still fresh, i.e., within 2–3 days.

POTTED SALMON

1 lb. cut of salmon (or tinned salmon)	½ tsp. ground cloves
Salt	½ tsp. ground nutmeg
½ tsp. ground mace	3 oz. butter
½ tsp. ground pepper	Clarified butter to cover

Skin and bone the salmon. Put a layer in a fireproof dish, seasoning with salt and spices, and put a liberal amount of butter on. Continue with the layers until the salmon is used up. Cover, and bake in a moderate oven for 1½ hours (or less if tinned salmon is used). Pound thoroughly in a mortar. Press into clean pots, and pour a layer of clarified butter over. This paste will not keep for more than a few days.

CREAM CHEESE AND PICKLED WALNUT

5–6 sweet pickled walnuts	¼ oz. cream cheese

Put the walnuts and cheese into a basin and blend together with a fork or wooden spoon.

Game Pie

6 oz. Shortcrust Pastry
FILLING *½ pint milk*
½ oz. Bournville Cocoa 1 tblsp. sugar 2 egg yolks ½ oz. margarine ½ oz. cornflour
MERINGUE *2 egg whites*
3 oz. castor sugar

Chocolate meringue pie

METHOD For this American style pie, line an 8″ flan ring and bake blind. Make sauce with cocoa, cornflour, sugar and milk, cool and add margarine and egg. Pour into cooked flan case. Bake in moderate oven 20-25 minutes, Regulo 6 or 375°F until firm. Whip egg whites until stiff, fold in sugar and pile on to chocolate. Set in cool oven. Serve hot or cold.

CADBURY'S BOURNVILLE COCOA

—perfect for all chocolate cookery

LOBSTER OR CRAB CREAM

2 oz. lobster or crab meat	Cayenne pepper and salt
1 tbsp. whipped cream or mayonnaise	Red colouring, if desired

Sieve or pound the lobster meat, blend thoroughly with the cream and season to taste. A little red colouring may be added to give a more attractive appearance.

MUSHROOM SPREAD

1 very small onion, chopped or minced	8 oz. finely chopped or minced mushrooms
4 oz. finely chopped or minced bacon	4 oz. breadcrumbs
	Melted butter to cover

Fry the onion and bacon lightly. Add the mushrooms and cook very gently for about 10 minutes, or until all the ingredients are tender. Add the breadcrumbs and stir until the whole is thoroughly blended. Pack into a basin or jar and cover with melted butter.

SAVOURY TOMATO

½ oz. butter	½ tsp. piquant sauce
2 tbsps. finely chopped onion	½ tsp. pepper
	2 tsps. salt
1 lb. tomatoes	2 eggs
2 tbsps. malt vinegar	2 tsps. finely chopped parsley
1 tbsp. tarragon vinegar	
1 finely chopped clove of garlic	A pinch of mixed herbs

Melt the butter in a saucepan and lightly fry the onion. Remove the skins from the tomatoes, cut them in four, and add to the onion. Add the vinegars, garlic, piquant sauce, pepper and salt, and simmer gently until the tomatoes are quite soft, stirring with a wooden spoon. Break the eggs and add them one at a time to the mixture, beating after the addition of each egg. Heat gently to cook the egg, stirring continuously, then add the parsley and powdered herbs and mix thoroughly.

PACKED MEALS

Although sandwiches are so often included in packed meals, they are by no means the only possibility. Particularly when the packed lunch must serve as the main meal, it should include a variety of well-balanced foods to maintain good health, with plenty of vegetables or salad, fresh fruit, fruit juice, milk, etc.

A vacuum flask is useful to carry soup in the winter months, while in summer a cold drink or fruit salad will be very acceptable. Use light-weight tins for cakes, pastries, buns or biscuits, to prevent crumbling. Any food that dries quickly can be wrapped in aluminium foil or put in a plastic bag. A sweet, such as a trifle (not too soft and runny), fruit in jelly, fruit whip, etc., can be carried in a waxed carton or plastic container.

Here are a few recipes specially suitable for packed meals:

CHEESE AND HADDOCK TRICORNES

6 oz. cooked smoked haddock	Cayenne pepper
	2 dessertsps. milk
2 oz. margarine	2 egg yolks or 1 egg
2 oz. grated Parmesan cheese	8 oz. cheese pastry
	Paprika pepper

Mash the haddock finely and add the margarine, cheese, cayenne, milk, and most of the egg. Roll out the pastry ⅛ inch thick and cut it into rounds 3½–4 inches across. Put a little of the mixture in the centre of each round, moisten the edges, and gather up to form a triangle. Tap up the edges, brush with egg, sprinkle with a little paprika, and bake in a hot oven (450° F., mark 8) for 10–15 minutes.

EGG AND HAM PASTIES

½ lb. shortcrust pastry	Pepper, salt, and a little made mustard
6 oz. ham	
2 hard-boiled eggs	Egg or milk to glaze
3 tbsps. white sauce	

Roll out the pastry until it is about ⅛–¼ inch thick and cut it into rounds about 4½ inches across. Mince the ham and mix with the roughly chopped hard-boiled eggs; bind together with sauce and season to taste. Divide the mixture evenly between the pastry rounds, damp the edges with egg or milk and form into crescent shapes. Knock up the edges, brush with egg or milk, and bake in a moderately hot oven (425° F., mark 7) for 20–30 minutes.

ONION AND TOMATO PASTIES

½ lb. shortcrust pastry	¼ lb. skinned sliced tomato
¼ lb. chopped cooked onion	Pepper and salt
2 oz. grated cheese	Egg or milk to glaze

Roll out the pastry ⅛ inch thick and cut into rounds 3–4 inches across. Arrange a layer of onion, grated cheese, and tomato in the centre of half the rounds. Season with pepper and salt, brush the edges with milk or water, and cover with a second round of pastry. Knock up the edges and make two slits across the top with a sharp knife. Brush over with egg or milk, and bake in a moderately hot oven (400° F., mark 6) for 15–20 minutes. Serve with watercress.

SAVOURY PASTRY ROLLS

8 oz. minced beef	Piquant sauce
¼ pint thick brown sauce	8 oz. shortcrust pastry
	Egg and crumbs
Seasoning	Fat for frying

Mix together the beef, brown sauce, seasoning, and piquant sauce. Roll out the pastry thinly and cut it into oblongs measuring about 4 by 2½ inches. Put some of the filling down the centre of each oblong and roll it up, sealing the edges well. Egg and crumb the rolls, then fry them in deep fat until golden-brown; drain well.

Other suggestions for packed meals are Scotch eggs, sausage rolls, meat loaf, Cornish pasties, individual mutton pies, and pork pie.

FISH ENVELOPES

8 oz. flaky pastry	1 tsp. lemon juice
8 oz. flaked cooked fish	Seasoning
	1 tbsp. chopped parsley
2 tbsps. white sauce	Egg to glaze

Roll the pastry out ⅛–¼ inch thick and cut it into 8 pieces about 6 inches square. Mix together the other ingredients and put a good spoonful of the filling into each square. Fold in the corners to make an envelope shape, using a little egg to join them. Decorate the joins with leaves cut from the pastry trimmings. Put on a baking sheet, glaze with egg and bake in a moderately hot oven (425° F., mark 7) for 10–15 minutes, until golden-brown and crisp.

SAVOURY SNACK ROLLS

Use long, thin French loaves or round rolls. Split open and butter, and if round rolls are used, remove a slice from the top. Fill with a variety of savoury ingredients, e.g., thinly sliced ham with French mustard, salami, Dutch cheese, olives, red or green peppers. If using round rolls, chop the filling ingredients coarsely and bind together with mayonnaise.

KEBABS AND SHASHLIK

(*See colour picture facing page* 417)

Miniature kebabs are ideal for the sort of picnic where you can build a campfire, or for a garden barbecue party. The Muslims who gave the dish its name (which can also appear in such forms as khubab, kibbab and qabab) used their swords to impale the food, but nowadays we usually employ a skewer. On each skewer thread small pieces of tender steak, mutton, bacon, sausage, liver, kidney or pre-cooked rabbit, using if possible a mixture of at least two or three kinds of meat, and interspersing them with mushrooms and tomatoes (whole or halved). Brush the food over with fat or oil, and season it, then suspend the skewers over the red-hot fire, supporting both ends on bricks or metal bars. Turn the skewers occasionally, so that the food is cooked on all sides. The pieces of meat, etc., should be thin enough to cook through in about 10–15 minutes; alternatively, the food may be partly cooked beforehand.

Shashlik, the Caucasian or Russian version of kebabs, requires tender lamb or mutton. (Traditionally, a very young animal, weighing not more than 5 lb., was the ideal choice.) Use best loin, if possible, and cut it into 2-inch squares, discarding the fat. If desired, marinade the pieces in seasoned oil and lemon juice for several hours; alternatively, rub them with salt. Put the meat on to skewers, brush with fat, and cook as above for about 20 minutes, turning the skewers and basting the meat occasionally. Whole tomatoes and sweet peppers (which take about 7–10 minutes to cook on skewers) may be served with the shashlik.

An Indian type of kebab is made from minced meat, which is seasoned, mixed with minced onion, dhal (lentil purée), garlic, green ginger, chillies, ground coriander and desiccated coconut, and formed into oblongs; place on skewers and cook as above.

For more ordinary occasions, the kebabs may be cooked under a very hot grill. Another method is to thread the meat (e.g., alternate slices of mutton and bacon) on skewers, place in a baking tin with a little fat and put in the oven until half-cooked. Drain off the fat, add a little butter and finely chopped onion, and bake until cooked through, basting constantly.

All types of kebabs are very good served on a bed of savoury rice. At an alfresco meal, where this is not practicable, offer instead plenty of crusty French bread, continental mustard and perhaps some olives to add piquancy.

HOT AND COLD DRINKS

TEA

There are many different kinds of tea, varying with the place in which it is grown and the parts of the leaf from which it is prepared. The kind of tea preferred is obviously a matter of individual taste, but generally speaking, it is best to buy good quality tea, as it has more flavour and is more economical in use than cheap tea.

Always buy tea in small quantities and keep it away from the air. Unless it is kept airtight, it loses some of its aroma and strength, and then has to be used extravagantly to obtain a good result.

The Teapot

There is nothing better than an earthenware or china teapot for making tea. It should be kept very clean, and rinsed out with boiling water just before use. When putting away a teapot which is used only occasionally, make sure that it is perfectly dry and free from tea leaves. If left damp, it is likely to go musty and to spoil the flavour of the tea.

Brewing and Serving the Tea

The water should be freshly drawn and freshly boiled, and used as soon as it is boiling; if it is kept on the boil for any length of time, the tea is likely to taste flat. Make sure that the water is really boiling, otherwise the stimulating property of the tea is not fully extracted.

Heat pot and put in the tea. It is usual to allow 1 heaped tsp. per person; when making tea for two or three people only, allow 1 extra tsp. Then pour on the boiling water and cover the pot with a cosy or stand it in a warm place to infuse.

The time required for infusing depends on the kind of tea. Household teas, which are usually full-flavoured blended Indian teas, require 3–5 minutes' brewing, and this also applies to Ceylon teas. More boiling water may be added if necessary after the first pouring out. On the other hand, teas from Darjeeling (which incidentally are more expensive than most other Indian teas) have a very aromatic and delicate flavour, which is not developed until the tea has brewed for 8–10 minutes. When making Darjeeling tea choose a pot large enough to hold all the water required, infuse for at least 8 minutes, and add no further hot water. Most China teas brew more quickly than Indian and may be poured out a minute or so after making, more boiling water being added as required.

In this country, tea is usually served with milk, with or without sugar, according to taste. Some people prefer "black" tea, in which case they usually like a squeeze of lemon juice, which has the effect of "softening" and clearing the tea.

RUSSIAN TEA

Russian tea is made very strong. Glasses are half-filled with the tea, to which hot water and slices of lemon are added. Jam or rum may be used instead of lemon.

AUSTRIAN TEA

Austrian tea is also made very strong. A little is poured into the cup and this is then filled up with warm milk.

ICED TEA—I

Prepare China tea in the ordinary way, strain, and pour into a tumbler filled with crushed ice. Add sugar with a slice of lemon. Re-chill before serving—quick chilling gives a clearer result and a better flavour.

ICED TEA—II

Strain hot China tea into glasses one-third full of crushed ice. Add orange juice and sugar to taste, and garnish with a slice of orange and a leaf of mint.

ICED TEA—III

Make tea twice as strong as usual, using about 4 heaped tsps. to 2 cups of boiling water. Strain into glasses one-third full of crushed ice, sweeten to taste, and put a slice of lemon into each glass. Chilling immediately after brewing retains the flavour.

LEMON OR ORANGE SUGAR FOR TEA

Take cubes of loaf sugar, and rub them on every side with the rind of a scrubbed orange or lemon. Store in a glass jar with a tightly fitting lid and use to sweeten tea.

MINT SYRUP FLAVOURING FOR TEA

4 oz. granulated sugar
2 tbsps. water
10 mint tips
1 tbsp. lemon juice
Green colouring

Boil the sugar and water together for 5 minutes. Cut up the mint very finely, add to the syrup, and bruise with the back of a spoon. Allow to cool and add the lemon juice and a little green colouring. Strain through muslin, and use with China tea to flavour and sweeten.

COFFEE

1. Be sure that the coffee is fresh—not only freshly ground, but also freshly roasted—so buy coffee in small quantities, put it immediately into a glass jar with a well-fitting lid, and use it up within a week. Never leave coffee in a bag or uncovered; the air destroys the flavour made by roasting the coffee and finally produces a stale flavour. If you do not live near a good coffee shop, you will probably find it better to buy a good brand of vacuum-packed coffee in ¼-lb. or ½-lb. tins. Never mix stale coffee with a fresh supply.

2. Roasting coffee is best left to experts, so buy your coffee already roasted. If, however, you have some berries which you think may be stale, you can freshen them by tossing them in a baking tin over a very low heat for a few minutes, until a good aroma comes from them; you can even place them in the oven for a short while. Some brands of coffee are "double roast," which gives a delicious nutty flavour, particularly suitable for after-dinner coffee.

3. Have the coffee suitably ground. Coarsely ground coffee should only be used in a percolator; for the jug or filter methods, finely ground coffee is much more satisfactory. You can, of course, buy coffee in the form of berries and grind it at home with a small coffee grinding mill: buy and store the berries in the same way as you would ground coffee, that is, see that they are freshly roasted, keep them airtight, and use them while still fresh.

4. Poor coffee may be caused by using a stale coffee-pot, so be sure that the coffee-pot or percolator is carefully washed in clean, hot, soapy water, using a brush for spouts, tubes, or narrow necks. Rinse well with hot water.

5. Use enough coffee. Many people are too economical with the coffee. For a good brew you need 2 oz. (2 heaped tbsps.) coffee to 1 pint of water. Good black coffee to serve after dinner may be made even stronger. Some people like to have a mixture of chicory in their coffee, but for many others this quite spoils the flavour. If used, it is added in the proportion of 1–2 oz. of ground chicory to 1 lb. of ground pure coffee. When brewing coffee from this mixture, use rather less than 2 oz. to the pint, otherwise it is likely to be bitter.

MAKING COFFEE IN AN EARTHENWARE JUG

Choose a jug of which you know the approximate capacity and put it to warm. Make sure that the jug is really hot, then put the coffee into it and pour on fast-boiling water in the proportions already stated. Stir vigorously for a moment, and leave in a warm place to infuse for at least 10 minutes, stirring once or twice during the first few minutes, then leaving it undisturbed for the grounds to settle. It is a good plan to cover the jug with a lid, a tea towel, or saucer, and to place it on the plate rack of a stove. If cooking is in progress or a very low flame is left burning, it will keep very hot.

When the coffee is ready, pour it gently off the grounds. Straining through muslin or a coffee strainer should not be necessary, though some people prefer to do it. If any grounds do appear to be floating on the top, stir the surface very lightly or sprinkle a few drops of water on the surface, and you will generally find that it sends the grounds quickly to the bottom of the jug. If the coffee has cooled during the process of settling, pour it off into a saucepan and reheat without actually boiling, then pour into a heated jug or coffee-pot. See that the milk to serve with it is brought almost to the boil, and warm the jug.

If you find it necessary to make the coffee some time before it is to be served, follow exactly the same procedure, allowing it plenty of time to settle. Then pour it off the grounds and reheat it when required, without letting it boil.

MAKING COFFEE IN A PERCOLATOR OR FILTER

With either of these devices, a perfectly clear brew is obtained with very little trouble. The method of procedure varies slightly with the different models, and the manufacturer's instructions should be followed carefully.

Percolators : In a percolator the boiling water circulates through the grounds, thereby extracting the flavour, and passes through a strainer which withholds the grounds. Percolators are economical and easy to use, and an advantage of making coffee in this way is that it is impossible to boil it, since the water is forced into the upper chamber of the percolator at a temperature slightly lower than boiling point.

Espresso Coffee Machines : It is now possible to buy domestic-sized espresso machines. They vary in design, but all work on the same basic principle—that is, steam is driven at pressure through the container which holds the coffee grounds. This is a quick and economical method of making strong coffee.

Filters : With the filter method, rather finely ground coffee is packed firmly into the filter, and boiling water is poured on so that it drips slowly through the coffee into the container below, extracting the flavour as it passes but leaving all the grounds behind in the filter. The chief advantage of this type of brewer is that it needs no stirring or other attention, but it is somewhat extravagant of coffee.

BLACK COFFEE (CAFÉ NOIR)

Black coffee should be clear and very hot. It is generally served alone without the addition of sugar, but cream, hot milk, or sugar may be served with it.

COFFEE WITH MILK (CAFÉ AU LAIT)

This beverage is strong black coffee to which hot milk is added, generally in a proportion of two or three parts milk to one part coffee. It is usual to pour milk and coffee into the cup at the same time.

COFFEE EXTRACTS AND POWDERED COFFEE

These are for people " in a hurry." Many of them contain chicory, but some are pure coffee extract and can be conveniently used for flavouring cake icings and sweets, as well as for a beverage. Follow the manufacturer's directions.

ICED COFFEE

Sugar syrup made in the proportion of 4 oz. sugar to ½ pint water
Clear, strong coffee
Ice
Whipped cream

Make the syrup by boiling the sugar and water together for about 10 minutes, then allow to become cold. Chill the coffee and pour into glasses, put a small lump of ice in each glass, sweeten with the syrup and top with cream.

COCOA AND CHOCOLATE

For 1 good breakfastcupful allow 1 tsp. cocoa, 2 tsps. sugar, 1 breakfastcupful of milk. Mix the cocoa and sugar, and blend to a smooth cream with a little of the cold milk. Bring the rest of the milk to the boil and pour it over the blended cocoa, stirring well. Return to the pan and boil for about 2 minutes, stirring. Pour back into the cup and serve plain or with whipped cream.

If necessary, cocoa may be made with half milk and half water. In this case, blend the cocoa and sugar with the cold milk, then fill up with boiling water, return to the pan and cook.

HOT CHOCOLATE

For 1 breakfastcupful allow ½–1 oz. block chocolate, or 2 tsps. chocolate powder, and 1 breakfastcupful of milk and a little sugar. Block chocolate (broken into small pieces or shredded down with a knife) or chocolate powder may be used. Put the milk into a saucepan, sprinkle in the chocolate and bring to boiling point, stirring. Strain into the cup and serve with sugar and whipped cream.

The exact amount of chocolate required depends on the variety and on individual taste. Milk and water may be used if preferred.

ICED CHOCOLATE

½ pint milk	Whipped cream
1 tbsp. chocolate powder	

Put the milk on to heat, sprinkle in the chocolate and bring to boiling point, stirring. Cover and allow to get cold, then chill in a refrigerator. Just before serving, stir in the whipped cream.

MILK SHAKES

To ½ pint milk and 1 portion of ice cream add 1 tsp. or so of fruit syrup or coffee essence. Mix thoroughly in a vacuum beater or with an egg whisk, and serve while still frothing.

CORDIALS AND SOFT DRINKS

APPLE CUP

2 dessert apples	1 lemon
4 tbsps. stock syrup	8 cloves
1 flagon cider	½ syphon soda water

Peel, core, and slice the apples. Heat the syrup with about ½ pint of the cider, and, when boiling, pour it on to the thinly peeled lemon rind, the juice, cloves, and apples. When cold, add the rest of the cider, chilled, and lastly, the chilled soda water.

APRICOT CIDER CUP

1 large tin of apricots	1 quart flagon cider
2-inch stick cinnamon	1 pint soda water
½ oz. sweet almonds	

Strain the syrup from the apricots, rub the pulp through a sieve and put into a large jug. Infuse the cinnamon and blanched almonds in a small saucepan with ½ pint of the cider for about 10 minutes. When cold, pour into the jug, add the remainder of the cider, chilled, and lastly, the pint of soda water.

BARBARY ALE

The juice of 8 oranges	1 tsp. finely grated nutmeg
1 pint water	1 tsp. ground cinnamon
6 oz. loaf sugar	½ tsp. mixed spice
The rind and juice of 2 lemons	6 bottles ginger beer

Mix all the ingredients, except the ginger beer, and let stand for 3 hours. Strain through muslin and add the ginger beer just before serving the Barbary Ale.

BLACK-CURRANT CORDIAL

1½ lb. black-currants	1 pint boiling water
½ lb. sugar	Thin slices of lemon
Juice of 2 lemons	

Cook the black-currants slowly with the sugar (reserving a tablespoonful of the berries); mash well, strain, and measure the juice, adding water to make up to 1 pint. Add the strained lemon juice and the boiling water. Allow to become cold, then chill and add the tablespoonful of fresh black-currants and some thin slices of lemon.

CHAMPAGNE CUP

1 bottle champagne	A bunch of borage
1 oz. crushed sugar-candy	1 quart bottle soda water (optional)
2 sliced oranges	
A bunch of balm	

Put all the ingredients, except the soda water, into a jug, cover and chill for 2 hours, then decant free from herbs. Add the soda water, although this may be omitted if preferred.

CIDER CUP—I

1 pint tea	A small glass of brandy
2 oz. loaf sugar	1 quart cider
2 oranges	1 lemon, thinly sliced

Infuse the tea and pour on to the loaf sugar, then allow to cool. Add the strained orange juice and brandy. Just before serving, add the cider and lemon.

CIDER CUP—II

1 quart cider	1 syphon soda water
½ lb. sugar	Grapes and slices of lemon for serving
Rind of 1 lemon	
Nutmeg	½ wine glass sherry

Mix together the cider, sugar, thinly peeled lemon rind, and a good grating of nutmeg, and chill for 2 hours. Strain, and add the soda water, fruit, and sherry.

CIDER CUP—III

1½ pints good home-made lemonade	1 quart flagon cider
A stick of cinnamon—about 4 inches long	½ a syphon of soda water

Prepare the home-made lemonade: peel the rind of 3 lemons thinly, put it into a jug, with the sugar to sweeten and all the juice of the lemons, and pour on boiling water, using ½ pint water to each whole lemon. Whilst the lemonade is still boiling, pour it on to the cinnamon in a large jug and allow to cool slowly. When quite cold, remove the cinnamon, and add the chilled cider and soda water.

CIDER CUP—IV

A bunch of balm
A bunch of borage
1 oz. crushed sugar-candy
1 sliced lemon
1 small glass brandy
1 quart cider
1 pint soda water

Bruise a few of the leaves of the balm and borage. Put both into a large jug, with the crushed sugar-candy and sliced lemon and brandy. Add the cider. Chill in a refrigerator or embed in ice for 1 hour or longer. Add the chilled soda water immediately before serving the cup.

CIDER MINT

A handful of fresh, young mint
1 quart flagon cider
2 tbsps. stock syrup
1–2 drops oil of peppermint

Wash the mint, shake it free from water and bruise some of the leaves. Put into a saucepan with ½ pint of the cider, allow it to infuse for ¼ hour, but do not let it boil. Put into a large jug with the syrup, and when cold, add the remainder of the cider and the oil of peppermint. Chill and strain before serving.

CIDER PUNCH

1 quart cider
¼ pint lemon juice
Sugar
Ice
1 syphon soda water
Fresh fruit
A sprig of mint

Mix the cider and lemon juice and sweeten to taste. Strain into a glass bowl over a large lump of ice. Just before serving, add the soda water and small pieces of fruit. Put a sprig of mint on top.

CLARET CUP

¼ pint water
4 oz. sugar
1 lemon
2 oranges
1 quart bottle claret
A sprig of borage
A few thin slices of cucumber
1 syphon soda water

Put the water, sugar, and thinly peeled lemon rind into a saucepan and boil gently for 10 minutes, then allow to cool. Strain into a jug and add the strained orange and lemon juice. Add the claret, borage, and cucumber. Chill, and add the soda water before serving.

EGG FLIP OR NOGG

1 egg, separated
2 tsps. sugar
1 cup of milk
A little brandy, rum, or sherry

Beat the egg yolk and sugar together, pour on the hot milk, add the brandy, rum, or sherry, and fold in the stiffly beaten egg white.

FRUIT LEMONADE

3 lemons
6–8 oz. sugar
1 quart boiling water
Fruit in season
Ice

Wipe the lemons, grate the rind of two and mix the grated rind thoroughly with the sugar. Pour on the boiling water, stir well and stand until cold. Add the lemon juice, strain into a glass jug, and add small pieces of fresh fruit and a lump of ice just before serving.

FRUIT NOGG

1 egg
2 tsps. caster sugar
1 orange
1 lemon

Beat the egg and sugar together thoroughly. Add the strained fruit juices, stirring all the time. Serve very cold.

FRUIT PUNCH

½ lb. sugar
¼ pint water
2 grapefruit
2 lemons
5 oranges
¼ pint crushed pineapple
1 syphon soda water
Thinly cut lemon

Dissolve sugar in water and boil for 5 minutes; allow to cool. Add the juice of the grapefruit, lemons and oranges, and the crushed pineapple. Chill the mixture for 2 hours. Add the iced soda water just before serving, and a few slices of thinly cut lemon.

GINGER BEER—I

1 gallon boiling water
1 lemon, sliced
1 lb. loaf sugar
1 oz. well-bruised ginger
½ oz. yeast
1 slice toast

Pour the boiling water on to the lemon, sugar, and bruised ginger, stir until the sugar is dissolved and cool until lukewarm. Spread the yeast on the toast and lay it on the liquor. Stand for 12 hours, remove the yeast, strain and bottle. Tie or cork down securely and put in a cool place. Keep for a week.

GINGER BEER—II

3 lemons
1½ lb. granulated sugar
1 tbsp. ground ginger
1½ gallons boiling water
1 oz. yeast
1 slice of toast

Slice the lemons, add the sugar and ginger, and pour on the boiling water. Cool until lukewarm, add the yeast spread on toast, and leave for 24 hours. Remove the toast, strain through muslin. Bottle and cork very lightly overnight, then make airtight. This is ready to drink in a few days' time.

GINGER CORDIAL

2 lb. 2 oz. loaf sugar	¾ oz. citric acid
3 quarts boiling water	1 drachm essence of lemon
	5 drachms essence of ginger
	1 drachm essence of cayenne

Melt the 2 oz. loaf sugar in a strong saucepan and heat until coffee-coloured, then carefully add 1 pint of the boiling water and re-dissolve the caramel. Put the rest of the sugar, the citric acid, and essences into a basin. Pour on the rest of the boiling water, and add the caramel. Stir occasionally, and bottle when cold. This cordial may be served hot or cold.

GINGER PUNCH

1 pint water	6 oz. chopped preserved ginger
1 lb. sugar	½ pint bottle ginger beer
6 lemons	
2 oranges	

Put the water, sugar, and thinly peeled rinds of two lemons in a pan; boil hard for 10 minutes, then cool. Add the strained orange and lemon juice and the preserved ginger. Chill for 2 hours; add the chilled ginger beer.

GRAPEFRUIT BARLEY WATER

2 oz. pearl barley	Sugar to taste
1 grapefruit	

Wash the barley, cover with cold water, and bring to the boil. Strain and rinse the barley, add 1½ pints cold water and boil slowly in a covered pan for 1½–2 hours. Strain into a jug and, when cold, add grapefruit juice and sugar.

STILL LEMONADE—I

1 lemon	½ pint boiling water
2 oz. sugar	

Wash the lemon and peel off the rind very thinly; put it with the sugar into a jug, pour on the boiling water, cover, and allow to stand until cool, stirring occasionally. Add the lemon juice, and strain.

STILL LEMONADE—II

3 lemons	1 oz. cream of tartar
12 oz. sugar	3 quarts water

Wash the lemons and peel them very thinly. Put the peel in a jug with the sugar and cream of tartar. Pour on the boiling water, cover, and cool, stirring occasionally. Add the lemon juice, strain, and serve cold.

EFFERVESCING LEMONADE

1 lb. 2 oz. caster sugar	2 egg whites
3 lemons	1 tbsp. rum
¼ oz. yeast	

Boil the sugar, 3¼ pints water and the thinly peeled lemon rinds together for 15 minutes. Beat the yeast to a cream with a little water. Whisk the egg whites stiffly and whisk them and the yeast into 7 quarts water, then strain in the lemon liquor and lemon juice and add the rum. Pour into bottles, and secure corks with wire or use patent stoppers. Keep for a week and use.

LEMONADE

(Using rinds only)

Rinds of 12 lemons	1 tbsp. citric acid
3½ oz. Demerara sugar	1 quart boiling water

Put the rinds in a basin. Add the sugar and acid and pour on the boiling water. Cover, and stir occasionally as it cools. Strain, and serve hot or cold.

LEMON SQUASH

Juice of 1 lemon	Soda water
Sugar to taste	

Put the lemon juice and sugar into a tumbler, and fill up with soda water.

LEMON SYRUP—I

1 pint lemon juice	1½ pints water
3 lb. sugar	

Wash the lemons and peel very thinly, or grate the rind. Add the rind to the sugar and water, warm, stir until the sugar has dissolved, and then strain. Add the lemon juice to the sugar syrup, mix well, bottle, and sterilise, bringing the temperature up to 170° F. and keeping it at this level for 30 minutes. Use diluted 4–5 times to make lemon drinks.

LEMON SYRUP—II

To 1 lb. lemons allow:—

3 lb. loaf sugar	¼ oz. citric acid
2 quarts boiling water	

Put the loaf sugar into a large jar or basin and pour the freshly boiled water over it.

Wipe the lemons, peel off the rind very thinly, and add it to the sugar and water. Dissolve the citric acid in a saucepan with a small quantity of water, and pour it also into the basin. Now remove all the white pith from the lemons (this is not used), slice the lemons thinly (removing the seeds), and add to the other ingredients. Cover the basin, and allow the syrup to stand for 2–3 days, stirring and pressing the lemons occasionally. Strain, bottle, and cork tightly. This syrup will keep for 2–3 weeks, and is used to flavour drinks and cold sweets.

MIXED FRUIT CUP

2 oranges
2 lemons
2 apples
1–2 peaches
1 tin raspberries
Small tin of strawberries
1 lb. sugar
3 quart flagons cider
1 pint soda water

Wipe the oranges and lemons and slice them thinly without peeling them. Peel, core, and slice the apples into rings. Skin and slice the peaches. Put the syrup from the tinned fruit into the saucepan with the sugar and 1 pint cider. Allow to boil for about 5 minutes, then pour on to the fruit. When cold, add the rest of the cider, chill, and just before serving, add 1 pint soda water.

MULLED WINE AND EGG

¼ pint water
3 lumps sugar
A small piece of stick cinnamon
2 cloves
1 glass claret or Burgundy
1 egg

Put the water, sugar, and spices into a saucepan, bring to the boil and simmer for 10 minutes. Add the wine and just bring to the boil. Beat the egg thoroughly and gradually pour on the hot mixture, stirring; serve hot.

ORANGEADE—I

2 oranges
1 lemon
1 oz. sugar
1 pint boiling water

Wipe the fruit and peel thinly. Put the peel and sugar into a jug, and pour on the boiling water. Allow to cool, then add the juice, and strain.

ORANGEADE—II

6 oranges
4 lemons
1¼ lb. sugar
2 quarts water

Wash and peel the fruit thinly. Put the rind, sugar, and half the water into a saucepan and boil gently for about 10 minutes, then strain through muslin. When cold, add the rest of the water and the strained juice of all the fruit. Chill before serving.

ORANGE CUP

1 pint orange juice
2 lemons
2 oz. sugar
¼ pint water
½ pint apricot syrup
1 pint iced water or soda water
Thinly cut orange

Put the orange and lemon juices into a jug. Boil the sugar and water together for 5 minutes, cool, and then add the apricot syrup and water or soda water to the fruit juices. Cut thin slices of orange and float them on top.

ORANGE PUNCH

1 large piece of ice
1 cup orange juice
½ cup lemon juice
Sugar syrup to taste
1 pint soda water
1 pint ginger ale
Slices of thinly cut orange

Put the ice into a bowl, strain the fruit juices over it, and add the syrup. Just before serving, add the soda water and ginger ale and a few slices of thinly cut orange.

ORANGE SQUASH

5 oranges
1 lemon
¼ lb. sugar
¼ pint water
1 egg white
Ice
1 syphon soda water

Peel the rinds of 1 orange and the lemon thinly. Put into a saucepan with the sugar and water, and boil gently for 10 minutes. Strain into a jug and leave to cool. Just before serving, add the strained lemon and orange juices, the stiffly beaten egg white and a few small pieces of ice, then the soda water.

ORANGE AND GINGER SQUASH

Rind of 1 orange
Rind of 1 lemon
3 oz. sugar
2 oz. glucose
1 oz. ginger
½ pint water
Juice of 2 oranges
Juice of 1 lemon
Soda water

Peel the orange and lemon thinly, and put the peel, sugar, glucose, ginger, and water into a saucepan. Heat slowly and infuse for 10 minutes. Cool, and strain into the fruit juices when cold. Serve with soda water.

PINEAPPLE CIDER CUP

1 tin crushed pineapple
Juice of ½ a lemon
A small strip of lemon rind
4 tbsps. sugar syrup
1 tbsp. brandy
1 quart flagon cider
½ syphon soda water

Put the crushed pineapple and juice in the bottom of a large jug. Add the lemon juice, rind, sugar syrup, and brandy. Now add the cider, and lastly, the iced soda water; chill.

RASPBERRY PUNCH

2 lb. bottle raspberries or 1 pint raspberries and juice	4 lemons
4 oranges	Cochineal
	Soda water

Prepare the raspberries if necessary. Squeeze the juice from the oranges and lemons, and strain on to the raspberries. Chill, and let stand for 2 hours, stirring occasionally. Add a little cochineal and chilled soda water just before serving.

RASPBERRY SYRUP

Wash the fruit and drain it thoroughly. Put it into a large double saucepan (enamel-lined) or into a china basin standing in a saucepan of hot water, and heat very slowly until the juice begins to flow. Remove from the heat and press and mash thoroughly, then strain through a jelly bag. Put the pulp into a clean linen cloth, fold over the ends and twist them in opposite directions to squeeze out as much juice as possible. Measure the juice, add ¾ lb. sugar to each pint, and stir until dissolved. Sterilise the syrup in fruit-bottling jars, raising the temperature of the water to 170° in 1 hour and keeping at this temperature for ½ hour. Seal in the usual way, test the next day. Wrap the bottles in brown paper to preserve the colour.

RHUBARB PUNCH

1 quart cut-up rhubarb (about 2 lb.)	1 inch of cinnamon stick
½ pint water	1 piece of root ginger
½ lb. sugar	Rose petals for decoration
6 cloves	

Wash the rhubarb, cut into small pieces without removing the skin, cover with boiling water and stand until cold. Boil the sugar, water, and spices together for 10 minutes. Strain, and add the strained water from the rhubarb. Serve chilled or with ice, with a few rose petals on the top.

SPICE CUP

¼ pint pineapple juice	4 cloves
½ pint orange juice	½ tsp. grated nutmeg
⅓ pint water	½ tsp. cinnamon
½ a lemon	¼ tsp. mixed spice
1½ oz. sugar	2 pints ginger ale or soda water
1 tbsp. honey	

Add the pineapple and orange juice to the water. Add the grated rind and juice of the lemon, the sugar, honey, and spices. Let stand for 12 hours. Strain, and add the ginger ale or soda water.

SUGAR SYRUP (STOCK SYRUP)

1 lb. sugar	½ pint water

Put the sugar and water in a pan, bring to a temperature of 200°–220° F., cool, and bottle. Use as required for sweetening fruit cups and other dishes.

COCKTAILS

General Hints on Making Cocktails

1. Follow the recipe closely. The quantities can of course be increased at will, but any variation in the given proportions will change the flavour of the drink. It is not necessary to follow any particular order in adding ingredients for cocktails, as they are shaken up well before being poured into the glasses.
2. Use only the best brands of spirits and flavouring ingredients.
3. Be sure that any ice used is clean and pure; failing ice, use a little cold water to dilute the cocktails slightly.
4. If possible, use a sugar syrup instead of sugar for sweetening. (The recipe is given on this page.)
5. Keep sliced fruit, cherries, or other garnishes in a cool but handy spot.

Recipes for a few of the best-known cocktails appear below. In some cases there is more than one accepted recipe, and which version you use is a matter of individual taste. For notes on planning a cocktail party, see the chapter on Serving Meals and Entertaining.

BRANDY COCKTAIL

1 part brandy	Lemon rind curls
1 part French vermouth	Maraschino cherries
Crushed ice	

Shake the brandy and vermouth with some crushed ice. Pour into a glass, and serve with a curl of lemon rind and a cherry.

BRONX COCKTAIL

Equal parts of dry gin, Italian vermouth and French vermouth	Juice of a ¼ orange or tangerine per cocktail

Shake all the ingredients well with ice, and strain into cocktail glasses.

CHAMPAGNE COCKTAIL

4 dashes Angostura bitters
1 small lump sugar
Lemon
$\frac{3}{4}$ glass champagne

Pour the bitters over the sugar and put into a glass. Add the strained juice of a quarter lemon and fill up with chilled champagne. Float a wafer-thin slice of lemon on top.

DRY MARTINI COCKTAIL

2 parts dry gin
1 part French vermouth
Cracked ice
Stuffed olives
Lemon rind curls

Shake the gin and vermouth together with some cracked ice. Pour into glasses and add a stuffed olive and a curl of lemon rind to float on top of each.

GIN AND VERMOUTH

Shake together equal quantities of Italian or French vermouth and dry gin. Strain and serve. (The proportions of this drink may be varied to suit individual tastes.)

MARTINI COCKTAIL

2 parts Italian vermouth
1 part dry gin
Orange bitters
Cracked ice

Add a few drops of bitters for each cocktail, shake all the ingredients together thoroughly, and strain into glasses.

SIDECAR COCKTAIL

2 parts brandy
1 part dry gin
Juice of $\frac{1}{4}$ lemon for each cocktail

Mix all the ingredients, shake well with cracked ice, and strain into cocktail glasses.

WHITE LADY COCKTAIL

1 part lemon juice
1 part Cointreau
2 parts gin

Put all the ingredients into the shaker with some crushed ice, shake well, and strain into cocktail glasses.

JAMS, JELLIES AND MARMALADES

Jam making by guesswork may be all very well—sometimes. But it is only by understanding the principles underlying the processes and carefully following the instructions that there is any certainty of consistent success. So be sure that you have a reliable recipe, and before you start to make the jam, you would be wise to study the following points :

EQUIPMENT FOR MAKING JAMS

Preserving Pan : If you intend to make jams, jellies and marmalades regularly, you would be well advised to invest in a good strong preserving pan. Cast aluminium, or a strong pressed aluminium of heavy gauge, or tin-lined copper pans, can be recommended. Whatever the material, choose a thick pan, otherwise the jam is likely to stick and burn. It should be fairly wide, particularly at the top, to give a large surface for evaporation and to enable the jam to boil up without frothing over.

The old-fashioned preserving pans made of brass or unlined copper, if in good condition, are quite suitable for jam, jelly and marmalade making, but must not be used for pickles or any preserve containing vinegar, since the acetic acid in the vinegar reacts with the copper to form a poisonous salt, copper acetate.

In the absence of a preserving pan, you can use an ordinary saucepan, but choose one that is thick, and do not more than half-fill it, otherwise the jam is likely to bubble over when it boils.

The following items, though by no means essential, will be found useful :

Skimming Ladle : A flat, long-handled, skimming ladle specially designed for the purpose so that a large flat surface can be skimmed speedily, and which allows the jam or jelly to drip through, is very useful.

Stone Basket : Removing stones from fruit preparatory to cooking is a tedious task, but a small wire basket, made to hang on the side of the preserving pan, simplifies the task considerably ; the stones can be removed with the ladle or spoon during cooking and put into the basket. Waste of jam is reduced to a minimum, as all the syrup drips back into the pan.

Jam-Pot Filler : Jam-pot fillers of 1 pint and 1 quart capacity, provided with a lip and handle, enable one to speed up the potting of jam very considerably.

Jam Funnel : A jam funnel with a wide tube for filling jam and chutney bottles is useful. These funnels serve also for filling bottles with small fruits and vegetables, such as currants, peas, and so on.

Cherry Stoner : Using a cherry stoner saves much time and prevents the hands from becoming stained with the cherry juice.

Jam Jars : You will need an adequate supply of large or small jars, which should be free from cracks, chips, or other blemishes. Wash them well in warm soapy water and rinse thoroughly in clean warm water. Then sterilise them by placing in a cold oven and heating gradually to about 250° F. Use while still hot.

THE FRUIT

Choose sound fruit that is just ripe. At this point the pectin content of the fruit is at its highest, and pectin is necessary for a good set. Slightly under-ripe fruit is possible for jam making provided it is well cooked before the sugar is added, but the fruit certainly should not be over-ripe or the jam will not set well. Ideally, the fruit should be picked on a dry day ; fruit picked on a moist, warm day quickly moulds and ferments. Use it as soon as possible after picking.

Pectin and Acid Content

A set will only be obtained if there is sufficient pectin, acid, and sugar. Some fruits are rich in pectin and acid, and so give a very good set ; these include apples, gooseberries, damsons, red-currants, black-currants, and of the citrus fruits, lemons, limes, and bitter oranges. Those of medium setting quality include plums, greengages and apricots, loganberries and raspberries. Fruits that lack acid and pectin, such as strawberries, cherries, pears, rhubarb, sweet oranges, and so on, require the addition of a fruit (or a fruit juice) that is rich in these substances; lemon juice is widely used for this purpose, since it aids the setting, at the same time bringing out, rather than masking, the flavour of the fruit to which it is added. Alternatively, an extract of apple or red-currant, etc. (see recipes in this chapter), may be used, or the whole fruit may be included, making a mixed fruit jam. Yet another method is to use a commercially prepared pectin, carefully following the manufacturer's directions.

Sometimes an acid only is added, such as citric or tartaric acid; these acids contain no pectin but help to extract this from the tissues of the fruit, and improve the flavour of fruits lacking acid.

Acid also acts on the sugar, and by changing part of the sugar into invert sugar helps to prevent the jam from crystallising.

JAM MAKING

Cooking the Fruit and Testing for Pectin

The preliminary cooking of the fruit is to break down the tissues and bring the pectin and acid into solution. Only a small amount of water, if any, is added (see recipes), and the fruit should be simmered rather than boiled, since rapid cooking breaks down the pectin. If extra acid is to be included it should be added to the raw fruit and cooked with it.

If there is any doubt as to the setting properties of the fruit, test the juice for pectin before adding the sugar: add 1 tsp. of the fruit juice to 3 tsps. of methylated spirit; a firm clot indicates a good pectin content.

The Sugar

For preference use preserving sugar or loaf sugar for jam making. It may be warmed slightly before adding it to the cooked fruit, though this is not essential. Always stir until the sugar is dissolved, before bringing to the boil. Once the sugar is dissolved, boil rapidly until a jell is obtained, stirring only occasionally to make sure the jam does not stick.

Skimming

This is necessary for clear jellies and also for jams such as strawberry which form a very frothy scum. The skimmings, which are quite wholesome, may be used in cooking.

To Test for a Jell

It is difficult to give the exact time for cooking after the addition of the sugar, as this will depend on the amount of water present, the juiciness of the fruit and its acid and pectin content, the rate of boiling, and whether a deep or shallow pan is used. It is advisable to start testing for a set a few minutes after adding the sugar, for it is easy to continue boiling, but once the jam is over-cooked the flavour and texture are spoiled.

For the saucer test, place a small teaspoonful of the jam on a cold saucer, and cool as quickly as possible. If a skin is formed that wrinkles when the finger is drawn across the surface, the jam is ready. If there is no skin, continue boiling, testing again.

A thermometer may be used for testing the setting point. Boil until a temperature of 220°–222° F. is reached. This method is only accurate for testing jams with full sugar content.

Measuring the yield of jam is a test which is sometimes found useful. Ideally, there should be 10 lb. of jam for every 6 lb. of sugar used. To make this test, the weight of the empty preserving pan must be noted and the pan plus jam weighed when it is estimated that the jam is cooked: the weight of the jam can then be easily calculated.

Potting, Covering, and Storage

Immediately a set has been obtained, remove the jam from the heat, skim if necessary, stir well, and pot in hot sterilised jars. Seal immediately to prevent the entry of bacteria, yeasts, and mould spores, using waxed circles (waxed side down) and parchment covers.

Jams containing whole fruit, such as strawberry, should be left to stiffen slightly in the preserving pan before potting—if potted while still boiling hot the fruit tends to rise to the top of the jars. In this case, cover the jam with a waxed circle immediately on potting, and leave until quite cold before covering with parchment.

Label the jars with the date and the variety of jam. Store in a cool, dry, well-ventilated place, and examine the jars from time to time.

HOME-MADE PECTIN EXTRACTS

Apple: Any sour cooking apples or crab-apples may be used for this purpose, also apple peelings and cores, windfalls, and those rejected on account of imperfections. The extract obtained may be added to fruit such as marrow, blackberry, etc., to supply the acid and pectin lacking in these fruits.

To prepare the extract, take 3 lb. fruit, wash, and cut up, without peeling or coring. Cover with 1–1½ pints water and stew gently for about ¾ hour, until well pulped. Strain through a jelly bag. Replace the pulp in the pan, add water to make a mash, then simmer a further ¾–1 hour, and strain. Mix the two extracts, and if watery reduce by boiling until slightly syrupy.

Gooseberry and Red-Currant: These can be made in a similar way, but slightly less water is necessary, and the fruit is stewed for ½–¾ hour.

JAM RECIPES

APPLE GINGER

4 lb. apples — 3 lemons
1 pint water — 3 tbsps. ginger syrup
8 oz. preserved ginger — 3 lb. sugar

Peel the apples and slice evenly. Tie the cores and peel in muslin. Add the water, and simmer all in a covered pan until soft. Remove the muslin bag, and mash the apples with a spoon or whisk. Add the cut-up ginger with the grated rind of the lemons, lemon juice, ginger syrup, and sugar. Bring to the boil, stirring constantly. Test on a cold plate after 10 minutes' boiling, then as soon as the jam sets, pot and cover immediately.

APRICOT JAM
(Made from dried fruit)

1 lb. dried apricots — 3 lb. preserving sugar
3 pints water — 2–3 oz. almonds (optional)
Juice of 1 lemon

Wash the apricots thoroughly, put them into a basin with the water, cover, and soak for 24 hours at least. Then put the fruit into a preserving pan with the water in which it was soaked, add the lemon juice, bring to the boil, and boil gently for ½ hour, stirring occasionally. Add the sugar and blanched almonds, and boil until the jam sets when tested on a cold plate. Stir almost constantly after the sugar is added. Pot, and cover immediately.

APRICOT JAM
(Made from fresh fruit)

4 lb. fresh apricots — Juice of 1 lemon
¾ pint water — 4 lb. sugar

Wash fruit, cut in half, and remove stones. Crack the latter to remove kernels, and blanch them by dipping in boiling water. Put the apricots into a preserving pan with the water, lemon juice, and blanched kernels, and simmer until they are tender and the contents of the pan somewhat reduced. Add the sugar, stir until dissolved, then bring to the boil, and boil briskly for about 15 minutes. Test on a cold plate for jelling, and continue to boil until the jam sets when tested. Pot, and cover immediately.

APRICOT JAM
(Made from tinned pulp)

3 lb. apricot pulp — 3 lb. sugar
1 lemon

Weigh the pulp, put it into a pan with the grated rind and juice of the lemon. Bring to the boil, and boil for 20 minutes. Then add the sugar, and boil again for 10 minutes. Test for jelling. As soon as it jells, pot and cover.

BILBERRY JAM

3½ lb. bilberries — ¼ oz. tartaric acid
¼ pint water — 3 lb. sugar

Pick over the berries and wash well, removing any leaves and stems. Put into a preserving pan with the water and tartaric acid, and stew until the fruit is tender and the pulp thick. Add the sugar. Bring to the boil, and simmer until it sets when tested on a cold plate. This jam never sets very firmly.

BLACKBERRY JAM

6 lb. blackberries — ¼ pint water
Juice of 2 lemons or 2 tsps. tartaric acid — 6 lb. sugar

Pick over the blackberries, which must not be over-ripe, and put them with the lemon juice or tartaric acid and water into a preserving pan. Simmer very gently until the blackberries are cooked and the contents of the pan reduced considerably. Add the sugar, bring to the boil, stirring, then boil briskly for about 10 minutes, and test on a cold plate for jelling. As soon as it jells pour into hot sterilised jars, and cover immediately.

It is important to use blackberries that are just ripe. Those that are over-ripe and soft do not make a good preserve.

BLACKBERRY AND APPLE JAM

8 lb. blackberries — 3 lb. sour apples
1 pint water — Sugar

Place the blackberries in a pan in ¼ pint of the water. Simmer slowly until tender, and sieve to remove the seeds. Peel, core, and slice the apples, add the remaining ¾ pint water, and cook until tender. Mash with a spoon or whisk. Add the sieved blackberries, weigh the pulp, and add an equal weight of sugar. Stir, bring to the boil, and simmer until the jam sets when tested on a cold plate. Pot, and cover immediately in the usual way.

If the preserving pan is weighed before cooking is begun, the weight of the pulp can easily be calculated.

BLACK-CURRANT JAM

4 lb. black-currants — 6 lb. sugar
3 pints water

Remove the stalks, wash the fruit, and put it into the preserving pan with the water. Simmer gently until it is tender and the contents of the pan reduced considerably. As the mixture becomes thick, stir frequently to prevent burning. Add the sugar, bring to the boil, boil hard for 10 minutes, and test on a cold plate for jelling. As soon as it sets, pot and cover immediately.

As the skins of currants are always very tough, it is important to cook the fruit thoroughly until tender before adding the sugar.

CHERRY JAM—I

4 lb. Mayduke or Morello cherries — ¼ oz. citric or tartaric acid
Cherry kernels — 3½ lb. sugar

Stone some of the cherries and remove the kernels. Put the kernels in a saucepan with the cherries and acid, and cook over a low heat to begin with; then bring to simmering point and simmer for ½ hour, or until the cherries are tender. Add the sugar, stirring while the contents of the pan come to the boil, boil fairly briskly for about 10 minutes, and remove the stones. Test on a cold plate for jelling. When a jell is obtained cool slightly in the pan before potting.

As cherries are lacking in pectin, this jam is only of light set.

CHERRY JAM—II

4 lb. cherries — 3½ lb. sugar
Juice of 3 lemons

Use the same method as for the first recipe, cooking the cherries with the lemon juice. The lemon juice has to be reduced, and consequently the preliminary cooking takes slightly longer than when citric or tartaric acid is used.

CHERRY AND RED-CURRANT JAM—I

2 lb. Morello cherries — ¼ pint water
1 lb. red-currants — 3 lb. sugar

Prepare and wash the fruit, then put into a pan with the water. Bring to the boil, and stew for 20 minutes. Add the sugar, stir until dissolved, then boil, testing after 10 minutes. When a jell is obtained, pot and cover as usual.

CHERRY AND RED-CURRANT JAM—II

2 lb. red-currants — 2½ lb. cherries
1 pint water — 3¼ lb. sugar

Wash the currants, and if they are in good condition do not trouble to pick them. Put them in a pan with the pint of water, and simmer very gently for about 1 hour. Then strain through a jelly cloth (about ½ pint red-currant juice should be produced). Put this, with the cherries, into a preserving pan, and simmer for about 20 minutes. Add the sugar, bring to the boil, and simmer for 10 minutes. Test on a cold plate for jelling. As soon as it sets when tested, pot and cover.

DAMSON JAM

4 lb. damsons — 4 lb. sugar
1¼ pints water

Wash the damsons, put them in a pan with the water, bring to the boil, and simmer until the fruit is cooked. Add the sugar, stir until dissolved, and bring to the boil. Boil quickly, removing the stones as they rise. After about 10 minutes' boiling test for jelling. As soon as it sets when tested, pot and cover.

GREENGAGE JAM

6 lb. greengages — 6 lb. sugar
1¼ pints water

Wash the fruit and cut in half, removing the stones. Crack the latter to obtain the kernels. Put the greengages, water, and blanched kernels in a preserving pan, and bring to the boil. Simmer until the fruit is tender and reduced (about ½ hour). Add the sugar, stir until dissolved, and bring to the boil. Boil for about 15 minutes and test for jelling. Pot and cover in the usual way.

GOOSEBERRY JAM

6 lb. under-ripe gooseberries — 2 pints water
6 lb. sugar

Top and tail and wash the gooseberries, then put into a pan with the water. Heat slowly at first, mashing the fruit as it softens, and continue to cook until the contents of the pan are reduced by about one-third. Add the sugar, stir until dissolved, and bring to the boil. Boil briskly for about 15 minutes, and test for jelling. Pot and cover as usual.

MUSCAT-FLAVOURED GOOSEBERRY JAM OR JELLY

A delicious and unusual flavour is given to gooseberry preserves by adding 3–4 elderflower heads to each pound of fruit or to each pint of juice. Cut off the stems close to the flower, tie the flowers in muslin, and add them to the jam or jelly when it comes to the boil, removing before the preserve is potted.

GREEN GOOSEBERRY JAM

Choose the variety of gooseberry that remains green even when fully ripe. Follow the above recipe and method, using the fruit under-ripe, and cook thoroughly before adding the sugar; prolonged boiling with the sugar darkens the jam.

RIPE GOOSEBERRY JAM

Fully ripe gooseberries, or even dessert gooseberries, may be used for making jam, the same recipe and method as for unripe gooseberries being followed. The jam is usually pink in colour and has a light set. It may be flavoured with elderflowers, if liked (see Muscat-flavoured Gooseberry Jam, above).

JAPONICA JAM

4 lb. japonica fruit — 2 tsps. powdered cloves or other spice
6 pints water
Sugar

Wash and slice the fruit, put it into a pan with the water, boil until tender, and then sieve. Weigh the pulp, add an equal weight of sugar, stir, and bring to the boil. Add the powdered spice. Continue to boil for 10 minutes, and test on a cold plate for setting. As soon as it jells, pour into hot, dry jars, and cover immediately in the usual way.

LOGANBERRY JAM

4 lb. loganberries — 4 lb. sugar

Hull and wash the berries. Heat gently at first, then cook for 20 minutes, stirring occasionally. Add the sugar, stir until dissolved, bring to the boil, and test for a jell. Continue to boil until a satisfactory set is obtained, then pot and cover the jars in the usual way.

MARROW JAM—I

(Using lemons)

4 lb. prepared marrow — Rind of 1 lemon
3 lb. sugar — Juice of 4 lemons
1 oz. bruised root ginger

Peel the marrow, remove the seeds, and cut into pieces about ½ inch square. Weigh, place in a basin, sprinkle with about 1 lb. of the sugar, and allow to stand overnight. Tie up the bruised ginger and the thinly peeled lemon rind in a piece of muslin, and place, with the marrow and lemon juice, in a preserving pan. Simmer for ½ hour, add the rest of the sugar, and cook gently until the jam sets when tested on a cold plate. Remove the muslin bag and pour jam into hot, sterilised pots, then cover immediately.

MARROW JAM—II

(Using apple extract)

2 lb. prepared marrow — 1 tsp. citric acid
2 lb. sugar — ½ oz. bruised root ginger
½ pint apple extract

Prepare the marrow by peeling, removing the seeds, and cutting into small dice. Weigh, put into a basin, and sprinkle with the sugar; cover, and leave overnight. Next day, put into a pan with the apple extract, citric acid, and bruised ginger, tied in muslin. Bring to the boil, and boil gently for 1–1½ hours, or until the marrow is clear and a jell is obtained on testing. Remove the muslin bag. Pot and cover as usual.

MARROW AND PLUM JAM

2 lb. marrow — 2 lb. purple plums
4 lb. granulated sugar

Peel the marrow, and remove seeds and rind. Cut into dice. Put into a bowl and sprinkle ½ lb. of the sugar over it and leave overnight. Next day, simmer the marrow gently till nearly cooked (about 35 minutes for above quantity), then add the plums, and cook till both are tender (about 30–40 minutes, according to the variety of plums). Add the rest of the sugar, and when dissolved, bring to the boil, and cook till it jells. Pot and cover immediately.

MULBERRY AND APPLE JAM

3 lb. mulberries — 1 pint water
2½ lb. apples — Sugar
2 tsps. tartaric acid

Wash the mulberries, and wash and slice the apples without peeling or coring. Put the fruit, acid, and water into a pan, bring to the boil, and simmer gently, mashing the fruit. Cook until the fruit is a thick pulp, then rub through a hair sieve, and weigh. Add an equal weight of sugar, stir until dissolved, and bring to the boil. Boil for about 10 minutes, and test for jelling. When a jell is obtained, pot and cover as usual.

PEACH AND RASPBERRY JAM

2 lb. stoned peaches — $\frac{1}{4}$ pint water
2 lb. raspberries — 3 lb. sugar

Skin, stone, and weigh the peaches, and cut into pieces. Crack the stones to obtain the kernels. Put all the fruit, water, and kernels into a preserving pan, and cook gently until tender. Add the sugar, and stir until dissolved. Boil for about 15 minutes, stirring occasionally, and test for jelling. Pot and cover as usual.

PLUM JAM

6 lb. plums — 6 lb. sugar
$1\frac{1}{2}$ pints water

Wash the fruit and cut in halves, removing the stones. Crack the latter to obtain the kernels. Put the water, kernels, and plums into a pan, and bring slowly to boiling point. Simmer gently until the fruit is cooked. Add the sugar, stir until dissolved, and bring to the boil. Boil briskly for about 10–15 minutes, and test for jelling. Pot and cover as usual.

QUINCE JAM

2 lb. quinces — $2\frac{1}{2}$ lb. sugar
$2\frac{1}{2}$ pints water

Peel, core, and slice the quinces. Cook slowly with the water in a preserving pan until the fruit is tender and mashed. Add the sugar, stir until dissolved, and bring to the boil. Boil quickly for 10–15 minutes, and test for jelling. Pot and cover as usual.

RASPBERRY JAM

4 lb. raspberries — 4 lb. sugar

Place the fruit in a pan, heat gently at first (if necessary adding a very little water), then simmer until the fruit is tender. Add the sugar, stir until dissolved, and bring to the boil. Test for a jell, and continue to boil until the preserve jells satisfactorily on testing. Pot and cover as usual.

RASPBERRY AND RED-CURRANT JAM

$1\frac{1}{2}$ lb. red-currants — 1 pint water
$1\frac{1}{2}$ lb. raspberries — 3 lb. sugar

Wash and string the red-currants, and put into a preserving pan with the raspberries and the water. Simmer gently until the fruit is cooked. Then add the sugar, stir until dissolved, and bring to the boil. Boil quickly for 10–15 minutes, and test for jelling. Pot and cover.

RHUBARB GINGER

$2\frac{1}{2}$ lb. rhubarb — 1 oz. root ginger
$2\frac{1}{2}$ lb. sugar — $\frac{1}{4}$ lb. crystallised ginger

Wash the rhubarb and cut it into small pieces; put it into a basin with the sugar sprinkled on in layers, and leave overnight. Put the contents of the basin into a pan, with the bruised root ginger tied in muslin. Bring to the boil, and boil hard for 15 minutes. Add the crystallised ginger, cut into small pieces, and reboil for 5 minutes, or until the rhubarb is clear. Test on a cold plate for jelling. As soon as it sets, pot and cover immediately.

RHUBARB JAM

4 lb. rhubarb — 1 oz. root ginger
4 lb. sugar — 1 tsp. citric acid

Wipe the rhubarb, and cut it into small pieces, then put into a basin with the sugar sprinkled on in layers, and leave overnight. Put the contents of the basin into a pan, add the bruised root ginger tied in muslin, and the acid, and bring to the boil. Boil briskly for 10–15 minutes, and test for jelling. When a jell is obtained remove the ginger, and pot and cover as usual.

SOFT FRUIT PRESERVE MADE WITHOUT HEATING

3 lb. soft fruit (raspberries, strawberries, currants, blackberries, etc.)
$3\frac{3}{4}$ lb. caster sugar
2 tsps. tartaric acid

Mash the fruit (which should be in good condition, not over- and not under-ripe) on a large dish. Put into a basin, and sprinkle each layer with the sugar and tartaric acid. Cover with two thicknesses of muslin and put aside for 24 hours, during which time the preserve should be stirred vigorously from time to time to mix the sugar with the crushed fruit. Then put into clean, sterilised jars, but avoid filling beyond the bottom of the neck. Tie down, and store in a cool place. Stir before use, to mix syrup and solid part.

STRAWBERRY JAM

(Using acid to aid setting)

4 lb. strawberries — $3\frac{1}{2}$ lb. sugar
$\frac{1}{4}$ oz. tartaric or citric acid

Place the strawberries and the acid in a preserving pan, heat gently at first, and then simmer for 30 minutes, or until the fruit is tender and the contents of the pan somewhat reduced. Add the sugar, stir until dissolved, and bring to the boil. Boil quickly for about 15 minutes, and test for jelling. Cool for about 15 minutes before potting, to prevent the fruit rising in the jars. Pot, then cover immediately with waxed circles. When quite cold, cover with parchment paper and tie down.

STRAWBERRY JAM

(Using red-currant juice to increase bulk and aid setting)

2 lb. red-currants — 4 lb. sugar
4 lb. strawberries

Wash the red-currants, put them into a pan with a little water, simmer gently until tender, then pass them through a hair sieve or strain through a cloth to obtain the juice. Pick over the strawberries and put them in a pan with the red-currant juice, and boil gently until tender. Add the sugar, stir until dissolved, and bring to the boil. Boil briskly for 10–15 minutes, and test for jelling. Cool about 15 minutes before potting, to prevent the fruit from rising in the jars. Pot, then cover immediately with the waxed circles. When cold, cover with parchment paper and tie down.

STRAWBERRY JAM

(Using lemons)

4 lb. strawberries — 3½ lb. sugar
Juice of 4 lemons

Remove the stalks and hulls of the fruit, put into the preserving pan with the lemon juice, and simmer until thoroughly well cooked. It is difficult to say definitely how long this will take, but about 30–45 minutes is generally sufficient. Add the sugar, stir until dissolved, then bring to the boil. After it has been boiling for about 15 minutes, test on a cold plate for setting. When it is sufficiently cooked, allow to cool, stirring occasionally. When half cold, pour into pots, cover immediately with waxed circles, and tie down when cold.

CONSERVES, CURDS, CHEESES, ETC.

APPLE BUTTER (OR CURD)

1½ lb. sharp-flavoured apples — ¾ lb. sugar
¼ pint water — 2 eggs
Juice of 1 lemon — ¼ lb. butter
¼ tsp. ground ginger

Peel, core, and slice the apples, and simmer gently in the water and lemon juice until they are thoroughly cooked. Beat until smooth, or rub through a sieve; add the sugar, beaten eggs, and butter. Blend thoroughly, and stir over a gentle heat until the eggs thicken, but do not boil. Add the ginger; pot and cover immediately.

Apple curd has not the same keeping qualities as apple jelly or jam, and should, therefore, be made in small quantities when required.

APPLE CONSERVE

Peel and core 2–3 lb. of apples, according to size of mould you wish to fill, and cook very gently without water; if the apples are very dry, 1 tbsp. of water can be added to prevent them sticking to the pan. Rub through a hair sieve when tender, and weigh the purée. Put in a saucepan with an equal weight of sugar, cochineal to colour, and juice and rind of 1 lemon. Allow to simmer from 20 minutes to 1 hour, until the conserve sets when tested on a cold plate.

Pour into the mould and cover like jam. To serve, turn out (if any difficulty is experienced, place the mould in hot water as one does with a jelly) and stick the shape with split, blanched almonds. It can be served alone or with cream or custard.

CRANBERRY ORANGE CONSERVE

1 pint cranberries — ¾ lb. sugar
1 orange — 2 oz. raisins
½ pint water — 2 oz. walnuts

Wash and pick the cranberries and cut the orange into small pieces. Put the cranberries and orange into a preserving pan with the water, and simmer until soft; allow about 40 minutes. Add the sugar, the stoned raisins, and chopped walnuts. Bring to the boil, stirring to prevent the mixture sticking to the pan, and simmer for 20 minutes; test on a cold plate for jelling. As soon as it sets, pour into sterilised jars and cover immediately.

CRANBERRY CHEESE

3 pints cranberries — 1½ lb. sugar
1½ pints water

Wash and pick the cranberries, put in a saucepan with the water, and simmer until they are thoroughly tender. If necessary a little more water may be added. When cooked, rub through a sieve with a wooden spoon. Wash out the saucepan, return the purée to the pan, add the sugar, and bring to the boil, stirring all the time. Boil for 5 minutes, pour into sterilised pots, and cover immediately.

Cranberry cheese can be used as a conserve, but is also excellent as an accompaniment to roast game or turkey.

DAMSON CHEESE

6 lb. damsons
1 pint water
1 lb. sugar to each lb. of fruit pulp

Wash the damsons and stew them in the water until tender. Then rub through a sieve, using a wooden spoon. Weigh the pulp obtained, place in the pan, and add an equal weight of sugar; stir until it comes to the boil, and simmer for 15–20 minutes. Test on a cold plate for jelling; as soon as it sets, pour into hot jars, and cover immediately.

GOOSEBERRY CONSERVE

3 lb. gooseberries
½ pint brown vinegar
4 lb. sugar

Choose gooseberries that are just turning red; top, tail, wash and drain them. Put in a pan with the vinegar and half the sugar, and simmer gently for 20 minutes. Add the remainder of the sugar and continue to boil for ½ hour, or until the mixture is syrupy. Pour into hot sterilised jars, and cover immediately. This is excellent to serve with meat or cheese and biscuits.

LEMON CURD

4 lemons
5 eggs
4 oz. fresh butter
1 lb. sugar

Grate the rind from the lemons very thinly after washing. Beat the eggs. Put the eggs, lemon rind and juice, and butter with the sugar into the top of a double saucepan. Stir until the sugar has dissolved, and the mixture cooks and thickens. When the mixture is thick, strain into small sterilised pots, and cover immediately in the usual way.

As home-made lemon curd contains a liberal proportion of eggs, it should be made in small quantities and it should be kept for only a short time.

MINCEMEAT—I

4 oz. currants
4 oz. raisins
4 oz. sultanas
2 oz. cherries, if liked
4 oz. apples, peeled and cored
2 oz. peel
4 oz. suet
2 oz. walnuts
8 oz. Demerara sugar
1 tsp. mixed spice
Brandy, rum, or raisin wine to mix the mincemeat.

Clean and prepare the fruit. Pass the suet and fruit through a mincing machine, or chop finely. (The sultanas and currants may be left whole if preferred.) Chop the walnuts, and add with the sugar, spice, and brandy to the minced fruit. Mix all thoroughly together. Cover, and let it stand for two days, then put into jars; cover, and set aside till required.

Mincemeat should be made at least a fortnight before it is required, to allow the flavour to mature.

MINCEMEAT—II

¾ lb. raisins
1 lb. currants
4 oz. mixed peel
1 lb. apples
Grated rind and juice of 2 lemons
¾ lb. suet
12 oz. caster sugar
1 tbsp. mixed powdered spice
¼ pint port
¼ pint brandy

The method is the same as in the previous recipe.

MINCEMEAT—III

1 lb. currants
1 lb. sultanas
1 lb. raisins
1 lb. apples
1 lb. peel
Grated rind and juice of 2 lemons
4 oz. sweet almonds
2 oz. bitter almonds
8 oz. suet
1 lb. dark brown sugar
1 tsp. grated nutmeg
1 tsp. powdered cinnamon

The method is the same as in the previous recipes.

MINCEMEAT—IV (ECONOMICAL)

¼ lb. sultanas
¼ lb. raisins
¼ lb. currants
1 oz. candied orange peel
¼ lb. cooking apples
3–4 oz. suet
2–3 oz. sugar
1 tsp. mixed spice
A little grated nutmeg
2 tsps. lemon juice
Rum or whisky (optional)

Prepare the dried fruits and mince them coarsely. Mince also the orange peel, and the peeled and cored apples. Add the finely chopped or shredded suet, the sugar, and the spices. Stir in the lemon juice and the spirits. Mix thoroughly, and put into a jar. Stir every day for a week. Keep the jar covered, and use the mincemeat as required.

You can make a more economical mincemeat by increasing the quantity of apple. Do not, however, add the extra apple when first making the mincemeat, otherwise it will ferment. Make the mincemeat as described above, and stir in the additional apple a day or so before the mincemeat is required for making tarts, etc.

HOME-MADE JELLIES

The process of jelly making is similar to that of jam making, but it is even more important that the fruit juice should have a good pectin and acid content, since the juice only is used, and a set is essential for success. Most English fruits can be made into jelly, except those that are poor in acid and pectin, such as strawberries and cherries, which must be combined with fruits that are rich in these two substances. If there is any doubt as to the suitability of a particular batch of fruit for jelly making, it is advisable to test the juice for pectin as described on page 461.

There are two processes in jelly making: firstly, to extract the juice, and secondly, to set it, by boiling with sugar. The fruit is put into a pan with enough water to cover it, and cooked gently to a mash, so that the tissues are broken down and juice extracted. It is then strained through a scalded jelly bag (of flannel or fine linen), allowing plenty of time for the juice to drip—it should not be squeezed through or the jelly will be cloudy. Fruits rich in pectin may be given a second boiling; the pulp in the bag is boiled again with more water, then strained, and the two extracts mixed together.

The next step is to weigh the extract and add an equal weight of sugar (or it may be measured and 1¼ lb. of sugar allowed for each pint of juice). Now boil briskly until the preserve jells when tested on a cold saucer. Any frothy scum that is thrown up during the boiling process should be taken off; if it gets stirred in and is difficult to remove, the jelly may be strained through a piece of muslin into the pots. The jelly is then covered in the same way as jam, and stored in a cool, dry place.

Here are recipes for popular and delicious jellies, including those made from the fruits, such as red-currants, which, on account of their juicy nature and high proportion of seeds, are most suitable for jelly, or, as in the case of crab-apples, are unsuitable for jam making.

APPLE JELLY

6 lb. cooking apples — Water
Juice of 2 lemons — Sugar

Windfalls can be used successfully, but sweet dessert apples do not contain sufficient pectin to produce a good set. Wash, and remove any bruised or damaged portions, and cut into thick slices without peeling or coring. Put them in a pan with the lemon juice and sufficient cold water to cover; 3 quarts is approximately the amount required. Bring to the boil, and simmer slowly until the apples are reduced to a pulp; then strain through a jelly cloth, leaving for several hours to drip. Weigh the juice, put into a preserving pan, and add an equal weight of sugar. Bring to the boil, stir until the sugar has dissolved, and continue to boil briskly for 10 minutes. Test on a cold plate for jelling. Skim, pot, and cover immediately.

As the colour of apple jelly is sometimes unattractive, it is a good plan to cook a handful of blackberries with the apples; or, if preferred, raspberries, red-currants, cranberries, or loganberries could be used instead.

BLACKBERRY AND APPLE JELLY

2 lb. blackberries — ½ pint water
2 lb. crab or other sour apples — Sugar

Wash the blackberries. Wash and cut up the apples, without peeling or coring. Put the fruit in a pan with the water and cook for about 1 hour, until the fruit is tender, mashing it with a spoon. Strain through a jelly cloth, and allow to drip for several hours. Measure the extract and put into a pan with 1 lb. sugar to each pint. Stir until dissolved, and bring to the boil. Boil quickly for about 10 minutes, or until it jells when tested. Pot and cover the jars in the usual way.

BLACK-CURRANT JELLY

4 lb. black-currants — Sugar
1–1½ pints water

Wash the currants, and remove any leaves, but it is not necessary to remove the stalks. Put into a pan with the water, bring very slowly to simmering point, and allow to simmer for about 1 hour, or until all the fruit is thoroughly mashed. Strain through a jelly cloth. Weigh the extract of juice and add an equal weight of sugar. Stir while bringing again to the boil, boil briskly for 10 minutes, and test on a cold plate for jelling. As soon as it jells, skim, pour into hot sterilised jars, and cover.

BRAMBLE JELLY

4 lb. blackberries — ½ pint water
½ oz. tartaric acid — Sugar

Wash the berries, which should not be over-ripe, and pick them over. Put them with the acid and water into a preserving pan, and bring to the boil. Cook slowly for about 1 hour, or until the fruit is quite tender, mashing it occasionally. Strain through a jelly cloth.

Measure the extract, and allow 1 lb. of sugar to 1 pint of extract. Put the extract in a pan, add the sugar, stir until dissolved, and bring to the boil. Allow to boil briskly for about 10 minutes, and test for jelling. As soon as it jells, pot and cover immediately.

CRAB-APPLE JELLY

6 lb. crab-apples — Cloves or ginger root
3 pints water — Sugar

Wash the crab-apples, and cut into quarters, without peeling or coring. Put into a pan, and add the water. Bring to the boil, and simmer about 1½ hours, or until the fruit is mashed, adding a little more water if necessary. A few cloves, or some ginger root, may be added while the apples are cooking, if the crab-apples are lacking in flavour. Strain through a jelly cloth. Measure the extract or juice, and put into a pan. Bring to the boil, then add 1¼ lb. sugar to each pint of extract. Stir while the sugar is dissolving, allow it to boil briskly for about 10 minutes, and test for jelling. As soon as it jells, pot and cover as usual.

CRANBERRY AND APPLE JELLY

3 lb. apples — Water to cover
2 lb. cranberries — Sugar

Wash the apples, and cut into thick slices without peeling or coring. Wash the cranberries, and put all the fruit into a pan; add sufficient water to cover, and simmer gently until the fruit is thoroughly tender and mashed. Then strain through a jelly cloth, allowing it to drip overnight. Weigh the extract, put into a pan, and bring to the boil. When boiling, add an equal weight of sugar, stir until dissolved, allow it to boil briskly for about 10 minutes, then test for jelling. As soon as it jells, pour into sterilised jars, and cover at once.

DAMSON AND APPLE JELLY

6 lb. apples — 2 quarts water
3 lb. damsons — Sugar

Wash the apples, and slice without peeling or coring. Put them with the damsons into a pan, add the water, and simmer gently until the fruit is thoroughly cooked and mashed. Strain through a jelly cloth, allowing it to drip for several hours. Weigh the extract, put into a pan, bring to the boil, and boil for 5 minutes, then add an equal weight of sugar, and boil briskly for about 10 minutes. Test on a cold plate for jelling. As soon as it jells, skim, pour into hot, sterilised pots, and cover immediately.

ELDERBERRY JELLY

2 lb. elderberries — 1 pint water
1 lb. crab-apples or other sour apples — 1 tsp. citric acid
Sugar

Wash the elderberries. Wash and cut up the apples, without peeling or coring. Put all the fruit into a pan with the water and citric acid, and stew gently for about 1 hour. Strain through a jelly bag, allowing it to drip for several hours. Measure the extract, place it in a pan, and bring to the boil. Add 1 lb. sugar to each pint, stir until dissolved, and boil briskly for about 10 minutes, or until a jell is obtained on testing. Skim if necessary, and pot and cover as usual.

GOOSEBERRY JELLY

3 lb. gooseberries — Sugar
Water to cover

Wash the gooseberries, but do not top and tail. Put them into a preserving pan, cover with water, and simmer gently until they are thoroughly tender and mashed. If the water boils away, a little more must be added. Strain through a jelly cloth, and allow to drip for several hours. Put the pulp from the jelly bag into a pan, add about 1 pint water; bring to the boil. Simmer for 20 minutes, stirring all the time. Strain as before. Put the two extracts together, and weigh. Add an equal weight of sugar, and simmer for 10 minutes. Test on a cold plate for jelling. As soon as it sets, skim, pour into sterilised jars, and cover immediately,

MINT JELLY

2 lb. tart green apples — A bunch of fresh mint
1 quart water — Sugar
Juice of 1 lemon or 1 tsp. citric acid — Green colouring

Wash the apples, and cut in slices, but do not core or peel. Put into a preserving pan with the water and lemon juice (or citric acid), and several sprigs of mint. Bring to the boil, and cook to a soft pulp, mashing occasionally. Strain through a jelly bag and allow to drip overnight. Measure the extract, bring it to the boil, and add 1¼ lb. sugar to each pint. If the flavour of the mint is not sufficiently strong, bruise the leaves of a well-washed bunch of fresh young mint and hold the bunch in the syrup for a few minutes while it is cooking. Chopped fresh mint may also be added, if liked. Continue boiling, test for setting, and as soon as it jells add a little green colouring. Skim if necessary, pot in small pots and cover.

RED-CURRANT JELLY

3 lb. red-currants   Sugar
¾ pint water

Wash the fruit, but do not remove the stalks, and put into a preserving pan with the water. Place over a very low heat, and simmer gently until the fruit is thoroughly cooked and all the berries pulped. Strain through a jelly bag, and allow to drip for several hours. Measure the extract, put it into a pan, and bring to the boil. Add 1 lb. sugar per pint of extract. Stir until dissolved, and bring to the boil. Then boil briskly for about 7–10 minutes and test for jelling. When the preserve jells, pot and cover.

MARMALADE

Marmalade making is very similar to jam making, except that the peel of oranges, lemons, and grapefruit requires a longer time to cook. During the cooking, which may take 2 hours or even longer, a considerable amount of moisture is evaporated: a relatively large amount of water, therefore, is put with the fruit in the first instance—by the time the peel is tender the bulk is much reduced, usually by about half. In other respects the same rules apply. Prolonged boiling should be avoided after the sugar has been added, as this not only darkens the colour but also breaks down the pectin, making it lose its jelling properties. As in the case of jam, the presence of acid is essential in order to bring the pectin into solution, and to help in changing part of the sugar into invert sugar, which is necessary to prevent crystallisation.

When large quantities of marmalade are made at home, a marmalade cutter is well worth while. Failing this, the peel can be put through a coarse mincer, but the effect is not so good as when a cutter is used. When slicing fruit by hand use a very sharp knife, otherwise it is difficult to cut the rind very thinly. The job of hand-slicing the peel can be greatly eased by cooking the fruit, partially if not completely, before attempting to slice it: merely cut the rind into quarters, put it with the amount of water stated in the recipe, and cook until soft enough to slice with ease, then return it to the pan and complete cooking, according to directions.

DARK THICK MARMALADE

2 lb. Seville oranges   4 pints water
1 lemon   4 lb. sugar

Wash the fruit, cut in half, and squeeze out the juice. Put the pips in a muslin bag. Cut the peel into thick shreds, and put into a pan with the pulp, pips, and juice. Mark the level of the contents. Boil for 2 hours, or until the depth is reduced by rather more than one-third. Remove the pips. Add the sugar, and bring to the boil, stirring constantly, until the sugar is dissolved. Boil for 1½ hours, or until the colour has darkened and the preserve sets firmly when tested on a cold plate. Pot, and cover immediately.

GINGER MARMALADE

5 Seville oranges   6½ lb. sugar
5¼ pints water   ½ lb. preserved ginger
3 lb. apples   ½ oz. ground ginger

Wash the oranges thoroughly, cut off the rinds, and shred thinly. Put the fleshy part of the fruit, and the shreds, into the pan. Tie the pips and stringy parts in muslin, and put into the pan. Add 5 pints water and boil for 1½–2 hours, until the contents of the pan are reduced considerably. Cool, squeeze the juice from the muslin bag, and discard the contents. Peel and core the apples, stew gently with the remaining ¼ pint water, mash well, and combine with the oranges. Add the sugar and gingers, boil for 10–20 minutes, and test on a cold plate. When the preserve is boiled sufficiently, pour into pots, cover immediately with waxed circles (waxed side down), and tie down.

GRAPEFRUIT AND LEMON MARMALADE

2 grapefruit   4 pints water
4 lemons   3 lb. sugar

Wash the grapefruits and lemons, and cut in half. Squeeze out the juice, and strain it into a preserving pan. Tie up the pips in a piece of muslin, and put them into the pan with the water, shredded peel, and juice. Boil until the shreds are tender and the contents of the pan reduced almost by half. Remove the bag of pips, squeezing out all the juice from it. Add the sugar, stir whilst it is coming to the boil, boil hard for 10 minutes, then test for setting. As soon as it jells, pour into hot, sterilised jars, and cover.

GRAPEFRUIT, LEMON AND ORANGE MARMALADE

2 grapefruit   6 pints water
2 lemons   5 lb. sugar
3 Seville oranges

Wash the fruit thoroughly, remove the rind with a peeler, cut into thin shreds with a sharp knife, and put into the pan. Remove the thick pith, cut up the fruit, and collect the juice. Put pith, pips, and stringy parts of the fruit into a piece of muslin, tie securely; put all the fruit, including the juice, into a preserving pan with the water. Boil rapidly until the rind is tender and the contents of the pan are considerably reduced. Cool, and squeeze muslin bag to remove as much liquid as possible, add the sugar, boil for 10–15 minutes, and test for jelling. Pour into pots, cover with waxed circles, and tie down immediately.

CLEAR SHRED MARMALADE

Proceed to cut up the fruit (as in the Seville Orange Marmalade), but put 2–3 oz. of very thin shreds into a clean muslin bag, in order to keep them separate from the bulk of the peel and pith. Boil until tender, then remove the bag of shreds and rinse them. Strain the remainder of the orange pulp through a clean scalded cloth or jelly bag. Put the extract in a pan, add the sugar, and stir until dissolved. Boil for 5–10 minutes, or until it jells, then stir in the rinsed and dried shreds.

Do not pot the marmalade until it has cooled somewhat, or the shreds will rise to the top.

LEMON MARMALADE

4 large lemons — 4 pints water
1 orange (sweet or bitter) — 4 lb. sugar

Slice the lemons and the orange thinly, and put them in a pan with the water and the pips tied in muslin; bring to the boil, and simmer until tender—about 2 hours. Remove the bag of pips. The pulp should then measure 3½ pints (if necessary add water to make it up to this amount). Add the sugar, stir until dissolved. then bring to the boil, and boil rapidly until the marmalade jells when tested. Pot, and cover immediately.

LIME MARMALADE

12 limes — 1½ lb. sugar
3 pints water

Peel the rinds off the limes, using a potato peeler, and shred them finely. Squeeze out the juice, then shred the rest of the pulp and tie it in muslin. Put the rind, juice, water and bag of pulp into a pan and boil gently for 1 hour. Add the sugar and stir until it has dissolved. Boil until a set is obtained on testing, and pot in the usual way.

SEVILLE ORANGE MARMALADE

2 lb. bitter oranges — 6 pints water
1 lemon — 6 lb. sugar

Wipe the fruit, cut in half, and remove the pips, tying them in a muslin bag. Slice the fruit and put it, together with the water and bag of pips, into a preserving pan. Boil until the rind is tender and the contents of the pan reduced by about half (1½–2 hours). Remove the bag of pips. Add the sugar, stir until dissolved, then boil briskly until the marmalade jells when tested on a cold saucer. Pot, and cover the jars immediately in the usual way.

PICKLES, CHUTNEYS AND SAUCES

To anyone with a garden, the making of pickles is almost as important a business as jam making or bottling fruit. Even if the vegetables have to be bought, it is worth taking the trouble to make a few jars of pickles and chutney that will add relish to many a savoury dish and make all the difference to corned beef, bread and cheese, or the remains of a joint.

In pickle making, the acid in the vinegar (which is essentially a weak solution of acetic acid), and the salt and spices used, all prohibit the growth of yeasts, moulds, enzymes, and bacteria, and so preserve the vegetables and fruits.

Unlined brass or copper pans must not be used for making any preserve containing vinegar; the acid in the vinegar is likely to react with the metal of the pan, forming a poisonous salt, copper acetate.

The Vinegar

Vinegar is an essential ingredient in all pickles, so before you start on the job, see that you have as much as you are likely to need.

For general purposes, brewed malt vinegar is satisfactory. Choose a good quality brand, then you can rest assured that the acetic acid content will be high enough (it should not be below 6 per cent.) to ensure that the pickle will keep.

When pickling a light-coloured vegetable, such as cauliflower or onions, you may prefer to use a white vinegar (or a pale variety, such as wine or cider vinegar), for the sake of the colour, but ordinary malt vinegar may be used, and indeed is preferred by some, since it usually has a more definite flavour than the white variety.

Spiced Vinegar

For many recipes "Spiced Vinegar" is recommended; this is vinegar in which spices have been infused. Take whatever kind of vinegar you decide to use, and to each quart of it add about ¼ oz. each of some or all of the following spices: cloves, peppercorns, allspice, chillies, blade mace, mustard seed, and root ginger. (If you don't keep the individual spices in stock, you can buy them already mixed, as pickling spice.)

Bring just to the boil in a covered pan, then remove from the heat and allow to stand until the vinegar is flavoured—about 2 hours is usually sufficient. Then strain, and the vinegar is ready for use. If a very spicy flavour is preferred, the spices may be included in the pickle, either sprinkled in between the layers of the vegetables, or placed in the top of each jar, tied in a small muslin bag.

Preparing and Brining the Vegetables

Use fresh, crisp vegetables. Wash them, peel if necessary, then cut into fairly small pieces; leave whole in the case of small onions, nasturtium seeds, and so on.

Brining is an important process. Its purpose is to draw out some of the water from the tissues of the vegetables; if this were not done the vinegar would be diluted too much and the pickles would not keep.

There are two methods of brining: Dry Brining, or sprinkling with salt, which is used chiefly for very watery vegetables such as marrow or cucumber, and Wet Brining, or soaking in brine, for drier vegetables such as cauliflower or onions. The brine is made in the proportion of 1 lb. salt to 1 gallon cold water. The time for brining varies from 12–24 hours according to the vegetable. Whichever method is used, it is advisable to rinse the vegetables after brining, or the pickle may taste too salty. Incidentally, though most vegetables are pickled raw, root vegetables such as artichokes are cooked until just tender in the brine (half-strength brine in this case) before pickling.

Packing and Covering the Jars

Pack the vegetables—brined, rinsed, and drained—into wide-necked jars to within an inch of the top. Then pour the vinegar over, taking care to cover the vegetables well. It is advisable to have a clear ½ inch of vinegar over the vegetables, to allow for the evaporation which is likely to take place unless the jars are very tightly covered. A small space at the top of the jar prevents the vinegar coming into contact with the cover. The vinegar is generally used cold for crisp, sharp pickles such as cabbage, onions, etc., and hot for the softer type of pickle such as plums and walnuts.

For sealing, use corks, sterilised in boiling water and lined with waxed paper, or just tie the jars down with a double thickness of parchment paper. If metal caps are used for covering, take precautions to see that the vinegar does not come into contact with the metal, otherwise corrosion will take place. Coat them inside with wax, or line them with waxed paper or with specially prepared kerosene paper.

Store in a cool, dry place. Keep for 2–3 months to mature before using, except for cabbage, which is nicer eaten while still crisp.

RECIPES FOR PICKLES

APPLE AND ONION PICKLE

¾ lb. tart apples	9 cloves
¾ lb. onions	1½ oz. chillies
2 oz. sultanas	1 tbsp. salt
9 peppercorns	¾ pint vinegar

Chop the apples and onions finely and pack them together with the sultanas in hot, dry jars. Tie the spices in muslin, add the salt to the vinegar, and steep the spices in it for ½ hour. Bring to the boil; simmer for 10 minutes. Pour on the boiling vinegar and tie down. This is ready for use the next day.

GREEN TOMATO PICKLE—I

3 lb. green tomatoes	1 pint brown malt vinegar
1 lb. cucumber or marrow	1 tbsp. mustard
2 oz. salt	1 tsp. allspice
½ oz. garlic	1 tsp. celery seed
1–2 red peppers	1 tsp. turmeric

Cut the tomatoes and cucumber in thin slices, sprinkle them with salt, and stand overnight. The next day, strain off the liquid, and turn the tomatoes and cucumber into a pan. Chop the garlic and red peppers finely, and add to the rest of the ingredients. Simmer until tender, for about 1 hour. Bottle, and tie down when cold, and keep for 4 months before using.

GREEN TOMATO PICKLE—II

4 lb. green tomatoes	2 tbsps. mustard
1½ lb. large onions	1 tbsp. curry powder
1 oz. salt	½ tsp. cayenne pepper
1 quart malt vinegar	2 tsps. mixed spice
¼ pint treacle or syrup	

Wipe the tomatoes, and cut in slices. Peel the onions, and cut in slices. Put tomatoes and onions in a bowl, and sprinkle liberally with salt. Leave for 24 hours, then drain and rinse. Put the vinegar, the treacle, and the spices into a saucepan, and bring them to boiling point. Add the vegetables, and cook very gently for 5 minutes. Pour into bottles, cover, and store.

MIXED PICKLES—I

The following vegetables make a good mixed pickle: Cauliflower, cucumber, green tomatoes, onions, and marrow.

Prepare the vegetables, with the exception of the marrow, and soak in brine for 24 hours. Peel the marrow, remove seeds, and cut into small squares, sprinkle with salt, and let stand for 12 hours. Drain the vegetables, rinse, pack, cover with cold spiced vinegar, tie down, and store for at least 1 month before eating.

MIXED PICKLES—II

1 lb. green tomatoes	1 cauliflower
6 cucumbers	Brine
2 lb. small onions	Spiced vinegar to cover the vegetables
½ small hard cabbage	

Slice the tomatoes, cut the cucumbers into thick slices without peeling, peel the onions, shred the cabbage, and separate the cauliflower into florets. Put the vegetables into a large bowl, cover with cold brine, and allow to stand for 48 hours. Drain, wash, and dry, arrange in jars, cover with cold vinegar. Cover, and store.

MIXED PICKLES—III

3 lb. green tomatoes	Brine
1 dozen small cucumbers	½ gallon vinegar
6 lb. small onions	Spices
1 small, hard cabbage	½ lb. sugar
3 cauliflowers	

Slice the tomatoes, remove the two ends from the cucumbers, and cut them in small pieces, peel the onions, shred the cabbage, and separate the cauliflower heads into little florets. Put all the vegetables into a large crock, cover them with cold brine, let them stand for 24 hours, then drain and dry. Pack them into hot jars or bottles, and well cover with boiling vinegar, flavoured with spices and with the sugar added. Cover, and store for several weeks before using.

All kinds of sharp pickles can be made in the same way.

PICCALILLI—I

3 lb. green tomatoes	1 lb. brown sugar
¼ of a cabbage	2 tsps. turmeric
2 large green cucumbers	½ oz. mustard seed
4 onions	¼ oz. celery seed
Salt	1 tsp. black pepper
1½ pints cider vinegar	¼ oz. mustard
½ pint vinegar	¼ cupful olive oil

Chop the vegetables, and place in layers in a basin, alternately with layers of salt. Let this stand overnight, then drain, discarding the liquid. Heat together the vinegars, sugar, and turmeric, and the seeds and pepper tied in a muslin bag. Pour over the vegetables. Leave this to stand for 48 hours, then drain off the liquor, removing bag of spices. Mix the mustard with this vinegar and the olive oil, and pour over the vegetables. Pack in sterilised jars. Cover, using corks dipped in melted wax.

PICCALILLI—II

1 large cauliflower	1 oz. bruised root ginger
2 cucumbers	
2 lb. shallots	1 oz. black peppercorns
2 lb. apples	1 quart vinegar
Brine	2 oz. cornflour
1 oz. chilli peppers	1 oz. turmeric
2 oz. garlic	1 oz. dry mustard

Prepare the vegetables and apples, and cut into neat pieces. Cover with cold brine. Leave overnight, drain, and pack into hot jars. Prepare the pickle by boiling the chilli peppers, garlic, ginger, and peppercorns in the vinegar for 5 minutes, and then pour in the cornflour, turmeric, and dry mustard, previously blended with a little cold vinegar. Stir, and boil for 10 minutes. Pour on to the vegetables and fruit. Cover, and store.

PICKLED ARTICHOKES (JERUSALEM)

Wash and scrape the artichokes. Cook in a half-strength brine (i.e., ½ lb. salt to 1 gallon water) until tender, but not too soft. Drain until cold. Pack in jars, cover with spiced vinegar, tie down, and store.

PICKLED CABBAGE

1 firm, red cabbage	1 dessertsp. allspice
Salt	1 quart vinegar
1 tbsp. whole pepper	

Quarter the cabbage, removing the outer leaves and centre stalk, and then cut each quarter very finely into strips. Place the cabbage on a dish, sprinkle plenty of salt over it, and leave until the next day. Tie the pepper and spice in a piece of muslin, and boil up in the vinegar. On the second day, place the cabbage in a colander, and allow it to drain thoroughly. Then put it in a large jar, and add the vinegar. Tie down, but do not store for much more than a fortnight, as it will lose its crispness.

PICKLED CAULIFLOWER

Choose young cauliflowers with close-flowered heads, and divide into florets, breaking rather than cutting. Cover with standard brine, and leave to steep overnight. Next day, rinse well, and drain thoroughly. Pack into jars, cover with cold spiced vinegar, and tie down.

PICKLED CAULIFLOWER (ITALIAN STYLE)

2 cauliflowers	Seasoning
Vinegar	¼ of a red pepper
4 tbsps. dried marjoram	Olive oil

Divide the cauliflower into florets, boil them in salted water for 5 minutes, drain well, put them in a bowl, and cover with boiling vinegar. Leave for 24 hours. Lift out the florets, and drain well, put them in layers in a jar, sprinkling the marjoram, seasoning, and chopped pepper between the layers. Put over a mixture of two-thirds olive oil and one-third vinegar until there is at least 1 inch of liquid over the last layer of cauliflower. Cover with oiled paper, and store in a cool place.

To serve, lift out the florets, pour over some of the liquid from the jar, and garnish with strips of red pepper and capers.

PICKLED GHERKINS

Gherkins	2 cloves
Brine	1 blade of mace
1 tsp. allspice	1 pint vinegar
1 tsp. black peppercorns	

Soak the gherkins in brine (made by dissolving 2 oz. of salt in 1 pint water) for 3 days. Drain them well, dry, and pack carefully in a jar. Boil up the allspice, peppercorns, cloves, and mace in the vinegar in the above proportions (sufficient being used to cover the gherkins) for 10 minutes. Then pour the vinegar over the gherkins, cover tightly, and leave in a warm place for 24 hours. Strain the vinegar, boil it up, and pour it over the gherkins, cover, and leave for another 24 hours, repeating this process until the gherkins are a good green. Pack in wide-necked bottles, cover with the vinegar, adding more if required; cork, and store.

PICKLED MUSHROOMS

1 lb. small young mushrooms	½ tsp. white pepper
	2 tsps. salt
Vinegar	2 tsps. ground ginger
2 blades of mace	¼ of an onion (chopped)

After removing the stalks, wash the mushrooms in salt water, and drain well. Peel them, put into a pan or casserole with sufficient vinegar to cover, and add the rest of the ingredients. Cook slowly (in the oven or on the top of the stove) until the mushrooms are quite tender and have shrunk, then lift them out, put into jars, and pour the hot vinegar over them. Cover as usual.

PICKLED NASTURTIUM SEEDS

Nasturtium seeds	1 bay leaf
½ pint white vinegar	3 peppercorns
1 tsp. salt	

Pick the seeds on a dry day, wash, and examine for insects. Dry well, and then put in a cool oven or the sun to dry. To prepare the vinegar, put the salt, bay leaf, peppercorns, and vinegar into a saucepan, bring to the boil, remove from the heat, and infuse for ½ hour at least, then cool. Pack the nasturtium seeds into jars, and cover with the cold spiced vinegar. Cork securely in the usual way.

PICKLED ONIONS

Use the small silver onions. With a stainless knife remove the skins, but avoid cutting the onions. Wash carefully, cover them with brine, and leave for 24 hours. Drain, wash, and dry, put them into jars, and cover with cold spiced vinegar. Tie down as usual.

PICKLED WALNUTS

Green walnuts	Spiced vinegar
Brine	

Wipe the walnuts, prick well, and put into a basin, rejecting any that feel hard when pricked. Cover with brine. Allow to soak for 7 days, throw away the brine, cover with fresh brine, and re-soak for 14 days. Wash, and dry well, spread the walnuts out, and expose to the air until they blacken. Put into pickle jars, pour over hot spiced vinegar, and tie down when cold. Store in a cool place for 5–6 weeks before use.

An interesting variation is obtained by pickling walnuts and onions together. Each should be prepared according to the directions given. Equal quantities of each should then be placed in jars, arranged in alternate layers, and cold spiced vinegar poured over.

SWEET PICKLES

Sweet pickles can be very delicious, and are often preferred to the sharper varieties. They usually contain more fruit than vegetable, and a fair proportion of sugar. These pickles are always cooked, any excess moisture is therefore evaporated during boiling, and brining is not usually necessary.

MELON PICKLE

4 lb. melon	8 cloves
1 lb. sugar	½ oz. stick cinnamon
1 pint vinegar	

Peel, and cut the melon into ½-inch slices, and soak overnight in a salt solution, using 1 oz. of salt to 2 quarts water. In the morning remove the melon from the salt water, put into fresh water, and bring to the boil; continue to simmer until the melon is tender and clear. Make a syrup by dissolving the sugar in the vinegar, add the spices, and boil for about 10 minutes, or longer if necessary. The solution must be really syrupy. Drop the melon into the boiling syrup, boil for 10 minutes, and bottle immediately in the usual way.

MINT PICKLE

½ lb. tomatoes
1 lb. apples
¾ pint vinegar
¾ lb. sugar
1 tbsp. dry mustard
1 tbsp. salt
1 stick of cinnamon
2 tsps. peppercorns
1 blade of mace
6 small onions
1½ oz. sultanas
1 teacupful mint leaves (pressed down)

Cut tomatoes into four, peel, core and slice apples. Boil the vinegar, sugar, condiments, and spices together very gently for about ½ hour, then strain. Add the tomatoes, apples, onions, and sultanas, and simmer for 10 minutes. When cold, pack the fruit and onions in pickle jars, sprinkling the chopped mint liberally between the layers. Cover with the spiced vinegar, cork, and leave for a month before use.

MIXED SWEET PICKLE

3 lb. mixed cucumber, water-melon rinds, and apples
1½ oz. allspice
1½ oz. cloves
1 stick of cinnamon
2 lb. Demerara sugar
3 pints vinegar

Cut the fruit and vegetables into neat pieces, and cook in a little water until nearly tender. Drain thoroughly. Tie the spices in muslin, and boil with the sugar and vinegar for 10 minutes. Add the fruit and vegetables, bring to the boil, and simmer for 5 minutes. Drain the fruit well, and pack into hot jars. Boil the vinegar for a further 10 minutes, remove the spices, and pour into jars. Cover as usual.

POPULAR SWEET PICKLE

¾ lb. cucumber
1 lb. tomatoes
1½ lb. prepared marrow
1½ pints brown malt vinegar
½ pint white malt vinegar
¾ lb. Demerara sugar
1 oz. salt
½ oz. turmeric
½ tsp. ground mace
½ tsp. mixed spice
½ oz. bruised root ginger
½ tsp. celery seed

Wash the cucumber, but do not peel it. Wash the tomatoes, cut in half, and remove the seeds. Pass the vegetables through a coarse mincer. Add the vinegars, sugar, salt, spices, and the ginger and celery seed tied in muslin. Stir, and boil for 3 hours until dark in colour, and of a fairly thick consistency. Cover carefully, as previously described, and store in a cool place.

SWEET PICKLE

2 lb. hard pears, hard plums or melon peel
2 lb. sugar
1½ pints white vinegar
2 cloves

Hard pears, hard plums, or melon peel may be used for this pickle. If melon peel is used, cut off the hard outside skin, and use the remainder. Boil the fruit or melon peel in water until tender, and drain well. Meanwhile, boil the sugar, vinegar, and cloves for ¼ hour. Put the fruit in this liquid, and boil for 15 minutes, pour into jars, and cover like jam. Keep for 6 months before using.

PICKLED BANANAS

12 bananas
1 tbsp. powdered mace
1 tbsp. powdered cinnamon
1½ tsps. powdered cloves
¾ pint vinegar
1 lb. Demerara sugar

Tie the spices in muslin, and boil with the vinegar and sugar for 15 minutes. Cut the bananas into slices about ¼ inch thick, add them to the vinegar, and cook gently until almost tender. Lift carefully into hot jars. Strain the syrup over, and cover.

PICKLED CHERRIES

Stoned cherries
1 oz. cinnamon
1 oz. cloves
2½ lb. Demerara sugar
1 pint vinegar

Tie the spices in muslin, and boil with the sugar and vinegar until syrupy. Pour over the cherries, and leave for a few days, stirring occasionally. Strain off the syrup, re-boil, and pour again over the cherries. Put into bottles or jars, and tie down.

PICKLED DAMSONS

3½ lb. damsons
2 lb. sugar
2 quarts vinegar
2 tsps. ground allspice
2 tbsps. ground ginger
2 tsps. ground mace
2 tbsps. ground cloves

Wash the damsons, and prick them in several places. Put into a preserving pan with the sugar. Add the vinegar and spices, and cook until tender, but not broken. Drain well, and put into the jars. Boil the syrup for a further ¼ hour, and strain into the jars. The next day, pour off the syrup, re-boil, and pour over. Repeat this process on four successive days, then finally cover the jars in the usual way.

PICKLED DATES

3 lb. dates
2¾ pints vinegar
1½ oz. pickling spices
¾ lb. brown sugar

Boil the vinegar, spices, and sugar together until a syrup is formed. Stone and halve the dates. Place in a jar, pour the hot syrup over them, and allow to get cold. Tie down, and keep 3 months before use.

PICKLED OR SPICED PLUMS

Victoria plums
$\frac{1}{2}$ pint vinegar
$1\frac{1}{4}$ lb. sugar
1 oz. powdered cinnamon
$\frac{1}{4}$ oz. allspice
$\frac{1}{4}$ oz. mixed spice

Wipe and pick over the plums, and put them in a jar. Boil the vinegar, sugar, and spices together until the mixture becomes syrupy, then allow to cool, and pour over the plums. The next day, strain the syrup from the plums, re-boil to make it safe for keeping, cool again, and pour over the plums. When quite cold, cover, and store. Keep 3 months before using.

PICKLED PEARS

7 lb. pears
1 piece of ginger root
1 stick of cinnamon
$\frac{1}{2}$ oz. cloves
$\frac{1}{2}$ tsp. powdered allspice
Rind of $\frac{1}{2}$ a lemon
4 lb. sugar
3 pints vinegar

Peel and core the fruit, and cut into equal-sized pieces. Crush the ginger, and tie with the other spices and lemon rind in a muslin bag. Dissolve the sugar in the vinegar, and add the bag of spices. Put the prepared fruit into the vinegar, and cook very gently until it is quite tender, then remove the fruit from the liquid and pack the pieces neatly into clean sterilised jars. Continue to boil the vinegar until it becomes slightly thick, then pour sufficient into each jar to cover the fruit. Tie down the jars securely, and store for 2–3 months before using.

CHUTNEYS

A good chutney should be smooth to the palate, with a mellow flavour. Two points to remember in making chutneys are :

1. Slice or mince the ingredients finely.
2. Allow long, slow cooking. This softens the fruit and blends the flavours. Cooking should be continued until the chutney is of a jam-like consistency.

The amount of salt and other seasonings can, of course, be adjusted as required to suit individual tastes.

APPLE CHUTNEY

2 lb. apples
$\frac{3}{4}$ lb. onions
1 clove of garlic
2 lb. tomatoes
$\frac{1}{2}$ lb. sultanas
1 lb. brown sugar
$\frac{1}{2}$ oz. mustard seed
Salt to taste
$\frac{1}{2}$ oz. curry powder
1 tsp. cayenne pepper
$1\frac{1}{2}$ pints vinegar

Peel and core the apples. Stew them in a very small quantity of water until they are tender and pulpy. Chop the onions and garlic, and cut up the tomatoes. Prepare and wash the sultanas. Add these, and the sugar, to the vegetables and fruit. Tie the mustard seed in muslin, and add, together with salt and spices, to the other ingredients. Add the vinegar, and cook gently for about 2 hours. Place in sterilised jars, and cover.

APPLE AND MARROW CHUTNEY

$1\frac{1}{2}$ lb. prepared marrow
$\frac{1}{4}$ oz. salt
$1\frac{1}{2}$ lb. apples
$\frac{1}{2}$ lb. onions
$\frac{3}{4}$ lb. brown sugar
$1\frac{3}{4}$ pints vinegar
$\frac{1}{4}$ oz. mustard seed
$\frac{1}{2}$ oz. root ginger and peppercorns

Peel and slice the marrow, and cut into small squares. Put into a large basin, sprinkling each layer with a little of the salt, and leave for about 12 hours, to extract some of the moisture, which must be strained off before cooking. Peel, slice, and chop the apples and onions, and put into a pan with sugar and vinegar. The mustard seed, ginger, and peppercorns should then be added, tied together in a small muslin bag. Bring to the boil, simmer gently until all the vegetables are tender and the vinegar reduced sufficiently to make the chutney of the correct consistency. Remove the ginger, mustard seed, etc., and pot immediately.

APPLE AND RAISIN CHUTNEY

3 lb. sour apples
3 onions
1 lb. seedless raisins
2 lemons
$1\frac{1}{2}$ lb. Demerara sugar
1 pint malt vinegar
1 tbsp. mustard seed
Pepper and salt

Peel the apples and onions, and mince them and the raisins. Put this mixture into a pan with the grated lemon rind and strained juice and all the other ingredients. Bring to the boil, and simmer slowly, stirring thoroughly until thick. Pot, and cover as usual.

GOOSEBERRY CHUTNEY

3 lb. gooseberries
$\frac{1}{2}$ lb. stoned raisins
4 onions, sliced thinly
$1\frac{3}{4}$ lb. brown sugar
$\frac{1}{4}$ oz. crushed mustard seed
$\frac{1}{2}$ tsp. turmeric
1 tsp. cayenne
1 oz. salt
$1\frac{1}{2}$ pints vinegar

Put all the ingredients in a pan, and cover with the vinegar. Bring to the boil slowly, and continue to cook for 2 hours, until the gooseberries are thoroughly pulped. If the vinegar boils away, add a little more. Put into warm jars, and seal immediately.

GREEN FIG CHUTNEY

3 lb. green figs
1 lb. onions
6 oz. dates
¼ lb. preserved ginger
1 quart vinegar
¾ lb. brown sugar
6 oz. raisins
½ tsp. cayenne
2 tsps. salt

Cut the figs and onions into rings, the dates and ginger into cubes. Boil the vinegar and sugar, and pour on to all the other ingredients, then leave all night. Next day, boil for about 3 hours, or until thick and dark.

GREEN TOMATO CHUTNEY—I

4 lb. green tomatoes
4 lb. apples
1 lb. shallots
1 lb. sultanas
3 pints vinegar
½ lb. granulated sugar
¼ oz. bruised ginger
½ oz. red chillies
Juice of 2 lemons
2 oz. salt

Pass the tomatoes, apples, shallots, and sultanas through a mincer. Put the vinegar and sugar into a pan, and boil to a syrup. Tie the ginger and chillies in muslin, add the minced ingredients, the lemon juice, and salt to the syrup. Simmer for 4 hours, adding more vinegar if necessary. Bottle, and cover when cold.

GREEN TOMATO CHUTNEY—II

2 lb. green tomatoes (weighed after peeling)
1 lb. apples (after preparation)
½ lb. onions
½–¾ lb. sugar or treacle
½ oz. salt
¼ lb. raisins or sultanas
½ oz. root ginger
2 tbsps. pickling spice
1 quart vinegar

Peel the tomatoes thinly, using a potato peeler, then weigh and slice them. Peel, core, and weigh the apples, and chop coarsely. Peel and slice the onions. Put all the ingredients into a pan, tying the bruised ginger and pickling spice in muslin. Bring to the boil, and boil gently (without a lid) until reduced to the desired consistency. Remove the bag of spice, then pot, and cover.

HOT INDIAN CHUTNEY

6 lb. apples
4 lb. plums or damsons
6 lb. marrow
6 lb. tomatoes
4 lb. onions
1 lb. shallots
1 lb. garlic
4 lb. sugar
10 oz. salt
¾ oz. chillies
¾ oz. cloves
¾ oz. white pepper
4 oz. mustard seed
1¼ oz. bruised root ginger
6 pints vinegar

Boil the apples in water first. Chop the rest of the fruit and vegetables, and sprinkle with sugar and salt. Leave for 12 hours. Tie the spices in a bag, then boil all the ingredients together slowly for 8 hours, or leave in the oven all night.

MARROW CHUTNEY

3 lb. marrow
Salt
½ lb. shallots
½ lb. green apples
12 peppercorns
¼ oz. bruised root ginger
½ lb. sultanas
4 oz. sugar
1½ pints vinegar

Cut the marrow in small pieces, and place in a basin with a sprinkling of salt between the layers; leave for 12 hours, then drain. Peel and chop the shallots and apples finely. Tie the spices in muslin. Put all the ingredients in a saucepan, bring slowly to the boil, and simmer gently until the chutney is cooked and of the correct consistency. Pot, and cover.

Cinnamon and allspice may be added to this chutney, if desired.

ORIENTAL CHUTNEY

2½ lb. dried apricots
1½ lb. dried peaches
1½ lb. stoned dates
2 lb. sultanas
1½ lb. seedless raisins
1½ lb. currants
6½ lb. Demerara sugar
2 oz. salt
¼ lb. garlic
1 oz. ground cloves
1 oz. cinnamon
1 tsp. cayenne pepper
2 pints vinegar

Mince the apricots, peaches, and dates, or cut up into small pieces. Wash all the dried fruits. Cover with water, and stew until tender and thick. Add the rest of the ingredients, and boil rapidly, stirring well, for about ½ hour, or until the contents of the pan are thick. Taste, and add more salt if required. Put into hot jars at once, cover, and store 6 months before using.

PEAR AND QUINCE CHUTNEY

4 lb. cooking pears
2 lb. quinces
2 lb. onions
2 lb. green tomatoes
1 lb. seeded raisins
1 lb. celery
3 lb. Demerara sugar
½ tsp. cayenne pepper
½ oz. salt
1 tsp. ground ginger
10 peppercorns
2 tsps. grated horse-radish
4 pints vinegar

Peel and core the pears and quinces, peel the onions, wash the tomatoes. Put these ingredients and the raisins through the mincer, and cook in a covered pan until tender. Add the finely chopped celery, sugar, pepper, salt, and ginger. Tie the peppercorns and horseradish in a muslin bag, add this and the vinegar. Cook slowly, stirring well, until the contents of the pan are thick—about 4 hours. Cool, pot, and cover.

PLUM CHUTNEY

3 lb. plums
1 lb. apples
1 lb. onions
1 lb. sultanas
½ lb. sugar
¼ tsp. cayenne pepper
1 oz. salt
2 tsps. allspice
2 tsps. cinnamon
2 tsps. ground ginger
1½ pints vinegar

Stone the plums, and cut in slices. Chop the apples, onions, and sultanas. Place all the ingredients in a saucepan, bring to the boil, and simmer until tender, and until the mixture is of the right consistency. Pour into hot jars, and cover as usual.

RED TOMATO CHUTNEY

4 lb. red tomatoes
1 oz. mustard seed
3 tsps. allspice
1 tsp. cayenne pepper
½ lb. sugar
1 oz. salt
¾ pint white malt vinegar

Peel the tomatoes by immersing in boiling water for 1–2 minutes, and then plunging into cold. The skins will then come off easily. Tie the mustard seed and allspice in muslin, and add with the cayenne to the tomatoes. Boil until reduced to a pulp (¾ hour), and add sugar, salt, and vinegar. Continue boiling until the right consistency is obtained (¾–1 hour), and bottle in hot sterilised jars. Care should be taken to reduce it sufficiently, otherwise it will be too liquid.

TOMATO AND APPLE CHUTNEY

4 lb. green tomatoes
2 lb. apples
1 lb. onions
½ oz. bruised root ginger
1½ lb. sultanas or chopped figs
¼ lb. sugar
¼ tsp. cayenne pepper
1 oz. salt
1 oz. garlic, finely chopped
1 quart vinegar

Slice and chop the tomatoes, peel and core the apples, and cut in thick slices; chop the onions. Tie the ginger in muslin. Put all the ingredients in a saucepan, bring to the boil, and simmer gently until the vegetables are tender, and the chutney of the desired consistency. Remove the ginger. Pot, and cover.

SAUCE AND KETCHUP RECIPES, ETC.

MUSHROOM KETCHUP

5 lb. mushrooms
2 oz. salt
½ pint vinegar
½ tsp. grated nutmeg
1 tsp. horseradish
3 cloves
2 tbsps. allspice
½ tsp. pepper
½ tsp. ground mace
1 small onion
1 clove of garlic

Mince the mushrooms, put the salt over them, and leave overnight. Add all the other ingredients, cook slowly for 2 hours, strain (or sieve), bottle, and sterilise at 186° F. for 30 minutes. Cork, and seal with paraffin wax.

GREEN TOMATO RELISH

3 lb. green tomatoes
3 small onions
1 pint malt vinegar
1 tbsp. salt
1 tsp. black pepper
2 tsps. made mustard
½ lb. brown sugar

Wipe the tomatoes and slice them. Peel and shred the onions. Place all the ingredients in a preserving pan, and cook gently for 3–4 hours, stirring occasionally. When all is soft, rub through a coarse sieve. Re-boil the pulp. Pour into jars or bottles, and cover immediately.

GREEN TOMATO SAUCE

6 lb. green tomatoes
1 lb. apples, peeled and cored
½ lb. sliced onions
1½ lb. Demerara sugar
3–4 oz. salt
1½ oz. peppercorns
2 tsps. cayenne pepper
6 cloves
A few blades of mace
2 tsps. celery seed
1½ pints vinegar

Slice the tomatoes and apples, add the onions, sugar, salt, and spices, etc., and pour the vinegar over them. Boil gently until the sauce is thick and dark. Rub through a hair sieve, adding more vinegar, if necessary. Re-boil, and bottle.

RED TOMATO SAUCE

12 lb. red tomatoes
1 lb. sugar
1 pint spiced vinegar
2 fluid oz. tarragon or chilli vinegar
A pinch of cayenne pepper
¼ oz. paprika pepper
1½ oz. salt

Wash the tomatoes thoroughly. Place in a pan over a low heat, stir until the contents of the pan become liquid, then reduce by boiling until the contents are thick. Rub through a sieve, add the sugar, vinegars, peppers, and salt. Continue stirring and boiling until the sauce is of a creamy consistency. Pour into hot sterile bottles. Have ready corks boiled in water, cork at once, and either cover with proper metal caps, or when the sauce is cold dip the necks of the bottles in melted paraffin wax.

MINT SAUCE

Mint leaves
½ lb. sugar
¾ pint vinegar

Use freshly gathered mint; wash, dry, and chop it finely, and half-fill small glass jars, Put the sugar and vinegar into a pan and stir over the heat until dissolved. When cool, pour over the mint and cover the jars.

PHILADELPHIA RELISH

3 lb. green tomatoes	¼ lb. salt
6 cucumbers	4 pints vinegar
3 heads of celery (stalks only)	½ lb. sugar
	½ oz. peppercorns
1½ lb. onions	½ oz. cloves
1 small cabbage	1 oz. mustard seed
2 small cauliflowers	

Chop the vegetables coarsely, then put alternate layers of the vegetables and of salt in a large basin, sprinkling about 4 tbsps. salt over each layer of vegetables. Allow to stand for 24 hours then drain, wash, and dry thoroughly. Put the vegetables, vinegar, sugar and spices in a pan, bring to the boil, pack into hot jars and cover.

TARRAGON VINEGAR

Gather a handful of tarragon leaves on a dry day, just before the plant flowers. Wash, remove the stalks, dry very thoroughly on a cloth. Put the leaves in a wide-necked bottle, and add 1 quart of vinegar. Cork tightly, and leave in a cool, dry place for about 8 weeks. Strain three times through fine muslin until it is clear, then taste, and add more vinegar if required. When bottled it is ready for use.

Other herbs, e.g., mint, thyme, marjoram, or basil, may be used in the same way.

elicious – HOT or COLD

Salad Hints

TRY fresh fruit; oranges, apples or pineapples with your green salad to give an unusual and attractive flavour.

A GOOD salad dressing can be made with vinegar and olive oil with a touch of red pepper. Rub bowl with cut clove of garlic for extra flavour. Ideally the dressing should be added at the table and the salad tossed in it.

ew Zealand Lamb

THERE'S NOTHING BETTER THAN THE BEST

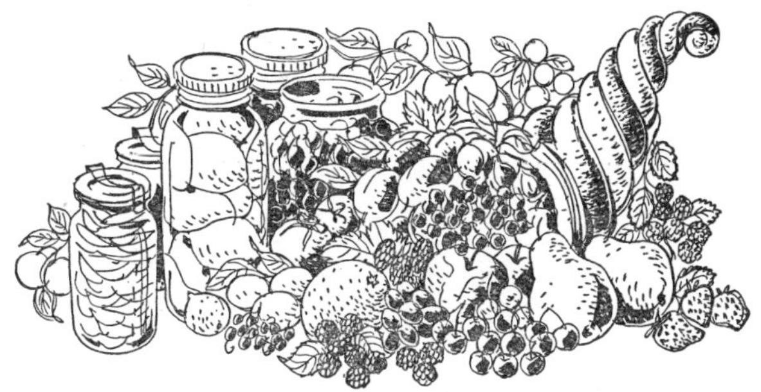

BOTTLING, CANNING, DEEP FREEZING

The joy of having a supply of delicious summer fruits ready for use in the winter-time amply repays the time given to the task of preserving.

FRUIT BOTTLING

When dealing with a large amount of fruit, and especially if you are new to fruit preserving, it is as well to set aside a whole day at a time when bottling can be the main preoccupation, so that you can give it all the necessary attention. But if your time is very limited, you can bottle in quite small and frequent batches, fitting it in with the routine cooking, and in this way build up a useful store of fruits with very little expenditure of time.

The two chief principles underlying the processes in fruit bottling are :

1. The destruction of the yeasts, moulds, enzymes and bacteria present in the tissues of the fruit, which if not destroyed would cause decay ; this is done by sterilising the fruit.

2. The hermetic sealing of the sterilised fruit, so as to exclude air and thus prevent the entry of any more of the organisms which cause spoilage.

So long as the fruit is adequately sterilised and the jars hermetically sealed, the fruit will keep indefinitely. Once the jars are opened the contents will, of course, keep only as long as will freshly stewed fruits, i.e., 2–3 days.

The above remarks apply whether the steriliser or the oven method of bottling is used.

Elaborate apparatus is not essential, but if you grow your own fruit, or intend to do a large amount of bottling, you will probably like to equip yourself with such apparatus as a steriliser, fitted with a thermometer ; a pair of tongs for lifting the hot jars ; a long-handled wooden packing spoon ; and a bottle brush.

The Bottling Jars

There are several types of jars made specially for the purpose of bottling. In principle they are all the same, that is, they are fitted with a rubber ring and a lid (of glass or metal) and are provided with some means of holding the lid firmly in position ; this may be a metal screw band, a clip or a metal spring cap.

The jars are made in sizes of 1 or 1½ lb., 2 lb. and 3 lb. It is a good idea to choose at least some jars with wide necks, for they are easier to pack, especially with large fruits such as Victoria plums or pears, and also easier to empty.

If you already have a stock of bottles, it is well to make a survey of them before the preserving season starts. This entails pairing them up with their lids and screws or clips ; testing rubber bands ; examining lacquered lids and making any necessary replacements or additional purchases.

As a general rule it is advisable to buy new rubber rings each season, but good quality ones may be used several times if necessary. As soon as they show signs of perishing or if they become in any way damaged, they must be discarded. Metal lids are lacquered on the inside to protect them from fruit acids. When using this type of lid, therefore, it is important to make sure that the lacquer film is intact. Lids with imperfections in the lacquer should not be used again.

There are several types of covers specially designed for use with ordinary jam jars, and if used with care these can be very satisfactory. The jars must be of standard size (1 lb. or 2 lb.) and the rims free from chips, bumps or other imperfections. The manufacturers' directions should be carefully followed.

Failing proper jars and covers, odd-shaped jars or jam jars can be utilised, being sealed with paraffin wax or clarified mutton fat, etc.; another method of sealing is to use layers of paper and paste (see page 484). These homely seals are only suitable to use with the oven method of sterilising.

Preparation of the Jars

Examine the jars to see that the rims are free from chips or other imperfections which would be likely to prevent them from sealing. Then wash thoroughly in warm soapy water, and rinse well. It is better not to dry the jars with a cloth, but just to shake them to remove any excess water, or place them upside down to drain.

Soak rubber bands in cold water.

The Syrup

Fruit may be bottled satisfactorily in water, but the flavour is much superior if syrup is used. A suitable syrup for most fruits is made with 4 lb. of sugar to a gallon of water, but as much as 6 or 8 lb. to the gallon may be used for very acid fruits. To prepare the syrup, put the sugar and water into a saucepan, cover and bring to boil; boil for 1 minute, strain through muslin.

The Fruit

Choose firm, dry fruit that is just ripe. For preference it should be picked on a dry day, though of course this cannot always be arranged. Bottle the fruit as soon as possible after gathering.

Prepare the fruit as for stewing, i.e., top and tail gooseberries; remove stalks from currants; hull loganberries, blackberries, strawberries and raspberries; halve and stone plums if very large; cut rhubarb into convenient-sized lengths. When necessary wash the fruit gently in plenty of cold water.

Apples, pears, peaches and some other fruits tend to discolour unless ascorbic acid tablets are added. Dissolve tablets in covering liquid and proceed in usual way. For each pint jar use 125 mg., i.e. 1¼ tablets of 100 mg. (2,000 i.u. potency), or 2½ tablets of 50 mg. (1,000 i.u. potency), or 5 tablets of 25 mg. (500 i.u. potency).

Apples and pears may, if preferred, be peeled into a bowl of salted water (1 oz. salt to 2 quarts cold water) to prevent discolouring. The fruit must be well rinsed after it is packed into jars.

Packing the Jars and Sterilising

Whenever possible, grade the fruit according to size and ripeness. Pack it tightly into the jars without bruising, using a packing spoon or the handle of a wooden spoon if necessary to push the fruit gently into place. Shake the fruit down by striking the bottom of the jar smartly with the palm of the hand.

Sterilise the fruit, either under water or in the oven, according to the directions given in the following pages.

To Test for a Seal

When the jars are quite cold, i.e., the next day, remove screw bands or clips. You should be able to lift the jars by the lids—this shows that a vacuum has formed on cooling and the jars are hermetically sealed.

Testing the Seal

Any jars that are not sealed must be re-sterilised before storing.

Storage

Bottled fruit should be stored in a cool, dry place. It is wise to re-check the seals a week or so after putting away, and occasionally during the storage period. If, as sometimes happens, sterilisation is not complete, or if a breakdown in the seal occurs, fermentation or mould growth will set in. If this is noticed in the early stages, while the fruit in the jars is still wholesome, it can be used at once, and need not be wasted.

Slight over-cooking, the use of a heavy syrup, or loose packing will cause fruit to rise in the jars during storage, which sometimes worries novices. It is often difficult to avoid over-cooking, especially when the oven method of sterilisation is used. It does not, however, affect the keeping quality of the fruit—provided that sterilisation is complete and the jars hermetically sealed, the fruit should keep.

STERILISING UNDER WATER

This is, on the whole, the most reliable method of bottling fruit. Special apparatus is not essential. A steriliser fitted with a thermometer is very convenient, but any deep receptacle such as a large saucepan, fish-kettle, clothes-boiler or even a clean pail will do quite well. The container should be deep enough to enable the jars to be covered with water, or for the water to be at least up to the neck of the jars. It must be fitted with a false bottom, which may be made of wire—such as the rack of a grill pan or a small cake rack—or of slatted wood. In the absence of these, several thicknesses of cloth or newspaper can be used. The rack, however, is better, as it allows the steam to escape and prevents excessive bubbling. Pack a cloth or a pad of crumpled paper between the jars to prevent their touching.

Packing and Sterilising

Prepare, wash and grade the fruit and pack it tightly into clean jars. Fill the jars to the top with cold syrup (or water) and put on the rubber rings, lids and clips or screw bands. Loosen the screw bands slightly, by about one half-turn.

Place the bottles in the steriliser or container, with cold water to cover them or to come well up to the neck. Cover with a lid to prevent evaporation. Heat very gently, so that after 1½ hours the water reaches the appropriate temperature for sterilising (see chart). Then adjust the heat and maintain this temperature—see chart.

Lift the jars out on to a wooden surface or folded newspaper. Tighten the screw bands immediately, and again after a few minutes' cooling. Leave undisturbed to cool. The next day, test the seals.

Temperatures and Times

When sterilising fruit by the under-water method, take 1½ hours to raise the temperature gradually to figure given, and maintain for time stated in last column. If no thermometer is available, heat very gradually to a slow simmering temperature, and maintain for 15–20 minutes.

Fruit	*Degrees F.*	*Minutes*
Apples	165	15
Apricots, Peaches	180	15
Blackberries, Loganberries	165	10
Cherries	190	10
Currants (black, red or white)	180	15
Gooseberries	180	15
Grapefruit	165	10
Grapes	180	15
Mulberries	165	10
Oranges, Tangerines, Lemons	165	20
Pears	190	30
Pineapple	180	15
Plums, Greengages, Damsons	180	15
Quinces	190	30
Raspberries	165	10
Rhubarb	165	10
Strawberries	180	15
Tomatoes	190	30
Whortleberries	180	15

Quick Method of Sterilising Under Water

The following method is useful when time is short, but the finished appearance of fruit sterilised in this way is slightly less good than when the more usual method is followed.

Prepare and grade the fruit and pack it into warmed jars. Fill up the jars with syrup or water heated to 140° F., and put on the rubber rings, lids and clips or screw-bands. Loosen screw-bands by about one half-turn.

Place the bottles in the pan or steriliser on a rack, folded cloth or paper, and just cover with warm water (100° F.). Cover the pan and raise the temperature of the water to 190° F. (or simmering point) in 25–30 minutes. Maintain this temperature for the following times:

Fruit	*Time*
Soft fruits (including gooseberries and rhubarb) for pies; apple slices (average pack)	2 minutes
Soft fruits (including gooseberries and rhubarb) for dessert; most whole stoned fruit (tight pack)	10 minutes
Apples (solid pack); nectarines; peaches; halved plums	20 minutes
Figs; pears	40 minutes

STERILISING IN THE OVEN

144 This simple method (which is useful when no deep receptacle is available for sterilising under water) can be used for all fruits except pears, some apples, peaches and apricots, which tend to discolour. It is quicker than the water sterilising method. There are two ways of carrying it out :

1. Liquid added after Sterilisation

The covering liquid is added to the jars when they are removed from the oven.

Prepare, wash and grade the fruit as described above and pack it tightly into clean jars. Do not add any syrup or water and do not put on the rubber rings, clips or screw bands ; but cover each jar with a patty-pan, or other lid to protect the top fruit from scorching, or put a baking tin over all the jars.

Place the jars on a baking sheet in a slow oven (325° F., mark 2) and keep them at this temperature until the fruit begins to shrink and appears cooked, and the juice begins to run—¾–1 hour (allow tomatoes 1–1½ hours). If the shrinkage is considerable, use the contents of one jar to fill up the others, replacing them in oven for another 5–10 minutes to complete sterilisation.

Have ready fast-boiling syrup or water, the rubber rings, lids, screw bands or clips. Remove one jar at a time from the oven and place it on a wooden surface or folded newspaper. Fill up with boiling syrup or water, place the rings and lid in position, and secure immediately with the screw band, clip or cap, according to type. Reboil the syrup or water and proceed with the next jar. Tighten the screw bands again after a few minutes' cooling. Leave the jars undisturbed to cool. The next day test the seals as described above.

2. Liquid added before Sterilisation

First heat the oven to 300° F., mark 1. Pack jars with fruit, fill up with syrup or cold water and put the rubber rings and covers in position. (If screw band jars are used, the bands must not be put on until after processing.) Put the jars in a baking tin containing about 1 inch of cold water, put into the oven and cook for 75–95 minutes, according to type : for most fruits 75–80 minutes is sufficient, but pears, quinces and tomatoes require 95 minutes. If at any point during the sterilising period the oven temperature drops below 300° F., a longer time will be required to complete the sterilisation.

Fruit	*Time, at 300°–320° F.*
1. Apples (in syrup) Apricots Blackberries Damsons Gooseberries Greengages Loganberries Raspberries Rhubarb Strawberries	75 minutes
2. Apples (solid pack) Cherries Currants (black, red or white) Grapes Peaches Plums	80 minutes
3. Pears Quinces Tomatoes	95 minutes

3. Quick Method

Prepare and grade the fruit as above, and pack into hot jars. Fill the jars with boiling syrup or water to within 1 inch of the top. Put on the rubber rings and covers, but do not put on screw-bands until after processing.

Place the jars 2 inches apart on a baking sheet lined with newspaper, and put them in the centre part of the oven, which must be pre-heated to 300° F., mark 1, and controlled to maintain this temperature. Process for times given in the following chart :

Fruit	*Time*
Soft fruits (including gooseberries and rhubarb) for pies ; apple slices (average pack)	30–40 mins.
Soft fruits (including gooseberries and rhubarb) for dessert ; most whole stoned fruit (tight pack)	40–50 mins.
Apples (solid pack), nectarines ; peaches, halved plums	50–60 mins.
Figs ; pears	60–70 mins.

BOTTLING PULPED FRUIT

Bottling fruit in the form of pulp is quick and easy. The fruit can be stored more compactly in this way, and the pulp is useful for puddings or can be made into jam at a later date. The pulp can be bottled with or without sugar.

First stew the prepared fruit in the minimum amount of water. When it is thoroughly cooked and mashed, and while still hot, pour at once into hot sterilised jars; seal immediately, as when bottling. Deal with one jar at a time, and reheat the pulp before filling the next jar. When cold, test the seal in the usual way.

Provided the fruit is boiling hot when poured into the jar, and the filling and sealing are quickly and carefully carried out, the fruit should keep satisfactorily without further sterilisation. As an extra precaution, however, the filled and sealed jars may be sterilised. Loosen screw bands by a half-turn, immerse bottles in hot water, standing them on a rack or folded cloth, and bring the water to the boil. Boil for 5 minutes, then remove, cool, and test as for bottled fruit.

For fruit purée, make and sterilise as for pulp, but when the fruit is tender, pass it through a stainless metal, nylon or hair sieve, then bring it back to the boil.

RESTERILISING

If any jars of fruit have failed to seal, remove the tops and rubber rings, and wipe off any pips or fruit fibres which may be adhering to them. "Top up" the jars with syrup or water. If the rubber rings are hard, replace with new rings, first boiling these in water for 5 minutes.

Resterilise by the under-water method, timing carefully. The water should not be allowed to boil, as this causes the fruit to taste stewed.

COLOURING FOR BOTTLED FRUIT

The addition of a little suitable colouring to the syrup used for bottling rhubarb, strawberries, cherries, etc., gives a better appearance to the fruit. Special powder colours are available for this purpose. Red-currant juice may also be used.

LEFT-OVER BOTTLING SYRUP

If any syrup is left over after all the jars have been filled, this may be strained, poured into a jar, sealed and sterilised at the same time as the fruit.

FRUIT JUICES AND SYRUPS

Sweetened and unsweetened juices are useful for winter sweets, sauces and drinks. The best fruits are blackberries, raspberries, strawberries, loganberries and black-currants, while rose-hips (see recipe below) make a syrup rich in vitamin C. The fruit must be really ripe and fresh.

Have ready some small jars and covers suitable for fruit bottling, or bottles with screw caps or corks. Heat the jars in a cool oven or by bringing them to the boil in water. Boil caps or corks for 10 minutes.

Put the fruit in a pan with little or no water (but for black-currants add ½ pint water per lb. and for blackberries ½ pint water per 5–6 lb.). Bring to the boil, stirring and crushing frequently but avoid over-cooking. Strain the pulp through a jelly bag.

For a very clear liquid, allow the juice to stand for several hours, so that any sediment can settle.

To make a syrup, add ½–¾ lb. sugar per pint of the strained juice, dissolving it well. Strain 145
through muslin.

Pour the fruit juice or syrup into the bottles to within 2 inches of cork or stopper, and seal tightly, fixing with wire, etc. Put in a deep pan, on a false bottom, and fill with cold water up to the base of the corks. Heat to 170° F. and maintain this temperature for 30 minutes. (If no thermometer is available, raise to simmering point and maintain for 20 minutes.) Remove the bottles and dip the corks into melted paraffin wax when partly cooled. If no screw caps are used, wire the corks on. Store in a cool, dry place.

ROSE-HIP SYRUP

The hips should be fresh, fully ripe and deep red. Crush or grate and put at once in boiling water, allowing 3 pints to 2 lb. hips. Bring back to boiling point, then set aside for 10 minutes. Strain through a jelly bag, and when it ceases to drip, return the pulp from the bag to the pan, with a further 1½ pints boiling water. Bring back to boiling point, leave for 10 minutes, then strain as before. Mix the two extracts, and reduce by boiling until the juice measures 1½ pints. Add 1 lb. sugar and stir till dissolved. Bottle, sterilise and seal.

FRUIT IN BRANDY

Fruits such as peaches, apricots, etc., are very delicious if preserved in spirits. The following recipe shows the general method used.

BRANDIED PEACHES

4 lb. peaches ¾ pint water
3 lb. sugar Brandy

Stew the peaches (which should be just ripe but not too soft). Meanwhile put the sugar and water in a preserving pan or large saucepan, stir until the sugar is dissolved, then boil hard for 5 minutes. Drop the peaches as they are peeled into the hot syrup and simmer gently until the fruit can be easily pierced with a skewer but is not over-soft. Drain off the syrup and continue to boil it rapidly for about 10 minutes, until it thickens, then pour it over the peaches and leave to stand. When the fruit is cold lift it out, using a draining spoon, and place in hot sterilised jars. Measure the syrup, add an equal quantity of brandy and pour over the fruit. Seal and leave to mature.

PRESERVING TOMATOES

Tomatoes intended for preserving must be fully ripe, but firm and sound. The choicest fruit is best for bottling or canning, while less well-shaped fruit can be used for tomato sauce or purée. Green fruit, though not suitable for bottling or canning, may be used in sauce or chutney (see separate chapter).

BOTTLED TOMATOES

Tomatoes may be bottled whole, if small, or can be quartered or sliced, if the fruit is large. It is best to skin them before bottling; to remove the skins easily, first put the tomatoes into boiling water for a few seconds.

Include 2 tsps. salt and 1 tsp. sugar in each 2 lb. jar of fruit, to improve the flavour.

To Sterilise under Water: After packing the jars as closely as possible, fill them up either with cold water or with tomato juice (prepared by rubbing stewed tomatoes through a sieve). Cover the jars in the usual way for sterilising, loosening screw bands by one half-turn. To sterilise, immerse the jars in water, raise the temperature to 190° F. (or simmering point, if no thermometer is available) in 1½ hours, and maintain for 30 minutes. Remove, cool, and test the jars next day in the usual way.

To Sterilise in the Oven: Prepare the fruit and pack as above, but avoid packing jars very closely when using this method; do not add any liquid. Cover each jar with a patty tin to prevent the top fruit from scorching during sterilisation. Do not put rubber rings, clips or screw bands in position. Place the jars on a baking sheet, put in a slow oven (325° F., mark 2) and leave until the fruit shrinks and appears cooked (1½ hours). As the shrinkage is usually considerable, the contents of one jar may be used to fill up the others. When this is done, replace the jars in the oven for a further 5–10 minutes to complete sterilisation. Finally, remove the jars from the oven one at a time, fill up with boiling water and cover immediately, finishing one jar before removing a second one from oven. Cool, and test jars for a seal next day.

QUICK METHODS OF STERILISING TOMATOES

Under-water Sterilising: Prepare as above, but pack the tomatoes into warmed jars, cover with hot brine (4 oz. salt to 1 gallon water; temperature 140° F.) and then with warm water (100° F.). Cover, and raise the temperature of the water to 190° F. in 25–30 minutes.

For whole tomatoes, in brine, maintain this temperature for 40 minutes; for solid-pack tomatoes, maintain the temperature for 50 minutes.

Sterilising in the Oven: Prepare as required. Pack into hot jars and fill to within 1 inch of the top with boiling brine. Put on rings and covers, but do not put on screw-bands until after processing. Stand the jars 2 inches apart on a baking tin lined with newspaper, and place in the centre of an oven pre-heated to 300° F., mark 1, and controlled to maintain this temperature.

Sterilise whole tomatoes in brine for 60–70 minutes, and solid-pack tomatoes for 70–80 minutes.

TOMATO PURÉE

Cut up the tomatoes and put into a saucepan with 2 tsps. salt to every 2 lb. tomatoes. Bring to the boil, stirring frequently, and cook gently until a thick pulp is obtained. Sieve this and pour into warmed jars. Cover as for bottled fruit. To sterilise, put the jars into a pan of hot water, bring to a temperature of 190° F. in 1½ hours (simmering point if no thermometer is available), and maintain this temperature for 15 minutes. This pulp is useful for soups and sauces in the winter months.

A quicker method, which dispenses with sieving, is to skin, cut up and stew the tomatoes and bottle them while still boiling hot, as for pulped fruit.

TOMATO JUICE

Simmer ripe tomatoes until they are soft, then rub through a sieve. To each 2 pints of pulp add ½ pint water, ½ oz. sugar, 2 tsps. salt and a shake of pepper. Put into jars or bottles and sterilise as for tomato pulp, above. Use for making tomato juice cocktails; a little lemon juice or piquant table sauce may be added to the bottled juice when it is served as an appetiser, etc.

BOTTLING VEGETABLES

Vegetables must be processed at a much higher temperature than is required for bottled fruit. Whereas fruits contain natural acids which, together with a moderate heat, will kill any bacteria present, vegetables lack these acids and may also be contaminated by soil bacteria, the spores of which are very resistant to heat. A temperature higher than 212° F. is therefore necessary to kill the bacteria and make the vegetables safe for storing. To achieve such temperatures the sterilising must be done under pressure, and the pan or cooker must be designed to operate accurately at a pressure of 10 lb.

Preparation : Only fresh, young vegetables in first-class condition should be bottled. Grade them for size, and wash and prepare them as for ordinary cooking. Cut into even-sized pieces, slice or dice when necessary. Mushrooms should be of the small button type; asparagus should be tied in bundles and packed with heads uppermost. Scald celery in water with $\frac{1}{2}$ tsp. of citric acid to 1 quart of water.

Blanching and Sterilising : Blanch the vegetables by tying them in muslin and immersing them in boiling water for the length of time shown in the chart below. Plunge them into cold water, pack them in jars (not too tightly) and cover with brine ($2\frac{1}{2}$ oz. salt to 1 gallon water). Place the tops in position, loosening metal screw bands by one half-turn.

TIME TABLE FOR BOTTLING VEGETABLES

Vegetable	*Blanching*	*Processing time (at 10 lb. pressure, 240° F.)*
Asparagus	2–3 mins.	30 mins.
Beans, broad (white-flowered variety)	2–3 mins.	35 mins.
Beans, French and Runner	2–3 mins.	35 mins.
Beetroot	10–30 mins.	35 mins.
Carrots	10–15 mins.	35 mins.
Celery	5 mins.	30 mins.
Mushrooms	5 mins.	35 mins.
New Potatoes	6–7 mins.	40 mins.
Peas	1–2 mins.	40 mins.
Peppers, red and green	5 mins.	35 mins.

Notes : Increase the time by 5 minutes if bottles larger than 1 pint are used.

Reduce processing times by 5 minutes when using size A-$2\frac{1}{2}$ cans.

Place the jars in the pressure cooker on the rack, over 1 inch of water, taking care that they do not touch the sides of the cooker or each other. Fix the lid of the cooker and heat gently to 240° F., i.e., until a pressure of 10 lb. is shown on the gauge. Adjust to maintain this pressure, and sterilise according to the times in the chart below. Finish as for bottled fruit, and test for a seal the next day.

USING HOME-PRESERVED VEGETABLES

Provided you preserve vegetables in good condition and follow the directions carefully, there is no reason why your bottled or canned goods should not keep well, but here are a few hints to guide you.

When the (cold) bottle or can is opened, there should be no sudden escape of air or liquid; the only odour should be the characteristic smell of the particular food, and the inside of a can should look smooth and clean and not markedly corroded. If there is the slightest trace of spoilage, discard the food at once—do not taste it to find out whether it is in good condition. A really " blown " can is, of course, easily recognised, for the ends bulge outwards owing to the pressure of gas from the fermenting food inside; such a can should be discarded unopened, and the contents should on no account be sampled.

Even when your home bottled or canned vegetables pass all the tests satisfactorily, it is still quite a wise precaution to boil them before serving them.

CANNING

FRUIT

Canning is a convenient method of preserving, if the quantity is large enough to warrant the purchase of a sealing machine and cans. Of the sizes of can available, No. $2\frac{1}{2}$ is most convenient for home use. Cans may be either tinned steel plate or lacquer-lined, the latter type being essential for red fruits such as raspberries, rhubarb, black-currants, etc. Unlacquered cans may be used for light-coloured green or yellow fruits.

The same rules concerning the choice and 146
preparation of the fruit apply as for bottling.

Rinse out the cans and fill one at a time with fruit, adding syrup or water to within $\frac{1}{4}$ inch of the top. Immediately each can is full, seal it on the machine, following the maker's special directions.

Quickly place the cans in a pan or steriliser

containing enough boiling water to cover them. Re-boil the water and sterilise according to the table below. (Note that the longer the time taken for the water to re-boil, the shorter the time needed for the cans to be kept in boiling water.) Cool the cans in cold water to prevent further cooking, and label and store as for bottled fruit.

Fruit	*Time taken to re-boil water (mins.)*	*Extra time in boiling water (mins.)*
Apples (in syrup), apricots, blackberries, damsons, gooseberries, loganberries, ripe plums, raspberries, red currants, rhubarb, strawberries	0–5 6–10 11–15 16–20	18–15 15–13 12–10 10–8
Apples (solid pack), black-currants, cherries, pears (ripe dessert), plums (under-ripe)	0–5 6–10 11–15 16–20	22–20 20–18 17–15 15–13
Tomatoes in brine (solid pack tomatoes should have 10 minutes extra boiling)	0–5 6–10 11–15 16–20	35–32 32–30 30–27 27–25

VEGETABLES

Vegetables must be processed under pressure, and only a person experienced in using a pressure cooker should attempt them. Cans lined with a sulphur-resisting lacquer are best for vegetables.

Blanch the prepared vegetables according to the chart for bottling vegetables. Pack the vegetables into cans and fill them with brine (2½ oz. salt to 1 gallon water) to within ½ inch of the top. Immediately place a lid on each can and put them into water at simmering temperature; it should come to within 1 inch of the top of the cans. Leave for 5 minutes, so that the contents of the cans are heated and the air is expelled, then remove the cans one at a time and seal in the usual way, as soon as they are removed from the hot water. Now sterilise the cans under pressure, following the chart for bottled vegetables, but if using size A-2½ cans, reduce time by 5 minutes. Cool, dry, label, and store as for canned fruit.

HOME PRESERVING OF MEAT, POULTRY AND FISH

The home bottling and canning of meat, poultry and fish, though possible, is not recommended, as very carefully controlled conditions must operate to ensure safety. Deep freezing (see this page) is becoming an increasingly popular method of preserving in this country.

DEEP FREEZE PRESERVATION

As mentioned in the chapter on Storing, deep freezing is ideal for those who have a large amount of fruit and vegetables to store. The following are some notes on the preparation of various types of food for storage in a deep freeze cabinet. The special deep freeze compartment which is incorporated in some types of ordinary refrigerator is also suitable for small quantities of fruit and vegetables.

Fruit : Usually frozen in a syrup or in sugar, without other treatment, though apples keep a better colour if blanched.

Vegetables : Dip them into boiling water and then cook for 1–4 minutes; cool, and place in a suitable packaging.

Flesh foods : When a deep freeze cabinet is available, flesh foods can be preserved. They must be packed in moisture-proof and vapour-proof materials (see below), so that air is excluded. Stockinette is sometimes used over this, to facilitate handling.

There is some doubt among commercial deep freeze processers as to whether birds should be drawn before freezing; since, however, there is a danger of spoiling the flavour of the flesh if the internal organs are left in, it is usually considered best to remove them. Poultry or game may be stored raw or cooked, but should only be frozen in the latter state where extreme care in handling can be ensured. Certain stuffings can be used: breadcrumbs, chicken fat, and sage keep well, but sausage-meat and onion are best avoided.

Eggs cannot be deep-frozen in their shells, but can be broken and stored in jars or waxed containers, preferably in the amounts needed for cooking purposes. Syrup or sugar should be added, in the proportion of 2 tbsps. to 8 eggs.

PACKAGING

All foods must be packed in moisture-proof and airproof material before freezing, the type varying according to the food. Pliofilm, aluminium, plastic, or cellulose wrappings are used for flesh foods, to prevent drying out; if used for cooked flesh foods, they should be sterilised before use. Wax-impregnated and plastic containers, tins, and glass jars are used for liquids.

COOKING HOME-FROZEN FOODS

Vegetables: Plunge these into the least possible amount of boiling water to cover, and cook for the minimum length of time to make them tender. If frozen in brine, use this as part of the cooking liquid.

Fruits : For use in salads, thawing only is necessary. If they are to be served raw, do not thaw until needed, then thaw them slowly in the unopened container in the kitchen or refrigerator : this may take 3 hours in the first case, and up to 8 hours in the second, but the exact time depends on the size and shape of the package.

Meat : This can be thawed before cooking, or cooked while in the frozen state. In the latter case, allow longer cooking time.

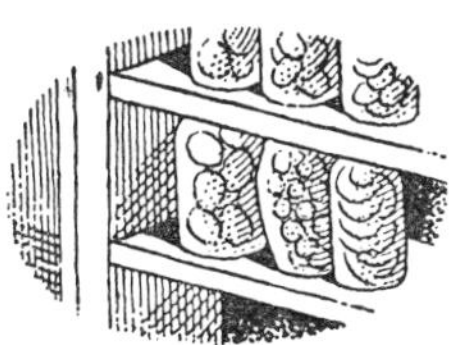

DRYING, SALTING AND EGG PRESERVING

FRUIT AND VEGETABLE DRYING

The method of preserving fruit and vegetables by drying is not used extensively in this country, owing to the fact that the climate is generally unfavourable for this process. However, certain fruits and vegetables, and of course herbs, can be dried by exposing them to artificial heat.

The fruit and vegetables must be spread out so that the air can circulate round them easily. Any of the following can be used for this purpose : a wooden rack, wire cake rack or oven rack, with a layer of muslin spread over if the mesh is very wide ; a wooden frame with muslin or coarse canvas stretched across, attached with tacks or drawing pins ; sieves ; canes or strings (for apple rings, mushrooms, etc.).

Drying must be carried out slowly and may be done in any of these ways : in a current of warm fresh air (e.g., by an open window) ; in a cool oven (not more than 140° F., between marks 0 and ¼ ; leave the door ajar for steam to escape) ; on the rack above a solid fuel cooker or boiler ; in an airing cupboard ; above hot-water pipes or a radiator.

The drying process may take anything from several hours to 2–3 days, but it may be done intermittently as and when convenient, e.g., after the oven has been used for cooking or in the range oven at night when the fire is out.

When drying is completed, leave the fruit and vegetables to cool for 12 hours before storing. Keep in a cool, dry, well-ventilated place, in store jars, tins or paper-lined boxes. There is no necessity to make these airtight.

DRYING FRUITS

Apples : Prepare the fruit by peeling, coring and slicing in rings about ¼ inch thick, using a stainless steel knife or peeler.

To prevent discoloration and to bleach the flesh, treat the rings with fumes of sulphur dioxide as follows :

Have ready a number of glass jars and invert these one at a time over burning flowers of sulphur, or a sulphur candle. (The fumes of burning sulphur are very suffocating, so this process should be done out of doors.) As each jar is filled with the gas, remove it and cover with a lid or saucer. Add the apple rings, not tightly packed, and leave for 15 minutes, shaking every 3–4 minutes to ensure that all cut surfaces come into contact with the fumes. Remove the rings, spread on trays or thread on thin sticks and dry in a slow oven (not above 180° F., mark ¼) until leathery in texture.

Note : The sulphuring process may be omitted if a darkish colour is not objected to, or alternatively, the sliced apples may be put into a weak brine—1½ oz. salt to 1 gallon of water—for a few minutes before drying.

Pears : These should be nearly ripe. Peel, core and cut into halves or quarters. Put into brine (made by dissolving 1½ oz. salt in a gallon of water) for 5 minutes to prevent discoloration, dry with a cloth, spread on trays and dry.

Stone Fruit : These can be dried whole, or large fruits, such as plums or greengages, can be cut in half and dried after the stones have been removed. Dry until no juice comes out when the fruit is squeezed.

Grapes : Spread out and continue drying until the grapes are no longer juicy.

DRYING VEGETABLES

Onions : Drying is an excellent way of treating onions which are unsuitable for harvesting. Peel the onions and slice them into rings, then steam for 1–2 minutes or blanch in boiling water for ½ minute. Plunge them into cold water, drain, and spread out to dry until crisp.

Mushrooms : Choose young and tender mushrooms, skin them and cut or slice if very big. Spread out or string (with knots between) to dry until leathery.

Runner Beans : String and slice the beans, then blanch in boiling slightly salted water for 3–5 minutes. Plunge them into cold water, drain and spread out to dry until crisp.

Broad Beans : Shell them and blanch in

boiling water for 3–5 minutes. Plunge them into cold water, drain and spread out to dry.

Peas and Haricots : These are best harvested. To do this, allow them to hang upon the plants until the pods become yellow. Then gather the pods, shuck them and spread the seeds out to dry before storing. Late crops (especially haricots) should be pulled up bodily and hung in a dry, airy place to ripen before shelling.

8 DRYING HERBS : See section on Herbs.

SALTING FRENCH AND RUNNER BEANS

Salting is a simple and excellent way of preserving French and runner beans for winter use. A glass or stoneware jar or crock is required —glazed earthenware is not suitable, as the salt impairs the glaze and renders the vessel porous.

1. Choose small, young beans and make sure that they are clean and dry. Break them in two if very long, but do not slice them. Arrange alternate layers of beans and cooking salt in the jar, allowing about 1 lb. of salt to every 3–4 lb. of beans. Finish with a layer of salt, press down firmly, and leave for a few days to settle down. More beans may be added as they become ready, always finishing with a layer of salt.
2. When the crock is full, finish with a good layer of salt.
3. Cover closely with a lid or several layers of paper.
4. Do not leave on a stone floor, but raise on a wooden shelf or board.

To use the salted beans, rinse well in cold water or soak for a few minutes only. Cook and serve as for fresh beans, omitting the salt when boiling. Long soaking tends to make the beans tough.

If the beans are old and inclined to be tough, add a pinch of bicarbonate of soda to the cooking water to soften them slightly. (This is not recommended as a general practice, as it tends to reduce the vitamin content of vegetables.)

PRESERVING EGGS

The season for preserving eggs is the springtime, for not only are they most plentiful then (and therefore at their cheapest), but also eggs laid in the spring keep better than those laid later in the year. For preserving they should, for preference, be non-fertile, though this is not essential.

Hens' eggs, when freshly laid, are free from harmful bacteria, and can safely be preserved by any of the methods outlined below.

Duck and Goose eggs, on the other hand, even when newly laid, may be contaminated with bacteria. Although egg-preserving solutions prevent the entry of bacilli into the egg, those already within it are not destroyed by their agency. By-products, set up over long periods, are harmful, and for this reason the preservation of these eggs cannot be recommended. (There need be no hesitancy, of course, in eating the fresh eggs : the products of putrefaction take some time to reach harmful proportions, and the bacillus itself is destroyed during cooking.)

Choice and Preparation of the Eggs

Eggs for preserving should be fresh, though not taken straight from the nesting box ; a minimum period of 24 hours should be allowed before preserving, in order that temperature and air pressure within the egg can reach equilibrium. Eggs more than three or four days old, however, are hardly worth preserving, for there is a risk that bacilli will by this time have found an entry.

The eggs should not be washed, but soiled ones may be wiped carefully with a clean, damp cloth. Do not preserve very dirty eggs, or any with a rough, uneven, very thin or cracked shell.

Waterglass Method of Preserving

A pail, galvanised iron bath or stoneware crock may be used, and it should have a lid. Sufficient waterglass will be required to fill the receptacle about three-quarters full. The exact proportion of waterglass to use for the solution depends on the brand used ; the manufacturers' directions should be carefully followed.

The pickling solution should be quite cold before the eggs are put in. If possible they should be arranged with the pointed ends downwards : this keeps the yolk to the middle of the egg. More eggs may be added as they become available, until the receptacle is full, but care must be taken to see that the solution completely covers the eggs. Cover the receptacle to keep out dust and to minimise evaporation. If the level of the liquid falls through evaporation, leaving the top layer of eggs exposed, cold water should be added until the original level is again reached. A fall in the level of the solution due to the removal of eggs should not be made good, except by the addition of more solution of the same strength.

Dry Pickling

This method consists of applying a protective coating of fat to the eggshell. It is a particularly convenient method to adopt if a move is anticipated, when storage space is limited, or when there is only a small number of eggs to be stored for a few months; (the time stated by the makers of the preservative is usually about 6–8 months). Keep the eggs in baskets or boxes till required. There are two methods:

1. The eggs may be treated with a special liquid preparation consisting essentially of a fat dissolved in a suitable solvent, which evaporates, leaving a coating of fat over the egg. Directions for this process are supplied with the preparation, together with a wire dipper for holding the eggs while coating.

2. The eggs may be rubbed over with a special greasy preparation, using the palms of the hands. Such preparations should be used according to the manufacturer's instructions.

Preserving in Lime Water

This method is preferred by some people, although it involves rather more labour. A solution of finely slaked lime is made in the proportion of 4 parts by measure of lime to 20 parts of cold water. This is stirred each day for a week, one part of common salt being added on the fourth or fifth day. Avoiding all sediment, the clear solution is poured over the eggs in a glass or glazed earthenware vessel. In time a crust forms on the surface of the liquid which checks evaporation.

Transporting Pickled Eggs

If it is found necessary to transport eggs that have been put down in waterglass, the best way is to remove them from the pickle, wrap them individually in soft paper (newspaper will do) for the journey, replacing them in waterglass immediately on arrival at the other end. The eggs should not be out of the pickle longer than is absolutely necessary—2 or 3 days at the most.

If the eggs have been in pickle for some time, a protective coating will have formed on the shell. Provided that this is not damaged in transit, it is likely that the eggs will keep satisfactorily when replaced in pickle. To preserve the coating, see that the eggs are carefully wrapped and firmly packed so that they do not come into contact with each other or rattle about inside the covering.

HOME-MADE WINES

Almost all cultivated fruits, edible wild berries and fruits, many flowers and root vegetables, make excellent wines, which are a useful addition to the store-cupboard. Once the basic methods have been mastered, many different varieties of wine can be produced by combining fruits and vegetables. All ingredients should be perfect, freshly gathered, and dry; any unripe or mildewed berries can spoil the result.

The natural yeast present in fruit and blossoms is sometimes sufficient to start fermentation. When making wine from root vegetables, however, yeast is usually added to help the fermentation; it also helps to increase the spirit content of the wine. Specially prepared wine yeast in tablet form is now obtainable which gives better results than ordinary compressed yeast. It is made up so that one tablet will ferment 1 gallon of wine, and it should be used according to instructions given. Compressed yeast should be added in the proportion of 1 oz. yeast to 1 gallon of wine, the best method being to blend it with a little of the warm vegetable juice.

Most recipes state the kind of sugar which gives the best results. Granulated is the type most generally used, but for a dark golden wine, Demerara sugar or barley sugar may be included. (Remember that these sugars tend to give slightly different flavours.) Poor quality sugar should not be used: it causes cloudiness, and filtering and fining are then necessary.

A very easy branch of wine making is the preparation of fruit liqueurs, for which fermentation is not necessary, as a spirit is used.

THE EQUIPMENT

Like most branches of cookery, wine making is easier if a certain amount of special equipment is available, but it is possible to obtain very good results with utensils found in the ordinary kitchen. Avoid using glazed earthenware containers, or metal containers, whether plain or enamelled (unless the latter are quite free from chips). Wooden, stoneware, or glass vessels, however, may all be used with absolute safety.

For the "working" or fermentation period you will need a wooden tub, glass vessel, stoneware crock or jar, new vinegar jars, or large bottles. For storing, a clean scoured barrel or clean bottles are needed. For straining the wine, use butter muslin or clean linen and a funnel, and if necessary, a jelly bag, unmedicated cotton wool, or filter paper.

All the equipment should be spotlessly clean. Wash all bottles with boiling water and soda, and rinse very thoroughly two or three times; if they are very dirty, leave them to soak for about a week, to remove any stubborn dirt which adheres to the inside. Make sure that the bottles used for storing are perfectly dry inside and out before being filled—moisture on the inside may cause the wine to sour. Always use new corks for each separate brew of wine, as stale ones can cause endless trouble. If the corks are hard, put them into a little boiling water to soften them and make them swell up, but dry them before use.

STAGES IN WINE MAKING

These general directions should be used in conjunction with the particular wine recipe, and modified as necessary.

1. Select dry, perfect, ripe fruit, vegetables or flowers, etc., prepare according to type or as the recipe directs, and weigh.

2. Place in large containers and pour hot or cold water over. Fruit is often crushed, and root vegetables are generally cooked beforehand, the strained juice being used. Cover the container with muslin to prevent dust or dirt entering, and leave for the required time. Avoid storing near anything strong-smelling.

3. Strain off the juice and add the sugar and yeast (if used), and cover with firmly tied brown paper. Have a little extra juice ready to add to the container during fermentation, as it must be kept full to overflowing all the time. A fermentation lock is useful for this process.

4. Leave to ferment in a warm place (65°–80° F.) till all bubbles have ceased. If fermentation is slow, move the container to a warmer place, and vice versa; the aim is to keep the fermentation even and continuous. Wines made with yeast are usually kept in a slightly cooler place than those made without it.

5. After fermentation has ceased, stir the wine gently and leave the sediment to settle for about 2–3 days. Strain as described, and if still very cloudy, "fine" it—see below.

6. Strain into casks or bottles and cork loosely (using new corks previously soaked in boiling water). If corked tightly at this stage, the containers may burst through the pressure of the gases formed during fermentation. When bottles are used, do not fill so full that the wine touches the corks.

7. When all signs of fermentation have ceased, cork tightly. If a sparkling wine is required, cork it tightly just *before* fermentation has ceased; a few grape leaves encourage a sparkle. The container should be full, as if the wine comes into contact with the air, it may become vinegary.

8. Leave to mature for at least 9–12 months. Remember that results do not come rapidly in wine making, and to obtain a well-matured wine it should, if possible, be left for about 12 months. Often, when a sample is taken after three months or so, the flavour is vinegary, but this effect will disappear in time. Examine the bottles occasionally—if a sediment has formed syphon the clear wine into clean bottles—this is known as "racking."

9. Decant into clean, dry bottles, cork tightly, and store in a cool, dark place.

TO CLEAR WINE

In many cases any sediment or cloudiness can be removed by simply straining the wine through a jelly bag, several layers of muslin, or filter paper, but if this is not satisfactory, the process of "fining" has to be followed.

Several methods of fining are recommended, involving the use of such substances as egg white, egg shells, and isinglass; whichever is employed, it should be used only in small quantities, or it may affect the colour and flavour of the wine.

Isinglass: Either (1) add a pinch of isinglass to each bottle, allow it to swell, and, when it has settled at the bottom, strain off the cleared wine; or (2) dissolve a pinch of it in a little warm wine and add this to the bulk of the wine; leave for 10–14 days before straining off.

Egg Shells: Allow 2–3 washed shells to each gallon of wine.

Egg White: One egg white will clear up to about 20 gallons of wine. Beat it until stiff, add to 1 pint of the wine, whisk to a froth, then add to the remaining wine. Leave to settle, and strain off the wine.

BLACKBERRY WINE

1 gallon blackberries
1 gallon boiling water
3 lb. sugar to each gallon liquid

Gather the fruit when ripe and dry. Put into a deep vessel and pour on the boiling water. When cool enough to handle, mash the berries with the hand, then cover, and leave to stand until the pulp has risen and formed a crust: this will take 3–4 days. Strain, and add the sugar in the above proportions. (If the wine is to be kept some time, allow 4 lb. sugar per gallon.) Leave to work till bubbles have ceased. When it has finished fermenting, cork or bung tightly, and keep for 6 months before racking off and bottling.

BLACK-CURRANT WINE

¾ gallon black-currants
¾ gallon boiling water
3½ lb. sugar to every 1 gallon of juice

Strip the currants, wash them very thoroughly, and put them into a large vessel. Bruise to extract the juice, and pour on the boiling water—there should be sufficient to cover the fruit. Leave until the next day, then strain through a coarse linen cloth, pressing the currants well. Measure the juice and add the sugar in the above proportion. When the sugar is dissolved, put into a clean stone jar or cask, and cover lightly. When it stops working, cork securely. Leave for 9 months before bottling.

CARROT WINE

4 lb. carrots
1 gallon water
4 lb. sugar
1 yeast tablet
1 oz. root ginger

Scrub the carrots, scrape and slice them. Put them into a saucepan with the water, and boil until tender. Strain the liquor on to the sugar, and add the yeast, prepared as directed, when the liquor is lukewarm. Leave to ferment as usual, then rack off and bottle. Store for 12 months or more.

HOME-MADE CIDER

1 gallon cooking apples
1 gallon boiling water
Sugar to taste

Wash the apples and mince or chop them, then put them into a tub and pour on the boiling water. Stir daily for a fortnight. Strain, and add sugar to taste. When the sugar has dissolved, put into a barrel, cork lightly at first, until fermentation ceases, then bung tightly. Store for 3 months, then bottle.

COWSLIP WINE

1 gallon cowslip flowers 2 lb. sugar
4 quarts water 2 lemons
1 oz. yeast

Pick the flowers, and remove the calyx from each. Boil the water and sugar for 30 minutes. Pour over the thinly peeled lemon rinds, and cool. Add the cowslip flowers and the strained lemon juice. Stir frequently during the day, then cover, and let stand for one week. Strain into stoppered jar or barrel, and ferment till bubbles cease. Bottle and rack off when the sediment has settled.

DAMSON WINE

4 lb. damsons 3 lb. sugar
1 gallon water, plus 1 pint for evaporation 1 oz. yeast or 1 tablet

Wash and prick the damsons and boil until tender in the water. Strain on to the sugar, and cool until lukewarm. Add the yeast and leave for 24 hours. Put the wine into a cask or bottle, and leave open to work. Fill up with liquid. When the fermentation has finished, cork tightly or bung. Rack off, and bottle after 6 months.

DANDELION WINE

½ gallon dandelion flowers 3 lemons
1 gallon boiling water 1 yeast tablet
3 lb. sugar ½ lb. raisins

Discard the green part of the flowers, and measure only the yellow petals. Pour boiling water over the flowers and leave for 3 days, stirring daily. Strain the liquid, and add sugar, the thinly peeled rind of the lemons, and the lemon juice, and bring to the boil. Leave to cool, then add the yeast and the cut-up raisins. Put into a cask or jar to ferment; when bubbles have ceased to appear, syphon off the wine, bottle and cork, and keep for a year before drinking, racking once or twice if necessary.

ELDERBERRY WINE

7 lb. elderberries 3 gallons boiling water

To each gallon of juice allow:

1 lb. raisins 1 yeast tablet
3 lb. sugar ¼ pint brandy (optional)
½ oz. root ginger

Pick the berries from the stalks, put them into a wooden tub, press well to mash the fruit. Pour on the boiling water, cover, and leave until the next day. Strain through a jelly bag, measure the juice, add all the ingredients except the yeast and the brandy, then bring to the boil, and simmer for ½ hour. Cool until lukewarm, add the yeast, cover and leave for a fortnight. Then strain into a clean jar, cork loosely till fermentation has ceased, add the brandy, then bung tightly. Bottle after 6 months.

ELDERFLOWER WINE

2 lemons 1 pint stripped elder blooms
2 oranges 1 gallon boiling water
2 pieces root ginger 1 oz. yeast
4 lb. Demerara sugar

Wash and slice the lemons and oranges, and put with the ginger, sugar, and elder flowers into a basin. Pour on the boiling water, cool to blood heat, and add the yeast. Allow to stand 4 days, stirring occasionally. Strain, and bottle. Keep for 6 weeks, then rack off.

GINGER WINE

1 gallon water 8 oz. sultanas
4 lb. sugar 2 tsps. yeast
1 oz. bruised ginger ¼ oz. isinglass
Rinds of 2 lemons ¼ pint brandy

Boil together the water, sugar, ginger, and the lemon rinds. When the liquid is lukewarm, put it into a cask, together with the sultanas and yeast. Stir daily for 10 days. When it has ceased to ferment, add the isinglass and brandy. Bung the cask closely and leave for 2 months.

GOOSEBERRY WINE

5 lb. gooseberries 2½ lb. granulated sugar
6 pints water 1 tablet of yeast to each gallon
¼ oz. root ginger (optional)

Top and tail the berries and wash them. Boil all the ingredients, except the yeast, for ¾ hour in a covered vessel. Strain, pressing the pulp to dryness. When the liquid is cool, add the prepared yeast tablet. Ferment as usual, and when fermentation ceases, cork tightly. Keep for 6 months before bottling.

GRAPE WINE

1 gallon grapes 3 lb. granulated sugar
1 gallon water ¼ pint brandy

Strip the grapes from the stalks, and wash thoroughly. Put into a vessel and mash thoroughly without crushing the seeds. Cover with water, and leave for a week, lightly covered. Strain through a jelly bag, add the sugar, and stir until it dissolves; add the brandy. Put the wine into a cask or bottle, bung loosely till bubbles cease, then cork tightly. Keep for at least 6 months before using.

LEMON WINE

20 lemons	6 lb. sugar
2 gallons water	2 yeast tablets

Wash the lemons thoroughly, and peel the rind very thinly off 10 of them. Boil the water and sugar for 1 hour without a lid, then strain the syrup through muslin on to the peel. Cool, and add the strained juice of all the lemons. Prepare the yeast and add it to the liquor; cover, and leave for 48 hours. Strain, bottle, and cork loosely until fermentation ceases, then cork securely. Leave for a year before using.

LOGANBERRY WINE

1 gallon loganberries	1 gallon of boiling water
5 lb. sugar to every gallon of juice	

Bruise the loganberries, and pour the boiling water over them. Cover, and allow to stand for 14 days. Strain, and to every gallon of juice allow 5 lb. of sugar. Stir until dissolved, then put into a jar, cover lightly, and allow to ferment till bubbles have ceased. Cork securely, allow to stand for 4 weeks, then bottle. Keep 6 months.

MIXED FRUIT WINE

1½ lb. red-currants	3 lb. Demerara sugar and ¼ pint of brandy to each gallon of liquor
1½ lb. black-currants	
1½ lb. cherries	
1½ lb. raspberries	
1½ galls. boiling water	

Wash, pick, and bruise the fruit well, then add the boiling water. Allow to stand for 4 days, stirring frequently. Strain through a jelly cloth, and press the pulp to dryness. Allow to stand for another 3 days, stirring frequently. Skim, and put into a jar with 3 lb. of Demarara sugar to each gallon. Ferment for several weeks, then add the brandy before closing down. Keep for 6 weeks before bottling.

ORANGE WINE

13 oranges	1 gallon boiling water
3 grapefruit	2 lb. sugar to each gallon
3 lemons	

Wash the fruit thoroughly and cut into slices, removing the pips. Pour on the boiling water, cover, and leave for a week, stirring frequently. Strain, and add the sugar, allow to dissolve, then pour into the cask. Allow to ferment, and when fermentation has ceased, seal up Bottle in 4 months' time.

PARSNIP WINE

5 lb. peeled parsnips	Sugar
1 gallon water	1 yeast tablet

Cut up the peeled parsnips and boil in the water until tender. Mash very well, then strain through a scalded jelly bag without pressing. Add sugar in the proportion of 3 lb. to every gallon of liquid, bring to the boil, cool, and add the yeast. Allow to ferment in a stone jar, fill up with surplus liquid, and cork securely when fermentation ceases. Leave for 6 months before bottling.

POTATO WINE

4½ lb. potatoes	3 oranges
1½ gallons water	1 oz. bruised root ginger
3 lemons	6 lb. Demerara sugar

Peel and slice the potatoes, cook in the water for ¼ hour, add the lemon and orange rinds and bruised ginger, and boil for another ¼ hour. Strain on to the sliced oranges, lemons, and the sugar. Stir until the sugar is dissolved, and allow to stand overnight. Strain and bottle, cork loosely until the working is finished, then cork tightly.

RASPBERRY AND RED-CURRANT WINE

4 lb. raspberries	4 lb. red-currants

To each gallon of juice allow:

1 yeast tablet	4 lb. sugar

Wash and pick the fruit. Press out all the juice. Boil the pulp with three times its measure of water for 2 hours. Strain, and press to dryness. Mix the liquids, add the yeast and the sugar in the above proportions. Ferment, and bung as usual. Keep for 6 months before bottling.

RHUBARB WINE

6 lb. rhubarb	Sugar
1 gallon boiling water	

Wash the rhubarb, cut it up, and bruise it, then pour on the boiling water. Cover, and let it stand for 10 days, stirring it occasionally. Strain, and add sugar in the proportion of 3½ lb. to each gallon. When the sugar has dissolved, put the liquid into a stone jar or a cask, and leave it to work. Skim it each day, and when it has finished working, cork, and leave for at least 6 months before racking it off and bottling.

SLOE WINE

1 gallon sloes	4 lb. sugar
1 gallon boiling water	

Pick the sloes when quite ripe, and pour the boiling water on them. Stand for a week, stirring twice a day. Strain, stir in the sugar, and when it is dissolved put into bottles or a cask to work. When the working is finished, cork down loosely at first, then tighten the corks after a day or two.

FRUIT LIQUEURS

APRICOT BRANDY

Cut 1 dozen apricots in small pieces; crush the kernels and put them with the fruit into a jar, adding 1 pint brandy and ½ lb. sugar. Cover, and leave for a month, shaking frequently. Strain, and bottle.

CHERRY BRANDY

Sound, ripe Morello cherries are required. Wash them, and either remove the stalks altogether or cut them to within ¼ inch of the fruit. Dry the fruit, and prick with a coarse darning needle. Weigh out 3 oz. of caster sugar for each 1 lb. of cherries. Put the fruit and sugar in alternate layers into a wide-necked jar, and cover with 1 pint good brandy. Cover the jar, and seal it closely. Leave for at least 2–3 months, shaking the jar occasionally, and finally strain off the liqueur.

PINEAPPLE LIQUEUR

Slice or scrape a pineapple very thinly, sprinkle with a little sugar, and leave for 24 hours. Press out the juice, measure it, and add an equal amount of brandy and sugar in the proportion of 2 oz. sugar to ½ pint brandy. Put in a jar with a few slices of fresh pineapple, and leave to infuse for 3 weeks. Strain, and bottle.

SLOE GIN

Half-fill some clean, dry wine bottles with the fruit, which should previously be pricked all over with a darning needle. To each bottle add 3–4 oz. granulated sugar or a few drops of essence of almonds or a little Noyeau liqueur Then fill up the bottles with unsweetened gin, cork securely, and leave in a moderately warm place for 3 months, shaking them occasionally. At the end of this time, open the bottles and strain the gin through muslin until clear. Re-bottle, and cork, and leave until required.

INVALID COOKERY

Invalid catering means more than simply placing meals before the patient. In many cases food is of more importance than drugs, and to those who have to spend their time in bed or in a sick room, meals are among the chief events of the day. The aim is to present to the invalid dishes which are enticing, and at the same time, nourishing and easily digested—a comparatively easy matter with a convalescent or one whose appetite seems to improve each day, but difficult indeed with those whose appetites grow more and more fastidious and the powers of digestion feebler.

Choice and Variety of Food

In many cases the doctor will prescribe the diet, often giving directions as to the quantity necessary for each meal; these medical directions must always be followed.

With serious illness, the very simplest foods are usually given, often of a liquid nature, but when this stage is over, the diet must be gradually built up to be as interesting and varied as possible. Even when the same ingredients must be given over and over again, they can be prepared differently and changes made in the manner of serving, in order to tempt the feeble appetite.

It is not, as a rule, a good plan to ask invalids what they would like, nor to discuss the day's menus in their hearing; it is better to let each meal be in the nature of a surprise. It is well worth studying the patient's tastes in the matter of food, for as a general rule, the meal that is fancied and enjoyed is the one which will do the patient the most good.

Preparation

Whether a meal is taken or not depends very largely on the way in which it is prepared. An unpalatable-looking dish will often be refused, while one that is daintily prepared will be acceptable for the sole reason that it is pleasing to the eye. Try, therefore, to make the dish look as attractive as possible. This is not always easy in invalid cookery—gruels, milk puddings and such-like do not lend themselves to artistic serving, but it is wonderful what a little thought and ingenuity will do in this matter. Dainty garnishes, the use of pretty individual dishes and the attractive arrangement of the tray, all help to create a good impression when the meal first appears.

Make only small quantities. In the following recipes the quantities given are in many instances just sufficient for one meal. In the case of soups and jellies and such dishes, a rather larger amount may be made, as dishes of this kind can generally be served twice—though with a little alteration.

All ingredients must be good and perfectly fresh: nothing of doubtful quality should be given to an invalid.

The greatest cleanliness must be observed in the preparation of invalid dishes. The senses of a sick person are often more acute than those of one who is in good health, and the slightest suspicion of anything disagreeable will be detected at once by the fastidious palate.

Seasonings should, as a rule, be very simple, highly spiced dishes being avoided, and wines or spirits not included except by the doctor's orders.

For preference, the cooking itself should not be done within sight of the invalid. If the fuss and smell of the preparation of the food must be endured first, there will be little appetite left to relish the results.

Serving the Food

Before the meal is brought in, it is a good plan to sponge the patient's face and hands and to make the bed and pillows comfortable.

Another important point is to serve the food punctually at the time it is expected, never allowing the invalid to become exhausted by having to wait too long for nourishment. A sick person has often little else to do but to lie and watch the clock, and sometimes the delay of even a few minutes may make the invalid impatient and fretful or cause the meal to be refused altogether. It is a good plan always to have some food in readiness, such as a little soup or jelly, in case it should be required at odd times.

Never serve too large a quantity of any one dish. It is better to keep some in reserve and to serve it if requested. If the dish is a hot one, let it be really hot and not just lukewarm.

Once the meal is over, the tray and any untouched food should be taken away at once and not left in the sick room.

We give here recipes for typically invalid dishes. Many other recipes in this book (such as the milk puddings, soups, egg dishes, and so on, included in the sections on those subjects) would also be suitable, particularly for convalescents.

MEAT TEAS, BROTHS AND SOUPS

BEEF-TEA—I

½ lb. beef — A little salt
½ pint cold water

Choose lean, juicy beef for the purpose. A piece from the buttock, rump, or top side is more suitable than shin of beef, as this is coarse gristle which requires long, slow cooking and produces gelatine, a substance of small value to an invalid.

Rub the meat lightly with a damp cloth to ensure that it is quite clean, and remove from it all fat and skin. Cut it in thin slices, cutting with the grain, and then shred down finely with a knife, in order to break the fibres of the meat and to enable the juice to escape more freely. If a large quantity of beef-tea has to be prepared, the meat may be put through a mincer.

Weigh the meat and put it into a strong jar or basin (or in a double cooker), with the above proportion of water and a little salt. Cover with a piece of strong white paper, or, better still, with a lid, and, if time permits, allow to stand for ½ hour, as the cold water will help to draw out the juice. Stir well before putting it on to cook, and place the jar containing the beef-tea in a saucepan with cold water to reach three-quarters of the way up the sides. Cover with the lid, bring to the boil, and simmer without boiling for 2–3 hours, adding more water if necessary.

When the meat is sufficiently cooked, remove the jar from the saucepan, stir the contents with a fork, and strain through a wire sieve or coarse strainer, pressing the meat as dry as possible. (The scraps of meat should be put in the stock-pot.) When clear beef-tea is ordered, the straining should be done through a hair sieve or piece of muslin. Remove all grease from the top of the liquid, and serve as required.

Beef-tea must not be made in large quantities, as (unless it is put into a refrigerator) it will not keep beyond 12–15 hours, or even less if the weather is hot or muggy.

BEEF-TEA—II

Prepare the meat as in the last recipe and allow the same proportion of water, but instead of steaming, place the jar containing the beef-tea in a slow oven and cook for 2–3 hours.

Made in this way, the beef-tea will be more savoury than when steamed, but it is not always appreciated by a delicate palate.

BEEF-TEA—III (QUICK METHOD)

½ lb. beef — A little salt
½ pint cold water

Prepare the meat as in recipe I, and if time permits let it soak in the cold water with the salt for ½ hour. Then turn it into a lined saucepan and heat it up very gradually, stirring and pressing the meat well with the back of a wooden spoon, in order to extract the juice.

The greatest care must be taken that the beef-tea does not boil, since the albumen, which is the flesh-forming element in the juice of the meat, will harden if heated above 150° F. It mixes freely with cold water, and remains soluble so long as the heat is not too great, but if once allowed to coagulate, it either hardens in the meat itself or forms a coarse sediment which is kept back in the straining, thus robbing the beef-tea of one of its most valuable properties.

When the meat becomes very pale in colour and the liquid a rich brown, the beef-tea is ready and must be strained as above. Remove all fat from the top, and serve as required.

RAW BEEF-TEA

2 oz. lean juicy beef	A pinch of salt
3 tbsps. cold water	

Free the meat from all fat and skin, and shred it down finely with a knife. Then put it into a breakfast cup, with the water and salt, and allow it to soak for ½–1 hour, pressing the meat from time to time with the back of a spoon or fork. Strain through a fine strainer and serve in a red glass, in order to disguise the colour.

This beef-tea is given in cases of great exhaustion. It is frequently added to other foods, such as gruel. It will not keep and must be made in small quantities only.

SAVOURY BEEF-TEA

1 lb. lean juicy beef	1 bay leaf
1½ pints cold water	¼ carrot
1 tsp. salt	¼ turnip
6 peppercorns	½ onion
4 cloves	A small piece of celery,
1 small blade of mace	or ½ tsp. celery seed

Make the beef-tea in the same way as in recipe I, putting seasonings and vegetables into the jar with the meat, water and salt.

The vegetables must all be carefully cleaned and prepared, and then cut into small pieces. Be careful not to have too much of any one, but try to have an agreeable blending flavours: one teacupful of the vegetables, cut up and mixed, will be quite sufficient. Any flavouring that is objected to may be omitted.

THICKENED BEEF-TEA

1 tsp. fine tapioca	½ pint beef-tea
A little water	1 egg yolk

Cook the tapioca in a small saucepan with a little water until it turns quite clear. Add the beef-tea to it and heat thoroughly, but do not boil. Beat up the egg yolk in a basin or cup with a fork, pour the beef-tea gradually on to it, stirring all the time, and it is ready for serving.

If too rich, the egg yolk may be omitted.

Arrowroot or cornflour may be used instead of tapioca, but in each case they must be cooked in water separately, as above, before the beef-tea is added.

BEEF-TEA AND MILK

The combination of beef-tea and milk con stitutes a very strengthening drink for an invalid, and will often be taken when milk alone is found too insipid. The proportions can be varied according to taste.

BEEF-TEA JELLY

½ pint beef-tea	¼ oz. isinglass

Add the isinglass to the beef-tea, heat, stirring, until just warm and leave until the isinglass is dissolved. Pour into small moulds rinsed with cold water and leave until set.

PURÉE OF BEEF

3–4 oz. juicy beef	½ pint beef-tea

Shred the meat finely, pound it in a mortar or in a strong basin, and then rub through a wire sieve, being careful to scrape the meat from underneath the sieve. Add this meat pulp to a cupful of hot and well-made beef-tea, stir well and serve at once. This is very strengthening.

CHICKEN BROTH

½ a chicken (or the carcase and trimmings of a chicken	Salt
	2 tsps. rice, fine barley or fine tapioca
1 quart cold water	1 tsp. chopped parsley

Wash the pieces of chicken thoroughly, cut the meat into small pieces and break up the bones. Remove any fat or soft grease, but not the skin. Put all into a deep saucepan, add the water, which should be sufficient to cover the meat, etc., and season with salt. Cover, and bring slowly to the boil. Then simmer for 4–5 hours, removing the scum from time to time, and adding more water if necessary. When all the goodness is extracted from the chicken, strain the liquid through a fine strainer and, if possible, leave till cold. Carefully remove all grease from the top and return the broth to a saucepan. Bring to the boil, sprinkle in the well-washed tapioca, barley or rice, and simmer until this is cooked. Add the chopped parsley a minute or two before serving.

Notes: A richer broth may be made by pouring it slowly on to a beaten egg yolk.

A more savoury broth may be made by adding a few small pieces of vegetable when making the stock.

Small pieces of cooked chicken may be served in the broth if a more substantial dish is required.

When economy has to be studied, the meat used may be half chicken and half veal; the flavour of the chicken will still predominate.

ESSENCE OF CHICKEN

Prepare and cut up the chicken in the same way as for Chicken Broth.

Put the meat, bones, skin, etc., into a large jar without any water, covering the jar with a tight-fitting lid or strong piece of white paper, greased. Place the jar in a saucepan, with cold water to come fully half-way up; put the lid on the pan and simmer slowly for 6–7 hours. If the water boils down, add more. When cooked sufficiently, remove the jar from the saucepan, and strain all the liquid away from the chicken through a fine strainer or hair sieve. This is just the pure juice or essence of chicken. When cold, it will be a jelly.

CHICKEN JELLY

1 chicken, or part of one	1 bay leaf
A pinch of salt	A few parsley stalks
Cold water	

The less choice joints will do very well for chicken jelly; the breast can be used for some other purpose. Cut the chicken into joints, and cut all the flesh from the bones. Wash any part that does not look perfectly clean, and keep back any fat. Cut the flesh into small pieces, and chop up the bones. The neck and gizzard may also be washed and used in the jelly, but not the liver, as it is too dark in colour. Put all into a lined saucepan with a little salt and cover with cold water; bring to the boil and skim well. Add the bay leaf and parsley stalks, and simmer slowly for 3–4 hours. Keep it well skimmed, adding more water if it reduces too much. When ready, strain through a hair sieve and leave till cold. Remove all grease from the top, and serve a little as required. More vegetable flavouring may be used in the making of the jelly if desired.

MUTTON BROTH—I

1 lb. neck or knuckle of mutton	2 tsps. salt
	1 tbsp. whole rice
2 pints cold water	2 tsps. chopped parsley

Wipe the meat well with a damp cloth to make it quite clean, and cut it into small pieces away from the bone. Remove as much of the fat from it as possible, and do not use this in the broth. Put the meat, bones, water and salt into a clean lined pan; put on the lid, and bring slowly to the boil. Remove all scum that rises: if this is allowed to boil again, the broth will have a cloudy appearance. Simmer slowly for 3–4 hours, skimming when necessary. Then strain through a fine strainer or sieve and let it stand till cold. When cold, remove all fat from the top with a spoon, or by passing pieces of kitchen paper over the top. Return it to a clean saucepan with the well-washed rice, and allow it to cook again until the rice is quite soft—about 20 minutes. Add the finely chopped parsley at the last, and it is ready for serving.

Crushed tapioca, or arrowroot blended with a little cold water, may be used for thickening the broth instead of rice.

MUTTON BROTH—II

1 lb. neck or knuckle of mutton	A small piece each of carrot, turnip, onion and celery
1 quart cold water	
2 tsps. salt	A pinch of pepper
1 tbsp. rice or barley	2 tsps. chopped parsley

Prepare the meat in the same way as for the last recipe. Put the meat, bones, water, and salt into a clean lined saucepan; put on the lid, and bring slowly to the boil. Add the rice, well washed, or the barley, well washed and blanched. Have the vegetables all carefully prepared and cut into small pieces, about one cupful altogether. Add them next to the broth, and simmer for 3–4 hours, until grain and vegetables are well cooked. Remove bones and any grease from the top, season to taste, add the finely chopped parsley and the broth is ready.

This makes a more substantial dish than the first method, and is better suited for a convalescent.

VEAL BROTH

A piece of knuckle or neck of veal may be prepared in the same way as for Mutton Broth, and makes a very delicately flavoured broth.

For variety, the broth may be made with half mutton and half veal.

CALF'S FOOT JELLY

This jelly takes two days to make; the stock must be made the first day, and the jelly finished the second.

To make the stock, cut 2 calf's feet into pieces and wash and scrape them well. Put the pieces into a saucepan, cover with cold water and bring quickly to the boil. Then pour off the water, rinse the feet and return to saucepan. Cover again with cold water—from 4–5 pints—put the lid on the pan and simmer slowly for 4–5 hours, until the liquid is reduced to half the quantity. Then strain and leave until cold, when the stock should be a stiff jelly.

To Make and Clear the Jelly

1 pint calf's foot stock	1½-inch stick of cinnamon
6 oz. loaf sugar	3–4 lemons
¼ pint sherry	2 eggs
3 cloves	2 tbsps. brandy

Remove all grease from the stock, measure 1 pint into a saucepan and add the sugar, sherry, cloves and cinnamon stick. Wipe the lemons with a damp cloth, and peel the rind very thinly off 2 of them. Then roll the lemons on the table to soften them, cut them in halves and squeeze out the juice. Strain this and measure ¼ pint. Wash the eggs before breaking them, separate the yolks from the whites, and crush up the shells. Add the lemon rind and juice, and the whites and shells of the eggs to the contents of the pan, and put on a slow heat. The pan should not be more than half full, as the jelly is very apt to boil over. Whisk the jelly over the heat until a good froth rises on it and it is just beginning to boil. Then draw gently to one side, where it will keep warm without simmering, cover it with a lid or plate and leave for 5–10 minutes, and then strain through a scalded jelly cloth. If the jelly is not clear the first time, change the basin, and pour the jelly back again into the cloth. Repeat this several times, until the jelly runs through perfectly clear. Cover the stand over with a piece of flannel or blanket, and let it stand until all the jelly has run through. Finally, add the brandy, and serve the jelly as required.

Notes : In hot weather, if the stock has not stiffened sufficiently, add a little gelatine or isinglass ; if it is too stiff, it must be diluted with a little water.

The amount of sugar can be altered to suit different tastes ; or the jelly may be made without sugar.

The amount of wine used can be altered. If less is used, more lemon juice should be added. A little orange juice may be used instead of some of the lemon juice, as a variation.

The jelly should be strained in a warm place and out of a draught. Should it stiffen in the cloth before it has all run through, place a small basin or cup in the centre, and fill it with boiling water. If this fails to melt the jelly, it must be returned to the pan, whisked up again, and strained as before.

COWHEEL JELLY

Make in the same way as Calf's Foot Jelly.

RICE SOUP

1 pint mutton, veal or chicken broth	1 tbsp. cream
2 tbsps. rice	Chopped parsley (optional)
1 egg yolk	

Remove any fat from the top of the broth, put it into a clean saucepan with the well-washed rice, and boil until this is perfectly soft. Then rub all through a fine sieve, rinse out the pan, and return the soup to it. Beat the egg yolk and cream with a fork, strain them into the soup, and stir carefully over the heat until thoroughly hot, but on no account let it boil or it will curdle. Milk (one teacupful—6 oz.) may be used instead of egg yolk and cream, and a little chopped parsley may be added. This soup may also be served without sieving.

FISH DISHES

STEAMED FISH

1 filleted fish—sole, whiting or haddock	A little butter
Pepper, salt and a squeeze of lemon juice	Sauce, if desired
	Parsley and lemon to garnish

The fish should be quite free from skin and bone, otherwise it is troublesome for an invalid to eat. Wipe it lightly with a damp cloth and season carefully, omitting the pepper if this is not allowed. Then either roll up the fillets or cut them in several pieces. Place them on a buttered plate, cover with greased paper, and place another plate or a saucepan lid on the top. Place this on the top of a saucepan of fast-boiling water, and cook in this manner until the fish loses its transparent appearance and looks white and creamy. The water must be kept boiling all the time, and any juice which runs from the fish must be served with it. This is one of the simplest methods of cooking fish for an invalid and is superior to boiling, as all the liquid and flavour are retained.

A sauce may be made separately, using the liquid from the fish, and may be poured over the fish before serving. A small sprig of parsley or one or two small pieces of cut lemon may be used as a garnish.

Serve the fish with dry toast or with creamed potatoes, and a serving of a vegetable such as creamed spinach, purécd peas, or asparagus.

FISH STEAMED IN MILK

1 small filleted sole or plaice
Salt
1 teacupful (6 oz.) milk
2 tbsps. breadcrumbs
1 tsp. butter
A pinch of nutmeg (optional)
Parsley to garnish

Wipe the fish with a cloth, season lightly with salt and make into little rolls. Put these into a basin with the milk, breadcrumbs, butter and, if liked, a pinch of nutmeg. Cover with a saucer or piece of greased paper, and steam for ½ hour. Serve on a hot dish, and garnish with a sprig of parsley.

FLAKED FISH IN SCALLOP-SHELL

Either a fireproof china or a natural scallop-shell can be used. Grease it well and coat the inside with fine breadcrumbs. Then lay in some flakes of nicely cooked fish that have been seasoned with white pepper, salt and a little lemon juice. Pour over the fish some well-flavoured white sauce, and sprinkle more crumbs over the top. Dot with small pieces of butter, then brown under the grill, or in the oven. Garnish with a sprig of parsley and a thin slice of lemon.

SOLE AU GRATIN

1 small sole
3 tbsps. milk
2–3 tbsps. breadcrumbs
A little parsley
Pepper and salt
2 tsps. butter

Fillet the fish and cut it in several pieces. Dip these in milk, and then in fine breadcrumbs in which a little finely chopped parsley, pepper, and salt have been mixed. Cover each piece rather thickly. Place the fish in a small greased fire-proof dish, pour the milk round, put a cover or piece of greased paper on the top, and bake quickly for 10–15 minutes. Then remove the cover, sprinkle some dry crumbs over the fish, put the butter over the top in small pieces, and brown lightly.

A small plaice or flounder may be cooked in the same way.

SOLE FOR AN INVALID

Put a small filleted sole into a saucepan with a light seasoning of pepper and salt and 4 tbsps. of water. Simmer slowly until the fish is cooked, and remove any scum. Then lift out the fish on to a serving dish. Stir a beaten egg yolk into the liquor in the pan, and whisk until it thickens. Strain this sauce over the fish, and garnish with sliced lemon and a sprig of parsley.

STEWED EEL

¼ lb. eel
½ oz. butter
1 tbsp. flour
⅓ pint stock
Salt and pepper
A squeeze of lemon juice
Port wine, if allowed

Wash the eel, dry it and cut into small pieces. Sauté these in the butter for a few minutes, then stir in the flour and brown it lightly. Add the stock gradually and bring to the boil, stirring. Skim well, then add salt, pepper and lemon juice, cover and stew gently until tender—1½ hours or even longer. Before serving, stir in a spoonful or so of port wine, if this is allowed.

MEAT AND POULTRY DISHES

BEEF CREAM

¼ lb. lean juicy beef
½ oz. butter
½ oz. flour
2 tbsps. stock
1 egg
Pepper and salt
2 tbsps. cream

Wipe the beef with a damp cloth and shred it down very finely with a sharp knife, as for beef-tea. Make a panada with the butter, flour and stock, as follows: melt the butter in a small saucepan, add to it the flour, and mix with a wooden spoon until smooth. Then pour on the stock (or beef-tea), and stir until boiling and thoroughly cooked. Put this panada into a mortar with the shredded beef, and pound well together. Add the whole egg and seasoning, and pound again until as smooth as possible. Then rub the mixture through a fine wire sieve into a basin, and scrape all the meat from underneath the sieve. Add the cream, and reseason if necessary. Have ready a small basin well greased, put the mixture into it and shake it well down. Cover the basin with a piece of greased paper, and steam the cream very gently for 15 minutes, or until it is firm to the touch. Lift from the pan, and let it stand a minute or two before turning it out.

Dish on a hot plate, with a piece of paper remove any grease which may be on the top of it, and serve plain, or with a little beef-tea heated and poured round it as a gravy.

MINCED BEEF

6 oz. best rump steak
3 tbsps. cold water
Pepper and salt
2 tbsps. breadcrumbs
Sippets of toast or fried bread

Select a nice juicy piece of beef. Either get the butcher to mince it for you, or remove all fat and skin from it, and put it through the mincing machine yourself. Do not buy for an invalid the ready-prepared mince from a shop, as it has too much fat about it. Take a small lined stewpan and put the minced beef into it, with half the water and the seasoning. Put the pan on the stove, and pound the meat well with a spoon for a few minutes, until it loses its red appearance. Then add the rest of the water, and simmer gently over a very low heat for 15–20 minutes. The greatest care must be taken that the meat is not allowed to cook too quickly. Remove any grease that may rise on it, and add the breadcrumbs 10 minutes before serving. Garnish the dish with some neat sippets of toasted or fried bread and serve very hot.

CREAMED CHICKEN OR VEAL

¼ lb. breast of chicken or ¼ lb. fillet of veal	1 tsp. cold water
A pinch of salt	1–2 tbsps. cream
	Toasted bread

Wipe the meat and cut it into small pieces, free from fat and skin. Put it into a cup or small basin, with a pinch of salt and the cold water. Tie over it a piece of greased white paper, and steam slowly for 1–1½ hours. Then lift out, and put the contents of the basin into a mortar; pound well, and rub through a fine wire sieve. Put the sieved mixture into a pan, add the cream, and heat through. This may be served on a piece of toast, or eaten cold. If considered too rich, use a little more water in the cooking and omit the cream.

CHICKEN CREAMS (COLD)

4 oz. cooked chicken	Rounds of bread and butter
2 tbsps. white sauce	Salad or aspic jelly to garnish
¼ pint aspic jelly	
Salt and pepper	
2 tbsps. cream	

Use cooked chicken (or prepare and cook some raw chicken as in the previous recipe). Mince it finely and pound it with the white sauce, then pass the mixture through a fine sieve. Mix with the liquid aspic jelly, season to taste and stir in the cream. Put into individual dariole moulds and leave to cool. When set, turn out on to small rounds of bread and butter, and garnish with a little salad if this is allowed, or with chopped aspic jelly.

A little cooked tongue mixed with the chicken makes a pleasant variation.

STEAMED CHICKEN MOULD

Prepare and cook some chicken as in the recipe for Creamed Chicken or Veal (see above) and either mince it or rub it through a sieve. To 4 tbsps. of this mince add 4 tbsps. fine breadcrumbs, a small piece of butter and a little pepper and salt. Pour over these 2–3 tbsps. hot milk or chicken stock, and let them stand a few minutes to soak. Then stir in a beaten egg and pour the mixture into a small greased basin or cup. Cover with greased paper, and steam slowly for 15–20 minutes, or until firm to the touch. Turn the mould on to a hot dish when required, and serve with or without sauce poured round it.

CHICKEN STEAMED IN MILK

½ a chicken	A small piece of butter or 1 tbsp. cream
¼ pint new milk	Bacon rolls to garnish (optional)
A small blade of mace	
White pepper and salt	
2 tsps. flour	

Cut the chicken into neat joints. Remove as much of the skin as possible and wipe the pieces with a damp cloth. Put them into a basin with the milk, mace, pepper and salt. Put a lid on the basin, or tie a piece of white greased paper over it, and place it in a saucepan with enough hot water to reach half-way up: alternatively, use a double saucepan. Put the lid on the pan, and simmer gently for 2–3 hours, or until the chicken feels quite tender. If the water boils down, more must be added. When sufficiently cooked, lift out the pieces of chicken on to a plate, and keep them hot. Pour the milk into a saucepan and remove the mace from it. Blend the flour with a little cold milk in a basin, and add it to the milk in the pan. Stir over the heat until it boils and thickens, and add more seasoning if necessary. A small piece of butter or 1 tbsp. cream may be added to the sauce before serving. Pour it over the pieces of chicken, coating them well. Small rolls of bacon may be served round the dish.

POTTED CHICKEN OR GAME

¼ lb. cooked chicken or game of any kind	Pepper and salt
2 oz. fresh butter	A little powdered mace
	Melted butter to cover

Take all the meat from the remains of cold roast fowl or game; remove all skin and gristle; then weigh the meat and allow butter in the above proportion. Mince the meat very finely, either with a sharp knife or by putting it twice through a mincing machine. Put it into a mortar with most of the butter (previously melted) and season to taste. Pound well together and rub through a fine wire sieve. Pack this mixture into little pots, and run a little melted butter over the top. Use within a few days. This potted meat makes nice sandwiches for an invalid's luncheon or supper, and will often tempt the appetite : spread between thin slices of brown or white bread and butter, or on toast or water biscuits.

Note : Almost any meat can be potted in the same way. Chicken by itself is rather tasteless, and when ham and tongue are allowed, a little piece of either used with the chicken is a great improvement. The same applies to other meat—two different meats used together are always more tasty than one. If a little ham fat is used, less butter will be required. The seasonings given in the above recipe are very simple, but of course, more can be added to suit different tastes.

QUENELLES OF CHICKEN

¼ lb. raw chicken	1 tbsp. thick cream or white sauce
1 small egg	Mashed potato, sauce and parsley to garnish
Salt and pepper	
A squeeze of lemon juice	

See that there is no skin or bone in the chicken. Mince it finely, then pound it with the beaten egg, seasoning, lemon juice and cream or sauce. Pass the mixture through a fine sieve and form into quenelles (i.e., shape like small eggs) using two dessertspoons dipped in water. Place in a shallow pan of nearly boiling water and poach for about 10 minutes. Drain well, then dish on a border of mashed potato and coat with a good sauce. Garnish with tiny sprigs of parsley.

GRILLED LIVER

Wash and dry the liver (calf's for preference, or pig's or lamb's) and cut it into slices ¼–½ inch thick, removing pipes or gristle. Brush over with melted butter (or with olive oil if preferred) and season lightly. Cook under a hot grill for 2 minutes on each side, then reduce the heat and continue heating gently under tender—7–10 minutes in all. Serve with creamed potatoes and small pats of Maître d'Hôtel butter, omitting the parsley if this is not allowed.

STEAMED LIVER

3–4 oz. calf's liver	1 tbsp. stock
¼ oz. butter	1 tbsp. cream (optional)
Seasoning	

Wash and dry the liver, then cut into neat slices about ¼ inch thick, carefully removing any pipes or gristle. Lay on a well-buttered plate, sprinkle with a little seasoning, then add the stock and cover with a second buttered plate. Cook over a pan of boiling water until tender—about 20 minutes. Serve with creamed potatoes. If liked, 1 tbsp. of cream can be poured over the liver two or three minutes before serving.

MINCED LIVER

¼ lb. calf's, pig's or lamb's liver	¼ pint stock
2 tsps. flour	1 tbsp. cream
Seasoning	A little finely chopped onion, if allowed
½ oz. butter	

Wash and dry the liver and cut it into small pieces, discarding any gristle. Toss them in the seasoned flour and sauté in the melted butter for a few minutes, without browning. Add the stock, cover and simmer gently until tender—about ½ hour. Pass the liver through a fine mincer, then return it to the pan with the cream and enough of the liver gravy to give it the desired consistency. Make thoroughly hot, but do not boil, and serve on toast or with vegetables.

If allowed, a little finely chopped or minced onion may be included in this dish : it should be sautéed in the butter with the liver.

QUENELLES OF LIVER

Follow the recipe for Quenelles of Chicken, substituting liver for chicken.

STEAMED MUTTON OR LAMB CHOP

Wipe the chop with a damp cloth. Trim off most of the fat and make the chop into a neat shape. Grease a plate with a little butter, place it over a pan half full of boiling water and put the chop on it. Sprinkle with a little salt, cover with a piece of greased paper and then with a basin or saucepan lid. Keep the water underneath boiling fast, that there may be sufficient steam, and replenish with more boiling water if necessary. Cook for 15–20 minutes ; then turn the chop and cook for about the same length of time on the other side. Serve at once, with any juice that has run from it.

STEAMED MUTTON AND RICE

1 mutton chop	2 tsps. whole rice
A pinch of salt	1 small stalk of celery
¼ pint cold water	

Wipe the chop with a damp cloth and trim off nearly all the fat. Put it into a jar or basin with the salt, water and well-washed rice. Wash and brush the celery, removing any brown parts from it; cut it into fine shreds, and put it in with the chop, etc. Cover all with a lid or strong piece of greased white paper, place the jar or basin in a saucepan with enough boiling water to come half-way up the sides, put the lid on the pan, and steam slowly for 1½–2 hours. If the water boils down, more must be added. When ready, lift the chop on to a hot plate and pour the rice, etc., round it.

STEWED SWEETBREAD

1 calf's sweetbread	2 tsps. cornflour
Cold water	1 tbsp. cream or
1 teacupful (6 oz.) light stock	1 egg yolk
	2 tsps. chopped parsley
Seasoning	Snippets of toast

Choose a very fresh heart sweetbread and let it soak for 1 hour in cold salted water. Then put it into a saucepan with fresh cold water, bring to the boil, and boil for 3 minutes. Put the sweetbread again into cold water, pull away from it all skin and fat, and break it in small pieces. (This preliminary preparation makes the sweetbread white.) When ready, put the prepared pieces in a small stewpan or earthenware casserole, pour in the stock, and add any seasoning desired. Simmer very slowly until tender, removing any scum that may rise. Then lift out the pieces of sweetbread and keep them warm.

Blend the cornflour with a little cold water and add it to the stock in the pan. Stir until boiling and cook for a few minutes. Add the cream and parsley, cook for 2 minutes longer, and then pour this sauce over the sweetbread. If an egg yolk is used instead of cream, the sauce must not boil after it is added. The dish may be garnished with a few snippets of toast.

LAMB'S SWEETBREADS

¼ lb. lamb's sweetbreads	½ oz. butter
¼ pint white stock or milk	2 tsps. flour
Seasoning	

Lamb's sweetbreads are usually cheaper than calf's and, although small, are very good and make an excellent dish for an invalid.

Prepare and blanch the sweetbreads as in the last recipe. After the skin has been removed, press them between two plates with a weight on the top for 1 hour or so. Then place them in a double saucepan with the stock or milk and seasoning, and let them cook until tender—½–¾ hour. Then drain, keeping the liquid. Make a little white sauce with the butter and flour and some of the liquid in which the sweetbreads were cooked, and season to taste. Put the sweetbreads into it and keep hot until required.

LAMB'S SWEETBREADS EN CASSEROLE

If preferred, the sweetbreads may be cooked in the oven. Prepare them as above and put them in a casserole, with the stock or milk and seasoning. Cover and cook in a moderate oven (350° F., mark 4) until tender—about ¾ hour. Make the sauce, using the liquor in which the sweetbreads were cooked, and pour it over the sweetbreads in the casserole.

STEWED PIGEON

1 young pigeon	Seasoning
2 tsps. flour	A piece of toast
A little butter	Parsley or watercress
½ pint light stock	

Prepare and clean the pigeon carefully, truss it as for roasting and dust it over with flour in order to make it dry. Melt a small piece of butter or a little bacon fat in a stewpan, put the pigeon into it, and cook until nicely browned on all sides. Then pour away any fat that may be left and add the stock. Season to taste and put the lid on the pan. Stew slowly by the side of the heat until the bird is tender, turning it over once or twice during the cooking and removing any scum that may rise. The time will depend very much upon the age of the pigeon—anything from 1–2 hours. When ready, lift it on to a neat square of toast, pour some of the gravy round, and garnish with parsley or a little watercress.

If preferred, this dish may be cooked in the oven. Place in a casserole, cover and cook in a moderate oven (350° F., mark 4) for 1–1½ hours.

HOT PUDDINGS AND FRUIT DISHES

CORNFLOUR PUDDING

½ pint milk	Flavouring as desired
½ oz. cornflour	1 egg
1 tbsp. sugar	

Put most of the milk into a saucepan and allow it to heat. Mix the cornflour into a smooth paste with the remainder of the milk and add it to the milk in the pan. Stir constantly over the heat until the cornflour boils and thickens, and allow it to simmer for at least 5 minutes. Then remove from the heat and add half the sugar and any flavouring desired. Next add the egg yolk and mix it in. Beat up the egg white to a stiff froth and stir it lightly into the mixture, pour all into a greased pie dish and wipe carefully round the edges of the dish. Bake the pudding in a moderate oven (375° F., mark 5) until it is nicely browned and well risen—about 20 minutes. Lift out, sprinkle with sugar, and serve as quickly as possible. A little cream and some stewed fruit might be served with it.

FRENCH CHOCOLATE CUSTARD

½–1 tbsp. chocolate powder	1 egg
	Sugar
1 teacupful milk	Vanilla

Dissolve the chocolate in a little of the milk, and when quite smooth add the remainder. Bring almost to boiling point, then pour slowly on to the beaten egg, stirring all the time. Add sugar and vanilla to taste, and strain into small fireproof dishes. Stand these in a tin with a little cold water round them, and cook in a moderate oven (350° F., mark 3) until custard is set.

FRENCH FRITTER

A French roll	Butter
A little milk or cream	Sugar
Flavouring	Jam or fruit syrup

Cut a slice of French bread about 1 inch thick. Trim it, making a neat shape. Soak it in a little milk or thin cream, adding flavouring to taste. Then melt some butter in an omelette pan, lift the bread carefully into it, and fry it a light brown on both sides. Sprinkle with sugar, and serve with jam or fruit syrup.

RICE AND APPLE PUDDING

Take equal quantities of well-boiled or steamed rice and lightly stewed apples. Grease a small pie dish or a fireproof dish, put the stewed apple at the bottom of it and the rice on the top. Sprinkle over some brown sugar or some cake crumbs, and dot with small pieces of butter. Bake in a moderate oven (375° F., mark 5) for about 12 minutes, or until nicely browned and hot through. Any other fruit, or even some good jam, may be used instead of the apples, if preferred.

RICE AND CHOCOLATE PUDDING

1 oz. whole rice	2 tbsps. water
½ pint milk	A little cream, if liked
2 oz. chocolate	

Steam the rice in a double cooker with the milk. Grate the chocolate, dissolve it in a little water, and add it to the rice. This may be served either hot or cold. A little cream served with it is an improvement.

BAKED BANANAS

Wash the bananas and cut off the ends. Put them on a tin or dish in the oven, and bake them until the skin bursts open like a baked apple. Serve hot with sugar and cream. A little lemon juice may be sprinkled over the banana if it is found lacking in flavour.

INVALID FRUIT TART

1 large apple	1 egg
2 tbsps. water	3 tbsps. milk
1 tbsp. caster sugar	1 tbsp. sugar for the meringue top
1 small sponge cake or 2 finger biscuits	

Stew the apple with the water and sugar until reduced to a pulp, and put it in the bottom of a small greased pie dish. Cut the sponge cake or finger biscuits in slices and place them on the top. Separate the yolk from the white of the egg. Beat up the yolk in a basin with the milk and pour it over the sponge cake. Let the pudding stand for a few minutes, and then bake in a moderate oven (350° F., mark 3) for about 10 minutes, until the custard is set. Have the egg white beaten to a stiff froth, add 1 tbsp. sugar and pile it on top of the pudding. Return to the oven until the white is set and very lightly brown; then lift out and sprinkle with sugar.

Any other stewed fruit may be used in this way instead of apples.

PRUNE SOUFFLÉ

¼ lb. cooked prunes	1 egg
2 tbsps. caster sugar	1 tsp. lemon juice

The prunes should be well cooked. Drain them from any syrup, remove the stones and cut them in pieces. Put the sugar and egg yolk into a basin, and beat them together with a wooden spoon until of a pale creamy consistency. Add the lemon juice (a little wine may be used instead of this) and prunes and mix them well in. Then beat up the egg white to a very stiff froth, and stir in as lightly as possible to the other mixture. Pour all into a greased fireproof dish and bake in a moderate oven (375° F., mark 5) about 15 minutes. Sprinkle with sugar, and serve it as soon as taken from the oven.

JELLIES AND COLD SWEETS

APPLE CREAM

2 baked apples	A squeeze of lemon juice
2 tbsps. thick cream	Sugar to taste

Remove the pulp from two baked apples, rub

it through a fine wire or hair sieve, scraping the sieve well underneath, and put the pulp into a basin. Add to it the cream and a squeeze of lemon juice, and sweeten to taste with caster sugar. Beat well for a few minutes, and serve in a small glass dish.

Custard may be used instead of cream in this dish.

BANANAS AND CREAM

Peel 1–2 bananas and cut them in very thin slices with a silver knife. Dust them over lightly with caster sugar and arrange in a small glass or china dish. Add the juice of ½ orange, or, if it is allowed, a little wine. Then whip 1–2 tbsps. cream until thick, sweeten to taste and pile this on the top of the bananas.

BAVARIAN CREAM

2 fresh eggs
2 tbsps. sugar
1 tbsp. brandy or sherry

Separate the yolks from the whites of the eggs. Put the yolks into a basin with the sugar and brandy and beat them for a few minutes. Then stir them over hot water until they thicken. Remove from heat, and when slightly cooled, stir in the egg whites, which had been beaten to a stiff froth, and pour into a glass or cup.

CURDS

Put 1 pint milk into a saucepan with a squeeze of lemon juice and heat very slowly until a curd has formed: the milk must not be allowed to boil. Turn on to a sieve lined with muslin and leave until the whey has drained away and the curd is dry. Serve with cream and caster sugar.

EGG JELLY

2 lemons
½ pint water
2 oz. sugar
½ oz. gelatine
2 egg yolks

Wash the lemons, peel off the yellow rind very thinly and put it into a saucepan with the water and sugar. Simmer by the side of the heat until some flavour is extracted from the rind, then add the gelatine and stir to dissolve it. Beat up the egg yolks in a basin, and strain the gelatine, etc., slowly on to them, stirring all the time. Return all to the saucepan and stir very carefully over the heat until the mixture thickens like a custard: it must not boil or it will curdle. When ready, strain again into the basin and strain in also the juice of the lemons. Mix, and set aside to cool.

A little wine is sometimes added to this jelly.

IRISH OR CARRAGEEN MOSS BLANCMANGE

½ oz. Irish moss
1 pint milk
Flavouring
Sugar
A little wine, if liked

Pick over the moss carefully, then weigh it and wash thoroughly in tepid water. Put it into a saucepan with the milk, and simmer very gently for ½ hour. Alternatively, a double cooker may be used and more time allowed. Flavour with vanilla, lemon rind, or a bay leaf, and sweeten to taste. Strain through muslin and set aside until cold. A little wine may be added.

IRISH MOSS JELLY

1 oz. Irish moss
1 pint water
2 oz. loaf sugar
Juice of 1 lemon
A little wine or brandy (optional)

Prepare the moss as above and then simmer it in the water for ½ hour. Put the loaf sugar into a basin with the strained juice of the lemon. Strain the moss through muslin over them and stir well, pour into glasses and leave to set. The result should be a clear amber jelly. Wine or brandy, with or without the lemon, may also be used.

LEMON SPONGE

1 lemon
¼ oz. gelatine
2–3 lumps of sugar
¼ pint water
1 egg white

Wash the lemon and peel off the yellow rind as thinly as possible. Put the rind into a small saucepan with the gelatine, sugar and water, and dissolve slowly over the heat. Then strain into a basin and cool slightly. Add the lemon juice (strained) and the egg white. Whisk all together until white and frothy, pile up on a small glass or fancy dish and serve very cold.

RICE CREAM

1 oz. ground rice
½ pint milk
½ oz. butter
Rind of ½ lemon
2 tbsps. sugar
2 tsps. powdered gelatine
2 tbsps. cream

Cook the rice in the milk, adding the butter and grated lemon rind. When ready, sweeten to taste and add the gelatine, dissolved in a little water. Cool and add the cream, lightly whipped. When set, serve with stewed fruit or fruit juice.

WHIPPED JELLY

Some calf's foot or gelatine jelly

Melt the jelly, put it into a large basin, and, with a whisk, whip it until cold, when it should be a firm froth and perfectly white. Pile up on a small glass dish and serve.

For JUNKET and other MILK DISHES, see the chapter on Milk Puddings and Custards.

DRINKS, ETC.

ALBUMEN OR EGG WATER

1 egg white — Sugar or salt
½ pint water

Beat the egg white stiffly, add the water and mix well. Let this stand for a short time, then strain through muslin and add sugar or salt to taste.

To serve, a little lemon juice may be added, or the solution may be added to different drinks.

ALMOND MILK

1 oz. sweet almonds — ½ pint water
2 bitter almonds — Sugar, if desired
Orange flower or rose water

Blanch the almonds in order to remove the brown skin. Chop them finely on a board and pound them in a mortar with a little orange flower or rose water. Then put them in a jug with the water, cover and stand for 12 hours, stirring occasionally. Strain, and add sugar if wished. This is used to dilute barley water and other drinks and to give flavour.

APPLE WATER—I

2 large apples — 3–4 lumps of sugar
Rind and juice of ½ a lemon — 1 pint boiling water

Select juicy apples with a sharp flavour and wash them well, but do not peel them. Cut them down in thin slices, and put them into a jug. Add to them the thinly peeled rind and juice of the lemon, and the sugar. Have the water freshly boiling and pour it over them. Cover and let stand till cold, then strain, and it is ready for serving.

APPLE WATER—II

2 large apples — 1 oz. sugar
1 pint cold water — Rind of ½ lemon

Wash the apples and cut them down in thin slices without peeling them. Put them into a lined saucepan with the water, sugar and thinly peeled rind of ½ lemon. Boil gently for 1 hour, until the fruit is soft. Then strain through muslin, and keep covered until cold.

ARROWROOT

¼ oz. arrowroot — 2 tsps. sugar
½ pint cold water

Put the arrowroot into a small basin, add to it 1 tbsp. of the cold water, and mix it with a wooden spoon until quite smooth. Add the rest of the water, mix well and pour into a saucepan. Heat gently until it boils and thickens, stirring constantly. Cook for about 10 minutes, sweeten to taste, and serve in a cup or basin.

If preferred, milk may be substituted for the water. A little nutmeg may be grated over the top, and wine or cream may be added.

BARLEY MEAL GRUEL

½ pint milk — A small piece of butter
1 tbsp. barley meal
Salt or sugar

Mix the milk very gradually with the meal, stirring until quite smooth. Take a small lined saucepan, rinse it out with cold water and pour the barley and milk into it. Stir constantly over the heat until boiling, and boil for 5–7 minutes. Season to taste with salt or sugar, and stir in a small piece of butter at the end. Serve very hot.

The gruel may be made thicker or thinner according to taste, and a little cream may be served with it.

Water may be used instead of milk, and wine or brandy added as required. A very good drink can be made by making the gruel with water, but rather thick, then thinning it down with port wine: heat thoroughly, but do not boil again. Barley gruel makes a change from the ordinary oatmeal gruel, and is very nourishing.

BARLEY WATER (CLEAR)

4 tbsps. pearl barley — ½ a lemon
2 cupfuls boiling water — Sugar

Wash the barley, put it into a lined saucepan and cover with cold water. Bring quickly to the boil and strain and rinse the barley: this whitens it and prevents the drink having a dark and cloudy appearance. Then put it into a jug and pour the boiling water over. Add the rind and juice of the lemon, and a little sugar if wished. Cover over, leave until cold, and strain ready for use.

BARLEY WATER (THICK)

4 tbsps pearl barley — ½ a lemon
2 breakfastcupfuls cold water — Sugar

Wash and blanch the barley as in the last recipe. Put the barley back into the saucepan with the water and rind of the lemon, peeled off very thinly. Allow this to cook slowly by the side of the heat for 1½–2 hours, adding more water if necessary. Then strain, add the lemon juice, and a little sugar if wished. Serve hot or cold.

This is considered to be a very light and nourishing drink, and having no decided taste, it is usually a favourite with invalids. It is often mixed with milk, the lemon in this case being omitted.

Patent barley may be used—it will take a shorter time to cook (see next recipe)—and grapefruit juice may be added instead of the lemon juice.

BARLEY WATER (QUICKLY MADE)

½ oz. patent barley — 2 lemons
3 pints boiling water — Sugar to taste

Blend the barley to a smooth cream with a little cold water and stir this into the boiling water. Cook for 2–3 minutes, stirring occasionally. Remove from the heat, add lemon juice (or other flavouring) and sugar to taste. Serve hot or cold.

BLACK-CURRANT DRINK

1 tbsp. black-currant jam — A squeeze of lemon juice
½ pint boiling water — A little sugar

Put all the ingredients into a jug, and stir well. Cover over, and stand by the side of the heat for 15–20 minutes. Strain through a fine strainer or piece of muslin, and serve hot.

CAUDLE

1 egg — Sugar
½ glass sherry — A pinch of nutmeg
1 cupful gruel — (optional)

Beat up the egg with a fork, removing the speck, and add the sherry. Make the gruel boiling hot, and pour it on to the egg and wine very gradually, stirring all the time. Add sugar to taste, and if liked, a little nutmeg. Serve very hot.

A CUP OF CHOCOLATE

½–1 oz. chocolate — ½ pint milk
A little water — Sugar and cream

Choose good plain chocolate and shred it down with a knife, or use chocolate powder. Put it in a small saucepan with a little water, and dissolve it over the heat. Add the milk, and bring to boiling point. Strain, and serve with sugar and a little whipped cream, if wished.

Notes: The amount of chocolate required depends upon the kind used and also upon individual taste.

Half milk and half water may be used in the making if the above proportions are found to give too rich a mixture.

CHOCOLATE WITH EGG

Make a cup of chocolate as above, and have it boiling hot. Break the egg, remove the speck from it, and put it into a jug. Whisk it with a wire whisk, strain the chocolate over it and whisk again until frothy.

CREAM DRINK

Put 2–3 tbsps. fresh, sweet cream into a tumber and fill up with soda water. This is both light and nourishing, and can often be digested when milk is found to be too heavy. A small piece of ice may be added when the weather is hot.

CREAM SOOTHER

1 tsp. cornflour — Sugar
1 cupful fresh milk — Flavouring
2 tbsps. cream — 1 egg white

Put the cornflour into a basin and mix the milk with it gradually. Turn it into a saucepan, stir until boiling, and cook for at least 5 minutes, stirring all the time. Add cream and sugar to taste. Flavour with vanilla or a little grated nutmeg, and stir in the egg white, stiffly beaten. Care must be taken not to make the cornflour too thick; it must be thin enough to drink.

This will be found very soothing and pleasant.

EGG DRINK

1 egg — 2 tsps. sugar
1 tbsp. sherry — 1 teacupful milk

Break the egg and remove the speck. Add to it the wine and sugar and beat together with a fork, but do not make too frothy. Heat the milk in a small saucepan, and when almost boiling, pour it on to the egg, etc., stirring all the time. Serve hot.

The wine may be omitted. The egg yolk only may be used, and soda water instead of milk.

See also EGG FLIP, in the Hot and Cold Drinks chapter.

LEMON COOLER

1 egg — 3–4 tbsps. shaved ice
Juice of 1 lemon — Soda water
½ teacupful water

Put all except soda water into a cocktail shaker,

and shake well for a few minutes until the ice is melted. Then strain into a large glass, fill up with soda water, and put a slice of lemon on the top. Serve with straws. Orange or grape-fruit juice can be used in the same way.

MILK LEMONADE

Juice of 1 lemon — ¼ pint boiling water
1 tbsp. sherry — ¼ pint milk
2 tbsps. sugar

Strain the lemon juice, and add to it the sherry and sugar. Pour on the boiling water, stir until the sugar is dissolved, add the cold milk and stir until the milk curdles. Strain through a piece of muslin that has been rinsed in warm water, and serve warm or cold.

MILK TEA

This is frequently ordered for an invalid, and it is more wholesome and nourishing than ordinary tea. It must, however, be properly prepared.

To make 1 breakfastcupful allow 1 breakfast-cupful of milk and 2 tsps. good China tea. First heat a small teapot with boiling water, pour away the water, and put in the tea. Heat the milk to boiling point in a small saucepan and pour it over the tea. Cover, and allow it to stand in a warm place for 20 minutes: the side of the stove or a cool oven will do, but the tea must on no account be allowed to boil. Then pour off carefully into another heated teapot or into a breakfastcup, being careful not to disturb the leaves and sediment. Serve at once.

This drink contains only the cream and the whey of the milk and the refreshing element of the tea. The casein, which is the heavy part of the milk, combines with the tannin, the bitter element of the tea, and forms a curd which sinks to the foot of the teapot. Hence the necessity for pouring off the tea carefully.

OATMEAL GRUEL

2 tbsps. oatmeal — A small piece of butter, if liked
½ pint milk — A little wine or brandy (optional)
A good pinch of salt or 2 tsps. sugar

Put the oatmeal and milk into a basin, and mix them together. Cover the basin with a plate or piece of paper and let it stand for at least ½ hour, stirring now and then. Then strain off the milk into a small lined saucepan, pressing the oatmeal as dry as possible. Stir the liquid over the heat until boiling, and simmer slowly for 10 minutes. If too thick, a little more milk may be added. Season with salt or sugar according to taste. A small piece of butter may also be added at the last, and wine or brandy, if desired. Gruel must be served very hot.

Oatmeal flour may be used instead of the meal, and water instead of milk. A little cream may be added.

OATMEAL GRUEL WITH BEEF-TEA

2 tbsps. fine oatmeal — ¼ pint beef-tea
¼ pint cold water or milk — Salt

Make the gruel with the oatmeal and water or milk, as above. When cooked add to it the beef-tea, and stir until quite hot, but do not boil again. Season to taste, and serve hot.

PRUNE DRINK

1½ oz. prunes — ½ oz. sugar
1 pint cold water

Wash the prunes and cut them in halves. If time permits, soak them for 1 hour in 1 pint of cold water, then put them into a lined saucepan with the water and sugar, and simmer slowly for 1 hour. Strain, and allow to stand until cold.

This makes a refreshing and excellent drink. A little lemon juice or port wine may be added.

RICE WATER

1 oz. Carolina rice — ½ inch cinnamon stick
1 pint cold water — A little sugar (optional)

Wash the rice well, and put it into a small lined pan with the water and cinnamon stick. Simmer slowly for 1 hour, then strain, and it is ready for use. It may be served hot or cold. If cold, stir it occasionally while cooling, or it will jelly. A little sugar may be added, if allowed.

If the patient has need of a stimulant, 1 tbsp. sherry or port may be mixed with the rice water. A piece of ginger may be boiled with the rice water instead of cinnamon stick.

RUM AND MILK

½ pint milk — A pinch of nutmeg (optional)
Sugar
½ glass rum

Make the milk very hot, sweeten to taste, and pour it into a glass. Add the warmed rum and a pinch of nutmeg (if liked).

TEA WITH AN EGG

Break the egg into a basin and add a little milk and sugar, if liked. Beat up with a fork and strain into a cup. Pour in the hot tea gradually, stirring all the time. If the whole egg is found to be too much, the yolk only may be used.

TOAST WATER

1 slice of stale bread or the crust of bread
1 pint cold water

The crust of bread is to be preferred for this, as it does not turn sour so soon. Toast it well on both sides until dry and nicely browned without being burnt. Have the water, which must be very fresh and cold, in a jug; break the toast into pieces, and add them to the water in the jug. Cover the jug and let the toast remain soaking until the water is the colour of sherry wine. Then strain and serve cold.

This makes a very refreshing drink. A little lemon juice may be added.

TREACLE POSSET

¼ pint milk
1 tbsp. treacle

Rinse out a small saucepan, put the milk into it, and bring to the boil. Add the treacle and boil up again. The acid of the treacle will curdle the milk. Strain through a piece of muslin, and serve hot. This is a pleasant drink to serve to anyone who has a cold.

WHEY

1 pint new milk
1 tsp. rennet

Warm the milk in a basin to a lukewarm temperature, or about the heat of new milk, and stir in the rennet. Let it stand in a warm place for about 15 minutes, until the curd forms and the whey is quite clear. Then let it cool; break up the curd and strain off the whey, which then forms a soothing drink that is very easily digested.

WINE WHEY

1 teacupful milk
½ glass sherry
A little sugar

Put the milk into a small clean saucepan with a lump of sugar if desired, and bring to the boil. Add the wine and heat until it curdles the milk. Stretch a piece of muslin over a glass or cup and strain the contents of the saucepan through. This keeps back the curd, which is the heaviest part of the milk.

Lemon Whey: Prepare in the same way as Wine Whey, using 1 tbsp. lemon juice instead of the sherry.

Cream Whey: This can be made according to either of the two last recipes. Add 1–2 tbsps. cream after straining.

VEGETARIAN COOKERY

Some people dislike eating meat and fish for humanitarian reasons ; others carry the principle still further and refrain also from taking milk, milk products and eggs, and for these people the daily meals must consist of cereals, vegetables, and fruits. The majority of vegetarians, however, merely eat no flesh foods. In contrast to these voluntary vegetarians, there are those whose doctor advises a temporary or permanent reduction of flesh foods, so that the patient for the time being has to fill the gap with vegetables or with vegetarian-type dishes.

To replace the meat and fish normally consumed, the vegetarian must eat nuts, haricot beans, peas, lentils, soya flour, etc., eggs, and cheese. Suet and lard will be replaced by vegetable or nut fats and peanut butter ; gelatine will be replaced by Irish (or carrageen) moss or Iceland moss. Vegetable soups and salads will play a large part in the menu.

From a nutritional point of view there are good and bad points in a vegetable diet. Firstly, it is a very bulky one, good for the over-fat, but with dangers for the emaciated. It contains a large amount of roughage, which relieves one type of constipation, but can aggravate another. It takes a long time to prepare and a long time to eat, though modern shredding and grating machines can overcome the first difficulty.

According to published tables of food values, there is a lower concentration of iron in vegetable foods than in meat, but wholemeal flour and bread and other whole grains, also eggs, if permitted, will help to fill this gap. Vitamin D may be slightly deficient even with fortified nut butter and cereal products. If vitamin A is deficient, a synthetic form is sometimes given. Any tendency to a deficiency of nicotinic acid is probably overcome in this country by eating brown, National, and fortified flours. Eating seeds and pulses which have been allowed to sprout helps to increase the riboflavin content of the diet, which might otherwise be lacking. Since the heights and weights of children on a vegetarian diet tend to be normal, they probably receive adequate calories and protein.

To omit meat, fish, and other flesh foods from daily meals obviously opens up a special field of cookery. Few ordinary main-meal dishes can be used as they stand, though some can be adapted ; for instance, bacon which has been added to a recipe merely for flavouring can be omitted, and animal fats can be replaced by vegetarian ones (extra salt may then be needed). To obtain variety in the vegetarian diet, however, it is advisable to have a range of recipes specially prepared for the purpose, and it is hoped that the suggestions in this chapter will prove useful to habitual vegetarians, and may also interest those who like to include a certain number of vegetable dishes in their ordinary menus.

Many of the recipes in the chapters on Soups, Vegetable Cookery, Salads, Cereals and Cheese Cookery, will also be found useful, though for strict vegetarians they may need some adaptation. Titles of books on vegetarian cookery, etc., may be obtained from the Vegetarian Society, 53 Marloes Road, London, W.8.

ARTICHOKES AU GRATIN

Peel some Jerusalem artichokes into water containing a little lemon juice (use a stainless knife and keep the artichokes under water as much as possible to prevent discoloration). Slice the artichokes thickly, add a squeeze of lemon juice to some boiling water and cook until tender—about 20–40 minutes. Make a roux with 1 oz. butter or margarine and 1 oz. flour, gradually add ¼ pint milk and ¼ pint water mixed, season well and cook for 15 minutes. Strain the artichokes and place them in a fireproof dish. Pour the sauce over, sprinkle the top with 2 oz. grated cheese and put the dish in a hot oven (450° F., mark 8) or under the grill for a few minutes, to brown the top.

BAKED EGGS IN TOMATO JUICE

1 small tin tomato juice   Creamed potatoes
4 eggs

Grease a shallow baking dish, pour in the tomato juice, and break the eggs whole into the tomato juice. Bake in a slow oven (325° F., mark 2) for about 20 minutes, until the eggs are firm. Serve with creamed potatoes.

BEETROOT AU GRATIN

1 large cooked beetroot	1 tsp. vinegar
1 tbsp. grated onion	2 oz. grated cheese
1–1½ oz. margarine	Pepper and salt
¾ oz. flour	2 oz. breadcrumbs
½ pint milk	Parsley to garnish

Dice the beetroot, and mix with the grated onion. Melt about half the margarine, stir in the flour, add the milk, and stir until boiling. Add the beet to this sauce, with the vinegar and a little of the grated cheese and seasonings. Pour into a fireproof dish, and cover with a thick layer of breadcrumbs and grated cheese and some small pieces of margarine. Bake in a moderate oven (375° F., mark 5) for 10–15 minutes. Garnish with parsley.

CATALINA PIE

2 Spanish onions	3 oz. grated cheese
4 tomatoes	Milk or egg to glaze
8 oz. pastry	

Slice the onions into rings, and boil in salted water until quite tender. Slice the peeled tomatoes. Line a pie plate with half the pastry, and put on a layer of onions, then a layer of tomatoes and then a layer of grated cheese. Continue to build up the filling in layers until it has all been used, then cover with the rest of the pastry. Glaze, and bake in a moderately hot oven (400° F., mark 6) until golden-brown.

GARDEN SURPRISE

A few handfuls of spinach	A handful of small broad beans
Some young carrots	6 tender cabbage leaves
Salt	
Shreds of fat	Large lettuce leaves
A cupful of green peas	Grated cheese
A handful of runner beans	Cooked potatoes

Wash the spinach carefully, removing coarse stalks, and lay it in the bottom of a fairly large casserole. Cover with a layer of young carrots, washed and left whole, and sprinkle with salt and a few shreds of fat. Next, prepare the peas and runner beans in the usual way, and the broad beans by cutting into small chunks (without podding). Wrap these in the cabbage leaves to make little parcels, including salt and a knob of fat in each one, and lay these on the carrots. Finish with a layer of the large lettuce leaves, then cover, and cook over gentle heat or in a moderate oven (350° F., mark 3) until tender—20–30 minutes. Serve with cheese and potatoes.

LENTIL PIE

½ lb. lentils	Salt
1 onion	Chopped parsley
A little water	A little tomato sauce
½ lb. mashed potatoes	

Wash the lentils thoroughly, and cook them with the sliced onion, with sufficient water to cover, until the lentils are quite tender and soft and the water absorbed. Pass the mixture through a sieve, add the potatoes, seasoning, parsley, and a little tomato sauce, and mix thoroughly. Put into a greased casserole and bake in a moderate oven (350° F., mark 3) for 15–20 minutes, till nicely crisped and browned.

CHEESE AND TOMATO PUDDING

1 large onion	2 tsps. sugar
2 oz. margarine	2 eggs
4 peeled tomatoes	3 oz. grated cheese
Salt and pepper	4 oz. breadcrumbs

Chop the onion, and cook in ¾ pint water till quite tender. Add the margarine and the sliced tomatoes, with seasoning and sugar, and cook for 5 minutes, until the tomatoes are cooked. Leave to cool, then beat the eggs and add to the mixture with half the grated cheese and breadcrumbs. Grease a pie dish and pour the mixture into it, sprinkle with remaining cheese, and bake in a moderate oven (375° F., mark 5) until set and brown on top. Serve with crispbread or toast.

CHEESE AND LEEK PIE

6 oz. shortcrust pastry	Seasoned flour
2–3 leeks or onions (parboiled)	4 oz. grated cheese
	2 tbsps. top of milk

Line a pie plate with pastry. Cut the leeks or onions into rings, put them on the pastry, and sprinkle with a little seasoned flour. Cover with the grated cheese and add the milk. Roll out the rest of the pastry and cut into strips. Plait them lattice fashion over the top, brush with beaten egg to give a glazed finish, and bake in a hot oven (450° F., mark 8) for about 10 minutes, until browned, then reduce heat and cook for a further 20 minutes.

CHEESE AND TOMATO PIE

¾ lb. tomatoes	6 oz. cheese
½ oz. margarine	Pepper
1½ oz. breadcrumbs	A pinch of allspice

Choose firm tomatoes and cut them into slices. Grease a pie dish, put a layer of breadcrumbs and cheese in the bottom of the dish, then a layer of sliced tomatoes, sprinkle with a little pepper and allspice, then add another layer of breadcrumbs and cheese. Continue until the dish is full, arranging for the top to have a good sprinkling of cheese. Bake in a slow oven (325° F., mark 2) till the tomatoes are cooked and the top brown. Decorate the dish with sippets of toast or fried bread.

CREAM CHEESE SALAD RING

½ pint aspic jelly	A shake of cayenne
½ cucumber, thinly sliced	½ lb. tomatoes, peeled and sliced
12 oz. cream cheese, salted	1 lettuce
¼ pint evaporated milk	Mustard and cress
A squeeze of lemon juice	

Mask a 6-inch ring mould with aspic jelly. Decorate with overlapping rings of cucumber, and just cover with more jelly. Mix the cheese with the milk, flavour with lemon juice and cayenne, and then fill evenly into the ring mould. Top with a layer of tomatoes. Cover with aspic jelly, and put in a cold place to set. Turn out on to a bed of crisp lettuce, and decorate with leaves of mustard and cress.

RICE AND CHEESE CASSEROLE

4 oz. rice	½ tsp. made mustard
½ oz. margarine	½ lb. tomatoes
½ oz. flour	Cooked celery
½ pint milk	2 oz. grated cheese
Pepper and salt	Parsley and toast

Wash the rice and cook till tender. Make an ordinary white sauce, using the margarine, flour and milk, season it well and add the mustard, then the rice. Pour half the mixture into a heat-proof dish, cover with a layer of thinly sliced skinned tomatoes and pieces of chopped cooked celery, and sprinkle with salt and pepper. Pour the remaining mixture over, and sprinkle with finely grated cheese. Bake in a moderate oven (350° F., mark 3) for about 20 minutes, or until golden-brown. Serve garnished with chopped parsley and crisp toast.

CHEESE AND POTATO CASSEROLE

1 lb. potatoes	A little powdered mace
2 onions	1 pint milk or vegetable liquor
2 oz. grated cheese	
Pepper	

Peel and slice the onions and potatoes, and partly cook them in boiling water, then strain off the liquid. Butter a pie dish or casserole, put in layers of the partly cooked potatoes and onions, and sprinkle with grated cheese, pepper, and mace, making the top layer potatoes, with a little cheese sprinkled on top. Cover with the liquid, put a lid on, or make a "cap" of greased paper, and cook in a slow oven (325° F., mark 2) for about 1½ hours. Before serving, take off lid and brown top.

NUT CROQUETTES

1 oz. fat	Chopped celery
Flour	1–2 tsps. salt
¼ pint milk	Pepper
4 oz. ground nuts	Breadcrumbs
1 small chopped onion	Fat for frying
1 tsp. yeast extract	

Make a panada by melting the fat, stirring in 1 oz. flour, removing the pan from the heat, and gradually adding the milk. Stir in the nuts, onion, yeast extract, celery, salt and pepper. Roll into cork-shaped pieces, and coat with a batter made from about 2 tbsps. flour, mixed with a little milk. Coat with crumbs, and fry in deep fat.

NUT FLAN

6 oz. shortcrust pastry	1 tsp. piquant table sauce
1 large onion	1 egg
½ oz. vegetable fat	1 tsp. salt
4 oz. Brazil nuts	
1 tsp. yeast extract	

Line a flan ring with the pastry, and bake blind in a hot oven (450° F., mark 8) for 10–15 minutes. Mince the onion, and fry it in the fat. Mince the nuts, reserving a few for garnishing. Mix the onion, nuts, yeast extract, sauce, egg, and salt, put the mixture into the flan case, garnish with the remaining shredded nuts, and bake in a moderate oven (350° F., mark 3) for ½ hour.

MARYLAND SOUFFLÉ

1 tin of sweet corn	Pepper and salt
1 oz. margarine	2 eggs
1 oz. flour	3 oz. finely grated cheese
½ pint milk	

Empty the corn into a fireproof dish. Melt the margarine, stir in the flour, add the milk, and stir until boiling. Season, and add the egg yolks and the grated cheese. Whip the egg whites to a stiff froth, fold lightly into the sauce, and pour the mixture over the sweet corn, leaving sufficient room for it to rise when baking. Bake in a moderate oven (375° F., mark 5) for 20–30 minutes, until golden-brown and firm.

Sliced tomatoes or cooked cauliflower can be substituted for sweet corn in this soufflé.

SAVOURY NUT LOAF

1 large onion	2 oz. breadcrumbs
8 oz. minced carrot	1 tbsp. chopped parsley
½ oz. vegetable fat	1 egg
4 oz. ground nuts	2 tsps. salt

Fry the onion and carrot in the hot fat. Add the nuts, breadcrumbs, chopped parsley, beaten egg, and salt. Roll into a loaf, brush over with fat, and bake in a moderate oven (375° F., mark 5) for about 30 minutes. Brown under the grill if necessary.

SAVOURY NUT ROLL

4 oz. nuts	1 egg
8 oz. boiled rice	1 tbsp. tomato sauce
2 tsps. chopped parsley	Tomato or brown sauce to serve
1 tbsp. chopped onion	
A pinch of diced herbs	Baked tomatoes to garnish
Salt and pepper	

Shell and mince the nuts. Mix the rice and nuts together, with the parsley, onion, herbs, and seasoning. Beat the egg, and bind the mixture with this and the tomato sauce, adding 1 tbsp. more sauce or more beaten egg if the mixture is too dry. Form into a roll, place in a floured cloth, roll up, and tie the ends. Put into a pan of boiling salted stock or water, and cook for 1½ hours. Remove the cloth, turn the roll carefully on to a hot dish, and pour tomato sauce or brown sauce over it. Garnish with baked tomatoes.

SCALLOPED NUTS

4 oz. minced nuts	2 tsps. salt
½ lb. tomatoes	½ pint water
2 tsps. dried sage	2 tsps. yeast extract
4 oz. breadcrumbs	2 tsps. horseradish sauce
1 onion, sliced	Vegetable fat

Put layers of minced nuts, sliced tomatoes, sage, and breadcrumbs in a pie dish. Cook the onion in the salted water, add the yeast extract and horseradish sauce, and pour over the contents of the dish. Dot the top with fat, and bake in a moderate oven (350° F., mark 3) for about ½ hour. Brown under grill if necessary.

POTATO CASSEROLE

2 oz. fat	1 lb. tomatoes
1 lb. potatoes	¼ pint stock or water
2 sticks of celery	Salt and pepper

Melt the fat in a casserole. Peel and slice the potatoes, cut up the celery, and slice the tomatoes. Fry the potatoes and celery in the fat until lightly browned. Fill the casserole with alternate layers of sliced potatoes, tomatoes, and celery. Pour the boiling stock or water over, add seasoning, put on the lid, and cook very gently in a moderate oven (350° F., mark 3) or over gentle heat until the vegetables are tender.

RAGOÛT OF BEANS

4 oz. butter beans	1 tbsp. tomato sauce
2 oz. fat	1 tsp. yeast extract
2 large onions	Pepper and salt
1 stick of celery	Chopped parsley and strips of fried bread to garnish
1 oz. flour	
½ pint stock	

Cook the butter beans until tender, then drain them. Put the fat in a saucepan, and heat until smoking hot, add the sliced onions and celery, and fry until golden-brown, then stir in the flour, and brown lightly. Add the stock, sauce, yeast extract, and seasonings, and stir until boiling. Heat the beans in the sauce, and serve in an earthenware dish, sprinkled with chopped parsley and garnished with strips of fried bread.

ONION AND CHEESE PUDDING

4 slices bread and butter	½ pint milk
3 oz. grated cheese	1 egg
1 tbsp. grated onion	Pepper and salt

Place alternate layers of bread and margarine, cheese and onion, in a greased fireproof dish, finishing with a layer of bread and margarine, spread on both sides. Heat the milk, and pour it over the beaten egg, season, and strain it into the pie dish. Bake in a moderate oven (350° F., mark 3) for ¾–1 hour, until firm and lightly browned.

ONION AND CHEESE TURNOVERS

½ lb. shortcrust pastry	¼ pint white sauce
¾ lb. cooked onions	Salt and pepper
3–4 oz. grated cheese	1 tsp. chopped sage

Roll out the pastry, and cut it into saucer-sized rounds. Cut up the onions, and mix with the cheese and sauce, season well, and add the sage. Put into the centre of the pastry, leaving ½ inch of pastry around the edge, fold the pastry over, and seal the edges well. Make some slits in the top of the pastry, and bake in a moderately hot oven (425° F., mark 7) for 25–30 minutes.

INDIVIDUAL SPINACH TIMBALES

(*See colour picture facing page* 97)

2 lb. spinach	1 oz. margarine
Salt and pepper	Fried bananas (see page 517)
1 egg	Cooked peas

Cook the spinach until tender, drain thoroughly, sieve or chop finely, and add salt and pepper, the beaten egg, and the margarine. Put into some greased dariole moulds, cover with greaseproof paper, and steam for 20 minutes. Turn out on to a hot dish, and add the bananas and peas.

FRIED BANANAS

3 bananas	Fat for frying
Egg and breadcrumbs	

Cut the bananas in half lengthwise, egg-and-crumb in the usual way, and fry till golden.

BAKED MARROW BALLS

6 oz. mashed cooked marrow	2½ oz. breadcrumbs
3½ oz. grated cheese	4 tbsps. ground nuts
1 large onion, minced and fried	A pinch of mixed herbs
	Pepper and salt
	Egg to bind

Drain the marrow well, mix it with the remaining ingredients, and form into balls. Arrange these in a greased casserole, and bake for ½ hour in a moderate oven (350° F., mark 3). Serve with carrot rings and buttered haricot beans.

MUSHROOM AND MACARONI SAVOURY

4 oz. macaroni	½ pint white sauce
3 oz. mushrooms	2 hard-boiled eggs
2 tsps. minced onion	Salt and pepper
Dripping or fat	1½ oz. grated cheese

Boil the macaroni for about ½ hour, or until tender. Fry the sliced mushrooms with the onion until cooked, and add to the sauce, with the diced eggs. Season to taste. Drain the macaroni and place it in a greased fireproof dish, cover with the sauce, sprinkle with grated cheese, and brown either in a hot oven (450° F., mark 8) or under a grill.

SPINACH AND MUSHROOM EN COCOTTE

1 lb. cooked spinach	Pepper and salt
4 oz. mushrooms	1 tbsp. unsweetened evaporated milk
1 oz. fat	
½ oz. flour	1 egg yolk (optional)
¼ pint spinach water	Parsley to garnish

Line 6 greased cocotte dishes with the finely chopped spinach. Peel, wash, and slice the mushrooms, keeping 6 small ones whole. Melt the fat, and add the sliced mushrooms. Stir in the flour, add the spinach water, and stir until boiling. Cool, season, and stir in the milk and the egg yolk, if used. Place 1 tbsp. of the mushroom mixture in each cocotte dish, and bake in a hot oven (450° F., mark 8) for 10 minutes, until lightly browned. Meanwhile, bake the 6 whole mushrooms with a small piece of fat in each, and use to garnish the cocotte dish, together with small sprigs of parsley.

VEGETARIAN STUFFED TOMATOES

4 large tomatoes	2 tsps. capers
2 hard-boiled eggs	1 tsp. salt
2 oz. ground nuts	Lettuce

Cut off the tops of the tomatoes, scoop out the insides, and mix with the chopped eggs, nuts, capers, and salt. Refill the tomatoes, and serve on a bed of lettuce leaves.

TOMATO PUDDING

2 oz. mushrooms	Pepper and salt
1 oz. margarine	Powdered mace
1 chopped shallot or onion	1 egg
1 lb. or 1 small tin of tomatoes	½ pint stock or liquid from tomatoes
4 oz. white breadcrumbs	Baked halved tomatoes to garnish

Peel, wash, and slice the mushrooms. Melt the margarine, and fry the mushrooms and shallot lightly. Slice the tomatoes if necessary. Put alternate layers of mushroom, tomatoes, and breadcrumbs in a fireproof dish, seasoning each layer with pepper and salt and a little mace. Beat the egg, add the stock or tomato liquid, and pour over the vegetables. Bake in a moderate oven (350° F., mark 4) for 45 minutes, until firm. Garnish with the baked tomatoes.

VEGETARIAN CURRY

½ lb. prepared mixed vegetables	2–3 cloves
1 oz. vegetarian fat	A pinch of ground cummin seed
1 onion	½ tsp. ground ginger
1 clove of garlic	A little mustard seed
1 tbsp. ground coriander	Tamarind water or water
1 tsp. ground turmeric	Seasoning
½ a bay leaf	
A pinch of chilli powder	

Dice the vegetables. Melt the fat and fry the thinly sliced onion and the garlic. Make a paste of the other ingredients, and fry it for 5 minutes, then add the vegetables and the liquid, and simmer until cooked. Season well, and serve.

If desired, 4 oz. minced nuts may be added.

VEGETARIAN RISOTTO

6 oz. rice	A pinch of saffron
2 large onions	1 red pepper or some paprika
2 oz. raisins	
3 oz. fat	6 tomatoes
1 pint stock	Grated cheese or scrambled eggs
Salt	

Wash and dry the rice. Slice the onions and stone the raisins. Melt the fat, and fry the onions and raisins until lightly brown, add the rice, and fry without browning. Add the stock, salt, saffron, sliced red pepper, and sliced tomatoes, turn into a casserole, and cook very gently for about 2 hours, until the rice has absorbed all the stock. Do not stir while cooking. Serve with grated cheese handed separately, or pile the rissotto on a hot dish with the scrambled eggs.

SPAGHETTI WITH WALNUTS

8 oz. cooked spaghetti	1 tbsp. chopped pickled walnuts
2 oz. margarine	Salt and pepper
A small piece of chopped garlic or 1 tbsp. chopped onion	Fried onion rings
	1 tbsp. chopped parsley

Cook the spaghetti in boiling salted water for about 30 minutes until it is tender, then drain it. Melt the margarine, and fry the garlic or onion and walnuts lightly. Add the spaghetti and seasoning, and toss until well mixed, pile in a hot dish, and garnish with fried onion rings and parsley. This makes a good accompaniment to scrambled eggs.

VEGETABLE FLAN AU GRATIN

Shortcrust pastry	1 cooked potato
2 cooked carrots	½ pint white sauce
2 cooked onions	Salt and pepper
2 tbsps. cooked or tinned peas	Grated cheese

Line a flan tin with the pastry, and bake it blind. Cut up the cooked vegetables and mix with the hot sauce, season well, and pour into the cooked flan ring. Sprinkle liberally with grated cheese, and brown under a hot grill.

VEGETARIAN STUFFED ONIONS

4 large onions	2 oz. nuts
¼ lb. carrots	1–2 tbsps. salad cream
1–2 oz. cheese	1–2 tsps. salt

Cook the onions until they are just beginning to go soft—½–¾ hour. Hollow them out, and save 1 oz. of the pulp for the filling. Grate the carrots and cheese, and chop the nuts and onion pulp. Mix together with the salad cream, reserving some of the cheese, season, and fill the onions, piling the mixture up if necessary. Sprinkle the tops with the remaining cheese, and bake in a moderate oven (350° F., mark 3) for about 30 minutes

VEGETARIAN FRITTERS

4 oz. lentils	1 egg yolk
½ oz. fat	1 tsp. yeast extract
1 small onion, finely chopped	Salt and pepper
	2 oz. flour
1 tsp. curry powder	2 tsps. salad oil
1 oz. breadcrumbs	1 egg white

Cook the lentils in 1 pint water until tender, strain, and sieve. Melt the fat, add the onion and curry powder, and fry lightly. Add the breadcrumbs, lentils, yeast extract, and egg yolk, season, mix thoroughly, and form into rolls. Make a batter by mixing the flour and a pinch of salt, stirring in the salad oil and enough tepid water to make a thick batter, and fold in the stiffly beaten egg white. Dip each lentil roll in batter, fry in the smoking-hot fat until golden-brown, drain, and serve piled in a dish.

TOMATO FLAN

¼ lb. finely chopped onions	Seasoning
	A pastry flan case
½ lb. skinned tomatoes	Grated cheese and breadcrumbs, mixed
½ a cucumber, finely chopped	Finely chopped parsley

Fry the onions, and when they are light golden-brown and soft, add the tomatoes and cucumber, and continue cooking until pulped. Season, and pour into the flan case. Top with cheese and breadcrumbs, place in a hot oven (450° F., mark 8) or under the grill to brown, and garnish with finely chopped parsley

VEGETABLE AND EGG PIE

1½ lb. spinach	2 spring onions
Margarine or fat	Salt and pepper
½–1 lb. mixed cooked vegetables	3 eggs
	3 tbsps. water

Cook the spinach and chop it finely, place in a fireproof dish, dot with small pieces of fat, cover with the diced mixed vegetables, and sprinkle with salt and pepper. Separate the eggs, beat the yolks till creamy, add seasoning and the water, and beat again; whisk the whites as stiffly as possible, and fold them into the yolk mixture. Pour this omelette mixture over the vegetables, and bake in a moderate oven (375° F., mark 5) for 20 minutes.

SWISS BREAKFAST DISH

2 oz. sultanas or seedless raisins	2–3 apples
	1 tbsp. cream, top of the milk or evapor ated milk
2 tbsps. flaked oats	
2 tbsps. brown sugar or honey	Lemon juice

Wash the dried fruit and mix with the oats, just cover with boiling water, and leave overnight. Add the sugar or honey and the apples (which should be grated without peeling), also the cream and a few drops of lemon juice. Blend well and serve at once. Extra cream may be handed separately.

SPICED EGGLESS SANDWICH CAKE

2 oz. margarine or fat	2 tbsps. golden syrup
3 oz. sugar	5 oz. flour
1 tsp. bicarbonate of soda	1 tsp. ground ginger
	1 tsp. ground cinnamon
5 tbsps. milk	Date filling (see below)

Cream the fat and sugar. Dissolve the bicarbonate of soda in the milk, add the syrup, and beat this mixture well into the fat and sugar. Add the flour and spices, and mix well. Pour into a 7-inch sandwich tin and bake in a moderately hot oven (425° F., mark 7) for 15–20 minutes. When cool, split, and spread with filling.

DATE FILLING

12 chopped dates	2–3 tbsps. water
½ oz. margarine	1 oz. sugar

Stir the ingredients together, and heat in a saucepan till thick enough to spread.

APPLE AND TANGERINE WHIP

¼ oz. gelatine	1 tsp. honey
½ cup water	½ tangerine (or ¼ of an orange)
1 apple, peeled and sliced	A few drops lemon juice

Soak the gelatine in the cold water. Stew the apple gently, and stir in the honey and soaked gelatine. When nearly cold, add the chopped tangerine sections (from which all tough pith has been removed) and the lemon juice, and whisk thoroughly. Serve in an individual dish, sprinkled with a little grated tangerine rind.

ORANGE FOAM

2 tsps. carrageen moss	1 egg yolk
1 pint water	2 tbsps. rose-hip syrup
1 orange	4 tbsps. evaporated milk

Mix the moss with a little of the cold water, and boil the remainder with the grated orange rind. Stir into the beaten egg yolk, and cook gently a few minutes. Stir in the rose-hip syrup, orange juice, and evaporated milk, whisk thoroughly, and place in individual dishes. Serve hot or cold.

BLACK-CURRANT FLUFF

2 tsps. carrageen moss	1 tbsp. black-currant purée
1 pint water	
2–3 tbsps. honey	1 egg white
Juice of ½ a lemon	

Soak the moss in a little cold water. Boil the remainder of the water with the honey and add to the soaked moss. Stir in the lemon juice and black-currant purée, and fold in the stiffly beaten egg white. Serve in individual dishes.

DIET AND WEIGHT

Many tables exist telling us exactly how much we should weigh. You look up your height, find the appropriate age column, and there is the "standard weight." It sounds very simple, but actually, the complications involved in arriving at a standard weight are tremendous. There are, for instance, racial differences, probably due at least in part to food habits and climate. There are the differences due to individual muscular development; a boxer, for example, might not fit into his niche in the standard table, but he would not be "overweight" in the bad sense of the term, since muscle, not deposited fat, would account for his extra pounds. Some people explain their plumpness or slenderness by declaring that their bones are large or small. In fact, we have no scientific data on this point, for the simple reason that it is difficult to carry out precise measurements.

The method of determining one's own real weight also presents difficulties. For various reasons our weight does not remain constant. A meal may weigh 2–3 lb. and two glasses of fluid about 1 lb.—in fact the scales may show an alarming increase when the stomach is full. Then we are continually losing water from all over the body through perspiration, the average amount being about 1 lb. per day, though on a hot day, after a busy morning of shopping or spring-cleaning, it can be very much greater. Again, just as the consumption of a meal will increase weight, so the elimination of waste products will cause a decrease. For all these reasons, it is important to weigh oneself at the same time every day or every week, and the same clothes should be worn, or an accurate adjustment should be made for necessary seasonal changes, etc.

All these points should be borne in mind when referring to the following table of weights. If, after making allowance for the relevant factors, you feel you are over or under weight, you will find in the rest of the chapter advice and recipes which will help you to adjust matters. However, if you are gaining or losing weight rapidly, you should seek medical advice.

AVERAGE WEIGHT TABLES

WOMEN AGED 25 AND UPWARDS

Height	*Weight*
5 ft. 0 in.	8 st. 10 lb.
5 ft. 1 in.	8 st. 13 lb.
5 ft. 2 in.	9 st. 3 lb.
5 ft. 3 in.	9 st. 6 lb.
5 ft. 4 in.	9 st. 10 lb.
5 ft. 5 in.	10 st. 0 lb.
5 ft. 6 in.	10 st. 3 lb.
5 ft. 7 in.	10 st. 7 lb.
5 ft. 8 in.	10 st. 11 lb.
5 ft. 9 in.	11 st. 0 lb.
5 ft. 10 in.	11 st. 3 lb.

MEN AGED 25 YEARS AND UPWARDS

Height	*Weight*
5 ft. 1 in.	9 st. 3 lb.
5 ft. 2 in.	9 st. 7 lb.
5 ft. 3 in.	9 st. 11 lb.
5 ft. 4 in.	9 st. 13 lb.
5 ft. 5 in.	10 st. 3 lb.
5 ft. 6 in.	10 st. 7 lb.
5 ft. 7 in.	10 st. 11 lb.
5 ft. 8 in.	11 st. 1 lb.
5 ft. 9 in.	11 st. 5 lb.
5 ft. 10 in.	11 st. 10 lb.
5 ft. 11 in.	12 st. 0 lb.
6 ft. 0 in.	12 st. 5 lb.
6 ft. 1 in.	12 st. 11 lb.
6 ft. 2 in.	13 st. 3 lb.

SLIMMING DIET

When the pointer on the scales indicates a figure ½–1 stone over the standard weight, the time has come to exercise a little more self-restraint. Far from being a question of vanity, such action is a definite means of preserving or regaining good health. Overweight is a potential danger to health, and any life assurance company contemplates with suspicion a waist measurement which exceeds that of the chest.

Cases of acute obesity, or these due to organic disorders, should, of course, be treated by a doctor, but many a severe case could be prevented by wise eating.

The whole basis of a sensible slimming diet is cutting down the calories. Calories, remember, represent the activity-value of food—they are used by the body in strict proportion to the amount of activity in which we indulge. Here are three examples of the number of calories needed daily by women doing different types of work :

A typist or office worker	2,000 calories
A housewife	2,400 calories
A housewife doing spring cleaning	3,000 calories

These figures would vary according to the type of person : some are lethargic in their actions and need fewer calories, others are excitable and extravagant in their movements, so need more. The office worker may indulge in gardening or some sport which would increase his calorie need to quite a large extent—half an hour's swimming, for instance, uses up 275 calories.

If we consistently take in more calories than we use up in our ordinary activities, the result is inevitable—unwanted fat and sugar (which is sometimes converted into fat by the body in as short a time as half an hour) are deposited under the skin, in the liver, around the kidneys, and so on. The outward effect varies from a " pleasing plumpness " to a really ugly obesity. Once this begins to happen, the only solution is to cut down the intake of calories, so that the stored fat is drawn upon for the body's daily activities, and thus gradually reduced, with a corresponding reduction in the body weight.

There are many different ways of cutting down the calories, one practical method being to follow the diet suggested in the table below. This table consists of three lists : eat as much as you like of the foods in the first list (A), take only moderate amounts of those in the second list (B), and, if possible, avoid altogether the very fattening foods in the third list (C). It will be noticed that fat itself is omitted from the lists. Fats have indeed a very high calorie value and are thus best avoided ; but they are also appetite-appeasers, and as such are sometimes included in moderation in a slimming diet.

(A) *Suitable Foods for Slimming*

Vegetables, vegetable dishes, and salads
Fruit and fruit juices (without sugar)
Lean meat, rabbit, poultry, fish (preferably white or shell fish)
Skimmed milk and yoghourt made from skimmed milk
Cheese (preferably made from skimmed milk)
Jellies, both savoury and sweet (sweetened with saccharin, not sugar)
Thin soups

(B) *Foods allowed in moderation*

Milk	Crispbread
Potatoes	Breakfast cereals
Bread	Cornflour and custard powder
Eggs, egg custards	Dried fruits
	Fatty fish

(C) *Foods to avoid*

Sugar	Steamed puddings
Jam	Cakes
Sweets and chocolate	Biscuits
Pastries	Cream

The following examples, giving the weight and the calorie value of an average serving of various foodstuffs, will show the contrast between the fattening qualities of the foods in the above tables. It will be noticed that although fish and meat have fairly high calorie values, they are included in the permitted foods ; this is because they are not " fattening " in the same sense as the starchy or sweet foods, since they help to speed up the " burning " of food in the body.

Calorie Value of Fattening Foods

Fried chop (4 oz.)	400
Chocolate bar (2 oz.)	300
Fish fried ($7\frac{1}{2}$ oz.)	300
Shortcrust pastry (2 oz.)	300
Boiled sweets (2 oz.)	210
2 sweet biscuits (1 oz.)	160
1 slice of Swiss roll (2 oz.)	150
1 slice of bread (1 oz.)	74

Calorie Value of Non-fattening Foods

Lettuce (1 oz.)	3
Boiled cabbage (4 oz.)	12
1 small tomato (3 oz.)	12
Boiled carrots (4 oz.)	20
$\frac{1}{2}$ a grapefruit (4 oz.)	24
1 orange (4 oz.)	40
1 banana (2 oz.)	44
1 eating apple (4 oz.)	52
Steamed fish (4 oz.)	112
Lean mutton, boiled (3 oz.)	180

Generally speaking, no one should aim at losing more than 2 lb. a week (unless under a doctor's supervision). The amounts to eat of the foods from the three different groups will therefore need to be adjusted to give this result.

Bread and Potatoes : Remember that these homely foods are a useful source of the essential vitamin B_1, so unless the supply of this vitamin is kept up in some other way (see notes on food values in Meal Planning chapter) a shortage may arise if bread and potatoes are drastically reduced. Starch-reduced bread rolls are of value in a slimming diet; although their calorific value is 106 per oz. as compared with 74 for ordinary bread, they are much lighter and seem to go further.

Fruit and Vegetables : All fruits, and all vegetables except potatoes, can be included in a slimming diet. Although these vary a little in calorie content, the amount is not enough to affect the weight unduly.

Sugar : Since this is very fattening it should be omitted where possible, and saccharin used instead. Present-day brands do not impart an unpleasant flavour to foods, and some types are made in convenient extra-small tablets. The amount required varies according to personal taste, and can be judged according to the amount one needs for, say, a cup of tea. A recipe giving four servings might need from 4–8 saccharin tablets, according to the type—whether acid or bland. Whenever possible, add saccharin to the food *after* cooking.

Skimmed Milk : Use this in recipes which include milk. It can be obtained by removing the cream from the top of the milk, preferably with the aid of a special device for this purpose. Alternatively, skimmed milk powder can be obtained from health food shops or departmental stores.

Soups : Those who have high-speed mixers can use them to produce excellent soups for slimming diets. Cook one or more vegetables until they are tender, then place them in the mixer, and after ½ to 1 minute's mixing, a purée soup is obtained. A little skimmed milk can be added before mixing, if desired. Ordinary thickened soups should be avoided.

Cornflour : It will be noticed that some of the recipes contain cornflour, which is used in very small quantities in this diet. Usually only about ¼ oz. per person is needed in the blancmange "cream" type of recipe, and this amount can safely be included in a slimming diet, unless of a drastic nature.

Liquids : Although the removal of water from a body does lessen its weight, the human body is planned to work with a certain amount of water in its composition, and it is dangerous to drop below this quantity. (Salt helps to retain water in the body, and for this reason some doctors tell their "slimming" patients to go slow on it, as excess salt may retain excess water.) Certain drinks help to increase weight, notably those containing much sugar. Beer and other slightly alcoholic drinks contain about 120 calories per ½ pint, and should be avoided by those who want to lose weight.

If you are genuinely anxious to reduce, you must take the diet seriously. It is no good relaxing the rules and hoping to catch up later by taking extra exercise. Exercise is in fact of considerably less slimming value than commonly supposed: it takes an astonishingly large amount of hard work to counteract an apparently small quantity of food. Two hours of washing, for example, can be done on half a bar (1 oz.) of chocolate, while a 1 oz. piece of shortbread will sustain one for 1½ hours' sweeping. Violent exercise, such as the swimming already mentioned, certainly uses up the calories, but it also has the disadvantage of resulting in a larger appetite, with increased temptation to eat the forbidden foods.

Although at first sight the weight-reducing diet may seem austere, it does include many enjoyable foods—crisp and colourful salads, fruits *ad lib.*, all fish except the fatty types, lean meat, rabbit, chicken, and game. The summer is obviously the ideal time to embark on such a diet, because of the abundance of fruit and vegetables, but even in winter one can, quite easily, devise attractive and tasty salad and vegetable dishes. Celery, raw carrot, shredded raw cabbage, chopped apple, watercress, orange, and grapefruit, help to make salad platters no less delicious than the summer combinations of tomatoes, garden lettuce, radishes, young beans, and so on.

MENUS FOR SLIMMING

The following are suggested lunch and dinner menus for a week in summer and a week in winter. Breakfast can consist of fresh fruit (without sugar), eggs, orange juice, tomato juice, etc. Afternoon tea is a meal best omitted from the daily menu.

Recipes for the dishes suggested appear in the following pages or in other parts of this book.

SUMMER MENUS

Sunday

Lunch	*Evening Meal*
Roast Meat (lean) Cabbage Carrots Holiday Sundae	Tomato Cups Salad Stewed Apples

Monday

Cold Meat Salad Fresh Fruit	Grilled Fish and Tomato Grapefruit Cocktail Salad

Tuesday

Ham and Tomato Salad Orange Jelly	Shrimps in Aspic Stewed Fruit

Wednesday

Tomato and Shrimp Salad Fresh Fruit	Mixed Grill (steak, tomatoes, apple rings, mushrooms, watercress) Milk Jellies

Thursday

Poached Egg on Spinach Chocolate Junket with Bananas	Cheese Salad Blackberry Whip

Friday

Mixed Vegetable Salad (lettuce, mustard and cress, tomato, apple, etc.) Fresh Fruit	Rabbit Casserole Raspberry Junket Stewed Fruit

Saturday

Jellied Rabbit Mould Fruit Salad	Stuffed Eggs Salad Blancmange

WINTER MENUS

Sunday

Lunch	*Evening Meal*
Lean Roast Meat Sprouts Carrots Coffee Junket	Vegetable Hors d'Œuvre Baked Apple

Monday

Savoury Meat Mould Winter Salad Steamed Custard	Poached Fish Peas Lemon Whip

Tuesday

Baked Stuffed Onions (with lean ham, cheese, parsley) Cabbage Stewed Fruit	Jellied Tomatoes Cabbage and Watercress Salad Apricot Cream

Wednesday

Scalloped Fish and Beetroot Apple Snow	Liver in Tomato Sauce Fruit Salad

Thursday

Onion Soup Egg Butterflies Watercress and Beetroot Chocolate Junket	Cold Luncheon Meat Salad Moderne Stewed Apples and Chopped or Grated Nuts

Friday

Rabbit Fricassee Carrots and Chopped Parsley Orange Fluff	Piquant Fish Jelly Cabbage and Celery Slaw Coffee Cream

Saturday

Baked Stuffed Tomatoes (with chopped celery and leeks) Yoghourt	Grilled Plaice Turnip Tops or Spinach Orange and Grapefruit Sections

RECIPES FOR SLIMMING

TOMATO JUICE WAKENER

½ pint tomato juice	A dash of pepper
1 tbsp. lemon juice	A sprig of mint

Combine the tomato juice, lemon juice, and pepper, and serve chilled, with a sprig of mint floating on top.

QUICK TOMATO SOUP

1 apple	½ oz. flour or cornflour
½ pint vegetable water	A little milk or water
1 small bottle of tomatoes	Seasoning

Chop the apple, and cook in a very little water until soft. Add the liquid and the tomatoes, bring to the boil, and put the soup through a sieve. Return it to the pan, and thicken by adding the flour or cornflour blended with a little milk or water. Season, and serve.

MIXED VEGETABLE SOUP

¾ lb. mixed vegetables (carrot, onion, celery, a little turnip, etc.)	Seasoning
	1 oz. oatmeal or rolled oats
1½ pints stock	¼ pint skimmed milk
A bouquet garni	2 tbsps. chopped parsley

Prepare the vegetables, and put them through a coarse mincer. Put in a pan with the stock, bouquet garni, and seasoning. Cover, and simmer gently until the vegetables are tender, adding more stock if necessary. Mix the oatmeal with the milk, add to the soup, and simmer about 10 minutes longer to cook the oatmeal. Add the finely chopped parsley just before serving.

ITALIAN SOUP

1 lb. carrots	2 pints stock
A small piece of turnip	Seasoning
2 sticks celery	A bouquet garni
¼ lb. artichokes	2 tbsps. macaroni
1–2 leeks or onions	A little ketchup
½ oz. fat	4 tbsps. chopped parsley

Prepare the vegetables, and cut into small, neat pieces. Melt the fat, and sauté the vegetables in it for 5–10 minutes. Add the stock, seasoning, and bouquet garni, cover, and simmer for about ½ hour, then add the macaroni, and continue cooking for a further ½ hour, or until the vegetables are quite tender. Reseason, and add a little ketchup to taste. Just before serving, remove the bouquet garni and add the finely chopped parsley. Serve with grated cheese handed separately.

LIVER IN TOMATO SAUCE

8 oz. liver	½ pint tomato purée
Salt	A small piece of bay leaf
Water	Seasoning
½ oz. cornflour	Parsley

Wash the liver in warm salt water, and simmer it gently in a little salted water until tender. Strain off the stock, remove the liver, and chop into small pieces. Mix the cornflour to a paste with a little of the tomato purée (made with 1 lb. tomatoes cooked in a little water and then sieved). Add the cornflour paste and bay leaf, and bring to the boil, boil for 10 minutes, then remove the bay leaf. Season to taste, stir in the cooked liver, and serve with chopped parsley.

SAVOURY MEAT MOULD

1 oz. gelatine	4 oz. diced corned beef
1 pint stock or water	4 oz. breakfast sausage
1 tsp. meat extract	Radishes, 1 tomato, cucumber
Seasoning	
4 oz. cooked peas	1 hard-boiled egg
2 tbsps. chutney	Lettuce, etc.

Dissolve the gelatine in ¼ pint water, and add it to the stock, meat extract, and seasoning. Place a little of this jelly at the bottom of a mould or cake tin, and put this in a cold place to set. Meanwhile, add the peas, chutney, diced corned beef, and the breakfast sausage (reserving some for garnish) to the rest of the stock. Slice the radishes, tomato, cucumber, and hard-boiled egg, and arrange them attractively in the set jelly in the mould, together with the rest of the breakfast sausage. Pour on the remaining jelly, and allow to set in a cold place. Turn out on to a dish, and garnish with lettuce, sliced tomato, and mustard and cress.

CHICKEN MOULD

1 small chicken	2 tbsps. cooked peas
1–1½ oz. gelatine	2 tbsps. chopped pimiento
¼ pint water	1 tomato, sliced
¾ pint chicken stock	1 hard-boiled egg, sliced

Cook the chicken, and remove the meat from the bones. Dissolve the gelatine in the water, and add to the hot stock. When the jelly is beginning to set, fold in the pieces of chicken and the peas and pimiento. Turn into a mould to set, and, when firm, serve cut in slices, and garnish with tomato and hard-boiled egg.

CHICKEN SOUFFLÉS

½ oz. gelatine	Salt
4 tbsps. aspic jelly	1 egg white
¼ pint white sauce	Parsley to garnish
¼ lb. minced chicken	

Fix stiff white paper firmly round some individual soufflé cases or one ½-pint one. Dissolve the gelatine in the aspic jelly, mix with the sauce, chicken, and seasoning, and leave until nearly setting; lastly, fold in the stiffly beaten egg white. When the mixture is on the point of setting, pour it into the soufflé cases, and put these in a cold place to set. Decorate the top with a little parsley, carefully remove the paper bands, and serve cold.

JELLIED EGGS

4 eggs	½–1 oz. gelatine
Seasoning	Watercress and stuffed olives to garnish
1 pint tomato juice	

First coddle the eggs: rinse a basin out with hot water, put in the eggs, in their shells, fill the basin with boiling water, and leave covered for 6–7 minutes, then plunge the eggs into cold water, and shell them carefully; the yolk will still be soft, but the white should be firm. Place the eggs in cups or individual moulds. Season the tomato juice, dissolve the gelatine in it, and fill up the moulds with this jelly. Leave in the refrigerator to set firmly, then unmould, and serve garnished with watercress and sliced stuffed olives. Alternatively, halve some hard-boiled eggs, sieve the yolks, and flavour with chopped chives, etc., fill the egg whites, and put together again. Set in small moulds in aspic jelly, with some carrot or peas.

PIQUANT STUFFED EGGS

3 hard-boiled eggs	1 tomato
Salad dressing	Paprika pepper
Pepper and salt	Lettuce and watercress

Shell the eggs, cut them in half lengthwise, and remove the yolks. Sieve these, and mix with a little salad dressing to a smooth consistency. Season with pepper and salt, and place the mixture in a piping bag fitted with a rose nozzle. Place a small piece of tomato in the centre of each egg white, pipe the yolk mixture on to it, and decorate with a little paprika pepper. Serve on a bed of lettuce and watercress.

EGG BUTTERFLIES

4 large firm tomatoes — Mustard and cress
2 hard-boiled eggs — Salad dressing

Wipe the tomatoes, and place them stem side down; with a sharp knife cut each tomato almost in half, and then in half again. Slice the eggs thinly, and put the slices very carefully between the tomato quarters. Arrange a little mustard and cress in the centre, and place on a salad plate. Garnish with mustard and cress, and hand salad dressing separately.

PIQUANT FISH JELLY

1 lb. white fish
½ oz. margarine
1 small onion
1 small carrot
1 tbsp. piccalilli
½–1 oz. gelatine
4 tbsps. water
½ pint fish stock
1 tbsp. chopped parsley
Seasoning

Poach the fish, then bone and flake it; reserve the stock. Melt the margarine, and fry the onion, carrot, and pickles. Dissolve the gelatine in the water, and mix with the fish stock. Add the fish, vegetables, and parsley, season, and pour into a wetted mould to set.

Vary the vegetables in this dish according to the time of year.

SHRIMPS IN ASPIC

½ pint aspic jelly
½ lb. green peas
2–3 new carrots
½ pint picked shrimps
Lettuce
Tomatoes or potato salad

Make up the aspic jelly. Cook the peas and carrots, and cut the latter into small dice or into fancy shapes with a small cutter. Decorate the bottom of a ring mould with shrimps and peas, and then add alternate layers of carrots and peas until the mould is full. Allow to set, and serve on a bed of lettuce, filling the centre with the rest of the shrimps and the tomatoes or potato salad.

FISH GALANTINE

1 lb. white fish
A little margarine
1 small onion
1 small carrot
1 tbsp. piccalilli
2 tbsps. finely chopped parsley
½–1 oz. gelatine
4 tbsps. water
½ pint fish stock
Seasoning
Tomatoes, cucumber, etc., to garnish the mould

Boil or steam the fish, remove the skin and bones, and flake with a fork. Melt the margarine, and lightly fry the chopped onion, carrot, and piccalilli. Remove from the heat, and add the parsley and the fish. Meanwhile, dissolve the gelatine in the water, add the fish stock, and season very well. Place a little of this mixture at the bottom of a mould, decorate with slices of tomatoes, cucumber, etc., and allow to set. Add the fish mixture to the rest of the jelly, and fill up the mould. When set, turn out, and serve with salad.

TOMATO AND SHRIMP SALAD

4 large tomatoes
2 dozen shrimps
2 tsps. chopped chives
2 tsps. chopped parsley
¼ of a cucumber
Salad dressing
Lettuce

Cut the tomatoes in half, scoop out the centres, and mix the pulp with the shrimps, chives, parsley, diced cucumber, and salad dressing. Put this filling back into the tomato cases, decorate the top of each with a whole shrimp, and serve with lettuce.

WHITE FISH SALAD

1 lettuce, washed and prepared
½ lb. cooked cod or other fish
2 tbsps. peas
2 tbsps. chopped cauliflower
2 tbsps. chopped gherkins
2 chopped tomatoes
Salad dressing

Arrange the lettuce round the edge of a dish. Mix all the other ingredients lightly together, and pile them in the centre of the dish.

HAM AND TOMATO SALAD

½ lb. tomatoes
½ lb. diced cooked ham
6 sliced olives
3–4 tbsps. sliced chicory
1–2 tbsps. chopped onion
Salad dressing to mix
Lettuce

Dice some of the tomatoes, keeping some back to garnish. Mix the diced tomatoes, ham, olives, chicory, and onion with the salad dressing. Arrange on a bed of lettuce, and garnish with the quartered tomatoes.

Note: Chicken may be used instead of ham.

CHICKEN AND MUSHROOM SALAD

2 oz. diced mushrooms
A little skimmed milk
¼ lb. diced cooked chicken
2 tsps. chopped parsley
Salad dressing to mix
¼ lb. thinly sliced tomatoes
Parsley sprigs for garnish

Cook the mushrooms in the milk until tender,

strain, and allow to cool. Mix the diced chicken and chopped parsley with the salad dressing, then add the mushrooms. Arrange on a dish with slices of tomato and sprigs of parsley.

GAME SALAD

½ oz. gelatine	Mixed salad
¼ pint water or stock	¼ pint salad dressing
½ pint thick apple sauce	Pieces of cooked game
Lemon juice	1 apple, diced
Salt and pepper	Slices of radish
Colouring (optional)	

Dissolve the gelatine in the water or stock. Add the apple sauce, a squeeze of lemon juice, seasoning to taste, and a few drops of colouring, if required. Pour the mixture into a wetted mould or cake tin, and leave to set. Turn out on to a bed of salad. Mix the salad dressing with the diced game, apple, and radish, and place in the centre of the ring mould. Chill before serving.

QUICK RUSSIAN SALAD

1 tin macédoine of vegetables	Salad cream to mix
	Chopped parsley

Drain the liquid from the macédoine of vegetables (reserving it for soup), toss the vegetables in salad cream, and sprinkle with chopped parsley.

CABBAGE AND WATERCRESS SALAD

1 white cabbage heart	2 tsps. chopped parsley
1 bunch of watercress	French dressing
1 small onion	

Shred the cabbage heart finely, and wash and trim the watercress. Chop the onion and the parsley separately. Arrange the ingredients in a large bowl, and pour the French dressing over the salad.

SPRING SALAD

2 spring onions	1 lettuce
6 oz. raw peas	1 bunch of watercress
1 lb. tomatoes, diced	6 radishes, sliced
Salad dressing	

Mix the chopped onion, peas, and tomato with the salad dressing and arrange in a bowl, with the lettuce leaves round the edge. Garnish with sprigs of watercress and sliced radishes.

BEETROOT AND ONION SALAD

Slice some cooked beetroot and chop a little onion finely. Arrange in layers in a dish, and dress with vinegar dressing.

BEETROOT MOULD

1 pint aspic jelly or 1 pint meat or vegetable stock, and ¾ oz. gelatine	2–3 sliced cooked beetroots
	3–4 tbsps. minced onion
	2 tbsps. chopped parsley
Salt and pepper	A little minced ham or meat, if available
Vinegar	

Make up the aspic jelly, or, if aspic is not available, dissolve the gelatine in some good meat or vegetable stock. Season to taste, and flavour with vinegar. Fill a mould with the beetroot, sprinkling the layers with the minced onion, chopped parsley, and minced ham or meat, if used. Other cooked vegetables may be added, if desired. Fill up the mould with the jelly, and allow to set. Serve with green salad.

VEGETABLE HORS D'ŒUVRE

1 small cauliflower	3 cooked potatoes
1 box mustard and cress	1 small bunch of radishes
1 lettuce	A few spring onions
3 tomatoes	4 oz. cooked peas
3 carrots	Salad dressing
1 cooked beetroot	

Divide the cauliflower into florets, and cook lightly in boiling salted water. Wash and pick over the mustard and cress and the lettuce, slice the tomatoes carefully, and grate the carrots. Peel and slice the beetroot, and dice the potatoes. Cut the radishes into roses or other fancy shapes. Chop the spring onions. When the cauliflower is quite cold, arrange it on a large dish, together with the other prepared vegetables, and dress with a good salad dressing.

JELLIED TOMATOES

1 oz. gelatine	2 tbsps. diced carrot
½ pint stock	2 tbsps. diced chicory
3 large tomatoes	1 lettuce
2 tbsps. cooked peas	2 tbsps. chopped parsley

Dissolve the gelatine in the stock. Cut the tomatoes in halves and scoop out the centres, adding the pulp to the stock. When the jelly is beginning to set, add the peas, carrots, and chicory, and leave until almost firm. Fill the jelly mixture into the tomato cases, piling it up as high as possible. Serve each tomato on a leaf of lettuce, garnished with parsley.

AMERICAN FRUIT SALAD

2 diced bananas	2 tbsps. clear honey
2 diced pears	1 tsp. lemon juice
2 diced apples	¼ pint red-coloured table jelly
2 tbsps. olive oil	

Mix the prepared fruit well together and turn into a glass dish or individual glasses. Mix together the olive oil, honey, and lemon juice, and whisk well. Pour this honey dressing over the fruit at once, and decorate with cubes of red jelly.

FRESH FRUIT SALAD

1 orange	½ lb. grapes
1 banana	Lettuce leaves
Walnuts	

Mix the orange sections, slices of banana, shelled walnuts, and stoned grapes, and serve on a bed of lettuce leaves.

SALADE MODERNE

A bunch of watercress, or 1 lettuce	1 banana (or 4 oz. skinned grapes)
1 celery heart	Salad dressing
1 apple	Paprika pepper

Tear the watercress into neat sprigs, or separate the lettuce leaves. Chop the celery and apple finely, and slice the banana thinly, then blend these three ingredients with the salad dressing. Serve on separate salad plates, on a bed of watercress or lettuce, and sprinkle with paprika pepper.

APPLE AND NUT SALAD

2 diced apples	Finely shredded raw cabbage
2 tbsps. chopped nuts	French dressing
2 tbsps. raisins	
Salad dressing	

Mix the apples, nuts, and raisins with the salad dressing, and serve on a bed of cabbage tossed in French dressing.

APPLE AND CELERY SALAD

2 apples	Finely shredded raw cabbage
4 tbsps. chopped celery	French dressing
1 oz. raisins	
Salad dressing	

Mix the apples, celery, and raisins with the salad dressing, and serve on a bed of finely shredded cabbage which has been tossed in French dressing.

GRAPEFRUIT COCKTAIL SALAD

1 grapefruit	Saccharin
8 glacé cherries	Sliced cucumber
1 orange	Lettuce

Using a pointed knife, cut the grapefruit in half, following a zigzag line so as to give a serrated edge. Remove the flesh and cut away the transparent skin from the segments. Chop 6 of the glacé cherries into pieces. Mix the grapefruit pulp, the orange segments, cut into halves, and the cherries, and return the mixture to the grapefruit cases, together with any fruit juice, sweetened with saccharin. Top with a whole cherry, and chill before serving. Place each grapefruit case on a small plate and decorate with sliced cucumber and lettuce.

SAVOURY GRAPEFRUIT CUPS

2 grapefruit	Salad dressing
1–2 sticks celery, diced	Lettuce leaves
1–2 apples, grated	Nutmeg or cinnamon

Cut the grapefruit in halves and take out the pulp, discarding the pips and skin. Chop the pulp, and mix with the celery, apple, and salad dressing. Fill the grapefruit halves and serve on lettuce leaves, sprinkling each cup with nutmeg or cinnamon.

GRAPE, PERSIMMON, AND CHEESE SALAD

¼ lb. grapes, cut in halves and stoned	1 oz. chopped walnuts
	¼ cucumber, diced
1 persimmon or tomato, diced	Lemon juice
	¼ lb. cottage cheese

Mix the fruit, nuts, and cucumber together, squeeze the lemon juice over them, and leave to chill in a refrigerator for about 1 hour. Serve in individual dishes, with a little cheese on top of each. (See recipe for Cottage Cheese on page 530.)

STUFFED PRUNE SALAD

1–2 sticks celery, diced	Lettuce leaves
1–2 apples, grated with the skins on	12–16 prunes, soaked in water for 12 hrs.
1 oz. chopped walnuts	2 portions cottage cheese
Salad dressing	

Mix the celery, apple, and walnuts with the salad dressing, and place on the lettuce leaves. Stone the soaked prunes, and stuff with the cheese. Arrange on the bed of lettuce.

FRUIT AND JELLY SALAD

½ a green table jelly	2 tbsps. olive oil
2 tbsps. boiling water	2 tbsps. clear honey
1½ tbsps. skimmed milk	1½ tsps. lemon juice
	Lettuce leaves
¼ pint hot water	2 oranges
4 sliced bananas	

Melt the jelly in the boiling water. Mix the skimmed milk with a little hot water, and stir in the remainder, cool, and add to the cooled jelly. Allow to set, then chop, and mix with the bananas. Add a honey dressing, made as follows: mix the olive oil, honey, and lemon juice together, and whisk well. Arrange the mixture on lettuce leaves, and decorate with orange segments.

APPLE BASKETS

4 red cooking apples	Watercress or celery
1–2 sticks celery, diced	Lettuce leaves
2 tbsps. chopped nuts	Lemon " butterflies "
Salad dressing	

Cut the apples in half and remove the centre part to form a cup. Chop the removed part and mix with the celery, nuts, and salad dressing. Fill each cup with the mixture, and make a handle with watercress or a piece of curled celery. Serve on lettuce leaves garnished with lemon " butterflies."

ORANGE COCONUT SALAD

4 oranges	½ pint green jelly
1½ oz. coconut	Grated orange rind

Arrange alternate layers of sliced orange, coconut, and chopped jelly in a glass dish, reserving a little of the coconut. Mix this with the grated orange rind, and use to decorate the salad.

BOILED SALAD DRESSING

1 tbsp. sugar	A pinch of cayenne
2 tsps. salt	A pinch of paprika
2 tsps. dry mustard	¼ pint skimmed milk
2 tsps. custard powder	3 tbsps. vinegar

Mix the dry ingredients with a little milk, beat well until all lumps disappear, add the remainder of the milk, and cook until the mixture thickens. Add the vinegar very carefully, and cook for a further 10 minutes. Remove from the heat. Strain and store, but do not keep for more than 2–3 weeks.

Note : The amount of custard powder may be increased or decreased according to the thickness required.

SLIMMING FRUIT SALAD

2 dessert pears	1 banana
1 dessert apple	A few cherries—fresh, bottled or glacé
1 orange or tangerine	
3 dessert plums	1 bottle of gooseberries or other fruit
1 peach	
4 oz. white and black grapes mixed	Saccharin
	Juice of 1 lemon

Prepare the pears, and remove the centres with the aid of a teaspoon ; peel and core the apple, and cut up into sections. Peel the orange or tangerine and divide into segments. Cut the plums and the peach in half and remove the stones, then slice into convenient-sized pieces. Place all these fruits in a chilled bowl, together with the grapes, sliced banana, cherries, and gooseberries. Sweeten ¼ pint water with saccharin to taste, add the lemon juice, and pour over the fruit.

SUNDAY MORNING APPLES

4 dessert apples	2 oz. nuts
2 oz. dates	

Wipe the apples with a clean cloth and core them, then notch the tops attractively to resemble a flower. Chop the dates, mix with the chopped nuts, and stuff the cavity in the apples with this mixture. Arrange on a dish, with pieces of celery heart and rolled bread and butter, if permitted.

STUFFED PEARS

2 large pears	3 tomatoes
Juice of 1 lemon	Lettuce
2 oz. grated cheese	Cress
2 tbsps. chutney	A few slices of cucumber
4 oz. cooked French beans or peas	1 hard-boiled egg

Peel and core the pears, and cover with the lemon juice. Combine the cheese, chutney, and French beans, and fill the centre of each pear with the mixture. Place a wedge of tomato on either side of the filling, place the pears on a bed of lettuce, and garnish with cress, cucumber, sliced egg, and the rest of the tomatoes.

BLACKBERRY WHIP

1 lb. apples	Saccharin
1 lb. blackberries	Gelatine, dissolved in water
2–3 tbsps. water	

Stew the peeled sliced apples with a very little water, and sieve or mash to a pulp and measure. (If the oven is in use, bake the apples and use the fleshy part.) Stew the blackberries, and strain off the juice. Dissolve gelatine in a little water, in the proportion of ½ oz. gelatine per pint of apple purée, add to the blackberry juice, and sweeten to taste, then mix with the apple purée. Pour the mixture into a large basin ; when cool, but not set, whisk thoroughly until light and frothy. Add the stewed blackberries or some juicy raw fruit, and pile in tall glasses.

APPLE FLUFF

1 lb. apples	2 egg whites
Juice of ½ a lemon	Angelica and glacé cherries to decorate
Saccharin to taste	

Cook the apples and sieve the pulp. Add the

lemon juice, and, when cold, add the egg whites and saccharin and whisk until the mixture is light and spongy. Pile into a glass dish, decorate, and serve as soon as possible.

COFFEE WHIP

1¼ oz. custard powder	Saccharin to taste
1 pint skimmed milk	Coffee essence

Blend the custard powder with a little milk. Heat the rest of the milk, and, when boiling, pour it on to the blended powder, stirring well. Add saccharin and coffee essence to flavour. Return the mixture to the pan and bring it to the boil, then whip it over cold water until cool. Pour it into glasses and serve cold, decorated, if desired, with whipped mock cream.

APRICOT CREAMS

1 packet of lemon jelly	1 pint skimmed milk
	Saccharin
1 small tin apricots	A few drops of vanilla essence
1½ oz. cornflour	

Dissolve the jelly in the apricot juice (made up to 1 pint with hot water). Cut up the fruit, stir into the jelly when almost set, and half-fill individual moulds. Blend the cornflour with a little of the cold milk, bring the rest to the boil, stir in the blended cornflour, and boil for 5 minutes, stirring continually. Add the saccharin and essence. Cool slightly, and fill up the moulds.

APRICOT WHIP

1 cup cooked and sieved dried apricots	1 egg white
	Saccharin
1 tsp. lemon juice	Custard sauce (see recipe on page 530.)
A few grains of salt	

Combine the apricot purée, lemon juice, and salt. Beat the egg white stiffly, fold into the apricot mixture, and sweeten with saccharin. Chill, and serve with the custard sauce.

FLORENTINE CREAM

1 lb. bottle or tin of cherries or raspberries	2 tsps. gelatine
	2 oz. cornflour
	A few drops of raspberry essence
Saccharin if necessary	

Strain the juice from the fruit, make up to 1 pint with cold water, and sweeten as required. Line a wet mould with the fruit. Add the gelatine to 4 tbsps. of the juice, and dissolve, pour into the mould and allow to set. Mix the cornflour with the rest of the juice and boil for 5 minutes, add the essence, pour into the mould, and allow to set firmly before serving.

LEMON JELLY

1 tbsp. lemon rind	1 egg
¾ pint water	2 oz. lemon juice
1 lemon table jelly	

Boil the lemon rind in the water, strain, and make up to ¾ pint. Melt the jelly in this, and stir into the egg yolk. Add the lemon juice, and, when cold, whip in the stiffly whipped white.

TINNED ORANGE JUICE JELLY

1 oz. gelatine	Colouring
1 pint tin orange juice	Saccharin to taste

Mix the gelatine with 4 tbsps. water, and melt over hot water. Stir in the orange juice, colouring, and saccharin.

GREENGAGE JELLY

1 greengage table jelly	3 tbsps. skimmed milk
⅓ pint boiling water	½ pint hot water

Melt the jelly in the boiling water. Mix the skimmed milk with a little hot water, and stir in the remainder. Cool, and add to the cooled jelly.

LIME JELLY

1 lime table jelly	3 tbsps. skimmed milk
¾ pint boiling water	3–4 tbsps. hot water

Melt the lime jelly in the boiling water and pour a little into individual moulds. Cool the remainder. Mix the skimmed milk with a little hot water, cool, and stir into the jelly. Pour on to the plain jelly in the moulds when this is set.

FRUIT JELLY

1 lb. bottle of fruit or equivalent	½ pint fruit juice
	Saccharin to taste
¾ oz. gelatine	Colouring and flavouring
½ gill water	

Strain the juice from the fruit and, if necessary, make up to ½ pint with water. Place the fruit in a large dish or in several individual dishes. Dissolve the gelatine in cold water, and add it to the warmed fruit juice. Sweeten, colour, and flavour to taste, pour over the fruit, and allow to set.

ORANGE JELLY

¼ pint orange squash (approx.)	¾–1 oz. gelatine
	Saccharin to taste
Hot water	

Mix the orange squash with ¾ pint hot water. Dissolve the gelatine in 2 tbsps. hot water by stirring it over a gentle heat. Add it to the warm orange squash, with saccharin if required.

Pour into a 1-pint mould. When it is quite set, stand the mould in a basin of hot water for a few seconds till the jelly just begins to melt round the edges, then turn out on to a dish.

LEMON CREAM JELLY

½ oz. gelatine (dissolved in ½ gill water)	Saccharin to taste
pint lemon squash mixed with ¼ pint water	1 oz. cornflour
	½ pint milk
	2–3 drops vanilla essence

Dissolve the gelatine in the ½ gill of water, add the lemon squash, and sweeten to taste. Pour this lemon jelly into the bottom of a wetted mould, and allow to set.

Meanwhile, make a blancmange with the cornflour and milk, sweeten, and flavour with vanilla essence. Stir while cooling, and when it is quite cold, pour it on to the set jelly. Turn out on to an attractive dish and, if liked, decorate with fresh fruit.

MILK JELLIES

1 lb. bottled fruit or 2 lb. fresh fruit	Saccharin to taste
1 oz. gelatine	Flavouring and colouring, if liked
½ pint milk	Mock cream

Strain off the juice from a bottle of fruit, or, if fresh fruit is being used, prepare it according to kind, and cook gently, taking care to retain the shape of the fruit. Dissolve ½ oz. of the gelatine in 2–3 tbsps. water, and stir in the milk; add sweetening and flavouring to taste. Dissolve the remaining ½ oz. gelatine in another 2–3 tbsps. water. Drain the fruit juice from the fruit, make it up to ½ pint with water, if necessary, and add the gelatine. Have ready 6–8 fruit glasses, half-fill each with milk jelly, and allow to set. Pour the fruit jelly into a basin or mould, and allow this to set. When the milk jelly is firm, cover it completely with some of the cooked fruit. Chop the fruit jelly and pile it on top of the fruit. Serve iced if possible, and decorate with mock cream.

CUSTARD SAUCE

2 eggs	Saccharin
A few grains of salt	1 tsp. vanilla essence
1 cup skimmed milk	

Beat the eggs slightly with salt, and add them to the scalded milk, then cook over hot water, stirring constantly, until the mixture thickens and will coat a spoon. Sweeten with saccharin, add vanilla essence to taste, and chill.

MOCK CREAM

1 tsp. gelatine	¾ cup skimmed milk powder
Water	Saccharin

Soak the gelatine in 2 tsps. water, and add to the milk powder, mixed with 1 cup water. Scald, then cool, and sweeten to taste. Whip for about 4 minutes.

COTTAGE CHEESE

Remove the cream from the top of the milk, and allow the skimmed milk to sour in a covered jar in a warm place until the whey separates from the curd. Drain through muslin, then remove from the muslin and whisk until smooth and creamy.

Note: Additional recipes will be found in other chapters of this book, e.g., Onion Soup, Savoury Sausage Flan, Rabbit Hot-pot, Cabbage and Celery Slaw, and many of the other salad dishes in the Salads chapter.

FOOD FOR FATTENING

There are many causes of excessive thinness. Some of these will be remedied if the ordinary rules of good diet are followed, but others need the advice and treatment of a doctor. Poor appetite, weak digestion, worry and upsets, or a nervous temperament may all contribute to the condition. Again, if one takes too little of the right kind of food, this can result in thinness: some foods both blunt the appetite and carry insufficient digestive elements, whereas others are in themselves appetisers, and also contain factors which help the body to make maximum use of food.

As already mentioned, there are no very exact and definite weight standards, and one can still be fit even with a weight that is less than the average, provided that it is maintained at a steady level, and there is no other sign of ill-health. However, a gradual and persistent loss of weight probably shows that medical advice is needed. (Sudden loss of weight in anyone, whether stout, normal, or thin, should always be investigated.)

The time when a fattening diet is most often required is after illness or a bout of worry and strain, if the weight does not soon go back to normal. Again, a woman who is so thin as to look "scraggy" will probably want from the point of view of vanity to put on a little extra flesh.

Anyone who comes into one of these categories should first of all study the rules for a balanced diet given in the chapter on Meal Planning, and make sure that the diet includes adequate amounts of vitamins. Lack of appetite is often due to a deficiency of vitamin A or B_1, or of nicotinic acid. A point to remember is that although sugar and sweet foods are fattening, they readily give a feeling of satiety and thus blunt the appetite for other and more important foods ; moreover, an excess of sugar can cause a deficiency of vitamin B_1. If you are fond of sweets and chocolate, therefore, eat them after a meal, rather than in between meals, and remember to include a plentiful supply of foods containing vitamin B_1.

Another important point to remember is that in order to tolerate larger quantities of food, the stomach must be trained gradually by taking just a little more at each meal. It is better at first not to include such things as heavy soups made with milk, as these tend to overfill the stomach, leaving little room and appetite for the more concentrated foods. These foods can be made even more concentrated by reinforcing them : use cream and evaporated milk in blancmanges, put dried milk or soya flour in cakes, scones, etc. ; add milk and margarine to mashed potatoes ; toss other vegetables in margarine. In the early stages, there is much to be said for taking only small servings of the bulky foods such as vegetables and fruits, and adding concentrated foods which are rich in vitamin C ; for instance, sweeten puddings with rose-hip syrup, flavour them with grated orange peel, make tea-time sandwiches of thickened black-currant purée or use it as a filling for cakes, perhaps combined with whipped cream ; take orange or grapefruit juice, sweetened with glucose, before breakfast.

It may be that the under-weight person is taking enough food, but that it is not being digested, or the body is not making full use of it. This is particularly the case with the highly-strung person during a period of worry and anxiety. Leisurely meal-times, with, if possible, a rest afterwards, are good for such people, and a soothing bed-time drink, with a biscuit or cake, will also help. The vitamins already mentioned are needed to enable the body to make full use of the food—in fact, the vitamins are rather like the key to a safe, the contents of which are of little use until the door is unlocked.

It is particularly desirable, when trying to increase weight, to avoid foods which cause indigestion. Fried and fatty foods and pastries are digested slowly, curries and pickled foods sometimes cause irritation, cabbage and cauliflower sometimes give rise to flatulence, especially when over-cooked. But each person will vary ; " To each according to his digestion " is the only safe advice.

Here is a suggested list which could form the basis of a day's meals for a person wishing to increase weight.

Breakfast	Fruit or fruit juice Egg, bacon, fish or meat dish Toast and butter Marmalade, syrup or honey
Mid-morning	Milk drink with meat or vegetable extract and a biscuit
Mid-day Meal	Cream soup Meat or fish Green vegetable Potatoes mashed with milk and margarine, or baked in their skins and served with butter or margarine Milk pudding or ice cream with fruit juice or cheese and biscuits
Tea	Sandwiches or scones, biscuits or rich cake Tea to drink
Evening Meal	Omelette or other egg or cheese dish, or a stuffed vegetable Tomatoes, spinach, or watercress Fruit whip and cream
Bed-time	Milk drink Biscuits, sandwiches, or buttered toast

Among the recipes in this book are many which are suitable for those who wish to put on weight. The following selection will also be found useful :

STEAK AND TOMATO DUMPLING CASSEROLE

1 lb. chuck steak	½ head celery
Salt and pepper	6 medium-sized onions
Flour	4 oz. self-raising flour
1½ pints water	1 oz. fat
½ lb. tomatoes (or 1 small bottle)	6 oz. tomato juice

Trim any excess fat from the meat and melt it down in a frying pan. Season 2 tbsps. flour. Wipe the meat and cut it into neat pieces, removing any bone, then toss it in the seasoned flour and fry until brown. Gradually add 1 pint water and stir continuously until boiling. Put into a casserole, cover, and cook gently in a moderate oven (350° F., mark 3) for ¾ hour. Add the tomatoes, celery, and onions, and cook for a further 30–40 minutes. Blend 1 tbsp. flour with ½ pint water, add to the stew, and continue to cook until thickened.

To make the dumplings, sieve the self-raising flour and 1 tsp. salt, rub in the fat, and mix to a fairly soft dough with the tomato juice. Form into small dumplings, add to the casserole, and cook with the lid off for a further 20 minutes.

BACON CHOP-SUEY

3 rashers of streaky bacon	½ pint water
3–4 onions	1 tsp. salt
5–6 outer stalks of celery	A pinch of pepper
2 oz. mushrooms, if available	1 tsp. soya sauce
½ oz. cornflour	1 small or ½ a large cabbage (shredded)
	6 oz. cooked spaghetti

Flatten the bacon, cut the rashers in half, and fry until crisp but not brittle, then remove from the pan. Add the cut-up onions, celery, and mushrooms to the pan, and fry until brown. Blend the cornflour with the water, and stir into the fried vegetables; bring to the boil, stirring well, and simmer for 10 minutes. Add the seasonings and the cabbage, and cook until just tender.

To serve, make a ring of the cooked spaghetti, decorate with the fried bacon, and pour the chop-suey in the centre.

MACARONI WITH MINCE

4 oz. macaroni	6–8 oz. minced cooked meat
1½ pints boiling water	1 tsp. mixed herbs
1 tsp. salt	2 tsps. meat extract
1 small onion	Finely grated sprouts
1 small tin meat soup	

Cook the macaroni in the boiling salted water with the onion. Make the soup up to ½ pint with macaroni water, and add the minced meat, herbs, meat extract, and macaroni, reserving some for garnish. Sprinkle with some finely grated sprouts just before serving.

BRAISED SAUSAGES

2 cupfuls diced cooked vegetables	1 lb. sausages
½ pint brown sauce	Seasoned flour
	Chopped parsley

Place the vegetables in a casserole and just cover with the well-seasoned sauce. Coat the sausages with seasoned flour, and prick well, place on top of the vegetables, cover with a lid, and braise slowly for 30 minutes in the top of a hot oven (450° F., mark 8). Garnish with the chopped parsley, and serve at once.

FISH, CHEESE, AND TOMATO CASSEROLE

2 medium-sized leeks	Seasoning
1 oz. dripping	1 small bottle of tomatoes
1 lb. potatoes	1 oz. grated cheese
1 tsp. dried mint	Browned breadcrumbs
½ pint stock	
1 lb. white fish	

Slice the leeks finely, put them into a pan with the melted dripping, and add the diced potatoes. Sauté, add the mint and stock, and cook for 5 minutes. Cut the fish into even-sized pieces, and season well. Place on top of the vegetables, cover, and simmer until quite tender. Just before serving, add the drained tomatoes and heat through. Serve the fish on top of the potatoes and leeks, surrounded by the tomatoes, well-sprinkled with grated cheese and a few browned crumbs.

COD À LA BERCY

4 cod steaks	Seasoning
1 oz. margarine	Juice of 1 lemon
2–3 shallots, sliced	2 tsps. chopped parsley
1½ oz. flour	1 oz. grated cheese
½ pint milk and water or cider and water	Parsley to garnish

Wash and clean the steaks thoroughly and put in a fireproof dish. Melt the fat and cook the shallots. Stir in the flour without browning, add the liquid gradually, stir, and bring to the boil, season, and add the lemon juice and parsley. Pour over the fish and sprinkle with the cheese. Brown in a hot oven (450° F., mark 8) and garnish with more chopped parsley.

CHEESE AND VEGETABLE FLAN

6 oz. shortcrust or savoury flan pastry	½ pint milk
Egg or milk to glaze	2–3 oz. grated cheese
1 small packet frozen mixed vegetables	Salt and pepper
1 oz. margarine	1 tsp. made mustard
1 oz. flour	1 hard-boiled egg
	Parsley

Line a flan ring with pastry, and use the trimmings to make a plait; damp the rim of the case and put the plait in position. Brush with egg or milk, and bake blind for 25 minutes in a moderately hot oven (425° F., mark 7). Cook the vegetables in boiling salted water. Make a white sauce with the fat, flour, and milk; add the cheese, seasonings, and cooked vegetables, and heat gently. Put into the flan case and decorate the top with slices of hard-boiled egg and chopped parsley, arranged in a pattern.

DEVILLED PILCHARDS

1 tin pilchards
1 tbsp. French mustard
1 tbsp. chutney
4 tbsps. piquant sauce
Salt and pepper
Breadcrumbs

Drain the pilchards. Blend the mustard, chutney, piquant sauce, and the seasoning well together and soak the fish in the mixture. Arrange in a fireproof dish, sprinkle with breadcrumbs, and bake in a hot oven (450° F., mark 8) for 15 minutes. A little additional sauce can be poured over the pilchards if desired.

CONTINENTAL SPAGHETTI

1 oz. dripping
1 oz. bacon or bacon rinds
1 small onion
1 lb. tomatoes
1 oz. flour
1½ pints stock
1 tsp. chopped garlic
2 tsps. chopped mixed herbs (sage, thyme, parsley)
Seasoning
4 oz. button mushrooms
8 oz. spaghetti

Melt the dripping in a stewpan or casserole, add the bacon fat or rinds and the peeled sliced onion, and sauté it until golden-brown. Slice the tomatoes, blend the flour with a little of the stock and add, together with the garlic, herbs, and seasoning. Simmer for 1–1½ hours, or until of a thick pouring consistency, stirring occasionally during the cooking. Rub through a hair sieve and return the mixture to the pan.

Meanwhile, peel the mushrooms, stew gently for 30 minutes, and add them to the tomato sauce when cooked. Cook the spaghetti in plenty of boiling salted water for about 20 minutes, drain, and pile round the edge of a flat oven dish, pouring the tomato sauce into the centre.

HARICOT LOAF

½ lb. haricots
2 oz. rice
1 onion
2 oz. breadcrumbs
1 tbsp. mixed herbs
2 tsps. yeast extract
2 tsps. chutney
Pepper and salt
1 egg, beaten

Soak the beans overnight, and the next day cook until tender and rub them through a sieve. Cook the rice to a mush and drain it. Mince the onion and add to the bean purée and the rice, together with the rest of the ingredients. Put into a greased loaf tin, and bake in a moderate oven (375° F., mark 5) for 20 minutes. Unmould, and serve hot, with a green vegetable.

MACARONI AND EGG CASSEROLE

4 oz. macaroni
2 oz. margarine or oil
1 oz. flour
1 pint milk
1 medium-sized onion
2 tsps. made mustard
Pepper and salt
1 tsp. piquant sauce
3 oz. grated cheese
1 packet frozen runner beans, cooked
2–3 hard-boiled eggs

Cook the macaroni in plenty of fast-boiling salted water, then drain, and rinse with boiling water. While it is cooking, make a sauce with the fat or oil, flour and milk. Add the finely chopped onion, seasonings, and table sauce. Remove the pan from the heat and stir in 2 oz. of the cheese. Arrange layers of macaroni, beans, and sliced egg in a casserole, pour the sauce over, and sprinkle with the remaining cheese. Bake in a moderate oven (375° F., mark 5) for about ½ hour, until well browned. Garnish with rings of hard-boiled egg white and a little sieved yolk.

CORINTHIAN PATTIES

4 oz. shortcrust pastry
½ oz. custard powder
½ pint milk
Ground ginger
1 apple
1½ oz. chopped dates and nuts
1½ oz. sultanas
Whipped cream

Make the pastry in the usual way, roll out thinly, and cover some inverted fluted patty tins with it. Bake in a hot oven (450° F., mark 8) for about 10 minutes. Make a sauce with the custard powder and milk, and flavour with ginger. Add the chopped apple, dates, nuts, and sultanas, fill the patty cases with this mixture, and top with whipped cream or marshmallow.

MERINGUED APPLES

3–4 even-sized apples
Raspberry jam
2 egg whites
2 oz. caster sugar

Peel and core the apples and put them in a fireproof dish with a little water, cover closely with a lid or a piece of greased greaseproof paper, and bake in a moderate oven (350° F., mark 3) for about 25–30 minutes, until tender but still unbroken. Put 2 tsps. jam in the middle of each apple. Whisk the egg whites stiffly and fold in the sugar, pile on top of the apples, sprinkle with sugar, and return the apples to the oven for about 10–15 minutes, until meringue is crisp and lightly browned. Serve with cream.

STUFFED APPLE DUMPLINGS

8 oz. shortcrust
Cooking apples
2–3 oz. sugar
Dried fruit

Cut pastry rounds large enough to cover the apples. Peel and core the apples, place on the pastry rounds, and fill with sugar and dried fruit; damp the edges of the pastry with cold water and gather it round the apples, pressing the joins. Put apples on a baking tin, joins underneath, brush with water, and dust with sugar. Bake in a hot oven (450° F., mark 8) till pastry is golden-brown; lower the heat to moderate (350° F., mark 3) and cook till apples are tender.

ORANGE MERINGUE PIE

6 oz. orange pastry	2–3 tbsps. orange juice
½ oz. custard powder	A pinch of salt
1 oz. sugar	1 tbsp. sugar for meringue
¼ pint water	
1 egg	1 orange

To make the pastry, add the grated rind of 1 orange to the flour, rub in the fat, and mix to a stiff dough with water. Roll out and use to line a sandwich tin, then bake blind in a hot oven (450° F., mark 8) for 10 minutes. Blend the custard powder and sugar, mix with the water, and boil for 1–2 minutes. Pour on to the beaten egg yolk and cook gently for a few minutes, then add the orange juice and pour into the pie shell. Beat the egg white until stiff but not dry, add the salt, and gradually add the sugar. Swirl this meringue on to the pie, and bake in a moderate oven (375° F., mark 5) for about 20 minutes. Cool slowly, and decorate with sections of orange.

GOOSEBERRY MERINGUE TART

6 oz. shortcrust pastry	3–4 oz. sugar
1 lb. bottle of gooseberries	¾ oz. cornflour
	Green colouring
1 tsp. grated lemon rind	2 eggs, separated
	Glacé cherries, etc.

Make a pie shell with the pastry and bake it blind. Stew the gooseberries in a little of their juice with the lemon rind and 2 oz. of the sugar until they are very soft, then pass them through a sieve, return the purée to the pan and bring slowly to the boil. Blend the cornflour and the rest of the fruit juice to a smooth paste and pour on a little of the boiling purée, then add the remaining purée, return to the pan, and boil, stirring all the time, for a further 2 minutes. Add a few drops of green colouring and allow to cool slightly. Add the beaten egg yolks to the thickened purée, then pour the mixture into the pastry case. Whip up the egg whites until stiff, fold in the remaining sugar, and pile on top of fruit. Decorate with cherries and angelica and bake in a slow oven (300° F., mark 1) until set.

STRAWBERRY CREAM FLAN

(*See colour picture facing page* 320)

2 eggs	½–¾ lb. fresh strawberries
2 oz. caster sugar	
2 oz. plain flour	¼ pint cream
1 tbsp. warm water	Button meringues
Sherry or fruit juice	Angelica

Grease a 7-inch sponge flan case. Whisk together the eggs and sugar until thick and creamy, and stiff enough to retain the impression of the whisk for a few seconds. Gradually fold in the sieved flour, and then add the water. Pour the mixture into the prepared tin, bake in a moderately hot oven (400° F., mark 6) for about 10 minutes or until well risen and light golden-brown, then cool. Soak with sherry and fruit juice. Hull the strawberries, sprinkle with caster sugar, and leave to stand. Lightly whip the cream and spread it over the sponge case. Top with whole strawberries, and decorate the edges with meringues and angelica, fixing them in position with cream.

PEAR AND COFFEE TRIFLE

Stale cake, diced or crumbled	½ pint coffee custard (see recipe below)
1 lb. cooked pears	A little crushed nut toffee for decoration
¾ pint vanilla table jelly or pear juice	

Place the cake in a glass dish. Cover with cooked pears, reserving one for decoration. Soak the cake with the liquid vanilla jelly or the fruit juice. Make the custard and pour it over the cake mixture. Decorate with the pear and the chopped nut toffee.

COFFEE CUSTARD

1 tbsp. custard powder	A knob of margarine
	Coffee extract to taste
½ pint milk	2 tsps. rose-hip syrup
A pinch of salt	

Make a custard in the usual way, adding the fat, coffee flavouring and syrup to the milk.

FRUIT AND NUT TRIFLE

Put some fruit in the bottom of a glass bowl and cover it with a layer of sliced sponge cake. Add more fruit and another layer of cake, and soak the whole with wine or fruit juice. Pour on a layer of custard, and top with shredded nuts, fruits, and piped cream.

Fresh, bottled, or tinned fruit, may be used for this trifle, or a mixture of two or more fruits which blend well together.

TANGERINE CHARTREUSE

$\frac{1}{2}$ pint orange jelly
6–8 tangerines
$\frac{1}{2}$–$\frac{3}{4}$ oz. gelatine
$\frac{1}{4}$ pint tangerine juice or orange jelly
$\frac{1}{2}$ pint evaporated milk
2 oz. caster sugar
Lemon juice
Chopped jelly, mock cream, and glacé cherries to decorate

Put a layer of jelly in the bottom of a 6-inch cake tin and allow it to set. Peel the fruit and divide into segments, dip each piece into the liquid jelly and decorate the bottom of the mould. Let this set firmly, then cover with another layer of jelly, and leave this to set. Dissolve the gelatine in the fruit juice or liquid orange jelly, and let it cool. Whip the evaporated milk until quite stiff, add the sugar, a few drops of lemon juice, and dissolved gelatine, and continue whipping till the mixture is nearly set. Pour it into the prepared tin, and again allow to set firmly. Turn out on to a dish, and decorate with chopped jelly, cream, and glacé cherries.

ORANGE FLUFF

2 oz. sugar
2 eggs
2 oranges
$\frac{1}{2}$ lemon
$\frac{1}{2}$ oz. gelatine
2 tbsps. water
Sponge cake, cut into fingers

Cream the sugar and egg yolks, add the grated rind of 1 orange and the half lemon, and mix thoroughly. Soak the gelatine in the water, then add the orange and lemon juice, and, when it is quite dissolved, strain the mixture into the egg yolks. Beat until just beginning to set, fold in the egg whites, and chill. Line the sides of some individual cups (or a glass dish) with the sponge cake fingers, and fill up with the orange mixture. Service with cream or custard sauce.

CORNFLOUR RING WITH FRUIT

$1\frac{1}{2}$ oz. cornflour
$\frac{3}{4}$ pint milk
2 oz. sugar
$\frac{1}{4}$ pint evaporated milk
Flavouring
Colouring, if required
Mixed fruit salad
Cream

Rinse out a 1-pint ring mould with cold water. Blend the cornflour with a little milk; heat the rest of the milk and pour on to the blended mixture. Heat, stirring, until it boils, and cook for 2–3 minutes. Add the sugar and evaporated milk, and flavour and colour to taste, pour into the mould, and allow to set. Turn out, fill with fruit salad, and decorate with a little piped cream, or as desired.

FROZEN MARSHMALLOW DELIGHT

4 oz. marshmallows
$\frac{1}{2}$ pint milk
$\frac{1}{4}$ pint whipped evaporated milk or cream
Vanilla essence
$\frac{1}{4}$ lb. fresh cherries
A few chopped walnuts or almonds
Marshmallows and cherries to decorate

Put the marshmallows into the milk, and heat gently until dissolved. Cool, and add the whipped evaporated milk or cream, vanilla essence, halved and stoned cherries, and chopped nuts. Put into the refrigerator trays and freeze until firm, stirring occasionally. Serve in sundae glasses, decorated with pieces of marshmallow and a few cherries.

COCONUT AND CHOCOLATE WHIP

1–2 tbsps. cocoa
2 oz. sugar
$1\frac{1}{2}$ oz. cornflour
A pinch of salt
1 pint milk
1 egg
1 tsp. vanilla essence
$\frac{1}{4}$ cup toasted desiccated coconut

Blend the cocoa, sugar, cornflour, and salt with a little of the milk, boil the remainder and add to the blended paste, then boil for a few minutes, stirring constantly. Stir a little of the mixture into the beaten egg yolk, return it to the saucepan, and cook for a few minutes. Add the vanilla essence, and cool. Just before serving, fold in the stiffly beaten egg white, pile lightly into individual dishes, and sprinkle with coconut which has been lightly toasted.

MARSHMALLOW AND PEPPERMINT SAUCE FOR ICE CREAM

$1\frac{1}{2}$ oz. golden syrup
2 tbsps. cocoa
$\frac{1}{4}$ pint milk
Peppermint essence to taste
1 egg white, stiffly beaten
8 marshmallows, cut in small pieces

Heat the syrup for a few minutes, add the cocoa, blended with the milk, and cook a little longer. Add the peppermint essence, and pour on to the egg white, beating constantly until the mixture is cool. Stir in the marshmallows. Serve with ice cream.

CHOCOLATE DECKER COOKIES

5 oz. flour
1 tsp. salt
3 oz. fat
2–4 tbsps. cocoa
A pinch of nutmeg
Milk to mix
Jam
Milk and brown sugar
Desiccated coconut

Sieve the flour and salt, and rub in the fat until the mixture is like breadcrumbs. Sieve the cocoa and nutmeg into two-thirds of the mixture, and mix to a paste with milk. Mix the remaining third of the mixture also to a paste with milk. Roll both out thinly. Spread half the chocolate paste with jam, and then put on it the plain mixture and the remainder of the chocolate paste. Cut into rounds, brush over with a mixture of milk and brown sugar, sprinkle with coconut, and bake in a hot oven (450° F., mark 8) for about 10–15 minutes

CRISPIE BALLS

1½ oz. sugar	1–2 tbsps. cocoa
½ oz. margarine	Cinnamon
6 oz. cake or bread-crumbs	Evaporated milk
	Chocolate vermicelli

Heat the sugar and margarine gently until golden-brown, then pour on to a greased baking tin so that it will form a thin layer, and leave to cool. Remove from the tin and chip into small pieces. (Almond rock can be used instead, if preferred.) Mix the crumbs with the cocoa, cinnamon, chipped toffee, and enough evaporated milk to bind stiffly. Make into balls about 1 inch in diameter, roll these in chocolate vermicelli or hundreds and thousands.

ORANGE NUT COOKIES

8 oz. self-raising flour	2 eggs
	6 oz. orange juice
A pinch of salt	2 tbsps. melted margarine
5 oz. sugar	3½ oz. Grapenuts

Sieve the flour, salt, and sugar. Beat the eggs well, add the orange juice and melted margarine, and combine the two with as little mixing as possible. Add the Grapenuts, and bake in greased individual tins in a hot oven (450° F., mark 8) for 15–20 minutes.

MARSHMALLOW FUDGE CAKES

3 tbsps. chocolate spread	2 oz. sugar
1½ gills water	1 egg
4–8 marshmallows, halved or chopped	6 oz. self-raising flour
2 oz. nuts	2–3 tbsps. milk
2 oz. margarine	

Combine 2 tbsps. chocolate spread and the water, and pour into a 6-inch square cake tin. Sprinkle the marshmallows and nuts on top. Cream the margarine and sugar until light and fluffy, and beat in the egg and then the remaining 1 tbsp. chocolate spread. Fold in the sieved flour and the milk alternately. Pour over the mixture in the tin and bake in a moderate oven (350° F., mark 3) for 35–45 minutes. Serve the cake hot, cut into squares.

ALMOND BALLS

5 oz. ground almonds	3 egg whites (small)
5 oz. caster sugar	½ tsp. almond essence
2 oz. icing sugar	3 tbsps. rose-hip syrup
1 tbsp. flour	Rice paper

Mix the dry ingredients and add the egg whites, whipped to a light froth, the almond essence, and the rose-hip syrup, and mix well. Shape into small balls and put on baking tins which have been covered with rice paper or greaseproof paper. Cover with a damp cloth for 5 minutes before cooking, then bake in a moderate oven (375° F., mark 5) about 20–30 minutes. Sandwich together in pairs with cream filling.

GRECIANS

4 oz. icing sugar	4 oz. margarine
7 oz. self-raising flour	Chocolate spread

Sieve the dry ingredients, rub in the fat until of a very crumbly consistency, and bind together with 1½ tbsps. chocolate spread—the mixture will be very stiff. Roll out thinly, cut into fingers, and bake in a moderate oven (375° F., mark 5) for about 20–30 minutes. When the fingers are cold, sandwich together with chocolate spread, and dust with icing sugar.

JAMMY SCONES

6 oz. self-raising flour	Milk and water to mix
2 tsps. baking powder	Milk and sugar to glaze
2 oz. margarine	Jam
1 tbsp. sugar	

Sieve dry ingredients, rub in fat, add milk and water to make a soft dough. Roll out about ¼ inch thick, and cut rounds with a fluted cutter about 2 inches in diameter. From half of the rounds cut out the centre with a 1¼ inch cutter. Moisten the edges of the bottom rounds with water, put the circles on top, brush with milk, and sprinkle with sugar. Bake in a hot oven (450° F., mark 8) for 15 minutes, and, when cold, fill each scone with 1 tsp. jam.

ORANGE TEA BREAD

1 egg	2 tbsps. grated orange rind
4 oz. sugar	
¼ pint evaporated milk	5 oz. self-raising flour
	½ tsp. salt

Beat the egg thoroughly and gradually add the sugar, beating continuously until the mixture is pale and thick. Add the evaporated milk and the orange rind to the egg mixture, alternately with the sieved flour and salt. Bake in a greased and floured 7-inch cake tin in a moderate oven (375° F., mark 5) for about 40 minutes. When cool, cut in slices and serve buttered.

ORANGE FOAM CAKE

6 oz. self-raising flour
2 oz. margarine
5 oz. sugar
2 eggs
¼ pint milk and orange juice (equal parts)

Sieve the flour. Cream the margarine and sugar, beat till fluffy and add 1 egg yolk. Sieve in some flour, and add the remainder alternately with the milk and orange juice, ending with flour. Fold in the egg whites quickly and thoroughly. Bake in a 7-inch greased tin in moderately hot oven (400° F., mark 6) 30–40 minutes. Cool, then top with icing (see below).

ORANGE EGG ICING

3 oz. sieved icing sugar
2 tbsps. cocoa
2 tbsps. orange juice
1 tbsp. softened margarine
1 egg yolk

Mix all the ingredients together and beat till of a spreading consistency—about 3 minutes.

ICY BANANA SHAKE

½ a ripe banana
¼ pint cold water
3 tbsps. sweetened evaporated milk
Ice cubes
1 tsp. cinnamon
A pinch of salt

Mash the banana. Mix the water and evaporated milk, combine with the banana, then add the crushed ice, cinnamon, and salt. Beat until the mixture is smooth and the ice melted, then serve immediately.

CHOCO-MILK SHAKE

2 tbsps. cocoa
3 tbsps. water
¼–½ tsp. peppermint flavouring
½ tsp. salt
¾ glass milk
1 large tbsp. ice cream

Mix the cocoa with the water and cook for a few minutes, then cool, and add the peppermint, salt, and milk. Just before serving, add the ice cream, and whisk thoroughly.

ECONOMICAL COOKERY

If a fairly strict budget has to be observed, there are certain recipes that cannot be closely followed because they contain costly ingredients such as cream, ground almonds, etc. Sometimes such recipes can be modified by cutting down or omitting some of the more extravagant ingredients; in other cases a substitute may be used. This chapter contains ideas for dishes in which as far as possible the more expensive ingredients are avoided, and also a number of recipes which help to eke out such things as meat and make them into nourishing and satisfying dishes. When following these economical recipes, it is important to pay special attention to the seasoning and the dishing—see the various notes on garnishes, etc., elsewhere in this book.

FISH DISHES

BAKED FISH CHARLOTTE

8 oz. cooked fish
½ lb. tomatoes
½ clove of garlic
4 oz. breadcrumbs
½ pint white or anchovy sauce
Salt and pepper
A little margarine

Flake the fish and slice the tomatoes. Crush the garlic and add to the sauce. Mix the flaked fish and sauce together and place in layers with the sliced tomatoes and breadcrumbs in a greased pie dish. Season each layer with salt and pepper. Cover with a layer of breadcrumbs and dot with margarine. Bake in a hot oven (450° F., mark 8) until heated through and golden-brown on top—about 20 minutes.

COSMOPOLITAN PIE

½ oz. margarine
1 oz. flour
½ pint milk
Pepper and salt
½ tsp. made mustard
3 oz. grated cheese
1 oz. chopped nuts
4 oz. cooked flaked fish
4 oz. cooked spaghetti

Make a sauce with the margarine, flour, milk and seasonings, then add the grated cheese and chopped nuts, leaving some of each for garnish. Grease a pie dish and fill with alternate layers of fish, spaghetti and cheese sauce, finishing with a layer of sauce. Sprinkle cheese and nuts on top, brown in the oven and serve with a salad.

FISH AND MUSHROOM ROLLS

1 lb. filleted fish
½ pint coating sauce
A little lemon juice
1 egg

For the Stuffing

2 oz. mushrooms
1 small onion
1 oz. margarine
4 oz. mashed potatoes
4 tbsps. finely chopped parsley
Seasonings

Prepare the mushrooms and the onion and chop them finely. Melt the margarine in a pan and fry the onion and mushroom mixture lightly for about 5 minutes. Add to the mashed potatoes with the parsley and seasonings and leave until cold. Wash, dry and skin the fillets of fish, spread some stuffing on each one and roll up. Pack closely into a greased fireproof dish, cover with a greased paper and bake in a moderately hot oven (425° F., mark 7) for 15–20 minutes or until the fish is cooked. Make the white sauce, cool slightly and add a little lemon juice and the egg. Recook without boiling. Coat the fillets with the sauce and serve at once.

FISH AND POTATO SCALLOPS

4 oz. cooked white fish
2 large cooked potatoes
¾ oz. flour
½ pint milk and fish stock
A small piece of margarine
Seasoning
Browned crumbs

Divide the fish into large flakes and dice the potatoes. Blend the flour with a little milk, heat the remaining liquid, and add the blended flour, stirring. Then add the margarine and seasoning, beat well, and simmer for several minutes. Put a spoonful of sauce into each greased scallop shell, half-fill with potato and fish, cover with the remaining sauce, sprinkle with crumbs, and bake in a moderately hot oven (425° F., mark 7) for 10 minutes, or brown under the grill.

HADDOCK ITALIAN STYLE

4 oz. spaghetti
1 lb. haddock fillet
Pepper and salt
Lemon juice
A little salad oil
1 oz. butter
1 chopped onion
2 tbsps. chopped pickles
8 oz. bottled or tinned tomatoes
Sugar to taste
1 oz. grated cheese

Cook the spaghetti in boiling salted water until soft. Meanwhile wipe the fish and cut it in even-sized portions. Season with pepper, salt and lemon juice, place in a greased fireproof dish, pour the salad oil over, cover with greased paper and bake in a moderately hot oven (400° F., mark 6) for about 20–30 minutes. To make a sauce, melt the butter in a pan, add the chopped onion and pickles and fry these until soft but not coloured. Sieve the tomatoes, add to the fried vegetables, with a little sugar, and simmer for about 20 minutes. Pour the sauce over the fish, pile the hot spaghetti round the edge and sprinkle with grated cheese.

MOCK WHITEBAIT

2 fillets of fresh haddock or plaice
2 oz. flour
Seasoning
Fat for frying
2 tbsps. chopped parsley
Lemon juice

Remove the skin and wipe the fish, then cut up the fillets in small strips about 2 inches long and ½ inch wide. Season the flour and toss the pieces in it. Shake well in a coarse cloth or in a sieve to separate the pieces and to remove surplus flour. Fry in hot fat until crisp and golden-brown. Drain well, pile in a hot dish, sprinkle with chopped parsley and lemon juice and serve at once with brown bread and butter.

POTATO FLAN WITH FISH

1 lb. sieved or finely mashed potatoes
A little margarine
Salt and pepper
2 eggs
⅓ pint milk and water
8 oz. cooked white fish
A pinch of grated nutmeg
2 tbsps. chopped parsley

Sieve or mash the potatoes while still hot. Add a knob of margarine, season with salt and pepper and beat until creamy. Shape into a round of about 7 inches diameter, making an edge 1–1½ inches high, and place on a greased baking sheet. Brush it with a little of the beaten egg and mark with a fork. Mix together the remaining eggs, milk and water. Pour on to the fish, season well and add the nutmeg and parsley. Put into the potato case and bake in a moderately hot oven (400° F., mark 6) until set and lightly browned—about ½ hour.

MADE-UP MEAT DISHES

BACON PUDDING

4 oz. fat bacon
8 oz. flour
1 tsp. salt
½ tsp. pepper
3 tsps. baking powder
2 tsps. chopped sage
Water, or milk and water to mix
Parsley sauce or gravy

Remove the rind and mince the bacon very finely, putting through the mincer twice if necessary. Mix the flour, salt, pepper, baking powder and sage together in a basin, add the minced bacon and enough cold water or milk and water to mix to a soft dropping consistency. Put into a greased basin, about three-quarters filling it, cover with a greased paper and steam for 2–2½ hours. Turn out and serve very hot with plenty of vegetables and parsley sauce (or gravy).

BACON RISSOLES

4 oz. bacon
1 lb. mashed cooked potatoes, peas and beans mixed
1 oz. flour
Salt and pepper
Mustard
Browned crumbs
Fat for frying, if required

Rind and dice the bacon and fry until golden-brown and crisp. Add the mashed cooked vegetables and the flour, and season well with salt, pepper, and mustard; mix thoroughly and form into small rissoles. Toss in the browned crumbs, then heat through under a slow grill or fry in a little fat.

BEEFSTEAK PUDDING (ECONOMICAL)

6 oz. flour
2 oz. breadcrumbs
1 tsp. salt
Pepper
2 tsps. baking powder
3–4 oz. suet
6 oz. minced steak and kidney
1 onion, minced
Milk to mix
1 egg (optional)
Gravy or sauce

Mix together all dry ingredients and add the minced steak, kidney and onion. Mix to a soft dropping consistency with milk, adding a beaten egg if liked. Put into a greased basin, cover with greased paper and steam for 2–3 hours. Turn out and serve with gravy or sauce.

CORNED BEEF HAMBURGERS

½ lb. corned beef
¼ lb. mashed potatoes
¼ lb. breadcrumbs
Pepper
A pinch of herbs
Piquant table sauce
Egg
Flour

Mince the beef and mix with the potatoes, crumbs, seasonings and sufficient egg to bind. Form into flat cakes and coat with flour. Bake in a well-greased tin in a moderately hot oven (400° F., mark 6) for about 30 minutes, until crisp and brown.

CURRIED MEAT BALLS

8 oz. minced cooked meat
1 small cooked onion
1 oz. dripping
2 tbsps. flour
1 tbsp. curry powder
¼ pint stock
4–6 tbsps. cooked rice
1 egg
Salt and pepper
Breadcrumbs
Fat for frying

Mix the meat and chopped onion together. Melt the fat and fry the flour and curry powder, add the stock and cook for several minutes, stirring all the time. Add this mixture to the meat, together with the rice, half the egg and the seasoning. When the mixture is cold, form it into balls, coat with egg and breadcrumbs and fry in smoking-hot fat until golden-brown. Serve with a green vegetable and chutney.

DUTCH BAKED BEANS

1 tin baked beans
4 rashers of bacon
1 large onion
A little fat for frying
Fried bread

Heat the baked beans. Fry the bacon, peel and slice the onion and fry it until crisp. Put the beans in a hot dish and arrange the onions and bacon on top. Garnish with fried bread.

MINCED MEAT ROAST

½ lb. minced meat
½ lb. mashed potatoes
1 oz. flour
Seasoning
Dripping

For the Filling

1 small onion
¼ lb. oatmeal
Seasoning
1½ oz. suet or dripping

Chop the onion and add it to the oatmeal, add the chopped suet or dripping and seasoning and mix all well together. Now mix together the minced meat, potato, flour and seasoning, and roll it out into an oblong shape. Spread the filling on it and fold over to form a roll. Place about 2 tbsps. dripping in a tin and heat it in the oven, then place the roast in the tin and baste well with the hot fat. Bake in a moderately hot oven (425° F., mark 7) for about ¾ hour, basting occasionally. Serve with hot gravy.

MEAT PORCUPINE

2 oz. trimmings of raw steak, minced
1 onion or leek, minced
½ lb. sausage-meat
1 rasher fat bacon
Mustard sauce

Mince the scraps of meat and the leek or onion and knead them into the sausage-meat. Form into a mound and place on a greased baking tin. Rind the bacon and cut into strips ¼ inch wide and about 1 inch long. Make holes about ½ inch deep in the meat mound and poke the strips of bacon into them. Bake in a moderately hot oven (400° F., mark 6) for ½–¾ hour. Serve with the mustard sauce.

MINCED MEAT HOT-POT

1 lb. potatoes
1 onion or leek
1 stalk celery
½ lb. carrots or parsnips
4–6 oz. minced meat
Pepper and salt
2 tbsps. chopped parsley
Water
Dripping

Prepare the vegetables: slice the potatoes and onion, shred the celery and mince the carrots or parsnips with the meat. Mix the carrot, meat, seasonings and parsley together. Line a casserole with potatoes and fill with layers of meat and vegetables, finishing with potatoes. Add water to three-quarters fill the dish and put some shavings of dripping on top. Cover, and bake 1½–2 hours in a moderate oven (375° F., mark 5).

MUSHROOM AND BEEF OMELETTE

3 oz. mushrooms
1 oz. margarine
4 oz. corned beef, diced
2 tsps. flour
¼ pint stock and vegetable water
Gravy browning
Salt and pepper
1 tsp. vinegar
1 tsp. piquant sauce or ketchup
3 eggs
Parsley and tomatoes to garnish

Peel and slice the mushrooms and fry them lightly in the margarine, add the diced corned beef, stir in the flour and add the liquid and gravy browning, stirring all the time. Bring to the boil and cook for 2–3 minutes. Season with salt and pepper, add the vinegar and piquant sauce or ketchup, cover and leave aside to keep warm. Lastly, cook the omelette, fill with the mushroom and corned beef mixture and serve at once on a hot dish, garnished with parsley and tomatoes.

NOODLE CORNED BEEF

4 oz. macaroni
4–6 oz. sliced corned beef
A little flour
Seasoning
1 oz. fat
1 large apple
Barbecue sauce

Boil the macaroni until tender in fast-boiling salted water. Dip the slices of corned beef in a little seasoned flour, fry, drain carefully, and arrange on a dish. Peel and slice the apple and dry it carefully in a cloth. Fry the apple slices and arrange on the corned beef. Drain the macaroni and arrange on the same dish. Make a barbecue sauce and serve separately.

POTATO TOAD-IN-THE-HOLE

1½ lb. potatoes
1 lb. sausages
Salt and pepper
A knob of margarine
A little milk and potato water
Made mustard

Boil the potatoes until very soft. Meanwhile, remove the skins from the sausages, divide the sausage-meat into small portions and roll into croquettes. Strain the potatoes and put through a sieve, or mash with a potato masher. Add salt, pepper and a knob of margarine, and beat in enough milk and water to make a soft, creamy mash, then spread this in a greased earthenware or ovenproof dish. Spread a little made mustard along each sausage croquette and lay them mustard side down on top of the potato, pressing them down slightly. Bake in a hot oven (450° F., mark 8) until the sausage croquettes are cooked through and the potatoes golden-brown—about 30 minutes.

PRESSED MEAT

¾ lb. sausage-meat
¼ lb. fresh minced meat
1 rasher bacon, chopped
1 large onion, minced or chopped
2 tbsps. chopped parsley
Pepper and salt
Water or stock
½ oz. gelatine dissolved in 2 tbsps. hot water
Cucumber, radishes and salad

Mix the sausage-meat, minced meat, bacon, onion, parsley and seasoning. Place in a pan with just enough water to prevent the ingredients from sticking to the pan and allow to cook gently for about ½ hour, until the meat is thoroughly cooked. Strain off any excess liquid, make up to ½ pint with water or stock, and add the dissolved gelatine. Add more seasoning if necessary. At the bottom of a wetted cake tin, place about 1 tbsp. jelly and set attractively cut slices of cucumber and radishes in this layer of jelly. Meanwhile, mix the remaining jelly with the meat mixture, and when the bottom layer in the tin is completely set and the meat mixture is cold, pack this tightly into the tin. When firm, turn out in the usual way and garnish with salad.

PUFTIES

3 oz. self-raising flour
Milk
Seasoning
Chopped cooked bacon
Fat for frying

Mix the flour to a very stiff batter with the milk and seasoning, and stir in the chopped cooked bacon. Heat the fat until smoking hot and fry tbsps. of the mixture in it, until golden-brown.

Any left-over vegetables or meat can be stirred into a batter and cooked like this.

SAVOURY POACHED EGGS

Mix 6 oz. of chopped ham or any left-over cold meat or mixture of meats, with ¼ pint white sauce and season with mustard, pepper and a little tomato ketchup. Put on to 4 rounds of hot toast and serve with a poached egg on top Add extra toast if required.

SNIPPET PIE

4 oz. minced cooked meat
12 oz. left-over savoury sandwiches or sandwich trimmings
¾ pint meat stock
½ lb. tomatoes
Pepper and salt
A little grated cheese
Parsley

Mince the meat and sandwich trimmings and put them into a basin. Pour on the hot stock. Bake in a moderately hot oven (400° F., mark 6) for 20 minutes, then put halved or sliced tomatoes on top, sprinkle with pepper, salt and a little grated cheese, replace in the oven and cook for a further 15 minutes, until the tomatoes are tender and the top browned. Garnish with parsley.

The same recipe can be used with cooked fish instead of meat, when the sandwiches or trimmings have a fish filling.

VEGETABLE DISHES

BAKED BEAN PIE

½ lb. haricot beans
1 pint water (approx.)
½ oz. margarine
½ oz. flour
2 tbsps. tomato purée
Salt and pepper
A little vegetable extract
2 oz. cheese

Soak the haricot beans overnight and cook them until tender in about a pint of water with a little salt added; then strain them, reserving the liquor. Melt the margarine in a pan, stir in the flour to make a roux, and add ½ pint of the liquor from the beans. Bring to the boil, stirring, then add the tomato purée and season well with salt and pepper and a little vegetable extract. Add the beans to this sauce, and when thoroughly hot pour into a greased pie dish or casserole and cover with very coarsely shredded cheese. Place in a hot oven (450° F., mark 8) for a few minutes, or under a slow grill to heat through, and brown slightly before serving.

CAULIFLOWER PLATE PIE

4 oz. shortcrust pastry
1 cauliflower
⅓ pint white sauce, coating consistency
2–3 oz. grated cheese
Seasoning
Mustard
1 egg yolk or ½ a beaten egg
A few drops of lemon juice
Breadcrumbs, if liked

Line a shallow fireproof dish with the pastry and bake "blind."

Meanwhile, remove the outer stalks from the cauliflower and cut them in very small pieces; break the cauliflower head into florets and wash thoroughly, with the stalks. Cook in boiling salted water until tender. Heat the white sauce and add the grated cheese, seasoning, beaten egg and enough lemon juice to flavour, then carefully stir in the drained cauliflower. Pour into the pastry-lined dish, sprinkle with breadcrumbs, if liked, and return to the hot oven (450° F., mark 8) until lightly browned (10–15 minutes).

FLORENTINE TART

4 oz. shortcrust pastry
½ lb. cooked spinach
2 anchovies
2 tbsps. white sauce
A little milk
A little grated cheese

Line a greased flan ring or sandwich tin with two-thirds of the pastry rolled very thinly. Sieve the spinach with the anchovies and stir in the sauce. Fill the pastry case with the spinach and cover with a lid of the remaining pastry. Glaze with milk and sprinkle with grated cheese. Bake in a hot oven (450° F., mark 8) for 30 minutes, until well browned. Serve hot.

FLUFFY POTATOES

1 lb. cooked potatoes
1 oz. butter or margarine
A little cheese or cooked ham
Salt and pepper
1 egg
¼ pint milk

Sieve the cooked potato and add the melted butter or margarine, the grated cheese or chopped ham and season with salt and pepper. Add the egg yolk and the milk and beat up well. Whisk the egg white as stiffly as possible and fold very lightly into the potato mixture. Put into a greased fireproof dish and bake in a moderately hot oven (425° F., mark 7) until risen and golden-brown—about ½ hour. Serve at once.

HARICOT BEAN CASSEROLE

4 oz. haricot beans
½ an onion or leek
½ a small head celery
1–2 tomatoes
2–3 artichokes
Salt and pepper
A bunch of herbs
1 pint stock or water
A little milk
1 oz. fat
1 oz. flour
A little grated cheese

Wash the haricot beans, and soak them overnight in cold water. Cook in boiling salted water until tender, then drain and place in a greased casserole. Peel and chop the onion or leek finely. Wash the celery, peel the tomatoes and artichokes and cut all into small pieces. Place all the vegetables in the casserole. Season well and add the herbs, tied in muslin, and the stock or water. Cover with a closely fitting lid and cook in a slow oven (325° F., mark 2) for 2–2½ hours. Reserve the liquid, making it up to 1 pint with milk.

Melt the fat, stir in the flour, season well and blend. Add the vegetable liquor and milk. Bring to the boil, stirring well, and cook for a few minutes. Pour over the vegetables, sprinkle cheese on top, and brown under the grill.

LEEK AND BACON SAVOURY

1 lb. leeks
Salt
Slices of buttered toast
2 rashers of fat bacon

Remove the roots and coarse tops from the leeks, cut in half lengthwise and wash thoroughly. Cover with boiling salted water and cook until tender. Drain, place on the buttered toast on a hot dish, and lay the rashers of bacon on the top. Put into a moderately hot oven (425° F., mark 7) and bake until the rashers are crisped —15–20 minutes. Serve hot.

OATMEAL RISSOLES

4 oz. medium oatmeal
1 oz. flour
A pinch of salt
2 tbsps. chopped leek or chives
2 tsps. chopped parsley
2 oz. melted margarine
Egg and breadcrumbs
Fat for frying

Mix together all the dry ingredients, then add sufficient melted margarine to bind the mixture. Leave it to become firm, form into rissoles and coat with egg and breadcrumbs. Fry in smoking-hot fat till golden-brown. Drain, and serve with creamy potatoes and mixed vegetables.

POTATO PANCAKES

12 oz. dry mashed potato
Salt and pepper
4 oz. flour
Fat for frying
Spinach purée or other savoury filling

Put the mashed potato through a sieve if at all lumpy, add seasoning, and work the flour into it to make a smooth dough. Divide into 4–5 portions and roll each one out about the size of a small frying pan. Heat a little cooking fat in the pan and fry the pancakes over a low heat until golden-brown on both sides. When cooked, place on a hot dish, spread with savoury filling, and keep very hot. Cover with the next pancake and more filling, etc., and finish with a pancake on top. To serve, cut into sections like a cake and hand gravy separately. Alternatively, spread each pancake with a little potted meat or other savoury filling, roll up, and serve with a good sauce.

PUMPKIN PIE (ECONOMICAL)

6 oz. shortcrust pastry	Sugar to taste
1 oz. margarine	½ tsp. salt
½ oz. flour	¼ tsp. ground ginger or nutmeg
¼ pint milk	A little lemon juice to taste
1 egg	
1 breakfastcupful steamed pumpkin	

Line a deep fireproof plate with the pastry, doubling the pastry round the edge and pinching with the fingers to give a crimped effect. Melt the margarine and add the flour to make a roux; stir in the milk and bring to the boil, stirring. Cool it slightly, then beat in the beaten egg. Put the steamed and strained pumpkin into a basin and mash it well. Add the prepared custard mixture, and sugar, salt, spice and lemon juice to taste. Put into the pastry case and cook in a moderately hot oven (400° F., mark 6) until the pastry is brown and the mixture set—30–40 minutes.

QUICK CURRIED POTATOES

1 lb. potatoes	1 oz. flour
1 oz. fat	½ pint milk and vegetable stock
1 finely chopped onion	Salt and pepper
2 tsps. curry powder	A few drops of vinegar

Scrub the potatoes and boil in their skins until tender, then peel thinly. Cut them in thick slices and lay in a fireproof dish to keep hot. Melt the fat and fry the chopped onion in it until lightly coloured. Stir in the curry powder and flour and mix thoroughly; then add the liquid, mixing it in gradually, and stir until boiling. Simmer for 5 minutes, season with salt, pepper and vinegar, and pour over the potatoes.

QUICK FRITTERS

2 rashers bacon	A little flour
½ lb. raw potatoes	Salt and pepper

Rind the bacon and cut the rashers in half. Fry until golden-brown and crisp, then draw to one side of the pan or lift out on to a plate to keep hot while cooking the fritters. Meanwhile, shred the potatoes on a coarse grater and stir in a little flour (about 2 tbsps.). If necessary, add a little milk or water to give the consistency of a thick batter. Season well, then drop in spoonfuls into the hot bacon fat. Fry gently until golden-brown on both sides. Dish with the bacon and serve at once.

QUICK POTATO DISH

Peel and slice about 1 lb. potatoes and 1 or 2 onions. Put into a pan with a good knob of margarine and salt and pepper. Just cover with equal quantities of milk and water. Put on the lid and simmer gently until the potatoes begin to break up. Throw in a handful of grated cheese and chopped parsley, and serve very hot, with slices of freshly made toast.

A SIMPLE TOMATO SOUFFLÉ

½–¾ lb. tomatoes	1½ oz. flour
Salt and pepper	¾ pint milk
A little finely minced onion	1 egg
1½ oz. margarine	A little grated cheese

Skin and slice the tomatoes and lay in an oven-glass dish or pie dish. Sprinkle with salt and pepper and the minced onion. Melt the margarine in a saucepan, mix in the flour and add the milk by degrees. Bring to the boil, stirring well, and cook for 2–3 minutes. Season with salt and pepper and allow to cool slightly, then add the egg yolk and leave aside. Whisk the egg white as stiffly as possible and fold it lightly into the sauce. Pour over the tomatoes, sprinkle with a little grated cheese, and bake in a moderate oven (375° F., mark 5) until golden-brown and risen—about 30 minutes.

Other vegetables (which should be cooked) may be used for this dish.

VEGETABLE DUMPLINGS

Minced cooked vegetables (carrot, onion, celery, etc.)	Mixed herbs
	A little grated cheese (optional)
Breadcrumbs	Egg to bind
Salt and pepper	A little flour

Mix the minced vegetables with an equal quantity of breadcrumbs (or dry bread, soaked and squeezed). Season liberally with salt, pepper and mixed herbs, and if liked add a little finely grated cheese. Add enough of the beaten egg to form a stiff paste, then roll into small balls and toss in flour. Serve with soups and stews, adding them to the liquid about 15–20 minutes before serving. If preferred, egg-and-crumb the dumplings and fry them.

VEGETABLE PIE

8 oz. shortcrust pastry
1 carrot
½ a parsnip
4 mushrooms
½ pint cooked beans
2 sticks of celery
½ tin of peas
2 tomatoes
½ a cauliflower
2 onions or leeks
½ pint water
A little margarine or dripping
A little meat extract
Pepper and salt

Make the pastry and prepare the vegetables, cutting them into neat pieces as required. Stew for 15 minutes in the water, adding the fat and meat extract. Place the vegetables in a pie dish, season and cover with pastry. Bake in a moderately hot oven (425° F., mark 7) 40 minutes.

CHEESE DISHES

BREAD AND CHEESE FRITTERS WITH SPINACH

4 slices bread
Butter or margarine
Sliced or grated cheese
Mustard, pepper and salt
1 tbsp. milk
Dripping
Cooked spinach

Spread the slices of bread lightly with butter or margarine and lay thinly sliced or grated cheese on top. Season, and sandwich the slices of bread together, pressing them lightly. Cut into fingers, dip in milk, drain and fry in a little smoking hot dripping until crisp and golden-brown. Serve with spinach or any cooked green vegetable.

CHEESE AND TOMATO FLAN

4 oz. shortcrust pastry
2 oz. grated cheese
A pinch of dry mustard
2 eggs
½ pint milk
Seasoning
Tomatoes

Line a sandwich tin with pastry. Mix together the cheese, mustard and eggs and blend with some of the milk until smooth, then add the rest of the milk. Add seasoning, and pour the mixture over the pastry. Bake in a moderate oven (375° F., mark 5) for about 35 minutes, until the custard is set. Slice the tomatoes thinly, cover the top of the flan with them and return it to the oven for a further 5–10 minutes.

CHEESE POTATOES

4 large even-sized potatoes
2 oz. grated cheese
Salt and pepper
A little milk
A knob of margarine
Brown crumbs
Parsley to garnish

Scrub the potatoes, prick with a fork and bake in a moderate oven for ¾–1 hour, until cooked, then cut in half and scoop out the middle. Mix this with the cheese, seasoning, milk and margarine. Return to the cases, fork the tops and lightly sprinkle with brown crumbs. Heat in a hot oven (450° F., mark 8) and garnish.

CRISPIE CHEESE PIE

For the Crust

3 oz. plain flour
Salt and pepper
1½ oz. cooking fat or margarine
4 tbsps. cornflakes

For the Filling

¾ oz. margarine
¾ oz. flour
½ pint milk
1 egg
3 oz. grated cheese
Salt, pepper, mustard, paprika

To make the crust, sift together the flour, salt and pepper and rub in the fat thoroughly. Mix in the cornflakes. With this mixture, line a pint-size pie dish, pressing the crumbs together and reserving some for the top of the pie. (No liquid is used for this crust, but it must be pressed well together.)

For the filling, melt the margarine and stir in the flour, then beat in the milk, adding a little at a time. Bring to the boil, stirring well, and boil for 2 minutes. Add the beaten egg, the grated cheese, salt, pepper, mustard and paprika pepper. Pour into the pie dish and cover the top with the crumb mixture. Bake in a moderately hot oven (400° F., mark 6) for ¾ hour. The top should be golden-brown and very crisp.

MOCK CRAB

2 oz. grated dry cheese
4 tbsps. fresh bread-crumbs
Salt and pepper
Mustard
About 1 tbsp. vinegar
A little milk
Watercress

Grate the cheese finely and mix it with the breadcrumbs. Season well with salt, pepper and mustard. Add the vinegar and stir in enough milk to make the mixture of the consistency of dressed crab. Fill into a clean crab shell and garnish with watercress. Serve with a good potato salad.

SAVOURY FLAN

6 oz. shortcrust pastry
1 rasher of bacon
1 small onion
Fat for frying
¾ pint milk
1 large egg
2 oz. grated cheese
1 tsp. made mustard
Salt and pepper

Line a flan ring with the pastry. Chop the bacon and onion and fry in the fat. Heat the

perfect coffee made right in the cup

ANOTHER OF NESTLÉ'S GOOD THINGS

SN46

she's bound to be a good cook— and save money *too*... with a *Kenwood* Chef!

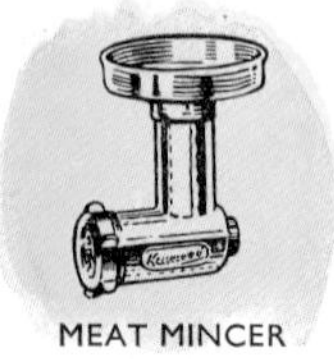
MEAT MINCER

LIQUIDISER

JUICE EXTRACTOR & OIL DRIPPER

COLANDER & SIEVE

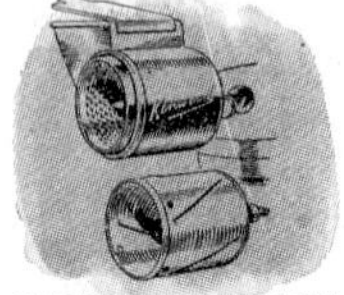
SLICER & SHREDDER

POTATO PEELER

COFFEE MILL

CAN OPENER

Also: CENTRIFUGAL JUICE-SEPARATOR
HIGH-SPEED SLICER & SHREDDER

No drudgery for *her*—no dull meals for *him*—there's a KENWOOD 'CHEF' in the kitchen! It does *all* the hard work of food preparation, turns complicated recipes into easy everyday delights, makes exciting new drinks and dishes that used never to be possible at home. Peeling, mixing, slicing, mincing, beating, shredding, juice separating, can opening—it's all done in a moment electrically, and far better than by hand. Look at the list of attachments (many of them have several uses) and you'll realise that the 1957 housewife simply cannot do without a KENWOOD 'CHEF', the world's most versatile Food Mixer. *Appointed electrical dealers and department stores stock the 'CHEF' and attractive easy terms are available.*

Note to him!

You can buy her a KENWOOD 'CHEF' for an initial payment of only £3.17.9 and eight monthly payments of £3.17.9. Cash price 31 GNS.

Mixing Bowl, taking 6 lbs. of mixture, K. Beater, Whisk and Dough Hook are included with every Kenwood 'Chef' as well as Plastic Dust Cover, Rubber Spatula and Recipe & Instruction Book.

The 'Chef' is available in White or Cream with choice of Red, Green, Blue, Yellow or Black plastic parts.

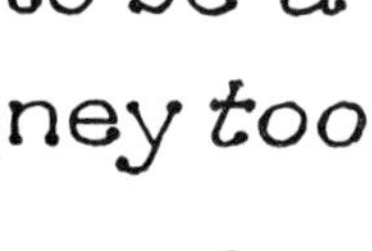

AFTER-SALES SERVICE

Kenwood Service Engineers call on all CHEF owners twice a year to ensure that their machines are kept in perfect running order. Sign up for Service.

YOUR SERVANT, MADAM!

KENWOOD MANUFACTURING CO. LTD · WOKING · SURREY

milk and pour it over the beaten egg, stir in the cheese, onion, bacon and seasonings, and pour the mixture into the pastry case. Put into a hot oven (450° F., mark 8), and reduce the heat to moderate (350° F., mark 3) after 15 minutes. Bake until golden, and serve cold, with salad.

The same mixture can be put in a pre-cooked flan case, and then needs to be baked for 20–30 minutes only, in a moderate oven (375° F., mark 5).

SIMPLE CHEESE SOUFFLÉ

1 pint milk and water	Salt and pepper
3 oz. breadcrumbs	Mustard
1 egg	2–3 oz. cheese

Heat the milk and water and pour over the breadcrumbs. Leave to soak for about 15 minutes and then beat up well with a fork, adding the egg yolk, salt, pepper, mustard and the grated cheese. Lastly, fold in lightly the very stiffly whisked egg white and put into a greased pie dish. Bake in a moderately hot oven (400° F., mark 6) until golden-brown and well risen—30–40 minutes. Serve immediately.

SPAGHETTI AND CHEESE CROQUETTES

2 oz. spaghetti	2 tsps. parsley
1 oz. margarine	Seasoning
1½ oz. flour	1 egg
¼ pint milk	Breadcrumbs for coating
3 oz. grated cheese	Fat for frying

Cook the spaghetti for about 20 minutes in boiling salted water, drain and chop it finely. Melt the margarine in a saucepan, add the flour, mix well until the fat is absorbed, add the milk gradually and cook until well thickened. Add the spaghetti, cheese, parsley, seasoning and half the egg. Mix well and turn on to a wet plate. When firm and cold, divide into ten or twelve pieces, shape into croquettes, coat with egg and breadcrumbs and fry in hot fat.

TOMATO RAREBIT

3 oz. grated cheese	1–2 chopped gherkins
1 oz. breadcrumbs	Salt, pepper, a little made mustard
1 tbsp. tomato ketchup	
1 tbsp. milk	4 rounds of toast

Place the grated cheese in a pan and melt very slowly with the crumbs, tomato ketchup, milk, chopped gherkins and seasonings. Pour on to the freshly made toast and serve immediately.

ECONOMICAL WELSH RAREBIT

¼ pint milk and water	2–3 oz. grated cheese
1 oz. breadcrumbs	1 tsp. sharp sauce
Seasoning	Toast

Heat the milk, add the fresh fine crumbs and stir until thick. Season, add half the cheese and the sharp sauce. Spread on slices of toast, sprinkle with the remaining cheese and brown under the grill.

HOT AND COLD PUDDINGS

APPLE SNOW (EGGLESS)

1 lb. apples	¼ pint boiling water
1–2 cloves	A few ratafias or sponge fingers
Sugar to taste	
½ pint pkt. lemon jelly	Mock whipped cream

Peel, core and slice the apples, adding 1 or 2 cloves if liked, and stew them to a pulp with a very little water. Remove the cloves and beat the apple pulp until smooth. Sweeten to taste and allow to cool.

Cut up the jelly and pour the boiling water over it. Stir until completely dissolved. Pour into a large mixing bowl and leave aside to cool. As soon as it is quite cold and just beginning to thicken, whisk briskly with an egg whisk, and when very light and spongy but not quite set, fold in the apple pulp lightly. Pile into a glass dish or individual glasses. Decorate with the ratafias or sponge fingers. Serve with cream.

BLACKBERRY AND APPLE UPSIDE-DOWN PUDDING

½ lb. blackberries	½–1 oz. margarine
½ lb. apples	1 oz. sugar

For the Pudding Mixture

5 oz. self-raising flour	1 egg
A pinch of salt	4 tbsps. milk or milk and water
2–3 oz. sugar	

For the Sauce

Juice from the fruit	Lemon juice
Cornflour	Sugar

First pick over and wash the blackberries, peel and slice the apples and stew together in a very little water until just tender. Then drain the fruit, saving the juice. Melt the margarine in a shallow fireproof dish, and tilt the dish so that the fat runs evenly over it. Sprinkle sugar over it and cover with the drained fruit, arranging it in a pattern if liked.

Mix the flour, salt and sugar together and stir in the beaten egg and milk to make a smooth, thick batter. Pour it over the fruit in the dish, and bake in a moderate oven (350° F., mark 4) until well risen and golden-brown—about ¾ hour.

When the pudding is nearly cooked, thicken the fruit juice with cornflour (2 tsps. to each ¼ pint of juice) and bring to the boil, stirring, then add a few drops of lemon juice and sugar to taste.

Loosen the pudding round the edge with a knife, and turn out, upside down, on to a hot dish. Serve with the hot fruit sauce.

BREAD PUDDING

8 oz. bread, preferably stale
4 oz. currants
2 oz. finely chopped peel
2 oz. chopped suet
2 oz. sugar
1 egg
Milk
Nutmeg (optional)

Remove the crusts, break the bread into small pieces, and cover with cold water. Leave to soak for ½ hour, then strain it, squeeze dry, and beat out the lumps. Add the cleaned currants, peel, suet, and sugar, and mix well. Add the beaten egg, and as much milk as is required to make the mixture of a dropping consistency. Pour it into a greased pie dish, grate a little nutmeg over, and bake in a moderate oven (375° F., mark 5) for about 1 hour. Dredge with sugar.

BUTTERSCOTCH CREAM

½ oz. margarine
2 oz. sugar
½ pint milk
2 tbsps. cornflour or 3 tbsps. flour
Syrup, chopped nuts, etc.

Melt the margarine, add the sugar and cook until golden-brown. Add the milk, and bring to the boil. Stir in the cornflour blended with 1 tablespoonful or so of water. Cook for 1–2 minutes, stirring continuously. Pour into a wetted mould, allow to set and turn out. Top with syrup and sprinkle with chopped hazel nuts, if available, or grated chocolate.

CANADIAN APPLE CRISPIE PIE

For the Crust

2 oz. crushed corn or wheat flakes
1½ oz. margarine
1 oz. sugar
A pinch of powdered cloves

For the Filling

½ lb. peeled and sliced apples
2 tbsps. water
Sugar
A knob of margarine
1 tsp. lemon juice
A pinch of powdered cloves
¼ oz. powdered gelatine
2 tbsps. water

Crush the corn or wheat flakes finely. Melt the margarine and the sugar in a saucepan and stir in the flakes and spice. Mix them well, then line a fireproof dish with the mixture, pressing it on with the back of a spoon to form a crust. Bake in a hot oven (450° F., mark 8) for about 15 minutes, until brown and crisp, then leave to cool. Stew the apples with the water and sugar until they are soft. Add margarine and flavour with lemon juice and powdered cloves. Beat until light and smooth, then stir in the gelatine dissolved in the water. When cold, but not set, pour into the crust. Chill and serve.

CHOCOLATE EVE'S PUDDING

¾ lb. cooking apples or dessert pears
1 tbsp. golden syrup
2 tbsps. water
2 oz. margarine
2 oz. sugar
1 egg
3 oz. self-raising flour
1½ oz. cocoa
Milk or water
Vanilla essence
Chocolate or custard sauce

Grease a 1½-pint basin. Cut the apples or pears into quarters and arrange decoratively at the bottom of the basin, together with the golden syrup and the water. Cream together the margarine and sugar until soft and white. Beat in the beaten egg gradually, then lightly fold in the sieved flour and cocoa, keeping the mixture moist by the addition of a little milk or water. The final texture should be such that the mixture just drops from the spoon when it is held over the bowl. Add a few drops of vanilla essence for flavouring. Place the chocolate mixture over the apples or pears (the basin should be about three-quarter full). Cover with a piece of greased paper and steam for about 2 hours. Turn on to a hot dish, and serve with the sauce.

CHOCOLATE PIE

6 oz. shortcrust pastry
1 pint milk or milk and water
1½ oz. semolina
1 tbsp. cocoa
Sugar to taste
A knob of margarine
Vanilla essence (optional)
A few sultanas

Make the shortcrust pastry in the usual way Bring the milk to the boil and sprinkle in the semolina, stirring continuously. Add the cocoa and boil gently until the mixture thickens considerably, stirring to prevent it sticking. Beat the sugar and the margarine and a little vanilla essence if liked. Place a layer of sultanas in the bottom of a pie dish and pour on the chocolate mixture. Cover with a thin lid of pastry and bake in a hot oven (450° F., mark 8) until golden-brown—20–30 minutes. Serve hot.

CRUNCHY PIE

1 lb. cooking apples
6 oz. breadcrumbs
3 oz. suet
3 oz. brown sugar
Grated rind of 1 lemon
A little margarine

Grease a pie dish. Prepare the apples and slice them thinly, then arrange them in the dish; if they are very sour, sprinkle with a little sugar. Mix thoroughly the breadcrumbs, suet, sugar and lemon rind, and sprinkle this mixture on top of the apples, press down and dot with a little margarine. Bake in a moderately hot oven (400° F., mark 6) for $\frac{1}{2}$–$\frac{3}{4}$ hour.

CUSTARD CREAM PIE

Corn or wheat flake crust (see Canadian Apple Crispie Pie, page 546)	$\frac{1}{2}$ oz. custard powder
	$\frac{1}{2}$ pint milk
	2 tsps. powdered gelatine dissolved in 2 tbsps. water
2 tbsps. jam	

Prepare the crust as described in the recipe for Canadian Apple Crispie Pie and line a dish with it. Bake in a hot oven (450° F., mark 8) for about 15 minutes. When cooked, spread with a thin layer of jam and then leave it to cool. Blend the custard powder with some of the milk and heat the remainder, then stir in the blended powder and bring to the boil, stirring all the time. Add the gelatine, dissolved in the water, whisk thoroughly, and leave to cool. When cold, but not set, whisk again, pour into the prepared crust and leave to set.

FLUFFY FRUIT FOOL

1 lb. plums (or other fruit)	$\frac{3}{4}$ pint milk
	1 egg white
2–3 oz. sugar	Fingers of sponge cake
1 oz. custard powder	

Cook the plums in very little water until pulpy. Add sugar to taste, stir until dissolved and rub mixture through a hair sieve. Blend the custard powder with a little of the milk. Heat the remainder of the milk and pour it on to the blended custard powder, stirring. Return to the pan and bring to the boil, stirring continuously. Combine the custard and fruit purée and allow to become quite cold. Just before serving, whisk the egg white as stiffly as possible and fold very lightly into the fool. Put into a glass bowl or individual glasses and serve with fingers of sponge cake.

FRUIT GÂTEAU

2 oz. margarine and lard mixed	Stewed fruit
	Sugar to taste
2 oz. sugar	About 2 tsps. cornflour or arrowroot
2 eggs	
Flavouring essence	Colouring, if necessary
4 oz. self-raising flour	A little lemon juice
Milk or water	Mock whipped cream

Prepare a ring mould or cake tin by greasing and dusting with flour. Cream the fat and sugar together very thoroughly, then beat in the beaten eggs, adding a little at a time. Add any flavouring essence (if oranges or lemons are being used, add the grated rind at this point). Stir in the flour lightly, together with enough liquid to give a dropping consistency. Put into the prepared mould—about three-quarters filling it. Bake in a moderately hot oven (350° F., mark 4) until well risen and firm to the touch (about 30 minutes). Turn on to a rack to cool.

Meanwhile, stew some fruit, sweeten it, and strain off the juice. Place the sponge ring on a glass dish and fill the centre with the fruit. Thicken the fruit juice slightly with 1 teaspoonful or so of cornflour or arrowroot, add a drop of colouring if necessary, and a little lemon juice to bring out the flavour. Pour over the sponge ring and leave to soak. When quite cold, decorate with mock whipped cream and a few pieces of the fruit.

LEMON SPONGE (WITHOUT EGGS)

1 pint pkt. lemon jelly	2 oz. crystallised ginger, cherries, angelica, etc., to decorate
$\frac{1}{4}$ pint boiling water	
$\frac{1}{2}$ pint cold water	
Juice of 1 lemon or orange	Custard sauce

Cut up the jelly and pour the $\frac{1}{4}$ pint boiling water over it. Stir until completely dissolved. Put into a mixing bowl with the $\frac{1}{2}$ pint cold water and the strained fruit juice. Leave until quite cold and just beginning to thicken; then whisk very briskly, if possible by an open window, so that the jelly is kept cool. Have ready the crystallised ginger, cherries, etc., cut into small pieces, and a wetted jelly mould. Continue whisking until the jelly is very spongy and beginning to set. Then quickly stir in the fruits and pour into the mould immediately. When quite set turn out and decorate with a few of the cherries and angelica leaves. Serve with custard sauce.

MINCEMEAT APPLE PIE

8 oz. shortcrust pastry	$\frac{1}{2}$ lb. cooking apples
4 tbsps. mincemeat	

Make the pastry in the usual way and divide it in half. Roll thinly and use one portion to line a pie plate. Spread with the mincemeat and cover with a thick layer of sliced apple. Moisten edges and cover with rest of pastry. Bake in a hot oven (450° F., mark 8) until the pastry is browned and the apple cooked—about $\frac{1}{2}$ hour.

MOCK MINCE PIE

10 oz. shortcrust pastry	1½ tsps. cinnamon
½ lb. cooking apples	½ tsp. ground cloves
1 tbsp. sugar	1 oz. currants
½ tsp. mixed spice	1 oz. candied peel

Make the pastry in the usual way. Divide it in two and roll each piece thinly. Use one to line a large pie plate. Peel, core and slice the apples, and mix them in a basin with the sugar, spices, currants and thinly shredded peel. Fill the pastry case with this mixture, moisten the edges and cover with the other piece of pastry. Bake in a hot oven (450° F., mark 8) until the pastry is well browned and the apple cooked—about ½ hour. Serve hot or cold.

ONE-EGG SWEET OMELETTE

1 oz. flour	Cooking fat
2 tbsps. milk	A little sugar
1 egg	2 tbsps. warmed jam

Mix together the flour, milk and egg yolk to make a batter and beat it thoroughly. Whisk the egg white very stiffly and fold it lightly into the batter. Meanwhile, heat a little cooking fat or clarified margarine in a frying pan or omelette pan. When smoking hot, pour in the omelette batter and spread it smoothly with a palette knife. Cook over a gentle heat for about 2 minutes, until lightly browned underneath. Have the grill hot, and hold the pan under it to finish cooking the omelette and to brown the top. Turn out on to a board or piece of paper, dust lightly with sugar, and spread with warmed jam. Fold in half, place on a hot dish, and serve immediately.

CHOCOLATE PEARS

1 lb. dessert or stewing pears	1 tbsp. cornflour or custard powder
1 oz. sugar or golden syrup	2 tbsps. cocoa
Lemon juice or a few cloves	

Peel and halve the pears and remove the cores carefully. Just cover with water and stew gently, using sugar or golden syrup for sweetening and lemon juice or cloves for flavouring. Great care should be taken to keep the pears unbroken. Strain off the juice carefully and use for the chocolate sauce.

Mix together the cornflour (or custard powder) and the cocoa. Blend with a little of the pear juice and bring the rest to boiling point. Pour the boiling juice on to the mixture, stirring meanwhile. Return to the pan and stir until thick and boiling, boil for 2–3 minutes, then cool. Arrange the cold pears on a round dish and coat each one with the chocolate sauce.

Chocolate Pears can be piped with a little mock whipped cream if liked.

POOR KNIGHT'S PUDDING

4–5 slices stale bread	2 tsps. sugar
About ¼ pint milk	Vanilla essence
1 egg	Frying fat

Cut the slices of bread into neat fingers, trimming off a little of the crust. Warm the milk slightly and pour on to the beaten egg, adding the sugar and vanilla essence. Dip the pieces of bread in the mixture, allowing time for it to penetrate thoroughly. Drain and fry in a little hot cooking fat or oil till golden-brown on both sides. Serve hot with jam or stewed fruit.

SIMPLE FRUIT SOUFFLÉ (HOT)

1 lb. plums or other fruit	1 pint milk and water
1½–2 oz. sugar	1 egg
1½ oz. custard powder	A few drops of vanilla essence

Wash the plums, cut in half and remove the stones, and arrange in the bottom of an oven-glass dish or pie dish. Sprinkle the sugar over the fruit. Mix the custard powder to a cream with a little of the milk and water. Heat the rest of the liquid, and when boiling pour on to the custard powder, stirring well. Return to the saucepan and cook for 2–3 minutes, stirring continuously. Allow to cool slightly, then add the egg yolk and vanilla essence, and reheat without boiling. Whip the egg white as stiffly as possible and fold it lightly into the custard. Pour the custard over the fruit and bake in a moderate oven (375° F., mark 5) until it looks well-risen and golden in colour—about ½ hour.

CAKES, BUNS AND BISCUITS

COFFEE CAKE

2 oz. margarine	1 egg
2 oz. caster sugar	2 tbsps. coffee essence
1 tbsp. honey or golden syrup	6 oz. self-raising flour
	3 tbsps. strong coffee

Cream together the fat and sugar until very light and creamy in texture and colour. Add the honey (or syrup) and the beaten egg a little at a time, beating thoroughly after each addition. Gradually beat in the coffee essence, then lightly stir in the flour, together with enough strong coffee to make mixture of a soft dropping consistency. Put into a crinkled paper baking case or a greased 6-inch tin, and cook in a moderate oven (350° F., mark 3) for 1 hour.

DUTCH APPLE CAKE

4 oz. flour	3–4 tbsps. milk or water
2 tsps. baking powder	½ lb. apples
1 tsp. salt	1 tsp. cinnamon
1½ oz. sugar	½ tsp. nutmeg
1 oz. fat	½ oz. melted margarine
1 egg	

Sift the flour, baking powder and salt together and add 1 oz. of the sugar. Cut in the fat with two knives or a pastry blender until the mixture is like coarse oatmeal. Stir in the combined egg and liquid with a fork. Spread in a greased tin approximately 10 by 6 inches. Arrange parallel rows of sliced apple on top. Sprinkle with the cinnamon and nutmeg, mixed with the remaining ½ oz. sugar. Drip the melted margarine over the surface. Bake in a moderately hot oven (400° F., mark 6) for 40–45 minutes, until the apples are tender and the mixture set. Serve warm.

This dish is very good made with plums in place of the apples.

EASTER BISCUITS (ECONOMICAL)

4 oz. margarine	9 oz. flour
3 oz. sugar	2 tsps. baking powder
1 egg	Milk or water to bind the mixture
2 oz. currants or sultanas	

Cream the margarine and sugar together until light. Gradually beat in the egg and add the fruit. Sift in the flour and baking powder, together with enough milk or water to make a stiff dough. Roll out ⅛ inch thick and stamp out with a large round cutter. Place on a greased baking tin and bake in a moderately hot oven (400° F., mark 6) for about 20 minutes, until evenly browned. Cool on a rack.

DROP SCONES (ECONOMICAL)

½ lb. flour	Approx. ⅓ pint sour milk (If the milk is not sour, double the cream of tartar)
1 tsp. salt	
1 tsp. bicarbonate of soda	
1 tsp. cream of tartar	1 tbsp. sugar or syrup
½ an egg	

Put all the dry ingredients into a bowl. Mix together the beaten egg, milk and syrup if used; add to the dry ingredients to make a smooth, thick batter the consistency of very thick cream. Grease a hot girdle, and drop the batter in spoonfuls on to it. When golden-brown on the under-side, with bubbles rising to the surface, turn the scones and cook until brown on the other side. Wrap in a clean cloth and serve while still hot, with butter.

HONEY BUNS

3 oz. margarine	2 oz. dates
3 oz. honey	8 oz. self-raising flour
1 egg	A little milk

Cream the margarine and honey very thoroughly. Add the egg by degrees and beat well. Add the chopped dates and stir in the flour, adding enough milk to give a dropping consistency. Half-fill greased and floured patty tins with the mixture and bake in a moderate oven (375° F., mark 5) for about 20 minutes.

HONEY GINGER NUTS

6 oz. flour	2 oz. margarine
1 tsp. ground ginger	1–2 tbsps. honey

Mix the flour and ginger and rub in the fat very thoroughly. Add enough honey to make a stiff dough. Roll into little balls about the size of a walnut, place on a greased baking sheet and flatten slightly with the hand. Bake in a moderate oven (375° F., mark 5) for 10–15 minutes.

HOT CROSS BUNS (ECONOMICAL)

¾ lb. flour	½ tsp. ground nutmeg
½ oz. yeast	½ tsp. ground cinnamon
1 oz. sugar	1½ oz. currants or sultanas
¼ pint tepid water or milk	1 egg
A good pinch of salt	1 oz. margarine

Put the flour in a bowl in a warm place. Cream the yeast with 2 tsps. of the sugar and stir in ¼ pint tepid liquid. Add the salt and spices to flour, also remaining sugar and dried fruit, and mix well. Make a well in the centre of the dry ingredients, pour in the beaten egg and melted margarine, and gradually add the creamed yeast, mixing with the hand to make a soft, sticky dough, adding if necessary a further 2 tbsps. of tepid water. Beat with the hand for 4–5 minutes, then cover with a cloth, and put in a warm place to rise until it has almost doubled its size—¾–1 hour.

Beat thoroughly again, then, flouring the hands, take out equal portions and shape into round buns. Place on a greased baking sheet, allowing room for the dough to spread. Cut a cross on top of each, then put in a warm place to prove—about 20 minutes. Bake in a hot oven (450° F., mark 8) for 15–20 minutes.

MARMALADE CAKE

½ lb. flour	3 tbsps. coarse marmalade
2 tsps. baking powder	
3 oz. sugar	1 egg
3 oz. margarine	A little milk

Sieve the flour, baking powder and sugar, and rub in the fat until free from lumps. Then make a well in the centre, and add the marmalade, beaten egg and enough milk to give a softish dough. Pour this into a well-greased shallow tin and bake in a moderate oven (375° F., mark 5) for about ½ hour, until firm to the touch.

PEANUT BUTTER LOAF

8 oz. plain flour	1–2 oz. sugar
1 tsp. salt	3–4 oz. dried fruit
1 tbsp. baking powder	½ pint milk (approx.)
3 oz. peanut butter	and water

Sieve the flour into a basin with the salt and baking powder. Add the peanut butter, and rub in with the finger-tips until no lumps can be felt—peanut butter takes rather longer to rub in than other shortening. Stir in the sugar and dried fruit (prepared according to kind). Make a well in the centre of the dry ingredients, pour in the liquid, and mix to a smooth, light dough. Turn into a greased bread tin and bake in a moderately hot oven (400° F., mark 6) for about 1 hour. Keep the loaf for about 24 hours before cutting.

SIMNEL CAKE (ECONOMICAL)

Mock marzipan (about ½ lb.)	1 tsp. ground ginger
4 oz. raisins, stoned or seedless	1 tsp. ground cinnamon
4 oz. sultanas	½ tsp. ground nutmeg
1 oz. candied peel, or grated orange rind	5 oz. flour
3 oz. margarine	2 tsps. baking powder
3 oz. sugar	Milk or water to mix
2 eggs	A little royal icing to decorate top of cake (optional)

Grease and line a 5-inch cake tin. Have ready the mock marzipan. Prepare the fruit and chop if necessary. Thoroughly cream together the fat and sugar and beat in the eggs a little at a time. Add the prepared fruit and stir in the mixed dry ingredients, together with enough milk or water to make the mixture of a stiff dropping consistency. Put half the mixture into the tin, smooth it flat, and cover with a round of marzipan about ½ inch thick. Place the remaining cake mixture on top, and bake in a moderate oven (350° F., mark 3) for 2–2½ hours, until well-risen, brown and firm to the touch. Turn out on to a rack, and when cold cover with another layer of marzipan; decorate with the remainder, made into little balls, then place under the grill to brown the top. Cool, and then run a little icing into the centre of the marzipan coating.

VINEGAR CAKE

2 oz. margarine	1 oz. mixed peel
¾ lb. flour	1 tsp. bicarbonate of soda
2 oz. sugar	½ pint milk (approx.)
¼ lb. currants	3 dessertsps. vinegar
¼ lb. sultanas or raisins	

Rub the fat into the flour and add sugar and prepared fruits. Mix the bicarbonate of soda with a little of the milk and add it with the rest of the milk to the dry ingredients. Lastly add the vinegar, mix very quickly, and put at once into a greased, lined tin and bake in a moderate oven (350° F., mark 3) for about 1½–2 hours.

SWEETMEATS, CAKE FILLINGS AND ICINGS

ALMOND SWEETS

2 oz. sugar	A few drops of almond essence
1 tbsp. water	Colouring, if liked
1 oz. butter or margarine	
2 oz. soya flour	

Put the sugar and water into a pan and heat gently until the sugar is dissolved, then beat in the fat. Stir in the soya flour and enough almond essence to give a good flavour. Add colouring, if liked. Form the mixture into a roll; cut off pieces the size of marbles and form into fancy shapes, fruits, etc.

CARAMELS

4 oz. sugar (white or brown)	¼ pint condensed milk
4 oz. golden syrup or treacle	Flavouring essences, if liked

Put the sugar, syrup and milk into a strong pan and heat gently until the sugar is dissolved. Then bring to the boil, and boil until it forms a hard ball when tested in cold water. Stir in a few drops of flavouring essence—vanilla or coffee essence if liked. Pour into a greased tin, approximately 8 by 6 inches. When cold, cut into squares with a sharp knife.

FUDGE

A small tin sweetened condensed milk (about ½ pint)	¾ lb. brown sugar
1 oz. margarine	½ tsp. vanilla essence or 2 tbsps. grated orange rind
2 tbsps. water	

Put the milk, margarine, water and sugar into a strong saucepan and heat gently until the sugar is dissolved. Then bring to the boil and boil steadily until the mixture forms a soft ball when a little is dropped in cold water. During cooking stir occasionally to prevent sticking. Remove from the heat, add the flavouring and beat vigorously with a wooden spoon. As soon as the mixture starts to granulate, pour quickly into a greased tin. When cold, cut into squares or fancy shapes.

White sugar can be used, if more convenient.

MOCK MARZIPAN—I
(*With Cake Crumbs*)

1 egg	5–6 oz. cake crumbs
2 oz. sugar	Almond essence

Put the beaten egg and the sugar into a bowl and whisk over hot water until thick and frothy. Remove from the heat, and work in enough sieved cake crumbs to give the desired consistency. Flavour with almond essence and use as required, within a few days.

MOCK MARZIPAN—II
(*With Soya Flour*)

3 oz. margarine	A few drops of almond essence
2 tbsps. water	6 oz. soya flour
4 oz. sugar	

Put the margarine, water and sugar into a pan and bring to the boil, stirring, then remove from the heat. Add a few drops of almond essence and stir in the soya flour, a little at a time. If the flavour is not strong enough, add more essence, kneading to mix it in evenly. This paste will keep well for several weeks.

CHOCOLATE FUDGE FILLING

2 tbsps. sweetened condensed milk (undiluted)	½ oz. margarine
1 tbsp. cocoa	1 oz. raisins, dates or figs

Put the milk, cocoa and margarine into a small basin and heat gently over hot water until well blended. Add the chopped dried fruit, stir well and allow to cool. Use as a filling for cakes or biscuits.

MOCHA FILLING

2 tsps. margarine	Strong coffee, or coffee essence
2 tbsps. caster sugar	
2 tbsps. cocoa	

Melt the margarine and work in the sugar until smooth. Stir in the cocoa and enough strong coffee, or coffee essence, to give a spreading consistency.

ORANGE FILLING

Juice and finely grated rind of ½ an orange	2–3 tbsps. water
1½ oz. sugar	1 egg yolk
2 tsps. cornflour	A knob of butter or margarine

Place the orange juice and rind in a saucepan and add the sugar. Blend the cornflour with the water, add to the juice, bring to the boil, and simmer for a few minutes. Cool slightly, then beat in the egg yolk and the butter. Leave to cool before using.

PRESSURE COOKERY

Cooking under pressure is a means of cooking foods at higher temperatures than are achieved by ordinary methods. Under normal conditions water boils at 212° F. and the steam escapes, whereas with a sealed pressure cooker the escape of steam is controlled, so that the temperature and the pressure inside the cooker are raised above normal levels, resulting in shorter cooking time (sometimes a matter of minutes) and consequent saving of fuel. This is particularly valuable in cooking tough cuts of meat, and poultry, soups, root, and pulse vegetables and dried fruit. For foods which in any case cook quickly, such as fish, soft fruit, and green vegetables, there is less advantage in using a pressure cooker.

There are two main groups of pressure cookers, though individual models vary in size and in the design of the separators provided.

1. Pressure saucepans, as the smaller ones are sometimes called, which have a capacity of 6–12 pints and which cook at pressures ranging from 5–15 lb. per square inch, as desired.

2. Pressure cookers with a capacity of 12–35 pints giving, cooking pressures between 5–20 lbs. per square inch. These larger cookers will cook a complete meal for several persons, or will accommodate several bottling jars or cans.

Some pressure cookers have lids which seal internally, fitting under a rim; other lids fit externally and are rendered steam-tight by the interlocking of a series of lugs. All cookers have safety devices—usually some form of plug which is designed to operate if the pressure rises above the maximum for which the cooker is intended. This may happen if the pan boils dry or the vent becomes blocked by dirt, grease or food. If the plug should blow, inspect the vent, cleaning it if necessary, and see that there is enough liquid in the pan, before replacing the plug.

A few cookers are fitted with pressure gauges. In the majority, the pressures can be controlled, and the regulator usually incorporates some form of warning mechanism such as a whistle, which operates when the desired pressure is reached. Separators to enable different foods to be cooked simultaneously, wire racks, and baskets are some of the accessories supplied with various cookers. Models are available for use on electric stoves as well as on gas and other cookers.

Choice of Cooker or Pan

Bear these points in mind when choosing a pressure cooker or pan:

1. Select the size of cooker that will suit your family. You will need an 8-pint model for 2–3 persons; a 10–12-pint one (or a model with a domed lid) for 4–6 persons; a family-size cooker (16 pints) for 8 or more persons. Two smaller pans may prove of greater use for a large family than one large cooker.

2. If the pan is to be used on a solid hotplate, see that it has a machined base.

3. For preserving, a three-pressure weight or lever control is required, and it is also useful for various other cooking purposes. Choose a pan with a domed lid to take 2-lb. bottling jars.

How to Use a Pressure Cooker

The instruction booklet supplied with each model should be carefully studied, and the directions for sealing the cooker and for controlling the pressure should be fully mastered. With most types of cooker the prepared food is put into the pan with the required quantity of liquid; the lid is then fixed into position, the cooker placed over a high heat and the contents brought to the required pressure. The heat is then reduced, and the cooking time is calculated from this moment.

The following points should be remembered:

1. The cooker should never be filled too full—not more than two-thirds full for solid foods and half-full for liquids, cereals, and preserves, though a model with a domed lid may be filled with solids to within 1–2 inches of the pan rim.

2. All cooking times are reckoned from the moment the required pressure is reached.

3. The times given in the charts should be followed, but there will probably be slight variations due to the weight, thickness, and quality of the food, especially with meat and poultry, etc.; sometimes the gas pressure or the loading of electric hot-plate varies.

If you are in doubt (e.g., when root vegetables seem particularly young and tender), cook the food for a slightly shorter time than usual; it can always be brought back to pressure and cooked for a little longer, if necessary, but nothing can restore food that has been really overcooked.

4. Always allow pressure to drop to normal before attempting to open the pan.

For the quick method, which is most generally used, hold the pan under cold water for 10–15 seconds. Lift the weight or lever slightly to ensure that there is no hissing, before raising it fully and opening the pan.

For the slow method (used for milk puddings, cereals, dried vegetables, steamed fruit, and some meat dishes) leave the pan at one side of the stove for 5–10 minutes, until the weight or lever can be raised without any hissing being heard.

5. Whatever type of pressure pan or cooker you use, the general methods given here will apply, but quantities and times quoted in recipes are for use with 8–12 pint pans. With a larger pan, increase the quantity of water till it reaches the level of the rack. For cookers operating at 20 lb. pressure, follow the manufacturer's instructions regarding times, etc.

Care of Cookers

Keep the cooker or pan thoroughly clean, washing it carefully after use; do not use soda, as the cookers are made of aluminium. Inspect and wash the vent after use, and see that the gasket or ring is kept free of grease and food particles. Store the cooker with the cover upturned, so that the air can circulate.

If steam escapes around the rim, remove the gasket, rub it with olive oil, stretch it slightly, and replace it in position. Renew gasket if steam continues to escape.

STOCKS AND SOUPS

When making stock or soup it is important to see that the pan is not more than half-filled. The recipes in this book can be used, the cooking time being reduced by two-thirds, and less liquid being required—usually $\frac{1}{2}$–$\frac{3}{4}$ of the usual amount. Cook at 15 lb. pressure. In the case of soups made with cereals or dried vegetables, care should be taken to bring the pan up to pressure gradually and to allow pressure to drop gradually; otherwise, reduce the pressure quickly. Do not use the rack when making soups.

COOKING MEAT AND POULTRY

You can boil, stew, braise, or pot-roast the meat or bird, choosing the method best suited to your particular purchase. The meat should be prepared as for ordinary cooking, and cooked as directed below and in the chart. The flavour is improved if the pressure is reduced slowly after cooking. Use the rack when pot-roasting or boiling.

POT ROASTING

This method is suitable for beef, lamb, etc., but not for pork, which is too fat. Wipe the meat and coat with seasoned flour. Heat 1–2 tbsps. fat in the pan (just enough to cover the bottom), and fry the meat on all sides to brown it. Remove the meat, pour off the surplus fat, and replace the meat on the rack. Add $\frac{1}{2}$ pint boiling water, fix the lid, and bring to pressure. Lower heat and cook for the required time. (See Chart.) Allow the pressure to drop gradually to normal. Gravy is made by adding stock or gravy browning after the meat is removed. The surface of the cooked meat may be crisped under a hot grill to give an appetising-looking finish, if desired.

Potatoes and other root vegetables can be cooked with the meat. Use vegetables which have the same cooking times, or else cut them in pieces to make the times the same. About 5 minutes before the meat is cooked, reduce the pressure in the pan, put in the vegetables, bring again to pressure and continue cooking in the same way.

STEWING

This is an excellent method for the tougher cuts of meat and poultry. Use your favourite recipes, but reduce the quantity of liquid by half (as there is no loss due to evaporation) and follow the times given in the chart. Include assorted cut-up vegetables, herbs, and spices to add flavour. For a brown stew, fry the floured meat and sauté the vegetables in hot fat before adding the liquid. Thicken a stew at the end of the cooking; do not use the rack.

Dumplings should be added to a stew after it has been pressure-cooked, and are cooked for 15–20 minutes, with the lid on but without pressure; allow extra liquid as required.

BOILING

This is suitable for cooking fresh or salted meat, and also poultry which may not be tender enough for roasting. Trim the fat from the meat, stand the meat on the rack and put in ¼ pint water for each 15 minutes' cooking time; add salt as required and cut-up flavouring vegetables according to taste. Follow times given below. Reduce the pressure slowly, if time allows.

Note: Soak salt meat in cold water for 1–2 hours before cooking it. Ham and tongue should be soaked overnight.

BRAISING

This form of pressure cooking is very suitable for tougher types of meat and poultry. Do not use the rack when braising. Brown the meat carefully, as for pot-roasting, remove it from the pan and pour off the surplus fat. At the bottom of the pan put a thick layer of cut-up root vegetables, with a bouquet garni and seasonings. Add about ½ pint of liquid, put the meat on the vegetables, fix the lid, bring to 15 lb. pressure, and cook as for pot-roasting. (See Chart.) Serve the meat on a dish with the braised vegetables, and hand the gravy from the pan separately.

TIMES FOR COOKING MEAT AND POULTRY

The following are the times to allow for cooking meat and poultry at 15 lb. pressure. (For braising allow the same time as for pot-roasting.)

Beef: For pot-roasting, 9–10 minutes per lb. plus 10 minutes; for boiling, 12–15 minutes per lb.; stewing, 15–20 minutes per lb.

Mutton, Lamb, Veal: For pot-roasting, 10–12 minutes per lb. plus 10–12 minutes. Other times as for beef.

Pork: (Not very satisfactory.) Pot-roast 12 minutes per lb. plus 12 minutes.

Hare: Pot-roast for 30–40 minutes, according to age; stew for 20–25 minutes.

Rabbit: Pot-roast for 20–25 minutes, according to the age and size of the rabbit; stew for 20–25 minutes.

Ox-tail: Pot-roast 30–35 minutes; stew 20 minutes.

Chops (Veal, Lamb, Pork, Mutton): Pot-roast for 6–12 minutes, according to the thickness of the chops.

Ham: Boiling time 12–15 minutes per lb.

Liver: Pot-roast for 6 minutes per lb.; stew 10 minutes.

Heart: Pot-roast 45–60 minutes, according to size; stew 40–60 minutes.

Chicken, Duck, Guinea Fowl, Pheasant, Grouse: Pot-roast 6–8 minutes per lb.; boil 8–9 minutes per lb.; stew 20 minutes.

Boiling Chicken: Pot-roast 30–35 minutes, according to size; boil 8–9 minutes per lb.; stew 20 minutes.

Partridges (and small birds)*:* Pot-roast for 15 minutes in all.

Ox-tongue: Boil 15 minutes per lb. plus 15 minutes.

FISH COOKERY

With whole fish or large pieces there is an appreciable saving of time when a pressure pan is used. With smaller pieces the saving is less obvious, but the pressure-steamed fish has a very good flavour.

Wrap fish in greased greaseproof paper or aluminium foil, to make it easier to handle, and put it on the rack. Use ¼ pint water for every 15 minutes' cooking time, allowing ¼ pint extra if greaseproof paper is used.

The following are the cooking times (after 15 lb. pressure is reached) for the various kinds of fish. The times refer to medium-sized pieces—make suitable allowance for extra thick or thin ones. Reduce pressure quickly under cold water.

Bream, Halibut, Fresh Haddock, Hake, Skate, Turbot: 3–4 minutes for cutlets; 4–5 minutes per lb. for whole fish. Serve with a well-flavoured sauce.

Cod: 3–4 minutes for cod steaks; 4 minutes per lb. for whole fish. (Take care not to over-cook cod, as it breaks easily.)

Haddock (dried), Golden Fillets: Cook in ½ pint milk with a knob of margarine, for 3–5 minutes, according to size.

Herrings, Trout, Mackerel: Melt a small knob of fat at bottom of cooker, dip fish in seasoned flour and cook rapidly on both sides in hot fat. Lift on to rack, add liquid, and cook, allowing 4–6 minutes, according to size.

Plaice or Sole : Whole fish, 2–4 minutes per lb. according to size; Fillets, 2–3 minutes.

Salmon Steaks : 6–7 minutes, according to thickness. Be sure to wrap this fish in well-greased paper.

Scallops : 4–5 minutes. Serve with a good cheese sauce.

VEGETABLES

Fresh vegetables cooked under pressure retain their valuable vitamin and mineral content; the method is particularly suitable for root vegetables. To get the best results, observe the following points :

1. Choose vegetables of about the same size, or cut large ones into small, even-sized pieces. Prepare in the usual way.
2. Cook at 15 lb. pressure, and time accurately : a minute or two more than the correct time will cause the vegetables to be very over-cooked. As they vary in size, age, and toughness, the cooking times should be adjusted accordingly.
3. Use the rack or separators when cooking vegetables, unless they are included as part of a meat dish.
4. Use ¼–½ pint of water (sufficient to reach level of rack) for all vegetables except beetroot, which requires 1 pint. Use only a small amount of seasoning, sprinkling salt over the food.
5. Bring quickly to pressure, and reduce pressure quickly.
6. Keep the vegetable stock, which is full of flavour and goodness, to use for sauces, soups, and gravy.

Vegetables with the same cooking times may be cooked together; stand them on the rack in separate piles, or wrap each kind in greaseproof paper or aluminium foil. (Allow an extra ¼ pint water if paper is used, as this is absorbent.) If your pan is fitted with separators, use these to keep the vegetables apart.

When the cooking times differ, put the vegetables needing the longest time in the pan first, and reduce the pressure part-way through the cooking to insert those taking a shorter time; e.g., potatoes take 10 minutes and leeks 3 minutes, so reduce the pressure after 7 minutes to put in the leeks. Sometimes the cooking times can be made the same by leaving some vegetables whole and cutting into smaller pieces those that take longer.

The following are the average times for cooking fresh vegetables at 15 lb. pressure :—

Vegetable	*Mins.*
Artichokes (Jerusalem)	8–10
Artichokes (Globe)	10
Asparagus	2–3
Beans (broad)	2–3
(French)	3
(runner)	2–3
Beetroot (according to size and age)	10–35
Brussels Sprouts	3–4
Carrots (diced or sliced)	2–3
(whole, young)	4–5
(large)	8–10
Cauliflower (sprigs)	3
(whole)	5–6
Celery	2–3
Corn on the Cob	4
Green vegetables	1–2
Leeks	3–5
Mushrooms	1–2
Onions (whole)	10
(sliced)	3–4
Parsnips	As for carrots
Peas	1–2
Potatoes (old)	8–10
(new)	6–8
Spinach	1–2
Swedes	4–5
Turnips	4–5
Vegetable Marrow	3–4

PULSE VEGETABLES

All pulse vegetables, except lentils, should be soaked for 1–2 hours in boiling water before cooking; discard this water. Put the vegetables straight into the cooker, and add 2 pints cold water and 1 tbsp. salt for every lb. of vegetables. Never fill the pan more than half-full, as these vegetables swell during the cooking. Bring up to 15 lb. pressure slowly over medium heat. Allow 15–20 minutes for beans, peas, and lentils, and 10–15 minutes for split peas. Reduce pressure gradually.

PUDDINGS AND CEREALS

STEAMED PUDDINGS

Christmas pudding, fresh fruit puddings made with suetcrust, steamed puddings made with suet (e.g., College, sultana, treacle, jam roly-poly, etc.) are suitable for cooking under pressure.

Pressure-cooked sponge puddings are not quite so light and spongy as the steamed version, but even so, good results can be obtained. Ordinary recipes for these and other puddings of a similar type may be used, the cooking time being one-third to one-half of the usual. The following points should be remembered:

1. The water in the bottom of the cooker should never be less than 2 pints, and must be at boiling point *before* the pudding is put in.

2. Fill basin not more than two-thirds full; cover with greased greaseproof paper and a cloth, tied so that the knot will not block the control valve.

3. Stand basin on the rack.

4. Steam without pressure (i.e., do not put weight on or control lever down) for first 15–20 minutes after steam appears from vent; keep pan over a low heat, then pressure-cook for required time. This method gives the lightest result.

5. Reduce pressure slowly.

MILK PUDDINGS

A milk pudding may be cooked directly in the actual pressure pan (do not fill more than half-full), or in a heat-resistant dish placed in the pan. It is important to bring milk puddings slowly to 15 lb. pressure over low heat, and to reduce the pressure slowly, otherwise the contents may froth up and block the pressure control. When using a dish, heat the milk, sprinkle in the cereal and cover with greaseproof paper. Stand dish on rack with ½ pint water, and increase cooking time by 10 minutes. The cooked pudding may be browned under the grill.

For Creamed Rice (see recipe in this chapter), allow 2 oz. rice to 1 pint milk, and pressure-cook for 15 minutes. With semolina, tapioca, and sago, allow 1½ oz. cereal to 1 pint milk, and pressure-cook for 10 minutes. Allow 20 minutes if cooked in a heatproof dish.

PORRIDGE

Use 2 oz. fine or medium oatmeal and ¾ pint water; add ½–1 tbsp. salt to the water, and bring to the boil in the open pan. Stir in the oatmeal and boil gently, stirring well all the time, for about 3 minutes. Fix the lid, bring slowly to pressure, and cook for 15 minutes at 10 lb. pressure or 10 minutes at 15 lb.; reduce pressure slowly.

Note: The brands of oatmeal specially prepared for quick cooking are not suitable for cooking under pressure, as no time is saved.

CEREALS, ETC.

Put the required amount of water in the pan (see table below), bring it to the boil and add salt in the proportion of 2 tsps. salt to every ½ lb. cereal. Do not use the rack, but sprinkle the cereal into boiling water, cover, and bring slowly to pressure. After cooling, reduce the pressure slowly.

Cereal (4 *oz.*)	*Amount of Water* *Pints*	*Cooking time* (15 *lb. pressure*) *Mins.*
Macaroni	1	5–8
Noodles	1	4–6
Spaghetti	1	6–8
Rice	1½	5–7
Pearl Barley	1½	20–25

Note: Increase the water in the proportion of ¼ pint to each 2 oz. cereal. Never more than half-fill the pan.

FRUIT AND JAM

Fruit cooked in a pressure cooker has a delicious flavour, owing to the quick cooking and the small quantity of water used. The method is particularly suitable for cooking pears and dried fruits.

Do not use the rack. See that the pan is never more than half-full, and bring to pressure slowly, otherwise soft fruits may froth up and block the pressure control. Add sugar to taste, either before or after cooking. With apple purée, reduce pressure slowly.

TIME TABLE FOR COOKING FRESH FRUIT

Fruit (1 *lb.*)	*Amount of Water* *Pint*	*Cooking time* (15 *lb. pressure*) *Mins.*
Apple purée	⅛–¼	3
Apples (sliced)	¼	½–1
Blackberries	¼	½–1
Black-currants	¼	½–1
Cherries	½	1
Gooseberries	½	1
Pears (hard cooking type)	½	6–7
Plums	¼	1–2
Raspberries	¼	Merely bring to pressure
Rhubarb	¼	Merely bring to pressure

DRIED FRUIT

Soak for 12 hours, and use the same water for cooking. See the time table on the next page.

TIME TABLE FOR COOKING DRIED FRUIT

Fruit (1 *lb.*)	*Amount of Water* *Pints*	*Cooking time* (15 *lb. pressure*) *Mins.*
Apple rings	½	5–6
Figs	½	10–15
Prunes	½	6–8
Apricots and Peaches	½	5–6

JAM AND MARMALADE

It is well worth while using a pressure cooker when making marmalade, and also for jam made from such fruits as black-currants, dried apricots, and damsons. Pressure-cook the fruit as described above, add the sugar, and then boil the preserve in the open pan till it sets. Never pressure-cook a preserve after the sugar is added. Use any reliable recipe, but reduce the liquid by one-half. Do not use the rack, and never fill the pan more than half-full (two-thirds full if using a pan with domed lid).

FRUIT AND TOMATO BOTTLING

Prepare the fruit in the usual way. Any type of bottling jar and closure may be used, except synthetic skin. Proceed as follows:

1. Pack the hot jars tightly with the prepared fruit and fill almost to the top with boiling syrup or water. Place the scalded rings and tops in position and fit the screw bands or clips, loosening screw bands slightly. Stand the jars in hot water, if there is any delay in processing.
2. Use 1–4 pints water, according to size of cooker. Place the rack in the pan, pour in the water and bring to the boil. Add a little vinegar to protect the pan from staining.
3. Stand the jars on the rack; see that they do not touch each other or sides of cooker.
4. Fix the lid, and heat pan quickly to 5 lb. pressure, taking 5–10 minutes and closing the vent immediately steam escapes. Process at 5 lb. for the time given in the table.
5. Remove the cooker from the heat and leave for 10 minutes before opening the pressure control and lid.
6. Carefully transfer the jars to a wooden surface. Tighten screw bands and leave jars to cool; after 24 hours, test for a seal.
7. Fruit for bottling should be prepared in the same way as for ordinary cooking. (Pineapple should be peeled, cored, sliced or diced, simmered in syrup for 5 minutes, then packed.)

TIME TABLE FOR BOTTLING FRUIT

Fruit	*Processing time* (*at* 5 *lb. pressure*) *Mins.*
Apples	1
Apples (solid pack)	1
Apricots	1
Blackberries	1
Cherries	1
Currants (black and red)	1
Damsons	1
Gooseberries	1
Peaches	3–4
Pears	5
Pineapple	3–4
Plums, Greengages	1
Raspberries, Loganberries	1
Rhubarb	1
Tomatoes (whole)	5

BOTTLING TOMATOES

Whole Tomatoes: Remove the calyx, skin the tomatoes if desired, and pack in hot jars with boiling brine. (Add 1 oz. salt and 1 tsp. sugar to 1 quart water.) Proceed as for fruit, and process for 5 minutes at 5 lb. pressure.

Solid Pack: Skin, and either halve or quarter; pack tightly in hot jars, sprinkling the layers with salt and sugar, allowing 2 tsps. salt and 1 tsp. sugar to every 2 lb. tomatoes. Do not add any liquid. Proceed as for fruit bottling, processing for 15 minutes at 5 lb.

VEGETABLE BOTTLING AND CANNING

Since pressure cookery is the only method possible for sterilising bottled and canned vegetables, instructions are given in the chapter on Bottling and Canning.

A MEAL IN A PRESSURE COOKER

With careful planning it is possible to cook a complete meal for two to eight persons using a pressure pan or cooker, but it is as well to make yourself expert at cooking the separate dishes before tackling this task. The number of people for whom you are cooking, and the size of your pan or cooker, will determine the quantities of different foods that can be cooked simultaneously. You may find it possible to cook two courses at the same time; otherwise, you can arrange to pressure-cook beforehand one or two of the courses comprising the meal, and these can either be served cold or reheated when required.

Cooking times vary, so try to cook together a selection of foods which take the same time (remembering that some vegetables can be cut small to make them cook more quickly). Where cooking times still differ, put foods needing the longest time in first; reduce the pressure part-way through their cooking, and insert the remaining foods. Plan the meal so that the cooker is not opened more than once, or at most, twice, during the cooking. Make use of separators, or wrap the foods in greaseproof paper or aluminium foil, or place them in small heatproof dishes to keep them separate.

The pressure should not be reduced during the cooking of a steamed pudding, or it will be spoiled.

Remember not to fill the pan more than two-thirds full (or to within 1–2 inches of rim, if you have a model with a domed lid). Some of the large cookers operate at 20 lb. pressure, in which case the cooking times must be reduced—follow the manufacturers' instructions, and see also menu given below. In any case, the general methods followed will be the same.

The following is a specimen menu showing the sequence in which to cook the dishes:

French Onion Soup
Cutlets
Potatoes Cauliflower French Beans
Peach Condé and Mock Cream

Cook the creamed rice for the Condé the previous day and finish the sweet well before the meal is required, making the Melba sauce and mock cream; if fresh pears are used, pressure-cook them first for 6 minutes.

Shortly before the main course is cooked, prepare and cook the French Onion Soup (see this page), and reheat it in a saucepan just before serving it. Prepare the vegetables, choosing medium-sized potatoes, and breaking the cauliflower into florets. Egg-and-crumb the cutlets, or toss them in seasoned flour, brown them in hot fat, wrap in aluminium foil, and place on rack in pan with the potatoes, using $\frac{1}{4}$–$\frac{1}{2}$ pint water. The cutlets and potatoes need 8 minutes' cooking at 15 lb. pressure; after 5 minutes, reduce pressure and insert the beans and cauliflower, in separators, then pressure-cook for a further 3 minutes. Dish up the vegetables, mash the potatoes, and, if desired, crisp the cutlets under the grill or in hot fat. Keep them hot while making gravy with stock from pan.

SOME PRESSURE COOKERY RECIPES

BONE STOCK

2 lb. bones (uncooked)	1 carrot, sliced
1 quart cold water	1 turnip, sliced
1 small onion	2 tsps. salt

Wash the bones, breaking large ones into small pieces. Put all the ingredients into the pressure pan, bring to the boil, skim, and fix lid. Bring slowly to 15 lb. pressure, reduce heat, and cook steadily for $\frac{3}{4}$ hour. Allow pressure to drop gradually to zero before removing the lid. Strain and cool the stock. When it is cold, lift off any fat from the top. In hot weather, boil stock every day, to keep it in good condition.

For white stock, use veal or chicken bones.

CREAM OF TOMATO SOUP

1 lb. tomatoes	Salt and pepper
1 onion	A bouquet garni
1 carrot	1 oz. flour or $\frac{3}{4}$ oz. cornflour
1 stalk of celery	$\frac{1}{4}$ pint milk
1 oz. margarine	A pinch of sugar
A little fat bacon	Chopped parsley
1 pint stock or water	

Prepare and slice the tomatoes and vegetables. Melt the margarine in the pan and fry the bacon to extract the fat. Add the prepared vegetables, and sauté all together for a few minutes. Add the liquid, seasonings, and bouquet garni, cover and pressure-cook for 5 minutes. Reduce pressure, sieve the soup, and return it to the cooker. Blend the flour or cornflour to a smooth cream with the milk, and stir into the soup. Bring to the boil and cook for 2–3 minutes, stirring all the time. Reseason with salt, pepper, and sugar; add chopped parsley just before serving.

FRENCH ONION SOUP

1 lb. onions	A French roll
1 oz. margarine	1–2 oz. grated cheese
1 pint stock or water	Fried onion rings and chopped parsley to garnish
Seasoning	

Peel and slice the onions and cook in the melted fat until golden-brown. Add the stock or water and the seasoning. Fix the lid, bring to pressure, cook for 5 minutes, and reduce the pressure. Place thin slices of the roll in a tureen and pour the soup over them, or float small pieces of roll on the surface of the soup; sprinkle with grated cheese, and garnish.

For Onion Cream Soup, cook onions in fat

until soft and yellow, add liquid, a blade of mace, a bay leaf and 4 peppercorns (tied in muslin), pressure-cook 5 minutes and remove herbs. Sieve the soup if desired, then add 1 oz. flour, blended with ¼ pint milk, bring to the boil and cook 3 minutes. Serve with diced toast, and hand grated cheese separately.

MINESTRONE

2 tomatoes, peeled and sliced
2 carrots
A small piece of turnip
2 stalks of celery
1–2 leeks or onions
1 rasher of streaky bacon
1 oz. dripping or butter
1½ pints boiling stock or water
Seasoning
A bouquet garni
4 tbsps. cooked macaroni
4 oz. grated cabbage heart
2 tbsps. chopped parsley
Grated cheese

Prepare the vegetables and cut them into very small, neat pieces. Rind and dice the bacon. Heat the fat and sauté the bacon, then the vegetables, for 4–5 minutes. Add the liquid, seasoning, and bouquet garni, the macaroni and the cabbage. Fix lid, bring to pressure, and cook for 7 minutes, then reduce pressure. Remove bouquet garni, and sprinkle in the parsley. Serve with cheese.

SCOTCH BROTH

1–1½ lb. scrag end of mutton
1 small carrot
1 onion
1 turnip
1 quart water
Salt and pepper
1 oz. pearl barley
Chopped parsley

Cut the meat into small pieces and remove any surplus fat. Dice the vegetables. Place the meat in pan and add water, seasonings, and barley. Fix lid and bring steadily to pressure, lower heat and cook for 20 minutes. Reduce pressure, open the lid and skim any fat off surface of soup. Add diced vegetables and pressure-cook for 5 minutes, then reduce pressure. Serve in a tureen, sprinkled with the parsley.

STEAK AND KIDNEY PUDDING

Follow the ordinary recipe, but first half-cook the meat and kidney with ¼ pint water in the pressure cooker for 15 minutes at 15 lb. pressure. Make the pudding, using the half-cooked meat (allow it to cool first). Put 1 quart water in pan, bring to boil, and put pudding on rack. Put on lid, but do not fix pressure control. Put over good heat and let steam come out for 25 minutes. Now cook under pressure for 25–30 minutes. Reduce the pressure quickly under cold water.

CURRY OF FRESH MEAT

2 oz. fat
1 large onion
1 lb. uncooked meat
1 tbsp. curry powder
2 tbsps. sultanas
2 tbsps. chopped coconut
¾ pint stock
Seasoning
Juice of ½ a lemon

Melt the fat in the pan, add the chopped onion, and cook for a few minutes. Then add the cut-up meat, curry powder, sultanas, and coconut, and stir well. Pour in the stock gradually, and season. Cook (at 15 lb. pressure) for 15–20 minutes, according to the meat used. Add the lemon juice, and dish up with a border of boiled rice. Serve with chutney.

FRICASSEE OF RABBIT

1 rabbit, jointed
¼ lb. streaky bacon
1 large onion, sliced
A bouquet garni
Seasoning
½ pint water
Diced mixed vegetables to garnish (optional)
2 oz. flour
½ pint milk
1 oz. margarine

Soak and wash the rabbit, and blanch it in boiling water. Drain, and put in pan with diced bacon, onion, herbs, seasoning, and water. Cook for 15–20 minutes at 15 lb. pressure and reduce pressure. Insert vegetables (in a separator) and pressure-cook 1 minute. Transfer rabbit to serving dish and keep hot. Blend flour with milk and add, with fat, to liquor; boil, and cook 3 minutes. Pour this sauce over the rabbit and garnish with the vegetables.

JUGGED HARE

Follow the ordinary recipe for ingredients and preparation, but use only ¾ pint stock. Pressure-cook for 30 minutes, and meanwhile, make the forcemeat balls and fry them. Reduce pressure of cooker, take out bag of herbs, stir in the flour, blended with a little stock, bring to boil, and cook for 3–4 minutes. Finish and serve as usual.

BOILED OX-TONGUE

Follow the ordinary recipe for the preparation of the tongue. After bringing it to the boil in water, add the sliced flavouring vegetables, peppercorns, salt, if required, and a bouquet garni (optional), bring to 15 lb. pressure and cook for the required time, allowing 15 minutes per lb. plus 15 minutes. Reduce the pressure and plunge the tongue into cold water to facilitate the skinning. Continue as usual.

BRAISED OX-TAIL

Follow the recipe for Stewed Ox-tail, but use only ¾ pint water. Pressure-cook the prepared meat with the diced vegetables, herbs, seasonings, and liquid for 30–35 minutes, reduce the pressure and remove the lid. Add the blended flour, bring to the boil, and cook till the gravy is thick. Serve in the usual way.

BRAISED LIVER

¾ lb. liver	1–2 rashers of streaky bacon
1 oz. seasoned flour	Seasoning
1 oz. dripping	½ pint stock
Sliced carrots, onions, leeks, celery	1 oz. flour

Slice and flour the liver and fry it in the hot fat, with the sliced onions and cut-up bacon, until brown. Remove from pan and sauté the remaining vegetables for about 2–3 minutes. Replace the liver, etc., season, add the stock, fix the lid, and cook for 10–15 minutes at 15 lb. pressure. Reduce the pressure, remove the liver, and keep it hot. Add the blended flour, bring to the boil, simmer for 3 minutes, season, and pour over the liver.

TRIPE AND ONIONS

1 lb. tripe	A little mace
2 large onions	½ pint water
A little dripping	¼ pint milk
1 tsp. salt	1 oz. flour

Blanch the tripe in the usual way. Grease the bottom of the pressure pan slightly with dripping, and put in the sliced tripe and onions, with the salt, mace, and water. Pressure-cook for 20 minutes at 15 lb., then add the milk and blended flour, bring to the boil, and simmer for 5–6 minutes. Garnish with toast snippets.

CHICKEN MARENGO

1 chicken	3 tomatoes
1 oz. seasoned flour	½–¾ pint stock
2 oz. dripping	1 oz. mushrooms
1 onion, sliced	Forcemeat
2 tbsps. tomato purée	Chopped parsley

Joint the chicken, dip the joints in seasoned flour, and fry them in the hot dripping till golden-brown; remove on to a plate. Fry the onion till brown, and add the rest of the flour. Stir well, and return the chicken joints to the pan. Add the tomato purée, tomatoes and stock. Pressure-cook at 15 lb. for 20–25 minutes. Reduce pressure, add mushrooms and tiny balls of the forcemeat, and simmer gently for 5 minutes with the lid off. Serve the chicken in a dish with the sauce poured over, and garnish with the whole mushrooms, the forcemeat balls, and the finely chopped parsley.

BOILED FOWL

1 small boiling fowl	2–3 sticks of celery
2 small onions	White sauce

Truss bird, or if too large to fit in pan, cut into sections. Pressure-cook (allowing 10 minutes per lb.) with 1 pint water, 2 tsps. salt, onions and celery, and skin it while hot. Keep it warm while making a white sauce with the liquor. Place bird on a dish, coat with sauce.

BRAISED PIGEONS

1–2 oz. dripping	A bouquet garni
2 onions, sliced	Seasoning
2–3 pigeons	¾ pint stock
2 carrots, diced	1 oz. flour
1 turnip, diced	¼ lb. mushrooms

Melt fat in pan and fry onions lightly; brown the pigeons, then remove them. Put in vegetables, herbs, seasoning, and stock. Add pigeons, and pressure-cook for 20 minutes. Put pigeons on a dish. Add blended flour, bring to boil, add mushrooms, cook 3–4 minutes, and strain over the pigeons. Garnish with the diced vegetables.

BRAISED VEGETABLES

The most suitable vegetables for braising are carrots, turnips, parsnips, celery, and onions. For every 1 lb. of vegetables, place 1 oz. dripping in the pressure pan, and sauté the vegetables over a low heat until the fat has been absorbed. Add ½ pint brown stock, and pressure-cook for the time required by the various vegetables. Reduce the pressure immediately, and thicken the stock, allowing 1 oz. flour to every ½ pint liquid.

HARICOT-STUFFED MARROW

1 short marrow	2 tbsps. chopped parsley
6 oz. haricot beans	2 tbsps. grated cheese
1 large onion	Salt and pepper
1 oz. margarine	1 egg, beaten
4–6 tbsps. bread-crumbs	A little milk

Peel the marrow, leaving it whole, halve lengthwise, and remove the seeds. Cook the

1

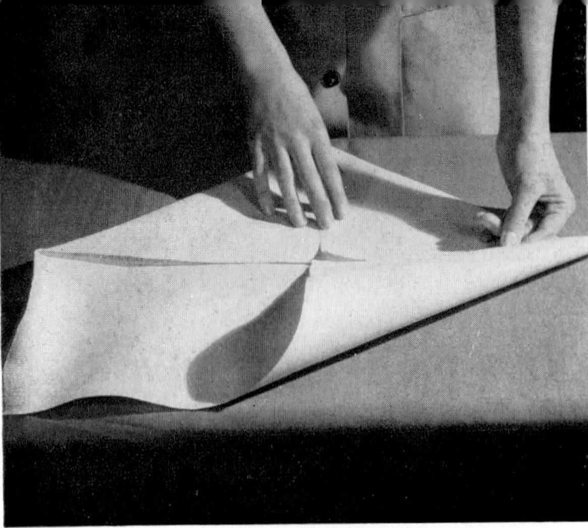

2a) Water Lily Napkin: Lay starched napkin flat, and fold all the corners in.

2b) Press these folds well in; repeat this whole folding process twice more.

2c) When each corner is folded in three times, turn napkin, and fold again.

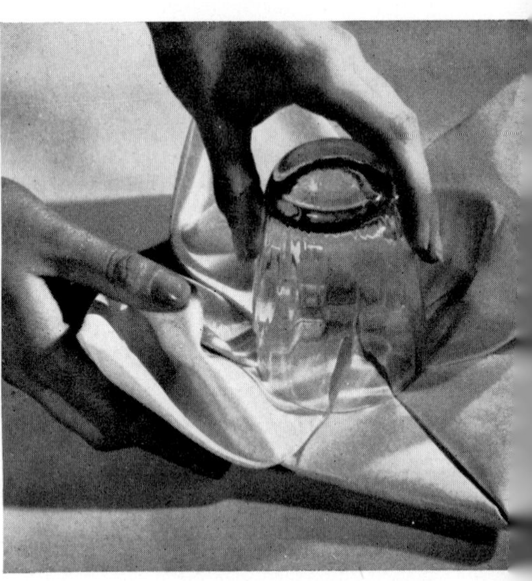

2d) Holding last folds with a tumbler, pull out the 8 points from underneath.

2e) Pull last 4 points up tightly, to hold other "petals" well in position.

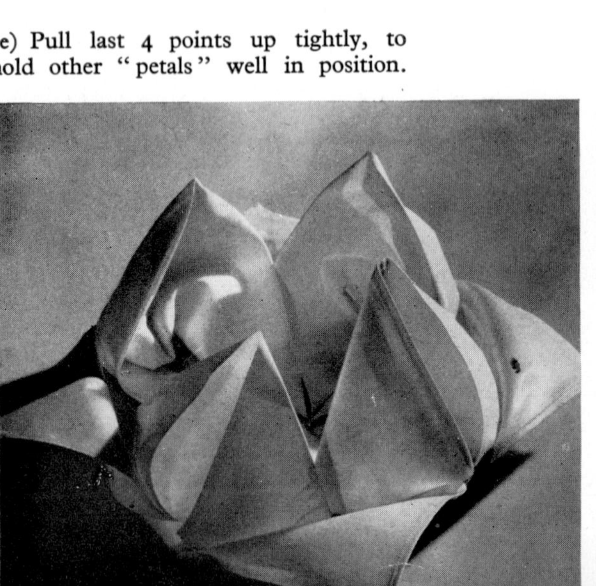

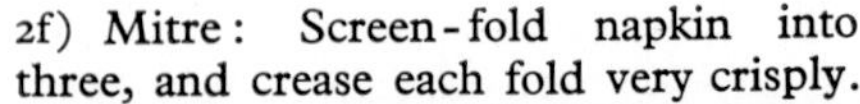

2f) Mitre: Screen-fold napkin into three, and crease each fold very crisply.

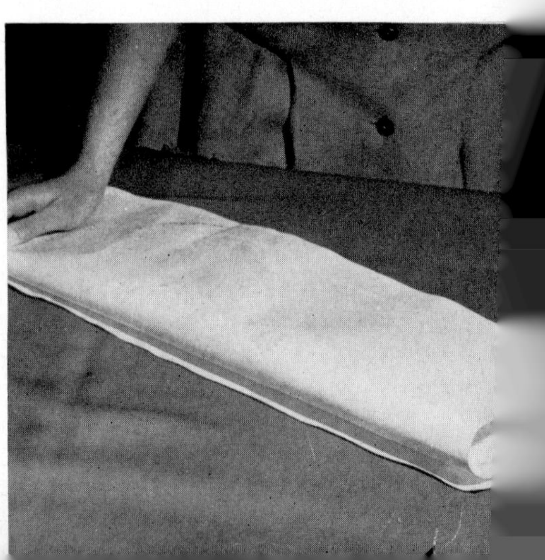

2

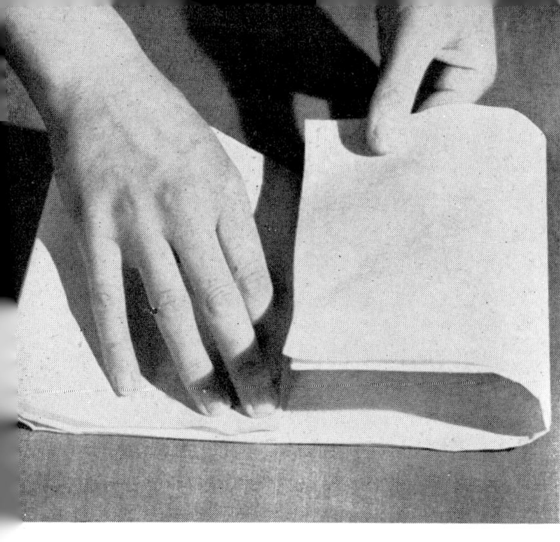

2g) Now fold two ends over to the centre line, and again crease the folds well.

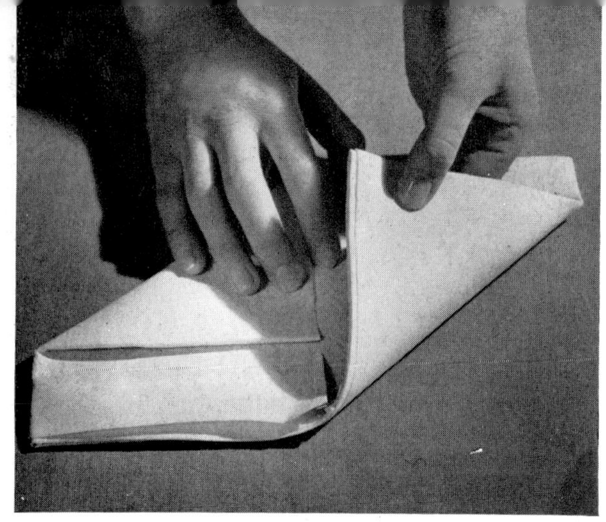

2h) Fold two opposite corners to meet down the centre, as seen in the picture.

2j) Turn napkin on to the other side, and fold it so that the long sides meet.

2k) Next tuck the left-hand base point well under the fold which lies on top.

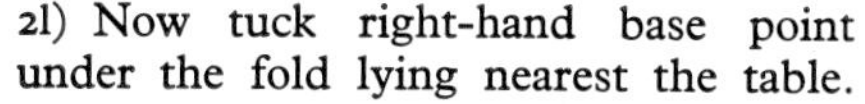

2l) Now tuck right-hand base point under the fold lying nearest the table.

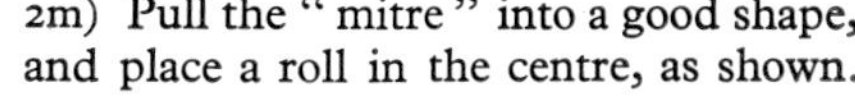

2m) Pull the " mitre " into a good shape, and place a roll in the centre, as shown.

3-7

3) Hors d'Oeuvre: Oysters should be bedded in ice, to chill them thoroughly.

4a) Rollmops, sardines, stuffed tomatoes and curried rice as Hors d'Oeuvre Variés.

4b) Smoked salmon, salads, peppers and onion rings in Hors d'Oeuvre Variés.

5) Grapefruit Ginger Cocktail. 7 (below): Fish Cocktails, garnished with cucumber.

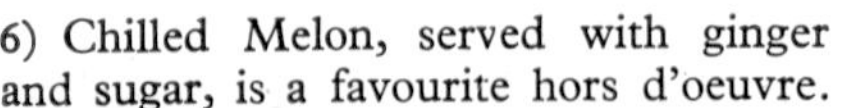

6) Chilled Melon, served with ginger and sugar, is a favourite hors d'oeuvre.

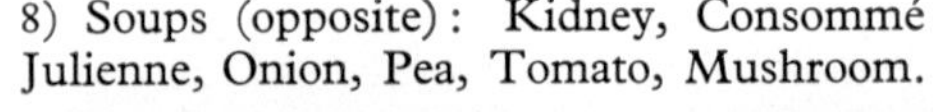

8) Soups (opposite): Kidney, Consommé Julienne, Onion, Pea, Tomato, Mushroom.

8

9-13

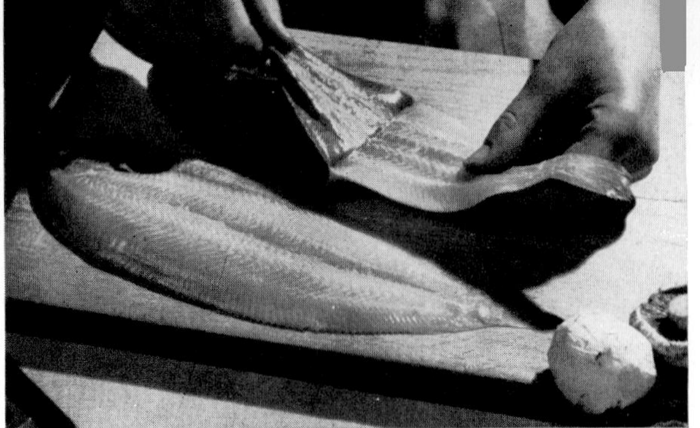

9) To Skin Soles: Loosen skin at tail end and then pull towards the head.

10a) To Fillet Plaice: First cut down the line of the bone, using a sharp knife.

10b) Remove fillets, inserting knife under flesh and using long, clean strokes.

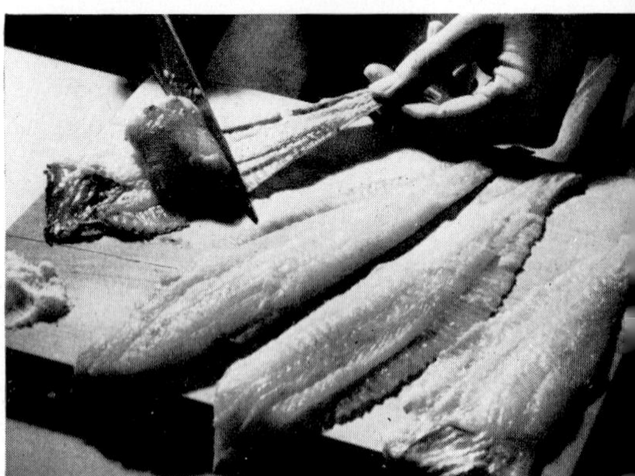

11) To skin, hold tail end, press knife against flesh and use a sawing movement.

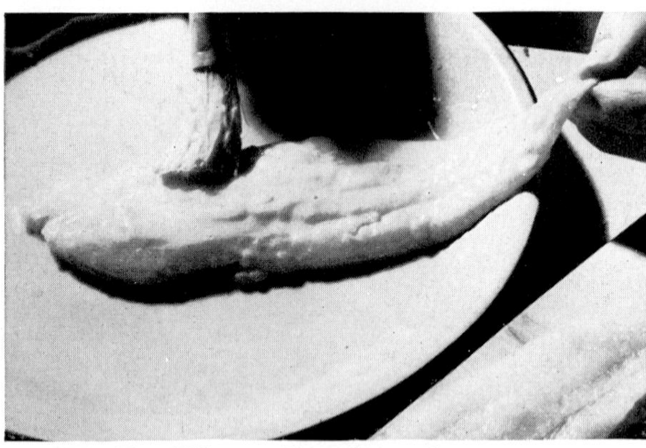

12a) To Fry Fillets: Dry them, then brush with beaten egg, or egg and milk.

12b) Coat with browned breadcrumbs and press these in well before cooking.

12c) Fry in smoking-hot fat, and drain on kitchen paper to remove surplus fat.

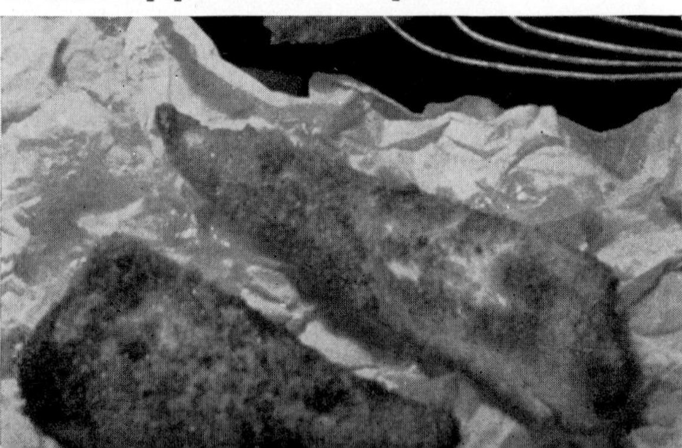

13) Serve very hot, with tomato lilies, lemon butterflies and button mushrooms.

14) Cod Cutlets, stuffed with forcemeat and baked with some halved tomatoes.

15) Haddock Soufflé, made in a large dish or individually, forms a tasty supper.

16a) To Prepare Herrings, first remove the head and inside, then clean the fish.

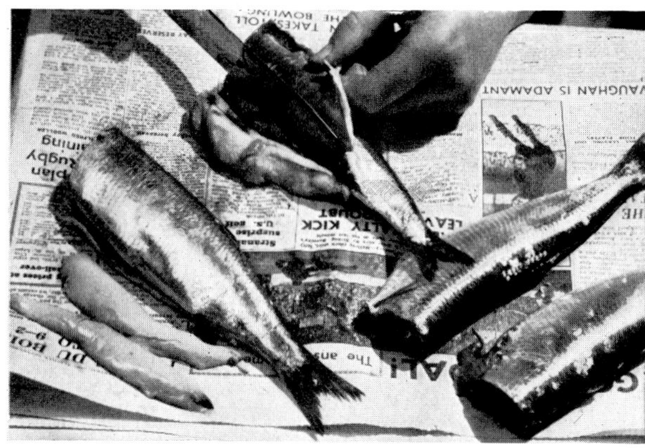

16b) Scale, and trim fins and tail. The roes may be reserved for another dish.

17) To bone, split underside, press along backbone and ease away with fingers.

18) To grill, put on a greased grid with roes, dot with fat and brown lightly.

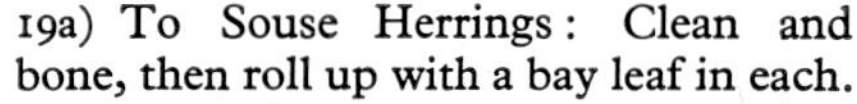

19a) To Souse Herrings: Clean and bone, then roll up with a bay leaf in each.

19b) Cook in a fireproof dish with vinegar and water. Serve either hot or cold.

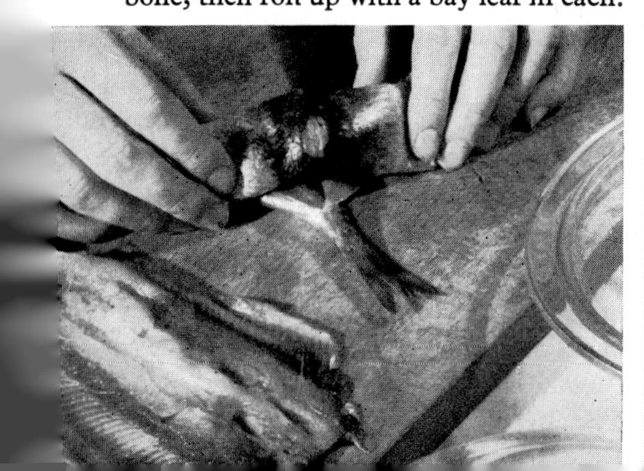

20
-
23

20) Steam Cutlets of Salmon, cool, coat with mayonnaise and serve with salad.

21) A creamy egg sauce is good with rolled poached Fillets of Sole or Plaice.

22) Sole à la Crème aux Champignons is a delicious rich dish for party occasions.

23) Crisp Fried Whitebait, served with lemon, makes an excellent hors d'œuvre.

24a) Dressed Crab : Pull top shell from the body. Now break off all the claws.

24b) Take out all the soft, dark flesh from inside the top shell, using a skewer.

24c) With skewer, detach stomach bag (found below eyes); break off surplus shell.

24d) Next discard all the greyish-white "dead men's fingers," which are inedible.

24e) Pick out the white flesh, keeping it separate from the dark ; use a skewer.

24f) Crack large claws and remove the flesh ; keep some small claws for garnish.

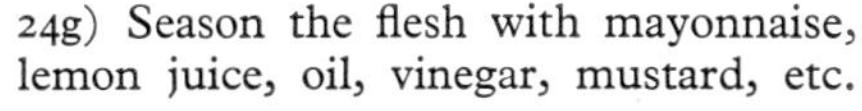

24g) Season the flesh with mayonnaise, lemon juice, oil, vinegar, mustard, etc.

24h) Wash and polish shells, replace meat, garnish with paprika and parsley.

25

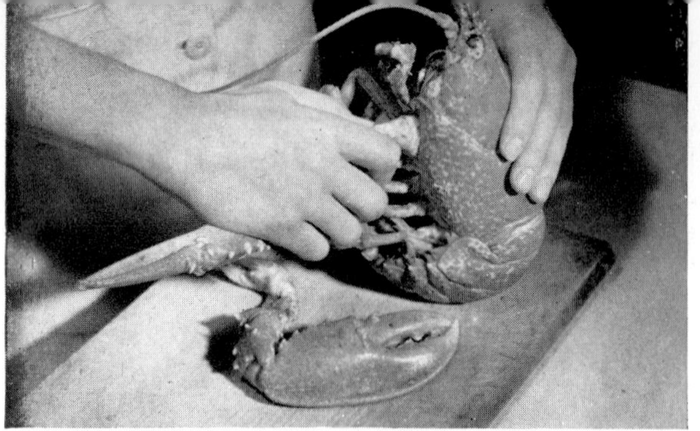

25a) Dressing a Lobster: Twist off all the claws and legs, and remove the "coral."

25b) Crack large claws carefully, using a weight or a hammer, and extract meat.

25c) Hold lobster as shown, and separate the body part from the tail section.

25d) Cut tail section in halves lengthwise from underside. Remove dark cord.

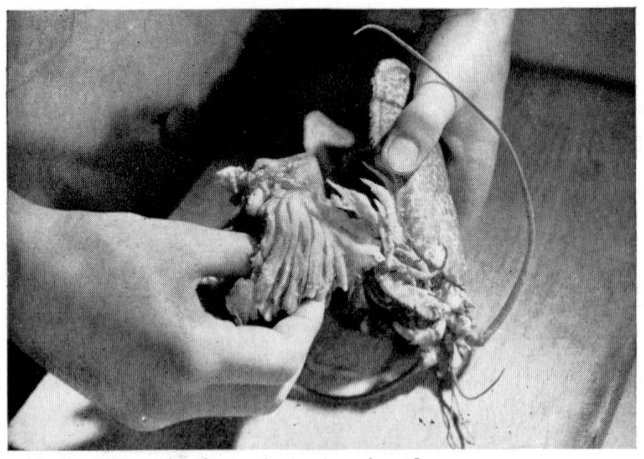

25e) Remove the large bony section from head, and discard the spongy-looking gills.

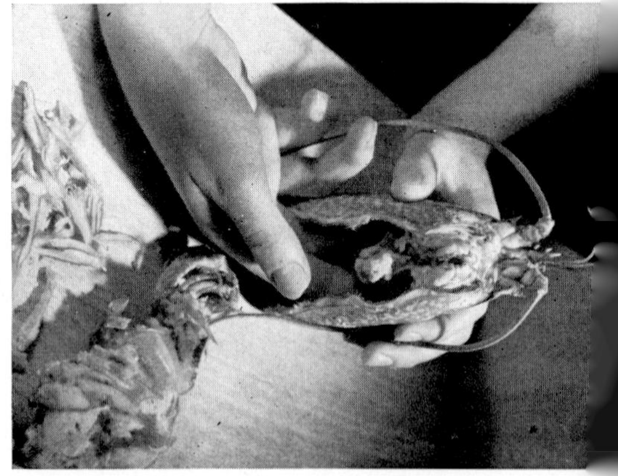

25f) Discard stomach bag, also found in the head. Keep the head for a garnish.

25g) Take out all other soft meat from the body, and mix with meat from claws.

25h) Mix meat with mayonnaise, and serve as shown, or on a bed of lettuce.

26
-
27

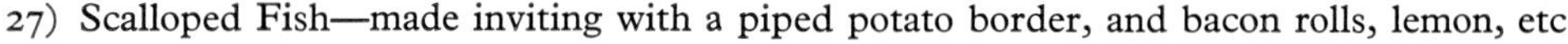

26) Fish in Jelly: Slice cooked rolled fillets of sole, and set in aspic, with slices of egg.

27) Scalloped Fish—made inviting with a piped potato border, and bacon rolls, lemon, etc.

28 - 33

28) Roast Beef, with individual Yorkshire puddings (also called popovers).

29) Mixed Grill, with slices of grilled pineapple included to give extra flavour.

30) Pressed Beef is easily made at home. Use pieces of cooked carrots for garnish.

31) Ragoût of Beef with a wide border of piped potato ; brown in a hot oven.

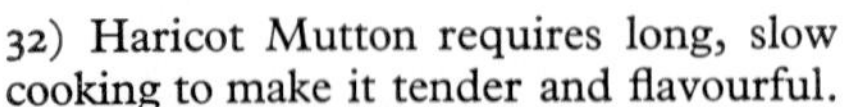

32) Haricot Mutton requires long, slow cooking to make it tender and flavourful.

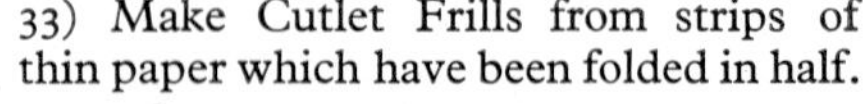

33) Make Cutlet Frills from strips of thin paper which have been folded in half.

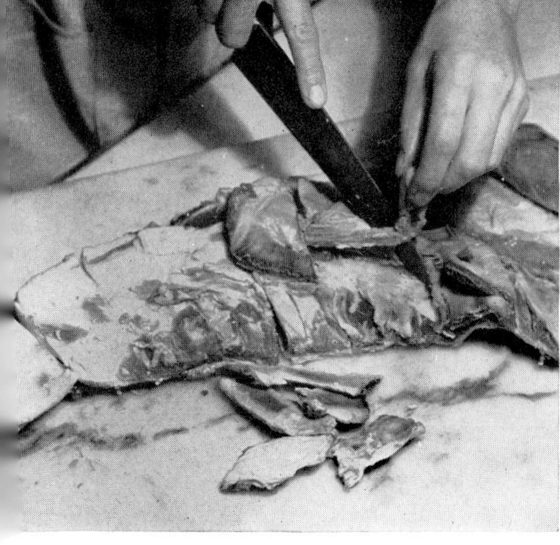

34a) Stuffed Breast of Lamb: Bone with a sharp knife, or buy ready prepared.

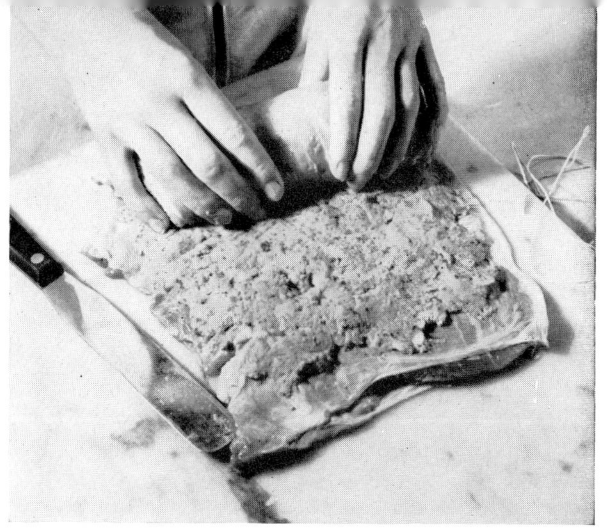

34b) Spread the stuffing over the breast, and then roll up from the narrow end.

34c) Tie the meat up like a parcel, using fine string. Spread with dripping.

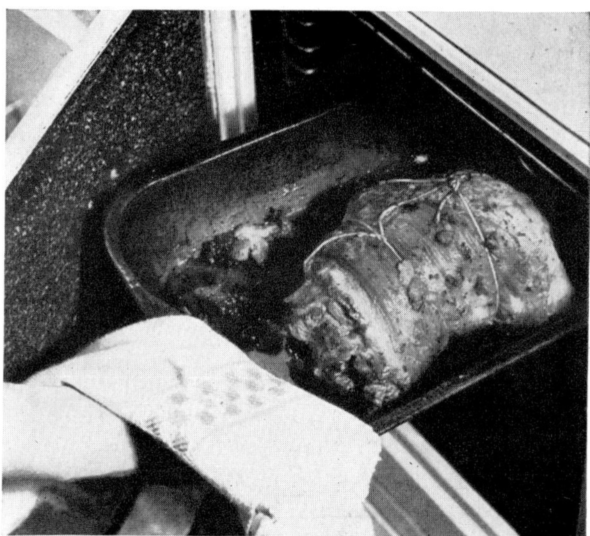

34d) Roast meat in moderately hot oven for 1–1½ hours, basting it occasionally.

35 - 40

35) Baked Ham, American style—glazed with brown sugar, studded with cloves.

36) Savoury Sausage Flan with an egg filling, topped with cooked mushrooms.

37) Piped Mashed Potatoes browned in the oven, with hot Rissoles in the centre.

38) Lamb Ring Mould with Russian Salad is a good choice for summer days.

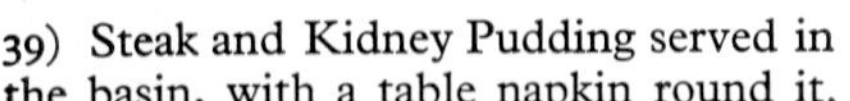

39) Steak and Kidney Pudding served in the basin, with a table napkin round it.

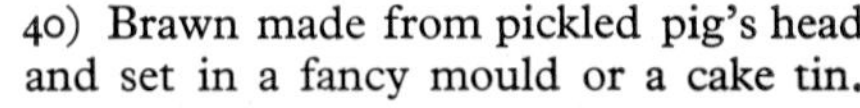

40) Brawn made from pickled pig's head and set in a fancy mould or a cake tin.

41a) Cooking a Tongue: Trim tongue, soak it, then simmer for several hours.

41b) Plunge the tongue into cold water. Skin, and remove any small bones.

41c) Put neatly into a tin. Cover with jelly stock and press with a weight.

41d) When tongue is pressed and jellied, use as required, cutting in thin slices.

42
-
43

42) Chicken Casserole, garnished with buttered asparagus and peas to give it a festive air.

43) Chaudfroid of Chicken, accompanied by tiny cooked sausages served on cocktail sticks.

44

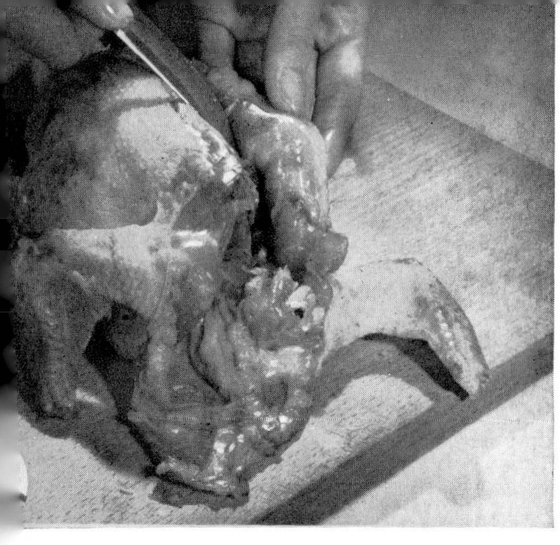

44a) Boning chicken for Galantine: Cut off neck, end joints of wing, and feet.

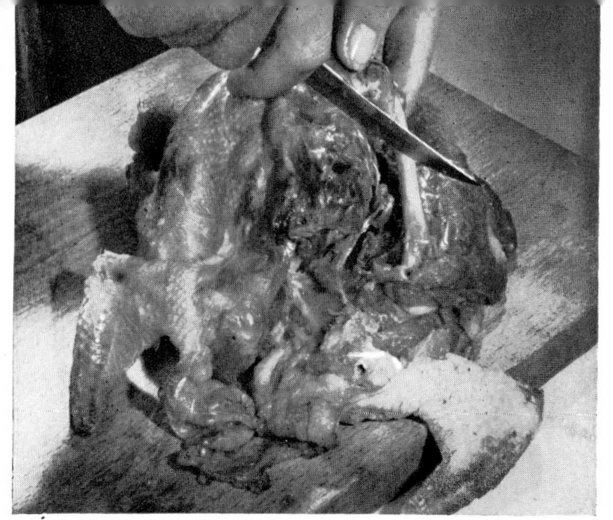

44b) Dislocate joints and separate flesh from bones. Scrape wing and leg bones.

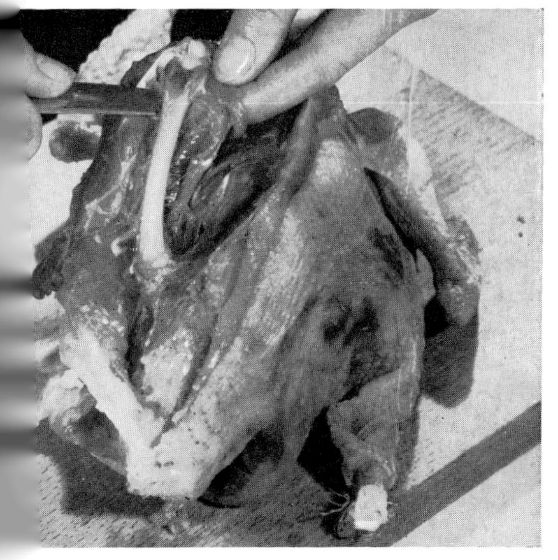

44c) Gradually turn flesh inside out. Remove bones as they are freed of flesh.

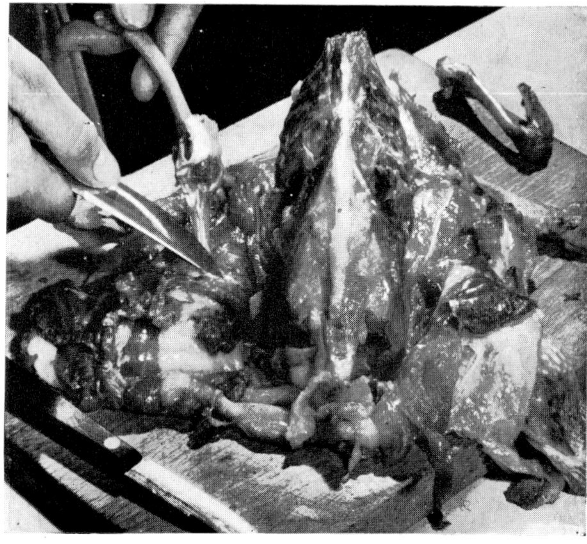

44d) Continue to breast-bone, working flesh from bones. Remove the carcase.

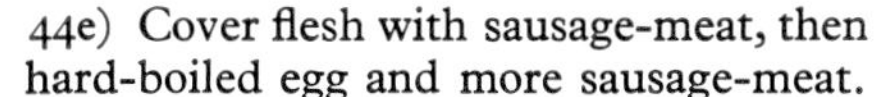

44e) Cover flesh with sausage-meat, then hard-boiled egg and more sausage-meat.

44f) Roll up, tie, and simmer till tender. Coat with glaze or chaudfroid sauce.

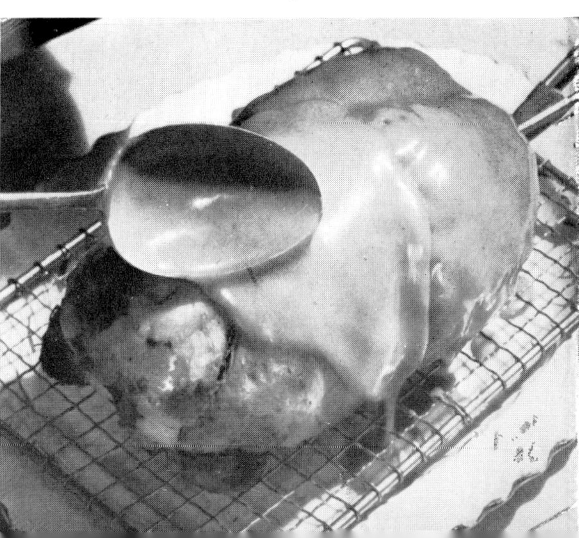

45
-
46

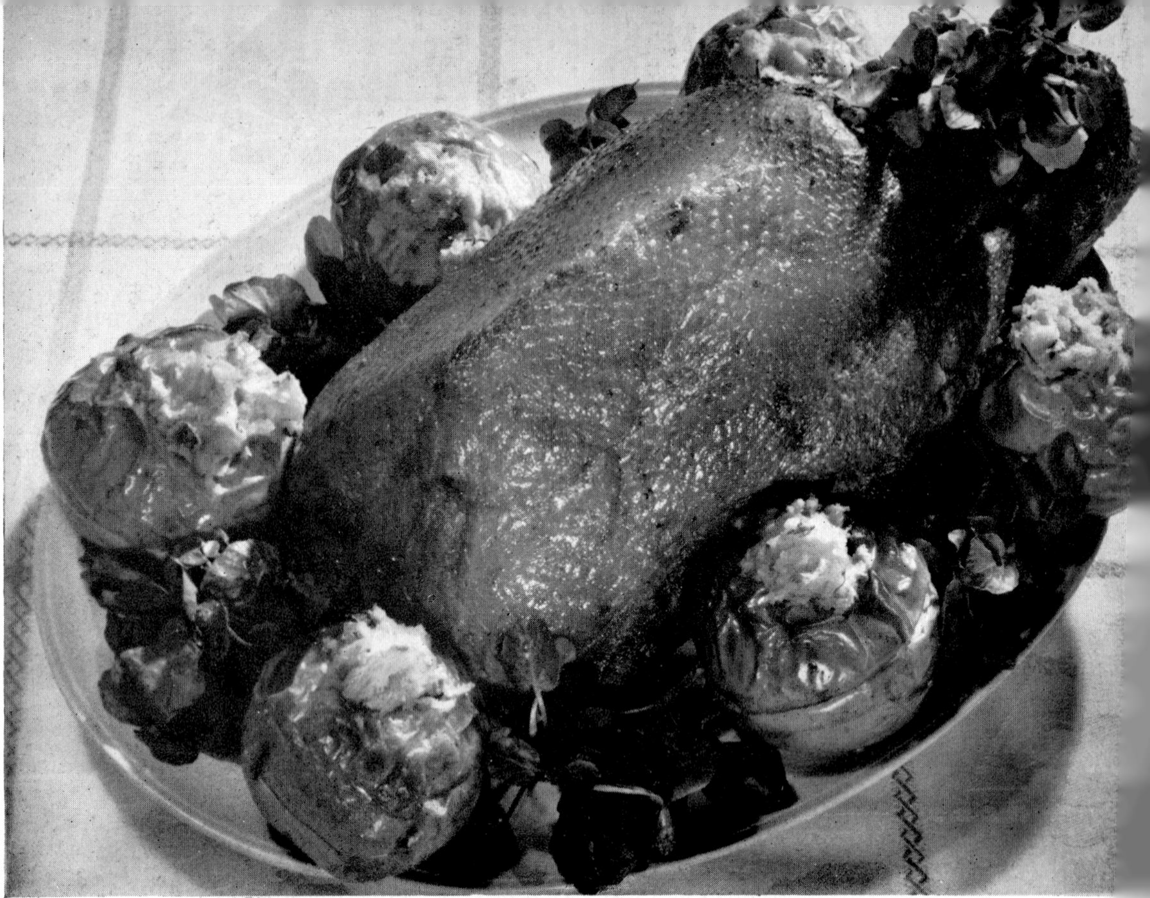

45) Roast Duck, served with stuffed baked apples, instead of the more usual apple sauce.

46) Duck with Orange Sauce, garnished with toast triangles and strips of the cooked rind.

47a) To prepare a Pigeon: Singe if necessary, then truss with skewer and string.

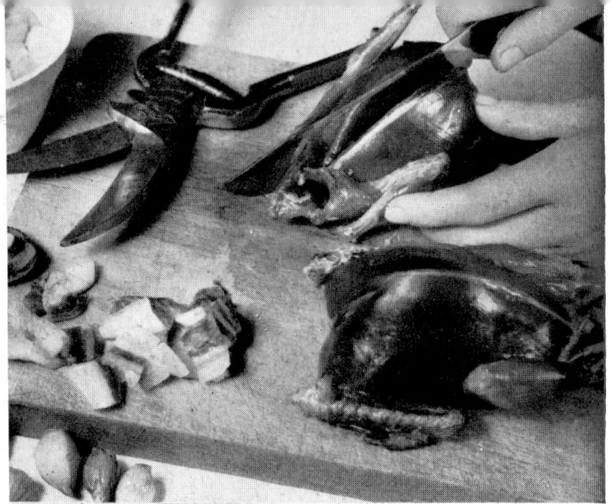

47b) For using in a stew, skin pigeons, and cut in half with knife or cutters.

47c) For roasting, bard breast with slices of fat bacon and spread with soft butter.

47d) Serve pigeons with watercress, game chips, tomatoes, mushrooms, gravy.

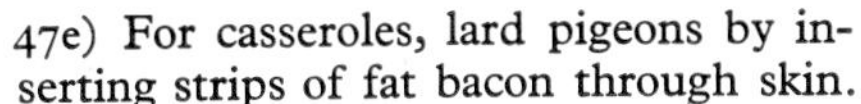

47e) For casseroles, lard pigeons by inserting strips of fat bacon through skin.

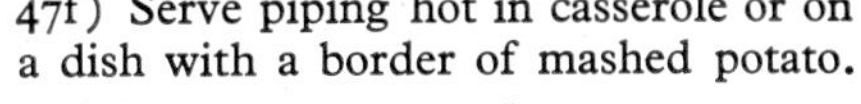

47f) Serve piping hot in casserole or on a dish with a border of mashed potato.

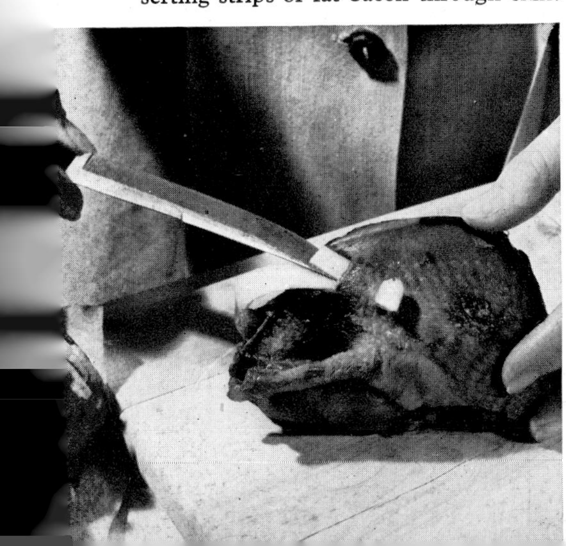

48

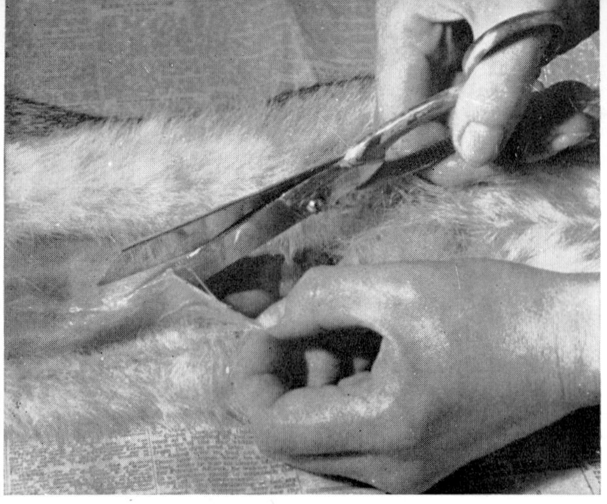

48a) Preparing rabbit (or hare): Cut skin from fork to breast-bone; ease off pelt.

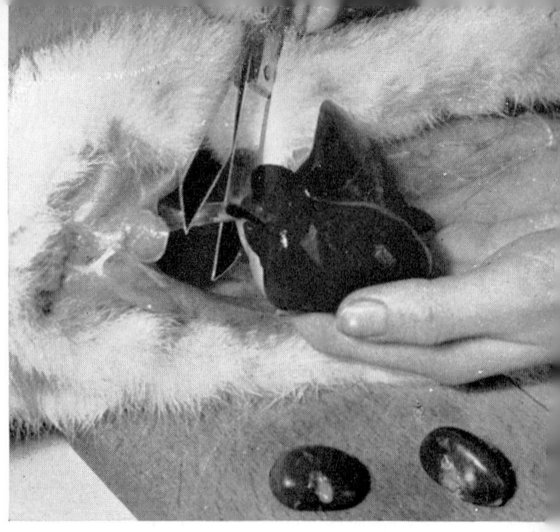

48b) Take out and burn the entrails. Remove kidneys, liver and gall-bladder.

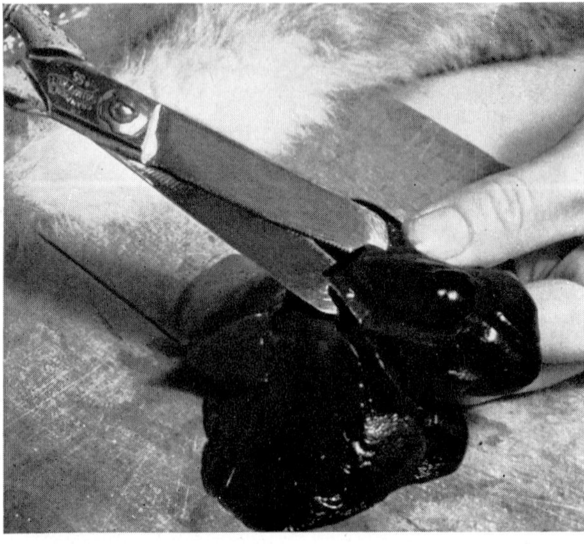

48c) Separate gall-bladder from liver and discard it and lungs. Keep the heart.

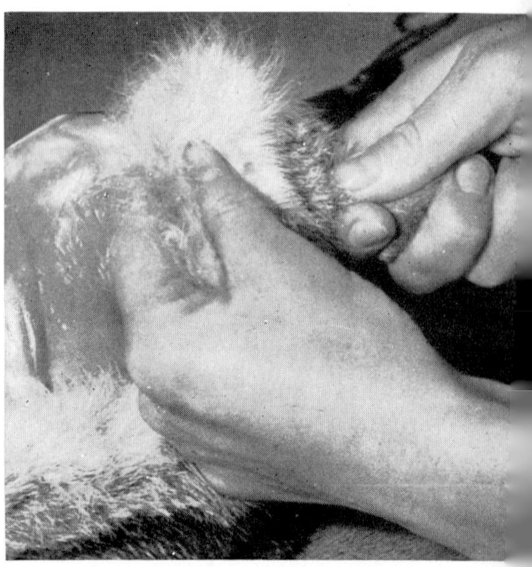

48d) Cut off feet at first joint, loosen and pull off skin, drawing it from the head.

48e) Soak rabbit in cold water; joint it, after cutting off fore and hind legs.

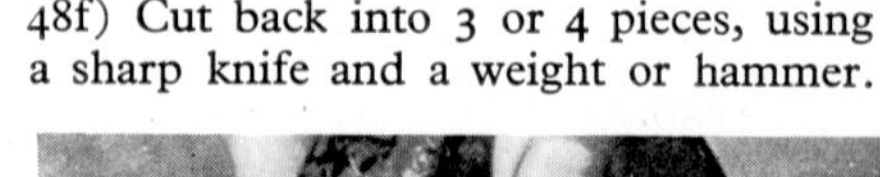

48f) Cut back into 3 or 4 pieces, using a sharp knife and a weight or hammer.

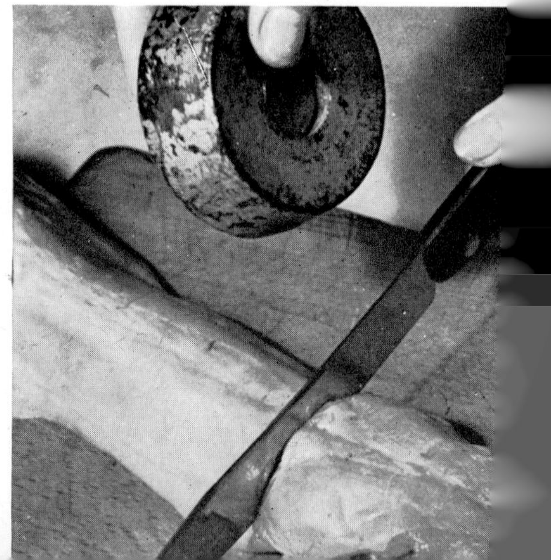

49
-
50

49) Roast Stuffed Rabbit with bacon rashers, served with baked stuffed tomatoes.
50) Jugged Hare is simple to cook for a dinner party; serve it with forcemeat balls.

51

51) (*opposite*) Individual Chicken Curry.
52) (*above*) " Belted " Celery with sauce.

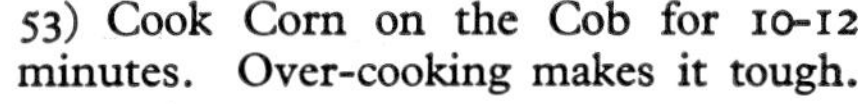

53) Cook Corn on the Cob for 10–12 minutes. Over-cooking makes it tough.

54) Serve Mushrooms à la Pompadour as entrée or accompaniment to a main dish.

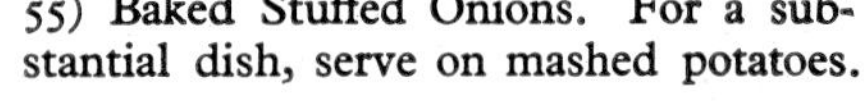

55) Baked Stuffed Onions. For a substantial dish, serve on mashed potatoes.

56 - 59

56) Shape Potato Galantine mixture (p. 223) into a case, bake, and add filling.

57) Sweet Peppers can be stuffed with a savoury mixture and baked in the oven.

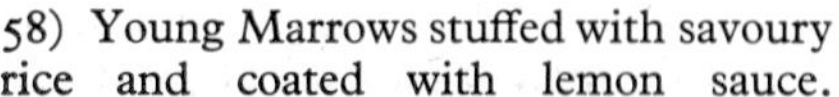

58) Young Marrows stuffed with savoury rice and coated with lemon sauce.

59) Cheese Dumplings make vegetable casserole into a substantial lunch dish.

60 - 65

60) Serve an Egg Salad in a glass platter or a shallow bowl, with French dressing.

61) Luncheon Salad, with tongue cut into thin slices and rolled into cornets.

62) Large and small Salads in Aspic, garnished with carrots, peas, cauliflower.

63) Sardine Salad, with a border of crisp lettuce and Parisian carrot balls.

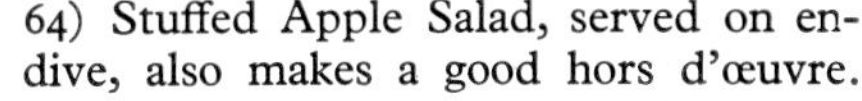

64) Stuffed Apple Salad, served on endive, also makes a good hors d'œuvre.

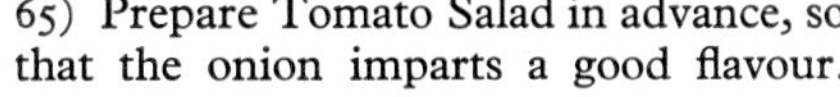

65) Prepare Tomato Salad in advance, so that the onion imparts a good flavour.

66 - 69

66) Serve Omelettes plain, with parsley or watercress, or with a suitable sauce.

67) A fluffy Soufflé Omelette, filled with hot jam and dusted with fine sugar.

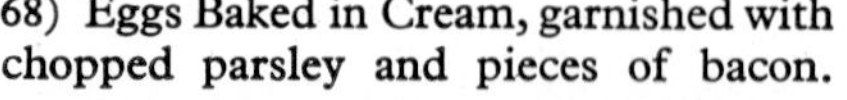

68) Eggs Baked in Cream, garnished with chopped parsley and pieces of bacon.

69) Curried Eggs, garnished with paprika, parsley, and lemon "butterflies."

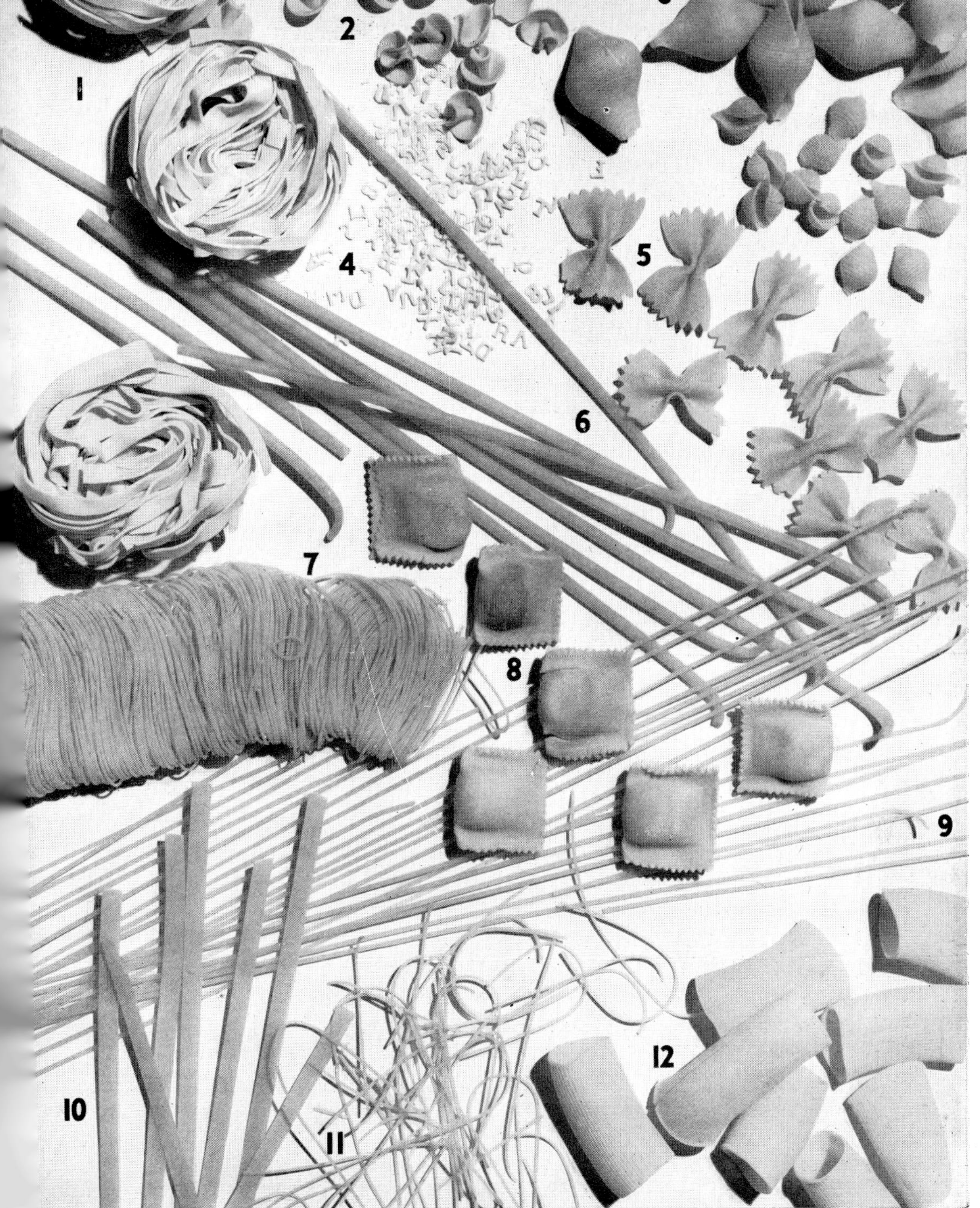

Italian Pastes : 1) Tagliatelle ; 2) Capellini ; 3) Conchiglie ; 4) Alfabeto ;
5) Farfalle ; 6) Maccheroni; 7) Taglialini ; 8) Ravioli ;
9) Spaghetti; 10) Lasagne; 11) Vermicelli ; 12) Cannelloni.

71

71a) Puff Pastry: For Cream Crisps roll an oblong, add sugar, fold in three.

71b) Fold in half, cut slices $\frac{1}{2}$ in. thick and place on baking sheet cut side down.

71c) For Cream Horns: Roll thinly round moulds, overlapping at each turn.

71d) Patty Cases: Roll evenly to $\frac{1}{2}$ in. thickness, stamp out and mark centre.

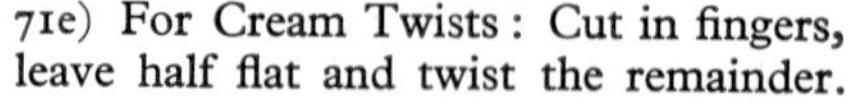

71e) For Cream Twists: Cut in fingers, leave half flat and twist the remainder.

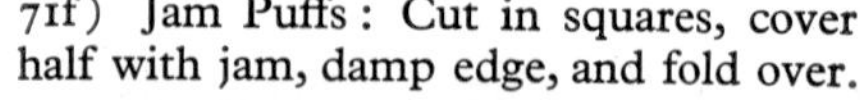

71f) Jam Puffs: Cut in squares, cover half with jam, damp edge, and fold over.

72a) Plum Pie: Pile fruit high in dish; damp edges and put pastry strip round.

72b) Damp edge of pastry lid and place over pie. Try not to stretch the pastry.

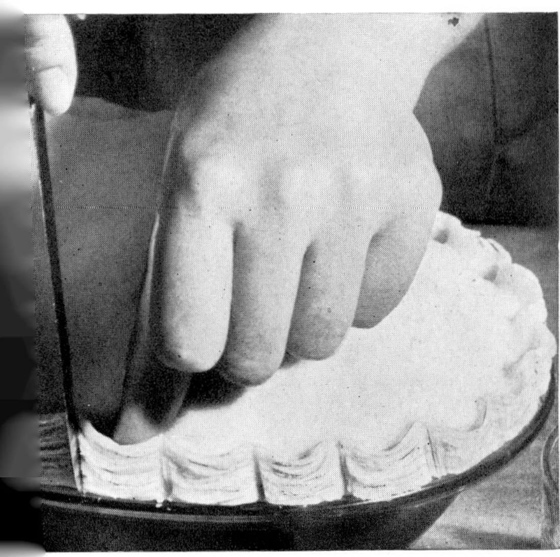

72c) Knock up edge with back of knife to seal; scallop with thumb and knife.

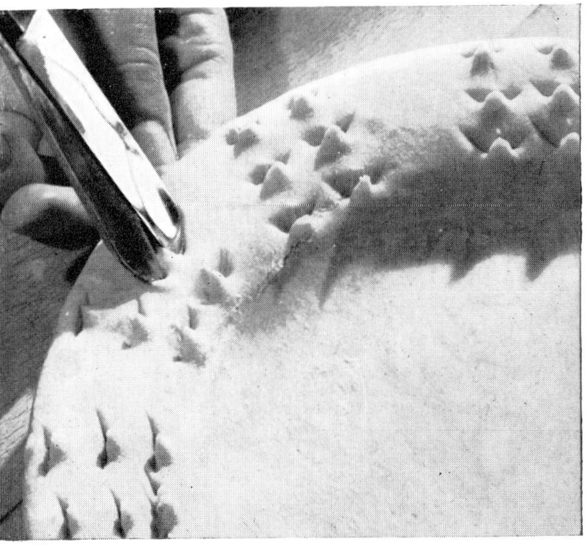

73a) Tart Edges: Use scissors to snip regular patterns round edge or on top.

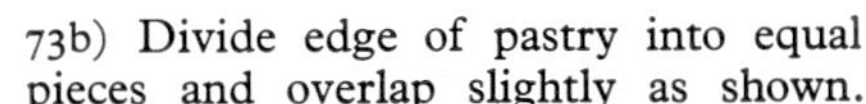

73b) Divide edge of pastry into equal pieces and overlap slightly as shown.

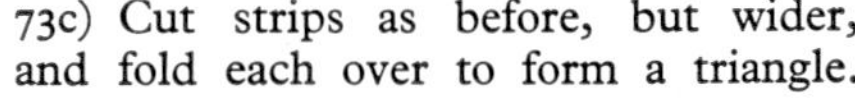

73c) Cut strips as before, but wider, and fold each over to form a triangle.

74a) Flan Case: Roll flan or shortcrust pastry slightly larger than flan ring.

74b) Press in place, making sure there are no air bubbles. Roll to trim edges.

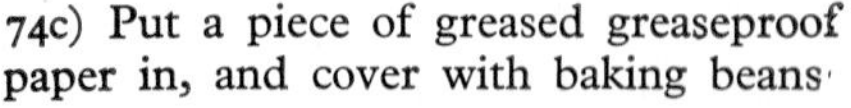

74c) Put a piece of greased greaseproof paper in, and cover with baking beans.

74d) Bake in a hot oven; when set remove beans and ring, and finish baking.

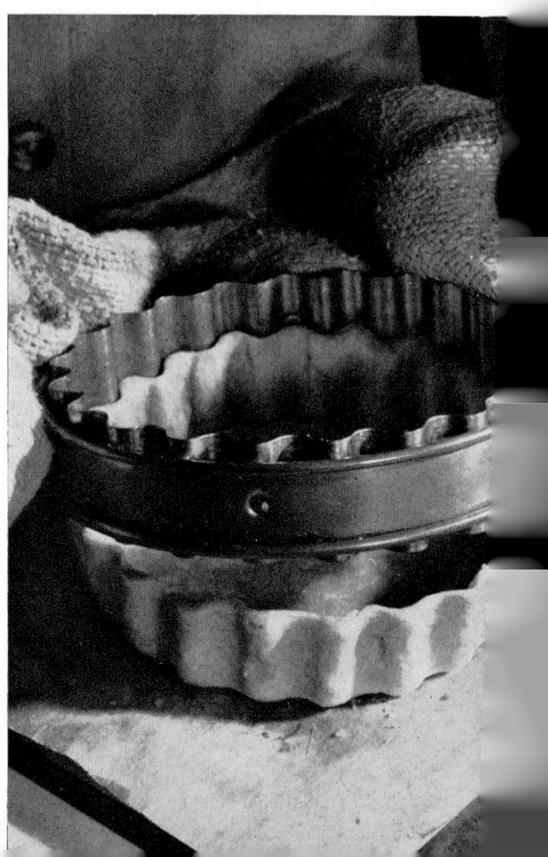

75) Eccles Cakes, with their delicious filling of currants, peel, butter and sugar.

76) Frangipan Flan, topped with apricots, lightly browned almonds and sugar.

77) Gay Fruit Flan, with rows of varicoloured fruit coated with clear glaze.

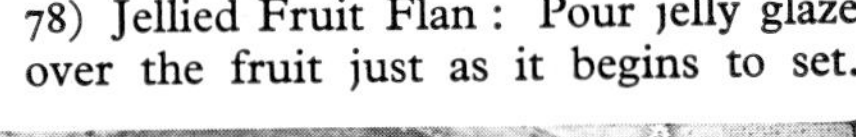

78) Jellied Fruit Flan : Pour jelly glaze over the fruit just as it begins to set.

79 - 81

79a) Jam Roly-poly: Roll suetcrust pastry in an oblong and spread with jam.

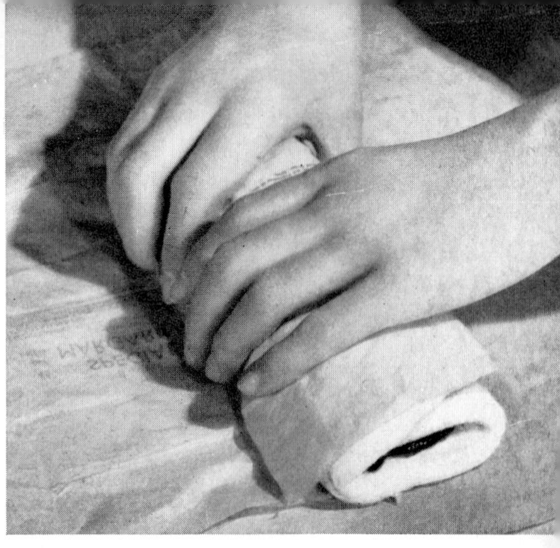

79b) Roll up, cover with greased greaseproof paper, then with a floured cloth.

79c) Secure ends with string; steam 2–2½ hours, or boil for about 1½ hours.

79d) Serve with jam sauce; if lemon curd is used in roll, serve with lemon sauce.

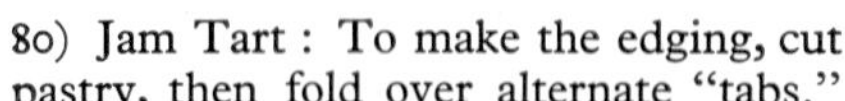

80) Jam Tart: To make the edging, cut pastry, then fold over alternate "tabs."

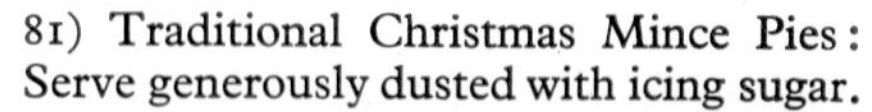

81) Traditional Christmas Mince Pies: Serve generously dusted with icing sugar.

82
-
87

82) Fruit Pudding : Line bottom of basin with dried fruit and some syrup or jam.

83) Spotted Dick : To make the roll shape, cook mixture in a cocoa or similar tin.

84) Canary Pudding mixture baked in ring mould, and served with fruit and custard.

85) These syrupy Baked Apples can be stuffed with prunes, sultanas or dates.

86) Fruit Cobbler is topped with fancy scones glazed with egg-white and sugar.

87) Chocolate Pudding made in fluted metal mould and decorated with almonds.

88
-
89

88) Little Batter Puddings (popovers) are served with the joint or as a sweet dish.

89) Sausage Toad in the Hole is best served straight from the baking dish.

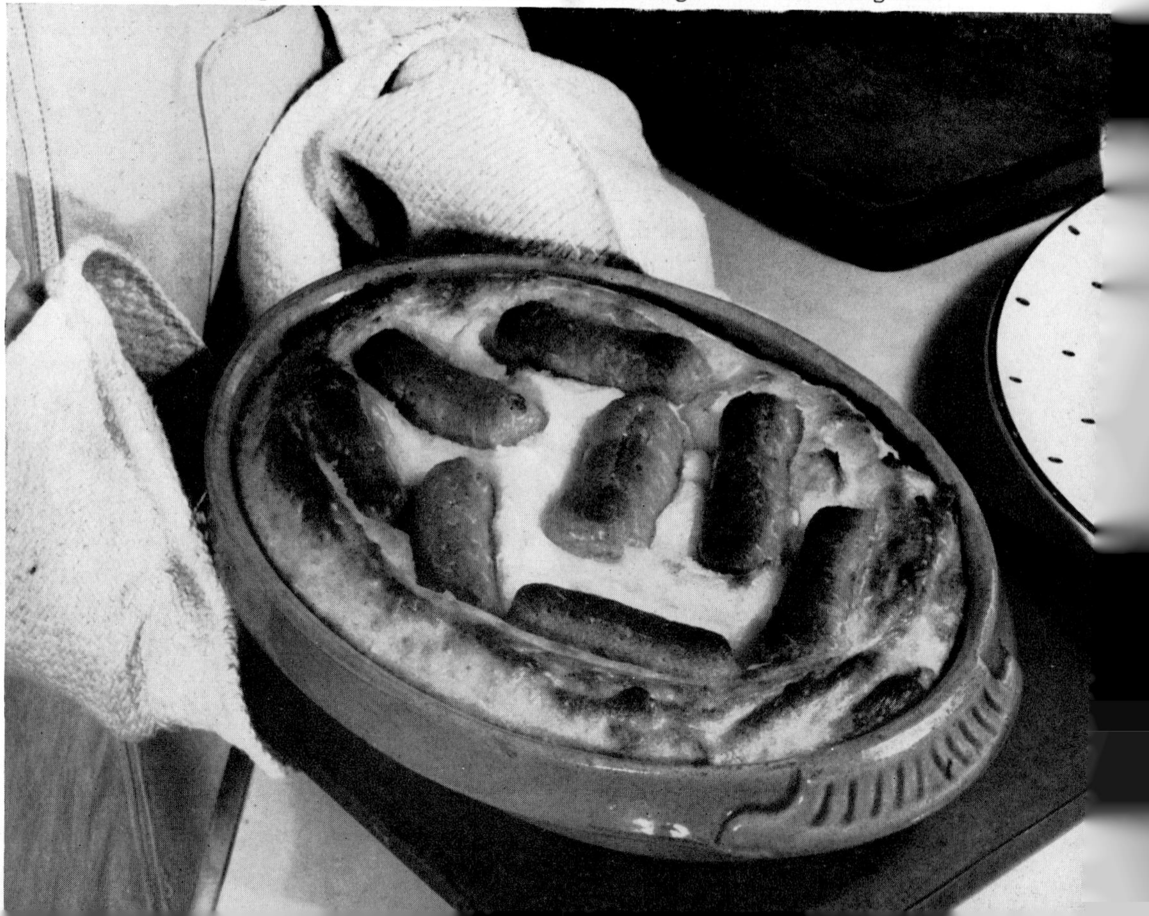

90a) Pancakes: Mix batter to a creamy consistency, working in flour gradually.

90b) Beat, using a wooden spoon, until bubbles appear and remain for a moment.

90c) Grease a pan very lightly and pour some batter from a jug into the centre.

90d) Tilt pan to work mixture to edge, and cook till golden-brown on underside.

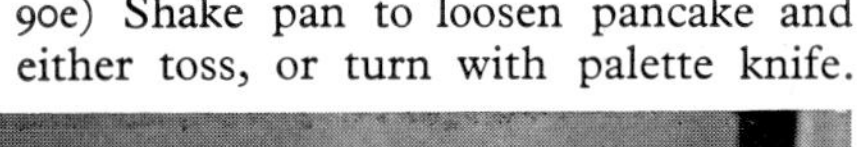

90e) Shake pan to loosen pancake and either toss, or turn with palette knife.

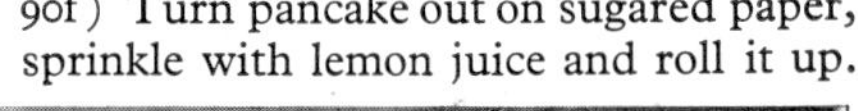

90f) Turn pancake out on sugared paper, sprinkle with lemon juice and roll it up.

91
-
92

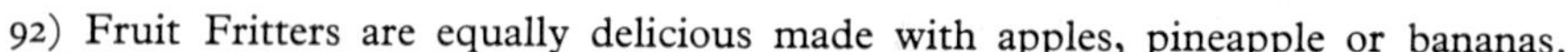

91) For a special dinner party, try Crêpes Suzette, made at table in a chafing dish.

92) Fruit Fritters are equally delicious made with apples, pineapple or bananas.

93a) Waffles: Prepare iron by brushing with oil or clarified fat and heating it.

93b) Just cover the surface of the iron with the waffle mixture and close the iron.

93c) Cook on both sides for the required time, open the iron and loosen the waffle.

93d) Serve sweet waffles with a suitable topping—jam, syrup, honey or cream.

94 - 95

94) (*above*): Hot Soufflé dusted with sugar.
95) (*below*): Cold Soufflé with piped cream.

96) (*opposite*): Cold Sweets—see the chapters on Fruits and on Jellies and Creams.

97
-
98

97) Fruit-filled Orange Baskets, pinked with scissors, and with angelica handles.
98) Crème Waflen, decorated with fruit and ratafia biscuits, tied with gay ribbon.

99
-
100

99) Nougat Pudding is a favourite with children, who love its texture and flavour.
100) Apricots in Brandy, made with fresh, bottled or tinned fruit and cream, etc.

101 - 102

101) Ice Cream Sundaes, with nuts, chocolate sauce, fruit, cream or jelly, and jam.

102) Peach Melba, topped with cream. Use a home-made or bought Melba sauce.

103
-
104

103) Baked Alaska, a delicious combination of ice cream and fluffy meringue.

104) Chocolate Refrigerator Cake, chilled, then completely masked with cream.

105 - 106

105) Cocktail Savouries, all arranged attractively around a centrepiece of cheese straws.

106) Hot Savouries, which include curried banana, prunes and bacon, piquant sardines.

107
-
108

107) Afternoon Scones, Malt Bread, Girdle Scones, and Scotch Pancakes for family tea.

108) Simple Yeast Breads are easily prepared, and taste excellent either plain or toasted.

109
-
111

109) Spicy-flavoured Hot Cross Buns are served warm for breakfast on Good Friday.

110) Savarin, marinated with fruit syrup, is served cold with fresh fruit salad.

111) Chelsea Buns, Croissants, Brioches, and an Iced Ring (a variation of Yeast Ribbon Cake).

112 - 113

112) " Cut-and-come-again" Cakes for hungry families. (See Cake-making chapter).

113) Cherry and Coffee Cakes, Raspberry and Rock Buns, from rubbed-in mixtures.

114
-
115

114) Rich Cakes, with a variety of simple finishes: glacé icing, American frosting, nuts, etc.

115) A selection of Small Cakes: Cherry and Lemon Slices, Gems, Queen Cakes, Madeleines

116

-

117

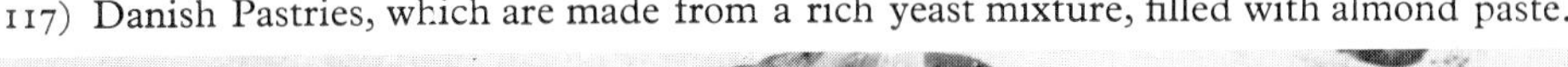

116) Rich Strawberry Gâteau, filled with crushed fruit and cream, dredged with sugar.

117) Danish Pastries, which are made from a rich yeast mixture, filled with almond paste.

118a) Forcing Bag: Fold a 9-inch square of greaseproof paper in halves diagonally.

118b) Fold paper into a cone as shown, wrapping the left-hand corner well round.

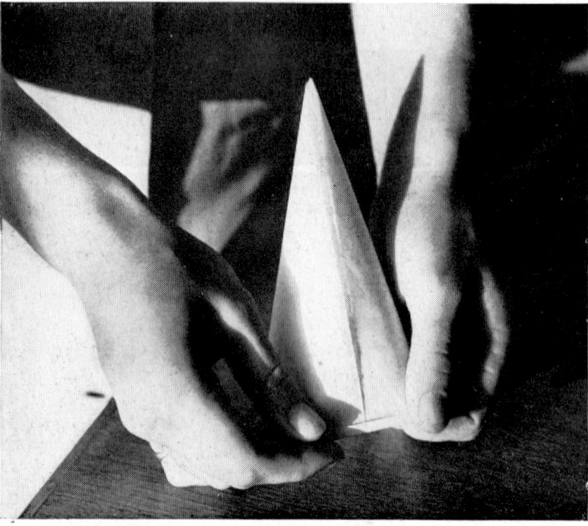

118c) Arrange paper so that the corners overlap, folding several times to secure.

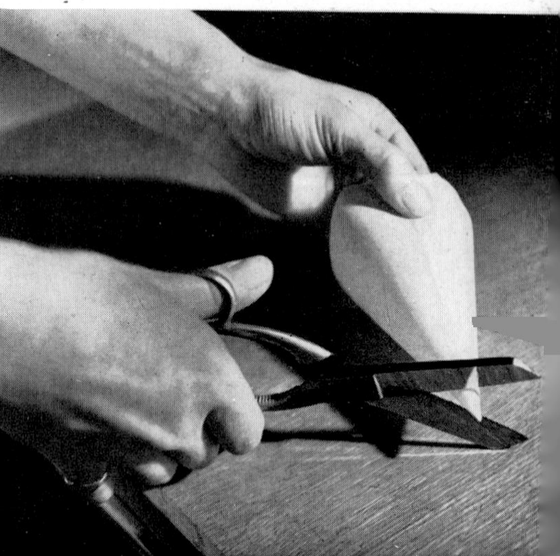

118d) Cut off the tip so that the metal nozzle protrudes from the end of the bag.

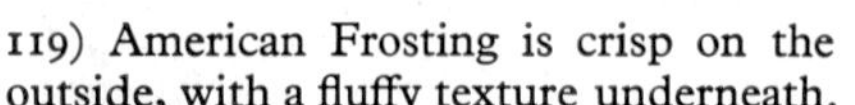

119) American Frosting is crisp on the outside, with a fluffy texture underneath.

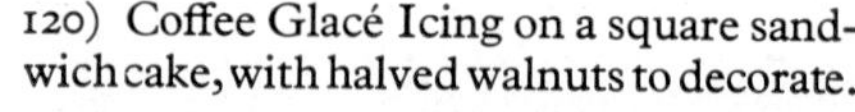

120) Coffee Glacé Icing on a square sandwich cake, with halved walnuts to decorate.

121a) Before piping Sugar Roses, attach a paper square to an icing nail with icing.

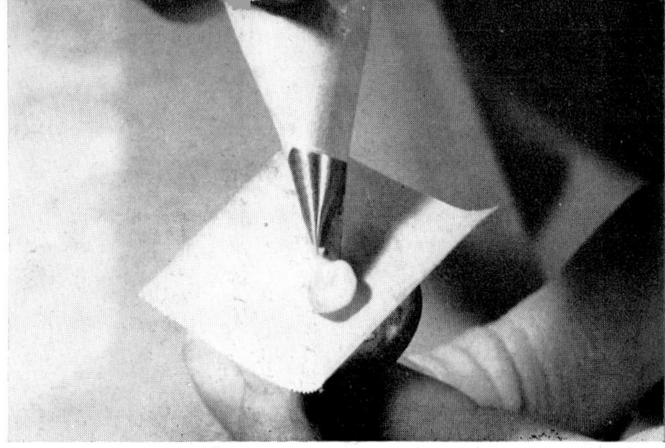

121b) Using a petal nozzle, with the broad edge next the paper, work the rose centre.

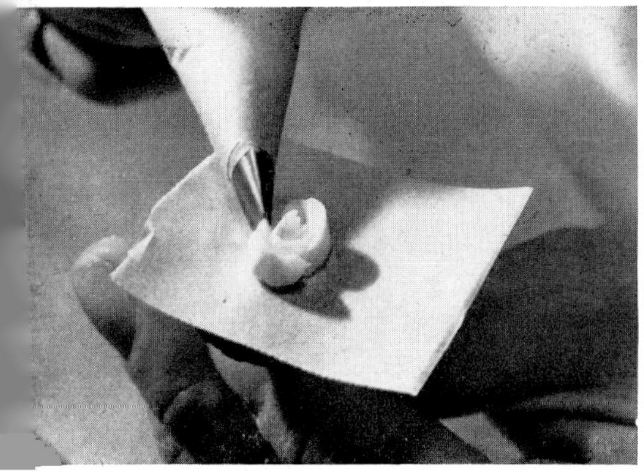

121c) Now pipe each petal separately, keeping the first few close to the centre.

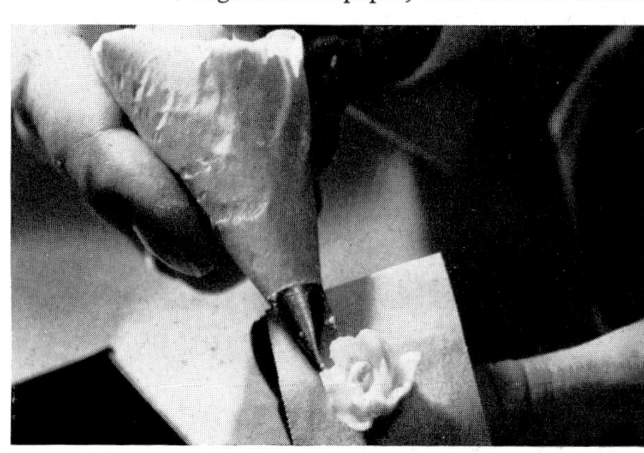

121d) Pipe larger petals round the outside, and gradually "open out" the flower.

122a) To work Flat Trellis Icing on the cake, pipe straight lines of royal icing.

122b) Many designs can be produced with trellis; a "check" effect is shown above.

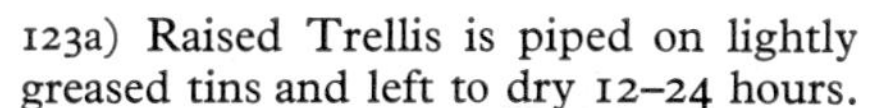

123a) Raised Trellis is piped on lightly greased tins and left to dry 12–24 hours.

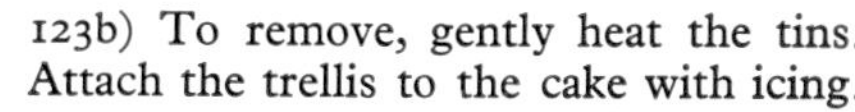

123b) To remove, gently heat the tins. Attach the trellis to the cake with icing.

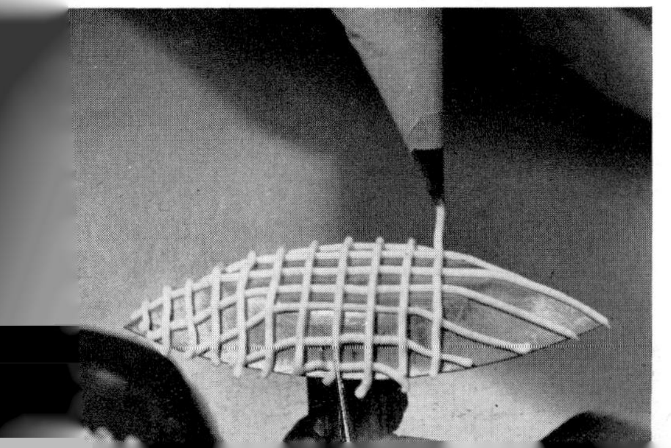

124

124, 125, 126) A Wedding Cake, Christmas Cake and Anniversary Cake, showing the use of different kinds of piped icing, combined with silver leaves and balls, coloured ribbons, etc.

127
-
131

127) Feather-icing in contrasting colours is used to decorate all kinds of cakes.

128) Coffee Yule Log: Pipe butter icing with a star nozzle, or rough up with fork.

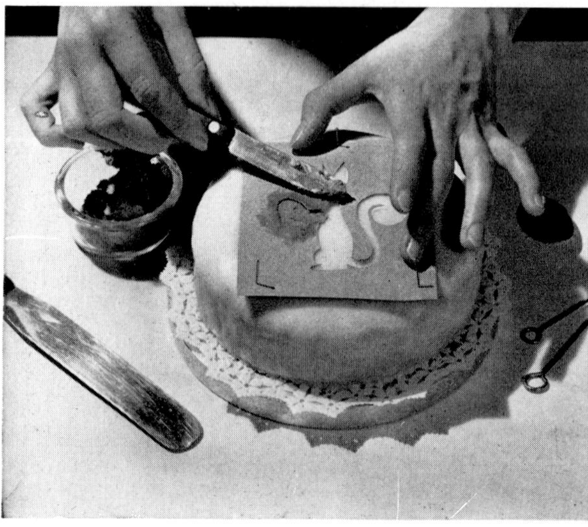

129a) Stencil Decoration; let the icing set, then apply some soft butter icing.

129b) Carefully remove stencil, add any extra touches, and finish with piped stars.

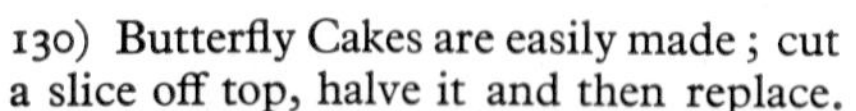

130) Butterfly Cakes are easily made; cut a slice off top, halve it and then replace.

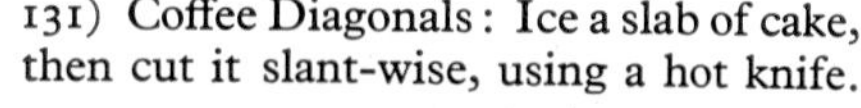

131) Coffee Diagonals: Ice a slab of cake, then cut it slant-wise, using a hot knife.

132
-
133

132) Meringues served with fruit and ice cream make an excellent sweet for parties.

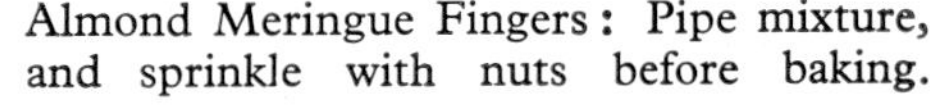
Almond Meringue Fingers: Pipe mixture, and sprinkle with nuts before baking.

133a) Éclairs: Add the filling, then coat with chocolate or coffee glacé icing.

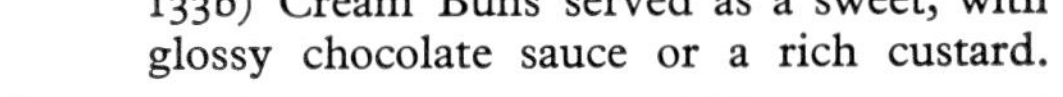
133b) Cream Buns served as a sweet, with glossy chocolate sauce or a rich custard.

134) Biscuit Dough is easily and quickly cut in shapes with a serrated pastry wheel.

135) Many different-shaped biscuits can be produced with a metal biscuit pump.

136a) Sugar Press Cookies can be left plain or iced. Keep them in airtight tins.

136b) These Piped Fingers can be sandwiched together with a filling, if desired.

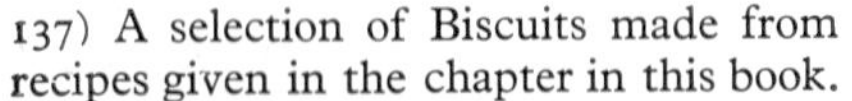

137) A selection of Biscuits made from recipes given in the chapter in this book.

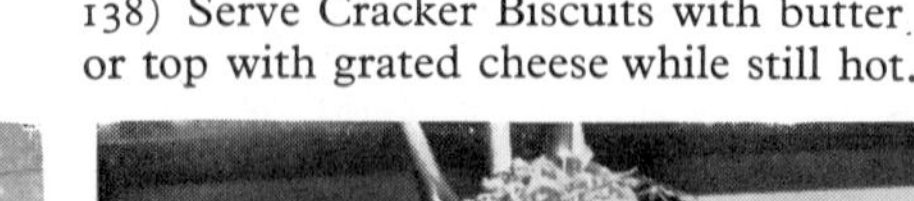

138) Serve Cracker Biscuits with butter or top with grated cheese while still hot.

139a) Fondants: Pour the syrup on to a wetted marble slab or suitable surface.

139b) When it is beginning to set at outside edge, " turn " with a palette knife.

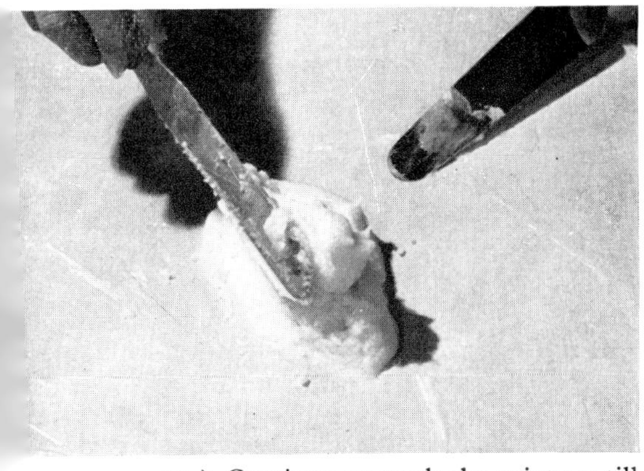

139c) Continue to work the mixture till it is pliable and cool enough to handle.

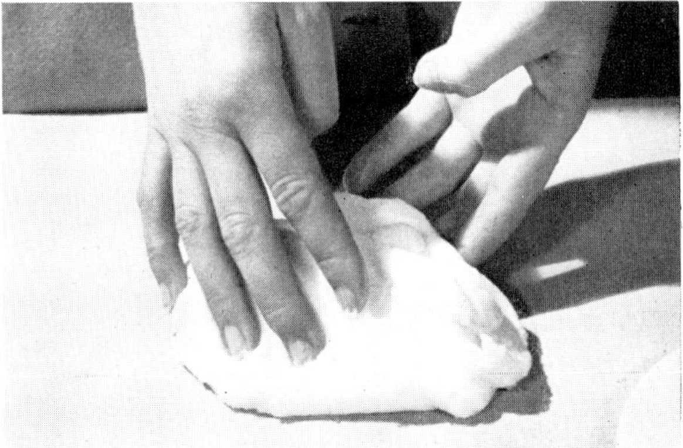

139d) Knead fondant in the hands till smooth and creamy; store in airtight jars.

139e) When the fondant is required for use, melt and then mould it—see page 428.

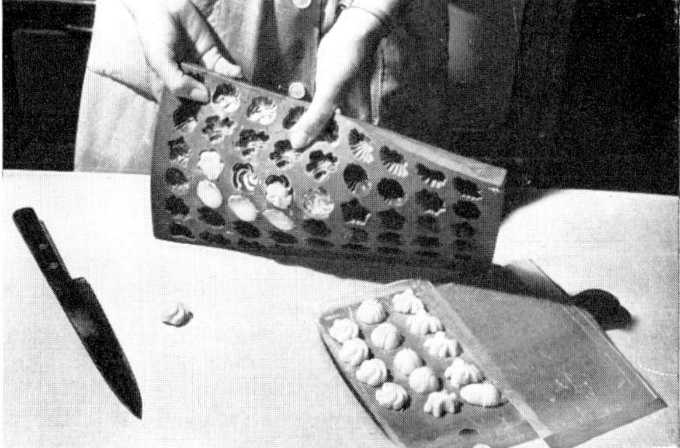

139f) Turn the fondants out when set, and decorate, or use as chocolate centres.

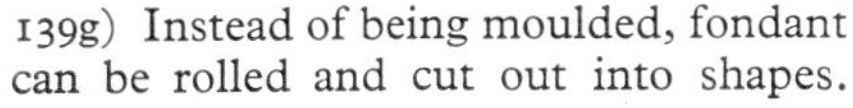

139g) Instead of being moulded, fondant can be rolled and cut out into shapes.

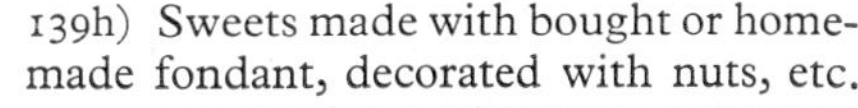

139h) Sweets made with bought or home-made fondant, decorated with nuts, etc.

WHAT IS POPCORN?

★ **POPCORN** was discovered by Red Indians who dropped grains of maize on their fire by accident. It has been a firm favourite in America ever since.

★ **POPCORN is easy to make.**
You buy the raw grain and pop it in fat on your cooker. One layer of grain bursts into a saucepanful of crisp, golden popcorn.

★ **POPCORN is versatile.**
Sprinkled with salt or grated cheese it is the perfect snack to go with drinks or TV. Toss it in melted chocolate or sugar, form it into different shapes and you'll always have a surprise up your sleeve.

★ **POPCORN is fun.**
Let your guests help pop it . . . it's an infallible ice-breaker. And for extra effect—you can always forget to put the lid on!

★ **POPCORN is health-giving.**
It contains more food energy than 96% of all foods. One pound of popcorn contains more protein than one pound of lean steak. And doctors in America have shown that popcorn when flavoured with salt and melted butter does real good to your children's teeth.

AMAZO cartons and BONNIE LEE cans *are available at leading stores or from the sole distributors:*
HOLBORN CEREALS LIMITED, 495, OXFORD STREET, LONDON, W.1

140a) Pulled Toffee: Pour the syrup out on to an oiled heat-resisting surface.

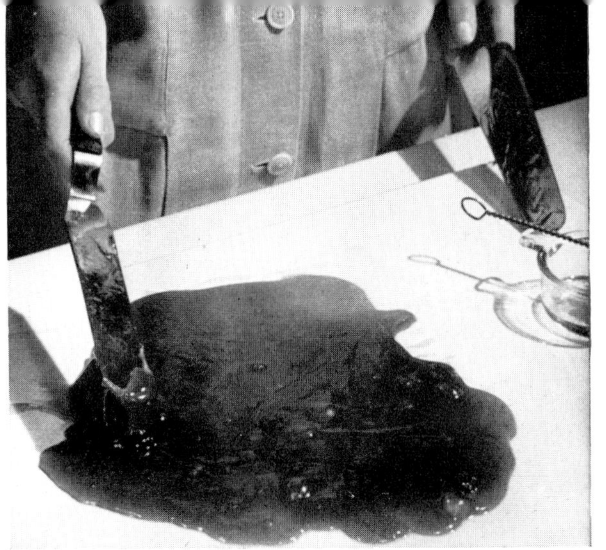

140b) When a skin forms on the surface, gradually "turn" mixture in at the edges.

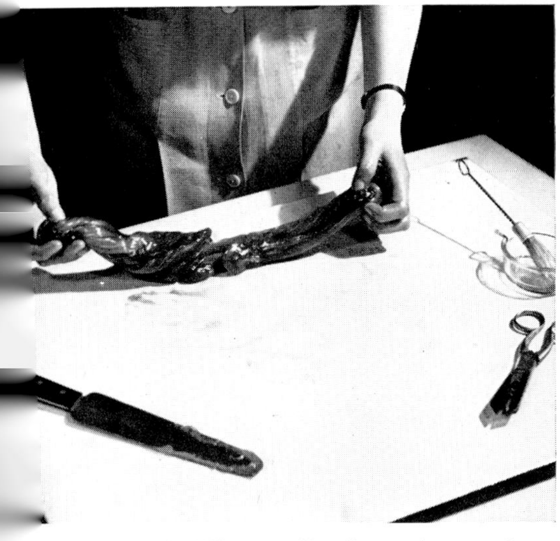

140c) When toffee is cool enough to handle, oil hands and form it into a rope.

140d) Pull and twist the toffee till it has a good sheen, and begins to harden.

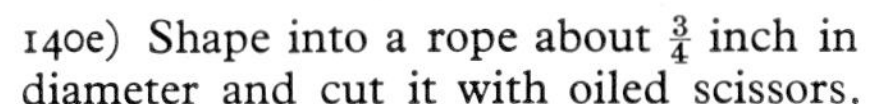

140e) Shape into a rope about $\frac{3}{4}$ inch in diameter and cut it with oiled scissors.

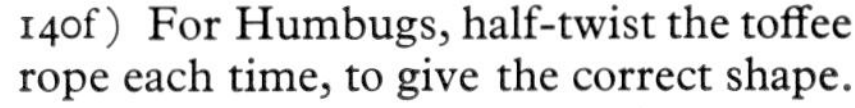

140f) For Humbugs, half-twist the toffee rope each time, to give the correct shape.

141
-
142

141 and 142) Wrap all toffee sweets in waxed or transparent cellulose paper. Store in airtight tins, or if the sweets are intended for a present, pack them in gay boxes.

143) Under-water method of Bottling: Use a steriliser or bucket, with water to cover.

144) Oven Bottling: If no liquid is added before sterilising, cover jars with tins.

145) Bottled Fruit Syrup: Fill bottles up to within about 2 inches of the top, and seal.

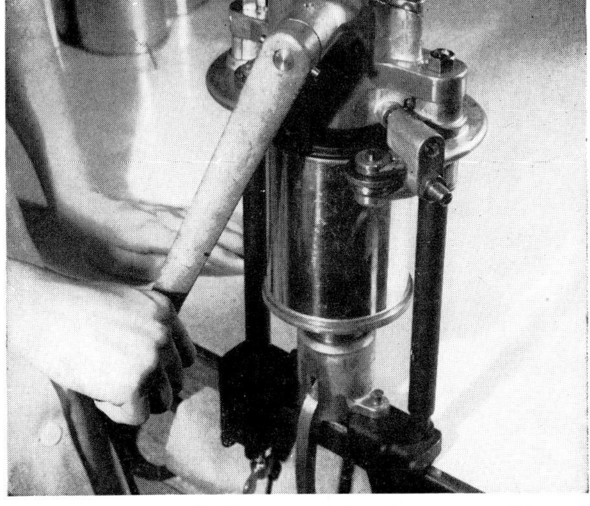

146) For preserving large quantities of fruit, a canning machine is invaluable.

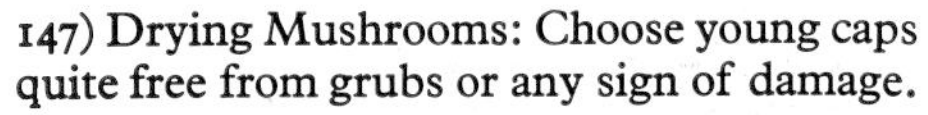

147) Drying Mushrooms: Choose young caps quite free from grubs or any sign of damage.

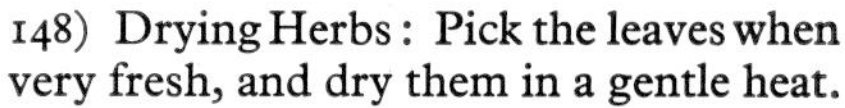

148) Drying Herbs: Pick the leaves when very fresh, and dry them in a gentle heat.

149a) Pressure-cooking: Put food on the rack with salt and water; do not fill pan.

149b) Fix lid, put over heat, and when steam flows, put on 15 lb. weight, or—

149c)—adjust pressure-control device as directed. (See chapter for cooking times.)

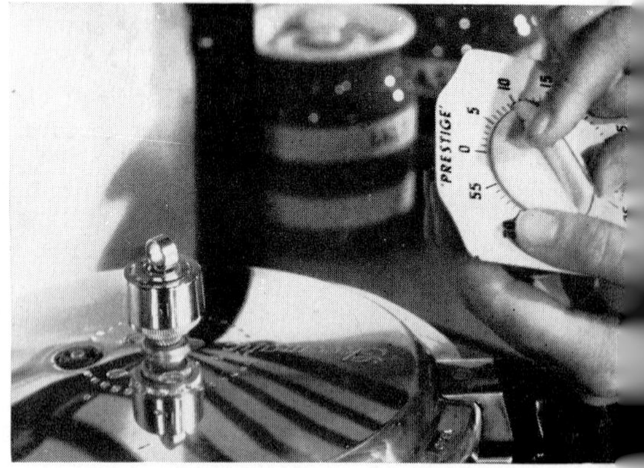

149d) Start timing when a loud hiss is heard, and then lower the heat somewhat.

149e) At end of the cooking time, reduce pressure as directed by the manufacturer.

149f) Lift control device slightly; if steam escapes, cool pan further before opening.

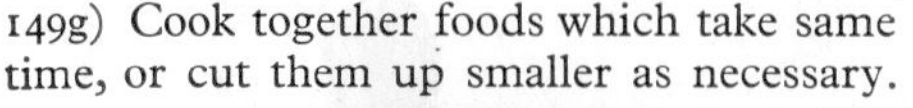

149g) Cook together foods which take same time, or cut them up smaller as necessary.

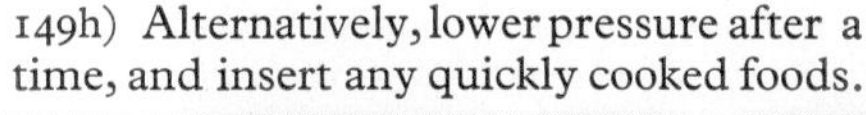

149h) Alternatively, lower pressure after a time, and insert any quickly cooked foods.

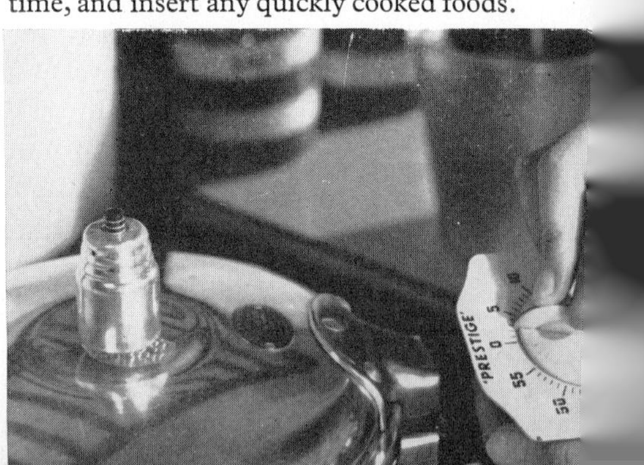

beans as given under Pulse Vegetables. Sauté the chopped onion and add the beans and remaining ingredients, mixing well. Fill the marrow with the stuffing, press the halves together, wrap in greased greaseproof paper, and tie. Put on the rack in the pan, add ½ pint water, and pressure-cook for 8–10 minutes, according to size. Reduce the pressure immediately. Serve on a hot dish, coated with cheese sauce.

LEEK AND CELERY CHEESE

1 lb. leeks	¾ pint milk
8–10 sticks of celery	¼ pint vegetable liquor
Salt	Seasoning
2 oz. margarine	½ tsp. mustard
2 oz. flour	2 oz. grated cheese

Wash and soak the leeks and cut in half lengthwise; scrub the celery and cut into convenient lengths. Put ½ pint water in the pan, stand the vegetables on the rack and sprinkle with salt. Pressure-cook at 15 lb. for 3 minutes. Reduce pressure and place the vegetables in a fireproof dish. Melt the margarine in a pan and add the flour gradually, then add the liquids, stirring all the time. Boil for 3 minutes, season well, and add the mustard. Remove from the heat and add the cheese, leaving a little to sprinkle on the top. Coat the vegetables with the cheese sauce, sprinkle with cheese and brown under the grill.

POACHED MUSHROOMS

Place the whole prepared mushrooms in ¼ pint hot milk in a small casserole and stand it on rack, with ¼ pint water in the pan. Pressure-cook for 4–5 minutes, and reduce the pressure slowly.

STUFFED ONIONS

Prepare 4 medium-sized Spanish onions, put them on a rack in the pan, add ¼ pint water, pressure-cook for 3 minutes at 15 lb., and reduce the pressure immediately. Remove the centre core from the onions, chop finely and mix with 4 oz. breadcrumbs, 1 beaten egg, 1 oz. grated cheese, and some seasoning. Fill the cavity in each onion with this mixture, wrap each in well-greased greaseproof paper and return to the rack in the pan. Pressure-cook for 5–6 minutes, according to size of onions. Reduce the pressure immediately, and, if desired, brown the onions under a hot grill for a few minutes. Serve with a white or cheese sauce.

SAVOURY MACARONI

4 oz. macaroni	1 pint tomato juice
2 oz. dripping	2 tsps. made mustard
2 medium-sized onions	A little vinegar
2 oz. mushrooms	Browned crumbs
2 rashers of streaky bacon	1–2 oz. grated cheese
2 tbsps. cornflour	Sliced tomato and mushrooms to garnish

Pressure-cook the macaroni in 1 quart water for 6 minutes and drain it. Meanwhile, melt the fat in a saucepan and fry the chopped onions, mushrooms, and diced bacon till golden-brown. Blend the cornflour with a little of the tomato juice, and pour the remaining juice into the pan; bring to the boil, and thicken with the blended cornflour, cooking it for 4–5 minutes. Season with the mustard, blended with the vinegar, and add the macaroni. Pour into a shallow dish, sprinkle with the crumbs and cheese, and garnish with tomato and mushrooms, brush these with margarine, then grill for 2–3 minutes.

CHRISTMAS PUDDING

Follow the directions given with the ordinary recipes for ingredients and preparation. Darken the mixture with black treacle, browning, or coffee essence. Place the mixture in one or more greased basins, but do not press down; cover tightly with greased paper and a cloth. Put 2½ pints boiling water in the pan, place the basin on the rack, and steam rapidly for ½ hour without pressure, then pressure-cook at 15 lb. for 1½ hours. Reduce pressure gradually. Store the puddings in usual way, and before serving them, pressure-cook for a further 25–30 minutes at 15 lb.

FRUIT SUETCRUST PUDDING

8 oz. self-raising flour	1½ lb. prepared apples, gooseberries, plums, etc.
A pinch of salt	4–5 oz. sugar
2–3 oz. margarine or chopped suet	
Cold water	

Sieve the flour and salt together. Rub in the margarine or add the chopped suet, and mix to a firm dough with cold water. Turn on to a floured board, cut off one-third of pastry and reserve for the top. Roll out the larger piece and line a greased basin with it. Fill up with fruit, sprinkle with sugar, and add a little water. Top with the remaining pastry. Cover with greased paper and a cloth, stand the basin on the rack in the pan in boiling water, fix the lid, and steam with the pressure control off for 15 minutes over low heat. Pressure-cook for 45 minutes at 10 lb. pressure, or 40 minutes at 15 lb. Reduce the pressure slowly.

GOLDEN SYRUP PUDDING

8 oz. self-raising flour
2 tsps. ground ginger
A pinch of salt
4 oz. prepared suet or margarine
2 oz. sugar
1 egg (optional)
Milk to mix
3 tbsps. syrup

Sieve the dry ingredients, add the suet or rub in the margarine, and add the sugar. Mix with the egg and milk, to give a soft dropping consistency. Put the syrup in a well-greased basin, add the mixture, and cover. Stand the pudding on the rack in boiling water, and steam it for 20 minutes, then cook for 35 minutes at 10 lb. pressure, or for 30 minutes at 15 lb. Reduce pressure slowly.

CREAMED RICE

$\frac{1}{4}$–1 oz. margarine
1 pint milk
2 oz. rice
1 oz. sugar
Flavouring, e.g. vanilla or lemon

Melt the margarine in the bottom of the pan, Add milk and bring to the boil in the open pan, then add the rice, sugar, and flavouring. Stir well, lower the heat, cover, and bring to pressure slowly over a low heat. Pressure-cook for 15 minutes, and allow the pressure to drop gradually. Serve hot or cold.

APRICOT JAM

$\frac{1}{2}$ lb. dried apricots
$\frac{1}{2}$ pint water
$1\frac{1}{2}$ lb. sugar
Juice of $\frac{1}{2}$ a lemon
2 oz. blanched almonds (optional)

Soak the apricots in the water overnight. Put the fruit and water into the pan and pressure-cook for 10 minutes. Allow pressure to drop gradually, then open the cooker and stir in the sugar, lemon juice, and almonds. Bring to the boil and cook without a lid until the jam sets when tested. Pot and cover immediately.

ORANGE MARMALADE

2 lb. Seville oranges
2 pints water
Juice of 2 lemons
4 lb. sugar

Wipe and halve the fruit, remove the pips and tie them in muslin. Slice the fruit finely and soak overnight in the water and juice, with the bag of pips. The next day, cook the fruit in the pressure pan at 15 lb. for 20 minutes, and reduce the pressure gradually. Remove the bag of pips, squeezing it dry, add the sugar, bring to the boil, and boil rapidly until a set is obtained. Leave to cool before filling into jars.

PLANNING THE KITCHEN

While good cookery does not depend on perfect surroundings, there is no doubt that a well-planned and equipped kitchen adds immeasurably to one's pleasure in cooking, and saves a vast amount of cleaning and of unnecessary running to and fro. Few housewives to-day have domestic help, and they must of necessity spend much time in the kitchen, so it is worth while giving thought and care to its planning, if necessary building it up bit by bit as circumstances and finances permit. Even if it is impossible to obtain new equipment, existing furniture and fittings can often be so re-arranged so as to give maximum convenience.

A good kitchen should be planned on paper first. The general underlying principles of kitchen arrangement, summarised below, are relatively simple, but there is such a vast range of equipment on the market to-day that it does take a certain amount of time and effort to gather together all the relevant information about available types and finishes.

The idea of work centres should always be kept firmly in mind when planning any kitchen. The food preparation centre, the stove, and the sink should be assembled in close vicinity to one another, and as far as possible everything required for the operations of mixing, cooking, washing up, and dishing should be close at hand. In the case of the food preparation centre, this can probably be best achieved by fitting wall cabinets for dry stores immediately above the work bench, and providing underneath it drawers and cupboards to accomodate small tools, gadgets, bowls, tins, etc.

Plans and illustrations of two modern kitchens are given at the end of this chapter.

GENERAL PRINCIPLES OF PLANNING

1. The kitchen should be made bright and cheerful, with wise use of colour and good lighting, and it should be well ventilated without being draughty.

2. The work centres should be well arranged, with the sink, the stove, and the main working surfaces close together, to avoid unnecessary walking about.

3. When planning a completely new kitchen, aim at a U-shaped one if possible, with equipment ranged round three walls, as this is on the whole the most convenient arrangement. When modernising an old one—possibly far too large for real convenience—it is often best to plan the new kitchen round a corner of the room, so as to get all the equipment reasonably concentrated, and so make for easier working and the minimum of walking to and fro.

4. Fittings and equipment should be of convenient height, and adapted if necessary to the height of the individual.

5. There should be ample and convenient storage facilities.

6. The equipment should be selected to suit the size and type of household.

7. The kitchen should be easily cleaned, with suitable grease-resisting finishes, and no mouldings and awkward corners.

LIGHTING, VENTILATION, COLOUR

Lighting : Equipment should be placed so as to make best use of daylight. When this can be arranged, it is usually found best to fit the sink or sink unit immediately in front of a window, and the cooker also should be in as good a light as possible. Where natural lighting is poor it is particularly important to choose the lightest of tints for the walls. The artificial lighting should, if possible, be planned to give light from the same direction as the daylight.

Ventilation : Good ventilation is essential in the kitchen to prevent condensation of moisture on walls and ceiling and to disperse cooking smells. It may be sufficient if the kitchen window is kept slightly open whenever cooking is in progress, but often this is not really adequate. A canopy with an outlet fitted over the cooker often makes all the difference, particularly if there is much cooking done. Alternatively, or even in addition to the canopy, an electrically operated exhaust fan fitted in the upper part of the window will help to ensure quick removal of cooking odours and steam.

Colour : For a kitchen with a cool outlook, cream and signal red look well together, and so do dusty pink and soft grey ; primrose yellow and silver-grey are other alternatives ; if you have a kitchen with a warm aspect, choose white and steel blue, or a silver-grey with blue.

Colour can be introduced in many ways. You may, for instance, like to keep the walls and woodwork white or neutral and install coloured cabinets, not necessarily all the same shade ; in this way a very gay effect can be given. You may, on the other hand, prefer to concentrate on brightly coloured working tops, tiles or glass panels. Indeed, there are endless possibilities for giving a free run to your fancy, and so achieving a kitchen which reflects your own tastes and personality. Incidentally, a few flowers on the window ledge, or on a high shelf, will improve even the most shining and attractive of kitchens, giving it a more " human " note.

SURFACES AND FINISHES

The most spectacular advances have occurred during recent years in regard to easily cleaned, non-absorbent surfaces, which are resistant to grease, and which require no more than a wipe over to keep them spotless. At the same time the various old and tried finishes should not be entirely overlooked or discarded, for many of them still hold their own successfully.

Walls : Where a relatively inexpensive wall finish is required, there is much to be said for glossy paint or enamel, or a semi-matt oil-based paint, which is particularly suitable if much condensation occurs. A washable, steam-resistant wall-paper can be used effectively in the part of the kitchen least exposed to steam and heat. Tiling is still a good choice round sinks and behind stoves ; the tiles may be of the standard type, which are now available for home fixing, or of the new plastic variety, which can be easily fixed by the housewife or the handyman. Another alternative is stoved enamelled panelling, in either a smooth or a mock-tile finish.

Ceiling : Like the walls, this should have an easily cleaned finish. Paint or enamel is more suitable than distemper or whitewash ; a rubber-based paint is a good choice, particularly if condensation is a trouble.

Floors : A reliable make of vinyl plastic flooring, in either sheet or tile form, is particularly suitable for the kitchen. Good Housekeeping Institute tests have shown it to be durable, resistant to marks and stains, and therefore, easily cleaned and maintained—with or without polishing as preferred. This type of flooring has the advantage of a slight resilience, which makes it less tiring than a too hard floor.

Linoleum makes an excellent and relatively inexpensive floor covering, provided it is fixed with waterproof adhesive, so that water does not penetrate the canvas backing and cause rotting and deterioration. In addition to the sheet form, linoleum tiles are now available, and if the makers' instructions are carefully followed, they can be laid by the amateur to give a very professional-looking floor, either in a single colour or to a special design. It is always worth while buying a reasonably good quality linoleum ; from the practical point of view, one with a broken, rather than a plain, pattern is advised, as it does not show footmarks so readily. To protect and preserve it, linoleum should be regularly polished, or treated with a plastic seal.

Quarry tiles make a satisfactory and easily cleaned flooring, but are rather cold to the feet unless fairly heavy shoes are worn.

Sheet rubber coverings are not grease-resistant, and are therefore not suitable for the kitchen. They become " tacky " in use and water-mark easily ; the surface is quickly damaged by grit from shoes, by coal dust, ash, etc., and it is not sufficiently resistant to heat when fitted under a gas stove or close to an independent boiler.

Polished parquet and hardwood floors are unsuitable for use in the kitchen, since they stain easily and are non-resistant to grease, unless treated with a floor seal. Unpolished wood also stains rapidly, and is dusty.

Tables and Working Tops : Laminated plastic sheets are perhaps the first choice here. Admittedly they are a little expensive, but they have many advantages : they look attractive, are available in a wide range of pastel and other colours, and can be used not only on new fitments but for bringing old ones up to date. For covering an old table, a cabinet, or low cupboard, etc., panels can be obtained with detailed instructions for fixing ; beading, etc., to neaten the edge is also obtainable.

For covering any surfaces that are not going to have very heavy use, flexible self-adhesive plastic sheeting is useful. This is made for home fixing, in two qualities—heavy for table tops, and a thinner one for covering shelves, etc. The sheeting comes in colours and designs to match some of the laminated plastics.

Stainless steel and vitreous enamel are among the other easily cleaned surfaces.

SINKS, CABINETS AND TABLES

The Sink or Sink Unit: This is such an important and constantly used item of kitchen equipment that its choice and installation demand the most careful consideration. As already mentioned, it is on the whole most practical to fit the sink immediately in front of a window, and for most people the top rim should be 35–36 inches from the floor.

Stainless steel sinks continue to increase in popularity. Grease does not cling to them, since steel is a good conductor of heat and is quickly warmed by hot liquids, and the rounded corners are very easy to keep clean. In addition to the ordinary rectangular type, bowl-shaped sinks are now obtainable for those who prefer them.

Glazed earthenware sinks are available in attractive pastel shades, in addition to white. They are a little more troublesome than metal to keep clean and free from stains, and it is important to avoid using scratchy abrasive cleaners; these soon roughen and impair the surface, with the result that not only is the appearance of the sink marred, but it is apt to become more readily stained as time passes.

There are two main types of vitreous enamel sinks—with an enamel finish on either cast iron or sheet metal. The former are more expensive, but harder wearing. However, good quality vitreous enamel on sheet metal will give reasonable wear, provided the sink is carefully used; the finish may chip if pans are dropped on it.

Sinks of moulded fibre-glass are now available in attractive colours. It is too soon to say how they compare in wearing quality with the above types; they have the advantage, however, of being relatively inexpensive. It is important to avoid scratching the surface of these sinks.

Complete sink units are available with cupboards underneath (often fitted with a removable garbage bin and vegetable rack).

Cabinets, Cupboards and Tables: Plenty of storage space is vital to every kitchen, and to-day this need is met by many makes of unit furniture, which considerably simplify kitchen-planning. A large variety of cabinets is available, some constructed of wood and others of metal. In most cases the range includes wall cupboards, floor cabinets with counter tops, and broom cupboards, as well as "fillers" and corner fitments. In many cases the fitments are available in green, blue, pink, and other colours, in addition to the more usual cream and white.

Before buying cabinets, it is essential to have a detailed plan worked out for your kitchen, so that you know exactly what you want. Even if you start with the minimum fitments and then add to them as required, it is just as important to have the complete plan drawn up first. When selecting cabinets, points to look for are well-fitting doors, drawers that run quietly and easily (one or two should be partitioned for cutlery and small gadgets), and ample shelving.

Don't forget to see that the height of your work table or bench is suitable. For mixing and creaming operations, etc., most people consider 32–33 inches convenient, but the standard counter fitment height, 36 inches, is, of course, suitable for many other jobs. Where space allows, a centre table at the slightly lower height usually meets requirements adequately.

REFRIGERATORS

There are two main types of domestic refrigerator. One is provided with a motor and compressor, which is of necessity electrically operated. The other, which is quite noiseless in operation, is of the absorption type, the compressor being eliminated and the necessary circulation of refrigerant gases being effected by the application of heat; the heat can be supplied by means of a small gas burner, an electric element, or even an oil burner. Bottled gas can also be used to operate the latter type, making it very convenient in country districts.

The size of refrigerator required depends not only on the number in the household, but also on whether or not the house possesses a good, cool larder. In the former case, a small refrigerator is sufficient to store most perishables. If the house contains no larder, however, it is generally recommended that one should allow, if possible, something like 1 cubic foot of refrigerator storage capacity for each member of the household.

Various internal fitments are provided with the leading makes of domestic refrigerator; these greatly facilitate the storage of foods and enable one to make the best possible use of the cabinet. Running costs are very moderate, and with electricity and gas at average rates, amount to only a few pence per week. (For notes on using the refrigerator see the chapter on Shopping and Storage.)

Cooking Stoves—see next chapter.

A MODERN KITCHEN—PLAN A

A well-planned kitchen which makes the best use of limited space. Note the corner-wise arrangement of the working area, which cuts down all unnecessary walking to and fro. The position of the sink under the window is a choice which appeals to all practical housewives. Two draining-boards are included, giving ample space for dirty crockery and a plate-drainer. A washing machine is stowed under the left-hand drainer so that it is ready for use near the sink. The cooker is placed between two working surfaces, which are covered with a soft pink laminated plastic. This arrangement facilitates the preparation and dishing-up of meals, and the plastic surface is easy to clean. Modern unit type cabinets provide ample storage space for dry stores, and for kitchen tools and gadgets. Racks for tools in constant use are fixed over the working surface and cut out unnecessary rummaging in drawers. Note the toe recesses at the base of the units—an essential for comfort when you are standing at the sink or work counter.

A well-shelved larder is conveniently near the working surfaces, and a small refrigerator will provide sufficient storage space for perishable foods. The broom cupboard is as near to the main part of the house as possible, and extra storage cupboards fill the remaining space on this wall.

The breakfast nook is slightly apart from the

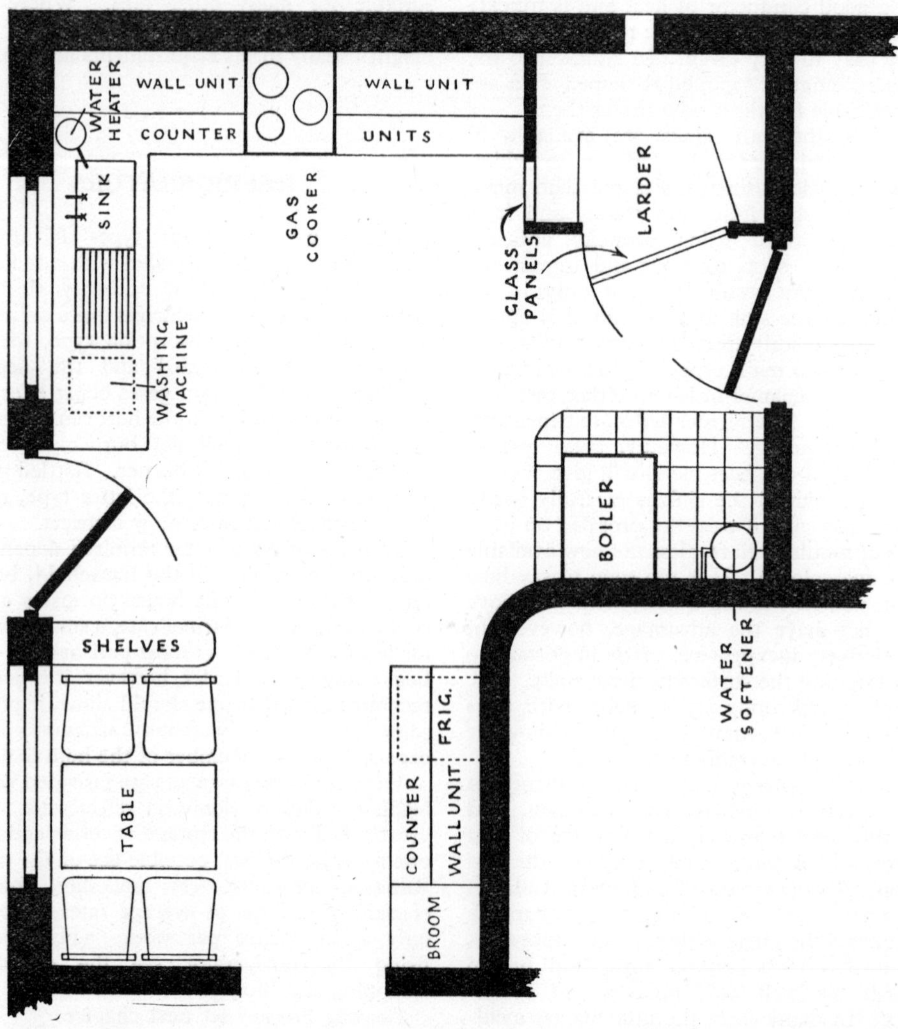

kitchen proper, and the shelved partition helps to segregate it from the main working area.

A solid-fuel boiler is used for domestic hot water, but a small sink heater has been installed as an alternative for the summer.

The floor is covered with plastic flooring which can be laid in sheet or tile form. A marbled grey is the colour chosen for this kitchen. The broken colour will not show the dirt as readily as a plain one. Quarry tiles round the boiler are easy to clean, and safe if hot ash should fall when the boiler is being attended to. There is ample room for fuel hods to stand, well out of the way, on this tiled area.

Plastic curtains add a note of gaiety to the kitchen. The south facing windows are shaded with coloured venetian blinds which can be adjusted to keep out the sun without excluding too much light. The central strip light should be sufficient for all working surfaces.

KITCHEN PLAN B

A modern kitchen with a new note. Although it undoubtedly has an air of individuality, this kitchen still remains an eminently practical and convenient workroom, with ample surfaces just where they are wanted by the busy cook. The colour scheme is good, as befits a present-day kitchen in which the housewife as a rule spends much of her time. The wall on the left inside is white, and the others red. An attractive paper has been used in the dining bay; this is the least steamy part of the kitchen, so wallpaper may be hung here. Soft brown laminated plastic makes a change for the counter tops, and the cabinets are white. The flooring is of green plastic tiles, which are easy to maintain without scrubbing or polishing, and reasonably warm to stand on.

Particular attention has been paid to the height of the working surfaces, which are provided at two levels. One is the standard height of 36 inches generally adopted for counter fitments, and the other a slightly lower height, which is less tiring and more practical for mixing and other operations. This lower level has been employed for the meal counter, which could also be used for working at when required.

Saucepans, etc. are all stored on slotted shelves near the sink.

The slow combustion stove is fitted to heat the

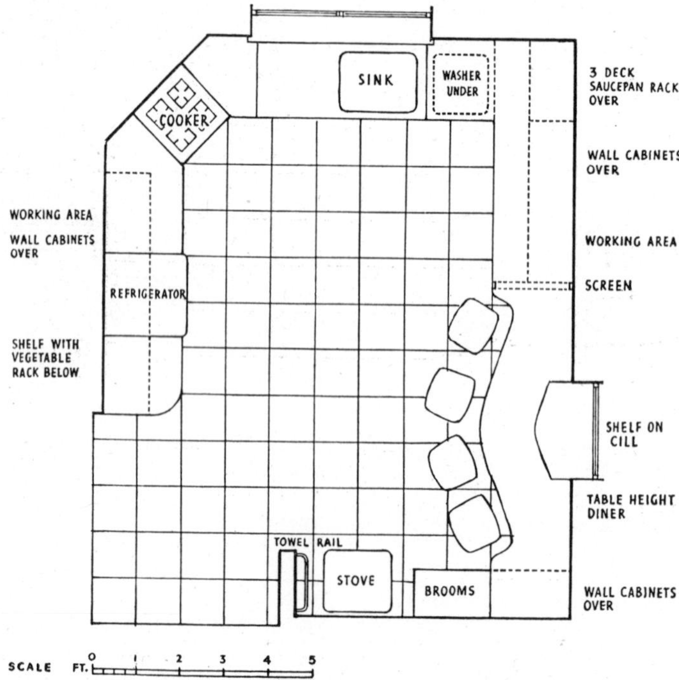

domestic hot water as well as the kitchen itself. When meals are taken in the kitchen the doors of the stove can be opened to show a cheerful fire. Towels can be dried on the rail near the stove.

A tall cupboard accommodates long-handled cleaning equipment and the ironing board, for which it is sometimes difficult to find a home. The vegetable rack and refrigerator are near the back door, so it is easy to put away groceries, etc. immediately on return from a shopping expedition.

Strip lighting over the sink and in the centre of the room will throw just the correct amount of light, and electric points for the washing machine, electric mixer, toaster, etc. are placed at convenient spots above the working counters.

A neat little rack holds any plates and other china likely to be used for meals taken in the kitchen, while the wide windowsill above the meal counter lends extra space to this area.

COOKERS AND COOKING TOOLS

THE COOKING STOVE

The housewife of to-day is fortunate in having available a very wide range of efficient cooking stoves and excellent cooking equipment.

Burnt cakes and pale, anaemic-looking pastries are seldom the fault of the modern cooking stove, and if the cook finds her baking a failure, she should first seek the cause of the trouble either in the faulty installation or adjustment of the cooker, or in her own management of it.

In the case of gas and electric cookers, if faulty adjustment is suspected the local supply authority should be called in. Solid fuel cookers, if properly installed, are unlikely to go wrong, though they must be managed correctly, the chimneys swept and flues kept clean. In case of maladjustment, consult the manufacturers.

Whether to select an electric, gas, solid fuel, or oil cooking stove obviously depends on individual circumstances and preference. Good Housekeeping Institute is satisfied that good service can be obtained from any of these types, provided a reliable make is selected.

ELECTRIC COOKERS

The advantages of an electric cooker are its extreme cleanliness, the absence of products of combustion, and the very even heat of the oven.

Boiling plates are of two main types :

1. The standard, solid type of plate, which is easy to clean and very durable. A refinement of this type is the lighter weight boiling plate with a central depression which offers faster adjustments of temperature ; with this type of boiling plate a six-heat switch offers a wider range of controlled temperatures.

2. Special radiant types of element, which have a metal-sheathed coil, and give variable visible red heat. These make quick boiling possible, and no special type of cooking utensil is needed.

An automatic time-switch, fitted to the oven and in some cases controlling one or more hot-plates, is a valuable feature of many new electric cookers. This means that the cooker can be set to switch itself on or off at the required time, and a meal left to cook without fear of spoiling. An automatic control unit can be fitted to an older type of cooker, if this is of suitable design.

An eye-level grill is incorporated in some electric cookers. Another type has a grill in the top of the oven, which is useful for people who like to have a large grilling space ; the grill cannot, however, be used at the same time as the oven. Both these arrangements permit the oven to be raised a little higher than in a standard cooker. Many electric cookers are fitted with a plate-warming drawer below the oven ; some of these are warmed by the heat from the oven, while others have a separate switch incorporating thermostatic control.

It is also possible to obtain separate oven and hot-plate units for building into a continuous working surface ; the oven is normally fixed at waist level, with the hot plates beside it.

Miniature electric cookers are especially suitable for people living in small flats. The table type also serves as an excellent auxiliary cooker ; the infra-red grill and the heat-controlled electric frying-pan are of particular interest.

The following notes will help you to get the best use from a standard electric cooker.

1. Use pans of the same size as the boiling plate or slightly larger. If the boiling plate is a flat one, use flat machine-based pans to make good contact with it.

2. Switch the current off several minutes before completion of baking and boiling.

3. Fill pans for vegetables, etc., from the hot water tap, and use only the minimum amount of water required.

4. Use the grill rather than the frying pan—grilling is the more efficient process on an electric range.

5. Avoid using the grill boiler unless the grill is also in use.

6. Make full use of the electric kettle for tea-making, etc.

7. Open the ventilator in the oven door (or, if no ventilator is provided, leave the oven door ajar) during the last stage of the cooling down ; this allows the steam to escape and prevents it condensing in the oven.

8. Try not to spill food or let pans over-boil on to the hot-plates—this is particularly important if the element is exposed. If spills do

occur, wipe them up immediately, first switching off the current—this is most important.

9. Wipe the cooker down after use, and clean it thoroughly as often as necessary. Switch off the current before beginning. The enamel boiling plate generally requires little more than a wipe with a damp cloth, with a little paste cleanser if needed. The oven should be washed over occasionally. Take care not to wet the element.

GAS COOKERS

Improvements are continually being added to the gas cooker. The stoves themselves are more streamlined, with easily cleaned, rounded corners, and coloured porcelain enamel finishes, while the burner grids are designed for easy cleaning, and are often in two sections only. A useful feature of the modern gas cooker is the level hot-plate, which enables a heavy pan to be drawn over the burner grid with no fear of its tipping. Good spillage trays are fitted under the burners.

Automatic ignition for the hot-plate is included on all new cookers. Safety taps and a fine adjustment of heat are common features. On some models the automatic ignition acts instantly, and should the flame accidentally blow out, the burner relights immediately. Many cookers have eye-level grills, some incorporating a rack for plate-warming.

The recently introduced automatic time control devices enable oven burners to be automatically ignited at a pre-selected time. Various types of these automatic devices are used, some being operated by gas, and others by a combination of gas and electricity.

With some makes of cooker a single row of burners is provided at the back of the oven instead of the two side rows. Tests prove that either arrangement can be perfectly satisfactory, but it must be remembered that with side burners the food must not be placed too near the sides of the oven, while with back burners the baking trays must not be pushed so far in that they touch the back of the stove and hinder free circulation of the heated air.

Here are some notes on using gas cookers :

1. Where a browning sheet is supplied use this (placed at the top of the oven) for baking ; remove it for dishes needing slow heat.

2. Keep the cooker clean by wiping it down after use. Occasionally—say, fortnightly—it must be cleaned more thoroughly. Wipe both burner grids and burners, then wash them in some hot water containing soapless detergent, taking care not to allow the water to get into the burners. Use a cocktail stick to clean any choked burner. Rinse well, dry, and replace in position.

3. If possible, wipe out the oven immediately after use, while still hot. Occasionally, the whole oven should be cleaned by removing the shelves and washing them, and the interior of the oven, with hot water and detergent. When the oven is specially dirty, a solution of caustic soda or a cleaning preparation containing caustic ingredients will be found effective. This should be used very carefully and applied with an old mop, brush or special applicator ; it is important that the caustic solution should not come in contact with the skin. After treatment, rinse the oven well with a cloth wrung out in fresh water. Any marks which remain may be removed by rubbing with fine steel wool.

GAS FOR THE COUNTRY HOME

" Bottled " gas is a substitute for coal gas which makes the country-dweller entirely independent of a town supply. This gas consists of a compound or compounds of carbon and hydrogen, and is supplied in liquid form in small cylinders. Special burners are required. The gas has a high heat-giving or calorific value of over 3,000 B.Th.U.s per cubic foot, compared with the 500 B.Th.U.s per cubic foot of coal gas from the Gas Board. It can be used not only for cooking, but also for heating domestic water, gas fires, gas-operated refrigerators, wash-boilers, laundry irons and lighting installations. Running costs are more than with town gas at ordinary rates.

SOLID-FUEL COOKERS

Very considerable advances have recently been made in the design and manufacture of this type of stove. All those which have passed the Ministry of Fuel tests will burn continually on smokeless solid fuel such as coke, anthracite, etc.

The majority of solid-fuel cookers are designed to heat domestic hot water in addition to providing cooking facilities for an average family. The hot water output varies according to the size and design of the cooker, some models being also capable of heating a radiator and towel rail.

Solid-fuel cookers of the following types are the most suitable choice for a modern home :

Insulated Cookers. The insulated range has been developed to save fuel, and at the same time avoid over-heating the kitchen, by conserving all possible heat for cooking and water-heating. This type of cooker does not therefore warm the kitchen enough for living-room use during cold weather; however, models are available with an open fire (which is closed while cooking is in progress).

Most insulated ranges are flexible in use, and can be fitted to provide an adequate supply of domestic hot water. One of the latest models has electrically operated thermostatic control.

Heat-Storage Cookers. These are very heavily insulated cookers designed to conserve the heat so that it is available when required. Although expensive to install, they are very economical to run; one well-known cooker of this type can do all the cooking for a household of 7–10 people with a daily consumption of only about 10 or 12 lb. anthracite or coke. Although these cookers can be fitted to provide domestic hot water, the output is usually lower than from an insulated cooker. Attempts are, however, being made to increase hot water output of heat-storage cookers, and also the flexibility of use.

Heat-storage cookers have insulated hot-plate covers, and when the stove is not in use it is essential to keep these down; if they are left open, considerable wastage of heat occurs.

The following points should be noted when using any type of solid-fuel cooker.

1. As far as possible, use the variety and grade of fuel recommended by the manufacturer, for this will give the highest efficiency.

2. Keep the flues clean. Brush them regularly—say, once or twice a week—as far as you can reach with the flue brush. (This is particularly important if the fuel is not smokeless.)

3. About once or twice a year, the flues must be thoroughly cleaned by the chimney sweep.

4. Use ground-based pans for preference. Such pans make good contact with the hot-plate and thus heat more rapidly.

5. Pans with two small handles (not plastic) are an advantage, since they can be put into the oven when desired.

OIL COOKERS

The modern oil cooking stove is economical in running costs, and if managed correctly, gives excellent results.

The most usual type of burner is provided with a circular wick, the heat being readily adjustable if a long-drum burner is selected.

The following are points to observe in managing these oil cookers:

1. Follow the manufacturer's instructions carefully.

2. Keep the stove level, or the burners will receive oil unevenly.

3. Protect the stove from draught.

4. Trim the wicks regularly, but avoid cutting; it is best to smooth them with soft paper or wick cleaner.

5. Clean the burners regularly.

6. Thoroughly heat up the oven before use, or the food will burn underneath before it is properly cooked through and browned on top.

Other types of burner used for oil cookers are the asbestos collar and the wickless pressure burner. Both give a clear, bright flame, which is, however, not so easy to adjust as the circular wick. The pressure burner, which is very economical in the use of oil, must be pre-heated with methylated spirit before use.

OVEN TEMPERATURES

The ovens of most modern electric and gas cookers—and to an increasing extent of solid-fuel cookers also—are thermostatically controlled. With such cookers, once the thermostat has been set, the oven heat will not rise above the selected temperature.

In the case of thermostatically controlled electric ovens, it is usually found that the thermostat scale is marked either in degrees Fahrenheit, or in serial numbers (1, 2, 3, etc.), corresponding with 100° F., 200° F., 300° F., and so on.

Oven heats in the recipes in this book are described by such terms as "Slow," "Hot," etc., with the corresponding temperatures and oven settings; the table below shows the various equivalents. If in doubt about settings for your own cooker you can ask advice from your electricity or gas showrooms, or from Good Housekeeping Institute.

Oven Description	*Approx. temp., and electric oven setting*	*Standard gas thermostat*
Very slow	250° F., 275° F.	¼, ½
Slow	300° F., 325° F.	1, 2
Moderate	350° F., 375° F.	3, 4, 5
Moderately hot	400° F., 425° F.	6, 7
Hot to Very hot	450° F., 475° F.	8, 9

Judging the heat of an oven which has no thermostatic temperature control is difficult for the beginner, though with experience this becomes easier. A portable thermometer is useful; this should be placed in the middle of the middle shelf when measuring the temperature of the oven as a whole; when a particular temperature is required for cooking a dish, the thermometer may be placed on the shelf to be used.

Failing a thermometer, the temperature may be roughly estimated with the hand. To do this, open the oven door gently, place the hand in the centre of the oven, and count slowly. If it becomes uncomfortably hot after counting three, the oven is Very Hot; after counting five, Hot; after counting ten, Moderately Hot; if it feels just comfortably hot and not unbearable, Moderate; if just warm, Slow.

When baking pastry, biscuits, and so on, it is a good idea to put a small piece of the trimmings of the dough in the oven to test the heat before putting in the main batch.

OVEN MANAGEMENT

In cases where a specific cooking temperature is required, allow time for the oven to reach it before putting in the food. Actually, it is best to heat the oven to a slightly higher temperature, to allow for the inevitable cooling which occurs when the oven door is opened and cold food is placed inside. This does not apply to dishes such as casseroles and milk puddings which can start from cold, i.e., may be put into the oven when it is lit, and brought gradually to the cooking temperature.

Ovens with automatic time control can be set in advance to reach the required temperature. Follow the manufacturers' instructions for use.

Place pie dishes, casseroles, cake tins, etc., on baking sheets before putting them in the oven. It is then easier to alter their position or to lift them from the oven for inspection, and they are less likely to spill.

Generally speaking, the top of the oven is the hottest part and the bottom the coolest. Place scones, rock cakes, Swiss rolls, small pastries, and dishes requiring quick cooking at a high temperature, near the top of the oven; large cakes, joints of meat, and dishes requiring rather longer time at a more moderate heat in the centre of the oven; those requiring long, slow cooking (milk puddings and casseroles, etc.), near the bottom.

When using the oven instead of the grill for browning dishes "au gratin" and so on, the oven should be very hot and the dishes placed at the very top, just below the roof or the browning sheet, if any. If the oven is not really hot the mixture is likely to boil instead of the top browning.

COOKING TOOLS

Having the proper tools greatly adds to the comfort, and therefore the enjoyment, of doing any job. So it is with cooking. Aim, not at a kitchen full of gadgets, but at a few well-made and carefully chosen utensils, and the right tool for the various kitchen jobs; then, if you use them properly and keep them in good condition, you will not regret the outlay, and you will find they give you increased pleasure in your cooking.

Not every newly invented domestic device is worthy of a place in the ideal kitchen, and the haphazard purchase of gadgets may prove a disappointing and expensive policy. However fascinating labour-saving devices appear at first glance, it is unwise to spend money and time on them without some assurance that they are sufficiently durable, and also—even more important—really effective and simple to use; it is obviously short-sighted to spend more time setting up and cleaning an appliance than is saved in the carrying out of the actual operation which it is designed to perform

Examples of all types of equipment and cooking tools are constantly being tested in Good Housekeeping Institute; when buying new kitchen utensils look for the Good Housekeeping Seal of Guarantee, shown below, which is an indication that the article fulfils the claim made by the manufacturers, and that it will be reliable and satisfactory in use.

The following is a comprehensive list of the utensils needed to carry out all the cooking processes described in this book. If you can purchase only a small amount of cooking equipment when you first furnish your kitchen, you will want to choose the most generally useful items and leave the more specialised ones till later, acquiring them as opportunity occurs. On this list, therefore, the items are graded according to their use, and those which are used only occasionally, or used exclusively for high-class cookery, are marked with an asterisk, so you will be able to see at a glance which tools you need to buy first. Refer back to this list from time to time, so that you can gradually fill the gaps in your equipment. It is well worth while also keeping a lookout for new types of equipment, such as an electric mixer, which is described in more detail at the end of this chapter. Although these labour-saving devices may seem at first to be a luxury, you will find more and more use for them as the amount of your cooking increases.

Knives

A sharp-pointed, stainless vegetable knife
A medium-sized cook's knife (6 to 8-in. blade), used for chopping
At least 1 ordinary round-ended knife, for mixing and for general purposes
Saw-edged knife, useful for cutting bread and tough-skinned fruits and vegetables
Palette knife, for lifting biscuits, etc., from the baking tin, turning fried foods, scraping out mixing bowls, and so on
Steel, stone, or patent knife sharpener

Spoons

Set of 3 wooden spoons
2 kitchen tablespoons
2 kitchen dessertspoons
2 kitchen teaspoons
Large metal spoon, for folding
Perforated or wire spoon, for frying, dishing, etc.
*Set of 3 measuring spoons, useful for measuring spoonfuls, ½ and ¼ spoonfuls

Forks

2 large kitchen forks
2 small kitchen forks
A 2-pronged fork, for turning bacon, for dishing, etc.

Other small items of cutlery, etc.

Pair of scissors, for rinding bacon and for general use
Potato peeler
Apple corer
Tin opener
Corkscrew
Bottle opener
Set of skewers
*Trussing needle
*Larding needle
*Parisian potato cutter } for cutting vegetable garnishes
*Pea cutter }

Utensils for general food preparation

Colander
*Bean slicer
Combined grater and shredder
Mincing machine
Potato masher
*Hair or nylon sieve
Wire sieve
Graduated quart measure
Set of measures, ¼, ½, and 1 pint
Lemon squeezer
2 wire whisks (1 large, 1 small) for whisking eggs, sauces, etc.
Funnel
Pointed strainer, useful for straining gravy, sauces, etc.
Small round strainer, to fit over a basin—useful for draining and for sieving small quantities
Chopping board
*Salad shaker

Saucepans, etc.

6 saucepans, assorted sizes (2 small, 2 medium, 2 large)
Double saucepan
*3-tiered steamer or single steamers
2 shallow frying pans (1 large, 1 small)
Deep fat frying pan and basket
Stock pot
Omelette pan
*Pressure saucepan or cooker
Kettle
*Girdle (see Girdle Scones, etc.)
*Waffle iron (see Batters and Waffles)

Utensils for Pastry Making

Pastry board
Rolling pin
Flour dredger
Set of plain pastry cutters
Set of fluted pastry cutters
1 or 2 pastry brushes
*12 deep patty pans
3 or 4 pie plates, assorted sizes
12 tartlet tins
*Bouchée cases
*Boat-shaped moulds
*Cream horn tins

Cake Tins, Moulds, etc.

2 sets bun tins
2 sandwich tins
2 or 3 baking sheets
*2 Swiss roll tins
4 cake tins, assorted sizes
2 wire cake trays
*12 dariole moulds
Jelly moulds
*Border mould
*Soufflé tin (for steamed soufflés)
*Shortbread mould
*Raised pie mould
*Muffin rings
2 meat tins
Trivet for meat

Kitchen China and Enamelware

2 mixing bowls
6 pudding basins, assorted sizes
3 or 4 pie dishes, assorted sizes
3 or 4 casseroles, assorted sizes
3 or 4 plates, assorted sizes
3 or 4 jugs, assorted sizes
*Soufflé cases (for baked soufflés)
Jelly moulds
*Pestle and mortar, useful for grinding nuts, praline, etc.

Other General Equipment

Kitchen scales	Bread bin
Store jars and containers	Flour bin
Cake and biscuit tins	*Oven thermometer
Refuse bin	*Sugar thermometer

**Equipment for Piping, Decorating, Cake Icing, and Decorating*

Star pipes, assorted sizes, for piping cream, butter icing, potato purée, etc.
Plain pipes, assorted sizes, for piping éclairs, meringues, etc.
Icing table and icing pipes
Dividing rings
Set of small fancy cutters, for cutting garnishes and decorations

**Equipment for Jam Making, etc.*

Preserving pans	Stone baskets
Jam spoon	Cherry stoner
Jam fillers	Jelly bag and stand
Jam funnel	Marmalade slicer

**Equipment for Bottling and Canning*

Steriliser	Bottling jars
Thermometer	Canning machine
Bottling tongs	Cans

**Equipment for Sweet Making*

Sugar thermometer
Chocolate dipping saucepan
Chocolate dipping forks
Wooden spatula
Marble slab
Caramel bars and cutter
Starch tray
Rubber fondant mat
Funnel and plug

Linen, etc.

Pudding cloths	*Piping bags
*Tammy cloths	*Meat cloths and muslin

* Items necessary only when high-class or specialised cookery is undertaken.

Electric Mixers

The modern electric mixer is a valuable piece of labour-saving equipment in any kitchen where a large amount of cooking is done, since on an average it will accomplish in about three minutes work which would take at least ten minutes by hand, even by a quick worker.

These machines can be used for making cakes and puddings with a creamed basis, and for all whisking processes. Some also have attachments for mincing and chopping, grating, blending, and liquidising, extracting fruit juices, puréeing, slicing, mashing, beating, mixing dough, and even a buff for polishing silver. Which model to choose must obviously depend on the money available, the household needs, personal preference, etc. Electric mixers are still somewhat expensive to buy, but running costs need hardly be considered, as the current consumption is negligible.

Success in using a mixer depends on following all the instructions provided, but it is always important to weigh or measure out all ingredients before starting mixing operations. For quick results, fats should be slightly softened first and they should not be used straight from the refrigerator, as the hard mass throws an unnecessary strain on the machine. If a mixture works up the sides of the basin, it should, when necessary, be scraped back into the centre with a spatula. A cake mixture should not be overbeaten after the flour has been added, or the cake will tend to be heavy; it is indeed often preferable to fold in flour with a spoon.

Potato Peelers

A good mechanical potato peeler is a worthwhile piece of equipment for a large family. Most models work on the same principle, and are usually operated by turning a handle, though some are turned by water power: for these it is necessary to have good water pressure. The potatoes are placed in a drum which has a roughened metal lining. The drum is then rotated, and this action rubs the skin off the potatoes. Water running through the machine washes the waste away during the process.

Household models hold 1 lb.–2 lb. potatoes, which can be dealt with in 2 or 3 minutes. To obtain even results select potatoes which are as nearly as possible the same size. It is necessary to look over the potatoes as you take them out of the machine, and to remove any eyes. Onions, apples and root vegetables of a suitable shape can also be peeled in these machines.

HOW TO USE THE INDEX

Make this Index work for you. It has been carefully planned, not only to save your time in looking up the particular recipes you want, but also to help you discover new ideas and new ways of cooking the food you may have in your larder. The Index has been kept as simple as possible, but these few notes may help you to use it to the best advantage.

Each recipe is indexed under the first word of its title, and cross-referenced under other main words. Thus, Brown Almond Pudding will be found under all three words. Names of foods used in both singular and plural form are found under one main heading. For instance, Apple Amber and Baked Apples are both listed under the heading Apple(s).

When information and recipes concerning a particular food extend over several pages, the entry in the Index reads thus : Page 280 *et seq.*

If you want ideas for cooking a particular food, look in the Index under its name. For example, look up the heading " Veal," and you will find listed over a score of recipes, some well-known and obvious, some unusual and capable of transforming a humble piece of stewing veal into a really sophisticated dish. Or if you are looking for a savoury to end a meal, or some new home-made biscuits for tea, look up " Savouries " or " Biscuits " in the Index and you will find a complete list of the pages on which they appear.

In many chapters alternative recipes are given for economical dishes that can be made from limited supplies. In addition there is a special supplement of Economical Recipes, useful for those who must manage on a restricted budget. The word " Economical " in brackets after an entry in the Index shows that the recipe is one of those included in that section. Similarly the word " Invalid " after an entry indicates that the dish appears in the chapter on Invalid Cookery, and the abbreviation " P.Ck." shows that the entry refers to the chapter on Pressure Cookery.

Sometimes a recipe may contain a word or phrase new to you (for example, " barding ") : in that case, look it up in the Index, and you will be directed to the page where it is explained—usually in the chapter on Cookery Processes and Terms.

Index